The West

combined
volume

The West
A Narrative History

A. Daniel Frankforter

The Pennsylvania State University

William M. Spellman

University of North Carolina, Asheville

with the assistance of John M. Cox, Florida Gulf Coast University

PEARSON

Prentice
Hall

Upper Saddle River, New Jersey 07458

VP/Publisher: Priscilla McGeehon
Executive Editor: Charles Cavaliere
Editorial Assistant: Lauren Aylward
Media Project Manager: Tina Rudowski
Marketing Manager: Laura Lee Manley
Marketing Assistant: Athena Moore
Managing Editor (Production): Lisa Iarkowski
Project Manager: Marianne Peters-Riordan
Senior Operations Specialist: Mary Ann Gloriande
Senior Art Director: Maria Lange
Interior and Cover Designer: K&M Design
AV Project Manager: Mirella Signoretto
Cover Photos: Tamar, "King" of Georgia: Charles Cavaliere/Library of Congress; Albert Einstein:

American Institute of Physics/AIP Meggers Gallery of Nobel Laureates/Emilio Segre Visual Archives
Cartographer: Pristine Graphics
Director, Image Resource Center: Melinda Patelli
Manager, Rights and Permissions: Zina Arabia
Manager, Visual Research: Beth Brenzel
Manager, Cover Visual Research & Permissions: Karen Sanatar
Image Permission Coordinator: Fran Toepfer
Composition/Full-Service Project Management: Heather Willison/S4Carlisle Publishing Services
Printer/Binder: Quebecor Printing

Credits and acknowledgments borrowed from other sources and reproduced, with permission, in this textbook appear on pages xxxi–xxxiii.

Pearson Education LTD., London
Pearson Education Singapore, Pte. Ltd
Pearson Education, Canada, Ltd
Pearson Education–Japan
Pearson Education Australia PTY, Limited

Pearson Education North Asia Ltd
Pearson Educación de Mexico, S.A. de C.V.
Pearson Education Malaysia, Pte. Ltd
Pearson Education, Upper Saddle River, New Jersey

10 9 8 7 6 5 4 3 2 1

Brief Contents

Introduction   **xli**

Part 1 Departure   2

1 **The Birth of Civilization**   4

2 **The Rise of Empires and the Beginning of the Iron Age**   32

Part 2 The Classical Era 2000 B.C.E. to 30 C.E.   60

3 **Aegean Civilizations**   62

4 **The Hellenic Era**   90

5 **The Hellenistic Era and the Rise of Rome**   118

6 **Rome's Empire and the Unification of the Western World**   148

Part 3 The Division of the West 300 to 1300   178

7 **The West's Medieval Civilizations**   180

8 **The Emergence of Europe**   208

9 **Europe Turns Outward**   236

10 **Europe's High Middle Ages**   266

Part 4 Challenges, Conflicts, and Departures   292

11 **Challenges to the Medieval Order**   294

12 **Renaissance and Exploration**   322

13 **Reformation, Religious Wars, and National Conflicts**   354

Part 5 The Revolutionary Impulse 388

14 **The Early Modern State** 390

15 **New World Views: Europe's Scientific Revolution** 418

16 **The Age of Enlightenment: Rationalism and Its Uses** 440

17 **Rebellion and Revolution: American Independence and the French Revolution** 462

Part 6 Europe Triumphant, 1815–1914 490

18 **Industry, Society, and Environment** 492

19 **The Age of Ideology** 518

20 **The Consolidation of Nation-States** 546

21 **Global Empire and European Culture** 576

Part 7 Europe in Crisis, 1914–1945 602

22 **World War I: The End of Enlightenment** 604

23 **The Troubled Interwar Years** 632

24 **World War II: Europe in Eclipse** 656

Part 8 The Postwar Western Community, 1945–2008 682

25 **Decolonization and the Cold War** 684

26 **Western Civilization and the Global Community** 714

Contents

Maps   xvii
Key Questions   xix
Preface   xxi
Acknowledgments   xxix
Photo Credits   xxxi
Note on Dates and Spelling   xxxv
About the Authors   xxxix
Introduction   xli

Part 1 Departure 2

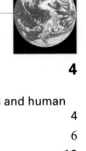

1 The Birth of Civilization   4

KEY|QUESTION: How do environments shape human communities and human communities alter environments?   4

The Evolution of Prehistoric Cultures   6
■ PEOPLE IN CONTEXT The Iceman   10
The Archaic States   13
The Origin of Civilization in Mesopotamia: Sumer   14
The Rise of Civilization in Egypt   23

2 The Rise of Empires and the Beginning of the Iron Age   32

KEY|QUESTION: Does civilization promote unity or intensify divisions among peoples?   32

The Transition States   34
Imperial Egypt: The New Kingdom (1550–1075 B.C.E., Dynasties XVIII–XX)   38
■ PEOPLE IN CONTEXT King "Tut"   42
The Indo-Europeans and the Clash of Empires   45
The Bible and History   51

Part 2 The Classical Era 2000 B.C.E. to 30 C.E. 60

3 Aegean Civilizations   62

KEY|QUESTION: When does civilization in the West become "Western"
civilization?   62
   Minoan Mentors   64
   The Mycenaeans, Greece's First Civilization   67
   The Aegean Dark Age   70
   The Hellenic Era   72
   ■ PEOPLE IN CONTEXT Hesiod, The Uncommon Common Man 74
   The Rise of the Mainland Powers   79
   The Persian Wars: Crucible of a Civilization   84

4 The Hellenic Era   90

KEY|QUESTION: What did the Greeks contribute to the development
of modern civilization?   90
   Persian Wars as Catalyst   92
   The Peloponnesian War   94
   ■ PEOPLE IN CONTEXT Aspasia, the Woman Behind the Great Man 96
   Intellectual and Artistic Life in the *Polis*   101

5 The Hellenistic Era and the Rise of Rome   118

KEY|QUESTION: What circumstances are likely to undermine governments
by the people?   118
   The Hellenistic Era   120
   The Origin of Rome   129
   The Roman Republic   132
   Rome's Civil War   139
   ■ PEOPLE IN CONTEXT Cornelia, Mother of the Gracchi 140

6 Rome's Empire and the Unification of the Western World 148

KEY|QUESTION: Do people prefer order to liberty?   148
   The Augustan Era   150
   Order and Continuity: The Dynastic Option   159

Order and Continuity: The Elective Option   163
■ **PEOPLE IN CONTEXT** **The Imperial Aristocracy: Pliny the Elder and Pliny the Younger**   **164**
Life in an Imperial Environment   169
The Decline of Rome   172

Part 3 The Division of the West 300 to 1300 178

7 The West's Medieval Civilizations   **180**

KEY|QUESTION: Should freedom of religion be limited?   180
The Christian Element   182
The German Element   189
The Byzantine Empire of Constantinople   193
Islam   197
■ **PEOPLE IN CONTEXT** **A'isha (614–678), Wife of the Prophet**   **200**

8 The Emergence of Europe   **208**

KEY|QUESTION: How did Europe build on its legacies from the ancient world?   208
The Merovingian Kingdom: Europe's Nucleus   210
The Franks' Neighbors   213
■ **PEOPLE IN CONTEXT** **Brunhild (d. 613) and Fredegund (d. 597): Powers Behind the Throne**   **216**
The Carolingian Era   217
Retrenchment and Reorganization   225
The Culture of Europe's Dark Age   231

9 Europe Turns Outward   **236**

KEY|QUESTION: Was conflict among the medieval civilizations inevitable?   236
Islam's Crest and Byzantium's Resurgence   238
The Reorganization of Europe   242
■ **PEOPLE IN CONTEXT** **Hroswitha of Gandersheim (fl. 935–1002)**   **252**
The Eleventh-Century Turning Point   254

10 Europe's High Middle Ages 266

KEY|QUESTION: Why are some societies more open to change than others?   266

The Renaissance of the Twelfth Century   268
Universities and Scholasticism   271
Religious Revival and Diversity of Opinion   274

■ **PEOPLE IN CONTEXT William IX, Duke of Aquitaine and Count of Poitou (1071–1127)** 276

The Artistic Vision of the High Middle Ages   278
The Nation-States of the High Middle Ages   283

Part 4 Challenges, Conflicts, and Departures 292

11 Challenges to the Medieval Order 294

KEY|QUESTION: What did the crises of the late medieval era reveal about the strengths and weaknesses of Europe's civilization?   294

Challenges from Nature   296
Turmoil in the Middle East   300
Spiritual Crises   305
Political Responses: The Burdens of War   312

■ **PEOPLE IN CONTEXT Christine de Pizan (c. 1364–1430), Professional Writer** 316

12 Renaissance and Exploration 322

KEY|QUESTION: How should a society use its history?   322

The Context for the Renaissance   324
The Culture of the Renaissance   329

■ **PEOPLE IN CONTEXT Elisabetta Gonzaga (1472–1526)** 334

The Northern Renaissance   338
The Middle East: The Ottoman Empire   341
Europe and Atlantic Exploration   346

13 Reformation, Religious Wars, and National Conflicts   354

KEY|QUESTION: How do civilized societies justify war?   354

The Lutheran Reformation   356
The Swiss Reformation   361
The Catholic Reformation   365
The Habsburg-Valois Wars   368
England's Ambivalent Reformation   369
Convergence of Foreign and Domestic Politics: England, Spain, and France   372
The Final Religious Upheavals   377
■ PEOPLE IN CONTEXT William Shakespeare (1564–1616)   378

Part 5 The Revolutionary Impulse 388

14 The Early Modern State   390

KEY|QUESTION: How do political systems reflect the structure of social and economic life?   390

Society in Early Modern Europe   392
Forging Centralized States   396
■ PEOPLE IN CONTEXT King James I as Political Theorist   398
Absolutism in France   399
Constitutionalism in England   404
Wars of Empire and Global Markets   406
Central and Eastern Europe   408
Europe's Declining Powers   411

15 New World Views: Europe's Scientific Revolution   418

KEY|QUESTION: How does the study of the natural world influence religious belief and the understanding of truth?   418

The Medieval World View   420
Anticipating the New Science   422
New Directions in Astronomy and Physics   424
New Approaches to Truth   427

Theory and Application   429
Politics as Science   432
Science and Religion   434
■ PEOPLE IN CONTEXT Locke as Natural Philosopher   435
Superstition and Its Victims   436

16 The Age of Enlightenment: Rationalism and Its Uses   440

KEY|QUESTION: How do people construct ideas of progress?   440
Critiquing the Traditional Way of Life   442
Formulas for Improving Material Conditions   449
Enlightened Despots   451
Critiquing the Enlightenment   453
■ PEOPLE IN CONTEXT Olympe de Gouges   456
The Arts in the Age of Reason   459

17 Rebellion and Revolution: American Independence and the French Revolution   462

KEY|QUESTION: Can political change occur without social and economic
upheaval?   462
America Rejects Europe   464
Revolution in France   470
■ PEOPLE IN CONTEXT Edmund Burke on Revolution   476
Napoleon Bonaparte and the Export of Revolution, 1799–1815   480
The French Revolution and the Americas   485

Part 6 Europe Triumphant, 1815–1914   490

18 Industry, Society, and Environment   492

KEY|QUESTION: How do technology and urbanization influence the relationship
between humans and nature?   492
From Rural to Urban Lifestyles in Europe   494
Agriculture, Demographics, and Labor   497
Innovations in Production   501
The Social Consequences of Industrialization   506
■ PEOPLE IN CONTEXT Alfred Krupp   510

19 The Age of Ideology   518

KEY│QUESTION: What leads people to challenge conventional ideas and
practices?   518

The Congress System and the Conservative Agenda   520
Ideological Ferment   523
The Revolutions of 1848   527
■ **PEOPLE IN CONTEXT** Giuseppe Mazzini   **532**
Britain and Reform   533
The Romantic Movement   536
Utilitarianism and Utopian Socialism   539
The Marxist Challenge   541

20 The Consolidation of Nation-States   **546**

KEY│QUESTION: Is nationalism a constructive force in the modern age?   546
Italian Unification   548
The Creation of Modern Germany   551
Constitutional Change in France and Britain   557
The Waning of the Habsburg, Russian, and Ottoman Empires   562
The United States and Western Europe   568
Nationalism and Race   571
■ **PEOPLE IN CONTEXT** Theodor Herzl and Jewish Nationalism   **573**

21 Global Empire and European Culture   **576**

KEY│QUESTION: How does the projection of power reflect wider
cultural values?   576
The New Imperialism: Motives and Methods   578
The Scramble for Empire: Africa   581
The Scramble for Empire: South and East Asia   584
Imperialism, Intellectual Controversy, and European Culture   589
Transformation in the Arts   595
■ **PEOPLE IN CONTEXT** Marie Curie and Modern Physics   **596**

Part 7 Europe in Crisis, 1914–1945 602

22 World War I: The End of Enlightenment 604

KEY|QUESTION: Are nation-states inherently adversarial?   604
   The Alliance System   606
   The Experience of Modern War   609
   The Eastern Front and Europe's Empire   612
   Naval War and American Entry   615
   The Impact of Total War at Home   618
   The Russian Revolution   620
   ■ PEOPLE IN CONTEXT John Reed and Bolshevism   624
   The Peace Settlement and European Consciousness   625

23 The Troubled Interwar Years 632

KEY|QUESTION: Can personal liberty be maintained
under conditions of material hardship?   632
   Postwar Problems in Western Europe   634
   The Price of Victory   635
   The Great Depression, 1929–1939   638
   Italy: The First Fascist State   641
   Authoritarian Regimes in Spain and Eastern Europe   643
   The Emergence of Nazi Germany   644
   ■ PEOPLE IN CONTEXT José Ortega y Gasset   645
   Imperial Japan   650
   The Soviet Union Under Stalin   651

24 World War II: Europe in Eclipse 656

KEY|QUESTION: Can the force of ideas sustain a civilization under attack?   656
   The Process of Appeasement, 1933–1939   658
   Nazism Triumphant, 1939–1941: Europe and North Africa   661
   ■ PEOPLE IN CONTEXT Charles de Gaulle and Free France   664
   The German Empire   666
   The Home Front and the Role of Women   670
   War in Asia and the Pacific   672
   The Tide Turns, 1942–1945   674
   Planning for the Postwar World   679

Part 8 The Postwar Western Community, 1945–2008 682

25 Decolonization and the Cold War   **684**

KEY|QUESTION: How does ideology shape public policy?   684

The Eclipse of Postwar Optimism   686

The End of European Empire   694

Expanding the Cold War   701

■ PEOPLE IN CONTEXT   Ho Chi Minh   **706**

The Cold War and Nuclear Threat   708

26 Western Civilization and the Global Community   **714**

KEY|QUESTION: Has the West defined the process of globalization?   714

The End of Communism   716

United Europe?   723

Science, Technology, and the Environment   731

Women and the Struggle for Equality   736

■ PEOPLE IN CONTEXT   Simone de Beauvoir   **738**

Religious Divides and Ethnic Nationalism   739

The Postindustrial West   744

Glossary   748

Suggested Resources   754

Index   765

DVD Table of Contents   791

Maps

Map 1–1......Early Agricultural Settlements 12

Map 1–2......The Fertile Crescent 14

Map 2–1......The Seats of the Ancient Middle-Eastern Empires 46

Map 2–2......Ancient Palestine 57

Map 3–1......The Bronze-Age Aegean World 65

Map 3–2......Greek Territories of the Hellenic Period 73

Map 3–3......The Persian Wars 85

Map 4–1......Competing Alliances: Athens (Delian League) and Sparta 95

Map 5–1......Alexander's Adventure 123

Map 5–2......The Rise of Rome 130

Map 5–3......Rome and Carthage 136

Map 6–1......Augustus's Empire 154

Map 6–2......The Pinnacle of the Roman Empire 166

Map 6–3......The Divisions of the Late Roman Empire 175

Map 7–1......Migrations into the Roman Empire 192

Map 7–2......Expansion of the Muslim Empire 201

Map 8–1......Western Europe in the Merovingian Era 213

Map 8–2......Growth of the Carolingian Empire 221

Map 8–3......The Ninth-Century Invasions 226

Map 9–1......The Medieval Muslim World 240

Map 9–2......England and the Viking Migrations 244

Map 9–3......Medieval France 247

Map 9–4......Medieval Germany and Italy 250

Map 9–5......Crusade Routes 259

Map 11–1....The Mongol Empire 303

Map 11–2....The Hundred Years' War 314

Map 12–1....Renaissance Italy 327

Map 12–2....The Ottoman Empire 345

Map 12–3....Europe's Initial Global Explorations 351

Map 13–1....The Empire of Charles V 359

Map 13–2....Religious Diversity in Post-Reformation Europe 366

Map 13–3....Europe After the Peace of Westphalia 381

Map 14–1....Europe in 1714 403

Map 14–2....Ottoman Empire Around 1600 412

Map 16–1....The Influence of Diderot's *Encyclopedia*   446

Map 17–1....North America in 1763   465

Map 17–2....Napoleon's Empire in 1812   484

Map 17–3....The Americas in 1828   487

Map 18–1....The Industrial Revolution in Europe   495

Map 18–2....Manchester, England   506

Map 19–1....Europe in 1815   522

Map 19–2....The Revolutions of 1848   528

Map 20–1....The Unification of Italy   549

Map 20–2....The Unification of Germany   553

Map 20–3....The Habsburg Multiethnic Empire   563

Map 20–4....The Decline of the Ottoman Empire, 1800–1913   567

Map 21–1....European Colonies in Africa in 1914   582

Map 21–2....European Colonies in Asia by 1914   587

Map 22–1....World War I in Europe   611

Map 22–2....Postwar Europe   626

Map 23–1....The Great Depression in Europe   640

Map 24–1....The Partitions of Czechoslovakia and Poland 1938–1939   660

Map 24–2....Axis Powers in Europe   666

Map 24–3....The Holocaust   669

Map 24–4....The Pacific War   674

Map 25–1....Postwar Decolonization   695

Map 25–2....Muslim Population of Western Europe, c. 2005   700

Map 25–3....The Cold War in Europe   702

Map 25–4....War in Vietnam   707

Map 25–5....The Cuban Missile Crisis   709

Map 26–1....The End of the Soviet Union   721

Map 26–2....The Growth of the European Union   726

Map 26–3....Comparative World Wealth, c. 2004   734

KEY | QUESTIONS

1 **The Birth of Civilization** How do environments shape human communities and human communities alter environments? 4

2 **The Rise of Empires and the Beginning of the Iron Age** Does civilization promote unity or intensify divisions among peoples? 32

3 **Aegean Civilizations** When does civilization in the West become "Western" civilization? 62

4 **The Hellenic Era** What did the Greeks contribute to the development of modern civilization? 90

5 **The Hellenistic Era and the Rise of Rome** What circumstances are likely to undermine governments by the people? 118

6 **Rome's Empire and the Unification of the Western World** Do people prefer order to liberty? 148

7 **The West's Medieval Civilizations** Should freedom of religion be limited? 180

8 **The Emergence of Europe** How did Europe build on its legacies from the ancient world? 208

9 **Europe Turns Outward** Was conflict among the medieval civilizations inevitable? 236

10 **Europe's High Middle Ages** Why are some societies more open to change than others? 266

11 **Challenges to the Medieval Order** What did the crises of the late medieval era reveal about the strengths and weaknesses of Europe's civilization? 294

12 **Renaissance and Exploration** How should a society use its history? 322

13 **Reformation, Religious Wars, and National Conflicts** How do civilized societies justify war? 354

14 **The Early Modern State** How do political systems reflect the structure of social and economic life? 390

15 **New World Views: Europe's Scientific Revolution** How does the study of the natural world influence religious belief and the understanding of truth? 418

16   **The Age of Enlightenment: Rationalism and Its Uses**   How do people construct ideas of progress?   440

17   **Rebellion and Revolution: American Independence and the French Revolution**   Can political change occur without social and economic upheaval?   462

18   **Industry, Society, and Environment**   How do technology and urbanization influence the relationship between humans and nature?   492

19   **The Age of Ideology**   What leads people to challenge conventional ideas and practices?   518

20   **The Consolidation of Nation-States**   Is nationalism a constructive force in the modern age?   546

21   **Global Empire and European Culture**   How does the projection of power reflect wider cultural values?   576

22   **World War I: The End of Enlightenment**   Are nation-states inherently adversarial?   604

23   **The Troubled Interwar Years**   Can personal liberty be maintained under conditions of material hardship?   632

24   **World War II: Europe in Eclipse**   Can the force of ideas sustain a civilization under attack?   656

25   **Decolonization and the Cold War**   How does ideology shape public policy?   684

26   **Western Civilization and the Global Community**   Has the West defined the process of globalization?   714

Preface

The Western civilization course, which was invented for American students, has evolved as students' educational needs have changed. Toward the end of the nineteenth century, when the traditional literature-based curriculum centered on Greek and Latin classics yielded to a new system of elective courses offered by a rapidly growing number of specialized academic departments, the Western civilization course was introduced to provide a foundation on which to erect a coherent program of study. At many schools the course became the centerpiece of a "general education program" that served as a required introduction to college for all students.

During the twentieth century, as thinking about higher education evolved, different rationales were offered for Western civilization courses and for general education requirements. Some instructors have presented these courses as essential instruction for novice scholars in a body of knowledge that all educated persons must have. In the environment created by the great wars that shaped much of the twentieth century, the Western civilization course was often perceived as training for citizenship and the defense of democracy. The history of the West was represented as the story of the rise of a rational and free way of life that was humanity's supreme achievement and universal aspiration—a precious legacy that had to be guarded against the forces of barbarism.

All of this was radically questioned during the 1960s. Many American schools abandoned the idea of general education and compulsory course requirements. In light of the growing specialization and professionalization of academic fields, faith in the unity of knowledge and the existence of a body of information with which every educated person should be familiar seemed naive. Given the complexity and diversity of intellectual life, academic reformers swept aside general education programs and insisted that students should be free to pursue their personal interests and define the contents of their own educations.

In this environment the Western civilization course was singled out for special criticism. It was accused of promoting provincialism and narrowmindedness by elevating European-American history to the status of universal history—the story of Earth's premier "high civilization." The realities of the emerging global community, it was argued, compelled the development of a new paradigm for higher education, one that did not "privilege" the West or represent its history as progress toward freedom and rationality. New courses in World civilization were proposed to take its place.

The critics of Western civilization courses make valid points—at least with respect to the way these courses have sometimes been conceived and taught. The Western civilization course has, at times, promoted Euro-American triumphalism and perpetuated colonialist attitudes, cultural intolerance, and racism. However, the fact that a subject can be badly taught does not suggest that it should never be taught. Any national history can degenerate into propaganda and be used to foster jingoism. The fault is less with the subject than with a loss of objectivity in its presentation.

Students at American colleges and universities are—regardless of their ancestral ethnic backgrounds—immersed in a culture deeply indebted to Europe and the

Mediterranean region. Other parts of the globe have made undoubted contributions to the culture of what is largely an immigrant nation, but these influences integrate with the values and institutions of a trans-Atlantic civilization that, for want of a better term, is invariably described as "the West." Despite this, most students begin their undergraduate careers with very little knowledge of the roots of their way of life. Those who come from American public schools have repeatedly been taught something of their national history, but they seldom have had more than a cursory exposure to its background. Their lack of understanding of the historical processes that shaped the West makes it difficult for them to situate the American experience in a global context. Having an inadequate knowledge of themselves, they are handicapped in their efforts to comprehend others. Far from narrowing their perspective, a course in Western civilization—which helps American students grasp how and why they have come to be what they are—can help them understand how and why other peoples have developed differently. Such understanding is essential if students are to appreciate other cultures, sympathize with their struggles, and value their integrity.

Approach

The West: A Narrative History is a unique text in its field in that it was conceived and developed as a brief introduction to the history of the West. The text is not a reduced version of a larger study, but a fully realized project in its own right. It defines *West* in the broadest terms as encompassing all the cultures that trace at least some of their ancestry to the ancient Mediterranean world. The text consistently reminds its readers of the links between the people who have come to define the West and those in other regions of the world.

In this respect as well, *The West: A Narrative History* distinguishes itself from many of the textbooks currently available for teaching courses in Western civilization. These books begin with brief treatments of ancient Mesopotamian and Egyptian civilizations and then largely abandon the Middle East. When they reach the medieval period, they mention the rise of Islam but leave students with the impression that Islam is an alien, non-Western phenomenon. This obscures the fact that both Christians and Muslims built on the same cultural foundations—Hebraic religious tradition and Hellenistic philosophy and science—and both borrowed significantly from the civilizations of India and the East. The importance of the help that the Muslim world gave medieval Europe in reclaiming the legacy both regions shared from the ancient era is often slighted; with the rise of the Ottoman Empire, Islam usually disappears from the narrative (except for brief references to later European encroachments on Ottoman territory).

Such minimal treatment of Muslim history poorly prepares students to understand the current international political situation and to evaluate critically common "Western" assumptions about what is, somewhat inaccurately, called "the East." The future of much more than the West may depend on Western civilization's Euro-American and Middle Eastern heirs re-examining their history of interaction and divergence and developing a deeper understanding of how much they have in common.

Organization

The volume of tourist traffic flowing through historical sites and the existence of a History Channel on TV prove that the public at large finds the past innately interesting for its own sake. Undergraduates, however, are often afflicted with "presentism," the assumption that the past is an alien land—a curious, but irrelevant realm. To encourage them to relate the experiences of long-vanished peoples to their own lives, each chapter of *The West: A Narrative History* begins by posing a "key question," a question of broad scope or general significance that is raised by something in the period the chapter treats. The chapter is not an essay on the question, and the chapter does not propose a definitive answer to the larger issue it asks students to ponder—though the problems it raises are reconsidered at the end of each chapter. The "key question" feature provides a springboard for wide-ranging class discussions of questions that have no simple answers. Debating the issues raised by the "key question" essays helps students discover for themselves that the past is more intriguing (and knowledge of its history more useful) than they may have realized.

Each chapter is equipped with features to assist its readers in grasping its structure and design. Quotations from primary sources, at the head of each chapter, introduce the chapter's theme—which is elaborated by the brief "key question" essay that follows. The topics covered in the chapter are then listed, and the text of the chapter is divided into sections and subsections with headings that make its content easy to outline. The text contains ample maps, illustrations, and timelines. Each chapter also has a sidebar that deals with an individual whose life illustrates something about the era the chapter discusses. The narrative unfolds chronologically and avoids shifting back and forth in time—something that many students claim makes a text confusing and difficult to understand. Politics often provides the skeleton of the story, but the traditional "names, dates, and battles" are fleshed out with materials from social, economic, and intellectual history. Attention is paid to segments of society (for example, women, slaves, and peasants) whose contributions sometimes receive insufficient recognition in survey courses. To help students grasp the overall design of the book, it is divided into eight parts that group related chapters. Numerous illustrations and maps, with detailed captions, supplement the primary narrative. A set of review questions, which can be used either for class discussion or written assignments, concludes each chapter, and an extensive list of resources that students can explore on their own is provided at the end of the text.

Changes to the Second Edition

In response to edifying comments and helpful suggestions from reviewers across the country, we have improved the book's organization and narrative flow and updated or enhanced the coverage of several important topics. We have also changed the book's subtitle to *A Narrative History* because it more accurately reflects the basic goal we set out to achieve when we embarked on this project—to provide students with a clear, concise, and provocative examination of civilization in the West.

Introduction
- Completely revised, the Introduction now examines "the West" in light of globalization. It offers an expanded discussion of the concept of "civilization."

Chapter 1
- A new "key question" focuses attention on relations between the environment and culture.
- The chapter provides an expanded discussion on the origins of agriculture and the rise of civilization on the Eurasian continents.

Chapter 2
- A new "key question" has been added on the dynamics of civilization—unity versus conflict.
- Expanded discussion is provided of the Bible and history.
- Increased coverage is offered of the roles of women.

Chapter 3
- Increased coverage is provided of Minoan civilization.
- Discussion of the values of classical civilization has been significantly revised.
- Expanded description is provided of Athens.

Chapter 4
- Coverage of military history has been clarified.
- Improved analysis is provided of the positive and negative aspects of Hellenic civilization.
- More emphasis is placed on Greece's ties with the Near East.

Chapter 5
- A new "key question" explores developments that undermine popular governments.
- Increased coverage is provided of the consequences of the Peloponnesian War.
- Expanded treatment is given of Alexander and the Hellenistic era.

Chapter 6
- A new discussion is offered of Augustus's strategy for ruling Rome.
- Treatment of Marcus Aurelius is expanded.
- Discussion of the political influence of the Roman military has been expanded.

Chapter 7
- A new "key question" examines the limits of religious freedom.
- Expanded discussion is provided of the status of women.
- Coverage of Byzantium and Islam has been increased.

Chapter 8
- A new "key question" focuses on the transmission of classical culture to medieval Europe.
- Increased coverage is offered of the Benedictines.
- Expanded discussion is provided of the manorial economy and agricultural innovations.

Chapter 9
- Updated discussion is provided of the concept of feudalism.

Chapter 10
- A new "key question" examines the ability of societies to confront change.
- Increased coverage is offered of religious heresies.
- Discussion of the artistic movements of the High Middle Ages is increased.

Chapter 11
- Expanded discussion is provided of medieval philosophers.
- Improved coverage is provided of military developments.
- More material is given on the Avignonese papacy and the resolution of the Great Schism.

Chapter 12
- Increased coverage is provided of the motives behind European exploration.
- Enhanced discussion is offered of the impact of European colonization.
- Updated analysis is given of the Ottoman Empire.

Chapter 13
- A new "key question" explores the rationales for war.
- Coverage of the Reformation has been increased.
- Increased coverage is given of the English Civil War.

Chapter 17
- Expanded analysis is provided of the French and American Revolutions.

Chapter 18
- To improve the narrative flow, Chapter 18 (formerly Chapter 19) examines industry and society in nineteenth-century Europe, while Chapter 19 (formerly Chapter 18) examines political, intellectual, and artistic developments during this same period.

Chapter 19
- Expanded discussion is offered of Marx and Engels.

Chapter 21
- Expanded discussion is offered of scientific racism.

Chapter 23
- Improved coverage of the Spanish Civil War and expanded treatment of Nazi theories of racism is provided.

Chapter 25
- Now entitled "Decolonization and the Cold War," this significantly revised chapter devotes more coverage to the end of European empire. It also includes a new section on domestic life in Western Europe after the war, with a special emphasis on the rise of American-style consumer culture, the rise and fall of the welfare state, and the place of the EU in world politics.

Chapter 26
- Significantly revised, the final chapter includes new consideration of demographic changes in Europe, the consequences of new immigration on Europe's domestic politics, and relations between Islam and the West.

In addition, this second edition of *The West* has been enriched with new maps and illustrations, a substantially revised and expanded "Suggested Readings," and a crisp and elegant full-color design.

Support Materials

The West: A Narrative History comes with an extensive package of support materials for teachers and students.

For Instructors and Students

 MyHistoryLab for *The West* offers instructors and students a state-of-the-art, interactive solution for Western civilization and can form the basis for administering an online course.

Features of MyHistoryLab

Instructor Resources
- Textual documents from the Primary Source DVD
- Images and captions from the Primary Source DVD in PowerPoint presentations
- Lecture Outline PowerPoint presentations
- Classroom-response system PowerPoint questions for *The West*
- Animations
- Maps from the text in PDF format
- Map Outlines
- The Prentice Hall Atlas of World History in PDF format
- Test-Item File

Student Resources
- Complete ebook for *The West*
- Chapter pretests
- Personalized study plans, which include review material for items missed on the pretests
- Flash cards of key terms
- "How to Read Primary Source" interactive tutorial

MyHistoryLab is available via an access code. Contact your Pearson/Prentice Hall representative for details or visit www.myhistorylab.com.

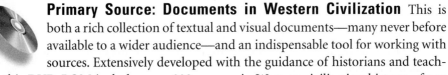

Primary Source: Documents in Western Civilization This is both a rich collection of textual and visual documents—many never before available to a wider audience—and an indispensable tool for working with sources. Extensively developed with the guidance of historians and teachers, this DVD-ROM includes over 800 sources in Western civilization history—from cave art, to text documents, to satellite images of Earth from space. All sources are accompanied by headnotes and focus questions, and are searchable by topic, region, or theme. In addition, a built-in tutorial guides students through the process of working with documents. Please refer to the back of the book for a complete listing of sources. The DVD can be bundled with *The West* at no charge. Please contact your Pearson representative for ordering information.

An abridged two-volume print version of *Primary Source: Documents in Western Civilization* is also available. Please contact your Pearson representative for more information or to receive an examination copy.

For Instructors

- **Instructor's Resource Manual and Test-Item File**

This supplement provides chapter outlines, detailed chapter overviews, discussion questions, lecture strategies, and essay topics. The test-item file contains over 1,200 multiple-choice, true-false, map, and essay questions, organized by chapter.

- **Test Manager**

This is a computerized test management program for Windows and MacIntosh environments. The program allows instructors to select items from the test-item file to create tests. It also allows for online testing.

- **Instructor's Resource Center (www.prenhall.com)**

Text-specific materials, such as the Instructor's Manual, the test-item file, PDF files of all the maps from *The West*, and PowerPoint™ presentations, are available for downloading by adopters.

For Students

- **CourseSmart Textbooks Online.**

This is an exciting new choice for students looking to save money. As an alternative to purchasing the print textbook, students can subscribe to the same content online and save up to 50% off the suggested list price of the print text. With a CourseSmart eTextbook, students can search the text, make notes online, print out reading assignments that incorporate lecture notes, and bookmark important passages for later review. For more information, or to subscribe to the CourseSmart eTextbook, visit www.coursesmart.com.

- **Study Guide (Volumes One and Two).**

The study guide provides students with chapter outlines, map questions, and practice tests.

 • **The Prentice Hall Atlas of Western Civilization, Second Edition.**

This popular atlas includes over 100 full-color maps, drawn by Dorling Kindersley, one of the world's most respected cartographic publishers. Copies of the Atlas can be bundled with *The West* for a nominal charge. Contact your Pearson sales representative for details.

- ***Lives and Legacies: Biographies in Western Civilization,* Second Edition.**

Extensively revised, *Lives and Legacies* includes brief, focused biographies of 60 individuals whose lives provide insight into the key developments of Western civilization. Each biography includes an introduction, prereading questions, and suggestions for additional reading.

Titles from the renowned **Penguin Classics** series can be bundled with *The West* for a nominal charge. Please contact your Pearson Arts and Sciences sales representative for details.

Acknowledgments

The only names that appear prominently on books are those of their authors. However, all books—particularly textbooks—are communal projects to which many people contribute their skills and expertise. The authors wish to acknowledge the debt they owe to all who have assisted them in bringing this project to completion, particularly the following individuals. Charles Cavaliere, executive editor at Pearson/Prentice Hall, sponsored this edition of the text and assumed the added responsibility of serving as its developmental editor. He deserves credit for many aspects of its design, its special features, and its supplements. Special thanks is owed to Jonathan S. Perry of the University of South Florida for the detailed reviews that guided the revision of Volume One, and John M. Cox of Florida Gulf Coast University, who provided major assistance with the preparation of Volume Two. Guy Ruggiero of Pristine Graphics redesigned and redrafted the maps. Credit for the book's attractive appearance belongs to Maria Lange, senior art director. Lauren Aylward, editorial assistant, took on many daunting assignments with grace and aplomb, while production editors Heather Willison and Marianne Peters-Riordan brought all the strands together to create the volume you hold in your hands.

A useful, accurate textbook owes much to the scholars who agree to review its contents from the perspective of their fields of specialization. Their willingness to take time from their own research and writing to enhance the value and utility of a textbook is a service to their profession that rarely receives the acknowledgment that it deserves. Their contributions to this project are hardly repaid by this brief expression of gratitude:

Stephen J. Andrews, *Central New Mexico Community College*

Thomas Behr, *University of Houston*

Beverly Blois, *Northern Virginia Community College*

April Brooks, *South Dakota State University*

Gregory Bruess, *University of Northern Iowa*

Laurel Carrington, *St. Olaf College*

Sara Chapman, *Oakland University*

John M. Cox, *Florida Gulf Coast University*

Peter L. DeRosa, *Bridgewater State College*

James Halverson, *Judson College*

Mark Herman, *Edison Community College*

L. Edward Hicks, *Faulkner University*

Charles Hilken, *St. Mary's College of California*

David Hudson, *California State University, Fresno*

Gary J. Johnson, *University of Southern Maine*

Sara L. Kimble, *University of Northern Iowa*

Christine J. Kooi, *Louisiana State University*

Jennifer M. Lloyd, *State University of New York at Brockport*

John W. Monroe, *Iowa State University*

Sean Moran, *Oakland University*

Michael G. Paul, *University of South Florida*

Jonathan S. Perry, *University of South Florida*

Mary Pickering, *San Jose State University*

Stuart Semmel, *University of Delaware*

Larissa J. Taylor, *Colby College*

William B. Whisenhunt, *College of DuPage*

Andrew D. Wilson, *Keene State College*

Photo Credits

Part 1: 2: NASA

Chapter 1: 5: "Ram in the Thicket." Ascension #30-12-702. University of Pennsylvania Museum Neg. #T4-1000; 8: Ministere de la Culture et de la Communication. Direction Regionale des affaires Culturelles de Rhone–Alpes. Service Regional de l'Archeologie; 10: Wieslav Smetek/Stern/Stock Photo/Black Star; 19: Brian Delft © Dorling Kindersley; 22: SCALA/Art Resource, N.Y.; 27: King Menkaure (Mycerinus) and Queen. Egyptian, Old Kingdom, Dynasty 4. Reign of Menkaure, about 2490–2472 B.C. Egypt, Giza, Menkaure Valley Temple. Greywacke. 142.2 × 57.1 × 56.2 cm (56″ × 22 1/2″ × 21 3/4″). Harvard University–Boston Museum of Fine Arts

Chapter 2: 33: © Cindy Miller Hopkins/ DanitaDelimont.com; 36: Stele of the Law Code of Hammurabi, from Susa (modern Shush, Iran). c. 1792–1750 B.C.E. Basalt, height of stele appx. 7″ (2.13 m), height of relief 28″ (71.1 cm). Musee du Louvre, Paris. RMN/Reunion des Musees Natioaux/ Art Resource, NY; 39: Petera A. Clayton; 41: ANCIENT ART & ARCHITECTURE/DanitaDelimont.com; 42: Getty Images/De Agostini Editore Picture Library; 48: Courtesy of the Library of Congress

Part 2: 60: Erich Lessing/Art Resource, N.Y.

Chapter 3: 63: Prentice Hall School Division; 67: Gianni Dagli Orti/Corbis/Bettmann; 69: Studio Kontos Photostock; 74: Nick Nicholls © The British Museum; 77: © ANCIENT ART & ARCHITECTURE/ DanitaDelimont.com; 86: Getty Images/De Agostini Editore Picture Library

Chapter 4: 91: Nigel Hicks © Dorling Kindersley; 94: With permission of the Royal Ontario Museum © ROM; 96: © ANCIENT ART & ARCHITECTURE/ DanitaDelimont.com; 104: National Archaeological Museum, Athens, Greece/The Bridgeman Art Library; 111: Getty Images/De Agostini Editore Picture Library; 113: Stokstad, Marilyn, "Art History Digital Image CD-ROM," 2002. Reprinted by permission of Pearson Education, Inc., Upper Saddle River, New Jersey

Chapter 5: 119: Nike of Samothrace. 3rd–2nd BCE. Hellenistic marble statue. H.: 328 cm. Inv.: 2369. Musee du Louvre/RMN Reunion des Musees Nationaux, France. SCALA/Art Resource, NY; 124: © ANCIENT ART & ARCHITECTURE / DanitaDelimont.com; 127: Vatican Museums and Galleries, Vatican City, Italy/The Bridgeman Art Library; 132: Sarcophagus of a married couple on a funeral bed. Etruscan, from Cerveteri, 6th B.C.E. Terracotta. Lewandowski/Ojeda. Musee Louvre, Paris France. RMN Reunion Des Musees Nationeaux/Art

Resource, NY; 140: Alinari/Art Resource, N.Y.; 143: Getty Images/De Agostini Editore Picture Library

Chapter 6: 149: Dagli Orti/Picture Desk, Inc./Kobal Collection; 151: Getty Images/De Agostini Editore Picture Library; 158: Ara Pacis Augustae, Rome/ Canali PhotoBank, Milan/SuperStock; 163: Getty Images/De Agostini Editore Picture Library; 164: Roger Ressmeyer/CORBIS; 172: Eric Lessing/ Art Resource, N.Y.

Part 3: 178: Moors and Christians play chess, altarpiece of San Nicolas, 14th c. Mallorca Spain. © Ancient Art and Architecture Collection, Ltd.;

Chapter 7: 181: Peter Scholey/Robert Harding World Imagery; 187: Araldo de Luca Archives/Index Ricerca Iconografica; 194: Walter. B. Denny; 196: San Vitale, Ravenna, Italy/Canali Photobank; 200: Kazuyoshi Nomachi/Photo Researchers, Inc.; 204: © Eddi Boehnke/zefa/CORBIS. All Rights Reserved

Chapter 8: 209: Musee du Louvre/RMN Reunion des Musees Nationaux, France. SCALA/Art Resource, NY; 215: The Board of Trinity College, Dublin/ The Bridgeman Art Library International; 216: Snark/ Art Resource, N.Y.; 222: Achim Bednorz; 224: Frits Solvang © Dorling Kindersley, Courtesy of the Universitetets kulturhistoriske museer/ Vikingskipshuset; 233: © Gianni Dagli Orti / CORBIS. All Rights Reserved

Chapter 9: 237: Robert Fried/robertfriedphotography. com; 241: Le Tresor de L'Abbaye de Saint-Maurice, France/The Bridgeman Art Library; 252: "The Emperor Otto I (912–73) Presenting a Model of His Church at Magdeburg to the Enthroned Christ in the Presence of Saints Peter and Mauritius (?) and Other Saints." One of a series of 17 ivory plaques known as the Magdeburg Ivories, possibly carved in Milan c. 962–68. Ivory, 5″ × 4 1/2″ (12.7 × 11.4 cm). The Metropolitan Museum of Art, NY. Bequest of George Blumenthal, 1941 (41.100.157). Phoograph ©1986 The Metropolitan Museum of Art; 257: Bibliotheque Cantonale, St. Gallen, Switzerland/The Bridgeman Art Library; 258: Getty Images/De Agostini Editore Picture Library; 263: Jonathan Blair/Woodfin Camp & Associates, Inc.

Chapter 10: 267: Sonia Halliday Photographs; 273: National Library, St. Petersburg, Russia/The Bridgeman Art Library; 276: Lebrecht Music & Arts/Lebrecht Music & Arts Photo Library; 279: Canali PhotoBank, Milan/SuperStock, Inc.; 281: SCALA/Art Resource, N.Y.; 282: © Achim Bednorz, Koln; 287: WILLIAM OSBORN/Nature Picture Library

Part 4: 292: Dagli Orti (A)/Picture Desk, Inc./Kobal Collection

Chapter 11: 295: Snark/Art Resource, N.Y.; 299: Canali Photobank; 306: Dagli Orti/ Picture Desk, Inc./Kobal

Collection; **310:** Dagli Orti/ Picture Desk, Inc./Kobal Collection; **316:** Dorling Kindersley Media Library; **318:** Marc Charmet/Picture Desk, Inc./Kobal Collection
Chapter 12: 323: John Heseltine © Dorling Kindersley; **333:** Bargello National Museum, Florence/Canali PhotoBank, Milan/SuperStock.; **334:** Dagli Orti (A)/ Picture Desk, Inc./Kobal Collection; **335:** Getty Images/De Agostini Editore Picture Library; **336:** Piero della Francesca (c. 1420–1492). Italian (Piero della Francesca?). View of an Ideal City. Galleria Nazionale delle Marche, Urbino, Italy. Photo credit: Scala/Art Resource, NY; **343:** © National Gallery Collection; By kind permission of the Trustees of the National Gallery, London/CORBIS; **349:** Courtesy of the Library of Congress
Chapter 13: 355: Getty Images/De Agostini Editore Picture Library; **362:** Erich Lessing/ Art Resource, N.Y.; **374:** Adam Wollfitt/ Robert Harding World Imagery; **376:** Hilliard Nicholas, Victoria & Albert Museum, London UK/The Bridgeman Art Library; **378:** Stock Montage, Inc./Historical Pictures Collection; **384:** Vatican Museums and Galleries, Vatican City, Italy/The Bridgeman Art Library
Chapter 14: 391: Royal Naval College, Greenwich, London, UK/The Bridgeman Art Library; **394:** Erich Lessing/Art Resource, NY; **398:** Lebrecht Music & Arts 2/Lebrecht Music & Arts Photo Library; **400:** Rigaud, Hyacinthe (1659–1743). Louis XIV, King of France (1638–1715) in royal costume. 1701. Oil on canvas, 277 × 194 cm. Louvre, Paris, France. Photo credit: Erich Lessing/Art Resource, NY.; **401:** Pierre Patel (1605–1676), "Birds Eye View of Versailles." Chateau de Versailles et de Trianon, Versailles, France. Copyright Giraudon/Art Resource, NY; **407:** Fur traders and Indians: engraving, 1777. c. The Granger Collection, New York; **409:** Library of Congress
Chapter 15: 419: Courtesy of the Library of Congress; **425:** The Granger Collection; **426:** Justus Sustermans (1597–1681), "Portrait of Galileo Galilei." Galleria Palatina, Palazzo Pitti, Florence, Italy. Nimatallah/Art Resource, NY; **427:** Sir Godfrey Kneller, Sir Isaac Newton, 1702. Oil on canvas. The Granger Collection; **428:** Rare Books Division, Special Collections, J. Willard Marriott Library, University of Utah; **431:** Rembrandt van Rijn (1606–1669). "The Anatomy Lesson of Dr. Tulp." Mauritshuis, The Hague, The Netherlands. SCALA/Art Resource, NY; **435:** The Granger Collection; **437:** "Three witches burned alive from a German Broaside," circa 1555. Courtesy of Stock Montage, Inc.
Chapter 16: 441: Monticello/Thomas Jefferson Foundation, Inc.; **445:** Nicolas de Largilliere. Portrait of Voltaire at age 23, bust length, 1728. Private Collection, Paris. Bridgeman-Giraudon/Art Resource, NY; **447:** Photo: AKG London, Gabriel Lemonnier, 1743–1824. "A Soiree with Mme Geoffrin" (with:

d'Alembert, Montesquieu, Diderot, Malherbes, Turgot, Rameau, Reaumur, Vanloo, Vernet). Painting. Malmaison, Castle; **449:** Herzog August Bibliothek, Wolfenbuttel, Germany/The Bridgeman Art Library; **451:** Sovfoto/Eastfoto; **452:** The Granger Collection, New York; **453:** Dagli Orti/Picture Desk, Inc./Kobal Collection; **456:** Musee de la Ville de Paris, Musee Carnavalet, Paris, France/The Bridgeman Art Library; **460:** Jacques-Louis David, "The Oath of the Horatii." 1784. Oil on Canvas. 10′10″ × 13′11″ (3.3 × 4.25 m). Musee du Louvre, Paris. RMN Reunion des Musees Nationaux/Art Resource, NY
Chapter 17: 463: Marquis de Lafayette by Francesco-Guiseppe Casanova, ca. 1781–85, oil on canvas, 18.5 × 16.5 in., accession 1939.9. Collection of The New-York Historical Society; **467:** The Boston Massacre, 5 March 1770: colored engraving, 1770, by Paul Revere after the drawing by Henry Pelham.The Granger Collection, New York; **472:** Courtesy of the Library of Congress; **473:** Getty Images Inc.—Hulton Archive Photos; **476:** © Bettmann/CORBIS; **477:** Giraudon/Musees Royaux des Beaux-Arts de Belgique, Brussels/Art Resource, NY; **479:** Private Collection/The Bridgeman Art Library; **481:** Jacques Louis David (1748–1825), "Consecration of the Emperor Napoleon I and Coronation of Empress Josephine," 1806–07. Louvre, Paris. Bridgeman-Giraudon/Art Resource, NY; **485:** Library of Congress
Part 6: 490: Gustave Caillebotte (French 1848–1894), "Paris Street: Rainy Day". 1877. Oil on Canvas. 83 1/2″ × 108 3/4″ (212.2 × 276.2 cm). Charles H. and Mary F.S. Worcester Collection, 1964.336. Photograph © 2006, The Art Institute of Chicago. All Rights Reserved.
Chapter 18: 493: Getty Images Inc.—Hulton Archive Photos; **498:** Walker Art Gallery, National Museums Liverpool/The Bridgeman Art Library; **500:** Chicago Historical Museum; **502:** The Granger Collection; **504:** Honore Daumier, French, (1808–79). The Third Class Carriage, Oil on Canvas, H 25.75 × 35.5″ (65.4 × 90.2 cm). The Metropolitan Museum of Art, Bequest of Mrs. H.O. Havemeyer Collection, 1929, (29.100.129). Photograph © 1992 The Metropolitan Museum of Art, Art Resource, NY; **509:** © Historical Picture Archive/CORBIS; **510:** Marc Charmet/Picture Desk, Inc./Kobal Collection; **512:** The Granger Collection, New York; **514:** Getty Images Inc.—Hulton Archive Photos
Chapter 19: 519: Museo Nacional Centro de Arte Reina Sofia; **526:** Eugene Delacroix (1798–1863), "Liberty Leading the People." July 28, 1830. Painted 1830. Oil on canvas, 260 × 325 cm. Photo: Hervé Lewandowski. Musée du Louvre/RMN Reunion des Musées Nationaux, France. SCALA/Art Resource, NY; **531:** Portrait of Giuseppe Garibaldi (1807–82) (b/w photo), Italian School, (19th century) Private Collection, Alinari /The Bridgeman Art Library;

Note on Dates and Spelling

Dates

Human beings struggle to orient themselves in a featureless sea of time. For much of their history the heavens have served as their primary clock. The Hebrew Bible claims that the Creator placed two "lights" in the sky, one to govern the day and the other the night. This sounds simpler than it turns out to be in practice, for the two lights divide time into cycles that are difficult to coordinate. Earth's journey around the Sun, which determined the annual revolution of the seasons, took 365.2424 days. The moon's revolution about Earth took 29.53059 days. A year could be divided approximately into 12 months by charting the waxing and waning of the moon—but only very approximately. The lunar year passed weeks faster than its solar partner; therefore, months originally associated with one season gradually drifted into another.

As ancient peoples improved accuracy in measuring the movements of the heavenly bodies, they devised a variety of increasingly sophisticated methods for computing calendars that better coordinated months and seasons. The Egyptians favored a year divided into 12 equal, 30-day-long months to which they annually added 5 days to complete the year. This still fell about 6 hours short of the actual length of the solar year, and as the centuries passed, those 6 hours accumulated, causing months gradually to slide from one season to another. The Babylonians devised a calendar based on cycles of 19 years—a combination of 7 years of 13 months and 12 years of 12 months. This was close, but still short enough to fall behind by several weeks each century. Julius Caesar drew on the best astronomical information of his day to decree a year of 12 months (some 30 and others 31 days long) with an additional "leap" day added every 4 years. This Julian Calendar was an improvement, but there was still a small discrepancy that eventually made a noticeable difference. In 1582 Pope Gregory XIII ordered a leap of 11 days (declaring that the day after October 4 be October 15) to synchronize months and seasons and added another refinement to calendar calculations. In the Gregorian calendar, leap years were to occur every four years but be omitted for years that marked centuries divisible by 400 (e.g., 2000). This, the calendar most widely in use today, is still several seconds out of sync with the Earth's orbit about the sun.

Not only did ancient calendars differ on how to calculate months and supplemental days, there was also no consensus on when a year began. The cycle of seasons disposed people to look on Spring, the season of rebirth, as the appropriate time to declare a new start. Therefore, in the northern hemisphere, March was often favored as the first month of the year. A memory of this survives in the names still used for some months: September, October, November, December—7th, 8th, 9th and 10th months (counting from March). About a century and a half before the birth of Christ the Romans decided to begin their year on January 1, the date on which their chief executives, the consuls), took office. The custom lapsed in many places during the Middle Ages and did not begin to win general acceptance until about 300 years ago.

The lack of a universal standard for measuring years and of agreement on when the year began made life difficult for ancient record keepers. A common strategy for keeping track of things was to associate an event with some memorable person or unusual development. For example: "This happened in the 8th year of the reign of King Sed, 17 years after the great famine." Greeks and Romans sometimes created "eponymous" offices and named each year for the person who held that office that year. For example: "In the year of the *praetor maximus* Livius Aurelianus." This system required public records offices to keep long and growing lists of names.

The modern way to chart a path through time is to choose a fixed point from which to count the sequence of years. The Jewish calendar begins with the date of the Creation of the world—calculated from information provided by the genealogies recorded in the Hebrew Scriptures. The Muslim calendar begins with an event in the Prophet Muhammad's life, an act that marked the birth of the *umma*, the community of Islam. As Christianity acquired status as the dominant faith of the region that had been the Roman Empire, the birth of Christ gained appeal as the pivot point of history. Dionysius Exiguous (c. 500–560) is said to be the first scholar to propose dating events from what he assumed (erroneously) to be the year in which Jesus of Nazareth was born. About a century and a half later, his system was popularized by the best historian of the day, an English monk named Bede (672–735), as a method for dating events both before and after Jesus' birth. This led to the custom of designating years as either B.C. ("before Christ") or A.D. (*anno Domini*, "in the year of the Lord")—e.g., "457 B.C." (457 years "before Christ") or A.D. 457 ("in the year of the Lord 457"). Writers today, who wish to be sensitive to the fact that not all their readers may share the Christian faith, use B.C.E. and C.E., which can be read as "Before the Common [or Christian] Era" and the "Common [or Christian] Era."

These dating conventions mean that years are counted down from the most remote eras to the birth of Christ and up to the present time from the birth of Christ. Thus in the pre-Christian or Common Era events become more recent as numbers grow smaller (i.e., 132 B.C.E. is earlier than 32 B.C.E.) and post-Christian events become more recent as numbers grow larger (i.e., 32 C.E. is earlier than 132 C.E.). Counting back from the birth of Christ, the 3rd century B.C.E. would begin in 201 and end in 300 (i.e., the 3rd century B.C.E. is the 200s). Counting forward from the birth of Christ, the 12th century would begin in 1101 and end in 1200 (i.e., the 1100s).

Spelling

Human beings are capable of making a wide range of sounds, and they have used their extensive vocalization skills to construct a myriad of different languages. Some are fairly monotone. Others are almost musical, using differences in pitch to indicate meanings. Some favor soft, mellifluous tones, while others emphasize harsher sounds. There are even languages that employ percussive, clicking noises that non-native speakers may find impossible to reproduce.

Writing systems invent symbols to represent the sounds of speech. Because not all languages use the same sounds, however, it can be difficult to write a language using a symbol system that has been developed for a different kind of speech. Letters may have to be combined in odd ways to suggest unique sounds (e.g., "kw"), "diacritical" marks may be added to indicate how a sound should be made (e.g., á, ä, or â), or entirely new symbols may have to be invented to supplement those that are normally sufficient. An added complication derives from the fact that a number of ancient languages were written only with consonants. Readers were expected to infer vowel sounds for themselves from context. A modern scholar who wishes to translate (and transliterate) these languages for English readers must make an educated guess as to what the sounds originally intended may have been. For instance, the seventeenth-century English translators of the Bible thought that the Hebrew consonants for God's name should be supplied with vowels and read as "Jehovah," but modern scholars generally prefer "Yahweh." The two English words render the same word in Hebrew, but they do not look much alike.

Linguists have devised sophisticated rules to promote consistency in moving from one writing system to another, but different traditions and customs have prevailed at different times and in different academic environments. For instance, because "c" in English can be pronounced like "s" or "k," a Greek name that begins with a hard consonant (kappa) might be spelled with either a "c" or a "k." British scholars might prefer one spelling of the name while Americans choose another. Classicists may favor one and historians another. Students must, therefore, be prepared to be flexible when they confront variant spellings in different texts.

About the Authors

A. Daniel Frankforter is Professor of History at the Pennsylvania State University, where he has taught for nearly four decades. His undergraduate work was in the history of ideas and philosophy at Franklin and Marshall College. He earned a Master of Divinity degree from Drew University, did graduate work at Columbia University and the University of Göttingen, and completed master's and doctoral degrees in medieval history and religious studies at Penn State. His research has focused on the medieval English Church and on the evolving role of European women throughout the medieval period. His articles on these topics have appeared in such journals as *Manuscripta*, *Church History*, *The British Studies Monitor*, *The Catholic Historical Review*, *The American Benedictine Review*, *The International Journal of Women's Studies*, and *The Journal of Women's History*. His books include *A History of the Christian Movement: An Essay on the Development of Christian Institutions*, *Civilization and Survival*, *The Shakespeare Name Dictionary* (with J. Madison Davis), *The Medieval Millennium: An Introduction*, *The Western Heritage*, brief edition (with Donald Kagan, Stephen Ozment, and Frank Turner), *The Heritage of World Civilizations*, brief third edition (with Albert Craig, William Graham, Donald Kagan, Stephen Ozment, and Frank Turner), an edition and translation of Poullain de la Barre's *De L'Égalité des deux Sexes*, and *Stones for Bread: A Critique of Contemporary Worship*. Over the course of his career he has developed 15 courses dealing with aspects of the ancient and medieval periods of Western civilization, Judeo-Christian studies, and gender issues. His work in the classroom has been acknowledged by the Penn State Behrend Excellence in Teaching Award and the prestigious Amoco Foundation Award for Excellence in Teaching Performance.

William M. Spellman is the Dean of Humanities at the University of North Carolina, Asheville. He is a graduate of Suffolk University, Boston, and holds a PhD from the Maxwell School of Citizenship and Public Affairs at Syracuse University. He is the author of *John Locke and the Problem of Depravity* (Oxford, 1988); *The Latitudinarians and the Church of England, 1660–1700* (Georgia, 1993); *John Locke* (Macmillan, 1995); *European Political Thought, 1600–1700* (Macmillan, 1997); *Monarchies, 1000–2000* (Reaktion Press, 2000); *Extraordinary Women of the Medieval and Renaissance World* (Greenwood Press, 2000); co-authored with Carole Levin et al.; *The Global Community: Migration and the Making of the Modern World, 1500–2000* (Sutton, 2002); *A Concise History of the World Since 1945* (Palgrave, 2006); and *Migration and the Nation State* (Reaktion Press, forthcoming).

Introduction

The Nature of History

History is not a natural phenomenon—something like gravity or the cycle of a plant's life. People "make" history in two ways: (1) by their actions in the present, and (2) by what they think about the past. Without the former, of course, there would be no past for historians to study. However, the present is also important to historians, not only because it becomes the past, but because it influences how they view the past. Each of us comes into a world that we did not make, and each of us is forced to live in circumstances that we, as individuals, cannot entirely control. A desire to understand the foreordained conditions that provide the context for our lives is often what makes us curious about the past. We want to know the origins of the problems, institutions, and values that are important to us—and even when we study remote eras or cultures that have no immediate or obvious ties with our own, we tend to interpret them in light of our concerns, assumptions, and experiences.

Before people become engaged in the study of history, they sometimes assume that history is a straightforward, objective narrative of dates, facts, and figures—and that, like most things that leave little room for imagination and intuition, it is "cut and (literally) dried." History can, of course, be badly written and taught so as to meet the lowest of expectations. But because historians write about the past from the perspective of the present, their work often stirs up strong feelings and invites controversy. It has a personal dimension for both its writers and its readers. Curiosity about ourselves plays a role in determining the books we choose to read or the topics we are drawn to research. We may identify ourselves and our issues with figures and events from the past and sit in judgment on what previous generations thought and did. Even the most rigorous scientists cannot entirely escape viewing the world through lenses shaped by their educations and life experiences.

The influence of the present on perceptions of the past makes any given historian's work a source of information on two sometimes widely separated eras—the one about which the historian writes and the one the historian writes in. For example: Edward Gibbon's *The Decline and Fall of the Roman Empire* is one of the most famous (if not one of the most read) works by an English historian. This immensely detailed description of Rome's decline rests on a mountain of evidence that Gibbon mined from the physical and literary remains of the ancient world. But it is also thoroughly imbued with the intellectual assumptions of Gibbon's own eighteenth century, Europe's "Age of Enlightenment." Gibbon ended his long narrative with a short and succinct summary of its conclusions: "In the preceding volumes of this History I have described the triumph of barbarism and religion. . . ."[1] Most European intellectuals of Gibbon's generation believed that reason

---

[1]Edward Gibbon, *The Decline and Fall of the Roman Empire,* vol. II (Chicago: Encyclopedia Britannica, Inc., 1952), p. 592.

held the key to understanding and solving all of humanity's problems and that rational thinking would inevitably spread—promoting knowledge of science and sweeping away every trace of supernaturalism. Rome, Gibbon argued, had been brought down by the opposite trend. It fell victim to the growth and convergence of two kinds of irrationality, ignorance and superstition—by which Gibbon meant German barbarism and the Christian religion, respectively.

Gibbon's argument appeared convincing at the time, and his study seemed destined to become the last word on its subject. But a century later the story of Rome's fall looked quite different to Russian-born and educated historian Michael Ivanovich Rostovtzeff (1870–1952). He lived at a time when the theories of Karl Marx had great influence. Marx believed that economic activities and class struggles were the engines that drove historical evolution, and in mid-life Rostovtzeff had witnessed an event that seemed to support Marx's theses. A popular revolution overthrew Russia's inept tsar and aristocracy and established a classless, but brutally oppressive, society in the historian's homeland. Something similar, Rostovtzeff believed, was what had destroyed first the Roman Republic and then the Roman Empire. He wrote:

> So long as Rome was fighting for pre-eminence in the ancient world, the division of classes within the state remained in the background or at least did not cause bloodshed. As soon, however, as she became mistress of the world, the power of 'the best men', the *optimates* or aristocracy, was assailed by the citizens in general. . . . [W]hen the empire was forced, after nearly two centuries of peace and tranquillity, to defend itself against enemies from without[, the] time called for a great display of enthusiasm. But the rich could not be roused from their indifference; and the poor, seeing the helplessness and weakness of their betters, and deprived of all share in their idle and indolent contentment, were filled with hatred and envy. [2]

The reasons Rostovtzeff gives for Rome's fall in the fifth century might serve almost as well as an explanation for the decline of tzarist Russia in the early twentieth. The fact that what seems important to historians in their own day often looms large in their view of the past does not mean that historians have no objectivity and simply write themselves into their narratives. It does, however, help us understand why history is never definitively written, but is always in the process of being rewritten. As time passes, newly evolving social contexts create new perspectives from which to view the past, and new perspectives suggest new ways of framing questions. Because people tend to see what they look for and ignore things they do not value, new questions prompt new discoveries. The modern feminist movement illustrates this dynamic. For centuries historians thought they could adequately explain the past by focusing only on the activities of men—and usually only a very few "great men." By demonstrating the importance of women to contemporary societies, feminism alerted historians to the necessity of understanding their activities in earlier periods. If the present could not adequately be understood without examining the

---

[2]Michael Rostovtzeff, *Rome* (NY: Oxford U. Press, 1960), pp. 321 & 323.

roles of women, neither could the past. This realization has resulted in the discovery of information that has caused many narratives to be rewritten.

The involvements, commitments, and loyalties that individuals embrace as fundamental to their identities can make them passionate about the past. They may, for instance, come to resent injustices that have been done to a specific category of people and write history to vindicate the importance of that group—to reveal its previously ignored contributions and to accord it what they regard as its due dignity. An Irish-American author, who is proud of his lineage, writes a book to explain *How the Irish Saved Civilization* (Thomas Cahill, 1995). Or an advocate for the peoples of the "developing world" writes to correct what he regards as a deliberate effort to conceal their historical significance (Martin Bernal, *Black Athena: The Afroasiatic Roots of Classical Civilization*, 1987). Advocacy for a cause is not necessarily bad. But if passions run too high, a historical inquiry can become an inquisition. Much history has been written to justify or convict, to claim credit for or to blame, to vindicate or to indict one party or another. It is up to its readers to decide how useful (or entertaining) this is, and it should not be allowed to get in the way of the primary reason for studying history: to understand.

The Divisions of History

Attempts are made to grasp human history as a whole, but broadly generalized surveys rest on a myriad of narrowly focused studies. There are political histories, gender histories, economic histories, intellectual histories, national histories, and numerous other kinds of approaches to the past. Different scholars have different preferences and vigorously debate the merits of different ways to develop narratives about the past.

One of the hottest arguments raging today concerns the legitimacy or usefulness of focusing attention specifically on a field defined as Western civilization. Many scholars believe that this implicitly continues a tradition of historiography that unfairly exalts European societies over the cultures of other peoples. And the current international political climate has made arguments about Western civilization especially intense. Hatred of "the West" (the European and American so-called "first world") is emerging as the major political problem of the twenty-first century. It has motivated appalling acts of terrorism and prompted a violent reaction—a "war on terrorism." The world—especially the academic world—seems increasingly to be divided between extreme critics (e.g., post-colonialists and post-modernists) and extreme defenders (e.g., Eurocentrists) of "the West." Each tars the other with a broad brush that makes orderly, fruitful discussion difficult.

The sins alleged to be the legacy of Western civilization are many: colonial exploitation, slavery, sexism, racism, heartless capitalist manipulation, wasteful consumption, and environmental degradation. There is no denying that Europeans, Americans, and their cultural kin have been guilty of these things, but it is less certain that all of these transgressions against humanity are innately or uniquely "western." A kind of racism justified by physical features was uncritically accepted by many eighteenth- and nineteenth-century Europeans, but many societies throughout history have drawn a sharp line between themselves and groups with characteristics (e.g., linguistic, cultural, and physical) that allegedly defined them as inferior "others." Imperialism, slavery, and abuse of women long predate the rise of European powers and can be found in many cultures around the globe. As for capitalism, China may have preceded Europe in its invention, and environmental degradation began with the technologies that supported Earth's first civilizations. What the West may not always get due credit for is its effort to promote the moral sensitivities, the self-critical attitudes, and the rational and scientific discourses that have been used to combat imperialism, slavery, sexism, racism, abusive capitalism, and ecological devastation.

Some students will be surprised to learn that courses in Western civilization are a relatively new idea and that they are an American innovation. They first appeared in the early twentieth century and were designed to lay a common foundation on which to build a coherent college education. Their content and design was profoundly influenced by the political environment of the first half of the twentieth century—particularly the First and Second World Wars. Americans and their European allies fought these bloody struggles in the belief that they were sacrificing themselves to save the world from tyranny. Wars create extreme conditions that can degrade patriotism into chauvinism, and scholars are not immune to their effects. At times Western civilization has been taught in ways that implied that it was the only true civilization—the goal toward which all other peoples should aspire and the standard by which their cultures should be judged. The triumphalism that accompanied this view of the West encouraged the belief that the West was innately superior and self-generating—that it owed little or nothing to inventions and ideas

The arrogance with which some Western nations have dealt with weaker countries is illustrated by this magazine cover from 1911. It asserts that the people of Morocco should yield gratefully to paternalistic dominance by France and the imposition of France's concept of civilized life. Abraham Lincoln's Emancipation Proclamation, however, is an icon for more enlightened behavior by Western powers, which have been in the forefront of movements to end social evils such as slavery.

borrowed from others. Its alleged native genius supposedly gave it a right to world leadership if not world domination.

The study of history is almost inevitably corrupted by the prejudicial assumptions and ethical blind spots of each generation that engages in it. This is certainly true of the ways in which Western civilization has sometimes been studied and taught. But things change, and the heirs of a tradition are free to correct the errors of its founders. Some people believe, however, that the whole enterprise should be abandoned. They insist that the current environment of globalization makes a focus on Western civilization obsolete and that world history should take its place. Others argue, however, that exploration of the world might best begin with an examination of one's own culture. Students at American colleges and universities are—regardless of their more or less distant ethnic backgrounds—products of a society that is still deeply indebted to Europe and the Mediterranean region. Other parts of the globe have made definite contributions to the life of what is largely an immigrant nation, but these influences are integrated with the values and institutions of what has been called, for lack of a better term, "the West."

Many students bring some knowledge of their nation's political and social history to college, but they have had few opportunities to consider that history in a larger context. One approach (and only one) that they might take to broadening their understanding is to situate the American experience in the older European-Mediterranean tradition before beginning to explore that tradition's links with, and indebtedness to, other regions of the world. Study of one's own culture need not inevitably lead back to oneself. It can equip an exploring intellect for the challenge of discovering meaningful patterns within the flux of information that is generated by an increasing complex and ever expanding global community.

Where Is "the West"?

One problem with the study of Western civilization is the slippery nature of the term *west*. It is hard to define or pin down just what historians mean when they speak about "the West." "West" is, after all, a direction, not a place. Dictionaries define it as the opposite of Earth's rotation (the English word *west* derives from a word that means "evening"). This makes "the west" relative to the point of view of the person who watches the sun set. Because this could be a source of confusion for navigators, geographers have arbitrarily fixed a line—the "prime meridian," running north-south through an observatory in Greenwich, England—to separate east from west. Therefore, technically most of the British Isles, a small portion of France, Spain, and a bit of the African continent are in "the west" while the rest of Europe and Africa are in "the east." This meaning of west is not very useful for historians. China, after all, is west of Japan and both these countries are west of the United States, but neither is thought of as part of what most people mean when they speak about "the West."

At first glance it might seem odd that books dealing with Western civilization begin in the Middle East and only slowly work their way across the Mediterranean to Europe and the Atlantic. But west and east are not simply geographical terms. They have always also had cultural implications. The Bible's Book of Genesis begins the human story in a garden that God plants "in the east"—the place where the sun rises being the appropriate symbol for "beginning." Similarly, the west has long been associated with death and ending. For these reasons, graves and places of worship (including medieval Christian churches) have often been oriented to the path of the sun.

The antagonism that developed between Christians and Muslims during the European Middle Ages created a "West" that was Christendom, a region under Christian control. During the sixteenth century, explorers made "the West" the "New World." For nineteenth-century Americans "the West" became a frontier, a wild land to be explored and tamed. During the Cold War of the second half of the twentieth century, "the West" indicated a political alliance—a block of states that opposed the communist east. Most people today think of "the West" as a term for countries that are, or once were, closely linked with those of western Europe. But this is not always an easy identity to determine. "The West" spans the globe, for it includes Europe, the United States, Canada, New Zealand, and Australia. But does it include the Catholic, Spanish- and Portugese-speaking nations of South America? Does it include English-speaking South Africa? Should it include post-communist Russia? Should it include Turkey, a majority Muslim state that has applied for membership in the economic alliance called the European Union? Should it include modern China because China has passionately embraced the "western" ideologies of capitalism and Marxism?

Confusion about the definition of "the West" today is not solely the result of the spread of its civilization. It also reflects the way in which that civilization has come into existence. Culturally speaking, "the West" did not give birth to itself. It is the child of many parents, and it has always existed in the context of diverse cultures exchanging goods and ideas over immense distances. The modern world has been compared to a "global village," but to greater and lesser degrees "the West" has always been part of a global community. It may too rarely acknowledge—or even realize—its debts to other civilizations, and at times it has drawn sharp distinctions between itself and cultures it viewed as "other" (and, by implication, inferior). But it has usually remained open to change and to learning from those with whom it comes in contact.

What Is Civilization?

If the definition of western creates problems for courses in Western civilization, so does the definition of civilization. The word's Latin root (*civis*) means "citizen," the resident of a city (*civitas*), and the common assumption is that urban institutions are central to civilizations. Civilizations are also said to be characterized by bureaucratic governments, stratified social systems, long-distance trade, and specialized technologies such as metal working and writing. Descriptions of this kind are, however, not very informative, for they merely assert that civilization appears when people begin to do what are thought of as civilized things. They do not explain what makes a behavior civilized, and the lists of civilized behaviors they propose are not definitive. This approach to defining civilization also begs the question of which and how many civilized attributes a people must manifest in order to be considered civilized. The Inca of ancient Peru, for example, had urban institutions, monumental architecture, and metal working, but no writing system. Did the absence of literacy mean they were not civilized?

Civilization is a tricky term, for its use sometimes implies a judgment about a society. There are ethical and aesthetic dimensions to civilized living. Despite romantic myths about "noble savages," people who live civilized lifestyles have often been regarded (or have regarded themselves) as superior to people who have not made the kind of progress that civilization supposedly represents. Not to be civilized is to be primitive, backward, and even barbaric—all emotionally charged descriptors.

Cultural relativists challenge the assumption that one society can legitimately be judged by the standards of another. They particularly object to the long tradition of historical writing that assumes the superiority of "western" (European-based) civilization, but it seems unduly contentious to question the value of civilization itself. The humane values articulated by great thinkers from many of the world's civilizations would seem to provide a scorecard by which all societies can justly be evaluated. If torture, slavery, human sacrifice, and cannibalism are authentic, indigenous practices of a society, does that make them acceptable—or do there seem to be ethical lines that no humane person should cross? There are, of course, costs to civilization that have to be weighed against its benefits, and a painful gap often yawns between the problems that civilization causes and the technologies it invents to deal with its effects. Civilization also offers no surefire way to prevent people from behaving barbarously, and it has in fact often helped human beings magnify their inhumanity.

Arguments about the relative merits of "high civilizations" versus "simple cultures" might benefit from contemplating what both forms of social organization have in common. They are best understood not as opposing conditions, but points on a continuum. Civilization is simply an elaborate form of the cultural behavior that is an innate characteristic of human beings and (to a lesser degree) the higher primates. The goal of that behavior is the preservation and enhancement of life. How that goal is best achieved depends very much on the context in which a population operates. The best outcome for the global community may not be to impose one way of life or set of institutions on everyone, but to find a way to reconcile diversity with a set of universal human values.

The West

Part 1
Departure
Prehistory to 1000 B.C.E.

The Earth from Space.

During the last half of the twentieth century, technology gave Earth's inhabitants their first opportunity to literally step back and view their home world in its totality. What they saw might prove to be the universe's rarest treasure: a planet that sustains a complex of delicately modulated systems without which the fragile phenomenon called life would not exist. Humanity has only just begun to unravel the mysteries of the great "blue marble" that gave it birth, for it has had relatively little time to explore its habitat. Earth is approximately 4.5 billion years old. The current human species did not appear until about 150,000 years ago, and it has been experimenting with civilization for, at most, 5,000 years. It is an infant species that has more energy than wisdom. To continue to thrive, it needs to grow in judgment and understanding. It has, however, no teacher other than itself and no choice therefore but to learn from experience. History is its classroom.

	ENVIRONMENT AND TECHNOLOGY	SOCIETY AND CULTURE	POLITICS
c. 4,500,000,000 B.C.E.	Earth's origin		
c. 4,000,000 B.C.E.	Hominid evolution begins	AUSTRALOPITHECINES	
c. 2,500,000 B.C.E.	Pebble tools	Lower Paleolithic era *Homo habilis*	
c. 1,600,000 B.C.E.	Pressure-chip tools	*Homo erectus*	Hunter–gatherer tribes
c. 200,000 B.C.E.	Migration out of Africa	Middle Paleolithic era Neanderthals *Homo sapiens sapiens*	
c. 130,000 B.C.E.	Composite tools	Upper Paleolithic era	
c. 30,000 B.C.E.	Cave painting Sculpture		
c. 10,000 B.C.E.	Agriculture Farming and herding	Neolithic era	Settled life: villages city-states, in Sumer
c. 3500 B.C.E.	Centers of population density Irrigation Metal working Writing	Bronze Age	
c. 3000 B.C.E.	Salinization of the Sumerian region		Unification of Egypt (3100 B.C.E.) Sumerian monarchy (3000 B.C.E.) Egypt, Old Kingdom (2700 B.C.E.) Egypt, Middle Kingdom (2025 B.C.E.) Sumer's fall (2004 B.C.E.)
c. 2000 B.C.E.	Domestication of the horse		Indo-European migration (2000 B.C.E.) Amoritic Babylon (1800 B.C.E.) Egypt, Hyksos invasion (1630 B.C.E.) Hittite Empire (1600 B.C.E.) Egypt, New Kingdom (1550 B.C.E.)
c. 1200 B.C.E.	Smelting and forging of iron	Iron Age	Sea Peoples invasion (1230 B.C.E.)
c. 1000 B.C.E.			Kingdom of Israel (1000 B.C.E.)

Topics in This Chapter

The Evolution of Prehistoric Cultures • The Archaic States • The Origin of Civilization
in Mesopotamia: Sumer • The Rise of Civilization in Egypt

1 The Birth of Civilization

And God blessed them and God said unto them, Be fruitful, and multiply, and replenish
the earth, and subdue it: and have dominion over the fish of the sea, and over the fowl
of the air, and over every thing that moveth upon the earth . . . And unto Adam he said,
. . . cursed is the ground for thy sake; in sorrow shalt thou eat of it all the days of thy
life; thorns also and thistles shall it bring forth to thee . . .

—**The Book of Genesis 1:28; 2:17–18 (Standard Version)**

KEY | Question

**How do environments shape human communities and human communities
alter environments?**

For thousands of years the human species was migratory. Men and women survived by hunting and gathering the foodstuffs that nature spontaneously provided. When supplies were exhausted in one area, they moved to another. About 10,000 years ago, some people began what
became a nearly universal shift from hunting and gathering to farming and herding. This forced
them to stay in place for longer periods of time and to confront the challenges that come with
settlement—everything from the construction of durable buildings to the engineering of new
social relationships. In a few exceptional locales environmental conditions and evolving food-
producing technologies contributed to the growth of unprecedented population density. The
informal, personal relationships that structure tribes and villages were insufficient for the management of the large settlements that began to appear. As societies grew more complex,
some communities established the institutions, created and improved the technologies, and
built the monuments that have customarily been regarded as signs of civilization.

　　The world's first civilization flourished some 5,000 years ago on the plains of southern
Iraq in a land called Sumer. Among the many achievements of the ancient Sumerians was the

Sumerian Artifact   This gold-encased wooden object was found in 1927 by excavators working near the ancient Sumerian city of Ur. Lively imaginations linked it with the biblical story of Abraham and Isaac and named it, "Ram Caught in a Thicket."

invention of writing. The documents they produced make them the first people who were able to leave behind a record of their reflection on the human condition—on the conundrum summarized by the biblical quotes that head this chapter. People "subdue" nature and alter the environment in which they live, but nature resists and compels them to adapt to its changing realities. The result is an endless interplay between human actions and the contexts in which humans act.

From the perspective of the natural world, the construction and maintenance of a civilization may be humanity's most radical act. Civilization's pioneers, the Sumerians, lived in large city-states ruled by kings, the most famous of whom is the quasi-legendary king of Uruk, Gilgamesh. His deeds are celebrated in what may be the earliest extant literary narrative, *The Epic of Gilgamesh*. This ancient poem describes its hero's superhuman efforts to subdue the Earth. In passing, it also reflects on the costs as well as the benefits of such behavior. Gilgamesh's subjects admired his strength, wisdom, and beauty. They boasted of the monsters he killed, the protection he offered them, the great walls and temples he built to foster their pride in their city, and his dangerous journeys to bring them treasures from foreign lands. But these good things came at a high price. Gilgamesh's ambitious projects compelled his people to sacrifice their sons to his wars and their daughters to his lusts.

Sumerian monarchies maintained order in large communities, coordinated labor on monumental public works, and helped ensure security and prosperity. But while they enhanced lives in some ways they limited them in others. They subordinated ties of family and kinship to hierarchies of class and institutionalized authority. They confiscated wealth, impressed labor, and limited freedoms. This enabled them to marshal unprecedented resources with which they literally redesigned their world. They altered humanity itself by altering the physical and mental environments in which human beings come to self-awareness. The assumption of such power entailed responsibilities of which they were only dimly aware and led to consequences they could not anticipate. In this, they resemble most people past and present. As you reflect on civilization's history, consider how the human struggle to survive by subduing the Earth alters the natural and cultural environments that, in turn, influence human actions.

The Evolution of Prehistoric Cultures

The human story has traditionally been divided into two phases. History is said to begin with the invention of writing and the accumulation of documents. Prehistory is the pre-literate era that preceded the innovation of writing systems. The division between the two periods is arbitrary and imprecise. Civilization can exist without writing, and people created and preserved vast amounts of information in oral traditions long before they began to write. When writing finally appeared, it was a very long time before it was used for any but a few narrowly specialized functions.

Humanity's prehistory is vastly longer than its recorded history. Hominids, the biological family to which human beings belong, may have evolutionary roots that go back 7,000,000 years. The modern human species, *Homo sapiens sapiens*, has existed for about 195,000 years. Anthropologists divide the immensely long prehistoric era into periods called Stone Ages, so designated because most of what is known about them has been inferred from the study of the stone implements that are their chief surviving artifacts. The characterization of the prehistoric eras as Stone Ages may, however, be somewhat limiting. It is, after all, likely misleading to judge an entire culture on the basis of only one of its products, particularly when that product may not reflect that culture's most sophisticated work. Stone is a difficult medium, and prehistoric people doubtless produced other—and possibly more elaborate—things from more tractable materials such as wood, leather, and fibers. Had more specimens of these crafts survived, we might have greater appreciation for the inventiveness of these peoples and the complexity of their cultures.

The Paleolithic Era   The **Paleolithic ("Old Stone")** era begins with the first evidence of hominids that displayed characteristically human cultural behavior (e.g., tool use), and it continues through the retreat of the last Ice Age (about 10,500 years ago). Tool use is not unique to the human species. Various kinds of animals and birds use and even make tools, but none relies on tools to the extent that humans do. Tools helped Paleolithic peoples support themselves by hunting and gathering. As hunters and gatherers, they had a passive relationship with their environment. They were dependent on whatever resources nature spontaneously offered them. Hunter-gatherer economies can be organized in different ways, and environmental conditions would have created differences among prehistoric societies. Locales with a rich variety of foodstuffs would have well rewarded gathering, while others, such as Arctic regions, would have increased dependence on hunting. In some modern aboriginal communities, gathering is often a female specialization and hunting an activity dominated (although not exclusively) by males. Scholars have speculated about the distribution of power between males and females in Paleolithic communities, but theories about prehistoric gender relations are more abundant than evidence to support them.

Our modern human species may have begun either as a single population arising in Africa or as the result of simultaneous development in several regions. About 30,000 to 40,000 years ago, signs of cultural activity exploded just as *Homo sapiens sapiens* was emerging as Earth's sole surviving member of the family *Hominidae*, which, like other families of animals, once had many branches. What happened to the other hominids—particularly the Neanderthals with whom *Homo sapiens sapiens* coexisted for a long time—is unknown. Some authorities believe that the modern human species exterminated the Neanderthals; others claim that the two species interbred and that *Homo sapiens sapiens* absorbed the Neanderthal line.

The people who lived in Europe as the Paleolithic era drew to a close were evolving increasingly complex cultures, as evidenced by the highly refined, specialized tools they produced. But their true breakthrough was the creation of a new genre of artifacts—things that modern scholars describe as art. The difference between an art object and a tool is not a simple contrast between a utilitarian instrument and an ornament. A tool can have aesthetic features, and an art object can be used for more than the pleasure of contemplation. Paleolithic sculptors and painters may have been less motivated by aesthetic impulses than by a hope that their works of art would help them manipulate magical or religious powers. The key distinction between a tool and an art object lies in art's symbolic functions. Human intellectual capacity took a great leap forward once people began to see things not just as themselves, but as symbols—as representations of something more or other than themselves. Higher level thinking rests on the ability to perceive and manipulate symbols.

What Paleolithic artists intended to symbolize by their work is uncertain. Scholars have, for instance, puzzled over the meaning of the numerous female figurines that have been found at Paleolithic sites from Europe to Siberia. Most of these follow a fairly standard design: an obese, pregnant female torso with full breasts. Some scholars claim that these images are evidence for a prehistoric mother-goddess cult. Others believe that this reads too much into them. Rather than serving as symbols of something as intellectually complex as religious belief, they may have been simple fertility amulets or charms to ensure safety in childbirth. Equally puzzling are the pictures that Paleolithic people began to paint on the walls of caverns about 30,000 years ago. The tradition they began continued for 15,000 years. Cave paintings were not decorations for places where people lived. They are found in deep caverns that were sometimes difficult and dangerous to access. There is evidence that rituals took place in some of the painted caves, but no one knows the purpose of the art or of the ceremonies that might have been associated with it. When cave paintings first began to come to light in the nineteenth century, scholars assumed that they were products of hunter magic—symbols used for ritual enactments that were intended to ensure successful hunts. But then it was noticed that the kinds of animals that Paleolithic people ate were rarely depicted. Some caves also seem to have been organized thematically—assigning different species of animals to different places. Cave artists lavished their greatest skill on realistic descriptions of animals. They rarely treated human figures, but they frequently covered walls with abstract shapes, hand prints, patterns of

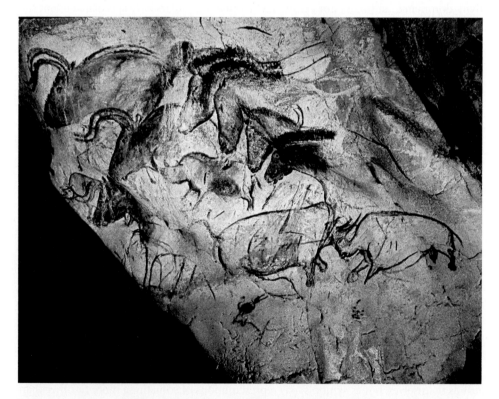

Prehistoric Painting of Multiple Animals, Chauvet Cave, Ardèche Gorge, France   When the first prehistoric painted caves were discovered in the nineteenth century, many people assumed that they were hoaxes. But scientific analysis has proven that they are genuine, and new ones continue to come to light. The Chauvet Cave was only discovered in 1994, and analysis of its contents has only begun. Portions of the cave have not been entered so as to preserve the ancient floors, which are littered with prints and detritus left by animals and ancient peoples. The paintings come from a wide span of time, but some may date as far back as 28,000 B.C.E.

dots, and clusters of lines. Some scholars speculate that cave art was linked with cycles of myths and legends that have long been forgotten.

The Paleolithic era phased into the **Neolithic** ("New Stone") at roughly the same time in perhaps seven different places around the world. The cultural innovations that marked the transition suggest that people were responding to a need to increase their food supplies. As the last Ice Age's glaciers retreated, the global climate became warmer and wetter, sea levels rose, the tundras favored by herd animals shrank and shifted northward, and plant and animal species redistributed themselves. Those stressed communities that could not migrate to the shrinking regions where their old way of life was still possible had to figure out how to wring more sustenance from their changing environment. This inched some of them toward the brink of civilization.

The Neolithic "Revolution"   As one of the Stone Ages, the **Neolithic era** is associated with the emergence of a particular kind of stone implement. In earlier periods, tools were manufactured by pressure chipping—by nicking flakes from pieces of flint, quartz, or obsidian (volcanic glass) to make instruments with sharp edges. Neolithic toolmakers worked tougher kinds of stone by grinding them into shape, but theirs was not the most important new technology of the New Stone Age.

The Neolithic has been described as a revolution, but some scholars object to this, pointing out that although the era had a revolutionary outcome, it was not the product of a revolutionary discovery. There is no disputing the fact that the Neolithic era witnessed a major lifestyle change that had wide-ranging implications for human development, for Neolithic people traded a passive relationship with nature for an active one. Instead of simply harvesting what nature spontaneously provided, they intervened in nature's systems to compel their environments to produce what they wanted. They ceased to rely exclusively on hunting and gathering, and began to farm and herd. Herding and farming revolutionized the context for human life, but they were not new ideas or inventions. Herders and farmers simply exploited what Paleolithic people had long since learned about the life cycles of plants and animals. Nomadic gatherers sowed seeds before they left a region to ensure a crop when they returned, and hunters, who sometimes trapped animals before killing them, knew that some species would feed and breed in captivity.

It did not take a stroke of genius to turn a hunter-gatherer into a farmer-herder. It did, however, take strong motivation, for farming did not make life easier. Farming probably required longer and more arduous labor than hunting and gathering. Farmers had a less varied and healthy diet. They staked their survival on fewer resources, and they ran a greater risk of disease from contact with domesticated animals and the wastes that accumulate when people remain in one place for an extended period of time. Anthropological evidence even suggests that the transition to farming reduced life spans. Why, then, was farming so widely adopted?

Farming offered one obvious advantage. It increased the yield of food from a finite amount of land. If climate change or population growth made it difficult for a people to feed themselves, they had to go on the offensive—that is, to force nature to yield more than it would on its own.

PEOPLE IN CONTEXT   The Iceman

The study of prehistory usually yields generalizations about groups of people, whereas historical records often preserve specific information about unique individuals. On September 19, 1991, hikers in the Alps, on the border between Austria and Italy, made a discovery that constitutes a rare exception to this rule. They stumbled across the corpse of a male who died about 3300 B.C.E. Because his remains (possibly the oldest known human mummy) had survived frozen inside a glacier, the media quickly dubbed him "the Iceman." He was 5' 4" tall and was in his early to mid-40s when he died. His clothes, weapons, and a few other possessions were preserved with his body: an axe with a copper head and yew-wood handle, a flint-bladed knife, a pouch filled with materials that may have been a fire-starting kit, an unfinished bow of yew wood (which is longer than its owner was tall), and a quiver with 14 arrows (two of which were finished with stone points and feathered shafts). He wore a fur cap, a vest of pelts stitched together, a leather loincloth, a leather belt, fur leggings, a cloak woven of grasses, and what appear to have been snow shoes—with bearskin soles and deer-hide upper portions. He used an insulating layer of grass as socks. His body bore 57 tattoos, and he sported an ornament or talisman suspended on a leather thong—a doughnut-shaped disk of white marble.

Chemical analyses of his remains suggest that he grew up in a region near a modern village called Feldthurns and that he probably never ranged more than about 40 miles from

The Iceman This manikin is a scholarly reconstruction of the appearance of the Bronze Age man whose mummy was found in the Alps in 1991.

his childhood home. The partially digested remains of a meal he had ingested about eight hours before his death were recovered from his gut. He had dined on meat (probably venison), some vegetable matter, and grain—einkorn, a form of domesticated wheat that is not native to Europe. Pollen grains consumed with his food were from trees that bloom in March and April, indicating the season when he died. He did not die from natural causes. A flint arrowhead about an inch long was lodged about three inches under his left shoulder near his lung. It traveled upward into his body, missing organs but severing blood vessels. He was involved in a fight before his death. Signs of bruises and cuts remain on his hands and chest, and there are traces of blood from four other people on his clothes and weapons. The shaft of the arrow that mortally wounded him had been pulled out. However, he may have done that himself, for he apparently died alone. His possessions were not looted, so he may have killed whoever shot him or escaped his enemy. He seems carefully to have stowed his equipment before lying down beside it to bleed to death or die of exposure. No one retrieved his body for burial. Perhaps he had been wandering alone or was the only survivor of an ill-fated hunting party. If he had friends and relatives who searched for him, they never found him, and his fate remained unknown for over 5,000 years.

Question: What do the Iceman's possessions and physical remains reveal about his environment and the cultural adaptations that helped him deal with the challenges it posed?

The agricultural economy that the Neolithic era pioneered has worked extraordinarily well for humanity. Some 500,000 years ago, Earth's hominid population may have numbered no more than a million. At the start of the Neolithic era, about 6 million people were spread around the globe. For eons population growth was moderated by plagues, wars, and famines, and it was not until the eighteenth century that the human species could boast a billion members. Another two centuries brought it to 6 billion, and there may be 9 billion humans by the mid–twenty-first century. Given that Earth's resources are limited and its environment is showing signs of stress, humanity may well be undone by its own success.

Prelude to Civilization   Farming appeared first where nature made it easiest. Pioneering farmers looked for fields that they could clear of undesirable vegetation, soil that they could work with simple tools, and a climate in which grains flourished. The thick forests of central and northern Europe, with their damp, heavy soils, were too challenging to till and lacked the desired indigenous species of plant life. The semi-arid grasslands of Asia Minor and the Middle East were, however, ideal, and many of the domesticated species on which Western agriculture came to depend (wheat, barley, pigs, sheep, goats, and cattle) were native to that region (see Map 1–1).

The earliest agricultural settlements appeared about 10,000 years ago. Most of them probably combined hunting and gathering with farming. (Some Native Americans still pursued this lifestyle in the nineteenth century.) The biblical city of Jericho, which appeared about 8400 B.C.E., is the oldest known continuously inhabited settlement in the world. By 7300 B.C.E., it had about 2,000 residents and was partially protected by a dry-stone wall equipped with a circular tower about 30' high. Whether the wall was meant to defend against human aggressors or flash floods is uncertain. The tower could have been used for observation or for exposure of corpses. (Some cultures retrieve the bones of their dead for burial after carrion-eating birds have stripped away the deceased's flesh.) During the eighth millennium, the people of Jericho collected skulls, which they coated with plaster and painted to represent flesh and hair. These artifacts suggest a cult of ancestor worship, but no one can be certain what inspired them.

Many early agricultural sites have been found in Syria and Palestine and in neighboring Anatolia (Asia Minor or modern Turkey). The most remarkable of these may be Çatalhöyük in central Turkey. It flourished for about 1,400 years (c. 7400 to 6000 B.C.E.), and at its peak it sprawled over 33 acres and was home to about 8,000 people. From a distance it probably looked like a huge adobe building, a cluster of 1,000 mud-brick houses. Each house was architecturally independent. Although each house had its own walls, these abutted those of its neighbors. There were a few open spaces in the town, which separated sections of settlement and provided dumping grounds for refuse, but there were no streets. People traveled over the roofs of buildings and used ladders to access their interiors.

Most houses at Çatalhöyük featured a large room for living space and one or more smaller storage rooms. They were furnished with mud-brick benches or sleeping platforms, woven floor mats, baskets, and various wooden and pottery vessels. Tools were made from obsidian. People clothed themselves with fur, leather, and cloth woven from plant fibers and animal hair. They wore jewelry made from bone and seashells,

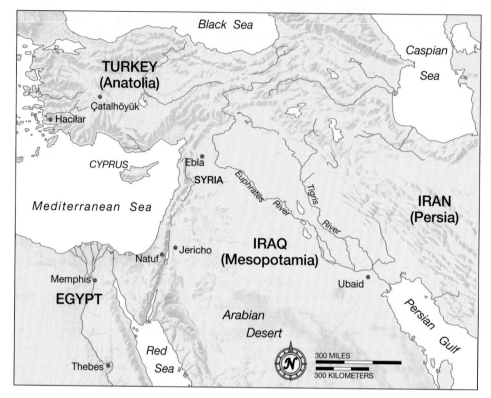

Map 1–1 Early Agricultural Settlements This map shows some of the earliest significant settlements and archaeological sites in the Middle East. The first civilizations arose along the Tigris, Euphrates, and Nile Rivers, but as the map indicates, that is not where the earliest farming communities were found.

Question: Why did the places where agriculture was first practiced not produce the first civilizations?

and figurines depict them wearing elaborately styled hair. The bodies of many of their dead were interred beneath the floors of homes where people continued to live. The remains of as many as 62 people have been identified from excavation of a single house site. Sometimes skulls were retrieved from previously buried bodies, and at least one plastered skull, similar to those found at Jericho, has come to light.

Many of the buildings excavated at Çatalhöyük are elaborately decorated. Domed ovens were standard features of each house. The walls of houses, soiled by soot from the fires that burned in these ovens, were frequently replastered and painted. Horns, skulls, and claws of cattle and wild beasts were embedded in walls. Bulls, leopards, vultures, and bears are common artistic motifs, and there are scenes that represent mass hunts or group baiting of wild animals. Human and animal figurines have been recovered, many of which have been mutilated, presumably for ritual purposes.

Some houses were a bit larger or more lavishly decorated than others. Some graves were a bit more richly equipped than others, but there is little evidence that the population of the town was divided into classes on the basis of wealth or privilege. No communal structures—that is, places for group activities—have been found. Although Çatal-höyük was tied into a wide-ranging trade network, its households appear to have been economically autonomous. Each may have produced what it needed for its own members, and there is not much evidence of specialized labor. The town was not fortified, and thus far archaeologists have found no evidence that it was presided over by kings, priests, or a warrior caste. Doubtless there were communal feasts and ritual celebrations that helped to integrate the community and enable so many people to live together in such close quarters. Çatalhöyük was a large, long-lived, and apparently stable settlement, but was it a truly civilized community or only an imposing agglomeration of households?

The Archaic States

Pottery appeared during the early seventh millennium in conjunction with the Neolithic lifestyle. Things made of fired clay were too heavy and fragile to be of much use to the Paleolithic era's nomadic hunters and gatherers, but pottery vessels were invaluable for the Neolithic's settled agricultural communities. They provided safe storage for the grains that were staple foods, and they facilitated the cooking that made these grains easier to consume. The invention of pottery was also a great boon for modern archaeology. Pottery can survive burial for eons, and shifting pottery styles and designs provide evidence that archaeologists use to establish chronologies for cultures and date the sites they excavate.

Civilization dawned as people added metals to their repertoire of stone and pottery artifacts. Nuggets of copper were being beaten into tools and ornaments as early as 7500 B.C.E., but it was not until about 5500 B.C.E. that copper began to be smelted from ore and cast in molds. Pure copper was too soft to make durable tools, but when it was alloyed with tin or arsenic, it became a much more serviceable metal called bronze. The technique was developed in Anatolia, and by 4000 B.C.E. it had spread throughout the Middle East.

Societies that were indisputably complex enough to be classed as civilizations arose in Sumer and Egypt well before 3000 B.C.E. Similar transitions to civilization took place somewhat later at other places around the globe. The Harappan civilization of the Indus River Valley emerged about 2500 B.C.E., and city-states ruled by the Shang Dynasty flourished along China's Yellow River sometime after 1800 B.C.E. A society capable of erecting monumental buildings was thriving on the coast of Peru as early as 2000 B.C.E., and the Olmecs pioneered civilization in Mesoamerica about 1500 B.C.E. The fact that peoples who lived on the Eurasian continent (in Egypt, Mesopotamia, India, and China) took the lead in founding civilizations may be explained by natural advantages they enjoyed. Compared to other parts of the world, Eurasia had a much greater abundance of native species of plants and animals (e.g., kinds of wheat, barley, rice, sheep, goats, oxen, horses, etc.) that could be domesticated. Unlike Africa and the Americas, Eurasia also has an east-west horizontal axis, which means that its people and species can easily diffuse throughout wide regions without having to adapt to extreme changes in climate and environment. Eurasians had the resources needed to support civilizations and unusual ease in sharing the domesticated species, inventions, and ideas that stimulated the development of civilizations.

The Origin of Civilization in Mesopotamia: Sumer

At first glance, it seems surprising that Earth's first civilization should have arisen in one of its more hostile environments. Average summer temperatures on the Mesopotamian plain hover around 104°F and may soar to 120°F or more. There is little rainfall, and no natural barriers offer protection from the windstorms and floods that sweep the flat, open landscape. Resources are few. The region has no stone, no metal ores, and no trees sturdy enough to provide lumber. However, it did have an abundance of deep, rich soil deposited and continuously renewed by the annual flooding of the Tigris and Euphrates Rivers. Many of the primal civilizations (e.g., Sumer, Egypt, India, and China) sprang up along flooding rivers. Once the Sumerians developed irrigation systems, water from their rivers unleashed the unique fertility of their land. The Sumerian farmer may have got 20 seeds back for every one that he sowed—two to four times what a Roman or medieval farmer earned thousands of years later (see Map 1–2).

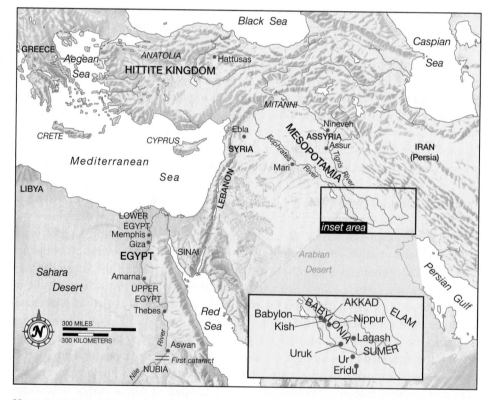

Map 1–2 The Fertile Crescent The arc of agriculturally productive land where civilization first took root is called the *Fertile Crescent*. Farmers in its eastern portion (Mesopotamia—Greek for "between rivers") relied on irrigation and the annual floods of the Tigris and Euphrates Rivers. Those inhabiting its center section (the Mediterranean coast) had enough rainfall to sustain their crops. The Nile's floods and irrigation ensured the productivity of the crescent's western segment.

Question: Would geography have facilitated contacts between the two primal civilizations or encouraged them to develop in isolation?

During the Neolithic era, farmers flourished in the Iranian highlands east of the Tigris River, but they were slow to move down onto the hot, dry Mesopotamian plain and confront its many environmental challenges. The Tigris River ran fast through a relatively deep channel that made its waters difficult to tap for use in irrigation. Early settlers preferred the banks of its partner, the shallower, slower-moving Euphrates. But it, too, presented them with problems. The sluggish Euphrates dropped silt that formed levees along its banks and raised its bed above the level of the surrounding countryside. The river sometimes broke through these levees, turning wide stretches of contiguous land into swamp. Its floods might carve new channels that altered its course, and these inundations came at an inconvenient time each year—in April, when grain crops were ripening. Skillful engineering and massive labor were needed to trap flood waters in reservoirs for distribution when and where they were needed during the growing seasons. However, once the Sumerians found solutions to these problems, their homeland was able to produce enough food to support a population of unprecedented density.

The Predynastic Era   We do not know where the Sumerian people originated or when they settled the lands north of the Persian Gulf. Language often provides a clue to a people's background, but in this case linguists can offer historians no help. Sumerian is not related to any known tongue.

The Sumerians probably entered Mesopotamia from the east, from the Zagros Mountains. Although they dominated the earlier periods in the history of the region, they were not alone. Sumer's population was multi-ethnic and multilingual. Settlers were drawn to southern Mesopotamia by the abundant foodstuffs that could be harvested from the marshes that lined the banks of the rivers and the coasts of the Persian Gulf. Agricultural villages appeared near the rivers as early as 6500 B.C.E., and by 6000 B.C.E. irrigation was enabling farmers to move farther out onto the plains. Pioneers in the region would have relied on a mixture of farming, herding, hunting, and gathering. Myths and archaeological evidence identify Eridu, near the site of the later and more famous Ur, as one of the area's earliest cities (c. 5400 B.C.E.).

During the early stages in Sumer's development, new kinds of settlements spread across the southern Mesopotamian plain. They were larger than Neolithic villages, and each boasted a major building, the construction and maintenance of which required a larger workforce and a more sophisticated supervising authority than was characteristic of a simple village. Given that most of the dwellings in these communities were about the same size, there is little evidence of significant differences in wealth or of occupational specialization. Clans may have owned land communally, and councils of elders may have provided government. The investment that these communities made in their public buildings suggests, however, that privileged social classes were appearing. The great structures they erected were probably temples, and temples of such size and grandeur usually indicate the presence of powerful priesthoods.

Sumerian city-states reached their full development between 3600 and 3000 B.C.E. The first to achieve some kind of regional dominance may have been Uruk (or Erech), home to the epic hero, Gilgamesh. Uruk owed its influence, at least in part, to its two great temples, one raised to the sky god Anu and the other to the goddess of fertility and war, Inanna. (The earliest known specimens of writing have been retrieved from the ruins of her shrine.) Uruk, like the dozen or so other urban centers that sprang up in Sumer during the fourth millennium B.C.E., grew by absorbing neighboring villages. At its peak it numbered about 50,000 inhabitants. Scholars have speculated about the motives that drove the Sumerians to congregate in cities. For a long time it was assumed that the creation and management of irrigation systems must have encouraged centralization of populations, but recent archaeological discoveries suggest that the expansion of irrigation systems actually followed the rise of cities. Sumer's cities were heavily fortified. Uruk, for instance, was encircled by six miles of defensive walls. Given that legends suggest that the threat of war was never far from the Sumerians' minds, they may have clustered together for protection.

The Dynastic Eras   Archaeology provides most of what is known about the early phases in Sumer's development, but a new source of information appeared when the Sumerians invented writing toward the end of the fourth millennium B.C.E. About the year 2100 B.C.E., a scribe compiled a list of the names of all the kings who were believed to have reigned in Sumer. Although buildings identifiable as palaces have not been found dating much before 2500 B.C.E., the Sumerian "king list" claimed that there were kings reigning in Sumer for about 240,000 years before a great flood nearly obliterated humanity. The Sumerian flood legend lies behind the Bible's account of Noah's ark, but there is no geological evidence for a universal flood. When Sumerian myth-makers imagined an event that would sweep the world clean and serve as a beginning point for their era, they naturally imagined a flood. Floods often swept across Sumer and forced its people to rebuild their lives literally from the ground up. The kings listed before the flood have impossibly long reigns of tens of thousands of years and are figures of myth and legend. The existence of some of the kings who are named after the flood can be documented. The earliest of these is Enmebaragesi, king of Kish (c. 2600 B.C.E.). Lavishly equipped graves at Ur, which are assumed to be those of royal men and women, also date to his era.

As villages grew into cities, several things may have fostered the development of monarchy. Sumer's early urban households, like those of villages, were economically self-sufficient and, therefore, fairly autonomous. But city life would have eroded their independence. Informal meetings of heads of families suffice to run small settlements, but not large cities—particularly when crises demand swift action. The records suggest that Sumer's cities were engaged in a perpetual struggle for supremacy. This must often have created military emergencies that left little time for groups to debate what to do. Success favored those who submitted to the authority of a single leader. After a crisis passed, such a leader might have surrendered his powers and returned to private life. (The Bible's Book of Judges suggests that the early Hebrew tribes had leaders of this kind.) But if one emergency followed quickly on the heels of another, people would come to depend on a permanent leader. The result would be enthronement of a king and possibly a **dynasty** (i.e., a family with a hereditary right to rule). Religion contributed to the authority and legitimacy of a Sumerian king, but unlike the Egyptians, the Sumerians seem not routinely to have deified their rulers. The king was generally believed to have a special relationship with the gods, but not to be a god himself. The story of the great king Gilgamesh centers on his futile search for immortality and his efforts to come to terms with the inevitability of death.

City Life   The security of a city required negotiation with heavenly as well as earthly powers. Priesthoods may have dominated Sumer's cities before dynasties of kings were permanently established. When modern scholars first began to delve into Sumer's history, they thought that Sumerian cities were religious communes in which everyone worked on temple estates and survived on rations doled out from temple granaries. Most authorities now believe, however, that this was an illusion created by the fact that most of the surviving documents come from temple archives. They provide insights into the organization and conduct of only one of Sumer's institutions, not the whole of its urban life.

Sumerian cities were complex societies, not hives of temple slaves. Artisans, merchants, priests, and government officials lived in cities, as did many farmers who commuted to the countryside to work their fields. Temples and kings had large estates, but much property remained in private hands. Title to this private land was often held by kinship groups rather than individuals, and it could be sold only with the consent of all the members of the family that had title to it. The prejudice against selling land away from the family was so strong that sellers sometimes adopted buyers to make the transaction more socially acceptable and legally secure. Personal property was passed down through the male line, and all a man's sons shared equally in his estate. Women, however, could own, buy, and sell land and testify in court cases. Monogamous marriage was the rule, but divorce and remarriage were possible. Women as well as men were impressed into labor gangs to carry out communal projects such as clearing irrigation ditches and building walls. The rations they received in exchange for their toil were smaller than those of the men with whom they worked.

Urban economies were complex systems to which farmers, traders, artisans, and various kinds of professionals all contributed. Some families prospered more than others, and class divisions and social stratification eventually became a fact of life. An aristocracy entrenched itself at the top of society, but it did not succeed in blocking social mobility. A few men from obscure backgrounds even became kings. Slave markets were supplied by war captives and persons who fell into debt. Slavery was taken for granted in this first civilization as it was in almost all of those that followed it until the modern era, but it was not essential to the Sumerian economy. Slaves usually worked as household servants, for it was hard to prevent their running away if they were sent out into the fields to do agricultural work.

By modern standards, Sumerian cities were uncomfortable. The tens of thousands who were sheltered behind the walls of a large town might be crammed into an area equivalent to about 20 football fields. Given that stone had to be imported, everything was constructed of mud brick. Major public edifices were sometimes protected with expensive facings of fired brick or sheets of copper. Their walls might be decorated with mosaics made from cones of colored clay set in plaster. With the exception of sacred structures, most buildings were only one or two stories high. They clustered along narrow (seldom more than nine feet wide) streets that followed no plan or pattern of organization. The expense of fortifying a town made space within it precious, so there were few open areas. Houses were jammed together and fronted directly on the street. They had few doors or windows on their outside walls and depended on interior courtyards for light and ventilation. This enhanced their security and cleanliness. The column of dust that was raised as the 50,000 or so residents of a city (and their animals) trod its unpaved streets must have been visible for miles. Homes were minimally furnished. Possessions were few and clothing simple. Men and women wore similar skirts or kilts and cloaks woven of wool.

Cities were unhealthy, for they had no sewers. Wastes were dumped into streets for animals to scavenge, and drinking water was drawn from the same streams and canals into which refuse was discarded or allowed to drain. One of the byproducts of civilization's urban lifestyle is epidemic disease. Dense human populations (particularly those that live in close association with domesticated animals) create ideal conditions for the spread of parasites and infectious agents. Trade and war also help disease spread quickly among population centers.

The most imposing features of a Sumerian city were its fortifications and its temples. Mud-brick walls encircled the greater cities, and temples soared above all other urban structures. Each city chose a deity as its special patron and provided him or her with lavish accommodations. Sumerian gods were assumed to want the same things that human beings crave: shelter, food, leisure, and amusement. Temples were literally homes for the gods, and their sacred images were cared for like living things. They were provided with changes of clothing, meals, and entertainment.

The Sumerians believed that a god's residence should be elevated above the ordinary human plane. Before 3000 B.C.E., lofty terraces were being built to serve as foundations for temples. Builders then began to layer terraces on top of terraces to create pyramidal structures called **ziggurats** (from an ancient Babylonian term meaning "pinnacle"). A ziggurat was an artificial mountain, a solid structure on whose top a temple perched. The largest ziggurats covered about two acres and may have been as tall as a seven-story building. Given that they were made of fragile, sun-dried bricks, considerable engineering skill was needed to stabilize them. They required constant maintenance, for fundamentally they were huge piles of dirt whose cores were weakened by the moisture they absorbed from the soil beneath them. Today they are so badly ruined that experts can only speculate about their original appearances.

Sumerian Trade and Industry   Sumer produced surpluses of grain that it traded for things that were not locally available. The merchants who dealt in goods from abroad did not necessarily make long journeys to obtain them. Items could reach Sumer's markets simply by being passed from hand to hand across great distances. Lapis lazuli, a blue stone used for jewelry, came from northern Afghanistan some 1,500 miles from Sumer. Carnelian, a red stone, was mined in equally remote India.

Sumerian artisans made skillful use of the materials merchants imported. They created splendid jewelry from beaten gold or silver and semiprecious gems. They carved statues from blocks of stone brought from distant quarries. They built furniture and musical

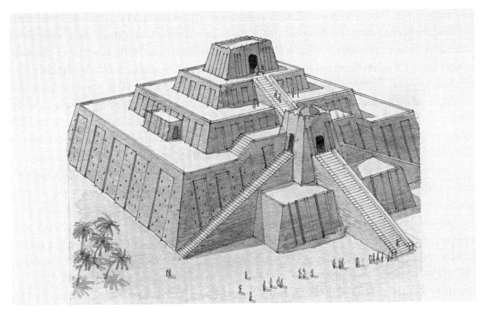

The Ziggurat of Ur   This is an artist's recreation of a ziggurat built by the city of Ur about 2111 B.C.E. Only the lowest level of the building survives, so the sketch represents an archaeologist's informed guess at the appearance of the intact structure.

instruments from rare woods and decorated these objects with subtle inlays. They wove garments from wool and linen for both domestic and foreign markets. (Cotton was not available to the Mediterranean world until the seventh century B.C.E., when an Assyrian king imported cotton plants from India to ornament his palace garden.) Sumerians knew how to make glass, and by 3000 B.C.E. their potters were using wheels to throw vessels. The Sumerians may have pioneered uses for the wheel; by 3500 B.C.E., they were replacing sledges with wheeled carts. The most distinctive Sumerian artifact was a small, but exquisitely carved, object called a cylinder seal. This was an engraved cylinder that was rolled across a clay tablet to imprint a design that served its owner as a signature.

Writing, Religions, and Intellectual Life
The challenge of managing Sumer's cities and their economies inspired the most famous Sumerian invention: writing. Fortunately for historians, the Sumerians wrote on tablets made from their country's most abundant, inexpensive, and durable material—mud. Many of these tablets, some sun-dried and some fired, have survived burial in the soil for thousands of years. As such, they are history's first true documents.

The earliest specimens of writing come from Uruk and may date as far back as 3500 B.C.E. Although they have not yet been deciphered, they support the theory that writing was invented by accountants. As early as 8000 B.C.E., people began to make small clay tokens whose size, shape, or design represented quantities of various commodities. By assembling piles of these tokens, a merchant or warehouse manager could keep track of how many, and what kinds of, items he or she had in stock. Frequent collection and distribution of things made it almost impossible to remember what one had on hand without some method for keeping and updating records. Eventually it dawned on some accountants that it was easier to draw pictures of their tokens than to make models of them. Some of the early tablets from Uruk have rows of lines beside these drawings that may indicate numbers. The evidence suggests therefore that writing was not first intended (or used) to preserve the words of scholars and poets, but it was inspired by the mundane needs of businesspeople. It was a long time before Sumerian scribes produced anything but business ledgers. Given the fact that only a small minority of people ever learned to read in the ancient world, most works of literature and learning were preserved, transmitted, and experienced as oral traditions.

Busy scribes were driven to speed up their work by making their writing systems more efficient. Because it took time to draw realistic pictures of objects or tokens, scribes began to strip these images down to a few essential lines. This made writing easier but reading more difficult. The meaning of simplified signs was not always self-evident. People had to be taught what each one represented. In addition to the invention of a more efficient script, speed and clarity were improved by reforming the physical act of writing. The Sumerians had nothing like paper, and given that most of the documents they produced were intended only for short-term use, they needed an inexpensive medium. Mud for making tablets was free and readily at hand, but linear drawings were difficult to make on mud tablets. Inscribed lines gouged furrows that had jagged edges and ended in messy clumps. It was cleaner and faster to poke a stylus (a reed) into a clay tablet than to push or pull it across one. Poking produced a triangular indentation instead of a line, but a quick series of jabs could create a clump of wedge-shaped impressions that approximated one of the older linear symbols. The triangular indentations with which the Sumerians covered their tablets constitute a script that modern scholars call **cuneiform** (from *cuneus*, Latin for "wedge").

The cuneiform writing system is complex, for its symbols can represent both objects and prominent sounds in the words for objects. The latter function allowed scribes to begin to think of writing as a method for recording what they heard rather than depicting what they saw. Once writing was viewed as a way to represent speech, its use spread to record anything that could be thought. Early cuneiform employed about 1,200 signs representing things and the syllables used to sound out the words of spoken language. Scribes steadily reduced the number of these signs, but the Sumerians never developed a true alphabet (a set of symbols for a language's elemental sounds). That was the achievement of Semitic-speaking Canaanites who lived in Palestine about 1600 B.C.E. The Phoenicians transmitted this invention to the Greeks and ultimately to us. The short list of symbols in the alphabet "democratized" writing by making it much easier to learn. Cuneiform was a script, not a language. Therefore, it could be—and was—adapted to record many tongues. It spread widely throughout the ancient Middle East and remained in use into the first century C.E.

Writing made history in every sense of the word. For the first time, thinking beings could leave an enduring, precise record of their thoughts. Most ancient cuneiform tablets are the byproducts of mundane transactions, but some record myths, legends, laws, proverbs, medical texts, astronomical charts, mathematical calculations, scientific treatises, dictionaries, letters, poems, and prayers. Knowledge of the development of Western literature and thought begins with the cuneiform legacy. It has been particularly enlightening for biblical scholars, for much of the material in the opening chapters of Genesis (the first book in the Bible) harks back to Sumerian or Mesopotamian sources.

The Sumerians worshiped gods who incarnated the powers of nature. They believed that although the gods were analogous to human beings, they were beyond human understanding. The wisest course, therefore, was not to try to understand them, but to curry their favor by offering them gifts and praise. The Sumerian pantheon numbered about 3,600 gods and goddesses, but only a few were of major importance—most notably: Anu, a remote high god; Inanna (also called Ninhursaga or Ishtar), a war and fertility goddess; Enlil, a storm god; and Enki, the god of the fresh waters that imparted life to Sumer's arid land. Myths depict Sumerian gods as all too human. They schemed, lied, loved, formed and broke alliances, sought revenge, and held grudges. The politics of heaven resembled those of a Sumerian city-state. Gods could be bribed, and they resorted to threats and influence peddling. A god who did a favor for another god—or a human being—expected something in return. When struggles broke out among the gods, the fates of the cities allied with them hung in the balance.

The major modern Western faiths all posit a connection between religion and ethics. They claim that how people treat one another has transcendent importance and that the deity they worship demands justice and judges their conduct. The Sumerians, by contrast, did not sense a moral principle at the base of reality. They believed that gods were interested primarily in themselves and were restrained by neither reason nor morality. Gods could, however, be swayed by offerings and magic spells. To guard against misfortune, therefore, it was important to try to anticipate what the gods might be intending to do. The Sumerians saw the world as filled with omens. All kinds of things (the livers of sacrificial animals, flights of birds, patterns of smoke, deformed births, etc.) hinted at what the gods were about, and it was a priest's profession to interpret these coded messages and recommend responses to them.

Some Sumerian myths taught that people should not hope for much from life. The gods were said to have created humanity for the sole purpose of laboring to keep their altars piled high with offerings. People were the slaves or the "cattle" of the gods. In practice, this meant that most men and women could expect to spend their lives in an unending struggle to win favor with heavenly, as well as earthly, powers. Ultimately, everyone suffered the same fate: death followed by a lingering, shadowy existence in the underworld. In *The Epic of Gilgamesh*, Enkidu, Gilgamesh's friend, has a deathbed vision of the underworld, a place where even kings and priests languish in darkness with nothing to eat but dust and clay.

The Mesopotamian environment may help to explain this gloomy outlook. Sumer was wealthy but insecure. The flooding rivers on which it depended periodically threatened to rout its people and destroy the monuments of its civilization. Violent storms swept the countryside. Epidemics and plagues decimated cities. Nomadic raiders pressed in on every side. Power struggles raged within and between cities, and innocent people were caught up in tumultuous events that were beyond their control or understanding. Even a superhuman hero like Gilgamesh was advised to yield to fate and to aspire to no more from life than enjoyment of its simple, transient pleasures—food, drink, friends, family, and sex.

Sumer's History   Sumer's cities probably began as independent settlements, but as they grew, they started to compete with one another for dominance. The king list claims that Eridu was the first state to achieve supremacy and that leadership passed to Kish after the great flood. The struggle went on, for the featureless plain that the Sumerians occupied provided no natural boundaries for a stable state and little encouragement for political centralization.

The Sumerian cities were subsumed into what has been called history's first empire by a man who called himself Sargon or "Rightful Ruler" (2371–2316 B.C.E.). He came from Akkad, a Semitic-speaking district on Sumer's northern border. Legend claims that he was a self-made man of obscure origin—allegedly abandoned as an infant and found floating in a basket on the Euphrates. (Similar stories were later told about the founders of other states, the Hebrews' Moses and Rome's Romulus and Remus.) Sargon rose to power in Kish, won sway over Sumer by defeating its high king (at that time, the ruler of Uruk), and then went on to build an empire that extended from the Persian Gulf up the Euphrates and across the caravan stations of northern Syria to the Mediterranean and Asia Minor. The site of the city he founded as the seat for his government has yet to be located, but it was near ancient Babylon (and modern Baghdad), a locale that remained politically important for millennia because of the communication links it commanded. The flow of information was such, however, that Sargon could not have exercised much direct control over the far-flung peoples who had submitted to him to greater or lesser degrees. The primary concern of his government may have been to exploit the trade routes that coursed through the lands over which he claimed jurisdiction. The soldiers he maintained for this purpose have been said by some to constitute history's first standing army. Sargon doubtless hoped that family ties would consolidate his government, and he assigned key posts to relatives—some of whom were women. His daughter Enheduana supervised the great temples of the cities of Ur and Uruk as their high priestess. Some of the hymns that she wrote have survived. They are the earliest literary compositions to which an author's name can be attached.

Sargon's empire collapsed following the death of his great-grandson about 2200 B.C.E. It may have been economically undermined by a three-century-long drought that began about 2100 B.C.E. Following a period of confusion, leadership of the region passed to the kings of the Third Dynasty of Ur. They presided over the last creative phase in Sumer's history (2112–2004 B.C.E.).

By the time that King Ur-Nammu founded Ur's third dynasty, the Sumerians had been a literate people for nearly a thousand years. Ur's kings were aware of the antiquity of their culture, and they assumed responsibility for preserving its legacy. They re-

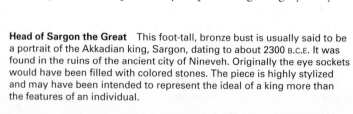

Head of Sargon the Great   This foot-tall, bronze bust is usually said to be a portrait of the Akkadian king, Sargon, dating to about 2300 B.C.E. It was found in the ruins of the ancient city of Nineveh. Originally the eye sockets would have been filled with colored stones. The piece is highly stylized and may have been intended to represent the ideal of a king more than the features of an individual.

built temples, collected ancient documents for safekeeping in their archives, and presided over a kind of Sumerian renaissance. In 2004 B.C.E., however, they were defeated by Elamite tribes, who invaded from southern Iran. The region fragmented politically, opening the way for Amorites, nomadic tribes native to the deserts west of Sumer, to spread throughout Mesopotamia. The Amorites who settled in Akkad founded the famous ancient city of Babylon, gradually restored order in Mesopotamia, assimilated Sumer's cuneiform culture, and rescued what they could from Sumer's fall.

The fall of a civilization that had endured for nearly 2,000 years cries out for an explanation. Many things could have happened. As governments age, they may develop rigid bureaucratic structures that resist adapting to changing conditions. States also fail when they cannot find leaders with talents equal to their responsibilities. Divisions between rich and poor (or other kinds of class conflicts) can destabilize societies, or shifting trade routes, military struggles, and natural disasters might pose ruinous economic challenges.

In addition to these problems, Sumer may have been the victim of an environmental disaster of its own making. Sumer depended on irrigation, and irrigation can degrade farmland. The minerals dissolved in irrigation water are left behind in the soil when that water evaporates. Ground water also contains minerals that are drawn to the surface. If these "salts" are not flushed out (which was hard to do on Sumer's flat, poorly drained terrain), the ground slowly becomes poisonous to plant life. The effect was mitigated by the new soil that the flooding rivers laid down, but as the years passed, the region suffered. Farmers developed strategies to deal with the changing conditions. They planted less wheat and more barley, for barley is more tolerant of salted soil than wheat. But the combination of declining harvests and political confusion may eventually have encouraged a critical mass of people to seek better conditions elsewhere. The fall of a civilization is not likely to have a single, simple explanation, but it is worth reflecting for a moment on the possibility that humanity's first civilization may inadvertently have engineered an ecological disaster that doomed it to destruction.

The Rise of Civilization in Egypt

At the start of the second millennium, the Middle East underwent wrenching transitions. Sumer disappeared. Small cities that had arisen in Palestine declined, and the first phase in the history of Egypt, the West's other premier civilization, also came to an end.

The Egyptian Environment
The Egyptians dealt with environmental conditions similar to those that confronted their Sumerian neighbors. It seldom rained in Egypt. Temperatures often hovered around 100°F, and permanent settlement of a large population would not have been possible without an annually flooding river that renewed fertile fields and supplied water for irrigation. An ancient Greek historian aptly described Egypt as "the gift of the Nile." Where the river's floods reached, Egypt was a "black land," formed by deposits of rich silt. A dramatically different "red land," an utterly barren desert, began where the river's reach ended and stretched to the horizons.

The Nile's bounty was so generous that prehistoric Egyptians were slow to take up agriculture. Along the river's banks plants and wildlife flourished, and nature needed little encouragement to meet human needs. As early as 5000 B.C.E., Egyptians had domesticated sheep, cattle, goats, barley, and wheat. But for over a thousand years, herding and farming simply supplemented hunting and gathering. Villages fully dependent on agriculture may not have appeared much before 3500 B.C.E., and no great feats of irrigation engineering were needed to support them. The Nile, unlike the Tigris and Euphrates, flooded predictably and at a convenient time for farmers. It rose in late summer following the harvest. Then it dropped a fresh layer of silt and saturated fields just in time for replanting. The Egyptians measured the flood's rise at their southern frontier, and the volume of water helped them predict how large the harvest would be. The floods of the Tigris and Euphrates were a mixed blessing for the Sumerians. They were essential for survival, but sometimes destructive, for Sumer occupied a vast flat land that offered no protection from surging rivers. The Egyptians, on the other hand, had little to fear from the Nile's flood, for much of Egypt was sheltered in a valley, whose walls kept the Nile's waters confined to natural flood plains.

The Nile rose in Uganda and flowed north toward the Mediterranean as if it were descending a huge staircase. When the river spilled over the edges of the higher steps, it created rapids or cataracts. Egypt's southern boundary was marked by what was, from the Egyptians' perspective, the First Cataract. From there to the Mediterranean—about 700 miles—there was no more white water. The Egyptians did not need roads to tie their country together. Given that the Nile Valley is only about 12 miles across at its widest, no one was ever far from the river. The river made trade and communication easy. Its current carried vessels north, and when boats raised their sails, prevailing winds pushed them south. The Nile provided such convenient transport that the Egyptians were slow to utilize wheeled vehicles.

Nature protected as well as provided for the Egyptians. On both sides Egypt's borders were defended by cliffs and deserts. The country was politically unified for over 1,300 years before it suffered a major foreign invasion. Metal ores and good building stone were also to be found in close proximity to Egypt's agricultural land. Wood was scarce, but it was easily imported by sea from the coast of Palestine. Egypt's generous environment may partially explain why many of its myths and legends seem to express more contentment with the human condition and more hope for life beyond death than some of Sumer's religious texts.

Egypt's Political Development   Nature divided Egypt into two distinct regions. The largest part of the country was Upper (up-river) Egypt, the long, narrow valley described previously. Lower (down-river) Egypt was the broad delta that accumulated where the Nile emptied into the Mediterranean. Lower Egypt was a flat, swampy land much like Sumer, and it was the part of Egypt most exposed to the outside world. Mediterranean sailors used its ports, and coastal routes linked it by land with Libya to the west and the Sinai to the east.

Settlement patterns help to explain why Egypt became a united country early in its history and was politically more stable than Sumer. Sumer's broad, featureless plain allowed people to cluster in fortified towns surrounded by farmland. Sumerian settlements, having originated as separate city-states, cherished independence, competed with one another, and resisted unification. Much of Egypt's productive land, by contrast, was confined to a narrow valley, which in many places was no more than two miles wide. Because lateral expansion was limited, Egyptians did not cluster in large cities. That would have forced many of them to make long commutes to their fields. This, together with the relative security from invasion their country enjoyed, encouraged the Egyptians to distribute themselves evenly in small villages throughout the valley. Patterns in the delta were probably different, but archaeological information from that part of Egypt is sparse. A damp environment and deep deposits of silt have worked against preservation and excavation of the earlier stages of human habitation.

Political divisions did exist in Egypt. The Nile Valley is composed of a series of flood basins, and long before the dawn of history, each of these was claimed by a tribe. Struggles among these tribes gradually led to the formation of separate kingdoms in Upper and Lower Egypt, and about 3100 B.C.E. a king of Upper Egypt conquered the delta. Egypt, therefore, became a unified country about the time when the first evidence for monarchies appeared in Sumer's city-states.

The writing of history was an invention of the ancient Greeks. After Alexander the Great conquered Egypt in 332 B.C.E., the country's Greek rulers charged scholars with organizing the records of Egypt's past. They grouped the names of the people who had ruled Egypt from its unification to its Greek occupation into 31 dynasties and dated events in Egypt's history by the reigns of its rulers. Although the ancient list of royal families is now known not to be entirely reliable, modern historians still use the numbers the Greeks assigned to Egypt's dynasties. In terms of historical development, Egypt's past can be divided into three major eras or "kingdoms" and a number of relatively brief periods of transition.

Early Dynastic Period (3100–2700 B.C.E., Dynasties I–II)   A clue to Egypt's origin as a unified state was found at the site of ancient Hierakonpolis in 1897—a palette (a ritual object used for grinding pigments) with inscriptions commemorating the victories of a ruler called Narmer (or Scorpion). On one side Narmer wears the crown of Upper Egypt and on the other the crown of Lower Egypt. If Narmer unified Egypt and launched its first dynasty, he can be called its first pharaoh. However, that title was not used until about 1400 B.C.E. It evolved because ancient peoples believed that naming something invoked its presence. The awe Egyptians felt for their ruler, who was literally the incarnation of a god, encouraged the custom of referring to him indirectly as pharaoh ("great house").

Key Events in Sumerian and Egyptian History	
SUMER	**EGYPT**
Predynastic Era (5300–3000 B.C.E.)	3500 B.C.E., agricultural villages appear 3100 B.C.E., unification of Egypt
Dynastic era (3000–2004 B.C.E.) monarchy appears	Early Dynastic Period (3100–2700 B.C.E.) Old Kingdom (2700–2200 B.C.E.) 2550 B.C.E., pyramids at Giza
Sargon's empire (2371–2200 B.C.E.)	First Intermediate Period (2200–2025 B.C.E.)
III Dynasty of Ur (2112–2004 B.C.E.)	Middle Kingdom (2025–1630 B.C.E.)

The early dynasties ruled from Memphis on the border between Upper and Lower Egypt. Memory of the delta's and the valley's origins as separate kingdoms survived, and pharaohs wore a double crown: the red circlet with a hooded cobra of the delta laid over the valley's white conical cap.

The institutions, artistic styles, and theologies that evolved early in Egypt's history established conventions that endured for 2,000 years. What began as a remarkably inventive society grew increasingly conservative as respect for tradition restrained the impulse to innovate. This may have been an effect of Egypt's rigorously centralized government. Pharaohs were worshiped as manifestations of an eternal god, and their courts were the chief markets for the products of Egypt's artists and intellectuals. Court taste favored repetition of symbols and images that by their unchanging nature expressed the pharaoh's timeless essence. Innovation may also have been inhibited, oddly enough, by the invention of writing. In modern societies writing stimulates development by facilitating communication and data collection. For ancient peoples, however, writing was an arcane and arduously acquired skill that few possessed. The mysterious markings that scribes made seemed magical. Many modern people share this primitive inclination to trust whatever is "in print" (or, worse, on the Web), and the word *scripture* ("writing") still connotes something holy—something that has authority and cannot be changed.

Archaeologists can trace the gradual development of Sumer's cuneiform writing system, but Egyptian **hieroglyph** ("sacred writing") has no comparable ancestry. Hieroglyphs began to appear about 3100 B.C.E., and a fully developed script quickly evolved. Egypt had trade contacts with Sumer, and Sumerian writing may have given the Egyptians hints that helped them quickly create a script of their own. Both the Sumerians and Egyptians based their writing systems on pictographs. As Sumerian scribes developed cuneiform's efficient clusters of wedge-shaped impressions, these early images became unrecognizable, but Egypt's hieroglyphs never lost their pictographic quality. Egyptian scribes did not inscribe clay tablets. They wrote with brushes and ink on a paper-like material made from the papyrus reeds that grew along the Nile. They had no difficulty making linear drawings. Hieroglyphs always remained in use for monuments and holy texts, but by 2000 B.C.E. a faster cursive script (called demotic) had been developed for ordinary documents.

The Old Kingdom (2700–2200 B.C.E., Dynasties III–VI)   The heart of ancient Egypt's civilization was its monarchy. The Egyptians believed that their pharaoh was their primary link with the supernatural powers on which life depended. He was an incarnate god whose power was absolute (in theory, if not always in practice). Egypt and all its people belonged to him, but he was not supposed to be a self-serving tyrant. He had a vital communal function. The Egyptians viewed the world as a dynamic place, a realm of order threatened by chaos. The pharaoh's task was to preserve *ma'at* ("justice"), the balance among competing forces that preserved a stable world order. His authority was so sweeping that Egypt, unlike many ancient kingdoms, did not develop a code of laws. Pharaoh's will was all the law that Egypt needed.

Pharaohs governed Egypt with the help of an elaborate bureaucracy. Some 2,000 titles have been identified for officials of the **Old Kingdom**. The pharaoh had to employ a horde of royal agents, for he had many functions. He was responsible for the religious ceremonies

King Menkaure and Queen Kamerernebti II   This regal couple from Egypt's IV Dynasty reigned about 2490 B.C.E. Their dress is simple, barely concealing their perfect bodies. The pharaoh sports a false chin beard, a mark of his rank. His rigid posture—facing forward, hands at sides, one foot advanced—illustrates one of the conventions of ancient Egyptian sculpture. The touch his queen gives him may not indicate affection. The inheritance customs of the early dynasties are uncertain, but some pharaohs may have claimed their thrones through marriages with important princesses—possibly their half-sisters. The queen's gesture might signal the king's legitimacy.
King Menkaure (Mycerinus) and Queen. Egyptian, Old Kingdom, Dynasty 4. Reign of Menkaure, about 2490–2472 BC. Egypt, Giza, Menkaure Valley Temple. Greywacke. 142.2 × 57.1 × 56.2 cm (56" × 22 1/2" × 21 3/4"). Harvard University-Boston Museum of Fine Arts

that placated the gods and regulated the cycles of nature. On a practical level, he handled defense, dispensed justice, oversaw planning for the Nile's flood, coordinated food production and distribution, erected buildings, provided patronage for artisans, handled long-distance trade, supervised public works projects, and oversaw the army of scribes who audited all this activity.

Egypt was highly centralized but minimally urbanized. Most Egyptians lived in small villages. For administrative purposes, the country was subdivided into units of local government called nomes (22 in Upper Egypt and 20 in Lower Egypt). In theory, all the land belonged to the pharaoh, and he could impress all his subjects into labor gangs to work for him. Actual slavery, however, may not have been all that common in the Old Kingdom. In the ancient world, slaves were often foreigners captured in wars, and the Old Kingdom was not very active in military campaigning in foreign lands.

The tombs of the Old Kingdom's pharaohs are the best surviving testimonials to their power. The investment that the Egyptians made in tombs throughout their history can create the mistaken impression that they were a grim people preoccupied with death. In reality, their preparations for death attest to their love of life. Egyptian burial practices were meant to guarantee that the deceased would continue to enjoy life's pleasures beyond the grave. So similar and so close were the worlds of the living and the dead that the Egyptians believed that support from this side of the tomb was important for happiness on the other. The dead were assumed to need all kinds of things. Supplies were buried with them, and they tried to arrange for a steady stream of offerings to flow in perpetuity across the altars of their funerary temples.

The Egyptian outlook on both life and death was more positive than the view described in some Sumerian texts. The Sumerians, on their exposed plain, were engaged in a constant struggle with one another and the seemingly arbitrary forces of nature. Life in the rich Nile Valley was easier and safer. The Sumerians conceived of the universe as a chaotic battleground for quarrelsome, incomprehensible gods, but the Egyptian universe was a realm in which a god, the pharaoh, was physically present and laboring to maintain balance and order. The eternal, unchanging nature of things caused death to be viewed as an event in life rather than an end to life. Experience with the dead tended to confirm this. The Egyptians did not waste agricultural land on cemeteries. They buried their dead in the deserts that bordered the Nile's flood plains—usually on the western frontier, the direction the sun took on its daily descent to the underworld. The desert's arid sands dehydrated corpses and shielded them from decay. Nature's reluctance to reclaim the physical remains of the departed may have inspired the Egyptian conviction that physical preservation of the dead was important. The methods the ancient Egyptians developed for embalming their dead imitated nature's technique. Bodies were gutted and the internal organs mixed with spices and sealed in jars. The corpse was then thoroughly dried, wrapped in bandages to preserve its shape, and dipped in pitch. The English word *mummy* derives from an Arabic word for tar or bitumen.

It was more difficult to provide a secure grave for a corpse than to preserve it from decay. Tomb construction evolved as the Egyptians experimented with ways to prevent bodies buried in desert sands from being exposed by the wind or dug up by animals. At the dawn of the dynastic eras, flat, rectangular structures made from bricks were being used to stabilize mounds of dirt over graves. This kind of a tomb is called a *mastaba* (from an Arabic word for a bench). Corpses could be interred in the ground beneath *mastabas,* but rooms were also created within them to house coffins and grave offerings. Royal tombs conformed to this pattern until about 2650 B.C.E., when the pharaoh Djoser, the second king of the Old Kingdom, departed from tradition. The result was a monument so impressive that later generations assumed that its architect, Imhotep, had been a god. Imhotep first built a *mastaba* for his employer, but then he began to tinker with its traditional design. He enlarged it, and then he piled levels of masonry on top of it to create a solid building resembling a square, six-layered wedding cake. Imhotep's "step pyramid" (a pyramid whose layers are not angled or filled in to create smooth sides) is the world's first monumental stone building. Around it was erected a model city in stone and the whole complex was enclosed within a wall a mile in circumference.

Djoser launched a fad for pyramid construction that lasted for centuries. The ruins of about 110 pyramids have been identified in Egypt, but the greatest are the earliest—those erected during the Old Kingdom. What pyramid designers strove to create was a soaring structure that rose at a steep angle. This was hard to do, for as any child who builds a sand castle at the beach discovers, gravity causes the sides of a steep mound to sheer off. By 2550 B.C.E., the Egyptians had developed engineering techniques that enabled them to erect what is still the world's most massive stone structure: the Great Pyramid at Giza.

The Great Pyramid, which was probably built for the pharaoh Cheops (or Khufu), is the supreme example of its kind. It anchors a sprawling complex of smaller pyramids, tombs, temples, and other monuments on the western bank of the Nile near modern Cairo. The statistics of the Great Pyramid are staggering. It covers 13 acres, rises to a height of 481 feet, and is constructed of 2,300,000 blocks of precisely cut and fitted stone. Some of the blocks of granite used for its interior chambers weigh 50 tons and were brought from quarries 500 miles away. Surveyors oriented the building precisely on a north-south axis and kept its sides in perfect alignment. When the Greek historian Herodotus visited the pyra-

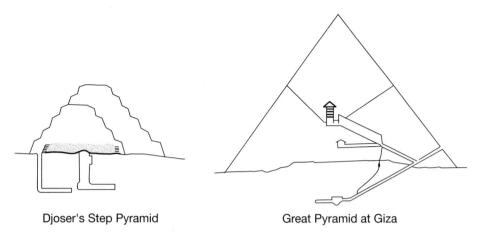

Djoser's Step Pyramid   Great Pyramid at Giza

The First Pyramid and the Greatest Pyramid   Most pyramids, like the first, were solid structures raised over subterranean tombs, or they had one small interior chamber. The Great Pyramid at Giza was not only the largest but it also had the most complex internal design. This has variously been interpreted as the result of changing plans or even the use of the building while it was under construction for purposes of astronomical observation. The straight passages leading directly to the primary chambers would not have done much to deter tomb robbers. No inscriptions or paintings have been found within the pyramids.

mid 2,000 years after it was built, he was told that it took only 20 years to complete. A modern authority has estimated that it might have been finished in as few as five.

Whatever the pyramids were built to contain was looted in antiquity, and what they symbolized for the ancient Egyptians is uncertain. Egyptian mythology envisioned the creation of the world as an island emerging from the waters of primal chaos. Pyramids may have represented this island, where life began, or their shape might have been meant to recall the slanting rays of the sun, the path that the pharaoh's spirit took as it returned to the heavens after his death.

The most mysterious thing about the pyramids may be the motive that persuaded the Egyptians to undertake the physically and logistically daunting labor of constructing them. They are sometimes dismissed as the work of megalomaniacal tyrants who enslaved thousands to build monuments to their personal glory. Pyramids were, however, not the work of slaves, and they may have done more than exalt an individual. A pharaoh could use only one tomb, but some pharaohs built more than one pyramid. This suggests that the process of building may have been as important as the end product.

Early Egypt did not have to fend off many invaders, but its creation was not bloodless. Texts praise pharaohs for being great warriors. Some led armies into the deserts to discipline nomads or up the Nile to intimidate Egypt's Nubian neighbors. Some fought to maintain internal order. The Old Kingdom was a relatively new monarchy that was attempting to do something that had never been done before—to consolidate a huge territorial nation. Pyramid building might have contributed to this. Great projects can strengthen a leader by inspiring awe for his power, and pharaohs may have used their construction to keep their subjects occupied at times when they might be inclined to cause trouble. Agricultural work is seasonal, and during the months when Egypt's fields required little tending, its idle men probably had a tendency to brawl. Pharaohs may have forestalled this by occupying their subjects on great projects that were sources of both employment and communal pride. Egypt certainly built pyramids, but pyramids may also have built Egypt.

First Intermediate Period (2200–2025 B.C.E., Dynasties VII–X)   The Old Kingdom continued for about 500 years. No one is sure why its centralized government ultimately lost control and allowed regional strongmen to begin fighting among themselves. A severe drought afflicted much of the Middle East about the time that both the Old Kingdom and Sargon's Mesopotamian empire fell. The drought may have depressed Egypt's economy, but the pharaohs of the Old Kingdom also may inadvertently have created the situation that contributed to their fall. Unless central governments moved their local officials from time to time, these men built regional power bases that increased their independence. But as governments took on greater responsibilities, a need for efficiency prompted them to leave experienced men at their posts for longer periods. The clever governor trained his son in the duties of his office and arranged for the boy to succeed him. If a family managed to do this for several generations, it acquired a kind of hereditary right to its office and enough local support to assert its independence if its royal overlord showed signs of weakness. The last pharaoh of the Old Kingdom lived to a great age, and his failing powers may have given Egypt's governors the opportunity they were waiting for.

The collapse of the Old Kingdom was followed by a period of political upheaval, internal warfare, and economic hardship called the First Intermediate Period. By then Egypt may have had over one million inhabitants, and it did not function well when divided against itself. Famine stalked the land, and confidence in the pharaoh was shaken. But the confusion was not entirely detrimental to Egypt's civilization. The destruction of the Old Kingdom's authoritarian government freed Egyptian society to evolve. When the country's unity was finally restored by the pharaohs of the Middle Kingdom, cultural creativity flourished with renewed vigor.

KEY QUESTION | Revisited

The belief that primitive societies thrive without disturbing nature is a romantic fantasy. Any hiker who has tried to "tread lightly on the land" and visit the wilderness without altering it knows how difficult that is. Nature is constantly adjusting to what its resident species consume, do, and produce. Prehistoric peoples changed the world around them by hunting and gathering. They drove some species toward extinction and encouraged the proliferation of others. The goal of a successful organism may not be to avoid having any impact on nature but to strike a sustainable balance with nature. This is difficult, for history and personal experience teach that actions have unintended, unpredictable consequences, particularly when they affect the complex symbiotic systems that make up the world of nature.

The people whose increasingly elaborate cultural activity culminated in the rise of the first civilizations exploited the potential of unique, but similar, environments—arid regions with annually flooding rivers. A major part of their strategy for adapting to these challenging environments was to adapt the environments to meet their needs. The result was acceleration of the cycle of action and reaction between communities and their contexts that continues throughout history.

Some of the most significant steps in the early stages of this process may have been taken in complete ignorance of what was happening. Civilization rests on the economic foundation laid by agriculture, and agriculture depends on the availability of domesticated species of plants and animals. The domestication of wheat, the staple food of the ancient world, may have come about largely by accident. Grains of wheat are the seeds of a kind of grass. In nature, grasses perpetuate themselves by scattering their seeds to the wind. This favors species in which ripened seeds are loosely tethered to a plant's stalk and can easily be blown free. Human gatherers may have begun to harvest grains by shaking their seeds into baskets, but it would have been difficult for them to avoid a lot of loss. When gatherers invented simple sickles for cutting clumps of grasses, their harvests improved. But they had most success collecting the seeds of plants that did not easily break loose and drift away. Planting these seeds encouraged the genetic evolution of a kind of wheat with seeds firmly attached to stalks. This is a domesticated species, for it is ill-adapted to survive on its own. Its reproduction depends on a human harvester gathering and planting its seeds. The ease and minimal loss with which such wheat could be harvested encouraged the ancient harvester to serve the plant that served him.

Environment for human beings is a context shaped by both nature and culture. The West's early civilizations created a previously unknown physical environment through technologies such as irrigation, agriculture, and metal working. The cities and states they built were not only new kinds of spaces in which to live; they constituted challenging new intellectual and social environments. The Sumerians and the Egyptians acted, and were acted upon, in ways that were similar and ways that were different. But each experienced the same thing: As they changed the world, the world changed them. To be civilized is to grasp a tiger by the tail and pin hopes for survival on the ability to cope with the consequences.

Review Questions

1. How did Paleolithic and Neolithic societies differ?
2. How did the first civilizations differ from the prehistoric cultures that preceded them?
3. Does environment explain why civilization appeared first in Sumer and Egypt?
4. How and why did Egypt's political evolution differ from Sumer's?
5. How and why did the Egyptian outlook on life and death differ from the Sumerian view?
6. What is the relationship between environment and civilization?

Please consult the Suggested Readings at the back of the book to continue your study of the material covered in this chapter. For a list of documents on the Primary Source DVD-ROM that relate to topics in this chapter, please refer to the back of the book.

Topics in This Chapter

The Transition States • Imperial Egypt: The New Kingdom • The Indo-Europeans
and the Clash of Empires • The Bible and History

2 The Rise of Empires and the Beginning of the Iron Age

You march forth to take your enemy's land, and he comes to take yours.

—**Mesopotamian Proverb**

KEY│Question

Does civilization promote unity or intensify divisions among peoples?

The word **civilization** and its cognates (civility, for example) conjure thoughts of peaceful, orderly behavior. Civilized persons, unlike barbarians, are supposedly possessed of self-control, rationality, and respect for life and standards of justice and decency. The history of civilization is, however, largely a history of wars and other atrocities waged by and among civilized peoples. This is puzzling, but when civilization is viewed as the most highly developed form of the cultural behavior on which the human species has pinned its survival, it becomes less so. Human beings do not just live their lives. They think about living them. They make themselves objects to themselves and describe themselves to themselves. This creates something called a personal identity. By locating a person in a context, it gives meaning to life and seems so essential to an individual's survival that people will go to great lengths to defend it.

A civilization shapes a people's view of "the right way to live," and it seems so natural that it is often difficult for persons from one civilization to appreciate the alternatives offered by another. All a leader may need to do to mobilize a people for war is to claim that their "way of life" is threatened by the "barbarism" of an alien culture.

But civilized life is a complicated phenomenon. The identity a civilization provides may unite millions of people on one level while simultaneously dividing them into groups with differing interests and concerns on others. In complex societies people acquire complex identities based on such things as wealth, occupation, gender, education, religion, ancestry,

Ramses II This statue from Egypt's Abu Simbel temple of an enthroned pharaoh, Ramses II (r. 1279–1213 B.C.E.), projects a sense of the majesty and power of the god-kings who presided over the ancient seats of civilization.

and so on. People can, therefore, feel tugged in contrary directions by their civilized lifestyle. Whether the values that unite them are strong enough to counter the tensions that divide them depends to a very large extent on their historical situation.

Individuals acquire their sense of identity as they become aware of how they resemble some people and differ from others. Unfortunately, people often tend to view persons different from themselves with suspicion, contempt, and hostility. One's identity is fundamental to one's sense of worth, and sometimes the mere existence of other lifestyles may seem to call into question the validity of one's own. A single difference (over a religious belief, for example) may be enough to set people who have everything else in common at one another's throats. The lives of small, scattered hunter-gatherer bands and farming villages may not have been much disrupted by this human tendency. But civilizations, the supreme products of the human capacity for invention and imagination, maximize potentials both for cultural differences and human contacts. They mobilize large populations and have often sought unity, stability, and self-affirmation through imperialism—that is, by imposing their way of life on others.

During the second millennium B.C.E., rulers in both Egypt and Mesopotamia began to use military force to build empires. This opened the way for a blending of cultures that produced sophisticated, cosmopolitan societies. But it also increased the risk of instability by raising questions about legitimate political authority and personal identity. Empires have always been easier to create than to maintain.

The Transition States

In 2004 B.C.E. the Third Dynasty of Ur was overthrown by the Elamites, tribesmen whose homelands lay east of the Tigris River. The Elamites were ill-equipped to maintain Sumer's urban institutions, and as the heartland of the West's first civilization declined, other groups took advantage of the political confusion. The Assyrians established the nucleus for a new state on the upper reaches of the Tigris River, but the immediate future lay with the Amorites. These nomadic tribes from the western deserts spread throughout Mesopotamia and Syria. Some of them settled in Akkad, north of Sumer, founded the city of Babylon, and gradually came to control much of the Middle East.

Babylon   The Babylonian empire was largely the work of the city's sixth king, Hammurabi (1792–1750 B.C.E.). He was about 25 when he inherited his throne, and he devoted the first 30 years of his reign to wars of conquest. At its height, Hammurabi's Babylon held sway from the Persian Gulf to northern Assyria. This was not a large state in comparison with later empires, but its population was diverse and hard to pacify. Hammurabi is memorable for his novel approach to dealing with this problem. He issued a common set of rules for all his subjects. That is, he published what is often said to be history's first code of laws, called the **Code of Hammurabi**. Fragments of earlier legal texts survive from the reign of the founder of Ur's Third Dynasty, Ur-Nammu, but they are probably records of decisions in particular court cases, not general principles meant to guide the administration of justice. Hammurabi's code, which contains almost 300 clauses, was much more ambitious and may have had a different purpose. Unlike modern legislation, it was not a set of statutes that lawyers cited when arguing cases. It was probably intended to provide judges with examples of the kinds of decisions the king wished them to make when dealing with various categories of disputes. By superseding local customs and establishing a common standard for justice throughout the empire, the king's law helped break down some of the cultural barriers that separated his subjects.

Hammurabi's laws provide historians with their first detailed description of an ancient Mesopotamian society. Hammurabi's code made separate provisions for three types of people: aristocrats, free commoners, and various kinds of dependents and slaves. People's legal rights were determined by their class standing. An injury done to an important person was more harshly punished than the same injury done to a less significant individual. Because ancient societies were not prepared economically or organizationally to maintain prisons, punishments took the form of fines, mutilations, and executions. Hammurabi's concept of justice followed the principle that the Bible succinctly characterizes as "an eye for an eye, a tooth for a tooth." It was not always easy, however, to make "the punishment fit the crime," and Hammurabi's attempts to establish exact equivalencies sometimes sought justice by mandating what are, from the modern perspective, unjust acts. For example, a builder who erected a house that fell down and killed its owner's son was punished by the execution of his own son. The boy might well have questioned the justice of this decree, but Hammurabi probably never thought about that. In his world sons were the property of their fathers. Fathers could sell them into slavery and lose them in property disputes.

Hammurabi's code gives significant space to property and family law. It spells out principles governing land ownership, rights of renters and tenants, and responsibilities for the maintenance of communal facilities such as irrigation systems. Some of its precepts would be judged enlightened by modern standards. It assumes that governments have responsibility for protecting environmental resources. The state was also to regulate money lending to prevent abuse of debtors, set fair standards for workers' wages, and protect the quality of consumer goods.

Hammurabi's code is especially noteworthy for the protection it offered the poor and the weak. It said that husbands could not abandon wives who were barren or ill without providing for their support. It gave women rights to property of their own and allowed them to run businesses—so long as they did not neglect their domestic duties. It granted wives the power to initiate divorce and reclaim their dowries, but it also enforced a sexual double standard. It allowed husbands to have sex outside of marriage, but it harshly punished adulterous wives. Babylonian society was patriarchal, and men were anxious to ensure that the children they raised were their own. The only way to do this was to limit the freedom of women.

In addition to women, the law protected slaves, another vulnerable segment of the population. Some slaves were war captives, but some were members of citizen families. A man could discharge his debts by selling his wife, his children, and himself. Slavery was, however, not inevitably permanent. A person could be enslaved for a specific term. A slave could also own property, go into business for himself, and earn the price of his freedom.

The rights Hammurabi's people had in theory no doubt exceeded those they had in practice, for it is unlikely that Hammurabi had the governmental machinery to enforce his laws and hold all his judges accountable. Public officials were legally liable for doing their duty. They were even supposed to compensate victims if they failed to find and punish thieves and murderers. However, given the difficulty modern governments

Hammurabi's Code   The seven-foot-tall stele (pillar) of black marble on which Hammurabi's famous laws are inscribed was found in the ruins of the ancient Persian city of Susa. It may originally have been set up as a boundary marker for Hammurabi's Babylonian state and later carted off as loot by Persian conquerors. *Stele of the Law Code of Hammurabi, from Susa (modern Shush, Iran). c. 1792–1750 BCE. Basalt, height of stele appx. 7" (2.13 m), height of relief 28" (71.1 cm). Musee du Louvre, Paris. RMN/Reunion des Musees Natioaux/Art Resource, NY*

have in meeting such high standards of justice, Hammurabi may have been legislating pious hopes.

In addition to progress in law and government, Babylonian intellectuals made significant advances in science—particularly astronomy and the mathematics needed to study the heavens. They used both decimal (base 10) and sexagesimal (base 60) systems. The latter survives in the conventional division of circles into 360 degrees and of hours into 60-minute segments of 60 seconds each. Babylonians did not distinguish astrology from astronomy. Their belief that celestial events influenced life on Earth may indeed have inspired their commitment to recording precise measurements of the movements of the heavenly bodies. The data they collected were used for centuries and greatly improved the accuracy of calendars.

Hammurabi's empire began to fall away shortly after his death, but his dynasty held on to Babylon for another 150 years. About 1595 B.C.E. the city fell to a group of northern raiders called the Hittites. They came to loot, not conquer. After they retreated to their base in Asia Minor, the Kassites moved down from the Zagros Mountains to occupy Babylon, Akkad, and Sumer. They ruled the lower Euphrates for the next 600 years and conscientiously guarded the region's cultural legacy. They restored temples, built libraries, and spread knowledge of cuneiform and its literary treasures.

Egypt's Middle Kingdom (2025–1630 B.C.E., Dynasties XI–XII)   Central government was reestablished in Egypt a few years before the fall of Ur's Third Dynasty and survived almost to the sack of Babylon by the Hittites. The pharaohs of this **Middle Kingdom**, contemporaries of Hammurabi's dynasty, presided over an era of prosperity and creativity. Many of the buildings they erected were torn down and replaced by grander structures by their successors, the rulers of the New Kingdom, but the Middle Kingdom's literary achievements proved more enduring.

The Middle Kingdom was founded by a warrior from Thebes in Upper Egypt. The pharaohs of both the Middle Kingdom and the New Kingdom claimed descent from Amun-Ra, the sun god of Thebes, and they preferred Thebes to Memphis, the Old Kingdom's seat near the juncture of the valley and the delta. The pharaohs of the Middle Kingdom seem to have cultivated a somewhat less remote image than their predecessors. The literature of the period calls them the shepherds of their people and praises them for defending the poor and equitably enforcing justice. They invested less in grandiose tombs and more in what might be described as economic development. They extended their power up the Nile into Nubia. They sponsored trading expeditions to distant lands. They dug canals to improve transportation and created reservoirs and irrigation systems that greatly expanded the agricultural productivity of the Fayum, an oasis in northwestern Egypt.

Historians have learned less from the monuments of the Middle Kingdom's pharaohs than from the private tombs of their officials. These are fairly numerous, suggesting that wealth was more widely distributed during the Middle Kingdom than in earlier eras. More people could afford to follow pharaoh's example and invest in tombs, and they even appropriated sacred texts that had previously been reserved for pharaohs. The cult of Osiris, the god of the dead, and his goddess wife Isis flourished during the Middle Kingdom and remained popular well into the Christian era. Osiris was a vegetation deity who, like the crops in Egypt's fields, died to be reborn with Isis's assistance. Each year, the inundation of the Nile restored life to Egypt, and Osiris and Isis promised worshipers a similar victory over death.

Because the Egyptians believed that in death they would want and need everything they had enjoyed in life, they stocked their tombs with their favorite possessions. Tombs were also well supplied with pictures and sculptures, for representations of things, like things themselves, were thought to have power to nurture the dead in their afterlives. Sometimes boxes filled with dolls representing servants at work were added to a tomb's equipment. They look like children's toys, but they had the serious adult purpose of supplying the deceased's needs for all eternity. They now provide invaluable information about the kinds of ordinary daily activities that usually go unrecorded.

The Middle Kingdom was remarkable for its literary productivity. Mythological and theological works, administrative tracts, letters, medical and mathematical treatises, and a great deal of less formal material survive from the era. The Egyptians were fond of morally edifying tales and proverbs, and they had an appetite for practical advice on how to get ahead in this world. The sages of the Middle Kingdom advised modesty, hard work, loyalty, and deference to superiors. They praised acts of charity and cursed officials who abused their offices and exploited the poor. They also warned young men to be especially careful in their dealings with women. The love poetry that survives from the era suggests that such advice may have been more readily given than heeded.

Second Intermediate Period (1630–1550 B.C.E., Dynasties XIII–XVII)

The Middle Kingdom had a strong government that cultivated a reputation for justice and worked hard to promote prosperity. It gave Egypt about four centuries of peace and stability before it was undone by a development that it understandably failed to anticipate. For eons, Egypt's location and terrain had protected it from foreign invasion, but now the defense these things provided was suddenly revealed to be inadequate. The delta was invaded and occupied by a people whom the Egyptian records simply describe as Hyksos ("foreigners"). These were bands of Semitic warriors who may have had links with the Amorites. It was their military technology and not their political connections, however, that enabled them to rout the numerically superior Egyptians.

The Egyptians of the Middle Kingdom had fallen behind in the development of military technology—thanks in part to their environment. Egypt had little need for wheeled vehicles drawn by animals. Simple sledges sufficed for men to drag things to the banks of the Nile, and the river provided most of the transport the country required. Some draft animals were used. Old Kingdom farmers plowed with teams of oxen. Donkeys served as pack animals, but horses may not have reached Egypt much before the end of the Middle Kingdom. (Horses had been domesticated in the Ukraine late in the fourth millennium, but they were not in widespread use in Mesopotamia until the second millennium.) The horse had greater speed and stamina than the ox or donkey, but it was more difficult to train and much more expensive to feed. By 1600, however, warriors from Asia Minor were demonstrating how useful horses could be on the battlefield. Archers who sped about in light, horse-drawn chariots could devastate companies of foot soldiers–cutting them down before they got within striking distance with their lances, spears, and clubs. Egypt's simple hordes of warriors were no match for Hyksos charioteers on the battlefield.

The Hyksos crossed the Sinai Peninsula, occupied Lower Egypt, and established their capital at Avaris in the eastern delta. Much of Upper Egypt remained in the hands of Egyptian chiefs who paid tribute to the Hyksos. Several generations passed during which the Egyptians learned to copy the weapons and tactics of their invaders. Finally, a leader emerged from Thebes who helped them begin the struggle to evict the Hyksos and reclaim their country (c. 1550 B.C.E.).

The Hyksos interlude taught the Egyptians that isolationism was a luxury they could no longer afford. Reasoning that the best defense is an offense, pharaohs developed a new interest in the outside world. They embraced expansionism and sent their armies into Nubia and Palestine to begin conquest of an empire.

Imperial Egypt: The New Kingdom (1550–1075 B.C.E., Dynasties XVIII–XX)

With the return of independence and unity, Egypt entered the period in its history known as the **New Kingdom**. Many of the New Kingdom pharaohs were warlords, and their conquests brought ancient Egypt to the pinnacle of its wealth and power. Thutmose I (1504–1492 B.C.E.), the third ruler of the eighteenth dynasty, led armies east to the Euphrates and farther south into Africa than Egyptians had previously ventured.

The New Kingdom produced some pharaohs who were great generals and some who did not fit the newly militarized image of their office. One of these was a woman. Six women are believed to have governed ancient Egypt at some point in its long history. Some served as regents who ruled during the minority of a male heir. Others were the last surviving members of their dynasties. The most significant were Egypt's last pharaoh, the famous Cleopatra VII, and a woman of the eighteenth dynasty named Hatshepsut (1478–1458 B.C.E.). The daughter of one pharaoh and the widow of another, Hatshepsut began her reign as regent for a stepson. She then shunted him aside, asserted a hereditary right of her own to the throne, and ruled Egypt for 20 years. Because the pharaoh's role was understood to be male, images of Hatshepsut conformed to tradition by depicting her wearing male dress and the pharaoh's false beard. The queen's chief ally was a man of obscure origin named Senenmut. He was her spokesman, the steward of her properties, and the supervisor of her many building projects. The most significant of the latter was her great mortuary temple at Deir el-Bahri, opposite Thebes, set against the cliffs of the western Nile Valley. Egypt had never seen anything like it—a series of ascending colonnades and terraces on which gardens

Mortuary Temple of Hatshepsut   The pharaohs of the eighteenth dynasty began the custom of separating their burial place from their mortuary temples. Hatshepsut's temple of terraced gardens and colonnades was a novel design. It marked the entrance to what became the customary burial place of the New Kingdom pharaohs. Tombs, such as pyramids, that were highly visible were open invitations to looters. By carving cave tombs into the walls of the Valley of the Kings, concealing their entrances, and providing the site with guards, the pharaohs hoped to provide themselves with a more secure final resting place.

were planted. For her burial, the queen may have prepared several tombs in the valley behind her temple. Her father, Thutmose I, was the first of the 62 pharaohs who were ultimately interred in what came to be called the Valley of the Kings. The location was probably chosen to provide greater security for royal tombs, the contents of which constituted an irresistible temptation for looters. Hatshepsut's multiple tombs may have been intended to throw grave robbers off the track. As it turned out, she had good reason to be concerned for the safety of her resting place. It is not clear how her reign ended, but following her death, an attempt was made to erase her name from her monuments and thus deny her the immortality they were erected to assure. Her burial place, like most of the other royal graves, was looted in the ancient era, but her remains appear to have been rescued and stowed without a coffin or treasures in the tomb of one of her servants. If forensic evidence confirms that the mummy now housed in the Cairo national museum is hers, she was an overweight woman who died in middle age—afflicted with diabetes and cancer.

Hatshepsut's successor, Thutmose III (1458–1425 B.C.E.), was a vigorous military man. He fought 17 campaigns to secure his hold on Palestine and Syria, and he brought all of Nubia under Egypt's control. The pharaoh was also something of a scholar. He collected plant specimens while on his military expeditions. He studied ancient literature, and he may have done some writing of his own. One of his strategies for consolidating his empire was to imbue the client kings who ruled its foreign provinces with enthusiasm for Egypt and its culture. The pharaoh took hostage the sons of kings he conquered and sent the boys to Egypt to be educated. By the time they returned home to inherit their fathers' thrones, they were thoroughly indoctrinated. Some of the New Kingdom's later pharaohs married foreign princesses to confirm treaties, and these women introduced alien cultural influences into Egyptian society at the highest level. Not until late in Egyptian history, however, did a pharaoh condescend to send an Egyptian princess abroad to marry a foreign ruler.

Egypt was managed by an army of bureaucrats that had to be closely supervised. Some reported to the pharaoh's chief wife, the high priestess of some of the state's most important temples, and others were directly accountable to the pharaoh. Vigilant attention was needed to preserve the empire. With the possible exception of Nubia, the Egyptians did not plant colonies abroad. Instead of occupation, they relied on periodic military expeditions to maintain the loyalty of native princes who governed as Egypt's clients.

The Amarna Period   The New Kingdom reached a pinnacle of power and prosperity during the reign of Thutmose III's son, Amenhotep III (1390–1352 B.C.E.). He made major additions to ancient Egypt's most imposing temple complexes, the shrines of the Theban god Amun-Ra at Karnak and Luxor. Egypt's temples were not churches designed to accommodate congregations of worshipers. They were private residences for the gods whose statues were enshrined in their innermost chambers. The pharaoh delegated his responsibility to tend the images of the gods to priests who maintained an elaborate round of daily rituals. From time to time, a sacred idol was taken out of its temple and carried in procession so that it could be seen and worshiped by the masses. Temples were branches of government, and their granaries provided a pharaoh with reserves of food for distribution to his subjects in time of need.

Wealthy priesthoods could occasionally threaten to impinge on the power of a pharaoh. By the end of his reign, Amenhotep III appears to have had reservations about the growing strength of the temple of Amun-Ra. Holding an endowment amounting to about a quarter of Egypt's arable land, its priests had immense resources at their disposal. Suspicion of the ambitions of Egypt's established priesthoods seems to have influenced the thinking of Amenhotep's son and successor, Amenhotep IV (1352–1338 B.C.E.), and motivated him to take a bold step. He closed many of the temples, confiscated their properties, and announced that henceforth Egypt would exclusively worship a new god—the Aten (the disk of the sun)—to whom only the pharaoh and his family were said to have direct access. In 1348 B.C.E. the pharaoh changed his name to Akhenaten ("Beloved of the Sun") and began construction of a new capital called Akhetaten ("Horizon of the Sun"). Akhetaten or **Amarna** (Tell el-Amarna, the modern name for its site) was situated between Thebes and Memphis on land that had no previous religious associations. It was strategically located opposite a cleft in the eastern walls of the Nile Valley through which the Aten's worshipers could glimpse the first signs of dawn, the daily rising of their god. The great temple at Amarna was not a dark sanctuary concealing a remote god. It was open

Akhenaten and Nefertiti Worship the Aten   This panel depicts the pharaoh Akhenaten, his wife Nefertiti, and their children worshiping the Aten. The royal family shared in the divinity of their god in that they were the unique mediators between him and Egypt's people. The sun disk of the Aten soars above them, and its descending rays end in hands bestowing blessings. Note the curiously distorted profiles, a characteristic of the art of the Amarna period.

to the heavens. Its god was depicted as a bright sun whose descending rays ended in open hands, a symbol of the blessings the sun generously bestowed on Egypt. The Aten was not a mysterious, hidden god but a power that everyone experienced.

Little is known about the theology of the Aten cult, for few of its monuments have survived. But given the spiritual powers it reserved to the pharaoh and his family, most scholars doubt that it was a true monotheism. It may have been an innovative attempt to revive and update the pharaoh-centered faith of the Old Kingdom.

Devotion to the Aten did not extend far beyond court circles, but it was sincere and powerful enough to inspire new artistic visions. One of the most famous of all Egyptian sculptures is a bust of Akhenaten's beautiful wife Nefertiti that was found in the ruins at Amarna. It realistically depicts the regal elegance of a queen, but much of the art of the Amarna period was expressionistic. Like some modern schools of art, it distorted forms to create graceful linear compositions. So odd are the jutting chins and protruding bellies that characterize the style's treatment of the human form that some people have speculated that it was intended to flatter a pharaoh whose body was misshapen by a glandular disease. It may be simplistic, however, to assume such a literal motive for the art of a faith that set out to transform so many of Egypt's traditions.

Akhenaten may have vowed never to leave the confines of his beautiful new city, and his preoccupation with his new religion may have caused him to neglect the management of his empire. Some 350 clay tablets inscribed in cuneiform with the Akkadian language

■ ■

PEOPLE IN CONTEXT King "Tut"

In 1922 British archaeologist Howard Carter realized every Egyptologist's fantasy. He discovered the intact tomb of an Egyptian pharaoh—the only one known to have survived into the modern era. The richness and elegance of the treasures found in the tomb of the pharaoh Tutankhamun, which include a 250-pound gold coffin, amaze visitors who view them in the Cairo Museum. (The pharaoh's mummy has been returned to his tomb for respectful reburial.) Staggering as the treasures of "King Tut's" tomb are, they only hint at the potential magnificence of Egyptian royal burials. The tomb Carter found was a small one that had been hastily furnished for a young, unnoteworthy king. Its occupant's insignificance may explain why his grave survived. Shortly after his funeral, attempts were made to loot his tomb, but they were foiled before the raiders did much damage. According to packing inventories found in the tomb, thieves made off with about half of the jewelry buried with the king, but some 5,400 items of various kinds were left in place. The tomb's entrance was then covered by debris from the excavation of another, larger tomb, and it was forgotten until Carter stumbled across it.

The Pharaoh Tutankhamun This magnificent gold bust (inlaid with lapis lazuli, obsidian, and turquoise) was created to serve as a mask for the pharaoh's mummy.

Tutankhamun, whose original name was Tutankhaten, may have been the son of Akhenaten by Kiya, a junior wife. If so, he was wed to his half-sister, Ankhesenpaaten, Akhenaten's third daughter by his primary queen Nefertiti, and he succeeded to the throne when he was 8 or 9 years old. Being too young to rule, Egypt was governed by a regency headed by Nefertiti's father Ay, who bore the title "God's Father." The new government returned to Thebes from Amarna, eschewed the Aten cult, revived the worship of the traditional sun god, Amun-Ra, and appropriately revised the pharaoh's name to Tutankhamun. The young man matured to a height of 5'6" and may have been athletic. He was probably trained for war, for he was buried with a horde of military equipment: 50 bows, 2 swords, 8 shields, 2 daggers, slingshots, and 6 chariots. Up until the time of his sudden death at the age of 18 or 20 (c. 1323 B.C.E.), he appears to have been in good health. He had sired no heir, but his young wife had had a miscarriage and a stillborn child (remains were buried with him).

It was far from unusual for a man to die young in the ancient world, but at one point archaeologists thought they had evidence that Tutankhamun had been murdered. A bone fragment within his skull (spotted by X-ray) appeared to have been caused by a blow to the back of his neck, something unlikely to be the result of an accident. It is now believed, however, that the fragment was a byproduct of the embalming process. The king's left thighbone is also broken, but it is uncertain whether that occurred while he was alive (perhaps leading to complications and death) or whether it was damage caused by rough handling of his mummy.

Murder conspiracies were fed by events that unfolded in the wake of Tutankhamun's death. His widow, Ankhesenpaaten, knew that she would quickly be remarried to confer legitimacy on an heir to her former husband's throne. Some remarkable letters have come to light in the archives of Suppiluliuma, ruler of the powerful Hittite empire based in Asia Minor. Scholars cannot be certain, but most believe that the correspondence was that of Ankhesenpaaten. She wrote to ask for the hand of one of Suppiluliuma's sons. Apparently under pressure to accept a husband she considered unworthy, she declared her determination never to wed one of her "servants." She urged the Hittite ruler to respond quickly, for she was uncertain how long she could hold out. Suppiluliuma was understandably suspicious, but he eventually sent a son named Zananza on the road to Egypt. The prince and his entourage were killed before they arrived, and Egypt's young queen was compelled to marry one of her "servants," her husband's former regent, Ay. Ay was in his sixties, and he may have been father to Nefertiti, Akhenaten's wife and Ankhesenpaaten's mother. If so, the young widow was forced to marry her grandfather. Ay survived on the throne for only three or four years. He may have been killed by a powerful general named Horemheb. Nothing more is recorded of the fate of his reluctant wife, and her tomb has never been found.

Question: How can religious belief in the divinity of pharaohs be reconciled with the ways in which the throne was passed from one person to another in ancient Egypt?

that was used for international diplomatic correspondence have been discovered at Amarna. Many contain appeals for help from client rulers, which suggests that trouble was developing in the eastern portion of Egypt's empire. The end of Akhenaten's reign is obscure, but it is likely that the old priesthoods joined forces with disgruntled military officers against their unconventional pharaoh. The identity of his immediate successor is uncertain. All the children of his chief wife, Nefertiti, were female. His male heirs may have been sons by minor wives who were wed to Nefertiti's daughters.

By 1336 B.C.E., a boy named Tutankhaten had been proclaimed pharaoh. He was controlled by a conservative political faction that was set on obliterating the cult of the Aten and returning Egypt to its traditions. The young pharaoh's name was changed to Tutankhamun (to honor Egypt's former high god), and the court returned to Thebes. Amarna, a city that had housed 20,000 people, was abandoned and dismantled. It had existed for only about 25 years. Fortunately for archaeologists, many of its inscribed stones were carted off for use in later buildings. Some 12,000 of them have been discovered at Karnak—pieces that help make up what is doubtless the world's most unwieldy and historically important jigsaw puzzle.

The three pharaohs who followed Tutankhamun were self-made men. Ay had been one of Akhenaten's most powerful officials. He was succeeded by a general named Horemheb, and at his death Ramses, another military man who rose through the ranks, became pharaoh. Ramses founded the nineteenth dynasty, which restored the glory and stability of the New Kingdom and guided Egypt through its final years as a powerful, independent nation. Ramses I's son, Seti, was a vigorous campaigner, and Seti's son, Ramses II, was both a warrior and ancient Egypt's most prolific builder. About half of ancient

Egypt's extant monuments were constructed during his reign (1279–1212 B.C.E.), one of the longest in Egypt's history. Ramses II did his best to ensure the future of his dynasty by fathering (with the aid of a large harem) about 160 children. However, by the time he died, threats to the power of his successors were materializing on the horizon.

Egyptian Society   No matter what happened abroad, Egypt's internal stability was rarely threatened. Life changed little from generation to generation. Security, a reliable economy, and the overwhelming authority of pharaohs moderated the development of the kinds of tensions that stressed societies in Mesopotamia and elsewhere. In theory, all Egyptians were on the same legal footing. They were the pharaoh's slaves. In practice, some families had opportunities for education and for government service that gave them advantages over others.

Most ancient Egyptians were peasants who lived in simple rural villages near the fields they farmed. Their ephemeral settlements have largely disappeared without a trace, making it difficult for archaeologists to find evidence to illuminate ordinary life. However, remains of villages that housed the artisans who worked on royal tombs have survived. They were in arid regions close to desert cemeteries, and their founders sometimes used their tomb-building and ornamenting skills to enhance their domestic environment. Although these communities served a unique class of specialized laborers, they give some impression of how most Egyptians lived. Villages were laid out in an orderly fashion. Some had walls to protect their residents from robbers. Houses were flat-roofed, rectangular structures constructed of mud brick and coated with painted plaster. They clustered closely together to shade narrow streets from Egypt's glaring sun. They contained five or six rooms, and their flat roofs provided additional living space— a cool place to sit or sleep after the sun went down. Furnishings were few. Villages maintained community shrines and cemeteries, but each home also had an altar dedicated to the worship of its household gods. The great temples served the state's gods. Each locality had its own patron deities and each family its own ancestral cult. Clothing was simple, and people sometimes dispensed with it entirely. The Egyptians valued bodily cleanliness. Soap had not yet been invented, but they scrubbed themselves with various compounds and applied unguents to protect their skin from the sun. They reduced the sun's glare by outlining their eyes with dark makeup (like some modern athletes). They shaved or plucked most body hair and wore wigs that were easy to clean and keep free of vermin. Males were circumcised.

Warlike peoples tend to exalt the status of males and to value sons more highly than daughters, but thanks to the protection that nature provided, Egypt was a fairly secure place. This seems to have fostered a milder form of patriarchy than found in other ancient societies. Egyptian men and women of the same class had nearly identical legal rights. Both could inherit, purchase, and sell property. Both could enter into contracts, make wills, and bring suits in court. Pharaohs had harems, but ordinary people were monogamous. Marriage was a private arrangement. The state did not impose regulations, but couples sometimes drew up contracts to define the terms of their relationship. A household's possessions were considered communal property, and divorce could be initiated by either a husband or a wife. People traced their ancestry through both maternal and paternal lines and inherited estates from both parents. Some Egyptians may have practiced brother–sister marriages, but evidence for this is sparse. Most documented examples come from the royal family and were motivated by its unique concern for establishing clear hereditary rights to the throne. The princes and princesses who married were usually half siblings, a pharaoh's son and daughter by different wives.

Women were associated with domestic environments and occupations. Artists painted women white and men brown to indicate that the former led sheltered lives in the home while the latter worked outside, exposed to the elements. Egyptians cherished their homes, and the home's female caretaker was highly respected. When Egyptian men composed epitaphs for their tombs, they often waxed sentimental about their mothers and bragged about both their matrilinies and patrilinies. The ancient Mediterranean world was, in general, not kind to women, but Egyptian women had a better lot in life than their sisters elsewhere.

The Indo-Europeans and the Clash of Empires

During Egypt's Second Intermediate Period (c. 1590 B.C.E.), as the country came under Hyksos domination, new peoples migrated into the Middle East and caused considerable upheaval. They were part of a vast movement that spread the **Indo-European** family of languages from Ireland to Iran and India. The Indo-European mother tongue no longer exists, but the distribution of its various offshoots suggests that it originated somewhere north of the Black Sea. People from this region began to migrate outward about 2000 B.C.E., and almost everywhere they went, their language dominated. It evolved to become the speech of the ancient Greeks, Romans, Persians, and Indians—and, ultimately, most modern Europeans and Americans (see Map 2–1).

The Hittites   An Indo-European people called the Hittites founded the most powerful of the Middle East's new states. Their base was in north-central Anatolia, but their influence was felt much farther afield. They sacked Babylon in 1595 B.C.E. but were prevented from immediately expanding into Syria and Mesopotamia by the Hurrians of Mitanni, a country north of Assyria. The Mitannians dominated Syria and northern Mesopotamia from about 1500 to 1360 B.C.E. and skirmished with the empire-building pharaohs of the early New Kingdom. About 1360 B.C.E. the Hittites defeated them. The Hittites then turned their attention to challenging Egypt's Middle-Eastern empire.

The contest between the Hittites and the Egyptians culminated in a battle that Ramses II fought in 1286 B.C.E. at a place called Qadesh. The pharaoh's monuments claim it as a great victory for Egypt, but it appears to have been a draw. At any rate, the rapprochement between the Egyptians and Hittites that followed Qadesh probably had little to do with the battle's outcome. The fall of the Mitannian Empire had liberated the Assyrians, a people who lived along the upper reaches of the Tigris River, and they had begun to pose a threat to the Hittites. The Hittites made peace with Egypt to avoid being caught between two enemies and dispatched a princess to Egypt to become one of Ramses' many wives.

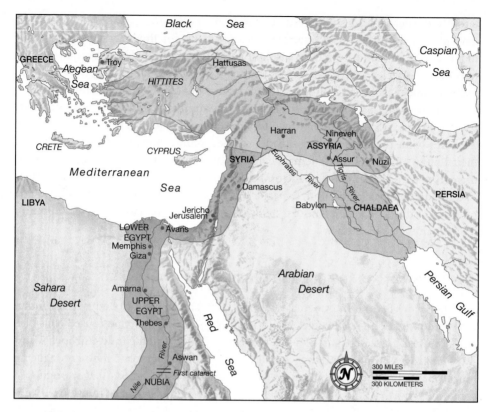

Map 2–1 The Seats of the Ancient Middle-Eastern Empires Many states appeared in the Fertile Crescent, and from time to time one would attempt to bring the others under its control and create an empire.

Question: How might the geography of the Middle East influence the region's military history?

The Hittites adapted cuneiform to write their language and assimilated the civilization they found already established in the Middle East. They lived in isolated, self-sufficient villages and established few cities apart from their heavily fortified capital, Hattusas. Theirs was a warlike society that was well mobilized to support a large, expensively equipped army. Their king shared power with a council consisting of the heads of his subjects' chief families, and their government was plagued by coups, assassinations, and disputed successions.

The Invasion of the Sea Peoples The Hittite empire collapsed about 1200 B.C.E. in the wake of events that also forced Egypt to retreat from its empire. Seafaring raiders attacked the coasts of the Mediterranean from Asia Minor to Libya. They were a polyglot band of pirates whom the Egyptians lumped together as the **Sea Peoples**. The invasion of the Sea Peoples was a mass migration that swept up different elements as it spread. It may have been triggered by the collapse of some small states in Greece and expanded as a growing crowd of refugees undermined and overwhelmed one community after another. Incursions into the Egyptian delta began in 1207 B.C.E. and continued for over 20 years. The Egyptians were not enthusiastic open-sea sailors nor adept at dealing with naval invasions. The Hittites were less exposed to attack from the sea, but they failed to cope with the waves of dislocated peoples who flooded across their borders. Famines may also have hampered the efforts of the established states to defend themselves. There is evidence that a prolonged drought afflicted much of the Mediterranean world at the end of the thirteenth century. A shift in military technology may also have played a role in the decline of the older empires. They had become heavily dependent on light chariots bearing archers to rout disorganized throngs of foot soldiers who fought with clubs and spears. But the invaders were armored men equipped with round shields, two-edged swords, and javelins. They may have developed a tactic for charging and disabling horse-drawn chariots. Whatever the causes, the result was widespread disruption and resettlement.

Assyria's Opportunity   The indigenous peoples who profited most from the confusion created by the Sea Peoples' invasion were the Assyrians, a Semitic folk who occupied the upper reaches of the Tigris River. Their difficult hilly homeland on the fringes of Mesopotamian civilization was under constant pressure from hostile tribes that dwelt in the mountains on its eastern and northern borders. The threat these people posed may explain the militarism that took hold of Assyrian society.

The fall of the Mitannian Empire (c. 1360 B.C.E.) removed the chief obstacle to Assyria's expansion, but the Assyrians advanced slowly. To the south they confronted the powerful Kassites of Babylon. In the west they faced the Aramaeans, desert nomads who were seeking places to settle. Their old enemies in the northern and eastern mountains remained a problem. On top of all this, Assyria wrestled with internal political problems that finally caused its drive toward empire to falter late in the thirteenth century.

Assyria languished until Tiglath-Pileser I ascended the throne in 1114 B.C.E. He subdued Babylon and drove through northern Syria to the coast of the Mediterranean. After his death in 1076 B.C.E., Assyria entered another period of decline. Its march toward empire resumed in the ninth century B.C.E., when it won control of most of Mesopotamia and Syria. A glorious new city called Nimrud was built south of the old Assyrian capital at Nineveh, and the ruins of the palace that Ashurnasirpal II (883–859 B.C.E.) built in Nimrud were among the first sites to be explored by the European adventurers who pioneered the science of archaeology in the nineteenth century. The great stone slabs covered with cuneiform inscriptions and bas-reliefs that formed the palace's walls were widely disbursed and can be seen in many European and American museums.

Disputed successions to the throne inaugurated another period of decline for Assyria in the late ninth century B.C.E. In 745 B.C.E. a general, Tiglath-Pileser III (745–727 B.C.E.), seized power and built an empire that extended from the Persian

The Assyrian Army Besieges a City   This bas-relief depicts Assyrian warriors battling their enemies, a task at which the Assyrians were notoriously adept. Note the weapons and shields, the prominence of foot soldiers, and the way chariots appear to be used.

Gulf north to Armenia and west to the Mediterranean coast and the borders of Egypt. In 722 B.C.E. the throne was usurped by Sargon II, who founded the last and greatest Assyrian dynasty. His grandson, Esarhaddon (681–669 B.C.E.), brought the empire to its height in 671 B.C.E. by conquering Egypt.

Egypt's Fading Glory   Egypt's New Kingdom began to decline following the raids of the Sea Peoples, and as local strongmen broke free of the central government and set up petty states, the country's vulnerability to invasion increased. Nubia, which had so often been invaded by Egypt, turned the tables on its old adversary. Nubian kings drove down the Nile, and by 727 they had become the pharaohs of a reunited Egypt. The Nubians then overreached themselves by invading Palestine in an effort to regain Egypt's former empire. This prompted an Assyrian counteroffensive that drove the Nubians from Egypt. The Assyrians then tried to govern Egypt with the help of native client rulers, but these men were chronically unreliable. The Assyrian kings, Esarhaddon and his successor, Assurbanipal (668–630 B.C.E.), repeatedly sent armies into Egypt to reassert their authority. Their empire was, however, overextended militarily, and they had pressing problems elsewhere that prevented them from consolidating their hold on Egypt.

By 655 B.C.E. the governors of Sais, a city in the delta, had restored Egypt's unity and independence. The Saite pharaohs sought allies and trading partners abroad and opened their country to the outside world. Foreigners established merchant colonies in Egypt and served the pharaohs as mercenary soldiers. The Saite dynasty tried to bolster its legitimacy (and maybe counter the influence of the alien cultures to which it had exposed its homeland) by restoring archaic Egyptian practices. Artists and architects resurrected the styles of the Old and Middle Kingdoms, and there was a literary renaissance. Egypt's destiny, however, was to be absorbed into a succession of empires: Persian, Greek, Roman, and finally Muslim.

Assyria's Culmination   Assyria relied on brute force and psychological intimidation to build and hold its empire, and its most significant cultural contributions were in the area of military science. Assyria maintained a standing army consisting of specialized units: infantry, cavalry, chariots, scouts, and engineers (to level roads, bridge rivers, and construct siege equipment). Progress in metallurgy made iron weapons and armor increasingly common, and breeders produced horses large enough to be ridden into battle. Most ancient armies were little more than armed mobs, but the units of the Assyrian army supported one another in the field and were trained to execute battle plans. Support structures were also devised to keep large armies well supplied during sieges and on the move.

An increasing supply of iron weapons may have contributed something to Assyria's success. During the eleventh century B.C.E. iron ceased to be an exotic metal and came into more general use in parts of the Middle East. Unlike copper, iron was seldom found in nature in a pure state—although meteors provided some highly prized specimens. The metal was so rare that it was sometimes set in gold and used as jewelry. Iron ore was much more plentiful than the copper and tin ores used to make bronze, but it was more difficult to smelt and forge into implements. Copper and tin melted at lower temperatures and could be cast in molds to create useful objects. But air had to be forced into furnaces to achieve the temperatures needed to smelt iron, and the resulting metal was too brittle for use. It had to be converted into steel by repeated heating, cooling, and hammering to combine it with carbon and to shape it. The first people to figure out the processes for working iron may have lived in Armenia. The Hurrians of Mitanni were using some iron as early as 1500 B.C.E. After the Mitannian Empire fell, its Hittite successor became known for iron production. One of the treasures found in Tutankhamun's tomb was an iron-bladed dagger that was probably a gift from a Hittite king. Hittite iron production was, however, limited. Not until about 900 B.C.E. did iron begin to become plentiful and cheap enough to equip large numbers of soldiers. The Assyrian military may have been the first to use it extensively, but soldiers were not the only people whose lives were affected by the new metal. Iron is plentiful, and iron implements were relatively inexpensive compared to bronze. Some peasant farmers began to acquire metal tools and to explore what these could do to make farming easier and more productive.

Assyrian emperors did not rely solely on well armed, elaborately equipped, and efficiently drilled armies to achieve victory. They resorted to terrorism to frighten their opponents into submission, and their monuments proudly catalogued the atrocities they committed: heads lopped off, eyes gouged out, limbs severed, skin flayed from living bodies, and the mass slaughter of women and children. Such treatment was not designed to win the loyalty and love of the peoples whom the Assyrians conquered, and their empire was plagued by revolts and rebellions. Some regions were pacified by deporting and scattering entire populations. This was the fate of the Bible's famous "ten lost tribes of Israel."

The creation and preservation of the Assyrian empire thoroughly militarized Assyrian society. Militarization sometimes promotes a kind of hyper-masculinization of a culture that makes life difficult for women. This is reflected in Assyrian law codes. Assyrian laws were more concerned with property rights than human freedoms, and they lavishly recommended mutilations and executions as punishment for all kinds of transgressions. The law declared women to be the property of their fathers and husbands, and a woman who dishonored the man who was responsible for her was fortunate if she lost only her ears, nose, or fingers. Some female offenders had their breasts ripped off. Because a man could get in serious trouble if he had contact with women belonging to another man, he needed to be able to recognize the status of each woman he met. Assyrian law, therefore, ordered respectable women to veil their faces whenever they left their homes and punished any prostitute who tried to hide behind a veil. The custom of requiring women to cover their faces when in public was widespread in the ancient world, and it is still enforced to greater and lesser degrees in some Middle-Eastern countries.

Assyrian civilization reached its height under the warlike, but cultivated, Assurbanipal (668–630 B.C.E.). He was a scholar and an aesthete as well as a general. He could read the long-dead Sumerian language and had a passion for collecting ancient texts. He searched his empire for documents and created a huge library at Nineveh. Some 30,000 tablets have been recovered from its ruins.

Things deteriorated rapidly during the reigns of Assurbanipal's two sons. The garrisons that had to be maintained throughout the empire to keep watch over its hordes of resentful subjects imposed a fatal drain on the empire's manpower, and this was probably a factor in its sudden collapse. The end came quickly after the Chaldaeans, an Aramaic-speaking tribe, seized Babylon and began to negotiate with their eastern neighbors, the Medes, an Indo-European people who had settled in Iran. In 612 B.C.E. the Chaldaeans and the Medes joined forces against Assyria and sacked Nineveh. By 610, the Assyrian empire was only a memory, and the Chaldaeans had become the rising power in the Middle East. The Chaldaean empire proved to be short-lived (612–539 B.C.E.), and it is remembered today primarily because of the role it played in biblical history. The Chaldaeans conquered Judah, destroyed Jerusalem and its temple, and forced the Jews into exile. The crisis created by the loss of their land and temple inspired the Jews to focus on the compilation of the Hebrew scriptures as one of several strategies they used to preserve the memory of their past, the rules of their cultic life, and their identity as a people.

The Bible and History

No ancient peoples have had a greater influence on what Western civilization became than a tiny group to whom the great Mesopotamian and Egyptian empires paid scant attention. All three of the West's major religions (Judaism, Christianity, and Islam) trace their origins, at least in part, to the sacred literature of a people who are known variously as Hebrews (from a Semitic term for nomad), Israelites (from Israel, the northern part of their territory), and Jews (from Judah, the region around their sacred city, Jerusalem).

The ancient Israelites' concept of divine power contrasted with the views prevalent in the ancient world. Over time, the Israelites came to embrace a monotheistic faith, but more original than their belief in one god was how they conceived that god. Most ancient peoples equated gods with forces of nature and assumed that gods were simply part of the created order. The gods may have designed and constructed this world, but they did not create existence itself. The God of the ancient Hebrews was different. He was the transcendent Creator who was the source of everything that was. He was not subject to time and space, the dimensions of the reality He called into being. He was the Other, an omnipotence beyond mere existence.

The exalted nature of Israel's God removed Him from the realm of ordinary human experience. He could be known, therefore, only if and where He chose to manifest Himself. The Israelites argued that as the Creator of nature, God was not revealed by the cycles of nature. The things of nature follow fixed laws. They are not free, whereas the Creator is absolute freedom. He is nature's master, not its prisoner. The suitable place for Him to reveal Himself, therefore, is in the kinds of phenomena where free wills manifest themselves—in the events of history. Because God is beyond all compulsion, however, He is no more a prisoner of history than of nature. He does not appear in all history, but only in the history He chooses to use. The ancient Israelites believed that God had elected their history as the vehicle for His self-revelation. This was what they meant by claiming that they were God's "Chosen People." God did not value them more than others, but for reasons He did not explain He invited them to become His human partners and to have a history that was to disclose Him to the world.

Many ancient cultures thought of time as an eternal, repetitive cycle of days and seasons. It went nowhere and had no significance. Most people had little awareness of time as a sequence of unique, significant events—of time as history. The Israelite conception of God fostered a different view of life's temporal context. It implied that the passage of time was a kind of journey filled with meaningful adventures and learning experiences that served to bring people a greater awareness of their Creator.

This journey, the Israelites believed, did not truly get underway until long after the world had been created. They did not think of themselves as one of the world's first (or even ancient) peoples. They traced their origin to a covenant (compact) that God made with a man named Abram ("honored father"), who was renamed Abraham ("father of many") as a sign of God's pledge to make him the founder of a nation. The Israelites were the "children of Abraham," descendants of a landless man who was born into a world that had long been occupied by other peoples.

The stories of Abraham and the creation of the Chosen People begin in the twelfth chapter of Genesis, the first book of the Bible. For the earlier chapters, which provide background for this event, the Israelites drew on the general religious mythology that circulated throughout the ancient Middle East. These chapters, with their stories of gardens of paradise, snakes, floods, arks, and heaven-scaling towers, derive from the myths of the Sumerians and Babylonians. There is little historical information in this material, but then the histories of most peoples begin with myths and legends. The Israelites recycled and transformed the tales provided by their cultural environment to explain their understanding of their mission in history and their God.

Sacred Myth and History   The Bible purports to derive, at least in part, from the experiences of a real people, the ancient Israelites. For generations scholars have sought to test this thesis by analyzing the Bible's narratives and comparing them with other ancient records. Because this undertaking has implications for the cherished convictions of both believers and nonbelievers, it has always excited great controversy.

The Bible claims that Abraham was an Aramaean nomad whose family came from "Ur of the Chaldaeans." Ur was gone long before the Chaldaeans appeared, but at the time when this text was written, the Chaldaeans ruled the Mesopotamian heartland where the Israelites believed their founding father's family had originated. After the collapse of the Third Dynasty of Ur in 2004 B.C.E., there was significant migration of Aramaean tribes into northern Mesopotamia, where the Bible locates Abraham at the start of his story. But no one can be certain if Abraham was a real individual or only a symbol representing the origin of a people and their unique sense of identity and destiny.

The Bible describes Abraham and his people as having virtually nothing on which to build a significant future. Their weakness was key to their mission. Any success they might have would obviously be due to God's strength and not their own. For several generations they remain *apiru* (Hebrews), landless nomads, a people who "dwell in tents." They wander about Syria, Palestine, and the Sinai following Abraham and his heirs, the patriarchs Isaac, Jacob, and Joseph. Archaeological evidence suggests that the Sinai was more hospitable to herders during parts of the second millennium than at other times, and Egyptian records from the fifteenth century B.C.E. document the presence of nomads in that region.

The Bible says that Joseph, the last of the patriarchs, persuaded a pharaoh to allow his people to settle in the "land of Goshen," a district on the border between Egypt's delta and the Sinai. If there is any truth to this, the Egyptian pharaohs who were most likely to welcome *apiru* immigration were Hyksos. The Hyksos, like the *apiru*, were Semites, and they may have wanted help with their occupation of Egypt. The Bible says that Joseph's people remained in Egypt for over 400 years, but it says nothing about these centuries.

The Middle-Eastern Empires of the Iron Age

THE MIDDLE EAST	EGYPT	BIBLICAL NARRATIVE
2004 B.C.E., Ur falls	MIDDLE KINGDOM (2025–1630 B.C.E.)	
BABYLONIAN EMPIRE Hammurabi (1792–1750 B.C.E.) {Indo–European migration}		Abraham and the Patriarchs
	SECOND INTERMEDIATE PERIOD (1630–1550 B.C.E.) {Hyksos invasion of Egypt}	
{1595 B.C.E., Hittites sack Babylon} Kassites occupy Babylon		Sojourn of the Israelites in Egypt
MITANNIAN EMPIRE (–c. 1360 B.C.E.) Hittite Kingdom	NEW KINGDOM (1550–1075 B.C.E.) Thutmose I (1504–1492 B.C.E.) Hatshepsut (1478–1458 B.C.E.) Thutmose III (1458–1425 B.C.E.) Amenhotep III (1390–1352 B.C.E.) Akhenaten (1352–1338 B.C.E.) {The Amarna Period} Tutankhamun (1336–1327 B.C.E.) Ramses II (1279–1212 B.C.E.)	The Exodus and Moses'
HITTITE EMPIRE (–c. 1200 B.C.E.) {1286 B.C.E., Qadesh} 1230 B.C.E., invasion of the Sea Peoples		Entrance into Canaan The era of Judges
		The Kingdom Saul (1020–1000 B.C.E.) David (1000–961 B.C.E.) Solomon (961–922 B.C.E.) ISRAEL and JUDAH
Ashurnasirpal (883–859 B.C.E.) Tiglath-Pileser III (745–727 B.C.E.) Esarhaddon (681–669 B.C.E.) Assurbanipal (668–630 B.C.E.) 612 B.C.E., Nineveh falls CHALDAEAN EMPIRE (612–538 B.C.E.) PERSIAN EMPIRE	Nubian pharaohs (–c. 656 B.C.E.) Saitic Dynasty (–c. 655–525 B.C.E.)	Israel falls, 721 B.C.E. 587 B.C.E., Judah falls The Exile

Abraham's descendants did not begin to become a distinct people with a unique identity, according to the Bible, until a man called Moses (the root of Egyptian names such as Thut-moses, "Son of Thut") led them out of Egypt. This event, which is called the **Exodus**, is described in some passages as a dramatic flight from a pursuing Egyptian army that drowned in the Sea of Reeds. There is no report of such a catastrophe in the Egyptian records. Some scholars have tried to connect Moses with the court of Akhenaten and to ground Hebrew monotheism in the cult of the Aten. Others favor a later date for the Exodus, during the reign of Ramses II (1279–1212 B.C.E.). All that the Bible says is that there was a change of dynasty that brought a new pharaoh to power, and he set the Hebrews to making bricks to build the cities of Pithom and Ramses. During the period of the New Kingdom, the residents of Egypt's eastern borderlands would have been impressed into service to construct the forts and depots (the Bible's "store cities") that were part of the empire's new military infrastructure.

The Hebrews who fled Egypt allegedly tried to break into the agricultural districts of southern Palestine, but were repulsed and forced to resume the nomadic life of their ancestors in the desert. Joshua, Moses' successor, finally led them across the Jordan River, past the city of Jericho, and into a land occupied by an urbanized people called the Canaanites. A likely time for desert tribes to breach Canaan's frontier defenses would be about 1230 B.C.E., when raids by the Sea Peoples were drawing defenders away from the inland borders to protect the coasts. Some Sea Peoples established themselves permanently in the region. The Bible knows them as the Philistines, the powerful enemies of the Hebrews. The Egyptians paid close attention to events in Palestine, and the first extra-biblical reference to a people called Israel is found on a monument erected by the pharaoh Merneptah in 1207 B.C.E. Merneptah, successor to Ramses II, defended Egyptian territory from incursions of invaders, and he claimed (erroneously, as it turns out) to have virtually exterminated Israel.

Although some biblical passages describe the Hebrews' invasion of Canaan as a war of conquest, examination of the details suggests something less dramatic. The Hebrews did not occupy any cities or claim the agriculturally rich Jordan Valley. They scattered into the mountains between the valley and the coast, and spent generations scratching out a precarious existence. They are said to have formed a loose federation of 12 tribes that was led, from time to time, by charismatic figures called judges. They were culturally backward folk, and although they survived, their existence was tenuous.

Archaeological evidence suggests an even less dramatic tale. Instead of a horde of people under single leadership spreading from Egypt and across the Sinai into Canaan, it implies that around 1100 B.C.E. small villages that relied heavily on herding appeared in the central hill country of Palestine. These were populated by people who had long lived on the margins of the Canaanite city-states. The Bible's description of the Jews as descendants of a single man who moved together through the Sinai to Egypt and ultimately left Egypt to claim Canaan as their "Promised Land" may well be an oversimplification—an effort by later generations to construct a story of origin for their people, a story that supported the sense of mission and political agendas of later generations.

Palestine   Urban settlement began very early (c. 7000 B.C.E.) along the eastern edge of the Mediterranean. The region had sufficient rainfall to support farming, and its rough terrain encouraged the formation of small city-states rather than large territorial kingdoms. The richest district was a strip of coast west of the Lebanese Mountains called Phoenicia. The Phoenicians, the West's first notable seafarers, derived their wealth from trade, for their ports (Tyre, Sidon, and Byblos) were ideally situated to mediate exchanges of goods between Mesopotamia and Egypt. Phoenicians were shipping wood from the Lebanese Mountains to treeless Egypt as early as the start of the Old Kingdom. They also trafficked in copper and manufactured a scarlet dye that was so costly that its color came to be identified with royalty. So many sheets of Egyptian papyrus passed through Byblos that the port's name became the Greek word for book (*biblos*), the source of the English word Bible.

The Phoenicians were explorers as well as traders. They traveled the length of the Mediterranean, colonized the coast of North Africa, and ventured onto the Atlantic. They may have reached Britain and, if a report in an ancient Greek history is accurate, circumnavigated Africa. They were the chief agents for diffusing the civilization that was evolving in the ancient Middle East throughout the Mediterranean world. Their influence lives on, for the Greeks adapted their letter forms and alphabet, and transmitted these things to the Romans and ultimately to the modern West.

In the biblical account, the Israelites who settled in the mountains between the Jordan Valley and the Mediterranean coast were less concerned with the Phoenicians than with the Philistines (who occupied the coast west of Jerusalem) and the Canaanites. The Canaanites were related to the Amorites who founded Babylon, and their urbanized culture was much more advanced than that of the Israelites. The Bible says that the Israelites had to trade with them to obtain metal implements, for they did not know how to make these things for themselves. Disillusionment with their inferior status finally convinced the Israelites that they needed to make changes in their way of life so that they could be like all the nations. This, they believed, required them to submit to the authority of a king.

The Bible says that religious leaders were reluctant to change tradition but finally agreed to appoint the Israelites' first king, a man named Saul (c. 1020–1000 B.C.E.). Saul's reign was not successful, and after Saul died in battle with the Philistines, his crown passed to an ambitious general named David (c. 1000–961 B.C.E.). David is said to have united the Israelite tribes, conquered Canaan, and created a state with its capital at Jerusalem. The new kingdom allegedly won international respect and grew extremely wealthy during the reign of David's son, Solomon (c. 961–922 B.C.E.). This was a time when small states like Solomon's might have flourished. The great empires of the Egyptians and Hittites had fallen, and no new superpower had yet appeared to threaten the independence of Palestine.

The Bible describes Solomon as a mighty ruler, but historians caution that no archaeological evidence confirms the Bible's picture of David's or Solomon's kingdom. An inscription mentioning the "House of David" has been found. Although it dates to about a century and a half after David's generation, there is no trace of great buildings or a great city at the site of Jerusalem. Some scholars believe that the first important Hebrew kingdom appeared north of Jerusalem in the territory the Bible calls Israel. Its capital was at Shechem. After this kingdom collapsed, the southern state, with its cult and political center at Jerusalem, may have rewritten history to magnify its own importance.

The Bible's narrative, however, describes a Hebrew state that, like Egypt, was a double monarchy: a northern kingdom of Israel and a southern kingdom of Judah. The Bible says that the ten northern tribes of Israelites refused to accept Solomon's heir and declared their independence under a king of their own. Solomon's dynasty retained only the smaller and more rural Judah. Both kingdoms were caught up in the international conflicts that accompanied the rise of the Assyrian empire. In 721 B.C.E. Assyria overwhelmed Israel and deported its people. Israel's ten tribes were "lost" in that they were scattered throughout the Assyrian empire. The tiny kingdom of Judah managed to outlast the Assyrian Empire, but it succumbed to the Assyrians' successors, the Chaldaeans. In 587 B.C.E. the Chaldaeans destroyed Jerusalem and deported its people. This began the **Exile**, the period that was, after the Exodus, the most theologically significant in Hebrew history (see Map 2–2).

Exile was intended to extinguish a people's identity, but the Jews escaped this fate. They were helped by the fact that for some of them the Exile was relatively brief. In 539 B.C.E. Cyrus the Great defeated the Chaldaeans, established the Persian Empire, and permitted a few Jews to go back to Jerusalem to rebuild its temple. Jerusalem was rarely independent of the empires that subsequently rose and fell in the Mediterranean world, but its continuing existence provided an anchor for Jewish identity.

A major thing that enabled the Jews to preserve their identity was the creation of the Hebrew Scriptures. The first five books, called the **Torah** (Law), probably assumed their present form during the Exile. Court scholars, who worked for the kings of Israel and Judah, had recorded several versions of the ancient oral traditions of their people, and these were integrated into a single narrative by Jewish scribes or rabbis (teachers) working during the Exile. They, of course, viewed the Hebrew past from the perspective of Judah. According to the Book of Ezra, the Jews who returned to Jerusalem were the first to hear a reading of the Torah. Its stories of Abraham and his descendants reminded them that it was a relationship with their God—not their land—that made them a people. This belief has helped them survive millennia of exile, *diaspora* (Greek for "scattering"), and persecution to become the only ancient people who have maintained their identity into the modern era.

The Biblical Faith   The land of Israel did not make the Jews a people, but its loss was a challenge to their faith. They believed that David's kingdom had been given to them in fulfillment of the promises that God made to Abraham. The loss of this "Promised Land" might have been taken as a sign that God had abandoned them, or that He was too weak to keep his promises, or that He was untrustworthy. Meditating on the experience, however, helped religious leaders, whom the Jews called prophets, articulate some of the Bible's most profound insights into the human condition.

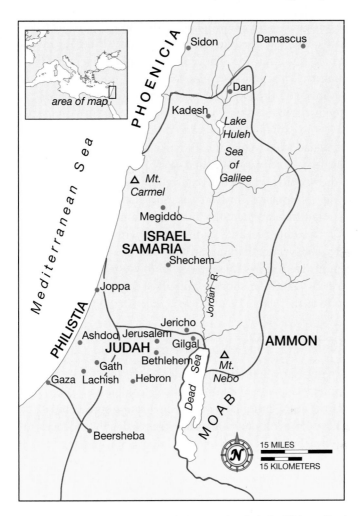

Map 2–2   Ancient Palestine   Although some scholars are skeptical, the Bible credits the establishment of the ancient Hebrew state to the second of Israel's kings, David. He is said to have conquered and united the Canaanite city-states and linked the Jordan Valley with a strip of coast bordered by Phoenicia in the north and the territory of the Philistines in the south. Following the reign of his son and successor, Solomon, the state he built allegedly split into rival kingdoms called Israel and Judah.

Question: Does geography support or provide grounds for questioning the Bible's description of the reigns of David and Solomon?

A twentieth-century philosopher has characterized the seventh and sixth centuries B.C.E. as the **Axial Age,** a crucial turning point for world civilizations. During these years, major religious leaders appeared in several parts of the world and changed how people thought about social relationships and the meaning of life. Greece produced the first philosophers. Zoroaster led a religious reform in Persia. Confucius and Lao-tzu taught in China. Buddha emerged from India, and a number of Hebrew prophets added their books to the Bible.

The Hebrew prophets were not prophets in the sense of fortune tellers. The Bible affirms the reality of human freedom and responsibility. If the future could be foretold, freedom would be an illusion. The Hebrew prophets operated like modern political commentators. Their mission was to explain the religious significance of contemporary events, and their predictions for the future were based on the lessons of history. For them, the loss of the Promised Land was part of a divine plan. God had given the Jews a law to explain how He wanted them to treat one another and honor Him. Instead, they had tried to placate Him, like a pagan god, with ritual and sacrifice. But what He demanded was justice and care for the poor and weak. The Jews had lost their land, the prophets claimed, because they had ceased to do God's will. But their situation was not hopeless, for God was more than a judge who punished transgressors. He was a faithful and merciful Father who somehow reconciled the requirements of justice (recompense and punishment) with those of love (mercy and forgiveness). The Bible's claim that human communities are accountable to transcendent standards of justice and charity sank deep into Western consciousness. Although Western societies have fallen far short in pursuit of this vision, they have never lost a sense of obligation to it.

KEY QUESTION | Revisited

Thanks to human ingenuity in finding multiple ways to adapt to environments (and to the new environments adaptation continually creates), human communities and cultural identities are of nearly infinite variety. As civilization spread and diversified in the ancient Middle East, drives for unity and order struggled with tendencies to disrupt and divide. Small political entities gave way to ever larger ones, and governments faced the challenge of wielding authority over great landmasses inhabited by diverse peoples. The states that appeared in ancient Mesopotamia and Egypt were the first to confront issues of this kind, and they developed a number of strategies for dealing with them. The most common plan was to impose order from above and to use the threat of force to suppress divisive tendencies. The need for efficiency in a world with relatively primitive means of travel and communication encouraged concentration of power in the hands of a monarch. But poor communications made the effective exercise of centralized authority difficult. It was hard for a king to know what was happening when he was not present in person to observe. To compensate for this, rulers sought to awe their subjects into obedience. The means they used to elevate themselves above the common herd of humanity were designed to persuade their people that their power was of supernatural origin and reach. But ideas about the accountability of monarchs to something beyond themselves also began to circulate in the ancient world. Egyptian pharaohs were responsible for maintaining *ma'at*. Babylonian emperors enforced laws decreed by their gods, and Hebrews inched their way toward faith in a humane principle of transcendent justice as the source of all things. Such beliefs could be used to justify the efforts of an individual civilization to expand the range of its dominance, or they could promote respect for diversity in the belief that all civilizations fell short of the ideal enshrined in the concept of civilization itself.

Review Questions

1. What challenges faced Hammurabi in consolidating his empire? How did he try to meet them?
2. How did religion and geography interact to unite Egypt and build its empire?
3. What strategies did the Assyrians employ to build and hold their empire?
4. What lessons about the construction of a viable society are taught by the biblical account of the rise, fall, and restoration of the Hebrew kingdoms?
5. Which of the strategies employed by the ancient empire builders was most successful? Why?
6. Is civilization one thing, or is it many?

 Please consult the Suggested Readings at the back of the book to continue your study of the material covered in this chapter. For a list of documents on the Primary Source DVD-ROM that relate to topics in this chapter, please refer to the back of the book.

Part 2
The Classical Era 2000 B.C.E. to 30 C.E.

Head of a man, from a bronze statue by the Athenian sculptor Phidias (c. 450 B.C.E.)

Many of the characteristics that distinguish Western civilization first emerged clearly during the era when the Greeks and the Romans dominated the Mediterranean world. Their moment in history therefore became the West's classical period. Western peoples are not, and have never been, a homogenous group with a single outlook, and they do not all honor, nor have they ever honored, identical institutions or sets of values. But certain ideas or attitudes have repeatedly surfaced in their societies and provided continuity for their history. A major Greco-Roman legacy was a faith in humanity itself—in reason, science, and human intellect as adequate tools for understanding the world and coping with its challenges. Associated with this was the assumption that ethics and morality have a basis in nature—a belief that has inspired noble concepts of human rights and drives to organize just societies. Respect for the past has paralyzed some peoples, but the West's recurring bouts of enthusiasm for its classical period have inspired innovation and renewal.

	ENVIRONMENT AND TECHNOLOGY	SOCIETY AND CULTURE	POLITICS
C. 2000 B.C.E.	Sea-faring ships Linear A script	Bronze Age Minoan Crete	Merchant-princes
C. 1800 B.C.E.	Linear B script	Mycenaean Greeks	Bureaucratic administration
C. 1230 B.C.E.	Geometric-style pottery	Aegean Dark Age	
C. 1200 B.C.E.		Iron Age	
C. 750 B.C.E.	Phoenician alphabet Social engineering Hoplite infantry	Greek Archaic era Etruscan expansion Rome founded Homer and Hesiod	Greek colonization *Polis* Spartan mobilization (650 B.C.E.)
C. 500 B.C.E.	Ionian natural science Black-figure pottery Red-figure pottery Doric and Ionic architecture	Hellenic era Sophist philosophers Athenian theater Socrates	Athenian democracy (510 B.C.E.) Roman Republic founded (500 B.C.E.) Persian Wars (492–479 B.C.E.) Delian League (477 B.C.E.)
C. 400 B.C.E.		Herodotus Thucydides Plato Aristotle	Peloponnesian War (432–404 B.C.E.) Philip of Macedon (359–336 B.C.E.) Alexander (336–323 B.C.E.)
C. 300 B.C.E.	Urban planning Alexandrian science The museum Euclid	Hellenistic era Pastoral and lyric poetry novels	Seleucid and Ptolemaic kingdoms
C. 200 B.C.E.	Roman legion Roman engineering: roads Latifundia	New Comedy	Punic Wars (264–202 B.C.E.) Roman civil war (133–30 B.C.E.)
C. 100 B.C.E.		Cicero Jesus of Nazareth Golden Age, Roman poetry Virgil, Horace, Ovid	Julius Caesar (100–44 B.C.E.) Octavian Augustus (63 B.C.E.–14 C.E.) Roman Empire founded (30 B.C.E.) Julio-Claudians (30 B.C.E.–68 C.E.)
C. 100 C.E.		Silver Age, Roman poetry	
C. 200 C.E.			Flavians (69–96 C.E.) "Good Emperors" (96–180 C.E.) Severans (193–235 C.E.) "Barracks Emperors" (235–285 C.E.)

Topics in This Chapter

Minoan Mentors • The Mycenaeans, Greece's First Civilization • The Aegean
Dark Age • The Hellenic Era • The Rise of the Mainland Powers
• The Persian Wars: Crucible of a Civilization

3 Aegean Civilizations

I would rather be a humble servant plowing fields for the owner of a tiny farm than the
greatest lord in the kingdom of the dead.

—Achilles, *The Odyssey*

KEY | Question

When does civilization in the West become "Western" civilization?

On his way home from the Trojan War, a Greek king named Odysseus paid a visit to the
mouth of the underworld to consult the ghost of Achilles, a friend who died in that war.
Achilles, who had been the greatest of Greece's heroes, used the occasion to explain the
facts of death to Odysseus. He said that he would rather occupy the lowest station in the
land of the living than the highest post in the world of the dead. Achilles' passion for life and
faith in the value of earthly existence, which are implied by this remark, help to explain the
achievements of the Greeks. The civilization they founded on the shores of the Aegean Sea
transformed the ancient world, and it continues to influence the modern world. People still
adapt the Greeks' architecture, imitate their sculpture, debate the theories of their philosophers, use their scientific vocabulary, and even go to the theater to be entertained by their
playwrights.

The influence of the ancient Greek thinkers and artists has been so pervasive
that some historians claim that the Greeks were the founders of Western civilization.
Others caution that the Greeks did not develop in a vacuum—that they had close ties
with Middle-Eastern states and borrowed much from them. A controversial school of
contemporary scholars has gone so far as to claim that most of Greek civilization was
derived from Egypt and Africa.

The Mask of Agamemnon   This gold mask was discovered in a grave at the ancient Greek city of Mycenae. Heinrich Schliemann, who excavated Troy, found it in 1876 and leapt to the unwarranted conclusion that it represented Agamemnon, leader of the Greek army in Homer's *Iliad*.

Advocates for all these positions make their cases by listing specific things that the Greeks are said either to have borrowed or to have originated. Arguments of this kind are not very persuasive, for a civilization is more than its component parts. The debate does, however, illustrate how difficult it is to draw hard and fast lines across the continuum of history, and it is a healthy corrective to the belief that Western civilization developed in isolation and entirely from its own intellectual resources.

The ancient Greeks' experience with civilization demonstrates how complex the interaction between people and environments can be. People inhabit two worlds simultaneously: one constructed by nature and one created in their minds. What they make of the former depends to a great extent on how they frame the latter. Different people react differently to similar sets of challenges and opportunities, and explanations for their behaviors are rooted in the mysteries of human psychology.

Greek history illustrates the role that imagination and creativity play in the human struggle for survival, for nature provided the Greeks with few resources. The Greek mainland was small (about the size of the state of Louisiana) and poor. It had no rivers like the Nile or Euphrates and no fields as productive as those of Egypt or Mesopotamia. Greek farmers could work only about 18% of their country's mountainous terrain. Greece's forests were depleted in prehistory, and even the seas off its coasts were not particularly rich in fish. The success the Greeks had in building a civilization under such circumstances proves that environmental resources alone are not enough to explain the rise of a great culture. The Greeks made extraordinary use of what they were given by their homeland, but they also profited from contacts with older civilizations. The fame of Greek civilization should also not obscure the fact that the role the Middle East played in the formation of "the West" did not end with the arrival of the Greeks.

Minoan Mentors

What has long been regarded as the West's most influential ancient civilization appeared in the Aegean, the part of the Mediterranean that is bound by the island of Crete on the south, Asia Minor on the east, and the Greek peninsula on the west and north. It was the work of a people who called themselves Hellenes, but who are better known as Greeks, the name the Romans gave them.

The Greeks were introduced to civilization by the inhabitants of ancient Crete. Archaeologists have named them Minoans after Minos, a legendary king of Crete. What they called themselves is unknown, for the documents they left us have not yet been deciphered. Scholars speculate that their language was related to one of the Semitic tongues of the Middle East. If so, significant elements in their population may have migrated from that region.

Minoan Civilization   Crete was inhabited as early as 7000 B.C.E., but the kind of monumental architecture that often signals the presence of a civilization did not appear until about 2000 B.C.E. Crete's great buildings, unlike those of Mesopotamia and Egypt, were not temples or tombs. They were palaces for merchant-princes, rulers whose major interest was trade, not conquest. Minoan civilization was forgotten until the ruins of the largest of these structures were discovered at a place called Knossos in 1899. No one knows whether the ruler of Knossos presided over all of Crete or was only one of several Minoan

Map 3–1   The Bronze-Age Aegean World   Two distinct but related civilizations (the Minoan and the Mycenaean) arose in the Aegean region between 2000 and 1200 B.C.E. Both were maritime powers whose wealth derived from Mediterranean trade.

Question: How would you expect Minoan civilization to differ from Mycenaean civilization given that the Minoans lived on an island and the Mycenaeans on the mainland?

princes. His court was certainly magnificent. The multistoried palace at Knossos had about 300 rooms arranged around its great courtyards—as well as lavishly decorated reception halls, ceremonial staircases, workshops, warehouses, and well-engineered ventilation, drainage, and sewage disposal systems. The fact that it was not fortified suggests that its owner enjoyed mastery of the sea and had no fear of invasion (see Map 3–1).

Seafaring funded Minoan civilization. Egypt had an insatiable appetite for northern products such as wood and olive oil (the all-purpose lubricant, fuel, and the chief source of fat in the ancient world's grain-based diet). Peoples such as the Minoans and Phoenicians, whose island and coastal homes oriented them to the sea, were eager to serve the Egyptian market. Minoan merchants were active in Egypt as early as the Middle Kingdom (2100–1700 B.C.E.), and Egypt greatly influenced Minoan culture.

Minoan trade supported the aristocrats who lived in palaces, such as Knossos on Crete's northern coast and Phaistos on its southern rim. It also enabled the residents of the towns scattered about Crete and on neighboring islands to erect comfortable homes. Little is known about its impact on the Minoan peasantry, for few traces of their villages survive.

Like other ancient peoples whose economic activities required them to maintain inventories of goods, the Minoans invented a system of writing. Crete's scribes may have been inspired by Egyptian hieroglyphs, but by 1800 B.C.E., they had evolved a distinctive script of their own. Scholars have named it Linear A to distinguish it from a later version, **Linear B**, that the early Greeks adapted for writing their language. Both scripts were drawn (using traced lines rather than cuneiform's imprinted wedges) on clay tablets and both were probably used exclusively for the purpose of compiling economic records. Because Linear A cannot yet be read, most of what we know about Minoan civilization comes from the study of its ruined buildings.

The frescoes that decorated the walls of homes and palaces provide windows into the Minoan world, for Minoan art was realistic. It described plants, animals, landscapes, and a variety of human activities. The paucity of military scenes in paintings and of weapons in graves has led some scholars to conclude that the Minoans were not a warlike people. No society that depended on the dangerous profession of long-distance trade could, however, have been indifferent to the martial arts, and myths and archaeological remains suggest that human sacrifices may have featured in Minoan religious ritual.

Minoan frescoes depict a slender, graceful, and athletic people. The men of Crete, like those of Egypt, wore short kilts. Female court costumes featured floor-length skirts and tight fitting bodices that left the breasts bare. Women are prominent subjects of a few frescoes, and Minoan religion featured a goddess, a young woman associated with snakes and birds. Some people claim that this is evidence that Minoan society was dominated by women, but many communities have honored a few privileged females and venerated goddesses while denigrating ordinary women. Minoan religious symbolism was also not exclusively female. Bulls represented the male element in what was doubtless a fertility cult. The horns of bulls decorated the walls of the palace at Knossos, and some frescoes depict young men and women engaged in a form of bull fighting that may have had religious significance. Recently what is believed to be a Minoan temple has been discovered, but the paucity of such sites suggests that Minoans may more commonly have worshiped at sacred places under the open sky, in caves, and at shrines in their homes.

Minoan History   Minoan civilization belonged to the Bronze Age and evolved in distinct stages. During the Early Minoan Period (2600–2000 B.C.E.), Crete developed its trade. The Minoans clustered into urban settlements and built their first palaces during the Middle Minoan Period (2000–1600 B.C.E.). The Late Minoan Period (1600–1125 B.C.E.)

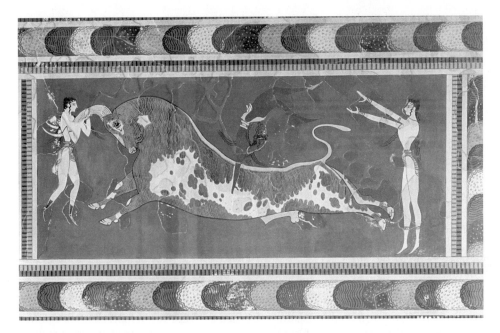

The Minoan Bull-Leapers   This much reconstructed fresco from the palace at Knossos illustrates what may have been a sport, a religious ritual, or an illustration of a myth. The participants leaped at charging bulls, grabbed their horns, and somersaulted over their backs. Similar frescoes have been discovered in a palace in the Egyptian port of Avaris. New Kingdom Egypt had close commercial ties with the Minoans.

emerged in the wake of a disaster that caused widespread destruction on the island. Because there was no change in Minoan culture, the damage was probably the result of a natural catastrophe, such as an earthquake, and not a foreign invasion.

About 1450 B.C.E., the scribes working at Knossos switched from Linear A to Linear B. The significance of this change became clear in 1952, when a young British scholar proved that Linear B recorded an early form of Greek. The use of Greek at Knossos suggests that warriors from the mainland conquered and occupied Crete. About 50 years later the whole island was again devastated by the hand of either man or God, and Minoan civilization began to fade from memory. The Minoans may have sowed the seeds of their own destruction by introducing the Greeks of the mainland to seafaring, trade, and civilization.

The Mycenaeans, Greece's First Civilization

The Greeks created two quite different civilizations. The one for which they are famous is the second, their Hellenic or "classical" civilization. Their first, which flourished from about 1600 to 1200 B.C.E., modeled itself on the Minoan example. Historians have named it for Mycenae, a city in the northeastern Peloponnese (the southern portion of the Greek peninsula) that Homer's *Iliad* says was ruled by Agamemnon, the leader of the Greeks in the Trojan War.

Origin of the Greeks   The ancestors of the Greeks were part of the great wave of migration that spread Indo-European languages from the Atlantic Coast to the Indian Ocean. They entered the Greek peninsula from central Europe between 2100 and 1900 B.C.E. and displaced its earlier inhabitants, villagers with cultural ties to Asia Minor. They were a warlike people with strongly patriarchal customs, and as nomadic herders from the northern plains, they had no maritime experience. Their language even lacked a word for sea.

The Greeks' appearance in the Aegean world roughly coincided with the rise of Minoan civilization on Crete. There is no evidence that the Minoans ever ruled the Greek mainland, but mythology suggests that the early Greeks were overawed by Crete's superior culture. The myth known as "Theseus and the Minotaur" narrates the adventures of a prince of Athens who was sent to Crete as human tribute. He negotiates a labyrinth, a maze that King Minos built to hold the Minotaur (Minos-bull), a beast born of a union between a bull and Minos's wife. Theseus kills the monster and escapes—with the help of Minos's daughter. The story suggests that the primitive Greeks knew that bulls featured in Minoan religious sacrifices and that Minoans erected mysterious buildings, such as the maze-like palace at Knossos, a "labyrinth," so-called because it was decorated with a sacred symbol, a double-headed axe called a *labys*. Another Greek myth claimed that in infancy the god Zeus had been hidden on Crete to prevent his father from killing him. When he grew up, he overthrew the older deities and established the reign of the Greeks. This may preserve a faint memory of the transition from Minoan to Mycenaean dominance in the Aegean.

The Mycenaean Kingdoms   Mycenaean civilization was the invention of mainland kingdoms that were tiny versions of the great states of Egypt and Mesopotamia. Mycenaean kingdoms had centralized governments administered by elaborate bureaucracies, and they were intensely militaristic. Their palaces were citadels into which besieged populations could retreat. Their art featured battle scenes. Their leaders were buried with weapons, armor, and chariots, and their merchants trafficked in armaments. The Mycenaeans had inherited a warlike disposition from their nomadic Indo-European ancestors, and Greece's environment did little to moderate it. The country's mountainous terrain hampered political unification, and competition for its scarce resources and commercial opportunities sparked vicious rivalries among its inhabitants.

Mycenaean kings were, like the Minoan rulers, merchant-princes. The professions of merchant and warrior were closely allied in the ancient world, for traders who ventured far from home had no protection other than what they provided for themselves. They were heavily armed, and only opportunity distinguished them from pirates. When they encountered the strong, they traded. When they met the weak, they looted.

The earliest evidence for the wealth and power of Mycenaean kings comes from offerings found in shaft-graves dating from about 1600 to 1500 B.C.E. Later, the Mycenaeans constructed imposing *tholoi* to house their dead. *Tholoi* were vaulted masonry chambers (shaped like bee hives) that were mounded over with soil and used for multiple burials. The **tholos** at Mycenae is 50 feet in diameter and 40 feet high. Young

The Lion-Gate at Mycenae   The gate that provided entrance to the citadel at Mycenae was formed from huge blocks of stone and decorated with a tympanum depicting two lions guarding a pillar, a motif found in Middle-Eastern art.

monarchies sometimes bolster their authority by acts of conspicuous consumption intended to overawe their subjects. *Tholoi* were probably shrines for the worship of royal ancestors. Unlike the later Greeks, the Mycenaeans seem not to have built temples. The fortress-palaces, which began to rise about 1400 B.C.E., were constructed of huge, irregularly shaped stone blocks that were fitted together like pieces of a puzzle. So monumental were their remains that later Greeks concluded that these "cyclopean" structures were the work of the Cyclopes, an extinct race of giants.

The reception rooms of the Mycenaean fortresses were decorated with frescoes and tiled floors and had furnishings made from exotic woods and precious metals. Like Minoan palaces, the Mycenaean royal residences housed the workshops, warehouses, and scribal offices essential to the livelihood of a merchant-prince. Mycenaean scribes developed Linear B, a writing system based on the Minoans' Linear A. Two major collections of their tablets have been found. One, as previously mentioned, is from Knossos. The other is from Pylos, a fortress on the southwestern coast of the Peloponnese (the mainland's southern peninsula). The 1,200 Linear B tablets from the archives of Pylos owe their survival to the destruction of the people who wrote them. Pylos fell to an attacker about 1200 B.C.E., and the flames that consumed the palace baked the fragile clay tablets in its scribes' offices into durable tiles.

The only things found on the Linear B tablets are inventories of supplies, but these reveal a great deal about Mycenaean life. Ration lists suggest that wheat and barley bread were the staples of the diet. Workers were also issued wine and figs. Meat is not often mentioned, but some must have been available. Many animals had to be slaughtered to produce the quantities of leather that palace craftsmen used to manufacture armor. Some agricultural products, particularly olive oil and honey, were cultivated for export. The 400 bronze smiths that Pylos's king employed would have turned out far more weapons than he needed, so he must have been an arms dealer. About 600 women were attached to the palace to weave linen and woolen cloth. The Pylos documents mention many specialized professions and list titles for numerous kinds of bureaucrats. The peasants who inhabited the kingdom's 200 villages may have been semi-free laborers who were legally dependent on a military aristocracy. Slaves, a byproduct of war, were plentiful. Most were female, for the males of defeated communities were usually slaughtered.

The Aegean Dark Age

Pylos was destroyed and abandoned about 1200 B.C.E., and within a few decades all the Mycenaean kingdoms had collapsed. Linear B, which was known only to the scribes who served the Mycenaean kings, was forgotten, and a Dark Age (an era without literacy) descended on the Aegean. Not until commerce revived in the eighth century B.C.E. did the Greeks again sense a need for writing. About 800 B.C.E. they adapted the Phoenician script for their own use.

Homer and the Fall of Mycenae   Although literacy disappeared from the Aegean with the Mycenaeans, an oral tradition preserved some memory of their existence and inspired the composition of the *Iliad* and the *Odyssey*, the first major pieces of Greek literature. Tradition attributes both these epic poems to a certain Homer, who supposedly flourished about 700 B.C.E., but stylistic features suggest that they may not have been the work of one man. The *Iliad* is the story of a quarrel between two Greek leaders, Agamemnon and Achilles, which took place in the tenth year of a Greek siege of Troy, a city in northwestern Asia Minor. The *Odyssey* catalogues the adventures of Odysseus, one of their companions, on his way home from the Trojan War. Both poems purport to narrate events from the Mycenaean era, but they read back into that period the conditions of the later and more primitive Dark Age.

It was once assumed that Homer's stories were entirely fictional, but in 1871 Heinrich Schliemann, a brilliant self-taught German archaeologist (who made a fortune in the California gold rush as a banker) discovered the site of Troy. His excavations there and on the mainland of Greece uncovered evidence for several Trojan wars and for the great Greek kingdoms that could have fought them. Scholars dispute which of Troy's battles may have given rise to the tales collected in the *Iliad*, but Troy's location explains why the Greeks would have fought a Trojan War. Troy commanded the entrance to the Hellespont, the waterway by which Greeks imported grain from the Black Sea. If anything could have persuaded the Mycenaean kings to set aside their differences and wage a joint expedition against a foreign power, it was a threat to their food supply. Troy was sacked sometime after 1250 B.C.E., not long before the Mycenaean kingdoms themselves began to fall. If the destruction of Troy was the last proud achievement of the Mycenaean era, stories about it would have come, during the Dark Age, to represent the glories of an increasingly mythic past.

A spate of fortification building on the mainland of Greece suggests that around 1250 B.C.E. the Mycenaean governments sensed a need to strengthen their defenses. Historians once postulated that the Mycenaeans confronted a second wave of Indo-European migration from the north, an invasion by primitive tribes that spoke the Dorian dialect of Greek. But no archaeological evidence confirms a Dorian presence in Greece until after the Mycenaean decline. An attack from without is not the only explanation for a civilization's fall. Internal problems can also bring it down. By the thirteenth century the Mycenaeans were struggling with overpopulation, declining agricultural production, and costly, unwieldy bureaucratic administrations. Under these circumstances, the fall of one shaky kingdom could have initiated a domino effect that brought them all down. As refugees flooded from a collapsing state into the territory of its neighbor, that neighbor would be pushed over the edge and its people would join a swelling tide of refugees. Greeks seeking new homes probably triggered the invasions of the Sea Peoples who descended on the coasts of Egypt and Palestine in the late thirteenth century. At this time Greeks also occupied the Aegean islands and the coast of Asia Minor.

The Homeric Era
The Mycenaean collapse cleared the way for the Greeks to reinvent themselves, but almost five centuries passed before the outlines of their great Hellenic, or classical, civilization emerged. These transitional centuries were not devoid of achievement. Iron came into widespread use. Pottery painters began to develop a distinctive and historically informative art. Religious traditions changed. New weapons and battlefield strategies were introduced. Novel political and social institutions appeared, and colonization scattered Greek cities throughout the ancient world.

Mycenaean trade, industry, and agriculture had been centrally managed by royal agents. Once these officials passed from the scene, a much simpler economy emerged. It centered on the village and the household. This is the world that Homer (or the school of poets he represents) knew and projected onto the Mycenaean past. It was far less wealthy than its Mycenaean predecessor. Few of its settlements had as many as a thousand residents, and the decline of trade in the Aegean meant that each community had to produce almost everything it needed for itself.

Conditions were difficult during the Dark Ages but not unpromising. A reduced population lessened competition for farmland, and an economy of self-sufficiency minimized class differences based on wealth and access to imported luxuries. The collapse of centralized political authority allowed local governments to flourish. The chieftains who headed these were called kings, but they were far less powerful than Mycenaean royalty. The simple equipment they took to their graves suggests that the economic gap between them and their followers was not great. The Homeric king was a first-among-equals in a band of military companions. He fought at the side of his men and shared their way of life.

Homeric society was dominated by warrior bands that were only nominally subservient to a hierarchy of regional overlords. The leaders of these bands constituted a hereditary aristocracy, but it was a working aristocracy. A king and his nobles defended their people and enriched them by raiding their neighbors' territory. The monarch's office passed to his son, but only if his men considered the heir to be competent. A leader was accountable to a warrior code that demanded demonstrations of strength, courage, and honor. He was expected to inspire his men by his superior prowess in battle and in the hunts and athletic competitions that proved his readiness for the rigors of combat.

A Homeric king's income consisted of locally produced consumable items (olive oil, grain, and wine). It made no sense to hoard such things, for they deteriorated in storage. However, if they were invested as social capital—that is, distributed among his followers—they returned rewards in the form of increased loyalty. Noblemen were supposed to be openhanded and hospitable, and to strive to outdo one another in the giving of gifts. A chief had to be as generous with time and patience as with property. The aristocratic warriors he led enjoyed freedom of speech in his councils and expected him to be capable of eloquent oratory. Men of less distinguished ancestry and reputation were, of course, required to show deference to their betters.

The works of Homer occupied a place in Greek society comparable to that of the Bible in the Christian communities of the medieval and early modern West. Most Greeks, regardless of their social status, identified with Homer's *aristoi* ("best men," aristocrats). Lineage and famous ancestors were important, but good bloodlines were not enough. Individuals were expected to earn respect through their achievements. The ideal man had to be both competent and handsome—a harmony of muscle, bone, brain, and spirit that excited the envy of the gods. The greatest of men could, in myths at least, become deities themselves.

The Hellenic Era

As things settled down in the Aegean world, trade revived and population increased. The Dark Age drew to a close, and the vague outlines of a new Greek civilization appeared. Its fundamental institutions were quite different from those of the Mycenaean era.

The Archaic Period (750–500 B.C.E.)   Population did not have to increase much before pressures on the limited resources of the Aegean environment caused social problems. Division of land among heirs reduced many farms to tiny plots that could not support families. This forced their owners either to become dependents of more prosperous neighbors or to sell their land and relocate. Both options transformed Greek society by concentrating land in fewer hands and widening class divisions. This caused political unrest, and many Greeks chose to leave the Aegean for new homes elsewhere. Emigration expanded trade networks, and entrepreneurs began to venture forth looking for new markets. City-states in the homeland eased their population crunch by sponsoring colonies, but they did not exploit their colonies for their own benefit. Each colony was independent and self-governing, and many were in locations that gave them opportunities to grow larger and richer than their mother cities (see Map 3–2).

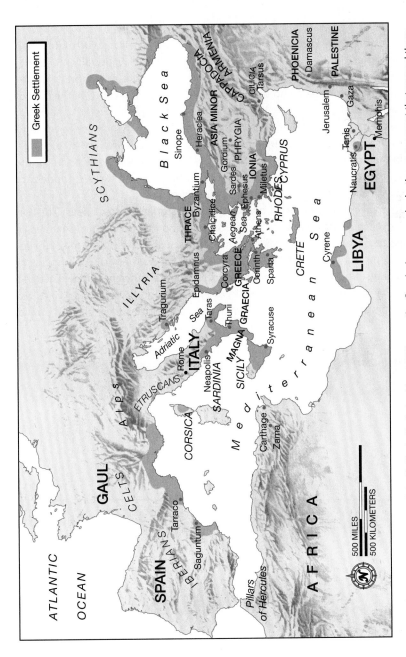

Map 3–2 Greek Territories of the Hellenic Period About 750 B.C.E. the Greeks began a colonization movement that spread them around the Black Sea and the Mediterranean. They looked for unoccupied harbors that could be developed as ports, and they prospered by trading with native peoples in the hinterlands.

Question: Why were the Greeks able to create a coherent civilization, given that their cities were so widely scattered?

PEOPLE IN CONTEXT Hesiod, The Uncommon Common Man

Homer may not have been a real person, but the poet Hesiod, whose work dates from the same period as the *Iliad* and *Odyssey*, probably was. He is especially intriguing, for while Homer, like most ancient authors, concentrated on the aristocratic warrior class, Hesiod was a common man who used his uncommon gifts to describe the lives of people like himself.

Hesiod is credited with two major poems: *Theogony*, a history of the Greek gods, and *Works and Days*, a description of the annual round of labor on a Greek farm. In the latter, Hesiod speaks in the first person about what he alleges to be personal experiences. Some scholars think that this may have been a literary device, but, if so, that does not detract from the accuracy of the picture of rural life that Hesiod paints.

Works and Days takes the form of an open letter to Hesiod's brother Perses. The two men had fought over the division of their father's estate, and Hesiod claimed that Perses bribed the judges to obtain the larger share (which he then squandered by mismanagement). Hesiod's letter is a species of "wisdom literature," a version of the collections of proverbs and secular sermons that were popular throughout the ancient Middle East and that made their way into the Bible as the books of Proverbs and Ecclesiastes. *Works and Days* lectures farmers and the agents of government on their duties and singles judges out for special attention. Hesiod warns that authorities who take bribes risk divine punish-

Hesiod's *Theogony* This painting from an ancient Greek vase depicts Hesiod's story of the birth of the goddess Athena. She emerges fully grown and armored from Zeus's head, which the god Hephaestus is shown splitting open with an axe.

ment, for there is a moral order in the universe that holds rulers accountable—a natural standard of justice to which human laws must conform. This was a conviction he unknowingly shared with his contemporaries, the Hebrew prophets.

Hesiod believed that justice was simply common sense. People should pay their debts, honor their obligations, and deal fairly and generously with one another. He also insisted that there was no substitute for hard work, that idleness was a personal disgrace and an offense to the gods. The small-property-holders whom he addresses are assumed to have a few slaves or hired hands, but they sweat in their fields alongside their servants. Hesiod saw in the work of these ordinary men the kind of nobility that Homer praised in the feats of aristocratic warriors. His definition of the good man is the self-sufficient individual whose unrelenting labor keeps his barns filled. Such a man, the poet warned, chooses a wife with care. Hesiod valued women as resources, not companions. He claimed that females were by nature deceitful, lazy, wasteful, and the source of most of mankind's problems. A man had to take a wife, for he needed children to care for him in his old age. But Hesiod advised the potential bridegroom to choose his fiancée not for her sex appeal but for her ability to pull a plow.

Hesiod was, in short, the champion of the frugal householder who kept a constant eye on the bottom line. The poet accused the upper classes of living off the backs of men like himself, but he was blind to his own exploitation of slaves and hired men. He advised that they be fed only enough to enable them to do a day's work. Hesiod was the spokesman for an emerging yeoman class that was destined to play a major role in shaping Hellenic civilization.

Question: Why might Greece, at the start of the Classical era, have produced a poet with interests like Hesiod's when Egypt and the Middle East did not?

Between 750 and 500 B.C.E., Greeks scattered colonies around the Black Sea, across Sicily and southern Italy, and along the coasts of Asia Minor, France, Spain, and parts of North Africa. They preferred sites where they could maintain contact with the sea. Although they generally avoided places occupied by other maritime peoples, some long-established nations, such as Egypt, welcomed Greek merchants and gave them land on which to build.

Greek colonists were exposed to alien cultural influences, but they resisted assimilation. The Greeks divided humanity into two categories: those who spoke Greek, and "barbarians" whose unintelligible babble sounded like "bar-bar-bar." They saw themselves as scattered members of a single culture and jealously guarded their Greek identity. Pan-Hellenic ("all-Greek") religious shrines (e.g., Apollo's oracle at Delphi) and festivals (e.g., the Olympic Games) helped maintain ties among them and spread Hellenism (Greek culture) far beyond the Aegean. Many of classical civilization's major artists and intellectuals were citizens of the colonies, not the Greek mainland.

The Greeks who spread throughout the world during the Archaic era took with them a unique institution called the **polis** (plural: *poleis*). *Polis* is often translated as city-state, but that captures only part of the word's meaning. The *polis* created the environment that nurtured Hellenic civilization. *Polis* is the root of the word *politics*, but a *polis* was much more than a political entity. It was an experiment in social engineering that used art, religion, education, sport, and entertainment—as well as governmental authority—to create model citizens.

Classical civilization embraced a philosophical point of view centered on the human being. It saw the world as a rational, humane place amenable to understanding and control. It taught that human beings were open-ended creatures who had the power and duty to invent themselves. The *polis* provided a means to this end. Most *poleis* were small states situated in sparse, competitive environments. Unlike the wealthy, populous kingdoms of the Middle East that could afford to squander manpower, *poleis* needed all their residents to contribute their best. Their small size also encouraged activism, for individuals were not lost in a mass of humanity. The impact they had on their communities was visible. This created a curious linkage in the Greek mind between what are often contrary drives: individualism and community spirit.

The Hoplite Infantry   Military technology powerfully influenced the development

of the *polis*. The Dark-Age battles that Homer describes were free-for-alls, simultaneous single combats fought by heavily armored champions who were carried about a battlefield in chariots. A horde of men from a chief's household accompanied him to war, but they did not fight in organized units. True infantry was an Assyrian invention of the eighth century. When it spread to Greece at the end of the Dark Age, it became uniquely lethal.

The Greek infantry soldier was called a **hoplite**—from his *hoplos*, a shield shaped like a round, shallow bowl that was his most distinctive piece of equipment. A hoplite was a foot soldier who was laden with about 70 pounds of equipment (about half the body weight of an average male in the ancient world). He had a helmet and breast plate, was armed with a thrusting spear and a short sword, and carried his *hoplos* on his left arm. The *hoplos* was made of wood and leather and was about three feet in diameter. It was carried on the left arm to protect its bearer's left side and shelter his neighbor's right. Hoplites fought shoulder to shoulder in a tightly packed company called a phalanx. A phalanx was eight ranks deep, and only the men in the front lines could wield their weapons. Men in the rear ranks used their shields to push into the backs of the men in front of them. Their strategy was to pool their strength, their weight, and the momentum of their charge so as to deal a crushing blow to their opponent's formation. Tactics were simple. Armies charged each other, smashed together, and the phalanx that first broke exposed its scattered men to slaughter.

Hoplite battles were intended to be brief and murderous. They relied more on strength, endurance, and courage than on skill with weapons. There was no room for fancy sword play, but any man who hoped to survive had to stay in peak physical condition and learn to control himself. Sports and athletic activities were not mere entertainments for the Greeks. They provided the physical training that prepared a man for the military duties of citizenship and preserved his life. The males of a *polis*

Warriors in Hoplite Armor This carving illustrates opposing soldiers in battle, each with hoplite equipment.

were liable for military service from their teenage years until the age of 60, and they could expect to be called into the field at frequent intervals. Because the strength of a *polis* literally depended on the physical condition of its men, the *polis* provided public facilities for training, made physical education part of their upbringing, and inspired them with art that celebrated the perfectly developed male body. The uniquely Greek custom of exercising in the nude spread after Homer's day and accompanied the rise of the *polis*. The Greeks themselves were not certain why this practice began, but it was consistent with the pressure the *polis* put on its men to demonstrate that they were keeping themselves in physical condition for combat. The gymnasiums in which people train today take their name from *gymnos*, a Greek word meaning "naked."

Hoplite Culture   As the Greeks came to rely on their new infantries, the balance of power shifted in their communities. Infantry armies depend on numbers for their strength, and the small circle of aristocratic families that had traditionally monopolized military power and political leadership could not provide all the manpower that they required. A *polis* needed every man who was competent to serve. Competence was determined by health, strength, and money. Simple governments were not equipped to collect taxes with which to finance armies. They expected their subjects to pay for their own arms and training. Only the rich could afford horses and chariots, but these were no longer all that important. Hoplite equipment was within the reach of men of moderate means, and they had good reason to invest in it. If their *polis* relied on them for its defense, it could not deny them some political recognition.

Service in the hoplite infantry enfranchised the male residents of a *polis*. Furthermore, because hoplite warfare put all soldiers on roughly the same footing, it promoted social egalitarianism. It turned the *polis* into a kind of military fraternity, a brotherhood of men who shared the bond of a common battlefield experience. The link the *polis* established between citizenship and soldiering also fueled intense patriotism and, like modern sports competitions, heightened rivalry among city-states. Greek *poleis* found it hard to coexist peacefully, and they often had more to fear from one another than from foreign invaders.

The militarized environment of the *polis* put women at a major disadvantage. The aristocratic women in Homer's epics are respected, influential people. There were some constraints on their activities, but they enjoyed freedoms that most *poleis* denied to women from their citizen families. Because women lacked the upper-body strength that would have enabled them to serve as hoplites (and earn citizenship), men regarded them as inferior creatures. They were declared unfit for public life and confined to their homes. A citizen woman had the same legal status as her children, but unlike her sons, she was a life-long dependent.

The legitimacy of children was extremely important, for citizenship in a *polis* was hereditary. The only way fathers could be sure that their offspring were their own was to limit the contact their wives had with other men. A woman's primary duty was to marry and produce the heirs that would perpetuate her husband's *oikos* (household). This was crucial, for a *polis's* strength depended on preserving the *oikoi* that provided its fighting men. Poor women had no choice but to go out in public and work to earn money to support their families, but their better-off sisters were confined to special quarters in their homes and expected to be as invisible as possible. A woman could visit family members, go to the neighborhood well to draw water, and attend some religious festivals, but she did not take part in social gatherings with her husband and his friends. Indeed, her husband may not have thought of her as a companion. Men often delayed marriage until they were about 30 years old and financially established. Their brides were usually girls just past puberty who were half their ages.

Men were seldom at home and invested little in making their homes impressive or comfortable. They spent their time out of doors or in the public facilities that were a *polis's* chief source of civic pride—its temple precincts or its *agora*, a place to conduct commercial and political business. A man had no opportunity to make female friends outside his family circle. When he desired female company, he turned to *hetairae*, professional entertainers who ranged from simple prostitutes to highly educated women who could engage a man in witty repartee and serious discussion. These women were usually slaves or foreigners. They entertained at *symposia* (drinking parties), feasts for male guests only that offered a citizen his primary opportunity for relaxed social interaction with his peers.

The Rise of the Mainland Powers

There were hundreds of *poleis* scattered throughout the Mediterranean and along the shores of the Black Sea. It is difficult to generalize about them, but we can gain insight into how *poleis* operated by examining the two quite different city-states that dominated political life on the Greek mainland.

Sparta   The Spartans possessed the most intimidating army in Greece. They created it by doing what the citizens of a *polis* were supposed to do. They decided what they wanted to be and then ruthlessly implemented a program of social engineering to achieve their goal.

The Spartans' ancestors were Dorian-speaking tribes that wandered into the Peloponnese during the Dark Age and settled along the Eurotas River. They expanded their territory by making war on their neighbors, and late in the eighth century they overran the plain of Messenia (the old Mycenaean kingdom of Pylos). This drastically changed the context for Spartan life. The war made Sparta the largest state on the mainland, but it left the Spartans outnumbered perhaps seven to one by people whom they had enslaved. The Spartans concluded that they would not survive unless they created a standing army that was so powerful it could frighten the *polis's* resentful *helot* (slave) population into submission. That meant that every male Spartan had to commit to becoming a superb, full-time soldier.

Legends claim that a sage named Lycurgos devised the system that kept Sparta in a state of permanent, total military mobilization. Sparta had to ensure that each of its citizens automatically accepted the lifetime of harsh discipline and regimentation that turned him into a professional soldier. It did so by making sure that it never entered his mind to be anything else. His training began at birth. State officials examined each newborn, and only those infants that were strong were allowed to live. Because all males were destined to serve the state as full-time soldiers, the state had to support them. Each boy was assigned a *kleros*, a farm worked by slaves, to maintain him, and the state did not invest in raising boys who could not fight.

At the age of 6 or 7, a boy left home and reported to a military camp. The army played a larger part in rearing him than did his family. He was taught basic literacy and subjected to trials that made him strong, courageous, and indifferent to hardship. At the age of 20 he saw front-line service. If he acquitted himself well in battle until the age of 30, he was granted full citizenship. Those who failed to measure up were publicly humiliated and shunned.

For most of his life, a Spartan lived in barracks as a member of a 15-man mess unit called a *sussition*. A man's mess mates were closer to him than were his family members. He was expected to marry and sire children, but he could not set up a household and live openly with his wife until he received his full citizen privileges. This created unique opportunities for Spartan women. Because their husbands were rarely at home and a man's time was taken up with military duties, women had both freedom and responsibility. Sparta could not afford, like other *poleis*, to confine women to their homes, and the interests of the state dictated that they be given much better treatment than most Greek women received. To ensure that they grew up to give birth to healthy children, Spartan girls were fed well, given physical training, and not married until they were fully mature at age 18.

The Spartan system produced the best army in Greece for the simple reason that the Spartans were the only Greeks who could devote all their time to training and physical conditioning. Most *poleis* were defended by part-time citizen militias, but the Spartans had a professional army. Sparta's primary weakness was the difficulty it had in maintaining its population. Birthrates were low, and the harsh conditions of Spartan life increased mortality.

The Spartans paid a high price for their system, but it gave them a tremendous sense of pride. They did not marry foreigners and kept a careful eye on visitors to make sure that outsiders did not spread alien ideas that caused citizens to question the Spartan way of life. The *polis's* economy ensured social stability by preventing the development of a gap between rich and poor. Some trade was necessary, but a primitive medium of exchange using iron bars kept it to a minimum. Each Spartan had his *kleros* to guarantee him a living wage. Private property existed, but the flaunting of wealth was discouraged. The Spartans boasted of their coarse food, rough attire, and indifference to comfort and luxury. Their educations taught them obedience to authority and tradition, and discouraged inquiry and speculation.

The Spartan *polis* had what the Greeks called a mixed constitution: that is, a government that combined aspects of different political systems. The monarchical element was represented by two royal families from whose princes the Spartans chose their kings. Spartan kings had little civil authority. Their chief function was to serve as commanders in the field. Sparta was a kind of all-inclusive aristocracy. Its chief organ of government was a council called the Gerousia. It was composed of 28 men over the age of 60 who held office for life. The Gerousia set policies that were implemented by five executives called *ephors*. The democratic element in the system was represented by a popular assembly to which all full citizens belonged. It elected the members of the Gerousia and the *ephors*, but had very limited powers. It met primarily to be advised of government decisions. It could ratify or reject proposals put to it, but it could not debate or suggest alternatives. Sparta also had a *krypteia*, a secret police corps that terrorized the *helots* and eliminated potential troublemakers.

Sparta had reason to be proud of its achievements. It was more stable than most *poleis*, and the other Greeks were in awe of its military might. But Spartan success came at a cost. By refusing to evolve and by turning their backs on the outside world, the Spartans lived through one of the most creative periods in Western history without being touched by it. In an era of unprecedented artistic and intellectual activity, the Spartans, with the exception of a few early poets, produced no great thinkers, authors, or artists. They focused exclusively on military matters and prided themselves on ignoring most of the things for which Greek civilization became famous. Worse, their decision to halt development, ignore change, and pin their survival on a single strength ultimately proved fatal.

Athens   The *polis* that is most associated with the achievements of Hellenic civilization is Athens, an Ionian-speaking community on the plain of Attica in the upper portion of the Greek peninsula. By the end of the Dark Age, its Mycenaean monarchy ("one-man rule") had been replaced by an aristocracy ("rule by the best," by those of elite lineage). Its chief organ of government was the Council of the **Areopagus**, a committee of leaders from aristocratic families. The council's mandates were enforced by three officials called *archons*, and it occasionally convened a popular assembly to publicize its edicts. At this stage in its development Athens resembled Sparta, but the two *poleis* steadily diverged. Sparta halted its economic and social evolution at this point by absorbing all its men into a single class and training them for the same profession. Athens allowed an unregulated economy to create divisions and tensions within its society, and these propelled further political development.

The citizens of Athens were not supported by the state. They had to earn their own livings. As trade began to revive in the eighth century B.C.E., new sources of wealth enabled some commoners to prosper, and they acquired the means to force the landed aristocracy to share its power with them. This delivered Athens into the hands of an oligarchy ("rule by the few"), a government dominated by the rich as well as the well born. Athenians who did not have large estates or commercial interests were at a serious disadvantage economically and politically. Each year, they had to raise enough grain on their small farms to feed their families and, if they hoped to accumulate any savings to fall back on, some surplus for sale. In years when harvests were poor, they could not make ends meet. They had to borrow from the rich and pledge to pay back their loans out of next year's crop. In effect, they mortgaged a portion of their labor for the following year and bound themselves to work their land for someone else's benefit. Over the long haul, the poor tended to dig themselves so deeply into debt that they were enslaved. Societies that allow wide gaps to develop between the few rich and the many poor flirt with disaster. The poor resent their condition, and when a leader appears to mobilize them, they have the strength of numbers to foment revolution. Revolutions are often begun by a member of the privileged class who rallies the people and uses them to drive his competitors from the city. This leads to a form of government the Greeks called tyranny ("rule by an individual who seizes power").

During the seventh century, many *poleis* passed into the hands of tyrants. The leading families in a *polis* were highly competitive and inclined to feud. When their fights threatened to destabilize a community, the lower classes often rallied behind a *tyrannos* ("a ruler who takes control by force") in an effort to restore order. Some tyrants abused their authority and oppressed their subjects. But if a tyrant was wise, he remembered the source of his power and courted the people by doing things that improved their lives. He funded buildings, festivals, and programs that provided jobs, promoted civic pride, and enhanced the reputation of his *polis*. In the process, he might encourage the growth of popular government. That, at least, was the Athenian experience.

In 632 B.C.E. the aristocrats of Athens thwarted an attempted coup by a popular Olympic victor named Cylon. He raised a private army and seized the Acropolis, the citadel at the heart of Athens. He hoped that the Athenian masses would join him, but they were not ready. The aristocrats put Cylon down, but the crisis alerted them to the danger they faced.

In 620 B.C.E. the Council of the Areopagus asked an elderly aristocrat named Draco to improve the enforcement of justice in Athens. Athens was governed by vague oral traditions that were subject to manipulation by powerful individuals, and rather than looking to the state for help, men often waged vendettas to punish those who wronged them. These private wars could easily get out of hand, and Draco sought to create a credible alternative to them. His plan was to publish a code of law and make neutral state officials responsible for enforcing a standard of justice that applied equally to everyone. Our word *draconian* ("extremely severe") derives from the harsh punishments that Draco decreed for even minor offenses. He may have hoped that fear would inspire respect for the novel idea of rule by law.

Legal reforms were a good thing, but they did not address the economic problems that were the chief source of discontent in Athens. In 594 B.C.E. the politicians in Athens took the remarkable step of granting a man named Solon absolute authority to reorganize the *polis*. Solon began by abolishing the debts of the farmers who had become enslaved agricultural laborers. This got both the rich and the poor out of what had become a mutually unprofitable situation. By cancelling their debts, Solon freed poor peasants to sell the small farms that could not sustain them, and he provided them with alternative forms of employment. He promoted trade, made loans to small businesses, and invited foreign craftsmen with valuable skills to settle in Athens. The rich were compensated by the opportunity this gave them to increase their estates and turn the land to more profitable uses. Poor farmers grew grain. They needed it to feed themselves, and it was the only crop that brought them a rapid return on the little capital they had to invest. Grain did not grow all that well in Attica, but olives and grapes did. It made more sense to import grain and devote Athenian land to the production of olive oil and wine for export. These were, however, capital-intensive crops. Only the rich could afford the decades that it took to bring an olive grove or a vineyard into production. Solon's reforms cleared the way for wealthy investors to convert Attica from minimally profitable grain production to valuable export crops and for Athens to become a thriving manufacturing center.

Solon also implemented political reform. He reserved archonships, the *polis's* most prestigious offices, to candidates from the wealthiest strata of society. Men who could afford hoplite armor qualified for lesser offices, and the poor (who had no equipment but who rowed the city's warships) were allowed to vote in the popular assembly and serve on juries. To help the assembly assert its authority, Solon created the **boule**, a council of 400 representatives chosen from the four tribes into which the Athenian electorate was divided. It prepared the agenda for meetings of the assembly.

Solon's reforms were well conceived, but they did not improve people's lives quickly enough to head off support for tyranny. In 560 B.C.E. a well-known military hero named Peisistratus won control of Athens. He cultivated the masses who had lofted him to power by providing loans for the poor, promoting trade, financing public works projects to provide employment, and sponsoring festivals. He commissioned a definitive edition of Homer's works for the city's archives, and his support for rites honoring the popular rural god Dionysus marked the dawn of one of the glories of Athenian civilization: the theater (see Chapter 5).

When Peisistratus died in 527 B.C.E., his sons Hippias and Hipparchus succeeded him. In 514 B.C.E. two men who had a personal grudge against Hipparchus tried to assassinate him and his brother. Hippias escaped, but fear turned him into a ruthless, suspicious dictator. In 510 B.C.E. the Alcmaeonids, an aristocratic family that Peisistratus had driven into exile, enlisted Spartan aid and forced Hippias to flee Athens. The Alcmaeonids' leader, Cleisthenes, became the city's next tyrant.

Cleisthenes set out to destroy the political machines on which the power of his aristocratic opponents was based by reforming Athens' electoral system. Each Athenian citizen inherited membership in a tribe through which he exercised his rights. These tribes were under the thumbs of the great families that had long dominated Athenian politics. Cleisthenes minimized their influence by limiting the four original tribes to religious functions and transferring their political duties to ten new and differently constituted tribes. Attica was divided into *demes* (counties or townships), and each of the new tribes was made up of *demes* from every region of the country. This meant that great landlords, who had always voted in tribes filled with their local dependents and retainers, now had to vote with strangers over whom they had no power. Cleisthenes may have gerrymandered the system for the benefit of his family, but it had the long-term effect of freeing up individuals to vote as they pleased. Aristocratic advantage was further diminished by the practice of filling many offices by casting lots. Each tribe chose 50 of its members by lot to serve on a new 500-member *boule* that led the assembly and oversaw state finances.

The assembly governed Athens, but it met only occasionally. When it or the *boule* was not in session, the aristocratic Council of the Areopagus was likely to assume power by default. Cleisthenes forestalled this by creating the *prytaneis* ("presider"). He divided the year into ten equal segments, each of which was assigned to one of the tribal committees that composed the *boule*. For the tenth of the year entrusted to it, each 50-man committee met daily as the *prytaneis*, the body that "presided" over Athens. Each day during their term, the members of the *prytaneis* cast lots to determine which of them would serve as Athens' chief executive that day.

The army was also reorganized to reflect the principles by which the state was to be governed. Each tribe provided a company for the army, and the soldiers elected their own leader, their *strategos* ("general"). Because soldiers much prefer to follow officers who have earned their trust, generals, unlike civilian leaders, could serve consecutive terms. The board of ten *strategoi* was able, therefore, to provide some continuity for Athens' government.

Finally, according to tradition, Cleisthenes instituted a special vote called an **ostracism** to prevent anyone from overthrowing the system he had established. From time to time the Athenian electorate was asked to take *ostraca* (fragments of pottery used as ballots) and scratch on them the name of any man suspected of posing a danger to the city. No trial was held, but if an individual garnered 6,000 votes, he was immediately exiled for ten years.

Cleisthenes's reforms launched Athens on an experiment with a radical version of an untested form of government that the Greeks called democracy ("rule by the *demos*," the people). All laws and major policy decisions were made by the people themselves, not by a small group of their representatives. The use of lots to select men for office meant that any individual, regardless of his talents and experience, had a chance of finding himself charged, if only briefly, with major responsibilities. Small villages could operate informally on similar principles, but Athens was no village. History was to prove if the unprecedented trust the Athenians placed in the masses was justified.

The Persian Wars: Crucible of a Civilization

The larger world did not stand still while Greek civilization reorganized itself in the Aegean. In the wake of Mycenae's collapse and the invasions of the Sea Peoples, successive empires rose and fell in the Middle East. The Assyrians built on the ruins of the Hittite and Egyptian empires. In 614 B.C.E. the Assyrians fell to the Chaldaeans, and in 539 B.C.E. Chaldaean Babylon surrendered to Cyrus the Great (r. 559–530 B.C.E.), founder of a gigantic Persian Empire that ultimately stretched from Egypt to the borders of India and the Himalayan Mountains.

Ionia and Marathon   In 547 B.C.E. Cyrus conquered the wealthy kingdom of Lydia in central Asia Minor and pushed on to the Aegean to subdue Ionia, a coastal district occupied by Greek cities. More important campaigns elsewhere and palace coups subsequently distracted him and his immediate successors from further adventures in the Aegean. In 499 B.C.E. the Ionian city of Miletus organized a rebellion that prompted the Persian emperor, Darius I (r. 522–486 B.C.E.), to return to the Greek world. Miletus asked the *poleis* of the mainland for assistance. Sparta refused, but Athens sent help. Athens was dependent on imported grain, and it feared that Persian control of the Hellespont might endanger its access to supplies from the Black Sea. The Athenians also worried that Darius might restore their exiled tyrant Hippias, who had fled to his court. The Greek rebels had some initial successes, but after they drove the Persians from the former Lydian capital at Sardis, their alliance fell apart. Darius then counterattacked, recovered Ionia, and inflicted a horrible punishment on Miletus as a warning to the Greeks.

In 492 B.C.E. Darius decided to make sure that a hope of support from the mainland never again tempted the Ionian cities to rebel. He demanded that the Aegean submit to Persia. Many of the Greek *poleis*, mindful of Miletus's fate, yielded, but Athens and Sparta refused. In 490 B.C.E. Darius's fleet landed an army of 20,000 men on the plain of Marathon about 20 miles north of Athens. Some Athenians wanted to surrender, but the *strategos* Miltiades persuaded the assembly to fight. A champion runner was dispatched to Sparta to ask for help, but the Spartans claimed that a religious festival prevented them from offering immediate assistance. The tiny *polis* of Athens (led by its new, untested democratic government) was left almost entirely alone to confront the superpower of its day (see Map 3–3).

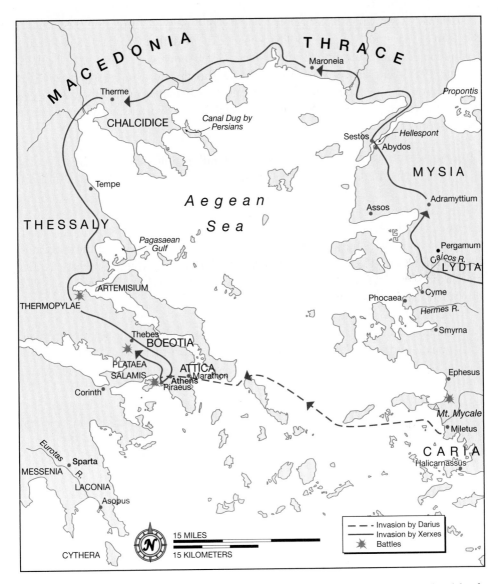

Map 3–3 The Persian Wars   The first of the Persian Wars was an attack from the sea on the plain of Marathon. The second involved a Persian army that was too large to be ferried across the Aegean. This map shows the routes taken by Xerxes' soldiers and the navy that accompanied them. (Stars mark the sites of major battles.)

Question: What advantages and disadvantages did each of these strategies offer for invaders of the Greek mainland?

Miltiades's army may have been half the size of the Persian force, but the battle on the plain of Marathon gave his hoplites a chance to prove that Greek training and discipline could compensate for inferior numbers. Greek sources claim that 6,400 Persians, but only 192 Greeks, died at Marathon. Whatever the statistics, the losses persuaded the Persians to withdraw. The delighted, but stunned, Athenians credited their victory to the patriotic morale generated by democracy, and like the Spartans, their confidence in the program of their *polis* soared.

Thermopylae and Salamis   The loss at Marathon angered the Persians far more than it hurt them, but a rebellion in Egypt and other problems prevented Darius from continuing the war. It fell to his son and heir, Xerxes (r. 486–465 B.C.E.), to determine the Persian response. In 484 B.C.E. Xerxes began to make highly visible plans for a massive assault on the Aegean. This had the intended effect of persuading a number of *poleis* to submit voluntarily, but 31 states pledged to cooperate in defending the mainland. Prospects for their success were not good. The Persian army was huge—perhaps a quarter of a million men. Even the sacred oracles to whom the Greeks turned for advice were intimidated and did not offer much encouragement.

The Greeks wisely chose to take their stand at Thermopylae, a narrow strip of beach in northern Greece that had mountains on one side and the sea on the other. The Persians had to pass through Thermopylae to reach their targets in Greece, but its confines prevented their great army from spreading out and using the advantage of its numbers. If the Greeks' navy prevented Persia's ships from landing soldiers behind the Greek lines, the allies could halt Persia's advance, and this alone might have forced Xerxes to retreat. Sanitation problems spread disease in large armies unless they stayed on the move.

The Greek allies mustered a mere 7,000 men to face the Persians at Thermopylae, but with the help of their commander, the Spartan king Leonidas, they repelled the Persians' assaults for three days. The battle was lost when a Greek traitor guided a troop of Persians through the mountains to a position behind Leonidas's lines. Realizing that his position was untenable, Leonidas dismissed most of his men. He, his 300 Spartans, and a handful of allies chose, however, to stay and fight to the death. Their willing self-sacrifice turned Thermopylae into a moral victory and made them the most celebrated heroes in Greek history.

The Greek army fell back to the Isthmus of Corinth, the land-bridge between northern and southern Greece. The plan was again to halt the Persian advance by blocking a narrow pas-

Spartan Warrior   Art objects from Sparta are rare finds, and this is one of the most famous. It dates to the early fifth century B.C.E. It has been called "Leonidas," after the famous Spartan commander at the battle of Thermopylae, but there is no proof that he was the intended subject.

sage. This had failed at Thermopylae, but the Spartan generals who commanded the army saw no alternative. Athens, which lay north of the Isthmus, was abandoned to the enemy. Its women and children were ferried to various islands, and its men took to their ships and watched as the Persians burned their city.

In 482 B.C.E. the Athenian voters had made a remarkably intelligent decision that now saved their homeland. A rich vein of silver was discovered in the state mines, and the assembly had to decide what to do with the profits. Some politicians courted popularity by proposing that the money be shared among the citizens, but Themistocles, the first non-aristocrat to rise to prominence in the young democracy, persuaded the

---

The Rise of Hellenic Civilization

THIRTEENTH CENTURY

1250 B.C.E., sack of Troy
1200 B.C.E., fall of Mycenaean
Civilization
Dark Age

EIGHTH CENTURY

776 B.C.E., first Olympic victor
750–700 B.C.E., Homer
750 B.C.E., Greek colonization begins
700 B.C.E., Hesiod
Hoplite warfare develops
Poleis appear

SEVENTH CENTURY

Spartan system established
Athenian system evolves:
632 B.C.E., Cylon's coup
620 B.C.E., Draco's law
614 B.C.E., Assyrian Empire falls

SIXTH CENTURY

594 B.C.E., Solon's constitution
560–527 B.C.E., Peisistratus tyranny
539 B.C.E., Chaldaean Empire falls
510 B.C.E., Cleisthenes exiles Hippias
Cyrus founds the Persian Empire
Democracy established

FIFTH CENTURY

499 B.C.E., Miletus rebels
492 B.C.E., Persian Wars: Darius
484–479 B.C.E., Persian Wars: Xerxes

voters to prefer their public to their private interest. He convinced them to use the money to expand their navy and make Athens a major sea power. The Spartans wanted the Athenians to use their navy to prevent the Persians from outflanking the Greek defenses on the Isthmus of Corinth, but Themistocles saw no advantage to Athens in sending its ships to protect the Peloponnese, which was Spartan territory. Because prospects for success on land were dismal, as Thermopylae had proved, he decided to risk everything on a battle at sea. Themistocles lured the Persian navy into the straits between Attica and the island of Salamis, and his smaller, faster ships, which were operating in familiar waters, outmaneuvered and sank many of the Persian transports. Xerxes could not afford to lose the navy that was his communications link with his empire. He chose to go home but to leave behind an army, under a general named Mardonius, to continue the fight.

Mardonius went into winter camp at Plataea, west of Attica, and prepared to resume the campaign the following spring. The Greeks used the time to amass the largest army they had ever assembled, and in the spring of 479 B.C.E. they took the offensive. Pausanias, the Spartan regent for the heroic Leonidas's infant heir, commanded the allied army. When he drove through the Persian line and killed Mardonius, the leaderless Persians scattered. The Greeks were again amazed to discover that they had succeeded against all odds. The conclusion seemed obvious: Their institutions were superior to all others, and there was no limit to what they might do.

KEY QUESTION | Revisited

The Greeks' victories over the Persians persuaded them that there was a wide gap between their civilization and that of their opponents. The Greek historian Herodotus (c. 484–425 B.C.E.), who wrote the first history of the Persian Wars, claimed that the Greeks won because they were free men fighting for their homeland, while the Persians were the dispirited subjects of an autocrat. The war had been a contest between freedom and slavery, and Greek liberty had proved its superiority.

There were obvious contrasts between Persia's empire and Greece's city-states, but there were also ties between the Greek and Persian worlds. The Mycenaean kingdoms had closely resembled and borrowed much from their Middle-Eastern neighbors. Many of the Greeks who fled their collapse settled in the Middle East, strengthened trade ties between the Aegean and the Middle East, and adapted Middle-Eastern technologies (such as writing and infantry warfare) as they emerged from their Dark Age. Trade with Egypt and the Middle East was extremely important to both the Mycenaean and the Hellenic civilizations, and Greek artists and intellectuals drew inspiration from, and had great respect for, the Middle East's older civilizations. There is no doubt that the Greeks were original and that they ultimately changed the course of civilization throughout the ancient world, but the long-popular assumption that they created a "West" that was independent of—and opposed to—an "East" can certainly be challenged.

Review Questions

1. What were the similarities and differences between the Minoan and Mycenaean kingdoms and those of Egypt and the Middle East? Do environments help to explain these?
2. Might people who live in a Dark Age be more open to cultural innovation than those who inhabit a fully civilized period? Why?
3. How did the Hellenic *poleis* differ from the Mycenaean kingdoms?
4. What explains the differences between the *polis* systems of Athens and Sparta?
5. What impact did the military have on the development of Hellenic civilization?
6. How did the Persian Wars affect the way the Greeks viewed themselves and their relationships with other peoples?

Please consult the Suggested Readings at the back of the book to continue your study of the material covered in this chapter. For a list of documents on the Primary Source DVD-ROM that relate to topics in this chapter, please refer to the back of the book.

4 The Hellenic Era

The monuments of the society that we have created are so great that future generations will be as awed by our achievements as are our contemporaries.

—Pericles

KEY | Question

What did the Greeks contribute to the development of modern civilization?

In the winter of 431 B.C.E., an Athenian politician named Pericles delivered a speech in which he made the following points:

1. We Athenians are grateful to our ancestors for creating a free country and bequeathing it to us;
2. Our greatness derives from our unique form of government, a democracy in which everyone is equal before the law;
3. We value people for their abilities, not their social class;
4. We do not despise the poor, but only men who do not try to better themselves;
5. We do not interfere in a man's personal affairs, and we are tolerant of one another;
6. We do not let our private goals and ambitions keep us from fulfilling our public responsibilities;
7. We obey our elected officials, our laws, and the unwritten standards that govern morality and human rights;
8. We enjoy an abundance of good things and relish our pleasures;
9. But our cultivated lifestyle does not make us soft;
10. Our society is open, for we are confident in the loyalty and courage of our people and do not need to resort to covert plotting;

Temple of Poseidon   This temple to Poseidon, Greek god of the sea, stands on cliffs overlooking Cape Sounion, five-and-a-half miles south of Athens. Dating to about 444 B.C.E., it is in the same style as the famous Parthenon in Athens.

11. Our selfless generosity wins us friends abroad;
12. And each one of us enjoys freedom and independence.

This ancient speech could be delivered today in the United States Senate. Indeed, Pericles would find much that seems familiar were he to visit one of the modern Western capitals. Most are filled with buildings, monuments, and sculpture in a style he would recognize. He would not be surprised by the scientific orientation of the modern world, for he witnessed the rise of theoretical science. References to history would not confuse him, for the study of history was pioneered by men he knew personally. He might even attend a performance of a drama that he had previously seen in Athens.

Pericles' speech celebrated the virtues of what has come to be known as "classical" civilization. The adjective implies that his Hellenic (Greek) civilization set the standards for the West. Hellenic societies were, however, far from perfect. They were plagued by wars, internal conflicts, and injustices (particularly in their treatment of women and slaves). Despite their stated commitment to reason, moderation, and self-control, they were capable of senseless, self-destructive acts and emotional excesses. Their moment of glory was brief, and the West may owe some of its weaknesses as well as its strengths to them.

Persian Wars as Catalyst

The defeats the Persians suffered at Salamis and Plataea hardly crippled Xerxes' empire, and the Greeks assumed that Persia had by no means given up hope of conquering the Aegean. The most pressing business of the mid-fifth century, therefore, was to evict the remaining Persians from Greek territory and to organize a defense that would prevent their return.

Sparta's Retreat   The Greek **poleis** had worked together to repel Xerxes' invasion, and they could defend the Aegean only if they continued to cooperate. No one knew, however, how to structure a permanent alliance. The Spartans had the best land army, and the Athenians were the strongest naval power. The military resources of both cities were needed, but neither *polis* trusted the other.

The immediate advantage was with the Spartans who had routed the last of Xerxes' forces at Plataea. The Athenians were temporarily homeless, for the Persians had burned Athens and leveled its walls. Sparta argued that Athens should not rebuild its defenses lest the Persians reoccupy the city and use it against the Greeks. They pointed out that Sparta's villages were unfortified, for Spartan men were all the "walls" Sparta needed. Themistocles saw things differently. He dragged out discussions with the Spartans while the Athenians hastily rebuilt their ramparts.

Pausanias, the Spartan general who had triumphed at Plataea, commanded the allied forces as they pursued the retreating Persians. But power apparently went to his head. The allies accused him of behaving like a Persian despot, and Sparta recalled him and convicted him of treason. When Pausanias sought sanctuary in a temple in order to avoid execution, the Spartan authorities—acting on a suggestion from his mother—bricked up the building's doors and windows and left him to starve.

The Spartans needed their men at home to guard against slave rebellions. Long-term, distant commitments of their soldiers made them nervous. As the Persian threat retreated, the Spartans returned to their accustomed isolation and left foreign affairs to Athens. Thanks to Solon's reforms, Athens had become a populous *polis* that was dependent on trade, and as a naval power, it was better equipped than Sparta to sweep the Persians from their outposts in the Aegean. Themistocles might have been the logical choice to be Pausanias's successor, but his increasing arrogance and a suspicion that he was engaging in foreign intrigues led the Athenian electorate to ostracize him in 471 B.C.E. He fled to Argos and finally found refuge in the Persian empire—and employment as a provincial governor!

Athens' Advance   In 477 B.C.E. the *poleis* that believed that a permanent defense had to be organized to protect the Aegean from Persia sent delegates to a conference on the island of Delos. The result was the formation of the **Delian League**, a military alliance that at its height numbered about 150 members. Athens dominated the league, but the league's treasury was headquartered on Delos, neutral territory sacred to all the Ionian Greeks.

Cimon, son of the Miltiades who had won the battle of Marathon, assumed leadership of the league's navy and did such a good job of pushing the Persians back that by 468 B.C.E. some members of the Delian League concluded that the organization had served its purpose. Cimon, however, used force to prevent them from withdrawing. The league had become too important to Athens to be allowed to disband. Cimon had urged the allies to supply him with money rather than men and ships, and their contributions had built what was fundamentally an Athenian navy. The Delian League was transformed into an Athenian Empire, and in 454 B.C.E. its treasury was moved to Athens. League money was even diverted from military programs to fund the construction of Athens' famous temples.

Cimon fell from power in 462 B.C.E. He was an aristocrat, and Athens' aristocrats tended to be pro-Spartan. (They equated Spartan discipline with the Homeric virtues of their presumed ancestors.) When Sparta asked Athens for help in putting down a slave revolt, Cimon persuaded the reluctant assembly to allow him to lead four thousand Athenians into the Peloponnese. They no sooner arrived than the Spartans changed their minds and ordered them to leave. The humiliated electorate promptly ostracized Cimon.

The political situation in Athens changed as the city used the resources of the Delian League to build its navy. The hoplite infantry, which was recruited from a relatively prosperous class, had been the original driving force behind the Athenian democracy. But the increasing prominence of the navy shifted power to the poorer element in the Athenian population, the men who rowed the state galleys. Athens' new generation of politicians, the most successful of whom was Pericles (c. 490–429 B.C.E.), cultivated this larger electorate. From 461 B.C.E. until his death, Pericles held the office of *strategos* and used his position to prod, manipulate, and lead his city first to the pinnacle of power and then to defeat.

The Parthenon and the Athenian Acropolis   Athens sprang up around the Acropolis, a rock-bound height that served the plain of Attica as a natural fortress. As the city grew rich and powerful, it adorned the Acropolis with monuments, the most famous of which was the *Parthenon*, a temple dedicated to the goddess Athena, Athens' patron deity.

The Peloponnesian War

Hellenic civilization was the product of a society that was almost constantly at war—more often with itself than with a foreign enemy. The Greeks' victories in the Persian Wars increased the threat of internal conflict by polarizing the Aegean world. Athens developed a maritime empire, and Sparta responded by expanding its league of Peloponnesian cities. This division of the Greeks into opposing armed camps set them up for civil war (see Map 4–1).

Precursor to Civil War   Great wars often begin with small conflicts. The first round in what was initially an undeclared war went to Athens. Corinth, the *polis* that occupied the narrow isthmus that connects northern and southern Greece, was Athens' major commercial competitor and Sparta's chief ally. Athens dominated the Aegean, but Corinth had access both to the Aegean and, through the Gulf of Corinth, to the Greek colonies in the western Mediterranean. About 460 B.C.E., Corinth's northern neighbor, the small *polis* of Megara, made a deal with Athens that allowed the Athenians to use Pegae, Megara's small port on the Gulf of Corinth. Corinth viewed this as a threat to its western trade.

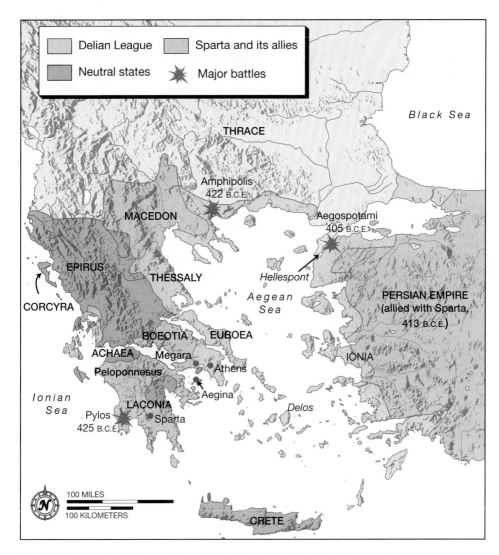

Map 4–1 Competing Alliances: Athens (Delian League) and Sparta This map illustrates the polarization of the Aegean region that developed in the wake of the Persian Wars.

Question: How did geography influence the formation of the Greeks' political alliances?

Corinth invaded Attica in 459 B.C.E. The attack failed, but it prodded the Athenians into making an important addition to their city's fortifications. Athens had sprung up around the Acropolis ("upper-town"), an outcropping of rock that served Attica as a natural citadel. The Acropolis was some four miles inland from the sea, and Athens' commerce passed through a small coastal port called the Piraeus. The obvious strategy for an invading army was to encircle Athens, cut its link to the sea, and starve it into submission. To prevent this, the Athenians built a fortified corridor (the Long Walls) to connect their capital with its port. So long as the Athenian navy ruled the sea and supplied the city through the Piraeus, land-based armies had little hope of taking Athens.

■ ■

PEOPLE IN CONTEXT   Aspasia, the Woman Behind the Great Man

The love of Pericles' life was his mistress, Aspasia, one of the few women who seem to have influenced Athenian politics. Unlike Sparta, Athens encouraged immigration to promote economic development, and it allowed its population to explode. However, as the city grew richer, more powerful, and more democratic, its citizens became jealous and protective of their privileges. In Pericles' day, about 50,000 of Attica's free male residents were citizens and about 25,000 were classed as metics (resident aliens). Metics could not own land, but many of them prospered as craftsmen and merchants. Their families lived in Athens for generations without acquiring citizenship. The sons of metic women who married Athenian citizens had always inherited citizenship from their fathers. But in 451 B.C.E. Pericles persuaded the assembly to limit citizenship to men whose mothers and fathers both came from citizen families. Pericles' motive probably had less to do with Athens' metics than with the dangerous alliances that were created by intermarriage of Athenian aristocratic families with nobles from other *poleis*. Whatever the law's purpose, it made Athens a more closed society and backfired on Pericles.

Pericles married a close relative who bore him two sons, but the union did not last. He divorced his wife and, a few years later (c. 445 B.C.E.), took up with Aspasia, a *hetaira* from Miletus. She lived with him for well over a decade (possibly until his death). After plague carried off Pericles' two older boys, his only surviving male child was a son that Aspasia bore him. To save his *oikos* (his lineage), Pericles had to plead with the assembly to give him an exemption from the law he had sponsored and to grant citizenship to Aspasia's son.

Pericles' bond with Aspasia was (or became in legend) a love match. Athenian gossips circulated the shocking rumor that he kissed her each morning when he left for work and again at evening when he came home. Such affection was considered a sign of an unmanly passion that made him vulnerable to manipulation by his foreign lover. In later years, she was even blamed for pushing him to take the actions that caused the **Peloponnesian War**.

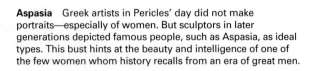

Aspasia was a convenient target for Pericles' opponents, and accurate information about her is difficult to disentangle from their xenophobic and misogynistic propaganda. She was born in Miletus about 470 B.C.E. and may have come to Athens about 450 B.C.E. with an older sister who had married an exiled Athenian aristocrat. Pericles' decree doomed any hope she may have had for a marriage that would have placed her on the same footing as a citizen-wife. Some

Aspasia   Greek artists in Pericles' day did not make portraits—especially of women. But sculptors in later generations depicted famous people, such as Aspasia, as ideal types. This bust hints at the beauty and intelligence of one of the few women whom history recalls from an era of great men.

sources refer to her as Pericles' concubine. Some maintain that she was a *hetaira*, a professional entertainer, and some simply call her a whore.

In comic plays from the period, Aspasia is a vamp, a seductress who uses sex to manipulate men. But elsewhere she is described as a highly educated, intelligent woman who taught rhetoric and held her own in debates with the city's philosophers. Several of Socrates' students remarked on his friendship with her and testified to her skill as a conversationalist and speech writer. If she was Pericles' most influential advisor, he might have done worse.

After Pericles' death, Aspasia was taken up by another of Athens' leaders, and his political career profited from her advice and connections. No one knows when or where she died, but unlike most Greek women of her generation, she was not forgotten. For good or ill, she—a foreigner and a woman—had helped to shape Athens' destiny.

Question: What does Aspasia's story imply about attitudes toward women in Pericles' Athens?

Athens' foreign policy in this era reflected the city's growing self-confidence and willingness to take risks. The most audacious decision the Athenian assembly made was to dispatch a fleet to Egypt to assist rebels who were trying to force the Persians out. The campaign bogged down, and in 453 B.C.E. the Persians cornered and obliterated the Athenian expedition.

The two hundred ships that Thucydides, an Athenian historian, says his city lost in Egypt sobered Athens, and in 451 B.C.E. the conservative politician Cimon returned to power and negotiated a five-year truce with the Peloponnesian League. At the same time, Callias, Cimon's former brother-in-law, seems to have come to an agreement with Persia. If so, it was not publicized, for a formal peace with Persia would have undercut the rationale for the Delian League. When the truce ended and a rebellion erupted among some of Athens' allies, Sparta seized the opportunity to invade Attica. Athens then abandoned most of its mainland holdings outside of Attica, and in 445 B.C.E. the two Greek superpowers signed the Thirty Years' Peace—a commitment that proved to be overly optimistic.

The Peloponnesian War   The Thirty Years' Peace gave the Athenians an opportunity to concentrate on trade contacts with the *poleis* of Italy and Sicily. This worried Corinth and Syracuse, a Corinthian colony that was the largest of the Sicilian *poleis*. Tensions increased in 433 B.C.E. when Corcyra, a Corinthian colony on an island off the western coast of Greece, quarreled with Corinth and asked for Athenian help. The ships Athens sent to observe developments intervened in a battle between Corinth and Corcyra, and this prompted Corinth to charge Athens with committing an act of war. Athens exacerbated the situation by ordering Potidaea, a *polis* in Chalcidice (the northern Aegean), to dismantle its defenses. Potidaea was a Corinthian colony, and Athens feared that if war broke out, it might provide the enemy with a base for attacking shipping through the Hellespont and cutting off supplies of grain to Athens. When Potidaea resisted Athens' order (with Corinthian encouragement), Athens had to undertake a lengthy, expensive siege of the city.

As the international situation heated up, the Athenians concluded that they had two options. They could back down, or they could mount a show of force that frightened their enemies into retreating. Pericles preferred the latter strategy and persuaded the assembly to take an action that some of his contemporaries later claimed caused the Peloponnesian War. As a warning to others, Athens closed the ports of its empire to merchants from Megara. This devastated Megara, for it cut off most of its trade.

Corinth appealed to Sparta, and Sparta summoned a meeting of the Peloponnesian League. Fighting did not immediately break out, for factions in both Sparta and Athens were opposed to war. The decision, however, was not left to the superpowers. Sparta's ally Thebes attacked Athens' ally Plataea, and that forced the two great cities to act.

Civil wars are among the most senseless of conflicts, for by squandering the resources of a country, they undermine both victor and vanquished. The Peloponnesian War was a particularly hopeless struggle, for neither combatant knew how to deal with the military strength of the other. The Athenian navy could not harm the Spartan infantry, and the Spartan army could not attack Athens' ships. Pericles assumed that once Sparta understood that it could not deal Athens a lethal blow, Sparta would give up. His trust in the fundamental rationality of human conduct proved to be misplaced.

The War's First Phase   Pericles' strategy for winning the war was to refuse to fight it on the enemy's terms. He talked the Athenians into abandoning the defense of Attica and retreating behind the walls of their city. Thanks to the Long Walls and Athens' control of the sea, Athens could outlast any Spartan siege. Initially, things played out as Pericles predicted. Sparta led an army into Attica and found nothing for it to do but chop down olive trees and uproot vineyards. Sparta's army was shown to be impotent against Athens, but instead of concluding what Pericles took to be self-evident (that is, that the war was unwinnable), Sparta refused to give up.

Pericles' strategy severely tested the discipline of the democracy, for it was as costly to individual citizens as it was to the state. Men were asked to stand idly by while an enemy torched their farms and taunted them with charges of cowardice. The resolve of the Athenian electorate was further tested in the second year of the war when plague spread through the crowded city. About a third of its inhabitants died. Among them were Pericles' elder sons and then Pericles himself.

As time passed and sacrifices mounted, emotion replaced reason in the deliberations of the Athenian assembly, and Athens' democracy began to deteriorate as voters were swayed by the self-serving rhetoric of **demagogues**. Calls for restraint were equated with treason as politicians fanned the flames of jingoism in their attempts to sway the citizenry. Still, the city was slow to lose its moral compass. In 428 B.C.E. four *poleis* on the island of Lesbos declared their intention to secede from Athens' empire. Athens' refusal to engage the Spartans might have led them to conclude that Athens would not fight. If so, they seriously miscalculated. Athens descended on Lesbos in force and quickly retook the island. In a fit of vindictive passion the assembly then dispatched a ship with an order directing the commander on Lesbos to slaughter his captives. Overnight, Athenian tempers cooled and consciences awoke. The assembly reconvened the next day, rescinded its decree, and managed to get word to Lesbos just in time to prevent genocide. The event provides a marker for measuring the effects of prolonged war on the ethics of a democracy. At the time of the Lesbos revolt, the Peloponnesian War was young, and its brutality had not yet lessened the Athenians' respect for the value of human life. Twelve years later, the situation was different. In 416 B.C.E. Athens ordered the tiny island of Melos to join its alliance. When Melos refused, Athens invaded, slaughtered its men, and enslaved its women and children. This time there were no second thoughts and no last-minute reprieves.

In 425 B.C.E. Athens scored a coup. A storm forced an Athenian fleet into the bay at Pylos, which had been abandoned since the fall of its Mycenaean kingdom over seven centuries earlier. Demosthenes, the admiral in charge, recognized the strategic importance of the site and decided to occupy it. The Spartans soon discovered his presence and sent an army to evict him. However, relief forces arrived from Athens and surprised and trapped 420 Spartans on an island in the bay. Sparta, fearing the loss of so many men, promptly sued for peace. But no Athenian politician was willing to urge moderation on an assembly that had a taste of victory. Athens sent enough men to Pylos to overwhelm the blockaded Spartans, and 292 of them were taken alive.

The capture of Spartan hostages at Pylos emboldened the Athenians to abandon Pericles' strategy and pursue the war on land. They attacked Thebes, Sparta's major ally in northern Greece, and were soundly trounced. An even greater loss followed in Chalcidice, where a Spartan general organized an uprising that cost Athens control of key ports on the crucial Hellespont grain route. The panicky assembly blamed the loss on an Athenian admiral named Thucydides and banished him. Posterity is grateful, for Thucydides devoted his enforced leisure to writing an extraordinary history of the war that preoccupied his generation.

Athens' ardor for war cooled. In the spring of 423 B.C.E. it endorsed a temporary cessation of hostilities. Two years later, Nicias, an Athenian general, negotiated a treaty that was supposed to end the war. Athens promised to withdraw from Pylos and Sparta from Chalcidice. Both states pledged to maintain the peace for 50 years. The treaty was a de facto defeat for Sparta, and several of its allies refused to sign. When ports in Chalcidice declined to submit to Athens, Athens refused to give up Pylos.

Interlude in Sicily   The treaty did not resolve the issues that had caused the war, so it was not likely to hold. Athens should therefore have proceeded with caution. Instead, it committed itself to a campaign on the distant island of Sicily. The chief advocate for the ill-advised expedition was Alcibiades (c. 450–404 B.C.E.), Pericles' nephew and one of the philosopher Socrates' students. Nicias, the elder statesman who had negotiated peace with Sparta, opposed it, but Alcibiades was the more appealing politician. Young, rich, handsome, intelligent, and totally unprincipled, he carried the day. The best that his opponents could do was to persuade the assembly to split command of the expedition among Alcibiades and two older generals, one of whom was Nicias. The night before the fleet sailed, many sacred images were vandalized in Athens. This blasphemy had to be punished lest the gods turn against the city, and the finger of suspicion pointed at a group of young rowdies led by Alcibiades. A ship was sent to Sicily to bring him home for trial. Rather than risk conviction, Alcibiades chose to defect to

Sparta. Nicias was left with responsibility for a campaign he had opposed, and the project's sponsor, Alcibiades, began to plot with the Spartans to bring about its failure.

Athens had committed about 25,000 men and 250 ships to the invasion of Sicily, but this was not enough. Nicias claimed that twice as many were needed, and he urged the assembly to allow him to withdraw. It chose instead to send him more troops. The Spartans countered by dispatching a general to organize the defense of Syracuse, the great Sicilian city that Nicias was besieging. Syracuse's navy first trapped the Athenian fleet in its harbor. Then Syracuse's army outflanked and began to encircle the Greek camp. Seeing that the situation was hopeless, Nicias ordered his men to scatter and try to save themselves. All of them (some 40,000) were captured. Nicias was executed, and his men were either enslaved or herded into a quarry and left to die from thirst and exposure. The loss of the army rendered Athens defenseless, but the city was unaware of that fact until a visitor to the port of the Piraeus casually mentioned the disaster to his barber.

Sparta could not pass up the opportunity presented by Athens' vulnerability. While Alcibiades moved through the Aegean urging members of the Athenian empire to revolt, Sparta established a fort on the edge of Attica as a retreat for runaway Athenian slaves. Some 20,000 defected and helped the Spartans lay Attica under permanent siege.

The War's Final Phase   Athens' fortunes had sunk suddenly and dramatically, but the city refused to give in. The war dragged on for another eight years and was finally ended by the intervention of Persia. The Spartans decided that they had to meet the Athenians on their own turf (metaphorically) by taking to the sea, and Persia financed the fleets with which Sparta pursued Athens' navy. Alcibiades may have arranged this, but when news of the hyperactive young man's affair with the Spartan king's wife leaked out, he fled Sparta for Persian territory. There he tried to make a deal that would allow him to return to Athens. The Persians were willing to offer Athens assistance, for it was to their advantage to help the Greeks destroy one another. All that was needed, Alcibiades said, was for Athens to replace democracy with a form of government that Persia regarded as more reliable. The Athenian elite promptly staged a coup that disenfranchised most of the *polis's* citizens. But when news of this reached the sailors of the fleet, they threatened to mutiny and elected new generals—one of whom was Alcibiades! Democracy was restored, and under Alcibiades' leadership the Athenians won several victories. However, suspicion of further double dealing prompted Athens to exile Alcibiades in 406 B.C.E. and replace him with incompetent admirals whose blunders assured the city's defeat.

In 404 B.C.E. Lysander, the Spartan admiral, destroyed the Athenian navy, blockaded Athens, and starved it into submission. Sparta allowed Athens to survive, for it wanted to block the expansion of Athens' ambitious neighbor, Thebes. But Sparta ordered the Athenians to tear down the Long Walls and limit their fleet to a mere dozen ships. Athens' days of military glory were over, but the city's fame as a cultural center endured.

Sparta profited little from its victory, for it was poorly equipped by tradition, experience, and manpower to lead the Aegean world. It also alienated the Greeks by ceding Ionia to Persia as repayment for its war debt. Persia, for its part, continued to fund the Greeks' internecine quarrels. Rebellions erupted against Sparta, and in 371 B.C.E.

Thebes, led by a brilliant general named Epaminondas, defeated Sparta and ended its hegemony. Thebes declined following Epaminondas's death a few years later, and without a dominant *polis* to maintain order, local wars proliferated. The Greeks continued to tear at the fabric of their civilization.

Only a little more than a century separated the victory at Marathon (490 B.C.E.) from the confusion that attended Sparta's fall (371 B.C.E.). From the military perspective, that century was bloody, wasteful, and disastrous. Surprisingly, however, the carnage did not impede the work of artists and intellectuals. In the midst of the tumult, they created the artistic and literary monuments that made these years a classic era in Western civilization.

Intellectual and Artistic Life in the *Polis*

Traditional wisdom held that the world was a product of divine forces and that the causes of things were mysteries hidden in the minds of gods. The explanation for earthly phenomena lay, therefore, in a realm that human beings could not explore. During the sixth century B.C.E. some Greek thinkers from Ionia began to question such beliefs. They demystified the world and conceived of it as an orderly place governed by intelligible principles that could be discovered by observation and rational analysis. For centuries people had collected data about the world in order to improve their ability to manipulate things, but the Greeks went further. They invented science, the disinterested search simply for an understanding of how things worked.

The rationality of the Greek mind should not be overemphasized, for Greek culture had its dark side. The Greeks believed that there were mysteries and truths that could be grasped only through intuition, feeling, or divine revelation. They invented potent myths and symbols that still engage our imaginations. They were capable of bloody deeds. They cultivated trances and ecstatic experiences, and they thrilled at stories of mutilation, incest, and cannibalism. They believed in magic, rituals, spells, visions, dreams, omens, and oracles, and they bowed before inexplicable forces they called fate or chance. Classical civilization was not a simple or even self-consistent phenomenon.

From Myth to Philosophy and Science   The *Iliad* and the *Odyssey*, which were composed in Ionia in the mid-eighth century B.C.E., belong to the most ancient of literary genres—the hero epic, the story of people who are larger than life. During the seventh and sixth centuries B.C.E., the Greeks began to produce a different kind of poetry—lyrics, short songs inspired by the personal feelings of real individuals. These intimate and sometimes confessional poems mark a shift of interest among the Greeks from fantasies about the past to the real situations people face in the present. The greatest lyric poet of the archaic period (750–500 B.C.E.) was an aristocratic woman named Sappho (fl. c. 600 B.C.E.), a native of the island of Lesbos. Only fragments of her work survive, but her passionate love songs were so exquisitely constructed that they joined Homer's epics as standard texts in ancient Greece's schools.

The lyric poets' interest in the real world was shared by their contemporaries, the first thinkers to seek rational alternatives to the mythic view of nature. Greeks called these people philosophers, "lovers of wisdom." They set aside stories about the gods and proposed natural explanations for natural phenomena.

Thales (fl. c. 550 B.C.E.), from the Ionian city of Miletus, pioneered the field of metaphysics, the search for the fundamental principles of existence. He was fascinated by the fact that things around us are constantly changing, yet the world remains a stable, permanent place. How, he wondered, could change and permanence, which are opposites, coexist in the same system? That the world maintains a balance between them suggested to Thales that there was a more fundamental reality, a single "substance" ("something standing under"), that controlled them. Such a substance had to be able to exist as a solid, a liquid, and a gas, for all these states are found in nature. Thales knew only one thing that fit the bill: water. He concluded, therefore, that everything that exists is a form of water. Things hold together because their contrasts are more apparent than real. In actuality, only one thing exists, a watery substance that naturally assumes different states of being.

Thales' followers, the **Monist** ("single principle") philosophers, taught that change was only a shift among the states that are natural to the one eternal substance that underlies all things. They disagreed, however, about the identity of that substance. Anaximander (c. 611–546 B.C.E.) objected that nothing we could experience with our senses (such as water) was complex enough to account for the variety of things found in nature. He postulated, therefore, that the ultimate substance was "the indefinite," a material that is never directly perceived in its pure essence, but only as it manifests aspects of itself in particular things. His successor, Anaximenes (d. c. 500 B.C.E.), was not convinced. He pointed out that an unknowable substance offered no better explanation for the world than an unknowable god. To explain anything, Anaximenes said, the ultimate substance had to be something identifiable. He proposed air. Just as the "breath of life" sustains the human body, he theorized that air maintains and activates the universe.

The problem with these theories was that they were unverifiable. This led some thinkers to suspect that their premise was incorrect. The Monists had begun by asking how opposites like change and permanence coexist, but what if change and permanence do not exist? What if only one of them is real and the other is an illusion?

Heracleitus of Ephesus (fl. c. 500 B.C.E.) argued that permanence was the illusion. Things that change more slowly than we do appear permanent to us, but in actuality everything is constantly changing. Being is analogous to a flowing river, and no one, he pointed out, can step into the same river twice. If we need to imagine a primal substance for the world, we should envision it as fire, pure energy. Parmenides of Elea (fl. fifth century B.C.E.) came to the opposite conclusion, for he regarded change as an illogical concept. Change implies that something new has come into being. There are only two ways this could happen, and neither is possible. If a change comes from what already exists, there is nothing new and therefore no change. If a change comes from something that does not exist, then nothing has created something, which is absurd. Nothing is the absence of being, not a kind of being with the power to cause something else to be. Therefore, Parmenides insisted the universe must be an inert solid. Empty space in which movement might take place cannot exist. Emptiness is nothingness, and nothingness means nonexistence.

The Classical Era

POLITICS	ARTISTS AND INTELLECTUALS
[600–500 B.C.E.]	
Solon (c. 638–c. 559)	Sappho (fl. c. 600)
Peisistratus (fl. c. 560)	Thales (c. 640–546)
Cyrus the Great (c. 600–530)	Anaximander (611–547)
Cleisthenes (fl. c. 507)	Anaximenes (d. c. 528)
	Pythagoras (d. c. 497)
	Aeschylus (525–456)
[500–400 B.C.E.]	
Miletus's rebellion (499–494)	Heracleitus (fl. c. 500)
	Parmenides (fl. c. 500)
	Hecataeus (fl. c. 550–480)
	Sophocles (496–406)
Darius invades Greece (492)	Empedocles (493–433)
	Protagoras (d. c. 421)
Xerxes' campaign (484–479)	Euripides (485–406)
	Herodotus (480–425)
	Socrates (469–399)
	Democritus (460–347)
	Hippocrates (460–377)
	Thucydides (460–399)
	Aristophanes (450–385)
Peloponnesian War (431–404)	Plato (429–347)
Pericles (490–429)	
[400–300 B.C.E.]	
Thebes defeats Sparta (371)	Aristotle (384–322)
Philip of Macedon (r. 359–336)	
Alexander the Great (r. 336–323)	

The rigorous logic of Heracleitus and Parmenides led to dead-end conclusions and a description of the world that defied common sense. The **Pluralist** ("multiple things") philosophers therefore hoped that by reconciling the arguments of these two thinkers, they might find a logically coherent explanation for the natural world that was consistent with ordinary experience. The Pluralists claimed that changing configurations of a number of different, but permanent, components create the world we experience. Empedocles of Agrigentum (fl. c. 450 B.C.E.) suggested that everything that exists is a product of the interaction of four fundamental elements ("irreducibles"): earth, air, fire, and water. The elements themselves never change, but their combinations do. Democritus of Abdera (c. 460–370 B.C.E.) felt that a few elements were insufficient to explain the great diversity of things found in the world. Like the Monists, he believed that only one substance existed, but that it existed in the form of discrete atoms ("indivisibles"). These were innumerable, eternal bits of a material that had only primary characteristics (size, shape, and location). All secondary attributes (such as color and odor) were mere impressions created by interactions among the atoms. Human beings and all they experience were the result of shifting agglomerations of atoms.

Democritus reduced the universe to a mechanism: a swirl of physical objects that randomly come together and split apart. This implied that existence has no meaning, but it encouraged the development of science by suggesting that mathematical measurements of physical changes might suffice to explain everything. A century earlier, Pythagoras, a contemporary of the Ionian Monists, had proposed something similar. Pythagoras concluded from the mathematical relationships that exist between sounds (pitches) and physical objects (lengths of plucked string) that mathematics provided the key to unlocking the mysteries of the universe.

Greek science developed these portentous theories largely by intuition and imagination, but speculation alone could carry science no further. Unless hard data could be found to confirm the existence of Empedocles' elements and Democritus's atoms, they were no more helpful in explaining the universe than were the gods. Two thousand years passed before the West invented instruments that could gather the information needed to test the ancient Greek hypotheses. Consequently, thinkers ended this line of inquiry and turned their attention to questions of a different kind.

Medicine   Greek science tended to trust rational argument more than observation and to be abstract and theoretical, but it also made advances in applied fields—particularly medicine. Hippocrates of Cos (c. 460–377 B.C.E.), Democritus's contemporary, acquired such a reputation as a healer that modern physi-

Ideal Humanity   The scientific and artistic interests of the Greeks converged in the production of the *kouros,* a free-standing statue of a nude youth. The sculptors of these works sought to depict the essence of real, if idealized, humanity: the male athlete at the peak of his development, devoid of all concealment, ornament, or artifice. The rigid standardized posture of these statues abstracted them from time and place. They represented male existence, not an individual man caught in a particular moment or action. The rigid posture was also doubtless influenced by the conventions of Egyptian painting and sculpture.

cians take a vow to honor the principles he allegedly established for the conduct of their profession. Almost no dependable information survives about him, but about 300 B.C.E. Greek scholars collected a body of medical literature that they claimed stemmed from his school. It influenced the practice of medicine for over two millennia.

Much ancient healing relied on spells and charms, but the Hippocratic tradition was relatively free of superstition. It sought natural causes for physical problems, relied on observation to diagnose them, and sought to cure them with drugs, surgery, and changes in diet and regimen. The treatment it offered was primitive, but its method had merit. Medicine did not make much more progress until the early modern era, when the microscope and advances in chemistry began to provide new clues to the mechanisms of disease and human physiology.

History   The invention of history was another sign of the Greek's preoccupation with science. The word *historia* ("inquiry") originally meant an investigation by a judge (a *histor*) into the facts of a dispute. A *histor* became a historian when he broadened his inquiry and searched for explanations for larger events.

It may seem odd to speak of the invention of something like history. Because human beings have memories, it is obvious that they have always been aware of the past. Early civilizations even compiled annals and lists of the names of kings or other officials and dated events by assigning them to years in the reigns of certain rulers or priests. The peoples of Egypt and the Middle East had accumulated much more of this material than the Greeks, whose civilization was comparatively young. But it was the Greeks who turned records of this kind into history by looking for patterns that made the past meaningful. Most of their neighbors dismissed history's panorama as transitory and meaningless or as a byproduct of mysterious struggles among the gods. Parts of the Hebrew Bible foreshadow history, but there, too, the past was of interest primarily as a revelation of God's will. Greece's historians, like its philosophers, were curious to see how far they could go in explaining the world in purely human terms.

History developed from geography. The Greeks of the archaic era were traders and colonizers who needed accurate information about foreign lands. Anaximenes, the Monist philosopher, was also a cartographer. He produced a map of the world, and one of his contemporaries was ancient Greece's first great cultural geographer, Hecataeus of Miletus (fl. c. 500 B.C.E.). Hecataeus believed that information of all kinds (topography, climate, plants, animals, religions, customs, and institutions) was needed to make foreign lands intelligible. (Hippocratic physicians agreed—maintaining that hard environments produced hardy people and that rich lands undermined both strength and character.) Herodotus of Halicarnassus (480–425 B.C.E.), the "father of history," began as a geographer building on the work of Hecataeus.

At a time when literate people were few and manuscripts rare, authors like Herodotus made their livings by giving lectures and public readings. They resembled Homeric bards and were regarded as entertainers. But what Herodotus offered his audiences was something different from Homer's epics. Poetry was the traditional medium for sacred myth and serious literature. Even secular leaders like Athens'

Solon wrote poems to explain their political agenda. But Herodotus composed prose. Anaximenes was the first major thinker from whom we have a few lines of prose. Prose signaled science's break with sacred myths and legends. Herodotus learned much about storytelling from Homer, but his use of prose declared his intention to depart from the epic tradition and view the past from the perspective of the new secular science.

Herodotus began by writing ethnographical studies in the style of Hecataeus—sketches of life in exotic locales like Egypt and Babylon. But when he visited Athens, he found the theme that transformed descriptive geography into history. The Athens Herodotus experienced was fresh from its victories over the Persians and riding the crest of a wave of self-confidence. The city's heady environment persuaded Herodotus that, thanks to the Greeks and particularly the Athenians, the world was on the brink of a glorious new age. He decided to try to explain how this had come about and suspected that the answer was to be found in a study of the Persian War. The war had pitted the might of a despotic empire against the will of a free people, and freedom had proved invincible. The Greek victory had changed the world by revealing for the first time what a free society could achieve.

The generation that had fought the Persian War was dying out by the time Herodotus arrived in Athens, and his history of it appeared during the early years of the Peloponnesian War. He may have wanted to remind his readers of what their ancestors had achieved by working together, but he probably did not expect this to divert them from their current path. Herodotus suspected that events were not entirely under human control. Individuals certainly affected what happened, but chance also played a role, as did a mysterious force that maintained a cosmic balance in the universe. Some outcomes seemed fated no matter what people did: Wealth and power undermined themselves; fortune and happiness did not last forever.

The era that invented history produced two of the West's greatest historians. Herodotus was about 20 years old when his future Athenian colleague, Thucydides (460–399 B.C.E.), was born. The two men not only worked in the same field; they treated complementary subjects. Herodotus told the story of the "good" war that launched Greece's Golden Age, and Thucydides narrated the sad tale of the willful conflict that frittered away Greece's opportunities. There were differences in their approaches to their common subject. Herodotus was not overly credulous. He went out of his way to check information and find reliable sources. Sometimes he warned his readers that they should not assume that he believed every story that he felt obliged to tell. He was, however, a religious man who trusted in omens and who felt that human agency alone could not explain history. For Thucydides, history was simply an account of human decisions and their consequences.

Thucydides was an aristocratic Athenian who was deeply immersed in his city's political and intellectual life. An intuitive sense of the importance of the time and place in which he found himself inspired him to do something that had never been done before: to record history as it unfolded. He had time and opportunity, for a few years after the Peloponnesian War began the Athenians blamed him for losing a battle and exiled him for 20 years.

Thucydides claimed that the proper subjects for a historian were politics and war, and he rigorously excluded everything else from his narrative. He believed that events could be explained as the outcomes of decisions that individuals made and that these decisions were rooted in the intelligence and character of their authors. No gods or mysterious powers intervened. An element of chance affected how situations played out, but chance was not a mystical force (a providence, fate, or destiny). Chance entered in because the human ability to anticipate developments and plan for every possible contingency is limited. Thucydides viewed human beings as fundamentally rational agents who are motivated by self-interest. Pursuit of power is part of their nature, and the strong always dominate the weak. The study of history has much to teach, he insisted, because human nature does not change. We learn about ourselves by analyzing the motives of our predecessors and the consequences of their actions. What ultimately counts is developing the skill we need to bring about the outcomes we want.

Philosophy, Psychology, and Politics Natural scientists and physicians work by observing phenomena and collecting and rationally analyzing data, but Greek thinkers of Thucydides' generation wrestled with the troubling discovery that what is observed depends, in part, on the observer. They knew that the unaided human senses (their primary scientific instruments) could deceive them. They concluded, therefore, that to learn more about the world, they had to learn more about themselves. In the interim between the Persian and Peloponnesian Wars (the 470s and 460s B.C.E.), Greek philosophers shifted their attention from the external world of the senses to the internal world of the human psyche. They began to analyze thought itself—to work out the mechanics of logic, explore the emotions, and ask themselves what "truth" meant. Some wondered if such a thing existed.

The earlier Greek philosophers, who focused their attention on the natural world, are called the "**pre-Socratics**." This suggests that the Athenian thinker Socrates (469–399 B.C.E.) was responsible for the major shift that took place in philosophy's focus, but philosophy's reorientation actually began with his teachers, professional educators called Sophists. Sophists taught public speaking and the arts of persuasion, valuable skills in a democracy. Their study of the uses of language led them to explore how the mind forms concepts and opinions and caused them to wonder what words like *justice*, *virtue*, and *truth* really signify.

Relativism was in the air that Socrates breathed. Colonization and trade had brought the Greeks into contact with all kinds of people, and the knowledge that alternative cultures existed was causing some Greeks to question their traditional values and institutions. Furthermore, the Sophist sellers of oratorical training claimed that truth, if it was even knowable, was irrelevant. A skillful speaker could make weak causes appear strong and black look white. There were no absolute standards or values, for as Protagoras (493–421 B.C.E.), one of the leading Sophists, succinctly put it, "Man is the measure of all things." One person sees things one way, and another sees them differently. Both are "right," for no one can rise above his or her individual perspective and grasp pure, objective truth. We might prefer one opinion to another, but only because it is useful or consistent with our preconceptions, not because it is true.

This radical skepticism had alarming implications. It undercut the possibility of shared values and objective standards and justified selfish individualism. If everything is simply a matter of personal opinion, how can people justify the laws and values that make it possible for them to form communities? How can they maintain a *polis?* The Greeks valued the individual, but believed that individuals were formed by community life. Citizenship in a *polis* made them what they were, and citizenship implied a duty to subordinate self-interest to the common good.

Socrates devoted himself to the search for an alternative to the relativism and skepticism of the Sophists. Because he never wrote anything, we know him today only through the reports of others—and those reports differ significantly. The most elaborate descriptions of his conversations (he would not have said "teachings") are dialogues penned by his devoted pupil Plato (c. 429–347 B.C.E.). These are imaginative recreations, not verbatim reports, and it is likely that they tell us more about Plato than Socrates.

In Plato's dialogues, Socrates is an ingenious debater who spends his life forcing people to justify their beliefs. He delights in revealing the absurd and contradictory implications of the commonsense opinions held by his fellow Athenians. He is adept at demolishing belief systems and unwilling to propose anything to take their place. Some people, like Plato himself, were devoted to Socrates for liberating them from sterile complacency and teaching them how to think; others considered him a nuisance or a threat to the beliefs on which the *polis* was based.

In the wake of the Peloponnesian War, the Athenians struggled with humiliation and self-doubt, and they had little tolerance for intellectual gadflies. Citizens of a democracy are responsible for what their government does. When it flourishes, they congratulate themselves; but when it blunders, they look for scapegoats on whom to place the blame. Socrates' habit of questioning the legitimacy of traditional values made him a convenient target. He may indeed have had little respect for democracy, a form of government guided by the kinds of commonly held opinions he delighted in demolishing. Socrates was indicted, tried, and convicted on a charge of corrupting the youth of Athens by undercutting their faith in the gods and the wisdom of their elders. This was a capital offense, but Athens, having made its point, was not eager to put a defenseless old man to death. Socrates was given an opportunity to flee, but he insisted on being executed. He told his friends that having been protected by Athens' laws all his life, he could not reject the authority of those laws just because they were now inconvenient. His death was perhaps his ultimate attempt to refute relativists and skeptics. It implied that rational people have an innate obligation to something more than personal self-interest.

Plato, Socrates' ardent disciple, was determined to justify belief in the existence of truth, and he thought he found the evidence he needed in the way our minds organize the things we perceive. When we encounter a thing, we assign it to a class of objects. A collie does not look much like a dachshund, but somehow when we see either of these animals (even the first time), we know that it is a dog. Plato believed that this was only possible if all the members of a class had something in common that our minds recognize—a defining reality that he called a form or an idea. Their form or idea makes them what they are even if it manifests itself somewhat differently in each individual. Plato claimed that the forms are eternal and exist apart from the particular things that we experience. We recognize dogs because our minds are born with some previous experience of "dogness," of the pure ideal that makes a dog a dog. Plato noted that our knowledge of a class of things becomes more accurate as we study more individuals belonging to that class. By combining multiple examples, we discover the higher category of being that each individual only partially represents. What is true of individual objects is also true of individual ideas. They, too, fit into categories, and those categories compose a hierarchy of increasingly abstract ideas. The class of dogs, for instance, is subsumed in the class of animals, and the class of animals, in higher and higher classes until we arrive at the ultimate idea—all-encompassing Truth. Plato's theory—that the world of sense experience is less real than a realm of pure intelligibility (which is accessible only to the mind)—has a mystical aspect that has long appealed to religious thinkers. Some of them have equated his ultimate Idea, which intuits all things, with what they mean by divinity.

Plato was born after the Peloponnesian War began, and the Athens he knew was a *polis* that labored, and finally broke, under the strains of that campaign. The great experiment with democracy that Athens had conducted was not an unqualified success. In the opinion of scholarly aristocrats, such as Plato and Thucydides, democracy tended to degenerate into mob rule. The ideal state that Plato conceived in his youth, therefore, was not a democracy like the one that had executed his beloved teacher Socrates. Plato hypothesized instead that power ought to be entrusted only to persons who had the knowledge and self-control to use it wisely. The best form of government was one that vested all authority in individuals whom nature had especially equipped to rule. When citizens of democratic societies (like Plato) lose confidence in themselves, they tend to look for a savior, a person with extraordinary gifts that will supposedly enable him or her to do for the people what the people have failed to do for themselves. The young Plato pinned his hope for the future on such saviors, and he even tried (and failed) to educate one. As he aged, he came to doubt that any individual could be trusted to use power disinterestedly. In his last work, he turned his attention from his earlier efforts to model an ideal state to drafting what he hoped would be a practical set of laws for a real community—one populated by people who struggle to reconcile their private desires with their obligations to society.

Among Plato's students was a youth named Aristotle (384–322 B.C.E.), who was destined to join him in the ranks of the West's greatest intellects. Unlike Plato, Aristotle was not an Athenian and not from an aristocratic family. His father was a physician who served the king of Macedonia. At about the age of 17 Aristotle came to Athens to work in Plato's school, the Academy. He remained there for 20 years, leaving only on Plato's death, when leadership of the school passed to Plato's nephew. About 335 B.C.E. he returned to Athens to found a school of his own, the Lyceum. He remained there until a year before his death, when a deteriorating political situation caused him to move to the nearby island of Euboea.

There were differences between Aristotle and Plato, but given their long association, these things should probably not be overemphasized. Aristotle followed Plato in believing that our knowledge of the world is the result of our ability to recognize the universal ideas or forms that are partially realized in individual things. He departed from his master, however, in rejecting the thesis that the ideas have a separate existence in a realm of their own. This disagreement reflected the differing intellectual preferences of the two men. Plato was drawn to the study of mathematics. He relied primarily on reason to develop explanations for the things that interested him. Consequently, he saw the world in terms of static abstractions. Aristotle, too, was intrigued by the processes of rational thought. He was the first to articulate the rules of logic that govern valid arguments. But Aristotle preferred to reason from information obtained by observation. His standard method was to collect and describe specific specimens and then propose general theories to explain their attributes. Like a modern scientist, he amassed data and looked for hypotheses that could make sense out of the information that he had collected. Consequently, he had a more dynamic view of the world than Plato. He saw it as an evolving place in which things strove to realize their innate potential—that is, to become rather than simply to be.

Aristotle believed the universe to be a coherent system of things moving toward ends or goals. Because motion cannot be perceived or defined without a fixed point of reference, he argued that the universe had its origin in what he called a "prime mover"—an unmovable reality that inaugurated the motion (or change) that characterizes existence. Christian theologians were later to find his argument for an "unmoved mover" a persuasive proof for the existence of the Bible's creator God. Aristotle was fascinated by every aspect of nature and human behavior. He brought order to the information he gathered by dividing it into separate fields or disciplines, and he produced treatises on everything from biology, zoology, and psychology to ethics, politics, poetics, logic, and metaphysics. The result was a vast amount of data organized and fit into a logical framework of explanation. Later generations of scholars were so impressed that many of them came to regard Aristotle's opinions as definitive.

Aristotle was, however, very much a man of his time, and reason did not prevent him from absorbing the common beliefs and prejudices of his day. He, for instance, thought that there was abundant evidence in nature for the inferiority of females. The male, he argued, was the human prototype. Females were produced when something went wrong with the processes of conception and gestation. The result of their failure to reach completion, Aristotle claimed, was the birth of a kind of diminished and castrated male, the physically weaker and intellectually inferior creature known as a woman. Its limitations necessitated its subordination to men and justified its exclusion from public life. What was true of women was also true of some categories of men. Aristotle agreed with Plato that human beings could reach their full potential only by participating in the life of a *polis*. But participation was possible and appropriate only for men rich enough to afford the leisure time needed for education and public service. Aristotle, like Plato and others of the post-Peloponnesian War generation, was no fan of the kind of radical democracy with which Athens had experimented.

The Arts and Politics   The Greeks practiced all the arts known to us and some that we no longer regard as fine arts. The influence of the remnants of their architecture and sculpture has been and remains incalculable, but their achievements in other media are harder to assess. We know that they produced skilled painters. Athens had a state art collection, which it displayed in a public gallery on the Acropolis. Fragmentary mosaic copies of a few paintings exist. But because none of the original work has survived, no one knows what it was like. Greek music and dance are also lost. The Greeks experimented with musical notation systems, but did not succeed in developing and standardizing an adequate one. Sculptors and vase painters depicted dancers, but it is difficult to infer choreography from frozen images. The texts of some ancient tragedies and comedies have survived, but words were only part of the experience of Greek theater. It was a multifaceted art that combined dance, music, costuming, and conventions of acting that are hard for us now to imagine.

Much Hellenic art was public art. That is, it was meant to educate and inspire citizens, to impress a *polis's* allies, and to intimidate its enemies. There was, however, an art that served private collectors: pottery painting. The Greeks turned the decoration of pottery into high art. Their jars, bowls, and cups were in demand throughout the ancient world, and they provide us with invaluable pictorial documentation of Hellenic society.

The Minoans and Mycenaeans produced sophisticated pottery decorated in multiple colors with naturalistic figures, but it was replaced during the Aegean Dark Age by a novel "geometric" style. Geometric pottery, as its name implies, featured bands of repetitive, abstract figures. It was an art that celebrated order and control, the preoccupations of a world struggling to rebuild. About 700 B.C.E., black-figure pottery appeared. Its images were painted in black glaze against a red background of fired, unglazed clay. Red-figure ware, the pinnacle of the Greek potter's art, emerged in the second half of the sixth century B.C.E. Its practitioners achieved greater realism by painting backgrounds in black

Red-Figure Pottery   Pottery painting is not usually regarded as a high art today, but it was much respected in the ancient world. This hydra (a container for water) was signed by one of the pioneer Athenian red-figure artists, Phintias (c. 525 B.C.E.). It depicts a teacher of a musical instrument called a lyre instructing a student. It is, therefore, a valuable historical document as well as a work of art.

glaze and letting the color of unglazed pottery represent the ruddy skin tones of their human figures. The drafting skills of the great pottery painters were extraordinary. Although they worked on curved surfaces, they were able to give figures volume, substance, and convincing proportions. They provide us with more intimate knowledge of the lives of the Greeks than we have for most other ancient people.

Greek sculptors worked in wood, stone, and bronze, and also assembled monumental figures from sheets of ivory and gold. Much of what they made survives today only in Roman copies. The principles of classicism (balance, restraint, simplicity, and harmony of proportions) are clearly apparent in their work (particularly in their treatment of their favorite subject, the human form). They did not record the idiosyncrasies of their models but created ideal human types. Males were more commonly represented than females. Greek science, as noted previously, maintained that the perfect human form was male. Female figures were usually clothed, but males were nude. Perfection was a matter of essence, not decoration or other enhancement.

The consummate examples of Greek architecture are temples. Greek temples were not analogous to modern churches, synagogues, or mosques, for they were not built to house worshiping congregations. They sheltered images of gods and goddesses and provided storage space for sacred treasures. Public religious ceremonies were held at outdoor altars, for which a temple's façade provided a backdrop.

Greeks practiced multiple religions simultaneously. Families maintained household shrines and venerated sacred objects inherited from their ancestors. Many individuals sought initiation into mystery cults whose secret rituals and teachings promised them spiritual support. Magicians cast spells to promote fertility or to curse enemies. Trust in omens and oracles was widespread. Greece's official pantheon consisted of relatives and courtiers of Zeus, an Indo-European sky-deity associated with Olympus, a mountain on Greece's northeastern frontier. The "Olympians" were the household gods of the state, the guardians of the *polis*, and their temples celebrated the principles on which it was founded.

Unlike the soaring complexity of a Gothic cathedral, a Greek temple was not meant to inspire a sense of transcendent mystery. Its purpose was to confirm the Greeks' belief that the world was fundamentally intelligible. The principles of a temple's construction—its stout pillars supporting horizontal lintels and a low-pitched roof—were meant to be immediately obvious and reassuring. Its symmetry, balance, and proportion reflected the stability and rationality that was fundamental to the order of nature.

Hellenic architects created three styles. The earliest, the Doric, featured sturdy, fluted pillars with plain, flat capitals and no bases. The pediments on the façades of its temples were filled with statuary. The second style, the Ionic, was inspired by the elegant arts of the Middle East. It was light, refined, and highly decorated. Its pillars were slender columns with bases and capitals sculpted to resemble curved ram's horns. The third style, the Corinthian, spread in the wake of the Peloponnesian War and reflected values associated with the decline of *poleis* and the rise of empires. Corinthian buildings were imposing and florid. Their pillars had capitals resembling sheaves of acanthus leaves (a plant common to the Mediterranean region).

Some Greek temples had no roofs or pillared façades. They were amphitheaters. Drama (comedy as well as tragedy) was a sacred ceremony, and actors had the status of

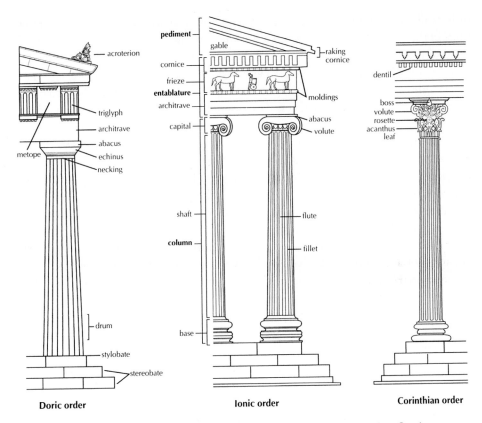

The Greek Architectural Orders   This drawing represents the three styles of ancient Greek architecture. The Doric was the earliest and simplest and the Corinthian the latest and most grandiose. Although Greek temples were often constructed from a pure, white marble, they, like the statues of the era, were frequently painted. They might, therefore, have appeared somewhat garish to the modern eye.

priests. The Greek plays were staged to honor Dionysus, the inebriated god of the vine-yard. His intoxication represented the power of the irrational—of ecstacy, inspiration, and feeling.

Theater's conventions evolved from rural holidays that featured dancing and singing. The tyrant Peisistratus may have introduced these celebrations to Athens. He is alleged to have established the **Great Dionysia**, a spring festival for which the plays that survive were written. The theater was not a mere entertainment. It was a civic duty. Everyone was expected to attend. Wealthy citizens were honored publicly for funding productions. Hundreds of men and boys took part as singers and dancers, and prestigious prizes were awarded to the playwrights who won the audience's favor. Theater-going was serious, arduous business. During the four days of the Great Dionysia, Athenians sat through 16 or more plays. Each playwright who won a slot at the festival had to create enough plays to fill the bill for an entire day.

Because Dionysus was attended by satyrs (men with the loins and legs of goats), hymns to him were called tragedies ("goat songs"). Originally, these took the form of dithyrambs, anthems sung and danced by choruses. Drama, as we know it, was allegedly born in the sixth century B.C.E. when a poet named Thespis made dialogue possible by separating a soloist from the chorus. (The modern term for actor, *thespian*, honors his memory.) Early Greek plays devoted a great deal of space to choruses and were written so that one or two actors could perform all the parts. Later plays reduced the role of the chorus, but authors of tragedies never employed more than three actors. The rules governing comedy were less strict. All performers were male, and because they wore masks and elaborate costumes, men could play women and take multiple roles as different characters. Masks were functional as well as traditional. Plays were staged in huge amphitheaters that seated thousands. Superb acoustical design meant that a trained actor's voice could be heard without difficulty, but many in the audience were seated so far from the stage that they could not have seen facial expressions and subtle gestures. Actors had to be magnified to make them visible. They performed on elevated stages above the level where the chorus danced and sang. Padded costumes, elevator shoes, and large masks enhanced their stature, but these ponderous outfits forced them to move carefully and to use choreographed, stylized gestures. They could not stage convincing fights or engage in violent action. Incidents of this kind took place offstage and were described to the audience by speeches from the actors or chorus. Scenery and props were limited, and Greek audiences (like Shakespeare's) were expected to use their imaginations to supply sets for the action.

The oldest complete plays we have from the ancient Greek theater are those of Aeschylus (525–456 B.C.E.), a veteran of the battle at Marathon. (It was this service to his *polis* and not his literary achievement that he ordered recorded on his tombstone.) Aeschylus was 26 when his first tragedy was produced. He continued to write throughout his long life, creating a total of 80 or 90 plays. Among the seven that survive is our only nearly complete bill for a day in the Athenian theater, the *Oresteia*, a trilogy (cycle of three plays) staged at the Great Dionysia in the year 458 B.C.E. Aeschylus's earliest extant play is unusual in that it treats a historical event (the Persian War). Playwrights customarily chose themes from sacred mythology. Aeschylus's dramas have long choruses, and his characters and plots deal with clashes of ideas more than with the behavior of realistic people. His gods harshly punish men who overstep human bounds, and the society he describes is preoccupied with codes of honor and duty to blood kin.

Sophocles (496–406 B.C.E.), Aeschylus's younger contemporary, was a member of the Athenian democracy's second generation, and his was a different mental universe. He was a politically active aristocrat, a friend of Pericles, who served as treasurer of the Delian League. Despite a busy public life, he found time to write 123 plays. Seven survive, some of which (particularly *Oedipus Rex* and *Antigone*) are perennial favorites with modern audiences. Sophocles reduced the role of the chorus, wrote compelling dialogue, and created characters that undergo psychological transformations. He was intrigued by competing moral obligations and by the fact that people never have enough information to know how the decisions they make will turn out. He pondered the relationship of society's laws to the higher obligations intuited by ethically sensitive individuals. He claimed that the moral order of the universe holds us accountable for the consequences of our actions—whether they are intended or not.

Euripides (485–406 B.C.E.), the youngest of Athens' three great tragedians, was socially and intellectually an outsider. His family was not prominent, and he did not hold major public offices. The Athenians had a love-hate relationship with his work. He wrote 92 plays, but won only five first prizes. The Greeks admired his poetry but found his plays troubling. Euripides' characters are psychologically complex, and his plots explore, but do not always resolve, morally ambiguous situations. In the year in which the Athenians voted to slaughter the people of Melos, for instance, Euripides produced a play about the Trojan War that described the brutalization of Troy's women by Greece's "heroes."

Euripides' work highlights the function of theater in the life of the Athenian *polis*. No modern state periodically suspends its activities and gathers all its citizens together for a week of theater. Why did Athens? Perhaps the answer lies in the importance of education to a democracy. Popular government requires an informed electorate—voters who are trained to think about serious issues and make sound judgments. Modern democracies use free public schools, newspapers, and electronic media to equip their citizens to govern themselves. None of these was available to the ancient Athenians, but the theater was. The theater regularly brought the Athenians together for a crash course in the problems posed by ethical dilemmas and the complexity of decision making. It created safe opportunities for the masses to vent—and learn to deal with—passionate feelings. Because each play was intended to be staged only once, its author wrote with the concerns of the moment in mind. Although most dramas were set in Greece's mythic past, playwrights chose stories with themes that had contemporary relevance and often made their connections with living issues pointedly obvious. Actors might wear masks with the faces of prominent politicians, name people in the audience, and refer to current events.

The topical relevance of Greek theater is most obvious in comedies, for the rules governing comedy were much more liberal than those for writing tragedy. Comedy was, however, as serious in its intent and function as tragedy. The only plays that survive to give us a sense of what comedy was like during the golden age of Greek theater are by Aristophanes (488–380 B.C.E.). He wrote about 40 comedies, 11 of which are extant.

Comedy derives from a word meaning "phallic song," a clear indication of its roots in fertility rituals. Not surprisingly, therefore, Aristophanes' plays feature broad humor, parody, and crude sexual references. His actors wore costumes that were padded to accentuate sexual characteristics, and what they did on stage might shock even the most sophisticated of modern audiences. While provoking hilarity, Aristophanes also prodded his audiences to think about serious issues, the most compelling of which for his generation was the Peloponnesian War. The hero of *The Acharnians* is a country bumpkin who, disgusted by the war, makes a separate peace with Sparta. In *Peace* the gods are asked why they inflict war on mankind, and they claim that they have nothing to do with it—that men make war and can stop whenever they want to. *Lysistrata*, a romping farce, proposed that the women of Athens and Sparta force their men to stop fighting by staging a sexual strike. Complications arise as the women discover that they find it as hard to do without sex as their men. Aristophanes concluded the play with a serious proposal for an exchange of territories to end the conflict. He also warned the Athenians of the continuing threat posed by Persia and reminded them of their cultural solidarity with other Greeks.

KEY QUESTION | Revisited

The speech that the historian Thucydides puts in the mouth of Pericles (which is referenced at the start of this chapter) reflects the confidence of a dynamic society at a pinnacle of its development. Pericles evidently had superb political skills. Athens was governed by a direct democracy, a system in which the masses made all decisions. The risk of such a system was that its electorate would be whipped about by emotional appeals and persuaded to make radical shifts of policy on momentary whims. But for decades Pericles (for good or ill) kept Athens committed to consistent goals. So great was his influence that historians have dubbed the period in which Athens reached the height of its power the "Age of Pericles." His fellow citizens were basking in the glow of their victories over Persia and their successful imperialistic ventures, but they had also suffered losses. His speech was a funeral oration for fallen soldiers, an address to a community of mourners who wanted to be assured that those who had died did so for a good cause. That cause, Pericles argued, was the defense of a unique and unprecedented way of life—a set of values and institutions that made Athenian society a model of justice and probity for the world.

There was much to admire about Pericles' Athens. The thinkers and artists of the Hellenic era, most of whom had ties to Athens, set in motion ideas that transformed the Mediterranean world and profoundly influenced subsequent civilizations. Indeed, the history of civilization in the West has been studded with renaissances, eras of cultural development stimulated by renewed interest in the art and literature of the classical era. The virtues of Athens, which Pericles listed, are worthy of emulation, but the splendor of the city's achievements should not obscure acknowledgment of its failings. Valuable things are learned from what goes wrong as well as what goes right.

There was a dark side to Greek civilization. Athens' prosperity rested on the twin pillars of slavery and imperialistic exploitation. The devotion of its famous intellectuals to reason and clear thinking did not prevent some of them from concluding that women were congenitally inferior creatures and that some men were naturally superior to others and therefore entitled to more privileges. Superstition was rampant, as was belief in witchcraft and participation in religions that cultivated emotional excess and violent behavior.

Readily apparent also is the fact that as Pericles' Athens grew stronger, it also became a more arrogant and closed society. Admission to the privileged rank of citizen was limited, and the democratic electorate endorsed aggressive actions that pushed Greece into the great disaster that was the Peloponnesian War. A popular theme of the tragic playwrights was *hybris*, the arrogant overconfidence that success creates and that leads ultimately to destruction. The Greeks knew the risks and dangers of the paths they chose, but one lesson their history teaches is that knowing that a behavior is self-destructive is often not enough to motivate people to abandon it.

The Greeks' interest in rationally examining the environments created by nature and human cultures produced considerable self-awareness. Greek writers analyzed both the strengths and weaknesses of their civilization. They were intensely proud of being Greeks, but that did not prevent them from admiring—indeed standing in awe—of some "barbarians." Egypt particularly intrigued them, and many Greek intellectuals would have freely acknowledged that they built on legacies from the older cultures of the Middle East and were stimulated by continuing contact with them. The Greeks were not solely responsible for what the West has become. The enduring influence of Greek philosophy, for instance, owes much to the uses to which the West's religions, which originated in the Middle East, have put it. The dynamism and creativity of Western civilizations spring from a multiplicity of sources.

Review Questions

1. Was civilization invented by the Greeks or passed to them?
2. How did Mycenaean Greek civilization differ from Hellenic civilization?
3. What contributed to the development of the *polis*?
4. Was Athens' experiment with democracy a success or a failure?
5. What does Greek history suggest about the influence of wars on civilization?
6. Was there a common theme or interest in the science, art, and literature of the Hellenic era?

Please consult the Suggested Readings at the back of the book to continue your study of the material covered in this chapter. For a list of documents on the Primary Source DVD-ROM that relate to topics in this chapter, please refer to the back of the book.

Topics in This Chapter

The Hellenistic Era • The Origin of Rome

• The Roman Republic • Rome's Civil War

5 The Hellenistic Era and the Rise of Rome

No one is so incurious or indifferent as not to want to understand how the Romans (in less than fifty-three years) conquered, and how they now govern, practically the whole inhabited world—an accomplishment that has no historical precedent.

—Polybius

KEY | Question

What circumstances are likely to undermine governments by the people?

Greek intellectuals tended to feel superior to non-Greeks, but Polybius (c. 201–120 B.C.E.) was an exception. He admired the Romans even though they repeatedly invaded his home-land, defeated its armies, and in 168 B.C.E. carted him and a thousand of his fellows off to Rome as hostages. In Rome he was treated more as a guest than a prisoner and was ad-mitted to the highest levels of Roman society. Publius Cornelius Scipio Aemilianus Africanus Numantinus (185–129 B.C.E.), whose imposing name catalogued his aristocratic connections and professional achievements, became his friend, and for 16 years Polybius enjoyed an insider's view of the workings of the Roman Republic.

Polybius's acute awareness of Greece's political problems contributed to his respect for his captor-hosts. The Greeks were better at the arts of war than those of peace. About 130 years before Polybius's birth, Alexander the Great had distracted the Greeks from fight-ing among themselves by turning their attention to the conquest of the Persian Empire. He led them on a triumphant march from the Aegean to Egypt and east to the Indus River Val-ley. At Alexander's death, his great empire came apart, and the Greeks returned to making war on one another.

The Romans shared Indo-European ancestry and many other things with the Greeks. Their civilization developed more slowly, but Polybius believed that they would ultimately

The Winged Victory of Samothrace   This statue of Nike, goddess of victory and daughter of the titan Pallas, was found on the Aegean island of Samothrace in 1863. The sculptor of this acknowledged masterpiece of Hellenistic art is unknown. *Nike of Samothrace. 3rd–2nd BCE. Helleninstic marble statue. H.: 328 cm. Inv.: 2369. Musee du Louvre/RMN Reunion des Musees Nationaux, France. SCALA/Art Resource, NY*

solve problems that had defeated the Greeks. Romans did not just conquer lands; they held on to them. In Polybius's day, they had no philosophy, science, art, or literature that compared to the products of Greek civilization (which they were eagerly assimilating), but Polybius thought that the world had much to learn from Rome's political and military institutions. Time has vindicated his faith. Rome created the largest and most long-lived empire the West had yet seen, and centuries after its fall, its memory continued to influence the course of Western societies. Leaders as different as feudal kings, medieval popes, French philosophers, Russian czars, German kaisers, and American revolutionaries have all laid claim to Rome's legacy.

The stability and longevity of Rome's empire was a hard-won prize for which the Romans paid dearly. The Romans began their climb to world domination by throwing off monarchy and embracing a form of government they called a Republic. It was not a direct democracy, such as Athens had established, but it gave significant power to its citizenry. The Romans developed a passionate affection for their republican system, and their patriotic military service in its defense led ultimately to the acquisition of a territorial empire. Administration of an empire proved, however, to be difficult for the Republic, and the methods the Romans devised simply set them up for a century-long civil war. Peace was not achieved until a skillful leader persuaded the Romans that submission to his monarchical leadership was essential to save their Republic. As the republican trappings of his system fell away, Rome became an openly autocratic Empire. The Empire limited freedoms but it delivered a long period of relative peace and prosperity.

As you reflect on Rome's history, consider the challenges that face democracies and republics as they try to reconcile the inherent inefficiency of government by the masses with a state's need for a swift and decisive executive.

The Hellenistic Era

The Peloponnesian War (432–404 B.C.E.) had no real winner. Athens yielded to Sparta, but Sparta collapsed under the burdens of victory. Sparta owed its military preeminence to a unique social system that enabled it to field the only full-time professional army in Greece. The lengthy Peloponnesian conflict neutralized that advantage by professionalizing the armies of many Greek *poleis*. Thebes finally dispelled the myth of Spartan invincibility by routing Sparta's armies in fair fights, but Thebes failed to fill the leadership vacuum left by Sparta's decline. Greece's *poleis* formed leagues and alliances, and fell to fighting among themselves. War became a major Greek industry— producing hordes of mercenaries who found employment at home and abroad.

This dismal situation convinced some Greeks that their compatriots were incapable of self-government. Men as different as the philosopher Plato (c. 429–347 B.C.E.), the soldier-historian Xenophon (c. 435–354 B.C.E.), and the Athenian orator Isocrates (436–338 B.C.E.) advocated some form of monarchy. Their hope was that an individual with a unique genius for leadership would unite the Greeks and protect them from their ancient enemy, Persia.

Macedonia Takes Control   When people decide that they need a savior, candidates for the job appear. Greece's savior emerged from an unexpected quarter, from the semibarbarous kingdom of Macedonia on the northern rim of the Greek mainland. The Macedonians were a tribal people who had not taken to life in *poleis* and who had even backed the Persians against their fellow Greeks in the Persian Wars. In the mid-fifth century B.C.E., however, Macedonian kings decided to Hellenize their subjects. They established a capital at Pella and ornamented their court with artists, craftsmen, and intellectuals imported from the more advanced Greek states. Men as distinguished as Athens' tragic playwright Euripides and the philosopher-scientist Aristotle entered their service. Despite this, Macedonia remained a rough, politically volatile country. The hereditary chiefs of its tribes were powerful, and coups and battles shortened the lives of its kings. Eight men ascended Macedonia's throne during the first four decades of the fourth century B.C.E.

In 360 B.C.E. King Perdiccas III died in battle, and his brother, Philip II (r. 360–336 B.C.E.), won the ensuing struggle for the crown. Philip spent two or three years of his youth as a hostage in Thebes which gave him a chance to observe Greek politics at close hand and to acquire training in the best Greek military techniques. Philip used what he had learned to transform the Macedonian army and unite his kingdom's tribal factions.

During the 350s B.C.E. some *poleis* sought Philip's help in their wars with their neighbors, and this gave him an excuse to intervene in the affairs of the Greek states. As one war led to another, the Athenian orator Demosthenes (384–322 B.C.E.) tried to rally opposition to Philip in the name of defending democracy, but in 338 B.C.E. the Macedonian army won a decisive victory over Athens and Thebes at Chaeronea. Further resistance seemed futile, so most of the mainland states accepted Philip's invitation to a peace conference to be held at Corinth in 337 B.C.E. At the meeting, Philip persuaded the Greeks to join him in an attack on Persia, but on the eve of this campaign he was assassinated. His son, Alexander (who may have been implicated in his murder), seized the Macedonian throne.

Alexander (III) the Great   Alexander was not cast in the mold of his father. Philip was a brute of a man who enjoyed physically and psychologically intimidating others. Alexander, who had the slight build of a runner, was distinguished by will and nervous energy more than muscle. His youthful appearance was enhanced by his habit of shaving, a custom that spread as his reputation grew. Alexander (r. 336–323 B.C.E.) was only 20 years old when his father died, but he had considerable military experience. He commanded the elite cavalry unit in Philip's army that carried the day for the Macedonians at the crucial battle of Chaeronea.

Alexander assured the Greeks that he intended to lead them in the Persian War his father had proposed, but he had to delay its start. He was not the only man with a claim to Philip's throne, and his survival was uncertain. Young, untried rulers face tests to their authority, and Alexander spent the first year of his reign eliminating potential rivals and fighting for control of his kingdom. Anti-Macedonian Greeks confidently anticipated his failure and began to scheme against him. This ended when he suddenly descended on Thebes, the rebels' ringleader, and destroyed the city. Similar acts of terrorism might have forced the Greeks to cooperate temporarily, but Alexander knew that he could not hold them against their will once he and his army were locked in combat with Persia far from home. The Greeks would inevitably rebel and isolate him in enemy territory. His survival, therefore, depended on inspiring them with genuine enthusiasm for him and his campaign.

Alexander left Greece, never to return, in the spring of 334 B.C.E. His army was ludicrously small for the task he set. He had about 37,000 men, but over 23,000 of these were Greek allies whose loyalty was doubtful. The core of Alexander's army consisted of 12,000 Macedonian infantrymen and 1,800 cavalry, most of whom were more closely tied to their hereditary chiefs (Philip's contemporaries) than to their young king.

Alexander was ahead of his time in understanding what skillful management of public relations can do for a ruler. At the campaign's start, he made a side trip to Troy to sacrifice at what was said to be the grave of Achilles, the hero of the *Iliad*. He wanted the Greeks to link the war on which they were embarking with him with the epic victory their Homeric ancestors had won over Greece's first eastern enemy. Alexander also began the development of something like the modern press corps. It consisted of a troop of scholars, headed by Calisthenes (the nephew of Alexander's boyhood tutor, Aristotle), whose job was to build enthusiasm for the campaign by providing the homeland with reports of its progress and descriptions of the exotic locales it discovered.

Alexander desperately needed a quick victory that would assure his men that he could deliver what he promised. The Persians might have defeated him by retreating. If they had drawn him deep into their territory, his soldiers would have grown increasingly fearful until they panicked, turned on him, and fled home. The Persians chose instead to give Alexander exactly what he had to have. They made a stand at the Granikos River in western Asia Minor (334 B.C.E.).

Alexander understood that he would have no second chances in this war. Only by appearing utterly self-confident and invincible could he distract his men from the odds they faced. At the first hint of failure, they were likely to lose heart and desert him. Therefore, he threw everything he had into every engagement. He commanded the most dangerous posts in each battle and performed heroic acts that inspired his men to comparable feats. The strategy worked, but it placed an all but unbearable burden on Alexander. The king's injuries mounted as the war progressed. He was often ill. The hardships of the march sapped his strength, and the stress of command tested his will.

At Granikos the ferocity of Alexander's attack swept the Persians from the field, but Alexander resisted the temptation to pursue them. He slowed the pace of the march and spent a year exploiting his victory, building the morale of his men, and picking up allies. It was the spring of 333 B.C.E. before he reached the Taurus Mountains and crossed from Asia Minor into Syria. The Persian emperor, Darius III (r. 336–330 B.C.E.), was eager to confront him, but faulty intelligence led the Persian army astray. By the time Darius found Alexander, impatience may have been clouding the emperor's judgment. At the Issos River on the Syrian coast he committed himself to a battle on a narrow field where he could not deploy his superior numbers. Alexander struck the center of the Persian line, and when Darius pulled back, his men panicked and fled (see Map 5–1).

Darius retreated from Issos in disarray, but Alexander did not go after him. Alexander could not risk proceeding inland, for the Persians controlled the sea. If Darius's navy had invaded the Aegean, Alexander would have had to go home to defend Greece. Because Alexander had insufficient ships with which to challenge the Persians at sea, the only way he could neutralize their fleet was to take all of the ports from which it oper-

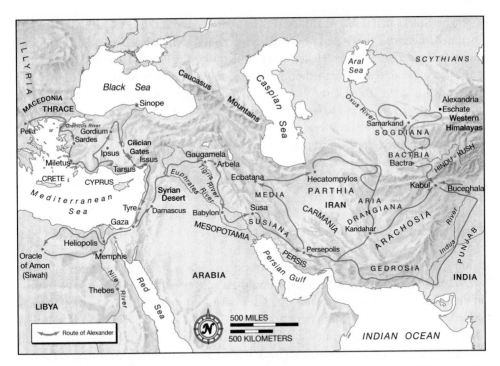

Map 5–1   Alexander's Adventure   Alexander led one of history's most extraordinary military campaigns. After winning the Persian Empire, the prize for which his men had signed on, Alexander persuaded them to march farther and farther east into territory unknown to the Greeks. He was preparing to invade China when he died and was rumored to have had a plan for the conquest of the western Mediterranean as well.

Question: Does Alexander's route suggest that he had a rational strategy for building an empire or that he was simply wandering about?

ated. This required arduous sieges of city after city until the whole coast as far as Egypt was in Greek hands.

By July 331 B.C.E., Alexander was finally free to leave Egypt and strike inland to challenge Darius. Darius wisely waited for Alexander to come to him and chose a battlefield that gave him all the advantages. The Persians dug in at **Gaugamela**, an arid plain north of Babylon. It provided ample space for them to maneuver and forced the Greeks to camp in a place that had no water. Despite the Persians' superior numbers and position, the Greeks triumphed at Gaugamela, but they were never entirely sure how. Dust and poor communications prevented anyone from having an overview of the battle.

Darius's army may have been too large for its own good. At any rate, it was thrown into confusion by Alexander's attacks, and Darius had to flee once again. Babylon submitted. The Greeks claimed the imperial treasury at Susa and made their winter camp at the Persian capital, Persepolis. The following spring, Alexander renewed the campaign. When Darius ordered another retreat, his disgruntled officers assassinated him.

The Greeks had done what they set out to do—conquer the Persian Empire. Most assumed, therefore, that it was time to go home, but Alexander persuaded them to continue the war a little longer. He led them farther and farther east into unknown territory. They wandered through the foothills of the Himalayan Mountains and finally descended into the Indus River Valley. At that point, they dug in their heels and refused to go on. Alexander agreed to lead them home, but only if they vowed: (1) to fight their way back through new territory, and (2) to return a year later to resume their conquests. The Greeks battled their way down the Indus River to the Indian Ocean and then endured a brutal march across the wastes of the Gedrosian Desert. A remnant of the army staggered back to Babylon, where Alexander threw himself into organizing his conquests and planning future campaigns.

Alexander did not have the manpower to occupy his huge empire and hold it by force. He had to induce his non-Greek subjects to submit to him voluntarily. His plan was to bolster his legitimacy in their eyes by adopting Persian court customs and adding Persian soldiers to his army. His Greeks and Macedonian followers strongly objected, but in the end Alexander got his way. He also tried to interfere as little as possible with the lives of his new subjects. The Persian Empire was composed of districts called *satrapies*. Their borders were drawn to respect the ethnic identities of their inhabitants. Alexander appointed a native governor (who knew the local customs) to handle each *satrapy's* civil affairs, a Greek to deal with its fiscal administration, and a Macedonian to provide for its defense. This gave the residents of a *satrapy* at least one leader with whom they could identify and made it difficult for any single official to take over a *satrapy* and use it against the central government.

Alexander demanded extraordinary things of himself, and he finally exhausted his physical resources. On May 29, 323 B.C.E., following an all-night drinking bout with his officers, he fell ill. His fever rose. He sank into a coma, and on June 10, 323 B.C.E., he quietly died. There were rumors that he had been poisoned, but no evidence of foul play was uncovered. Fevers were

Portrait of Alexander No one can be certain of the accuracy of ancient portraits, for they were often idealized for purposes of propaganda or meant to represent a type of person rather than an individual. Alexander's statues broke with the conventional representation of a king by depicting him as a beardless youth rather than a mature man. This bust dates to the late fourth century B.C.E., the same century as Alexander's death.

common in swampy Babylon, and Alexander's arduous lifestyle must have sapped his strength and weakened his resistance.

The Hellenistic Environment   Alexander was only 32 when he died, and he was not the kind of man who cared to think about mortality. Death surprised him before he had provided himself with a successor. Alexander's primary emotional attachments were homosexual. He delayed marriage, and he had no children by mistresses. In 327 B.C.E. he had wed an Iranian princess named Roxane, and after returning to Babylon, he had also married one of Darius's daughters. Both women may have been pregnant at the time of his death. The Persian princess did not long outlive Alexander, but Roxane made him the posthumous father of a son, Alexander IV. Alexander's generals declared themselves regents for the infant, dispatched him to Macedonia to be raised, and set about carving up his empire. This inaugurated a period of shifting alliances and bloody conflicts. By 317 B.C.E. the surviving generals had disposed of Alexander's son, wife, and mother, and the outlines for a lasting division of his empire had emerged. The Aegean and the Macedonian throne went to Antigonus the One-Eyed (d. 301 B.C.E.). **Seleukos** (c. 358–280 B.C.E.), governor of Babylon, claimed the Persian heartland, and **Ptolemy** (d. 285 B.C.E.), one of Alexander's boyhood friends, made himself pharaoh of Egypt. Ptolemy also highjacked Alexander's body and enshrined it in a mausoleum in Alexandria, a great port in the Egyptian delta that Alexander had founded.

Alexander's empire did not survive, but his imperial conquests had lasting significance. They marked the end of the Hellenic (Greek) period and the beginning of the Hellenistic (Greek-like) phase in Western civilization. Greeks had always avoided mixing with "barbarians" (non-Greeks), but Alexander believed that a blending of peoples and cultures was essential for the survival of his empire. He promoted intermarriage between his men and his eastern subjects, and he was willing to learn from the peoples he conquered and to adapt to their expectations.

The garrisons that were posted throughout Alexander's empire grew into Greek towns that spread Hellenic culture as far east as India. It is debatable how much influence the Greeks had on indigenous peoples, but these peoples clearly influenced the Greeks. As thousands of Greeks migrated to the new towns that had been founded in the wake of Alexander's armies, they became a more cosmopolitan people. Their widening view of the world even affected their language. Its grammar and syntax simplified, and its vocabulary grew much richer as it assimilated words from other tongues. The result was a flexible new *koine* ("common") Greek that was so adaptable that it became the international medium of communication. When the Romans added the eastern rim of the Mediterranean to their empire in the first century B.C.E., they found Greek so well established that they used it rather than imposing Latin on their subjects. Many Romans were bilingual, and the early Christians (even those who were born Jews) wrote their New Testament in *koine* Greek instead of the language of the Hebrew scriptures.

The Hellenistic era witnessed the decline of the *polis*, the institution that had nurtured Hellenism. This signaled a significant change in the environment for civilized life in the Mediterranean world. Small, self-governing city-states had failed to maintain order in the Greek world. As they succumbed to the builders of empires, political power shifted from their citizens to the bureaucrats who administered those empires. The Hellenistic era preferred professionals to citizen-volunteers. This was not necessarily bad, for the highly trained specialists who served Hellenistic rulers were extremely competent and able to plan and execute great projects. They laid out orderly cities and equipped them with magnificent temples, monuments, baths, theaters, and arenas. They built sewage systems. They constructed aqueducts to convey fresh water over great distances. They organized police forces, regulated commerce and food supplies, and generally made urban life far more comfortable, clean, and secure than it had ever been.

Hellenistic communities were as prosperous as they were well run. Alexander returned to circulation a great deal of gold that had been sealed away in Persia's coffers, and the consolidation of large territorial states by his successors made trade easier and promoted economic growth.

There was, of course, a cost for the comforts of the new societies. As governments grew larger and specialists assumed responsibility for more governmental functions, the power of popular assemblies and elected officials declined. A citizen's vote meant little to a huge, centrally managed state, and it had no use for his amateur military service or advice. Even his labor was not all that important, for wars replenished the supply of inexpensive slaves who did much of society's essential work.

Hellenistic Civilization   The subjects of the Hellenistic states were prosperous and well cared for, but they were pawns of forces beyond their control. For those who came from *poleis* proud of their democratic traditions, this required some emotional adjustment. The Hellenic *polis* affirmed the worth of the individual by demanding much from him, but a Hellenistic empire reduced the individual to a replaceable cog in the machinery of a great state. The world of the *polis* was human in scale and amenable to control, but empires rendered their subjects small and impotent.

The art and literature of the Hellenistic era reflect the period's new sociopolitical environment. Theater flourished, but playwrights steered clear of political issues and focused on entertainment. Aristophanes, the master of Hellenic Old Comedy, used laughter to make people think, but Hellenistic **New Comedy** was the ancient world's equivalent of a television "sit-com." It relied on stock characters and plots that were as silly as they were predictable. Persons who wanted comparable entertainment at home turned to the era's new literary genre, the novel. The most popular novels were erotic romances set in exotic places or idealized bucolic locales. They conjured up fantasy worlds and provided escapist entertainment for literate urbanites.

Hellenistic architecture and visual arts, like the era's literature, appealed to emotion more than to intellect. Buildings grew large and imposing. The first skyscraper (a 400-foot-tall lighthouse) was erected on an island in the harbor of Alexandria. The city of Ephesus on the coast of Asia Minor built a temple to Diana that was almost five times the size of Athens' Parthenon, the largest of the mainland's Hellenic temples. The port of Rhodes erected a bronze statue of the sun god that may have been 120 feet tall, about the height of America's Statue of Liberty. Sculptors developed incredible technique that imparted stunning realism to their work, and they expanded their range far

Laocoön and His Sons   Unlike their Hellenic predecessors, Hellenistic sculptors sought to convey drama, complexity, emotion, and movement in their work. This literally writhing statue depicts an episode from Homer's *Iliad*, the destruction of the priest Laocoön and his sons. Laocoön tried to thwart the will of the gods by persuading the Trojans not to drag into their city the wooden horse the Greeks had mysteriously left on the battlefield.

beyond the Hellenic era's idealized male athletes. They sought out subjects that were novel and emotionally stirring: portraits of individuals, erotic female nudes, cute children and animals, persons suffering the ravages of age and poverty, and men and women in the throes of death or extreme passions. The human ideal, the art of the democratic *polis*, lost some of its relevance for the subjects of the Hellenistic empires. They lacked the political freedoms that gave dignity and meaning to *polis* citizenship and made Hellenic ideals worth striving for. What they wanted was art that dispelled boredom and affirmed the values of uniqueness and individuality that the imperial context threatened.

Most schools of Hellenistic philosophy focused on developing "philosophies of life" that were designed to help individuals come to terms with their new cultural and political environment. The most popular of these urged people to distance themselves in some way from the world around them. Zeno (335–263 B.C.E.), the founder of the Stoics, preached acceptance of the inevitable. He maintained that everyone had a preordained place in the universe's unalterable, rational system. Fulfillment lay in doing the duties of one's station while cultivating an emotional detachment that preserved inner peace. Stoics warned that people could not control what happened to them but claimed that they could control their emotional responses to life's vicissitudes. Zeno's contemporary, Epicurus (341–270 B.C.E.), believed that everything that existed (including the human soul) was the result of random, temporary conjunctions of atoms and that nothing, therefore, had meaning or permanence. Because lasting achievements were impossible, life's only purpose, he concluded, was the enjoyment of pleasure. However, true pleasure was not ecstasy and sensual indulgence, but tranquility, a state undisturbed by extreme emotions of any kind. Individuals who retreated from the world to "cultivate their gardens" had the best chance of achieving happiness, for they avoided situations that might stir the emotions. The followers of Diogenes of Sinope (c. 400–325 B.C.E.) were called Cynics ("dogs"). Diogenes claimed that fulfillment derived from self-sufficiency, and self-sufficiency was achieved by minimizing one's needs and obligations. The Cynics were likened to dogs because, like animals, they spurned all social conventions and freely and openly did whatever came naturally. Diogenes lived in the street, expressed contempt for authority, and performed intimate bodily functions in public. The Cynics, Epicureans, and Stoics all agreed that individuals had no mastery over the world; the best they could do was to master themselves. This was a far less ambitious assessment of human potential than the visions that had inspired the social engineers of the Hellenic *poleis*.

Hellenistic Greeks still had confidence in the superiority of their civilization, and their desire to explore and to learn only grew as their empires broadened their horizons and stimulated their curiosity. Hellenistic monarchs provided unprecedented patronage for intellectuals—particularly the Egyptian dynasty founded by Alexander's friend, Ptolemy I (r. 323–285 B.C.E.). The Ptolemaic pharaohs established a library in Alexandria and set the goal of obtaining a copy of every important book. They dispatched agents abroad in search of rare volumes. They funded translations (including one of the Hebrew scriptures), and they even searched the baggage of travelers entering Egypt, hoping to find interesting texts. The result was a collection that may have numbered a million items.

A research institute was attached to Alexandria's library. It was called the Museum, the home of the Muses (the nine female deities who, according to the poet Hesiod, preside over the arts). Some of the Museum's scholars devoted their lives to refining the library's collection and building on its contents. They compiled dictionaries and catalogues, and wrote commentaries on classic texts. What their work lacked in originality, it made up for in quantity. A certain Didymus of Alexandria is said to have written 3,500 books—not one of which survives!

Pedantry did not characterize all the work at the Museum. Some of its scholars pioneered new literary genres. The most popular of these was a sophisticated pastoral poetry that romanticized rural life and reveled in obscure, learned references. The Museum was especially noted for encouraging progress in the sciences and mathematics. Euclid (fl. c. 300 B.C.E.) wrote the text that has made his name synonymous with geometry, and Archimedes of Syracuse (c. 287–212 B.C.E.) laid the groundwork for calculus. Eratosthenes of Cyrene (c. 270–194 B.C.E.) calculated Earth's circumference with remarkable accuracy. Hipparchus of Nicaea (c. 160–125 B.C.E.) made precise calendar calculations. Aristarchus of Samos (fl. c. 275 B.C.E.) advanced the theory that Earth was a globe that rotated on an axis and revolved around the sun, but for the next 1,500 years, most astronomers supported the contention of a non-royal Ptolemy of Alexandria (fl. c. 130 C.E.) that the sun revolves around Earth. The Hippocratic medical texts were edited at the Museum, and some of its physicians conducted important anatomical research. Herophilius of Chalcedon (fl. c. 270 B.C.E.) mapped the sensory nerves and identified the brain as the center of a nervous system. Although capillaries were too small to be seen by the naked eye, Erasistratus of Ceos (fl. c. 260 B.C.E.) hypothesized that veins and arteries were connected, a prelude to the discovery of blood circulation and the function of the heart.

Alexandrian technicians and engineers produced marvelous gadgets that ranged from useful pumps and astronomical instruments to amusing toys (one of which was a working model of a steam turbine). To the modern mind, the most puzzling thing about all of this activity is that so little of it found practical application. The fact that Hellenistic society was slave-based may have something to do with this. Its educated classes were not motivated to think of ways to make work easier, and its workers had little freedom to innovate.

The Origin of Rome

Hellenistic civilization spread to, and was spread by, the Romans. The Latins (Rome's founders) took to it readily, for they had much in common with the Greeks. Both peoples had Indo-European ancestry, and their languages were related. They settled in their respective homelands at about the same time (c. 1900 B.C.E.), and their cultures evolved in similar environments. The Greeks, however, got off to an earlier and faster start, for they had the stimulating advantage of close contacts with the civilizations of the Middle East.

The Italian Environment   The Aegean Sea and its many islands facilitated communication between Greece and the Middle East, but Italy faced west. Like the Greek mainland, Italy is a mountainous peninsula. All its major agricultural plains and most of its natural harbors are on its western coast, and the Apennine mountain chain forms a spine along its eastern edge that makes access from the Adriatic Sea difficult.

The Greeks planted Naples (Nea-polis, "New Town") and other colonies in Campania, Italy's southwestern plain, in the mid-eighth century B.C.E. At the same time, the Etruscans, a people whose origin has been much debated, built prosperous city-states on the plain of Etruria (Tuscany) north of the Tiber River. The Latins took their name from the small plain of Latium ("flat land") that lay between Campania and Etruria. North of Etruria and the Apennines was the great basin of the Po River. It was inhabited by Celtic tribes and considered by the Romans to belong to Gaul more than Italy (see Map 5–2).

The Kingdom of Rome   The Romans were aware that their Latin ancestors had lived in Latium for a long time before they established the city of Rome, but they knew little about them. Homer's epics provided the classical world with what it assumed to be its earliest history, so the Romans looked to Homer to supply them with a past. Because Romans were not Greeks, they sought an ancestor from the *Iliad*'s other nation, the Trojans. The attention of Roman myth-makers centered on a Trojan prince named Aeneas, who escaped Troy's fall. After several adventures, he allegedly landed on the plain of Latium and married Lavinia, daughter of the native king, Latinus. Thirteen generations of their descendants reigned over Latium before

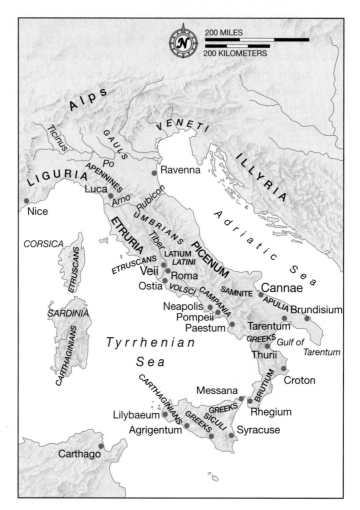

Map 5–2   The Rise of Rome   The Apennine Mountains form a crescent-shaped wall running the length of the Italian peninsula. They impede access to Italy from the east and cradle the three western agricultural plains (Campania, Latium, and Etruria) where urban communities first appeared in Italy. The ancient Romans considered the Po Valley north of the Apennines part of Gaul, not Italy.

Question: Did Rome's location inevitably make it the seat of a great empire, or was its location inconvenient for an imperial capital?

Rome's founders, the twins Romulus and Remus, were born to a Latin princess and Mars, the Latins' god of war. The city that Romulus founded (and that bore his name) was said to have begun as a rough frontier post populated by outcasts and women abducted from the surrounding region. Although this colorful myth of Rome's origin is fanciful, it nonetheless contains some truth.

The traditional date for Rome's founding is April 21, 753 B.C.E. Archaeological evidence confirms the existence of several primitive villages on the hills next to the Tiber in the mid-eighth century B.C.E. and suggests why the Latins might have planted them there at that time. Rome came to occupy the first spot inland from the coast (about 20 miles) where the Tiber River narrowed enough to be easily bridged. In the mid-eighth century B.C.E., when the Greek and Etruscan civilizations that flourished on either side of Latium developed trade routes converging at the Tiber crossing, the Latins hastened to occupy this corner of their territory.

Seven kings are said to have reigned over Rome from 753 B.C.E. to 509 B.C.E. They ruled in tandem with an aristocratic council called the Senate (*senex*, "elder"). Most of the stories told about the monarchy are legends, but some historical information can be gleaned from them. Etruscan names are recorded for two of Rome's kings, and it is unlikely that the Romans would have invented a memory of a time when outsiders ruled their city if this had not been the case. There is ample evidence of Etruscan influence on Roman institutions and customs, but this does not necessarily imply Etruscan occupation of Rome. The Romans may have chosen Etruscan leaders to strengthen commercial or political ties with Etruria.

The Etruscans   Much that was unique about Rome can be traced to the Etruscans, but the Etruscans themselves remain something of a mystery. Their language is not related to any known tongue and, apart from words whose meaning has been provided by ancient Latin authors or can be inferred from context, it is largely untranslated. Most surviving specimens are short inscriptions. Etruscan cities developed very quickly (possibly in response to the trade that was increasing between Italy and the eastern Mediterranean in the eighth century B.C.E.). Etruria had a benign climate, fertile fields, and accessible deposits of metal ores. The skills of its gold and bronze workers were second to none. Etruscan traders had much to offer, and they took to the sea to compete with Greek and Phoenician merchants.

Stories circulated in the Greek and Latin worlds about the luxury and permissiveness of Etruscan society. The Greeks were shocked by the freedom enjoyed by Etruscan women, and the Romans, who wrested austere livings from small plots of poor land, insisted that the Etruscans' self-indulgent custom of feasting twice a day was evidence of their moral laxity. Some Etruscans were undeniably rich, for they built expensive subterranean chamber-tombs that replicated their lavishly furnished homes and banqueting halls. The favorite design for a sarcophagus was a dining couch with an effigy of the deceased reclining on its lid—at ease in festive clothes, wine cup in hand. Etruscan graves have yielded some of the finest specimens of pottery, jewelry, and bronze work to survive from the classical era.

The Etruscans may have been connoisseurs of life's pleasures, but wealth did not make them soft. They dominated Italy until the mid-fifth century. Their decline was caused, at least in part, by the failure of their independent city-states to cooperate in countering competition from the Greeks. The Greeks planted colonies on both sides of Etruria and battled the Etruscans for control of the sea.

The Romans owed many of their political symbols and social customs to the Etruscans, but it was in the area of religion that they were most aware of their debt.

An Etruscan Couple This sarcophagus from the sixth century B.C.E. depicts what are probably an Etruscan husband and wife resting at ease on a dining couch. Greeks and Romans often reclined while eating. In early Rome, however, women sat while men reclined. Although a Roman woman of the republican era had more freedom than her Greek sister, neither may have enjoyed as much independence as a contemporary Etruscan lady. *Sarcophagus of a married couple on a funeral bed. Etruscan, from Cerveteri, 6th BCE. Terracotta. Lewandowski/Ojeda. Musee Lourve, Paris, France. RMN Reunion Des Musees Nationeaux/Art Resource, NY*

Throughout Rome's history, colleges of priests perpetuated ancient rituals and sacrifices of Etruscan origin. Romans saw omens everywhere and studied them before undertaking any project. They were especially in awe of the presumed skills of Etruscan diviners and soothsayers. Long after the Etruscan civilization disappeared, the Romans preserved Etruscan as a dead language used primarily in arcane religious rites. A similar fate was, of course, one day to befall Latin.

The Roman Republic

Rome made significant progress under the leadership of its later kings, one or more of whom had ties with the Etruscan city of Tarquinia. The Romans drained the swampy lowland that separated the hills on which they lived to create the Forum, a place for markets and assemblies. They built the largest temple in Italy on the Capitoline hill, and archaeological evidence suggests that they enjoyed a rising standard of living.

Kings may not deserve all the credit for early Rome's progress, for they operated under the watchful eye of the city's Senate. Relations between the monarch and the aristocratic families represented in the Senate must often have been strained. Few of Rome's kings (including the city's founder) were said to have died peacefully in their beds, and eventually the Senators decided to dispense with kings and govern the city themselves.

The Roman Revolution   Legends blame Sextus, the aptly named son of King Tarquinius Superbus (Tarquin the Proud), for the fall of his father's throne. In 509 B.C.E. Sextus supposedly raped a virtuous Roman matron named Lucretia, a deed that so infuriated the Romans that they drove out the Tarquins and vowed never again to submit to a king. The story may be fanciful, but the revolution was real.

The republic that the revolutionaries established to govern Rome was not a democracy. It limited political privileges to the male members of the city's "**patrician**" families. Early Rome was a federation of extended families, and for reasons that even the Romans could not explain, citizen families were divided into two classes: the noble patricians and the common **plebeians**. In the early republic, only the former could hold political offices and priesthoods.

Family was such an important determiner of status that each Roman male needed three names to indicate the place he occupied in the social order. His first name was one of a few common names used only by close friends. His second identified his *gens*, the great clan to which his paternal ancestors belonged. His third indicated his birth family. If his achievements were notable, the city might commemorate them by granting him a fourth name. The winner of a war in Africa, for example, bore the ponderous name Publius Cornelius Scipio Africanus.

A Roman *familia* included not only immediate blood kin but all the dependents of a household—including slaves. The male head of a *familia*, the *paterfamilias*, had

TABLE 5–1   The Greek and Roman Pantheons

GREEK GODS	ROMAN EQUIVALENTS	
Zeus	Jupiter	The Greeks and Romans both were Indo-European people, so it is not surprising that their state religions were similar. However, few of their gods and goddesses had Indo-European ancestry. Zeus or Jupiter (Deiw-pitar, "Father of the Bright Sky") had impeccable Indo-European credentials, but some of his children (Apollo, for instance) had Middle-Eastern origins.
Hera	Juno	
Athena	Minerva	
Apollo	[Apollo]	
Artemis	Diana	
Hephaestus	Vulcan	
Aphrodite	Venus	
Ares	Mars	
Demeter	Ceres	Comparable gods did not always have the same significance for Greeks and Romans. Mars, for example, loomed large in the Roman pantheon as the god who brought victory in war. Ares, his Greek double, was a far less respected deity, a symbol of the negative passions that spark conflict.
Poseidon	Neptune	
Hades	Pluto	
Hestia	Vesta	
Hermes	Mercury	
Dionysus	Bacchus	

absolute authority over all its members. His sons never outgrew his power, and he could, if he wished, order their execution.

Some of Rome's plebeian families were as ancient as (and richer than) their patrician superiors. The Senate expected them to contribute their men to its army, but it refused to allow them any role in government. Not surprisingly, they refused to accept this, and a "struggle of the orders," the challenge they mounted to the patrician monopoly of political power, dominated the early history of the republic. The plebeians were able to force concessions from the Senate because the patrician Senate needed plebeian help to defend the city. Whenever the Senate balked at the demands of the plebeians, they threatened a military strike. These confrontations usually ended in compromises that, over the course of two centuries, forged a complex constitution for the republic.

In 471 B.C.E. the plebeians set up an assembly of their own headed by ten magistrates called tribunes. In 451 B.C.E. they won acceptance of the Twelve Tables, a law code establishing a common standard of justice for all citizens. In 445 B.C.E. marriage between patrician and plebeian families was legalized, and elective offices began to be opened to plebeian candidates. In 287 B.C.E. the Hortensian Law made plebiscites (votes by the people) binding on all Romans. This granted legislative authority to the people, but the result was hardly a triumph for democracy. The effect of the new laws was to permit intermarriage between wealthy patrician and plebeian families and to create a complicated system of checks and balances that allowed these wealthy families to dominate the republic.

The republic's complex organization was designed to prevent any individual from acquiring enough power to reestablish monarchy. All elected magistrates served terms of only one year, and they were forbidden to seek immediate reelection. The duties of the chief executive were shared by two consuls—the expectation being that each would keep the other in check. The consuls' authority over soldiers in the field (their *imperium*) was absolute, but their power in the city was limited. To prevent them from seizing control of Rome, their armies were strictly forbidden to cross the *pomerium*, the city's sacred boundary. If the Senate wished to honor a general, it showed its trust by suspending this rule and granting him a "triumph" (permission to parade his men through the city).

The diffusion of power in Rome made alliances necessary and encouraged influence peddling and a system of patronage. The poorer citizens needed the support and protection of those who were richer and more powerful. A patron advertised his importance by parading through the streets accompanied by a crowd of his clients. They gave him political clout, for they voted as he commanded or risked losing his support. (The secret ballot was not introduced until 139 B.C.E.) No poor man could marshal enough votes to be elected to an office, and if he had, he could not have afforded to serve. The republic's magistrates were not paid, and they were expected to fund the costs of their offices from their private fortunes. A man who wanted a major office also had to spend years pursuing it. The *cursus honorum* ("path of honors") decreed a sequence of lower offices that a man had to win before he qualified to run for higher ones.

The Roman Republic was so far from what most people today would regard as an equitable government that one wonders why the Romans were so attached to it. They, of course, did not have the advantage of a modern perspective and did not feel deprived of rights they had never imagined. But they also had a good reason to be proud of their republic. It won them an empire.

The Republic Acquires an Empire

At the start of the fifth century B.C.E., Rome was a tiny, landlocked city-state that had no obvious potential to become an imperialistic power. Its survival was threatened by enemies that attacked from every direction: Etruscan, Greek, Latin, and Celtic. Time and again, however, the Romans rose to the challenge and built on their victories by generous treatment of those whom they defeated. The republic annexed some territory and garrisoned some places with military colonies, but it created more allies than subjects. One by one, Italy's city-states (some eagerly and others lacking alternatives) joined Rome in a federation. They retained control over their domestic affairs, but submitted to Rome's foreign policy and contributed to its armies. The rights some allies were given to trade with Rome, to migrate to Rome, and to marry Romans helped spread Roman customs and language and create a common culture for Italy.

Rome's consolidation of Italy was viewed with suspicion by the western Mediterranean's other major power, the Carthaginian empire. While the Greeks were planting their colonies in Sicily and Italy in the mid-eighth century B.C.E., their seafaring competitors, the Phoenicians, were colonizing the Mediterranean's southern rim. Their chief outpost, the North African city of Carthage, emerged as the administrative center of a self-sufficient empire that closed the southwestern corner of the Mediterranean to outsiders. The primary threat to the Carthaginians came from the Greeks on the island of Sicily. Carthage believed that it had to hold the western end of Sicily to protect its sea lanes (see Map 5–3).

Sicily was perpetually at war. Its Greek *poleis* fought among themselves and with the Carthaginians, and Syracuse, the largest Greek city on Sicily, sought to unite the island under its control. In 265 B.C.E., the Romans added to the confusion by acceding to a request from the Sicilian city of Messana for military assistance. (Messana commanded the narrow strait between Sicily and Italy through which Italy's shipping passed.) Carthage and Syracuse were both alarmed by Rome's intervention in their sphere of influence, and the situation quickly escalated into a major conflict called the First Punic (Phoenician) War (264–241 B.C.E.). The war dragged on because Carthage and Rome were incompatible military powers. Carthage fought at sea with its navy, and Rome campaigned on land with its army. Neither made much progress until Rome built a navy and set out to meet Carthage on its own terms. Carthage finally decided that the war was not worth its cost, and it ceded Sicily to Rome in exchange for peace.

The Romans had not set out to conquer Sicily, but the war convinced them that they had to hold the island to prevent anyone from using it as a base for invading Italy. Because their interests in Sicily were primarily defensive, they declared it a military

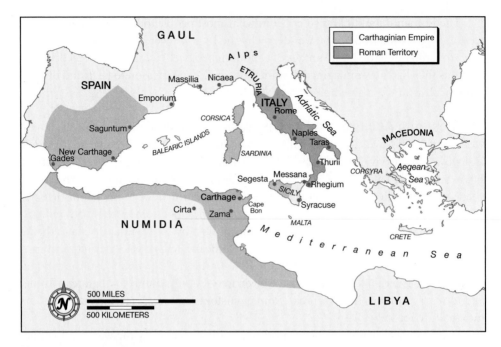

Map 5–3   Rome and Carthage   The lines drawn on maps seem to imply that the Romans and Carthaginians controlled large blocks of contiguous territory, but such was not the case. Borders were vague, jurisdictions overlapped, and governmental power was more effectively imposed in some places than others.

Question: Does the map support Rome's belief that Carthage was a threat to its security?

province and turned it over to a Roman general. This first province in what was to become a Roman Empire altered the politics of the republic in unanticipated ways. Rome refused to shoulder the expense of maintaining its army in Sicily and ordered its commander to raise the funds he needed from the Sicilians themselves. This gave him an opportunity to loot the province and return to Rome much richer than when he left. He could then pour his new wealth into a campaign to win more offices and honors. As Rome's leaders discovered the advantages a provincial governorship gave a man in the game of Roman politics, the republic's foreign policy began to change.

By expanding into Spain, Carthage recovered from the First Punic War much more quickly than Rome expected. Its leading general, Hamilcar Barca (c. 270–228 B.C.E.), believed that things were not settled between his people and the Romans, and his suspicions increased in 238 B.C.E., when Rome ordered Carthage to surrender the island of Sardinia. Rome may only have wanted to make sure that Carthage could not use Sardinia to attack Italy, but by annexing Sardinia, it confirmed Carthage's fear that Rome was bent on its destruction. Hamilcar Barca's son, Hannibal (247–182 B.C.E.), inherited his father's belief that war with Rome was inevitable. The Romans, for their part, felt fairly secure. Control of the seas around Italy gave them confidence that if war came, it would be fought on Carthaginian territory.

When the Second Punic War (218–202 B.C.E.) broke out, the Romans dispatched their armies to Spain and Sicily to confront Hannibal and his forces. But Hannibal was not where they expected to find him. When Publius Cornelius Scipio, the Roman commander of the Spanish expedition, landed to take on supplies on the coast of Gaul, he was shocked to discover that Hannibal had already departed Spain with an army of 30,000 men (and 60 famous elephants), crossed Gaul, and was heading over the Alps into northern Italy. Scipio sent his soldiers on to Spain while he hastily returned to Italy to patch together another army, but the ease with which Hannibal routed him gave the Romans their first hint at the danger they faced. Hannibal won every major battle the Romans risked giving him (except the last). He devastated Italy and slaughtered its men. But Rome refused to admit defeat, and the war dragged on for 14 years. Hannibal had made a serious miscalculation. He had expected Rome's Italian allies to defect and join him, but most remained loyal to Rome. If Italy's cities were subjects of a Roman Empire, they were not eager to seize the chance Hannibal gave them to escape their subjugation.

Rome finally defeated Hannibal by refusing to fight him in Italy while opening new fronts against the Carthaginians elsewhere. One Roman army dogged Hannibal's tracks in Italy and harassed his rearguard. Another overwhelmed his bases in Spain and his allies in Sicily, and a third finally took the war to North Africa. In 204 B.C.E. Hannibal was forced to pull his men out of Italy and take them home to defend Carthage. He fended off the Romans for two more years, but he was finally defeated by Scipio "Africanus," the son of the Scipio who had tried (and failed) to stop him when he first entered Italy. Carthage surrendered, and Hannibal fled to the Middle East, where ultimately he committed suicide to avoid capture by Rome's agents.

Carthage was allowed to survive—stripped of most of its territory and ships, and burdened with a huge war indemnity. Rome annexed Spain but ceded much of North Africa to Numidia, its ally in the war with Hannibal. The western Mediterranean was now indisputably Roman territory, but only portions of it were directly administered by Rome (which still had no plan for organizing an empire).

The Second Punic War had exhausted the Romans, but they leaped immediately into new campaigns in Greece. In 215 B.C.E. Philip V of Macedon (r. 221–179 B.C.E.) had allied with Hannibal because he was afraid that Rome might use its naval bases at the mouth of the Adriatic to invade his realm. A war with his Greek neighbors prevented him from sending help to Hannibal, but that made no difference to Rome. Rome declared war on Philip in 200 B.C.E., and three years later he surrendered. Curiously, Rome annexed no territory but contented itself with liberating the Greek city-states from Macedonian control. So long as the Greeks were disunited and fighting among themselves, they posed no threat to Rome.

When a warring Greek faction invited the Seleucid emperor, Antiochus III (r. 223–187 B.C.E.), to come to its aid, Rome sent its armies back to Greece. Antiochus beat a hasty retreat. The Romans pursued him across the Aegean, and in 188 B.C.E. he yielded most of Asia Minor to Rome. Rome fought two more wars with Macedonia and the Greeks, and in 168 B.C.E. it tried to pacify Greece by taking a thousand prominent Greeks hostage (the historian Polybius among them). In 148 B.C.E. Rome finally turned Macedonia into a province, and in 146 B.C.E. Rome sacked the city of Corinth and put down the last of the Greek rebellions. In the same year, a Third Punic War (149–146 B.C.E.) ended with the obliteration of Carthage. Rome emerged as the dominant power in the Mediterranean world, but its imperial territory did not yet have an imperial government.

The Stress of Success Rome's republican institutions were barely adequate for a city-state, and they were certainly not designed for the responsibilities of a vast empire. The new lands that Rome had acquired altered life for both the rich and the poor in ways that did neither class much good. Lax oversight of the provinces meant that most of the profits from the empire went into the pockets of military governors who used them to corrupt republican politics. The custom developed of giving a Roman magistrate a provincial command at the end of his year-long term in office. This prevented him from scheming to stay in power by getting him out of the city. But it also gave him a chance to recoup his finances and return to Rome with enough money to run for another office that would bring him another governorship. Because it was virtually impossible for an outsider to break into this system, about 50 families appropriated much of the empire's wealth and monopolized the republic's offices.

As the few rich grew richer, the empire's new provinces impoverished many of the soldiers who had conquered them. The Hannibalic War devastated Italy's farms, and long terms of military service prevented many men from caring for their land. When Rome's farmer-soldiers finally returned home, many lacked the capital to rebuild their farms and those who had the money found that the kind of farming they could do was no longer profitable. Grain was the small farmer's cash crop, but the Italian market was flooded with cheap grain from the provinces. Small domestic producers could not compete and had to sell out to wealthy investors who could afford to convert the land to more profitable uses. Rich families consolidated huge blocks of land and created **latifundia**, plantations that produced commercial crops (such as olives, wine, and cattle) for the international market. These *latifundia* provided no employment for the Roman farmer whose land they absorbed, for Rome's wars created an excess of cheap slaves. As slaves took over much of the agricultural work, rural freemen had little choice but to flood into cities like Rome. The government distributed bread to keep them quiet, and they earned handouts by joining the armies of clients with which the great families fought their political battles.

The situation was so corrupt that by the middle of the second century B.C.E. even wealthy Romans feared that the republic might collapse. There were calls for reform, but two things made changing the system difficult. No one was sure what would work, and no one wanted anyone else to get credit for a program that did work. Matters came to a head in 133 B.C.E., when Tiberius Gracchus (168–133 B.C.E.), a tribune, proposed confiscating the excess from anyone who had appropriated more than 320 acres of what was designated as public land, dividing the surplus into small farms, and giving these to the poor. The office of tribune had been created to protect the plebeians, and each tribune had the power to block legislation that he thought was not in the people's interest by standing up in the assembly and saying *veto* ("I forbid!"). When Tiberius presented his land redistribution proposal, its opponents induced another tribune to cast a veto. Tiberius, however, was prepared for this. He persuaded the assembly to throw the man out of office—on the theory that he had not used his powers for the purpose for which they had been granted. Land reform passed, but at the cost of destroying one of the crucial checks and balances of the Roman constitution. If the mob could instantly depose any politician who displeased it, the republic would degenerate into mob rule. When Tiberius's opponents finally ran out of legal ways to counter his maneuvers, they simply murdered him.

Tiberius's land redistribution plan was implemented, but it failed. Like many reforms, it addressed the symptom of a problem while ignoring its causes. It did nothing to change the situation that had forced small farmers off their land in the first place. Returning them to the land only set them up to fail again.

The strategy Tiberius invented to pass his reform program had a greater impact on the republic than did the reform itself, for it caused a new division in Roman politics. The **populares** ("people's party") sought power, as Tiberius had, by championing ideas that appealed to the mob. The **optimates** ("aristocrats") defended the prerogatives of the Senate by affirming Rome's conservative traditions. Neither party had a platform of proposals designed to cure the ills of Roman society. Each was defined by the method it used for gaining political advantage.

In 123 B.C.E. Tiberius Gracchus's younger brother, Gaius (159–121 B.C.E.), took up the *populares'* cause and made considerable headway until the *optimates* again employed force to destroy a rival politician. Rome's next leader, Gaius Marius (157–86 B.C.E.), learned a lesson from the fate of the two Gracchi that profoundly affected the course of Roman history. He concluded that to survive in the Roman political arena, a man had to have an army at his back.

In 107 B.C.E. Marius won a consulship by promising to bring a war with Numidia to a speedy conclusion. He proposed beefing up the army by dropping the traditional property qualification for service. This was welcomed by the impoverished Roman masses who had no jobs and no prospects, for it gave them a chance to vote themselves military careers. The soldiers Marius created in this way were, however, more his than Rome's. To secure their own continued employment, they were determined to keep him in office. Marius's reform turned Rome's army into a political machine that, contrary to tradition, won one consulship after another for its general.

Rome's Civil War

No one could compete with a man like Marius without building an army comparable to his, so every Roman politician who hoped to stay in the game set about winning a military command. That meant that aspiring politicians needed wars, for armies were

PEOPLE IN CONTEXT Cornelia, Mother of the Gracchi

I n theory Roman women, like Greek women, were subject to male authority, but in practice they had much more freedom. Roman girls could attend school, and Roman women were not confined to their homes. They followed politics and sometimes demonstrated in the streets to push for legislation they wanted. Women from prominent families were well-known public figures who exercised considerable influence. The most respected of these from the republican era was the Gracchi brothers' mother, Cornelia. Roman women bore only one name, the feminine spelling of their father's *gens*. (All of a man's daughters had the same name.) Cornelia (c. 180–105 B.C.E.) was the daughter of Publius Cornelius Scipio Africanus, the victor in the Second Punic War. The husband to whom Scipio gave her (at age 12) was a distinguished Roman considerably her senior, Tiberius Sempronius Gracchus. The marriage was fruitful. Cornelia bore him 12 children, alternating boys and girls. Only three survived to adulthood: Tiberius, Gaius, and their sister Sempronia (who married a Scipio to reaffirm the links between her parental families).

Mother of the Gracchi   This statue is of a woman from the era of Rome's Empire, not the Republic. But its design follows a convention believed to have been established by the lost republican-era statue of Cornelia (i.e., depicting Roman matrons seated in chairs).

After her husband's death in 154 B.C.E., Cornelia chose to remain a widow and declined a proposal of marriage from the pharaoh of Egypt. She devoted herself to the education of her sons and was said to have fired their political ambitions by telling them that she was ashamed to be known as Scipio's daughter rather than the Gracchi's mother. Given their bloody fates, she may have come to regret her words. Ancient historians cited letters (the authenticity of which modern scholars doubt) that she wrote to Gaius, urging him to moderate his radical politics. She was so well known and admired that her sons could score points with their audiences simply by mentioning her in their speeches, and her popularity was such that she became the first Roman woman, other than a priestess, to whom the republic erected a statue. The bronze effigy has disappeared, but its inscribed base survives. We know what it looked like, for statues honoring other women took it as their model. It is hard to imagine such a monument being raised in Athens, where, according to Pericles, the best women were those who were totally invisible.

Question: What explains the fact that women were more liberated in the Roman republic than in the Athenian democracy?

only justified when there were wars. After years of being slow to acquire provinces, Rome's foreign policy changed. Its leaders began to look for lands to conquer as a means to the ultimate conquest: Rome itself.

Sulla   In 88 B.C.E. Sulla (138–78 B.C.E.), one of Marius's officers, revealed the danger at the heart of the new power politics. He raised an army and marched on Rome to force the Senate to legitimate his command. After a profitable campaign in Asia Minor, Sulla retook Rome, assumed dictatorial powers, and executed thousands of citizens. Although Sulla used the *populares'* strategy to win control of Rome, he was an *optimate* reformer. He believed that Rome's difficulties had been caused by *popularis* demagogues, and to prevent any more of them from appearing, he emasculated the popular assembly and restored the traditional dominance of the Senate.

Sulla's reform was as unrealistic as the Gracchan land redistribution scheme. The Senate could not defend the empire with magistrates who were hobbled by the traditional restraints of the republican constitution. A government in which every office changed hands every year lacked continuity and could not successfully wage lengthy foreign wars. Almost immediately, therefore, the Senate began to appoint "special commanders" to deal with its more difficult problems. What made a command "special" was its freedom from the legal limitations imposed on the regular magistrates. Ambitious men immediately recognized that the fastest route to power was not through the old *cursus honorum* but via a series of special commands.

The first of the great special commanders was Pompey (106–48 B.C.E.), a young *optimas* who was one of Sulla's supporters. His conservative credentials persuaded the Senate that he could be trusted, and his loyal service lulled the Senators into granting him one special command after another—culminating in a commission to sweep pirates from the Mediterranean. This warranted a massive army and navy, which Pompey used not only to suppress piracy but to extend the empire in the east to the borders of Egypt. The Senate ultimately awoke to the possibility that it had created another Sulla, and the only strategy it could think of to block him was to make more like him. The Senators decreed special commands for Crassus (115–53 B.C.E.), reputedly Rome's richest man, and an ambitious and talented blue blood named Julius Caesar (100–44 B.C.E.).

When Pompey returned from the east in 62 B.C.E., he surprised everyone by leaving his army behind. He was a conservative man who would have been content simply to be showered with lavish praise for his services to the republic. The Senators chose instead to try to bring him down. They delayed the grants of land he requested as retirement pay for his veteran soldiers in an attempt to undermine his troops' loyalty to him. The Senators also concluded, somewhat prematurely, that they could handle Pompey on their own and that they had no further need for Crassus and Caesar. This had the effect of forcing Pompey, Crassus, and Caesar to bury their differences and join forces to defeat the Senate. In 59 B.C.E. they formed an alliance called the First **Triumvirate** ("rule by three men").

The First Triumvirate   Together, Pompey, Crassus, and Caesar were invincible, but they had no common objective for the use of their power. Each man had a private agenda that reflected his suspicion of his allies. Because Pompey's army made him the dominant member of the triumvirate, Crassus and Caesar wanted assignments that would enable them to build up comparable forces. Crassus set out to conquer the Parthian Empire, a great Iranian state on the eastern edge of Rome's territory, and Caesar stirred up trouble with the Gauls in northern Europe. Caesar pushed Rome's frontier to the Rhine River and the English Channel and whipped up enthusiasm in Rome by publishing an account of his campaigns (*The Gallic Wars*). Pompey, who stayed in Rome, was distrustful of both his colleagues, and the Triumvirate unraveled after the Parthians killed Crassus in 53 B.C.E. The Senate concluded that Pompey, an *optimas*, was a lesser threat to its interests than Caesar, a *popularis*, and it joined with Pompey in an attempt to end Caesar's career.

The situation came to a head in 50 B.C.E. Caesar's term as governor of his provinces expired, and the Senate refused to extend his command of his army. Caesar then marched on Rome and Pompey, and many of the Senators fled to Greece where large numbers of Pompey's troops were quartered. Although Caesar's army was much smaller and short of supplies, it went in pursuit, and in June, 48 B.C.E., Caesar routed the Senatorial forces at the battle of Pharsalus. Remnants of Pompey's army scattered to Africa and Spain, and Pompey sought refuge in Egypt, the only Mediterranean state still outside Rome's empire. Fearing Caesar's retribution, the Egyptians killed Pompey, embalmed his head, and sent it to Caesar as a token of their friendship. Caesar then invaded Egypt to avenge Pompey's murder. Egypt owed its survival as an independent country to the skill with which its young queen, Cleopatra VII (69–30 B.C.E.), a descendant of Alexander's general Ptolemy, handled Caesar.

Cleopatra In the popular imagination Queen Cleopatra VII of Egypt, mistress to both Julius Caesar and Mark Antony, has become a seductress whose beauty men found irresistible. However, the most reliable of her portraits suggest that she was not remarkably handsome. The formalized example shown here was probably executed during her lifetime. The legend of her beauty may in large part be a product of misogyny—of the assumption that a woman's only power and appeal derive from her sexuality.

It took some time for Caesar to clean out pockets of resistance, but by 45 B.C.E. he was master of Rome. Caesar was a good historian, and he probably concluded from his study of recent events that a republic could not govern an empire. Rome's urban mob had neither the wisdom nor the right to rule the world, and there was no way (given the primitive means of communications that were available) to enfranchise all the free men of the empire. Because monarchy was the only form of government efficient enough to run a large state in the ancient era, Caesar probably planned to establish kingship of some kind. That, at least, is what the Senate suspected, and to prevent it, some 60 Senators mobbed him at a meeting on March 15, 44 B.C.E. (the ides of March), and stabbed him 23 times.

Brutus and Cassius, the plot's leaders, had no plan to replace Caesar. They saw themselves as reformers who were defending the republic, and like previous reformers, they mistook a symptom for a cause. They assumed that Caesar was the problem and that when he was removed, the republic would automatically thrive. It was the republic's inadequacy, however, that had brought Caesar to power. His death did not correct that. It simply created a vacuum to be filled by a new Caesar.

The man best poised to succeed Caesar was his popular second-in-command, Mark Antony (c. 83–30 B.C.E.). Antony's plan was to stage a showy funeral for Caesar and distract Caesar's men until their desire to avenge themselves on the Senators abated. If they remained under his control, the Senate would be forced to rely on him for protection and he would be Rome's master. The problem with Antony's strategy was that Caesar had an heir. Caesar had no son, but he had adopted a nephew, Octavian (63 B.C.E.–14 C.E.), to carry on his name. Octavian was only 18 when Caesar died, and he had little military or political experience. But when he charged into Rome demanding vengeance for the murder of his "father," Caesar's soldiers cheered. The Senate was perversely delighted. Even though Octavian was vowing to punish the senatorial assassins, the Senate granted him a military command. It assumed that he was too young to be a threat and that his mere existence would divide Caesar's men and set them to fighting among themselves. Octavian was too smart for that. As soon as he had something to offer, he joined forces with Antony and Lepidus (d. 13 B.C.E.), another of Caesar's officers. They formally established the Second Triumvirate, a legal joint dictatorship, and in 42 B.C.E. they defeated the armies of Brutus and Cassius at Philippi in Greece.

The Second Triumvirate   The triumvirs had assumed dictatorial powers allegedly to restore the republic, but they were in no hurry. After Philippi, they divided up responsibilities for governing the empire. Antony's military reputation made him the dominant member of the triumvirate, and he awarded himself the best assignment. He headed east to prepare an invasion of Parthia. A successful Parthian campaign would provide him with a huge army with which he hoped in the end to sweep the other triumvirs aside. Octavian remained in Italy and oversaw efforts to track down rebel armies led by Pompey's sons. Lepidus governed Africa until 36 B.C.E., when Octavian placed him under house arrest (which continued until Lepidus's death 24 years later).

Octavian was a poor general but a superb politician, and when Antony committed a public relations blunder, Octavian moved in for the kill. Like Julius Caesar before him, Antony struck up a relationship with Egypt's Cleopatra. It was personal. (He fathered three of her children.) But it was also a sensible strategic alliance between two level-headed rulers. Antony needed Egypt's support for his invasion of Parthia, and Cleopatra extracted a promise of land in exchange for her aid. Octavian, however, convinced the Romans that the unpopular eastern queen had used her sexual wiles to captivate Antony—as she had previously captivated Caesar—and that Antony had become her pawn and the instrument through which she intended to rule Rome.

Octavian's charges would have had little effect if Antony's attack on Parthia had succeeded. But when it failed, Octavian made his move. In 32 B.C.E. he persuaded the Italians to swear a personal oath of loyalty to him and to support him in attacking Antony—allegedly to save the Roman Republic from overthrow by Cleopatra. The opposing armies again met in Greece, but they had little enthusiasm for the fight. The issue was decided by a sea battle off the western coast of Greece at Actium (31 B.C.E.). Antony and Cleopatra retreated to Egypt where they committed suicide rather than submit to Octavian.

Octavian's victory confronted him with the challenge that had cost Caesar his life—the responsibility for creating a stable government for Rome's empire. Octavian had already publicly eliminated the option of monarchy, for he had risen to power by promising to restore the republic. His ingenious strategy for reconciling what Rome wanted with what Rome needed was to create an "invisible monarchy,"

GREECE	ROME
Greece and Rome, 750 B.C.E.–31 B.C.E.	
750 B.C.E., colonization movement	750 B.C.E., foundation of the city of Rome
510 B.C.E., Cleisthenes and Athens' democracy	509 B.C.E., Roman Republic founded
492–479 B.C.E., Persian Wars	"Struggle of the Orders"
432–404 B.C.E., Peloponnesian War	Rome fights in Italy
336–323 B.C.E., Alexander the Great	
323 B.C.E., Antigonids, Seleucids, Ptolemies (Zeno, Epicurus, Euclid)	
	287 B.C.E., Plebiscite established
(Archimedes)	264–241 B.C.E., First Punic War
	218–202 B.C.E., Second Punic War
200–196 B.C.E., Rome's war with Philip V of Macedonia	
190 B.C.E., Rome defeats Antiochus and occupies Asia Minor	
(168 B.C.E., Polybius deported to Italy)	
	146 B.C.E., Corinth and Carthage sacked
	133 B.C.E., Tiberius Gracchus's tribunate
	123 B.C.E., Gaius Gracchus's first tribunate
	107 B.C.E., Marius's first consulate
	88 B.C.E., Sulla's first march on Rome
	67–61 B.C.E., Pompey expands empire in the east
	60 B.C.E., First Triumvirate
	45 B.C.E., Caesar defeats Pompey (d. 48 B.C.E.)
	43 B.C.E., Second Triumvirate
	31 B.C.E., Octavian defeats Antony

an imperial administration masked by a republican façade. By allowing the Romans to indulge the illusion of living in a republic, he was able to subject them to a monarchy. Sometimes governments increase their power by seeming to repudiate the very things that they are doing. Citizens of modern republics and democracies need to keep that in mind.

KEY QUESTION | Revisited

Imperialism and monarchy have largely fallen out of fashion in the modern West, and Americans generally view some form of government by the people as the only reliable guarantor of what they hold to be God-given, inalienable freedoms. Americans have, from time to time, felt that it is the obligation of their country to defend democracy and spread it around the globe.

Government by the people may, however, not always be a people's highest priority. A potential conflict can arise between two things that citizens want from government: they want protection for individual liberties, but they also want security for person and property. If circumstances force them to choose between these things, history suggests that the desire for safety often wins out. The Greeks' experiment with democracy led to an era of civil war and chaos that ended in foreign occupation. The Romans repeatedly tinkered with their republic in an effort to make it work, but in the end they sacrificed the reality of government by the people for its illusion. For many Romans the price must have seemed worth paying. The imperial administration that took over from Rome's quarrelsome republic unified Europe, North Africa, and much of the Middle East and maintained something like world peace for over three centuries.

An autocracy can provide a more efficient response to a crisis than a government that depends on numerous people reaching consensus about what to do. Given that efficiency can mean the difference between life and death in wartime, people may willingly sacrifice liberties to achieve it. Consequently, wars—particularly long ones—are dangerous for democracies. The struggle for victory usually drives them to increase the power and reduce the number of their leaders.

The size of a state has also often been a factor in determining the success or failure of a citizen-run government. Consensus is usually easier to reach in small communities than large ones, and citizens of small communities develop emotional bonds that sometimes inspire them to remarkable acts of self-sacrifice in defense of their homeland. Such was the experience of Athens in the Persian Wars, as well as the behavior of the Romans in the early days of their republic. In the ancient world, however, when the scale of social life grew beyond a certain point, government by the people tended to falter and to allow autocracy to take its place. Given the limited means of communication then available, an autocratic hierarchy provided the only efficient way to govern a large area. Orders could quickly be sent down from the top, but it was difficult for opinions to be gathered up from the bottom. In this respect the modern world is different. It is often said that communications technologies have shrunk the world and made it the equivalent of a global village. If so, can great territorial states now be successfully and permanently governed by the masses, or are governments by the people still fated, when pressured by war and conflict, to surrender to small coteries of powerful leaders?

Review Questions

1. What were Alexander's strategies for conquering an empire and for making that conquest permanent?
2. What do the arts, sciences, literatures, and philosophies of the Hellenistic empires imply about the sociopolitical environments these empires created?
3. Why did the discoveries and inventions of Hellenistic scientists have so little impact on their world?
4. How did Rome's republican system of government differ from Athens' democracy?
5. Did Rome intentionally build an empire, or was its empire an unintended consequence of its attempts to defend itself?
6. Why was the Roman Republic unable to manage its empire?

Please consult the Suggested Readings at the back of the book to continue your study of the material covered in this chapter. For a list of documents on the Primary Source DVD-ROM that relate to topics in this chapter, please refer to the back of the book.

6 Rome's Empire and the Unification of the Western World

[Octavian Augustus] seduced the military with gifts, the civilians with cheap food, and everyone with the benefits of peace. Then he gradually took over the functions of the Senate, the magistrates, and the law itself. The prominent men who had survived [the civil war] found that the best way to prosper politically and financially was slavishly to support him.

—Tacitus

KEY | Question

Do people prefer order to liberty?

In 1937 a skillful feat of engineering recovered fragments of the Altar of Peace (*Ara Pacis*), a first-century monument that lay buried beneath a sixteenth-century Roman *palazzo*. It had been erected about 9 B.C.E. to commemorate the *pax Romana* ("Roman peace") that descended on the Mediterranean world after Octavian's victory over Antony and Cleopatra. The altar stood on a platform open to the sky, and it was surrounded by a wall on which carvings depicted Octavian (63 B.C.E.–14 C.E.) and his family in a religious procession. Its style so brilliantly synthesized Greek idealism and Roman realism that it inspired artists for centuries.

Near the end of his life, Octavian published a testament cataloguing his services to Rome. In addition to bringing peace, he noted that he had used his personal fortune to see the state through fiscal crises. He had rebuilt the city of Rome and entertained its residents with races and games. He had provided free food during famines. He had reduced the size of the army while expanding the empire, securing its frontiers, and maintaining its internal order. But the achievement of which he said he was most proud was the restoration of Rome's republican government.

Portrait of a Roman Woman   Portraits on planks of wood, such as this one, were commissioned to cover the faces of mummies. Their style may be a little rough, but they can be compelling in the way they capture the individuality of their subjects. *Dagli Orti/Picture Desk, Inc./Kobal Collection*

In truth, Octavian had not restored the republic. He had used republican rhetoric to engineer Rome's transition to monarchy. At the time, few objected, for it seemed safe to trust him with overwhelming power. Few thought about what might happen when that power passed to other hands. Within a few years, the historian Tacitus (c. 55–120 C.E.) and other members of the senatorial class were so disillusioned that they even denigrated the peace the emperors created for Rome. It was purchased, they said, at the cost of the republican liberties that they had long enjoyed (and abused). Tacitus claimed that the victim sacrificed on Octavian's Altar of Peace was freedom.

Just societies aspire to reconcile the freedom of the individual with the desires of the group for security and stability. This is difficult. Too much freedom leads to chaos, and too much control to tyranny—and fear of one may bring on the other. Octavian rescued Rome from a century-long civil war and established a peace that brought undeniable benefits. There was, however, a cost. As you examine the history of imperial Rome, reflect on what it implies about the problem of balancing liberty against the risk of anarchy.

The Augustan Era

The Roman Republic was able to conquer an empire, but not to rule one. The republic's strategy for heading off tyranny was to divide power among its magistrates. This risked disorder, for men often yielded to the temptation to use the resources of their offices to fight among themselves for supremacy. A monarchy, which set one man far above all others, promised more stability, but the Romans equated monarchy with servitude. They were so attached to the image of themselves as free citizens (not subjects of a king) that they clung to their faulty republic—even though it condemned them to a century of recurrent civil war.

An Invisible Monarchy   When Octavian returned to Rome from his eastern campaigns in 29 B.C.E., he was hailed as the savior of his country. He knew that its salvation would be short-lived unless fundamental changes were made in its political institutions, but he was acutely aware of the danger of making any changes that might be interpreted as threats to the republic. Suspicions of monarchical ambitions had cost Julius Caesar and Mark Antony their lives.

Rome's immediate need for a leader strong enough to restore order bought Octavian a period of grace. For eight years, he provided a legal basis for his authority by monopolizing one of the consulships, but this was risky. It looked suspiciously like a step toward monarchy. In January, 27 B.C.E., he secured his position by threatening to give it up. He convened the Senate and offered to surrender all his powers and fully restore the republic. There was no risk that the Senate would accept his offer. The Senators realized that things would fall apart if he loosed the reins of power. So instead, they thanked him for his services to the republic by granting him a title—Augustus ("majestic")—and prevailed on him to continue as consul and accept a ten-year term as governor of 18 of the empire's 28 provinces. The army had been split up and posted to trouble spots in the provinces, most of which, coincidentally, were the ones assigned to Octavian.

As the holder of **imperium** *maius* ("supreme military authority"), the new Augustus was Rome's *imperator* ("emperor"). This was an ancient republican term for a victorious general, not a monarch, but Augustus preferred to use a civilian title that the grateful Romans had lavished on him to recognize his record of public service: *princeps civitatis* ("first of citizens"). All of Augustus's titles were republican in origin, but they, like his adopted family name, Caesar (the origin of Kaiser and Tsar), soon came to signify regal authority.

Augustus believed that the Romans would tolerate a *principate* (a government in which one man had the power to keep things on track) if it brought the blessings of peace and if its prince honored their republican traditions. He scrupulously avoided anything that looked monarchical. His home on the Palatine Hill was a typical upper-class residence. (Parts of it have survived.) He wore ordinary civilian dress, and he claimed that his togas (the garments that symbolized Roman citizenship) were home-spun by his wife, Livia, and daughter, Julia. He did not surround himself with armed men or throw his weight around needlessly. He wandered the streets, entered into the fray of elections, solicited votes for candidates he backed, took part in debates, and treated his senatorial colleagues as equals.

Augustus's stated affection for republican tradition was not entirely insincere. He shared as much power as he thought he safely could with the Senate and the republican magistrates. He reduced the Senate from 1,000 to about 600 members and filled its ranks with experienced men of good reputation. His preference was for members of Rome's old families, but the civil war had taken a toll on these. They were dying out and a new aristocracy with roots in other Italian cities and the provinces was in the making. The reconstituted Senate had real responsibility. It managed the treasury, served as a kind of supreme court, and had the power to legislate. Augustus assembled a small company of trusted Senators and magistrates to serve as his personal advisors, and during his sometimes lengthy absences from Italy, the Senate was left to manage (or mismanage) on its own.

In 23 B.C.E. Augustus increased his republican cover by resigning the office of consul. His successive terms were unpopular, for they violated tradition and kept other men from enjoying the prestige of the office. Thereafter, he based his authority on his privileges as an honorary tribune and the periodic renewal of his provincial governorships. From time to time, he also held the office of censor, which allowed him to create Senators and "equestrians" (Rome's second highest social class), and he served as *Pontifex maximus*, the head of the state religion. Throughout his career he was careful to make sure that his powers derived from republican offices or precedents. By skillfully combining and prolonging these, he exercised mastery over Rome. His example suggests that the greatest danger to a modern republic with separated branches of government may not be an overt attack on its constitution, but a covert strategy that quietly and behind the scenes amasses privileges and bits of authority.

Octavian Augustus   Octavian Augustus, unlike Julius Caesar, was not a soldier or talented general. His skills were political, and he was a master of propaganda. He claimed that his goal was the restoration of the Roman Republic, and he carefully avoided any of the trappings of monarchy. This statue depicts him as a good republican citizen. He wears the toga Roman men donned on formal occasions. He has no crown or jewelry, and he carries nothing more threatening than a scroll.

Reorganization   The republican cloak that shrouded Augustus's monarchy rendered it officially "invisible," and this allowed his fellow Romans to submit to it without sacrificing pride or patriotism. Even those who understood what was happening were inclined to play along with Augustus. The benefits of his administration were obvious but alternatives to it were not. On several occasions the Senate and the people of Rome begged him to take charge and see the state through an economic or political crisis.

The Augustan peace owed a great deal to Augustus's military reforms. Since the days of Marius, Rome's politicians had repeatedly involved its armies in their power struggles, and the empire's military had grown to immense size. At each stage in the civil war, the victor had added his defeated opponents' legions to his own. The army of which Augustus took command after Antony's fall was more than twice as large as the one that he estimated Rome could afford, and he was eager to shrink it for other than fiscal reasons. A smaller army meant fewer threats from fewer generals. Augustus appropriated Egypt as his personal domain and used its wealth to retire about 300,000 men. This reduced the standing army from 60 to 28 legions.

Augustus limited the legionnaires' opportunities to intervene in Rome's politics by posting them to camps along the frontiers. An elite troop of about 4,500 men, the Praetorian Guard, was created to maintain order in Italy. Its name derived from a term for the loyal soldiers who guarded the tents (*praetorii*) of republican generals. In later years, the Praetorian Guard's proximity to the city of Rome tempted it to intervene in the empire's politics, but Augustus hoped that by professionalizing military service he could eliminate some of the motives that previously had politicized Rome's armies. Legionnaires signed on for tours of duty lasting from 16 to 20 years. They were paid according to a fixed scale and could earn promotion from the ranks to the officer corps (although the higher commands were reserved for men from the Senatorial and equestrian classes). In short, Rome's defenders became state employees and no longer were dependent on their generals for their pay and retirement benefits.

Augustus's military reforms helped to consolidate, as well as pacify, the empire. His 28 legions enrolled about 160,000 men—just barely enough to maintain Rome's 4,000-mile-long frontier. To back up the legions (membership in which was limited to Roman citizens), Augustus created auxiliaries, companies of men recruited from the provinces. The legions and auxiliaries together provided about a quarter of a million men to protect and police a population of about 100 million. Auxiliaries were less well paid than legionnaires, but a term of honorable service earned citizenship for the veteran of an auxiliary unit and qualified his sons to join the legions. The army thus provided entry into Roman society for provincials.

Cities were central to the administration of the empire, for its primitive systems of communications meant that most government had to be local government. The army literally built Rome's famous network of roads to facilitate its movements. Augustus began to extend the roads beyond Italy to the headquarters he established for the legions in the provinces. Many of these new military camps became permanent cities that assumed responsibility for administering the districts in which they were located, and they helped to spread Latin language and culture—particularly in the west. The eastern half of the empire already had many cities, but much of the west (particularly in Spain,

North Africa, and trans-Alpine Europe) was still rural territory divided among tribes. Augustus sponsored about 100 colonies, many of which were settled by his veterans. Part of a soldier's pay was banked for him so that when he retired at about the age of 40 he had a nest egg with which to begin a new career. Many men invested in farms and businesses in the provinces in which they had served.

The Roman Empire became a kind of federation of city-states. Each of its urban centers operated within parameters set by the central administration, but each also accommodated local customs. The schools that towns supported and the opportunities for political participation they provided helped to Romanize the provincial elites and foster their loyalty to the empire. As these elites learned Latin and Greek, the empire's upper classes acquired a common culture. The cities in which they lived were similar, no matter where they were located. Each had temples, arenas, theaters, schools, monuments, baths, and public buildings, many of which Augustus and his successors funded. Each had its councils of local leaders. Romanization spread widely, but in many places classical civilization was only a thin veneer over native cultures that outlasted the empire.

Augustus turned the republican hodgepodge of territories into a coherent empire. He redrew the boundaries of provinces and standardized their governments. He reduced corruption by establishing fixed rates of taxation and by appointing state officials, rather than private contractors, to collect and audit taxes. He waged campaigns to extend the empire to what he believed were defensible frontiers. In the east he set up a string of client kingdoms dependent on Rome. In the west he suppressed resistance in Spain and the Alpine region and extended Roman territory in the Balkans north to the Danube Valley. He planned to cross the Rhine and conquer more of Germany, but he failed in his attempt. In 9 C.E. the Germans ambushed and exterminated three legions. Augustus recovered enough to hold the line and maintain order, but the historian Tacitus grumbled about the emperor's heavy-handed methods. The peace in some provinces, Tacitus said, was only the quiet of a man-made desert (see Map 6–1).

Augustus's administrative reforms also helped to turn Rome's diverse holdings into a true empire. The republic had largely been run by amateurs who improvised ad hoc policies to govern its provinces. But Augustus created an imperial bureaucracy of salaried, specially trained professionals to manage the empire. Wealthy Romans often relied on well-educated freedmen and slaves to run their plantations and political offices, and Augustus followed a similar practice when staffing the administration of the empire. Service in the government gave some men, who were legally or socially handicapped, considerable power over people who were otherwise their superiors. Senators and equestrians were enlisted to oversee a growing list of government services. They supervised grain and water supplies, police forces, courts, treasuries, public entertainments, and construction projects.

Moral Regeneration   Augustus, like many Romans, believed that Italy had been able to build the empire because of the unique strength and virtues of its people—their **Romanitas**. It was vitally important, therefore, to preserve Italy's traditions and cultural dominance. This was not a new idea. The Roman Senate had from time to time sought

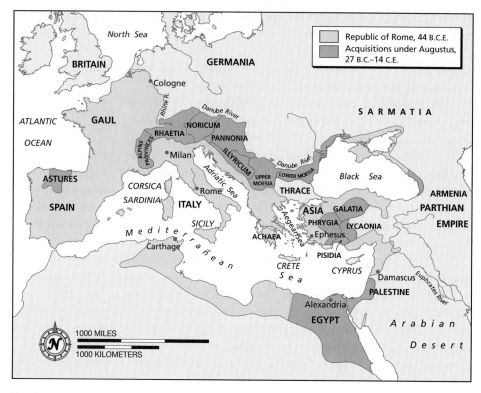

Map 6–1 Augustus's Empire   Under Augustus Rome completed its encirclement of the Mediterranean, but the empire had not yet reached its full extent. His successors added territory in Britain, Germany, Central Europe, and the Middle East.

Question: Were there natural geographic boundaries for Rome's empire?

to limit the spread of eastern religions that it viewed as detrimental to Roman character, and Italy had supported Augustus in his fight with Mark Antony because Mark Antony was seen as having succumbed to evil eastern influences.

To guarantee Italy's supremacy and the continued integrity of Roman culture, Augustus believed he needed a large pool of disciplined, patriotic upper-class Romans from which to recruit a staff for governing the empire. The civil war had devastated the citizen population, and Rome's upper classes preserved their fortunes by limiting the number of their offspring. Augustus tried to solve the manpower problem by passing laws aimed at strengthening families, increasing birthrates, and restoring commitment to traditional values. He financially penalized women below the age of 50 and men younger than 60 who failed to marry early and remarry promptly when widowed or divorced. Bachelors and sterile couples were heavily taxed, and families with three or more children were given honors and preferential treatment by the government. Adultery for women and for men who had affairs with married women became a crime against the state, punishable by fine, exile, or death. Temples were restored and archaic patriotic ceremonies revived as part of a program to promote patriotism and civic virtue.

Augustus's social legislation was a failure. He and his family even failed to set a good example for others. He sired only one child, a daughter named Julia, and her flagrant immorality ultimately drove him to exile her to a remote island.

Latin High Culture   The arts played a part in Augustus's program for the moral and patriotic regeneration of his fellow citizens, and Roman literature reached the pinnacle of its development during his reign. Ironically, given Rome's condemnation of eastern influences, Romans did not produce much in the way of art, literature, or serious thought until they were stimulated by contact with the Greeks during the last century of the republican era. As Rome's armies moved east, Rome was flooded with looted objects and trade goods that Italian craftsmen eagerly imitated. Much classical Greek statuary survives today only in Roman copies. Influential upper-class Romans, such as the Scipios who led the city during the First and Second Punic War, were infatuated with all things Greek. They learned Greek, dressed as Greeks, bought Greek furniture and slaves, and sat at the feet of Greek philosophers. Some Roman intellectuals and politicians insisted that Greeks were effeminate, untrustworthy, and otherwise lacking in the stalwart virtues of *Romanitas*, but Rome thoroughly succumbed to the blandishments of Hellenistic civilization.

Romans followed the Greeks more closely in some fields than in others. They also adapted what they copied and made some original contributions of their own. This is most evident in architecture. The Romans shared the classical taste for symmetrical designs, but their buildings were often larger and more complex than those of the Greeks. They added curves—arches and domes—to the linear elements (columns and lintels) characteristic of Hellenic buildings. They invented concrete and used it to construct new kinds of imposing but graceful structures. Sulla built Rome's first major building (a temple) in the Greek style. Pompey and Caesar added a few more, but when Augustus came to power, his empire's capital still had few notable buildings. He set about changing that—claiming in the end that he found Rome a city of brick and left it a city of marble.

Related to architecture was the Romans' unique gift for engineering. They drove arrow-straight roads across rough terrain, tunneled through mountains, and created immense systems of aqueducts to supply their cities with lavish amounts of water. Over 200,000 gallons a day eventually flowed into Rome to supply its fountains and baths. A leisurely daily bath was an indispensable ritual of civilized life for a Roman, and Roman cities were equipped with luxurious public bathing facilities.

Latin literature was pioneered by comic playwrights. Twenty-one plays by Plautus (c. 254–184 B.C.E.), an Italian, and six by his successor, a former Carthaginian slave named Terence (c. 195–159 B.C.E.), have survived. Both men imitated Greek models, but Terence's work was the more refined. Plautus served a Roman appetite for farce and slapstick, as serious playwrights with literary pretensions were not much in demand.

The authors of the early republican period were handicapped by the immaturity of the Latin language. The first Romans to try their hands at prose writing wrote in Greek. Cato the Elder (234–149 B.C.E.), a Senator remembered primarily for his political activities, attempted a history of Rome in Latin. It has been lost, but a book he wrote on agriculture survives to provide us with our earliest extended specimen of Latin prose.

Latin poetry began to flourish in the middle of the first century B.C.E. as Romans became acquainted with the work of Greeks associated with Alexandria's Museum. Among the best and earliest extant examples are the poems that Catullus (c. 85–54 B.C.E.) penned to describe his passionate, stormy, and disillusioning affair with the promiscuous wife of a prominent Roman politician. Lucretius (c. 94–55 B.C.E.), the republican era's other major poet, chose a more serious theme for his work. He wrote to convince his countrymen that Epicurean materialism provided escape from the stress and anxiety of the wars that plagued his generation. He claimed that the universe was nothing more than bits of matter randomly colliding in empty space and that when people came to understand this, they would lose their fear of death and the gods and begin to behave rationally. Reason would persuade them of the wisdom of avoiding strong feelings—the pleasurable as well as the painful—by distancing themselves emotionally from a world that was essentially random and meaningless.

At about the same time when Romans were discovering Greek poets, they were introduced to Greek philosophy. In 155 B.C.E. Athens dispatched a number of its prominent teachers to Rome as ambassadors. The traditional values of Roman culture disposed the Romans to reject philosophies that flirted with atheism and religions that undercut moral rigor. In 186 B.C.E. the Senate outlawed the worship of Dionysus (Bacchus), a cult associated with orgiastic excesses. In 173 B.C.E. it banished Epicurean philosophers for teaching what it regarded as self-indulgent quietism. The Greek philosophy that most appealed to the Romans was Stoicism, and Rome produced two of the best known Stoic authors: Epictetus (b. c. 50 C.E.), a Greek slave, and Marcus Aurelius (r. 161–180 C.E.), an emperor (both of whom wrote in Greek). Stoics provided a rationale for the traditional Roman virtues of duty and self-discipline. They taught that the world is a great material organism animated by a rational principle. Because it is a rational system, all of its parts serve essential purposes in the functioning of the whole. Individual freedom is, therefore, an illusion. Peace of mind comes from realizing this— from accepting the duties of one's station knowing that everyone (from emperor to slave) is on the same footing. All obey necessity. The only thing within their power is their attitude toward life, and the only real evils are the painful emotions (such as anger, frustration, disappointment, and jealousy) that are aroused when the world cannot be made to serve one's personal desires. Reason frees the virtuous individual to serve the community dispassionately and disinterestedly.

Because republican politicians had to solicit support from voters and sway the thinking of popular assemblies, they were attracted to the study of rhetoric, the art of persuasive speaking pioneered by Greek philosophers. The oratorical skills of Cicero (106–43 B.C.E.) helped him overcome the handicap of undistinguished ancestry, earn a consulship, and serve as one of the Senate's leaders during the era of the First and Second Triumvirates. Cicero was less an original thinker than a popularizer of Greek philosophy. He favored the Stoics and maintained that the infighting that plagued the republic would end if men allowed themselves to be guided by the rational laws that Stoics claimed governed nature. A rational society would grant uniquely talented people (such as Cicero) special privileges and elevate them to positions of leadership no matter what their family backgrounds. Cicero claimed that, from time to time, the republic needed a **princeps,** an extraordinary citizen whose natural charisma, wisdom, and moral authority equipped him to guide the Senate and the popular assemblies in discharging their respective duties. To his dismay, Cicero discovered that a *princeps* might not be all that rational and benevolent. He attacked Mark Antony in a series of fiery speeches, and when the Second Triumvirate came to power, Antony murdered him and exhibited his head and right hand (the orator's instruments) on the speaker's platform in the Forum.

Greeks were certainly capable of the kind of viciousness that Mark Antony displayed, but only the Romans turned slaughter into entertainment for the masses. By the Hellenistic era, most towns had arenas and theaters in which to stage public spectacles. The Greek and Roman religious calendars were replete with festivals celebrated with games. But where the Greeks had a passion for athletic competitions, the Romans loved to witness the shedding of animal and human blood.

The politicians of the Roman Republic competed for office by bribing the voters with lavish games, and this was one of the many traditions Augustus honored. When he totted up his services to Rome, they included sponsorship of 18 gladiatorial combats involving 10,000 men and 3,500 animals. Later emperors outdid him. Tens of thousands of men and beasts were offered up during holidays that sometimes continued for months. Exotic animals were imported at great expense simply to be destroyed. To find men to kill, jails were emptied of criminals, slaves purchased, and captives taken in war. Contests between odd pairings of animals (a bear versus a bull, for example) or men with different weapons were invented to prevent the slaughter from becoming routine and boring.

Some of Rome's educated elite (including a few emperors) despised the games, but they knew that it was politically unwise to insult the masses by expressing contempt for the public's entertainment. The delight Romans took in witnessing bloodshed and death might tempt a modern American to look down on them, but no Roman was ever able to relish the kind of elaborate atrocities that Hollywood simulates. Contemporary audiences excuse their appetite for mayhem by pointing out that what they spend billions of dollars to watch is not real. But if the Romans had had special effects artists at their disposal, they too might have been content with make-believe. The real question is why such spectacles appeal to anyone in any age.

Art and Augustan Propaganda
The Golden Age of Latin literature dawned with Augustus's empire. The leading authors of his day helped promote his reforms, but their propagandistic works were inspired by sincere belief in his vision of Rome's strengths and his faith in its destiny. They were deeply grateful for the Augustan peace and brimming with patriotic enthusiasm. They shared Augustus's faith that cultivation of the sturdy agrarian virtues that had enabled their ancestors to win an empire would equip them to lead the world into an era of peace and plenty.

Virgil (70–19 B.C.E.) was Rome's greatest poet. His father, a northern Italian landowner, wanted him to practice law. His work, however, came to the attention of one of Augustus's close associates, a wealthy equestrian named Maecenas (c. 63–8 B.C.E.) whose patronage freed Virgil to pursue his writing. Virgil's earlier poems, *Eclogues*, were mostly romanticized descriptions of the Italian countryside and the simple pleasures of

The Altar of Peace   The altar Augustus commissioned to express gratitude for the end of the civil war was surrounded by a wall on which a religious procession (featuring members of Augustus's family) is depicted. It is a masterpiece both of classical sculpture and Augustan propaganda. The public ceremony it celebrates is very much an idealized family affair. The women have their heads modestly covered, the toga-clad males wear wreaths indicating honor and public service, and they have produced children who are being raised in traditions of Roman patriotism and piety.

rural life. He followed these with the *Georgics*, patriotic poems giving thanks for the Augustan peace and celebrating the yeoman farmer, the type of hard-working citizen that Augustus claimed was the source of Rome's strength. Virgil's greatest project, one he did not live to finish, was the *Aeneid*, the story of the Trojan prince Aeneas, the legendary founder of the Roman people. Virgil intended the *Aeneid* to provide Rome with an epic account of its origin comparable to the *Iliad* and the *Odyssey*, and to tie the story of Rome's founding into Homer's mythic history. The poem justified the Roman Empire by claiming that the gods destined the Roman people to rule the world and establish universal peace. That was why the gods endowed the Romans with *Romanitas*, their characteristic virtues of self-sufficiency, strength, courage, devotion to duty, patriotism, and simple piety. Virgil's description of Rome's past was Augustus's vision for Rome's future.

The second major poet of Rome's Golden Age was Horace (65–8 B.C.E.), a freedman's son who saw military service in the civil war. Virgil recommended him to Maecenas, who gave Horace a rural estate on which to live and write. Horace worked on a smaller scale than Virgil (producing satires, odes, epistles, and hymns,) but joined Virgil in exhorting the Romans to practice the hardy, sober virtues that Augustus championed.

Augustus was less pleased with the third of the Golden Age's great poets, Ovid (43 B.C.E.–17 C.E.). Ovid's prolific output dealt largely with sensuous subjects that appealed to the dissolute young aristocrats whom Augustus was trying to reform. Among his works was a textbook for seducers, *The Art of Love*, which was especially likely to offend the *princeps*. Scarcely less titillating were some of the 250 or so tales he retold in *Metamorphoses*, a kind of encyclopedia of classical mythology. In 8 C.E. Ovid's involvement (with Augustus's granddaughter) in a sexual scandal led to his banishment to a remote, barbarous town on the shores of the Black Sea. His pleas for forgiveness went unanswered, and he died in exile.

The greatest prose writer of Augustus's generation was the historian Livy (59 B.C.E.–17 C.E.), who produced a monumental survey of Roman history from the city's founding to his own day. The 35 of its 142 books that survive constitute a virtually unique source of information relating to Rome's early development. Like the poets, Livy was an advocate for the Augustan virtues. He believed that history's purpose was to teach moral lessons, and his history was filled with tales of Roman valor, self-control, piety, patriotism, and moral rectitude. For centuries, schoolteachers have used Livy's inspirational stories in their struggle to turn unruly children into disciplined adults.

Order and Continuity: The Dynastic Option

Augustus avoided assassination, gave Rome over 40 years of stable government, and died in his bed at an advanced age. He knew that the empire needed someone like him to oversee it. However, because Rome was still officially a republic, it had no provision for appointing a successor to carry on his work. An invisible monarchy had to be passed on secretly. This was not hard to do, for Romans were not particular about the line that separates public from private authority.

In the testament Augustus wrote to review his life's work, he gave an accounting of his private expenditures on behalf of Rome. On several occasions, he had distributed 400 or more sesterces to at least a quarter of a million men. During famines, he had fed Rome at his own expense. He had spent 400 million sesterces to settle veterans from the army, and he had donated 150 million sesterces to the public treasury. Given that a laborer's daily wage was about four sesterces and that Augustus by no means impoverished his heirs, his fortune must have been staggering. By using it to fund public services, Augustus blurred the distinction between government agents and his personal servants. This created confusion between his household and the state bureaucracy that allowed the latter to pass to his heirs when they inherited the former. The easiest way to perpetuate his invisible monarchy was to make it the hereditary property of his family.

Augustus's popularity and the length of his reign helped smooth the path for his heir. By the time he died, there were few Romans left who had experienced life under the old republic and who had painful memories of the civil war. The Romans did not want to return to the past, but they were not ready to repudiate their republican traditions and acknowledge the new political reality. This meant that they, in effect, surrendered to Augustus's heirs, for they could not control the choice of their monarch until they admitted that they had a monarchy. Hereditary systems of succession are risky. An heir may not be qualified to handle his inheritance, or a ruler may fail to produce an heir. Augustus's family confronted Rome with both problems.

The Julio-Claudians   Augustus's only child was his daughter Julia, and his hopes for an heir were pinned on the two grandsons she gave him. When both these boys died, he had to make an arrangement that displeased all concerned. He compelled his estranged stepson Tiberius, the son of his wife Livia and her first husband (Claudius Nero), to divorce a wife he loved, marry Julia, and assume the duties of heir. Because Augustus was a Julian by adoption and Tiberius a Claudian by birth, historians refer to Rome's first imperial dynasty as the Julio-Claudians.

Augustus owed much of his success to his ability to cultivate the fantasy that he was only a first among equals in the game of republican politics. On his deathbed he reportedly asked a group of friends, "In life's farce have I acted my part well?" Tiberius (r. 14–37 C.E.) initially tried to follow Augustus's example, but Tiberius was a moody man who lacked Augustus's patience and ability to connect with people. He was soon loathed by both the masses and the Senators.

In 26 C.E. he left Rome and took up permanent residence on the island of Capri in the Bay of Naples. By now the imperial bureaucracy was so well entrenched that Rome's imperator could ignore the Senate and popular assemblies and run the empire from any location he chose. This humiliated and infuriated the Senators, whom Tiberius disliked as much as they disliked him. He characterized them as "men eager to be slaves." To be fair, Augustus had put the Senators in the difficult position of having responsibility without power, and they reasonably feared being set up to take the blame for things that were beyond their control. Having few alternatives, they took up their pens and vented their frustrations by writing histories. Modern readers need to keep in mind that the descriptions of Rome's emperors in these sources are far from objective.

If Tiberius failed at public relations, he succeeded at government. He surrounded himself with good advisors and trained specialists, paid close attention to the administration of the provinces, reduced their taxes, built roads, economized by cutting back on Rome's gladiatorial games, and racked up a huge surplus in the imperial treasury for his successor.

Tiberius's only son died in 23 C.E., and his heir was a grandnephew, Gaius Caesar. He is better known by the childhood nickname his father's soldiers gave him when he strutted about their camp in a tiny military uniform: Caligula ("Little Boots").

Caligula (r. 37–41 C.E.), who is remembered as one of Rome's worst emperors, began well. He returned to Rome, was deferential to the Senate, courted the Roman populace with games, and recalled exiles. Then something went terribly wrong. Some historians believe that a serious illness disturbed his already precariously balanced mind. He was frenetic, high strung, given to insomnia, and plagued by insecurities. Many of the outlandish stories about him that are found in hostile senatorial histories defy belief. If Caligula was mad, there may have been a logic to his insanity. His extreme behavior makes some sense if it was an attempt to force the Romans to recognize that their republic was a farce and that they had become the subjects of rulers similar to the god-kings of Egypt, Persia, and the Hellenistic East.

Caligula made the mistake of alienating those closest to him, and disaffected officers of the Praetorian Guard murdered him, his wife, and his only child (an infant daughter). The Praetorians then elevated his uncle, Claudius, to the throne.

Claudius (r. 41–54 C.E.) was a bookish man who studied with the historian Livy and wrote on subjects ranging from Etruscan history to the alphabet. He was just what the faltering empire needed. Although the strength of the imperial bureaucracy and sheer momentum had carried Rome through Caligula's years of mismanagement, inertia would not preserve order indefinitely. Rome needed a conscientious leader, and Claudius had the right qualifications. He was a well-educated workaholic who enjoyed the details of administration. He had extensive knowledge of Roman law, which he put to work in the courts. He financed new colonies and public works—the most important of which was the rebuilding of Ostia, the port (at the mouth of the Tiber River) that served the city of Rome. He authorized the campaign that added Britain, which Julius Caesar had twice invaded but never conquered, to Rome's empire.

Claudius's fourth and last wife was his niece, Agrippina the Younger. The unusual marriage was probably intended to safeguard the dynasty. Claudius was aging and ill and unlikely to live long enough to see his only son, Britannicus, reach maturity. The other possible heir to the throne was Nero, a son Agrippina had by an earlier marriage. Claudius's union with Agrippina and adoption of Nero joined the surviving branches of the imperial family and created two potential heirs. Because both boys were young, Agrippina was groomed for the role of regent. Claudius gave her the title "Augusta" and minted coins in her honor. Ancient governments used coins to communicate with the masses. As they passed from hand to hand, people absorbed the messages the government had stamped on them. By accustoming the Romans to an Augusta, Claudius prepared them, should it become necessary, for a situation they had never faced before: rule by a woman.

When Claudius died in 54 C.E., Nero (r. 54–68 C.E.), the senior heir, was 17 years old. He, like Caligula, has often been dismissed as a madman, but that may be too simplistic an interpretation of the ancient sources. On the one hand, he is accused of wanton murder of countless persons (including his half-brother, his mother, and his wife) and absurdly self-indulgent, self-deluding behavior. But on the other hand, Suetonius, an ancient Roman historian who never heard a scurrilous rumor he was not eager to repeat, claims that after Nero's death people raised statues to him in the Forum, annually decked his grave with flowers, circulated his edicts, and even claimed that he was not dead but would someday reappear to reclaim his throne.

The Roman concept of leadership was essentially military, but Nero was no soldier and was unwilling to pose as one. His strange behavior may have been an attempt to establish a new kind of authority over Rome. An imperator was a general, a warrior who led by intimidating his subjects. Nero, a poet, may have embraced the romantic idea that an artist could lead by inspiring his followers. His education convinced him that Greek civilization set the standards to which Romans should aspire. He adopted Greek dress, promoted Greek customs, and tried to persuade the Roman mob to accept Greek athletic competitions in place of Roman gladiatorial combats. The more the Romans resisted his efforts to convert their tastes, the more extreme his behavior became.

In 64 C.E. Nero proved that he was capable of governing effectively. When news reached him that a fire had destroyed 10 of Rome's 14 city districts, he hastened to Rome to supervise relief efforts. He then drew up plans for rebuilding Rome on a grander scale and issued new construction codes to make it a safer city. He also confiscated a large tract of land at the eastern end of the Forum on which to build a new palace-garden complex, the Golden House. His enthusiasm for these projects prompted rumors that he had started the fire to clear the way for them. Fires often swept through crowded ancient cities, and Rome's fire was doubtless accidental. However, suspicion of arson fell on a band of Christians, followers of a new eastern religion that preached the imminent destruction of the world. In the midst of Rome's holocaust, some Christians had probably taken to the streets to celebrate the apparent fulfillment of their prophecies and urge last-minute conversions. Nero seized on this circumstantial evidence and made Rome's Christians scapegoats for the fire. It is important to note, however, that it was their alleged arson, not their faith, that led to their persecution and that only the small group of Christians in the city was affected. The Christian movement was not yet large enough to exert much influence on the course of Western history or attract much attention from the imperial government.

Nero's neglect of the army finally brought him down. In 68 C.E. the governor of one of the Gallic provinces organized a revolt that spread by fits and starts. Nero had no idea how to respond, and his confusion soon turned to panic. Assuming that all was lost, he ordered one of his servants to slit his throat.

The Flavian Dynasty Nero was the last of the Julio-Claudians. Rome had become dependent on an emperor, but because it had created no constitutional machinery to govern succession to its throne, it had no legal way to fill the power vacuum left by the extinction of its first dynasty. The crisis reignited the civil war, but Rome was lucky. Three generals won and lost the city in rapid succession, and the fourth, Vespasian (r. 69–79) restored order and established a new dynasty, the Flavian.

The Julio-Claudians were aristocrats of ancient lineage, but the Flavian family had a far less exalted equestrian background. The new emperor was a 60-year-old career soldier with a lifetime of command experience acquired from postings to every corner of the empire. He was a tough, pragmatic man who spoke plainly and cracked crude jokes. The trappings of power did not seduce him into taking himself too seriously. On his deathbed he mocked the Roman custom of deifying dead emperors by quipping, "I think I'm becoming a god!"

Vespasian helped the empire recover from the colorful excesses of the Julio-Claudians. He had used his army to seize power, but he was careful not to revive the soldiers' political aspirations. He broke up dangerous concentrations of troops and transferred men frequently so that they did not put down roots and develop greater loyalties to specific regions and commanders than to the empire. Augustus had envisioned an empire run by Italians, but Vespasian (and later rulers) bridged the gap between Italy and the provinces. He encouraged Romanization of the provinces, promoted provincials to the Senate, and added them to his administration. He established a budget for his government based on a census that estimated income from taxes. He funded the construction of roads, bridges, and public buildings throughout the empire and gave Rome a new temple to Jupiter on the Capitoline hill and its famous amphitheater, the 50,000-seat Colosseum.

Vespasian's successor was his elder son Titus (r. 79–81 C.E.), whom he had groomed for the responsibilities of the imperial office. Titus was a seasoned general. At the start

Ruins of Herculaneum   Pompeii is the most famous site devastated by the eruption of Vesuvius on August 24, 79 C.E., but it was not the only place that suffered that day. Pompeii was covered with ash, while the nearby coastal town of Herculaneum was inundated by volcanic mud. The mud hardened into stone, with the result that many of the more perishable materials, such as wood or other organic substances, that burned or rotted away at Pompeii have been preserved at Herculaneum. Excavation there is very difficult, but it has yielded such unexpected things as the contents of an ancient Roman library.

of his father's reign, he had put down a rebellion by Jews seeking independence for Judea. A triumphal arch at the eastern end of the Forum commemorates his victory and depicts the treasures the Romans sacked from Jerusalem's temple. Titus died before he could do much, but his reign was marked by a memorable event. In August of 79 C.E., Vesuvius, a volcano near Naples, erupted and (to the delight of generations of archaeologists and tourists) buried the towns of Pompeii and Herculaneum.

Titus's heir was his younger brother Domitian (r. 81–96 C.E.), an arrogant autocrat. The splendid residence he built on Rome's Palatine hill gave us the word *palace*. He lived in constant fear that plots were being hatched against him, and his wanton executions of suspects ensured that they were. Thanks to his wife's cooperation, one of these conspiracies finally succeeded.

Order and Continuity: The Elective Option

Domitian had no obvious heir, and his assassins had no candidate of their own whom they wished to see succeed him. Instead, they asked the Senate—Rome's most prestigious political assembly—to legitimate what they had done by appointing a new emperor. By now there was no question of reestablishing a true republic, and the Senate knew that if it did not act to fill the throne, the army would.

PEOPLE IN CONTEXT   The Imperial Aristocracy: Pliny the Elder and Pliny the Younger

The Roman Republic had belonged to the aristocratic families that monopolized its political offices, commanded its armies, confiscated its wealth, and charted its destiny. The empire diminished their power. Emperors utilized a few men of senatorial rank as advisors, provincial governors, heads of departments of state, and military officers, but they kept a close eye on them. Association with the court or a too successful military career could be dangerous for a man from a prominent family. Most of the blood shed by Rome's "bad" emperors was the blue blood of upperclass men who were suspected of plotting against the throne or who simply had fortunes their ruler wanted to confiscate. Given the risks of exposure, wealthy men often preferred the security of their country villas to life in Rome. Shut out from the world of politics, they devoted themselves to the safer pursuits of literature and to entertaining one another. Those who published took care not to write anything that might offend their emperor.

Prominent among the literary lights of the day were an uncle and a nephew, both named Pliny. The uncle, Pliny the Elder (c. 23–79 C.E.), was a close friend of Vespasian's, who found time in a busy military career to write poems, histories, and a huge encyclopedia of the ancient world's scientific and pseudoscientific lore. His passion for research led to his death. He was living near Pompeii when Vesuvius erupted. The temptation to view the mountain up close was simply too great, and he was killed by a surge of volcanic

The Ruins of Pompeii   Pliny the Younger has left us an eyewitness account of the eruption of Mount Vesuvius that buried the city of Pompeii in 79 C.E.

gas. His nephew, Pliny the Younger (c. 61–113 C.E.), has left us a description of the eruption and the circumstances of his uncle's death.

Pliny the Younger studied rhetoric with Quintillian (35–95 C.E.), the author of Rome's leading text on the art of oratory. By the age of 18 he was representing clients in Rome's courts. He did not follow his uncle into the military, but he held a few prestigious offices. He was briefly a consul (a largely empty honor by his day), and the emperor Trajan (r. 98–117 C.E.) appointed him governor of Bithynia, a province on the southwestern coast of the Black Sea.

Pliny was an enthusiastic correspondent who was proud of his literary style and who edited his letters for publication. He wrote to and about many important people, among whom was his emperor. An emperor's servant was well advised to show deference and proceed with caution, and Pliny took no chances. As governor of Bithynia, he referred every decision about which he had the least doubt to the emperor, for, as he explained to Trajan, who "could better guide my ignorance." If every Roman governor did likewise, Trajan's flow of paperwork must have been overwhelming. Among the issues that puzzled Pliny was what to do with some practitioners of a new religion called Christianity. His letters reveal how little the Roman authorities knew (or cared) about the faith that would one day transform Western civilization.

Question: How might a society's concern to maintain order affect the work of its artists and intellectuals?

The "Good Emperors"   Not surprisingly, the new emperor the Senate chose was one of its own, an elderly man named Nerva (r. 96–98 C.E.). Nerva knew that there was little chance that the army's generals would allow a senatorial appointee to deprive them of the opportunity to make a bid for the throne, but he had a strategy for ensuring his survival. Nerva had no children and at age 66 was not likely to produce any. So like Julius Caesar, he adopted an heir. In this case the choice was not a teenaged relative, but a 45-year-old man named Trajan. Trajan commanded the legions along the Rhine, and he was the general who was most likely to win should a battle for Rome break out. The adoption set a valuable precedent. From 96 to 180 C.E. no emperor had a son, so each was free to choose his own successor. All chose wisely, and the result was the longest period of consistently excellent rule that the empire enjoyed.

Trajan (r. 98–117 C.E.) was eager to expand the empire. He created a new province called Dacia north of the Danube—a Latin-speaking enclave that lay a cultural foundation for the modern nation of Romania. His other campaigns humbled Parthia; conquered Armenia, Assyria, and Mesopotamia; and brought the Roman Empire to its height (see Map 6–2).

Italy was the preferred recruiting ground for Trajan's legions, and his government implemented an ingenious program to boost its population. Italy's small farmers and artisans suffered as producers in the empire's western provinces began to compete with Italian products on the world market. To enable poorer Italians to raise more children, Trajan established the **alimenta**, an endowment that provided food and education for

Map 6–2 **The Pinnacle of the Roman Empire** Augustus conquered territory that he thought would provide the empire with defensible frontiers. Claudius added Britain, but the major and final additions to the empire were the work of Trajan. Hadrian, his successor, concluded that some of the land Trajan had won was too difficult to defend, and he relinquished it.

Question: What portions of Rome's frontier were most vulnerable to attack?

impoverished children of both sexes. The money came from interest that landowners paid on loans the government provided to help them improve their estates. Instead of handing out money, Rome funded its welfare program from investments that promoted economic growth.

Trajan was succeeded by a distant relative, Hadrian (r. 117–138 C.E.), who spent most of his reign away from Rome, touring the provinces and cultivating close ties with his troops. He was popular with his army even though he fought few wars. He concentrated on strengthening the empire's frontiers by retreating to defensible positions. Where terrain offered no help, he built elaborate fortifications (the largest of which was a 72-mile-long wall backed up by a string of forts that spanned northern Britain).

Hadrian was a multifaceted person, a soldier and athletic outdoorsman as well as an aesthete and a scholar. He reformed Roman law to reflect Stoic principles of justice and protect slaves from abuse. He reorganized the empire's administrative system and held its bureaucrats accountable to high standards. He had such a passion for Greek literature and art that he was nicknamed "the Greek." He studied architecture, experimented with novel designs, and lavished buildings on provincial cities. The only major ancient temple still standing in Rome is one of his: the Pantheon, a drum-shaped hall roofed by a dome 141 feet in diameter.

Hadrian's last years were spent wrestling with a painful illness, but he outlived the first man he chose as his heir. When he finally died in 138, he commended the empire to the care of a senatorial aristocrat known for his cultivation of the Roman virtues of dignity, sobriety, and simplicity: Antoninus Pius (r. 138–161 C.E.). Rome faced no wars or other crises throughout Antoninus's long reign, but the quiet was deceptive. Beyond the empire's northern frontiers, hostile German tribes were training in the use of Roman arms and tactics. Shortly after Antoninus passed the reins of government to his successor, Marcus Aurelius (r. 161–180 C.E.), the storm broke.

Marcus Aurelius was 17 when Hadrian arranged for Antoninus Pius to adopt him, but he did not inherit the throne until he was 40. He was serious-minded and drawn to the study of philosophy—particularly Stoicism. Over the period of a decade he composed a series of essays reflecting on life from the Stoic perspective. Collected into a book now entitled *Meditations*, they have been variously praised as exhortations to duty and self-discipline and condemned as the musings of an unrealistic dreamer and dilettante. But whatever their possible shortcomings as philosophy, as history, they provide modern readers their only opportunity to engage a Roman emperor through his own words.

Marcus Aurelius's Stoic detachment was severely tested, for his reign was a long series of crises: plagues, earthquakes, floods, famines, and wars. When he ascended the throne, he anticipated the practice of later emperors by sharing the imperial honor with a colleague, Lucius Verus. The long frontiers of the empire were threatened in the west by Germans and in the east by Parthians, and there was plenty of work for two emperors. Verus's army succeeded in stabilizing the eastern frontier, and in 166 he returned to Rome to celebrate a triumph. Unfortunately, among the spoils his men brought back to Rome was a plague that spread throughout the empire.

After Verus's death in 169 C.E., Marcus Aurelius ruled alone. He spent most of the remainder of his reign campaigning against the Germans on the Danube frontier. He was largely successful, but at the time of his death in Vindobona (Vienna) there was still work to be done. Unfortunately, responsibility for that task passed into incompetent hands.

Alone among the five men whom history remembers as the "Good Emperors," Marcus Aurelius sired a son, Commodus (r. 180–192 C.E.). He was the only male to survive from the 13 children the emperor and his wife Faustina had in 30 years of marriage. Commodus's defects may have been apparent to his father, but Roman traditions of family and the inheritance rights of sons were strong. An attempt to deny him the throne might well have invited a succession struggle and civil war. Commodus spent his reign in dissipation and may have descended into madness. When those around him began to fear for their lives, they assassinated him and, like Domitian's killers, asked the Senate to appoint his successor. This maneuver had inaugurated the era of the Good Emperors, but this time it did not work. The armies mutinied, and the empire was again torn by civil war.

Military Rule   The winner of the civil war was Septimius Severus (r. 193–211 C.E.), commander of the Danube legions. He restored order, but his methods augured poorly for Rome's future. He increased the army's size and nearly doubled its pay. His deathbed advice for his heirs was, "Enrich the troops, and despise everyone else."

The army may always have been the basis of an emperor's power, but it was dangerous for an emperor to acknowledge this too openly. Once the soldiers realized that they were in control, it was impossible to maintain their discipline. They killed the officers who tried to keep them in line and supported those who promised to do their bidding. Of the five emperors of the Severan dynasty, only one died of natural causes. The others were killed by their own men.

Following the murder of the last Severan emperor in 235, the army spun out of control. Over the next 50 years, approximately 25 men claimed the imperial title. They have been called the "**Barracks Emperors**," for most began their careers as common soldiers. The administration of the empire languished while military factions fought among themselves, and large blocks of territory in both the east and west seceded and

---

The Imperial Dynasties

JULIO-CLAUDIANS (31 B.C.E.–68 C.E.)

Octavian Augustus (31 B.C.E.–14 C.E.)
Tiberius (14–37 C.E.)
Caligula (37–41 C.E.)
Claudius (41–54 C.E.)
Nero (54–68 C.E.)
"The Year of the Four Emperors" (68–69 C.E.)

FLAVIANS (69–96 C.E.)

Vespasian (69–79 C.E.)
Titus (79–81 C.E.)
Domitian (81–96 C.E.)

"THE GOOD EMPERORS" (96–180 C.E.)

Nerva (96–98 C.E.)
Trajan (98–117 C.E.)
Hadrian (117–138 C.E.)
Antoninus Pius (138–161 C.E.)
Lucius Verus (161–169) & Marcus Aurelius (161–180 C.E.)
[Commodus (180–192 C.E.)]

SEVERANS (193–235)

Septimius Severus (193–211)
Caracalla (211–217)
[Macrinus (217–218)]
Elagabalus (218–222)
Alexander Severus (222–235)

"THE BARRACKS EMPERORS" (235–285)

set up governments of their own. From 267 to 272 the eastern rim of the Mediterranean from Asia Minor to Egypt was ruled by a woman, Zenobia, queen of the desert city of Palmyra.

Life in an Imperial Environment

Geography helped make Rome's empire, the ancient world's largest and most enduring, a viable entity. Although the empire's frontier was long, much of it needed minimal defense. The Atlantic Ocean protected the west, and the Sahara the south. There were wars with the Parthian Empire in the east, but most trouble on that front was stirred up by the Romans themselves. The frontier that needed the largest military investment was the northern line defined by the Rhine and Danube rivers. Communication, travel, and trade for the people who lived within these boundaries were facilitated by the empire's numerous rivers and its great central sea.

An Imperial Economy   Once the Romans secured the empire's frontiers, swept pirates from the Mediterranean, and began to spread urban institutions throughout their territory, the stage was set for the West's economy to thrive. The empire was abundantly supplied with natural resources. Most regions could provide themselves with fundamental necessities, but once secure trade routes were established, some districts began to specialize in what they could do best. Olive oil was exported from Spain, grain from North Africa and Egypt, and wine from Gaul and Greece. Metal ores were mined in Britain, Spain, Dacia, and Cyprus, and manufacturing centers sprang up in many places. Glass was shipped from Egypt and the Rhineland. A popular line of red-glazed pottery was mass produced in northern Italy. Textiles came from Asia Minor, and bronze work from Italy. Despite the success of some of these enterprises, shipping problems forced most industries to remain small and to produce for local markets. Water offered the only economical means for transporting goods. Wine brought from Gaul to Rome by sea (about 450 miles) was less expensive than wine carted to the city from Italian vineyards only 50 miles away.

The economies of inland districts lagged far behind those of regions on coasts and waterways, and the empire's overall economy began to show signs of weakness as early as the Flavian period. Romans imported large quantities of luxury goods from India and the Far East and paid for them with gold and silver. This drained bullion from the West, and as the productivity of its mines decreased, emperors were hard pressed to find the precious metals they needed to mint an adequate supply of coins. The empire's success in suppressing war also had an economic downside. It diminished the supply of cheap slaves, an important element in its workforce.

Social Developments   Romans were generous in freeing slaves, and many of Rome's citizens were freedmen and their descendants. This may have given some of them sympathy for slaves. Philosophers urged respect for the humanity of slaves, and some emperors passed laws to protect them. But ideals and laws were difficult to enforce.

The gap that steadily widened between rich and poor in the Roman world blurred the line between freedom and slavery. Many of the free poor became **coloni**, tenant farmers who took over the work of slaves on the *latifundia* (large estates) of the rich. Lack of opportunity made them a virtually captive workforce. Large numbers of the indigent and unemployed also flooded into the empire's major cities and eked out livings on the public dole.

The distinction between Italy and the provinces that Augustus wanted to maintain steadily eroded. By the end of the Julio-Claudian period, most of the old republican families were dying out and a new aristocracy, drawn increasingly from the provinces, was taking their place. The settlement of Roman veterans on the frontiers, their intermarriage with local women, and the acquisition of citizenship by non-Italians who served in the auxiliaries all helped to create a larger, more inclusive class of people who identified with the empire. In 212 the Severan emperor Caracalla granted citizenship to all the free residents of the empire. Stoic philosophers preached a doctrine of universal brotherhood, and Roman jurists posited the existence of a natural law that gave equal rights to all men. Roman law is one of the great legacies of the empire, for the principles of justice it articulated have had tremendous influence on the development of Western thinking about courts, the rights of accused people, and the proper use of evidence in determining guilt and innocence.

Although citizenship and legal rights were usually viewed from a male perspective, women were not passive pawns in Roman society. They were required to have guardians to handle their legal affairs, but this had already become a mere formality by the end of the republic. Aristocratic women had great power and influence, and despite Augustus's attempt to revive some version of the patriarchal family of the early republican period, women added to their rights. Romans had long regarded marriage as a private matter that did not involve the state. Tradition had established two kinds of marriage—one that transferred the bride entirely to her husband's *familia* and another that preserved her relationship with her father's household. The second kind of marriage made divorce easier, for the bride and her family retained more power over her dowry. By the beginning of the empire, it had become the standard form of marriage, and divorce and remarriage, at least in aristocratic circles, were common. Augustus believed that this contributed to the decline of the Roman family, and he tried to reverse it by increasing the state's power over marriages. Legal procedures were instituted for divorces, and adultery became a crime prosecuted by the state. A sexual double standard was accepted. Husbands had nothing to fear from the law so long as they did not debauch another man's wife or conspire in the misconduct of their own mate. Because men could safely conduct affairs with women who were licensed as prostitutes, some aristocratic women, who wished to continue their amorous dalliances in safety, got around the law by registering as prostitutes. Augustus's laws had little effect, and his successors made few attempts to legislate morality until the fourth century, when Christian emperors began to impose the moral principles of their faith on society.

Intellectual Life Virgil, Horace, Ovid, and Livy—Augustus's contemporaries—ended the dependence of Roman authors on Greek sources by providing them with

Latin models for the composition of poetry and prose. However, the growing power of Rome's emperors created an intellectual environment that prevented later authors from writing in the same spirit as the giants of the Golden Age. The *Romanitas* that inspired them was a vision of an idealized republican Rome, and this dream of liberty faded as the reality of life under autocratic emperors became clear. Scholars did not have to wait long for a warning about the danger of speaking too freely. Tiberius, Augustus's successor, convicted the author of a history of the civil wars of treason and burned his books. Elections and popular assemblies also lost much of their meaning during Tiberius's reign as the imperial bureaucracy took over more and more functions of government. This struck at the heart of Roman literary education—the study of rhetoric. Without opportunities to debate real issues and influence important decisions and elections, rhetoric became a pointless exercise. Students continued to be trained in the techniques of debate, but debate became not a means to an end but an end in itself. People wrangled over abstract hypothetical problems that had no connection with contemporary politics. As style came to be more important than substance, formal writing became increasingly elaborate, convoluted, and verbose.

Things temporarily improved when the scholarly Claudius took the throne and appointed the Stoic philosopher Seneca the Younger (c. 4 B.C.E.–65 C.E.) tutor to his heir, Nero. Literary activity revived and began what historians refer to as Rome's Silver Age. The empire produced many good writers, but none as influential as those whom Augustus had encouraged. Many of the new voices came from the provinces—a testimony to Rome's success in spreading Hellenistic civilization.

The first flush of the Silver Age was brief. During the course of his long literary career, Seneca produced plays, essays on Stoic philosophy, treatises dealing with ethical issues, and a book on natural science. Although he tried to tread carefully, his Stoic moralism needled the libertine Nero, and the emperor finally ordered him to commit suicide. Seneca's nephew, Lucan (39–65 C.E.), joined him in self-murder, leaving unfinished a passionately republican epic poem dealing with the war between Caesar and Pompey. Petronius (d. 66 C.E.), another of Nero's victims, wrote a novel, *The Satyricon*, from which only fragments survive. It wittily mocked the falsity, pretentiousness, and crass self-indulgence of wealthy Romans and their sycophants. Satire appealed to a generation of cynical, disillusioned artists. The *Epigrams* of Martial (c. 40–104 C.E.) commented ironically on a wide spectrum of Roman society, and the *Satires* of Juvenal (c. 55–130 C.E.) are as amusing as they are filled with anger and scorn.

Nero's sensitivity to criticism and paranoia suppressed literary activity, and conditions did not improve much under later emperors. The Flavians funded libraries and schools, but silenced philosophers of whose teachings they disapproved. A few historians thrived, however, despite the politically sensitive nature of their material. Tacitus (c. 55–120 C.E.) reflected on the empire from the hostile perspective of the senatorial aristocracy. His elegant prose is replete with pithy, memorable phrases that sum up (often pessimistic) insights into human character. Josephus (c. 37–95 C.E.), a Jewish author, wrote to provide the Romans (and his Flavian patrons) with background

The Roman Forum   The city of Rome acquired a number of forums, but the first and most famous was the swampy lowland beside the Palatine hill that the Etruscan kings drained. Over the years it filled with temples, public buildings, and monuments. This view is from the western end looking east to the Arch of Titus. The forum reverted to swamp and pastureland during the Middle Ages, and its buried ruins were not completely excavated until the twentieth century.

on his people. Biblical scholars have found his work an invaluable source of information on the period between the testaments and the environment into which Jesus of Nazareth was born. Suetonius (c. 69–135 C.E.), the most colorful of the era's historians, wrote biographies of Rome's rulers from Julius Caesar to Domitian. He relied heavily on amusing tales and titillating gossip. Plutarch (c. 45–120 C.E.), a Greek author, produced a large set of biographies in which he compared Greek and Roman leaders whom he thought had similar careers. His work is as accurate, or inaccurate, as the literary sources on which he relied, and it reflects the belief of his age that the purpose of history was to provide lessons in morality.

The Decline of Rome

A famous historian has said that the question that should be asked about the Roman Empire is not why it fell, but how it managed to last as long as it did. His point is that the empire was inherently fragile, and to speak of its fall may be misleading. It did not come to a sudden end, and no single thing brought it crashing down. The way of life that Rome represented was incrementally transformed until the world had changed so much that it no longer made sense to call it Roman. The western provinces of the empire were economically weaker, less populous, less urbanized, and more exposed to invasion than the eastern, and by the fifth century the empire was fast becoming for them more a memory than a reality. But a region of vacillating size in the eastern Mediterranean continued to be ruled by a line of Roman emperors for another thousand years.

Rome's Weakness   Like most ancient societies, the Roman Empire's resources barely sufficed to meet its routine needs, and crises caused by invasions, civil wars, plagues, or crop failures could push it to the brink of collapse. Rome's longevity owed much to the absence of a major foreign enemy who might have taken advantage of the empire's internal problems. Parthia was the only civilized state with which Rome shared a border, and it seldom posed a threat. Rome's most vulnerable front was its 1,500-mile-long Rhine–Danube frontier. Occasional localized campaigns were enough to hold this line until the third century, when the German tribes began to consolidate and adopt Roman military practices.

The Roman Empire was handicapped by the ancient world's failure to make more technological progress. The empire was an agrarian state supported by fairly primitive methods of cultivation. Some plantations and manufacturing industries produced products for the world market, but waterways provided the only cost-efficient transportation. The residents of coastal districts and regions near navigable rivers could trade profitably, but people who lived inland had to be self-sufficient. Wheat brought by sea from Egypt and southern Gaul, for instance, sold more cheaply in Rome than did Italian grain raised 50 miles from the city.

Some of the empire's trade depressed its economy. Romans had an appetite for luxury goods from the Far East, but the West produced little that India and China could not provide for themselves. The West, therefore, had to pay with gold and silver for the silks and spices it imported. The bullion this drained from the empire undermined its monetary system. By the second century, the West's mines were being worked out, and gold and silver from which to mint coins were becoming scarce. Emperors stretched the shrinking money supply by debasing coins (that is, by mixing gold and silver with cheaper metals), but this backfired. Because these coins had less innate value, sellers demanded more of them for their goods. Prices rose, and the empire faced the problem of inflation. Overall, the costs of administering and defending the Roman Empire steadily increased, while the economy that sustained the empire declined.

From a modern perspective, the ancient world's failure to grow its economy may appear perplexing. Hellenistic scholars made scientific breakthroughs that, if they had been exploited, could have transformed the ancient way of life. Physicists worked out the principles of levers, gears, and pulleys, and they built working models of steam turbines. Some slave-staffed businesses utilized assembly-line techniques. The Romans possessed key ingredients for an industrial revolution, but somehow they never put them together. Slavery and an aristocratic intelligentsia preoccupied with literary and philosophical pursuits probably contributed to the absence of any motivation to find ways to make work easier and more productive.

Diocletian and the *Dominate*   The rapid turnover of leaders during the half century (235–285) when the Barracks Emperors squabbled over the throne created such confusion that Rome's imperial government lost control of huge stretches of territory. But the last of the Barracks Emperors, Diocletian (r. 285–305), restored the empire's unity and stability. His policies preserved the empire for another century, but at the cost of many aspects of its traditional way of life. Augustus's title of *princeps* ("first citizen") acknowledged his commitment to civilian government. But Diocletian was called *dominus* ("lord"). He ruled as a divine king over the **dominate,** a system of government ruled with the power of a military autocrat.

Diocletian's first priority was to secure the person of the emperor, for the empire could not function if its leaders continued to be frequently overthrown. To reduce the number of potential competitors for the imperial office, Diocletian divided and dispersed political authority. He doubled the number of the empire's provinces and gave each both a civilian and a military governor. This greatly diminished the strength of the provincial commanders, but at the cost of quadrupling the size of the imperial bureaucracy.

It was too dangerous to divide the army, so Diocletian consolidated an elite, mobile force under his direct command and settled a class of militarized peasants along the empire's frontiers. These farmer-soldiers were supposed to fend off attacks on their home districts long enough for the emperor to bring up the main army and restore order. Generous pay and preferential treatment (such as special legal privileges and exemption from taxes) ensured the loyalty of the emperor's troops, his *comitatenses* ("companions"). Diocletian may have had half a million men under arms, and their maintenance imposed a tremendous burden on his treasury.

Similarly costly was Diocletian's court. A *dominus* ruled by intimidation—by projecting an aura of awe-inspiring majesty. He was a remote being insulated from contact with his subjects by court functionaries and elaborate protocols. When he appeared in public, he wore elaborate robes, jewels, and the golden diadem of the sun-god.

Diocletian concluded that one emperor was not enough to defend Rome's frontier, and he shared the empire with a colleague named Maximian (286–305). He stationed himself in Asia Minor to watch the Parthian and lower Danube borders, and Maximian established a base in northern Italy from which to guard the upper Danube and the Rhine.

Having no son to inherit his throne, Diocletian tried to revive the practice of adopting successors that had worked so well throughout the second century. He decreed that each "augustus" (the emperor's title) was to choose a "caesar" (a second-in-command) to assist him, and at the end of a 20-year term, the augustus was to retire and the caesar ascend to his office. This tetrarchy ("four-man rule") gave four powerful men a vested interest in working together and it promised an orderly transmission of power to experienced, competent successors (see Map 6–3).

North
Sea

Baltic
Sea

Prefecture
of
Gaul

Prefecture
of
Italy

Prefecture
of
Illyricum

Prefecture
of
the East

BRITANNIA

Rhine R.

GERMANIA

BELGICA
Trier

LUGDUNENSIS

SEQUANIA

RHAETIA

NORICUM

PANNONIA
SUPERIOR

AQUITANIA

Milan VENETIA
HISTRIA

PANNONIA
INFERIOR

Sirmium

SCYTHIA

Danube R.

500 MILES
500 KILOMETERS

NARBONENSIS

TUSCIA

FLAMINIA

Ravenna DALMATIA

Salonae

PRAEVALITANA

MOESIA
SUPERIOR

MOESIA
INFERIOR

Black Sea

TARRACO-
NENSIS

UMBRIA

PICENUM

Rome CAMPANIA

CORSICA

SAMNIUM

APULIA

CALABRIA

DACIA

DARDANIA

MACEDONIA

RHODOPE

THRACIA

BYZANTIUM

Constantinople

EUROPA

PAPHLAGONIA

Nicomedia PONTUS

BALEARES

SARDINIA

LUCANIA

EPIRUS

THESSALIA

ASIA

BITHYNIA

PHRYGIA

GALATIA

ARMENIA
MINOR

SICILY

ACHAIA

INSULAE

LYDIA

CARIA

PISIDIA

LYCIA PAMPHYLIA

CAPPADOCIA

CILICIA

NUMIDIA

Mediterranean

CRETE

CYPRUS

COELE-
SYRIA

MAURETANIA

TRIPOLITANIA

Sea

PHOENICIA

300 MILES

300 KILOMETERS

N

LIBYA

AEGYPTUS

PALESTINE

ARABIA

Map 6–3   The Divisions of the Late Roman Empire   Diocletian's creation of separate governments for the eastern and western halves of the Roman Empire forecast a division that became permanent.

Question: Why were all the empire's administrative centers (Trier, Milan, Sirmium, and Nicomedia) on its northern rim rather than in a central location?

The Transformation of Roman Society
Government policies often have unintended consequences. Diocletian's innovations certainly did, for they all increased Rome's economic difficulties. Diocletian quadrupled the size of the empire's bureaucracy, built a larger and more expensive army, and established four imperial courts. Rome could not afford the burdens this imposed, for its simple agrarian economy may have required the labor of six farmers to support each soldier, bureaucrat, and court functionary who did not till the soil.

Diocletian tried to deal with this problem by careful budgeting. He conducted censuses at five-year intervals to estimate the wealth of the empire and set tax rates. He debased the coinage to increase the money supply and encourage economic activity. He tried to halt the inflation that resulted by issuing an Edict of Prices, which decreed what could legally be charged for about a thousand items and services. All this did, however, was to force goods onto a black market that the government could not regulate.

Diocletian was finally driven to confiscate the property of his subjects to meet the expenses of his government, and this transformed the empire's social structure. Its wealthier citizens fled its cities, where they were too exposed to its tax collectors, and took up permanent residence on their rural estates. It was impossible for the government to track them all down, and to do so could be dangerous for tax collectors. This migration had a devastating impact on the empire's cultural institutions, for urban life was the dynamo that powered classical civilization. Without their rich and powerful citizens, cities went rapidly downhill.

Lesser individuals had fewer options for protecting their resources than the wealthy. When government confiscations bit into the working capital of farmers and artisans, they had little choice but to abandon their fields, close their shops, and resort to banditry or go on the public dole. Each year the number of productive individuals declined. This increased the burden on those who remained and drove yet more people out of business. The state tried to maintain production of essential goods by taking over industries and conscripting laborers to work on state plantations. To maintain the workforce, men were required to teach their trades to their sons, and sons were forced to take up their father's professions. What had been, theoretically at least, a free society became a caste system. As masses of peasants (*coloni*) were bound to the lands they worked for the state and wealthy aristocrats, the empire began to break up into quasi-independent rural fiefdoms.

KEY QUESTION | Revisited

The Romans often faced the unhappy choice between freedom and order. Theirs was never a democratic, egalitarian society in which everyone enjoyed the same liberties, but they honored ideals of citizenship and patriotism. These ideals have had a positive influence on the development of Western nations, but Roman history also illustrates what happens to such values when societies are under stress or delivered into the hands of unscrupulous or inept leaders. The insecurity of life in Rome's turbulent republic induced its citizens to submit to a powerful imperial government. For a long time, that government maintained stability and prosperity, and the majority of its subjects may have been content with the balance it struck between freedom and order. It is important to realize that its eventual decline into oppressive autocracy was neither inevitable nor accidental. It was the outcome of decisions that the Romans convinced themselves they were compelled to make.

Review Questions

1. Why was the Roman Republic unable to govern an empire?
3. Did Augustus save the Roman Republic or destroy it?
3. How did relationships between the military and the civilian elements in society change during the era of the empire?
4. Why might residents of the provinces and ordinary Romans have disagreed with the Roman Senate on which of Rome's emperors were good and which bad?
5. Could the Roman Empire have been saved?
6. Is government by the people a luxury that only relatively secure societies can afford?

Please consult the Suggested Readings at the back of the book to continue your study of the material covered in this chapter. For a list of documents on the Primary Source DVD-ROM that relate to topics in this chapter, please refer to the back of the book.

Part 3
The Division of the West 300 to 1300

Muslims and Christians playing chess, ca. 1300, Mallorca, Spain.

During the ancient phase in the history of the West, the peoples whose homelands encircled the Mediterranean shared cultural influences and grew closer together, and for several centuries the whole of the Western civilized world was united under one government: the Roman Empire. There were significant differences among the subjects of that empire. They spoke a variety of languages, practiced numerous religions, and preserved some ethnic distinctions, but at least for the governing classes, the things they shared were more important than the things that divided them. The Mediterranean Sea lay at the center of "a world" that was politically unified, economically interconnected, and intellectually in agreement.

The decline of Rome's empire was more than the end of a political system, for it inaugurated an epoch in Western history in which the ancient trend toward unification reversed. The Mediterranean ceased to tie civilized peoples together, and the West divided against itself. During the ensuing Middle Ages, three distinct civilizations appeared: Latin Catholic Europe, Greek Orthodox Byzantium, and the Arab-Persian Muslim empire. Although all three shared common legacies from the ancient world, they were more alert to their differences than to their similarities. The defensiveness, misunderstanding, and hostility that came to characterize their relationships have yet to be overcome.

	ENVIRONMENT AND TECHNOLOGY	SOCIETY AND CULTURE	POLITICS
c. 300	Urban decay *Coloni* Two-field cultivation	Christian persecution Edict of Toleration (311) Council of Nicaea (325) Monastic movement begins Christianity mandated (395)	Diocletian: the Dominate (305) Constantine (306–337) Visigoths at Adrianople (378) Roman Empire divided
c. 400	Heavy, wheeled plows	Augustine (354–430)	Sack of Rome (410) Rhine frontier (406) Attila the Hun (d. 454) Romulus Augustulus (476)
c. 500		*Comitatus* Benedictine Rule (ca. 529)	German kingdoms Clovis (d. 511) fds. the Merovingian dynasty
	Hagia Sophia	Byzantine civilization	Justinian (d. 565)
c. 600			Muhammad (570–632)
		Islam and the *umma* (622) Shi'ite Islam (660)	Caliphate (est. 632) Umayyad dynasty (660–750)
c. 700			Isaurian dynasty (fd. 717) Charles Martel (d. 741) Abbasid dynasty (fd. 750) Carolingians (fd. 751)
	Stirrup and heavy cavalry Mold board plow	*Capitularies*	Charlemagne (768–814)
c. 800	Three-field cultivation system	Carolingian Renaissance	
	Minuscule Byzantine *theme*	Feudalism Manorialism	Viking–Magyar invasions Macedonian dynasty (fd. 867)
c. 900			Fatimid caliphate (fd. 909)
	Horseshoe	Ottonian Renaissance Cluniac Reform (910)	Saxon dynasty (fd. 919) Capetian dynasty (fd. 987)
c. 1000	Capitalism		Spanish crusade begins
		Towns and trade revive	Salian dynasty (fd. 1024) Seljuk sultanate (fd. 1060) William the Conqueror
		Investiture Controversy (1075)	Battle of Manzikert (1071) Kingdom of Sicily (fd. 1092) I Crusade (1095–1099)
c. 1100		Twelfth-Century Renaissance Peter Abelard (1079–1142)	II Crusade (1144) Hohenstaufen dynasty Henry II (1154–1189)
	Scholastic method Romanesque architecture Gothic architecture	University of Bologna (1158)	III Crusade (1189–1192) Philip Augustus (1180–1223) Innocent III (1198–1216)
c. 1200		University of Paris (1200) troubadour lyric, romance	IV Crusade (1204) *Magna Carta* (1215)

Topics in This Chapter

The Christian Element • The German Element

• The Byzantine Empire of Constantinople • Islam

7 The West's Medieval Civilizations

We were sentenced to be thrown to the beasts, and we returned rejoicing to prison. . . .
A few days later the prison warden realized that we had a great power within us, and he
began to treat us with respect.

—**Vibia Perpetua,** *Memoir*

For all the differences that exist among the world's many peoples . . . there are only two
kinds of societies, which . . . we have accurately characterized as two "cities." One is
the "city of men," inhabited by people who are governed by the appetites of the flesh.
The other is [the city of God], composed of people who live according to the spirit.
Each of these communities decides what will make it happy, and when each gets what
it wants, it lives with the consequences of its choice.

—**Augustine of Hippo,** *The City of God*

KEY | Question
Should freedom of religion be limited?

Religion is often a major contributor to the shared identity that defines a people as a people.
But for this reason it also divides the human community—inspiring controversy, persecution,
and warfare. The ancient world had not had to wrestle much with the divisive potential of religion, for the pagan gods were not jealous. Their polytheistic worshipers welcomed new deities
to the pantheon as they became aware of them. With the spread of monotheistic faiths, such
as Christianity and Islam, however, the situation changed. Early Christians like Vibia Perpetua,
a 22-year-old Roman matron who dictated a memoir shortly before her martyrdom in 203,

Emperor Constantine This bust of the Roman emperor Constantine may be a fragment from a gigantic statue that was raised in Rome during his lifetime to commemorate a battle that won him control of the western Roman Empire.

believed that they alone had the truth. They willingly courted death in the confidence that their sacrifice would be rewarded and vindicated by a higher power. There was, they believed, no room for compromise in matters of faith. Certain of her righteousness, Vibia almost eagerly abandoned a new-born son; turned a deaf ear to the desperate pleas of her aged, loving father; and spurned the traditions and institutions of her people.

By the time that Augustine (354–430), bishop of the North African city of Hippo, was born a century and a half later, Christianity was no longer a religion of martyrs. It had become the state religion and had begun to persecute its pagan predecessors. In this changing world, faith was assumed to require hard choices between clear alternatives. Augustine did not become a Christian until midlife, and he wrestled with the decision to convert for a long time. To be true to the Christian faith, he felt that he had to give up his flourishing secular career, break off a socially advantageous engagement to marry, separate from a mistress with whom he had lived for years and by whom he had a son, take a vow of celibacy, and embrace a life of ascetic self-denial. Halfway measures would not do, for Augustine believed that people had to decide whether their allegiances lay with the "city of God" or the "city of man." There was no middle ground. Those who trusted in Christian revelation were destined for eternal life in communion with God. Unbelievers were damned beyond hope of redemption. These two groups mingled on Earth, but ultimately God would sort them out—and the consequences would be eternal.

The Roman Empire unified the West and held it together for about three centuries. But as the empire came apart, three new civilizations, whose identities were largely shaped by religion, staked claims to Rome's territorial and cultural legacies: Latin Christian Europe, Greek Christian Byzantium, and an Arab-Islamic empire that extended from Spain across North Africa and the Middle East to India. Each of these civilizations championed different (if related) faiths, and their respective religions profoundly influenced their internal politics and their foreign relations.

The pagans of the ancient world were generally predisposed to religious tolerance, for they believed that divinity was a multifaceted reality that manifested itself in many ways. As polytheists, they were open to the discovery and veneration of new gods. Their governments might go to war to win control of shrines and their treasures, or they might outlaw cults that inspired what they viewed as immoral or treasonous behavior. But they did not usually regard religion as a source of contention. This changed as the West entered the Middle Ages (the fifth through fifteenth centuries), for the religions to which the three medieval civilizations were committed were monotheistic faiths. The exclusive allegiance that each demanded to its own understanding of God created the potential for disagreements that escalated into bloody conflicts. Given that religion can divide a people as well as unite them, how should societies handle it?

The Christian Element

The steps that Diocletian took to save the Roman Empire changed it so much that it is reasonable to wonder if the empire he saved was still Roman. Its government was headed by a god-king and staffed by soldiers. Barter began to replace the use of money in its economic transactions. Many of its cities were declining. In some regions, powerful landlords were carving out quasi-independent domains, and people everywhere were being subjected to the restraints of a rigid caste system. Most of this was probably unintentional, for Diocletian did not set out to separate Rome from its past. However, his successor, Constantine (312–337), struck a purposeful blow at the roots of classical civilization by shifting his allegiance from paganism to Christianity.

The Origin of the Christian Faith   Jesus of Nazareth, arguably the most influential individual in Western history, lived and died virtually unnoticed by his contemporaries. His brief career as the leader of a small band of Jewish disciples ended when he was crucified in Jerusalem during the reign of Emperor Tiberius. After his death, some of his acquaintances claimed that he had risen from the grave and that he was the **messiah** (or, in Greek, "the Christ," "the anointed"), a savior whose appearance the Jews had been anticipating. Their proclamation of this *gospel* ("good news") was not met with instant success. As late as the fourth century, when Emperor Constantine legalized Christianity, scholars estimate that only 5% (or perhaps as few as 1%) of his subjects were Christians.

Jesus never strayed far from Galilee, a rural district north of Jerusalem that was populated by conservative Jewish peasants. Nothing is known about his activities until, at about the age of 30, he began to wander about Galilee, preaching and healing. He continued this work for one to three years before going to Jerusalem to die on a Roman cross.

Jesus' history remains elusive. He wrote nothing, and no firsthand reports of his activities have come down to us. The oldest Christian writings are the letters of Paul (the former Saul of Tarsus) that form part of the New Testament, the Christian scriptures. Paul was a Jew from Asia Minor who came to Jerusalem sometime after Jesus' crucifixion. He never met Jesus personally, but was converted to faith in Christ by a mystical experience. He could have learned much about Jesus' earthly ministry from people who had been Jesus' companions, but this apparently did not interest Paul. His letters focus on the resurrected Christ, not the historical Jesus. The major sources of information about Jesus' life are the New Testament's four Gospels: Matthew, Mark, Luke, and John. They were written between 30 and 65 years after Jesus' death, and none of their authors claims to have been an eyewitness of the events he narrates. The Gospels were testimonials of faith, not objective histories. They were written, as the Gospel of John (20:31) says, to persuade those who read them to believe that Jesus is the Christ.

Jesus and his disciples were all Jews, and Jesus is never said to have sanctioned a break with Judaism. His brother James, the head of the Christian community in Jerusalem, was well known for his scrupulous observation of Jewish religious law. As Jews, the first Christians seem to have assumed that gentiles (non-Jews) who wished to join their community ("the **church**," from Greek for "lord's house") would convert to Judaism. If gentile Christians did not become Jews, Jewish Christians could not associate with them without transgressing Jewish religious law. Paul, although he too was a Jew, saw things differently. He condemned any effort to impose Judaism on the church's gentile converts, and his position ultimately prevailed.

Although missionaries like Paul believed that the messiah's appearance meant that the era governed by Jewish religious law had come to an end, they clung to the Hebrew scriptures. The witness of this "Old Testament," as Christians began to call it, was needed to understand the Christ, for the messiah was the fulfillment of the promise God had made to Abraham. God had said that Abraham's descendants would someday become a great nation. For generations the Jews had assumed that this meant that they would acquire land and political power. However, by the second century B.C.E. their expectations had changed. They concluded that on their own they were too few and weak ever to triumph over the great gentile empires. God, therefore, would fulfill His promise by intervening in history on their behalf. He would send them a messiah, an agent who was commissioned (anointed) to act with His authority. Some Jews expected the messiah to resemble the prophets, kings, or priests who had led them in the past. Others claimed that he would be an angel, a supernatural manifestation of God's power. No one anticipated a messiah like Jesus—a humble laborer who was crucified as a common criminal and whose passing left the world apparently unchanged.

Many Jews were shocked by the Christian claim that the transcendent and majestic deity of their faith had incarnated His power in a man like Jesus. Gentiles, on the other hand, were less likely to find this implausible. Pagan religious mythology was full of stories of gods who appeared as all-too-human men and women—and of human beings who became gods. Jesus' crucifixion was, in Paul's words, a "stumbling block" to the faith of both Jew and gentile. However, all things considered, conversion may have been easier for gentiles than for Jews.

The Church's Reception   As the first century C.E. unfolded, Judaism and Christianity grew further and further apart. Jewish leaders condemned Christianity as a distorted version of their faith, and the political situation in Palestine made Christians eager to distinguish themselves from Jews. Palestine was restive under Roman control, and a radical Jewish faction, the Zealots, incited riots against the Roman authorities. (The Romans may have executed Jesus on the assumption that he was a Zealot.) Full-scale war finally broke out in 66 C.E. It took Rome seven years to suppress the Jewish revolt, and in the process Jerusalem was stormed and its temple destroyed. Given these circumstances, Christians were eager to assure the Roman authorities that they were on the empire's side in the conflict. The Gospels were written in this context, and that may explain their eagerness to place as much responsibility as possible for Jesus' crucifixion on the Jews and to shift it from the Romans who actually carried it out.

Rome's objectives in the Jewish conflict were political, not theological, for the Roman practice was to adopt religions rather than suppress them. Romans worshiped simultaneously on multiple levels. The state honored numerous gods: classical mythology's Greco-Roman Olympians, foreign deities such as Asia Minor's Magna Mater and Egypt's Serapis and Isis, and, of course, the emperors themselves. Countless localities had sacred caves, groves, and springs. Families maintained household shrines for their own private guardian spirits, and many individuals were devotees of mystery cults. A mystery cult was a secret society that initiated its members. Its doctrines and rituals were inspired by the story of a divine savior who defeated the forces of evil and opened the way for human beings to obtain personal immortality. These cults sometimes required converts to be baptized before admitting them to the key ritual: a shared meal that united worshipers with one another and their god.

Christianity's resemblance to the popular mystery cults doubtless helped it to grow, but it also had unique features that gave it advantages over these competitors. Its savior was not a fantastic being from a mythic past, but a real man from recent history. It accorded women and slaves the same spiritual standing as free men, and its conviction that the appearance of the Messiah heralded the imminent end of the world motivated it to proselytize with unusual zeal. The chief source of the young religion's friction with Roman society was its commitment to Hebrew monotheism—its insistence that its God was the only god.

Pagans feared that Christian blasphemy against the gods would anger the gods and prompt them to punish everyone. If a disaster occurred, the people affected might spontaneously rise up and attack their Christian neighbors. But there was no empire-wide effort to eradicate Christianity until the reign of Decius (r. 249–251), one of the Barracks Emperors. Decius was fighting to save an empire that was on the verge of collapse, and he had no patience with disloyalty. Christians incited suspicion because they refused to perform a simple patriotic ritual—the sacrifice of a pinch of incense before the statue of the emperor. Their apocalyptic preaching, which maintained that the world (including Decius's empire) was soon to come to an end, also did little to assure the emperor that they supported his efforts to save civilization.

Some Christians may have courted persecution, for **martyrs** were honored as heroes of faith whose salvation was assured. The earliest account of a Christian martyrdom is a description of the death by burning of Polycarp of Smyrna (c. 69–155), a bishop who was said to have been a disciple of Jesus' apostle John. It says that his followers recovered his charred bones and treated them like precious jewels. The medieval church vigorously promoted this kind of piety, and the veneration of relics—of anything that had been associated with a martyr or saint—became a staple of Christian worship. People made arduous pilgrimages to visit places where relics were enshrined, for these sacred objects were believed to work miracles.

The Church's Organization

Persecution of the church was counterproductive. The willingness of Christian martyrs ("witnesses") to go to their deaths rather than compromise their allegiance to their deity made the strongest possible argument for the uniqueness and power of Christian faith. The threat of persecution also weeded out the weak, recruited the strong, and forced Christian communities to organize and work together.

Many religions fragment as they spread, but Christian congregations resisted this tendency. An increasing threat of persecution encouraged them to work together, but so did a sense of mission that was part of their faith from its beginning. Early Christians believed that the messiah's appearance meant that the end of the world was near. Christ would soon come again, and every human being would face God's final judgment. Christians believed that God, in His mercy, was granting them a brief period in which to take this message to the world. The urgency of the situation forced them to invest their limited time where it promised to do the most good. They ignored the people who were scattered thinly across the countryside and focused their attention on those who clustered in cities. Consequently, Christianity became an urban religion, and paganism, the religion of pagani ("rural villagers"), lingered for a long time in the countryside.

As Christianity spread, the organization of the church began to mirror that of the empire. The empire was divided into territorial units centered on cities. The Christian missionaries who worked in these cities created ties among them. When a church in one town sponsored a mission to another, it forged an enduring link between them.

Gradually, a network of such ties spread across the empire. It had no center, but it could diffuse information and financial aid widely. As the number of congregations grew in a town, a **bishop** (*episcopus*, "overseer") would be elected to coordinate their work. Bishops of neighboring communities corresponded and occasionally convened meetings (synods or councils) to discuss doctrinal and disciplinary issues. This helped create and maintain some consistency of faith and practice. Inevitably, the bishops of the larger and more important towns came to dominate their lesser brethren, and an administrative hierarchy began to evolve. No single bishop was ever recognized as the head of the whole church, but one had a unique claim to distinction. Peter, the chief of Jesus' disciples, was said to have been Rome's first bishop and to have been martyred in Rome. In the Gospel of Matthew (16:18–19) Jesus calls Peter "the rock" on which the church is founded and promises that whatever Peter does on Earth will be ratified in heaven. Rome's bishops insisted that, as Peter's successors, his status passed to them, but it was a long time before they could lay exclusive claim to the title pope (*papa*, an affectionate word for a father) or any other privilege.

Constantine and Imperial Christianity   Diocletian launched the empire's most concerted attack on the church. However, his successor, Constantine (r. 312–337), reversed course, embraced Christianity, and encouraged the process of converting the empire. Constantine was not supposed to be Diocletian's successor. He became emperor by the tried and true method of persuading a portion of the army to help him eliminate other candidates for the office. Early Christian historians claim that he was converted by a vision on the eve of the battle that won him control of the western half of the Roman Empire. His faith was doubtless sincere, but it was also politically motivated. Persecution had been a conspicuous failure, and Constantine thought that the shaky empire might gain more by winning the church over than by continuing to oppose it. He did not go so far as to declare Christianity the empire's sole religion, but his policies made his intentions clear. He poured money into the construction of great basilicas, welcomed bishops into councils of state, and gave favorable treatment to Christians in the imperial bureaucracy. After he won control of the whole empire, he took a dramatic step that indicated his expectations for the empire's religious future. He moved its capital east to a new city called Constantinople, which was modeled after Rome. However, where Rome had pagan temples, Constantinople had Christian churches.

The church benefited greatly from Constantine's patronage, but it did not do as much to shore up the empire as he might have hoped. Once the threat of persecution was removed and church offices became stepping stones to wealth and power, Christians began to fight among themselves. The young faith had yet to resolve many theological questions, and now that it was safe for Christians to air their differences, fissures widened in the Christian community. Factions accused one another of promulgating heresy (false teaching), and each claimed that, as the sole arbiter of orthodoxy (correct belief), it ought to lead the church. Mobs took up the cause of one party against another, and religiously inspired violence erupted on the streets of Roman cities.

Constantine's first impulse was to use the power of the state to resolve theological disputes, but his experience with the Donatists, a group of North African Christians

The Arch of Constantine   By Constantine's day Rome had not been the administrative capital of the empire for decades. The seats of imperial government had moved to places that had better communications with chronic trouble spots. However, Rome still had enough importance as a symbol of the empire that emperors continued to adorn it with monuments. Constantine followed the tradition of erecting an arch to celebrate his victory over his competitors for the throne, but his monument suggests that the glory of the ancient world was fading. Its best components were looted from earlier buildings, and its new elements are of inferior quality.

who had withstood Diocletian's persecution, taught him that this was unwise. The Donatists claimed that priests who had yielded to Diocletian's demands had forfeited the power to perform valid sacraments (the sacred rites that imparted God's grace to believers). The only valid priests who remained, therefore, were the Donatists' own. Their opponents disagreed, for, as they saw it, a priest's powers derived from his office, not from his personal merit as a Christian. A sinful priest could forgive other sinners their sins, for a priest did not act on his own authority. He was an agent of the church and therefore of God. Constantine's judges accepted this argument and ordered the Donatists to stop making trouble. The Donatists, however, refused and rejoiced that the state was again giving them the opportunity to validate their faith through martyrdom. Constantine's efforts to heal the split within the African Christian community had only made things worse.

When an Egyptian priest named Arius (c. 250–336) initiated a furious debate over the relationship between Christ the Son and God the Father, Constantine was ready with a different strategy. At issue was whether the Son was the Father's equal or His first creation—a subordinate agent through whom the Father had created the world. Constantine decided to force the church to take responsibility for working this out for itself. In 325 he invited all the bishops of the empire to a council in the city of Nicaea (near Constantinople) and ordered them to resolve the dispute. The bishops hoped to unify the church by providing it with a creed (a statement of essential beliefs) that all Christians could profess. The council ratified a creed, but it failed to bring the warring factions together. Each group interpreted the creed as affirming its position, and the squabbling continued. The exasperated emperor finally resorted to force and even tried switching from one side of the argument to the other, but the Arian debate raged on and spawned other doctrinal controversies.

The church did not unify Rome's crumbling empire, but it rescued much from the empire's decline. The eastern half of the empire survived longer than the western half, and Constantinople's powerful emperors treated the eastern church much like a department of state. The situation was different in Rome's western provinces, where fading imperial governments thrust freedom and responsibility onto the church. Each Roman city had a secular administration staffed by civil magistrates and an ecclesiastical administration headed by a Christian bishop. But as the empire declined in the west, the agents of secular government disappeared. Christian bishops, who were supported by the church's endowments, were the only public officials left in many cities. People inevitably looked to them for leadership. Cities came under the control of bishops, and they labored to preserve some of the administrative machinery of the former Roman state. When new kingdoms eventually began to rise from the ruins of the western empire, their rulers turned to the church's bishops for help in organizing them.

The church that bishops led served "the world"—the realm where men and women raised families and struggled to survive. As the empire declined, however, a kind of church within the church sprang up. It was populated by religious ascetics who wanted nothing to do with the worldly concerns of ordinary people. They believed that by disciplining their flesh, they could strengthen their spirits and draw closer to God. This was not exclusively a Christian impulse. The secular philosophies of the era also tended to be world-denying, and the speed with which the ascetic movement spread suggests that it matched the mood of the age.

The church's first ascetics were hermits—people who fled human company to live alone in remote, desolate places. This idea seems to have struck fire first in Egypt, and a biography of an Egyptian hermit named Anthony (c. 250–355) helped to publicize it. Religious asceticism spread rapidly through the eastern empire, but was somewhat slower to find a foothold in the west. It soon became so popular, however, that large numbers of hermits began to cluster in some places. They were often drawn by the fame of a holy man (like Anthony) from whom they hoped to receive spiritual counseling. Practical concerns forced these spontaneous gatherings to organize themselves, and they evolved into institutions called monasteries—communities of **monks** (from a Greek word meaning "solitary"). The earliest monasteries were set up by one of Anthony's younger contemporaries, a former Egyptian soldier named Pachomius (292–346).

The growth of monasticism accelerated after Constantine legalized Christianity and made the faith both safe and popular. Early Christians expected the world to resist their call for repentance and their warning of an imminent apocalypse. When the world suddenly capitulated and embraced their faith, some Christians were unsure how to respond. Many believed that faith required a witness against the world, and they were shaken when the world not only refused to martyr them, but offered them wealth and power. Fearing seduction, they literally fled into the wilderness and substituted voluntary ascetic disciplines for martyrdom. They became the spiritual heroes of the post-Constantinian church, and crowds of pilgrims sought their prayers and advice. Church officials saw this as a potential problem. Few hermits and monks were ordained priests, and their religious enthusiasm was not a reliable substitute for training in theology. To prevent them from drifting into heresy, church leaders devised rules to govern their communal lives. A **rule** penned by Basil of Caesarea (330–379) won wide acceptance in the eastern empire, and a century later an Italian hermit named Benedict of Nursia (480–542) wrote the rule adopted by most of western Europe's monks. Western monasticism emphasized ascetic disciplines less than eastern monasticism and focused more on a precisely regulated regimen of work and prayer.

Although the hermit's flight from the human community ended with the formation of new communities, the monks who set up these communities still sought to isolate themselves from the world. They raised their own food and established schools to give their recruits the educations they needed to read the scriptures and chant the liturgies of worship. As the empire declined, its urban classes faded away—taking with them the schools and libraries that depended on their patronage. Monasteries survived, however, for they were largely self-sufficient, and the schools they maintained became, by default, the primary institutions keeping literacy alive in the West. Paradoxically, the men and women who fled the civilized world saved its civilization.

The German Element

Constantine was survived by three sons who divided the empire he had spent much of his life uniting. One of these men, Constantius (r. 337–360), outlived his brothers, reunited the empire, and passed it on to his cousin Julian (r. 360–363). Early Christian historians dubbed Julian "the Apostate," for he withdrew state support from Christianity and tried to reform and revive paganism. Julian's reign was too brief to enable him to reverse the tide of events, and his successor, a soldier named Jovian (363), restored the church's privileged status. Jovian reigned for only eight months, and at his death a coalition of military and civilian officials elevated another Christian soldier, Valentinian I (r. 364–375), to the throne. Valentinian divided the empire, taking the western half for himself and assigning the government of the east to his brother Valens (r. 364–378). Valens made a decision that precipitated a crisis from which the empire never recovered.

Invaders and Immigrants   The Germans who began to flood into the western Roman Empire in the fourth century have been called barbarians, but the term is misleading. They were not primitive people or strangers with an alien culture who suddenly appeared to threaten Rome. They had been the empire's neighbors for centuries and were thoroughly familiar with its civilization. They traded with Romans, worked inside the empire, and moved peacefully back and forth across the empire's vague boundaries. Roman diplomats even helped some German chiefs consolidate their tribes, for this stabilized turbulent regions and raised up kings with whom Rome could negotiate treaties. Roman merchants and Christian missionaries worked among the Germans, and some tribes converted to Christianity (albeit to the heretical Arian version) while still outside the empire. Germans envied Rome's wealth and power, and many were attracted to the empire in hopes of sharing the benefits of its civilization. Unfortunately, they came so quickly and in such numbers that the fragile, poorly governed empire could not absorb them.

The Germans were not only drawn to Rome; they were pushed against its frontiers by the migration of the Huns. The Huns had long preyed on China from their homeland in Mongolia. But when an aggressive dynasty arose in China and stiffened its defenses, the Huns were deflected to the west. They were formidable warriors whose equestrian skills were legendary, and they had invented a technique for making powerful bows that were small enough to be shot from horseback. In the mid-fourth century, they reached the lands north of the Black Sea, where they encountered and subdued their first Germans, the Ostrogoths (East Goths). In 375 they routed the Ostrogoths' neighbors, the Visigoths (West Goths), who then fled to the Roman border and begged permission to enter the empire.

This forced Valens, the eastern emperor, to make a difficult decision. As many as 80,000 Visigoths were massed on his frontier. No ancient government could handle that many refugees, but if Valens refused the Visigoths entry, they were likely to attack and cost him soldiers he needed to fend off the Huns. Valens admitted the Visigoths to the empire (hoping perhaps to use them to bolster its defenses), but things did not work out well for the eastern empire. The Visigoths soon faced starvation in their refugee camps, and they were infuriated by the Roman profiteers who tried to exploit them. In desperation, they began to forage for supplies in the region north of Constantinople. Valens pursued them, and on August 9, 378, he blundered into an ambush near the city of Adrianople. He and Rome's eastern army were slaughtered. By then, the western half of the empire had passed to Valentinian I's son, Gratian (r. 375–383). He gave Theodosius, a family friend, the job of restoring order in the eastern empire. Theodosius made peace with the Visigoths and enlisted them as **foederati**—independent allies resident within the empire and pledged to defend it.

By 394 various usurpers had overthrown Gratian and his brother Valentinian II (r. 378–392), and Theodosius (d. 395) had emerged as sole emperor. He was the last man to govern the whole empire and the first to proclaim Christianity its state religion (392). At his death, the empire was divided between his sons. The west passed to Honorius (r. 395–423), who was only 10 years old, and the east to Arcadius (r. 395–408), who was 18. The shortsighted policies of their inept administrations were soon to extinguish the last vestiges of Roman power in the western half of the Mediterranean world.

The Decline of the Western Empire   About the time of Theodosius's death, the Visigoths acquired an ambitious young leader named Alaric (c. 370–410). When he began to press Constantinople for new opportunities for his people, the eastern empire took the easy way out. It rid itself of the Visigoths by urging them to move west into Italy. Italy's defense was managed by Stilicho (c. 365–408), a German general who commanded Emperor Honorius's army. He repulsed Alaric's initial assaults, but fear of the Visigoths caused Honorius's government to make some fateful decisions. Milan, the seat of the western empire, seemed too vulnerable to siege, so the court moved to Ravenna, a small port on the Adriatic. Ravenna owed the honor of becoming the last capital of the western Roman Empire to swamps that protected it from landward assault and to its proximity to the sea. The emperor wanted to be able, if need be, to take to his ship and flee Italy. Honorius's advisors also chose to beef up Italy's defenses by recalling the troops that guarded the Rhine and Danube frontiers. This cleared the way for large numbers of Germans from several tribes to cross the Rhine unopposed on the last day of year 406 and begin to loot their way through Gaul.

In 408 the bad situation grew worse. Honorius became suspicious of Stilicho's ambitions and ordered the general's execution. This disrupted the defense of the western empire and gave the Visigoths a chance to break into Italy. Ravenna's swamps prevented Alaric from assaulting Honorius directly, but Alaric had a plan for putting pressure on the western emperor. He ordered the Visigoths to march on Rome. Honorius could not ignore this assault on the symbol of his authority. He opened negotiations with Alaric, but when he failed to implement their agreements, Alaric lost patience and made good his threat. On August 24, 410, he sacked Rome. This was of little practical consequence, for the city was no longer the seat of the western empire. However, Rome's humiliation was a blow to the morale of the ancient world. It had been 800 years since the city last fell to an enemy, and its defeat was an ominous portent. Pagan intellectuals blamed the disaster on the rise of Christianity and the empire's neglect of the gods that had long protected it. The western empire's leading Christian thinker, Augustine (whose words are quoted at the head of this chapter), defended Christianity by putting the event in the broadest possible historical context. It was, he claimed, not all that significant, for it was simply one in a long series of painful consequences of humanity's sinful rebellion against God (see Chapter 8).

The Visigoths did little serious damage to Rome. They were Arian Christians who respected the city's churches, and after three days of looting, they left Rome and marched south along Italy's coast. Their plan was to collect ships and eventually to sail to North Africa. When a storm destroyed the flotilla they had gathered, they turned around and headed north to Gaul. Alaric died somewhere near Naples and was buried in a grave hidden beneath the bed of the Busento River.

Once the Visigoths were out of Italy, Honorius recognized them as *foederati*, and they settled in southern Gaul and Spain. They were far from the only Germans to stake claims to parts of the western empire. Many tribes had entered Roman territory in 406, when Honorius stripped troops from the Rhine frontier. The Vandals were part of the vanguard. As they looted their way across Gaul, others followed in their wake. Scattered bands of Franks occupied northern Gaul, and the Burgundians founded a kingdom in eastern Gaul. When the Visigoths pushed into southern Gaul, the Vandals wandered into Spain. In 429 they crossed the Straits of Gibraltar, conquered North Africa, established a capital for a kingdom at Carthage, and built a navy with which to raid Sicily and Italy. In 455 they sacked Rome. By then, Britain, whose defense Honorius had abandoned in 410, was being taken over by Angles and Saxons. Many other less significant tribes also grabbed bits and pieces of what was still, in theory at least, Rome's empire (see Map 7–1).

The western empire prolonged its existence as a legal entity by recognizing many of the Germans who settled within its boundaries as *foederati*. Rome had little power over these allies, but they responded to its calls for help when it was in their interest to do so. The last major occasion on which they served Rome was in 451, when Attila (c. 406–453),

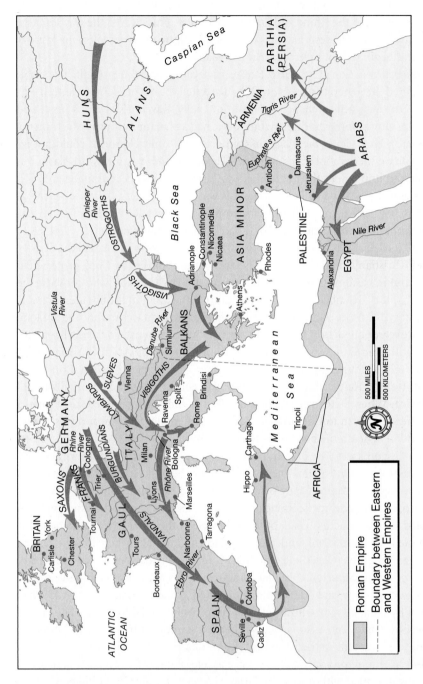

Map 7–1 Migrations into the Roman Empire Between 376 and 406, the western Roman Empire let down its defenses, and German tribes wandered freely throughout its territory. Constantinople blocked them from spreading into the eastern empire, but in the eighth century the east had to contend with invaders from Arabia and the rise of Islam.

Question: Did geography pose different challenges for the defenders of the eastern and western halves of Rome's empire?

king of the Huns, led his people into Gaul. Aëtius (c. 390–454), a Roman general who served the emperor Valentinian III (r. 425–455), met the Huns at Châlons, south of Reims. With the aid of his German allies, he fought the Huns to a draw, and Attila retreated to Germany. The following year, when the Huns struck south into Italy, Rome was abandoned by its allies. They fought only when their own lands were threatened. Papal diplomacy or a timely outbreak of malaria in Attila's army saved the city of Rome from another sack. The Huns withdrew to Germany's healthier environment, and Attila died the following winter. His empire did not survive him, but its sudden collapse did not guarantee Rome's security. It only freed Germans whom the Huns had enslaved to seek their fortunes in Roman territory.

By now, the western emperors controlled little more than Italy, and that was often only nominally theirs. The real power had passed to generals who were usually of German descent. In 476 one of these, Odovacer (c. 493), deposed the last of the west's figurehead emperors, a 15-year-old boy who bore the name of Rome's founder, Romulus, and who was mockingly called Augustulus ("Little Augustus"). The eastern emperor championed another claimant for the western throne, but he was powerless to seat his candidate.

After Attila's empire fell, the Ostrogoths advanced on Constantinople, and it dealt with them as it previously had the Visigoths—by diverting them to the west. In 489 the eastern emperor commissioned the Ostrogothic king Theodoric (r. 489–526) to invade Italy as his agent and restore it to the empire. Although Theodoric theoretically served the eastern emperor, he was an independent monarch who gave Italy a few decades of peace, during which attempts were made to rescue the West's faltering civilization. Two notable scholars, Boethius (c. 480–524) and Cassiodorus (c. 490–580), worked at his court, and the books they produced became staples of education throughout Europe during the early Middle Ages. Theodoric gave Italy a valuable, if brief, respite from the confusion of a chaotic era. An attempt by an eastern emperor to regain control of Italy after Theodoric's death inflicted far more damage on the heartland of the ancient empire than anything the German "barbarians" had done.

The Byzantine Empire of Constantinople

When people speak of the fall of the Roman Empire, they are usually thinking only of its western half. The eastern Roman Empire, with its seat at Constantinople, was relatively undisturbed by the German invasions, and its succession of emperors continued until 1453, when the city was conquered by the Ottoman Turks and renamed Istanbul. However, once the western Roman Empire was gone, Roman elements in the eastern empire diminished. It became an ardently Christian state with a largely Greek-speaking population and a partially Persian culture. Historians distinguish this emerging medieval civilization from its Roman predecessor by referring to it as the Byzantine Empire (from the Greek name for the site of its capital).

Justinian   In 518 a military coup elevated Justin (r. 518–527), an illiterate soldier of peasant origins, to the eastern throne. He governed with the assistance of a gifted and well-educated nephew named Justinian. Justinian (r. 527–565) eventually succeeded his uncle and assembled a team of remarkable people to help him run his empire. Chief among them was his wife and virtual co-regent, Theodora (c. 500–548).

As the only surviving Roman emperor, Justinian believed that it was his duty to recover the western territories that had been lost to the Germans. The empire had previously come apart on several occasions and been restored. Justinian had no reason to assume that history could not repeat itself. In 533 his loyal general, Belisarius (c. 505–565), made a promising start by quickly overwhelming the fragile Vandal kingdom and restoring North Africa and Sicily to Justinian's control. Diplomatic negotiations then persuaded some places along the coasts of Gaul and Spain to submit, but the Ostrogoths vigorously resisted Justinian's efforts to gain control of Italy. War there raged on until 552, when the Ostrogoths finally gave in and agreed to evacuate Italy. Justinian's victory was, however, Pyrrhic. His war had devastated Italy. The city of Rome suffered great damage, particularly to the aqueducts that supplied its water. During the sixth century it lost nine-tenths of its population. The Byzantine Empire was left so exhausted by the struggle that it could not hold the prize it had won. In 568 another wave of Germans, the Lombards, swept into Italy from the north, and the Byzantines retreated to Ravenna and outposts in southern Italy. Rome's bishop defended his city and preserved its independence. But most of Italy was divided up among Lombard chieftains. The peninsula was to remain politically fragmented for the next 1,293 years.

Justinian could not concentrate all his attention on his western wars. Slavs, Germans, and various Asiatic peoples flooded into his Balkan provinces, and he faced a formidable opponent on his eastern frontier. Khusro I (r. 531–579), the Persian shah of the Sassanid Empire, devoted much of his reign to preying on Byzantine territory. Justinian kept him at bay, but the fight drained both Byzantium and Persia, and made them easy targets for Arab Muslim armies in the seventh century.

The eastern half of Rome's empire had always been more prosperous, populous, and urbanized than the western, and the east was not disrupted, as was the west, by the migrations of German tribes. The eastern emperors, therefore, still had formidable resources at their disposal—as Justinian's reign demonstrates. In addition to his costly wars, he had the wealth to fund so many building

The *Hagia Sophia* Justinian's palace church is one of the world's architectural and engineering masterpieces. The walls and domes of its great hall, which is nearly as long as a football field, were originally covered with colorful mosaics. These were destroyed or covered when the building was converted to a mosque in the fifteenth century. Today it is a museum, and some of its original art has been restored.

projects that his court historian, Procopius, devoted an entire book to describing this aspect of his employer's reign. The most famous of his monuments is the massive Church of Holy Wisdom (the *Hagia Sophia*) that he erected next to his palace in Constantinople. It is an engineering marvel—a vast rectangular hall roofed by a system of interconnected domes, the greatest of which soars to a height of about 180 feet. Its innovative design and skillful construction prove that the eastern Roman Empire was capable of highly original and significant achievement during the era of the ancient world's "fall."

Byzantine Culture   Constantine designed Constantinople to make it a worthy successor to Rome as the capital of a renewed empire. From the city's site on the waterway that connected the Aegean Sea and Black Sea, its rulers could watch both of the late Roman Empire's trouble spots: the German and Persian frontiers. Its location was also economically advantageous, and it became a focal point for major international trade routes. It had access to Mediterranean markets through the Aegean Sea. Via the Black Sea and the Russian rivers that emptied into it, the city had a route to the Baltic region. Goods reached it along "the Silk Road" from China, from India up the Persian Gulf and the Mesopotamian rivers, and from Africa through the Red Sea and the empire's Egyptian ports.

Constantinople's virtually invulnerable fortifications added to its attractions. As conditions in the western empire deteriorated, many of the empire's wealthy families moved themselves, their art collections, and their libraries to the new capital. Emperors stripped other cities to adorn their new seat, and a steady stream of valuable records and objects flowed to "New Rome."

Among the things that Justinian's government inherited was a mountain of legal documents—judicial records, imperial and senatorial edicts, and lawyers' commentaries—that had been accumulating in the imperial archives for centuries. Justinian set up a commission to comb through this material, organize it, and distill from it the essence of Roman law. The result was a set of volumes, the *Corpus juris civilis* (*Body of Civil Law*), that was to have a major influence on the formation of Europe's medieval kingdoms and subsequently on some modern European nations.

Byzantine scholars produced encyclopedias and library inventories that make fascinating, if depressing, reading. They document how much ancient literature once existed and how much has been lost. Byzantine intellectuals are not remembered for much original work, but a few of them made significant contributions to history and theology.

Religion was at the heart of Byzantine civilization, and it both strengthened and stressed the eastern empire. A declining level of education and literacy in the west had the effect of diminishing theological disputes, but arguments over faith flourished in the more highly cultivated east and divided Christians against themselves. There was such an insatiable appetite for theological debate among Byzantines of all classes that it was said that a man could not get his hair cut without receiving a lecture on an obscure doctrinal point from his barber. It is hardly surprising that Constantinople dedicated its most important church to the wisdom (or intellect) of God. Byzantines were fascinated by the intellectual challenge of making sense of the mysteries of faith. They pursued

their arguments with such passion, however, that their rulers concluded that maintenance of a viable empire required them to stamp out dissent (heresy) and enforce conformity of religious opinion (orthodoxy). This preoccupation with purity of doctrine
led to the characterization of eastern Christianity as the Orthodox tradition. The Roman Catholic Church that emerged in western Europe evolved differently, and the eastern and western versions of Christianity formally separated in the eleventh century.

As the western half of the empire sank into confusion and the authority of its emperors faded, the power of their eastern colleagues increased. The eastern emperors
were able to build on the foundation Diocletian had laid for autocratic government and
the command Constantine had acquired over the church. A vast gulf separated the emperor of Constantinople from his subjects, but an elaborate governmental bureaucracy
kept him fully informed and fully in charge. The emperor was the source of all authority, and his agents had a hand in managing (and taxing) all industry and commerce. His
army was recruited from self-sustaining rural peasant villages that dealt directly with
him rather than through a hierarchy of aristocratic overlords. And there was no separation of church and state in the eastern empire. The clerical head of the eastern church
was the "patriarch" of Constantinople, but he reported to the emperor, who was him-

Byzantine Art Byzantine artists excelled in the production of mosaics, pictures executed in tiny
pieces of colored stone and glass. This panel from the Church of San Vitale in Ravenna, Italy, depicts
the empress Theodora, attended by splendidly costumed courtiers, presenting a chalice to the
church. A companion scene shows her husband Justinian offering bread for the mass. By setting the
figures in two-dimensional space, the Christian artist has lifted them from the ordinary world and
placed them in a spiritual environment. He has minimized their human corporeal natures and set
them in a timeless, heavenly realm.

self a quasi-clerical figure. The emperor presided at church councils, and on occasion he took part in liturgies, representing Christ. Such role-playing was consistent with the tendency of eastern Christianity to try to incarnate the divine and make it part of human experience. The overwhelmingly lavish decorations and elaborate services of the Orthodox churches were intended to give worshipers a foretaste of heaven. The desire for a physical link between the realms of heaven and earth, such as Jesus had provided during his earthly existence, found expression in powerful devotion to sacred objects called icons. Icons were usually paintings representing figures from scripture or saints. (Sculptures in three dimensions were less common, doubtless because of their association with pagan idols.) Icons were not worshiped in themselves, but were seen as a medium through which the spiritual realities they represented could be contacted. In this they functioned much like the sacred relics that were eagerly collected and passionately venerated by all medieval Christians.

Islam

About five years after Justinian died, a man named Muhammad ("Highly Praised," c. 570–632) was born in Arabia. At about the age of 40, he began to have religious experiences that transformed his life and the history of the world. He became "the Prophet," the man chosen to reveal the will of Allah, to found the religion known as Islam, and to set in motion events that rapidly created an empire larger than Rome's.

The Arabian Context   At the start of the seventh century, no one could have predicted that the next great world power would arise from Arabia. Most of the million-square-mile Arabian peninsula, with the exception of some oases and coastal districts, was desert inhabited by primitive nomads called Bedouins (*badw*, "desert"). Although Arabia was exposed to civilizing influences from Egypt and Mesopotamia, none of the ancient world's empires paid it much attention. The land was too barren to be worth the cost of conquest. Geography, however, gave Arabia some economic significance. Trade routes that connected the markets of the Mediterranean with those of India and east Africa passed around or through Arabia. As herdsmen wandered from place to place with their flocks, they could easily form caravans and move goods through their territory. Trade brought them into contact with Jews, Christians, Persians, Greeks, and Romans, and enhanced the importance of Mecca, Muhammad's birthplace.

Pre-Islamic Arabia was a politically chaotic country. It had no central government and no coordinated leadership. Arabs acknowledged few loyalties beyond those to blood kin. Scarcity of resources forced them to prey on one another and live by harsher codes than those that governed life in wealthier regions. Such order as existed in Arabia was maintained by fear of vendettas—by the knowledge that a man's kinsmen would avenge any harm done to him.

Trading was risky in a country where there was no governmental protection and in a culture where to display valuable items was to challenge others to try to take them from you. Fortunately, religion helped to compensate for the weakness of political institutions. Awe motivated people to restrain their behavior at sacred sites. Acts of violence or bloodshed were often believed to pollute holy ground, and those who commited them risked divine punishment. Mecca was one of Arabia's sacred places, the site of a rectangular stone building of ancient, but uncertain, origin called the Ka'aba ("cube"). Various Arab tribes had deposited some 300 holy images in the Ka'aba, and they venerated a black stone in its eastern corner. It was said to have been placed there by the Hebrew patriarch Abraham from whom the Arabs, like the Jews, claim descent. The Arabs believe that their ancestor was Ishmael, Abraham's son by his maid Hagar, and that their cousins, the Jews, descend from Isaac, the son Abraham had with his wife Sara. Respect for the Ka'aba created a space around Mecca where a powerful taboo forbade the kinds of fights that were routine elsewhere. Mecca was therefore a good place to trade.

Muhammad's tribe, the Kuraish, bore special responsibility for Mecca and the Ka'aba, but Muhammad was not born to a life of rank and privilege. He was orphaned at a young age, raised by a grandfather and then an uncle, and compelled as a youth to make his own way in the world. He worked on caravans, and about 595 he married a wealthy widow named Khadija, who was his elder by a decade or more. She may have borne her husband seven children, but only one lived: a daughter named Fatima. After Khadija's death Muhammad acquired a harem of nine wives, but Fatima was his only descendant. The lack of a male heir may have confirmed his conviction that he was meant to be God's final prophet.

The Origin of Islam   In 610, when Muhammad was about 40, he began to receive visions that conveyed the precepts of a new faith. An angel (said to be Gabriel, the messenger who had previously inaugurated Christianity by announcing the news of Christ's birth to Mary) ordered him to speak, and he was inspired to recite the first of the 114 **suras**, or divine messages, that compose Islam's sacred book, the Qur'an (the "Recitation"). Muhammad's Arab audiences were stunned by the poetic beauty of his utterances, and they committed them to memory and circulated them as an oral tradition. About 20 years after Muhammad's death, the *suras* were collected, and an authorized text of the Qur'an was compiled. A collection of **hadiths**, "traditions" about the Prophet handed down by his acquaintances, provided additional religious guidance.

In the beginning Muhammad's visions alarmed him, and he was reluctant to make them public. He had good reason. When he began to preach in 615, he set himself on course to collide with the Meccan authorities, the leaders of his tribe. Muhammad was disturbed by the growing materialism of the Meccan merchants, and he called for a return to traditional social values. He insisted that the rich had a duty to care for the poor. He personally had no taste for wealth or luxury and lived so frugally that he repaired his own clothing and helped his wives with household tasks. He advocated egalitarianism. All his followers were to be on the same footing, and no one was to claim superior social or spiritual status. None of this struck Mecca's leaders as new or alarming, but in 616 Muhammad crossed the line. He repudiated the polytheistic beliefs of his ancestors and embraced a radically consistent monotheism. This was an attack on the Ka'aba, and an attack on the Ka'aba was a blow at the foundation of Mecca's economy.

Muhammad claimed that his revelations came from *al-Ilah*, "the God," an ancient Arab term for a remote high god. Muhammad, however, declared Allah the sole deity—a unique, all-encompassing, transcendent divine power that defied human comprehension. Human beings could not hope to understand this ultimate reality; they could only surrender to it. Muhammad's core message was a call to submit (*salama*, "islam") to God's will. Muhammad repudiated every doctrine or image that might compromise Allah's unity or transcendence. He was acquainted with Judaism and Christianity, and he accepted their validity to a point. He said that the Hebrew prophets and Jesus were true spokesmen for God, but that their messages had been misinterpreted. He honored Jesus as a major prophet, but insisted that he was only a man and not an incarnation of God. He also forbade his own followers to pay him divine honors, and he claimed no miraculous powers. He was "the Prophet," God's final messenger, but that did not make him anything other than a mortal man.

By 620 the Prophet's situation in Mecca was deteriorating rapidly. As Muhammad pondered what to do, he had a vision in which he was carried to Jerusalem to the mountain where the Jewish temple had stood. From there he rose into heaven to meet the earlier prophets and to enter the presence of Allah. This experience confirmed his faith—as did a development that marked the turning point in his fortunes. He made six new converts from Yathrib, an oasis 200 miles north of Mecca. Yathrib subsequently came to be called Medina ("city" of the Prophet), but it was not an urban community. It was a 20-square-mile patch of arable land inhabited by tribes of both Arabs and Jews. The people of Yathrib were having a hard time living together. They needed an outsider to mediate their disputes, and in 621 they offered Muhammad the job. Having found a safe haven, Muhammad instructed his followers to prepare for the **hijra** ("departure"). The *hijra* was a spiritual as well as a literal journey, for it meant a break with the tribe of one's birth and a commitment to a new **umma** ("community"), whose members were bound by faith, not blood.

Umma **to Empire**   Because the *hijra* of 622 marked the start of Islam as an independent religious movement, it became the pivot point for Muslim historiography—the event from which all other events are dated. However, it took more than a move to Yathrib to secure Islam's survival. At first, life in Yathrib was as challenging for Muhammad as it had been in Mecca. Some of the oasis's inhabitants were not happy about his arrival, and he had to find some way to support himself and his people. Yathrib's location near the caravan routes that served Mecca solved the latter problem. Muhammad ordered his men to prey on Mecca's trade, and he may have led as many as 25 raids in person. Christians find it hard to imagine Jesus doing such a thing, but Jesus lived in a different world. Muhammad's situation was more like the one that Moses faced as he forged the Jews he had led out of Egypt into a people and helped them to survive by waging wars with competing tribes.

In 627 Mecca dispatched a large army to evict Muhammad from Yathrib, but the campaign backfired. The Prophet won a stunning victory over Mecca's superior forces, and as the news spread, converts to Islam multiplied. In 630 the Meccan authorities came to terms with the man whose spiritual vocation they had ridiculed. It was agreed that all pagan shrines throughout Arabia would be destroyed except Mecca's Ka'aba. The Ka'aba would be purged of its idols, but the building itself would be honored as marking the most sacred place on Earth.

Muhammad's insistence that loyalty to Allah superseded all other allegiances provided a way for the Arabs to transcend their tribal divisions and come together as a people. The

PEOPLE IN CONTEXT A'isha (614–678),
Wife of the Prophet

In 620 a girl named A'isha was informed that her father had arranged for her to marry his best friend and spiritual mentor, Muhammad. She was 6 years old, and her future husband was about 50. The wedding took place three years later, and despite the gap in age between the bride and groom, the marriage was a great success. A'isha bore her husband no children, and he had other wives, but she became his favorite. He may have been intrigued by her independent spirit and her audacious sense of humor. (She once told him that she was amazed at how willing Allah was to do his will!) She narrowly avoided divorce when she blundered into a misadventure that raised doubts about her sexual fidelity, and on another occasion she led a harem revolt that brought Muhammad to the brink of repudiating all his wives. Despite occasional conflicts, the Prophet's affection for his feisty wife never waned, and when he was overtaken by his final illness, he asked to be taken to her room. He died with his head in her lap and was buried beneath her bed.

Muhammad's death committed A'isha, at the young age of 18, to perpetual widowhood, for the Prophet proclaimed his wives "Mothers of Believers" and forbade them to remarry. A'isha did not, however, sink into obscurity. As the only one of Muhammad's wives in whose presence he had received revelations from Allah, the leaders of the Muslim community turned to her when they were uncertain what to do. Her memories of what Muhammad had said and done served as precedents for deciding difficult questions. Tradition credits her with some 2,210 *hadiths*, the quasi-scriptural verses that supplement the Qur'an. A'isha knew how to make the most of her situation. She amassed wealth, dispensed influence, and intervened in the struggles that broke out for control of the Islamic community. At the start of Islam's first civil war, she raised an army and was captured on the battlefield when her men were defeated. Her reputation as the Prophet's beloved protected her, and she remained a force to be reckoned with until her death in 678. Clearly the early Islamic community was not exclusively a man's world.

The Prophet's Mosque, Medina, Arabia
Muhammad spent the later portion of his life in Medina, and he died and was buried there.

Question: Given that priestesses were common in the ancient world, why did female religious leadership decline when the medieval West embraced Christianity and Islam?

new faith that the Prophet revealed founded a new community, but Muhammad had little time to turn the *umma* into a state. He died in Medina on June 8, 632. His death did not shake the faith of his followers, for he had never denied his own mortality. It did, however, pose a problem. Muhammad had insisted that there would be no more prophets after him, and he had said nothing about choosing a new leader for the *umma*. Some tribes concluded that their allegiance had been to Muhammad, and that his death dissolved their ties to the *umma*. However, Abu Bakr (632–634), the first of Muhammad's prestigious converts and a long-time friend, stepped in and prevented Islam's dissolution. Muhammad had sometimes chosen Abu Bakr to stand in for him and lead the *umma*'s communal prayers. The precedent that this had established and Abu Bakr's close association with the Prophet made him the logical choice to become Islam's first **caliph** ("successor"), the heir to Muhammad's duties as leader of the *umma*.

Abu Bakr, being about the same age as Muhammad, outlived him by only a few years, but this was long enough to secure the *umma*'s future. Faith helped preserve its unity, but so also did material success. Under Abu Bakr's leadership, Muslim raiding parties thrust into the lands of the Persians and Byzantines that bordered Arabia. Their timing was excellent, for both these empires had been locked in combat for decades and were reeling with exhaustion. Raids quickly became conquests, and Islam began to acquire an empire (see Map 7–2).

Muhammad had forbidden his people to fight among themselves and decreed instead that they devote their energies to waging *jihad* ("holy struggle"). The word is difficult to

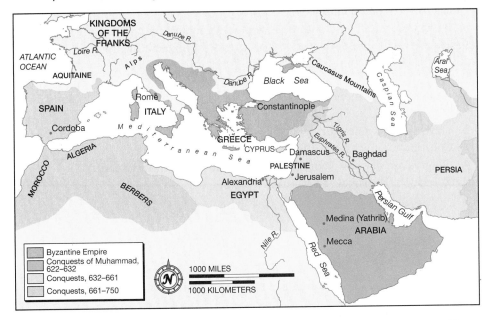

Map 7–2 Expansion of the Muslim Empire This map shows the stages by which Islam spread (in little more than a century) from the interior of Arabia west to the Atlantic, north into France, and east to India and the frontiers of China.

Question: Given that Islam originated on the periphery of the Roman Empire and Muslims claimed much of Rome's former territory, was the Islamic empire a "Western" empire?

translate and has often been misunderstood by non-Muslims and abused by Muslims. It asserts the *umma's* right to defend itself, but it also extends to the religious duty to fight for a just society and do whatever is necessary to defeat evil in one's own character. It can involve taking up arms against others, but it also entails the difficult spiritual struggle that all believers are called to wage against their darker impulses. There was no strain of pacifism in Muhammad's teaching, but he insisted that wars be fought only for just causes, that they be as brief as possible, and that they cease as soon as opponents offer honorable terms. He did not send his people forth to convert the world at the edge of a sword. Islam's rapid spread owed little to compulsion and much to its innate appeal.

Islam and Christianity   The church, in its various forms, had virtually captured the West by the seventh century. Then, Islam suddenly emerged to challenge Christianity's religious monopoly. The result was a division in Western and world civilization that has had—and continues to have—troubling consequences.

A history of conflict obscures the fact that Islam and Christianity have much in common. Both claim Hebraic ancestry. Both are monotheistic, and both have relied on Greek philosophy for help in developing their theologies. Many of the individuals who appear in the Bible are also found in the Qur'an. More is even said about some Christian figures (Jesus' mother, the Virgin Mary, for example) in the Qur'an than in the New Testament. The Qur'an praises Jesus as a highly respected prophet. It affirms his virgin birth (but not his role as an incarnation of God) and describes him performing some miracles that are not mentioned in the Bible.

It is extremely difficult to summarize the faith and practice of a major religion with fairness and accuracy, but the traditional scheme for highlighting the fundamentals of Muslim belief is something called the "Five Pillars of Islam":

1. Affirmation of a monotheistic creed: "There is no god but Allah, and Muhammad is his prophet";
2. Prayer at fixed times during the day;
3. Contribution to charities that care for the poor;
4. Observation of a season of fasting during the month of Ramadan;
5. At least one pilgrimage to Mecca in a lifetime.

What is too seldom noticed is that medieval Christianity can be described in similar terms. Medieval Christians affirmed monotheistic creeds—although theirs tended to be much longer and more detailed. Christian monks prayed at fixed times during the day, and churches rang their bells at certain hours to encourage laypeople to pause in their labors and pray. The medieval church, like the Muslim state, had the power to levy taxes to support charitable works. Christians observed Lent, a longer period of fasting (40 days) than the Muslim month of Ramadan. Medieval Christians were also enthusiastic pilgrims, many of whom endured great hardship to fulfill the dream of visiting the Holy Land, the birthplace of their faith.

The most blatant contrasts seen today between the practices of Muslims and Christians reflect the gulfs that have widened between secular cultures in different parts of the modern world. There are also some significant differences between the faiths that reflect the particular environments in which their founders worked. The Christian church arose within the Roman Empire. This meant that responsibility for protecting and policing the society within which the church operated belonged to Rome's secular government and that the church could confine itself to a narrowly defined religious mission. As the empire declined, the church was sometimes forced to fend for itself and take on political responsibilities. This created problems during the Middle Ages. Kings and popes sometimes disagreed as to which powers belonged to which leader, but the church and state were still assumed to be different entities. The *umma*, on the other hand, was a religious community that sprang up in a place where there was no state. It had to provide itself with the services of secular government. Consequently, the distinction between sacred and secular authority was far less clear in Muslim than in Christian societies. Islam did not create a priesthood at the head of an independent religious organization. It has no sacraments that require priestly intermediaries, and its mosques (*masjid*, "place of worship") have no altars. In this, Islam resembles Judaism. Mosques, like synagogues, are places for prayer, preaching, and study, and the duties of Islam's imams ("leaders" of prayers) are similar to those of Jewish rabbis. Islamic clergy interpret sacred texts and define **shari'a** ("required path"), laws for the *umma*. The rules for governing a Muslim society reflect a belief that Muhammad shared with the Hebrew prophets and Jesus—that God cares about how people treat one another and that He holds communities and individuals accountable to standards of social justice. Muhammad taught that God's justice would ultimately be revealed by a final judgment. Good people would be separated from bad, and individuals would receive the eternal reward or punishment their conduct merited. Many Muslims are convinced that because human actions have such transcendent significance, *shari'a*, or religious law, should govern every aspect of life and determine the policies of states.

The Muslim World   The Byzantine Empire was in bad shape when Muslim armies erupted from Arabia in the mid-seventh century. Justinian's costly projects had driven taxes so high that some of Constantinople's subjects in Syria and Egypt welcomed the Arabs as liberators. Plagues had depopulated much of Asia Minor, and wars with Slavic invaders of Byzantium's Greek and Balkan provinces had drained the Byzantine Empire's resources. Fights over the throne and palace coups added to the confusion, and in 611 the Persians pushed through Byzantine territory to the Mediterranean coast, cut the empire in half, and sacked Jerusalem (614).

The Byzantine Empire's decline was reversed when an army from its North African province staged a military coup and placed its commander, Heraclius (r. 610–641), on the throne. By 627 Heraclius had driven the Persians back to their capital at Ctesiphon (near ancient Babylon), and regained the empire's lost provinces. He then, however, had to face the Muslims who were surging out of Arabia. In 636 they routed his army at the battle of Yarmuk and occupied Syria, Egypt, and Armenia. Constantinople then enjoyed a respite, for the Muslims shifted their attention to Persia. After the Persian Empire collapsed in 651, Constantinople's days also appeared to be numbered. Dynastic squabbles and brief reigns crippled the Byzantine Empire for the rest of the seventh century. The Muslim threat temporarily diminished, however, for divisions emerged within the *umma*.

As close associates of Muhammad's, the early caliphs were obvious choices for their office. But after Muhammad's generation died out, agreement had to be reached on a system for passing down the leadership of the *umma*. On November 4, 634, Umar (r. 632–634), the man to whom Abu Bakr had bequeathed the caliphate, was stabbed by an assassin. He lived just long enough to charge a committee with responsibility for choosing his successor. Two candidates emerged, each representing different political philosophies. Ali, Fatima's husband and father of the Prophet's grandsons, was the favorite of those who believed that the caliphate should descend in Muhammad's family. Uthman, his opponent, was the head of the prestigious Umayyad family, the first of the great Meccan clans to convert to Islam. Wealth and connections won Uthman (r. 644–656) the prize, but he had little aptitude for the office. In 656 a company of disgruntled soldiers from Egypt besieged his residence in Medina and killed him.

Uthman's assassins tried to save themselves from punishment by claiming that Uthman was unworthy of the caliphate and by offering it to Ali. Ali's acceptance infuriated Mu'awiya, governor of Syria and leader of the Umayyad family. Fighting broke out, and a schism developed within the *umma* that has never been bridged. In 660 a panel of judges declared that Mu'awiya was the legitimate caliph, and he inaugurated an Umayyad dynasty that monopolized the caliphate for a century (660–750). The **Shi'a** (the "party" of Ali), however, refused to acknowledge the Umayyad caliphate. When its leader, Ali, was killed in 661, the *Shi'a* split into factions that championed the rights of various individuals who claimed connections with Muhammad's family. Some Shi'ites insisted that the true caliph was a "hidden imam," an unknown messianic figure who would eventually emerge from obscurity to unite the *umma*. Today, *Shi'a* Islam is centered in Iran and Iraq, but the larger Muslim community, the Sunnis ("orthodox" believers), accepts the legitimacy of Islam's historic dynasties.

The Umayyads settled in Damascus, a far more convenient location for running an empire than the remote religious centers of Mecca and Medina. Once in power, they resumed Islam's wars of conquest. The North African port of Carthage fell in

The Lion Court, the Alhambra Palace, Granada, Spain Pre-Islamic Arabs were nomads who did not burden themselves with works of art, but as the empire of their Muslim descendants grew, Islam drew from a multitude of cultures to develop a unique artistic tradition. For some time, beginning in the eighth century, artists were forbidden to represent living things, for this was considered a mockery of God's creative powers. The art and architecture of this period explored the aesthetic potentials of geometric abstraction and elaborate calligraphy. Muslim aesthetics reached a high point of grace and refinement in the construction of the palace for the rulers of Spain's last Islamic state, Granada.

698, and by 714 most of Spain was under their control. Muslim navies patrolled the western Mediterranean, and in 718 Muslim armies pushed into France. Islam's eastward expansion was equally rapid. In 711 the Muslims reached the Indus River Valley and began the conquest of what is now Pakistan. In 714 a Muslim expeditionary force probed the frontiers of China.

The Umayyads' empire was too large, given the technologies of its day, to be administered by a central government. Local officials had considerable discretionary authority, and some of them established independent states. Arab rule was not unpopular. Muslims did not force conversions to Islam. Jews and Christians were respected as "People of the Book." They were viewed as inferiors and paid a special tax (*jizya*) to acknowledge that position, but they enjoyed *dhimma* status (that is, recognition as a tolerated religious community). They could practice their faiths (with some limitations) and have a degree of autonomy under their own religious leaders, but they could not bear arms. The Umayyads, indeed, thought of Islam as a privilege Allah bestowed on Arabs. They did allow non-Arabs to convert, but often regarded such converts as second-class Muslims. Separate mosques were provided for them. They paid taxes from which Arabs were exempt, and Arabs were discouraged from intermarrying with them. This discrimination created tensions within the Muslim community that eventually unseated the Umayyads.

In 747 a family that claimed descent from Muhammad's uncle, Abbas (d. 653), rallied non-Arab Muslims and launched a revolution that nearly exterminated the Umayyads. The Abbasid dynasty left Damascus for a new capital called Baghdad ("Gift of God") near the ruins of Ctesiphon, the seat of the former Persian Empire. Baghdad's Abbasid court became legendary for its luxury and sophistication, and the civilization it represented was the most progressive of the early Middle Ages. The caliphs supported scholars who collected and built on the works of the Greeks, Persians, and Indians. As a consequence, the Islamic world began to make significant progress in philosophy, mathematics, and science.

The Abbasid dynasty survived for a long time, but its power steadily eroded. Initially (in 750) it failed to destroy all its Umayyad competitors, and one Umayyad prince escaped to Spain, where his descendants established a rival caliphate. Another sprang up later in North Africa and Egypt. The Abbasid caliphs, like the last of the western Roman emperors, became figureheads for governments run by their soldiers, and the dynasty was finally extinguished in 1258, when a Mongol army destroyed Baghdad.

KEY QUESTION | Revisited

By bringing the peoples of the Mediterranean region and Europe together, the Roman Empire helped to create a unified "Western" civilization. As that empire declined, however, the political and cultural ties that held this "West" together weakened. Differences among regions became more pronounced than things held in common, and fissures widened in the fabric of the empire. Communication between Latin- and Greek-speaking districts diminished. The economy of the western half of the empire declined as it struggled with political upheaval and invasion. Meanwhile, the east, which suffered less from the changing situation, turned in on itself. Religion added a new level of complexity to the situation.

The Three Medieval Civilizations

EUROPE	BYZANTIUM	ISLAM
Romulus Augustulus (476)		
Merovingian dynasty (fd. 481)		
Clovis (d. 511)		
	Justinian (d. 565)	
	Heraclius (610–641)	Muhammad (570–632)
		Abu Bakr (632)
		Omar (632–634)
		Uthman (644–656)
		Ali (d. 661)
		Umayyad dynasty (fd. 660)
		Mu'awiya (d. 680)
[Charles Martel (d. 741)]	*Isaurian dynasty* (fd. 717)	
	Leo III (d. 740)	
Carolingian dynasty (fd. 751)		*Abbasid dynasty* (fd. 750)
Pepin III (d. 768)		
Charlemagne (r. 768–814)		
		Harun al Rashid (786–809)

Constantine had hoped that religion would strengthen the state by compensating for the weakening of other ties. His predecessors had never questioned their right and duty to promote and oversee the religious practices of their people. And given the tolerant attitudes and widespread moral consensus fostered by classical paganism, religion seldom conflicted with state policies. But Christianity had evolved in opposition to the state (and to the world, which Christians regarded as doomed by sin to destruction), and it saw no virtue in tolerating other faiths. Doctrinal disputes among Christians added to the tensions with which the empire had to deal, and Constantine's effort to maintain order created a precedent for the church to claim a degree of autonomy from the state.

The Christian church triumphed over its competitors and was recognized by the empire as the West's sole legitimate faith. As such, it exercised overwhelming influence on the development of Western civilization. It acquired a monopoly over education and literacy, and its precepts were written into law. The result, however, was not universal concord and agreement. Although Christians professed the same faith, they did not all understand that faith in the same way. It divided as well as united them. Quarrels over heresies continued, and as the eastern Roman Empire became the Byzantine Empire, it evolved a Christian culture distinct from, and sometimes opposed to, that of the Latin west. In both east and west, serious disputes arose over the division of powers between secular and religious leaders.

Islam's experience was somewhat similar. Muhammad's preaching unified the Arab peoples and kept them working together long enough to build a huge empire. But like Christianity, Islam soon developed internal divisions—both cultural and theological—

that spawned intense hatred among persons who professed allegiance to the same faith. Islam's spread into territory occupied by Christians created another cause for war and for the fragmentation of the world that Rome had united.

The fact that Islam, Christianity, and Judaism all spring from the same tradition and all honor many of the same sacred figures and shrines has often, paradoxically, made it difficult for them to tolerate one another or even dissident members of their own faith communities. As monotheistic faiths, they share a tendency to assign people to opposing categories: the saved versus the damned, the sheep versus the goats, the citizens of the city of God versus the inhabitants of the city of man, true-believers versus heretics—some version of "us versus them." The West's three great religions saved its civilization. They trained and supported its scholars. They commissioned and inspired its arts, and they provided the ideologies that helped to integrate its political communities—but at the cost of great bloodshed.

Religion has not invariably promoted justice, tolerance, and moral progress. It has a history of provoking wars, pogroms, and lesser conflicts. In light of the current international situation, some commentators have insisted that the world would be better off without religion. Their opponents argue that civilization would be impossible without the grounding that religion provides for values. Religion is not likely to disappear, and much of value would be lost if it did. Freedom of conscience and of religion are fundamental Western values, but can such liberties exist without accountability?

Review Questions

1. Edward Gibbon, an important British historian of the eighteenth century, said that the fall of the Roman Empire was brought about by the triumph of barbarism and religion. Is this a fair assessment of Rome's decline?
2. How did the eastern half of Rome's empire come to differ from the west? Why did the two have different fates?
3. How does Jesus' career compare with Muhammad's?
4. How does Christianity compare with Islam? How is the church different from the *umma*?
5. Why did religion become the most powerful cultural influence shaping Western societies in the early Middle Ages?
6. Are Islam and Christianity both Western religions?

Please consult the Suggested Readings at the back of the book to continue your study of the material covered in this chapter. For a list of documents on the Primary Source DVD-ROM that relate to topics in this chapter, please refer to the back of the book.

8 The Emergence of Europe

I am convinced that no one can describe these deeds [of Charlemagne's] more accurately than I can, for I was there when they transpired and, as people say, witnessed them with my own eyes. What is more, I cannot know for sure that anyone else will record these things. Therefore, I have concluded that it would be better to produce an account myself . . . rather than permit the amazing life of this most remarkable king, the leading man of his generation, to fade from memory.

—Einhard, *Life of Charlemagne*

KEY | Question

How did Europe build on its legacies from the ancient world?

The explanation Einhard (c. 770–840) gave for his decision to pen an account of the life of his king, Charlemagne, reveals how different his world was from ours. In our abundantly documented age, it is unthinkable that a man like Charlemagne, who ruled much of Europe, might be forgotten. Einhard, however, was right to be concerned. He was a member of Charlemagne's inner circle from 793 until the emperor's death in 814, but he had no information about his subject's birth and youth. There were no public records, and no one who knew Charlemagne as a boy was still alive. Only a few years had passed, but already part of the great man's history was lost. Under such circumstances, even the memory of extraordinary events could fade quickly. This worried Einhard, for he believed that his generation had witnessed one of history's turning points—the emergence of Europe as a world power.

Although Einhard and his contemporaries had a very limited knowledge of history, the past was a potent force in their lives. No emperors had reigned in the western half of the Roman Empire after the deposition of Romulus Augustulus in 476, but on Christmas Day 800, the people of Rome had ended a 324-year-long interregnum by reviving the imperial title and bestowing it on Charlemagne. Charlemagne bore little resemblance to Rome's previous emperors, and

Emperor Charlemagne   No contemporary portraits of Charlemagne, one of the greatest medieval kings, survive. However, this small bronze figure from the ninth century might have been intended to represent him. *Musee du Louvre/RMN Reunion des Musees Nationaux, France. SCALA/Art Resource, NY*

his lands were not coterminous with those of their empire. His domain extended from the Pyrenees (the mountains between France and Spain) to the Oder River in eastern Germany and from the North Sea to Naples. Much of the territory that Rome had formerly governed, from Spain in the west across North Africa to Egypt and Syria in the east, had come under Muslim control. The Balkans, Greece, and Asia Minor were ruled from Constantinople, whose emperors' line of succession stretched back to the Roman Caesars.

The Greeks coined the word *Europe* (perhaps from an Assyrian term meaning west), but they knew little about the region to which it referred. Much of the land that lay to the north and west of Greece was of peripheral importance to the civilized world even after the Romans added Gaul, Britain, and part of Germany to their empire. This changed following the western empire's collapse. Rome's former northwestern provinces began to expand, coalesce, and develop a sense of identity. Their emerging self-awareness is reflected in the title that one of Einhard's colleagues, Alcuin (c. 737–804), bestowed on Charlemagne: *Europae pater* ("father of Europe").

Charlemagne believed that the great continental state he had created entitled him to the prestige that the imperial title conferred. His coronation was also meant to put the world on notice that Europe was emerging from the decline into which it had slipped in the fifth century and was asserting its claim to the civilization that was Rome's legacy. Charlemagne's subjects were culturally inferior to the ancient empire's other heirs, the Byzantines and Muslims, but history more than vindicated Charlemagne's confidence in his people's future. Rightly or wrongly, Europeans would one day regard themselves as the sole guardians of Western civilization.

When the Roman Empire broke up, what had been a politically unified territory with a veneer of common culture split into regions with ever more diverging identities. As distinctions between east and west—and north and south—increased, shared traditions diminished, and memories of common origins faded. Initially, the inhabitants of the lands along the eastern and southern shores of the Mediterranean, the Byzantines and Muslims, did the best job of preserving and building on the foundations laid by the ancient world. But by the end of the Middle Ages, the peoples who lived north and west of the Mediterranean had taken the lead (thanks in no small measure to help they had received from their eastern and southern neighbors) and were poised to spread the West's civilization around the globe. Much of the modern world, therefore, has experienced Western civilization in a form mediated by Europe. Because Europe's physical and cultural environments were different from those of the ancient Mediterranean region, Europeans had both continued and diverged from the legacies of the ancient world to create a version of its Western civilization appropriate to their context.

The Merovingian Kingdom: Europe's Nucleus

When the Franks, for whom France is named, first appeared in history, they were a gaggle of German tribes inhabiting the eastern bank of the lower reaches of the Rhine River. Emperor Constantine's father, Constantius I, settled some of them (the Salian, or "Saltwater," Franks) in the Netherlands to create a buffer between the empire and wilder folk to the north. Some of the Franks who remained in the Rhineland (the Ripuarian, or "River," Franks) also entered Rome's service. In 406, after Honorius (r. 395–423) recalled Rome's legions to Italy to fight the Visigoths, the Franks tried to hold the Rhine frontier for the empire. Franks were part of the army with which the Roman general Aëtius blocked the Huns' advance into Gaul in 451. Thirty years later, a Frankish chief named Clovis united his people and founded a dynasty that turned Roman Gaul into medieval Francia.

Clovis and the Franks   Clovis (c. 466–511) was about 10 years old when the last western Roman emperor was deposed, and he was still in his teens when he succeeded his father as one of many Frankish tribal chiefs. His people lived near Tournai in Austrasia ("Eastern Lands"), a region between the Rhine and Somme rivers. Clovis's early campaigns extended his power south beyond Paris to the Loire Valley. The Franks called this territory Neustria ("New Lands"). Clovis pushed the Visigoths south to the Garonne River, eliminated rival Frankish chiefs, brought much of Germany under his control, and married to form an alliance with the Burgundians, whose kingdom lay on his southeastern border.

Two decades after Clovis's death in 511, the Byzantine Emperor Justinian still dreamed of regaining control of what had been the western Roman Empire. He succeeded in temporarily occupying Italy, but by then, much of western Europe was firmly established on the road to independence. This was thanks in large part to Clovis, who did more than conquer territory. He helped unify a world that had been culturally fragmented by the events that brought down the western empire. Germans, such as Clovis's Franks, constituted a small minority of the population of the new lands their kings aspired to rule. Most of Gaul's residents were Romanized Celts, Catholic Christian descendants of the subjects of the old empire. Religion was especially important to them, for their leaders were their bishops. The clergy had inherited responsibility for Rome's *civitates* (the city-states that composed the old empire) when the empire's secular government crumbled. Clovis's Gaul was a loose association of regions headed by Catholic bishops from powerful aristocratic families, and German kings, like Clovis, had to come to terms with these native magnates.

This could be difficult for several reasons. Some Germans, Clovis and the Franks among them, were pagans who worshiped ancient tribal gods. Others, such as the Visigoths and Burgundians with whom the Franks competed for control of Gaul, were heretics—Arian Christians. The Catholic clergy despised the Arian faith as a perversion of their religion, but they viewed pagans more positively as candidates for conversion. Clovis, therefore, had a slight advantage in negotiations. Like Constantine a century and a half earlier, he understood the political advantages of conversion, and like Constantine, he justified abandoning his ancestral gods by claiming that the Christian God gave him victory in a crucial battle. The church, which welcomed him as its defender and patron, had much to offer him. It supported him in his wars with the Arian kings and helped him create a more effective monarchy by utilizing what was left of the imperial tax and administrative systems.

Many of the German tribes remained aloof from the peoples whose lands they occupied, but not the Franks. The conversion of the Franks made it possible for them to intermarry with the Romano-Celts and join them in developing a common culture. This required compromises on both sides. The Christian religion and Roman practice altered some German traditions—particularly those governing marriage, the status of women, inheritance, and property rights. Frankish customary law influenced courts and enforcement of justice—the prosecution and punishment of crime becoming a private matter rather than the duty of the state. Government's function was primarily to restrain the vendettas that threatened to break out among quarreling families. Accused persons could clear their names by undergoing physical ordeals or by compurgation (that is, finding a number of individuals who would swear to their innocence). The guilty could avoid physical punishment by paying **wergeld** ("man money"), monetary compensation. Amounts were determined by the nature of the injury and the status of the person who had been harmed. As more formal governmental procedures evolved under Roman influence, the German laws, which had been preserved as an oral tradition, were translated into Latin and written down. Latin survived as the language of scholarship and formal documents, but the "street" Latin spoken by the majority of Gaul's residents was gradually transformed into the Romance ("Roman") dialects that are the ancestors of modern French. As the Frankish and Romano-Celtic peoples fused, Gaul's cultivated, literate nobility disappeared, and the new aristocracy that emerged at the top of society adopted the lifestyle of the German warrior elite. In short, the features of a new medieval civilization began to appear in western Europe.

The Merovingian Succession   Clovis's kingdom was a collection of separate regions that he kept together by force. He did not think of his domain as a state, a political entity to be handed down intact from generation to generation. He understood it to be a private estate—the property of his family, the **Merovingians** (descendants of a quasi-mythical Merovech). This had major consequences for the future of Francia. German tradition dictated that private property be divided among all a man's heirs. Consequently, the Frankish kingdom was repeatedly divided and recombined—giving each generation of Merovingian princes an excuse to fight among themselves and fatally weaken their dynasty (see Map 8–1).

Clovis divided his kingdom among four sons. Fortunately, they were more interested in wars of conquest than in fighting among themselves. One of the boys outlived the others and briefly reunited the realm, but he divided it again for his heirs. From about 570 to 613, civil war raged between the two original Merovingian courts, Austrasia and Neustria. The survivor of the conflict laid claim to all of Francia, but by then the power base of the Merovingian kings was seriously eroded.

The Franks viewed their kings less as administrators of territorial states than as tribal leaders. Their king was a warlord who was supposed to settle disputes among his followers and lead them on profitable raids. A Frank expected his loyalty to his king to be rewarded by a steady stream of gifts. This custom had developed when the Franks were bands of semi-nomadic warriors who made their livings by dividing up the cattle and movable goods they captured from their neighbors. But once they settled down and land became the source of their wealth, their kings had difficulty meeting their expectations. A king who acquired new lands through conquest was able to enrich himself and reward his men. But when conquests ceased, kings sometimes had to give away their own lands to maintain the support of their followers. Over time, important nobles greatly enriched themselves at the expense of the royal family, and the balance of power shifted to them and away from their impoverished monarch.

A proliferation of heirs also helped to weaken the Merovingians and encourage their tendency to fight among themselves. Royal marriages were fluid, and the distinction between a wife and a concubine vague. Kings often had children by many women, and because there was no tradition of primogeniture ("first born") mandating that the whole kingdom pass to a king's eldest son, every male with a bit of Merovingian blood could claim a share of the royal estate. This played into the hands of the Frankish nobles, for rival can-

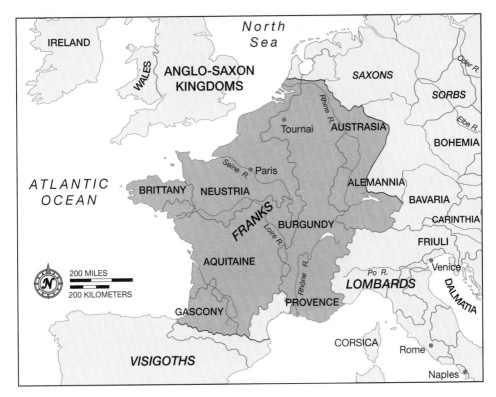

Map 8–1   Western Europe in the Merovingian Era   Clovis and his descendants assembled what might have become the core territory for a continental state, a united Europe. But they failed to overcome centers of regional power and develop a stable monarchy.

Question: Did geography work for or against Francia's development into the country of France?

didates had to offer them gifts in exchange for their support. The last significant Merovingian monarchs were Chlotar II (d. 629) and his son Dagobert (d. 638). After them, the throne passed to youths and weaklings whose fortunes steadily diminished until the last Merovingian kings were reduced to living modestly on a small farm outside of Paris.

The Franks' Neighbors

The Franks were not the only Germans to try to build new states amid the ruins of Rome's western empire. Other groups made promising starts, but like the Franks, they suffered reversals. The political contours of a new Europe were slow to emerge.

Italy and the Lombards   While Clovis was building a Frankish domain in Gaul, the Ostrogoths, under the leadership of their king Theodoric (r. 489–526), were taking control of Italy. Theodoric restored political stability to Italy, protected its Roman inhabitants, and safeguarded its classical culture. After his death, the Byzantine emperor, Justinian (r. 527–565), invaded Italy, and the peninsula was devastated by a war that dragged on to

552. The Ostrogoths ultimately yielded and left Italy to join the Visigoths in Gaul and Spain (see Chapter 7).

In 568 the exhausted Byzantines fell back as another wave of German invaders, the Lombards, descended on Italy. Alboin, their king, established his seat at Pavia (south of Milan) in what came to be known as Lombardy. The Lombard kingdom was weak, and it failed to impose its authority throughout Italy. Lombard chiefs carved out independent duchies, and the Byzantines hung on to Ravenna and a few outposts in southern Italy. The peninsula was divided up among small states that preyed on one another and kept the region in turmoil.

Spain: The Visigoths and the Muslims

After sacking Rome in 410, the Visigoths settled in southern France and began to spread into Spain. Fighting among factions kept them weak, and in 507 Clovis and the Franks seized much of the land they had occupied in Gaul. Their hold on Spain was not much more secure. The Visigothic nobles elected their kings, and their preference was often for a weak candidate who posed no threat to their independence. The Visigoths' Arian religion was also a problem, for it drove a wedge between them and their Catholic subjects. The Visigoths finally converted to Catholicism in 589, but the continuing reluctance of the Visigoths to marry native Spaniards kept Spain's two peoples divided. The Visigoths spent much of their time fighting among themselves, and in 711 a group of rebels asked Tarik, the Muslim governor of North Africa, to help them overthrow their king. The army that Tarik landed at "Tarik's Mountain" (Jebel el-Tarik, or Gibraltar) chose instead to conquer Spain. Spain's Christians lost everything but the tiny state of Asturias in the northwest corner of the Iberian Peninsula. Spain became, and was for a long time to remain, a Muslim country.

In 720 the Muslims crossed the Pyrenees bent on the conquest of Francia. By then the authority of the impoverished Merovingian kings had all but disappeared, and the Franks found a new leader in Charles Martel, the head of a powerful noble family. In 732 he halted the Muslim advance near the city of Tours. The Muslims retreated but retained control of a strip of France's Mediterranean coast until about 750. In that year the Abbasids overthrew the Umayyad caliph. He and most of the members of his family were slaughtered, but one Umayyad prince escaped and fled to Spain. He waged a bloody struggle that culminated in Spain's repudiation of the Abbasids and the establishment of a rival caliphate with its seat at Córdoba.

England

The Franks and Goths who founded kingdoms in Gaul and Spain got their starts as *foederati* (allies) of Rome's empire. They were influenced by Roman culture, and they tried to save some of the empire's institutions. The situation in the Roman province of Britain was different. The cities the Romans founded in Britain failed to flourish, but the rural villas they scattered about the countryside thrived. During the fifth century, when the migrations of the Germans disrupted production on the continent, demand for British goods soared and Britain's economy prospered. The island's Romano-Celts, the Britons, were understandably dismayed when, about 406, Rome withdrew its troops and told the people of Britain that they would have to defend themselves. Their situation was precarious. They faced raids from Ireland and Scotland, and the wall that the emperor Hadrian had built across northern England was useless without an army to back it up.

Local strongmen emerged to fill the political vacuum left by Rome's departure, and some of them raised armies by recruiting German mercenaries from the tribes of Angles and Saxons who roamed the continent's North Sea coast. These soldiers-for-hire turned on their employers, and by 450 the homeland of the Britons was becoming Angleland (England).

The Anglo-Saxons, in contrast to other Germans, had been little exposed to Rome's civilizing influence, and the Britons gave them no help. The Germans who established the new kingdoms on the continent came from tribes that had a history of involvement with Rome, and when they settled in their new territories, they had the advantage of mixing with Rome's former subjects. But as the Anglo-Saxons moved into Britain, the native Britons either fled or were exterminated. So many emigrated to northwestern Gaul that the area came to be called Brittany. Others moved to Ireland and Spain. Few stayed behind to try to convert the Anglo-Saxons to Christianity or instruct them in the arts of civilization. This period in England's history is largely undocumented, but the memory of at least one battle in which Britons triumphed over Anglo-Saxons survived into the twelfth century. It inspired a cycle of romantic tales about a King Arthur and a legendary land of Camelot. Scholars have proposed various Latin and Celtic roots for the name Arthur, but Camelot's king is a creature of mythology.

Ireland   As civilization declined in Britain, it began to flourish in Ireland, a land that had never been part of the Roman Empire or had much contact with its civilization. Ireland was divided into clan territories headed by petty kings. It had no cities and no literate culture until a chance event set in motion a chain of events that fundamentally altered its way of life.

In the fourth century Irish raiders sacked the coast of Britain and abducted a youth named Patrick, the son of a Roman official. Patrick spent six years as a slave in Ireland before escaping to the continent. For two decades, he studied in various monasteries, and about 432 he was consecrated a bishop and sent back to Ireland. He was phenomenally successful at converting the Irish to Christianity, and the new faith promoted the spread of monasticism and literacy.

Because Ireland was, for some time, cut off from the rest of the Christian world, it evolved some unique religious customs. Ireland did not have cities like those that provided seats for bishops in former

The Book of Kells   This page from an illuminated (decorated) text of the gospels was probably created about 750 at Iona, an Irish monastery on the western coast of Scotland. It lavishly ornaments the Greek letters that begin a verse from the first chapter of the Gospel of Matthew. Celtic and Germanic arts featured complex designs that utilized abstract geometrical forms.

PEOPLE IN CONTEXT Brunhild (d. 613) and Fredegund (d. 597): Powers Behind the Throne

n 567 Sigibert, king of Austrasia, made a prestigious marriage that threatened the balance of power in Francia. He wed Brunhild, daughter of the Visigothic king of Spain. This gave him a major ally in his competitons with his brother, Chilperic, king of Neustria. But Chilperic quickly checked Sigibert's move by winning the hand of Brunhild's sister, Galswinth. For some unknown reason, Chilperic then turned against his bride, murdered her, and returned to a former wife, Fredegund (d. 597), a woman of humble origin with whom he was apparently infatuated.

Merovingian princes often wed commoners to avoid the troublesome entanglements associated with aristocratic marriages, but a match with Fredegund did not make life any easier for Chilperic. She became a power at his court and cleared the way to the throne for her children by eliminating his sons by other women. The only one of her boys to outlive Chilperic was an infant named Chlotar II. Although his paternity was questioned, Fredegund successfully defended his claim to the throne and served as regent during his minority.

War erupted between Austrasia and Neustria after Galswinth's murder, but no contemporary source claims that it was caused by Brunhild's desire for vengeance. Dynastic ambitions may be enough to explain the bloody conflict that raged between her and Fredegund and Chilperic. In 575 Fredegund engineered the assassination of Brunhild's husband, Sigibert. Childebert II, Brunhild's young son by Sigibert, retained control of Austrasia with the help of an uncle, but Brunhild fell into Chilperic's hands. She tried to recoup her fortunes by marrying Merovech, one of Chilperic's sons who was attempting to unseat his father. When their coup failed, Merovech committed suicide, and Brunhild escaped to her son's court. Two of Fredegund's agents, both clergymen, then tried but failed to assassinate Brunhild and Childebert.

Gold Fibula This pin for a cloak was cast for a wealthy Merovingian who lived in the seventh century.

Although one of the Merovingian queens was a foreigner and the other a commoner, both wielded great power. The sources depict them as scheming behind the scenes, but both were highly visible figures. Fredegund's assassination of Sigibert reversed the course of a war, and the queen dominated her husband's successor until her death in 587. Brunhild received flattering letters from Pope Gregory the Great (r. 590–604), who assumed that she had the power to reform the Merovingian church, and her husband and her son were both accused of being under her thumb.

Brunhild manipulated the feuds that divided Francia's aristocratic families, and by 585 she and her son Childebert were firmly in control of Austrasia and busily eliminating their opponents. In 584 Brunhild avenged Fredegund's assassination of Sigibert (Brunhild's husband) by murdering Fredegund's husband, Chilperic I. By 589 Brunhild and Childebert had become the dominant powers in Francia, and the death of an uncle in 592 allowed Childebert to add Burgundy to his possessions. Childebert died four years later, and Brunhild ruled as regent for his sons, Theudebert II and Theuderic II.

When Theudebert reached his majority (c. 600), a coalition of Austrasian nobles forced Brunhild to flee to Burgundy, Theuderic's territory. She then announced that Theudebert was the bastard child of a palace gardener and that Theuderic was the legitimate heir to Austrasia. Her influence over her grandson increased as she encouraged his sexual affairs and dissuaded him from a marriage that would have raised up a rival queen. Reform-minded clergy were scandalized, and declared Theuderic's offspring illegitimate. Brunhild then had the kingdom's bishops denounce the reformers.

In 612 Brunhild finally persuaded Theuderic to attack Austrasia. Theuderic killed Theudebert and his son, and he was on the verge of invading Neustria to unseat Fredegund's son Chlotar II when he died of dysentery. Brunhild prevented the division of Theuderic's estate among his sons, and arranged for the eldest, her great-grandson Sigibert II, to inherit a unified kingdom. At that juncture, a block of aristocrats defected to Neustria and helped Chlotar II capture Brunhild and Sigibert. Chlotar claimed that Brunhild had been responsible for the deaths of ten kings, and he condemned the elderly woman to be torn apart by wild horses.

Question: What do the careers of Brunhild and Fredegund suggest about the roles that other less well-documented aristocratic women may have played in medieval politics?

Roman territory. Its church was organized around monasteries established in the territories of the Irish clans. The abbots who presided over these houses were more important leaders of Ireland's church than its bishops.

Christianity brought literacy to the Irish, and Irish monks became renowned for their superior scholarship at a time when learning was declining on the continent. Irish monasticism also placed a great deal of emphasis on ascetic self-denial. Some monks embraced self-exile as an ascetic discipline. Some became missionaries to England and the continent. They helped to convert the Anglo-Saxons. They planted monastic outposts as far afield as Gaul and Italy, and one of them even tried to reform the morally lax court of the Merovingian queen Brunhild.

The Carolingian Era

In 751 the last of the Merovingians was deposed, and the Franks transferred their allegiance to the family of the **Carolingians**, whose most famous king was Charlemagne (a contraction of the French for "Charles the Great").

A Transition of Dynasties The Carolingian family was formed by the intermarriage of the heirs of the two most powerful men at the Austrasian court of the Merovingian king Dagobert (d. 638). The Carolingians controlled the office of "mayor of the palace," a kind of prime ministry, and were more powerful than the rulers they theoretically served. In 679 Pepin of Heristal, the Carolingian mayor of Austrasia, extended his authority over Neustria and united both Frankish homelands under a Merovingian puppet king. When he died in 714, his illegitimate son, Charles Martel, dispossessed his half-brothers, who were minors, and assumed control of the family's enterprises. It was Martel (c. 688–741) who repulsed the Muslim invasion of Francia in 732. Further military successes won him the submission of Aquitaine and Burgundy, and new lands in Germany.

Some of Martel's contemporaries called him *rex* ("king"), but this was only a courtesy or flattery. It was Martel's son and heir, Pepin III, "the Short" (r. 741–768), who formally elevated the Carolingian family to royal status. He might simply have appropriated the Merovingians' title, but that would have diminished its worth. Titles are only significant when people believe that they are legitimate, and it was hard for Pepin to challenge the Merovingians' legitimacy. Because the Franks had no memory of a time when they had not been ruled by Merovingians, the Merovingians' right to the throne appeared to be part of the divine order of creation.

Given that the Franks had embraced Christianity and no longer worshiped the gods who had reigned at the start of the Merovingian era, Pepin reasoned that they would accept a change of dynasties if it were approved by the Christian God. The difficulty, of course, lay in finding someone who could speak for God. The bishop of Rome claimed that right, and it was in Pepin's interest to support his claim.

The Christian community had never acknowledged a supreme leader. The emperor dominated the church in Constantinople, and the groups of Christians that were scattered and cut off inside the Muslim empire attended to their own affairs. The church in western Europe was far from unified, but one of its bishops could make a case for precedence over the others. The bishop of Rome (the pope) headed the only diocese in the region that had been founded by one of Jesus' apostles, and its founder, Peter, was a very special apostle. Jesus (in the sixteenth chapter of Matthew's Gospel) had granted him the "power of the keys." Jesus had said that whatever Peter "loosed" or "bound" on Earth would be "loosed" or "bound" in heaven. Catholic dogma holds that this authority passed to Peter's successors in Rome—giving them the right to speak and act for God. A wide gap existed, however, between the powers the early medieval popes claimed and the powers they actually exercised.

The church came of age as one of the institutions of the Roman Empire, and its leaders clung to the empire as long as they could. After the line of western emperors ceased in 476, the bishops of Rome looked to the eastern emperors for protection. But this was not a satisfactory arrangement. Byzantine emperors and popes quarreled over doctrine, and the military assistance that Constantinople could offer Rome steadily diminished as the Lombards moved into Italy. Rome's Senate is not recorded as meeting after 579, and as the city's secular government faded away, responsibility for defending and administering Rome fell to its bishop. During the seventh century, some popes had courted Frankish rulers in hopes of winning their help, but the Franks were reluctant to be drawn into a war with the Lombards.

In 751 the Lombards conquered Ravenna, Constantinople's major base in Italy, and the danger they posed to Rome increased. Pope Zacharias (r. 741–752) made a desperate appeal to Pepin for help. Pepin was willing to negotiate, for the pope now had something of value to offer a Frankish leader. Zacharias endorsed Pepin's argument that the man who had the responsibility of king ought also to have the title, and he urged the Franks to elevate Pepin to their throne according "to their custom." Pepin, supported by the clergy, deposed the last Merovingian king and confined him to a monastery. Pepin was then crowned in a ceremony that included a new ritual—an anointing, a spiritual consecration. This added dignity and awe to the new dynasty, but it raised troubling questions. Did it give kings clerical status and authority over the church? Or did it imply that the church, because it consecrated kings, also had the right to depose them? A serious struggle between church and state was to break out in the distant future, but in Pepin's day kings were so much stronger than popes that the possibility of a conflict between secular and spiritual authorities may not even have occurred to them.

Pepin's sons were both married to Lombard princesses, and his reluctance to offend his Italian allies delayed repayment of his debt to the papacy. In 754 a desperate Pope Stephen II (r. 752–757) came to Paris to plead with Pepin in person—and to reconsecrate him as king. Pepin finally took his army to Italy, drove the Lombards back from Rome, and ceded the lands that he liberated to the pope. This "**Donation of Pepin**" confirmed the existence of a papal kingdom (the Papal States). The pope had conferred spiritual status on Pepin, and Pepin had reciprocated by shoring up the pope's secular power. The pope doubtless needed a base of his own so that he could resist domination by lay lords and kings, but the papacy's temporal interests inevitably conflicted with its spiritual role—at considerable cost to both church and state.

Charlemagne Builds an Empire

When Pepin died in 768, his throne was well established. However, his decision to divide his kingdom between his two sons, Carloman (r. 768–771) and Charles (Charlemagne, r. 768–814), cast doubt on its future. Carloman's premature death in 771 prevented the outbreak of civil war, for Charlemagne quickly deprived Carloman's young sons of their inheritance and reunited the Frankish kingdom. He then set about building an empire.

Charlemagne's first acquisition was the Lombard kingdom in northern Italy. Its ruler, Desiderius, was Charlemagne's father-in-law, but that did not prevent Charlemagne from responding to another appeal from the papacy (in 774) for help against the Lombards. He defeated Desiderius, imprisoned him, and appropriated the Lombard crown. This removed one threat from the papacy, but posed another. With much of France, Germany, and Italy under the control of the Frankish king, the pope had little latitude for independent action.

The papacy's concern for its independence may account for the appearance in the eighth century of a forged document called the "**Donation of Constantine**." In fairness, the forging of documents was not the crime then that it is today. The decline of literacy meant that many people lacked documents confirming rights to which they were entitled. Often the forger's motive was to create records that should have existed but did not. The popes believed that, as the only officials of the Roman Empire left in western Europe, they took precedence over the new German monarchs. The Donation of Constantine made their case by appealing to a popular, but groundless, legend that claimed that Pope Sylvester I (r. 314– 335) had cured the emperor Constantine of leprosy. The grateful emperor had supposedly repaid the pope by ceding the empire to the church, but the pope had graciously decided to allow Constantine to continue to rule the eastern half. The medieval popes did not claim, on the basis of this story, to be emperors. As early as the fifth century, Pope Gelasius I (d. 496) had declared the church and state to be separate and equal partners. He said that kings, like popes, were established by God. The former was given a secular, and the latter a spiritual, "sword." Ideally, each was to assist the other without transgressing on his colleague's turf. In practice, however, popes had a difficult time preventing royal encroachments on the church, and the Donation of Constantine was an attempt to intimidate kings by implying that popes were the final arbiters of the legitimacy of the West's monarchs.

The Donation of Constantine complicated disputes between popes and kings until it was proved to be a forgery in the fifteenth century. Charlemagne was far too powerful to worry about its implications for church-state relations, and he may actually have found it useful in improving his position. His father, Pepin, wanted to become a king, and Charlemagne sought recognition as an emperor. The church helped both men reach their objectives.

If any German leader deserved recognition as an emperor, it was Charlemagne, for he came to control most of western Europe. Following his victory over the Lombards, he turned his attention to Muslim Spain. Spain seemed vulnerable, for the Muslims were fighting among themselves. But as soon as the Franks appeared, the Muslims closed ranks and forced Charlemagne to withdraw. As his army retreated over the Pyrenees, the native Basques attacked its rearguard. This was an inconsequential event that did not alter history, but for some reason it captured the popular imagination. Stories began to be told about a Roland, an alleged duke of Brittany and favorite of Charlemagne's, who died in the encounter. In the late eleventh century these inspired the first major piece of French literature, an epic poem entitled *The Song of Roland*.

Although Charlemagne's first Spanish campaign failed, he continued to probe Muslim territory, and by 801 he had taken Barcelona and created the Spanish **march** (a frontier military district). The march provided Christians with a base south of the Pyrenees from which they launched crusades in the eleventh century to reconquer Spain (see Map 8–2).

Most of Charlemagne's wars were aimed at winning German territory. From 772 to 804 he waged annual campaigns in Saxony (the region south of the Danish peninsula). Mass executions and deportations were needed to pacify Saxony, which became one of Germany's stronger duchies. In 787 Charlemagne put down a rebellion in Bavaria, and a subsequent campaign culminated in the founding of the East March (Ostmark, or Austria). Next, he drove down the Danube Valley into the territory of the Avars, invaders from the Russian steppes who had grown wealthy extorting tribute from Constantinople and the Balkans. In 796 the Franks secured Germany's eastern border by defeating and dispersing the Avars, and Charlemagne returned home with massive amounts of treasure.

Charlemagne wanted the imperial title as a recognition of his achievement in uniting much of western Europe, but its quest confronted him with the same problem his father Pepin had faced. If the title was to be more than a presumptuous affectation, he could not simply assume it. His right to it had to be confirmed by an appropriate au-

Map 8–2   Growth of the Carolingian Empire   By spreading their civilization and government across much of Europe, the Romans created a tradition of European unity that was never forgotten. It inspired repeated efforts to reunite the peoples of Europe under a single political authority.

Question: Does geography work for or against the formation of a continental European state?

thority. The most obvious authority was the surviving Roman emperor who ruled in Constantinople, and in 780 Charlemagne began to negotiate with the Byzantine Empire for recognition as the eastern ruler's western colleague.

To bolster his claim to the imperial title, Charlemagne embarked on a program that would make him look as imperial as possible. German kings tended not to have fixed, permanent seats for their governments. They found it easier to feed their court by moving it from one royal estate or monastery to another than by shipping food from distant farms to a central location. Poor communications also meant that the king had to travel to stay in touch with his subjects. The lifestyle of Roman and Byzantine emperors was different.

Charlemagne's Chapel at Aachen   The palace complex at Aachen was laid out as a rectangle covering an area of about 50 acres. Charlemagne's palace occupied one side of the rectangle, and the church the other. A long covered gallery connected the two. The church was rebuilt and added on to by later generations, but the center portion remains much as Charlemagne knew it.

They resided in capital cities ornamented with monuments testifying to their power. Charlemagne, therefore, decided to construct a grand palace complex as a permanent seat for his court. The site he chose revealed, however, that his capital was to be more a symbol than a center of government. Charlemagne settled in Aachen (Aix-la-Chapelle), an old Roman spa. Its appeal was not its potential as a center for a communications network, but a pool fed by hot springs in which the king enjoyed swimming. The centerpiece of the new capital was a church in Byzantine style. It was as magnificent as the best European artists could make it. They looted Ravenna, the old capital of the western Roman empire, for architectural elements to use in its construction, but the finished building fell far short of the splendors of Constantinople's *Hagia Sophia.*

Charlemagne's negotiations with Constantinople dragged on for over 20 years without making much progress. The delay was due in part to political confusion in the eastern empire. In 797 the eastern emperor's mother, Irene, overthrew him and became the first woman to assert a claim of her own to either a Roman or a Byzantine throne. Because there was doubt about the legitimacy of a female emperor, a case could be made that the office was vacant and therefore available for someone else to claim. The situation might have had some influence on Charlemagne's decision to go to Rome in 800 to extricate Pope Leo III (r. 795–816) from some political difficulties. He stayed on to celebrate Christmas, and at the holiday mass the pope and the Roman populace hailed him as emperor. Einhard, Charlemagne's biographer, claims that the pope did this without Charlemagne's prior knowledge and that it infuriated Charlemagne. That seems unlikely. Leo was on shaky ground and could hardly have risked taking such a momentous step without Charlemagne's approval. It is also hard to imagine how he could have carried out a coronation ceremony without Charlemagne's cooperation. The story of Charlemagne's displeasure may have been circulated to smooth things over with Constantinople. It provided diplomatic cover for Charlemagne by shifting responsibility for the event to the papacy.

The patriarch of Jerusalem acknowledged Charlemagne's status as an international Christian leader of the first rank by sending him the keys to the Church of the Holy Sepulcher, the site of Christ's tomb. Harun al-Rashid (r. 786–809), the Abbasid caliph of

Baghdad, addressed him as an equal and sent him a gift befitting an emperor, a war elephant. Constantinople grumbled, but in 813 it accepted the *fait accompli* in exchange for resolving a dispute over some Balkan territories. A few months after Byzantine ambassadors hailed Charlemagne as an emperor (but not explicitly a Roman emperor) in Aachen, he shared his title with his son and heir in a ceremony that pointedly excluded the clergy. Charlemagne did not want his coronation to set a precedent for the papacy to claim an exclusive right to crown emperors. However, his successor undid his work by subsequently seeking papal confirmation of the title, and thereafter it was firmly established that the imperial title was assumed only with a papal blessing.

The Nature of the Carolingian Empire   Charlemagne's empire was held together by personal relationships that were maintained by the judicious use of carrots and sticks. The emperor was a daunting man who could physically intimidate his subordinates or seduce them with gifts, as the situation warranted. Their loyalty was essential to the functioning of his government, for primitive communications prevented Charlemagne from knowing much about what was occurring in his far-flung domain. Because he had to grant his officials a great deal of discretionary authority, he bound them to him with oaths and personal obligations. He filled most key offices with Austrasian nobles whose families had ties with his. He required all his male subjects over the age of 12 to swear personal oaths of loyalty to him, and he persuaded his leading men to take oaths of vassalage. His father was the first to impose vassalage on the nobility as a sign of their subservience to their king. *Vassus* (or *vassallus*) was a Celtic term for a servant or slave, but by the end of the eighth century, it had come to designate a far more exalted status.

The empire had seven marches (militarized frontier districts) and about 300 counties. A duke (*dux*, "general") or count (*comes*, "companion") headed each of the territorial divisions of the empire, and he was responsible for all aspects of the government and defense of his district. Left largely on his own, he was, in effect, a mini-king, but there were safeguards to prevent him from abusing his power. A man was usually assigned to a region where he did not have influential relatives to back him up, and he was moved from time to time to prevent him from building a power base that he might use against his emperor. Charlemagne frequently summoned his officials to court to remind them of their dependent status, and an annual mustering of the army at the beginning of the campaigning season (the Mayfield) gave him another chance to reinforce ties with them. He circulated open letters called capitularies to establish guidelines for good government, but it was difficult for him to know if his orders were followed. About 779 he began to send out teams of auditors (**missi dominici**, "emissaries of the lord") to check up on his governors and hear complaints against them, but it is doubtful that this did much to stem corruption or halt abuse of power. Most of Charlemagne's subjects thought of their emperor as a remote figure who had little to do with their lives. Their fates were decided locally.

The Division of the Empire   Charlemagne's empire was held together by the vigilance and energy of its leader, and as age sapped his strength, it too declined. The emperor had a bevy of wives, concubines, and children. He avoided some dynastic complications by refusing to allow his daughters to marry, but he planned to divide his realm among his sons. The civil war that this invited was avoided when he outlived all but one of them. Unfortunately, the survivor, Louis the Pious (r. 814–840), may have been the heir least suited to be an emperor.

Louis was a well-educated man who, had he not been destined for a throne, probably would have chosen a life in the church. In childhood he had been dispatched to the French region of Aquitaine to serve as its titular king. Raised there under the tutelage of a monk, he became a sober man who was appalled by the moral laxity of his father's court. One of his first acts upon becoming emperor was to purge the court of everyone (including his sisters) whose conduct was not up to his strict standards. He believed that the church was also in need of reform, but he was overly deferential to his clerical advisors. When his vassals realized that their lord was as weak-willed as he was pious, they began to take liberties. His own sons ultimately turned on him and on one another. After Louis died in 840, his three surviving sons fought for another three years before agreeing to a settlement of their father's estate. In 843 the Treaty of Verdun, which ended their war, foreshadowed the emergence of Europe's major nations. The youngest of Louis's sons, Charles the Bald, became king of western Francia. His brother, Louis the German, got the empire's eastern territories, and the oldest of the three princes, Lothair, claimed the imperial title and a long, narrow kingdom that ran between his brothers' realms from the North Sea down the Rhineland to Italy. The new kingdoms represented regions that were already evolving separate ethnic cultures. Evidence for this is preserved in a chronicle that describes a meeting between Louis and Charles at Strasbourg in 842. Each swore an oath in a tongue that the other's followers could understand, and the text of Louis's oath is the earliest specimen of a Romance language.

Lothair's kingdom was divided among his heirs and eventually disappeared. The rulers of Francia and Germany appropriated parts of it. (France and Germany were still quarreling over Lorraine—Lotharingia—as late as the mid-twentieth century.) No new royal dynasty appeared in Italy, and the imperial title itself was allowed to lapse in 924. By then it meant little.

Invasions and Fragmentation

The western Roman Empire had fallen to the migrations of Charlemagne's German ancestors, and now a similar fate was to befall his empire. Signs of what was to come appeared during the closing years of his reign.

In the second half of the eighth century, Viking fleets began to sally forth from

A Viking Ship   Viking chiefs were sometimes buried in their ships, and well-preserved specimens have been excavated and preserved in Norway's museums. This vessel dates to about 820. *Frits Solvang © Dorling Kindersley, Courtesy of the Universitetets kulturhistoriske museer/Vikingskipshuset.*

Scandinavia, driven by overpopulation or by opportunities for pillage. These Norsemen (Northmen, or Normans) had developed the best seafaring technology of their day. Viking ships could handle the high seas, but their shallow drafts also enabled them to navigate Europe's many rivers and strike deep inland.

While the Vikings attacked from the north, the Muslims renewed their assault from the south. In 800 the Abbasid caliphate ceded Algeria to the Aghlabids, a dynasty of local princes. The Aghlabids ended a long fight between Berber and Arab Muslims in North Africa by diverting their quarreling subjects to Christian targets. In 827 they began the conquest of Sicily, which was still Byzantine territory. From Sicily they raided Europe's Mediterranean coasts. They assaulted Rome in 846, and in 888 they established bases in the south of France from which they attacked traders who used the Alpine passes.

By then, a third threat to the Carolingian kingdoms had appeared on Germany's eastern frontier. The Magyars migrated westward from the Russian steppes and began to push up the Danube Valley into the heart of Europe (see Map 8–3).

The Carolingian states were poorly equipped to counter simultaneous attacks on multiple fronts, for they had little infrastructure to support centralized government. Some paved roads existed in those parts of Europe that had once belonged to Rome, but neither information nor troops could travel quickly. A king could not respond rapidly enough to fend off raids to his realm that might come from any direction or hit different places simultaneously. It made more sense to disperse resources and command authority, for every part of a kingdom needed a strong leader who was permanently in residence and prepared to defend it. Kings did not disappear, but power shifted decisively to their military vassals. Kings became firsts-among-equals who reigned rather than ruled. Their status was superior to that of their vassals, but their primary responsibility, like that of an ordinary lord, was to govern and defend their own estates.

Retrenchment and Reorganization

The medieval era in Western history is one of the most difficult to understand, for it had no central focus—no city like Athens or leaders like the Roman emperors to give structure to its narrative. The radical political fragmentation of Europe that followed the invasions of the ninth century confronts students of history with a special challenge. Scholars rely on models and generalizations to create an overview that helps to make sense out of the past, but the people they study actually lived in particular situations. They were concerned with survival, not conforming to a theory. They did whatever they deemed best to adapt to the specific circumstances they confronted. The European continent has many diverse environments, and its medieval inhabitants had a rich legacy of traditions and customs to draw on when exploiting them. Consequently, it is difficult for historians to say much that is equally true of all medieval people—particularly during the years of their most extreme political and cultural fragmentation.

In the Early Modern Era (post-sixteenth century), scholars sought explanations for the institutions and conventions of European society by delving into the medieval past. Untold numbers of legal documents were preserved in their countries' archives, and many of these dealt with rights to a piece of property or revenue called a **feudum** or fief. This led to the

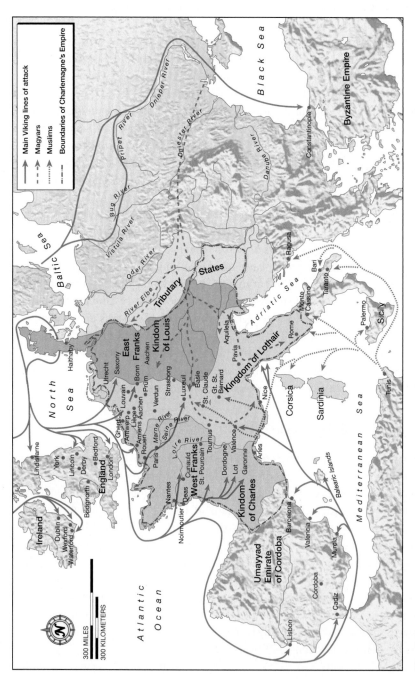

Map 8–3 The Ninth-Century Invasions The invaders who descended on Europe in the ninth century did not coordinate their attacks and did not have a common objective. Europeans also had no single strategy for opposing them. Rather than the invasions inspiring Europeans to unite to mount a defense, the people of Europe opted to divide their forces.

Question: What challenges did geography pose for the defense of the European continent?

belief that a coherent "feudal system" had structured the lives of medieval people. But over the years, scholars have defined feudalism in so many different ways and found so many exceptions to its supposed "system" that the current trend is to dispense with the term entirely.

Medieval societies did, however, have some distinguishing features, and some generalizations about them can be useful as points of reference and comparison. Students should always keep in mind, however, that generalizations are only approximations of reality. Local and regional studies of medieval peoples will continue to turn up innumerable variations in the ways they arranged their lives, for people are pragmatists when it comes to the struggle for survival. They do what works, not what a theory or the pursuit of rational consistency may dictate.

Political Model   A *feudum* or fief was a resource (often land) given to a vassal to support him while he served his lord. The minting of coins dwindled drastically following the decline of the Roman Empire, and there was little money in circulation. Therefore, rulers in early medieval Europe did not collect most of their taxes in coin and pay their officials' salaries from a public treasury. Most financial transactions involved exchanges of consumable or otherwise desirable items. Because it was too cumbersome to collect all the goods produced on the state's lands for redistribution to the state's servants, governments parceled out the land itself. A lord paid his vassals by giving them the use of fiefs (usually farmland equipped with laborers). They did not own the lands that supported them while they served their lord. They owned only the right to the income from those lands—and that, technically, only so long as they rendered the services that their fiefs were meant to fund.

Once a vassal had a fief in his possession, however, it was hard for his lord to reclaim it. If the vassal had an heir who could perform the tasks for which his fief had been granted, the easiest thing was to pass it to him. But this risked creating precedents that might give the vassal's family a hereditary claim on its fief. To remind an heir of who owned the fief, when he received his inheritance the heir was required to pay his lord "relief" (*relever*, "to pick up again"), a fine that might amount to the first year's income from the fief. If there was no competent mature male heir, a compromise between the rights of the lord and the family had to be worked out. The fief's purpose was to support a soldier. If the heir was a minor, the lord obtained his soldier by making the boy the ward of a man who could provide knight service for him. If the heir was a female (either a daughter or widow), the lord could require her to marry a man of his choice. If the family died out, the fief returned to the lord who originally granted it.

Because a vassal enjoyed all the income from his fief, it made sense that he (not his lord) bore the costs of providing government services for the people who lived on it. As the individual on the scene, he was also much better situated to do this than a distant lord. Land ownership, therefore, came to entail "jurisdiction" (the right to enforce justice and to rule) over those who lived on one's land. There were, however, some restraints on the authority of a fief's owner. In simple, illiterate societies, custom acquires the force of law, and traditions could be quite explicit about the rights and duties of all members of society.

Medieval political and social arrangements had deep roots in the Roman and German pasts. Both the Roman patron-client system and the German warrior band, the **comitatus**, had used oaths of allegiance to structure society, and personal arrangements of this kind were fundamental to the organization of early medieval society. Citizenship had no meaning once the Roman Empire ceased to provide protection for legal rights. Without a state to rely on, individuals had to make private arrangements to ensure their survival. This usually involved commending oneself to the service of a protector. To commend oneself was to surrender some autonomy in exchange for help. Commendation applied to every rank on the social scale from lord and vassal down to the level of serf (a peasant farmer bound to the land). These categories of people had different functions in society, but their legal status was the same. None was free, for freedom was not a desirable condition in a chaotic world where power was more important than right. Free persons had failed to find a niche in society. They had no claim on a protector.

Reliance on oaths was a way of organizing society by means of contracts. Contracts were promises of mutually beneficial exchanges—for example, land for military service. The preservation and enforcement of these promises required special arrangements in what was in the early Middle Ages a largely illiterate world. Most of the contracts that military men and the lords entered into were probably oral agreements that existed only in the memories of witnesses. It was important, therefore, that witnesses understood the precise meaning of the events they were called on to witness. This led to development of rituals and symbolic actions that were widely understood to have specific meanings. Texts describing these ceremonies have survived. They often involved a lord enclosing within his hands the hands of a man doing homage to him. That man would swear an oath of fealty (fidelity) and then be given a clod of earth or some object to "invest" him with his fief.

In the early medieval world as in the modern one, birth often determined a person's options. Children of vassals had the chance to become vassals and those of serfs usually remained serfs. Individuals did, however, personally have to take the oaths their roles required, and there was some social mobility. Noble families could lose their wealth and standing, and talented people of humble origins might rise to great heights, particularly if they pursued careers in the church. Not every man born to a knightly family and trained for military service received a fief. The number of fiefs was limited, and if a fief was divided among all a vassal's sons, the portions soon became too small to support a knight, which defeated the purpose of the fief. This encouraged inheritance rules that passed the fief intact to one son, usually the eldest. His brothers had to find heiresses to marry or employment as mercenaries. There was a large number of career military men who survived by finding employment with a lord rich enough to maintain them as part of his household. They helped to man the private armies that proliferated as royal government declined. These armies provided protection, but they were also often disruptive elements in medieval society.

Militarized local governments took control throughout Europe as Carolinigian rule weakened, but they did not assume the same form everywhere. What worked in the rich grain-growing districts of northern France may not have made as much sense in the different cultural and economic environments of southern France, Germany, or central Europe. In unique regions, such as Switzerland, the terrain may have provided enough protection to minimize the need for much political and military organization at all.

Many places, however, witnessed the rise of a professional military class that enjoyed significant political authority. This class owed its origin to the increasing importance of a new kind of warrior, a heavily armed cavalryman called a knight (*cniht*, "boy" or "servant"). He was the product of medieval inventions that exploited the military potential of the horse in new and highly effective ways. Scholars debate when these inventions took hold in Europe and when the fully developed knight appeared. At the start of the Middle Ages, Frankish soldiers appear to have used horses for transportation to the field of battle, but then to have dismounted for combat. Saddles were in use in the West prior to the first century, but they had no stirrups. This made it hard for a rider to thrust a spear or swing a sword without lofting himself off his horse. The Koreans had stirrups by the fifth century, and the Byzantines were using them by the sixth century. They had certainly reached Francia by the eighth century, but it took time for their potential to be recognized—and other things were needed before that potential could be realized. Larger, stronger horses that could withstand the rigors of battle had to be bred. These animals needed the protection provided by horseshoes, which may not have appeared until the late ninth century. New weapons and armor had to be designed, and men had to devise and master new methods of combat. The fully equipped medieval knight may, therefore, not have charged onto the battlefield much before the late ninth century.

A lance driven by the combined weight and momentum of a charging horse and rider delivered a lethal blow, and a knight could slice through a company of foot soldiers like a tank. The knight marked an advance in military technology that every lord who wanted to remain competitive had to match. The process of making the transition to the new technology was, however, not easy, for knights were extraordinarily expensive. One knight might represent an investment equivalent to the cost of about 20 plow teams. As early as the generation of Charlemagne's grandfather, Charles Martel, Frankish leaders had begun to mobilize the resources of their society for the support of their expensive armies. The church, as well as holders of secular property, was compelled to provide lands for the maintenance of soldiers, and the use of land for this purpose created an association in some places of landownership with military service. It also signaled a change in the status of the ordinary man. The peasant foot soldier ceased to be of much importance as cavalry came to dominate infantry in medieval warfare. Hordes of men on foot might still be marshaled to attend the knights, but fighting—the politically empowering function of providing protection—was increasingly a job for professionals.

Economic Model   Given the economic burden that the new military technology imposed on medieval society, transition to the new kind of warfare would not have been possible if advances in agriculture had not been made to support it.

The methods used to work the thin, dry soils of the Middle East and the Mediterranean's shores did not translate well to northern Europe. Farmers in Francia, Britain, and Germany had to contend with heavy, wet soil and short growing seasons. A simple "scratch plow" (a pointed stick) worked well in southern regions where the ground was easy to break up, and farmers wanted to conserve the moisture it contained by disturbing the land as little as possible. A much heavier, animal-drawn wheeled plow was needed to cultivate northern Europe's fields, and plowshares had to be invented that did not merely break the soil but turned it over to promote drainage. It may have been the sixth century before such farming equipment was widely available.

Draft animals and metal plowshares were expensive. In regions where they were useful, farmers banded together to afford them. They established what have been called **manors** (*manere,* "to dwell"), medieval agricultural cooperatives. Manors differed from most modern communes in that they combined private ownership of land with common ownership of the tools that worked the land. Each serf (*servus,* "servant") who was commended to a manor held title to certain fields on the manor. He did not receive a percentage of the total production of the manor, but was entitled only to the crops that grew on the fields designated for his maintenance. Furthermore, his holdings were not concentrated in one part of the manor, but divided up into strips that were scattered throughout its arable land. This "open-field" system helped spread the risk involved in farming with communal equipment. It prevented fights over who got to use the plow first and ensured that everyone had a bit of land in whatever part of the manor plowing began and ended. This was important, for growing seasons were short in northern Europe. Serfs who had to sow their crops late ran a greater risk of starvation than those who could plant early.

Medieval farmers developed new methods as well as new tools to enhance their productivity. They understood the use of fertilizers (chiefly, lime and animal manure), but these were in short supply. The common method for maintaining the fertility of fields was fallow farming—plowing, but not planting, land, so that it "rested" for a season. Ancient farmers and medieval farmers in the Mediterranean regions employed a two-field system. That is, they plowed all their land, but planted only half of it—alternating halves annually. The kind of land worked by many of medieval Europe's farmers could support more intensive cultivation by a three-field system that combined fallow farming with crop rotation. They divided their land into thirds and planted one-third in the fall with a grain crop, another in the spring with beans and peas (that restored nitrogen to the soil), and left the third fallow. This reduced the amount of nonproductive plowing, provided some protection in case one of the crops failed, and increased harvests. Farmers made no major improvements on these early medieval techniques until the eighteenth century.

Serfs were not free people. In 332 an edict of Emperor Constantine, which was designed to counter the shrinking of the empire's workforce, had required agricultural laborers to stay on the lands they worked. But the ancient Roman *coloni* and the medieval serfs were not slaves. They had rights. They could not be separated from the land and sold like chattel. They were better off than many free people, for they were at least guaranteed a chance to earn a living. They also had a good deal of autonomy in the conduct of their affairs, for a vassal to whom a manor was given as a fief did not supervise his serfs' work. He was a soldier, not a farmer. His serfs managed their own affairs (guided by the customs of their manors). The vassal was supported in the same way as his serfs. He received whatever grew on his **demesne** (domain), the fields assigned to him. The serfs' chief obligation was to work those fields for him. His serfs might also have to pay for the use of a mill and oven he provided, and he profited from fines levied by his manorial court. Serfs were sometimes assessed a head tax as a sign of their inferior status. Payments from their estates were due to their lords when they died, and they were taxed for the support of the church. In some regions they may have had to forfeit half their annual income.

It is important to remember that not all medieval peasant farmers lived on manors and that many owned property outright. In some regions, the land was best worked by scattered, individual farmsteads, and many of Europe's peasants may have continued the ancient custom of working fields until their fertility declined and then moving to new locations. It might not have been until the eleventh century that the ruling classes began to force them into more stable, permanent village communities.

The Culture of Europe's Dark Age

Some people mistakenly assume that the whole medieval era was a dark age—and many Hollywood movies have depicted the Middle Ages as literally dark and dismal. A dark age, however, is so-called because it is dark to historians, not to those who lived it. It is a period that left few, if any, written records to inform later generations about its history. By this standard Europe's early medieval period might best be described as shady rather than dark. Literacy declined in what had been the western Roman Empire, but it did not disappear. Scholarly work continued in scattered places, and there were even flashes of creative genius.

Scholarship in a Period of Transition   The fifth century produced a trio of great Latin intellectuals who laid the foundation for medieval Europe's Christian culture. Augustine (d. 430), bishop of the North African city of Hippo, remains one of the West's most important theologian-philosophers, a figure who is studied today not just for his historical significance but for the continuing relevance of his ideas. Bishop Ambrose of Milan (c. 340–397), who converted Augustine, shaped the preaching and liturgical practices of the Latin church. Jerome (c. 340–419), an ascetic scholar, produced the Vulgate, the Latin translation of the Bible that was used throughout the Middle Ages.

During the years immediately following the deaths of these men, the confusion created by the migrations of the Germans into the western empire peaked, and intellectual activity in the Latin world declined. Whenever German kings restored a bit of stability, however, scholarly work resumed. The 30 years of order that Theodoric the Ostrogoth (r. 489–526) maintained in Italy gave Boethius (480–524) and Cassiodorus (490–580) the opportunity to create translations and textbooks that influenced education in Europe for centuries (see Chapter 7). Benedict of Nursia (c. 480–543), their contemporary, was no scholar, but he was largely responsible for the survival of schools and libraries in Europe. The rule that Benedict wrote for the monastery he founded in southern Italy at Monte Cassino spread throughout Europe and was ultimately mandated by the Carolingian monarchs for all the monasteries in their empire. The rule owed its success to the skillful balance it struck between the radical asceticism of the eastern hermits and monks and the more pragmatic values of western Europeans. Benedict's monks did not just strive for individual, personal salvation. Their vocation, they believed, was to pray and intercede with God for the sinful world while caring for its poor and needy. Benedict believed that monks should support themselves, so he divided their day into periods for work as well as worship, recreation, and rest. Although Benedictine monks, in the early years, did manual labor, many of their working hours were eventually devoted to the study and production of books.

Turmoil returned to Italy following Theodoric's death in 526, but by then his contemporary, Clovis (c. 466–511), had founded Francia's Merovingian dynasty. Over the

Cultural Leaders of the Early Middle Ages

TRANSMITTERS OF CLASSICAL CULTURE

Ambrose of Milan (c. 340–397)
Jerome (c. 340–419)
Augustine of Hippo (354–430)
Patrick (c. 380–c. 461)
Benedict of Nursia (c. 480–c. 550)
Boethius (c. 480–524)

MEROVINGIAN ERA

Columba (521–597)
Fortunatus (c. 535–605)
Gregory of Tours (c. 538–594)
Gregory the Great (c. 590–604)
Bede (c. 672–735)
Isidore of Seville (c. 570–636)
Augustine of Canterbury (d. 604)
Cassiodorus (c. 490–c. 580)

CAROLINGIAN RENAISSANCE

Alcuin (c. 735–804)
Paul the Deacon (c. 720–c. 800)
Peter of Pisa (744–799)
Theodulf of Orleans (c. 750–821)
Einhard (c. 770–840)

years, several scholars surfaced at, or corresponded with, the Merovingian courts. The elegant Latin poetry of Fortunatus (535–605), an Italian who was supported by Merovingian patrons, proves that excellent literary educations could still be obtained in Europe. Fortunatus's Frankish contemporary, Bishop Gregory of Tours (c. 538–594), complained, however, that standards of literacy had declined dramatically in his part of the world. The Latin of his *History of the Franks* supports this, but scholars debate whether the obscurity that plagues the text is the fault of its author or of the copyists who transmitted it to us. Despite its literary weaknesses, Gregory's book is a major achievement. In his day, the writing of history was a nearly forgotten art. Had he not revived it, we would know very little about the Merovingians.

Gregory of Tours had a contemporary, also named Gregory, who was one of Rome's most important popes. Gregory I, the Great (r. 590–604), defended Rome from the Lombards, laid a foundation for the Papal States, and still found time for literary work that earned him the title "Europe's schoolmaster." Gregory became pope at a time when the church in the Latin world was in near total disarray. His correspondence with bishops throughout Europe during an era of great confusion helped sustain them and retain a semblance of Christian unity. In addition to his many letters and sermons, he wrote several influential books. *Dialogues,* the most popular of his works, is a collection of stories about saints and miracles that had a tremendous impact on medieval preaching and spirituality. Gregory struggled to raise the standards of the church and further the spread of Christianity. He tried to interest the Merovingian queen Brunhild in church reform, and in 597 he sent missionaries to England to convert the pagan Anglo-Saxons. Augustine (d. 604), the Benedictine monk who led the mission, set up headquarters in Canterbury, the capital of the Anglo-Saxon kingdom of Kent. The archbishops who head England's church today still have their cathedral there.

By the time the pope's emissaries arrived in England, Irish missionaries were already at work. About 565, a monk named Columba (521–597) had established a monastery on the island of Iona, off the coast of Scotland, and launched a mission that spread into northern England. The schools that the Irish and Roman missions established in England produced some of the era's greatest scholars. The most notable of these was a remarkably original thinker named Bede (672–735). His interests ranged from natural science to theology and history. His major contribution to history, *The Ecclesiastical History of the English People*, is noteworthy for research methods that were far ahead of its time. Bede searched out evidence to document historical events and carefully critiqued his sources. He also helped establish the custom of dating historical events from the birth of Christ.

Visigothic Spain produced a notable scholar in this period, Isidore of Seville (c. 570–636), a contemporary of Pope Gregory. Isidore's major work, *Etymologiae* (or *Origines*), was a cross between an encyclopedia and a dictionary. It drew material from many ancient sources to suggest explanations for the meanings of words, and it provided medieval readers with an immense amount of useful information and dubious speculation. Typical was Isidore's claim that the word *medicine* derived from "moderation" because excess causes disease.

Spain's intellectual life received a great boost about 75 years after Isidore's death. The Muslim conquest of the Iberian Peninsula exposed Spaniards to influences from the Islamic world, the seat of the most dynamic of the early medieval civilizations. Muslims, Christians, and Jews rubbed shoulders in Spain. They learned each other's languages, traded literatures, and engaged in learned conversations. The vibrant intellectual life that evolved in Spain eventually drew students from northern Europe and stimulated Europe's recovery from the cultural slump into which it fell at the end of the Roman era.

The Carolingian Renaissance   About the time that Bede died (735) another scholarly Englishman was born. His name was Alcuin, and the excellent training he received at the cathedral of York from a student of one of Bede's students prepared him to become

Bust of Charlemagne   No contemporary portraits of Charlemagne survive—if indeed, any were ever made. But in the medieval literary tradition he was honored as a model king, and artists imagined him as the embodiment of majesty.

Europe's most prominent educator. Charlemagne persuaded him to move to Francia and undertake the leadership of a project that historians call the Carolingian Renaissance.

Charlemagne knew that the level of civilization in Europe had declined dramatically since the days of the Roman Empire. The church was in a particularly lamentable condition, for many clergy were illiterate. Village priests, who were often peasants without formal educations, could not chant the mass accurately. Even some bishops could not read and found preaching a challenge. Charlemagne hoped to correct this by ordering monasteries and cathedrals to establish schools. To provide these institutions with teaching materials, curricula, and a model, he asked Alcuin to set up a school at court, and he combed Europe for scholars to staff its faculty. Italy yielded a historian, Paul the Deacon, and a Latin grammarian, Peter of Pisa. Spain sent Theodulf, a poet. A couple of Irish scholars were in residence, and the most prominent Frank was Charlemagne's biographer, architect, and master of the palace works, Einhard (who was quoted at the beginning of this chapter).

The Carolingian Renaissance did not aspire to much original work. Its objective was to rescue literacy so that Europeans could access the intellectual legacy of the ancient world. Given the situation Charlemagne's scholars faced, their achievement was considerable. Following the example set by Roman textbooks, they designed an educational curriculum divided into seven liberal arts, the areas of knowledge needed by a *liber* ("freeborn man"). A liberal arts education emphasized literary skills. It began with the study of the **trivium** (grammar, dialectic, rhetoric), instruction in reading and writing Latin. The **quadrivium** (arithmetic, geometry, astronomy, and music), which followed, taught clergy what they needed to know to manage estates, calculate dates for church feasts, and sing liturgies.

Alcuin and his colleagues wrote textbooks for their schools. They sought out manuscripts of neglected works to build library collections, and they published improved editions of ancient texts. They even reformed the mechanics of writing. So many different scripts had evolved in so many places in Europe that it was difficult for scholars from one region to read what those in another had written. Charlemagne's schools standardized shapes for the letters of the alphabet and taught students to leave spaces between words to make reading easier and more efficient. Our system of writing is based on this Carolingian "minuscule."

The Carolingian Renaissance had some notable successes. It reformed the liturgy of the church by building on Roman customs that it believed went back to the generation of Pope Gregory the Great. The tradition of Gregorian chant, which the renaissance promoted, thrived for centuries and produced music that still moves worshipers. Charlemagne's scholars also halted the loss of books and rescued what was left in Europe of the literary legacy of the ancient world. Few major works exist today in copies older than those made by Carolingian scribes. Primarily, the renaissance's claim to be a decisive moment in European intellectual history rests on the fact that it halted the cultural decline that began with the passing of the Roman Empire and put western Europe back on the road to recovery. The political confusion that broke out after Charlemagne's death was a setback, but things were never again to be as bad as they had been before Charlemagne.

Charlemagne may have hoped for more than he got from his investment in Europe's re-education. The schools that he ordered monks and bishops to establish were not always able to fulfill their missions. His nobles ignored his call to educate themselves, and he may secretly have empathized with them. Einhard says that Charlemagne learned to read but that he started too late in life to master the motor skills that writing requires. He did not give up trying, however. He kept a slate under his pillow and practiced the alphabet before falling asleep.

KEY QUESTION | Revisited

Despite a healthy dose of barbarian ancestry, the inhabitants of early medieval Europe believed that they were legitimate heirs to the civilization of the ancient Mediterranean world, and they were determined to assert their claim to their legacy. They revered Rome's memory, the shreds of classical literature that had survived in their shrunken libraries, and the Christian religion. But they struggled with harsher and more primitive conditions than had faced most of the subjects of Rome's Mediterranean empire. They survived by innovating new technologies. They integrated information from their tribal oral traditions with classicism's literary legacy and their understanding of the Christian faith. They adapted to a challenging physical environment, to an economy that offered little more than basic sustenance, and to a society that had nearly lost all order and structure. Their unique needs and resources shaped what they did with their inheritance from the past. For a long time, the culture they were pioneering remained inferior to the civilizations of Islam and Byzantium, but they were slowly feeling their way toward a great future.

Review Questions

1. When did the northwestern provinces of the Roman Empire cease to be Roman and become European? What changes mark the transition between the two eras?
2. How did the problems that brought down the Merovingian dynasty differ from the problems that caused the fall of Rome's dynasties?
3. How did Charlemagne's empire differ from the realm of the Roman emperors whose title he claimed?
4. Why were medieval Europeans unable to sustain progress toward a continental empire?
5. How did Europeans adapt politically and economically to the Carolingian empire and its decline?
6. How did the civilization of early medieval Europe differ from the classical civilization of the ancient Greeks and Romans? Was it at all similar?

Please consult the Suggested Readings at the back of the book to continue your study of the material covered in this chapter. For a list of documents on the Primary Source DVD-ROM that relate to topics in this chapter, please refer to the back of the book.

Topics in This Chapter

Islam's Crest and Byzantium's Resurgence • The Reorganization of Europe

• The Eleventh-Century Turning Point

9 Europe Turns Outward

You Franks, the beloved of God whom He has chosen (as your many victories prove) and set apart from other peoples by the location of your country, your Catholic faith, and your respect for the church—on you we call! There is grievous news from Jerusalem and Constantinople. A race from Persia—an accursed people who are totally opposed to God—has stormed Christian lands and depopulated them by looting and burning. . . . On whom does the task of avenging these crimes fall . . . if not on you, you on whom God has conferred—more than on any other nation—outstanding military valor, great courage, vigor, and strength with which to overwhelm all who oppose you?

—Pope Urban II

KEY | Question

Was conflict among the medieval civilizations inevitable?

On November 27, 1095, Pope Urban II (r. 1088–1099) allegedly addressed the words quoted above to a crowd of knights assembled on a field at Clermont in central France. The knights who heard him may have been surprised to find themselves exhorted to fight, for they had come to Clermont to pledge themselves to the Truce of God. The Truce of God and an earlier movement called the Peace of God were efforts by the church to persuade feudal warriors to exercise self-restraint. The Peace, which originated in 989 at a council at Charroux in Aquitaine, decreed that knights should do no harm to noncombatants (clergy, women, and peasants). The Truce further curtailed bloodshed by declaring that no fighting should take place on sacred days: Sundays, religious festivals, and during the penitential seasons of Advent and Lent. Urban's call for a holy war was not, however, inconsistent with the objectives of the Peace and Truce. One way to pacify the home front was to divert Europe's military resources to foreign campaigns.

Cathedral of Cordoba This interior view of the cathedral of the Spanish city of Cordoba testifies to the cultural complexity of the medieval world. Now a Christian church, it was at one time the world's second largest mosque.

Urban's war is now known as the First Crusade, but the word **crusade** ("war of the cross") did not exist in his day. In fact, it was not coined until the thirteenth century. Urban called his holy warriors pilgrims. Pilgrims were not supposed to bear arms, and the church had always said that it was a sin to shed blood, but Urban assured the knights who responded to his call that his was a new kind of war that merited new rules. The enemy Christians faced was so heinous—and such an anathema to God and civilization—that killing him was an act of self-sanctification. The crusader's sword purified a warrior's soul, for by wielding it against the enemies of the faith, he fulfilled the mission for which God had created him.

Urban believed—correctly, as it turned out—that Europe had reached a turning point in its history. God, he claimed, had kept the Franks in reserve, tucked away from other peoples on the edge of the world. He had given them the true faith and the superior military virtues needed to defend that faith. The time had come, the pope said, for Europe's soldiers to be loosed on the enemies of God. For centuries Europeans had been in retreat and on the defensive. They had lost territory and suffered humiliating raids and invasions. Finally, however, they were ready to realize their destiny—to take the offensive and destroy all that they regarded as alien.

Urban's crusade was an early manifestation of the European impulse to thrust outward, both territorially and culturally. The descendants of his pilgrim-soldiers would one day build globe-spanning colonial empires and attempt to make their civilization universal. In the process, they divided the world between "the West" and "the Other" and spawned resentments and misunderstandings with which modern nations still struggle. Viewing events simplistically as a battle between the virtuous and the vicious seldom produces an adequate picture of reality. In the case of warring cultures, it absolutizes their differences and makes it difficult to build on whatever common ground they might share.

Islam's Crest and Byzantium's Resurgence

The pan-European empire that Charlemagne hoped to build did not materialize. Europe lacked the infrastructure and cultural ties needed to support political unification, and the invasions of the Vikings, Magyars, and Muslims forced it to decentralize its governments and defenses. The tendency toward political fragmentation was, however, not confined to Europe. The momentum of conquest preserved the Muslim empire until the mid-eighth century, but once expansion ceased, the Muslim world, like Christian Europe, came apart.

Caliphs and Sultans   The Muslim empire was torn by ethnic tensions, new and old. The Umayyad caliphs did not impose Islam on all their subjects or even encourage them to come together to form a single people. They viewed Islam as a gift God intended primarily for Arabs, and they wanted Arabs to remain aloof from the natives of the lands they conquered. Umayyad "racism" had fiscal as well as cultural motives. The empire's non-Muslim subjects paid taxes from which Muslims were exempt. Many non-Arabs were, however, sincerely drawn to Islam. Although it was impossible to deny their wish to convert, Arabs often discriminated against them, and this created tensions within the *umma* (the Muslim community).

In 739 fighting erupted between Berber and Arab Muslims in North Africa, and in 750 Persian converts helped the Abbasids overthrow the Umayyad caliphate. In 756 Abd al-Rahman (731–788), an Umayyad prince who had survived the coup, wrested control of the Iberian Peninsula from the Abbasid caliphs and declared Spain an independent emirate. In 788 a Shi'ite leader won over the Berber Muslims and founded the Aghlabid dynasty in North Africa. In 800 the Abbasids acknowledged its virtual autonomy. The Aghlabids clashed with Spain's Umayyad emir, and they kept their Arab and Berber followers from feuding among themselves by sending them to raid southern Europe. In 902 they drove the Byzantines from Sicily and brought Islam to the island. Sicily, like Spain, developed a thriving Muslim society that eventually helped to stimulate a revival of intellectual life in Europe by acquainting Europeans with the fruits of Muslim scholarship.

In 909 the Aghlabids were overthrown by a Berber faction that supported a Shi'ite who claimed to be a descendant of Muhammad's daughter, Fatima. The Fatimid dynasty that he founded established a Shi'ite caliphate in opposition to the Sunni Abbasids. In 929 Spain's Umayyad emir rallied the Sunni Muslims in the western Mediterranean to his side by declaring himself their caliph. Baghdad's response was weak, for by then the political authority of the Abbasid caliphs was fading (see Map 9–1).

The Abbasid dynasty had reached its peak during the reign of Charlemagne's contemporary, Harun al-Rashid (r. 786–809). Harun al-Rashid's court in Baghdad was probably the most splendid and sophisticated of its day, but ominous developments shadowed the future of his empire. He had lost Spain to the Umayyads, and in 800 he relinquished North Africa to the Aghlabids. Wars between Harun al-Rashid's sons cost the Abbasid dynasty more territory, and in 820 a Persian prince wrested the eastern province of Khurasan from its control.

In the mid-ninth century, the beleaguered Abbasid caliphs tried to secure their position by creating an army of Turkish slaves. The theory was that foreign slaves, who had no powerful families or local allies to support them, would be totally dependent on, and loyal to, the caliph. The Turks, however, rallied behind leaders of their own and wrested territory in Persia, Syria, and Egypt away from their caliph. Some Abbasids put up a good fight, but in 945 Baghdad's caliph submitted to the Persian Buyids. While the Buyids brought Persia and Iraq under control, the Fatimids moved across North Africa to Egypt. In 969 they evicted a Turkish ruler from Egypt and relocated the seat of their caliphate to a new city, which they named Cairo (al-Kahira, "Victorious"). Sporadic warfare raged inconclusively between the Buyids and Fatimids for about a century, and in the end, both succumbed to a third Muslim power, the Seljuk Turks.

The Turks, like the early Germans, were an assortment of nomadic tribes that spoke related languages. They first made contact with Islam about 653, when the Arab armies that were sweeping across the Persian Empire reached the Oxus River. The Turks' relationship with Islam's new empire resembled the one the Germans had with Rome's old empire. They absorbed its religion and were attracted by its wealth, power, and culture. Some immigrated and integrated peacefully. Some were enslaved, and some set up their own states on its territory. During the tenth century, Islam's eastern lands were overrun by Turks. Some of these planted Islam in northern and central India, and others, the Seljuks, took over Persia.

The Seljuks came from the region of the Jaxartes River and converted to Islam in the second half of the tenth century. After occupying Khurasan, they set their sights on the Buyids, and in 1060 they took Baghdad. The Seljuks allowed the Abbasid caliph to serve as a religious figurehead, but their **sultan** (*shultana*, "governor") assumed responsibility for running Baghdad's empire and defending Sunni Islam against its primary enemies, the Shi'ite Fatimids and the Christian Byzantines.

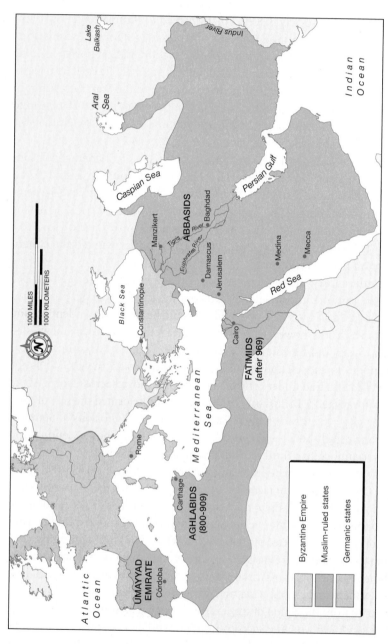

Map 9–1 The Medieval Muslim World The Muslim Empire grew so quickly that it had little opportunity to consolidate before it began to break up into a variety of states with different religious, ethnic, and political identities. The three caliphates that emerged (Umayyad Spain, Fatimid Egypt, and Abbasid Baghdad) created tensions within the Muslim world similar to those that divided the Christian region between the Orthodox and Catholic traditions.

Question: Today the "Muslim world" is sometimes contrasted with "the West." Does that description make historical or geographical sense?

Harun al-Rashid's Court The magnificence of Harun al-Rashid's Baghdad is hinted at by this gift of an ewer that the caliph sent to Charlemagne. Its lavishly embossed gold surface is studded with jewels and decorated with vividly colored enamels in a technique called cloisonne.

The Fatimid dynasty was the lesser threat. Although Fatimid Egypt had been a strong state with a powerful navy, it had failed to make much progress against the Buyids, the Byzantines, or even rival Shi'ite groups. The Fatimids' early victories had raised unrealistic expectations among their Shi'ite followers. The Shi'ite faith was apocalyptic. It awaited a messiah—the revelation of a secret descendant of the Prophet who would miraculously reunite the *umma* and complete Islam's triumph. As the tenth century dragged on, hope diminished that the Fatimid caliphate would produce such a savior. Wealth and privilege gradually had a corrupting effect on Fatimid rulers, and by the eleventh century, internal power struggles and inept caliphs were costing the Fatimids both followers and territory. The dynasty survived until an unexpected event altered political arrangements throughout the Muslim world. Constantinople triggered an invasion of the Middle East by western Europeans.

Constantinople When the Arab armies first erupted from their homeland, they descended on a Byzantine Empire that had been weakened by a long war with Persia. In 636 the Byzantine emperor Heraclius (r. 610–641) lost a major battle to the Muslims, and by the time of his death, his empire had been reduced to Asia Minor, parts of Greece and the Balkans, and nominal authority over Sicily, North Africa, and a few outposts in Italy. Then things got worse. Arabs annually raided throughout Asia Minor—sometimes threatening Constantinople itself. They challenged the Byzantine navy's power at sea, and in 670 they began a triumphal march through the Byzantine province of North Africa. Then things got much worse. In 679 the Slavs, who had long posed a threat to Constantinople's possessions in the Balkans, were joined by the Bulgars, a people similar to the Huns. Byzantium's efforts to deal with all these external threats were complicated by internal fights over its throne.

In 717 (just as Charles Martel was laying the foundations for Europe's Carolingian Empire) a great general, Leo III (r. 717–740), seized power in Constantinople and drove the Muslims back from the city. Leo and his heirs, the Isaurian dynasty, restructured Byzantine government and society to mobilize support for a stronger military. They divided the empire into regions called **themes.** A regiment of soldiers was assigned to each, and each was governed by the commander of its regiment. Some soldiers were salaried; however, many were supported, like Europe's vassals, by grants of land. Repeated Muslim raids had broken up many of the great estates and undercut the institution of serfdom. By redistributing lands among free peasants, the Isaurian dynasty created a class of independent farmers from which to recruit stalwart defenders for its empire.

Leo issued a new code of civil law—in Greek instead of Latin, the official language that had been used since Constantinople's origin as the capital of the Roman Empire. He also forced through a controversial religious reform that marked another break with tradition. In 726 he promulgated the first in a series of edicts that forbade the use of icons in worship. Repugnance for religious art was widespread in the Middle East, for both Muslims and Jews regarded it as a temptation to idolatry. Leo apparently believed that veneration of icons was indistinguishable from blasphemous worship of icons, but he also had political motives for ordering their destruction. He wanted to diminish the influence of overly powerful monasteries whose sacred images attracted devotion and support from the masses. Leo's iconoclasm ("destruction of sacred images") sparked revolts among his subjects and was roundly denounced by theologians who believed that a ban on religious images was tantamount to the denial of Christ's humanity. If, as the iconoclasts claimed, material images could not mediate spiritual realities, then Christ could not have been truly incarnated as a human being. Church councils in western Europe also objected to Leo's policy, and opposition to iconoclasm was probably a factor in the papacy's decision to distance itself from the Byzantines and strengthen its ties with the Frankish kings. The issue continued to make trouble for Constantinople until its rulers gave in and repudiated iconoclasm in 843.

In 867 Basil I (r. 867–886), who had risen from slavery to become an imperial advisor, assassinated his emperor and seized the Byzantine throne. The Macedonian dynasty he founded restored the glory of Constantinople and reclaimed territory the Byzantines had lost to the Muslims and Bulgars. The ruthless Basil II (r. 963–1025), "the Bulgar-slayer," brought Russia within the orbit of Constantinople and Christianity. Vikings who worked the river systems that linked the Baltic Sea with the Black Sea joined the Slavs of central Europe to form a people called the Rus ("Russians"), after Ruric, a Viking who ruled Novgorod about 862. Dominance of the region passed to the city of Kiev, whose ruler, Vladimir I (r. 980–1015), accepted baptism in exchange for the hand of Basil's sister. The marriage forged strong commercial and cultural ties between Constantinople and Russia and began the spread of Orthodox Christianity and Byzantine civilization to Russia.

In 1057 a coalition of Byzantine aristocrats and clergy overthrew the last of the Macedonian emperors. Their coup was ill-timed, for it weakened Constantinople's defenses just as the Seljuk Turks were beginning to revive Islam's martial spirit. In 1071 the Byzantine emperor Romanus IV Diogenes (r. 1068–1071) lost a decisive battle with the Seljuks near an Armenian fortress called Manzikert, and the victorious Seljuks seized most of Asia Minor—the region from which Constantinople recruited its armies. The city survived, for it had strong fortifications and continued to prosper as a depot for international trade. The Seljuk threat also quickly receded, for the Turks began to fight among themselves for shares of the lands they had conquered.

The Reorganization of Europe

Europe, which had borne the brunt of the devastation caused by the German invasions that brought down the Roman Empire, lagged behind the Byzantine and Muslim worlds for centuries. Charlemagne had tried to close the gap, but the invasions of the

Vikings, Magyars, and Muslims in the ninth and tenth centuries set Europe back once again. Charlemagne's successors were weak kings whose effective authority did not extend far beyond their own estates. However, once the invasions ended and things began to settle down, the surviving monarchs began to give some attention to building centralized governments and consolidating the states that were to become the nations of modern Europe. This was a difficult project that did not always meet with success. By the end of the Middle Ages, England and France had emerged as stable, unified countries under different kinds of royal authority, but Germany and Italy remained politically fragmented until late in the nineteenth century.

England and France   England was a small country (only a little larger than the state of New York) situated on an island, but geography was not enough to guarantee its political unification. The Anglo-Saxons, who occupied it in the fifth century, may have divided it among as many as seven kingdoms. The Viking invasions of the eighth and ninth centuries obliterated all but one of these—the kingdom of Wessex, England's southwest corner. A young heir to the throne of Wessex, Alfred the Great (r. 871–899), pushed the Vikings (Danes) back and confined them to the Danelaw (the northeastern half of England). The strong Anglo-Saxon state he founded endured for about a century. Alfred, like Charlemagne, was a patron of scholars and a sponsor of a palace school. He was particularly eager to promote Anglo-Saxon literature, and was better educated than the Frankish emperor. He translated a number of books into Anglo-Saxon, updating some of them with information about his part of the world.

In 954 one of Alfred's successors brought all of England under his control and converted the Vikings who had settled on the island to Christianity. Churches and monasteries were restored, but the opportunity to rebuild and consolidate was brief. At the end of the century King Ethelred the Unready (r. 978–1016) confronted a second wave of Viking invaders. He tried to buy them off with the proceeds of a national tax called the **Danegeld**, but in 1013 a Danish army forced Ethelred to flee England (see Map 9–2).

England then became part of a North Sea empire headed by a king who also ruled Denmark, Norway, and parts of Sweden. The island's new ruler, Cnute (r. 1016–1035), was no unlettered barbarian. He visited Rome to consult with the pope and earned a reputation as an able monarch. Europe's history might have been quite different had his empire survived, but fights among his potential heirs destroyed it. Once England regained its independence, Edward the Confessor (r. 1042–1066), the Anglo-Saxon heir to its throne, returned from exile.

Edward, England's last Anglo-Saxon king, had Viking blood. His mother was the sister of a French duke, who was a descendant of a Viking chief named Rollo. In 911 the French king, Charles the Simple (r. 893–929), had tried to limit his losses to the Vikings by coming to terms with Rollo. Rollo swore an oath of fealty to Charles in exchange for the title of duke and a fief consisting of the lower Seine Valley and much of the French side of the English Channel. The king hoped that Rollo's Vikings, the barons of the newly created duchy of Normandy (from Norsemen or Normans), would prevent other Vikings from raiding farther into French territory. The Normans acculturated quickly—adopting Christianity, the French language, and the heavily armed cavalry fighting techniques that

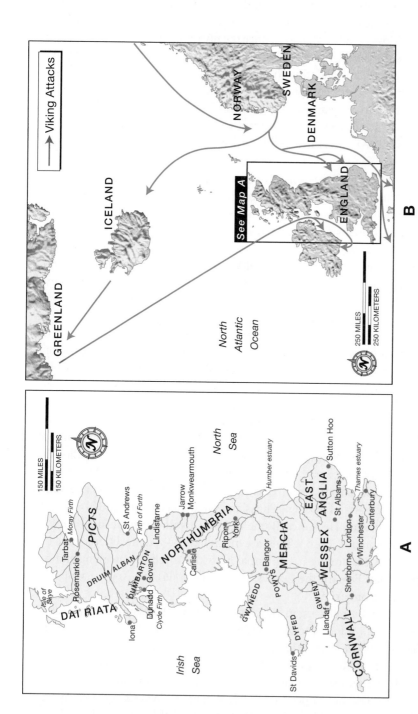

Map 9–2   England and the Viking Migrations   The sea can protect an island country or render it vulnerable to attack depending on the technologies its enemies possess. Invaders with minimal sailing skills could cross the narrow channel between the continent and England, but so long as the island was vulnerable along only parts of its coast it was relatively easy to defend. The Viking migration was, however, much broader in scope and relied on something more closely resembling true marine forces than anything Western Europeans had previously confronted.

Question: Given that the Mediterranean Sea had bound much of the Roman Empire together, could a northern empire have developed around the North Sea?

were evolving on the continent. Normandy produced a remarkable number of famous soldiers and adventurers who spread the duchy's influence from Ireland to the Holy Land.

Edward the Confessor had spent most of his life in Normandy and had no personal power base in England. He wed the daughter of the most influential man in his kingdom, an earl (an English title of nobility) named Godwin, but sired no heir. He achieved little, and his death in 1066 set off a three-way race for England's vacant throne. The native Anglo-Saxon candidate was Edward's brother-in-law, Harold Godwinson. Harold Hardrada, king of Norway (r. 1045–1066), asserted the Viking claim. Edward's distant relative, William, duke of Normandy, also entered the lists. In September 1066 Harold Godwinson defeated Harold Hardrada in northern England. But his involvement there gave William a chance to ferry the Norman army across the English Channel and land unopposed in southern England. Harold Godwinson dashed from one campaign to another, and England's fate was decided by a battle fought near the port of Hastings. Godwinson and most of the Anglo-Saxon leaders were killed, and Duke William became King William I, "the Conqueror" (r. 1066–1087).

William—as a conqueror, not a native king—was not bound by English tradition. He was free to impose any kind of government he wanted on his new subjects. He built on institutions with which he was familiar in Normandy, but he wisely preserved some unique English customs that strengthened the monarchy. Medieval kings not only had to work at keeping the masses in line, but also had a struggle to control the men through whom they governed. The nobles who served in a king's government often preferred him to be weak. The less power he had, the more they could appropriate for themselves. But England's new Norman aristocracy found itself in a different situation. It consisted of a small number of French-speaking foreigners who were unpopular with the masses of their Anglo-Saxon subjects. It needed the support of a powerful monarch. William limited the number of castles his nobles were allowed to build, lest they be used against him. He also preserved the Anglo-Saxon division of his kingdom into shires supervised by non-noble officials called shire-reeves (sheriffs). They were responsible for collecting a national tax (which had begun as the Danegeld ransom) and marshaling a peasant army called the **fyrd**. Unlike continental states, England had continued the German tribal custom of requiring all adult males to bear arms should they be needed to defend their country. Sheriffs and the *fyrd* freed the king from having to rely exclusively on the nobles as agents of his government.

William succeeded in establishing a Norman ruling class in control of England, but his victory led to a struggle between the kings of England and France that dragged on for 400 years. If William's estate had been divided as he ordered, however, the problem might have been avoided. At William's death, the duchy of Normandy passed by right of inheritance to his eldest son, Robert "Curthose." Robert showed little promise as a leader, and this may have entered into William's decision to separate the duchy he had inherited from the kingdom he had won. England needed a strong king, and the best candidate was William's second son, William II, "Rufus" (r. 1087–1100). In 1095 Robert pawned Normandy to his brother to raise the money he needed to join the First Crusade. He survived that adventure, but he lost his duchy and his freedom to William's successor, their younger brother Henry. The duchy's reunification with the English crown might have seemed like good policy at the time, for many Norman lords owned lands on both sides of the English Channel. However, it created a diplomatic situation rife with confusion. Henry, as duke of Normandy, was the vassal of the king of France, but as king of England, he was the French monarch's equal.

William the Conqueror's third son became Henry I (r. 1100–1135), king of England, under suspicious circumstances. His brutal and unpopular brother, William Rufus, died in what was represented as a hunting accident but may well have been an assassination. Few lamented his death, but his demise by no means assured Henry's succession. His surviving older brother Robert had the stronger claim to England's throne. Henry therefore set about courting support. He dismissed William's unpopular officials, and at his coronation he issued a Charter of Liberties in which he pledged not to abuse his power. The proclamation had little effect at the time, but it set an important precedent.

The church maintained that a king's power derived from God, not his subjects, and that subjects therefore had no right to sit in judgment on kings. Henry's pledge, however, implied that a monarch was accountable to his people for how he governed them. A century later the famous Magna Carta reaffirmed this principle. Other events helped to keep it alive, but until the English Parliament was firmly established, there was no way to enforce it. Efforts to limit the power of England's monarchs faded during the reigns of strong kings and revived when weak rulers mismanaged the country. As fate would have it, throughout the medieval period strong kings tended to alternate with weak ones in England—leading ultimately to modern Britain's parliamentary government headed by a powerless royal figurehead.

The power that the Conqueror and his sons, William and Henry, had carefully guarded was nearly lost in a struggle for succession to their throne. The only one of Henry's legitimate children to survive him was a daughter, Matilda (1102–1167). Henry forced his reluctant vassals to promise to accept her as his heir. But the idea of a reigning queen was so unconventional that it was easy to rationalize breaking such a pledge. A medieval king was a warlord, and few people thought that a woman could do his job. Some of England's nobles repudiated Matilda (and her French husband, the count of Anjou) and declared her cousin Stephen the rightful heir to Henry's throne. Matilda had the advantage of descent from the Conqueror through the male line, but she was a woman. Ordinarily, Stephen's claim would have been weak or nonexistent, for his link with the Conqueror was through his mother, William's daughter. However, Stephen was a male, and his supporters argued that this tipped the balance in his favor.

Civil war erupted, and for 20 years the nobles had the advantage of being able to play one royal claimant off against another. Stephen finally offered Matilda a compromise. In exchange for her recognition of his right to live out his life in peace as England's king, he acknowledged her son, Henry, as his heir. Stephen died a year later, and England's battered crown passed to a man who had the skill and resources to refurbish it.

Henry II (r. 1154–1189) was the right man in the right place at the right time—intelligent, well educated, crafty, physically vigorous, and charismatic. His family connections positioned him to make the most of his gifts. His uncle bequeathed him the kingdom of England. His mother and father left him duchies and counties covering much of northern France, and his wife, Eleanor (c. 1122–1204), brought him the duchy of Aquitaine, a large portion of southern France. Henry's sprawling Angevin (from Anjou) Empire made him a more powerful man in France than France's king (see Map 9–3).

The English monarchy began strong and was forced by circumstances to accept limits to its authority. The French monarchy headed in the opposite direction. France's early kings were weak, but by the end of the Middle Ages, they were well on their way to becoming absolute monarchs.

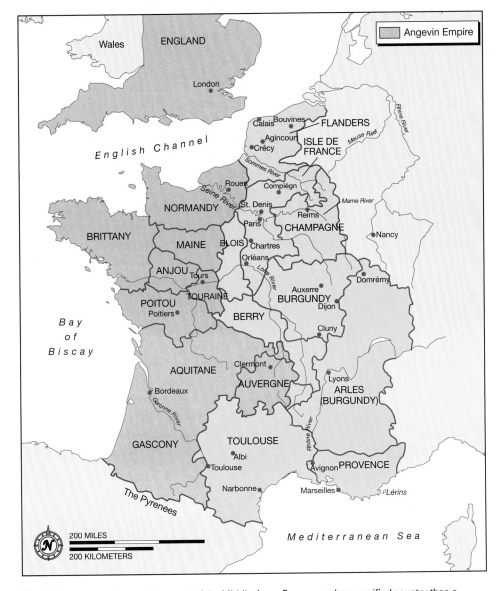

Map 9–3 Medieval France For much of the Middle Ages, France was less a unified country than a collection of separate entities. Each of its regions had a distinct dialect and culture, and the kinds of nationalistic sentiments that seem natural to modern people had not yet appeared to bind them together.

Question: Did geography make the unification of France easy or difficult?

William, as England's conqueror, had the freedom and power to get his dynasty off to a strong start, but the French monarchy had a very different beginning. The invasions of the ninth and tenth centuries cost its kings considerable power and prestige. Because France was four times the size of England and exposed to attack on multiple fronts, a king could not offer as much protection as a strong local lord, and the competition France's kings faced from powerful landed nobles rendered them extremely weak.

In 987 the French nobles switched their allegiance from Charlemagne's ineffectual descendants to Hugh Capet (r. 987–996), count of Paris. Hugh's county was the front line in the war with the Viking invaders, and it was in the self-interest of his fellow nobles to help him defend his small estate. The early kings of the Capetian dynasty, which Hugh founded, had no power to compel obedience from France's nobles, many of whom controlled much more territory than their monarch. The Capetians also had to be careful not to offend their vassals by trying to assert their rights as kings. They were not born kings with a hereditary claim to the crown. They were elected kings by men who could, whenever they wanted, shift their allegiance to someone else. Little could be done to strengthen the monarchy in France until the Capetians established an unchallengeable right to the throne. To do this, they simply had to prolong their possession of the prize. For generations, they threatened no one and always had a viable candidate (an adult son) ready for election before his father's death. Because the Capetians seemed a safe choice and none of the powerful lords wanted a competitor to have the royal title, the Capetians were repeatedly elected kings. Eventually, the succession of a Capetian became a foregone conclusion, and the nobles dispensed with pointless elections. Vassals, who based title to their fiefs on generations of family occupancy, could hardly challenge the Capetians' right to lay claim to the crown on the same grounds.

The first member of the Capetian dynasty who was secure enough to assert his authority was Louis VI, "the Fat" (r. 1108–1137), a contemporary of England's powerful Henry I. Louis did little more than exercise the rights that all lords were traditionally understood to have over their vassals, but he also cultivated allies who wanted a stronger monarchy. France's nobles preferred a weak king who could not threaten their autonomy, but its clergy and many of its ordinary people wanted a king who could restrain its marauding lords and their private armies of knights. The residents of the new towns that sprang up in France in the eleventh and twelfth centuries were particularly eager to promote the development of centralized government. Townspeople depended on trade, and they wanted a king who could make the countryside safe for travelers and limit the tolls local lords imposed on merchants.

A medieval monarchy was inherently weak because it ruled through subordinates whose self-interest was to make it weak. If a king hoped to increase his effectiveness, he had to find an alternative to working through the landed nobility. Townspeople and clergy could help him by giving him money with which to hire salaried officials. It was hard to evict a vassal from his manors, but it was easy to cut off a salary. Salaried officials therefore tended to be more loyal than vassals, and they wanted a strong employer. The stronger the king, the more secure their wages.

Louis VI used the customary privileges of an overlord to tip the balance of power in France decidedly in his dynasty's favor. When the huge duchy of Aquitaine passed to an heiress, Eleanor of Aquitaine, Louis exercised his prerogative to choose her husband.

He wed her to his son and heir Louis VII (r. 1137–1180). The young king was, however, never able to compel his bride or her duchy to submit to his authority. In 1152 the flagrantly incompatible couple persuaded the pope to annul their union, and Eleanor immediately chose as her second husband the man who posed the greatest threat to her first. She wed Henry of Anjou who, in 1154, became King Henry II of England, the architect of the Angevin Empire. Louis spent the rest of his life in an unequal struggle with Henry, but in the next generation the tide turned in the Capetians' favor. Henry's sons, Richard I, "the Lionhearted" (r. 1189–1199), and John (r. 1199–1216), were no match for Louis's heir, Philip II, "Augustus" (r. 1180–1223). Philip recovered many French fiefs from the English kings and kept much of what he won for the royal domain. He bequeathed his heirs a much stronger throne than the one he had inherited, but he did not resolve France's problems with England.

Germany, Italy, and the Papacy   The medieval monarchy that made the most promising start (and the most dismal finish) was Germany's. In 911 the last of Germany's Carolingian rulers died, and the German dukes chose Conrad, duke of Franconia (r. 911–918), to be their king. His primary achievement was to pass the crown to a more viable candidate, Henry I, "the Fowler" (r. 919–936), duke of Saxony. Saxony was a much larger and more powerful duchy than Franconia. Thanks to its location in northwestern Germany, it had been spared the Magyar raids that had weakened the rest of the country. Germany's dukes submitted to Henry's authority because they needed the help he could give them in their fight with the Magyars. In 955 Henry's son and successor, Otto I, "the Great" (r. 936–973), decisively defeated the invaders and reestablished Austria (Charlemagne's Ostmark) as a buffer state protecting Germany's eastern frontier. This contained the Magyars in a land of their own and encouraged them to settle down. Missionaries, whom Otto sponsored, quickly converted them, and in the year 1000 the pope recognized the existence of the new Christian kingdom of Hungary by sending its leader, Stephen (r. 997–1038), a crown.

As Europe's most powerful monarch and the ruler of its largest kingdom, Otto saw himself as picking up where Charlemagne had left off. In 951 he began a war to bring Italy under his control, and in 962 the pope revived the imperial title and bestowed it on Otto. Romantic visions of Roman and Carolingian empires were not the only reasons for Otto's interest in Italy. His home duchy was in northern Germany, and he would have had difficulty holding his kingdom together if the leaders of either of its southern duchies, Swabia and Bavaria, had crossed the Alps and added Italy to their possessions. Otto and most of his successors believed that Germany and Italy (where monarchy had died out) had to be united, but some Italians saw things differently. The papacy and the wealthy towns that flourished in northern Italy feared German domination and put up stiff resistance (see Map 9–4).

Constantinople was persuaded to accept Otto's coronation as emperor, and in 972 a marriage was arranged between his heir, Otto II (r. 973–983), and a Byzantine princess named Theophano. She and her cosmopolitan entourage elevated life at the German court, and the close ties with Constantinople that the marriage established stimulated a burst of artistic and literary activity, which historians call the Ottonian Renaissance.

Map 9–4 Medieval Germany and Italy   Although the Roman Empire had never extended far into German territory, medieval Germany was haunted by the memory of the empire. German monarchs claimed the Roman title and believed that it gave them the right to rule Italy. Italians disagreed and viewed the Germans as invaders. The failure of Germany's kings to overcome the combined resistance of the Italian towns, the papacy, and their own feudal nobles sapped their authority and led to the political fragmentation of both Germany and Italy.

Question: Did geography encourage or hamper the attempts of the German kings to unify their country and join it with Italy?

In the process of creating his empire, Otto had acquired a lot of territory for the crown, but he knew that kings often had difficulty hanging on to the lands they won. Land made a king powerful by giving him the resources he needed to support his agents and soldiers. But when he granted land as fiefs to those who served him, it became more theirs than his. Men who possessed land also controlled the source of their income. Economic independence meant that they might not remain as loyal as men who were totally dependent on the king's favor. Otto hoped to solve these problems by granting the bulk of his lands to the church. The church, like a secular lord, owed the king military service for its lands. The advantage was that the leaders of the church could not marry and pass their offices down to their sons. Germany's bishops and abbots were appointed by its king. He could therefore make sure that the lands he gave the church remained in the hands of men he trusted. His power was safe so long as his authority over the church was unquestioned, but in the late tenth century challenges began to be mounted to the power laity had over clergy.

In 910, shortly before Otto's Saxon dynasty was founded in Germany, the duke of Aquitaine funded an ecclesiastical experiment in France. He endowed a new Benedictine monastery called Cluny and gave its monks the privilege of choosing their own abbot and managing their own affairs. This was unusual, for the wealthy families that donated to ecclesiastical institutions usually assumed that they had the right to appoint the clergy who were supported by their gifts. The reformers who sponsored Cluny claimed that this practice had resulted in the corruption and weakening of the church, for a lay patron who had a church office to give away tended to be more influenced by applicants' political connections than by their spiritual qualifications. The result was a lot of unworthy appointments and a general decline of religion. Things would improve, the Cluniacs insisted, if clergy were freed from secular interference and allowed to decide for themselves who was suited for a religious post. Cluny bore this out, for it quickly became the most respected monastery in Europe. Other cloisters asked Cluny to reorganize them, and before long Cluniacs were spearheading a drive to reform the whole church, a movement known as the **Cluniac Reform**.

The Saxon dynasty died out in 1024 before the Cluniac movement had become powerful enough to cause kings much trouble. The Salian dynasty (1024–1125), which succeeded the Saxon, was not so lucky. In 1049 its king, Henry III (r. 1039–1056), appointed his cousin, Leo IX (r. 1049–1054), to the papacy. Leo was a vigorous reformer. He traveled throughout Europe, convening councils to encourage spiritual renewal, and he improved the machinery of papal government by making more use of the cardinals ("primaries," the Roman clergy who reported directly to him). By the time Henry III's son, Henry IV (r. 1056–1106), came to the throne, the German king faced an ecclesiastical hierarchy that was determined to establish the papacy's independence of secular monarchs and to end the tradition of laymen appointing clergy.

Henry was crowned king at a young age, and the regents who governed for him were weak. This gave Pope Nicholas II (r. 1059–1061) an opportunity to establish a new procedure for papal elections that would exclude interference by kings. No formal procedure for choosing popes had ever existed. Some men had been elevated to the papal throne by political factions in the city of Rome. Others had been chosen by whatever emperor, king, or lord had sufficient influence in Rome at the time. Nicholas decreed that

PEOPLE IN CONTEXT   Hroswitha of Gandersheim (fl. 935–1002)

The most original of the Ottonian Renaissance's authors was a Benedictine nun, Hroswitha of the Benedictine cloister at Gandersheim. Her personal history, beyond the little that can be inferred from her works, is a blank. She was probably an aristocrat, for Gandersheim was an elite house to which women from the royal family occasionally retreated.

Hroswitha was deeply grateful for the education she received at Gandersheim, and her teachers must have been women of considerable erudition. Hroswitha wrote excellent Latin and was a student of classical literature. Some of her works were what one might expect from a nun: saints' legends, apocryphal tales about the life of the Virgin Mary, and an account of the foundation of her cloister. But Hroswitha also ventured into unusual literary territory. She tried her hand at a history of Otto I's reign (the first attempt, as far as we know, by a medieval woman to write secular history). But her crowning achievement was a set of six plays that she said she wrote to counter the negative image of women found in the comedies of Terence, a playwright from the era of the Roman Republic. Hroswitha's plays are surprising because we might not anticipate that anyone in remote medieval Saxony would know of Terence, that a nun would be drawn to his work, that she would write fine Latin, that she would decide to write plays, and that she would use theater to rehabilitate the image of women. Hroswitha is the only

The Magdeburg Ivories   Hroswitha of Gandersheim tried her hand at writing a history of the reign of Otto the Great. This is one of a series of ivory plaques executed in Italy for Otto. It depicts the king presenting the church of Magdeburg to the enthroned Christ. "The Emperor Otto I (912–73) Presenting a Model of His Church at Magdeburg to the Enthroned Christ in the Presence of Saints Peter and Mauritius (?) and Other Saints." One of a series of 17 ivory plaques known as the Magdeburg Ivories, possibly carved in Milan c. 962–68. Ivory, 5" × 4 1/2" (12.7 × 11.4 cm). The Metropolitan Musuem of Art, NY. Bequest of George Blumenthal, 1941 (41.100.157). Photograph © 1986 The Metropolitan Museum of Art

playwright known to have worked in the long period between the fall of Rome and the gradual emergence of religious drama from the liturgy of the church in the twelfth century. It is unclear whether she intended her plays to be staged or simply read, but at least one of them seems to call for comic action to flesh out its dialogue.

Hroswitha was that rarest of medieval authors, a woman who wrote about women. Her world offered women only three roles: wife and mother, consecrated virgin, and whore. Hroswitha's plays illustrated how women in each of these situations could become spiritual heroines. She believed that females were physically and mentally inferior to males, but this, she argued, gave them a spiritual advantage over men. In her opinion, the male's strengths of body and intellect subject him to powerful temptations that women find easier to resist. The male is also likely to succumb to sin unless women, with God's help, courageously guard their virtue. Hroswitha's ingenious reinterpretation of the common gender stereotypes of her era challenged medieval religious tradition by placing women at the center of humanity's struggle for salvation.

Question: On what did women base their self-respect in the male-dominated medieval world?

henceforth only clergy could participate in a papal election. Because it was impossible to poll clergy throughout Europe, Rome's cardinal clergy were given the job of choosing popes. In 1073 they elected an avid Cluniac reformer who took the name Gregory VII (r. 1073–1085). The new pope immediately made his position perfectly clear. He claimed that popes were the highest authorities on Earth, that no one had the right to judge how they used their office, and that they even had the right to depose secular rulers.

It was some time before Henry IV was able to respond to the papacy's challenges to his authority, for the Salian dynasty had difficulty bringing Germany's landed nobility under control. Once the king had Germany more or less in hand, however, he turned his attention to Italy and to Gregory. The result was the **Investiture Controversy**, a major episode in the ongoing struggle between church and state.

In 1075 Gregory ordered laymen to discontinue the practice of "investing" clergy (that is, appointing candidates to church offices). Henry promptly called the pope's bluff by investing an archbishop for Milan, a major Italian see. This inaugurated a series of escalating events. Gregory denounced Henry. Henry then convened a council of German bishops that declared Gregory deposed, and Gregory reciprocated by excommunicating and deposing Henry. Gregory's deposition decree posed a real threat to Henry, for it gave Germany's nobles an excuse to repudiate a king whose growing strength threatened their freedom. The nobles asked Gregory to come to Germany to give their rebellion an aura of legitimacy, but Henry forestalled this by crossing the Alps in midwinter and ostentatiously begging the pope's forgiveness. Gregory had no choice but to reconcile with a king who made such a flamboyant public show of regret. But when he did so, the German nobles concluded that he had betrayed them, and they turned on him. Henry recovered his hold on Germany, and in 1084 he descended on Rome and forced the pope to flee.

Gregory was humiliated and died in exile, but this did not end the Investiture Controversy or solve the problem of church–state relations. The church was endowed with about one-third of the land in Europe, and kings would not relinquish the right to a say in the choice of the clergy who administered so much territory within the boundaries of their kingdoms. The church therefore settled for a face-saving compromise. Kings agreed not to take part in the ceremonies that invested clergy, but candidates for investiture had first to take oaths of homage to kings for the secular services they owed for the church's land. This gave kings a chance to veto candidates whom they did not like without seeming to violate the church's independence. The resolution of the Investiture Controversy was an example of the strategy the church pursued throughout the Middle Ages. By consistently claiming more power in theory than it settled for in practice the church was able slowly to make practice catch up with theory.

The Salian dynasty did not long survive Henry's victory over Gregory. The death of its last king in 1125 nearly extinguished the monarchy in Germany, and a generation passed before a new dynasty was established. Despite the advantage of an early, strong start, Germany's kings were still a long way from providing their subjects with effective, centralized government.

The Eleventh-Century Turning Point

The shift of resources from centralized monarchies to local lords had succeeded in helping Europe weather the invasions of the ninth and tenth centuries. The fragmented government that resulted tended to be chaotic, but it provided enough security to prevent the loss of the cultural gains made during the Carolingian era. In addition, as the situation slowly stabilized, Europeans returned to the world stage. Europe had largely been on the defensive since the fall of the western Roman Empire, but in the eleventh century that changed. Europe took the offensive, expanded territorially and economically, and developed an environment in which artists and intellectuals flourished.

The Spanish and Sicilian Crusades   The most obvious sign that the eleventh century marked the start of a new phase in Europe's history was the threat Europeans began to pose to their neighbors. After centuries of being invaded, Europe became the invader. It waged crusades—holy wars motivated (at least in part) by a fervent desire to destroy persons whom it regarded as enemies of its church. Crusades primarily targeted Muslims in foreign lands, but they also triggered pogroms in Europe—massacres of Jews that continued to erupt sporadically well into the twentieth century. The hatreds, misunderstandings, and suspicions the crusades nurtured still complicate international relationships.

Europe opened its first front against the Muslim world in Spain, the point of closest contact between western Christendom and Islam. In the middle of the tenth century, the Umayyad caliph of Córdoba united Spain's Muslims and attacked the tiny Christian states on the northern rim of the Iberian Peninsula. In 997 alarm spread throughout Europe when the caliph's vizier, al-Mansur, sacked Compostela, a pilgrimage center that ranked in importance only behind Jerusalem and Rome. Al-Mansur died in 1002, and no comparable Muslim leader was found to take his place. This created an opportunity for Sancho III, "the Great" (r. 1000–1035), the ruler of Navarre, a kingdom on the slopes of the Pyrenees. He appealed to Europe's Christian knights for help in mounting a counteroffensive. The church blessed his campaign as a holy war, and the monks of Cluny vigorously promoted it. The Christian forces advanced steadily, and in 1085 they captured the old Visigothic capital of Toledo in the heart of Spain. At this point, their Muslim opponents received reinforcements from North Africa, and the war bogged down. The Christian reconquest of Spain dragged on for four more centuries, for neither the Muslims nor the Christians could resist fighting among themselves.

Europe's Christians launched their second offensive against Islam in the central Mediterranean. In 1017 a group of Norman knights stopped off in southern Italy on their way back from a pilgrimage to Jerusalem. The Normans discovered that Italy's petty wars provided plentiful employment for mercenaries, and as word spread, recruits poured in from France. Among these were Robert Guiscard ("Cunning") and his brother Roger, two of the numerous sons of Tancred de Hauteville, a minor Norman nobleman. They subdued or evicted the native lords of southern Italy and drove the Muslims from Sicily. In 1130 the pope conferred a royal title on Roger's son, Roger II (r. 1105–1154), and recognized the existence of a Norman monarchy (the future Kingdom of the Two Sicilies) ruling Sicily and southern Italy. Robert Guiscard also tried to conquer Byzantine possessions in the Balkans and Greece, but his dream of building a Mediterranean empire proved too ambitious. Still, the recovery of Sicily greatly strengthened Christian Europe's position in the Mediterranean region. The ports of Italy profited especially from enhanced security and opportunities for trade.

The Crusades to the Holy Land   While the first crusades were altering the balance of power in the western Mediterranean, the situation in the Middle East was also changing. Constantinople had ceded most of Asia Minor to the Seljuk Turks after its defeat at Manzikert in 1071. A decade later, however, it saw a chance to recoup its losses. The Seljuks had broken up into mutually hostile states, and a competent military man, Alexius Comnenus (r. 1081–1118), had ascended the Byzantine throne. Alexius's diminished empire was short on manpower, but there were plenty of Christian knights in western Europe. Alexius therefore asked Pope Urban II (r. 1088–1099) to use the church's communication network to help him recruit soldiers.

Alexius's goal was the recovery of the Byzantine territory that had been lost in 1071, but Urban decided to represent the emperor as proposing something much grander— nothing less than the eviction of Muslims from Jerusalem, a city they had held for almost 500 years. Urban had several motives for endorsing and expanding the scope of Alexius's project. He hoped that by assisting Constantinople, he could heal a **schism** that had erupted between the eastern and western churches in 1054. (They had quarreled over a doctrinal issue—the nature of the relation of the Holy Spirit to the Father and to the Son in the Trinity.) Urban further reasoned that by rallying an international army to wage a universal holy war, the pope would strengthen his claim to be Christendom's supreme leader. The diversion of Europe's soldiers to foreign lands also might help to pacify European society, a cause for which the church had been working for over a century.

By Urban's day, an abundance of underemployed soldiers was posing a threat to the stability of European society. Europe's population was increasing, and the number of

The Three Medieval Civilizations: Leaders and Events		
MUSLIM WORLD	**BYZANTIUM**	**EUROPE**
	Leo III (717–740)	
	Iconoclasm Controversy (726–843)	Pepin III (741–768)
Abbasid dynasty (750)		
Umayyad Emirate of Spain (756)		
Aghlabids (800)		Charlemagne (768–814)
		Vikings attack (860)
	Macedonian dynasty (867)	*England-France-Germany*
		Alfred the Great (871–899)
Fatimid dynasty (909)		Cluny founded (910)
		Saxon dynasty (919)
Umayyad caliphate of Spain (929)		
Buyids take Baghdad (945)		
		Capetian dynasty (987)
	Schism: Greek and Latin churches (1054)	
		Cnute (1016–1035)
		Salian dynasty (1024)
Seljuks take Baghdad (1060)		
		William I (1066–1087)
	Manzikert battle (1071)	
		Investiture Controversy (1075)
		Toledo reconquered (1085)
		Sicily reconquered (1092)
	First Crusade (1095–1099)	

knights exceeded the number of fiefs available to support them. A knight did not just train his heir. He trained all his sons to be knights. Lacking other educational opportunities, medieval men usually learned their fathers' professions. By the eleventh century, primogeniture (the right of the eldest male to inherit the whole estate) was becoming the preferred method for preserving both fiefs and a family's fortune and status. It, however, forced the younger brothers of heirs to leave home and fend for themselves. They might find heiresses to marry, enter the church, become soldiers of fortune, or take to the road as brigands. Many found employment in the private armies of local lords. Given that there was little point in a lord supporting knights if he did not use them, these companies of professional soldiers were a standing threat to the peace and order of the countryside.

The church, partly out of self-interest and partly out of a sense of duty, looked for ways to pacify the unruly military elements that threatened to destabilize society. One

The Medieval Knight This page from an illuminated manuscript illustrates episodes from the medieval epic poem *The Song of Roland*. It depicts knights in action, and the slaughter that could result. The soldiers wear chain mail and surcoats, wield spears and long swords, and carry shields that taper to a point (and provide protection for the legs of a man on horseback). Chain mail guarded against sword cuts, but it was vulnerable to penetration by missiles (e.g., arrows or spears). Bit by bit, metal plates were added to reinforce chain mail until, by the end of the Middle Ages, a knight could be entirely encased in a suit of steel.

of its strategies was to persuade knights that honor required them to discipline themselves. The Peace of God and Truce of God movements (see Key Question) appealed to the idealism of young soldiers by declaring knighthood a sacred vocation—a divine commission to protect others. To drive this point home, the church urged that quasi-religious dubbing ceremonies be used to admit men to knightly status. This was helpful, but Urban's plan to divert western Europe's excess soldiers to wars outside Europe was a more direct way of promoting peace in their homelands.

On November 27, 1095, Urban preached a wildly successful sermon at a church council held at Clermont, France. It urged Europe's knights to go to the aid of the east's Christians and offered them all the spiritual and practical assistance the church could provide—primarily, full forgiveness for all their sins and protection for their property at home. The pope toured France for eight months, whipping up enthusiasm for the campaign, and numerous preachers were dispatched to fan the fires he lit. The result was not just a crusade, but a crusading movement that continued for the rest of the medieval era to inspire repeated European assaults on the Muslim world. Historians recognize seven or eight major crusades, but many more European armies departed for the Middle East before the impulse finally died out.

No European king, at the end of the eleventh century, could risk leaving home for an adventure in the Holy Land, and the First Crusade did not have a supreme commander. It was managed (or mismanaged) by a committee of nobles who put themselves at the head of about 4,000 knights, 26,000 foot soldiers, and a horde of pilgrims and camp followers. Some who enlisted hoped to make new lives for themselves in the east, but most planned to return home once the campaign was over. The families of crusader knights endured financial hardship to equip them, and few seem to have made money from the venture.

Before the official crusade got underway, a charismatic preacher called Peter the Hermit led a horde of soldiers and pilgrims to Constantinople. The passions they inspired as they marched across Europe excited Christian mobs to slaughter their Jewish neighbors. Jews were lumped together with Muslims as infidels—as were, in the opinion of some Europeans, the Orthodox Christians of the Middle East. Peter's so-called Peasants' Crusade suffered a disastrous defeat as soon as it crossed into Asia Minor. It was not what Alexius had expected, nor were the French barons, who arrived later with their armies. They did not want to work for him; they had plans of their own (see Map 9–5).

If the Muslims had ceased fighting among themselves and joined forces to defend their territory, the First Crusade could never have succeeded. The Europeans knew little about the Middle East, and they were poorly equipped to deal with its geography and climate. They suffered from heat, thirst, hunger, and disease. Their leaders quarreled. Units defected from the main army to grab lands for themselves. But despite horrific blunders and misadventures, a remnant of the army reached Jerusalem on June 7, 1099. On July 15 they forced their way into the city and slaughtered everyone they found—including Jews and eastern Christians. An eyewitness reported that on the Temple Mount the knights' horses waded up to their bellies in blood and gore.

The crusaders declared Jerusalem the seat of a new Latin kingdom and established a string of crusader states along the Palestinian coast. These fragile European outposts owed their brief survival to the fact that the Muslims continued, for some time, to fight among themselves. In 1144, however, the Muslims recovered Edessa, the first state that the crusaders had claimed. The loss so alarmed Europe that two kings "took the cross" (that is, they wore the image of a cross that marked a man as having made a crusader's vow). The Second Crusade set out under the leadership of Louis VII of France and Conrad III

Krak des Chevaliers To preserve their tenuous hold on their conquests, Europe's crusaders invested heavily in the construction of massive stone fortresses. This castle, which dates to the twelfth century, belonged to an order of crusader monks called the Hospitalers. Sites such as this have kept memories of the crusades alive in the Middle East to a degree that might surprise a European or American.

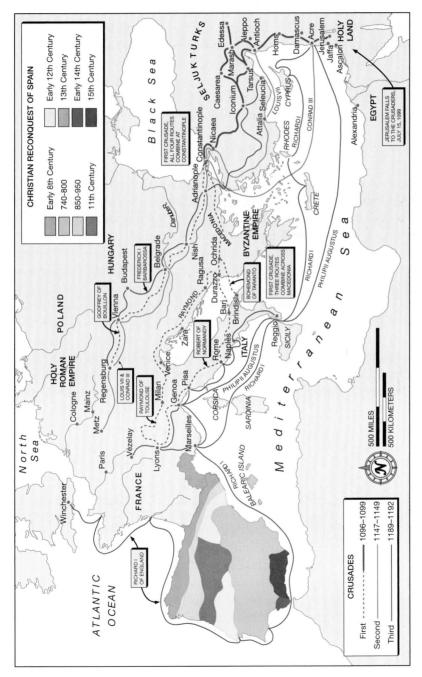

Map 9–5 Crusade Routes The earlier crusaders marched overland to Constantinople. The faster and easier sea route did not become popular until the twelfth century—after Sardinia and Sicily were in Christian hands and Italy's commercial cities had begun to wrest control of the Mediterranean from the Muslims.

Question: Why did the Mediterranean unite the Roman Empire but separate the medieval civilizations?

(r. 1138–1152) of Germany. Louis's strong-willed wife, Eleanor of Aquitaine, insisted on accompanying them on what proved to be a costly and embarrassing debacle. This crusade and the ones that followed are distinguished primarily by the ways in which they failed.

The Cultural Environment   It is often assumed that if people from different cultures are given a chance to mingle, they will become more understanding and tolerant of one another. This, alas, is not always the case. However, Europeans learned a great deal from the Muslims who became their subjects in Spain and Sicily and their neighbors in the Holy Land. Muslims introduced Europeans to Arabic, Greek, and Hebrew texts that revolutionized intellectual life in the Latin west. Arab poets inspired the knightly **troubadours** ("inventors"), who appeared in the wake of the First Crusade and invigorated European literature, music, and popular culture. The monastery of Cluny was curious enough about the Christian world's rival faith to sponsor a Latin translation of the Qur'an, but none of this made Europeans any more sympathetic toward Islam.

An eleventh-century epic poem, *The Song of Roland*, assumed that Muslims worshiped an odd trinity of gods that included the Greek deity Apollo. The ludicrous picture of Islam it paints reveals how ignorant many Europeans were of Islam on the eve of the crusades. A generation or two later, they were better informed but, if anything, less tolerant. They could not connect the Muslim scholars whose books they admired with the Muslim faith that they regarded as the enemy of truth. Some Europeans were exceptions to this rule, of course, but their generous attitudes could, paradoxically, deepen prejudices against Islam. The longer Latin Christians lived in the Holy Land, for example, the more their lifestyles came to resemble those of their Muslim neighbors. This horrified visitors from Europe and confirmed their suspicion that Islam was an insidious heresy that had to be exterminated to prevent the spread of its infection. Some Europeans took Muslim texts and practices out of context and unfairly used them to create the impression that Islam was a religion of carnal self-indulgence and wanton blood lust. The many things that encouraged Europeans to fear that their Christian faith was engaged in a life-and-death struggle with Islam submerged the pacific elements in Christ's teachings. European Christianity became a militant faith that mirrored the violence that it imagined to be a characteristic of its enemy.

Europe's Economic Revival   The collapse of the western Roman Empire had sent Europe into an economic decline that dragged on for centuries. Rome's western provinces had never been as wealthy or productive as its eastern ones, and although trade across the Mediterranean continued after Rome's fall, the west produced little that the east wanted. The repeated waves of attackers and migrants that swept across Europe disrupted commercial activity, and people adapted to the chronically chaotic environment by becoming as self-sufficient as possible. They never entirely abandoned trade, for vital supplies (salt and metals, for example) were not available in every locality. The church and the wealthy also wanted luxuries (such as spices, silks, and incense) that had to be imported from the east.

When the Viking, Magyar, and Muslim invasions passed and commercial activity began again to revive, two foci for international trade appeared at opposite ends of Europe. Trade flowed into the continent from the city of Venice in the southeast and from the region of Flanders in the northwest.

At the start of the Middle Ages, Christians had ceded most of the Mediterranean to Muslims, but they retained control of the Adriatic Sea. This gave Venice, at the head of the Adriatic, an early advantage over other Christian cities. It commanded a sea route to Constantinople, and the goods it imported could be shipped over nearby Alpine passes to markets in northern Europe. Most of Italy's other ports were on the western coast of the peninsula. Pisa and Genoa began trading along the French and Italian coasts in the tenth century, and in 1016 they drove the Muslims from Sardinia. A half century later, the Norman conquest of Sicily (1072) secured more of the Mediterranean for Italian sailors, and the success of the First Crusade created bases for them in the Middle East.

Flanders, the northern hub of economic activity, developed in response to the voyages of the Vikings. While some Vikings sailed west to raid England and the coast of France, others headed east across the Baltic Sea and down Russia's rivers. Navigable river systems nearly converge in Russia, so that with a little portage overland from one to another, it was possible to sail from the Baltic to the Black Sea. The Vikings established bases at Novgorod and Kiev. From the latter, they sailed down the Dnieper River to the Black Sea and Constantinople. By the eleventh century, Kiev was, after Constantinople, Christendom's largest city. Goods could flow profitably between the Byzantine capital via Scandinavia and the North Sea to Flanders.

Constantinople's merchants were primarily interested in western Europe's raw materials and agricultural products, but Europe had at least one industry that served both foreign and domestic markets. Europe's climate produced a superior quality of wool, and the manufacturers who turned it into cloth played an economic role in the Middle Ages analogous to that of the makers of automobiles in twentieth-century America. Cloth was an ideal product for trade under medieval conditions. Everyone needed it, but not everyone could produce it. It was lightweight and could be transported over long distances without excessively increasing its cost to consumers. Europe's major cloth-producing centers were the cities of Flanders and northern Italy.

Commercial activity built slowly in the early Middle Ages, for merchants faced many obstacles. Their customers were widely scattered. There was little money in circulation to serve as a medium of exchange, and workers produced little surplus with which to trade. So long as opportunities to trade were limited, people had no motivation to produce surpluses. If a community produced more of something than it could consume and it had no way to sell the excess, it had uselessly expended its labor. The goal of an economically isolated community, therefore, was self-sufficiency, not increasing productivity. If commerce was to grow, merchants had to change the way Europe's laborers thought about their work and their economic goals.

In the tenth century nature began to make things a bit easier for Europeans. Europe's climate entered a warming phase that lengthened growing seasons and extended the ranges of some crops. The improving environment and the spreading use of new farming techniques (the three-field system) and tools (collars and shoes that allowed horses to be used as draft animals) encouraged agricultural productivity. Europe began to expand internally by bringing more of its land under the plow. Forests were cleared, wetlands drained, and farmland was even reclaimed from the sea. More food and increasing political stability encouraged population growth. Between 1000 and 1300 Europe more than doubled its population, and the expanding pool of producers and consumers greatly stimulated economic activity.

Europe's economy did not just grow; it changed. Originally, Europeans had assumed that wealth was a finite resource and that the fundamental economic challenge was to figure out how to share it. That belief governed the thinking of the medieval craft **guilds** that monopolized production for local markets. Only members of a guild were allowed to manufacture and sell its product in its market area. The guild limited production to prevent saturation of its market. It regulated prices so that each guild member could make a living, but it also policed manufacturing to ensure that shoddy goods did not alienate its customers. A wise manufacturer understood the necessity of maintaining a healthy market of satisfied consumers.

Guilds could not establish monopolistic control over international markets, and the producers who traded internationally behaved more like capitalists. Capitalism maintains that wealth is not a finite resource, but something that can be increased by human effort. Capitalists try to maximize the production of surplus goods and then find markets in which to sell them at a profit. This profit becomes capital when, instead of being consumed, it is invested in the production of more goods to be sold to generate more profits. Scholars debate whether true capitalism appeared in Europe during the Middle Ages, but the medieval cloth industry was at least a forerunner of the system. Its investors employed a salaried workforce supervised by managers who ruthlessly served "the bottom line." When competition among them led to overproduction and market saturation, they simply fired their workers and ceased business until demand returned. One product of the commercial revolution of the eleventh century was a proletarian underclass of industrial workers who were vulnerable to such exploitation. During economic downturns, these hungry masses threatened social upheaval.

The Rise of Towns and the Middle Class   The early medieval merchant had to search far and wide for customers. The cities that had survived Rome's passing were ghosts of their former selves, and Europe's reduced population was thinly dispersed about the countryside. Few places had enough people to support a permanent market. Many medieval merchants were therefore simple peddlers who wandered about looking for people to buy their goods.

Commercial activity increased as peddlers learned to entice customers to meet them part way. Life in the medieval countryside offered little excitement. Most Europeans lived in small, isolated communities or farmsteads where the arrival of an itinerant merchant would have been a major event. He offered a new face, desirable merchandise, and news from abroad. Peddlers gradually figured out how to exploit this. They discovered that if they let it be known that they would be in a certain place at a certain time, people would travel some distance to meet them. They also discovered that by working together, they could create greater excitement and draw larger crowds. For safety's sake, they preferred to display their merchandise near a castle or monastery that offered them protection, and the best time to appear was when the people who lived nearby congregated at these places to celebrate a holiday, a **fair** (*feria*, "feast day"). Fairs were exciting events that provided entertainment as well as opportunities to stock up on goods that were otherwise unattainable. Medieval people shopped by the calendar, not by whim, and annual cycles of fairs constituted medieval Europe's primary distribution system. Some fairs served retail customers. Others—particularly those of the French county of Champagne, which was a convenient place for traders from Venice and Flanders to meet—primarily provided opportunities for merchants to restock their wares.

As population grew and the customer base increased, fairs in some places stretched out for longer and longer periods of time. By the eleventh century, some merchant encampments were becoming permanent. If merchants wanted to settle down, however, they had to come to an agreement with the lord on whose land they were squatting. To do so, they formed a commune (a kind of corporation) and sought a charter from the lord that gave them title to land and legal freedom to manage their own affairs. The founders of a *bourg* (a fortified settlement), the **bourgeoisie**, sometimes took up arms to win their privileges, but often they simply purchased their land and rights.

Medieval merchant communes reinvented urban life. Some of Europe's new towns occupied the same sites as old Roman cities, but they bore little resemblance to their predecessors. Most ancient cities served military or administrative purposes, but medieval towns owed their origin to commerce. They were created by traders and craftsmen who had no power over anyone but themselves. Their inhabitants were, in the opinion of the scholars of the day, exceptions to the divinely ordained social order. God,

Carcassonne, France   A few medieval towns have survived in Europe. Their walls, buildings, and twisting streets give modern people some impression of what medieval urban life was like, but a visitor who wants to avoid romantic misconceptions should keep in mind that medieval cities had no sewage systems. Their streets were clogged with people, animals, and refuse, and their air was tainted with fumes from ubiquitous cooking and heating fires. They were neither comfortable nor healthy places.

it was alleged, had (with consummate efficiency) created three kinds of people to perform the three tasks essential to human survival. Protection was the work of knights, provision was the duty of serfs and peasants, and prayer was the responsibility of clergy. There was no place in this system for artisans and merchants, but ultimately they grew so powerful that they could not be ignored. Because their wealth and influence placed them somewhere between the lords and knights of the upper class and the agricultural laborers of the lower class, they became the "middle class."

Townspeople may never have accounted for more than 10% of the population of medieval Europe, but they drove the evolution of medieval society by injecting a new kind of freedom into the social order. Free persons were legal outsiders, for they had not commended themselves to the service of a lord nor been bound to the land. Townspeople, however, found ways to make their freedom of movement and self-determination profitable, and their self-governing towns gave people in the surrounding countryside options that had not previously existed. Lords who wanted to keep the serfs who cultivated their fields had to be careful how they treated them, for oppressed serfs might flee into a town. Because a town was an independent entity, a lord had no right to enter it to retrieve fugitives from his lands. Tradition decreed that if a serf stayed in a town for a year and a day, he became legally free. If a serf opted to remain on his lord's land, a town in the neighborhood could still give him a chance to improve his lot. Townspeople did not raise their own food. Serfs who produced surpluses could sell them in a town's market and use the profits to buy privileges from their lords. Lords were inclined to negotiate, for they wanted to keep their workers—and they needed money. Conspicuous consumption was essential to maintaining a lord's aristocratic status, and the expanding economy created a rising standard of living that put him in a bind. He lived on a fixed income, for his serfs owed him only what grew on his *demesne*, the fields assigned him on his manors. As his expenses increased, it made sense for him to give up his rights to labor services and simply rent his lands to his serfs. Tradition limited labor services, but rents were negotiable. As the new economy took hold, serfdom faded away, and other kinds of ties began to take the place of commendation as a way to organize society.

KEY QUESTION | Revisited

By the end of the eleventh century, a newly assertive Europe was preparing to take on the world. As the weakest of the West's three medieval civilizations, it had come to regard its cultural inferiority as a sign of moral superiority. It spurned the Greeks as devious quasi-heretics and the Muslims as enemies of God. It saw itself as the defender of true faith and authentic civilization—of the real West.

Today, the expression "the West" is usually reserved for European-American cultures, but limiting its use in this way obscures the memory of the West's historical development. The European institutions and attitudes that were transplanted to the Americas had deep roots in the ancient Middle East where the Christian religion was born from the much older Hebrew faith. The classical components of Western civilization also owed much to the ancient Middle East. Islamic, Byzantine, and medieval European cultures were all nurtured by the same Hebraic and classical sources. Medieval

Europe would also have had a much more difficult time rebuilding its version of Western civilization if it had not had the help of Muslim and Byzantine scholars.

The people who inhabited the Roman Empire were culturally and ethnically diverse, but they were aware of a common identity, a shared understanding of what constituted civilized life. However, after the empire was split into eastern and western sections and the culture of its western portion went into steep decline, the contrast between east and west was magnified. The rapid rise of a dynamic Muslim empire did more to turn difference into division. The result was that the peoples who lived at opposite ends of the Mediterranean in the early Middle Ages became more aware of things that separated them than of things they shared.

Cultural contrasts became grounds for cultural opposition in the eleventh century as Europeans evolved a stronger sense of identity and acquired the resources to assert themselves. The crusades they inaugurated widened fault lines into gulfs. The kind of future that might have been built on the friendly exchanges that had taken place between Emperor Charlemagne and Caliph Harun al-Rashid no longer seemed possible or desirable. Economic, political, and military contacts among Europeans, Muslims, and Byzantines multiplied during the second half of the Middle Ages, but they did not bring these peoples closer together. At the end of the Middle Ages, when Europe shifted its attention from the Mediterranean to the Atlantic, they grew even further apart. The result is a legacy of alienation, resentment, and misunderstanding that may constitute the most serious threat to the peace of the modern world. For people who do not understand the history of the development of the concepts of a "Christian West" and an "Islamic East," war between them may seem unavoidable. War is always an option, but it is also always a choice. Better alternatives may occur to those who question the inevitability of conflict and understand the origins of cultural differences.

Review Questions

1. How did the European environment differ from that of the Islamic world during the early Middle Ages?
2. Why were the Christians of medieval Europe suspicious of their fellow Christians in Byzantine and Muslim regions?
3. What things did the three medieval civilizations of the Mediterranean world have in common?
4. Were the political struggles faced by the English, French, and German monarchies unique to Europe or similar to developments elsewhere in the medieval world?
5. Why were the crusades launched? How did they affect the three medieval civilizations?
6. What developments made the eleventh century a turning point for western Europe?

Please consult the Suggested Readings at the back of the book to continue your study of the material covered in this chapter. For a list of documents on the Primary Source DVD-ROM that relate to topics in this chapter, please refer to the back of the book.

Topics in This Chapter

The Renaissance of the Twelfth Century • Universities and Scholasticism
• Religious Revival and Diversity of Opinion • The Artistic Vision of the High Middle Ages
• The Nation-States of the High Middle Ages

10 Europe's High Middle Ages

Bernard of Chartres used to say that we resemble dwarfs riding on the shoulders of
giants in so far as we see more and farther than they do—not because we are
physically or intellectually their superiors, but because their greatness lifts and
supports us.

—John of Salisbury, *Metalogicon*

KEY | Question

Why are some societies more open to change than others?

Although John of Salisbury (c. 1115–1180) was an Englishman, he became bishop of
Chartres, a diocese southeast of Paris. It would be unusual today for a man who was not
French to occupy a major ecclesiastical office in France, but such appointments were
common in the Middle Ages. Two of the medieval archbishops of Canterbury, the heads
of England's church, were Italians recruited from a French monastery. When a job is important enough to a community, talent outweighs almost any objection that might otherwise be made to an individual's employment. Following World War II, for instance, the
United States eagerly embraced the German scientists who had developed rockets for
Nazi Germany—ignoring not only the indiscriminate slaughter their weapons had caused,
but the vicious exploitation of slave labor that had occurred in the facilities they ran. Because modern Western societies give science and technology the kind of priority that
religion had in the medieval world, our scientific institutions are more likely to be staffed
by persons with diverse backgrounds than our places of worship.

The remark quoted above, which John of Salisbury credited to his teacher Bernard of
Chartres, captures the combination of humility and self-assertion that characterized scholars of
John's generation. They were by no means prepared to claim equality with the great thinkers

Chartres Cathedral The great church of the small town of Chartres, just south of Paris, is one of the earliest and best examples of Gothic architecture. Its architect is unknown, but he was a pioneer in the use of the "flying buttresses" that are a hallmark of Gothic style.

of the ancient world, but they were also no longer constrained by excessive respect for them. They assumed that by studying the works of their predecessors they could pick up where "the giants" had left off, make more progress, and even correct the mistakes of the past.

As the intellectuals of the twelfth century shifted from merely assimilating the past to critiquing it, ideas and disagreements proliferated. Instead of recoiling in fear that this might lead to confusion and undermine traditional values and institutions, they scrambled to develop techniques of analysis and inference that would reconcile conflicting opinions. Some warned about the risks of doubt and skepticism, but most had faith that they could work through the tangle and arrive at a more adequate and comprehensive understanding of life and the world. The dream that motivated many of the period's scholars was the creation of a **summa**—a rationally consistent summation of all truths.

Medieval civilization hit its stride in the twelfth and thirteenth centuries, the High Middle Ages. States evolved more sophisticated instruments of law, justice, and government. Architects conceived radically new designs, and awe-inspiring buildings of a type never before seen rose all across Europe. New kinds of schools promoted a new kind of learning, and innovation in the arts and vernacular literatures flourished. These advances required some painful adjustments, for some of them challenged traditional beliefs and institutions. Critics feared that heresies would multiply, respect for authority would diminish, and confidence in truth itself would be lost. But overall, the positives were deemed to outweigh the negatives, and the pioneers forged boldly and rapidly ahead.

The Renaissance of the Twelfth Century

Europe's intellectual history is studded with renaissances—eras when a surge of interest in ancient Greek and Roman literature promoted cultural advances. Most Greek literature had disappeared from western Europe by the twelfth century, but there were enough Latin classics available to sustain a renaissance. The intellectuals of the twelfth century took Virgil and Cicero as their mentors. They wrote elegant poems, letters, and treatises studded with allusions to Greco-Roman myth and history, and the artistic programs they designed to decorate churches spread their esoteric learning to the unlettered masses.

The twelfth-century renaissance was also stimulated by a flood of scientific and philosophical information from Arabic sources. Muslim scholars had made significant advances in science and philosophy, and Latin translations introduced Europeans to their work and important Greek and Hindu thinkers. Muslims also produced commentaries on ancient texts that helped Europeans understand what they were reading and acquire the intellectual tools they needed to strike out on their own.

Christian Europe was preoccupied with theology, but it was the lure of science that first drew its scholars to Muslim libraries (the nearest of which were in Spain). Constantine the African (d. 1087) specialized in translating Arabic medical texts. Adelard of Bath (d. 1126), an Englishman, made a Latin translation of an Arabic version of Euclid's *Elements of Geometry*. He also published an edition of the astronomical tables of the Arab mathematician al-Khwarizmi (d. 850) that introduced Europeans to trigonometry. About 1145 another Englishman, Robert of Chester, translated al-Khwarizmi's *On the Restoration and Opposition of Numbers*—a text that was so fundamental to the study of mathematics that it came to be known simply as "algebra" (*al Gebra*, "the book"). A generation later, Italian mathematician Leonardo Fibonacci (1170–1230) introduced

Europeans to "Arabic" numerals and the concept of zero, both of which Muslims had appropriated from Hindu sources.

The Popularity of Dialectic   The intellectuals of the High Middle Ages exalted **dialectic** (the craft of constructing logical arguments) over the other liberal arts that structured the medieval educational curriculum. This was due in part to the influence of Gerbert of Aurillac (c. 940–1003), who was reputed to be the most learned man in Europe. Gerbert rose from humble origins in a French monastery to become the head of an influential school, tutor to an emperor, and (despite allegations of witchcraft) a pope (Sylvester II, r. 999–1003). He studied mathematics and astronomy in Barcelona, Córdoba, and Seville; constructed scientific instruments; and revived the use of the abacus (the ancient and medieval world's premier calculating device).

The great thinkers of the Middle Ages, which included Gerbert, turned language into a tool for scientific research. Scientific breakthroughs in the modern era are often the result of new data provided by instruments or techniques that improve on the human senses. Researchers can now look more closely at the world and more deeply into the universe than ever before in history. Medieval scholars did not have this option. Because they could not improve on the information simple observation provides, their only hope for progress lay in improving what their minds did with that information—on refining the language they used to describe it and think about it. They defined terms with technical precision and then explored the logical implications of their words. They focused on a task that scientists still acknowledge to be important: understanding how the mind represents the world to itself.

Gerbert taught his students dialectic with the help of what came to be called the Old Logic, the philosophical treatises that Boethius (see Chapter 8) had assembled and translated in the sixth century. This was familiar material, but it inspired a change of attitude for Gerbert's generation. Earlier scholars had been taught that truth rested on authority—that something was true because a respected source said that it was true. The most important source of truth was revelation (enlightenment by God). The study of dialectic prompted men like Gerbert, however, to suspect that truth needed the support of nothing beyond itself. A true belief appeared to have an inherent rationality that made its validity self-evident.

A famous debate between two eleventh-century theologians, Berengar of Tours (d. 1088) and Lanfranc of Bec (d. 1089), encouraged dialectic's advocates. At issue was what happened when a priest consecrated bread and wine in the sacrament of the mass. The church had not yet taken a stand, but it was widely believed that consecration turned the bread and wine into Christ's body and blood (the Roman Catholic Church's doctrine of transubstantiation). Berengar claimed that this could not be so, for human senses could discern no difference between consecrated and unconsecrated bread and wine. The traditional method for dealing with skeptics like Berengar was to remind them that human understanding was limited and that because some truths could only be grasped by faith, they had to be accepted on the authority of the church. Lanfranc, however, opted to use dialectic to argue for the rationality of faith. Philosophers, Lanfranc noted, distinguish between substance and attribute. A *substance* is the essential nature of a thing, while an *attribute* is a feature of that thing that can change without affecting its identity. (A cloak, for example, remains a cloak no matter what color it is dyed.) In ordinary experience, Lanfranc argued, attributes change but substances do not. Logic dictates, however, that an omnipotent God could make an exception in the case of the mass—changing the substances of consecrated bread and wine but not their attributes. Lanfranc did not claim to have proved that this was the case, but only to have shown that what faith believed was not a logical absurdity.

Lanfranc's reconciliation of faith with reason had a significant implication. If the truths that come from revelation are, as he suggested, compatible with those acquired by ordinary human experience, the universe must be fundamentally intelligible and its mysteries should yield to dialectical analysis. Theologians quickly discovered, however, that reason was a two-edged sword that required skillful handling.

Reason and Authority   Europe's dialecticians were fascinated by a problem that the Old Logic raised but left unresolved: the status of words that refer to classes of things versus those that refer to individual things. Nominalists maintained that a word that referred to a category of objects (*chair*, for example) was a mere *nomen* ("name") that the mind invented for its own convenience. Their opponents, the realists, insisted that the fact that the mind can assign individual things to classes (that is, identify this particular thing as "a chair") means that it perceives something that transcends the separate existences of things—something that is really in them. Chairs can be designed in many ways and made of many different materials, but we recognize them all as chairs because there is an eternal reality (an essential "chairness") that defines them as chairs. Both these positions had unfortunate theological implications. **Nominalism** suggested that the Trinity was only a name for a group of three deities: the Father, the Son, and the Holy Spirit. **Realism**, in contrast, led to the heresy of pantheism (the belief that God is simply the sum total of everything that exists—pure being, the pinnacle of a hierarchy of increasingly general and comprehensive classes). Neither of these alternatives was acceptable to Christians, and the search for a rational alternative to them inspired exploration of the subtleties of logic.

The dialectical method's most famous advocate was Peter Abelard (1070–1142), the eldest son of a minor Breton nobleman. Abelard relinquished his patrimony to a younger brother and, freed of family obligations, left home to seek an education. He drifted from school to school immersing himself in the debate between the nominalists and the realists and soon began to challenge prominent spokesmen for both sides. As his brilliantly constructed critiques revealed the flaws in the arguments of one famous scholar after another, he earned enemies, followers, and (in 1115) a position as a teacher at Ste. Geneviève in Paris. Abelard was a brilliant, charismatic educator who enthralled his students with poetry as well as dialectic. The crowds of scholars who flocked to Paris to hear him established the city's reputation as Europe's premier center of intellectual activity. At the height of his popularity, however, Abelard made a serious blunder.

One of Paris's prominent clerics had a niece named Heloise (d. 1163). He sent her to a convent school where she mastered Latin, Greek, and (possibly) Hebrew and earned a reputation as an intellectual prodigy. Because it was impossible for a girl to mix with the rowdy adolescent males who populated Paris's schools, Heloise's uncle was at a loss as to how to continue her education—until it occurred to him to ask Abelard to tutor her privately. Abelard was intrigued by her intellect (more than her looks, he said), and she fell passionately in love with him. They became sexually involved. After she became pregnant, he persuaded her (although she argued against it) to marry him. His plan was to keep the marriage secret. Medieval scholars were considered clergy, and the rewards they aspired to were appointments to well-funded offices in the church. Because clergy had to be celibate, an acknowledged wife would have ended Abelard's career. Heloise's uncle, however, concluded that Abelard was sacrificing Heloise's reputation to protect his own, and he took drastic steps to avenge her and his family's honor. He hired thugs who broke into Abelard's rooms and castrated him.

Abelard sought refuge in a monastery, and Heloise (for love of him and not God, as she explained to him in her letters) entered a convent. The cloister, however, brought Abelard no peace. New controversies arose, and his situation became precarious when his enemies accused him of attacking the church. Abelard had written a book called *Sic et Non* (*Yes and No*) which listed conflicting opinions on points of doctrine ("yes" affirming and "no" negating) cited from the works of famous theologians. By showing that authorities sometimes disagreed, the book was intended to demonstrate that scholars had to do more to establish the truth of an opinion than quote respected thinkers. Abelard urged his contemporaries to use dialectical methods to critique all opinions, even those of the most revered fathers of the church. The church hierarchy, however, saw this as an attack on traditional beliefs that would result in the proliferation of heresy, and in 1141 a council of clergy condemned Abelard. He immediately set out for Rome to appeal to the pope, but he died on the way. His career might have been less stormy if he had been less brash, for the spirit of the age was with him. Dialectic was in the ascendancy, and his younger contemporary, Peter Lombard (d. 1160), produced a book (*Sentences*) similar to *Sic et Non* that became one of the medieval world's standard student texts.

Universities and Scholasticism

Monasteries dominated education in the early Middle Ages, but during the twelfth century leadership passed to cathedral towns (the seats of bishops). The move reflected a fundamental change in the nature of education. Monks were taught to respect authority and tradition and to sacrifice individuality to a communal ideal. Twelfth-century Europe, however—with its flourishing economy, rising towns, more complex institutions, and increasing contacts with the wider world—needed men who were trained to innovate, solve problems, and take individual initiative. The urban schools that trained church administrators and that had access to the wealth and the new information flowing into Europe were better situated than monasteries to meet this need.

The Academic Guild   Universities developed from local schools that became famous enough to attract an international clientele. The situation in which this clientele found itself prompted its organization as a university. The medieval world had no embassies or consulates and no international agreements to assist travelers and protect resident aliens. Foreign students and faculty had no legal rights in the towns where they studied and

taught. They were, therefore, vulnerable to exploitation by landlords and abuse by government authorities. To strengthen their position, they banded together to form a guild or union—a *universitas* ("university"). Together, they had considerable leverage in negotiations with local leaders, for students were a source of income for a town. They rented rooms and bought food and other supplies. Because schools had no campuses or buildings, students and faculty could easily pack up and threaten to take their business to another community. Many of Europe's famous universities were created by migrations of disgruntled academics.

The earliest known charter according legal recognition to an academic *universitas* was issued in 1158 to a school in Bologna, Italy, that was governed by students. The student council employed the university's professors, oversaw its curriculum, and even regulated methods of instruction. Bologna emphasized the study of law and attracted older, career-driven students. Most medieval universities, such as the famous one chartered in Paris in 1200, were faculty guilds.

Teachers and students in the first medieval universities made do with whatever facilities they could find. A man who was licensed by a university guild to teach would set up a lectern (reading desk) in the side aisle of a church or some other public building. His students would stand or sit on the floor around him. Latin was used for instruction and much casual conversation, for it was the only language that all members of the academic community had in common. Many students had no books or writing materials, for these things were expensive. They might use wax-covered boards for taking notes, but medieval scholars trained themselves to memorize what they heard and read. They carried prodigious amounts of information in their heads. Professors (*profiteor*, "to educate") taught by glossing texts. That is, they read a passage from a book and then commented on it, explaining its meaning and spelling out its implications. There were no course exams and no grading system. Students (sometimes as young as 10) were completely on their own. They drifted from teacher to teacher and school to school until they felt that they were ready to apply for membership in the teachers' guild. As with any guild, those who aspired to join (that is, become "masters") were required to produce a masterpiece that demonstrated their command of their craft. An aspiring master shoemaker, for instance, submitted a pair of shoes for examination by the officials of the shoemakers' guild. Candidates for academic guilds submitted theses—propositions that they were prepared to defend in public debate before the whole university community. Graduate programs in modern universities perpetuate this custom. Candidates for degrees conduct original research, write theses or dissertations, and then defend their ideas before committees composed of experts in their fields.

Entry level students in medieval universities were "bachelors of arts," young males who were learning the basics of medieval education, the seven liberal arts of the *trivium* and the *quadrivium* (see Chapter 8). The members of the guild who taught these subjects were "masters of arts." A lengthy course of advanced study in a specialized field earned a scholar the highest academic title, *doctor* ("teacher"). The most prestigious degree was the doctorate in theology. Medieval society was organized hierarchically, and people dressed to reflect their social rank. Academics wore gowns appropriate to their place within the university, and on ceremonial occasions faculty and students of American universities still don the

Medieval Scholar This miniature from a fifteenth-century manuscript illustrates a twelfth-century scholar, Matthaeus Platearius, at work writing a medical text. It is likely idealized, for few medieval scholars may have been able to afford such comfortable quarters and expensive clothing.

robes and hoods that served their medieval predecessors as overcoats and head coverings.

Scholasticism and the Influence of Aristotle
Medieval scholars never completely threw off their respect for the authority of ancient texts. They took it for granted that the Bible, the church fathers, and the great ancient philosophers all spoke the truth, and they sometimes trusted what these sources said more than the evidence of their own eyes. Universities, however, promoted a more liberal way of thinking that diminished reliance on authority and valued independent investigation. Their scholars were struggling to organize a flood of information from Muslim and Byzantine sources, and rational critiques seemed to offer the best hope for reconciling the diversity of opinions found in their sources. The medieval university nurtured the open-minded spirit of inquiry that characterizes modern Western civilization at its best.

The men who worked at the new schools are called Scholastics. Modern students may find their dialectical methods and arguments tedious, but the great Scholastics were exciting, original thinkers. Although some of them wrote beautiful poetry, their scholarly interests were in the use of language as science, not art. They sought solutions to problems by refining definitions of terms and spinning out incredibly subtle logical arguments. They used language with the precision of mathematics.

The Scholastics owed much to the arrival in Europe during the second half of the twelfth century of the New Logic, previously unknown treatises on logic by the ancient Greek philosopher Aristotle. Europeans' appetite for Aristotle had been whetted by their study of the works of his great Muslim interpreters Avicenna (Abu ali ibn Sina, 980–1037) and Averroës (Ibn-Rushd, 1126–1198). During the thirteenth century, all of Aristotle's works that had survived from antiquity gradually became available to European scholars in Latin versions taken directly from the original Greek. Their impact was revolutionary. Aristotle was the fulfillment of a medieval scholar's dream. He was the primary authority on the rules for constructing logical arguments, and he wrote on a huge range of subjects.

The church was initially alarmed by the enthusiasm scholars manifested for Aristotle, for some of his ideas were incompatible with Christian theology. Aristotle, for instance, maintained that the universe had to be eternal and uncreated, for the alternative (i.e., something arising from nothing) was a logical absurdity. In 1210 a church council tried to protect faith by censoring Aristotle's works and limiting their use, but it was impossible to force the Aristotelian genie back into his bottle. Aristotle quickly became required reading for every serious scholar. Some medieval thinkers simply accepted the conflict between his philosophy and the church's teachings and declared that there were two kinds of truth—one of faith and one of reason. But the era's greatest thinkers—notably, Albertus Magnus (1193–1280) and his student Thomas Aquinas (1225–1274)—devoted their lives to reconciling Aristotle's insights with Christian doctrine. Aquinas did such a masterful job that the Roman Catholic Church has endorsed his theological *summae* as definitive explications of its faith. Aquinas believed that reason and faith were complementary methods for understanding reality. Reason began a journey that only faith could complete. Some medieval scholars attacked Aquinas's work, but the logic of his *summae* was so compelling that they were difficult to undermine. The *summae* were also so comprehensive that Aquinas's followers had little left to do but to comment on and explicate his insights.

Not all medieval intellectuals were equally enthusiastic about dialectic and the influence of Aristotle. John of Salisbury, among others, complained that dialectic substituted narrow vocational training for true education. He championed a broader humanist curriculum based on the study of classical literature. Even at the peak of **Scholasticism**'s popularity, there were critics who used the tools of dialectic to counter what they regarded as the Scholastics' excessive rationalism.

Religious Revival and Diversity of Opinion

A surge of religious enthusiasm energized the cultural creativity of the High Middle Ages by creating a constructive intellectual tension between feeling and reason. The passionately faithful stressed the importance of experience and intuition and cautioned against the era's drift toward excessive rationality. Curiously, however, the religious enthusiasts' exaltation of the practice of faith and direct experience of God over mere speculation about divine mysteries sometimes inspired challenges to traditional beliefs and institutions similar to those that the rationalists posed.

Monastic Innovations   The religious fervor of the High Middle Ages sparked a renewal of interest in monasticism. But recruits did not flock to the older Benedictine houses that Cluny had reformed in the tenth century. They were drawn to new, stricter orders that restored the asceticism and simplicity of the original Benedictine Rule.

The emergence of new monastic ideals was forecast by a hermetical movement at the end of the eleventh century that was officially recognized (about 1130) as the Carthusian Order. Carthusians worshiped as a community but lived alone as hermits in isolated cells where they worked with their hands and practiced rigorous self-denial. Their order was too strict to attract large numbers, but it was so disciplined that it never needed reform. Far more popular was the Cistercian order that sprang up in the first half of the twelfth century. Cistercians eschewed the richly ornamented sanctuaries and elaborate rituals characteristic of the old Benedictine houses. They refused gifts of rich estates worked by serfs and established their houses on wasteland where they labored to support themselves. Many survived by herding sheep and supplying wool to Europe's thriving cloth industry. They were such successful developers that the barren lands to which they fled in pursuit of simplicity and spirituality made them rich and powerful.

So many monastic orders appeared during the twelfth century that the papacy finally decided to authorize no more. But in the early thirteenth century, it made an exception for some orders that redefined the monastic vocation. Monks traditionally withdrew from the world to devote themselves to prayer. Their vocation was to beseech God's mercy and forgiveness for the world's sins, but not to change a world that God had destined for final judgment and destruction. The confident atmosphere of the High Middle Ages, however, nurtured a greater sense of responsibility for working to improve the world. Some people who felt called to devote their lives totally to God wanted to embrace traditional monastic asceticism but not retreat to a cloister. They wanted to stay in the work-a-day world and engage in a struggle to ease suffering and save souls. A man who embraced this new kind of religious vocation was called a **friar** (*frater*, "brother"). The pattern for the life of a friar was set by the son of a prosperous Italian cloth merchant, Francis of Assisi (1181–1226).

Francis initially immersed himself in all the pleasures life offers handsome, wealthy young men. But at some point a religious conversion convinced him that God was calling him to model his life on the example set by Jesus and the Apostles. Francis believed that Jesus and his companions had no possessions and trusted entirely to God to provide for them while they went about preaching and healing. He, therefore, gave away everything he had and became a mendicant, a wandering beggar. Francis drifted about preaching and doing what he could for the poor. He ordered his followers never to keep anything in reserve for the future, but immediately to share everything they were given or earned with the needy. His radical vision of a religious fellowship that pinned its survival entirely on a constant stream of charitable offerings was soon moderated by church authorities. They devised a legal fiction that allowed the friars to enjoy the kinds of endowments that supported traditional monasteries while still claiming not to own any property. Endowments were forthcoming, for the friars' highly visible work among the laity made them the most popular and respected of medieval clergy.

In 1216 a second order of friars was founded by a Spanish priest named Dominic de Guzmán (1170–1221). Dominic was attracted to evangelism, and his plan was to become a missionary. The pope, however, sent him to southern France to deal with another product of the religious revival of the twelfth century—heresy. The Dominicans—officially, the Order of Preachers (or Black Friars, from the color of their robes)—were educators. They were trained to preach and to supplement the limited religious instruction and pastoral care the laity received from parish priests. They hoped that by engaging people's intellects and by setting them an example of Christ-like living, they could combat religious error. The Franciscans' founder was a poet who imbued their order with a deep appreciation for the emotional, mystical aspect of faith. The Dominicans, in contrast, appealed to people who preferred a cooler, more intellectual religion. Although the Dominicans recruited some of the era's most important scholars, others were drawn to the Franciscans, and both orders played major roles at the medieval universities. Their work and popular appeal may have served to mitigate, but it did not halt, criticism of the regular clergy and the spread of heresy.

PEOPLE IN CONTEXT William IX, Duke of Aquitaine and Count of Poitou (1071–1127)

S aints and scholars were not the only contributors to the robust civilization of the High Middle Ages. The era had a thriving popular culture that produced innovative art, music, and literature. Early medieval entertainers had chanted epic poems featuring stolid, one-dimensional warrior-heroes, such as Beowulf and Roland. But the audiences of the High Middle Ages had a taste for something more individual, passionate, and intimate. They were attracted to lyric poetry, music, and romance. Students at universities composed Latin lyrics (on both sacred and profane themes), but the pioneers of vernacular poetry were the troubadours (*trovar*, "inventor") who appeared first in southern France. The names of about 460 troubadours (some of whom were women) have survived.

Troubadours were either aristocrats or artists who depended on the nobility's patronage. Prominent among the early notables was a lord of exalted rank, Duke William IX of Aquitaine. As duke of Aquitaine and count of Poitou, he presided over about one-third of France. His domain was not only large, but it boasted a uniquely rich and sophisticated culture—thanks, in part, to contact with Muslim Spain (whence the inspiration for the new poetry may have come). William was a worldly man who was more inclined to enjoy this life than prepare for the next. The great adventure for noblemen of his generation was the crusade, and the success of the First Crusade prompted him to raise an army and set off for Jerusalem. Unfortunately, he blundered into an ambush while crossing Asia Minor and lost most of his men. He and similarly ill-fated, freelance campaigners were blamed for restoring the confidence of the crusaders' Muslim opponents.

William was not a man to dwell on setbacks. His poetry is enlivened by a sense of humor, self-mockery, and sheer physical joy at being alive. The songs he composed celebrate the pleasures of rides through the sunny Provençal countryside and his delight in the company (apparently intimate) of beautiful women. The troubadour's primary theme was love—a passionate emotion but one to be governed by elaborate etiquette. Modern literary critics call the fad that troubadour poetry began "**courtly love**," an elegant game of courtship played by

Troubadours This illustration from a medieval manuscript depicts a band of entertainers: a singing troubadour accompanied by a viol and a flute player.

medieval aristocrats (courtiers). The courtly lover placed the woman he adored "on a pedestal." He praised her as a paragon of beauty and virtue and pledged to endure any hardship in exchange for the slightest sign of her favor. His love for her drove him to realize the best in himself. William's granddaughter, the Eleanor of Aquitaine who became England's queen, continued the duke's tradition of providing patronage for poets, and the troubadour culture that she and her daughters spread through Europe did much to turn its rude feudal warriors into civilized, cultivated gentlemen.

Question: Would the kind of praise that troubadours heaped on women have contributed to the empowerment of women in medieval society?

Return of Heresy   The general decline of European culture during the early Middle Ages had reduced the threat of heresy by diminishing intellectual speculation of all kinds. But as levels of education and literacy rose in the twelfth century, heresy returned. People who learned to read could access the Scriptures and decide for themselves what they believed God required from the church and its clergy. Inevitably, some concluded that the conduct of the religious establishment fell far short of Christ's standard. Glaringly obvious was the fact that the lives of the popes, who claimed to be Christ's vicars on Earth, and many of the clergy bore little resemblance to those of Christ and his disciples. The Franciscans and Dominicans were able implicitly to criticize the church on these grounds without breaking with it, but others were less successful at steering such a delicate course.

In the 1170s (a decade or more before Francis of Assisi's birth) a merchant from the French city of Lyons named Peter Waldo heard the Scriptures' call to live the Christ-like life and responded in ways that anticipated Francis and the friars. He gave away his property and devoted himself to serving the poor. When local clergy objected to what they regard as Peter's transgression on their turf, he and his followers became more radical. Like the Protestants produced by the Reformation of the sixteenth century, the Waldensians insisted that the Bible was the only authority binding on Christians. They repudiated the pope and the priesthood and claimed that faithful lay people could administer the sacraments (the Christian rituals that mediate God's saving grace) for themselves. The pope condemned the Waldensians in 1184, but the movement spread and survived. Waldensian churches can be found today in Europe, South America, and the United States.

A more extreme form of religious dissent rooted itself in the south of France. Some historians believe that the religion of the Cathars ("the Pure") or Albigensians (from Albi, a town that a contemporary may have unfairly branded as a center of the heresy) spread into western Europe from the Balkans with the trade that surged in the eleventh century. The Cathars preached a dualistic faith similar to the Gnostic cults that had competed with Christianity during the last centuries of the Roman Empire. They claimed that an evil demon, not the true God, had created the material world and imprisoned souls in flesh. They taught that extreme asceticism could free the soul from a cycle of reincarnation and return it to the realm of pure spirit where God reigned. The Cathars attracted a large following, for their ascetics were more admirable spiritual exemplars than many of the church's clergy. When preaching and threats failed to counter the heresy, the church resorted to force. In

1208 the pope called for a crusade to root out the Cathars, and the lords of northern France seized on it as an excuse to grab rich lands for themselves in the south. The war raged for 20 years and devastated what had been one of Europe's most culturally advanced regions.

Mysticism and the Limits of Reason   Mystical currents have always coursed through Christianity, but they flowed with great vigor at the start of the twelfth century. Mystics have experiences of God that transcend reason and understanding and that give them, in the opinion of other Christians, a kind of prophetic authority. The twelfth-century renaissance produced one of the greatest of the medieval mystics, Bernard of Clairvaux (1090–1153). Although he was abbot of a Cistercian monastery, he was no recluse. He advised kings and popes and was the driving force behind the Second Crusade (see Chapter 9). He devoted some of his considerable energy to destroying the pioneering scholar, Abelard, and to opposing the kind of dialectical approach to theology that Abelard advocated. Bernard believed that knowledge of God came from an encounter with God—that it was mediated by love, not reason.

Many of Bernard's contemporaries shared his passionate approach to faith, and mysticism was not confined to monks and clergy. It influenced the pious practices of the laity. It inspired artists, motivated reform movements, and helped some women escape the constraints that medieval society imposed on their gender. Female mystics and visionaries were particularly plentiful during the second half of the Middle Ages. Some earned such respect that kings, popes, and prominent male intellectuals sought their advice. Bernard held women in low regard, but even he made an exception for two: the Virgin Mary and Hildegard of Bingen (1098–1179). The latter was a visionary nun, a poet, a composer, a physician, and an astute dialectician who carried on a large correspondence with the leading men of her day. In recent years, modern audiences have rediscovered the pleasures of the music she wrote for her sisters to perform.

Mysticism was not willful ignorance. Some of the great thinkers of the High Middle Ages were mystics who used dialectical methods to argue their positions. Bonaventure (1221–1274), a Franciscan scholar and faculty colleague of Thomas Aquinas's, was one of the most influential of these. He, like the early Latin theologian Augustine of Hippo (354–430), believed that human reason is untrustworthy because it, like the rest of human nature, is corrupted by original sin. Reason, he argued, describes the surface of things and provides superficial knowledge unless it is enlightened by love and divine grace. Only an individual who has had an experience of transcendence can intuit truth—the ultimate divine reality that the created world merely symbolizes. Aquinas himself may have come around to Bonaventure's point of view. Toward the end of his life Aquinas is said to have had a mystical experience that so overwhelmed him that he ceased to write.

The Artistic Vision of the High Middle Ages

For medieval mystics such as Bonaventure, the world was filled with visible things that symbolized the invisible truths of faith. That was the purpose of much ecclesiastical architecture, and nothing better captured the spirit of Europe's medieval civilization than the great churches that were erected during the High Middle Ages.

New churches sprang up everywhere during the twelfth and thirteenth centuries. In France, where much of the era's architectural innovation took place, more than 80 cathedrals and thousands of lesser churches were built. A town of 5,000 people might have as many as 50 parish churches, and some cities built cathedrals large enough to house their entire populations. The sheer volume of construction was remarkable, but so were its products. The new churches of the High Middle Ages so perfectly expressed Christianity's transcendent faith that even today they continue to influence the design of Christian houses of worship.

Origin of Christian Architecture   Early Christianity had no architecture of its own. The first Christian congregations were small, poor, and met in the homes of their members or in the open air. So long as persecution threatened, it was not safe for Christians to design buildings that advertised their presence. Only after Emperor Constantine legalized the faith in the fourth century were conditions right for Christianity to evolve an architectural vocabulary of its own.

The church grew so rapidly after Constantine endorsed it that there was no time to invent a new kind of space to house its proliferating congregations. Bishops simply appropriated and consecrated existing public buildings. The Roman Empire's standard

The Basilica of Santa Maria Maggiore   Rome's Church of Santa Maria Maggiore dates to the fifth century and is a splendid example of an early Christian basilica. Its lavish decoration tends to obscure the simplicity of its design—a flat-ceilinged rectangular building consisting of a nave, apse, and side aisles.

multipurpose building was the basilica, a simple rectangular hall (nave) with a rounded bay (apse) at one end to house the office of the building's administrator. Additional floor space was sometimes created by running parallel corridors (aisles) down the side-walls of the building. Basilicas had low-pitched roofs and were lit by windows cut in the wall above the level of the aisles (the clerestory).

The basic basilican design evolved to serve the needs of Christian worship. When more room was needed for the increasing number of clergy who chanted the liturgy, the apse was pushed out to create a space called the choir. Altars multiplied along the walls of the nave, and some expanded into side chapels. When large chapels appeared on op-posing sides of a nave, they created a transept or "crossing" that gave the floor plan of a church the shape of a cross. The blank walls and flat ceilings of basilicas were often en-livened with frescoes, mosaics, or other kinds of decoration.

In addition to rectangular basilicas, a circular church design also appeared in the late Roman period. It probably evolved from shrines built over the graves of saints. The design was particularly popular in the Middle East, and its association with some of the lavish sanctuaries of the Byzantine Empire may explain why Charlemagne chose it for his great church at Aachen. It appealed to the crusaders as well. The Templars, one of the orders of warrior monks, often built round churches.

Romanesque Style   Basilican churches spread to northern Europe in the early Middle Ages, but they were not well adapted to its environment. Their low-pitched wooden roofs were prone to rot in climates damper than those of the sunny Mediter-ranean. The weight of northern snows stressed them, and they were vulnerable to fires. A pious desire to honor Christianity's eternal God with eternal buildings may also have motivated the search for ways to replace wooden roofs with vaults of stone, the most durable building material then available.

Medieval architects began by copying the vaulting techniques used by the Romans. Roman buildings employed round arches. The simplest way to vault a nave was to line up lots of these arches, one next to another like slices of bread. This created a barrel vault, a tunnel-like room that was difficult to light. Because each part of the vault was supported by the wall immediately beneath it, it was risky to cut holes in the walls for windows. Walls also had to be very thick to counterbalance the lateral thrust from the arches that rested on their tops. The use of round arches also imposed design limita-tions. The ratio between the span and the height of a round arch was fixed. The only way to make a barrel-vaulted nave wider was to make it higher, but a point could soon be reached where the weight of the vault became too great to manage.

The medieval architect's **Romanesque** style featured round arches, thick walls, and small windows. It was popular in Italy, Spain, and southern France, for hot, sunny regions welcomed the shelter of dark, cave-like buildings. Romanesque churches continued to be erected in southern Europe long after the north had switched to the later **Gothic** style.

Romanesque architects tried to make their heavy buildings look less ponderous by covering them with elaborate decoration. False arcades were cut into walls to lighten their appearance, and blank spaces were filled with paintings, mosaics, and sheets of colored stone arranged in geometric patterns. But the Romanesque's fortress-like ap-

Romanesque Interior   This view of the nave of the early twelfth-century Church of St. Sernin, Toulouse, France, illustrates the environment typical of a Romanesque church. Its effect is imposing, but also dark and, despite the height of its vault, somewhat oppressive.

pearance fit the defensive mood of the early Middle Ages, and it served well for monastic retreats from the world. The confident, expansionist spirit that pervaded the towns of the high Middle Ages, however, called for something more open and audacious.

Gothic Style   The first church in the Gothic style (the supreme achievement of the medieval architect) was erected about 1140 at France's royal monastery, St. Denis, near Paris. It was the work of the cloister's abbot, Suger (1081–1151), chief counselor to King Louis VI (r. 1108–1137) and King Louis VII (r. 1137–1180). (For their reigns, see Chapter 9.) By integrating a series of structural innovations, some of which dated back to the eleventh century, Suger invented a new kind of sacred space—one designed to maximize light as a symbol of God's presence. The inscription Suger placed on the door to his new church explained the purpose of the artistry that went into its creation: "Meditation on material things lifts the intellect from lethargy and enables it to grasp the truth."

The most distinctive feature of Gothic architecture is the pointed or broken arch. Gothic architects escaped the limitations imposed by the geometry of the Romanesque's round arch by "breaking" it at its apex. A pointed arch has no fixed ratio between its height and span—its apex can be pitched at any height. It serves as a kind of hinge for halves of an arc that can be widened or narrowed as a builder wants.

By combining pointed arches with rib-vaulting (a technique that Romanesque architects developed), Gothic architects could erect vaults over rectangular or irregular spaces. Rib-vaulting was a significant improvement over the simple barrel vault. If the nave of a church was divided into squares, each square could be vaulted by running round arches not from side to side, but between diagonal corners. These arches (the ribs) intersected over the center of the square and light masonry was used to fill in the spaces between them. They functioned as a built-in scaffolding that bore much of the vault's weight. They also gave an architect more control over the thrust from a vault, for ribs focused the weight they carried on the points where they intersected with the walls. Walls had to be buttressed (thickened) at these places to compensate for that weight, but the reduction of pressure on the wall between the buttresses meant that more of the wall could be cut away to create a window.

Gothic architects allowed even more light into their churches by preventing buttresses from shading the windows near them. They planted buttresses some distance from their

Gothic Interior   Paris's Sainte-Chapelle illustrates how effective Gothic architects could be at lighting the interior of their buildings. Here walls have been replaced by a nearly continuous circuit of window.

buildings and used arches to link them to the pressure points where ribs intersected with walls. These "flying buttresses" turned a Gothic building into a kind of stone tent. The sheet of stone (the vaulting) that roofed it was held in place by stone "ropes" (arches) anchored to stone "pegs" (buttresses) around its perimeter. Because the ribs and buttresses carried most of the weight of the building, its walls could be replaced by vast expanses of window. Well-designed Gothic churches were so filled with light that medieval people called them glass houses.

During the second half of the twelfth century, the Gothic style spread rapidly from its birthplace in northern France throughout Europe. Towns spent phenomenal sums to construct ever larger, brighter, and more awe-inspiring sanctuaries. The record was set by the builders of the cathedral at Beauvais who, after several failed attempts, pitched a vault at the height of 157 feet—high enough to shelter a 14-story building.

The Gothic style captivated medieval people because it was so congruent with their faith and spiritual experience. The easiest way to understand this may be to compare Gothic churches with the temples of the ancient Greeks. Classical architecture reflected the belief that the world centered on the human being. A Greek temple, like Athens' Parthenon, was meant to assure people that the world was an intelligible place that affirmed human nature. The principles of its construction were not intended to be mysterious and awe-inspiring, but immediately obvious and comfortable. Vertical pillars supported horizontal lintels. Stone did what stone was expected to do.

A Gothic church creates the opposite impression. To convey Christianity's faith in a transcendent reality quite different from our own, it offers an experience of a supernatural world. A Gothic church encloses a divine space where nature's laws appear to be transcended. The Gothic architect conceals the principles of his building's construction so that the logic of its design is hidden from those who enter it. Vertical lines dominate the interior and pull the eye upward. The ribs of the vault seem to converge at infinity, and far overhead tons of rock apparently float on walls of light. There are windows on every side. However, their tinted glass prevents the worshiper from connecting the interior with the ordinary world outside and fills the sanctuary with unnatural light. From the engineering point of view, a Gothic church is a supremely rational structure, but one that uses reason to create the experience of irrational space. It is a place where nature, by seeming to behave supernaturally, fulfills Suger's mandate and turns the intellect from the seen to the unseen. A Gothic church is not just a place to hear about God's transcendence; it is a place to experience it.

The Nation-States of the High Middle Ages

The High Middle Ages witnessed decisive events leading to the formation of modern Europe. Carolingian dreams of empire receded, but so did the radical political fragmentation that set in with the decline of the Carolingian dynasty. As powerful states emerged and ethnic enclaves consolidated, Europeans' growing awareness of their diverse political and culture identities struggled with their heritage of a common religious faith.

England   A pattern of alternating strong and weak reigns helped define the institutions of the English monarchy. William the Conqueror (r. 1066–1087) and his sons, William Rufus (r. 1087–1100) and Henry I (r. 1100–1135), exploited the opportunity that conquest gave them to lay the foundations for a powerful royal government in England. Their work was undermined by the 20-year-long civil war (1135–1154) that raged between Matilda (1102–1167), Henry's daughter and only surviving legitimate child, and her cousin Stephen (r. 1135–1154). The truce that ended that war and brought Matilda's son, Henry II (r. 1154–1189), to the throne reversed England's course once again and restored the authority of its throne.

The French lands that Henry II inherited from his parents and acquired by marrying Eleanor of Aquitaine (c. 1122–1204) gave him immense resources, but he was no autocrat. His grandfather, Henry I, had implicitly conceded that England's king was accountable for the use of his powers, and Henry II affirmed the "liberties" that Henry I had promised the English people. Henry's attention was not focused exclusively on England. He had not been raised there and, like many of medieval England's kings, he did not speak English. He ruled a vast Angevin Empire (see Chapter 9) that included about half of France, and he was eager to expand his holdings on the continent.

Although Henry was often abroad, he did not neglect England. He stabilized its frontier with Scotland, brought parts of Wales under control, and invaded Ireland to win recognition of his lordship over the outposts that enterprising Norman warriors had taken the initiative to establish there. In 1172 the pope recognized the English king's claim to Ireland, but the Irish and English are still disputing their relationship.

Henry I greatly improved his kingdom's machinery of government, and Henry II continued his grandfather's work. William I had got off to a strong start by claiming all the land in England by right of conquest and requiring all property owners to contribute to the support of the crown. By preserving the Anglo-Saxon system of shires administered by sheriffs (commoners whom the king appointed), William also freed England's king from total dependence on landed aristocrats to carry out his will. Henry II staffed his government with professional bureaucrats who were trained in Europe's new schools, and he raised enough money to salary most of the men who worked for him. Instead of fighting in the king's army, his vassals were encouraged to pay scutage ("shield money"). This gave the king funds with which to hire professional soldiers, and it had the added benefit of pacifying noble warlords by turning them into a class of tax-paying landowners.

Henry courted support for the monarchy by increasing the services his subjects received directly from the crown. A king was expected to protect his people. This involved not only guarding frontiers from invasion, but preserving internal order by enforcing justice. The right to hold a court and administer justice was a privilege landowners coveted, for the fees and fines a court levied were a significant source of income. Henry took business away from the courts of his vassals by reserving some categories of crimes to the royal justice system. To make it easier for people to access the king's justice, he ordered judges to ride circuits about England. He also expanded the use of writs, documents that people could purchase to order royal officials to take action on their behalf.

The royal courts imposed a "common law," a single standard of justice, in England and developed procedures that are still used today. Henry's courts empaneled two kinds of juries. In order to ferret out criminals, grand (large) juries put local men under oath and ordered them to report any crimes that might have occurred in their communities. This created business for petit (small) juries, which heard cases and rendered verdicts. Juries could usually settle disputes about property, for local people could provide evidence about who owned what and for how long. It was often impossible, however, to gather evidence in criminal cases, so other methods were used to resolve them. **Compurgation** allowed the accused to clear their names by finding a certain number of people who would swear to their integrity. By identifying the most trustworthy party in a dispute, it increased the probability of rendering a just verdict. Sometimes suspects were forced to undergo ordeals—physical tests that risked injury or death. The theory was that God would protect the innocent, but by Henry's day enlightened governments were reducing their reliance on ordeals. In 1215 the pope contributed to the demise of the ordeal by prohibiting priests from receiving the oaths of innocence that ordeals supposedly tested.

As royal governments became more effective and assumed broader responsibilities, the potential for conflict between the church and the state increased. In England, the fight was triggered by Henry's efforts to improve enforcement of justice. In 1164 Henry's **Constitutions of Clarendon** clarified the relationship between his courts and those of the church. Two years earlier he had thrust priesthood and the office of archbishop of Canterbury on his friend, Thomas Becket (1118–1170), a commoner who was serving as England's chancellor (chief minister). Ordination changed Becket's loyalties and led him, in the opinion of some of his fellow bishops, to make extreme claims for the church. At issue was the treatment of clergy who were accused of crimes. Henry did not dispute the church's right to judge their cases, but he insisted that the guilty should be stripped of their clerical status and turned over to the state for punishment. This would ensure that lay and clerical criminals received the same penalties for the same crimes. Becket refused to accept this, fled England, and spent six years trying to turn international opinion against Henry. In 1170 he and Henry declared a truce. But when Becket returned to England, he infuriated Henry by excommunicating some royal officials. When Henry received this news, he made an intemperate remark that a few of his men interpreted as an order to kill Becket. On December 29, 1170, they forced their way into the cathedral of Canterbury and profaned its sanctity by slaughtering its archbishop. The scandalized medieval world instantly hailed Becket as a martyr. Miracles were credited to him, and three years after his death he was officially declared a saint. His tomb at Canterbury became a major pilgrim shrine, and Henry submitted to a whipping by Canterbury's monks as a penance for his part in Becket's murder.

The Becket defeat was humiliating, but the greatest threat to Henry came from his family. Queen Eleanor bore him five sons, and she and they plotted against him. Henry placed Eleanor under house arrest in 1174, and he managed to outlive three of their boys. But the remaining two (with the help of the French king) disrupted the last years of his reign.

Henry's heir was Richard I "the Lionhearted" (r. 1189–1199), a king whose popularity in English literature and folk memory far exceeds his achievements. Richard spent only eight months of his reign in England, and he was interested in his kingdom primarily as a source of revenue for foreign wars. Chief among these was the Third Crusade. In 1187 Saladin (1137–1193), a warrior of Kurdish descent, united the Muslims of the Middle East and retook Jerusalem. The people of Europe clamored for a new crusade, and Richard eagerly responded. He compelled France's young king, Philip II, "Augustus" (r. 1180–1223), to take the cross with him. Frederick I, "Barbarossa" (r. 1152–1190), Germany's aging emperor, agreed to go as well. The venture yielded little for all that was invested in it. Barbarossa drowned on his way to the Holy Land, and Philip Augustus withdrew as soon as possible. Richard lingered in the east, while Philip and Richard's brother, John, worked to undermine his position at home. In 1193 Richard tried to hurry back to his kingdom through the territory of a German enemy and was captured. Eleanor raised a huge ransom to win his release, and he spent his remaining years fighting to regain the French lands he had allowed to slip from his control. He died from a wound received in a skirmish with one of his own vassals.

Richard's successor was his disloyal brother, John (r. 1199–1216). John was neither stupid nor cowardly, but he was headstrong and had a talent for alienating people. He was also no match for Philip Augustus, who took Normandy from him. After he picked a needless quarrel with Pope Innocent III over the appointment of an archbishop for Canterbury, the pope closed all the churches in England and excommunicated John. John held out for six years, but in 1213, when the pope threatened him with deposition, he suddenly reversed course and took an oath of vassalage to the pope. John was developing an elaborate plan for winning back his French lands, and he did not want his vassals to use his quarrel with the church as an excuse to repudiate him.

In 1214 John, his cousin Otto of Brunswick, and the count of Flanders joined forces to invade France. Philip Augustus decisively defeated them at the Battle of Bouvines, and John fled back to England where his disgusted vassals were finally on the brink of revolt. He met them at Runnymeade, west of London, and agreed to terms spelled out in the famous Magna Carta ("Great Charter"). Within two months, the document was a dead letter. The pope absolved John from his oath to honor it, for the pope believed subjects had no right to limit the authority of the kings God gave them. John's barons, however, believed that they could persuade God to give them a new king by inviting Philip Augustus's son, Louis, to invade England, depose John, and claim his throne.

The **Plantagenet** dynasty was saved by John's timely death. His heir was his 9-year-old son, Henry III (r. 1216–1272). England's rebellious barons, who preferred a weak child king to a powerful French prince, promptly switched their allegiance back to the English royal family. Henry's reign was one of the least successful in England's history, but its weakness had the effect of inching England further toward limited monarchy. Henry mismanaged England so badly that civil war broke out under the leadership of the king's brother-in-law, Simon de Montfort. In 1264, when the rebels captured Henry, Simon decided to convene a council to rally national support for an act that technically was treason. He invited the barons and church leaders who usually attended such meetings, but he also included representatives of England's shires and boroughs (towns). The result was the first session of what the French-speaking English court called **Parliament** (parler, "to speak").

Henry's son Edward, who was far more competent than his father, rallied the royalist forces, killed Simon (d. 1265), restored his father to the throne, and reversed the monarchy's decline. Edward was open to learning from his enemies. Although the first Parliament had been a rebel organization, Edward continued to convene parliaments for purposes of his own. England's kings were expected to meet the costs of government from their own incomes. If they needed more money, they had to ask their subjects for it. Parliament was an expedient way to do this. Medieval Parliaments were weak. Only the property-owning classes were represented in them, and they met only at the king's pleasure. But they survived, grew in importance, and ultimately became a model that has influenced the design of institutions of popular government throughout the modern world.

Edward I (r. 1272–1307) accomplished a great deal. He brought Wales under his control. He strengthened England's hold on parts of Ireland, and he was on the brink of subduing Scotland when he died. On the civilian front, he promulgated so much legislation that he has been called "the English Justinian." His interest in law and justice did not prevent him from raising money by expelling the Jews from England and confiscating their property. He also destroyed Italian banks by failing to repay the money he borrowed from them.

France   France's Capetian dynasty made slow progress, for its kings were often opposed by powerful English rulers and their own vassals. But the French monarchy reached a turning point in 1214, when Philip Augustus (r. 1180–1223) defeated England's King John at the Battle of Bouvines. Philip's victory secured his hold on northern France and tripled the royal estates and income. In 1208, when the pope called for a crusade against the Cathar heretics of southern France, Philip's soldiers answered and extended his influence into that region.

Philip reorganized royal government to enhance its ability to administer the lands he won. One of his major reforms was an improved method of tax collection. Earlier kings had relied on tax farmers to collect their dues. These men paid the treasury a fixed sum in exchange for the right to collect what was owed to the crown. Whatever additional money they extracted, they kept for themselves. Philip ended the corruption, abuse, and cheating this system invited by replacing tax farmers with salaried government officials.

When Philip died and passed the crown to his mature, experienced son, Louis VIII (r. 1223–1226), the future of the Capetian dynasty seemed secure. Philip had dispatched Louis to protect the crown's interests in the crusade against the Cathars, and Louis had extended royal influence to the shores of the Mediterranean. Despite this strong start, Louis

Caernarfon Castle   To secure his hold on the British Isles, Edward I invested heavily in the construction of castles. His most imposing were built in newly conquered Wales. To encourage the Welsh to accept the legitimacy of English rule, he arranged for his wife to give birth to his heir in Wales and dubbed the boy "Prince of Wales," the title the first in line to Britain's throne still bears.

ended by doing two things that endangered the future of his dynasty and the French monarchy. He died young—leaving the throne to a minor (a first for the Capetians), and his will carved out appanages (quasi-independent territories) from the royal estates for the boy king's three younger brothers.

Louis IX (r. 1226–1270) was only 12 years old when he inherited the throne. He faced a horde of powerful nobles who relished the opportunity a weak regency government gave them to cripple a monarchy that had become too strong for their tastes. Fortunately, the young king had an able defender—his mother, Blanche of Castile (1188–1252), granddaughter of Eleanor of Aquitaine and England's Henry II. Her job was made easier by the tendency of France's nobles to squabble among themselves. England was small enough that its barons knew one another and sometimes agreed to form a common front against their king. This was less likely in France, which was four times England's size. Regionalism was strong in France, and awareness of common interests developed slowly among nobles from different districts.

Louis IX grew up to become the most popular and respected of France's kings, and his reputation obliterated whatever doubts remained about the Capetians' divine right to the throne. Twenty-seven years after his death, the church declared him a saint. Louis was pious and inclined to personal asceticism, but these traits did not diminish his effectiveness as a king. He was a strong, courageous military man who sincerely believed that it was a Christian monarch's duty to protect the poor and weak and deliver justice. Louis restrained France's nobles and limited the private warfare that ravaged its countryside. He made himself accessible to the humblest of his subjects and acted to right their grievances.

He sent out *enquêteurs* ("investigators") to audit the accounts of his officials and hear complaints against them. He relied on the *Parlement* of Paris (a group of legal advisors) to help him improve the professionalism of his administration. He settled territorial squabbles with neighboring kingdoms by making generous concessions, and his reputation for fairness was so great that other countries asked him to adjudicate their internal disputes.

France flourished under Louis's leadership, but the Christian principles that inspired his virtues as a leader also clouded his judgment. He persecuted Jews and persons accused of heresy, and he squandered his country's resources on two crusades that had little likelihood of success. In 1249 he led an elaborately equipped expedition into Egypt. The Muslims cut off his supply lines. Disease broke out in his army, and it was forced to surrender. A huge ransom had to be paid to win Louis's release, but even then he was reluctant to give up and return to France. He never relinquished the dream of winning back Jerusalem, and in July of 1270 he set out on a second crusade. This time he attacked Tunis, intending to work his way across North Africa and Egypt to the Holy Land. Seven weeks into this campaign, he died of a disease that ravaged his army.

Louis had prepared his son, Philip III (r. 1270–1285), for the duties of kingship, but Philip lacked his father's talent and charisma. Philip was overawed by his forceful uncle, Charles of Anjou (1227–1285), who was determined to carve out a kingdom for himself in Italy and Sicily. Philip died shortly after leading a futile expedition into Spain in support of his uncle. The throne then passed to Philip's much more competent son, Philip IV, "the Fair" (r. 1285–1314)(see Chapter 11).

Germany and Italy   France, like Germany, was tempted to try to expand into Italy, but the German experience should have warned the French of the risks of such a policy. Two strong German dynasties, the Saxon and the Salian, tried to join Italy to Germany, and both were defeated by the combined efforts of popes, Italian cities, and truculent German nobles.

The premature death of Henry V (r. 1105–1125) ended the Salian dynasty and began a quarter-century-long tug of war for the German throne. Two factions contended: the Welfs (**Guelf**s) who backed the duke of Saxony-Bavaria, and the Waiblingens (**Ghibelline**s) who supported the duke of Swabia. Kings were chosen, but none was more than a figurehead.

In 1152 the Waiblingen candidate, Frederick I, "Barbarossa" ("Red Beard"), won out over the young Welf duke, Henry the Lion (1129–1195). Frederick (r. 1152–1190), whose mother was Henry the Lion's aunt, was a compromise candidate, and it was hoped that his ties to both ducal factions would persuade them to work together. Frederick established his authority and broke up some of the German duchies. But whereas France's Capetian kings added the lands they conquered to the royal domain and ruled them directly, the German nobles forced Frederick to grant his acquisitions as fiefs. Germany, therefore, remained a fragmented collection of baronies over which the king had only indirect control.

The Hohenstaufen dynasty that Frederick founded pinned its hopes on Italy. Its base, the duchy of Swabia, in the southwestern corner of Germany, was poorly situated to be the capital of a German kingdom, but it was ideally located to become the center of a Roman Empire that united Germany and Italy. Frederick expanded his control of territory on Italy's northern frontier by marrying the heiress to the kingdom of Burgundy, which lay west of his duchy. In 1161 he forced the rich towns of northern Italy (Lombardy) to come to terms. However, as soon as he turned his attention back to Germany, they and the pope colluded against him. In 1176 he lost a battle to the Lombards and was forced to compromise. The cities recognized his overlordship, but retained the right of self-government. A decade later a bit of luck tipped the balance of power in Italy in the Hohenstaufens' favor. Frederick's daughter-in-law, Constance, inherited the kingdoms of Sicily and Naples from her nephew, William II (r. 1166–1189). This surrounded the Papal States with Hohenstaufen territory and opened the way for Frederick to consolidate his hold on Italy. At this point, however, the Third Crusade distracted the aging king, and he headed for Constantinople at the head of the greatest crusading army ever assembled. He drowned before reaching the Holy Land.

Frederick's son, Henry VI (r. 1190–1197), was a competent king, but his reign was brief. His heir (another Frederick) was only 2 years old when he died. The Hohenstaufens' enemies seized the opportunity this gave them to try to topple the dynasty. The young heir's claim to the throne was ignored. He was shunted aside in Sicily while Philip of Swabia, his uncle, and Otto of Brunswick (c. 1174–1218), the head of the Guelf party, battled each other for control of Germany. Pope Innocent III (r. 1198–1216), whose reign began just as their war was breaking out, tried to prolong the fight in order to keep them out of Italy. This worked until Philip was assassinated in 1209. When the victorious Otto then staked a claim to Italy, the pope remembered Frederick, the forgotten Hohenstaufen heir.

Frederick II (r. 1215–1250) was such a remarkable man that his contemporaries nicknamed him *Stupor Mundi*, "Wonder of the World." The young king was an athlete, a warrior, and an intellectual. He was fluent in six languages. He sponsored scientific research, wrote a book on the art of falconry (which survives), founded a university, and gave Sicily a constitution that was a model of centralized monarchy. Frederick believed that a king's duties extended beyond policing and protecting his people. Frederick managed Sicily's economy and even issued environmental regulations to protect air and water quality.

In exchange for the church's support, Pope Innocent elicited a promise from Frederick that he would not rule both halves of Italy, but Frederick had no intention of keeping his word. He grew up as a Sicilian and had little experience of, or interest in, Germany. After defeating Otto and claiming the crown, he allowed the German barons to do as they wished in order to be free to concentrate on Italy. In hopes of distracting Frederick from Italy, the pope persuaded him to go on crusade. But he was so slow to act on his crusader vow that by the time he finally sailed for the Holy Lands in 1228, the pope had excommunicated him. When he arrived in the Middle East, he negotiated with the Muslims and persuaded them to hand Jerusalem over to him without a fight. The pope was appalled that an excommunicate had succeeded where so many faithful crusaders had failed and responded by declaring war on Frederick. Frederick spent the rest of his life battling with the papacy and the Lombard cities. He forced the pope to flee Italy, and its cities would probably have yielded to him had he been a bit more compromising. In the end, his opponents were saved when the king contracted dysentery and died.

Frederick had so alarmed his enemies that they joined forces, tracked down his heirs, and exterminated his dynasty. Germany's empty throne once again became a prize for which many were eager to compete. However, the German barons, who fattened on bribes from candidates, were in no hurry to choose a new king. From 1254 to 1272 the throne remained in dispute, and without a strong king, there was no hope of countering Germany's drift toward political fragmentation.

As Germany retreated, a new threat to Italy's cities and the papacy appeared. Louis IX's brother, Charles of Anjou, invaded and seized control of southern Italy and Sicily. In 1282 the Sicilians drove the French out and offered themselves to one of Spain's monarchs, the king of Aragon. The French held on to Naples, but instead of focusing on Italy, they invested their resources in futile attempts to conquer Hungary and the Balkans.

The progress that artists and intellectuals made during the High Middle Ages was only partially matched by kings and politicians. Rulers sought and received help from scholars and university-trained lawyers that enabled them to construct and staff the most effective governments Europe had seen since the passing of the Roman Empire. But the results were mixed. The English and French monarchies flourished and advanced the consolidation of their realms, but the story was very different in Italy and Germany.

KEY QUESTION | Revisited

A society consists of many things (economic, political, and social) that must work together if it is to remain viable. A change in any one of them forces the others to adjust. Because coordination and accommodation can be difficult and outcomes can be uncertain, people tend to fear change. When their traditional institutions and values begin to fail, their first impulse may not be to try something new, but to reaffirm the past—to try harder to make the old ways work. Familiar things are reassuring, for they have a record of success. A new thing often stirs up anxiety, for it has not been tested. Commitment to it requires an act of faith. Ideally, this faith is an informed belief that has grounds for probable success. But a society's attitude toward change is always determined to some degree by how much it is willing to trust—by how much confidence it has in its ability to understand the world and rise to its challenges.

The dominant intellectual faith that gave thinkers of the High Middle Ages the courage to innovate was a belief that existence would ultimately be discovered to be a rationally coherent, unified system—that everything that human beings learned from experience or received by revelation and faith could be integrated into an intelligible, universal order.

This faith was encouraged by progress toward rationalization and integration on numerous fronts. An international intellectual community appeared, using a common language and training itself in similar schools. It developed methods of research that enabled it to organize, analyze, and exploit the flood of information from Muslim and Byzantine sources that threatened to inundate Europe in the twelfth and thirteenth centuries. The radical fragmentation that had overtaken governments and societies in the wake of the invasions of the Vikings, Magyars, and Muslims began to be reversed—at least in parts of Europe. Clearer rationales for institutions and policies were developed. More sophisticated governments provided a wider range of services. Artists and poets created new forms of entertainment that stimulated the popular imagination and encouraged new codes of conduct. New kinds of religious vocations earned new respect for the clergy and

Political Leaders of the High Middle Ages

ENGLAND	FRANCE	GERMANY	THE PAPACY
Henry I (1100–1135)	Louis VI (1108–1137)	Henry V (1106–1125)	
Stephen (1135–1154)	Louis VII (1137–1180)	[Civil War, 1125–1152]	
Henry II (1154–1189)		Frederick I (1152–1190)	
	Philip II (1180–1223)		
Richard I (1189–1199)		Henry VI (1190–1197)	
John (1199–1216)		Philip & Otto (1198–1214)	Innocent III (1198–1216)
Henry III (1216–1272)	Louis VIII (1223–1226)	Frederick II (1215–1250)	
Edward I (1272–1307)	Louis IX (1226–1270)	[Interregnum 1254–1273]	
	Philip III (1270–1285)		
Edward II (1307–1327)	Philip IV (1285–1314)		

focused some of the church's resources on dealing with social ills. And architects created environments that had never before been experienced—churches in which the rational skills of engineers superbly served the transcendent visions of religious faith.

Bernard of Chartres's "dwarfs" had much of which they could be proud, but their *summae* remained incomplete. The presumed coherence of the world proved frustratingly difficult to capture in a simple rational model. Dialecticians fought among themselves and with mystics. Skeptics questioned reason's ability to search out truth. Reformers and heretics rebelled against traditional institutions and authorities. Consolidation of states led to larger wars, not peace, and promising crusades ended in defeat. None of this, however, persuaded Europeans to alter course. Their faith in their ability to master a changing world was, however, soon to be severely tested.

Review Questions

1. How did intellectual life change in Europe with the appearance of universities?
2. What was dialectic? Why were the scholars of the High Middle Ages preoccupied with it?
3. How did religious enthusiasm affect the cultural and political environments of the High Middle Ages? Were its effects positive or negative?
4. How did Romanesque architecture differ from Gothic? Did theology influence the differences between the two styles?
5. How did the development of the French and English monarchies differ?
6. Why did German kings persist in trying to conquer Italy?

Please consult the Suggested Readings at the back of the book to continue your study of the material covered in this chapter. For a list of documents on the Primary Source DVD-ROM that relate to topics in this chapter, please refer to the back of the book.

Part 4
Challenges, Conflicts, and Departures
1300 to 1700

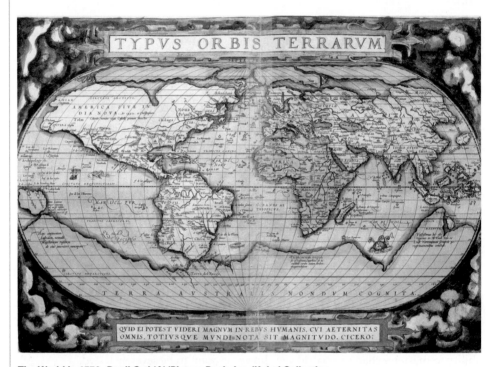

The World in 1570. *Dagli Orti (A)/Picture Desk, Inc./Kobal Collection*

Throughout the Middle Ages, Europeans believed that they were tucked away in the northwestern corner of the world. People had known at least since the time of the ancient Greeks that the world was round, but geographers argued that nature blocked avenues for exploration. They assumed that the Arctic wastes limited movement north and that it was impossible to sail far west across the trackless Atlantic. They also believed that because temperatures grew warmer as one headed south, a zone of intolerable heat formed a barrier between the northern and southern hemispheres. Europe's only access to the lands of the Far East (the source of exotic silks and spices it desired) was therefore through Russia and the Middle East, journeys of thousands of miles across hostile territory. A few European merchants and missionaries made the trip, but direct contact with these fabled places was rare.

All of this changed at the end of the fifteenth century when Europeans discovered that the Atlantic was not a barrier to their exploration of the wider world, but a highway providing them with access to lands both known and unknown. They were amazed to discover that the world was much larger than they had ever imagined, and the initiative they took in exploring it gave them a new sense of their place in it. The Mediterranean and the Middle East became less important to them, as they began to envision a new world order centered on their western European homelands.

	ENVIRONMENT AND TECHNOLOGY	SOCIETY AND CULTURE	POLITICS
c. 1200	Marco Polo (1254–1324) Dante (1265–1321)	Western Europe: Population Growth and land clearance	Ayyubid Empire Mamluk sultanate Mongol invasions *German Interregnum* (1254–1273) Habsburg dynasty
c. 1300	Giotto (1226–1337) **Italian Renaissance** Petrarch (1304–1374) Chaucer (1340–1400)	"Little Ice Age" commences The Great Pestilence (1347–1350) First appearance of Cannons	Estates General (1302) Avignese papacy (1305–1377) Timur the Lame (1336–1404) Hundred Years' War (1337–1453) Golden Bull (1356) Great Schism (1378–1415) Ottoman dynasty
c. 1400	Conciliarism Joan of Arc (1412–1431) da Vinci (1452–1519) Erasmus (1466–1536)	Portuguese explorations (1430) Printing press (1446)	Council of Constance (1415) Constantinople falls (1453) Ottoman Empire Tudor dynasty
c. 1500	Michelangelo (1475–1564) Martin Luther (1483–1546) **Protestant Reformation** Diet of Worms (1521) English Reformation (1534) Council of Trent (1545–1563) Edict of Nantes (1598)	Columbus's first voyage (1492) Disease ravages the Americas Global circumnavigation (1522) Exports from the Americas change Europe	Safavid dynasty Aztecs fall (1519) Charles V (1519–1556) Süleyman (1520–1566) Incas fall (1529) Habsburg-Valois Wars (1525–1544) St. Bartholomew's Day Massacre (1572) Spanish Armada (1588)
c. 1600	Shakespeare (1564–1616)		Thirty Years' War (1618–1648) English Civil War (1642–1646) Puritan Republic (1649–1660)

11 Challenges to the Medieval Order

Age of sorrow and temptation, of tears, jealousy and torment,
Time of exhaustion and damnation, declining to extinction,
Era filled with horror and deception, lying, pride and envy,
Time without honor and meaning, full of life-shortening sadness.

—Eustache Deschamps

KEY | Question

What did the crises of the late medieval era reveal about the strengths and weaknesses of Europe's civilization?

The verses quoted above are from a poem by Eustache Deschamps (c. 1346–1406) in which he laments the dismal prospects of his generation. His disillusionment is understandable. He trained for the law at a university, won royal patronage, traveled in the service of his king, and held a series of important political offices. But his career unfolded against a background of disasters that would have undercut the confidence of the most determined optimist. Deschamps was born about the time that a great plague carried off a third of the population of Europe, and those who survived were never free of the threat of its return. A devastating war between England and France also disrupted his life. He endured sieges, his home was burned, and he lost his job. From his perspective, the world was drifting toward anarchy, and he had no confidence in the leaders whose duty it was to maintain order and provide justice.

During the twelfth and thirteenth centuries, Europe had expanded on all fronts. Population grew. Commerce, cities, arts, and intellectual life flourished. Then, early in the fourteenth century, things began to go wrong—some suddenly and dramatically, others

grans seigne que chun voucloit
monstier sa puissance. Si nest
nul homme combien qil fust
present a la tonce qui sceust
ne peust ymagmer ne recor
der la verite. Espraalement
de la partie des francois tant
y eut peuple arroy et petite
ordonnance en leurs grans
contorps qui estoient sans
nombre. Et ce que le scay
de leurs besongnes et ordon
nances et ce que le dise
ray et determineray en ce

laur de lay sceu et apprins
le plus pur moult vaillans
sommes dingleterre sanges
et dysaetz tant chevaliers
comme aultres qui moult
ententifuemet auiserent
leur contenant. Et aussi
pur les gens de messi. Iehin
de haynault qui furent
tousiours delez le Roy
phle de france. Cy ple de la
bataille de crecy entre le roy de
france et le roy dingleterre.

Battle of Crécy This painting, an illustration for a medieval manuscript, depicts the Battle of Crécy, the first major engagement in the Hundred Years' War between England and France.

slowly and insidiously. Food shortages became common. Epidemics spread. Europe was threatened with invasion. The leadership of the church broke down, and the efforts of government leaders to cope with these crises often made them worse.

People of Deschamps' generation had reason to believe that their world was in decline, but it would be inaccurate and unfair to accuse their civilization of having failed them. The stresses of the fourteenth and fifteenth centuries certainly forced Europeans to make painful adaptations, but many of their problems were signs of evolving circumstances more than cultural failure. Some were the dark side of the achievements of the twelfth and thirteenth centuries, and others were the result of natural and historical processes that were beyond human control.

Historians have rightly described the late medieval period as the Age of Anxiety, a time characterized by pessimism, skepticism, and self-doubt. But the fourteenth century also witnessed the flowering of Italy's Renaissance, a movement associated with a surge of optimistic humanism (see Chapter 12). Some of Deschamps's contemporaries shared his belief that they were sorely afflicted, but they also anticipated the dawn of a glorious new era. It was their destiny to be born at a time of testing for the institutions that the dynamic High Middle Ages had created. The crises they weathered revealed weaknesses in Western civilization but also signs of future strengths.

Challenges from Nature

Because most modern people live in artificial environments, they forget how dependent even an advanced civilization is on the processes of nature. Such forgetfulness is dangerous, for scientists have discovered that the natural environment that sustains all life is not fixed and stable. Earth has experienced such drastic shifts in climate that tropical plants have flourished in what is today the arctic, and glaciers once reached the Mediterranean. The whole history of civilization has unfolded during an unusually warm and stable period in Earth's cycle of climates. This is a sobering fact, for even minor shifts in climate can threaten the viability of human institutions. And consensus is building among scientists that the energy consumption associated with twenty-first-century civilization is accelerating the rate of climate change.

Climate Change   From 1000 to 1300 Europe enjoyed a benign climate, but then the Little Ice Age, an era of slowly diminishing average temperatures, set in and continued into the nineteenth century. This had a serious impact on medieval Europe's largely agrarian economy. Weather patterns changed. Precipitation increased. Growing seasons shortened, and in some places, crops that had once thrived would no longer grow.

Much of Europe lies at the latitude of Canada. (Paris is farther north than Nova Scotia.) Western Europe's climate is moderated by the Gulf Stream and warm seasonal winds from Africa. Any change in these phenomena can have serious repercussions for all forms of life in Europe.

Sporadic famines had always been a part of medieval life, but in the fourteenth century they came more frequently and affected larger areas. In 1309 there was a continentwide famine, the first in 250 years. Crops failed throughout northern Europe in 1315, 1316, and 1317, and there was another widespread famine in the 1330s. Death by starvation was not unusual. People ate dogs, cats, and rats, and there were even rumors of cannibalism. Medieval governments could do little to respond to such crises. Even if they found supplies of food, they lacked the distribution systems to get emergency relief to afflicted regions.

Food supplies were critical, for increasing political stability and economic growth had allowed Europe's population to triple between the eleventh and the fourteenth centuries. Although population density was not great by modern standards, it reached previously unprecedented heights. There were perhaps 80 million Europeans in 1300 compared with 732 million today. But given the available agricultural technologies, Europe began, by the fourteenth century, to exceed the carrying capacity of its land. During the eleventh, twelfth, and thirteenth centuries, Europeans had brought more and more land into production. They drained swamps, reclaimed fields from the sea, and cleared so much forest that Europe may have more trees today than it did then. Europeans eventually reached the limit of their arable land. And when the climate began to cool, the poorer land stopped producing, and society's agricultural base started to shrink. The demand for food outstripped supply, and people went hungry.

Wealth was unevenly distributed in medieval societies, and there was no social safety net. In any age, economic depressions can trigger migrations from the starving countryside into cities by people who are desperate for food and work. But as large numbers of destitute, chronically malnourished people crowded into Europe's medieval towns, they increased their vulnerability to the second blow that nature struck the West in the fourteenth century: plague.

Plague   Between 1347 and 1350 a great epidemic spread across the world and carried off between 30% and 50% of Europe's population. Medieval people called it simply "the pestilence." The name Black Death appeared in the sixteenth century, and the term *Bubonic Plague* only describes one symptom of the disease. A bubo is a swollen, infected lymph node, usually in the groin or armpit. Plague can rupture blood vessels, causing bleeding from bodily orifices and subcutaneous bleeding that turns the skin black with bruised blotches. It can also infect the lungs and assume a form spread by coughs and sneezes.

The diseases that afflicted the ancient and medieval world are hard to identify, for the records describing symptoms are often inadequate. Diseases also mutate over time, and modern diseases may differ from their earlier versions. For a long time, historians have assumed that the pestilence that afflicted Europe in the fourteenth century was caused by a bacterium called *Yersinia pestis*. It is indigenous to parts of China and Africa and lives in the digestive tracts of fleas that infest certain species of rats. When the bacteria multiply excessively, they block their host flea's digestive track. The starving insect then begins indiscriminately to bite other warm-blooded creatures, and its bite injects them with infected material from its blocked gut. Recent research has raised doubts about the cause of the great medieval pandemic, for it did not conform in many ways to modern plague. Its behavior bore some resemblance to the virulent strain of influenza that swept the globe in 1918.

The fourteenth century was not the first to confront an epidemic. Smallpox spread through the Roman Empire about 180. Measles erupted in 251. *Yersinia pestis* may have spread from Africa north through the Byzantine Empire and into western Europe around 540 and burned itself out by the eighth century. From then until the fourteenth century, Europeans suffered few epidemics, for once the pool of diseases to which they were regularly exposed stabilized, their immune systems were able to adapt. So long as no new infectious agents appeared, they were reasonably secure.

If the fourteenth-century plague was a version of *Yersinia pestis*, the global climate shifts that were taking place at that time may help to explain its arrival in Europe. Humidity and temperature affected the activity of the fleas that were the plague's hosts. As Europe's climate grew wetter, central Asia suffered drought, and flea-infected rodent populations migrated into regions inhabited by nomadic tribes of Turks and Mongols. The medieval epidemic began in China in approximately 1330 and reached Samarkand in 1339, the Crimea in 1345, and Sicily in October 1347. Within months the disease had spread throughout Europe as well as the Islamic world. Muslim countries may also have lost 30% to 50% of their populations. The rapidity with which the epidemic spread, however, is one of the reasons for doubting that it was caused by *Yersinia pestis*.

Modern people are all too familiar with acts of genocide and natural disasters that devastate limited regions, but it is hard to imagine what it was like to experience a universal onslaught of a mysterious, lethal illness. Medieval people were baffled. They knew that the pestilence was infectious, but they did not know how it spread. There were no effective treatments for it, and it was almost always fatal. There seemed to be no logic to its behavior. It struck unevenly, decimating some places and skipping others. Thousands of villages disappeared. Tightly packed communities such as monasteries and nunneries were obliterated. The general upheaval reduced the number of universities from about 30 in 1349 to 10 in 1400. Disease and deteriorating climate led to abandonment of the country of Greenland, and Europe did not recoup its population losses until the mid-sixteenth century.

Social Consequences   Frightened people often turn on one another, and the plague prompted persecution of Europe's resident outsiders, the Jews. Despite the fact that they were dying along with everyone else, rumors spread that Jews were causing the plague by poisoning wells. The physicians who taught at the universities of Paris and Montpellier dismissed this, and Pope Clement VI (r. 1342–1352) ordered the clergy to protect the Jews. However, panicked mobs destroyed over 200 Jewish communities.

Lacking any earthly explanation, university scholars fell back on astrology and attributed the disease to an unfortunate alignment of planets. It was widely assumed that God had sent the plague to chastize humanity for its sins. In desperation, people

The Last Judgment   In the early fourteenth century, Giotto di Bondone, a pioneering Italian artist, covered the entrance wall of the Arena Chapel in Padua with his vision of the final judgment. The condemned occupy the lower right quadrant of the composition.

fasted and made pilgrimages. They increased their acts of charity, and some tried to appease God by tormenting their flesh. Processions of flagellants whipped one another into bloody, ecstatic frenzies. The church condemned such excesses, but it had no effective alternatives to propose for dealing with the crisis. It may have lost 40% of its clergy in the first onslaught of the epidemic, and there was no evidence that sacraments, intercessions, and traditional acts of piety did much good. Some Christians responded to the crisis by turning inward and cultivating a private faith that helped them come to terms with their mortality. This and other developments in late medieval societies accustomed people to assuming more personal responsibility for their spiritual lives.

The era was preoccupied with death. Artists covered the walls of churches with depictions of the Last Judgment, and they lavished imagination on devising horrid punishments for the damned. Grave monuments warned about the tenuous frailty of earthly life. Earlier generations had favored tomb effigies that represented the deceased in the full bloom of youth and vigor, but now the dead were depicted as corpses in an advanced state of decay. The intent was to abase pride and affirm that this life was dust and ashes compared to what awaited the faithful beyond the grave.

Every cloud is said to have a silver lining, and this held true even for the fourteenth-century epidemic. Many of those who survived it found their prospects improved. The disease potentially reduced pressure on Europe's food supply by shrinking its population. The deaths of so many property owners freed up land for the landless, and enabled small holdings to be combined as larger, more viable farms. Wages rose, for a diminished population created a labor shortage that put workers in a good position to bargain. Prior to the epidemic, overpopulation had glutted the labor market and driven wages down. Now, as the process was reversed, employers had to give their workers better terms to keep them. In western Europe the wage-laborer replaced the serf, but in central Europe, where towns and strong kings were few, serfdom spread. The powerful landowners of that region were able to exploit their peasants, for they had no place to flee to and no alternative sources of employment.

The propertied classes did not want to pay the higher wages that workers on their lands demanded, and they had political power that they could use to restore what they regarded as the status quo. The poor had no representation in government, for medieval governments paid attention only to those whom they tapped for money. The rich, therefore, were able to pass laws designed to prevent the poor from profiting from the situation the plague had created. Sumptuary laws preserved class distinctions by regulating how people were allowed to dress and by limiting indulgence in certain luxuries to the aristocracy. More galling, no doubt, were ordinances that kept wages low by imposing caps.

People tolerate bad situations if they assume that misery is inevitable. The dangerous time for a society is when improving conditions raise hopes that are subsequently dashed. Europe was little troubled by popular uprisings so long as its economy was flat or slowly improving. But the economic adjustments necessitated by the plague and the political class's response to them prompted a series of peasant revolts. In 1358 the first of a number of Jacquerie rebellions (named for a kind of cheap leather jacket the poor wore) erupted in France. In 1381 the English throne was shaken by the Peasants' Revolt in which a mob occupied London and executed some royal officials. Similar uprisings took place later in Spain and Germany. Although the commoners, especially in England, sometimes won concessions, the upper classes remained in control. The aristocracy was, however, not a closed order. Wars, feuds, dangerous sports, and political executions put medieval male nobles at great risk. The average life expectancy of a male born into an English ducal family in the fourteenth and fifteenth centuries, for instance, was only 24 years. His sister could anticipate living into her thirties. Aristocratic families had difficulty preserving their male lines for more than a few generations, which created opportunities for new families to climb the social ladder. Commoners broke into the upper class by intermarriage and by acquiring fortunes with which to purchase titles and estates.

Turmoil in the Middle East

During the thirteenth century, a series of events disrupted the Byzantine and Muslim worlds, but few western European leaders may have grasped the dire significance of what these developments portended. They did try to take advantage of the situation to regain footholds in the Middle East, but their interventions backfired disastrously. They weakened Constantinople to the point where it could no longer protect Europe's eastern frontiers from Muslim incursions. The Muslim region was temporarily thrown into a state of upheaval by invaders from the east. But the newcomers converted, reenergized Islam, and set it on the road to building a new empire. The Middle Ages were to end as they had begun—with Muslim and Christian powers contending across the Mediterranean Sea. The crusaders' repeated thrusts into Muslim territory were all repulsed, but Islam's late medieval counteroffensive partially succeeded. Muslim armies seized Greece, the Balkans, and parts of central Europe, and held them for centuries.

Constantinople   The crusades cast a lengthy shadow over Europe's relations with its eastern neighbors. Byzantine emperor Alexius Comnenus (r. 1081–1118) had unintentionally launched the Holy Land crusades by asking Pope Urban II (r. 1088–1099) to help him recruit soldiers for Constantinople's wars (see Chapter 9). What seemed a good idea at the time proved in the long run to be a disaster for Alexius's empire. Constantinople lost trade as the crusaders took control of ports on the eastern coast of the Mediterranean, and Constantinople itself became a target for Europe's crusaders.

In 1202 the armies of the Fourth Crusade gathered in Venice. They planned to sail to the Holy Land. But when they could not raise the money to pay for their passage, they agreed to earn their way by selling their services to Venice. Venice diverted them to Constantinople to support an exiled Byzantine prince's bid for the imperial throne. Once the Venetian candidate was in power, Venice expected to control trade with Constantinople. The intimidated Byzantines crowned the prince, but he soon fell victim to a plot. A series of palace coups increased the confusion and frustrated the crusaders, who finally stormed the city and took it by force on April 13, 1204. The Christian city that for centuries had withstood multiple attacks by barbarian and Muslim armies fell for the first time—and not to its religious enemies, but to soldiers who fought in the name of Christ. The crusaders sacked Constantinople, claimed it for themselves, and enthroned a Latin emperor. Many of the treasures the city had preserved from antiquity were lost in the fires and looting that ensued.

The triumphant crusaders forgot about Jerusalem and rushed to stake claims to Byzantine territory. However, a rival Greek emperor established a base in Asia Minor and rallied resistance to the Catholic Latins, who were loathed by their Orthodox subjects. The Latin Byzantine Empire, like the earlier crusader states, was a weak kingdom whose ruler had little power and few resources. The last of Constantinople's Latin emperors was so desperate for money that he hawked relics from the city's churches and sold the lead that roofed his palace. In 1261 Venice's competitor, the Italian city of Genoa, helped the Greek emperor, Michael Palaeologus (r. 1261–1282), regain control of a depopulated and impoverished Constantinople. Michael's Byzantine Empire was a shadow of its former self, and it faced a world in turmoil. Europe's crusaders had set in motion events that were to lose Christians their last outpost in the eastern Mediterranean. For centuries, Constantinople had blocked Muslim advances into Europe, but its ability to do so was now seriously compromised. However, the city survived in Christian hands for almost another two centuries, for the Muslims had more important matters to attend to.

The Islamic Middle East   The First Crusade succeeded because the Muslims of the Middle East were fighting among themselves. They continued to squabble until a Kurdish warrior named Saladin (1138–1193) brought them under his control. In 1174 he terminated the Fatimid caliphate and occupied Egypt. Syria and Mesopotamia were his by 1186, and in 1187 he took Jerusalem. After he repulsed Richard the Lionhearted's Third Crusade (see Chapter 10), he built an empire that stretched from Tunisia in

North Africa to Armenia and the Caspian Sea. His Ayyubid dynasty reigned over a loose federation that posed no threat to the Christian West. It wanted good trade relations with Italy's cities and was primarily interested in maintaining stability.

The Muslim lands east of the Ayyubid Empire (roughly modern Iran) passed from the Seljuk sultans to the shahs of Khwarazm, the region south of the Aral Sea. There, in 1218, the Muslims first encountered a threat that renewed hope in Europe for their ultimate defeat. The shah's lands were invaded by the Mongols, nomadic tribes who roamed the vast stretch of grasslands bordering northern China. The Mongols were not Muslims. European leaders thrilled at the prospect of converting them to Christianity and enlisting them in a joint effort to exterminate Islam.

Mongols   The Mongols owed their entrance onto history's stage to the leadership of Temujin (c. 1167–1227), who is better known by his well-deserved title, Genghis Khan ("Universal Lord"), and to a unique and highly effective military technology. Mongol craftsmen bonded different materials together to make powerful bows that were small enough for use by mounted soldiers. Mongol bowmen were able to cut opponents to pieces before their enemies' weapons got within striking range. Temujin created an army with a unified command and trained it to execute strategic maneuvers on the battlefield. This enabled him to rout much larger opponents who had little grasp of tactics and who lacked the mobility of Mongol bowmen. Temujin focused his attention on northern China while his generals made progress on other fronts. In 1221 a Mongol army overthrew the shah of Khwarazm and then split into two branches. One headed north of the Aral and Caspian Seas into Russian territory, and the other moved south across Persia (see Map 11–1).

In 1258 the Mongols took Baghdad (in a siege of only four days) and slaughtered all its inhabitants—including the last Abbasid caliph. They met no effective resistance until they reached the shores of the Mediterranean, where the Mamluks, Turkish slave soldiers who had overthrown Egypt's Ayyubid ruler in 1250, made a successful stand. After the Mongols withdrew to Baghdad, the Mamluks emerged as the dominant Muslim power in the Middle East. In 1291, they took the last crusader outposts on the Palestinian coast.

The pope and France's crusader king, Louis IX, tried to establish contact with the Mongols in hopes of converting them and allying with them against the Muslims. In 1245 they dispatched a Franciscan friar, John of Piancarpino, to Mongolia. He returned two years later, bringing Europeans their first eyewitness account of the exotic Far East. In 1255 a second Franciscan, William of Ruybroek, repeated his feat. Late in the century another Franciscan, John of Montecorvino, established a Christian bishopric in Peking. The most famous account of the Mongol Empire derived, however, from the autobiography of a Venetian merchant named Marco Polo (1254–1324). He claimed to have visited the Mongol court with his father and uncle in 1275, to have spent 17 years in China, and even to have been an official in the Mongol government. Some historians question whether Marco Polo ever visited the East and suggest that he may only have cobbled together stories about China that sifted back to Venice along its trade routes. Their doubts arise not so much from what he said about China

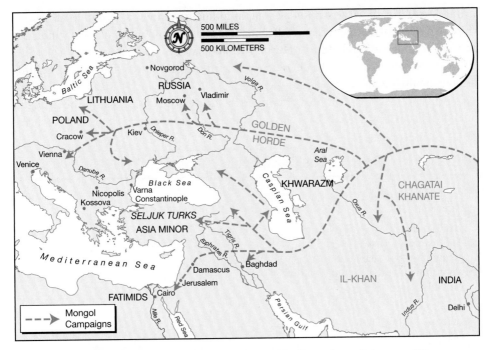

Map 11–1   The Mongol Empire   The Mongols resembled the Huns, Avars, Bulgars, and Magyars who had earlier emerged from the Russian steppe to threaten Europe, but their military organization was much more sophisticated than that of their predecessors.

Question: How did Eurasian geography facilitate the Mongol invasions?

but from prominent Chinese customs (tea drinking and foot binding, for example) that he failed to mention.

European hopes for a Mongol alliance were dashed late in the thirteenth century when the Mongols converted to Islam. By then, Europeans had come to view the Mongols more as potential enemies than friends. The northern branch of the Mongol army had charged almost unopposed through the territory north of the Black and Caspian Seas. In 1238 the Mongols sacked the Russian cities of Vladimir and Moscow, and in 1240 they took Kiev. By 1241 they were nearing Cracow in Poland and pushing up the Danube to the gates of Vienna, Austria. Here their momentum was broken by Vienna's Christian defenders and by the confusion that followed the death of their khan.

The Mongols organized the territory north of the Black and Caspian Seas as the khanate of the Golden Horde (named for the color of its ruler's tent). They commissioned the prince of Moscow to collect the tribute their Russian subjects owed them, and this gave him a chance to establish his authority over the Russians. In 1480 Moscow's Ivan III, "the Great" (1462–1505), threw off the Mongol yoke and laid the foundation for a Russian state.

In the late fourteenth century, another Mongol army under the command of a Timur "the Lame" (Tamerlane, 1336–1404), who claimed to be a descendant of Temujin, erupted from the east. He raided across Russia as far as Lithuania, struck south into India, leveled the city of Delhi, and then occupied Baghdad, Damascus, and much of Asia Minor. Europe, with a population diminished by plagues and famines, had reason to anticipate the worst. But when Tamerlane suddenly died, his numerous descendants fell to fighting among themselves for the spoils of his empire.

Far from assisting Europe's Christians in the destruction of Islam, the Mongols added vigorous new blood to the ranks of Muhammad's followers. Their advance thrust

---

The Crusading Movement

The Iberian Crusade (1015–1492)—Spain
The Sicilian Crusade (1059–1091)—Kingdom of the Two Sicilies

First Crusade (1095)—Holy Land
"The Peasants' Crusade"
Conquest of Jerusalem (1099)
Establishment of the Crusader States
{Fall of Edessa, 1144}

Second Crusade (1145)—Holy Land
Louis VII, king of France
{Fall of Jerusalem, 1187}

Third Crusade (1187)—Holy Land
Richard I, the Lionhearted, king of England
Philip II, king of France
Frederick I, Barbarossa, emperor of Germany
"The Northern Crusades" (1193–c. 1300)
Finland, Estonia, Lithuania

Fourth Crusade (1204)—Holy Land
Diverted to the conquest of Constantinople
"The Albigensian Crusade" (1209–1229)
"The Children's Crusade" (1212)

Fifth Crusade (1218)—Holy Land
Cardinal Pelagius, Papal Legate
Fought in Egypt
"The Prussian Crusade" (1226–c. 1300)
Teutonic Knights
Crusade (1229)—Holy Land
Frederick II, excommunicated emperor of Germany, regained Jerusalem by negotiation

Sixth Crusade (1249)—Holy Land
Fought in Egypt
Louis IX, king of France

Seventh Crusade (1270)—Holy Land
Fought at Tunis
1453 {Fall of Constantinople}
1464 Final call for a crusade to the Holy Land fails
Pope Pius II

Europe back on the defensive and raised the specter of yet another charge by eastern peoples into the heart of the continent. A weakened Constantinople, disillusionment with crusades, and loss of the initiative in foreign affairs added to what plague, famine, and social unrest did to make the late medieval era truly an Age of Anxiety.

Spiritual Crises

Even in the modern world, where religion is far more marginalized than it was in medieval society, people often look to religious institutions for help in stressful times. Unfortunately, when the Europeans of the late Middle Ages turned to their church, they found an institution that was in disarray. Instead of offering aid and comfort, it added to the problems of an anxious age.

Innocent III and Papal Monarchy   The pope who most successfully exercised the exalted rights that medieval pontiffs claimed for their office was Innocent III (r. 1198–1216). Innocent was a Roman aristocrat with relatives in the papal court. He studied law at the University of Bologna and theology at Paris. He wrote several books, one of which was a piece of devotional literature that enjoyed great popularity. He was only 37 when he became pope, and in addition to youth, he had the advantage of good timing. For most of his reign, the Germans were too busy with a civil war to intervene in Italy and threaten the papacy's independence.

The text on which Innocent preached at his coronation made plain his understanding of the powers of his office: "I have set you today over nations and kingdoms" (Jeremiah 1:10). Innocent maintained that all Christians, including kings, were subject to the spiritual authority of the pope. He agreed that kings derived their power directly from God. However, as Christ's representative on Earth, the pope was charged with holding kings accountable for how they used the office God entrusted to them. Innocent urged Europe's kings to become his vassals. This would not have made him Europe's ruler, but as overlord of Europe's kings, he would have had the right to adjudicate their disputes. Innocent wanted the church to become a kind of high court in which nations could resolve their difficulties without resorting to war.

Few kings accepted the pope's invitation to become his vassals, but Innocent, on several occasions, challenged great monarchs and forced them to back down. He owed his success to the care with which he chose his fights. He confronted kings when they blundered and made themselves vulnerable. His victories had the effect of making the papacy look stronger than it was.

Like his predecessors, Innocent hoped that by sponsoring crusades, he could strengthen the pope's role as Christendom's supreme leader. This was the least successful of his undertakings. The first army he intended for the Holy Land (the Fourth Crusade) ended by sacking Christian Constantinople in 1204. The crusade he called against the Cathar heretics in 1208 devastated southern France. The Fifth Crusade (1218–1221), an attack on Egypt that he was planning at the time of his death, was a debacle.

Innocent III and St. Francis Although Pope Innocent III was opposed to the proliferation of monastic orders, he showed remarkable wisdom in making an exception for the friars. This fresco from the Basilica of St. Francis in Assisi depicts the pope endorsing the work of St. Francis. *Dagli Orti/Picture Desk, Inc./Kobal Collection*

Innocent's greatest achievement was the strengthening of papal authority over the church and its clergy. In 1215 his Fourth Lateran Council affirmed that the church was a papal monarchy, endorsed the doctrine of transubstantiation as the explanation of the Eucharist (see Chapter 10), enforced clerical celibacy, and imposed new pious duties on the laity. Innocent bluntly asserted that the state had no power over the church and denied kings the right to tax or exercise judicial authority over the clergy. Given the growing strength of some of Europe's monarchies, Innocent committed his successors to a position that they were ill-equipped to defend, and their failure produced a century-long crisis for the church.

Humiliation of the Papacy In 1295 France's powerful king, Philip IV (r. 1285–1314), informed the French clergy that he was imposing taxes on the church. The clergy appealed to Pope Boniface VIII (r. 1296–1303), and the pope informed Philip that the church (as the Fourth Lateran Council had made clear) was totally independent of the state and not subject to taxation by kings. When Philip responded by blocking funds flowing from France to the papal treasury, the financially strapped Boniface tried to make a face-saving retreat. He explained that although kings had no right to tax the church, the church would, of course, help out a king in an emergency—and that a king had the right to decide when an emergency existed.

Having won de facto taxing authority, Philip next challenged the pope's claim that clergy did not fall under the jurisdiction of the state's courts. In 1301 he charged a French bishop with treason and threw him into prison. Boniface fired off a letter to Philip, warning him of the spiritual penalties awaiting him if he continued to attack the church. Philip circulated a distorted version of the letter to inflame his subjects against the pope, and then (in 1302) he convened a national assembly to see where they stood. This first meeting of France's Estates General, like England's Parliament, represented only a minority of the population—the higher clergy, nobility, and townspeople. But with its assurance that France was solidly behind him, Philip dispatched troops to Italy to arrest Boniface. The French held the pope captive for three days, and he died a few weeks later.

The cardinals who met to elect a new pope had learned a hard lesson. If people were forced to choose between their king and their pope, they were likely to side with the king. It was also clear that Europe's leaders would not unite and take action to punish a king who assaulted the head of their church. The cardinals therefore concluded that they had to make peace with France. Boniface's short-lived successor, Benedict XI (r. 1303–1304), lifted the spiritual penalties Boniface had imposed on Philip. At the end of his brief reign, a French archbishop was elected pope.

Clement V (r. 1305–1314) was in France at the time of his election, and he stayed there to negotiate with Philip. There was much for him to do, for he hoped to head off a war that was looming between France and England, and in 1307 Philip attacked the Knights Templar, one of the richest and most prestigious of Europe's military orders. The king arrested as many Templars as he could and tortured them to force them to confess to everything from witchcraft to sexual deviance. The pope, powerless to defend them, acquiesced to the order's dissolution, but did what he could to minimize the king's appropriation of its property.

Clement established what was supposed to be a temporary residence at Avignon, a city in southern France on the border of Philip's territory, but he never had an opportunity to go to Rome. At his death, the College of Cardinals, which was now largely French, elected another French pope who opted to remain in Avignon. The pattern repeated itself, and for more than 70 years (1305–1377) the bishop of Rome never visited the city of Rome. Lavish facilities were built for the papal court at Avignon, and it began to appear that the pope had no intention of ever returning to Rome.

Critics branded the papacy's sojourn in Avignon a "**Babylonian captivity**," a reference to the Bible's account of the Chaldaeans carting the Jews off to exile in ancient Babylon. They accused France of having abducted the papacy. French influences were strong at Avignon, but the Avignese popes were no one's puppets. Many were excellent executives who improved the power and efficiency of the church's central government. Having lost control of the Papal States, they were ingenious at finding other sources of income. They claimed the right to appoint candidates to all major clerical offices, to collect the revenues of those offices during periods when they were vacant, and to hear appeals from all ecclesiastical courts. They created an elaborate bureaucracy dedicated to attracting as much business as possible to the papal court, and they collected fees (and bribes) for all services. The papal administration at Avignon became a model of efficiency for Europe's secular governments, but the popes' fiscal skills hardly enhanced their reputations for sanctity. Holy men were not supposed to be so preoccupied with— and good at—raising money.

As the crises of the fourteenth century mounted, the church on which Europeans depended for spiritual comfort seemed to become ever more worldly and materialistic. Saints—notably Bridget of Sweden (1302–1372) and Catherine of Siena (1347–1380)— begged, and reformers demanded, that the popes return to Rome before they irreparably damaged the church. In 1378 Pope Gregory XI (r. 1370–1378) yielded to the pressure and took the cardinals back to Rome.

Papal Schism   The Papal States were out of control, and the Roman buildings that housed the papacy had been neglected for 70 years. Gregory and the cardinals, who were accustomed to the comforts of their elaborate palace in Avignon, soon concluded that Rome was not livable. Gregory decreed a return to Avignon, where the papal bureaucracy was still headquartered. Death, however, intervened, and Gregory's demise forced the cardinals to stay in Rome until they had chosen his successor. This proved difficult, for the College of Cardinals split in support of rival French candidates. To break the stalemate, the cardinals decided to placate the Roman people by elevating an obscure Italian, Urban VI (r. 1378–1389), to the papacy. The cardinals expected to be able to dominate Urban, and prior to his election they required him to promise to take them back to Avignon. Once seated on the papal throne, however, Urban changed his mind. He knew that in Avignon, as a lone Italian in a sea of Frenchmen, he would have little power.

When Urban informed the cardinals that they would stay in Rome, they refused and returned to Avignon without him. In Avignon they declared his election invalid and chose a new pope, Clement VII (r. 1378–1394). Urban responded by appointing a new College of Cardinals in Rome. Europe suddenly had two papal courts, and because there was no way to decide which one was valid, kings simply supported the pope who best suited their political agendas. France and its allies endorsed Avignon. England, France's enemy, favored Rome, and other states lined up accordingly.

This division of the papacy—the **Great Schism** (1378–1415)—plunged a generation of Europeans into spiritual confusion. Catholic doctrine maintained that allegiance to the true pope was essential for salvation, but there was no way to determine which of Europe's rival popes was Christ's authentic representative. A Christian's salvation depended upon receiving valid sacraments, but a sacrament—the power to act in God's name—was something delegated by Christ to the clergy through their superior, the pope. If the pope was really an anti-pope, the clergy who served him had no authority to act for God. Because the sins they forgave were not truly forgiven, the souls of the best intentioned and most obedient of Christians could be in great danger. A divided papacy posed a major threat to medieval Christian faith and practice.

Prominent Europeans pressed the popes to settle the issue between themselves. But neither man was willing to resign and sacrifice himself for the good of the church. Attention next shifted to the cardinals. They were urged to repudiate both popes and unite behind a new one. The cardinals welcomed this plan, for it confirmed their belief that they were the arbiters of papal legitimacy. In 1409, when they met in the Italian city of Pisa and chose a new pope, the popes they had forsaken in Rome and Avignon appointed new Colleges of Cardinals. Ironically, the strategy for resolving the schism multiplied the number of popes.

Conciliarism and Popular Government   The Avignese papacy and the Great Schism forced Europeans to think seriously about the nature of authority—secular as well as sacred. To end the schism, they needed a justification for forcing popes, who claimed to be accountable only to God, to do what they did not want to do. More was at stake here than restoration of the church's unity. The development of a rationale for sitting in judgment on a pope would have wide-ranging political ramifications, for the same argument could easily be adapted to apply to kings.

William of Ockham (1285–1349), an English Franciscan philosopher, insisted that because popes were human, they were as prone to error as anyone else. The most reliable way for fallible human individuals to determine the truth about an issue, he insisted, was to seek a consensus of opinion from all persons qualified to comment. Ockham warned, however, that even experts make mistakes and that it was important, therefore, that minorities be listened to and coercion minimized.

Marsiglio of Padua (c. 1278–1342), an Italian philosopher, claimed that the church was not some supernatural entity, but only a name for groups of Christians. It should be subordinate to the state, for the state was charged with responsibility for defending the peace on which life itself depends. Furthermore, given that Aristotle had logically demonstrated that whatever affected the whole should be decided by the whole, both the church and the state should be subject to the will of the people—or at least to the will of the more responsible element in the general population.

The Englishman John Wyclif (d. 1384) offered a different justification for empowering the masses. He admitted that dominion (the right to rule) had long been believed to be a sacred power delegated to men by God. But he argued that this logically implied that dominion was to be used for the purpose God intended—for the welfare of God's creatures. If popes (and kings) failed to use the authority God gave them for the good of their subjects, they forfeited legitimacy. The subjects of an ungodly ruler, therefore, had a duty to replace him, for he had no right to dominion over God's people. Wyclif also denied that the pope had sole authority to interpret the Scriptures. He urged that the Bible be translated from Latin into the vernacular languages so that laypeople could study it and make up their own minds about what it taught. The church had forbidden vernacular translations, for it claimed that simple folk, who were not trained in theology, would misread the text and fall into error. Wyclif's championing of the rights of ordinary people may have contributed to the Peasants' Revolt that erupted in 1381. Despite the fact that his theories were inherently revolutionary, a powerful patron protected him until his death. Ultimately, however, the church branded him a heretic and condemned his writings. This drove the popular preachers and religious dissidents whom he inspired (the Lollards) underground, but their movement may have endured and helped to prepare the way for England's break with the papacy in the sixteenth century.

Critiques of papal authority and arguments justifying action by the masses led to the proposal that finally ended the Great Schism. A group of scholars known as the Conciliarists argued that a universal church council would have the authority to end the schism. **Conciliarism**, their theory, held that final authority in spiritual matters belonged to the whole community of Christians as represented by a general church council, not the pope alone. Church lawyers objected that only a pope could summon a council and that no council had exercised power over a pope, but the Conciliarists found ways around these obstacles. They pressured the weakest of the

Council of Constance A fifteenth-century chronicle compiled by Ulrich of Richental provides valuable insight into the work of the Council of Constance. This miniature, which decorates the manuscript, represents Pope Martin V sitting with cardinals and other members of the council. *Dagli Orti/Picture Desk, Inc./Kobal Collection*

popes, the one in Pisa, to convene their council, and they argued that if an essential institution (such as the church) breaks down, logic gives its members the right to do whatever is necessary to save it. The alternative would be to ignore the natural right beings have to exist and to claim that they have no choice but irrationally to will their own destruction.

In 1415 the Swiss city of Constance hosted a council at which most of the powers in Europe—kings, cardinals, bishops, abbots, lawyers, and prominent scholars—were represented. The council had a number of items on its agenda. To demonstrate that it was staunchly orthodox, the council violated a safe conduct it had given to a religious dissident named John Hus and tried him for heresy. Hus had been inspired by John Wyclif's arguments to raise a popular revolt against the papacy in his homeland, Bohemia. His execution at Constance only served to inspire his followers, the Hussites, to take up arms. They defeated the imperial armies sent against them, and peace was restored only after the church made major concessions to satisfy their demands.

The chief business at Constance was the resolution of the Great Schism. This proved to be easy once all the European powers agreed to withdraw their support from the rival popes and unite behind one chosen by the cardinals at the council. The new pope, Martin V (r. 1417–1431), was eager for the meeting to adjourn, for the Conciliarists wanted the delegates next to debate reforming the reunited church. Martin feared that if this happened, the council would replace the pope as the ultimate authority over the church.

Once the schism was healed, much of the excitement went out of the meeting, and its members were eager to go home. Before the council disbanded, however, it passed two potentially revolutionary decrees. The first, *Sacrosancta*, declared that the church was to be governed by councils—implying that popes were simply the church's chief executive officers, agents who were accountable to councils and subject to their supervision. The second decree, *Frequens*, ordered popes to summon councils at regular intervals. If these decrees had succeeded, the church would have become an institution governed by a representative assembly. This did not happen, because kings knew that what was done to popes might be done to kings. In 1431 a council that met in Basel, another Swiss city, made a fatal mistake. It quarreled with the pope, deposed him, and elected a rival. To prevent a new schism from developing, Europe's kings withdrew their support for councils and did not object when popes ignored the schedule for convening them. In 1460 Pope Pius II (r. 1458–1464) declared it a heresy to claim that anyone or any council has authority over a pope. In 1870 Pope Pius IX (r. 1846–1878) confirmed this at the First Vatican Council by promulgating the doctrine of papal infallibility. The church emerged from the crises of the fourteenth century with the claims it made for the authority of its leader intact, but its reputation as a spiritual institution tarnished.

Private Faith, Mysticism, and Skepticism The medieval church claimed to be the sole intermediary between God and His people. Pope Boniface VIII had clearly stated to King Philip IV of France (and to the world) that there was no salvation outside the communion of the church. Yet for much of the fourteenth century, the church did not inspire trust as a mediator between God and sinners. Rival popes excommunicated one another and insisted that their opponents' sacraments were invalid. Faithful Christians had no way to determine the truth. They were therefore thrust back on their own spiritual resources: private prayer, study, and meditation. Laypeople took the initiative and invented new kinds of religious communities and disciplines that had little to do with the church and clergy. The mystical element in medieval religion thrived, for mysticism was an avenue to a direct, personal communion with God. The breakdown of the church forced people to assume more responsibility for themselves, and the autonomy to which they became accustomed in the religious sphere spilled over into other areas of their lives.

Even the authority of reason, the standard in which medieval dialecticians placed their greatest trust, was questioned by late medieval philosophers such as William of Ockham. Ockham denied that reason could be used to support faith. He argued that the only realities of which the mind can be certain are the things of which the body's senses make it aware. Ockham was a philosophical nominalist (see Chapter 10) who believed that the mind infers classes and abstractions from the specific bits of data that the senses provide. In his opinion, there was no evidence that classes and abstractions actually exist outside the human mind. Reasoning from particular things to general abstractions helped people understand how the natural world operates, but it did not lead to an understanding of God or of ultimate spiritual truths. The truths of faith are not deduced by reason, he insisted, but grasped by intuition. The fact that God created a rational universe does not mean that God is bound by the rules of logic. If God were, logic would be greater than God. Faith in the Bible's omnipotent Creator transcends reason and understanding. Ockham's skepticism severely limited what human beings could hope to know. But by separating faith from reason, he created a justification for liberating science from constraints imposed by theology.

Political Responses: The Burdens of War

The governments of the young states that were taking shape in the late Middle Ages faced the challenge of managing populations unsettled by plague and famine. The tools available to them were as limited as their experience. Kings were still primarily warlords, but war was an unlikely cure for the problems of their unstable world.

France and England   England and France were late medieval Europe's most fully formed states. Both had well-established dynasties and at least a start toward a centralized bureaucratic government. Unfortunately, however, they also had an unresolved territorial dispute. Ever since 1066, when the Norman dukes became kings of England, the jurisdictions of the French and English monarchies had overlapped. Henry II of England had ruled about half of France. His son, John, lost much of his father's Angevin Empire (see Chapter 9), and by the fourteenth century, England's holdings on the continent had been reduced to Gascony, the region around Bordeaux in southwestern France. England's kings were, however, not yet ready to give up hope of recouping their losses on the continent.

Edward I (r. 1272–1307), the warrior-king who conquered Wales and nearly subdued Scotland, reopened war with France to support his allies in Flanders. Flanders and England had close economic ties, for English wool merchants supplied the Flemish cloth industry. France evened the odds by helping the Scots fend off the English king. In 1308 the French and English dynasties agreed to a truce, and a royal marriage was arranged to seal peace between the two kingdoms. Edward's son and heir, Edward II, married Isabella, daughter of Philip IV of France. The union was supposed to ensure future good relations between France and England, but instead it created grounds for a conflict between them called the **Hundred Years' War**.

Edward II (r. 1307–1327) was as weak a king as his father had been strong. He led his army to disastrous defeat in Scotland, and his excessive devotion to a few unworthy friends alienated his barons and his wife, Isabella. In 1325 she traveled to Paris on a diplomatic mission to her brother's court, and there she began an affair with an exiled English nobleman, Roger Mortimer, the Earl of March. Isabella and Mortimer raised an army, returned to England, and forced Edward to abdicate in the name of his son, Edward III (r. 1327–1377). The ex-king died, or most likely was murdered, a few months later, and Isabella and Mortimer governed England as regents for his son. In 1330 Edward III overthrew them and at age 18 began his independent rule.

Edward II had seriously damaged the prestige of the monarchy, but Edward III was just the man to restore it. He was a handsome, athletic young man who looked like a king, and he had a gift for what the modern world would call public relations. Enthusiasm for the Arthurian romances was at its height when Edward came to the throne, and he encouraged his subjects to think of him as a new Arthur. He hosted feasts and tournaments at which he and his friends played at being knights of the round table, and in 1348 he founded the Order of the Garter, a fraternity of knights like the one that the legendary King Arthur had assembled at Camelot.

Hundred Years' War: Opening Phase

Although ceremonies help build a royal image, a medieval king who aspired to glory had to win his spurs as a warrior. Edward led several forays into Scotland, but his men were not excited by the prospect of plundering such a poverty-stricken land. Much more tempting were the rich provinces of their traditional enemy, France. Moreover, Edward believed that he had a justification for a war with France—He claimed to be the rightful heir to the French throne.

Ever since its founding in the tenth century, France's Capetian dynasty had enjoyed remarkable biological success. Whenever a king died, there was always a son to take his place. Philip IV had seemingly ensured the future of the dynasty by siring three sons: Louis X (r. 1314–1316), Philip V (r. 1316–1322), and Charles IV (r. 1322–1328). Each succeeded to the throne, but surprisingly, none produced a male heir who survived his father. When Charles died in 1328, the senior line of the Capetian house died with him. The Capetian family, however, did not die out. It had a collateral branch founded by Philip IV's brother, Duke Charles of Valois (1270–1325), who had a son named Philip. When Charles IV died, the throne passed to his cousin Philip of Valois, France's King Philip VI (r. 1328–1350).

Edward did not protest when Philip was crowned in 1328. However, in 1337 the English king's eagerness for an excuse to invade France prompted him to claim that the French throne should have come to him. Philip VI was only Philip IV's nephew. Edward was Philip IV's grandson, a more direct heir. The French disagreed. They pointed out that Edward's link with the Capetian line was through his mother, Isabella, and they claimed that ancient Frankish tradition—the so-called Salian Law—barred women from occupying France's throne or transmitting title to it. This legal wrangling was only a smoke screen. Edward hardly expected France to turn itself over to him. Nor was he likely to conquer it with the resources of a kingdom that was one-quarter its size. His claim to France's throne, however, provided the English with a high-minded justification for looting and pillaging the French.

Edward could do little more than harass the French by staging quick raids on their territory, but in 1346 one of his forays turned into a major battle. A large French army surprised Edward while he was charging across Normandy and forced him to take a stand near the village of Crécy (see Map 11–2). The English were outnumbered, but an unconventional strategy saved them. Edward took up a defensive position and waited for the French to charge him. Archers armed with a uniquely English weapon, the longbow, were stationed on both wings of his army. Their arrows reduced the heavily armored French cavalry to a flailing heap of wounded horses and men before its charge reached the English lines. Edward's knights then dashed in, completed the rout, and won a victory that was as complete as it was unexpected.

The lesson of Crécy was that the era of cavalry's dominance on medieval battlefields was coming to an end, and the reluctance of the French feudal aristocracy to accept this explains why the Hundred Years' War dragged on for so long. Small English armies using new methods repeatedly defeated larger French forces that insisted on

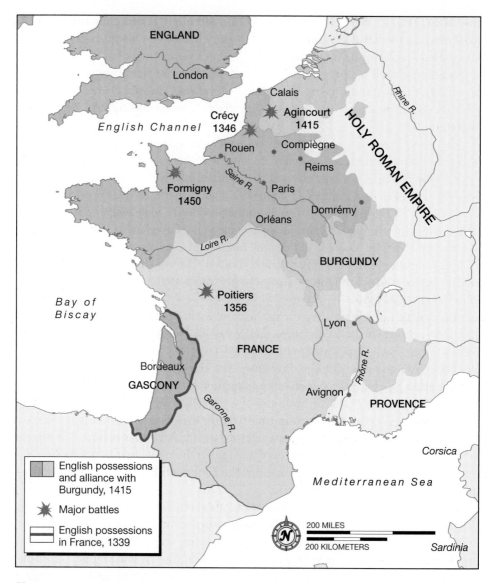

Map 11–2 The Hundred Years' War   France was politically divided at the start of the Hundred Years' War not only between the kings of England and France, but among France's powerful nobles. One of the effects of the war was to increase the power of the French king within his own realm.

Question: What role did geography play in determining the outcome of the Hundred Years' War?

fighting with outmoded techniques. England, however, did not have the strength to exploit its victories and occupy France. All the English could do was go home and celebrate their victories while the French prepared for the next round. The result was periods of combat separated by periods of peace, but no progress toward a resolution of the war.

The medieval aristocracy owed its social and political supremacy to its military technology, but by the fourteenth century new weapons were making expensive aristocratic training and equipment anachronistic. Minimal training was needed to teach a man how to shoot a crossbow—a small bow that was bent by a crank and released by a trigger—and it was so lethal that the church tried to outlaw its use. It cost little to arm large numbers of men with longbows. Their six-foot length gave them great range and power, but a lot of practice was needed to master them. They were therefore used primarily by men from Wales and England who grew up with them. The Swiss developed a weapon called a pike—a combination long-handled spear, axe, and grappling hook. With it, a company of infantrymen could halt a cavalry charge in its tracks, pull knights off their mounts, and slaughter them. By the fourteenth century, gunpowder was also bringing primitive cannons and small arms onto battlefields—although these weapons were not yet very effective. Knights defended themselves against the new weapons by increasing their armor, but heavier armor meant less mobility and therefore vulnerability of a different kind.

Infantry had dominated the battlefields of the ancient world. At the start of the Middle Ages, inventions such as the stirrup had permitted cavalry to gain the upper hand. By the fourteenth century, new inventions were again reversing the balance of power. This was clear to objective observers, but people are reluctant to abandon behaviors that are fundamental to their sense of identity and way of life. France's knights resisted acknowledging that the hard-won traditional military skills of their class were no longer effective, and their obduracy nearly cost France its independence.

As Edward aged, his son and heir apparent, Edward "the Black Prince" (1330–1376), took over the reins of government. In 1356 at Poitiers the prince won a second major victory over the French that was nearly a repeat of his father's triumph at Crécy. He captured the French king, John II, "the Good" (r. 1350–1364), and carted him off to captivity in England. John was a dubious prize. The rules of chivalry required that his English hosts foot the bill for maintaining him in a style appropriate to his rank until his French subjects ransomed him. After an appropriately kingly sum was promised to the English, John went back to France. But when he discovered that it could not be paid, he decided that honor required him to return to captivity in England. He died there a few months later.

During John's absence, France was governed by his far more competent son, Charles V, "the Wise" (r. 1364–1380). Charles earned his reputation for wisdom by giving up pitched battles with the English and turning conduct of the war over to a guerilla fighter, Bertrand du Guesclin (1320–1380). Bertrand's army was composed of mercenaries who valued victory and survival more highly than chivalry. The long war multiplied the numbers of men who fought for pay, and this added to the problems of the Age of Anxiety. Governments hired mercenaries for specific campaigns and then discharged them. Between bouts of employment, these professional soldiers, who had no other sources of income, supported themselves by freelance looting and raping.

PEOPLE IN CONTEXT Christine de Pizan (c. 1364–1430), Professional Writer

Christine de Pizan This late medieval manuscript illumination depicts Christine de Pizan in the act of writing one of her popular works. For companionship she has a lap dog, a pet associated with aristocratic ladies.

In 1368 France's King Charles V (r. 1364–1380) offered Tommaso di Benvenuto da Pizzano, a professor of medicine and astrology at the University of Bologna, the post of royal astrologer, and Tommaso moved his family to Paris. His daughter Christine surely absorbed much from the conversations of the learned men who were her father's colleagues and friends, but her only formal education was the elementary training that medieval society gave middle- and upper-class girls.

Christine anticipated a conventional life. At about the age of 16 she married Etienne de Castel, one of the king's secretaries. The couple produced two sons and a daughter, and then the family's fortunes began to fail. Charles V died, leaving the throne to a more frivolous monarch, Charles VI (r. 1380–1422), who provided little patronage for the scholars who had adorned his father's court. Christine's father died in poverty about 1387, and three years later her husband followed his father-in-law to the grave. Christine, at the age of 25, was left alone to support herself, three young children, a mother, and a niece.

Christine had no training for a trade or profession, but she was literate. She appears, at first, to have maintained her household by working as a copyist. In the days before the printing press, book sellers got their wares from scribes who wrote them out by hand. One benefit of being a copyist was the opportunity the job provided for self-education. A copyist was lent books to work with that otherwise might have been hard to come by, and copying a book meant reading it. This provided Christine with sufficient education to become an author herself.

In 1402 Christine published her first collection of poems, and she soon established herself as one of France's more popular and prolific writers. Some of her works dealt with the theme of love and drew on the romances that were staples of late medieval popular literature. But she also treated more serious themes. She discussed politics and education and advised kings, dukes, and princes. She was particularly interested in the condition of women. She wrote extensively about the roles they had played in history and offered them advice on how to make the best of their current opportunities. Fittingly, Christine's last poem was a celebration of the deeds of a female contemporary who vindicated her faith in the potential of women: Joan of Arc.

Question: What does the career of a woman like Christine de Pizan suggest about the role of women in late medieval society?

There was a long lull in the Hundred Years' War in the second half of the fourteenth century while England struggled with internal problems. The Black Prince, who had been raiding France from his base in Gascony, diverted his attention to civil wars in Spain. By 1367 his overtaxed Gascon subjects were in revolt, and he was suffering from an illness that slowly killed him. Edward turned his duties over to his brother, John of Gaunt, the Duke of Lancaster (1340–1399). He then retired to England, where he died in 1376. By then, the aging Edward III was mentally incompetent. Because the Black Prince's son Richard (his heir) was still a minor, John of Gaunt (the boy's uncle) governed England as a regent. But given the anomalous situation, he was barely able to restrain the quarrelsome English nobility.

When Richard II (r. 1377–1399) reached maturity, he was determined to exercise what he believed was his God-given right to autocratic power. This necessitated the destruction of some of England's great noblemen—particularly Henry of Lancaster, John of Gaunt's son and Richard's cousin. Richard's attempt to strip Henry of his estates was a major mistake. England's barons realized that if Richard succeeded in humiliating the powerful Duke of Lancaster, none of them would be safe. Therefore they rallied to Henry's side and forced Richard to abdicate. Given that Richard had no son, the campaign cleared the way for Henry to claim his cousin's crown.

The Hundred Years' War: Concluding Phase There were other English nobles with royal ancestry who could have claimed Richard's crown. Consequently, the new Lancastrian monarch, Henry IV (r. 1399–1413), was forced to spend his reign shoring up support for a somewhat shaky throne. His son, Henry V (r. 1413–1422), decided that the best way to promote the young dynasty's popularity with its subjects was to revive the war with France. In 1415, in what was virtually a repeat of Crécy and Poitiers, a large French army cornered the English invaders at Agincourt and was decimated by the English longbow. This time, however, the aftermath of the battle was different, for the situation in France had changed.

In 1392 France's king, Charles VI (r. 1380–1422), began to suffer violent bouts of insanity that required him to be restrained and confined. His uncle Philip, Duke of

Burgundy, and his brother Louis, Duke of Orléans, contested control of the regency for the disabled king. In 1407 Philip's heir, John "the Fearless," assassinated Louis, and war broke out between the Burgundian and Orléanist (or Armagnac) factions. The army that Henry V defeated at Agincourt was Orléanist. After their loss, the Orléanists tried to heal the breach with the Burgundians, but at the peace conference a disgruntled Orléanist avenged Louis's death by assassinating the Burgundian duke. The infuriated Burgundians promptly allied with Henry and gave Agincourt's victor the help he needed to occupy Paris and capture Charles VI. Henry married Charles's daughter, Catherine, and in due course the union produced a male infant—the future Henry VI—who was declared heir to both England and France.

There was another claimant to the French throne, Charles VI's son, Charles "the Dauphin" (the title of the heir to the French throne). As the English advanced, the Dauphin fled to safety in a region that was still controlled by Orléanists, but his sup-

Joan of Arc   The art of portraiture began to be revived in the late Middle Ages. One of the earliest reliable royal portraits is one painted of France's King John the Good about 1350. This picture of Joan of Arc is found in a manuscript from the late fifteenth century. Although it dates to Joan's era, no one can know if its artist had any idea of what she looked like. *Marc Charmet/Picture Desk, Inc./Kobal Collection*

porters were too dispirited and disorganized to put up much of a fight. Their prospects improved in 1422, when both Charles VI and Henry V died. The regents who governed for the infant King Henry VI (r. 1422–1461) were his two English uncles. Although it was soon apparent that they were not working well together, another seven years passed before the Dauphin's party took advantage of England's weakness. The Orléanists were finally prodded to action by a 17-year-old peasant girl, Joan of Arc (c. 1412–1431). On her own initiative she made her way to Charles's court to inform him that God had sent her to save France. Charles was skeptical, but he had little to lose by backing her. His soldiers responded enthusiastically to her confident assertion that God was with them, and they began to roll back the poorly led English. In 1429 they regained Reims, the city in whose cathedral France's kings were crowned, and the Dauphin was enthroned as King Charles VII (r. 1429–1461). Confident that England's defeat was now only a matter of time, Charles concluded that Joan had served her purpose, and he began to shunt her aside. When the Burgundians captured her in 1430, he declined to ransom her, and her captors sold her to the English. England hoped to demoralize the French by convicting Joan of heresy. After a lengthy trial, they burned her at the stake, but her death did not improve their situation. (The pope declared Joan's innocence in 1455, but the church did not canonize her until 1920.)

In 1435 Duke Philip "the Good" of Burgundy sealed England's fate by making peace with Charles VII. England had no hope of resisting a united France, and by 1453, it had lost everything on the continent but the port city of Calais (which it retained until 1558). The French monarchy emerged from its humiliation stronger than ever. The long war, which was fought entirely on French territory, convinced the French that they needed a strong royal defender. The king's subjects knew that he had to have the power to act quickly and decisively. Therefore, they did not resist his efforts to tax them or force him to consult with them on major decisions. Wartime conditions prevented the Estates General from aspiring to the kind of political and fiscal authority the English Parliament sought and promoted development of absolute monarchy in France.

The situation in England was different. After a century of famous victories, the English king had to admit to his subjects that he had won the battles but lost the war. This damaged the prestige of the crown, and Henry VI lacked the talent to rebuild it. He was a weak, distracted ruler, and in 1453 he suffered a mental breakdown. A powerful faction formed in support of his more competent cousin, the Duke of York, and in 1455 civil war erupted. The heraldic symbol of the king's Lancastrian family was a red rose, and that of his Yorkist cousins was a white rose. The conflict between them has therefore been dubbed the **War of the Roses**.

The Yorkists triumphed over the Lancastrians, but their tenure on the throne was brief. Edward IV (r. 1466–1483), who deposed Henry, left a 13-year-old heir who disappeared shortly after his father's death. The boy and his brother had been entrusted to an uncle who claimed their inheritance and declared himself King

Richard III (r. 1483–1485). Richard's title was quickly challenged by the exiled leader of the Lancastrian faction, Henry Tudor. Henry invaded England, and Richard died in battle, deserted by his followers. With Richard, the Plantagenet dynasty and England's medieval era came to an end. The new king, Henry VII (r. 1485–1509), founded the Tudor dynasty and began to rebuild the battered monarchy. Much was yet to happen, however, before England settled on what kind of royal government it would have.

KEY QUESTION | Revisited

Periods of stress pose challenges that reveal the weaknesses and prove the strengths of individuals and institutions. The civilization that blossomed in Europe in the twelfth and thirteenth centuries was tested by the crises of the fourteenth and fifteenth. The church did not fare well. But the lapses in its performance gave the faithful the freedom to assume more responsibility for themselves and motivated scholars to think deeply about the nature of legitimate authority. Plagues and economic difficulties confronted states with problems that were beyond their understanding and control, and the use to which they put the tools of government—legislation and war—probably made bad situations worse. The outcome, however, may have been progress toward a stronger, more open society. Economic opportunities improved for the masses. Wars decimated the ranks of the aristocracy, and popular uprisings hinted at new assertiveness on the part of ordinary people. Few persons outside of university circles were probably familiar with the philosophical treatises that developed rationales for individual autonomy, free inquiry, and representative government, but these characteristic features of modern Western civilization were beginning to have some effect on people's lives.

Review Questions

1. What environmental and geographical factors helped make Europe vulnerable to plague?
2. Was religion the only source of medieval Europe's hostility to Islam?
3. How did the problems Europe faced in the late Middle Ages affect its traditional institutions, the church and state?
4. How did reformers justify sitting in judgment on popes (and kings) who were believed to be established on their thrones by God?
5. Why was tiny England able to win so many victories and sustain such a long war with the much larger nation of France?
6. Was Europe strengthened or weakened by the crises of the Age of Anxiety?

 Please consult the Suggested Readings at the back of the book to continue your study of the material covered in this chapter. For a list of documents on the Primary Source DVD-ROM that relate to topics in this chapter, please refer to the back of the book.

Topics in This Chapter

The Context for the Renaissance • The Culture of the Renaissance • The Northern Renaissance • The Middle East: The Ottoman Empire • Europe and Atlantic Exploration

12 Renaissance and Exploration

God gives man the power to have whatever he wants and become whatever he decides to be. At birth animals have—from their mothers' wombs—all that they will ever have. At the Creation (or shortly thereafter) the angels became what they will forever be. But when man appeared, God the Father bestowed on him all of life's possibilities. Therefore, whatever each individual cultivates will mature and bear fruit as his nature.

—**Giovanni Pico della Mirandola,** *Oration on the Dignity of Man*

KEY | Question

How should a society use its history?

Giovanni Pico della Mirandola had high ambitions for himself and for all humanity. The youngest son of the ruler of a tiny state in Italy's Po Valley, he studied at the universities of Bologna, Padua, and Paris, where he was particularly attracted to Hebrew literature. Pico believed that the insights of major thinkers from all the ancient Western civilizations—Greek, Latin, Hebrew, and Arabic—could be reconciled, and at the young age of 23 he set out to prove this by defending some 900 theses. When the church condemned 13 of his propositions as heretical, Pico fled to France. A powerful patron interceded for him, and he was allowed to return to Italy to live out the remainder of his short life in Florence, the capital of the Renaissance.

Pico's celebration of human potential—his faith in the power of people to shape their own destinies—signaled a shift in European intellectual history. Early medieval thinkers, such as Augustine of Hippo (354–430), claimed that sin rendered human nature impotent and turned the world into a worthless realm doomed to extinction. They denigrated earthly life as something from which people waited to be rescued by God's grace. There was much

Michelangelo's *David* This photo is of a replica of one of the most famous statues from the era of the Italian Renaissance, Michelangelo's *David*. When the original was moved indoors, the replica took its place on Florence's Piazza della Signoria.

in both pagan philosophy and sacred literature to support their view, but Renaissance optimists like Pico believed that these thinkers had missed a more fundamental truth. The Bible's Creator-God had declared His Creation good, imparted His image to the people He made, and ordered them to go forth to populate and subdue the world. God's prime directive was a command that human beings share the divine work of perfecting Creation—themselves included.

Pico was not alone in proclaiming the "dignity" and "excellence" of humanity. The architect Leon Battista Alberti (1404–1472) spoke for many when he asserted that "man can do everything that he sets his mind to." This, the Renaissance's proponents argued, was not a groundless faith but a truth taught by Scripture and the Greek and Roman sages. What set men like Pico and Alberti apart from their medieval predecessors and made them "modern" men, they believed, was their rediscovery of this ancient wisdom.

Some clergy and conservative scholars of the Renaissance era urged caution. They warned that it was a mistake to put too much trust in human virtue, rationality, and self-sufficiency, for the true ancient wisdom was that history offered little support for the kind of confidence in human nature that Pico and Alberti preached. In light of the human record therefore, bold departures from tradition and attacks on the status quo were unwise.

Western civilization has repeatedly reengaged its own history. Sometimes the past has served as a "dead hand," a legacy that caps what people permit themselves to think and do. It inspires a kind of religious fundamentalism, a belief that certain ideas or institutions transcend history. They are eternal absolutes that never change and must not be challenged. Veneration for the past can retard development, but it can also provide security during turbulent times. Conversely, a revival of interest in a historical era can prompt people to think about the present in new ways. It can inspire critiques of received truths and launch reform movements. Either way, the past shapes the present and the future. Much depends on what people do with their history.

The Context for the Renaissance

The Renaissance is a controversial period for historians. They debate when it began, how it should be defined, and even its importance. Some scholars stress the Renaissance's role in ending the medieval era and launching the modern world. Others emphasize its continuity with the Middle Ages and note that its effects were limited. There is, however, widespread agreement that its origin is to be found in medieval Italy's unique urban institutions.

Formation of City-States in Italy   The commercial activity that flourished during the High Middle Ages scattered towns across the map of Europe, but city life flourished more vigorously in Italy than elsewhere. Most of Europe's trade via Mediterranean routes passed through Italy's ports and generated employment for large urban populations. By 1400, four of Europe's five largest cities (Genoa, Florence, Milan, and Venice) were to be found in Italy. Only Paris (at about 80,000) was their equal. Italy had about 20 cities in the second rank with populations of about 25,000. In the rest of Europe, there were only four.

Size and number were not all that made Italy's cities noteworthy. In most parts of Europe a city's jurisdiction ended at its walls, and a city was an isolated island of special political privilege operating inside a larger governmental entity such as a kingdom or the domain of a noble. Italy's cities, however, acquired power over the lands around them and became city-states. The territory a town controlled was often small. Its farthest frontier might be only a day's ride from its urban center. But wealth from trade and industry gave some Italian city-states influence comparable to the much larger countries of northern Europe.

Geography—a mix of mountains, valleys, and plains—encouraged the political division of the Italian peninsula, and some of its city-states had their origin as *civitates* of Rome's former empire. Others, however, owed their rise to medieval Italy's unique political situation. The division of the Carolingian Empire in the ninth century was followed by the rise of royal dynasties in France and Germany, but not in Italy. The Italians had no native king around which central government could coalesce, and at least one Italian power was determined to prevent the establishment of a secular monarchy in Italy. Rome's bishop, the pope, ruled an Italian state, but he also claimed jurisdiction over all Europeans. If a secular ruler succeeded in uniting Italy, the pope would have come under his control and lost credibility as a universal religious leader. He was convinced therefore that the only way to preserve the church was to prevent Italy's political unification. (Popes are still the heads of a state—the 105-acre Vatican City—that is independent of Italy's government.)

For much of the medieval period, it was Germans and not Italians who sought unification of Italy. When Germany's kings assumed the imperial title and invaded Italy, Italy's landed aristocracy had no native king behind whom to rally in defense of their estates, but they had allies close at hand. The urban communities that flourished as trade began to revive in the eleventh and twelfth centuries shared the nobility's opposition to German domination. In addition to political objectives, town and country also had economic concerns in common. Townspeople bought the food raised on the nobles' rural estates, and nobles bought the products manufactured and imported by towns. Over time, self-interest brought urban and rural leaders closer and closer together. Nobles moved into town, intermarried with bourgeois families, and integrated into urban life. As the families and properties of merchants and landowners intermingled, the town's authority spread over the countryside, and it became a city-state.

Many of Italy's city-states began as communes—associations of tradespeople who voluntarily banded together for mutual benefit. A commune was often governed by a town council (of a hundred or more members) assisted by a pair of executive officers. Checks and balances and short terms in office were relied on to prevent individuals or political parties from monopolizing power, but these strategies were not very effective. Family and clan groups competed for dominance. They built fortified towers inside towns and sallied forth to battle one another in the streets. Trade and merchant guilds and various kinds of fraternities also jockeyed for advantage. Consequently, a commune's leaders were engaged in a never ending struggle to persuade numerous self-interested groups to work together. If a hopeless stalemate developed, it became common by the second half of the twelfth century for a town to suspend its constitution and temporarily turn itself over to a *podestà*. A **podestà** was an outsider who was empowered to govern a town for a limited period of time. Because he was a neutral stranger, factions trusted him to arbitrate their disputes and get their community back on track. The danger, of course, was that a *podestà* might make his lordship permanent.

This happened frequently, for republics were far less efficient and less able to defend themselves than states ruled by autocrats. Sometimes the autocrats openly reveled in their power, as did the Visconti and Sforza despots who ruled Milan. Sometimes they masqueraded behind a republican facade, as did Florence's Medici family. The exception was the "Serene Republic" of Venice. It was governed by a small number of families who alone had hereditary right to political office, but a constitution that headed off suicidal factional fighting among these families and an adequate distribution of wealth prevented the kind of internal upheaval that brought strongmen to power in many of Italy's states.

Italy's Political Development

The Italian peninsula was divided into political zones of different types (see Map 12–1). A kingdom centered on Naples governed the southern portion of the peninsula. Its rulers won and lost Sicily several times and occasionally crossed the Adriatic to try to conquer portions of the Balkans. The popes' realm, the Papal States, spanned the center of Italy and extended up the Adriatic coast into the former Byzantine exarchate of Ravenna. It was a large, but inherently unstable, entity. Entrenched aristocratic families fought among themselves for control of the papacy, and popes, who were often elderly men with short reigns, had difficulty maintaining order. Northern Italy was divided among major and minor city-states that experimented with different kinds of governments. Some (primarily Venice, Florence, Genoa, Lucca, Pisa, and Siena) called themselves republics. Others (Milan, Ferrara, Mantua, and Modena) were duchies. Functionally, all were oligarchies dominated in different ways by wealthy minorities.

International trade gave the Italian city-states more wealth and influence than small territories might be expected to possess. Milan, a large northern duchy, lacked access to the sea but controlled approaches to vital passes through the Alps. Genoa, Milan's western neighbor, was a small coastal republic controlled by a powerful merchant oligarchy. It had a large navy and was one of Italy's richest ports. Venice, a city built on lagoons and islands at the top of the Adriatic, was Genoa's chief competitor for Mediterranean trade. Its wealth derived from its commercial ties with Constantinople and the Byzantine Empire. Venice, like Genoa, was formally a republic and functionally an oligarchy. With the exception of Venice, factionalism plagued the Italian city-states—none more than Florence, the cultural capital of the Renaissance.

Florence was an inland town on the Arno River that traded through the port of Pisa (which it conquered in 1406). Its wealth, which derived from textile manufacturing, banking, and international finance, was immense, but unevenly distributed. A few Florentine families amassed huge fortunes, which they used to fight among themselves. Lesser persons were drawn into their disputes, and unruly factions formed behind the major contestants. Social and economic conditions periodically increased the volatility of the situation. Well over half the city's residents were wage laborers whose economic condition was perilous. Their employment depended on the wildly fluctuating international cloth market. When it boomed, they worked. When it crashed from overproduction or was otherwise disrupted, they starved. The Great Pestilence that spread through Europe in 1347 created a major crisis. It may have reduced the city's population by more than a third in a few months. Florence, along with the rest of the world, was thrown into

Map 12–1   Renaissance Italy   This map simplifies the complicated political geography of Italy during the era of the Renaissance. The boundaries of its states shifted with their military fortunes, and alliances and leagues further altered the configuration of the political landscape.

Question: How did geographical features divide the Italian peninsula? What were the political implications of its division?

economic confusion. By 1350 Florence's first banks, those of the Riccardi, Frescobaldi, Peruzzi, and Bardi families, had all failed—due in large part to the refusal of kings to repay their loans. The city's government was unprepared to deal with the situation. It was controlled by trade and merchant guilds that looked out for the interests of the propertied classes. Humble laborers had no representation. In 1378 poverty and frustration with an unresponsive system triggered a rebellion by the city's wool workers. Their so-called "Ciompi Revolt" was put down, and political infighting among the great families continued.

A new era began in 1434 with the ascendancy of Cosimo de Medici (1389–1464). The bank his father, Giovanni de Medici (1360–1429), founded laid the foundation for a staggering fortune that Cosimo used to oust his opponents and bring the republic under his control. After Francesco Sforza, a **condottiere** (commander of a mercenary army), came to power in Milan in 1450, Cosimo ended a war with the duchy. This was followed in 1454 by a treaty, the Peace of Lodi, that established a balance of power among Italy's greater states: Florence and Milan on one side and Venice and Naples on the other.

Florence owed much of its cultural as well as its political influence to Cosimo de Medici, who began his family's custom of providing patronage for scholars and artists. His grandson, Lorenzo "the Magnificent" (1449–1492), attached some of the period's greatest artists (the young Michelangelo, for example) to his household. Medieval artists often labored in anonymity as humble craftsmen, but the Medici broke with tradition and treated the artists and intellectuals they supported more as honored guests than as servants. The Renaissance highly esteemed talented individuals, no matter what their origin, and the princes who competed for their services believed that their own reputations were enhanced by the genius of the people they attracted to their courts.

The Italian cities' willingness to agree to the Peace of Lodi in 1454 may have owed something to an event that occurred in May of 1453. Constantinople fell to the Ottoman Turks, who had previously moved into the Aegean, Greece, and the Balkans. They were eventually to occupy Hungary, besiege Austria, attempt a direct assault on Italy, and replace Venice as the dominant naval power in the eastern Mediterranean. The fear they inspired was ultimately, however, not great enough to persuade the Italian states to form a united front and cease squabbling among themselves. In 1494 the Papacy joined Naples and Florence in an alliance aimed at Milan, and Milan sought aid from France. The armies of King Charles VIII (r. 1483–1498) swiftly swept through Italy, and the French laid claim to Naples. The Pope and Venice responded by appealing to Germany's Holy Roman Emperor for help. The conflict among Italy's city-states grew to include France, Germany, and Spain. The event that is sometimes seen as marking the end of the Renaissance was a sack of the city of Rome by German forces in 1527 (see Chapter 13).

Italy's troubles during this period prompted the composition of one of the most influential books ever written about politics: *The Prince* by Florentine historian Niccolò Machiavelli (1469–1527). It purports to be a primer for the instruction of a young Medici heir in the arts of government. The lesson Machiavelli draws from history is that a ruler should allow nothing—religion, morality, law, or conscience—to stand in the way of the pursuit of power. The "Machiavellian methods" the book so bluntly advocates (manipulation, brutality, hypocrisy, and treachery) are so extreme in their ruthlessness and amorality that some readers believe that Machiavelli intended his book as a joke. It is likely, however, that Italy's turbulent history convinced the Florentine scholar that nothing mattered more than the establishment of a government strong enough to maintain order.

In 1516 (three years after *The Prince* appeared), Machiavelli's English contemporary, Thomas More, published a witty satire that was similarly pessimistic in its assessment of politics. More called his book and the mythical society it described *Utopia* (Greek for "No-place"). More's Utopians behaved completely rationally. The contrast between their customs and those of More's contemporaries revealed that Europeans clearly did not. Like Machiavelli, More was acutely aware of the painful gap between what human beings are and what they might aspire to be.

Italy's Economy and the Renaissance   The leaders of the Renaissance broke with the ascetic, world-denying ideals of the Middle Ages by stressing the nobility of human existence and the legitimacy of earthly pleasures. They gloried in the creation of beautiful things, the possession of rare objects, esoteric scholarship, courtly refinements, and various forms of conspicuous consumption. All of this was supported and encouraged by the great wealth that accumulated in Italy. Much of that wealth came from Italy's dominance of trade between Europe and the Middle East. Profits from this commerce provided capital to fund banks, and Italy's bankers multiplied their wealth by becoming Europe's leading financiers, industrialists, and (what today would be called) venture capitalists.

Much of the wealth that Italians earned stayed in Italy, for they had to spend little of it abroad. Italy had sufficient raw materials to supply its home industries, enough agricultural production to feed its population, and monopolies on the manufacture of many (but certainly not all) of the luxury goods its people consumed. More money entered Italian markets with invading German, French, and Spanish armies, and the papal treasury in Rome siphoned funds from every corner of Europe.

Political fragmentation prevented any one ruler or government from monopolizing these resources. Wealth was always concentrated in the hands of small elites, but Italy's chronic instability—shifting political fortunes, economic crashes, and onslaughts of plague—kept society open and provided opportunities for some social mobility. Italy, in short, had an ideal environment for the growth of an entrepreneurial middle class of pioneering capitalists who respected talent, industry, and ambition. The Renaissance was, in many ways, an affirmation of the politically engaged, family oriented, secular lifestyle of a prosperous, powerful, and self-aware bourgeoisie.

The Culture of the Renaissance

Most people today associate Italy's Renaissance with the arts—sculpture, painting, and architecture. But the Renaissance was above all a literary movement devoted to the study of ancient Greek and Latin texts. Its scholars searched out forgotten manuscripts, and they found some long-disregarded works in Europe's libraries. Cicero's letters and Tacitus's histories were significant additions to the Latin corpus. A surge in Greek studies also made texts by Homer and Plato widely available to western Europeans. But the Renaissance owed less to the discovery of new documents than to the development of a new way of reading familiar ones. Medieval scholars had long mined classical literature for useful ideas. But Renaissance scholars valued this literature for its own sake and did their best to grasp the original intent of its authors. As they read, they were excited to discover what they thought was an ancient way of life that confirmed their own.

Most historical eras are named by later generations looking back at the past, for it usually takes time for the significance of events to become clear. But the Renaissance was an era named by the people who lived it. The poet and scholar, Petrarch (1304–1374), witnessed a world convulsed by plague, war, and the breakdown of the church, but he was convinced that his generation was on the brink of a glorious new age—that it was emerging from a long dark period during which civilization had languished. Petrarch defined civilization as the way of life pioneered by the ancient Greeks and Romans, and he believed that it was being reborn in Italy's city-states, in communities that he assumed resembled ancient Athens and Rome. For Petrarch, the previous millennium had been "the middle ages," a period of cultural retreat and retrenchment between the ancient and modern worlds, the eras of true civilization.

The Humanist Agenda   The intellectual leaders of the Renaissance were called humanists, for they advocated the study of humanity (**studia humanitatis**). This should not be taken to imply that they embraced what some Americans have called "secular humanism," an atheistic ideology. That the Renaissance was far from hostile to religion is demonstrated by the abundance of religious paintings from the era that can be found in the collection of any major museum. The humanists did, however, value the material world and secular life more highly than many of their medieval predecessors.

Renaissance humanists were often professional scholars who specialized in rhetoric, the study of language—particularly the works of ancient orators such as Cicero and Seneca. Their more traditional faculty colleagues, the scholastic dialecticians who worshiped Aristotle, believed that the function of language was to construct logical arguments. The humanists, in contrast thought of language as an instrument for persuasion. Reason was all that mattered for the scholastics. But humanists maintained that will and passion were also important, for people were more than reasoning machines. Logic and detached contemplation were not enough; to be convinced of truths and fulfilled as individuals, people needed action, empathy, and engagement with the world.

The humanists' philosophy of life affirmed the values of Italy's urban classes. Humanists believed that people should marry, have families, shoulder political responsibilities, develop their individual talents, and enjoy the beauties and pleasures of the material world. They maintained that a fully human life was packed with action and achievement, and that a fully developed human being was a multifaceted individual who was interested in everything and able to do all things well. This was more than a theory; it was a reasonably accurate description of some of the giants of the Renaissance.

Poets and Prose Writers   Early signs of the Renaissance appear in the work of the poet Dante Alighieri (1265–1321) and emerge more clearly in the writings of two of his fellow Florentines of the next generation: the aforementioned Petrarch and Boccaccio

(1313–1375). All three, as was the medieval custom, wrote in Latin when addressing the scholarly community, but their fame derives in large part from what they wrote in Italian. Humanists were enthusiastic students of the classical languages, but they understood that Latin and Greek had been the speech of ordinary people in the ancient world. They concluded therefore that poets and serious thinkers ought to use the tongues common to the eras in which they live.

Dante's thought was deeply rooted in the Middle Ages, but he lived like a Renaissance intellectual. Most medieval scholars took clerical orders, but not Dante. He married, had a family, and pursued a political career. He became a professional man of letters after his party's fall from power forced him to leave Florence and spend the rest of his life in exile.

Among Dante's Latin works was a treatise (*De vulgari eloquentia*) that urged scholars to break with tradition and write in the vernacular so that a wider audience might profit from their work. Dante practiced what he preached—with phenomenal success. About 1293, while he was still living in Florence, he finished *La Vita Nuova* (*The New Life*), a cycle of lyric poems and prose narratives celebrating his passion for a woman called Beatrice. She was not his wife or mistress, but a woman whom he adored as a feminine ideal—like a medieval courtly lover—from afar. His masterwork was a huge poem written during his years in exile. He called it *Comedia*, not because it was funny, but because—unlike a tragedy—it was a story with a happy ending. *The Divine Comedy*, the title Dante's readers gave his poem, purports to describe a dream in which the poet journeys through Hell and Purgatory to Heaven, where he is granted a vision of God. Dante's guide during the first stages of his trip is the pagan Roman poet Virgil (70–19 B.C.E.). Because medieval scholars interpreted one of Virgil's poems as a prediction of Christ's birth, Virgil served Dante as a symbol for the truths that reason can intuit without the help of faith. Because reason does not require Scripture or revelation to grasp society's need for laws and the enforcement of justice, Virgil can lead Dante through the realms where sinners are punished—Hell and Purgatory. But because reason cannot grasp the mysteries of divine grace, Virgil turns back at the gates of Heaven. Beatrice, Dante's love, then appears to lead him into Paradise. *The Divine Comedy*'s cosmology and theology are medieval, but its respect for the dignity of human nature and human love hints at the emerging Renaissance. Dante has a higher opinion of some of the sinners whose punishments he describes in Hell than of spiritless people who go to their graves having done nothing either good or bad.

Petrarch studied at a university, was ordained a priest, and sought ecclesiastical stipends to support his work. At first glance therefore, his scholarly career looks more conventional than Dante's, but the two men had much in common. Although he did not marry, Petrarch formed an attachment with a woman and was a family man with a son and daughter. He shared Dante's interest in the poetry of courtly love, and his equivalent of Dante's Beatrice was an unidentified woman whom he called Laura. The sonnets she inspired him to write in Italian are his most popular compositions.

The Renaissance shines more clearly in Petrarch's work than Dante's primarily because of the role Petrarch played in sparking the Renaissance's passion for classical literature. He has been called "the father of humanism." Petrarch believed that intellectual darkness had descended on Europe after Rome's fall, but that the light of civilization was being rekindled for his generation. Progress, he argued, required an educational reform based on a curriculum that polished literary skills (Latin grammar, rhetoric, and poetry) and promoted moral edification (Roman history and Greek philosophy). He urged scholars to comb through libraries for forgotten works by ancient authors, and he believed that he and his contemporaries could train themselves to pick up where these giants of the past had left off. He encouraged the use of classical Latin rather than the ecclesiastical Latin that had evolved during the Middle Ages. His most ambitious attempt to honor the classical tradition was a poem entitled *Africa*, a Latin epic on the life of the Roman republican general, Scipio Africanus (237–183 B.C.E.) which dealt with the struggles leading to the Roman Republic's victory over Carthage. In 1341 the people of Rome gathered on the Capitoline Hill to award Petrarch the ancient symbol of achievement, a crown of laurel. Petrarch's love for the classics persuaded him that fame was a noble pursuit, but it did not override his Christian concern for the sin of pride. He took his pagan trophy to the Vatican and dedicated it to God. The people of Rome were less deferential to traditional religious authority. They rose up in 1347, took control of the city, and tried until 1351 to govern it as a new Roman Republic.

Boccaccio, the illegitimate son of a Florentine banker, was Petrarch's devoted disciple. Petrarch's influence persuaded Boccaccio to abandon the poetry and storytelling of his youth and take up classical studies. He wrote a number of books in Latin that served his contemporaries as useful compendia of information culled from ancient sources. The most popular of these were a genealogical encyclopedia of the pagan gods and collections of biographies of famous men and women. His more well-known compositions, however, are his earlier vernacular works, the most famous of which is a collection of bawdy and serious tales entitled *Decameron* (a combination of Greek words for ten and day). It is a fictive record of a hundred stories that ten young Florentine men and women allegedly told to entertain themselves while they hid from the plague in the comfort of a luxurious country house. Like Dante and Petrarch, Boccaccio was inspired to write poetry by love for a woman. But unlike Dante and probably Petrarch, he had a physical relationship with Fiammetta, the lady whom he idolized. When she deserted him, he poured out his anguish in his poetry. The intimacy and personal nature of these poems illustrate the humanist's confidence that the emotions and interior life of the individual are worthy of study and documentation.

Boccaccio's contemporary, the English author Geoffrey Chaucer (c. 1340–1400), shared this faith. Chaucer, like many of the great Renaissance artists and scholars, was a son of the middle classes with a background in business and experience in politics. He is not usually thought of as a Renaissance figure, but he read Italian and modeled some of his poems on Boccaccio's work. Italy's Renaissance would not have spread so readily to the rest of Europe if cultures north of the Alps had not, on their own, been evolving similar values and interests. Chaucer's most popular work, *The Canterbury Tales*, describes a company of pilgrims en route to the shrine of St. Thomas Becket at Canterbury. Chaucer introduces each pilgrim and then narrates the stories each tells to amuse the others. In this way the book resembles Boccaccio's *Decameron*. The characters in *The Canterbury Tales* are not the kinds of abstract or allegorical types found in much medieval literature. They are unique, memorable persons, and Chaucer bestows individuality on his pilgrims by matching descriptions of them with the stories they tell.

Sculptors Vernacular literature helped to spread the Renaissance beyond the narrow circle of humanist scholars, but literature was not the only thing that helped the Renaissance extend its influence. Artists and architects created urban environments that exposed ordinary men and women to the spirit of the new age.

Artifacts of Roman civilization were more abundant in late medieval Italy than they are today, and their influence on Italy's sculptors was apparent as early as the thirteenth century. Real bodies seem to exist beneath the classical robes with which the sculptors Nicola Pisano (c. 1220–1284) and his son Giovanni (c. 1250–1320) draped their figures. Renaissance artists did not, however, simply copy ancient models. They combined the idealism of classical art with a new realism that reflected the humanists' emphasis on the individual. Many ancient Greek statues have a detached, timeless quality that renders them static. Renaissance sculptors tried to convey a greater sense of their subjects existing not in timeless eternity, but in a particular moment. They portrayed ideal types, but with a novel vibrancy. Their medieval predecessors had conceived of statuary as architectural ornament and subordinated it to the lines of the buildings it decorated. But the Florentine sculptor Donatello (1386–1466) revived the art of carving statues that, like many of those in the ancient world, were meant to stand alone and be viewed in the round. They were so natural and imbued with life that some people found them shocking. The early work of Michelangelo (1475–1564), particularly the gigantic *David* he created to stand in front of Florence's town hall, represents the humanist ideals of the Renaissance at their best. *David*'s heroic nudity proclaims the glory of an idealized human body, but the statue's proportions were not dictated by slavish imitation of nature or some mathematical theory about ideal form. The statue's outsized head and hands impart tension to its design, and the intense look on David's face hints at the youth's thoughts as he heads into his unequal contest with the giant, Goliath (I Samuel 17).

Architects The Gothic style that originated in France in the twelfth century had some influence in Italy, but the Mediterranean region clung to the older Romanesque tradition and the elements of classical style which it preserved. The Renaissance's architects drew both inspiration and, unfortunately, building materials from Italy's abundant Roman ruins. Marble, columns, bronze ornaments, and simple bricks were plundered from the remains of ancient buildings for use in new structures. A book on architecture by Vitruvius, a first-century B.C.E. Roman engineer, that came to light in the fifteenth century also helped spread knowledge of the principles underlying classical designs.

Donatello's *David* Cosimo de Medici, the banker and leader of Florence, built a magnificent palace for his family, and in 1430 commissioned the sculptor Donatello to create a statue for its courtyard. Donatello's subject was the biblical account of the fight between David and Goliath. He represented David as a very young man, nude except for elaborate boots, and standing over the head of his slaughtered enemy. *David*, the first free-standing nude human figure to be sculpted since the end of the Roman Empire, is sometimes said to be the first true Renaissance sculpture. *Bargello National Museum, Florence/Canali PhotoBank, Milan/SuperStock*

■ ■

PEOPLE IN CONTEXT Elisabetta Gonzaga (1472–1526)

Feminist historians have pointed out that the Renaissance did not affect men and women in the same way. The respect the period accorded individual talent and achievement in the secular realm—in politics, business, and family life—opened doors for some men. But the ancient Greek and Roman societies that the Renaissance admired were thoroughly patriarchal, and their attitude influenced the humanist perspective on the family. It gave new currency to the ancient belief that women (despite the independence some of them enjoyed in the Roman era) should be confined to the domestic sphere and subordinated to the male heads of their households. Economic reality had more to do with the status of women in most poor and middle-class families than did humanist ideology. These women had to work to help support their families, while the upper class could afford to curtail the activities of its women. This deprived aristocratic women of some of the rights and opportunities they had enjoyed during the medieval era. Their fate ultimately affected their lesser sisters, for the upper class set the standards that the middle class adopted whenever it could afford to. This gave Elisabetta Gonzaga's life an importance she could never have anticipated.

Elisabetta's family, the Gonzaga, ruled the tiny Italian state of Mantua. At the age of 16, Elisabetta wed Guidobaldo da Montefeltro, the duke of Urbino. Her husband was a friend of humanists, an art collector, and the owner of one of the larger libraries in Italy. As the duchess of Urbino, Elisabetta presided over a court famous for its refinement and elegance.

Baldassare Castiglione (1478–1529), the count of Novellata and a distinguished papal diplomat, spent his early career in the service of Urbino's duke. Near the end of his life, Castiglione drew on his extensive experience with court life to write *The Book of the Courtier*, a kind of guidebook to the upper reaches of Renaissance society. The volume, which was translated into numerous languages and remained a best seller for over a century, made Elisabetta famous.

The Book of the Courtier purports to be an account of conversations at Elisabetta's court. It describes a kind of salon

Elisabetta Gonzaga The art of portrait painting flourished during the Renaissance, for it was consistent with the era's celebration of the value of the individual. Scholars have tentatively identified the subject of this painting as Elisabetta Gonzaga. *Dagli Orti (A)/Picture Desk, Inc./Kobal Collection*

where Elisabetta and her guests debate the nature of gentility and, not surprisingly, come to the conclusion that their hostess is the ideal Renaissance lady. Elisabetta is praised for her humanist education—for a knowledge of literature, art, and music that ensures that cultured men find her conversation worthy of their time. But her special vocation as a woman is to keep her court running smoothly and, by her charm and elegant behavior, elevate its tone. The physical activities in which men indulge—riding, hunting, and warfare—are beneath her. She attends to the domestic sphere and serves the wider world by civilizing the men who run it.

Some of Elisabetta's aristocratic female acquaintances were cut from different cloth. They governed states and did not shrink from violence and bloodshed. She, however, actually appears to have been the kind of gracious, but submissive, woman that Castiglione described as the period's ideal. Thanks to the success of his book, generations of Europeans thought of her as the embodiment of a model that all women should aspire to emulate.

Question: To what extent are a society's theories about gender roles an accurate guide to how its people actually behave?

The first of the great Renaissance architects was Filippo Brunelleschi (1377–1446). The dome he designed for Florence's cathedral is an engineering marvel, and it still dominates the city's skyline. Brunelleschi intensively studied Roman buildings, but, like the sculptors of the Renaissance, he did not merely copy his models. He admired their symmetry, simplicity, and proportions, and he used their standard design elements (pillars and round arches). However by the way in which he manipulated these things, he mated Renaissance energy with classical stability.

The most ambitious of the Renaissance's building projects was the reconstruction of Europe's largest church, St. Peter's at the Vatican. The first St. Peter's was a basilican church that Emperor Constantine built for the popes in the fourth century. By the fifteenth century it had deteriorated so badly that Pope Nicholas V (r. 1447–1455) was determined to tear it down and replace it with an entirely new building. The work dragged on for two centuries and involved over a dozen architects, the most

Church of St. Andrea   The facade of the Church of St. Andrea, Mantova, Italy, illustrates the conventions of Renaissance architecture: classical motifs, symmetry, and abstract geometrical forms. It was designed about 1470 by Leon Battista Alberti.

important of whom were Donato Bramante (1444–1514), Michelangelo (1475–1564), and Gianlorenzo Bernini (1598–1680). Michelangelo was not only a superb sculptor, but also a brilliant architect, an extraordinary painter, and a competent poet. The frescoes he created for the vault and altar wall of the Vatican's Sistine Chapel (named for its builder, Pope Sixtus IV, r. 1471–1484) are a miracle of design and execution.

Painters   Unlike sculptors and architects, Renaissance painters had few ancient examples of their art to study. They were inspired by classical sculpture. But to imitate it, they had to invent the techniques to represent three-dimensional figures on the flat surfaces of their paintings.

Medieval artists thought of paintings as pages of text. They drew two-dimensional figures against blank backgrounds and suggested depth and distance simply by painting one figure in front of another. They often combined different scenes from a story in the same composition. A single painting of the Virgin Mary might, for instance, depict the Annunciation, the birth of Jesus, and the Virgin's ascent to heaven. Its overall design could be aesthetically pleasing, but its meaning only became clear when its elements were separated and read like words on a page. Renaissance paintings were not pages, but windows. They framed a scene—a view of a realistic, three-dimensional world into which a spectator could imagine stepping.

The Florentine painter Cimabue (c. 1240–1302) worked in a style that was heavily influenced by Byzantine frescoes and mosaics, but he anticipated the Renaissance by experimenting with ways to suggest three-dimensional space and by giving the faces of his subjects individuality and emotional intensity. Giotto di Bondone (1267–1337), his student, had greater success in achieving these objectives. His human subjects manifest strong feelings and move in real space—like actors in theatrical scenes. The plague that began to spread through Europe in 1348 may explain why Giotto (like his younger contemporary, the poet Dante) had no immediate successor. Eventually, however, a Florentine called Masaccio (1401–1428) picked up where Giotto left off, and an extraordinary number of great artists appeared over the course of a few generations.

Perspective   This painting by Piero della Francesca was executed for the ducal palace in Urbino, Italy. It represents an idealized city-scape and illustrates how Renaissance artists created the illusion of space and depth. The rigor of the composition compels viewers to see the scene from the artist's perspective and is consistent with the humanist's vision of a rationally ordered world. *Piero della Francesca (c. 1420–1492). Italian (Piero della Francesca?). View of an Ideal City. Galleria Nazionale delle Marche, Urbino, Italy. Photo credit: Scala/Art Resource, NY*

Research into how to represent **perspective** (that is, create the illusion of three-dimensional space) began with the study of vision and a search for mathematical formulae that would describe how light enters the eye. Brunelleschi's research into the design of architectural space led to the discovery that if lines are traced along the profiles of buildings and extended as far as possible, they all converge at one point on the horizon. Renaissance artists quickly began to orient their compositions around this so-called "vanishing point." Another architect, Alberti, worked out and published the mathematics governing the projection lines that meet at a vanishing point.

Renaissance painters added a new medium to their art. Medieval and early Renaissance painters usually worked in tempera—that is, with pigments mixed with a binder such as egg yolk. They painted on wooden boards or walls covered with wet plaster.

Leading Artists and Authors of Italy's Renaissance

ca. 1220 Nicola Pisano . . .1284
1240 Cimabue 1302
1250 Giovanni Pisano   . . .1320
1265 Dante 1321
1267 Giotto 1337
1295 Andrea Pisano 1348
1304 Petrarch 1374
1313 Boccaccio 1375
1377 Brunelleschi 1446
1378 Ghiberti 1455
1386 Donatello 1466
1395 Fra Angelico 1455
1399 Della Robbia 1482
1400 Jacopo Bellini 1470
1401 Masaccio 1428
1406 Filippo Lippi 1469
1407 Lorenzo Valla 1457
1415 Piero della Francesca 1492
1429 Gentile Bellini 1507
1430 Giovanni Bellini .1516
1431 Mantegna 1506
1435 Verrocchio 1488
1444 Bramante 1514
1445 Botticelli 1510
1452 da Vinci 1519
1457 Filippino Lippi 1504
1469 Machiavelli 1527
1475 Michelangelo 1564
1475 Giorgione 1510
1483 Raphael 1520
1485 Titian 1576
1500 Cellini 1571
1518 Palladio 1580

Tempera was a restrictive medium, for it dried quickly and its colors did not blend well. Northern European painters were the first to discover that these difficulties could be overcome by mixing their pigments with oils. Oils dried slowly, and translucent oil-based paints could be applied in multiple layers to produce an infinite variety of intense, glowing colors. There is literary evidence for oil painting as early as the twelfth century, but the first great practitioners of the art were the Netherlanders, Hubert (c. 1366–1426) and Jan van Eyck (c. 1390–1441) and Dirk Bouts (1415–1475). They filled their pictures with a wealth of detail—precisely describing the physical world and representing the gleam or texture of all kinds of materials. Northerners also pioneered landscape painting. Medieval artists had sometimes sketched landscapes as background for human activities, but the respect that Renaissance humanists had for the material world made that world a fit subject for study and description in its own right.

Artists working in Venice introduced oil painting to Italy in the late fifteenth century, along with a second northern invention: the use of a canvas on stretchers as a surface for a painting. This expanded the market for art by reducing the cost of pictures and improving their portability. The church's dominance of patronage declined as the prospering urban classes began to commission paintings, and artists found plenty of work producing decorative objects to satisfy the Renaissance's taste for luxury and self-promotion. The era's renewed respect for the individual created a strong demand for a kind of art that had languished during the Middle Ages: portraiture.

The Northern Renaissance

Germany and the Politics of the Holy Roman Empire   Frederick II had largely ignored Germany as he struggled vainly to win control of Italy. After his death and the extermination of his Hohenstaufen dynasty, the German nobles were slow to seat a new king. The German throne remained vacant from 1254 to 1274. In the interim, the country's hundreds of political entities enjoyed independence. Some regions were governed as hereditary duchies, some were ruled by the church, and many were tiny feudal baronies or urban republics and oligarchies. The most interesting political organization that emerged to counter the confusion of the era was a powerful league of cities.

The German merchants who operated in the Baltic region compensated for the absence of a royal protector by forming a corporation (Hanse) and working together to defend themselves. The cities that established the **Hanseatic League** in 1359 did not occupy contiguous territories, but the army and navy they maintained policed the land and sea routes that connected them. At the league's peak, it had about 170 members and exercised a virtual monopoly over Baltic and North Sea commerce. The league dominated the Scandinavian kingdoms, and England and France treated it as if it were a sovereign state. The development of Atlantic trade routes eventually eroded its economic clout, but it survived into the seventeenth century.

A development with more significance for Germany's future took place on the region's eastern borderlands. In 1248, when the family that ruled Austria died out, the duchy of Austria should have returned to its overlord, the Hohenstaufen emperor, Frederick II. However, he was too preoccupied with wars in Italy to assert his claim. A year after Frederick II died, Ottokar II (r. 1253–1278), heir to the kingdom of Bohemia (the region around Prague), annexed Austria. So long as Germany had no king, there was no one to challenge his usurpation of lands that doubled the size of his kingdom.

The situation changed in 1273 when Pope Gregory X (r. 1271–1276) persuaded the German barons to end the squabbling over their vacant throne by electing a king. They chose a minor nobleman, Rudolf of Habsburg (r. 1273–1291) and assumed he would pose no threat to their independence. Because Rudolf's barons feared the powerful king of Bohemia more than their new Habsburg leader, they agreed to help Rudolf reclaim the duchy of Austria for the crown. When the Bohemians withdrew, Rudolf left his tiny ancestral barony on the Aar River east of the Swiss city of Bern and moved his family to Vienna. The Habsburgs reigned there until 1918, when World War I ended their regime.

The German monarchy was elective, and the nobles' preference for weak rulers turned them against the rapidly rising Habsburg family. After Rudolf's death, the electors transferred the royal title to less consequential men. However, in 1310 their attempt to preserve the weakness of their king was frustrated when history repeated itself. Ottokar of Bohemia's family died out, and the Bohemians offered their throne to the son of Germany's king, Henry VII (r. 1308–1313). Henry's family, the Luxemburgs, followed the example set by the Habsburgs and relocated to their new Central-European domain. In 1347 Charles IV (r. 1347–1378), the Luxemburg ruler of Bohemia, became Germany's Holy Roman Emperor. In 1356 he issued a decree that virtually guaranteed that his descendants would keep the imperial title. Charles's Golden Bull (from *bullum*, the seal that ratifies a document) helped to stabilize Germany by limiting participation in imperial elections to the heads of seven great principalities (four secular lords and three archbishops). This established a rough balance of power among the German magnates and ended the pope's meddling in Germany's affairs. Because Charles recognized the independence of the electors, they felt safe in allowing the crown to remain with the Luxemburg family.

In 1440 the Luxemburgs died out and the throne passed to the Habsburgs with whom they had intermarried. By then, the imperial title was largely an empty honor, and the Habsburgs were far less interested in Germany and Italy than in an empire they were building in Central Europe. On their eastern frontier, they faced the rising power with whom the Italians were attempting to come to terms in the late fifteenth century: the Ottoman Turks. As the Ottomans charged up the Danube valley—the route that the Huns, Avars, and Magyars had taken into the heart of western Europe—Habsburg Vienna was the primary obstacle in their path.

The Arts   Political confusion was no more antithetical to cultural progress north of the Alps than it was to their south. But a vibrant medieval tradition lingered in the north that affected how northerners appropriated aspects of Italy's Renaissance. Gothic architecture was far from dead in the late fifteenth century, particularly in England where a refined and delicate "Perpendicular Gothic" style flourished. The minutely detailed realism that characterized the work of northern oil painters (such as Hubert and Jan van Eyck) owed more to the tradition of medieval manuscript illumination than to Renaissance classicism.

Albrecht Dürer (1471–1528) was the first major northern artist to intensively study Italy's Renaissance. He was a citizen of Nuremberg, an independent German city that had extensive commercial ties with Italy. Many of Italy's Renaissance artists were trained in the shops of goldsmiths. Dürer's father was a goldsmith, and Dürer practiced one of the goldsmith's arts: engraving. His interest, however, was not in ornamenting objects, but in the artistic potential of one of the great technological breakthroughs of the era—the printing press, which Johannes Gutenberg had perfected about 1455. Dürer made a name for himself not only as a painter but as an engraver of plates for printing pictures. It was probably a desire to study the works of the Renaissance artists who were pioneering techniques for drawing in perspective that drove him to make several trips to Italy. Dürer immersed himself in the rapidly growing literature dealing with the laws of perspective, and his reading of classical authors and study of ancient statuary convinced him that art should be informed by a close, scientific study of nature. He filled files with detailed sketches of plants, animals, and people and worked these elements into superbly executed woodcuts and engravings. Prints from his blocks and plates were inexpensive enough that, for the first time, people of modest means could purchase the work of an important artist. The printing press not only encouraged the growth of literacy in early modern Europe, but it also acquainted an ever widening spectrum of European society with the arts of the Renaissance.

Northerners came to Italy to study the Renaissance firsthand, but some Italian artists also migrated to northern regions. Leonardo da Vinci (1452–1519), whose *Mona Lisa* may be the most famous portrait from the Renaissance era, was employed by King Francis I (r. 1515–1547) of France. Francis's political aspirations probably explain why he was the first of northern Europe's kings to become a patron of the Renaissance. Whenever the Germans retreated from Italy, the French were tempted to move in. After the extermination of Frederick II's Hohenstaufen dynasty, Charles of Anjou (brother of France's King Louis IX) had seized the kingdoms of Naples and Sicily. Sicily rebelled and broke free in 1282, and France's attempt to establish an outpost in southern Italy eventually came to nought. But in 1525 Francis mounted another expedition in the hope that acquisition of Italian territory would help him balance the growing power of the Habsburgs. He failed spectacularly, but even futile military ventures were culturally significant, for the hordes of foreign soldiers they brought into Italy absorbed Italy's Renaissance culture and took it home.

Northern Humanism The environment of northern Europe shaped the kind of interest that northerners took in the Renaissance. Northern Europe had few inspiring Roman ruins to remind people of the grandeurs of classical civilization. Unlike Italy's powerful urban communities, its towns did not see themselves as successors to the classical world's great city-states, and it was not the pagan past that drew northern scholars to the work of Italy's humanists. The northerners were intrigued by another of the ancient civilization's legacies: the Bible and the church.

The northern Renaissance was energized by a religious revival—the **Modern Devotion**—that originated in the Netherlands in the fourteenth century. It inspired the foundation of quasi-monastic organizations dedicated to charitable work and education. The schools maintained by the most famous of these, the Brethren of the Common Life, were noteworthy for the training they provided in the ancient languages. Italy's humanists had pursued the study of classical Latin and Greek in order to better understand the civilization of ancient Rome and Greece. The northern humanists sought the same linguistic competence, but applied it to intensive study of the Bible.

Desiderius Erasmus (1466–1536), the most prominent of the northern humanists, was the illegitimate son of a learned priest who developed an interest in humanism while visiting Italy. Erasmus was educated by the Brethren of the Common Life and entered the church, which was the traditional way for a scholar to further his career. He became a monk and was ordained a priest, but soon realized he had made a mistake. He found monastic life stultifying, and he was no happier when his superiors sent him to study theology at the University of Paris. The medieval scholasticism that still held sway in Paris repulsed Erasmus and drove him into the humanists' camp.

Erasmus's greatest achievement was a superior edition of the Greek New Testament based on a critical analysis of ancient manuscripts, which scholars used to improve the accuracy of Latin and vernacular translations. Erasmus was, however, much more than an arid philologist whose studies were ends in themselves. Like others of the Renaissance period, he believed that intellectuals should not keep their work to themselves, but rather should use it to benefit the masses. His close examination of the Scriptures inspired him with a vision of early Christianity, and he urged the church to jettison much of the baggage it had accumulated during the Middle Ages and revert to the simplicity of the New Testament era. Authentic Christianity, he believed, was a charitable and selfless way of life guided by a personal experience of God. The best way to restore and build faith, he argued, was to give ordinary people a Bible they could read for themselves. He had little sympathy for clergy who wanted to keep their congregations ignorant and subservient. One of his most popular books, *Praise of Folly*, was a social satire that targeted the clergy. Erasmus was such an outspoken critic of medieval Catholicism that his contemporaries joked that he laid the "egg" that the Protestant reformers hatched. When the Reformation broke out, however, Erasmus—like his friend, the English humanist Thomas More (1478–1535)—was unwilling to leave the Catholic Church. He agreed with the Protestants that the church should be reformed to bring it in line with the New Testament model. However, as a humanist, he preferred a more tempered and rational faith than the leading Reformers preached (see Chapter 13).

The Middle East: The Ottoman Empire

The states that the Seljuk Turks had established in the Middle East in the eleventh century were undermined by the Mongol invasion in the thirteenth century. As they crumbled, other Turks who were pushed west by the Mongol advance took their place. The Ottoman Turks were named for Osman (r. 1299–1326), a chief who settled them in Asia Minor close to the Byzantine city of Nicaea. In 1301 he defeated a Byzantine army, and he and his successors steadily detached territory both from Constantinople's crumbling empire and from neighboring Turkish chiefdoms. The Ottomans' location on the frontier of the Byzantine Empire enabled them to recruit men for a popular holy war with Islam's Christian opponents. In 1331 they took Nicaea. By 1340 they had brought most of Asia Minor under their control and had crossed the Dardanelles into Europe. In 1354 a contender for the Byzantine throne, who wanted their help, allowed them to establish a base at Gallipoli, a fortress commanding a choke point on the channel that links the Black and Aegean Seas. From there they moved into the Balkans and began to encircle Constantinople. In 1389 they defeated the Serbs at the first battle of Kosovo, and a year later the remaining parts of Asia Minor as far east as the Euphrates submitted to them.

Expansion of Ottoman Power   In 1402 Timur the Lame (Tamerlane), the greatest Mongol conqueror since Genghis Khan (see Chapter 11), routed an Ottoman army and killed the sultan Bayezid I (r. 1389–1402). However, the Mongols soon turned their attention elsewhere and left the Ottomans to fight among themselves. A decade of confusion ensued until Mehmed I (r. 1413–1421) finally won the upper hand and began to restore Ottoman unity and territory. His son, Murad II (r. 1421–1451), conquered Greece and the Balkans, and pushed into Hungary. The defeats he gave the Hungarians at the battle of Varna in 1444 and at the second battle of Kosovo in 1448 crippled the Christian state and opened the way for the Ottomans to drive deep into Catholic territory.

Murad's son, Mehmed II, "the Conqueror" (r. 1451–1481), secured the Ottomans' position by winning a prize that had eluded Muslim armies for nearly 800 years. On May 29, 1453, the 20-year-old Turkish sultan took the city of Constantinople—with the help of some European technology. In 1452 a Hungarian gunsmith offered to construct a huge cannon for the last Byzantine emperor, Constantine XI (r. 1448–1453). When Constantine failed to raise the money for the project, the Hungarian approached the Ottomans, who commissioned several pieces of artillery. The largest was a cannon 26 feet long that fired missiles weighing 800 pounds. With weapons like this, it took only a few weeks to pound the impoverished and depopulated capital of eastern Christendom into submission. Venice and Genoa might have helped Constantinople, but they did not want to do anything that risked harming the good commercial relations they wanted to establish with the Ottomans.

The Turks renamed Constantinople Istanbul and turned its great church, the Hagia Sophia, into a mosque. The loss of the last great Christian outpost in the Middle East was a shock to Europe, but it had little practical significance. Constantinople had ceased to protect the eastern frontiers of Christendom, and its new Muslim rulers had no intention of severing its mutually profitable commercial ties with Europe. In fact, Italy actually profited from the disaster that befell Constantinople. Greek scholars fleeing the Ottomans sought refuge in Italy, and their linguistic expertise and libraries helped fuel the Renaissance. Cultural influences also flowed in the opposite direction. Mehmed employed Italian artists and architects. Despite Islam's occasional hostility to representational art, he sat for portraits by one of Italy's great Renaissance painters, Gentile Bellini (1429–1507).

Several things contributed to the Ottomans' success. For one, they never seem to have considered dividing their conquests to provide domains for all a ruler's sons. The sultanate passed intact to only one heir (not inevitably the eldest), and to ensure safety and stability his brothers were killed. Mehmed II formalized this tradition as the Ot-

Mehmed II This portrait of the conqueror of Constantinople is ascribed to the Italian Renaissance artist, Gentile Bellini. The classical style of the arch with which the painter has framed his subject may seem somewhat at odds with Mehmed's eastern dress and appearance, but he obviously would not have thought so. Istanbul and Venice had a long history of close association, and the Ottomans were well informed about developments in Italian politics and culture.

toman law of fratricide. Unique customs also governed how sultans sired their heirs. Their marriages were celibate, and they had their children by concubines. Once a concubine had borne a son, the sultan ended relations with her. This motivated her to focus on the care and preparation of her son to be the winner in the life-and-death struggle for succession to the throne. The relationship that this built between a woman and her son meant that a sultan's mother could become an extremely powerful influence on his government. Once the Ottoman royal house settled in Constantinople and built its lavish residence, the Topkapi Palace, its princes were confined to quarters and raised in luxurious seclusion. This, of course, meant that heirs came to the throne with very little experience of the world. In 1603, due to concerns for the survival of the dynasty, the execution of its princes ended. It then became customary for the throne to pass to the eldest Ottoman prince—often the brother of the previous sultan.

The Ottoman Empire had an extremely diverse population. Although the Ottomans were Muslims, they were exposed to multiple religious influences, for there were different kinds of Islam just as there were different kinds of Christianity. Given that the Ottomans first expanded into Byzantine territory, more of their subjects may initially have been Greek Orthodox Christians than Muslims. Many of the former preferred Muslim rule to domination by the Latin Catholics who had staked claims to Byzantine lands after the Fourth Crusade sacked Constantinople in 1204. Europe's Christians viewed eastern Christians as near heretics and pressed them to submit to the papal church. The Ottomans, by contrast were tolerant of both Christians and Jews. They continued the long-standing Muslim practice of according "the people of the book" a kind of second-class citizenship. Christians and Jews paid special taxes, but were protected and allowed a limited degree of autonomy. Among the taxes they paid, however, was a unique kind of human tribute. Christian boys were taken at a young age, converted to Islam, and educated for special military and governmental service in the corps of Janissaries ("new troops"). Murad I (r. 1362–1389) was said to have founded the Janissaries to counter the influence of the Turkish cavalry. The horse soldiers were supported by grants of land which gave them a degree of independence from the sultan, but Janissaries were the sultan's slaves. Slave armies had a long history in the Middle East. The Seljuk and Mamluk regimes had been founded by formerly enslaved soldiers. The trust the Ottoman sultan placed in the Janissaries led to their occupying many of the posts in his government. The result was a Muslim empire largely managed by recent converts from Christian families.

Mehmed and his successors did not concentrate all their attention on European targets, for they had much to do in the divided Muslim world. In 1502 Shah Ismail I (r. 1502–1524) founded the Safavid Empire in Persia (Iran). Religion complicated the situation, for the Ottomans were Sunni Muslims and the Safavids were Shi'ites (see Chapter 7). Each empire regarded the other as heretical and tried to purge its territory of inhabitants who professed its opponent's faith. In 1514 Selim I (r. 1512–1520) routed a Safavid army and took control of Egypt and the Muslim holy cities of Mecca and Medina. This brought the Arab homeland into the Ottoman Empire, and in 1517 Selim was hailed as caliph, a title implying religious as well as governmental authority (see Map 12–2).

The Ottoman Empire reached a peak of power and magnificence during the reign of Selim's successor, Süleyman (r. 1520–1566). His domain extended east into Iraq and north and west to Hungary and the walls of Vienna, which he besieged in 1529. In 1522 he drove the Knights of St. John from the island of Rhodes and established the dominance of his navy in the eastern Mediterranean. The Ottoman juggernaut rolled on without serious reverses until 1565, when a great armada failed to take the island of Malta south of Sicily.

Ottoman Civilization   The civilization of the Ottoman Empire was shaped by the Turks' devotion to Islamic religious law, the Shariah. Muslims believe the Qur'an literally records God's words. As such, it is a source of immutable laws for human conduct. All such laws are, in theory, already revealed in the life and teachings of the Prophet Muhammad. Additions to the law are therefore impossible, but religious scholars can interpret the law to deal with new situations. The Ottoman ruler's function was not to make law but to enforce the divine law with the help of **muftis** (religious jurists). Islam has no priests, for it has no sacraments. Its religious leaders, like Jewish rabbis, are specialists in the interpretation of sacred texts and laws. Muslim faith in a revealed code of divine laws did not stifle change, but it did make change problematic. New things had to be justified as extensions of Islamic principles.

Paradoxically, the Ottomans' concern for Muslim orthodoxy did not lead to intolerance. The Ottoman Empire was, in fact, far more religiously tolerant than most contemporary European states. The empire had many Jewish, Christian, and even some Shi'ite Muslim subjects, and there were variations within its official Sunni faith. Muslims who found the legalism and formal liturgies of their state religion emotionally unfulfilling turned to Sufism. Sufis were mystics who used music, song, poetry, and dance to cultivate ecstatic trances and visions.

Culturally, the Ottoman Empire was sandwiched between two quite different peoples: the Shi'ite Safavids in the east and the Catholic Europeans in the west. Both were enemies, but the Ottomans absorbed influences from both. Protection and promotion of commercial relations was a priority of Istanbul's government, and the empire allowed Europeans to establish residency in its ports and to travel within its boundaries.

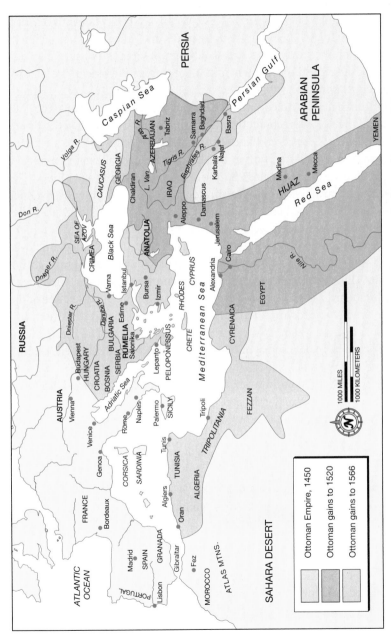

Map 12–2 The Ottoman Empire After the conquest of Constantinople, the Ottoman sultan maintained, as his Byzantine predecessors had, that he stood in a line of rulers that began with Rome's emperors. The lands he controlled included and exceeded those of the ancient eastern Roman Empire.

Question: Given the amount of European territory and Mediterranean shoreline within the Ottoman Empire, should it be classified as a western or an eastern state?

Few Muslims, however, toured Europe. The empire's trade outposts in Europe were usually manned by its Jewish or Christian subjects.

The Ottoman Empire survived into the twentieth century. Its longevity is proof of its ability to evolve and adapt, but whether such adaptation should be viewed as success or decline depends very much on one's perspective. As early as the seventeenth century, some Turkish historians judged their empire to be in decline. The fault, they claimed, lay with sultans who allowed unworthy favorites and corrupt servants to usurp their authority. The power of the central government, if not the empire, did fade in the late sixteenth and seventeenth centuries.

In 1571 the Ottoman navy suffered a major defeat in a battle off Lepanto in the Gulf of Corinth. Although the fleet was rebuilt, the nature of naval warfare changed. The era of great armadas and struggle for dominance of the Mediterranean came to an end as the European states shifted their attention to the Atlantic and global exploration. New and faster kinds of ships, designed for use on the oceans, replaced heavy galleys. The poorly policed Mediterranean was infested by pirates, privateers, and enterprising buccaneers. Ottoman merchants faced problems of a different kind in the Red Sea and Indian Ocean where Portuguese traders were beginning to compete.

The Ottomans continued military activity on some fronts. In 1669 they took over Crete, and in 1683 they staged their final assault on Vienna. But the strain of fighting wars on two fronts (Europe and Persia) sapped the empire's resources. Manpower shortages lowered standards of training, and even the organization and discipline of the elite Janissaries suffered. Warlords appeared in the provinces, raised private armies, and compelled Istanbul to grant them greater degrees of autonomy. The bullion that flooded through Europe from its colonial outposts contributed to inflation. The sultan's government scrambled to meet expenses and resorted to tax farming. The weakening of centralized government did not, however, lead to the fall of the empire. Local governments strengthened and assumed greater responsibility for preserving peace, prosperity, and stability. Rebels did not seek the overthrow of the empire but only to win greater freedom to operate within it.

Europe and Atlantic Exploration

The rise of the Ottoman Empire meant that once again western Europe was under siege from the east. By the late sixteenth century, however, the anxiety this initially created was receding (except perhaps in central Europe, which was directly threatened by Ottoman armies). Europeans had discovered that the Atlantic was not, as their ancestors assumed, an impassable obstacle at their backs. For the first time in history, they shifted their attention from the Mediterranean and the Middle East to the Atlantic and to a much larger world than they had ever imagined existed.

A long tradition of technological and scientific invention lay behind the ships, weapons, and tools that equipped Europeans to embark on the adventures that ultimately spread the influence of their civilization around the globe. Many of the inventions that enabled them to explore and to transform their world were made by eastern peoples and diffused across the Eurasian continents. New farming tools and techniques appeared early in the medieval era. By the eleventh century, the horse's potential for use on the farm and on the battlefield was being fully realized for the first time. The Romans had watermills, but medieval people may have improved on them with ideas from the Chinese. They also harnessed the winds and tides and invented crankshafts and camshafts to improve on machines driven by these powers of nature. They built sawmills to make lumber and water-powered hammers to pulverize ore and full cloth. By the fourteenth century, water-powered bellows—which the Chinese had developed as early as the first century C.E.—were easing the work of ore smelting and forging.

Some societies resist learning from others, but medieval Europeans readily appropriated (and improved on) ideas from many sources. They learned paper-making from the Muslims, and then created a product that competed successfully on the world market. The Chinese or Koreans pioneered printing with inked blocks of wood. The earliest Chinese printed book dates to the ninth century. Europeans adapted ink, paper, metal casting, and die cutting, and Johannes Gutenberg combined these things with a press similar to those used to crush grapes and olives to begin a revolution in European literacy. There may have been only about 100,000 books in all of Europe in 1450, but by 1500, there were probably nine million. Gutenberg may have been preceded in the invention of movable type by the Chinese. But if so, the Chinese did not find the innovation as useful as did the Europeans (perhaps because the Western languages could be printed with a handful of letters, while the Chinese script employed thousands of characters). The Chinese invented gunpowder, perhaps as early as the ninth century, and they may have cast the first metal cannon in the late thirteenth century. These weapons appeared in Europe in the early fourteenth century and led to the armaments that gave later generations of Europeans unsurpassed success in building colonial empires. A Chinese astronomer of the eleventh century is believed to have constructed a mechanical clock. However, his invention, like the model steam turbines built by the Hellenistic Greeks, initially had little impact. Yet, when the clock appeared in Europe at the start of the fourteenth century, it revolutionized human behavior. Once time could be accurately measured, the activities of whole communities could be coordinated and work planned with unprecedented efficiency. Towns all across Europe began to erect clock towers as a public service. The Chinese discovered the properties of magnetized needles and used them as compasses. Compasses and the astrolabe, an ancient Greek invention for making celestial measurements that was improved by medieval Muslims, made voyages easier for sailors. By the thirteenth century, Europeans had ships that relied entirely on sails (not oars). By the fourteenth, they had large vessels with multiple masts and lateen rigging—a Muslim invention that permitted a ship to sail against the wind. A host of innovations that improved sailcloth, rope, carpentry, metals, and navigational instruments contributed to the creation of the ships that enabled Europeans to undertake global exploration late in the fifteenth century.

Portuguese Explorations   The tiny Iberian state of Portugal pioneered European Atlantic exploration. It was highly motivated, for its only access to the Mediterranean (the center of the medieval world's trade network) was through the Straits of Gibraltar, which were controlled by Spanish and Muslim competitors. In 1415 Prince Henry "the Navigator" (1394–1460), third son of Portugal's king, John I (r. 1385–1433), earned his knight's spurs in a battle that won Portugal the Muslim port of Ceuta on the African coast opposite Gibraltar. Henry's subsequent military campaigns were inconsequential, but his sponsorship of voyages of Atlantic exploration paid huge dividends.

The Portuguese initially worked their way down the Atlantic coast of Africa, searching for the source of the gold that Muslim caravans brought across the Sahara Desert from Africa's interior. By 1432, they had discovered the Atlantic islands: the Canaries, Azores, and Madeiras. When these proved suitable for growing sugar, the nearby African continent was raided for slaves to work island sugar plantations. (Slaves were to be found in Renaissance Europe employed as household servants, but it was in regions where plantation systems were profitable that slavery truly flourished.) Successive expeditions inched farther and farther down the African coast until Bartolomeu Dias (c. 1450–1500) rounded the southern tip of the African continent in 1488. In 1498 Vasco da Gama (c. 1460–1524) explored the east coast of Africa and, with the help of Muslim sailors, charted a sea route across the Indian Ocean that linked Portugal to the port of Calicut. News of his return with a cargo of spices (particularly pepper) sent shock waves through the markets of Europe. By importing directly from India, the Portuguese could compete with merchants who used the older overland routes. The Portuguese wasted no time in exploiting their advantage. They dispatched a fleet of ships, negotiated access to Indian ports, and then pushed farther east to Indonesia, China, and Japan.

However, Vasco da Gama was not the first to sail around the African continent. An ancient Carthaginian may have done so, and Arab and Chinese vessels had worked their way down the eastern coast of Africa and into the Atlantic before the Portuguese charted the continent's western coast. One of the puzzles of world history is why Europeans rather than Chinese exploited the sea route between the West and the Far East. The third emperor of the Ming dynasty (1386–1644) built ships that were many times larger than any that his European contemporaries were capable of constructing, and between 1405 and 1433, he dispatched fleets of 60 or more vessels to Africa's eastern coast. His successors, however, terminated the project, and China ceased to explore. What the Chinese had learned of the outside world evidently did not intrigue them, and they may have concluded that the costs of exploration outweighed its potential profits. China did not withdraw from trade and contact with the outside world, but to bolster the claims of its emperor to a unique mandate from heaven, foreign trade was officially described as tribute.

Spanish Explorations   Italy, with centuries of seafaring experience to draw on, produced excellent navigators and cartographers, some of whom were eager to take part in the Atlantic adventure. About 1478 Christopher Columbus (1451–1506), a Genoese sailor and map maker, emigrated to Portugal, where he married the daughter of a ship's captain who had sailed for Prince Henry.

Columbus's study of the geographical information available in his day led him to grossly underestimate the size of the globe. Otherwise, he never would have proposed trying to reach the Far East by sailing west across the Atlantic. Had the Americas and certain Pacific islands not been where they are, no ship of Columbus's day could have survived a journey directly from Europe to the other side of the world. Columbus tried to persuade the Portuguese government to fund an expedition to prove his theory that the shortest route to the Far East lay west. However, Portugal decided that its African explorations, which were just beginning to pay off, were a better investment.

Columbus considered going to France next, but he finally decided to try his luck at the Spanish court. Spain was a new nation, which had been formed in 1469 by the marriage of Queen Isabella I of Castile and King Ferdinand V of Aragon (joint reign, 1474–1504). The royal couple was intrigued by Columbus's proposal, but the time was not propitious for a new project. In 1484 Ferdinand and Isabella had set out to conquer Granada, Spain's sole remaining Muslim state. Until that costly campaign was resolved, they were not prepared to take on anything else. Granada finally surrendered on January 2, 1492. Thereafter, things moved quickly. Columbus received his commission on April 17, set sail with a fleet of three small ships on August 3, and 70 days later planted Spain's standard on what was probably one of the Bahamian islands—although he was certain that it was not far from Japan. Columbus had been lucky. By striking south to avoid the Portuguese, he had discovered the prevailing winds that offered the easiest passage across the Atlantic.

Columbus's largest ship ran aground in the Caribbean, and he was forced to leave half his crew (44 men) behind when he hastened back to Spain to announce that he had reached outlying portions of India and contacted "Indians." He received a hero's welcome, a title of nobility, and a much larger fleet for a return to what he claimed, until the end of his days, was the perimeter of Asia. The four expeditions Columbus led explored the Caribbean and the coast of Central America, but they never found the passage to Japan that their admiral was certain had to be in the vicinity.

England occupied the extreme western end of the lengthy medieval trade routes that linked Europe with the Far East. The shorter Atlantic passage that Columbus claimed to have found promised to be an economic godsend for England. News of his discoveries therefore persuaded King Henry VII (r. 1485–1509) to fund an expedition by another Genoese explorer, whose anglicized name was John Cabot (1450–1498). In 1497 Cabot reached islands off the coast of Canada and returned to England to inform the king that he had made contact with Asia somewhere north of Japan. A second voyage in 1498 took Cabot as far south as Labrador.

The Discovery of the New World   This woodcut is from a series created (c. 1493) to publicize Columbus's discoveries. Columbus was never shaken in his belief that he had reached the outer rim of the orient. The exotic look of the boat and the eastern costumes of the men who are exchanging items with the naked natives may have been intended to support this claim.

England's financiers contemplated more expeditions, but because Cabot had found nothing of value aside from some furs, investors and plans were slow to materialize.

In 1500 a Portuguese fleet bound for India via the African route went off course and sighted a land its leader named Brazil (for a species of tree that grew there). A year later, the Portuguese dispatched a follow-up expedition piloted by Amerigo Vespucci (1454–1512), one of Columbus's associates. Vespucci was among the first to suggest that what the Europeans were exploring was not the outer reaches of Asia, but a "New World"—new to Europeans that is, but obviously not to its indigenous peoples. The geographers who used his reports labeled the continent whose outline was emerging on their maps "the discoveries of Amerigo" ("America"). Any lingering doubts about the place America occupied on the globe were resolved in 1522 when the remnants of a Spanish fleet that had set out under the command of Ferdinand Magellan (1480–1521) completed the first circumnavigation of the Earth (see Map 12–3).

Columbus never found the gold he promised his Spanish sponsors, but in 1519 the longed-for wealth finally began to flow. Hernán Cortés (1485–1547) invaded Mexico and looted the treasures of the Aztec Empire. Ten years later Francisco Pizarro (c. 1475–1541) overthrew the New World's other major civilization, the empire of Peru's Inca. Small companies of Spanish soldiers subdued large native populations with surprising ease, for the invaders had advantages that more than compensated for their inferior numbers. Their weapons were vastly superior, and they had horses—animals that were new to the Americas, which had no comparable indigenous species. Native armies had never before confronted anything as formidable as a force of mounted warriors with guns. But an unanticipated development further tipped the scales in favor of the Europeans. Whether they intended to or not, they became practitioners of germ warfare. Migration and trade among the peoples of Asia, Africa, and Europe had exposed the inhabitants of these regions to many diseases. Over time, their descendent's evolved the ability to minimize the effects of what became familiar infections. Lack of similar exposure meant that the peoples of the western hemisphere had different immune systems that left them defenseless against diseases that were minor childhood afflictions for Europeans. Smallpox, chicken pox, measles, and other illnesses swept ahead of the European invaders and cleared the way for their conquests. Native populations were quickly reduced to such a low level that the European entrepreneurs who established plantations and mines in the New World had to reconstitute its workforce by importing slaves from Africa—people who shared the Old World immunities. It is difficult to reconcile the brutality with which Columbus and Europe's later explorers treated Native Americans with their sincere desire to baptize them and bring them into the Christian community. Some missionaries did protest the Europeans' excesses and abuses, but the profits to be made from slave labor in mining and plantation agriculture proved too tempting even for the church to forego.

In 1494 the pope presumed, as Christ's vicar on Earth, to draw a longitudinal line that divided the globe into Portuguese and Spanish spheres of influence. Territories east of his "**Line of Demarcation**" (which ran through Brazil) were declared Portuguese, and anything to the west was declared to be Spain's property. Other European

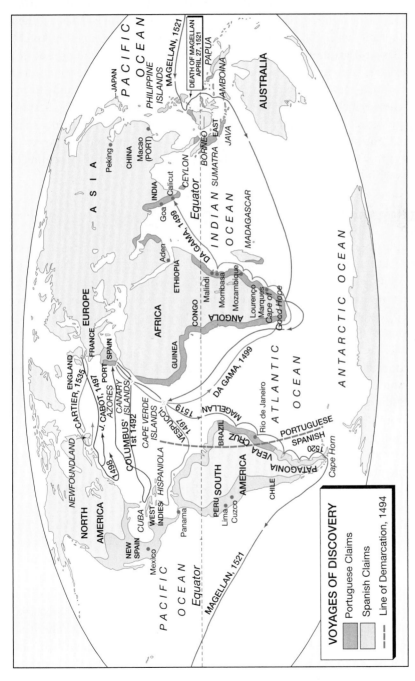

Map 12–3 Europe's Initial Global Explorations This map shows the routes taken by the Portuguese, Spanish, English, and French explorers as they ventured into the Atlantic and beyond.

Question: What effect would the increasing attention that Europe gave to global exploration have on relations between the Christian and Muslim worlds?

351

nations with access to the Atlantic refused to be restrained by the papal decree. Three years after the pope's proclamation, John Cabot staked England's claim to the New World, and in 1534 France sent out the first of its explorers, Jacques Cartier (1491–1557). He made four trips to a land he thought the natives called Canada (their word actually meant "village"). Cartier searched for a waterway through the Americas to the Far East and a rumored North American kingdom that was said to be as rich in gold as Mexico's Aztec Empire. Although he found neither, France sent out more explorers and added the Mississippi watershed and some Caribbean islands to the American territories it claimed. In 1595 tiny Holland established bases in the East Indies to compete with the Portuguese. England and France eventually followed. As Europeans moved out into the world, they spread their civilization and the power of their colonial empires around the globe. The twenty-first century is still struggling to come to terms with the consequences.

KEY QUESTION | Revisited

A handful of European explorers needed only a few decades to change the course of world history. They cleared the way for Europe's civilization and the political and economic power of its colonial empires to transform life for peoples around the globe. European society was as profoundly affected as any of the alien cultures its colonizers encountered. The gold, silver, and raw materials that poured into Europe greatly expanded its economy. Luxury consumables, such as sugar, rice, and spices, became much more affordable. The new plants that explorers brought back for cultivation in Europe revolutionized society at every level. Europeans tasted maize, squash, and tomatoes for the first time and discovered the pleasures of tobacco and chocolate. They eagerly took to coffee, an Ethiopian beverage that spread through the Muslim world in the fifteenth century. Tea from the Far East likewise entered the European market in the sixteenth century. The potato, which was indigenous to Peru and Chile, flourished in Europe's cool, wet climate and began to replace wheat as the staple food of the poor. This eased famines and encouraged population growth. The national cuisines for which European countries are famous today feature foods, drinks, and flavors that were unknown to Europeans until relatively recently.

The New World's creation of a new Europe caused Europeans some anxiety. The flood of information that suddenly became available to them about peoples, places, and things whose existence they had not previously suspected posed immense challenges. For the first time, they became aware of viable alternatives to their way of life, and this forced them to rethink the fundamental assumptions of their civilization and religion. There was no hint in their histories and traditions of anything that would prepare them for what they were discovering and experiencing. The past, therefore, began to seem less reliable as a guide for comprehending the present and plotting the future. Europeans were, however, accustomed to dealing with change. Their late medieval Renaissance, despite its name, was less a rebirth of the past than a creative response to it. It revived beliefs and institutions of an earlier age, but treated these things as the beginning, not the end, of its search for understanding and a better life.

There was always, however, a tempting alternative that has never lost its appeal for some people. Change is costly. What one person counts as gain another experiences as loss. The common strategy for opposing change is to insist that all essential truths have been revealed and are already known. The responsible thing to do, therefore, is to cling firmly to traditional beliefs and values and reject anything that might challenge them. There is wisdom in warning people not to let an appetite for novelty obscure the hard-won lessons of earlier generations. However, excessive reverence for the past diminishes curiosity about the world, acquiesces when limits are placed on intellectual freedom, and hampers experimentation and exploration. It can lead to stagnation and ultimate irrelevance. What people do with their past—their history—goes a long way toward determining their future.

Review Questions

1. Why did the Renaissance originate in Italy before spreading elsewhere?
2. What is humanism? What medieval ideas and values did it challenge?
3. What features do the different arts of the Renaissance—sculpture, architecture, and painting—have in common? How do they relate to humanism?
4. How did the Renaissance change as it moved into northern Europe?
5. Is the history of the Ottoman Empire and Islam part of Western history?
6. How did the discovery of the New World change the way Europeans thought about themselves?

Please consult the Suggested Readings at the back of the book to continue your study of the material covered in this chapter. For a list of documents on the Primary Source DVD-ROM that relate to topics in this chapter, please refer to the back of the book.

Topics in This Chapter

The Lutheran Reformation • The Swiss Reformation • The Catholic Reformation • The Habsburg-Valois Wars • England's Ambivalent Reformation • Convergence of Foreign and Domestic Politics: England, Spain, and France • The Final Religious Upheavals

13 Reformation, Religious Wars, and National Conflicts

Why should we tear the world apart arguing over obscure things which are incomprehensible or arguable or useless? The world is filed with anger, hostility, and strife.

—Desiderius Erasmus, *Sponge to Wipe Away the Aspersions of Hutten*

KEY | Question

How do civilized societies justify war?

The humanist scholar Erasmus (c. 1466–1536) was dismayed to witness the unintended fruits of his labors. His critical studies had revealed errors in the traditional Latin text of the Bible, and his witty satires had lampooned corrupt clergy. But he had intended to promote reform, not rebellion, and his expectation was that rational debate would lead to a new and better consensus on matters of faith. Instead, he found himself witnessing the birth of an era of warfare in the name of religion. Wars are not rare in human history, but a congruence of forces (rivalry among monarchies, the class struggles of a capitalistic economy, opposing belief systems, and a host of other things) made them especially abundant in sixteenth- and seventeenth-century Europe. People in almost every era have grievances that might lead to war, but they do not always act on their sense of wrong or always find the same issues worth fighting for. Therefore, it is important for them to learn what history can teach about motivations for shedding blood. How can it be that a war that seems senseless to some is, to others, worth the sacrifice of life itself?

The Reformation of the sixteenth century ended the medieval church's monopolistic control over the practice of the Christian faith in Europe. Confronted for the first time with religious pluralism, Europeans reacted violently. Wars flared on all sides as they took up arms to defend one variety of Christian faith from another. Catholics warred with Protestants,

Queen Elizabeth I England's first Queen Elizabeth (1533–1603) struggled to navigate the currents of an extremely turbulent era. She was about 47 when she sat for this portrait by the Italian painter Federico Zuccari (c. 1542–1609).

but sometimes Protestants sided with Catholics against other Catholics or other kinds of Protestants. Sometimes the leaders of opposing factions made suspiciously opportunistic conversions. Wars fought for sincerely held religious reasons could obviously also have other causes.

The explanations that people give for their quarrels are not always accurate or sufficient. Because civilized people have consciences that require them to justify violent acts, they prefer to think that when they commit mayhem, they do so for a noble purpose. The personal advantage a victory may bring is only a pleasant (if well-deserved) byproduct of their action. The most exalted of motivations is fidelity to God or, in secular terms, commitment to an ultimate value. Although the West's major religions—Judaism, Christianity, and Islam—urge people to live together in love and peace, they have often inspired hatred and slaughter. Secular ideologies, such as communism, fascism, nationalism, and democracy, have done the same. It is reasonable, therefore, to ask whether faith (in either a sacred or secular ideal) is a cause for war, a pretext for war, a precondition for war, or a preventative of war. A civilized state promotes specific religious and secular ideals to provide its people with a context that gives their lives meaning. Sometimes, however, a society resorts to barbarism in the name of its civilizing ideals. It is vitally important to understand how human beings come to terms with this morally ambiguous situation.

The Lutheran Reformation

The Reformation sprang from ground tilled by the humanists of Italy's Renaissance. The humanists believed that Western civilization and Christian faith had been corrupted over the centuries, but that their original natures could be restored by studying ancient texts. Humanism was, however, largely confined to an intellectually elite segment of society, while the Reformation was a mass movement—something that would not have been possible before the invention of the printing press and the subsequent rapid spread of literacy. The Reformation's theologians shared the humanists' belief that ancient wisdom would correct the errors of the recent past. But their enthusiasm was not for paganism's classical culture. It was for the "apostolic" Christianity of the early church.

Luther   Martin Luther (1483–1546), the man whose personal religious struggle became a catalyst for the Protestant Reformation, was not inclined to rebellion by either nature or education. Until middle age, he led a very conventional life, and he never abandoned a certain fundamental conservativism. Although he claimed peasant origins, his father was actually an upwardly mobile member of the middle class who could afford to give his son a good education. Luther completed his arts degree at the University of Erfurt in 1505 and then began to study law in preparation for a secular career. But after a few months, a growing anxiety for the state of his soul led him to do what highly motivated medieval Christians had been doing for centuries. He turned his back on the world, dropped out of school, and entered a monastery. He completed the novitiate, took the vows of an Augustinian monk, and in May 1507 was ordained a priest. He earned a doctorate in theology, and his order assigned him to lecture at the University of Wittenberg in Saxony.

Luther was 34 years old before anything caused him to question his medieval Catholic faith. He had been taught to think of himself as a sinner destined for judgment by a righteous and angry God. Fear of God and of eternal punishment had driven him to take monastic vows, but the fasts, prayers, and disciplines of the monastic life failed to bring him an assurance of salvation. Sometime after 1512, however, he had a kind of conversion experience—a burst of insight prompted by reading the letters of the Apostle Paul (particularly the Epistle to the Romans). Paul, according to the New Testament's Book of Acts, had not wanted to become a Christian and was actively persecuting the church when God suddenly intervened, bestowed faith on him, and made him a Christian. Luther concluded that what had been true for Paul was true for all Christians. They did not earn salvation by doing good works; salvation was a gift God freely gave them while they were still sinners. It could not be earned, and human beings could not comprehend God's motives in bestowing it.

Luther's resolution of his personal crisis of faith did not turn him into a reformer or a critic of the church, for he did not believe that he had discovered anything revolutionary. He had only understood what was plainly laid out for everyone in the Bible. Therefore, he settled back into his routine as a college professor and might never have been heard of had it not been for a chance encounter in 1517 with a Dominican friar named Johann Tetzel (c. 1465–1519).

In 1514 an ambitious German clergyman, Albert of Brandenburg, sought a favor from the pope. At the age of 23, Albert was already bishop of two dioceses, but now he wanted a third: the archdiocese of Mainz, one of Germany's most important sees. Pope Leo X (r. 1513–1521) agreed to sell Albert the office and to license a sale of indulgences in Germany (by men like Tetzel) to help raise the money to pay for it. An **indulgence** was a dispensation from the need to do penance for one's sins. Church doctrine held that while God freely forgave the guilt of sin, sinners still owed compensation for the moral damage caused by their sin. The souls of the dead who had not fully atoned for their sins in life were sent to Purgatory to complete their penances before being admitted to heaven. Originally, the church granted indulgences as an act of mercy or as a reward for self-sacrificial service. An indulgence would release a Christian from a penance that proved too severe or protect a crusader who died fighting for the faith in a foreign land without receiving absolution. In 1343, however, a pope opened the way for indulgences to be granted with unprecedented liberality. He declared that the church possessed an infinite "treasury of merit," a vast spiritual reservoir of grace, that it could draw on to pay the debts of individual sinners—both dead and alive. The temptation for the church was then to begin to grant indulgences from this inexhaustible source for more and more reasons. When it showed its gratitude to generous donors by dispensing them from the penalties of their sins, it opened itself to the charge that it was selling salvation.

Martin Luther certainly believed that Johann Tetzel was doing this, for Tetzel devised a thoroughly modern marketing campaign to sell Pope Leo's indulgences. He dispatched advance men to whip up customer demand. He organized parades with banners and songs, and composed what may be history's first advertising jingle: "When a coin in my coffer rings, a soul from Purgatory springs!" Luther's understanding of the Christian faith rested not only on the tradition of the church but on his study of the New Testament. He believed that Tetzel, by claiming to be able to sell what God freely gave, was committing fraud and endangering souls. He also believed that it was his duty as a pastor to expose Tetzel, whom he assumed was operating on his own initiative without sanction from the church. Following medieval scholastic tradition, he proposed debating 95 propositions relating to indulgences. Tradition holds that he nailed them to the door of his Wittenberg church. If he did, this was not an attack on the church. Church doors served as community bulletin boards, and all sorts of notices were posted on them. The fact that Luther wrote his 95 theses in Latin suggests that they were intended for his fellow scholars and not meant to rouse the populace.

When the debate Luther stirred up began to hurt the sale of indulgences, Archbishop Albert asked the pope to silence the annoying monk. The pope was willing, but there was a complication. Luther's overlord was Frederick the Wise, the Elector of Saxony (r. 1486–1525), one of the princes who chose the Holy Roman Emperor. Frederick was no proto-Protestant. (He had one of the largest collections of holy relics in Europe.) He was, however, not about to let the pope compromise his sovereignty by intervening in his territory. He took Luther under his wing, and Luther suddenly found himself in a theological dispute that was also a high-stakes political struggle.

The Political Context   In June 1519 the election of the Habsburg heir, Charles V (r. 1519–1556), as Holy Roman Emperor created a situation that gave men like Frederick reason to be protective of their sovereignty. The 19-year-old emperor's sprawling domain included Austria, Hungary, Bohemia, the Netherlands, Spain, Sicily, Sardinia, the Kingdom of Naples, and overlordship of Germany and Italy (see Map 13–1). Charles posed a threat to every ruler in Europe, and Germany's lords were particularly worried about maintaining their independence. The Reformation provided them with an excellent justification for challenging the authority of the Catholic emperor.

In 1521 Charles summoned Luther to appear before a **diet** (Germany's equivalent of England's Parliament and France's Estates General) in the city of Worms. Luther had never intended to break with the church, but a series of pamphlets he wrote to explain his beliefs argued for positions that were at odds with medieval Catholic tradition. They articulated three principles common to most forms of Protestantism. The first was that salvation is by faith alone—that it is a gift from God that cannot be earned by human effort. The second was that the Bible (not the pope or the tradition of the church) is the primary authority a Christian must obey. And the third maintained that every Christian has a direct relationship with God that does not depend on the church and mediation by its priests. When the church ordered Luther to recant these beliefs, he refused. To do so, he claimed, would be to violate his conscience, the highest court to which each individual is ultimately accountable.

The emperor and the diet condemned Luther as a heretic, but Frederick the Wise saved him by spiriting him away to a remote castle. He passed his time in hiding by translating the New Testament into colloquial German. His insistence at Worms that private conscience and the Bible were the highest authorities to which a person should be held accountable implied that ordinary men and women were entitled to have Bibles they could read for themselves. Vernacular translations of the Scriptures already existed,

Map 13–1   The Empire of Charles V   Charles's empire was the product of a series of carefully plotted dynastic marriages that made him the heir to lands scattered across Europe.

Question: Can an empire consist of scattered states, or must it consolidate its territory in order to survive?

but they were based on the Vulgate, the Latin translation of the Greek text that Saint Jerome had made in the early fifth century. The Renaissance humanists had labored to recover and improve the accuracy of the ancient texts that were the primary sources of Western civilization, and Luther built on their work. He based his translation on the best Greek text available—an edition that Erasmus published in 1516. Luther's German New Testament appeared in print in 1522, and it was an instant success. Within a decade, nearly 200,000 copies had been sold. A companion version of the Old Testament did not appear until 1534, however, for its preparation required delving into Hebrew manuscripts with the assistance of other scholars. Luther's German Bible had tremendous influence on the development of the German language.

During Luther's absence from the public stage, the Reformation proceeded without him. Events took an alarming course. Luther's opponents had warned him that his insistence on the autonomy of each individual's conscience threatened the breakdown of society by undermining respect for authority, and Luther feared that they might be right. Some of his self-proclaimed followers vandalized churches and monasteries, seized their property, and made radical changes in traditional religious practices.

In the spring of 1524 the situation threatened to spin completely out of control. A peasant uprising spontaneously erupted in southwestern Germany. It found leaders among the mercenary soldiers employed by the empire and rapidly spread. The authorities were caught off guard, for many of their regular troops had been committed to campaigns in Italy. Early in 1525 negotiators considered a multiple-point plan for restoring order. The peasants wanted the abolition of serfdom and burdensome dues and taxes, and they also wanted the right to choose their own clergy. Luther had justified his rebellion against the church by an appeal to Scripture, and the peasants seized on his arguments to ground their revolt against the state. They even offered to submit their demands to Luther and a board of mediators and relinquish any that were proven to be contrary to Scripture.

The uprising was initially restrained, but became increasingly violent as it spread. A particularly radical faction materialized around Thomas Müntzer, a university-educated man whom Luther had recommended for a pastorate. Müntzer challenged the authority of scholars like Luther by claiming that the inspiration of the Holy Spirit could give simple people religious knowledge in addition to that derived from the study of Scripture. He urged his followers to seize control of towns, drive out their opponents, and establish communities governed by leaders who were directly inspired by God. Müntzer preached the imminence of the Apocalypse and the bloody struggles that were prophesied to precede Christ's return. Luther initially tried to steer a middle course between the peasants and Germany's princes, but he became alarmed as the increasing radicalism of Müntzer and the rebels threatened to undermine support for the Reformation. In 1525 he published an intemperately worded pamphlet, *Against the Robbing and Murdering Hordes of Peasants*, that urged the German nobles to "smite, slay, and stab" the peasants—claiming that nothing is more "devilish than a rebellious man." God had empowered princes, he said, to maintain order and they were justified in doing whatever was necessary to stamp out rebellion. As their troops began to return from Italy in mid-1525, the princes quickly put down the divided and poorly led rebels. Müntzer was executed, and thousands of peasants were hunted down and killed.

Luther's fundamental instincts were conservative. He feared disorder, and there was much about the medieval church to which he was emotionally attached. Seeing no other option, he concluded that the head of the state, whom he believed was charged by God with maintaining order in society, had the right to decide what kind of church he would tolerate and to use force to require his subjects to conform to its practices. Luther therefore filled the void of leadership he had created when he repudiated the pope by endorsing state control of the church.

Luther had inadvertently unleashed disorder and instability on the world. As he aged and struggled with illness, he became increasingly intolerant of opposition and continuing conflicts. He refused to compromise with other Reformers, and he turned against the Jews, who he had once hoped would convert to his renewed version of Christianity. In 1543 he published a series of harshly worded pamphlets, with such titles as *The Jews and Their Lies*, that have caused some people to brand him, fairly or unfairly, as an anti-Semite.

The power to suppress rebellion that Luther said God gave to secular leaders might have been used by Emperor Charles V to squelch the Reformation had crises on other fronts not distracted him. However, a decade passed before Charles could give his full attention to events in Germany. In the interim, Lutheranism spread widely, particularly in urban areas. Its empowerment of the individual appealed to humanist scholars and their students at universities, and these men scattered through Germany preaching and leading public discussions of Luther's call to return to the religious practices described in the New Testament. Luther had poetic gifts, and the hymns he composed were effective instruments for proselytizing the masses. He authored a flood of pamphlets that poured off the new presses, which also issued woodcut prints and cartoons—a new form of highly effective propaganda. Some rulers were attracted to Protestantism by the excuse the Reformation provided for confiscating church property and setting up state-controlled churches. In the 1530s, the king of Sweden—the dominant Scandinavian monarch—established Lutheranism as his country's official religion, and Denmark and Norway soon followed suit.

In 1530 Charles convened a diet at Augsburg and gave the Lutherans a year in which to return to the Catholic faith or face dire consequences. This prompted some of the Lutheran states to form the Schmalkaldic League, a military alliance named for the town where its leaders met. Civil war was averted when problems elsewhere in Charles's sprawling empire prevented him from acting on his threat. He was not able to return to Germany until 1546. A year later, he defeated the armies of the Schmalkaldic League, but Catholic France helped the Lutherans recover. Catholic rulers were no more eager for Charles to unite and control Germany than were their Lutheran colleagues.

Charles finally concluded that his huge empire could not be governed by one person. When he retired in 1556, the eastern Habsburg territories were being administered by his brother Ferdinand (r. 1558–1564), and he assigned responsibility for his western possessions—including Spain and the Netherlands—to his son Philip II (r. 1556–1598). In 1555 another diet that met at Augsburg arranged a truce between Lutherans and Catholics. On the assumption that people of different faiths could not live together, it decreed that each prince should decide for himself whether his state would be Catholic or Lutheran. His subjects would then have to either conform or emigrate to a place where their faith was legal. The **Peace of Augsburg** lasted until 1618, but by polarizing Germany, it created the conditions for one of Europe's most devastating conflicts, the **Thirty Years' War** (1618–1648).

The Swiss Reformation

Martin Luther was neither the first nor the only person to challenge the authority of the papacy on the basis of a reading of the Scriptures. Peter Waldo had done so in the twelfth century. A group of Franciscan friars, the Spirituals, had done so in the thirteenth century. The English theologian, John Wyclif, had followed suit in the fourteenth century, and his writings inspired the Bohemian reformer, John Hus, to launch a successful reform movement in the early fifteenth century. It was, however, one thing for the church's critics to agree that Christians should be guided by Scripture and another for them to agree on what the Scripture said. Luther's conservative practice was to allow traditional customs that were not mentioned in the New Testament to continue in use so long as they did not contradict Scripture. However, an independent

Martin Luther The printing press made leading figures of the Reformation, such as Martin Luther, the first media stars. This likeness of the reformer is from the workshop of Lucas Cranach the Elder (1472–1553), painter to the court of Luther's protector, Duke Frederick of Saxony. It may have been executed about 1529. Oil portraits were sometimes copied in engravings or woodcuts to produce inexpensive prints for distribution to the masses.

reform movement that began in Switzerland was more radical. It insisted on wiping the slate clean and restoring only what the Bible mandated, but even this rigorous approach failed to produce consensus.

Zwingli

Ulrich Zwingli (1484–1531), the first major figure of the Swiss Reformation, became a reformer thanks in large part to the humanist education that prepared him for the Catholic priesthood. Like the great humanist biblical scholar Erasmus, he believed that the study of the New Testament would sweep away medieval superstition and bring about the moral regeneration of Christian society. Zwingli was a powerful orator, and his gifts served him well when, in 1519, he was assigned to fill the pulpit of the chief church in the Swiss city of Zurich.

Zwingli used sermons that explicated biblical texts to persuade his congregation to embrace reform. His study of the New Testament led him to question traditional pious customs (such as fasting and priestly celibacy) that had no scriptural basis. It also led him to the conclusion that churches should be purged of art and musical instruments, for there was no New Testament precedent for the presence or use of such things. Zwingli could also find no support for the Catholic doctrine of transubstantiation. He argued that the Eucharist, the ritual meal that Jesus directed his disciples to celebrate, was not a sacrament (a divine mystery in which people literally partook of the body and blood of Christ) but only a symbol, a ritual commemoration that reminded the faithful of Christ's work. Luther passionately disagreed, and his opposition to Zwingli hampered the attempts of Protestant leaders to cooperate against their enemies. In 1529 Philip of Hesse (r. 1509–1567), the leader of the Lutheran princes, arranged a meeting between Luther and Zwingli. Charles V was preparing to attack Germany's Lutherans. (They had begun by then to be called Protestants because of their protestations against Charles's policies.) Philip hoped that a united front would strengthen the Protestant cause, but it was not to be. Luther insisted that Christ's flesh and blood were in some sense truly present in the Eucharist, and he was appalled by Zwingli's reduction of the central Christian mystery to a mere symbol. Swiss and German Protestants declined to work together, and in 1531 Zwingli died in a war with Swiss Catholics. Luther did not lament his passing.

The Anabaptists   Luther considered Zwingli a radical, but some of Zwingli's fellow Swiss did not think that he was radical enough. Zwingli convinced them that the Bible was the sole authority in faith, but they were frustrated by his cautious approach to enforcing its precepts. In 1523 they took matters into their own hands and alarmed the authorities by smashing religious art and demanding an immediate end to the Roman mass. When they met resistance, they withdrew from society into communities of their own. They called themselves the Swiss Brethren, but their opponents dubbed them Anabaptists (Rebaptizers). They insisted on baptizing adult converts who had been baptized as children because they considered infant baptism to be unbiblical and therefore invalid.

The Anabaptists advocated separating from society and establishing elite communities of "saints" governed solely by Scripture. Their eagerness to recreate biblical societies led some of them to endorse practices, such as polygamy and communal ownership of property, that are in the Bible but that were out of step with the widely held convictions of their contemporaries. A literal reading of the Bible's apocalyptic passages also convinced some Anabaptists that the end of the world was at hand, and this prompted more radical behavior. In 1534 a group of Anabaptists seized the German city of Münster and purged it of all people who did not profess their faith. Lutherans and Catholics joined forces to retake the city, and the determination of the authorities to suppress the Anabaptist movement caused some Anabaptists to moderate their behavior. They gave up hope of mastering the world and retreated to parts of Europe where they could live unmolested. Some (the Mennonites, Hutterites, and Amish) eventually emigrated to North America and established communities that have endured and that still continue the way of life that their founders decreed to be godly.

Calvin and the Reform Tradition   Lutheranism did not spread as widely as the brand of Protestantism named for John Calvin (1509–1564), a Frenchman who eventually settled in Geneva. Like Luther, Calvin was the son of a family newly risen to the middle class, raised a Catholic, and educated for the priesthood. At the University of Paris, he made the acquaintance of humanists, but in 1528 his father ordered him to give up his theological studies and enter the law school at the University of Orléans. Unlike Luther, he completed his degree, and legal training shaped his work as a theologian and reformer.

On May 21, 1534, at the age of 25, Calvin took a step that radically altered his circumstances. Having been persuaded of the truth of Protestantism by an experience that he described as a burst of insight, he resigned the posts in the Catholic Church that provided his income. His change of mind owed much to humanism, but he did not share the humanists' optimism about human nature. Like Luther, the Apostle Paul, and the early Latin theologian Augustine of Hippo, he believed that human beings were captive to sin and lost unless God intervened to save them.

Calvin was a subject of the French monarch, Francis I (r. 1515–1547). Francis was a patron of the Renaissance and was sympathetic with aspects of humanism, but he had no motive for backing the humanists' push for radical church reform. The papacy had ceded the French king virtual control over the Catholic Church in France, and Francis did not want anyone to interfere with an institution that had become one of the instruments of his power. In October 1534, after militant reformers plastered Paris with posters attacking the mass, the king struck hard at suspected Protestants.

Calvin fled and found asylum in the Swiss city of Basel, and there, in August 1535, he published a rigorously rational explication of Protestant faith, *The Institutes of the Christian Religion.* The book was immediately popular and influential. Luther was a brilliant polemicist who dashed off thoughts in response to specific situations. This resulted in some gaps and inconsistencies in his writings that make their interpretation difficult. Calvin, however, was a systematic thinker who, in lawyerly fashion, developed a complete, succinct, and tightly reasoned case for Protestantism. Catholics, with centuries of scholarship to draw on, were well-prepared for theological debates; Calvin suddenly leveled the playing field by providing Protestants with cogent arguments for their beliefs.

Calvin and Luther agreed that the Bible was the sole guide to faith and that salvation was entirely a gift from God. Both endorsed **predestination**—the idea that humans could not affect God's decision about their ultimate fate. But they differed on the implications of this principle. Luther believed that God's laws were meant to convince people of the depth of their sin and the impossibility of earning salvation by their own efforts. Once they accepted that salvation was God's gift, they were freed from all concern for themselves and able to do good works. Only then were they truly able to devote themselves to serving others. Luther believed that if the church imposed rules governing behavior, people would slip back into thinking that obedience to these rules would earn them salvation. Calvin disagreed. He claimed that God's law was eternally valid. It did not earn anyone salvation, but it was binding on everyone (the damned as well as the saved) simply because it was God's law. It had to be enforced because God is God and human beings are His creatures.

Catholics insisted that the Protestant doctrine of salvation by faith undercut the motive for moral striving. Why, they asked, should anyone be good if good deeds are not rewarded? Contrary to Catholic expectation, however, Calvinist doctrine did not turn Calvinists into amoral libertines. It tended instead to produce dour moralists and ascetics—people who embraced "the Protestant work ethic," the sober lifestyle of the pleasure-averse laborers who, some scholars claim, have been major contributors to the success of the West's capitalist economy. The Calvinists' behavior makes some sense when viewed from a psychological perspective. If people believe that the most important decision that could ever be made about their lives has already been made, they will want desperately to know what this decision is. Calvin warned that no one could be certain that he or she is among the "elect" whom God had chosen for salvation. But it was reasonable to assume that those whom God had saved would do His will, and the Bible promised that "you will know them by their fruits" (Matthew 7:16). The desire to assure themselves that they were saved encouraged Calvinists to be moralistic and hardworking—and introspective. To see into their own hearts, they began to compile diaries in which they recorded their deeds and analyzed their motives.

In 1527 the people of Geneva expelled their Catholic bishop, and in 1534 they invited Calvin to reorganize their churches. The rigorous discipline he imposed was not popular, and the town's governing councils refused fully to empower the Consistory, a board of clergy and lay elders that Calvin set up to police public morals. Calvin was dismissed in 1538, but in 1541 Geneva recalled him and submitted to his reform program. With Calvin in charge, Geneva quickly became a haven for Protestant refugees from every corner of Europe. About 5,000 of them entered the city between 1549 and 1559—a huge number for a town that originally had about 12,000 inhabitants. When it was safe for them to go home, the Calvinism they absorbed in Geneva went with them. John Knox (1513–1572), Scotland's reformer, claimed that Geneva was "the most perfect school of Christ that ever was in the earth since the days of the Apostles."

The lessons people learned in Calvin's "school" extended beyond the practice of faith to the realm of politics. Luther endorsed a state church which submitted to the authority of a secular government. However, **Reform** (Calvinist) congregations followed what they believed was the custom of the early church. They elected councils of presbyters ("elders"), consisting of both clergy and laity, to lead them. The bodies of representatives that ran their churches increased pressure on states to accommodate a similar form of popular government.

The emphasis that Calvin placed on individual conscience and participatory decision making did not lead him (any more than it had Luther) to sanction rebellion against established authority. He drove those who opposed him from Geneva and even burned a Spanish refugee, Michael Servetus (1511–1553), at the stake for denying the doctrine of the Trinity and the divinity of Christ. However, when the shoe was on the other foot and Calvinists were the persecuted rather than the persecutors, they readily rationalized revolution—as England and France soon learned (see Map 13–2).

The Catholic Reformation

At the start of the Reformation, most of Europe's Christians belonged to a church that was—at least in their frame of reference—literally catholic ("universal"). But within a few years of Luther's excommunication, the church headed by Rome's pope was Catholic only in name and struggling to defend traditions and institutions that previously had seemed unassailable. Its response to the Protestant challenge has been characterized as a Counter-Reformation. However, it would be more accurate to call it a Catholic Reformation, for it was more than a reaction to the rise of Protestantism. It owed much to a reform movement that was active within the church before Martin Luther spoke out. In 1517, the year in which Luther attacked indulgences, an organization called the **Oratory of Divine Love** was established in Rome to promote religious renewal among both clergy and laity. Its influential members advocated reform, but they faced a serious obstacle in the Renaissance papacy.

The Renaissance Popes   In the years leading up to the Reformation, the papacy was preoccupied with rebuilding its power. The Great Schism (1378–1417) had lessened respect for popes, and the Conciliarist movement had questioned the basis for

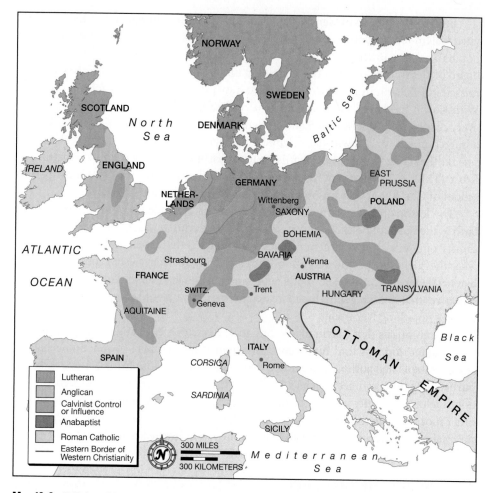

Map 13–2 Religious Diversity in Post-Reformation Europe   By the middle of the sixteenth century the region that medieval people thought of as Christendom was no longer united in allegiance to a single church. This affected the policies of the states that were emerging in many parts of the continent.

Question: Does the map suggest any explanation for where the various kinds of Protestantism spread?

their authority (see Chapter 12). Secular governments were also limiting a pope's right to operate within the boundaries of the emerging territorial states. The popes responded to these challenges abroad by building up their home base, the Papal States. Many of the popes were members of the aristocratic families that jockeyed for power in Italy, and they were well-schooled in the use of the tools of Renaissance governments: bribery, deception, assassination, and war. Their eager participation in Italy's convoluted politics made it difficult to distinguish them from the secular lords with whom they contended.

Popes, like the Renaissance's secular rulers, used patronage of the arts to bolster their image, and therefore their power. Pope Nicholas V (r. 1447–1455), the founder of the Vatican library, launched a program for reconstructing Rome that continued for generations. The city filled with buildings designed to bestow majesty on the papacy. Churches multiplied. Cardinals erected lavish palaces, and the old Vatican basilica, which Emperor Constantine had given to Rome's bishops, was pulled down to make way for construction of what was intended to be the grandest ecclesiastical building in Christendom. Kings embarked on similar programs of conspicuous display to nurture similar claims to status and respect, but behavior acceptable for a king was less so for a spiritual leader. The schemes popes devised to fund their pursuit of power earned them a reputation for greed and worldliness.

The worst popes had few aspirations beyond living like kings and enriching their relatives. Sixtus IV (r. 1471–1484) devoted most of his energies to the wars that raged among the Italian states. He was even implicated in a plot to assassinate the Medici family during mass in Florence's cathedral. The ironically named Innocent VII (r. 1484–1492) had 16 children, whom he richly rewarded from the spoils of the papal office. Alexander VI (r. 1492–1503) won the papacy by bribing the cardinals and used the church's wealth to fund wars that he hoped would win an Italian duchy for his son, Cesare Borgia (1476–1507). Julius II (r. 1503–1513) was determined—as he made clear by the name he chose when he became pope—to emulate the conquests of Julius Caesar. He donned armor and personally led troops in battle. But he was also a knowledgeable patron of the arts who commissioned Raphael to decorate the papal apartments and Michelangelo the Sistine Chapel. It fell to a Medici prince, Leo X (r. 1513–1521), to deal with Martin Luther. Not surprisingly, the aristocratic Italian pope failed to take the ranting of an obscure German monk seriously.

The papacy did not begin to mount a serious offensive against Protestantism until the reign of Paul III (r. 1534–1549). Paul appointed reforming cardinals and established a commission to draw up a plan for renewing the church. In 1537 his agents issued a report that documented many of the abuses of ecclesiastical authority of which Protestants complained. Three years later, Paul authorized the establishment of the Society of Jesus (the Jesuits), a religious order dedicated to serving the papacy and winning converts for the church. In 1542 he gave the Court of **Inquisition** authority to hunt down heretics everywhere in Europe, and in 1545 he convened the body that was primarily responsible for rebuilding the Catholic Church, the **Council of Trent**.

The Council of Trent worked with the Society of Jesus to effect the Catholic Reformation. The Jesuits were founded by Ignatius Loyola (1491–1556), a Basque soldier who discovered his spiritual vocation while recuperating from a war injury. The order accepted only the most gifted men, and it subjected candidates for admission to a 12-year-long course of study and testing that prepared them for the church's toughest assignments. Jesuits reversed gains the Reformation initially made in southern Germany, Poland, and Hungary. They spread the Catholic religion to the Americas, the East Indies, Japan, and China, and they founded hundreds of schools, colleges, and universities to provide Catholics with a firm intellectual grounding in their faith.

The Council of Trent, which met intermittently from 1545 to 1563, set the church on the path that it has (with some adjustments) followed ever since. The council affirmed that faith was based not only on Scripture, as Protestants claimed, but also on the traditions of the church. It rejected the idea that salvation was by faith alone and asserted the importance of good works. It reaffirmed transubstantiation as the explanation for the mystery of the Eucharist and asserted that each mass was an offering of Christ's sacrifice on the cross. The council's decrees were not meant to invite a dialogue that would lead to reconciliation with Protestants. They were intended to strengthen the Catholic cause by making it perfectly clear where the church stood in opposition to Protestantism. Having decided on its position, the church vigorously defended it. The Inquisition weeded out dissenters, and in 1559 the papacy imposed censorship. It forbade the reading of vernacular translations of the Bible and published an Index of Prohibited Books. So strict were the Index's standards that it condemned works by Erasmus, the loyal humanist biblical scholar who had opposed the Reformation.

The success of the Reformation should not be assumed to imply that sixteenth-century Catholicism was a moribund faith. While the Reformation spread in some parts of Europe, elsewhere a surge of enthusiasm for monastic vocations and passionate, mystical piety reflected renewed devotion to traditional religious life. Commitment to the defense and advancement of Catholicism was strongest in Spain, where Ferdinand and Isabella, "the Catholic kings," presided over the last phase in the long Iberian crusade. They crowned their conquest of Granada, Spain's last Islamic state, by banishing Jews as well as Muslims from Spain and by establishing an Inquisition that mercilessly policed the Catholic orthodoxy of their subjects. Spain's inquisitors were so alert to any whiff of heterodoxy that they briefly incarcerated the Jesuit's founder, Ignatius Loyola, and cast a wary eye on Teresa of Ávila (1515–1582), a Carmelite nun who was the era's leading mystic. Loyola's *Spiritual Exercises* and the works of Teresa and her disciple, John of the Cross (1542–1591), have become classics of Christian mystical literature. All three of these influential authors were eventually canonized (that is, acknowledged to be saints).

The Habsburg-Valois Wars

The Protestant and Catholic reformers did not work in a social vacuum. Because it was widely assumed that peoples of different faiths could not live together, one's allegiance to a religion implied one's support for—or opposition to—a government and the faith that it endorsed. This made religious and political issues inseparable.

The collapse of the German monarchy that followed the death of the Hohenstaufen emperor Frederick II in 1250 (see Chapter 12) cleared the way for France to move into Italy. Charles of Anjou, brother of Louis IX of France, conquered the Kingdom of Naples and founded a dynasty that survived until 1435. In 1494 King Charles VIII of France (r. 1483–1498) led an army into Italy to reclaim Naples for France, but a league of Italian states defeated him. In 1499 his successor, Louis XII (r. 1499–1515), occupied the duchy of Milan. However, by 1512 the French had once again been forced to retreat from Italy.

The election of Charles V as Holy Roman Emperor in 1519 made control of Italian territory a high priority for France's king, Francis I (r. 1515–1547). Charles held lands on every side of France, and Francis hoped that by occupying Italy he could avoid encirclement by the Habsburg Empire (see Map 13–1). Francis's first campaign ended in 1525 with his defeat and capture by Charles. No sooner was the king free, however, than he began a second war that also ended disastrously—particularly for his ally, Pope Clement VII (r. 1523–1534). In May 1527 Charles's imperial army broke out of control and sacked Rome—making the pope a virtual prisoner. Francis still refused to give up. In 1533 he strengthened his ties with the pope, who was eager to get out from under Charles's thumb. Francis arranged for Clement's niece, Catherine de Medicis (1519–1589), to marry his heir, Henry II (r. 1547–1559). Francis then shocked Europe by establishing diplomatic relations with the Ottoman sultan, Süleyman the Magnificent (r. 1520–1566), who had occupied most of Hungary and besieged Habsburg Vienna in 1529 with 200,000 men. Süleyman attacked Vienna again in 1532, and Francis wanted him to keep up the pressure on Charles V while the French navy assisted the Turkish fleet against the Habsburgs in the Mediterranean.

Francis began a third war with Charles in 1535. Fighting erupted in Italy, southern France, and the Habsburg Netherlands and dragged on until 1538. A fourth war broke out in 1542. Francis invaded Spain, and Charles thrust into France nearly to the gates of Paris. But by 1544 mutual exhaustion forced the opponents to agree to a truce. Both men were dead by the time the Treaty of Câteau-Cambrésis established peace between France and Spain in 1559.

England's Ambivalent Reformation

Apart from the Scandinavian states, England was the only major country to break with the papacy. Its decision to do so owed more to politics than to religion. As nation-states consolidated in the late medieval era, their governments increasingly regarded the papacy as a foreign power whose right to intervene in their affairs had to be curtailed. In the mid-fourteenth century, the English Parliament limited the pope's authority to fill offices in the English church and hear appeals from English courts. In 1438 the **Pragmatic Sanction of Bourges** declared that the French clergy (actually their king) would choose the bishops who headed the French church. Even the Court of Inquisition that the papacy established to root out heretics in Spain in 1477 served the interests of Spain's rulers, Ferdinand and Isabella. The decision to break with the papacy and make England a nominally Protestant country was similarly inspired by a desire to secure the kingdom by ensuring the future of its Tudor dynasty (1485–1603).

Henry VIII   England's civil war, the War of the Roses, ended in 1485, when Henry Tudor, a Welsh noble, defeated Richard III, the last Plantagenet king, and ascended the throne (see Chapter 11). England did not yield easily to its new ruler, Henry VII (r. 1485–1509). He spent much of his reign suppressing rebellions, but his clemency, intelligent government, and sound fiscal policies laid a solid foundation for his Tudor dynasty.

England had long cultivated alliances with the Spanish kingdoms against France, and in 1501 Henry reaffirmed this foreign policy. He obtained the hand of Catherine of Aragon (1485–1536), daughter of Spain's Ferdinand and Isabella, for Arthur (1486–1502), his son and heir. When Arthur died less than six months after the wedding, Henry decided to maintain the tie with Spain by obtaining papal permission for

Catherine to wed his new heir, his second son, the future Henry VIII (r. 1509–1547). A dispensation from canon law was required, for a biblical text (Leviticus 20:21) forbade a marriage between a man and his brother's widow.

Catherine endured many pregnancies, but only one of her children survived, a daughter named Mary. Henry doubted that England would accept a female heir to his throne and feared that after his death, the country would lapse back into the civil war from which it had recently emerged. He believed that the security of his kingdom depended on his having a son. When Catherine, who had not had a pregnancy in seven years, turned 40 in 1525, Henry—who was 34—decided that his only hope for a son lay in obtaining a younger wife.

Henry hoped that the pope would void his marriage on the principle that God had rendered sterile a marriage that the Bible had forbidden. The church had a long history of finding reasons to dissolve inconvenient marriages for influential people, but Clement VII, the pope to whom Henry appealed, was in no position to oblige England's king. Catherine opposed Henry's petition, and her nephew, Charles V—whose troops had recently sacked Rome—dominated Italy. When the pope prolonged the negotiations to buy time, Henry turned to Parliament for help in pressuring Rome. Parliament obliged by enacting a series of laws that began to sever ties between England and the papacy.

Events came to a head in 1533. Henry had fallen in love with Anne Boleyn (1504–1536), the daughter of one of his courtiers. Near the close of 1532 Anne became pregnant. Henry, who was desperate to assure the legitimacy of her child, secretly wed her in January 1533. In May his compliant archbishop of Canterbury, Thomas Cranmer (1489–1556), declared that he had never been validly married to Catherine and that Anne was therefore his legal wife. To the king's great disappointment, however, Anne bore him another daughter, Elizabeth.

In 1534 the pope came to Catherine's defense and declared her to be Henry's legitimate wife. Parliament responded by passing the **Act of Supremacy**, which severed ties with the papacy and recognized the king as the head of England's church. The break with Rome was not motivated by any royal sympathy with Protestantism. Henry had made his antipathy to the Reformation clear in 1521 by publishing an attack on Luther. The pope had been so grateful for Henry's support that he had awarded him the title: "Defender of the Faith." England's monarchs still list this among their titles although the faith they defend has changed.

A few prominent individuals, most famously the humanist Thomas More (the king's former chancellor), refused to swear allegiance to the new church and were executed. Although some modern scholars believe that anticlericalism was on the rise in England, most of Henry's subjects considered themselves to be Catholics. In 1536, when Henry began to suppress England's monasteries and confiscate their vast properties, there was a rebellion (the Pilgrimage of Grace) in the north of England. However, this was not solely a religiously motivated protest. It was also a reaction by the numerous tenants who lived on monastic estates to Henry's disruption of their lives. The strongest support for reforming England's church came from the merchant class, which had close commercial ties with those parts of Europe where Protestantism was spreading. This segment of English society was well represented in the Parliaments that met in 1536, 1537, 1538, 1539, and 1543 to draw up regulations for the new church. However, apart from suppressing monasteries and endorsing the use of vernacular Scriptures, Henry made few concessions to Protestantism. The Anglican (English) church over which he presided was to be nationalized, but not to depart significantly from its Roman Catholic model. It was to be ruled by bishops (whom the king appointed) and staffed by a celibate clergy who celebrated seven sacraments, and continued most medieval liturgical practices.

The king had risked much to marry Anne, and when her second pregnancy miscarried, he lost faith in her. He accused her of adultery, beheaded her, and took a third wife, Jane Seymour (1509–1537). On October 12, 1537, she died not long after giving birth to the long-sought male heir, the future Edward VI. Henry's next bride, a German Lutheran named Anne of Cleves (1515–1557), was chosen to forge an alliance between England and Germany's Lutheran princes. Thomas Cromwell (c. 1485–1540), Henry's chief minister, had argued that this would dissuade France and Spain from heeding the pope's call for a crusade against England. Henry, however, disliked Anne so much that their (allegedly unconsummated) marriage was annulled. In 1540 he wed Catherine Howard, a sprightly young niece of the duke of Norfolk. Her flagrant promiscuity with young men at court prompted her execution in 1542. A few months later, Henry married his sixth wife, Catherine Parr (1512–1548), a sensible widow with strong Protestant sympathies. She provided her aging husband with domestic comforts and took charge of the education of his children.

The Tudor Succession   When Henry died in January 1547, his 9-year-old-son, Edward VI (r. 1547–1553), ascended the throne. Edward was afflicted with chronic ill health but was intellectually precocious and (thanks to his stepmother and the Lutheran tutors she provided) a sincere Protestant. The chief monument of his brief reign was a new liturgy for the Anglican Church, *The Book of Common Prayer*. It tried to reconcile the various religious factions that were developing in England by being ambiguous on contentious issues.

The course of the English Reformation was nearly reversed when the young king died. His father's will named his half-sister Mary, Catherine of Aragon's Catholic daughter, next in line to the throne. Edward's Protestant advisors persuaded the dying boy to disinherit Mary, but the English people refused to accept this and rallied to her side.

Mary I (r. 1553–1558) shared her Spanish mother's conservative Catholic faith and was eager to restore England's allegiance to the papacy. She imprisoned some prominent Protestant clergy at the start of her reign but preferred to rid England of Protestants by urging them to reconvert or emigrate. Hundreds fled to the Netherlands, Germany, and Switzerland. There, under the influence of Calvinism, many became **Puritans**—sober, but passionate, Protestants who were filled with contempt for Catholicism and dedicated to "purifying" England's church of every taint of "Romanism."

Mary's first Parliament revoked some of her brother's religious legislation but balked at rebuilding England's monasteries. This would have necessitated the restoration of their confiscated lands, many of which had been acquired by members of Parliament. The thing that alarmed Parliament most about its new queen was not religion but her intended marriage. Mary was 37 years old, and she was desperate to bear an heir who would guarantee a Catholic succession to the English throne. The mate she chose was Charles V's son, Philip II, heir to Spain and the western half of the Habsburg Empire. Premarital agreements could limit the rights of the queen's husband over her kingdom, but not those of any child she and her spouse might have. It would have inherited both their thrones and made England, the weaker country, a Spanish dependency.

Four months after she became queen, Mary swept Parliament's objections aside and married Philip by proxy. Nine months later Philip arrived in England to meet a bride who was 11 years his senior. With Philip's encouragement, Mary sought formal reconciliation with Rome, which was granted on November 30, 1554.

Fear of Spain undercut support for Mary and encouraged her Protestant opponents. She reacted by searching out and executing Protestant sympathizers. She may have burned about 280 men and women at the stake (the standard punishment for heretics), which caused later Protestant historians to blacken her reputation. Some scholars point out that she was responsible for fewer deaths than her successor, her Protestant sister Elizabeth, but Elizabeth's record as an executioner was compiled over a much longer reign.

After less than a year of marriage, Philip left England. He did not give Mary a child, but he did draw her into the Habsburgs' wars with France. This misadventure cost England its last continental possession—the French port of Calais. Mary, isolated and disillusioned, lost touch with reality. When she died on November 17, 1558, Elizabeth—Mary's hated half-sister and the daughter of Anne Boleyn, whose marriage to Henry VIII had humiliated Mary and her mother—ascended her throne.

Convergence of Foreign and Domestic Politics: England, Spain, and France

The religious diversity the Reformation created greatly complicated political life in Europe, for it was widely assumed that a state could not survive unless all its citizens shared the same faith. Subjects who differed with the religion of their ruler were suspected to be traitors, particularly when wars broke out between Catholic and Protestant states.

Elizabeth's Compromises   In 1558 John Knox (c. 1505–1572), a Protestant exile from Scotland who found refuge in Geneva, published *The First Blast of the Trumpet Against the Monstrous Regiment of Women*. Knox blamed the ills of his generation on the women who, contrary (he claimed) to the laws of God and nature, were presuming to govern kingdoms. Mary Tudor, an ardent opponent of Protestantism, ruled England. In addition, Mary of Guise (1515–1560), a daughter of a powerful French Catholic family, governed Scotland as regent for her daughter, Mary Stuart (r. 1542–1567). What Knox considered a bad situation was destined, from his point of view, to get worse. France soon came under the thumb of its queen mother, Catherine de Medicis, and in 1558 England's throne passed to its second female heir. There were, however, no more blasts from Knox's trumpet, for timing made his book something of an embarrassment for his Protestant allies. The *First Blast* was intended to deafen a Protestant enemy, Mary Tudor, but it actually grated on the ears of Europe's most important Protestant monarch, Mary's sister Elizabeth I (r. 1558–1603).

Because Catholics did not recognize the validity of the marriage between Henry VIII and Anne Boleyn, they believed that Elizabeth's birth was illegitimate and that she therefore had no right to England's throne. But political objectives could trump religious scruples, and Europe's Catholic powers did not immediately attack the new queen. The pope held out hope for her conversion, and Philip II, Mary's widower, considered proposing to her. Elizabeth's position was precarious. England was nearly surrounded by Catholic states, and there was a Catholic claimant to her throne: Mary Stuart, a granddaughter of a sister of Henry VIII's who had married the king of Scotland. She was Scotland's hereditary queen and, as spouse of France's short-lived King Francis II (r. 1559–1560), briefly queen of France. Religious divisions were also increasing among Elizabeth's subjects. Some opposed her father's Reformation, and some—particularly the radicalized Puritans who returned to England from exile after Mary Tudor's death—believed that his Reformation had not gone far enough.

Elizabeth survived by making it difficult for everyone to figure out where she stood. She was adept at depriving potential opponents of clear targets and keeping alive their hopes for reconciliation. She flirted with, but never committed to, the many men who sought her hand in marriage. She endorsed some Catholic practices and some Protestant ideas. Gradually, she eased her country toward a "settlement" of religion—a church with a Catholic hierarchical structure and ritual and a partially Protestant theology. This did not end religious conflict in England, but it postponed a showdown until the 1630s.

Philip II and Spain's Golden Age
Elizabeth hoped to maintain England's alliance with Spain against France, but Spain's ruler had other plans. Philip II (r. 1556–1598) inherited the western half of Charles V's empire: Spain, Spain's New World possessions, and the Habsburg Netherlands (modern Belgium, Holland, and Luxembourg). Control of the commercially rich Netherlands and a steady flow of gold and silver from America gave Philip great resources, and he was willing to spend whatever it took to bring more of Europe under his control.

The weakest point in Philip's empire was the Netherlands, a small but highly urbanized and wealthy country whose independent townspeople were notoriously difficult to govern. The Netherlands was a loose collection of culturally diverse provinces. The ten southern provinces were French or Flemish, and the seven northern ones were linked by the Rhine River to Germany and Switzerland. Protestant influences (predominantly Calvinistic) spread to the Netherlands and there, as elsewhere, appealed to urban populations. Townspeople had, throughout the Middle Ages, been predisposed to self-government, and they responded to Luther's defense of the rights of the individual and Calvin's arguments for representative institutions. Philip concluded, therefore, that to strengthen his hold over the highly urbanized provinces, he had to purge them of Protestantism. This only increased the determination of some Netherlanders to resist Spanish domination.

El Escorial   The greatest monument from Spain's Golden Age is the huge palace-monastery complex that Philip II erected in honor of St. Lawrence, El Escorial. The structure reflects the wealth, power, and ardent faith of its builder. Philip's austere quarters were placed next to its great church and featured a window through which the king, who was sometimes bedridden, could witness the celebration of mass.

In 1567, after lesser measures had failed, Philip sent an army into the Netherlands to compel conformity to his religious policies. This heavy-handed action roused nationalistic passions, and a resistance movement formed around a native nobleman, William of Orange (1533–1584). William tried to unite all the provinces, but religious disputes doomed his efforts. In 1579 the largely Franco-Catholic southern provinces sided with Spain, while the north's more easily defended Dutch-speaking provinces formed a Protestant alliance (the United Provinces) and continued the fight for independence. Because the United Provinces received help from England's Protestant queen, Philip decided to try to subdue both these enemies in a single campaign. Developments seemed to favor his success. William of Orange was assassinated in 1584. A pro-Spanish faction won ascendancy at the French court, and a plot unfolded in England to place Mary Stuart on Elizabeth's throne.

England's Henry VIII had tried to win Mary Stuart's hand for his son and successor, Edward. But the Scots, who had long relied on France's help to maintain their independence from England, preferred that their queen wed the heir to the French throne. As a young child, Mary (1542–1567) was sent to France to be educated for her future role as its queen. Her mother, Mary of Guise (a member of an extremely powerful and ardently Catholic French noble family), governed Scotland as her regent. Although some Scots favored the French alliance, others feared French dominance. In 1559 a cadre of nobles, with an agenda that mixed religion and politics, overthrew Mary of Guise and recalled a native son, John Knox, from exile in Geneva. Knox, a former Catholic priest who had embraced Calvinism, was charged with reforming Scotland's church. A year later, Mary Stuart's husband, Francis II, died. The young widow of the French king was then sent back to Scotland to govern a country she had not seen since early childhood. Mary, who was accustomed to the luxury and sophistication of the elegant French court, was ill-prepared for life in a much poorer and less urbane society. Her manner offended men like Knox, and she was soon at odds with powerful members of her court. She worsened her situation by conducting an affair with—and ultimately marrying—the man suspected of killing her second husband, a great-grandson of England's Henry VII. In 1566 she gave birth to a son (Scotland's James VI and England's future James I), and a year later she was compelled to abdicate her throne to him. She then fled to England to ask for help, despite the fact that she was a strong potential rival for its Protestant queen's throne. Elizabeth was uncertain what to do with her. Not wanting to kill her or trusting what she might do if she were free, the English queen kept Mary in confinement for 20 years. Rumors of plots to overthrow Elizabeth and enthrone Mary multiplied, and in 1587 evidence for Mary's involvement in one of Philip II's schemes persuaded Elizabeth to order her beheading.

Elizabeth had good reason to fear for her throne, for Philip was assembling a great fleet for an invasion of England. His plan was to sail to the Netherlands with an army, pick up additional troops there, and then cross the channel to England. Various setbacks delayed the departure of the so-called **Spanish Armada** until the summer of 1588, and then the expedition was undone by a combination of bad planning, worse weather, and the skills of English sailors. After the Armada's destruction, Philip continued to threaten England, but his resources were diminishing as his problems were multiplying. The struggle in the Netherlands continued, and in 1589 he attacked France. The English also devised an effective way to undermine him. Privateers (government-licensed, privately funded pirates) raided Spanish shipping. The queen herself invested in these highly profitable ventures, over a hundred of which sailed in some years. England did not yet have a navy, but it was on its way to becoming a major sea power.

After Philip's death in 1598, Spain entered a long period of gradual decline. The gold and silver that Spaniards had extracted from the Americas had not been invested in building a productive economy. Instead, the bullion had flowed through Spain to fund Philip's numerous wars. The church controlled about half the land in Spain and supported a huge number of clergy. Most of the rest of the country was in the hands of an entrenched aristocracy that clung to its medieval prerogatives. Portraits of Spain's grandees by the artist El Greco (c. 1541–1614) proclaim their sense of entitlement, and the paintings by Velázquez (1599–1660), a generation later, suggest a royal court that had drifted into the realm of fantasy. In addition to major artists, Spain's Golden Age also framed the career of its greatest writer: Miguel de Cervantes Saavedra (1547–1616). Cervantes' groundbreaking novel, *Don Quixote*,

Mary, Queen of Scots   This portrait is the work of Nicholas Hilliard (1547–1619), the leading painter of miniatures at the court of Elizabeth I. A number of prominent figures from the Elizabethan age, including the queen herself, had likenesses drafted by Hilliard.

affectionately lampooned his countrymen's romantic devotion to an archaic way of life that was dooming them to irrelevance.

France's Wars of Religion
Spain was not Elizabeth's only concern. A war between Catholic and Protestant factions raged in France for much of her reign and complicated her foreign policy. In France, as elsewhere, the Reformation attracted people who were critical of established authority and who saw religious change as part of a broader program of reform. Many of these came from the professional and middle classes and the lower nobility—educated people who chafed under the restraints of institutions that they regarded as outmoded. France's Protestants were Calvinists called Huguenots. Scholars are uncertain of the origin of their name.

For most of the sixteenth century, France's royal government left much to be desired. Francis I used the French Catholic Church as a source of political patronage and squandered his country's resources in futile wars with his Habsburg rival, Charles V. Francis's son, Henry II (r. 1547–1559), achieved little before an accident in a tournament bout ended his life and delivered France into the hands of his Italian wife, Catherine de Medicis (1519–1589). Catherine was the power behind a throne that passed in succession to three of their sons. Francis II (r. 1559–1560) survived his father for only a year. He was succeeded by his 10-year-old brother, Charles IX (r. 1560–1574). The third brother, Henry III (r. 1574–1589), was an adult when he became king, but debauchery subverted his effectiveness as a ruler.

It was all that Catherine could do simply to preserve the Valois dynasty, for France was less a unified kingdom than a league of powerful principalities. Whenever its kings were weak, aristocratic factions led by great noblemen fought for dominance at court. During the sixteenth century, religious differences defined the opposing camps. The Catholic party was led by the dukes and cardinals of the Guise family and the Protestants by the Bourbons, a cadet branch of the royal house. In 1562 the duke of Guise began a war with the Protestants by slaughtering 70 Huguenots whom he surprised at worship. In 1572 Catherine's attempt to reconcile France's Catholic and Protestant factions backfired and led to a mass murder that shocked Europe. The French aristocracy gathered in Paris for the wedding of Catherine's daughter, Margaret, to Henry of Navarre, the Bourbon head of the Huguenot faction. The marriage was intended to bring Catholics and Protestants together, but on the eve of the ceremony someone tried to assassinate one of the Huguenot leaders. Fear of Protestant reprisals prompted the crown to act quickly and with great force. Early on the morning of August 24, the feast of St. Bartholomew, the king's army fell on the unsuspecting Huguenots. The slaughter spread to other cities, and some 70,000 Protestants may have perished before the purge ended. The **St. Bartholomew's Day Massacre** poisoned relationships between Protestants and Catholics throughout Europe and diminished hope that the faiths could coexist peacefully.

Spain and England encouraged civil war in France by providing aid to the combatants, and the bloodshed continued until 1589, when a monk extinguished the Valois dynasty by assassinating Henry III. This cleared the way to the throne for the Bourbon heir, the Protestant Henry of Navarre, France's King Henry IV (r. 1589–1610). After a prolonged struggle, Henry concluded that his largely Catholic country would not accept a Protestant king, and he converted—allegedly quipping, "Paris is worth a mass." Henry IV, a nominal Catholic with Protestant credentials, had enough credibility with both sides to negotiate a truce between them. In 1598 he issued the **Edict of Nantes**, which declared France a Catholic country but designated places where Huguenots could worship and ceded some towns to their control. Since 1555, a similar arrangement (the Peace of Augsburg) had maintained order in Germany, but events there were about to demonstrate that religious segregation was not a permanent solution.

The Final Religious Upheavals

By the end of Elizabeth's reign (1603), a lull was developing in Europe's conflicts. England was fairly secure. Spain's struggles in the Netherlands were winding down, and France was recovering from its long internal bloodletting. There were, however, problems on the horizon. Despite all the killing, Europe's population had increased by

■ ■

PEOPLE IN CONTEXT William Shakespeare (1564–1616)

Literature flourished in Elizabethan England as never before, and the period's greatest author was, as one of his contemporaries put it, "not of an age, but for all time." He might have added "and for all cultures," for William Shakespeare's plays have been translated into many tongues, staged as operas and Broadway musicals, and produced as commercially successful films. Given their fame, it is surprising that so little is known about their author.

Shakespeare, for all his talent, seems to have led a fairly conventional life. John Shakespeare, his father, was a glove maker, money lender, and commodity trader in the town of Stratford-on-Avon. He and his wife, Mary Arden, had eight children. Will, the eldest of their four sons, was born in a terrifying year in which about 250 of Stratford's 800 inhabitants died of the plague. John served a term as mayor of Stratford and applied for a coat-of-arms to bolster his social aspirations. But by the time Will was 11, his father was suffering serious financial reverses and could do little to help his son make a start in life.

Shakespeare's formal education appears to have been in Stratford's free school. Unlike other famous playwrights of his generation, there is no evidence that he studied at one of England's universities. His plays testify to his familiarity with the major classic authors (Ovid, Plutarch, Seneca, etc.) but do not suggest that he was unusually well read. This background has caused some to doubt that he could have written the works ascribed to him. Various more distinguished individuals (including noblemen and rival poets) have been proposed as writers for whom he fronted. Although his works have been minutely combed for clues to

the identity of an anonymous author, there is no convincing evidence that Shakespeare did not write the plays and poems his contemporaries credited to him. Genius such as he displayed is not unprecedented, but it usually seems inexplicable.

At the age of 18 Shakespeare married Anne Hathaway, a woman eight years his senior. Six months after the wedding, their daughter Susanna was baptized, and three years later they had twins—a boy and a girl. No one knows how young Shakespeare supported his family or what drew him to London and the theater in the late 1580s.

William Shakespeare This portrait of William Shakespeare is from an engraving that was made for a 1623 edition of his work.

Somehow he learned to act and to write plays, and by 1592 his work was attracting envious notice from his competitors. By 1597, he was rich enough to purchase the second largest house in Stratford, and by 1599, he was part owner of a new London theater called "The Globe."

Shakespeare's family may have secretly clung to the old Catholic faith, but Shakespeare was no propagandist or overt advocate for a cause. He was a professional playwright whose goal was to please his audiences without overtly taking sides in contentious political or religious debates. He dealt with universal themes of perennial human concern: love, jealousy, ambition, deceit, treason, and the meaning of life. He wrote to make a living, and when he could afford to (in 1613), he laid down his pen and devoted the rest of his life to managing his business interests. He appears to have given little thought to preserving his work for posterity. He died on April 23, 1616, and seven years passed before a group of admirers gathered up scattered manuscripts of his plays and edited them for publication.

Shakespeare wrote exclusively for his own company at the rate of about two plays a year. Scholars credit him with 154 sonnets, several longer poems, and about 40 plays. The latter span the genre of theater: comedies, tragedies, histories, romances, and fantasies. The great characters he created for the stage—Romeo, Juliet, Hamlet, Macbeth, Lear, Othello, Falstaff, and many others—have become prototypes in world literature. Lines from his plays (e.g., "Neither a borrower nor a lender be," *Hamlet*) are commonplace quotations that are sometimes mistaken for verses from Scripture. It is likely no other single author has had more influence on the development of the English language and its literary canon.

Question: Does Shakespeare's work support the common assumption that artists reflect the dominant values and concerns of the eras in which they live?

■ ■ ■ ■ ■ ■ ■

about 40% during the sixteenth century. The gold and silver that had flooded in from the New World had caused inflation to soar. Widespread poverty and unstable economies inspired riots and rebellions. Governments strained to control their subjects, and some failed conspicuously.

The Thirty Years' War By separating Germany's Lutherans and Catholics, the Peace of Augsburg diminished opportunities for the two faith communities to learn to trust one another. Some people were also determined to undermine Augsburg's arrangements. The Jesuits reclaimed much of southern Germany for the Catholics. The Calvinists, who were rivals of the Lutherans and who had not been accorded legal recognition in the Augsburg agreement, were equally aggressive in their recruiting. In 1608 the Calvinist ruler of the Palatinate, Frederick IV (r. 1592–1610), established the Protestant Union, an alliance of Protestant states. Duke Maximilian of Bavaria (1573–1651) countered by recruiting members for what was called the Catholic League. France, England, and Holland supported Frederick, and the Habsburgs—both Spanish and Austrian—backed Maximilian.

The only thing needed for war to break out was an incident to trigger hostilities. That was provided by a colorful event that took place in Prague in 1618 in the wake of the ascension to the Bohemian throne of the Austrian archduke Ferdinand (1578–1637), the Catholic heir to the Holy Roman Empire (as Ferdinand II). The kingdom of Bohemia had accommodated religious heterodoxy at least since the early fifteenth century, when the followers of John Hus fought for and won a degree of independence from the papacy (see Chapter 11). Bohemia had subsequently provided refuge for Anabaptists, and Calvinism had spread in some aristocratic circles. The Jesuit-educated Ferdinand, however, had no sympathy with his new kingdom's tradition of tolerance, and he broke pledges he had made to his Protestant subjects by mandating their return to Catholicism. The Bohemian nobles reacted to the orders he sent them by tossing his messengers out a window onto a dung heap. Ferdinand treated this "Defenestration of Prague" as a declaration of war and prepared to invade Bohemia. The Bohemians responded by turning to the son and successor of Frederick IV of the Palatinate, Frederick V (r. 1610–1632), for help. The German states quickly chose sides—not allowing their religious preferences to stand in the way of their political interests. Some Lutherans, who despised Calvinists, supported Ferdinand. In contrast, some Catholics, who did not want the Catholic Habsburgs to grow stronger, sided with Frederick.

In the first phase of the war, the Catholic forces swept through Germany and routed Frederick, but that only widened the conflict. The possibility of a Germany united under a Catholic monarch so alarmed Germany's neighbors that they intervened on the Protestant side. Denmark was the first to attack, but its campaign foundered and enabled the Catholics to seize additional ports on the Baltic. That, however, brought Sweden into the fray. In 1630 Sweden's great warrior king, Gustavus Adolphus (r. 1611–1632), forced Ferdinand to retreat from northern Germany. Catholic France then allied with Lutheran Sweden. After Gustavus Adolphus was killed in battle, France directed the course of the war against the Catholic emperor. France was governed by Cardinal Richelieu (1585–1642), chief minister for Henry IV's son, Louis XIII (r. 1610–1643). Richelieu was a sincere Catholic and a "prince" of the papal establishment, but he put the interests of his country above those of his church. The last thing France wanted was to face a unified Germany along its eastern frontier. Therefore, Richelieu had little choice but to help Germany's Protestants fend off their Catholic emperor. The intervention of foreign powers turned Germany into an international killing ground. By the time the war ended, battles, raids, plagues, massacres, and famines had resulted in the deaths of about eight million people, roughly 40% of Germany's population.

The **Peace of Westphalia** that concluded the war in 1648 ensured that Germany would remain an impotent collection of hundreds of tiny states and that the Holy Roman Empire would be an empire only in name. The victors rewarded themselves with bits of German territory, and the Habsburg defeat cleared the way for the Swiss cantons and the Dutch Republic to be recognized as independent states. Germany's collapse and Spain's humiliation also meant that France now had a chance to dominate the continent (see Map 13–3).

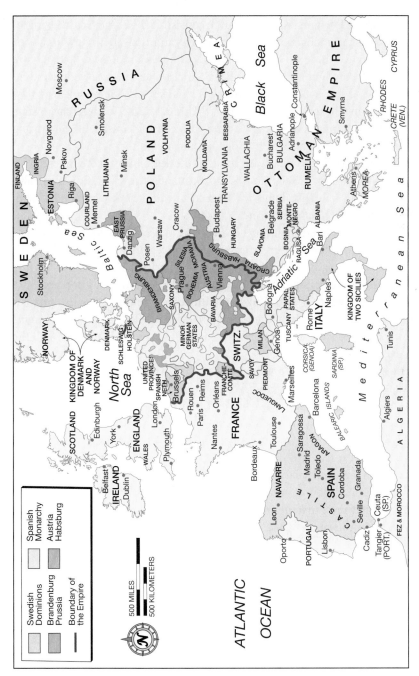

Map 13-3 Europe After the Peace of Westphalia The Treaty of Westphalia redrew the map of Europe. France and Sweden acquired additional territory. The United Provinces and the Swiss cantons were recognized as independent states, and Germany's political fragmentation was assured to continue.

Question: To what extent were the political borders that the treaty drew on the map of Europe determined by geography?

England's Civil War   By the time Westphalia brought the continent's religious wars to an end, a conflict between Puritans and Anglicans was raging in England. England's religious factions had different political visions for both their country's church and its government. The Puritans wanted a church consisting of self-governing congregations overseen by a national synod to which congregations elected representatives. The secular equivalent for this ecclesiastical organization was a monarchy headed by a king who ruled in consort with Parliament. Elizabeth and her successors understood the political implications of Protestant church order, which was one reason why they insisted on an Anglican Church modeled on the traditional Catholic hierarchy. A state church governed by bishops appointed by the crown was more consistent with strong monarchy than the alternatives favored by England's Protestants.

Elizabeth never married, and her death brought the Tudor dynasty to an end. Her heir, James I (r. 1603–1625), was Mary Stuart's son, Scotland's King James VI. Ironically, centuries of war waged by English kings who hoped to conquer Scotland ended with Scotland's king ascending England's throne.

James's experience with Presbyterians in Scotland did not inspire him with enthusiasm for either Protestantism or representative government. In 1598 he published a book, *A True Law of Free Monarchies*, that clarified his stance. It firmly embraced the medieval principle that God appointed kings and that kings were accountable only to God, which was out of step with recent trends in English history. The Tudor dynasty had needed Parliament's help to effect the Reformation and manage its consequences, and Parliament had come to think of itself as a partner with the monarch in governing England.

Parliament met only when the monarch called it, and what kept its tradition alive was its control of taxation. England's kings could not levy taxes without parliamentary approval. To avoid calling a Parliament that might try to limit his authority, a king had to find other ways to meet the expenses of government, and James was ingenious in devising these. He imposed customs duties, sold titles of nobility, licensed monopolies for a fee, and did everything he could think of to fill the royal coffers without resorting to Parliament. He had no sympathy with any aspect of Puritanism and even sponsored a national campaign to encourage the recreations, games, and sports that the Puritans condemned as frivolous and ungodly pastimes. His major concession was to commission a new vernacular translation of the Scriptures. The result was the eloquent Authorized Version (or as it is popularly known, the King James Version) of the Bible.

James's policies and dissolute court were so offensive to Puritans that some of them gave up hope for England's reformation and decided to make fresh starts elsewhere. In 1593 a small group of radical Puritan separatists left London for the Netherlands, and in 1620 they emigrated again to found a colony called Plymouth in North America. They were the vanguard of a much larger migration that eventually brought thousands of more mainstream Puritans to New England and the islands of the West Indies. As it turned out, they were somewhat premature in anticipating the decline of the Puritan cause in their homeland.

Leaders of the Reformations and the Wars of Religion		
RELIGIOUS LEADERS	**POLITICAL LEADERS**	**EVENTS**
Luther (1483–1546)	Charles V (1519–1556)	Diet of Worms (1521)
Leo X (1513–1521)	Süleyman (1520–1566)	
Zwingli (1484–1531)	Francis I (1515–1547)	Habsburg-Valois Wars (1521–1544)
Clement VII (1523–1534)	Henry VIII (1509–1547)	
Calvin (1509–1564)	Catherine of Aragon (1485–1536)	English Reformation (1534)
		Geneva reformed (1541)
Ignatius Loyola (1491–1556)	Edward VI (1547–1553)	Peace of Augsburg (1555)
Paul III (1534–1549)	Mary Tudor (1553–1558)	Council of Trent (1545–1563)
Knox (1505–1572)	Philip II (1556–1598)	Scotland reformed (1559)
Theresa of Avila (1515–1582)	Elizabeth I (1558–1603)	Spanish Armada (1588)
	Mary Stuart (1542–1567)	
	Catherine de Medicis (1485–1536)	French Wars of Religion (1562–1589)
	Henry IV (1594–1610)	Edict of Nantes (1598)
	James I (1603–1625)	
	Frederick V (1596–1632)	
	Ferdinand II (1578–1637)	Thirty Years' War (1618–1648)
	Gustavus Adolphus (1611–1632)	
	Richelieu (1585–1642)	
	Charles I (1625–1649)	English Civil War (1642–1646)
	Cromwell (1599–1658)	English Republic (1649–1660)

James's son and successor, Charles I (r. 1625–1649), shared his father's determination to rule without interference from his subjects. After a Parliament early in his reign forced him to acknowledge that he had no unilateral right to levy taxes, he avoided convening another session for 11 years (1629–1640). He was even less willing than his father to compromise with Protestants, and the Puritans suspected him of being a Catholic at heart. His French wife enjoyed the privilege of hearing mass at court, and his archbishop of Canterbury, William Laud, had his support in promoting liturgical reforms that Puritans regarded as a reversion to Roman worship.

Puritans who criticized him in print or from their pulpits were dragged into court, speedily convicted, and harshly punished. What precipitated his fall, however, was not his quarrel with England's Puritans but his determination to force Scotland's church to conform with Anglican practice. In 1637 Charles ordered Scotland's Presbyterian clergy to use the Anglican prayer book. When the Scots refused, Charles took up arms against them. The small army he was able to raise without Parliament's assistance failed to do anything but goad the Scots into invading England in 1640. This forced Charles to call a Parliament, but that only worsened his situation. When members of Parliament insisted that he carry out extensive governmental reforms before they granted new tax levies, he dissolved the meeting (the "Short Parliament"). A few months later, a victory by the Scots forced him to reconvene Parliament. This meeting passed a law to the effect that a parliamentary session could only be ended by vote of its members. Given that no resolution for adjournment was passed for the next 20 years, this became the era of the "Long Parliament." The Long Parliament moved rapidly to curtail the power of the king. It dismissed his archbishop, punished some of his councilors, repealed his taxes, and decreed that the king had to call future Parliaments at regular intervals. Charles believed that Parliament was vastly overstepping its boundaries and curtailing his royal prerogatives. The reforms it demanded were in fact similar to those that later limited the powers of the throne and established Parliament as the dominant body in Britain's government. In 1642 the exasperated king made the mistake of sending soldiers to break up Parliament. When Parliament's leaders resisted and London rose to support them, the king left London and began to rally his supporters in the west and north of England.

This was the prelude to a civil war that raged for four years (1642–1646). Its turning point came in 1645 with Parliament's institution of the **New Model Army**, a reorganized military recruited from committed Protestants called "Roundheads." (Their closely cropped hair contrasted with the flowing locks of the king's courtiers, the "Cavaliers.") Unlike earlier armies, the New Model Army was commanded not by aristocrats, but by experienced officers who advanced by merit. Its men were strictly disciplined, passionate about their

Oliver Cromwell   This unfinished miniature is a likeness of the enigmatic Puritan leader, Oliver Cromwell. He allegedly had a religious experience in his youth that convinced him that he was one of God's elect—a man destined to serve God in unique ways. His confidence in his calling may explain the forceful means he often employed to impose his will on others.

cause, and respected for their moral rectitude. They routed armies larger than their own and did not indulge in the rape and pillage that had traditionally been the prerogatives of victorious soldiers. Parliament was also fortunate in finding a brilliant military strategist among its members. Oliver Cromwell (1599–1658), a member of the House of Commons, was an obscure individual from the ranks of the country gentry. He raised a company of cavalrymen whose spirit and discipline spread through the parliamentary forces, and he quickly rose in the chain of command.

The king's army was broken at the Battle of Naseby in June 1645, but Charles eluded capture and survived as a fugitive in his own country for a year. In May 1646 he surrendered to the Scots who held him for eight months before turning him over to the English.

Parliament was better at winning wars than governing England, for victory cleared the way for its numerous religious factions to begin to fight among themselves. A rift also opened between politicians and soldiers when Parliament attempted precipitously to disband the army. Parliament's Presbyterian majority was more conservative than many of the soldiers. A faction known as the Levelers demanded that the current Parliament be dissolved and that every adult male citizen be given the right to vote for a new Parliament that would govern without restraint by a king or House of Lords. Freedom of religion was also to be guaranteed.

In November of 1647 the king escaped, and the war flared up again. This had the effect of strengthening the army and draining whatever respect the soldiers still had for the monarchy. The army recaptured the king, occupied London, and purged Parliament of its Presbyterian majority. The much reduced "Rump Parliament" then convicted the king of treason and—on January 30, 1649—beheaded him. The monarchy was declared at an end, and England was henceforward to be governed as a republic. In reality, Cromwell became the new head of state. His support derived in large part from his ability as a military leader to restore order to a country that was desperate for stability. He stuck to a Puritan middle path—suppressing both the radical Levelers and the Anglo-Catholics. He dealt harshly with critics and opponents, and mounted new military campaigns. He put down revolts in Ireland, brought Scotland back under England's control, and waged war at sea with the Dutch. The taxes he imposed were more onerous than those that Charles had levied, and in 1653 this prompted Parliament to consider disbanding his army. He prevented this by using the army to disband the Rump Parliament. Cromwell wanted to rule in cooperation with a Parliament, but when debates in the meetings he subsequently convened grew too radical for his tastes, he sent their delegates home. He leaned heavily on the army to maintain himself in power and in May of 1657 he assumed the title of hereditary Lord Protector—a king by a new title. He survived for another year, dying on September 3, 1658.

Cromwell's son, Richard, briefly assumed his father's office, but he was unable to maintain control of a divided army and a country that had been disillusioned by both Republicanism and Puritan extremism. A period of confusion ensued in which civil war again threatened. Finally, a powerful general arranged for the election of a new Parliament. In April of 1660 it invited Charles I's son, Charles II (r. 1660–1685), to return from exile in France and restore the monarchy and the Anglican Church. England embraced its former institutions, but the Puritan revolution had not been a complete failure. Mindful of Charles I's fate, England's kings moderated claims to absolute authority and conceded Parliament a role in their governments. Britain's "constitutional" monarchy was not yet complete, but it was on the brink of the final stage in its development.

KEY QUESTION | Revisited

During the sixteenth and seventeenth centuries, Europeans worked to resolve power struggles of various kinds. Emerging states jousted for advantage. Within states, there were tugs of war between regional and centralized authorities. Nobles resisted the growing power of kings. Social and economic classes and rural and urban areas were in conflict. The long-standing tension between the two visions for Europe—imperial unity and religious homogeneity or political fragmentation and cultural diversity—came to a head.

Religious convictions, both sincere and opportunistic, provided moral justification for decisions to shed blood that was spilled for many other reasons as well. The ethical context for the wars of the Reformation era may have been more complex than for the religious wars of earlier generations. Unlike the crusades, which were wars of foreign aggression waged in defense of European Christianity against what was thought to be a hostile, alien faith, Europe's "wars of religion" were civil wars within European Christendom. Their rationale involved differing views of orthodoxy and heresy—of what constituted fidelity to God and what was to be fought as a perversion of true faith.

Combatants championed different belief systems, but they were sometimes willing to ignore religious differences when it was to their advantage. The determination of the German princes to defend their separate sovereignties had much to do with their decisions to embrace or combat the Reformation. Fear of the potential power of the Catholic Habsburg Empire drove some into the Protestant camp, and the expectation of help from Catholic authorities kept others loyal to the papacy. In France, religion split an aristocracy that had a long history of struggling within its own ranks for ascendancy at court. In England, most openly of all, political motives and perceived national interests lay behind the initial decision to break with Rome.

Opportunism aside, religion had a direct link with politics, for it affected how people thought about authority and legitimate government. The sovereignty that Protestantism claimed for individual conscience predisposed Protestants (particularly Calvinists) to favor some form of popular or representative government. Catholics, who were inclined to the traditional belief that authority was a gift God bestowed on rulers of His choice, supported monarchy and hierarchical systems of administration. Partisans from both camps faced the same dangerous temptation—to equate the defense of particular human institutions with the survival of transcendent principles. When opponents make that leap, they risk disaster. By absolutizing their positions, they persuade themselves that mediation and compromise are equivalent to treachery. All means, no matter what the human cost, seem justified when "the Truth" is at stake.

Review Questions

1. What key beliefs forced Luther to separate from the Catholic Church?
2. How were Calvinists different from Lutherans? From Anabaptists?
3. Was the English Reformation a reformation or a revolution?
4. What effect did the Reformation have on Catholicism and the power of the papacy?
5. What roles did religion play in the wars of the sixteenth and seventeenth centuries?
6. How did religion affect political developments in Spain, France, Germany, and England?

Please consult the Suggested Readings at the back of the book to continue your study of the material covered in this chapter. For a list of documents on the Primary Source DVD-ROM that relate to topics in this chapter, please refer to the back of the book.

Part 5
The Revolutionary Impulse

Joseph Wright of Derby, *An Experiment on a Bird in the Air Pump,* **1768.**

During the seventeenth and eighteenth centuries, Europeans were confronted with unprecedented challenges to conventional political thought and practice, to their picture of the physical universe, and to established social and religious values. In politics, ambitious monarchs consolidated their power through the expansion of royal bureaucracies and the formation of large standing armies. In both its absolutist and constitutional forms, monarchy made important strides toward the enhancement of state authority.

For almost two millennia, the accepted understanding of the cosmos placed humans at the center of God's creation. This Earth-centered and hierarchical cosmology was embraced by church authorities as reflecting the centrality of the human drama in creation. By 1700 this model of physical creation had been replaced by a sun-centered and mathematically ordered cosmos. Leading eighteenth-century thinkers extended the principles of order and rationality at the heart of the Scientific Revolution to new areas. Calls for reform were predicated on a new assumption: If the physical world operated according to natural laws, then comparable laws could be discovered and implemented in the social, religious, economic, and political spheres. A colonial political revolt in Britain's American empire in 1776 set the stage for a sweeping revolution in France in 1789. In both settings the institution of monarchy was eventually rejected, and efforts to build civil society anew on the basis of assumed laws of nature were carried forward.

ENVIRONMENT AND TECHNOLOGY	SOCIETY AND CULTURE	POLITICS
1543 1543 Copernicus, *On the Revolution of the Heavenly Spheres* 1543 Vesalius, *On the Fabric of the Human Body*	1611 *King James Bible* 1633 Trail of Galileo 1637 Descartes, *Discourse on Method*	1643–1715 Reign of Louis XIV 1642–1649 Civil War in England
1650 1609–1619 Kepler's laws of planetary motion 1610 Galileo, *Starry Messenger* 1620 Bacon, *Novum Organum*	1662 English Royal Society founded 1666 French *Academie des Sciences* founded 1690 Locke, *Essay Concerning Human Understanding*	1660 Restoration of English monarchy 1689 Revolution in England 1689–1725 Reign of Peter the Great 1690 Locke, *Two Treatises of Government*
1700 1687 *Mathematical Principles of Natural Philosophy*	1751 *Encyclopedia* 1764 Beccaria, *Of Crimes and Punishments*	1740–1786 Reign of Frederick the Great 1762–1796 Reign of Catherine the Great
1776 1700 European population reaches 100 million 1712 First steam engine 1733 Flying shuttle invented 1760 Spinning jenny invented 1780s–1850s Britain becomes first industrial nation 1790 European population reaches 250 million	1776 Smith, *Wealth of Nations* 1700–1750 Height of Baroque Music 1791 Death of Mozart at age 35	1776 American Revolution 1789 French Revolution 1792 *Vindication of the Rights of Women* 1793 France becomes a republic
1815		

Topics in This Chapter

Society in Early Modern Europe • Forging Centralized States

• Absolutism in France • Constitutionalism in England

• Wars of Empire and Global Markets • Central and Eastern Europe

• Europe's Declining Powers

14 The Early Modern State

A well conducted government must have an underlying concept so well integrated that it could be likened to a system of philosophy. All actions taken must be well reasoned, and all financial, political, and military matters must flow towards one goal, which is the strengthening of the state and the furthering of its power. However, such a system can flow but from a single brain, and this must be that of the sovereign.

—Frederick II

KEY | Question

How do political systems reflect the structure of social and economic life?

Frederick II (r. 1740–1786) of Prussia, also known as Frederick the Great, viewed himself as one of a new breed of European monarchs. In his *Political Testament,* written in 1752, he observed that a king must be the "first servant of the state" and not an arbitrary ruler. Still, as the previously quoted passage indicates, Frederick refused to acknowledge that his subjects had any right to help formulate state policy. "Just as it would have been impossible for Newton to arrive at his system of attractions if he had worked in harness with Leibnitz and Descartes, so a system of politics cannot be arrived at and continued if it has not sprung from a single brain." For Frederick, and for many of his royal contemporaries, absolute monarchy was necessitated by the flaws inherent in human nature. The leading Protestant reformers had reminded their followers that sinfulness and disobedience lay at the core of the human predicament. Apologists for absolutism maintained that social order and political harmony were impossible without the steady hand of divine-right rulers. In the wake of the Protestant Reformation, as political leaders claimed greater autonomy from Rome, the theory of absolutism found fertile ground in an intellectual climate that emphasized human frailty.

William and Mary Detail from the Painted Hall in Greenwich, England showing the resplendent English monarchs King William III (1650–1702) and Queen Mary II (1662–1694). William and Mary assumed the English throne in the bloodless "Glorious Revolution."

During the approximately 200 years from 1600 to the French Revolution that began in 1789, Europe's social structure, family traditions, and behavioral patterns remained largely unchanged, but some countries saw the stirring of new values and practices. Just as the hierarchy that had characterized the physical universe was challenged by Copernicus, Galileo, Kepler, and Newton, so too did Europe's hierarchical social and political structures come under increased scrutiny. In mid-seventeenth-century England, the old model of rulership under king, priest, and noble was temporarily upset during a protracted civil war, while in England's North American colonial empire a combination of environmental and geographical factors aborted efforts to transfer Europe's hierarchical social and political order to a new setting.

Monarchy was restored in England in 1660 after a troubled 11-year experiment in quasi-republican government, and in France a powerful form of centralized rule was forged under the leadership of King Louis XIV (r. 1643–1715). However, the experience of government without a king in England, the emergence of elected assemblies in Britain's North American colonies, and the acceleration of new forms of economic activity brought about by overseas exploration and colonization contributed to the emergence of a new and dynamic society in Western Europe. It was a society where material wealth began to displace hereditary status, titles, and landholding as the key measure of political power. By the last quarter of the eighteenth century, challenges to political absolutism reflected the emergence of a more confident picture of human nature and human potential. Individuals were assumed to possess certain rights that could not be abridged by either civil or religious authorities.

Society in Early Modern Europe

Status and Authority   For centuries European society had been divided into *estates* or status groups. Most people identified themselves with membership in occupational, religious, and regional groups that looked to the past for guidance in determining how to conduct life. The notion of individual rights, especially individual rights against public authority, was largely absent. Corporate assumptions—the well-being of the community before the advancement of the individual—informed the texture of everyday life. As late as the mid-eighteenth century most of Europe's population lived in rural settings, worked the land for subsistence, and rarely traveled more than a few miles from their place of birth. Society's natural leaders were identified by their lineage, not by their talents. Even leaders of popular revolts against high taxes and brutal landlords accepted the hierarchical social order and its traditional leaders. Indeed, most rebels called for a restoration of traditional practices and relationships, not a fundamental change in the economic and social fabric of life.

Aristocracy   Historians often refer to the period between 1650 and the third quarter of the eighteenth century as the *ancien régime* (Old Regime). Europe's aristocrats, a tiny fraction of the overall population, continued to dominate the political, religious, economic, and social life of the continent even though the growth of overseas trade and urban commerce was producing fundamental economic changes. Members of the titled aristocracy (dukes, marquises, counts, barons, etc.) considered themselves to be the natural leaders of society, their wealth derived from rents on lands worked by serfs or heavily taxed free peasants. Titled aristocrats were privileged subjects of the crown, serving as local political and military leaders, responsible for maintaining good order in the countryside, and monopolizing leadership positions within the established churches. In most European countries, aristocrats enjoyed a political voice at the national level through their residence at court or their membership in a parliament, diet, or assembly. In England, for example, the aristocracy consisted of a mere 400 families, but they enjoyed exclusive control over the upper chamber of Parliament, the House of Lords. In France, where there were 400,000 nobles out of a population of almost 20 million, the aristocracy exercised political influence through their monopoly over high positions in the church, the military, the courts, and the bureaucracy.

The fiscal privileges the aristocracy enjoyed were enormous. In France they were exempted from paying the *taille* or land tax, nor could they be obliged, as the peasants were, to contribute to the *corvée* (forced labor) on public works projects. Polish nobles were exempted from taxes after 1741, while various exemptions were available to the aristocratic class in the German states, Russia, Austria, and Hungary. Holding the exclusive right to bear arms, members of the aristocracy were expected to come to the aid of the poor who lived around their estates because status was thought to entail responsibility to one's inferiors. However, compassion for the poor was combined with wide-ranging power and legal discretion. Polish nobles held the power of life and death over their serfs, while in Prussia, Russia, England, and France manorial courts placed enormous judicial power in the hands of aristocrats. In return for humane treatment, the poor were expected to show deference and gratitude toward their wealthy benefactors. In reality, much resentment was directed against the privileged, especially against those who lived lavishly and employed large contingents of servants and military retainers. There were, for example, over 50 peasant revolts in Russia during the 1760s alone, and while this number was unusually high, peasant grievances were many and serious across Europe.

Peasants and Serfs   It is impossible to generalize about the condition of the common people in Old Regime Europe other than to say that their numbers increased significantly during the eighteenth century. The period from 1600 to 1700 was characterized by slow demographic growth in some areas and stagnation in others, with famine, war, and disease near constants of daily life. However, populations increased after 1700, mainly because of improved agricultural techniques and more effective use of land. In 1700 an estimated 110 million people lived in Europe; by 1800 the total had reached 190 million inhabitants. The largest increases occurred in Eastern Europe, especially in Russia and Hungary. The introduction of fodder crops such as clover added important nutrients to the soil, while turnips were grown to feed livestock during the winter. New crops from the Americas, especially maize (corn) and potatoes, afforded high nutritional content while yielding more food per acre than many traditional crops, such as wheat and rye. Poverty and malnutrition continued in the countryside, while urban underemployment led to much suffering in the cities. However, the steady growth in aggregate population across Europe signaled the enhanced ability of eighteenth-century society to provide for the basic necessities of life.

In England and France, most peasants enjoyed personal freedom. Further to the east, however, in the German states, Poland, and Russia, most peasants were **serfs**, legally bound to an estate and a particular landlord—often an aristocrat. Regardless of one's status, however, across the continent the class that owned the land dominated the class that worked it; social dependency in an overwhelming rural economy constituted the parameters of life for most men and women from the English Midlands to Russian Siberia. As population and food prices rose, and as farmland was consolidated in the interests of efficiency, the displacement of rural laborers and widespread urban poverty became two of Europe's most serious social problems. Charity hospitals and workhouses expanded their services in cities, but these institutions were often overwhelmed by the demand for assistance. A few hospitals resorted to lotteries to determine who would gain admission.

Conditions of work for common people varied markedly in each country, but in general more people often meant more hardship. French peasants typically owned a small piece of land, but it was seldom enough to provide for their families. Employment under the supervision of a landlord or the rental of additional land from a powerful aristocrat placed the peasant in a precarious economic position. Local fees *(banalites)* had to be paid to landowners to use their mills, ovens, and tools, and landlords had a monopoly on these items. Uncompensated work on the landlord's holdings and mandatory labor on public works projects—called the *corvée* in France—also strained the peasant's economic and physical resources. In England the emergence of commercial agriculture, initiated by a handful of improving landlords but subsequently affecting the entire kingdom, meant heavy labor demands on landless peasants and those who rented. Russian serfs, who were the virtual property of the nobility, experienced the harshest conditions. Both Peter the Great (r. 1682–1725) and Catherine the Great

Peasant Laborers in France   The *corvée* system in France required peasants to engage in public works projects like the building of roads and bridges. This mandatory labor system came to an end only after the French Revolution in 1789.

(r. 1762–1796) granted the aristocracy total control over the lives of their serfs. A Russian noble's wealth came to be measured in terms of the number of serfs (called "souls") in his possession, not the amount of land that he owned. The serf's travel, housing arrangements, and even marriages were ordered according to the wishes of the landlord.

Family Life   Western Europeans tended to work as family units, and families rarely exceeded six to ten members. Children normally resided in their parents' home and helped till the soil. Some would leave in their early teens to become servants in other families or apprentices under skilled craftsmen. Few persons lived alone, and those who did were regarded with the suspicion often associated with the rootless and the criminal. Marriages normally occurred when men and women were in their mid-twenties, and newlyweds established their own household and had children as soon as possible. In Eastern Europe family units tended to be much larger, and young married couples were more apt to reside with parents. Landlords sometimes forced serfs to marry or to remarry after the death of a spouse. Arranging marriages for serfs was intended to enhance the economic position of the lord of the manor.

The role of women in the family unit was defined largely by their child-bearing capacity and their economic acumen. Young girls often left home to become paid servants in other households. However, once they accumulated a sufficient dowry and a marriage was arranged for them, brides were expected to bear children who would become assets to the rural economy. Women and men worked together in the fields, plowing, planting, and producing sufficient crops to pay taxes and rent. Usually, this left only enough (in a good year) to survive until the next growing season. For the small minority of women who were married to traders or artisans and who lived in towns or cities, the death of a husband often meant that the widow would assume control of the business and even employ male apprentices. Although they were excluded from the political life of the urban center, these women could acquire economic independence after the death of a spouse.

Mortality   In this culture people were intimately familiar with the prospect of sudden death from one of a variety of causes. Even though the population of Western Europe increased sharply in the 1700s, mortality rates remained high. Perhaps the most difficult thing for us to understand about what life in the past must have been like is the experience of living and dying in a world without efficacious medicine. From the mid-eighteenth century until today, the development of narcotics and therapies capable of lessening the pain of death has altered the end-of-life experience for most people in the West. The narcotic effects of opium and its derivatives began the process that has culminated in the insensible death that millions experience in modern times. It is a death removed from public view and lacking the least element of personal oversight. By contrast, in early modern Europe most deaths occurred in the home. Immediate family and close friends assumed, in a way that could be exceptional today, a direct and continuous role in the physical and spiritual care of the person. The doctor's job, if his costly services were secured at all, was to diagnose the illness and offer a prognosis of how it would develop. He was not expected to provide a cure through aggressive intervention.

Eighteenth-century Europeans, like all humans around the world at that time, lived with sickness and death as close companions.

Forging Centralized States

While life conditions might differ enormously for the poor, peasant allegiances were fiercely local throughout Europe. Everyone was aware that a rigidly stratified social structure in which appearance, diet, housing, and speech reflected one's place in the order of creation was firmly endorsed by society's religious and secular leaders. Unlike modern society, status was still largely associated with education, birth, title, legal privileges, and office, not with wealth. Loyalties to lord, priest, and community were largely taken for granted and were much stronger than any feelings toward the ruling monarch. Indeed, taxes paid to the central government provoked the greatest resentment among the peasantry, especially because these taxes rarely seemed to benefit the local community.

Political Fragmentation   Unlike the world's other major civilizations in China, Japan, India, and the Ottoman and Persian empires, the political map of late sixteenth-century Europe was characterized by hundreds of independent and semi-independent units. No European head of state enjoyed the strong centralized authority of the Ming emperors in China and the Mughal emperors in India, for example. There were hereditary kings and queens in Spain, France, England, and Scandinavia, but elective monarchs in Poland and Hungary. The Holy Roman Emperor, perhaps the most powerful European head of state in terms of lands under his nominal control, was also elected by a select group of German churchmen and princes. Important ecclesiastical cities and principalities existed in parts of Germany, and the pope ruled over a large sweep of territory in central Italy. At the regional level, hundreds of nobles and city councils dominated the political life of their respective locales. In much of Europe, the monarch was only a distant and bothersome figurehead. Most rulers found themselves leading multilingual and multicultural collections of people, all of whom were eager to protect their long-established habits of autonomy.

This localism and provincialism largely ended during the seventeenth century. The wars of religion between Catholics and Protestants that had occupied European leaders since the 1550s not only caused enormous physical destruction and human dislocation, but also contributed to the rapid enhancement of centralized state power. Royal courts expanded during this period, taxes increased, and military spending absorbed a greater percentage of national revenue. In 1500 European governments were tiny, with a small number of full-time advisors and officials. Two centuries later, the major kingdoms employed thousands of bureaucrats and professional soldiers, each one committed to enhancing the authority of the crown. Local aristocrats, clerics, regional assemblies, and urban leaders lost portions of their autonomy as monarchs moved decisively to strengthen their position as leaders of consolidated states. Sending tax collectors, military recruiters, and judicial officers into the countryside, Europe's princes transformed their office. Abandoning the old medieval model in which they had been "first among equals," Europe's kings and queens served as divine-right agents of God on Earth.

The Church and Political Power   The most significant casualty of the sixteenth and seventeenth-century wars of religion and the subsequent enhancement of royal power was the Catholic Church. Before the Reformation, the medieval papacy enjoyed its own international sources of revenue, its own administrative bureaucracy, its own system of courts, and a centuries-old claim to jurisdictional superiority over individual Christian princes. The Church was the only truly transnational European institution, and its clergy were encouraged to accept the authority of their ecclesiastical leaders over the wishes of their respective monarchs. The success of the Reformation in northern Europe by the mid-seventeenth century—in England, Scandinavia, parts of the Netherlands and Switzerland, and many north German states—put an end to the Roman Catholic Church's pretensions to universal religious and political authority. In Protestant territories, monarchs claimed leadership over state-supported churches, while in powerful Catholic countries like France and Spain, kings and queens played a key role in the selection of bishops and archbishops.

Political Theory and the State   Two distinct models of political authority emerged during the seventeenth century to further the goal of centralization. The theory behind each model differed, but the practical outcomes were similar. France followed the path of **absolutism** under the leadership of a powerful king. England, in contrast, curbed the monarch's discretionary authority and accorded greater political power to a Parliament dominated by aristocrats and landowners. Ironically, one of the most compelling books in support of the monarch's absolute power was written by the English King James I (r. 1603–1625), while some of the strongest arguments against absolutism were written by late sixteenth-century French authors.

In *The True Law of Free Monarchies* (1598), King James insisted that hereditary monarchs enjoy their elevated status because God chose them. The book acknowledged that the monarch held a sacred trust to advance the material and spiritual well-being of his subjects. In addition, it held that kings and queens were accountable to God alone, and that subjects had a sacred duty to obey even if the monarch violated God's law. In France the period of religious wars and monarchical weakness that began in the 1560s occasioned the publication of important anti-absolutist works. Soon after a terrible attack by Catholics against French Protestants in 1572 that left 10,000 dead in the country's major cities, an event known as the St. Bartholomew's Day Massacre, the Protestant Francois Hotman (1524–1590) published *Francogallia* (1573). Hotman believed that the dissolute young French King Charles IX (r. 1560–1574) had ordered the attacks. In his book Hotman claimed that history showed the French crown was not hereditary. Instead, it was conferred by the people on "those who were reputed just."

Six years later another French Protestant author wrote *Defense of Liberty Against Tyrants* (1579), a book that claimed that magistrates had the right to remove a king who failed to enforce God's law. These and other resistance theorists—some of whom were Roman Catholic—had a strong impact on political theory in seventeenth- and eighteenth-century Europe. The Spanish Jesuit Juan de Molina (1536–1624) captured the essence of their position when he wrote in *The King and the Education of the King* (1598) that monarchs and magistrates were only the representatives of the people.

PEOPLE IN CONTEXT   King James I as Political Theorist

When he succeeded Queen Elizabeth I of England in 1603, James I was already a mature and experienced monarch. One year after his birth in 1566, James's mother, Mary Queen of Scots (1542–1587), was forced to abdicate the throne of Scotland due to a series of scandals. Not the least of these was her reputed involvement in the suspicious death of James's father, Henry Stuart, Lord Darnley (1545–1567). Scotland was completely independent of England during the sixteenth and seventeenth centuries, as King James faced an uphill struggle to consolidate his authority against independent-minded Gaelic-speaking highland clans and lowland nobles who commanded their own fighting forces. After a long regency during which his advisors jostled for power, James began to rule Scotland directly in 1585 at the age of 21.

As King James VI of Scotland, James's intellectual pursuits reflected his desire to strengthen the power of the monarchy. In 1598 he published two books whose objective was to explain and defend divine-right monarchy. In *The True Law of Free Monarchy* and *Basilikon Doron (Royal Gift)* James insisted that only a strong executive could end the civil and religious conflict tearing Europe apart. For a monarch to be effective, however, subjects must acknowledge that royal power is a divine gift. According to James, kings represent God on Earth, and human laws could not constrain them. The sovereign must be obeyed in all things, for royal commands are the commands of God's minister. No subject had the right to resist, for only God could judge an errant king. The wise king would always try to obey human law, "yet he is not bound thereto but of his good will, and for example-giving to his subjects."

TO THE MOST HIGH AND MIGHTIE Prince, IAMES by the grace of God King of Great Britaine, France and Ireland, Defender of the Faith, &c.

THE TRANSLATORS OF *THE BIBLE,*
wish Grace, Mercie, and Peace, through IESVS CHRIST *our* LORD.

Reat and manifold were the blessings (most dread Soueraigne) which Almighty GOD, the Father of all Mercies, bestowed vpon vs the people of ENGLAND, when first he sent your Maiesties Royall person to rule and raigne ouer vs. For whereas it was the expectation of many, who wished not well vnto our SION, that vpon the setting of that bright *Occidentall Starre* Queene ELIZABETH of most happy memory, some thicke and palpable cloudes of darkenesse would so haue ouershadowed this land, that men should haue bene in doubt which way they were to walke, and that it should hardly be knowen, who was to direct the vnsetled

The King James Bible   Title page to the 1611 English translation of the Holy Bible, commissioned by James. The Bible is dedicated to the king and the translators make it clear that he rules "by the grace of God."

James's absolutist political theory was not well received after he became king of England. His long reign (1603–1625) was marked by repeated disagreements with Parliament. But James attempted to live by some of the more temperate advice contained in his two books. The *Basilikon Doron* was a best-selling advice book written for the king's elder son Henry. Soon after its publication, it was translated into Latin, French, Dutch, German, and Swedish. In the book, James admonished his son to "think not therefore that the highness of your dignity, diminisheth your faults (much less give you license to sin) but by the contrary your fault shall be aggravated, according to the height of your dignity." Absolute monarchy did not mean arbitrary monarchy. For James I of England, obedience to national law and tradition strengthened the crown and legitimized the king's right to rule.

Question: How did the political theory of absolutism seek to enlist the support of Christianity?

Absolutism in France

King Henry IV (r. 1589–1610) struggled mightily to bring an end to the religious divisions that had wracked France since the 1560s. With his promulgation of the Edict of Nantes in 1598, Henry granted religious toleration to the kingdom's minority Protestant population. Henry also attempted to limit the political privileges of the regional judicial courts, called *parlements,* staffed by the provincial nobility. The government introduced the labor tax, or *corvée,* and created monopolies over the production of gunpowder and salt. In the wake of his efforts to defuse religious tensions, however, the king was assassinated by a Catholic fanatic in 1610. His death left the throne to a 9-year-old male heir, Louis XIII (r. 1610–1643).

Cardinal Richelieu   During the minority of Louis XIII, his mother, Marie de Medici (d. 1642), appointed Armand Jean de Plessis, Duke de Richelieu (1585–1642), as principal advisor to the crown. This brilliant and shrewd Roman Catholic cardinal set about to strengthen the king's position within France and to enhance French power across Europe. Cardinal Richelieu assigned new government officials, called *intendants,* to each French province. These men served as the eyes and ears of the crown throughout the country, making sure that royal edicts were obeyed and taxes were collected fairly and efficiently. Richelieu also curbed the political autonomy of the Huguenots. He sent royal armies to occupy their strategic cities and abolished their separate law courts. He did not, however, interfere with the practice of their religion.

On the international front, Cardinal Richelieu was convinced that the Catholic Habsburgs represented the greatest threat to France, and he assisted the Protestant states opposed to the Habsburgs during the final decade of the Thirty Years' War (1618–1648). In particular, Richelieu helped to fund the armies of King Gustavus Adolphus of Sweden (r. 1611–1642) in an effort to curb the ambitions of Habsburg Spain. Throughout his long tenure as chief minister (1624–1642), Richelieu embraced the principle of "reason of state" when formulating and implementing policy. The greater glory of France and the consolidation of royal power always superceded the interests of local officials, nobles, and even the international Catholic community.

The Personal Rule of Louis XIV   When Louis XIII died in 1643, France was left with another child king, 5-year-old Louis XIV (d. 1715). Richelieu had died just five months before Louis XIII. The regency government set up to administer affairs during the new monarch's minority was led by another leading churchman, the Italian-born

Louis XIV   In this 1701 portrait of Louis XIV by Hyacinthe Rigaud, Louis XIV appears in his coronation robes projecting an image of wisdom, strength, and resolve. The portrait communicates the importance of divine-right monarchy to the stability of the kingdom. *Rigaud, Hyacinthe (1659–1743). Louis XIV, King of France (1638–1715) in royal costume. 1701. Oil on canvas, 277 × 194 cm. Louvre, Paris, France. Photo credit: Erich Lessing/Art Resource, NY*

Cardinal Mazarin (1602–1661). Efforts to further Richelieu's state-building campaign involved the imposition of new taxes. In 1649 members of the Parisian nobility, led by the highest court of the land, the *Parlement* of Paris, refused to endorse a new round of taxation. Barricades were erected in the capital city, and Mazarin and the young king had to flee. The uprisings, collectively known as the *Fronde* after the slingshots used by street children, continued sporadically until 1652. Urban riots involving the poor and dispossessed so alarmed the aristocracy that they reaffirmed their support for the young king. Members of the Paris *Parlement* wanted a greater role in the formulation of royal policy, not the destruction of the existing social and political order.

Shocked by the actions of his leading subjects during the *Fronde*, Louis XIV worked throughout his long reign to transform the monarchy into the unchallenged center of political power in France. From the early 1660s until his death in 1715, he ruled without consulting a representative assembly. He made laws and appointments directly, and he built and repeatedly employed a large professional army of over 200,000 men. In 1685 he transformed France into a confessional state by rescinding the limited toleration that the Edict of Nantes granted to the Huguenots in 1598. He also banned a splinter Roman Catholic movement known as Jansenism. Gallicanism, the idea that the French Catholic church should be a separate entity under the French crown within the Roman Catholic fold, gained increased support after 1650. The king's wish became the law of the land. Under Louis's careful guidance, France became Europe's premier political and military power during the second half of the seventeenth century.

Versailles and the Projection of Power   Constructed under the direction of King Louis XIV, the enormous palace of Versailles was a powerful symbol of royal rule from 1682 until the start of the French Revolution in 1789. Located just 12 miles outside Paris, the property was first used by King Louis XIII as a small hunting lodge. Louis XIV committed vast resources to the construction of his new residence, employing architects, painters, decorators, and landscapers to create a palace and gardens of unrivaled scale and beauty. That Versailles was an open palace, missing the walls and battlements of medieval castles, testifies to the king's unique position in the country's political order. Construction and expansion of the palace began in 1669 and continued until Louis's death in 1715. Over 30,000 laborers were engaged in the project during the reign of the "Sun King," as Louis XIV was known. The palace could accommodate more than 5,000 people, and over 10,000 servants and soldiers were quartered in the nearby town of Versailles.

Louis XIV obliged the great nobles of the realm to spend much of the year at Versailles. This enabled the king to keep a close check on potential rivals while simultaneously denying his most powerful subjects opportunities to build independent support in the countryside. The nobility became servants of the crown at Versailles, and Louis's daily routine was carefully planned to take full advantage of this aristocratic entourage. Rising at 8:30 in the morning, Louis was bathed, dressed, and fed by those fortunate enough to be admitted into the royal bedchamber. At 10:00 the royal party attended mass, and at 11:00 the king convened his various councils of state—foreign affairs, the military, finance, state, and religious affairs. A private dinner was usually served at 1:00 in the afternoon and after 2:00 the monarch would typically promenade in the palace gardens or hunt on the expansive grounds.

On these occasions even the most humble of the king's subjects could observe the court routine. Once again noble courtiers would compete with each other for the right to accompany the king, for it was in these informal settings that influence was won and lost. According to one participant, Louis de Rouvroy, Duc de Saint-Simon (1675–1755), "the frequent fetes, the private promenades at Versailles, were means on which the king seized in order to distinguish or mortify the courtiers, and thus render them more assiduous in pleasing him." More work or a social gathering would occupy the king until around 10:00, when a supper would be served to members of the royal family.

The Palace of Versailles   Built during the reign of Louis XIV, the gigantic Palace of Versailles conveys the power and opulence of French absolutism. Located a few miles west of Paris, the palace was the home of the French monarchs and the administrative center of the *ancien régime. Pierre Patel (1605–1676), "Birds Eye View of Versailles." Chateau de Versailles et de Trianon, Versailles, France. Copyright Giraudon/Art Resource, NY*

Royal palaces like Versailles—and monarchs built versions of the palace across Europe—were designed to showcase political power. Royal emblems and portraits of the monarchs filled the public spaces of the palace. On the ceiling of the magnificent Hall of Mirrors at Versailles, Louis commissioned paintings depicting the great events of his reign. He is portrayed as a Roman emperor, an expert administrator, and a military commander. In this imposing space the king would receive foreign ambassadors and other high dignitaries. It would have been impossible for the guest not to be impressed by the opulence and solemnity of the space. In choosing the sun as his official emblem, Louis XIV wished to evoke references to Apollo, the god of peace and the arts who was associated with the sun, while also emphasizing the sun's status as lifegiver. Royal complexes like Versailles served a variety of functions associated with a form of political control in which subjects would accept their place in a fixed social hierarchy.

Royal Bureaucrats   Louis XIV chose many of his most dedicated servants and officials from among the ranks of the middle class or bourgeoisie. These men of modest means were unlikely to build independent bases of power for themselves while serving the crown. Their success was based exclusively on loyal service to the king, and in the case of the *intendants,* they were regularly reassigned to new provinces to ensure their loyalty to the government at Versailles. The king's talented chief finance minister, Jean-Baptiste Colbert (1619–1683), encouraged the formation of new industries and adopted an unrelenting protectionist policy known as mercantilism. Under mercantilist practice, exports were expanded and imports curbed while the government protected French industries from foreign competition. By increasing the *taille* and better regulating its collection, Colbert gave the king the fiscal resources to pursue an ambitious military agenda (see Map 14–1).

The Wars of Louis XIV   Louis was a man of war, dedicated to securing what he defined as France's natural borders—the Pyrenees, the Alps, and the Rhine River. The king's many military campaigns led to the emergence of strategic alliances against France. Beginning in 1667 and continuing with little interruption until the end of Louis's reign, French forces attacked Spain's Belgian provinces (1667–1668), the United Provinces of Holland (1672–1679), and the free city of Strasbourg (1681). The latter assault eventually led to the exhausting nine-year War of the League of Augsburg (1688–1697) and pitted France against England, Spain, the United Provinces, and much of the Holy Roman Empire.

Finally, between 1700 and 1714, Louis pressed a claim on behalf of his grandson, Philip of Anjou (1683–1746), to the Spanish throne. The rival claimant was an Austrian Habsburg prince, and Louis feared Habsburg domination of the continent if the Austrian became king of Spain. Once again, a large coalition, including England, Holland, and the Holy Roman Empire, united against the French. During this long conflict, French resources were stretched to the limit, and English forces under the superior leadership of John Churchill, the duke of Marlborough (1650–1722), defeated a poorly organized and led French army in two decisive battles. The first took place at Blenheim in

Map 14–1 Europe in 1714 At the end of the War of the Spanish Succession in 1714, Louis XIV was able to secure Bourbon control of the Spanish throne, but the French king failed to realize his territorial ambitions along the frontier with the Holy Roman Empire.

Question: What territories did Louis XIV claim as part of France's "natural" eastern frontier?

August 1704, and the second at Ramillies in 1706. Despite these setbacks, and in the face of increasing unrest at home, Louis XIV refused to concede defeat. Absent an organized political opposition in his absolutist state, his will again prevailed. At the end of the war Louis's nephew was recognized as Philip V of Spain (r. 1700–1746), although Spain had to cede its territories in Belgium and Italy to the Habsburgs and their allies.

By the time of Louis's death in 1715, France had suffered a series of agricultural disasters and a serious financial crisis. The worst years for the king's subjects were 1708 and 1709, as widespread famine and high taxes led to revolts throughout the country. Louis had lost the admiration of his people. He had failed to follow the Machiavellian and Hobbesian injunction to provide for the peace, security, and material improvement of his subjects. His successors continued to involve the country in a series of debilitating continentwide and imperial overseas conflicts against England, Austria, and Prussia during the eighteenth century. All of these conflicts led to a final reckoning for the monarchy in 1789.

Constitutionalism in England

The Early Stuarts England followed a very different political path. The political and religious consensus that Queen Elizabeth I (r. 1558–1603) had established began to fray almost immediately after her death. The new monarch, James I, infuriated religious reformers. The reformers were convinced that the Church of England, with its reliance on bishops, elaborate rituals, and arbitrary religious courts, too closely resembled its discarded Roman Catholic predecessor. Their opponents called these would-be reformers Puritans. The Puritans attempted to use their influence in Parliament to force the king's hand. James and his successor, Charles I (r. 1625–1649), refused to make concessions, however, convinced that the Puritan demand for the abolition of the bishops would be followed by even more radical calls for the end of the monarchy.

When Charles succeeded his father in 1625, he attempted to strengthen the power of the monarchy along French lines. A protracted clash with Puritan members of Parliament led the king to dissolve the House of Commons in 1629. For 11 years Charles refused to call this representative assembly into session, leading thousands of disgruntled Puritans to strike out across the Atlantic for a new life in Massachusetts Bay colony. During the 1630s, crown revenues were raised by a variety of extra-parliamentary means, and the Church of England further alienated members of the middle class and landed gentry.

Civil War Full scale civil war erupted in 1642 after the king unsuccessfully attempted to impose the Church of England's official prayer book on the Scottish Presbyterian Church. The Puritan forces were led by the skilled military commander Oliver Cromwell (1599–1658). They repeatedly accused King Charles of taxation without the consent of Parliament, imprisonment of subjects without cause, and the illegal transformation of the Protestant Church of England into a replica of Roman Catholicism. The war continued intermittently until the Royalist supporters of the king were decisively defeated in 1649. Charles was executed, episcopacy was abolished, and the hereditary House of Lords was suspended. The country was then ruled as a semi-republican Protectorate under the heavy hand of Cromwell as Lord Protector and the army leadership until 1660. During this period the Puritan leadership found itself unable to institute meaningful political reform, and Cromwell emerged as a de facto military dictator. Taxes escalated and general disillusionment with the Protectorate led to a restoration of the monarchy under Charles II (r. 1660–1685) in 1660.

Monarchy Restored   The civil war had resolved few of the main issues separating crown and Parliament. The period 1660 to 1689 was marked by ongoing constitutional debate over the limits of royal authority and the role of the two Houses of Parliament in the direction of national affairs. Charles II was a skilled political operative who, while envious of the power wielded by his cousin Louis XIV, was also a realist who acknowledged the historic role of Parliament in the political life of the kingdom. While sympathetic to the difficulties faced by England's small Roman Catholic minority (Charles declared himself to be a Catholic on his deathbed), the king refused to alienate his Protestant subjects by fighting for religious toleration.

His brother and successor was less adept at navigating the troubled waters of religious bigotry. King James II (r. 1685–1688) was a Roman Catholic in a Protestant country. His subjects were prepared to accept his inaugural pledge that he would not allow his religious preferences to influence his decisions as king of a Protestant nation. Unfortunately, their trust was almost immediately betrayed. James appointed Roman Catholics to leadership positions in the military and in the colleges at Oxford and Cambridge. He also tried to alter the process by which members of Parliament were elected from urban constituencies, and he attempted to secure religious toleration for his Roman Catholic subjects. In November 1688, just three years after James had assumed power, a group of aristocrats encouraged the king's Protestant daughter Mary and her husband Prince William of Orange to invade England on behalf of Protestantism and parliamentary government. James was accused of having attempted to abridge the rights of Parliament while forwarding a design to establish a French-style absolute monarchy.

Bloodless Revolution   In the aftermath of the successful invasion, James II fled to France, and William and Mary accepted the constitutional compromise influenced by the ideas of John Locke (1632–1704; see Chapter 15, "New World Views: Europe's Scientific Revolution"). A Bill of Rights, passed by Parliament and signed by William III (r. 1689–1702) and Mary II (r. 1689–1694) as joint monarchs, solidified the contractual nature of civil society. The Bill of Rights recognized the rights of the political elite to share in the kingdom's governance. Religious toleration for all Protestants who accepted the doctrine of the Trinity was secured in 1689, and king and Parliament agreed on an orderly mechanism for the peaceful succession of Protestants to the throne. While the Church of England continued to receive state support well into the nineteenth century and is still the official church of the English part of the United Kingdom, the business of government had taken a decisively secular turn in 1689.

Perhaps the clearest measure of this increasing secularization can be seen in the shifting precipitants to war. While conflicting religious outlooks had been at the heart of military confrontations in England for most of the seventeenth century, King William III engaged the enormous fiscal and military resources of England in a monumental struggle against Louis XIV's territorial ambitions. The eighteenth century would be marked by wars for empire and for trade, not for souls. In this area of human activity, religious belief was of lesser moment than the furs of North America, the sugar of the Carribean islands, or the spices of India.

Wars of Empire and Global Markets

Beginning in the 1680s, the wars between France and the Grand Alliance in Europe involved a wider colonial dimension. In particular, the British repeatedly challenged French power in North America, the Caribbean, South Asia, the Mediterranean, and the Pacific. At the end of the War of the Spanish Succession in 1714, Britain acquired Nova Scotia, Newfoundland, and Hudson Bay territories from the French. They also received the strategic entrance to the Mediterranean at Gibraltar from the Spanish. British maritime supremacy, coupled with government support for trade and commerce, enabled this small island kingdom to become the dominant power in Europe during the second half of the eighteenth century. Whereas military conflict led to mounting debt and a weakened monarchy in France, in Britain the engagement of the aristocracy, the rising gentry, and the urban elite in the process of policymaking enhanced the power of the crown. In particular, greater access to political power strengthened the commitment of investors to fund the considerable cost of overseas warfare.

Commercial Conflict   By the start of the eighteenth century, Western Europe's colonial empires in the Americas and parts of Asia were firmly established. Non-Western peoples from Japan and the Indian subcontinent to West Africa and across the Atlantic in the Americas were forced to respond to the intrusive designs of the Europeans. Only China and Japan continued to rebuff Western efforts to secure uncontrolled trade relations. Elsewhere, the success of Western traders, settlers, and missionaries to extend their influence and to reduce the significance of cultural differences was without precedent. For good or ill, the world was becoming "Europeanized" by the eighteenth century, beginning a process that has continued with ever greater acceleration into our own day.

In particular, overseas exploration, trade, and colonization won the enthusiastic support of Britain's political elite during the eighteenth century. This alliance of commercial capital and government military power facilitated the process of "making the world one" on European terms. Joint stock companies, the increased use of paper currency, sophisticated credit arrangements, and insurance plans all facilitated the movement of people and goods across the oceans. Beginning with the Treaty of Utrecht (1713), which ended Britain's participation in the War of the Spanish Succession, the boundaries of the respective empires were clearly established. A weakened Spanish monarchy reaffirmed its control over all of mainland South America, with the exception of Portuguese-held Brazil. Spain also held territory in Florida, New Mexico, California, and the Caribbean islands of Cuba, Puerto Rico, and that part of Hispaniola that today is the Dominican Republic. Britain controlled the eastern coastline of North America together with the sugar-producing islands of Jamaica and Barbados. The French, despite their losses in the War of the Spanish Succession, remained in possession of the lucrative sugar islands of Saint Dominique (modern Haiti), Guadeloupe, and Martinique. French traders also operated along the St. Lawrence River Valley in New France, or Canada, at the mouth of the Mississippi around the city of New Orleans, and west of the Appalachian mountain range in North America. The Dutch, now pushed to the margins as a trading power in the Americas, still ruled over Surinam (Dutch Guiana)

The Fur Trade   A Native American hands a pelt to a European buyer. By 1700, the fur trade had decimated the beaver population in southern Canada and New England. *Fur traders and Indians: engraving, 1777.* © The Granger Collection, New York

in South America and a few Caribbean islands. The Dutch, French, and British also held lucrative trading stations along the west coast of India, and the Dutch had begun the conquest of the rich spice islands that today make up the Republic of Indonesia.

Global Clashes   Following mercantilist economic theory, colonies were valued mainly for their potential economic benefit to the home country. Each of the major powers prohibited rivals from trading with its colonies. While widespread smuggling persisted throughout the eighteenth century, colonial wars were normally fought to protect overseas markets and natural resources. The rivalry between the British and the French was especially bitter. Clashes along the lower St. Lawrence River Valley, in the Ohio River Valley, in the West Indies, and in India cultivated deep and lasting animosities. In addition to the War of the Spanish Succession (1702–1714), two mid-century clashes in central Europe had their counterparts in the colonies. The War of the Austrian Succession (1744–1748) and the Seven Years' War (1756–1763) drew the French and British overseas colonies into what were initially localized European conflicts. The War of the Austrian Succession began when King Frederick the Great of Prussia seized the province of Silesia from Austria's Empress Maria Teresa (r. 1740–1780). Britain, seeking to uphold the continental balance of power, supported Austria while the French, traditional enemy of the Habsburgs, sided with Frederick. During the war,

French and British colonists clashed repeatedly in northern New England, New York, the Ohio River Valley, the Caribbean, and India.

The decisive Seven Years' War actually began in the Americas in 1754, two years before the outbreak of hostilities in Europe. British colonials fought with the French and their Native American allies over lands deemed to be important in the lucrative fur trade. Confronted with about one and one-half million English colonists, the 90,000 French settlers desperately needed the assistance of their skillful Native American allies. When British Prime Minister William Pitt (1708–1778) decided that the defeat of France on the continent demanded a global strategy, he decided to send a fighting force of over 40,000 men to the colonies. It represented the largest army ever employed in colonial warfare up to that time. After initial setbacks, the British captured Quebec City in 1759 and soon won control over all French territory in Canada. The British navy also captured most of the French sugar islands in the Caribbean. In India, British Commander Robert Clive (1725–1774) won a key victory over the French in 1757 at the Battle of Plassey. In the aftermath the British secured control over the province of Bengal in northeast India. By the end of the conflict in 1763, French colonial trade had plummeted to a fraction of its prewar level, leaving Britain the undisputed leader in global commerce. In terms of mercantilist economics, Great Britain was now the predominant power in Europe.

Consequences for France   Louis XV ascended the French throne in 1715 at the age of 5, and he reigned for nearly 60 years until 1774. Like his predecessor Louis XIV, the king claimed to rule by divine mandate, but the fiscal pressures on the government undermined royal authority. The crown wished to raise taxes to meet its mounting military obligations, but the 13 *parlements* refused to endorse any plan that would oblige the wealthy aristocracy to help reduce the national debt. All efforts to reform government finances failed, and by the early 1770s the king had become deeply unpopular. Louis's reputation for lavish spending at court and his involvement with a succession of young women further alienated his subjects. When he died in 1774, few of his subjects mourned his passing.

Central and Eastern Europe

Russian Absolutism   The dramatic overseas expansion of Europe's Atlantic kingdoms during the seventeenth and eighteenth centuries was matched by Russia's continental drive to the east. Beginning in the 1580s and continuing into the nineteenth century, Russian merchants, soldiers, adventurers, and political prisoners moved across the Ural Mountains. They gradually transformed Siberia, one of the world's key centers of mineral wealth and other natural resources. By the mid-eighteenth century, Russians had penetrated over 6,000 miles east of Moscow, first toward the fertile lands of the Ukraine and subsequently east toward the Pacific. The subjugation of Siberia alone was comparable in scale, economic impact, and strategic significance to contemporary Spanish, Portuguese, Dutch, English, and French incursions into the Americas. Siberia was a central feature of the conversion of a landlocked regime centered around Moscow into a powerful absolutist state under the leadership of the Romanov dynasty, which would rule Russia until 1917. By 1700 Russia had become the largest territorial kingdom on Earth.

Michael, the first Romanov tsar (caesar or emperor), was chosen by a group of leading nobles in 1613. They elected the 16-year-old grandnephew of Ivan the Terrible, the tsar who had ruled Russia with an iron fist from 1533 to 1584. Tsar Michael (r. 1613–1676) came to power after a period of civil unrest known as the Time of Troubles that had followed Ivan's death. Michael and his Romanov successors consolidated their power during the seventeenth century despite a number of unsuccessful revolts from the 1640s through the 1670s. Contacts with the West increased during the late seventeenth century, and when Peter I, "the Great" (r. 1689–1725), ascended the throne, the stage was set for a dynamic assertion of royal power and display.

Peter the Great   Peter I had traveled to Western Europe early in his reign, and he was deeply impressed by Western technology, military organization, and political practice. He invited numerous Western technicians and advisers to Russia and instituted government protection for new industries and commercial enterprises. The tsar insisted that his nobles become engaged in lifelong state service—either civil or military—and he created a system of bureaucratic advancement based on merit. Taxes imposed on the peasantry paid for the needs of the military, while serfs were assigned to work in state-owned factories and mines. When the leaders of the Russian Orthodox Church objected to the tsar's reforms, he attacked the church's wealth and replaced the Patriarch of Moscow, who had been the head of the church, with a new administrative office called the Holy Synod. Significantly, the leader of the Holy Synod was a lay official appointed by the tsar.

Military reform was a top priority for the energetic and ruthless tsar. Peter built a professional army of nearly 200,000 men armed with modern muskets and artillery. Engagements against the Ottoman Turks in lands adjacent to the Black Sea were unsuccessful, but after a protracted struggle (1700–1721) against Sweden, Peter secured control over the Baltic provinces of Estonia and Latvia. Confirming his gains in the Treaty of Nystad (1721),

Peter the Great   A youthful Peter the Great appears in this portrait wearing armor. The image of determination and self-confidence enhanced his claims to absolute power.

the tsar proceeded to build a new capital on the shores of the Baltic. This modern capital, called St. Petersburg, provided the Russians with an opportunity to imitate the contemporary Baroque building style of Western Europe. Peter's reforms cost both money and lives. Taxes escalated fivefold during his reign, and tens of thousands died in his wars and in the building of St. Petersburg. The condition of the serfs became increasingly desperate. Serfs became the personal property of their lords, and the official distinction between a slave and a serf was ended.

Catherine the Great   Peter's male offspring predeceased him, and upon the tsar's death in 1725, Russia was subject to a period of serious political instability marked by palace coups and assassinations. In 1741 the tsar's youngest daughter, Elizabeth, ascended the throne. Elizabeth then named her nephew Peter her heir and chose an obscure German princess to be Peter's wife. Her name was Catherine, and when her weakling husband came to power in 1762, Catherine plotted his deposition and murder in collusion with a group of disgruntled military officers. With the support of aristocratic army leaders, Catherine ruled successfully until 1796. During the first decade of her reign, the empress corresponded with leading Enlightenment figures and made a range of cultural, educational, and legal reforms. But after a large revolt by Russian peasants in 1773 in which hundreds of influential landlords were slaughtered, Catherine's interest in reform waned. During the remainder of her reign, the condition of Russia's serfs became even more onerous even as their masters increasingly imitated the lifestyles of Western aristocrats. In 1785 Catherine extended the institution of serfdom into new areas of the empire and freed the nobility from all state taxes.

In foreign affairs Catherine was more successful than Peter the Great. The empress launched a war against the Ottoman Turks in 1768, and after six years of fighting, the Turks ceded to the Russians strategically important territories along the northern coast of the Black Sea and in the Balkans. Catherine also sought to extend Russia's frontier in the West. In a series of assaults against Poland, Russia joined with Prussia and Austria in three partitions that eventually wiped that large country off the map of Europe. When Catherine died in 1796, Russia had taken its place as one of the great powers in Europe.

Prussian Militarism   The hereditary rulers of Prussia first emerged in the German territory of Brandenburg during the early fifteenth century. The Hohenzollern family gradually added more lands to its realm. By the start of the eighteenth century, the Hohenzollern electors of Brandenburg (so called because they were one of the German ruling families who helped elect the Holy Roman Emperors) had become the kings of Prussia. They ruled over a variety of German duchies, bishoprics, counties, and provinces that constituted a total area second in size in Germany only to the Habsburg domains. During the mid-seventeenth century, Elector Frederick William (r. 1640–1688) built a strong and disciplined military establishment and a loyal administrative bureaucracy capable of uniting Prussia's disparate lands. Career officers replaced mercenary commanders, and troops were called up for specific tours of duty before returning to their agricultural pursuits. His successors, especially King Frederick William I (r. 1713–1740) and Frederick II, "the Great" (r. 1740–1786), were competent and dedicated rulers who built on these initial efforts. Service to the state became a central characteristic of Prussian aristocratic culture during this period.

Frederick William I began the Prussian royal practice of always appearing in public in military dress, and he built the continent's third largest army (over 80,000 men). The king was reluctant to use this army, however, preferring to maintain this well-equipped fighting force as a symbol of Prussia's arrival as a great power. His son, Frederick II, demonstrated no such reservations about the employment of force. During the first two decades of his reign, he fought wars against a variety of coalition powers, including Austria, Russia, and France. During the Seven Years' War (1756–1763), Frederick's kingdom was almost destroyed. Only British financial support and Russian withdrawal from the coalition in 1762 saved Prussia. During the second half of his reign, Frederick introduced agricultural improvements, put an end to torture and capital punishment, and codified the laws of the realm. He also encouraged commerce and industry through the recruitment of enterprising refugees who were fleeing religious or political persecution in other European countries.

Key Developments in the Rise of the Early Modern European State	
1558–1603	Reign of Elizabeth I
1598	King James I, *The True Law of Free Monarchies*
1618–1948	Thirty Years' War
1642–1949	English Civil War
1643–1715	Reign of Louis XIV
1689–1725	Reign of Peter the Great
1740–1786	Reign of Frederick the Great

Europe's Declining Powers

Ottoman Decay   Russia's victory over the Turks in 1774 was symptomatic of the once mighty Ottoman Empire's long descent as a European power. At its height in the sixteenth century, the Ottoman-controlled territories stretched over an area larger than the Roman Empire. Suleiman I, "the Magnificent" (r. 1520–1566), ruled over 14 million subjects at a time when there were only two and one-half million people living in Queen Elizabeth I's (r. 1588–1603) England. The Ottoman capital of Istanbul was much larger than any city in Western Europe, and the Ottoman bureaucracy—part of a vast military establishment—was both dedicated and competent. Ottoman military power was unrivaled in Western Europe until the late sixteenth century,

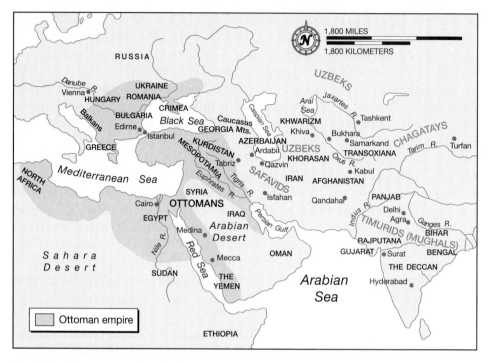

Map 14–2   Ottoman Empire Around 1600   The Ottoman Empire spanned from North Africa to the Caucasus and north to the gates of Vienna. As this map indicates, there were a number of powerful Muslim empires to the east of the Ottoman-dominated lands, but few rivaled Ottoman power, and none could match the level of often hostile contact the Ottomans had with Western Europe.

Question: Why did the Habsburgs fear the Ottoman Turks?

when a combined Venetian, Spanish, and papal naval fleet defeated a Turkish force at the Battle of Lepanto in 1571. This military reversal was closely related to a wider set of economic, cultural, and political problems facing the Empire at a time when Western Europe was becoming innovative and aggressive (see Map 14–2).

After the death of Suleiman in 1566, Ottoman political leadership was compromised under a series of undistinguished sultans. These men failed to encourage change and risk-taking in agriculture, trade, or manufacture. In fact, manufacture declined sharply as the government curbed exports and as businessmen abandoned trade and instead purchased the right to collect taxes for the central government. The Empire's foreign trade gradually fell into the hands of Europeans resident in Istanbul. The Ottoman ruling elite lost touch with the concerns of the common people, as the bureaucracy, the military, and the sultan's courtiers preferred to exploit domestic producers. The dissemination of new ideas was hampered by conservative religious leaders who, for example, successfully destroyed an astronomical observatory on the grounds that human curiosity about divine secrets had caused a plague. Despite the brilliance of high culture at court and in the cities, a chasm developed between the elite ruling class and the producers of wealth. While Ottoman power remained formidable within a global context until the nineteenth century, Europe's rapid economic development after 1500 placed Ottoman accomplishments in an unfavorable light by the eighteenth century.

Poland: The Failure of Elective Monarchy

At the start of the eighteenth century, Poland was the third largest country in Europe (only France and Prussia were bigger). Situated between the expansive Russian empire to the east and the German states of the Holy Roman Empire to the west, Poland lacked any natural river or mountain frontiers. The Polish nobility clung to its privileged status, enjoying the right to elect the monarch through their control of the legislative assembly, or diet. Each new monarch found himself confirming and even expanding the legal privileges and exemptions of the aristocracy. Individual noblemen could even veto legislative initiatives in the diet. Rivalries among the nobility undermined the crown's ability to maintain state sovereignty in the face of aggressive neighbors, while waves of domestic anti-Semitism during the seventeenth century decimated the Jews who were among Poland's most enterprising communities.

Military, political, and economic weakness led to the first partition of the country in 1772. Frederick the Great initiated the aggression, suggesting to Russia and Austria that all three powers combine in the assault against Polish sovereignty. Prussia took the important Baltic port city Gdansk and surrounding territory, which allowed the Prussians to unite East and West Prussia for the first time. Russia received a large portion of Poland's agricultural northeast together with 1 million inhabitants, while Austria seized the southern region known as Galicia, an area containing over 2 million inhabitants. In the wake of this initial carve-up, the aristocratic Polish diet voted to strengthen the powers of the crown. Unfortunately, the call for greater centralization came too late. Two more partitions, in 1793 by Russia and Prussia and in 1795 by Russia, Prussia, and Austria, led to the complete dissolution of Poland. The country would not be restored until the end of World War I in 1918.

Spanish Decline

The Spanish government remained largely decentralized even during the height of empire in the sixteenth century. In particular, the provinces of Catalonia and Aragon hesitated to support the expansionist ambitions of the Spanish crown that was resident in the province of Castile. Regional aristocratic assemblies called *cortes* enjoyed considerable autonomy. Despite these challenges, Philip II (r. 1556–1598) was able to employ the enormous revenues of Spain's New World empire in a monumental struggle against Protestantism in the Spanish-ruled Netherlands and in England. Both enterprises failed badly. The rebellion in the Netherlands began in the 1550s and dragged on for decades, while the massive Armada sent to destroy Queen Elizabeth I was turned away by storms and a smaller English force in 1588.

Philip's overextended government was bankrupt by the time of his death. Portugal, which had been united with Spain in 1580, reestablished its independence in 1640, and the northern Netherlands secured its freedom in 1648. During the long reign of the last

Spanish Habsburg, the ineffective King Charles II (r. 1665–1700), France eclipsed Spain as Western Europe's major power. Charles, who had no children, even selected Louis XIV's grandson, Philip of Anjou (r. 1700–1746), to succeed him on the Spanish throne. At the end of the War of the Spanish Succession in 1714, Austria won control over most of Spain's Italian and Belgian possessions, while Britain secured the exclusive (and highly lucrative) right to transport African slaves to Spain's American colonies.

Although the new dynasty instituted significant military and administrative reforms, Spain never recovered its leading position in European affairs. The country's economic base remained too fragile. Relying for too long on revenues from its enormous New World colonies, the Spanish crown and the nobility failed to encourage agricultural innovations, industry, and internal commerce. The aristocracy and the church dominated Spanish society, and for these two groups manual labor and commercial enterprise were disreputable undertakings. An inventive and ambitious middle class, or bourgeoisie, never emerged as a vital force in early modern Spanish society. The French Bourbons may have replaced the Austrian Habsburgs on the Spanish throne in 1700, but the transition only temporarily arrested the process of political and economic slump that continued unabated well into the twentieth century.

The Dutch Republic

Alone among the major powers of Europe during the seventeenth century, the mainly Protestant Netherlands managed to combine a quasi-republican form of government and a small geographical base with great commercial power, political resilience, and artistic genius. All of this was achieved in the face of repeated aggression from its monarchical neighbors. The Habsburgs had controlled the Netherlands (Holland and Belgium) since the fifteenth century. In the sixteenth century it had become a vibrant manufacturing and trading center. However, during the reign of Philip of Spain, who had inherited the Netherlands from his father, the Emperor Charles V (r. 1519–1556), Holland's Calvinist minority used its naval resources to challenge the Spanish monopoly over the seaborne carrying trade. Philip responded by introducing the Inquisition accompanied by a large standing army, triggering a large-scale Dutch revolt against Habsburg rule. Once the seven northern provinces (Holland) had secured effective independence in 1609, a vibrant bourgeois republic of only one and a half million people—mostly urban dwellers—set out to dominate international shipping and manufacturing. The seventeenth century was the "golden age" of the Netherlands, as Dutch ships penetrated markets around the globe.

Under the leadership of a federal assembly, or States General, with the Princes of Orange as hereditary commanders or stadtholders, the Dutch replaced the Portuguese as Europe's main goods carrier to the Far East. Capturing the overseas spice trade propelled Dutch traders into the foreground of European commercial enterprise. Within 30 years of its founding, the Dutch East India Company was paying its investors healthy returns of 25% a year and more. In 1638 the Portuguese were expelled from Japan, and the Dutch replaced them as the only Westerners permitted to trade with the country. A small Dutch colony was planted on the Cape of Good Hope in Southern Africa in 1652 as a supply point for ships headed to Asia. By the early eighteenth century, Dutch carriers enjoyed trading supremacy in the Indian Ocean and in the Far East. In addition to overseas trade, the Dutch also became Europe's most accomplished bankers and creditors, providing capital for many commercial and industrial ventures. Religious toleration throughout the provinces encouraged foreign investment in a wide range of business enterprises.

Despite these successes, the Dutch were unable to match their English competitors in terms of establishing permanent colonies throughout their global empire. The long and costly defensive wars against Louis XIV that began in the 1670s drained fiscal resources, and a comparatively small population base diminished the need for colonial settlements. Small Dutch colonies in North America and India could not withstand the intrusive power of the English. While they maintained their presence in Indonesia, the Dutch gradually lost their position as Europe's premier shipbuilders and traders under competitive pressure from larger neighboring kingdoms. By the 1720s, the Netherlands was no longer a major European power.

Austrian Habsburg Empire   After a century of struggle to return northern Germany to the Catholic fold, the Austrian branch of the Habsburg family accepted the autonomy of over 300 states within the Holy Roman Empire. The Treaty of Westphalia, signed at the conclusion of the Thirty Years' War in 1648, reaffirmed the Habsburgs as Holy Roman Emperors. But it was difficult for the emperor to coordinate policy over his multinational domains. A variety of languages, customs, and cultures frustrated royal efforts to centralize government, even in the Habsburg hereditary lands of Austria and Bohemia. What kept the empire together was the threat of a common enemy. The German, Czech, Magyar, Croat, Slovak, Slovene, Italian, Romanian, and Ruthenian subjects of the Holy Roman Emperor struggled repeatedly to roll back the Ottoman Turks who threatened the empire's southern flank. Emperor Leopold I (r. 1657–1705) was able to strengthen his hold over his lands by defeating the Turks in a long war (1683–1689), and imperial forces subsequently extended Habsburg authority as far south as the Balkan peninsula.

Under the terms of the Treaty of Radstadt (1714), Emperor Charles VI (r. 1711–1740) secured additional territories in Italy and Belgium from Spain. However, Charles was obliged to spend much of his long reign winning the support of Europe's other major powers to recognize the right of his daughter, Maria Teresa, to succeed him. The document that was designed to guarantee a smooth succession was known as the Pragmatic Sanction. Soon after the emperor's death, however, Frederick the Great of Prussia violated the agreement and invaded the Habsburg province of Silesia. Maria Teresa successfully defended her title but failed to recover Silesia. Both she and her son Joseph II (r. 1780–1790) worked diligently to bring unity and consistency to the laws of the empire, but their scattered provinces remained divided by a range of differences large and small. Although the dynasty survived until 1918, the Habsburgs were never able to create a strong centralized monarchy capable of coordinating the considerable material resources of the empire. Instead, the emperors were constantly engaged in a series of negotiations with leaders of the constituent kingdoms, especially Hungary. With a strong Muslim enemy to its east, the Habsburgs never became a global colonial power.

KEY QUESTION | Revisited

The early modern European state-building enterprise involved, first and foremost, a contest between landed aristocrats who wished to preserve their local autonomy and new monarchs committed to enhancing centralized power. For the monarchs of the seventeenth and eighteenth centuries, royal control over national churches, the building and equipping of standing professional armies, the efficient collection of tax revenues, the creation of bureaucracies whose members were dedicated to the crown, and the formation of a system of rewards for loyal members of the nobility all served to enhance the power of the national government. Most rulers aspired to follow the model of French absolutism. In England, however, a form of limited monarchy in which the aristocracy and the gentry participated in the political process set the stage for unprecedented global power by the second half of the eighteenth century.

Throughout the course of this state-building enterprise, the condition of Europe's poor remained largely unchanged, with free peasants in Western Europe struggling to maintain a subsistence lifestyle. In Eastern Europe, the expansion of serfdom meant that the lives of most of the population deteriorated sharply. As European monarchs successfully coerced and co-opted the aristocracy to unite in defense of the traditional political hierarchy, new political forces were stirring in the cities, in the merchant houses, and in the overseas colonies. As we shall see in Chapter 17, "Rebellion and Revolution: American Independence and the French Revolution," the Old Regime was ill-equipped to confront these unprecedented challenges.

Europe's absolutist states were organized around the assumption that only the leader and his or her closest advisors were competent to manage the affairs of the country. Monarchy itself assumes the propriety of human inequality, privilege associated with birth, sacred status, and the purity and intelligence of the one against the sinfulness and incapacity of the many. Absolute monarchy infers that one individual alone has special access to an eternal set of rules governing society: No one has the right to challenge the ruler, even if that ruler violates his or her sacred trust. The political theory of absolutism was predicated on a very somber estimate of human nature and human potential. It also reflected the structure of much social and economic life in Europe. By the mid-eighteenth century, this centuries-old political system came under increasing scrutiny on both sides of the Atlantic, and the challenge had a good deal to do with the emergence of a more sanguine estimate of humans as rational beings. It also had much to do with the emergence of a more fluid and dynamic social and economic order, an order deeply at odds with traditional notions of hierarchy based solely upon heredity.

Review Questions

1. What privileges did the European aristocracy enjoy during the seventeenth and eighteenth centuries, and on what grounds were these privileges defended?
2. How do we explain the rapid growth of Europe's population during the eighteenth century?

3. Describe the role of peasant women in the economic life of early modern Europe.
4. How did Europe's sixteenth-century wars of religion contribute to the formation of strong centralized states?
5. Describe the key steps taken by Louis XIV of France to build an absolutist state.
6. How did mercantilism contribute to Western Europe's colonial wars of the eighteenth century?
7. Why was Peter I of Russia attracted by Western Europe, and how did he attempt to remold Russia along Western lines?

Please consult the Suggested Readings at the back of the book to continue your study of the material covered in this chapter. For a list of documents on the Primary Source DVD-ROM that relate to topics in this chapter, please refer to the back of the book.

Topics in This Chapter

The Medieval World View • Anticipating the New Science

• New Directions in Astronomy and Physics • New Approaches to Truth

• Theory and Application • Politics as Science

• Science and Religion • Superstition and Its Victims

15 New World Views: Europe's Scientific Revolution

Yet certainly there are diverse things in nature, that do much conduce to the evincing of a Deity, which naturalists either alone discern, or at least discern them better than other men.

—Robert Boyle

KEY | Question

How does the study of the natural world influence religious belief and the understanding of truth?

During the seventeenth century, the question just posed was much on the minds of educated Europeans. The Englishman Robert Boyle (1627–1691), for example, was easily one of the most distinguished experimental scientists of the second half of the century. Today he is remembered for his contributions to science in general and to chemistry in particular. However, Boyle's preeminent interest throughout his adult life was theology, not science, and in his will he left a considerable sum of money to endow academic lectures for the defense of Christianity against its opponents. Boyle was always troubled by what he saw as the "great and deplorable growth of irreligion, especially among those that aspired to pass for wits, and several of them too for philosophers." He was convinced that the most powerful way to counter this growing trend among educated people was to demonstrate the power and glory of God in His handiwork. The "Boyle Lectures" were designed to do just that.

It is easy to see why we find Boyle the scientist an attractive figure. The desire to know, to understand the unfamiliar, to be freed from mystery and arbitrary authority, is a commonplace of the modern human condition. We are restive with uncertainty, impatient with external authority, troubled by the unexplained. Over the past 400 years, Western culture has been interested, like Boyle, in observation, experiment, and analysis, with an approach to

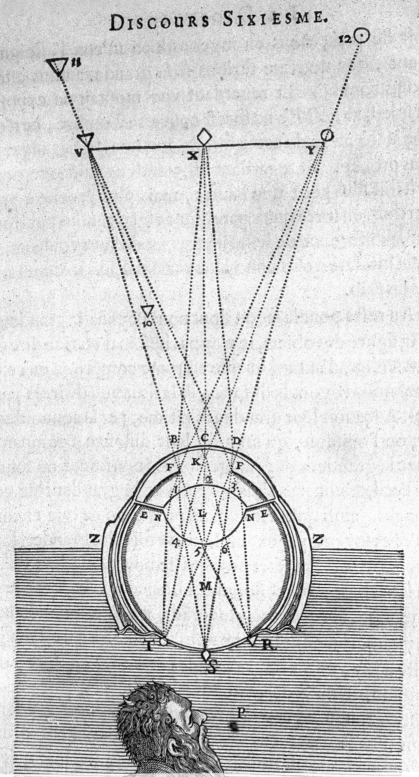

Illustration from *Optics* (1637) by René Descartes Though better known for his *Discourse on the Method,* the great French philosopher made many contributions to mathematics and science, including the problem of refraction, as illustrated by this drawing from the original edition of his essay, *Optics.*

the natural world that we have come to call the scientific method. That approach has had a global reach. In terms of larger influences, the world's many peoples have embraced Western political forms and religious systems with varying degrees of enthusiasm, and Western economic models have had a significant impact outside of their European point of origin. Yet, virtually all cultures have eagerly embraced European science and the Western scientific outlook.

The modern world has become closely identified with science, with a belief in progress anchored in the advancement of this new way of thinking. Indeed, the foundations of our secular, materialist, and utilitarian culture are situated firmly in the Western scientific world picture. Over the past 400 years, Westerners have come to expect certain types of explanations and answers to their questions; today, the fruits of scientific investigation offer some of the most compelling responses to basic human needs. Optimism about the future, despite the horrors of two world wars and the threat of nuclear annihilation during the twentieth century, hinges largely on humanity's fascination with science and with the expectation that the fruits of scientific research will bring us closer to a mastery of the natural world.

The Medieval World View

Explanations, if they are to claim the assent of individuals, must provide both intellectual and emotional satisfaction. Humans respond best to interpretations of phenomena that fit closely with their dispassionate feelings about the structure or true nature of things. In the medieval West, where the influence of the church and its theological view of creation dominated local and national cultures, a picture of the cosmos where humans occupied center stage in a divinely ordered drama of salvation was accepted as simple common sense. The dignity of its subject matter made theology the foremost science on the eve of the Reformation in the early 1500s. First and last things, human purpose and destiny, the particulars of the divine mandate—all came under the heading of theological studies. Religion even shaped the contours of more mundane subjects, from diet and marriage relations to business and banking practices. Lending money at interest, for example, while common practice across late medieval Europe, was still considered a sin by church authorities.

The world of nature, in contrast, involved subjects of lesser moral significance, and religion offered little assistance in explaining how the physical world operated. Nature as experienced through the senses was, in the end, a place of trial and a temporary abode for sinful humanity. This lower world, while open to limited investigation, was also a region of perpetual change, decay, and death. In the Christian hierarchy of value that informed all things, the student of physical nature was inferior to the student of Scripture.

Church Authority and the Natural World   Historians once criticized medieval church leaders for their lack of interest in the natural world, but such a position is no longer sustainable. Christian intellectuals of the High Middle Ages were genuinely interested in questions about the material environment, and the original Christian position on the nature of God's creation was central to explaining this curiosity. Unlike South Asian Hindus and Buddhists, who viewed the material world as ultimately illusory, and unlike earlier pagans, who identified the gods with particular aspects of nature such as wind, fire, and water, Christians had a different view of the Deity and creation: God was separated from and superior to his material handiwork. Since God had created it, the material world was both good and open to human investigation.

The standard interpretation of God's command to Adam to fill, subdue, and have dominion over Earth was a powerful guide to daily Christian action. Nor did theological proscriptions hinder methodology. St. Thomas Aquinas (1225–1274) celebrated the place of reason in every compartment of human activity, and in his great poem *The Divine Comedy* Dante Alighieri (1265–1321) made the abuse of this God-given faculty subject to the severest eternal penalties. Rational inquiry was no threat to orthodoxy for most medieval thinkers, nor was the thoughtful assimilation of Arab and Greek contributions in mathematics, optics, and medicine. Aquinas built his reputation around an effort to demonstrate that Christians had nothing to fear from pagan thought.

Non-Western Contributions

Humans have always been curious about their habitat, and important intellectual breakthroughs had occurred in a variety of fields outside of the West long before a burst of activity took place in Europe beginning in the sixteenth century. Scholars in Muslim kingdoms had made essential contributions in geometry and algebra, in astronomy and in medicine, and in the overall observation of natural phenomena. Chinese advances in technology—from the simple wheelbarrow to navigational techniques, printing, and gunpowder—all were adopted by Europeans as examples of innovation based upon observation, experiment, and a desire to manipulate nature for human purposes.

Early medieval Europe had only a handful of scientific works from the ancient world, but eventually many Greek and Arab texts, copied and maintained by Byzantine and Muslim scholars, were translated into Latin. Most of the translations were made where Muslim and Christian cultures intersected in Spain and Sicily. By the thirteenth century, Christian scholars began to argue for the intrinsic value of investigations into natural phenomena. Churchmen like Albertus Magnus (c. 1206–1280) at the University of Paris and the English monk Roger Bacon (c. 1214–1294) emphasized the propriety, if not the supreme value, of rational inquiry into God's creation. By the fourteenth century, leading European universities had established new professorships in astronomy, natural philosophy, and mathematics. Still, medieval science never disengaged itself from the theological underpinnings that informed its larger world view. These underpinnings would come under direct assault during the *Scientific Revolution* of the sixteenth and seventeenth centuries.

An Intimate Creation

Medieval thinkers saw the cosmos as limited in scale, hierarchical in structure, and monarchical in leadership. It was firmly under the providential direction of an active God, the biblical king of kings, whose knowledge and power were unlimited. The accepted picture, which most educated persons embraced because it reflected observable forces in nature, placed sinful humans and their environment at the center of a divine but ultimately mysterious creation. Building on a combination of Christian teaching, theories articulated by Aristotle (384–322 B.C.E) and further refined by the Greco-Egyptian mathematician Ptolemy (c. 90–168), the medieval cosmology comforted people whose lives were buffeted by hardships in an environment where material want was a constant close companion. Animated by angels, spirits, and the workings of unmerited divine grace, the entire physical universe was alive with energy and activity. The activity of all phenomena could be traced, in the end, to the immediate power of a God who micromanaged his handiwork. Just as the ancient Greeks believed that the god Apollo drove the sun across the sky in his chariot, so too medieval Christians witnessed the hand of God in events both mundane and exceptional.

The Authority of Aristotle   Church authorities found much to admire in the cosmic speculations of the pagan Aristotle, not least because this Greek thinker argued that everything in nature had an individual purpose, or *telos,* that directed objects to move in certain ways. Before the investigations of the seventeenth century, educated Europeans assumed that a body remained in motion only so long as a mover was impelling it. The first or prime mover, of course, was God, but unseen hands or key intermediaries were required for the moment-by-moment action of bodies throughout the cosmos. The four elements that made up the accessible natural world—earth, water, air, fire—each had properties conducive to particular ends. For example, in the Aristotelian cosmology or world view, heavy objects made of earth naturally sought their rest at the center of the universe. Thus stones, because they are heavy, seek their repose on Earth's surface, and since the exceptionally heavy Earth did not maintain properties tending toward motion, this special planet served as the focal point of every other object.

The sun, the moon, and the other planets all revolved in perfect concentric circles around Earth, the human home. Many Christians believed that the planets, kept in motion by the labors of angels, influenced everyday lives. The planet Venus, for example, was thought to affect lovers by a special power transmitted through invisible rays. Humans might learn something about the set of physical laws that governed the region below the moon (sublunary sphere), but the larger sphere that lay above the moon (superlunary) was not subject to investigation. There, an unapproachable physical reality—a fifth element, or *quintessence*—that informed the laws of motion. According to Aristotle, then, creation was dualistic at its core, with the larger portion of physical creation forever beyond human understanding. This was yet another reason, he believed, that humans should not place excessive faith in "natural philosophy," as it was known. In a cosmos informed by purpose and value, the real goal of humans was to seek the higher realm, the abode of the heavenly bodies and of the divine home itself.

Anticipating the New Science

The Aristotelian-Ptolemaic-Christian picture of the cosmos was, for almost 2,000 years, a fairly obvious and natural way of looking at observable data. After all, the sun does appear to be in motion, while no one can actually feel or experience Earth's orbit. A great conceptual and intellectual hurdle, what the modern historian of science Herbert Butterfield once called "a transposition in the mind," was required before the modern explanation for the motion of heavenly bodies was established. Fundamental shifts in how a civilization views its place in creation do not occur suddenly, and it is fair to say that in the year 1600, despite the challenges posed by a handful of thinkers who called themselves natural philosophers, most people, even educated people, continued to accept the Aristotelian–Ptolemaic model as the most coherent explanation of observed phenomena.

This should not surprise us, especially given the deep religiosity of Europeans and the ongoing power of state authorities to coerce the unorthodox. Most countries did not enjoy genuine religious toleration until the start of the nineteenth century. Despite this serious handicap, however, by 1700 a new, less anthropomorphic or human-centered, world picture had taken hold. Social, cultural, and intellectual developments helped to set the stage for this monumental challenge to the medieval world view, fostering dissatisfaction with explanations offered solely on the grounds of tradition and ancient authority.

Renaissance Contributions As we saw in Chapter 13, "Reformation, Religious Wars, and National Conflicts," Renaissance humanists had successfully promoted a naturalistic understanding of and appreciation for the human body, and their focus on perspective in art, where natural objects are represented on a plane surface, contributed to a more realistic rendering of the natural environment on canvas. Painters and sculptors were among the first to question established authority and to call for a more systematic observation of nature. In addition, sixteenth-century Europe's growing urban population fostered an innovative and risk-friendly approach to commercial undertakings, while transoceanic explorers exhibited a sense of curiosity about the unknown world that emboldened investigators in other areas of inquiry. Finally, the problem-solving approach of medieval artisans and craftsmen nurtured a basic interest in observation and inventiveness in the service of labor-saving devices. From windmills and plows to horseshoes and weapons, the practical labor of people who measured and mastered small corners of the natural environment promoted interest in explaining the natural world.

Voluntary Associations Beginning in the sixteenth and seventeenth centuries, new institutions and associations began to emerge that contested the intellectual monopoly that the church and Europe's few universities had enjoyed for so long. Learned societies were founded in several capital cities; normally sponsored by wealthy patrons and attracting the educated urban middle class, their inquiries focused on the utilitarian aspects of how nature worked. England's Royal Society for Promoting Natural Knowledge (1662) and the *Academie des Sciences* in Paris (1666) were leaders in what had become a Europe-wide trend by the early eighteenth century. Some of the members of these organizations were also associated with an older magical and alchemical tradition. Astrologers, village "wise men," and alchemists who worked with herbs, metals, and powders all believed that nature was an organized system and that uncovering its secrets would produce practical advantages. Working out of their homes or studios on a part-time basis, natural philosophers acquired greater social prestige as the seventeenth century progressed, and more educated Europeans joined the quest for new knowledge.

Expanding Literacy Much of the intellectual ferment after 1500 was due to the simple expansion of literacy and the growth of a reading public. Encouraging literacy was a key goal of the early Protestant reformers; if nothing else, the Reformation represented a massive dissent from religious authority. While rates of literacy were highest in Renaissance Italy during the early sixteenth century, Protestant England and the Netherlands moved ahead after 1600. English Puritans in Massachusetts and Connecticut placed a premium on education and literacy, while in eighteenth-century Prussia and Austria, the government sponsored experiments in primary education. The diffusion of new ideas in books, almanacs, journals, newspapers, and broadsheets was extensive in many urban settings, despite the continuing censorship of church and state. New knowledge could be disseminated quickly thanks to the printing press, making Western Europe arguably the most literate civilization on Earth after 1700.

Recalling Plato One more variable, again originating in ancient Greece, profoundly influenced the unfolding of the Scientific Revolution. In their recovery and dissemination of ancient texts, Renaissance scholars in Italy, such as Marsilio Ficino (1433–1499) and Pico della Mirandola (1463–1494), had developed a strong appreciation for Plato's (c. 427–c. 347 B.C.E.) notion of a realm of ultimate reality, one located beyond everyday sensory appearances and situated in the world of forms and ideas. This invisible reality was thought to be simple, rational, and comprehensible. For scientific thinkers, the possibility that universal laws of nature lay within the grasp of human reason was enormously liberating. The belief that nature, once understood, might be manipulated for human good proved to be an enormous spur to the expansion of natural philosophy, alchemy, and even astrology.

New Directions in Astronomy and Physics

Ironically, the Polish mathematician and astronomer who first seriously challenged the Aristotelian–Ptolemaic model of the cosmos was also a Roman Catholic priest. After studying at the University of Krakow in Poland and in Renaissance Italy, Nicholas Copernicus (1473–1543), possibly influenced by neo-Platonic ideas, expressed serious concerns about the mathematical complexity of the Ptolemaic system. In particular, Ptolemy had accounted for the apparent irregular motion of some heavenly bodies by adding a series of additional mini-circles to the main path of each planet as it revolved around the sun—orbits within orbits, in effect. Copernicus insisted that these epicycles cluttered a cosmic order, which, if Plato were to be trusted, was supposed to be a work of simplicity and harmony. Copernicus was not the first to raise objections. The fifteenth-century churchman Nicholas of Cusa (1401–1464) had suggested that the world might be in motion, and the ancient Greek thinker Aristarchus of Samos (c. 310–230 B.C.E.) had proposed a heliocentric (sun-centered) model of the universe. Reaffirming this bold conceptual leap, Copernicus placed the sun at the center of the universe and then attempted to assemble the mathematical proofs he needed to support a hypothesis that defied commonsense evidence.

Challenging the Church In 1543, as the first shock waves of the Protestant Reformation countermined centuries of church influence on the theological front, Copernicus published his groundbreaking *On the Revolutions of the Heavenly Orbs*. Suddenly, the church was confronted with a profound dissent on matters involving the structure

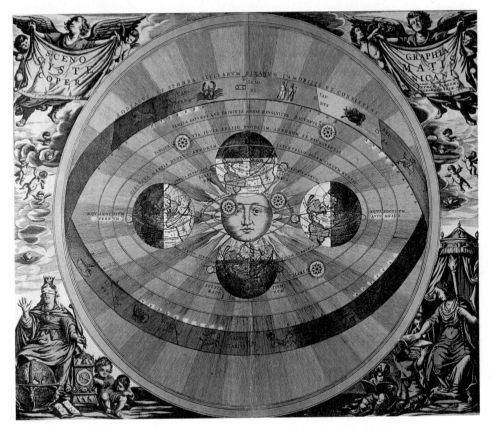

The Copernican Universe   This seventeenth-century Dutch engraving illustrates Copernicus's revolutionary "heliocentric" theories, which placed the sun—rather than the Earth—at the center of the universe.

and operation of God's handiwork. The dissent was every bit as serious as the Lutheran and Calvinist challenge to the definition of what constitutes the true church. Just as a Catholic monk—Luther—had repudiated the apostolic and monarchical authority of the pope, now a Catholic priest who was highly respected for his mathematical skills was attempting to decenter humanity and make Earth just another planet among many, all in orbit around a fiery lantern. Biblical authority employed in the defense of the Aristotelian–Ptolemaic model of the universe now came under close and damaging scrutiny by men who wished to uncover nature's rudimentary elegance.

Tycho Brahe and Johannas Kepler   The first empirical evidence in support of the Copernican theory came, surprisingly, from a man who adhered to the older Aristotelian–Ptolemaic model. The Danish astronomer Tycho Brahe (1546–1601), working for over 20 years from an observatory on the island of Hven in the Baltic that was paid for by the king of Denmark, collected an enormous volume of astronomical data on the movements of the heavenly bodies, including the planets. His student, Johannas Kepler (1571–1630), used Brahe's observational data to demonstrate that the planets moved not in perfect circles, as Aristotle and even Copernicus believed, but in ellipses, following irregular velocities depending on the planet's distance from the sun. Kepler was a deeply mystical man and a product of the neo-Platonic tradition, which saw nature as a single explanatory system. At one point in his career he served as court astrologer and mathematician to the Holy Roman Emperor Rudolf II (1576–1612), one of Europe's leading patrons of the occult. Like so many other early scientists, Kepler was convinced that the language of nature was mathematics and that humankind had a religious duty to investigate the world machine. What eluded him in his major work, *The New Astronomy* (1609), was a plausible explanation for what kept the planets in their respective orbits. Kepler died in obscurity, reduced to telling fortunes for his income while simultaneously laboring on the frontiers of modern science.

Galileo's Breakthrough

Galileo Galilei (1564–1642) was a contemporary of Kepler who employed the newly invented (c. 1608) telescope and mathematics to confirm the Copernican heliocentric theory. He wrote his major statement on the subject, *Dialogue on the Two Great Systems of the World* (1632), in Italian, not Latin, and dedicated it to the pope. Like the Protestant Kepler, the Roman Catholic Galileo believed that the Platonic conception of a world of universal truth lay close at hand. He was also convinced that mathematical expression was the appropriate language for investigating the natural world. As an experimental scientist whose first interest was the motion of bodies, Galileo's major contribution to physics involved his discovery of the law of inertia. The established theory of dynamics claimed that the natural state of all bodies was at rest and that motion was due to an agent impelling a body. Galileo insisted that there was no natural state; if a body was in motion, it would remain in motion until another force deflected it. Working over a long career before he was silenced by the church, Galileo's contributions were varied; employing the telescope, for example, he observed the rough surfaces and mountains on the moon

and spots on the sun, and discovered three moons around Jupiter. In 1610 he published *The Starry Messenger,* which provided empirical evidence for his case that the moon was not the perfect sphere that the Aristotelians posited, but instead a body whose rough surface, filled with craters and mountains, was not unlike the face of Earth.

Galileo overthrew the medieval hierarchy of the heavens and the incorruptibility of so-called superlunary matter that sup-

Galileo   A true "Renaissance man," Galileo Galilei excelled in many fields, but made his most lasting contributions in science and physics. This famous portrait by Giusto Sustermans captures the haunted expression that Galileo may have worn in his later years, when he was persecuted for his defense of heliocentrism. *Justus Sustermans (1597–1681), "Portrait of Galileo Galilei." Galleria Palatina, Palazzo Pitti, Florence, Italy. Nimatallah/Art Resource, NY*

Sir Isaac Newton Newton was appointed Lucasian Professor of Mathematics at Cambridge University before he was 25 years old. He made original contributions in mathematics, optics, physics, and astronomy, but like his friend John Locke, he was also deeply interested in the study of Scripture. *Sir Godfrey Kneller, Sir Isaac Newton, 1702. Oil on canvas. The Granger Collection*

posedly lay above the moon. The telescope did not lie, and according to *The Starry Messenger,* "truly demonstrated physical conclusions need not be subordinated to biblical passages." Galileo was not a modest man, but in his efforts to understand the movement of bodies through the application of mathematics, especially in statics and dynamics, his labors complemented the efforts of Kepler to establish a single system of physical laws for the terrestrial and celestial realms.

Newton's Orderly Universe   The capstone to the flurry of work on physics and mechanics occurred when an English professor of mathematics at Cambridge University offered a compelling physical explanation of the heliocentric theory. Isaac Newton (1642–1727) was a devout Christian who shared a strong interest in the study and explanation of Scripture with the philosopher John Locke (1632–1704). Both men belonged to the Royal Society for the Advancement of Knowledge, and both approached the study of nature as an exercise of Christian piety. Newton's law of universal gravitation demonstrated that all bodies in motion were intimately connected. His main work, *The Mathematical Principles of Natural Philosophy,* was first published in Latin in 1687. He introduced and clarified the role of gravity and motion in all aspects of physical creation, offering answers to the key issues in astronomy and physics that scholars had debated since Copernicus. His picture of the forces in play throughout the cosmos remained central to physics until the contributions of Albert Einstein (1879–1955) in the early twentieth century. Newton attributed the presence of gravity to God's eternal power. His great breakthroughs were palatable to men of faith largely because in Newton's world machine, God was constantly tending to his creation. In a letter to a friend, Newton affirmed that the state of the heavenly bodies can only be explained by reference "to the counsel and contrivance of a voluntary agent." In 1705 Newton became the first scientist to be knighted by an English monarch, thus enhancing the role of the specialist academic in the broader cultural life of the nation.

New Approaches to Truth

Alternative modes of inquiry or methodology were also key components of Europe's Scientific Revolution. Whereas Aristotle had assumed that a purpose, or *telos,* was inherent

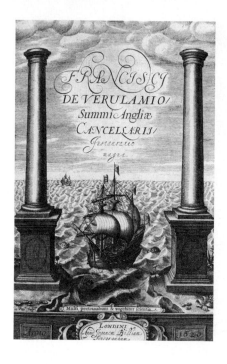

Title Page from *Novum Organum* Title page from *Novum Organum* (1620) by Sir Francis Bacon. Bacon established the principles of the "scientific method," placing induction and observation ahead of traditional methods of scientific reasoning. The illustration on the title page shows a ship striking out for the unknown territories seeking, as did Bacon, for a new understanding of the natural world.

in all physical and spiritual matter, the temper of Renaissance skepticism was unwilling to rest on the authority of the ancients, no matter how exemplary their contributions had been to Western thought. Talented amateurs began to investigate the practical application of natural phenomena. A more systematic approach to scientific inquiry, one devoid of respect for precedent, reputation, or grand general systems, took hold outside the walls of the medieval university, where the emphasis on tradition and hallowed authority remained firmly entrenched.

Francis Bacon Leadership emerged from some unlikely quarters. In early seventeenth-century England, an ambitious and grasping high government official, Francis Bacon (1561–1626), popularized the experiential and collaborative outlook. In *The Advancement of Learning* (1605) Bacon offered a sharp critique of the old medieval scholastic method and the standard pedagogy of the universities. Urging his contemporaries to look into the nature of things themselves without respect for tradition, Bacon wished to master nature to improve the human condition. He was convinced that the sole end of scientific investigation was the enrichment of human life in concrete, even quantifiable terms. Much enamored of what later generations would label technology, Bacon held that improvements in this field could only be secured by rigorous induction, working from particular examples and experiments, and avoiding grand generalizations. He offered a method of inquiry based firmly on careful collection and observation of empirical data together with a strong commitment to collaborative work and peer criticism. His ideal society, described in *The New Atlantis* (1627), placed equal value on the work of manual laborers and highly educated theoreticians. Both contributed to the "relief of man's estate."

René Descartes In France the brilliant Catholic philosopher and mathematician René Descartes (1596–1650) sought to bypass the bitter theological controversies of the day by focusing on a method of inquiry that began with rigorous skepticism and strict reliance on reason. Perhaps more than any other person, Descartes helped to forge an understanding of nature as mechanism and of God as the supreme artisan who worked within the boundaries of mathematical laws and rational exposition. In his influential *Discourse on Method* (1637) Descartes called upon his contemporaries to scrutinize all past and current claims to truth. Questions sublime and mundane were equally open to the new mode of inquiry. For Descartes, whose important contributions to mathematics, optics, and analytic geometry distinguish him from gentleman amateurs like Bacon, the universe was analogous to a machine that operated according to inflexible principles. The key to genuine understanding, he felt, centered on the discovery of general laws revealed through mathematics in alliance with logical deduction. Clear and distinct ideas were the building blocks of knowledge in every compartment of life. Truth about the world and humankind's place in it could be extracted from the study of God's handiwork in addition to or in place of his written word.

Theory and Application

Science involved much more than signal breakthroughs in astronomy and physics. More terrestrial concerns, especially those related to human health and longevity, had the greatest impact on the largest number of people during the seventeenth and eighteenth centuries. For the people of sixteenth- and seventeenth-century Europe, food and nutrition stood at the top of the basic needs list, as they had since time immemorial, and it was here that Bacon's counsel was followed to good effect.

Food Supplies and Mortality   Approximately 60 million people were living in Europe in 1500, and this total grew slowly to around 110 million by 1700. The latter figure represented about one-fifth of the world's overall population. Before 1500, indeed ever since the calamity of the Black Plague of the 1340s, Europeans rarely produced more food than they needed for survival, and in the sixteenth century Europe's economy was overwhelmingly agricultural. It was a fragile foundation; epidemic disease destroyed communities and ravaged countries well into the 1700s. Italy, Germany, Spain, and England all suffered outbreaks of plague during the 1600s, and every European state wrestled with periodic crop failures and the resulting malnutrition and even starvation.

Indeed, the expectation of severe want was a constant of human life, something that most people experienced during their normal lifetime. Lowered resistance to disease brought on by poor or inadequate diet was compounded by the depredations of opposing armies that tended to live off the land as they crisscrossed the countryside. Further, Europe's armies had more deadly military hardware thanks to innovations in cannon and rifle manufacture. Placed in the hands of larger armies, the scale of battlefield casualties increased. And finally, global climate patterns changed. From Beijing to Berlin, cooler temperatures and wetter summers prevailed. This "little ice age" of the late sixteenth and early seventeenth century may have reduced average temperatures by 1 degree centigrade. Such a shift would have abbreviated the typical growing season by three to four weeks, while also reducing the maximum altitude at which crops would ripen by some 500 feet. The result was a smaller crop yield and additional hardships for growing families.

The overall result was, from a modern perspective, a life of enormous hardship, dearth, and, comparatively speaking, brevity. Few people survived into their fifties, while poor diet meant that small stature and a generally debilitated physique were the lot of older peasants across Europe. Infant mortality rates were roughly 25% before the first year of life. Short life spans were a worldwide phenomenon: In 1500 the overall life span of European and non-European peoples averaged in the mid-twenties.

Agronomy and Land Management

Enhancing the quality and length of life began with improvements in the quantity and quality of food. Once agriculture began to orient itself toward production for urban and overseas markets, research and innovative experiment started to make significant headway. Improved animal husbandry, the selective breeding of domesticated animals, draining and reclamation of marginal lands, bigger farms, better seed, improved plows, and the widespread employment of wage laborers all facilitated the growth of output. This was especially the case in the Netherlands, England, and to a lesser extent in France. The consolidation of small, inefficient farms often meant additional hardship for the peasants who lost their own farms and became employees of a market-oriented landowner. However, increased output at least reduced the frequency and severity of crop failures from weather and blight. By the eighteenth century, the introduction of turnips, clover, and legumes improved the supply of fodder, allowing farmers to maintain more food-producing animals over the long winter months. The new crops also returned precious nitrates to the soil, which increased its fertility and enabled peasants to abandon the practice of leaving parts of their land fallow for an entire growing season. The widespread acceptance by European farmers of the American potato that began in the seventeenth century also enhanced caloric intake substantially. This allowed overall agricultural output to keep pace with Europe's expanding population.

Medical Thought and Training

Another human science that the new method of study influenced was biology. Renaissance painters were careful students of human anatomy, but strong religious injunctions against desecrating the material temple of the soul after death hampered knowledge about how the internal body operated. As in physics and astronomy, ancient Greek authority dominated medical thought and practice. Galen (c. 130–c. 201), the foremost medical authority of the ancient world, had dissected animals and studied human skeletons in an effort to explain the workings of the human body. His conclusions lay at the core of university medical training well into the seventeenth century. Key to Galen's system was the concept, based on Aristotle, that the human body consisted of four fundamental elements or humors (blood, choler, phlegm, and black bile). Sickness was rooted in an imbalance of these elements. The standard curative practice involved various purges, including bloodletting, designed to bring these elements into balance. As might be expected, recovery rates were not high. Galen also held that the human body had two kinds of blood. One ran from the liver through the veins to all parts of the body and supplied nutrients, and the other flowed through the arteries to enliven or vivify the body.

Formal medical education at the university level normally involved a professor of anatomy reading from Galen's works, or notes based on Galen, while a humble surgeon—usually trained as a barber—dissected the cadaver to confirm the Galenic principles. The professor himself would never stoop to dissect a body, and students of medicine would also often avoid it. The seventeenth-century English philosopher John Locke, who held an advanced medical degree from Oxford University, shared this disdain. Like so many of his contemporaries, he distinguished between manual labor and true intellectual work. It was an age-old attitude.

New Practitioners   Breaching the social divide separating the doctor from the barber-surgeon, however, a handful of medical practitioners across Europe eagerly embraced both physical and mental production. The maverick German physician and alchemist Paracelsus (1493–1541) had experimented with chemicals in lieu of purges to cure common illnesses, but the medical establishment sharply criticized his methods. Those who dared to challenge the ancient texts slowly made headway against this powerful opposition. Ironically, inhumane developments in military technology furthered their efforts. The gruesome transformation of warfare made possible by the widespread use of artillery and guns enhanced the value, if not the ability to cure, of the physician and surgeon.

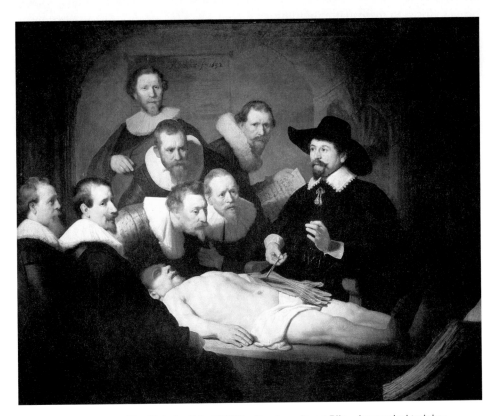

The Anatomy Lesson of Dr. Nicholas Tulp (1632) by Rembrandt van Rijn   Anatomical training became an important feature of medical education during the seventeenth century. Physicians increasingly recognized the value of direct observation in the treatment of illness. *Rembrandt van Rijn (1606–1669). "The Anatomy Lesson of Dr. Tulip." Mauritshuis, The Hague, The Netherlands. SCALA/Art Resource, NY*

In Belgium the surgeon Andreas Vesalius (1514–1564) called for rigorous anatomical investigation in his precedent-setting book, *The Structure of the Human Body* (1543). This work contained the first set of modern anatomical drawings available for students of medicine. Subsequently, the Englishman William Harvey (1578–1657), who, like Vesalius, Galileo, and Copernicus, had studied at the university of Padua in Italy, discovered the circulation of the blood and the major function of the heart thanks to the invention of the microscope. The historian William McNeill believes that the microscope led to discoveries like microorganisms in water that were just as surprising as Galileo's identification of moons around Jupiter. Harvey approached the heart as a sophisticated mechanism, and the microscope enabled him to detect the vessels through which the blood flowed. Clinical observation and prolonged experiment, together with advances in technology, transformed the human body into a rational and comprehensible machine not unlike the cosmos in its entirety. At the close of the seventeenth century, Robert Boyle dismissed Galen's theory of the four bodily humors. Boyle argued that everything in the material world consists of tiny particles that behave in a regular, predictable fashion. Changes in the particles, not invisible spirits, spurred changes in matter. The medieval consensus, with its intelligent spirits and angelic influences, was being reduced to mere matter in motion.

Major Contributions to the Scientific Revolution

1543	Copernicus, *On the Revolutions of the Heavenly Orbs*
1605	Francis Bacon, *The Advancement of Learning*
1609	Johannas Kepler, *The New Astronomy*
1610	Galileo, *The Starry Messenger*
1632	Galileo, *Dialogue on the Two Great Systems of the World*
1637	Descartes, *Discourse on Method*
1687	Isaac Newton, *The Mathematical Principles of Natural Philosophy*

Politics as Science

The skepticism, empiricism, and rationalism that marked the investigation of nature after 1500 found its counterpart in the political world as Renaissance authors began to look anew at the constitutional compromises of the late medieval period. As we read in Chapter 14, "The Early Modern State," few rulers wielded effective centralized control over their respective territories during the Middle Ages. Allegiance and resentment centered on the village, the manor, and the city, as taxes and labor obligations originated with local elites. Niccolo Machiavelli's *The Prince* (see Chapter 13, "Reformation, Religious Wars, and National Conflicts") was informed by the author's deep sense of frustration over Italy's lack of political unity. Drawing conclusions from an acute observation of contemporary life, *The Prince* ignored traditional moral and religious justifications for the exercise of political power, arguing that for rulers "it is safer to be feared than loved."

Thomas Hobbes and the State of Nature   Under not entirely different political circumstances one century later, the English philosopher Thomas Hobbes (1588–1671), amid a bitter civil war and soon after the execution of King Charles I (r. 1625–1649) by his Puritan opponents, published his *Leviathan* (1651). Hobbes was a widely traveled intellectual who had met Descartes in France and Galileo in Italy. In his political writings he sought to discover natural laws of civil organization comparable to those uncovered in physics and astronomy. The experience of civil war and the chaos it unleashed propelled Hobbes's inquiries.

A dark view of human nature outside the confines of political society, where "every man is enemy to every man," obliged Hobbes to call for the creation of a social compact in which individuals surrender their right to absolute freedom in return for security and domestic peace. Humans were innately self-interested creatures who would trample the rights—and the lives—of others in pursuit of their own pleasures. In the *Leviathan,* each person surrenders the liberty that he or she enjoys in the natural state to an absolute monarch who is charged to do whatever is necessary to maintain the polity. Hobbes was no apologist for *divine-right* monarchy; instead, he felt that the ruler's success in avoiding the worst aspects of the state of nature legitimized a government's power. His daring image of a secular society where peace and personal security, not salvation and the preservation of natural social hierarchies, were the most important obligations of government anticipated many of the positions that Enlightenment thinkers advocated in the eighteenth century.

John Locke and Limited Government   John Locke also experienced the mid-century breakdown of civil order in England, but he drew different conclusions from Hobbes. Locke argued that no single individual was competent to rule in an unrestrained manner, even if, as Hobbes proposed, the ruler had been raised to his position of supreme authority by an agreed social contract. Locke was troubled not only by the arbitrary tendencies of English monarchs but also at a deeper philosophical level by the question of how humans acquire knowledge.

For Locke, divine-right monarchy assumed that one individual was somehow uniquely fitted to know, interpret, and enforce God's will in the wider community. In his *Essay Concerning Human Understanding* (1690) Locke firmly rejected the argument that any one person was privileged with special innate knowledge of the divine mandate. Instead, each child was born as a blank slate, *tabula rasa,* and the sole source of human knowledge was experience of and in the world. Combined with the reflective powers of the rational mind, the raw data of sensory experience provide each person with the building blocks of knowledge, including knowledge of God and of a wider moral order. Locke was contesting the traditional Christian view that innate moral knowledge, while not fully developed in the child, was nonetheless present at birth. Absent innate knowledge, no one had the right to claim unmediated access to truth. Even kings and religious leaders were denied singular privileges in this crucial area, and it is no coincidence that the harshest critics of Locke's *Essay* were leading theologians in the Church of England.

Locke published his major political work, *Two Treatises of Government,* in the immediate aftermath of the 1688 Glorious Revolution that overthrew King James II. The same challenge to arbitrary authority that informed his theory of knowledge guided his approach to the problem of establishing a durable civil society. Locke accepted Hobbes's contract theory of government, but he imposed strict limits on the power of the sovereign. While not opposed to the institution of monarchy, Locke called for a strong legislative assembly with concrete law-making authority. The purpose of government, according to Locke, was to protect property, preserve political freedoms, and advance religious toleration. In one stroke, *Two Treatises* disengaged the state from the centuries-old enforcement of religious orthodoxy and secularized the civil order. Religion was a private matter, Locke stated in *A Letter Concerning Toleration* (1689). Six years later, in *The Reasonableness of Christianity* (1695), he argued that religious belief could be reduced to a few simple precepts. His title suggested that the rationalist outlook of the Scientific Revolution had now intruded itself permanently into the affairs of the spirit.

Science and Religion

Replacing the concept of a universe that God governed directly and in which he regularly intervened did not mean that proponents of the new science were hostile to religion. In fact, men like Galileo, Kepler, Harvey, and Newton celebrated God's power and knowledge in the economy and exquisite order of creation. The Christian God became the great watchmaker. While humans no longer occupied the center of creation, they remained the most elevated of God's creatures by virtue of their rational nature and their ability to comprehend and utilize nature's bounty. The natural philosophers categorized their own investigations as acts of intense piety.

Medieval churchmen had been leaders in the study of the natural world for centuries, but even though the key figures in the Scientific Revolution were either devout clerics or pious laymen, Roman Catholic authorities were deeply upset with the broad theological and social implications of the new discoveries. The story of Galileo's troubles at the hands of church leaders is well known: forced to recant his acceptance of the Copernican system and placed under house arrest in Florence for the final decade of his life (1632–1642), the aged and nearly blind scientist worked in silence as the church condemned his theories and placed his publications on an index of forbidden books. When Galileo's countryman Giordano Bruno (1548–1600), a former Dominican monk, embraced the new learning and declared that there were innumerable planets in what amounted to an infinite universe, he was arrested, tried as a heretic, and burned at the stake. Bruno's confinement and execution, while an unusually barbaric exercise of coercive power, became a powerful rallying cry for all future advocates of freedom of thought across Western Europe.

PEOPLE IN CONTEXT   Locke as Natural Philosopher

In many respects John Locke's training and interests reflect the many changes taking place in the study of nature during the seventeenth century. The son of Puritan parents of middle-class background, Locke's father fought against King Charles I in the English Civil War of the 1640s. The younger Locke attended Westminster School in London and Oxford University. Like many promising undergraduates, Locke was destined for a clerical career, but after much deliberation he declined to take holy orders, continuing on at Oxford instead for a medical degree.

Just as Bacon had done before him, Locke grew weary of what he took to be the uncritical and authority-bound nature of traditional academic life. From his journals we know that the bulk of his reading before leaving Oxford in 1667 was in medicine and chemistry. In 1666 he supervised a dangerous operation to remove an abscess of the liver. The patient, Anthony Ashley Cooper, later Earl of Shaftesbury, credited Locke with saving his life. It was the start of a close friendship that would take Locke into the center of English political life.

Soon after relocating to London with Shaftesbury, Locke was duly elected a fellow of the Royal Society. He was on friendly terms with the chemist Robert Boyle. He later befriended Isaac Newton, and toward the end of Locke's life Newton would visit his friend not only to discuss science, but also to study and to write commentaries on the Bible. Both men believed firmly that science and religion were complementary undertakings. While Locke was often criticized by religious leaders who believed that his *Essay Concerning Human Understanding* threatened belief in an unalterable moral order, Locke insisted that his study of the mind was akin to the study of nature and that there was no inherent tension between faith and reason.

John Locke   Trained as a physician, Locke authored works in the fields of economics, educational and political theory, and Scripture commentary. In each area of endeavor, he emphasized the importance of empirical observation.

Question: How can the study of nature claim an affiliation with religion?

Skepticism   Official religious opposition to the new science was not simple obscurantism, however. Scientific inquiry involved a deeper challenge to centuries-old habits of thought and belief respecting intellectual authority. The Baconian and Cartesian claims that knowledge was the end product of ardent skepticism undermined the central premise of the religious view of life. That premise was simple, and for centuries it had been compelling. It held that truths revealed to the world in canonical texts were sufficient to guide the earthly enterprise. Even Luther and Calvin, no great admirers of institutional authority and tradition, affirmed that God had communicated all that humans needed to know in the Bible. The new claim that reason was key to understanding how the world works and that it alone was sufficient in this life struck at the core of the faith traditions, Catholic and Protestant alike. The possibility that skepticism might, in the end, lead people to maintain that nothing could be known with certainty, even the existence of a creator-God, left many churchmen fearing the complete breakdown of an agreed moral order.

Blaise Pascal   Church officials were not the only ones whom the claims and implications of the new science troubled. Talented thinkers like the French mathematician Blaise Pascal (1623–1662) cautioned that the claims of science were exaggerated. He believed that the human condition remained one of enormous ignorance and sinfulness, that central truths were forever beyond the grasp of frail reason. For Pascal, organized religion and reliance on the operation of unmerited grace remained essential to the overall well-being of God's special creation. Science and reason were valuable components of Christian living, but by themselves they could not offer humans a satisfactory picture of creaturely purpose and destiny. "The God of the Christians is not simply the author of geometrical truth," pleaded Pascal in response to the ambitions of Descartes. Scientism would destroy all spiritual values if left unchecked, fostering a misplaced sense of confidence in human power and autonomy. Pascal's admonitions retain their power even today, in a world where material ambitions and values often outpace otherworldly perspectives on life.

Superstition and Its Victims

The rationalist outlook of the Scientific Revolution may have upset church authorities and thoughtful laymen like Pascal, but for Europeans outside of the intellectual elite, the reality of a realm of power and influence beyond the purview of reason was compelling and frightful. Most Europeans continued to believe in the power of demonic forces, while occult practices and magic maintained their hold on the educated and uneducated alike. While the privileged paid astrologers to identify propitious days for marriages, common people turned to sorcerers when a crop was endangered. In periods of social and political dislocation, blame was often ascribed to the practitioner of magic. Parallel with the growth of natural science during the sixteenth and seventeenth centuries was the intensification of witchcraft persecution.

Charging one's neighbors with the practice of harmful magic and witchcraft seemed to provide the accusers with an explanation for a wide variety of natural misfortunes and harmful occurrences. Preliterate village cultures in every global setting have accepted the claims of certain individuals to special powers over nature. "Cunning folk" were expected to protect communities from the worst effects of natural disasters and to serve as healers for the sick and infirm. The practices associated with the magician often had ancient, pre-Christian roots. In some cases the peasant who engaged in such practices and claims to special powers was seeking to establish a modicum of social respectability in a sharply hierarchical society. However, their claims came into direct conflict with the institutional church. The sacramental power of the Roman Catholic clergy was a form of magic, and while church authorities had always stressed the reality of demonic power in the world, it did not allow the laity a special role in combating that power. "Cunning folk" were unwelcome rivals.

Women and Witchcraft   Thousands of people were accused of witchcraft during the age of great scientific discoveries, and the majority of the accused were women. Most of the victims of witch hunts were single or older widowed women. They were vulnerable targets in a society dominated by men and where the accused were often seen as burdens on the community. Such women served as convenient scapegoats during a period of religious upheaval and conflict, where the older certainties of religious orthodoxy were under attack. By the mid-sixteenth century, Catholic and Protestant religious leaders were equally strident in their condemnation of witchcraft and magic for evil. Witches were accused of using their special access to the devil to undermine the fabric of Christian society. The accusation, prosecution, torture, and execution of women who were associated with destructive forces beyond the reach of rational understanding allowed communities under strain to demonstrate that they could take to the offensive in an inhospitable world.

Combating Witchcraft   Three women are burned to death as witches in Baden, Germany. Their alleged crimes are depicted on the right, where they are seen feasting with demons. *"Three witches burned alive from a German Broaside," circa 1555. Courtesy of Stock Montage, Inc.*

KEY QUESTION | Revisited

The controlling feature of the cosmic structure as formulated by the ancients and endorsed by the medieval church was its hierarchical structure. Multiple layers of value, dignity, nobility, and purity were associated with various types of matter and motion. The analogy between the human body and the cosmos was a popular one for the medieval mind. Microcosm and macrocosm were integrated; from thunderstorms and the appearance of comets to the death of a child or defeat in war, all physical phenomena were interrelated in a complex web of meaning. Of deeper significance was that this value-laden hierarchy of the heavens was thought to be the natural counterpart of hierarchies in the social and political domains, in the realm of personal relations (especially the family), and in the institutional church. Equality was a distant concept for most medieval thought, while rank and accompanying privilege based on sex, birth, and office defined access to social, economic, and political power.

The anti-authoritarianism of the scientific outlook had little immediate social impact. Women, for example, continued to be excluded from university life and from the new scientific societies. Most men considered women their intellectual inferiors, and the developing physical and biological sciences were all but closed to them. In fact, the period of the Scientific Revolution, with its appeal to reason and truth, was also an age of heightened witch hunts, with upwards of 100,000 people (mostly women) sentenced to death for their alleged involvement in black magic and witchcraft. Similarly, little political or religious freedoms were extended to the peasants. Most Europeans remained illiterate, devoid of access to political power, and firmly committed to their traditional religion.

But even after taking account of these significant limitations, by 1700 the hierarchical world view—a cosmic and terrestrial "great chain of being" linking all creation—was under sustained and probing attack. Attempts to understand the component parts of the physical world in terms of purpose or ends had been confidently discarded, and the aesthetic or even emotional assurances provided by the older world picture were forever abandoned. The Scientific Revolution introduced a mechanical picture of creation and described an inert physical order that humans could understand, especially in mathematical language. The closed and finite universe of medieval consciousness was replaced by an expansive and perhaps infinite clockwork. A secular and rational approach to life began to shape the thought and habits of the educated elite, and science as a realm of inquiry separate from theology gained significant new ground.

Newton had demonstrated that everything in the known universe influenced everything else, that one set of physical laws kept the constituent parts of creation neatly in their proper places. God as workman had erected a knowable mechanism. The study of nature prompted a significant challenge to traditional authority during the sixteenth and seventeenth centuries. If Francis Bacon was correct and the artisan was as essential as the aristocrat to the advancement of the human condition, if God could be known through his works alone, and if the ancient biblical injunction calling for dominion over Earth was still valid, then the next century, the century of Enlightenment, offered tremendous potential for human transformation.

Review Questions

1. Why was the medieval cosmos intellectually and emotionally satisfying for over 1,500 years?
2. In what respects did the medieval church encourage the investigation of nature?
3. Why were many leading figures in the Scientific Revolution strongly influenced by the occult, magic, and alchemy?
4. How do we explain the genuinely international character of scientific discovery?
5. How was the scientific method extended to the realm of political thought and practice?
6. What are the common threads in religious and scientific reformation?

Please consult the Suggested Readings at the back of the book to continue your study of the material covered in this chapter. For a list of documents on the Primary Source DVD-ROM that relate to topics in this chapter, please refer to the back of the book.

Topics in This Chapter

Critiquing the Traditional Way of Life • Formulas for Improving Material Conditions
• Enlightened Despots • Critiquing the Enlightenment
• The Arts in the Age of Reason

16 The Age of Enlightenment: Rationalism and Its Uses

I have sometimes been ready to think that the passion for liberty cannot be equally strong in the breasts of those who have been accustomed to deprive their fellow creatures of theirs.

—**Abigail Adams to John Adams, March 31, 1776**

KEY | Question

How do people construct ideas of progress?

As the spouse of one of the leading revolutionaries in the struggle for American independence against Great Britain, Abigail Adams (1744–1818) knew a great deal about the ideas that inspired the resistance to Old World monarchy. There was much talk about human equality and the right to national self-determination within Britain's 13 colonies in the years before 1776. But Adams was perceptive enough to realize that the rhetoric of men like her husband was directed solely toward their educated male peers. Women, landless laborers, African-American slaves—all were excluded from the debate over what Thomas Jefferson termed "inalienable rights."

When eighteenth-century men used the word **Enlightenment** to describe their own age, they were eager both to separate themselves from what had gone before and to emphasize a firm commitment to the improvement of the human condition without reference to religious systems. Plans for the improvement of political institutions, reform of the criminal code, enhancement and expansion of education, economic development, and religious toleration all assumed a more optimistic view of human nature, or at least human potential. The possibility that institutions might be organized in harmony with what were believed to be universal principles of human reason led many thinkers to call for reform irrespective of tradition and authority. While the Enlightenment focused on practical change in the interest of efficiency and material improvement, it also promoted the idea that progress was a law of nature. Enlightened thinkers

Monticello Thomas Jefferson's estate in western Virginia is one of the most striking examples of the Enlightenment in North America. Pictured here is Jefferson's bedroom, which was modeled on classical sources and featured several innovative design elements. A few hundred yards away, Jefferson's African American slaves slept in much more modest quarters. *Monticello/Thomas Jefferson Foundation, Inc.*

believed that the enhancement of the human condition was possible through the discovery and application of scientific principles in every sphere of human activity. This was a new outlook on life, one that was not shared by the overwhelming majority of Western Europeans who for centuries had lived in conditions where change and improvement were unfamiliar.

Critiquing the Traditional Way of Life

Life in the Old Regime   The eighteenth century in Europe did not signal a basic transformation in the way most people lived. They continued to cultivate the land, worship in a traditional Christian church, and pay land and labor taxes without any expectation that they would either choose their leaders or influence political decisions. Most would remain illiterate, working in harmony with the seasons and preparing their simple meals in a one-room cottage of timber, thatch, wattles, and dirt. More often than not, these Europeans spent their lives in an isolated village or hamlet where news of great events was neither offered nor expected. Most people were more concerned about the impact of influenza, typhoid, smallpox, intestinal worms, infantile diarrhea, and dysentery than they were about the decisions of administrators in Berlin or members of Parliament in London. It is difficult for those of us used to the insatiable drives of a consumer culture, where university-trained advertisers sell products to an eager public, to understand a world where it was the demands of the natural environment that dictated abstinence and restraint, self-sufficiency, and artisanal competence. Villages of a hundred or so inhabitants, often coinciding with a parish, might be located miles from the next area of population, and roads, if they existed at all, were in the best of times rutted, muddy, and frequented by bandits.

These isolated farming archipelagos lacked even the idea of personal privacy. The individual and the community were one in terms of labor on the land, use and maintenance of tools and livestock, dress, diet, language, and, perhaps most importantly, the struggle for collective security. Community feeling, unlike anything our intensely individualistic modern culture knows, was, in the words of historian Michael Kamen, "perhaps the most powerful social force in early modern Europe." Eating, sleeping, entertaining, praying, quarreling, loving, and dying in their anonymous cottages, regulating their lives around the seasons, the weather, and the church's ritual year, the eighteenth-century peasantry knew nothing about concepts of change and innovation.

The general impoverishment of the peasant majority had never been a deep concern of Europe's political elite. In fact, some believed that the deprivation of the majority actually enhanced social order. Cardinal Richelieu, chief minister to King Louis XIII of France from 1624 to 1643, wrote that "all students of politics agree that when the common people are too well off it is impossible to keep them peaceable." If they are not constantly engaged in securing the bare necessities of life, the poor "find it difficult to remain within the limits imposed by both common sense and the law." Here was a harsh estimate of the human potential for peaceable improvement. It was this very perspective that would be overturned, at least in the minds of a distinct minority, during the eighteenth century. The two great political upheavals of the century, the successful

American colonial revolt against Britain and the more radical French Revolution of 1789, together pointed toward the potential for change through education and a new outlook about what formal human associations like government were supposed to do.

\multicolumn{2}{c}{**Key Figures and Texts of the Enlightenment**}

1690	Locke, *Two Treatises of Government* and *An Essay Concerning Human Understanding*
1721	Montesquieu, *Persian Letters*
1733	Voltaire, *Letters on the English*
1739	John Wesley begins open-field preaching
1751	Diderot, first volume of *Encyclopedia*
1759	Voltaire, *Candide*
1764	Beccaria, *On Crimes and Punishments*
1764	Rousseau, *Discourse on Inequality*
1776	Smith, *Wealth of Nations*
1790	Paine, *Rights of Man*

The Community of Philosophes It is difficult to associate the eighteenth-century Enlightenment with a set of firm, easily delineated ideas. What united a wide range of thinkers (most of whom, interestingly, were not associated with Europe's intellectually conservative universities) was a more general attitude toward the human condition. This attitude reflected confidence in the possibility of progress through the application of human reason to a variety of fields. Most seventeenth-century Europeans did not believe that the future could be better than the past. Western culture had always looked backwards for models of the good society: The Greeks recalled a mythical world of gods and heroes, and Romans of the later Empire remembered the vanished Republic. Christianity had its Garden of Eden, the Middle Ages turned to the rugged simplicity of the early faith, and the Renaissance looked to Greece and Rome for inspiration and imitation. The achievements of natural philosophy—the belief that the environment could be understood, measured, and mastered—helped to transform this retrospective outlook. In a protracted literary debate around the turn of the eighteenth century, what has come to be known as the quarrel between the ancients and the moderns, the latter group, led by the Frenchman Bernard de Fontenelle (1657–1757), asserted that contemporaries could build on the collective wisdom of the past. They could utilize an established core of knowledge to exceed the accomplishments of all previous ages.

Emerging in part out of the Scientific Revolution, the most recognizable figures of the Enlightenment were less original thinkers than their predecessors. But they were enormously effective popularizers of new ideas, new methods of intellectual inquiry, and new views on educational theory. Like the Scientific Revolution, however, the Enlightenment was an international undertaking. It was centered in France but included figures as diverse as the Scottish professor of political economy Adam Smith (1732–1796), the German philosopher Immanuel Kant (1724–1804), the French satirist and advisor to kings Voltaire, and the American president Thomas Jefferson. Most were from either aristocratic or middle-class backgrounds and had received the benefit of a traditional university education. Collectively referred to by the French word **philosophes** (philosophers), these men—and a few, mainly aristocratic women—took all fields of knowledge under their charge. In an essay titled "What Is Enlightenment?" Kant described the movement as a call to think for oneself, to question and reflect, to understand the world according to one's own rational lights. If followed closely, the injunction would subject a wide range of institutions to scrutiny: the church, the state, the universities, the legal system, and, more generally, the whole design of authority.

The Power of Environment

When John Locke died in 1704, the major breakthroughs in physics and astronomy had been consolidated by his compatriot and fellow Christian Isaac Newton. In a short work titled *Some Thoughts Concerning Education* (1693), Locke had argued that "all the men we meet with, nine parts of ten, ninety-nine of one hundred, are what they are, good or evil, useful or not, by their education." Here was an emphatic affirmation of the argument for nurture over nature that lay at the heart of the better-known *Essay Concerning Human Understanding*. Locke's claim that education was key to shaping the student's character as well as informing the content of his mind called into question a long-standing consensus about humanity's inherent depravity and sinfulness. Locke even included sections on the education of women, insisting that no one was exempt from the influences of family, community, and formal instruction. Environment determined human character.

This radical empiricism or environmentalism spurred a reexamination of many established precedents and practices in religion, ethics, politics, economics, and social life. Extending the belief in natural laws that lay at the core of the Scientific Revolution to the realm of human affairs, the *philosophes* claimed that progress was itself a general law. They believed that the application of reason to all human activities could accelerate the march of progress. In the late 1690s, the French Protestant Pierre Bayle (1647–1706) condemned the religious intolerance of Louis XIV's government on the grounds that alleged "truths" beyond the test of reason were inherently unstable. In his *Historical and Critical Dictionary* (1697), Bayle maintained that the only legitimate test of truth is conformity with rational understanding. Dogmas that transcended the embrace of human reason could never be obligatory. More controversially, Bayle asserted that morality and religion were separate spheres. He held that one could reject divine revelation and still conduct oneself in harmony with a rational standard of morality. Bayle was fond of saying that "errors are none the better for being old," and he articulated the internationalism of the Enlightenment when he stated that the true scholar "should forget that he belongs to any country. . . . I am neither French nor German, nor English nor Spanish, etc., I am a resident of the world."

The argument that individuals might be good without the oversight of religious authorities and nationally based institutions encouraged eighteenth-century reformers to leave no organization, system, or custom outside the purview of independent reason. In an effort to reach the widest possible audience, many of the *philosophes* deliberately adopted a popular and accessible form of exposition. They wrote philosophy to fit the tastes and the comprehension of a growing urban middle class. Journals, fiction, histories, satires, plays, letters—all avenues were exploited in a broad effort to subject hallowed conventions to the test of reason. One of the more influential strategies for expanding readership in this growing republic of letters was the exotic traveler's tale, stories written from the perspective of the non-Western visitor to Europe.

The Literature of Reform Two Frenchmen excelled in the use of this genre, even deriving significant income from the sale of their works. Baron de Montesquieu's (1689–1755) widely popular *Persian Letters,* published in the Netherlands in 1721 (French censorship was still strong), critiqued European customs from the perspective of two Persian travelers. Anticlerical in tone and sympathetic to non-Christian traditions, the book capitalized on Europe's growing awareness of divergent world cultures. On a more regional level, Francois Marie Arouet, better known to the world under his pen name Voltaire (1694–1778), contrasted English freedoms with French autocracy in his influential *Letters on the English,* first published in 1733. The book popularized the work of Locke and Newton for a French reading public. It also championed the English constitutional system in which Parliament limited the monarch's powers. Voltaire's immensely popular novel *Candide* (1759) focused on the adventures and troubles of a single young character in order to chastise more radical thinkers who thought that progress in this world was somehow predestined. In Ireland the Protestant churchman Jonathan Swift (1667–1745) wrote satirical essays decrying England's treatment of its Irish colony. His *Gulliver's Travels* (1726), another work of fantasy literature with a strongly moralizing tone, reached a broad audience.

Efforts to classify, systematize, demonstrate, and disseminate new knowledge became a central goal of the Enlightenment. Pierre Bayle's *Dictionary* was in fact the first encyclopedia, organized alphabetically by topic and offering synopses of the most up-to-date scholarship on a wide range of topics. It was followed in the 1720s by an English-language production, stressing the arts and sciences, under the authorship of the Scotsman Ephraim Chambers (1680–1740). But no one person could write a truly comprehensive encyclopedia. Beginning in the 1740s, a new effort was undertaken by a group of Parisian publishers. They appointed Denis Diderot (1713–1774) as

Voltaire Voltaire was the most influential critic of Europe's religious institutions during the eighteenth century. He was a historian, dramatist, and poet whose works reached a wide readership. *Nicolas de Largilliere. Portrait of Voltaire at age 23, bust length, 1728. Private Collection, Paris. Bridgeman-Giraudon/Art Resource, NY*

Map 16–1 The Influence of Diderot's *Encyclopedia* This map indicates where subscriptions were taken out for Denis Diderot's *Encyclopedia*. This huge endeavor at compiling scientific, technological, and mathematical knowledge expressed the Enlightenment beliefs in reason and progress.

Question: Why were the largest numbers of subscribers found in France?

general editor for what would become a multivolume collaborative effort to distill recent learning, especially in science, technology, and mathematics. In a preface co-authored by Jean le Rond d'Alembert (1717–1783), Diderot announced that the project was designed to "contribute to the certitude and progress of human reason." Thanks in no small measure to the indulgent attitude of the French government's chief censor, the first volume of the great *Encyclopedia* appeared in print in 1751. Six more volumes were issued annually until 1759, when a royal decree quashed the release of volume eight. France was at war with England by this date, and the government suspected that many of the contributors to the *Encyclopedia* were Anglophiles with little loyalty to the French state. Yet Diderot persisted, recruiting a wide range of *philosophes* as contributing authors. Eventually, in 1766 the 17 volumes were finished. Another 11 volumes of plates and additional volumes containing supplementary material and an index reached the bookshops in the 1770s. By the start of the French Revolution in 1789, over 20,000 full sets of the *Encyclopedia* had been sold (see Map 16–1).

Masonic Lodges and Salons   In addition to the popular *Encyclopedia*, new ideas were discussed in Masonic lodges that were located in every major European city by the

Salon of Marie-Therese Geoffrin   Salons provided a forum for Enlightenment thinkers to bring their ideas to the attention of a larger audience. Wealthy women often provided the patronage needed to sustain writers and reformers.

mid-1700s. The first Grand Lodge had been established in London in 1717, bringing together a number of smaller discussion circles. The movement known as Freemasonry offered alternatives to traditional religious houses of worship. Complete with their own rituals, fostering a sense of intellectual community, and even engaging in charitable activities, the Masons attracted members who were eager to share their engagement in the world of new ideas with like-minded men. Also key to the dissemination of knowledge during the Enlightenment were the aristocratic *salons,* or discussion circles, held in private homes and provincial literary academies. In Paris the *salons* were the center of activity. Normally hosted by influential women and serving as places where writers and their aristocratic patrons could interact, these meetings helped to make the French capital the center of Enlightenment thought.

Jesuit Education   The Roman Catholic Society of Jesus, or Jesuit Order, was established in 1540 during the Reformation era Council of Trent. Dedicated initially to reconverting Protestants to the Catholic faith, by the 1700s the Jesuits had become the premier educators in most Catholic countries, and in particular within France. The Jesuits were men of the world, counselors to kings and missionaries to distant lands such as India, China, and the Americas. In seventeenth- and eighteenth-century China, Jesuit missionaries even served as astronomers and cartographers at the Ming and Qing courts.

Many of the intellectual leaders of the Enlightenment were educated at Jesuit schools. Francis Bacon, although a Protestant, had spoken highly of Jesuit education in the early seventeenth century. The Jesuits were clearly the most influential teachers in the Age of Enlightenment. Students received rigorous training in the classics, rhetoric, and the latest sciences. The virtues stressed by Jesuits—discipline, self-control, intellectual exactitude—were endorsed by the *philosophes.* However, some former students turned their skills against their teachers. René Descartes was trained in mathematics by Jesuits, but he later rejected their steadfast position on authority and obedience. Voltaire, another Jesuit student, had been expelled as a ne'er-do-well.

The Church as Enemy   One of the most bitterly contested issues during the eighteenth century was the status of revealed religion and the power of the church to regulate people's lives. Outside of England and the Netherlands, official state churches afforded little toleration to religious minorities. Orthodoxy was enforced through censorship and the courts, and civil authorities employed the coercive power of the state to support the official faith. The Inquisition, for example, remained active in Spain, and non-Catholics were prohibited from traveling to Spain's colonies in the Americas. The same proscription applied against French dissenters; Protestants were banned from New France (Canada). National churches controlled vast tracts of land, and church leaders, especially within the Roman Catholic tradition, were often drawn from the aristocracy. In many ways, state churches were the chief buttresses of the Old Regimes across Europe, utilizing the power of the pulpit to inculcate obedience to civil authority and deference to superiors. The *philosophes* equated such power and control with bigotry and decried intolerance as the root cause of human divisions.

Deism   For Voltaire, established religious institutions stood squarely in the path of human freedom and progress. Some of his most vitriolic attacks were reserved for the Roman Catholic establishment in France. Censorship authority and control over education were the two areas where the malevolent influence of the hierarchical church was most pronounced. Opposing the creeds, dogmas, legal systems, and rituals of Europe's Protestant and Catholic churches, Voltaire spoke for an increasing number of educated believers who sought to simplify Christianity while bringing it in line with the mandate of universal reason. In his *Philosophical Dictionary* (1764), he articulated the essential position of those who referred to themselves as Deists (Voltaire preferred the word "theist"). God exists, and in the end He rewards and punishes His creatures on the basis of their conduct in this life. But He is a remote Creator who does not intervene in the daily affairs of individual believers, and He has certainly not saddled humanity with the incapacitating burden of original sin; each person enjoys the freedom to choose or reject salvation. There exists one universal and primitive religion, embracing Muslims, Buddhists, Hindus, Jews, Christians—indeed people of all faith traditions. Differences between these eclectic paths are only unfortunate human contrivances.

Deism rejected the incarnation and the doctrine of the Trinity, accepting Jesus as a great moral teacher but not God. Worship the one transcendent God and deal justly with others: This was the simple creed of most Deists from the plains of central Europe to the plantations of Virginia. A handful of thinkers took the critique of religion one step further. The Scottish philosopher David Hume (1711–1776) concluded that miracles, which by definition eluded

Benedict Spinoza The great Jewish philosopher Spinoza (1632–1677) was a major influence on the deists and other Enlightenment thinkers of the next century. Spinoza sought to reconcile faith with reason and challenged many deeply held theological beliefs of both Judaism and Christianity.

the confines of rationality, lay at the core of Christianity. Hume's claim that even reason could not demonstrate the existence of God led to charges of atheism and, among other hardships, cost him a coveted professorship at Edinburgh University. The Jewish philosopher Baruch Spinoza (1632–1677) believed that all sacred texts should be scrutinized at the bar of reason. In his best-known book, titled *Ethics,* he seemed to approach a pantheistic faith in his identification of God with all of nature. This, at least, is how his many critics interpreted his arguments, and he was excommunicated from his synagogue. Other influential figures, including Denis Diderot, Julian Offray de la Mettrie (1709–1751), and the German Baron d'Holbach (1723–1789), concluded that the idea of God was the great superstition of the ages.

Formulas for Improving Material Conditions

The social sciences as a distinct area of study were born during the Enlightenment, and the issue of wealth creation received special attention as Europe's colonial holdings matured and the Industrial Revolution began in Britain. Mercantilism, the belief that the total amount of wealth in the world was finite and that a country's share of this wealth depended on its ability to protect its own agricultural and manufacturing sectors from foreign competition, was the leading economic theory. Its impact reached across Europe and the Americas from the 1500s to the late eighteenth century. Dissenters from the orthodox model included merchants in Britain's North American colonies who were eager to trade with every European state, whether friend or foe of Britain, and a group of French reformers known as *physiocrats.* Arguing that the only genuine measure of wealth lay in the agricultural sector, these theorists, led by Francois Quesnay (1694–1774), physician to King Louis XV (r. 1715–1774), called for the state to promote human happiness and its correlate individual liberty. The state could do this by refraining from interference with the operation of natural economic forces except to protect agricultural property. This meant that for the first time in Western history, getting and consuming—an ethic of private appropriation—was being championed as one of the principal objectives of civil society, and governments were now to be judged according to how well they advanced this hedonistic ethos.

Adam Smith   The case for government noninterference on economic activities was taken into the industrial age by a professor of moral philosophy at the University of Edinburgh, Adam Smith (1723–1790). In 1776 he published a groundbreaking work that would have enormous influence into the twentieth century. In *The Wealth of Nations* Smith argued that society as a whole is best served when individuals are permitted to seek, secure, and hold their private material gains under conditions of minimal state interference. Only when government abandoned mercantilist protectionism, which in Smith's mind amounted to a discriminatory subsidy for one group of businessmen and a handicap against all other subjects, would broad-based material progress occur. In concrete terms, Smith's pioneering work called for an end to all tariffs, protective duties, subsidies to particular industries and enterprises, and the privileging of domestic over foreign manufactures.

A hands-off, or *laissez-faire*, approach to economic development would also lead to true social harmony. Smith posited the operation of an "invisible hand" or universal law of economics. According to Smith, freeing individuals to pursue their own rational, selfish interests would in fact further the material well-being of the entire community, both at the local and national levels. He rejected the mercantilist idea that total global wealth was limited, arguing instead that opportunities for wealth creation were as varied as the talents of the world's many peoples. Freeing those many talents, celebrating self-reliance, allowing the pressures of the marketplace to determine product, quantity, and price, were the inflexible laws that, if adhered to, would best serve every people irrespective of cultural differences. In this respect Smith was a proponent of the essential equality of economic man. Although after his death he became the darling of liberal capitalism and big business, Smith was no apologist for the uninhibited business tycoon. Indeed, he believed that employers who conspired to hold down wages often oppressed workers. Removing the heavy hand of government from economic affairs, he was convinced, would improve workers' ability to negotiate with their wealthy employers.

Crime, Punishment, and Reform   The problem of crime and the treatment of criminal offenders were also priorities of Enlightenment discourse. The conventional wisdom held that crime was to be equated with sinfulness, the fruit of human depravity. Once tried and convicted, the prisoner should be exposed to a regime of corporal punishment, torture, and, for many offenses, the death penalty. Europe's legal systems drew few distinctions between what today would be called misdemeanors and serious felonies, while in prisons murderers were held alongside debtors and petty thieves. The Italian reformer Cesare Beccaria (1738–1794) led the field in questioning the accepted wisdom. He called for a reform of irrational legal systems and focused on the need to rehabilitate the offender. In his popular *Crimes and Punishments* (1764), Beccaria condemned the use of torture and capital punishment as counterproductive vengeance, not deterrence. He called for new law codes that would enhance human happiness, what he termed "the greatest happiness of the greatest number," and not just reflect someone's personal understanding of divine law. More controversially, Beccaria alleged that criminality was not unrelated to wide disparities in wealth, leading the poor to operate outside of a legal system that they could not change.

Enlightened Despots

Just as there were many targets of the overall Enlightenment critique, so too there were differences of approach to the common problems that reformed thinkers identified. This was especially true of the political arena. On one hand, a few of Europe's monarchs encouraged and supported those *philosophes* who endorsed absolute rule. On the other hand, a thinker like Jean-Jacques Rousseau (1712–1778) put the good of the community before that of the individual and attacked society itself for corrupting human nature.

Catherine the Great   None of the *philosophes* endorsed democratic rule. Despite broad agreement over the importance of education to rational living, few envisioned an age when most people would be fitted to exercise political rights. This was no small comfort to Europe's crowned heads. As we read in Chapter 14, "The Early Modern State," Catherine the Great (r. 1762–1796) sought to transform a state that had lacked strong leadership since the reign of Peter the Great (r. 1689–1725) into a model of monarchical efficiency and innovation. During the first 15 years of her reign, the empress subsidized the publication of the French *Encyclopedia,* supported the foundation of schools, encouraged the fledgling Russian publishing industry, and created a legal reform commission that included commoners as well as noblemen. Catherine's program for legal reform was influenced by her reading of Beccaria's work, and the final document or "instruction" she gave her commission was translated into a number of European languages. Voltaire even received a personal copy from the empress (thanks to Catherine's interest, most of Voltaire's manuscripts today reside in Russia). Sadly, aristocrats and commoners on the special commission quarreled endlessly over serfdom, and in the end few reforms were implemented.

Frederick the Great   The most celebrated "**enlightened despot**" was the Prussian king Frederick the Great (r. 1740–1786). Fond of describing himself as the "first servant of the state," he was never directly accountable to his subjects, but he acknowledged a moral obligation to work for the good of the broader national community. Frederick was one of only a handful of rulers who, from an early age, developed an appreciation for and interest in music, literature, and philosophy. As king, he continued to perform in private concerts as a flutist and exchanged letters with Europe's leading

Catherine the Great of Russia   After securing the throne in 1762, Catherine worked to create an efficient government informed by Enlightenment ideas. During the early years of her reign, the empress supported legal and educational reform, but she was reluctant to surrender any of her powers as an absolute monarch.

Frederick the Great Frederick II valued his exchanges with Enlightenment thinkers, but he was committed to reform only within the context of enhancing state power. In this painting, the king performs on the flute during a private concert.

thinkers. His first correspondence with Voltaire dates from 1736, and the stormy friendship that developed between the two men culminated in Voltaire's residence at Frederick's court in Berlin from 1750–1753. Frederick's official actions early in his reign reflect the essential Enlightenment belief that problems and errors are man-made, not cosmic constants of the human condition. The king reformed the criminal code and abolished torture. He embraced religious toleration at a time when few rulers were willing to accept dissenters, and he promoted agricultural reform in the tradition of the physiocrats.

However, Frederick the Great, like Catherine the Great, was not solely interested in lessening misery and increasing happiness. Neither ruler hesitated to go to war when the opportunity arose to expand his or her territory and power. A series of partitions from 1772 to 1795 dismembered Poland, as Russia, Austria, and Prussia divided up the spoils. Neither Frederick nor Catherine was committed to reform at the cost of alienating the nobility. Frederick had little faith in the abilities of his non-noble subjects. When the French Revolution broke out in 1789, Catherine firmly rejected the position that the masses were equipped to carry out reforms similar to the ones she had enacted. Soon after Frederick died in 1786, almost all of his unique alterations, including the unprecedented edict against serfdom, were swiftly overturned.

Joseph II The only "enlightened" eighteenth-century ruler who dared to take on fundamental questions of social rights and economic reform was Emperor Joseph II of Austria (r. 1780–1790). Joseph had become Holy Roman Emperor in 1765 after the death of his father. However, he had to wait for the passing of his strong-willed mother, Maria Teresa (r. 1740–1780), before he could begin to reform his far-flung, diverse, and economically backward empire. The emperor's Italian, Flemish, Magyar, Polish, Czech, Croatian, and German subjects had little in common, but Joseph was undaunted by the scale of the task before him. During his ten-year reign, he issued thousands of royal edicts in an effort to realize some of the key goals of Enlightenment thinkers. Censorship was relaxed, religious toleration was declared, and Jews were given more freedom to worship and greater civil rights. The legal system was transformed as torture was abolished and capital punishment restricted. Most importantly, equality before the law was enforced. In the most dramatic decision of his brief reign, Joseph abolished serfdom within the empire, ending with the stroke of a pen centuries of social and material oppression. The opposition of the privileged classes and the church was both unanimous and loud, and after a decade of frenetic activity, the emperor had earned for himself the disdain of his nobles, priests, and the provincial legislatures that these social groups dominated. Absent this support, most of his innovations could not be sustained.

Critiquing the Enlightenment

Jean-Jacques Rousseau   The troubled loner Jean-Jacques Rousseau would have little to do with the top-down reforms of enlightened despots. Born in the Republic of Geneva in French-speaking Geneva, Rousseau's mother died soon after his birth, and his father abandoned him ten years later. The poor and ill-educated young man served several apprenticeships before leaving his natal land for France. Involved in a number of romantic affairs, Rousseau, like his father, abandoned his own children. In the midst

of this erratic personal life, he began to critique the very foundations upon which his society rested. In his *Discourse on the Origin of Inequality* (1755), *Emile* (1762), and *The Social Contract* (1762), Rousseau denied that humans were inherently evil or corrupt at birth. He insisted instead that society itself was to blame for the poor state of human relations.

Jean-Jacques Rousseau   "Man is born free, and everywhere is in chains," wrote the great Enlightenment thinker. Rosseau diverged from many of his fellow *philosophes* in his advocacy of a "social contract." Rosseau's writings and example would serve as an important inspiration for the French Revolution. *Dagli Orti/Picture Desk, Inc./Kobal Collection*

Rousseau overturned the Hobbesian description of the hypothetical state of nature, claiming that before the imposition of rules of property and formal institutions of government, self-interest and materialism were not central features of human comportment, that a genuine communism prevailed on Earth.

But since the fateful step had been taken to create civil society, Rousseau was prepared to offer his own model of the best possible polity. He disavowed the widespread assumption, shared by most of the *philosophes,* that society was simply an aggregate of individuals seeking personal goals and protected in their quest by a government of laws. Locke was wrong: Property was no natural right but a curse. Instead, Rousseau demanded that people enter into a social contract whereby they surrender their individual wills for the greater "freedom" of the common good. A *general will,* the embodiment of what each person would will for himself if he were thinking in a truly rational manner, must be the guiding principle around which the just society is constructed and maintained. Many of Rousseau's erstwhile friends saw in the concept of the general will not the liberation of the individual but the seeds of despotism and stultifying conformism. Rousseau's pursuit of the just society, his critics alleged, came at too high a price. Minorities and dissenters would find little solace in the unlimited power of the general will.

Montesquieu and Law   A more modest approach to the "science" of politics, but one equally troubling to the Enlightenment faith in universal natural laws, was provided by Montesquieu. Like his compatriot Voltaire, Montesquieu had traveled to England and was an admirer of Locke. He titled his study *The Spirit of the Laws* (1748), and in true Baconian fashion the author advanced his novel thesis only after assembling broad comparative data on governments around the world. In this respect it could be considered an early work in sociology as well as political science. For Montesquieu, no one formulaic model of government was applicable everywhere. Rather, a country's size, climate, population, religious and social customs, together with its economic structure, provided keys to the form of government that was best for current conditions. France, for example, was ideally situated to be organized under a limited monarchy, where the regional aristocratic courts or *parlements* (of which Montesquieu was a member) checked the ruler's powers. The guiding spirit or informing principle of limited monarchy was honor. The city-states of Geneva and Venice, in contrast, where virtue and moderation were the animating ideals, could function effectively under a republican system due to their modest size and cultural homogeneity. Montesquieu sharply disparaged despotisms, where fear prevailed, although they had once served well in large, heterogeneous empires like Rome.

Montesquieu's typologies for government even helped to inform thinking in Britain's former North American colonies. The framers of the Constitution of the United States, a document first drafted in 1787, embraced the idea of separation of powers (dividing executive, legislative, and judicial functions) contained in *The Spirit of the Laws.* While Montesquieu made many naive assumptions on the basis of climate and geography—northern peoples, he concluded, were more courageous than their southern neighbors, and Asians were less vigorous than their Western counterparts—his efforts to uncover a set of invariable laws (as opposed to a single law) of political evolution boosted interest in the study of society as a fledgling science.

Women and the Age of Reason   Wealthy patronesses frequently provided essential financial support for writers like Rousseau, and politically connected aristocratic women also facilitated contacts and helped controversial works get published. King Louis XV's mistress, Madame de Pompadour (1721–1764), for instance, helped to temper official criticism of the multivolume *Encyclopedia*. She even wrote an article on cosmetics for one of the volumes. Émilie du Châtelet (1706–1749) was wealthy and highly educated, and her marriage to another man did not prevent her from forming a close bond with Voltaire. She was interested in physics and translated Newton's *Principia*; her early death was a crushing blow to Voltaire.

Overall, however, the major Enlightenment thinkers were not champions of sexual equality or what would later be termed women's rights. Married women had few property rights, and the conduct of husbands within the household was virtually unassailable, no matter what abuses took place. Locke had questioned the biblical grounds for the ascendancy of the father in his *Two Treatises of Government,* but the *philosophes* did not share his judgment. The great *Encyclopedia* did not bother to address the contributions of women. Emmanuel Kant felt that too much education overtaxed the female intellect. Rousseau believed that women were the natural inferiors to men and should be confined to the home. He unapologetically stressed that the education of women ought to center on domestic and child-rearing responsibilities. Rousseau was a man of his word in this respect, regularly mistreating and then abandoning the many women with whom he fathered his offspring. A few, like Locke and Montesquieu, were sympathetic to greater educational opportunities for women and disputed the notion that unbridgeable intellectual differences existed between the sexes. However, none envisioned women playing an equal role with men in the political realm. The double standard in sexual conduct remained firmly in place, and child-rearing duties continued to be associated exclusively with the mother.

The Scotsman David Hume, with characteristic bluntness, alleged that men were led to repress women to preserve their own power. However, he was not troubled enough by this analysis to call for any change. The American Abigail Adams felt no such inhibitions. Upon hearing from her husband John that the 13 colonies were set to declare their independence from Britain, she reminded him that "in the new code of laws which I suppose it will be necessary for you to make, I desire you would remember the ladies and be more generous to them than your ancestors."

Three years after the start of the French Revolution, one extraordinary woman indicted the wholesale hypocrisy of the Enlightenment project with respect to the place accorded one-half of the population. Olympe de Gouges (1748–1793), the daughter of a butcher, boldly extended the revolutionary *Declaration of the Rights of Man and Citizen* (1789) to females with her 1791 *Declaration of the Rights of Women and Citizen*. Calling for equal rights before the law and in property relations, she spoke for many working-class women who were active in the early years of the French Revolution.

The English author Mary Wollstonecraft (1759–1797) followed the work of de Gouges with her widely read *A Vindication of the Rights of Women* (1792). The London-born daughter of a weaver, Wollstonecraft traveled to Paris in 1792, just before King Louis XVI was executed by his republican opponents. Her book set out to demonstrate that the progress of humanity could not occur so long as women remained the virtual

PEOPLE IN CONTEXT Olympe de Gouges

Olympe de Gouges (1748–1793) was born in humble circumstance and managed to educate herself before relocating to Paris after the death of her husband in the late 1760s. Once in the capital, she set out to become a playwright and political pamphleteer. By all accounts, she was a quarrelsome personality, and other writers tired of her efforts to dominate literary gatherings. She wrote on many subjects, including the abolition of slavery, but she is best remembered as an early champion of women's rights. Her *Declaration of the Rights of Women* was composed in a climate of enormous social and political upheaval, when women were enjoying newfound influence.

Despite her strident call for women's rights, de Gouges was a royalist who even dedicated the Declaration to the embattled Queen Marie Antionette. She called upon the Queen "to give weight to the progress of the rights of women, and to hasten its success." In 1792 she came to the defense of King Louis XVI, attacking the radical leader Maximillien Robspierre, and referring to him as an "egotistical abomination." In 1793 de Gouge called for a national plebiscite to determine the government of France. Arrested, tried, and convicted of sedition by the new republican government, she attempted to delay her execution by feigning pregnancy. In one hostile obituary, Olympe de Gouges was not only labeled a traitor, but condemned "for having forgotten the virtues which befit her sex."

Women's Patriotic Club   Women's clubs, such as the one depicted here, flourished during the revoluntionary period in France and focused mainly on philanthropic work.

Question: Can human equality be secured under traditional political institutions?

slaves of men. Wollstonecraft called for equal educational opportunity for boys and girls, and she insisted that existing social norms were the exclusive cause of women's alleged incapacities. Not content with mere assertions of equality absent empirical evidence, Wollstonecraft forwarded the Baconian call for rigorous experiment and data collection. "Let [women's] faculties have room to unfold, and their views to gain strength, and then determine where the whole sex must stand in the intellectual scale." Men constantly complain about the frivolity and intellectual weakness of women while simultaneously keeping women "in a state of childhood."

Slavery and Inequality   Europeans were latecomers to the African slave trade, but their involvement, while comparatively brief to that of native African rulers and Arab slave traders, was unrivaled with respect to the demographic, physical, and psychological impact it caused. The movement of black slaves northward across the Sahara Desert began more than 500 years before the first Portuguese traders arrived on the west coast of the continent in the mid-fifteenth century. These early centuries were dominated by Muslim middlemen who sold their captives as concubines, eunuchs, and domestic servants in Muslim lands across North Africa, the Near East, and as far east as India. Over the centuries, millions of African men and women were forced to trek thousands of miles in harsh desert conditions to reach their ultimate destination. Islam forbade the enslavement of other Muslims, but infidels could be denied their freedom with impunity. While slaves in the Muslim world could occasionally rise to positions of considerable authority, disparaging assessments of Africans based on race were not the monopoly of later Europeans. The fourteenth-century Arab historian Ibn Khaldun expressed a commonplace view when he wrote that "the only people who accept slavery are the Negroes owing to their low degree of humanity and their proximity to the animal stage."

Ironically, it was just as human bondage was disappearing in Europe that the horrific black African slave trade began in earnest. Africans were first brought to Portugal for sale in 1444. Thereafter, the sale of captive Africans expanded dramatically in the wake of Europe's colonization of sugar-producing islands off the west coast of Africa and subsequently in the Americas. The extremely high mortality rates from disease that Amerindians suffered soon after the arrival of whites from across the ocean opened up an acute need for labor in cash-crop, plantation-based economies.

The Spanish crown began licensing slave traders to the Americas in the 1550s. Before it was brought to a close in the late nineteenth century, upwards of 22 million Africans had been forcibly removed from their homes and transported to the Americas. Historian Philip Curtin estimated that 42% of all African slaves lived and worked in the small sugar-producing islands of the Caribbean. Another 38% engaged in plantation agriculture in Brazil, and 5% resided in North America. Plantation labor was so harsh that the slave population died faster than it could reproduce itself. In 1800 there were about eight and one-half million Africans born in the Americas, which was less than the total number of Africans that had been brought across the Atlantic since the year 1600. Despite European willingness to pay for slave labor, the sale of slaves by African rulers to European traders contributed nothing to the economic or social advancement of nascent West African states. Indeed, the scale of the trade undermined the ability of African governments to begin the process of agricultural reform or manufacture. Handicrafts never evolved into viable manufacture for export, and not a single West African kingdom transformed itself into a cash-crop exporting area comparable to the West Indies. Africa's main export product became the essential labor force for Europe's transformation of the New World.

Most of the *philosophes*, while perhaps opposed to the institution of slavery, declined to take a strong stand against slavery. Nor did they reflect seriously on the impact that the removal of so many able-bodied young men and women had on the indigenous peoples of Africa. Voltaire attributed the institution to humanity's penchant for power and domination. A strongly worded essay in the *Encyclopedia* condemned the institution, and the volume's wide readership may have contributed to the growth of a movement in favor of emancipation. By the third quarter of the eighteenth century, more voices were being raised in opposition. In Britain's American colonies, the pamphleteer Thomas Paine (1737–1809) rebuked his countrymen for tolerating the nefarious system at the very time that they were calling for their own freedom from royal authority. However, it was not the *philosophes* who led the antislavery drive, but dissenting Protestant religious groups.

Challenging the Enlightenment Faith

In many respects, the enthusiasm of the Age of Reason, the intoxicating effects of progress, and the conviction that social phenomena were amenable to scientific analysis and manipulation prompted a sharp reaction from a variety of thinkers. In particular, those who found the arid rationalism of the *philosophes* both emotionally unsatisfying and intellectually arrogant voiced the strongest objections. Rousseau suggested that feeling was of greater value than raw intellect in his novels *The New Heloise* (1761) and *Emile* (1762). Samuel Richardson's popular novel *Pamela* (1749) elevated sentiment and habits of the heart above rational understanding. However, it was in religious circles that the biggest response to the ascent of reason took place, and especially among dissenting voices within the established Protestant churches.

Efforts by select churchmen to harmonize reason and revelation left many believers with little sense of the beauty and mystery, the emotive and transformative side of essential faith. By the mid-eighteenth century, a number of restorative movements were underway. In Germany it was Pietism, in England Methodism, and in North America the Great Awakening. Each of these corrective endeavors took aim at the rigidity and complacency of the state-sponsored religious establishments, calling for a return to revelation absent rationalist interpretations. The Moravians in Germany were a Pietist group who found refuge in North America, and one of their number had a powerful influence on the Church of England cleric John Wesley (1703–1791). Wesley, along with his brother Charles (1707–1788), founded a dissenting branch of the official Anglican church that became known as Methodism. In America the evangelist George Whitefield (1714–1770) transformed the message of unmerited free grace and the need for personal transformation into a mass movement called the Great Awakening during the 1740s. While most popular in rural areas, even growing cities like Boston embraced the spirit of revival Whitefield fostered. For the religious leaders of these grassroots journeys, the power of human reason was as nothing compared to the glory and majesty of the personal God of Christianity.

The Arts in the Age of Reason

In terms of original thought and creation, one area of artistic endeavor reached new levels during the eighteenth century. European music entered an exceptionally vibrant and diverse period after 1700. The major royal courts and *salons* commissioned a stream of works while patronizing various composers, and a growing number of public concert halls offered a wide range of religious and secular music to urban audiences. While opera remained popular, new forms of instrumental and orchestral music appeared. Perhaps most significantly, eighteenth-century Western music began to reflect the rationalism of the age in its emphasis upon formality, harmony, control, and studious adherence to the original composition at each performance. Spontaneity, emotion, and improvisation in performance, central to musical traditions in the non-Western world, were discouraged in favor of balance and order. While compositions dedicated to religious themes and ritual observances remained at the forefront of artistic endeavor in music, composers also began to write secular works for entertainment.

Classical Music   A new musical style, described as "classical" both for its enduring as opposed to ephemeral impact and for its efforts to imitate the symmetry, clarity, and measured restraint of Greek and Roman art, emerged around mid-century. It continued to dominate the compositional arena until the early 1800s. As in so many Enlightenment endeavors, the movement was international in scope, although the leading composers came from Germany and Austria. The central performance innovation was the birth of the orchestra, complete with groups of related instruments (strings, brass, woodwinds, and percussion). Musical instruments evolved rapidly, with the piano enjoying primacy of place. The Austrian Franz Joseph Haydn (1732–1809) rose from humble circumstances to music director for a wealthy and powerful Hungarian noble family, the Esterhazy. Over a long career, Haydn composed operas, string quartets, music for religious services or liturgies, and symphonies. During a stay in London in the early 1790s, he composed additional symphonies for large orchestra (some 60 players) and won the acclaim of a large urban public.

Mozart   The preeminent artist of the century was doubtless the Austrian-born Wolfgang Amadeus Mozart (1756–1791). He began to compose at the age of 6, and his overall output when he died at age 35 included more than 600 works, among them 41 symphonies and 22 operas. In 1788 alone, Mozart composed three symphonies in six weeks. Like so many of his contemporaries, the young Mozart supported himself by seeking private appointments to play and compose in the courts of Europe's noble families. However, despite the quality and quantity of his artistic output, Mozart never amassed great wealth and was buried without circumstance in an unmarked grave.

Architecture, Painting, and Sculpture   In architecture, the fascination with ancient Greece and Rome that had informed the spirit of the Renaissance grew, especially after fresh archeological studies gave scholars more artifacts from early sites. Excavations at two buried Roman towns near Naples, Herculaneum and Pompeii, fascinated the reading and traveling public and became "must see" for aristocratic gentlemen making the "grand tour" of Europe's cultural sites. For those who could not

Oath of the Horatii   Jacques-Louis David rendered several of the most famous paintings of his era. This 1782 painting—which covered a huge canvas, measuring 14 by 10 feet—invokes an ancient Roman ritual in order to promote self-sacrifice and patriotism. David would later turn his attentions to contemporary affairs, while retaining his flair for the dramatic. *Jacques-Louis David, "The Oath of the Horatii." 1784. Oil on Canvas. 10'10" × 13'11" (3.3 × 4.25 m). Musee du Louvre, Paris. RMN Reunion des Musees Nationaux/Art Resource, NY*

travel to original sites, sketches and engravings offered architects a wealth of ideas. A "neoclassical" style began to inform design and construction across Europe and even reached the United States by the early nineteenth century. Eighteenth-century designers believed that buildings should reflect the reason, order, and clarity that purportedly lay at the heart of the Enlightenment project. Gone was the riotous detail and elaborate ornamentation of an earlier Baroque style. No longer projections of mystery and absolute power, the neoclassical buildings—public and private—of the eighteenth century emphasized mathematical proportion and refined taste.

Even painting, portraiture, and sculpture began to respond to the Enlightenment call for directness, realism, balance, and harmony. In Jacques-Louis David's (1748–1825) famous *Oath of the Horatii*, three brothers swear to fight a rival family in a struggle to determine the fate of Rome. The enormous canvas, completed in 1782, was 14 feet by 10 feet, and the viewing public embraced it with enthusiasm. Life lived in earnest, the virtues of self-sacrifice and patriotism, the ascendancy of principled intellect over the varied and unreliable emotions—these were the themes extracted from David's work. The artist's equally well-known and popular *The Death of Socrates* appeared in 1785. Here the great philosopher is unflinching in his acceptance of an unjust sentence, resolute and composed as he consumes the deadly hemlock. Working in a different genre, the English engraver William Hogarth's (1697–1764) many explorations into the lives of common people offered unadorned, if sometimes highly satirical and moralistic, portrayals of eighteenth-century urban existence at every social level.

KEY QUESTION | Revisited

How do people construct ideas of progress and human flourishing? During the Enlightenment these ideas were built on the foundations of a new view of human potential. Some seven decades ago, the historian Carl Becker alleged that the *philosophes* had dismantled St. Augustine's otherworldly City of God, the city of Christian believers, as part of a larger effort to rebuild that city on Earth with more up-to-date materials. What Becker meant by this analogy was that the Enlightenment thinkers were just as clearly men of faith as those whom they so publicly disparaged. Faith in progress, in reason, in secular versions of human flourishing, and in humankind's ability to fashion a self-referential heaven on Earth placed the *philosophes* on the same level of intellectual rigor as the churchmen and "mystery-mongers" whom they so disparaged in their writings.

Becker's views were challenged and amended by scholars like Peter Gay in the 1960s, and today our estimate of the Enlightenment is much more complex—confusing even. The movement consisted of varied streams of thought, and the family of enlightened thinkers, like all large families, was replete with problem children and stubborn debate. Yet there were important areas of consensus, and these included a suspicion of emotion and intuition, a desire for efficient and orderly institutions of governance, a willingness to place all traditions under the critical lens of rational inquiry, and, perhaps most eventfully, a willingness to broaden the circle of discussion beyond the confines of the university and the courts of princes. Abigail Adams was part of Enlightenment discourse even though she was denied political rights. While no democrats, the *philosophes* had made an enormous intellectual concession to the idea of human equality, if only in principle. For them, progress and human flourishing were the product of the application of reason to the affairs of daily life. Before the century concluded, serious revolutionaries on both sides of the Atlantic would attempt to translate this belief into action.

Review Questions

1. Why did the *philosophes* object to the influence that traditional religions exercised?
2. How did the Enlightenment affect the lives of common people?
3. Can one really speak of a firm Enlightenment project or agenda?
4. Is it fair to argue that modern social science began in the eighteenth century?
5. Was *Enlightened Absolutism* a serious institutional mechanism for reform?
6. What did human equality mean in the Enlightenment?
7. What were the main features of an "Enlightenment style" in the arts?

Please consult the Suggested Readings at the back of the book to continue your study of the material covered in this chapter. For a list of documents on the Primary Source DVD-ROM that relate to topics in this chapter, please refer to the back of the book.

17 Rebellion and Revolution: American Independence and the French Revolution

Having it at last in my power to visit my American friends, I hastened to the well known, and heartily beloved shores of this continent, and now feel happy to think, I once more am within the limits of the United States.

—Marquis de Lafayette, 1783

KEY | Question

Can political change occur without social and economic upheaval?

In 1776, the Marquis de Lafayette (1757–1834) signed an agreement to serve as a major general in the Continental army of the newly established United States of America. Lafayette was a wealthy French aristocrat who had begun his military career as a cavalry officer at age 16. In America he fought and distinguished himself under the command of General George Washington (1732–1799). In letters home to family, friends, and government officials, Lafayette faithfully promoted the America cause, and he was a key figure in forging a military alliance between the monarchy of King Louis XVI and the American republic. After returning to France in 1781, Lafayette served as a liaison between the French government and two American ambassadors to France, Benjamin Franklin (1706–1790) and Thomas Jefferson (1743–1826).

Why did this member of the European nobility risk his life in defense of a republic that repudiated both monarchy and titled aristocracy? When he first agreed to fight in America, the 20-year-old Lafayette saw only an opportunity to enhance his professional skills and to win renown on the battlefield. Writing in 1779, he admitted that he could recall "no time in my life when I did not love stories of glorious deeds, or have dreams of traveling the world in search of fame." But upon his arrival in the rebellious colonies, Lafayette was almost immediately inspired by the principles that had rallied the American patriots. "Never before

The Marquis de Lafayette The great French military officer (1757–1834) played leading roles in both the American and French revolutions. *Marquis de Lafayette by Francesco-Guiseppe Casanova, ca. 1781–85, oil on canvas, 18.5 × 16.5 in., accession 1939.9. Collection of The New York Historical Society*

had such a glorious cause attracted the attention of mankind; it was the final struggle of liberty, and its defeat would have left it neither asylum nor hope." In the years leading up to the French Revolution of 1789, Lafayette worked on behalf of a range of liberal causes: the liberation of African slaves, religious freedom for French Protestants and Jews, and the creation of a constitutional monarchy for France. When the Revolution broke out, this aristocratic friend of the United States drafted a statement of rights modeled after the Declaration of Independence. The revolutionary French National Assembly incorporated many of Lafayette's ideas into the *Declaration of the Rights of Man and Citizen* (1789), the central text of the French Revolution. That same year, now serving as commander of the Paris National Guard, a newly formed citizen militia, Lafayette sent the symbolic key of the old royal fortress-prison of the Bastille to his "adoptive father," President Washington. Today that symbol of what Lafayette called the "fortress of despotism" hangs in Washington's home in Mount Vernon, Virginia.

America Rejects Europe

Rebellion or Revolution?   In certain respects, the American colonial revolt against Britain that began in 1776 was fundamentally different from the French Revolution. Strong social and economic grievances (except among African Americans) were absent from the American conflict, religious issues were insignificant, and the post-independence political system remained unchanged except for the withdrawal of American allegiance to the British crown. In short, the American break with Britain was not a genuine revolution, if one associates revolution with profound social, economic, religious, and political upheaval. All of these factors were present in the uprising that began in France in May 1789.

Conversely, ideas and events in America from the end of the French and Indian War in 1763 to the successful conclusion of the American war of independence in 1783 had a profound impact on developments in France. Political leaders in America were familiar with French Enlightenment thought, while America's successful experiment in republican government inspired antimonarchical elements in France during the 1790s. Eager for an opportunity to avenge its loss in 1763, the French government of Louis XVI exploited the differences between Britain and its North American colonies; when the American war effort began to falter, French financial and military assistance enabled the rebellious colonists to prevail in their struggle against the world's greatest power. However much the French government disliked American **republicanism**, it decided that the opportunity to strike a blow against British power was worth the risk involved in assisting the rebels.

Britain's Fiscal Crisis   The British national debt had doubled during the French and Indian War. At the start of the eighteenth century, that debt stood at 14 million pounds; in 1763 it totaled nearly 130 million pounds. With the successful conclusion of the war in 1763, King George III (r. 1760–1820) and the leaders of Parliament decided to raise crown revenues and service the debt. They planned to do this by enforcing mercantilist trade regulations on the colonies and by imposing new tax measures designed to relieve the burden on English taxpayers. The British expected the Americans to cooperate with these measures because the war had largely been fought to increase the security and prosperity of

Map 17–1   North America in 1763   Britain's victory over France in 1763 presented authorities in London with two difficult challenges: how to pay for the cost of the empire and how to administer newly acquired North American territories.

Question: Why did British authorities seek to restrict settlement to lands east of the Appalachians?

Britain's American colonies. The costs associated with administering the empire stood at about 70,000 pounds in 1756. After the war, those costs increased five times, largely because the imperial government stationed troops along the Appalachian frontier (see Map 17–1). British attempts to redefine the relationship between the colonies and the home country precipitated a crisis of trust less than a decade after the defeat of the French.

A New Tax Regime   Beginning with the establishment of the Virginia House of Burgesses in 1619, most of the original 13 British colonies in North America had created legislative assemblies that were modeled after the Parliament in London. By the mid-eighteenth century, colonial governors, all appointed by the king, led bicameral assemblies. The governor appointed the members of the upper house, and property-owning white males elected the lower house. Despite their extensive executive powers, most governors worked closely with their legislatures. The British government had allowed the colonial governments to administer their own affairs as long as the colonies obeyed the laws of trade. However, ambitious colonial merchants grew increasingly restive with restrictions that prohibited them from trading with other European powers. Extensive smuggling with the French West Indies occurred during the French and Indian War, and in response the British authorized the use of general search warrants in an effort to confiscate smuggled goods. Some British colonists insisted that such actions violated Britain's unwritten constitution and the "rights of Englishmen." The move to define the extent of Parliamentary authority in the colonies had begun.

In 1764 the British enacted the first of a series of tax plans. Under the leadership of Prime Minister George Grenville (1712–1770), the so-called Sugar Act became law. In addition to expanding the list of products subject to tariffs, the legislation called for customs agents in all colonial ports to rigorously enforce procedures for collecting revenue. Smugglers were to be prosecuted in military courts. Assemblies in nearly every colony officially protested the adoption of the Sugar Act, sending petitions to London asking for repeal. The following year Parliament approved the Stamp Act. This law required that revenue stamps be affixed to all legal documents and even to newspapers and playing cards. Grenville's government hoped that the excise would raise around 60,000 pounds annually. Outspoken colonists declared that the Stamp Act amounted to "taxation without representation," a claim that members of Parliament in London vehemently denied. In fact, English politicians claimed that all subjects of the crown, irrespective of where they resided, were "virtually" represented in the House of Commons by members who placed the interests of the British Empire before provincial concerns. The government of George III believed that American objections to the Stamp duties represented simple tax evasion, a selfish unwillingness to assume some of the costs of administering the British Empire to which the colonists belonged and from which they benefited.

The Americans countered by insisting that from the period of the earliest colonial settlements, representatives lived in the districts that they served. The idea that a member of Parliament who had never been to America could adequately represent local interests was incomprehensible to the colonial mind. Colonial assemblies passed resolutions condemning the Stamp Act, angry mobs threatened and intimidated Stamp tax collectors, and most businesses and legal transactions took place absent the hated tax. American merchants then began boycotting British goods. Under extreme pressure from irate British merchants, moderates in Parliament decided to withdraw the tax in March 1766. Colonial politicians and merchants were jubilant, but when British lawmakers coupled the withdrawal of the tax with a Declaratory Act stating that Parliament could enact any law it wished to bind the colonies, the issue of sovereignty was again placed in dispute.

Constitutional Conflicts   By the 1760s, the colonial understanding of *representation* and *constitution* diverged significantly from the interpretations put forward in London. The same words were used, but the opposing sides attached different meanings to them. While representation in colonial assemblies meant advocacy on behalf of one's local constituency, in Britain it meant a more comprehensive view of imperial interests. In the colonies constitutions were written documents that delineated the specific powers granted to the government. The British constitution, however, was not a single charter or document but the totality of laws, customs, and institutions basic to the life and culture of a people. In effect, the constitution was fluid, always changing and responding to the needs of the kingdom.

As Parliament attempted to assert its sovereignty over the North American colonies, this semantic divide compounded the differences between a provincial outlook and its imperial counterpart. Leaders in the colonies were increasingly convinced that the liberties and "rights of Englishmen" that had been secured in the Glorious Revolution of 1688 were under attack by corrupt politicians who were determined to erect a tyrannical state. This, at least, was the view of a group of republican writers called the Commonwealthmen who saw England as the only state in Europe not governed by an absolutist monarch. Especially active at midcentury, their arguments resonated in the colonies, and all plans to tax the colonies were viewed through this ideological prism. When the English radical John Wilkes (1727–1797) was expelled from the House of Commons in the 1760s for his criticism of the king and his ministers in the newspaper *The North Briton*, colonists who followed these developments saw a sinister pattern developing. England was slipping into tyranny, with the royal executive attempting to emulate his peers on the continent. The Commonwealth perspective was represented throughout the colonies in newspaper articles, in public demonstrations, and in mob actions against "corrupt" representatives of the crown.

In 1767 the new British finance minister, Charles Townshend (1725–1767), imposed fresh tariffs on glass, lead, tea, and paper imported into the colonies. Again, the Americans organized boycotts of British goods. Troops were sent to Boston to protect the customs agents who were charged with collecting the levies, and in March 1770 clashes between townspeople and soldiers led to an exchange in which five civilians were killed. This so-called "Boston Massacre" temporarily galvanized colonial public opinion against the crown, and Townshend's tariffs were withdrawn (with the sole exception of the tariff on imported tea). For the next two years, there were no major incidents, and British imports

Boston "Massacre"   Just as the Declaration of Independence would unfairly portray King George III as a tyrant, this view of the Boston Massacre by Paul Revere was an effective piece of propaganda to generate support for the colonial resistance effort. The innocent civilians who were being fired upon were actually members of a violent mob who had provoked the British troops.

returned to their preboycott levels. Not until a group of Bostonians destroyed a shipment of imported East India Company tea in May 1773 did the government of King George III take robust and determined action against the colonies.

This Boston "Tea Party" outraged the British government. The king resolved that "we must master them or totally leave them to themselves." The port of Boston was ordered closed, and the Massachusetts colonial assembly was suppressed until reparations were paid to the East India Company. For the first time in almost two centuries, the Bay Colony had lost its right to self-government. In 1774 Parliament also passed the Quebec Act, extending the boundaries of that mostly French-speaking Catholic territory into the Ohio River Valley. The Quebec Act also put the province under a royal governor with no assembly (which was how Quebec had been ruled by France). Together the actions in Massachusetts and Quebec seemed to confirm the worst fears of colonial radicals that Britain wished to destroy self-government in America.

Continental Congress and Independence   Representatives from each of the 13 British colonies maintained close lines of communication throughout 1763–1774. In September 1774 these political figures organized the First Continental Congress in Philadelphia to plan a joint strategy. The following summer pitched battles between British troops and colonial militia took place at Lexington and Concord in Massachusetts. A Second Continental Congress met in May 1775 in an attempt to work out a compromise with the British. Failing in this effort, the Congress moved to organize a unified government for the colonies. King George III declared the colonies in open rebellion in August 1775, and over the winter a short pamphlet called *Common Sense* helped to build broad public support for an American repudiation of British rule. The author was Thomas Paine (1737–1809), an English-born artisan who had been in America for less than one year and who would later relocate to France during the French Revolution. In July 1776 the Continental Congress adopted a Declaration of Independence written by Thomas Jefferson, a 33-year-old delegate from Virginia.

The spirit of the European Enlightenment informed the American Declaration of Independence. With the Declaration, monarchy was nullified, aristocracy renounced, and the equality of white male citizens established as the basis of national sovereignty. Consisting of two parts, the general statement of the right to revolution, a right that Jefferson based on natural law, "self-evident" reason, and the defense of "certain inalienable rights," has inspired people around the world for over 200 years. The second part, a personal indictment of King George III, served as a brilliant polemic during the course of the war for independence. Together they provided an unprecedented public justification for political rebellion, a statement designed as much for a Europewide audience as it was for the 10% to 15% of colonists in America who opposed independence.

War and Republican Rule   During the first year of fighting, Britain employed a seasoned and well-trained army, together with German mercenaries, against an inexperienced colonial militia led by George Washington. In addition to large numbers of Tories (colonists who supported the British), thousands of colonists were indifferent to the outcome of the struggle, making Washington's task extremely difficult. After a series of setbacks on the battlefield, the American Continental army finally won a crucial victory at Saratoga, New York, in October 1777. Almost 6,000 British troops surrendered to American forces. King Louis XVI, whose government had been sending arms and supplies to the American patriots, now quickly recognized the independence of the United States. Within six months, France signed a formal treaty of alliance with the fledgling republic. The French loaned the U.S. government over 8 million dollars and sent a large fleet and army to North America. In October 1781 Washington and his French allies won a decisive victory over British forces at Yorktown in Virginia. In 1783, the British signed a formal treaty in Paris acknowledging American independence and ceding some colonial possessions to France and its ally Spain.

Constitution Building   The Continental Congress had served as America's national government during the war with Britain, and in 1781 its legal basis was established with the ratification by each state of the Articles of Confederation. Under its provisions, states retained their sovereignty and independence, with the federal government denied the power to tax or print money. No executive office was created under this instrument of government, and judicial power remained at the state level. Each state enjoyed one vote in the unicameral Congress, and unanimity was required before important legislation could become law. The Articles of Confederation reflected American fear of coercive central government under the leadership of a single British executive. But decentralized power was not a complete success; by the mid-1780s, many political leaders were calling for the formation of a stronger national government. Foreign affairs, military preparedness, and internal development all required a government with the power to raise revenue and print money. The loose alliance of 13 states, while preserving sovereignty at the local level, hindered the formation of mutually beneficial trade policies and weakened the ability of the United States to negotiate successfully with foreign powers.

In 1787 the Congress approved a meeting in the city of Philadelphia, where delegates were to work on revisions to the Articles of Confederation. Broadly interpreting their mandate, the assembled delegates jettisoned the Articles and drew up a new instrument of government. The final product was sent to the states for ratification, and it was approved by late 1788. The Constitution of the United States established a presidential system, with a separate judiciary and a strong legislative branch. A Bill of Rights was added to the document in order to protect individual citizens from possible government abuse of power. The new Constitution permitted the national government to tax citizens, regulate interstate and foreign commerce, and raise and maintain an army and navy. States lost their right to issue money or to make treaties with foreign governments. The framers of this second Constitution believed that the new instrument of government provided an adequate set of checks and balances to prevent any single branch from abridging the "natural rights" of the citizenry.

Key Developments in the American and French Revolutions

AMERICA		FRANCE	
1763	Britain victorious in Seven Years' War	1789	Meeting of Estates General
1765	Stamp Act	1789	Fall of the Bastille
1770	Boston "Massacre"	1792	Outbreak of war with Austria
1774	First Continental Congress	1793	Execution of Louis XVI
1775	Second Continental Congress	1793–1794	Reign of Terror
1776	Declaration of Independence	1799–1804	Napoleon's Consulate
1778	France joins American war effort against Britain	1802	Napoleonic Code
		1804	Napoleon declared Emperor of the French
1781	British defeated at Yorktown		
1783	Treaty of Paris recognizes American independence	1814	Collapse of French Empire

Impact in Europe and Latin America   Leading figures in America's successful bid for independence, men like Thomas Jefferson, Benjamin Franklin, and John Adams (1735–1826), embraced the Enlightenment's call for the critical evaluation of all institutions and ideas. The American adoption of religious toleration, the insistence upon trial by jury, freedom of speech and religion, an expansive franchise, and government by the consent of the governed all served to animate European and Latin American reformers and revolutionaries during the next century. The success of the American republic encouraged opponents of the Old Regime across the European continent and in Spain's American empire; for European royalty and the titled aristocracy, however, the United States stood as a dangerous challenge to the inviolability of the hierarchical social order, to the belief that only a chosen few were born to rule. The government of Louis XVI had taken a huge gamble by backing the American cause. Britain may have been humbled by America's successful colonial revolt, but over the next 20 years, its government would weather the upsurge in European republicanism while the Old Regime in France would be overturned.

Revolution in France

Crisis of the Old Regime   When Louis XVI (r. 1774–1793) assumed the French throne upon the death of his grandfather, the country was facing a pronounced fiscal emergency. The unsuccessful French and Indian War (1754–1763) had been largely funded by loans secured against a government guarantee of military victory. New sources of taxes were desperately needed, but those individuals and institutions most able to pay—the aristocracy and the church—consistently refused to register royal decrees thanks to their control over the 13 regional *parlements*. French peasants, who were better off than peasants elsewhere in Europe, shouldered the bulk of the tax burden in the country. Louis XVI compounded the financial crisis by supporting the American war of independence. By the time that the Americans had secured their freedom from Britain, more than half of the French national budget was dedicated to interest payments on loans taken to support earlier military ventures.

Louis XVI appointed a series of reform-minded finance ministers, but each man was forced to resign in the face of strident aristocratic opposition. When one of these ministers, Charles Alexandre de Calonne (1734–1802), proposed a tax on land and the sale of church property, the wall of privileged opposition reached new heights. Nobles spoke of the "rights of man" and the government's attack on individual freedom. Clearly, the first two orders or estates of the realm, the clergy and the nobility, were attempting to use the rhetoric of Enlightenment in a base effort to maintain their varied financial exemptions. In frustration, the king agreed to call a meeting of the Estates General, a medieval advisory body that had not convened since 1614. The king's advisors hoped that this assemblage, which included representatives from all three estates—nobility, clergy, and commoners—could muster the required moral authority to break the deadlock.

A troubling set of demographic and economic indicators compounded the fiscal crisis. Population grew at a brisk pace during the eighteenth century, and while food production managed to keep up with the increases, long-term inflation made food more expensive and undermined the ability of poor peasants to maintain themselves. As the population expanded, landlords attempted to protect themselves against inflation by holding down wages while simultaneously raising rents and dues. A series of bad harvests during the 1780s aggravated conditions; thus, when elections to the Estates General were held in 1789 a mixture of anger, resentment, and high expectations influenced the outlook of millions of French men and women.

From Estates General to National Assembly   The meeting of the Estates General provided the Third Estate, which included urban laborers, peasants, artisans, businesspeople, lawyers, bankers, and financiers, an unprecedented opportunity to influence national politics. Delegates arrived at Versailles with a list of grievances *(cahiers de doleances)* drawn up by their local constituencies. A more perceptive monarch than Louis XVI would have realized that decades of pent-up frustration over the high cost of food, inequitable tax and service burdens, urban underemployment, and chronic government inefficiencies would result in a contentious meeting. The impact of books, political pamphlets, and broadsides published during the Age of Enlightenment was bound to be significant, at least in shaping the outlook of the reading public. During the 1790s, France's political, social, and religious institutions would be shaken to their foundations. Millions of French men and women would become involved in some form of political action, and their status as subjects would be transformed into the role of citizen.

REVEIL DU TIERS ETAT.

Ma feinte, il etoit tems que je me réveillisse, car l'opreforion de mes fers me donnions le cochemar un peu trop fort.

"The Third Estate Awakens" An illustration from the early days of the French Revolution shows the "third estate" awakening—and arming itself—while the First and Second Estates (the clergy and the nobility) recoil in horror. The violence of the Revolution is further suggested by the destruction of the Bastille in the background.

When the Estates General first assembled at Versailles in early May 1789, the Third Estate had already received royal permission to double its delegation. According to the protocol of the last meeting in 1614, each estate was allowed to elect 300 delegates. Because it represented most of the French population, the Third Estate sent 600 delegates to Versailles. How each estate was to vote was a more difficult issue. Traditionally, each estate cast one vote, a procedure guaranteed to enable the clergy and nobility to defeat all reforms originating with the commoners. For weeks, the first two Estates refused to amend the voting process. Finally, on June 17, 1789, the Third Estate, together with a handful of sympathetic clergy and nobility, declared itself the National Assembly of France and pledged not to disband until the country had a new constitution. As newspaper accounts and eyewitness reports of the events at Versailles spread throughout the country, peasants and urban workers were suffering after an especially harsh winter and faced escalating food prices. They looked upon the actions of the Third Estate with a sense of renewed hope for change.

The Storming of the Bastille   The attack on the Bastille on July 14, 1789, marked the first time that ordinary Parisians shaped the course of the French Revolution.

Fall of the Bastille
Initially, King Louis XVI was unwilling to accept the legitimacy of the National Assembly. When he began to increase the number of troops at Versailles and in Paris, fears of a violent crackdown grew. Some 800 Parisians responded on July 14 by storming the Bastille, a royal armory that doubled as a debtor's prison. After overwhelming the handful of troops stationed at the Bastille, the enraged mob killed the governor of the fortress and some of his soldiers. Subsequently forming a citizen militia called the National Guard and led by Lafayette, the radicalized Parisians—most of whom were members of the middle class—instantly became the military wing of the Third Estate. Lafayette suggested an insignia for the Guards, a tricolor of blue, white, and red stripes that became the new flag of revolutionary France.

Declaration of the Rights of Man and Citizen
Similar urban revolts took place in cities throughout France. The formation of regional militia groups modeled after the National Guard led to the resignation of many royal government officials who feared for life and limb. In the countryside, landless, hungry, and desperate peasants began to attack the homes of local nobles, pillaging and destroying any legal papers related to dues and services owed by local peasants to their superiors. Their actions led liberal nobles and churchmen in the National Assembly to renounce their feudal privileges. Equality before the law had been conceded in the face of direct action by the peasantry. On August 27, 1789, the National Assembly approved the *Declaration of the Rights of*

Man and Citizen, a statement of political principles modeled after America's Declaration of Independence. All men were declared free and equal citizens, religious toleration was adopted, and taxation based on the ability to pay was accepted as a basic constitutional principle. Women were not mentioned in this watershed document, but women were coming to play an important role in the Revolution. In Paris the high price of bread—the staple food of the urban poor—led some 7,000 women (armed with knives, swords, and pikes) to march on Versailles in early October. After skirmishes in which a few royal guards were killed, the women compelled Louis and his queen, Marie Antoinette (1755–1793), to accompany them back to the capital. The king was now forced to recognize the *de facto* power of the National Assembly, whose bourgeois delegates were committed to the formation of a constitutional monarchy.

A Written Constitution for France

In 1791 the Assembly created a constitutional monarchy whereby the king now exercised a delaying, but not a permanent, veto over legislation passed by a unicameral Legislative Assembly. The members of the new legislature had to meet high property qualifications in order to serve, although all males who paid local taxes equal to three days' labor wages could vote for electors who then picked the legislators. In effect, only about 50,000 of France's 25 million people could hold public office under the new constitution. However, the criterion for officeholding had shifted from birth to wealth, opening new opportunities for non-noble citizens to shape public policy at the national level. In fact, all titles of nobility were abolished. A uniform court system staffed by professional judges replaced the feudal *parlements*, and 83 administrative regions called *departements* of roughly equal size replaced the medieval provinces. In an effort to rationalize economic policy, free trade policies were adopted and restrictive guilds were suppressed. French women were denied political rights under the new constitution, and some, like the self-educated commoner Olympe de Gouges (d. 1793), called for an extension of civil rights. In her *Declaration of the Rights of Women*, de Gouges rephrased the *Declaration of the Rights of Man* by inserting the word *woman* wherever the initial document used the word *man*. Her efforts to make natural rights language more inclusive failed, but the active role played by women in the Revolution kept the issue of human equality alive.

Attacking the Church

Unlike most revolutionary regimes in recent centuries, the French National Assembly reluctantly assumed all of the debts of the previous royal government. To address the acute financial crisis, the new government ordered the confiscation of the property of the Roman Catholic Church. In addition, all clergy were required to take loyalty oaths to the new government, in effect transferring their allegiance from the pope in Rome to the national state. The Assembly also reduced the number of bishops to conform to the new administrative *departments*. Church property was offered to investors, and *assignats*, or government bonds, were sold to the public on the expectation that revenue generated from sales of church land would service the bonds. However, the income derived from this one source failed to make a significant impact on the gigantic debt. In addition, the actions taken against the church enabled opponents of the Revolution to rally common people to their cause; the revolutionaries were increasingly portrayed as destroyers of traditional religious values, and the Roman Catholic Church set out on a course of opposition to liberalism and revolution that would continue for most of the nineteenth century.

The Radical Revolution and End of the Monarchy, 1792–1794   During the first two years of revolutionary change, King Louis XVI had reluctantly assented to the measures taken by the National Assembly, even approving the shift to constitutional monarchy. Equality before the law, careers open to talent, a written constitution—liberals were pleased with the accomplishments of the Revolution and wished to build upon these moderate reforms. However, many French aristocrats, including the king's younger brothers, the counts of Provence (1755–1824) and Artois (1757–1836), fled to neighboring countries and worked to build a counterrevolutionary movement. In June 1791, Louis XVI, feeling increasingly insecure in Paris and opposed to the measures taken against the church, was persuaded to join them. Disguised as commoners, the king and his immediate family attempted to flee the country but were discovered at Varennes in eastern France. They returned to Paris as virtual prisoners. Sympathizing with Louis's predicament, Queen Marie Antoinette's brother, Emperor Leopold II of Austria (r. 1790–1792), together with Prussia's King Frederick William II (r. 1786–1797), threatened intervention if the French royal family was harmed. Within a year the French government declared war on both countries (ostensibly for harboring French aristocrats who were plotting against the government), confident that military conflict in defense of the homeland would rally the French people to the revolutionary cause.

Middle-class property owners had been the chief beneficiaries of the moderate stage of the Revolution. However, poor laborers, shopkeepers, and artisans had less to show for their efforts. Beginning in 1792, these **sans-culottes** (referring to the long trousers that workingmen wore instead of aristocratic knee breeches) called on the government to address the problem of economic inequality by increasing wages, controlling food prices, and raising taxes on the wealthy. The *sans-culottes* also called for a more democratic political order in which the voice of the common citizen would be heard. In their view the middle-class leaders of the Revolution were content to slow reform down now that they enjoyed political privileges once held by the aristocracy of the Old Regime.

The outbreak of war with Austria and Prussia in April 1792 worsened the economic situation and led to dissension within the ranks of the Legislative Assembly. Lacking strong military leaders in the wake of numerous defections by aristocratic officers (among them Lafayette, who was afraid of the increasing radicalization of the Revolution), the French army fared poorly on the battlefield. As enemy troops penetrated deeper into France, panic spread in Paris. Acting on wild rumors that disaffected priests and nobles who had been arrested were about to break out of custody, mobs attacked prisons and murdered over 1,000 inmates. Earlier, the people of Paris had also assaulted the royal residence, killed hundreds of the royal guards and servants, and demanded universal manhood suffrage,

■ ■

PEOPLE IN CONTEXT Edmund Burke on Revolution

Edmund Burke (1729–1797) was born in British-controlled Ireland and attended Trinity College, Dublin, before moving to London in 1750. During Britain's conflict with its American colonies, Burke was a member of Parliament who took the unpopular position that the king and Parliament should work to conciliate the colonists by trying to understand their constitutional grievances. In speeches before Parliament, Burke appealed for the abandonment of colonial taxation and the promotion of colonial freedoms as consistent with the history of British involvement in North America. In a "Speech on Conciliation with the Colonies" (1775) Burke stated that English settlers "have turned a savage wilderness into a glorious empire, and have made the most extensive and the only honorable conquests, not by destroying, but by promoting the wealth, the number, the happiness of the human race. Let us get an American revenue as we have got an American empire. English privileges have made it all that it is; English privileges alone will make it all it can be." For Burke, the essence of political wisdom lay in a respect for precedent, the accumulated wisdom and traditions of centuries. He believed that government efforts to enforce new tax schemes on the colonists after 1765 smacked of innovation and constituted a violation of English liberties.

This same conservatism, the defense of tradition and custom, led Burke to come to the defense of Irish Catholics (Burke's mother was Catholic) who sought to practice their religion in freedom and Irish merchants who sought to trade on equal terms with their English counterparts. Once again, Burke took an unpopular stand in pleading for colonials, whom most English politicians considered troublesome. When the French Revolution began in 1789, many liberals in England and America applauded the efforts of the National Assembly to curb the power of the crown and to establish a new constitution. But at this juncture Burke broke with many in his own political party, the Whigs. In *Reflections on the Revolution in France* (1790) Burke denounced the revolutionaries even before the radical stage had begun. He doubted whether

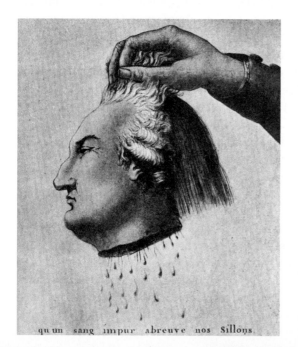

qu un sang impur abreuve nos Sillons.

Severed head of Louis XVI The instability and radicalism of the French Revolution greatly disturbed Burke. The line at the bottom of the drawing reads: "May an impure blood water our furrows."

the newly elected French assembly could control the forces of change in a manner consistent with order and tranquility. "The objects of society are of the greatest possible complexity," he maintained, and hastily drawn up blueprints for the good society, implemented without regard for a particular nation's heritage, were a formula for disaster.

Thomas Paine responded to Burke's *Reflections* with *The Rights of Man* (1794). Burke was opposed to the Enlightenment language of "natural rights" and claimed that "Government is not made in virtue of natural rights, which may and do exist in total independence of it." Instead, "Government is a contrivance of human wisdom to provide for human wants," and only men who worked within the framework of existing national institutions and practices could successfully guide the state. He believed that the French Revolution would go violently wrong because its leaders sought to do away with a centuries-old political system. Effective political systems were for Burke akin to organic systems, complicated and delicate, and while these systems should evolve over time, forcing change through revolution was self-defeating. During the nineteenth century, Burke's ideas were influential in conservative circles across Western Europe and in America.

Question: Is Conservatism always opposed to change?

decentralized government, and economic justice. Radicals succeeded in forcing the Legislative Assembly to "suspend" the king and call for elections to a new national government. This "Convention" government, named after the American Constitutional Convention of 1787, was elected on the basis of universal male suffrage and charged with drawing up a more radical constitution. Almost immediately, the newly elected delegates proclaimed France a republic and moved to prosecute the monarch for conspiring against the liberty of the French people.

Louis XVI, derisively referred to by his accusers as "Citizen Capet" after the Capetians who had founded the dynasty in 987, was tried and convicted in December 1792. On January 21, 1793, he was beheaded by the newly invented guillotine. Marie Antoinette, the frivolous queen who had become the supreme symbol of royal indifference to the suffering of the French people, followed her husband

Marat   Jean Paul Marat was one of the most radical of the revolutionary leaders. He published a newspaper called *The Friend of the People* and was popular among Paris's *sans-cullotes*. This painting by the great French artist Jacques-Louis David depicts Marat's 1793 assassination, in his bathtub, by a royalist named Charlotte Corday.

to the guillotine in October (Olympe de Gouges, who had spoken out for the queen, was executed in November). The war with Austria and Prussia intensified, and the Convention government's difficulties were compounded when the anti-French coalition expanded to include Britain, Holland, Portugal, Spain, Sardinia, and Naples. For the leaders of the Revolution, the European conflict was now about the defense of new political principles and fundamental social transformation. Europe's monarchs and titled aristocrats, they believed, were committed to the destruction of their enlightened republic, and extreme measures were justified in the heroic struggle ahead.

Jacobin Rule and the Reign of Terror In June 1793 a group of radical leaders in the Convention, known as **Jacobins** (after the name of a former Dominican monastery in Paris where they met informally), began to dominate the proceedings. The Jacobins favored strong central control over the *departements* and emergency powers to address the economic and military crisis. The urban *sans-culottes* supported the Jacobin leaders, and in early June 1793 a mob surrounded the Convention and demanded the expulsion and arrest of the more moderate members, known as Girondins (from the *departement* of Gironde), who were seized and executed. The Jacobins were now emboldened to pursue their revolutionary plans. In the face of emerging peasant counterrevolution in the countryside, foreign invasion from the east, and economic breakdown everywhere, the Jacobins persuaded the Convention to delegate executive power to the 12-member Committee of Public Safety, which they dominated.

These fervent republicans instituted an unprecedented draft of unmarried men between the ages of 18 and 25 and built a citizen army of over 800,000 men. Women and children were called upon as well, stitching clothing and manufacturing bandages for the troops. These citizen-soldiers were inspired by French nationalism to fight for the revolutionary ideals of liberty, equality, and fraternity, not for a divine-right monarch who cared little for their plight. Fired by patriotism and led by battle-hardened officers who had risen through the ranks, the rejuvenated army managed to roll back the enemy and even take the offensive in Belgium and the Rhineland by the summer of 1794.

The Committee of Public Safety fought an even more bloody war on the domestic front. Led by Maximilien Robespierre (1758–1794), the radical leaders were intent on creating a "republic of virtue" in which ignorance and superstition would be expelled and there would be no extremes of wealth and poverty. A Law of the Maximum, designed to control the price of bread and flour, was instituted in order to appease the *sans-culottes,* and a new draft constitution (never implemented) promised rights to education and basic subsistence. Influenced by the thought of Rousseau and convinced that they alone understood the general will of the French people, Robespierre and his colleagues on the Committee of Public Safety attacked Girondin critics of the regime, peasant opponents of centralized rule, royalist priests, nobles, and their supporters—anyone who disagreed with Jacobin leadership. A brutal terror campaign was inaugurated against the varied "enemies of the people." It began with royalists in the capital and eventually consumed members of every social class and most political

Maximilien Robespierre   Known as "The Incorruptible" for his austere lifestyle and revolutionary ethics, Robespierre emerged as leader of the Committee for Public Safety during the "Reign of Terror." Robespierre was eventually claimed by the Terror; he was beheaded in July 1794.

perspectives. Upwards of 30,000 people, most of them peasants and workers, were put to death before Robespierre turned against his own allies. In self-defense, members of the Convention arrested Robespierre and his key lieutenants and executed them—by guillotine—in July 1794.

The End of the Terror   With the invading enemy armies defeated and internal rebellion contained, few French citizens saw any justification to continue the type of idealistic political extremism sponsored by the Robespierrists. The **Reign of Terror** began in an effort to forge a rationalistic republic of virtue and ended by repudiating the humane ideals of the Enlightenment. The property-owning bourgeoisie quickly regained control of the government, imprisoned and executed Jacobins, purged the army leadership, and removed many of the restrictive measures imposed by the previous regime. A new constitution, adopted in 1795, limited the right to vote to wealthy property owners. All executive functions were reserved for five individuals—named the Directory. Over the next four years (1795–1799) the government continued to face challenges from disgruntled royalists on the right and Jacobins on the left, the war dragged on, and finances remained precarious. The role of the army in maintaining the authority of the increasingly corrupt Directory became greater each year, creating an opportunity for ambitious military commanders to influence state policy.

An Assessment in 1795   The Directory government wished to refocus the revolutionary impulse back to the reform agenda of the early years. The accomplishments had been significant: the formal abolition of feudalism, an end to legal privileges based on status and title, the repudiation of divine-right monarchy, government accountability to property-owning males, the dramatic fall of church influence in affairs of state, the emergence of citizen armies, and anticipations of modern patriotic nationalism. For the first time in European history, a significant number of common people—wage earners, shopkeepers, peasants—had become political actors capable of influencing the national agenda in a significant manner. The ideas generated by the *philosophes* during the eighteenth century, especially their discussion of natural rights and liberties, religious freedom, and the accountability of magistrates, were now implemented. These ideas animated a kingdom where economic hardship was acute and where society's traditional leaders seemed out of touch with conditions experienced by the majority of the population.

In some respects the Americans had paved the way for the French Revolution. Many French soldiers—like Lafayette, who had fought in the American war for independence—returned home with a new sense of possibilities for their own country. However, Americans before 1776 did not have to contend with a titled aristocracy, an entrenched state church, grinding poverty in the countryside, and high urban unemployment. The French Revolution undermined the corporate and hierarchical nature of society. In its place a society emerged where talent, not title, mattered, where the mandate of the people, not the mandate of God, legitimized civil authority. There is perhaps no better illustration of the new principles in action than the meteoric career of Napoleon Bonaparte (1769–1821).

Napoleon Bonaparte and the Export of Revolution, 1799–1815

Born on the Mediterranean island of Corsica just after it became French territory, Napoleon Bonaparte attended a French military school and received a commission as a second lieutenant at age 16. As a commoner, he was resentful of the aristocratic officers who secured their positions on the basis of status. When the French Revolution began, Napoleon quickly sided with the Revolutionaries. His successes on the battlefield brought him to the attention of the National Convention, and in 1795 he was charged with suppressing a crowd of royalist insurgents in Paris. He was then assigned to lead a French army fighting in Italy, where he won a series of important victories over the opposing Austrians and Sardinians. Napoleon established a number of Italian republics in the wake of his military successes. He then accepted command of an expeditionary force of 35,000 troops whose task was to attack British interests in Egypt. Although Napoleon was victorious on land, the British prevailed at sea, with Admiral Horatio Nelson (1758–1805) crushing the French fleet at the Battle of the Nile on August 1, 1798. Stymied, Napoleon was able to slip back into France, and he carefully controlled the reports coming out of Egypt.

When he arrived in France, conservative factions were planning to overthrow the government of the Directory. The conspirators needed a popular general to serve as a figurehead leader, and Napoleon was recruited to lead the coup d'etat. The French population, wearied by a decade of political instability, economic hardship, and for-

Coronation of Napoleon On December 2, 1804, Napoleon crowned himself Emperor of the French in Notre Dame Cathedral. In this painting by Jacques-Louis David, Pope Paul VII raises his hand in blessing as Napoleon places a crown on the head of his wife, Josephine. *Jacques Louis David (1748–1825) "Consecration of the Emperor Napoleon I and Coronation of Empress Josephine," 1806–07. Louvre, Paris. Bridgeman-Giraudon/Art Resource, NY*

eign war, accepted the appointment of the popular military commander as "first consul" under a constitution created in 1799. Two additional consuls initially served as executives with him. However, Napoleon quickly consolidated support, and by 1802, he was made first consul for life with the exclusive right to name his successor. Two years later, in an elaborate ceremony at Notre Dame Cathedral in Paris, Napoleon crowned himself Emperor of the French, restoring the hereditary monarchy. Shrewdly, Napoleon called for plebiscites (popular votes) to ratify his many changes, thus allowing him to claim that he ruled by popular will. Thanks to the opportunities presented by the Revolution, the obscure commoner had risen to the heights of political power in less than a decade.

Domestic Reform Napoleon recognized that his past military accomplishments would soon be forgotten if he failed to address pressing needs at home. He won the support of the conservative peasantry by his reconciliation with the Roman Catholic Church in 1801. By the terms of the Concordat, or agreement, concluded with the papacy, Napoleon recognized Catholicism as the faith of the majority of the French and allowed the pope to consecrate all new bishops. The Emperor was not a devout man, but he recognized the value of religion for its potential extrinsic function: It served to keep the people quiet and obedient. In return for official recognition, the French clergy were to be paid by the state, and land confiscated from the church during the 1790s would remain in the hands of its new owners. Napoleon also permitted freedom of worship for Protestants and Jews.

On the economic front, the Emperor supported businessmen with protective tariffs and government loans, while large public road, canal, and bridge-building projects enabled goods to move more freely around the country. The Bank of France was established to handle government funds and to regulate the currency. Hard-pressed peasants and workers were provided with subsidized bread, and the old feudal obligations were not restored. The principle of careers open to talent meant that enterprising common people could rise through the ranks in Napoleon's army, in the bureaucracy, or in private enterprise. These and other policies won Napolean wide support, even though political liberties and freedom of the press had been eliminated by a ruler whose power was now more absolute than that enjoyed by any Old Regime king of France.

Legal Reform The legal systems in prerevolutionary Europe were both many and arbitrary. In most countries, traditional practice and the preference of the ruling monarch normally set the parameters of civil and criminal law. In France what passed as law varied from province to province, with over 350 different codes in place when the Revolution began in 1789. In the north of the country customary Germanic law tended to dominate, while in the south Roman law was more widespread. Voltaire once quipped that in France travelers change legal codes as often as they changes horses. The early reforms of the French Revolutionaries added thousands of additional decrees to the existing laws, making some sort of overhaul necessary.

In an effort to streamline and rationalize French law, the National Convention attempted to frame a new system of law in 1793. It was rejected, however, and the governments of the 1790s never succeeded in revamping the existing patchwork. In 1800 Napoleon undertook to complete the project. He appointed a commission of influential jurors to examine all French civil (not criminal) laws and to synthesize these into one code that the average citizen could understand. Bonaparte presided at many of the meetings, and the Code received its legitimacy through his dictate. The final version of the Civil Code (popularly known as the Code Napoleon) consisted of over 2,000 articles with sections covering persons and property. It became the law of the land in 1804.

The Code recognized the inherent equality of males, freedom of religion and separation of church and state, the inviolability of property, and freedom for the individual to choose a career. It represented a great victory for the property-owning middle class, and it boosted Napoleon's popularity at home and abroad. The export of the Code's provisions throughout Napoleon's European empire effectively destroyed the feudal system of privilege and private jurisdictions that had dominated life for centuries. Napoleon later sponsored reform of the Code of Civil Procedure (1806), Commercial Code (1807), and the Penal Code (1808), bringing greater system and order to these three areas.

The Code also reflected Napoleon's deep distrust of women in public life. Not only were women denied the vote, but husbands enjoyed complete control over family property, and divorce, while allowed in limited cases, was difficult for women to secure. Napoleon believed that civil marriage "should contain a promise of obedience and fidelity by the wife. She must understand that in leaving the guardianship of her family, she is passing under that of her husband." Unmarried women had few rights, with the Code emphasizing the importance of the traditional male-dominated household. The children of divorced parents remained in the custody of the father, while illegitimate children were denied rights of inheritance.

Despite these weaknesses, the Code Napoleon emphasized the modern conception of a free and equal citizenry, sanctity of contract and property rights, the secularization of civil society, and unified standards of conduct irrespective of location or circumstances of birth. The Code also contributed to the enhancement of nationalism within each country where it was adopted. Its influence spread far beyond France, shaping the civil codes in the Low Countries, Northern Italy and Germany, parts of South America, the state of Louisiana in the United States, and Quebec Province, Canada. The Enlightenment ideal of a society guided by reasonable law and not by arbitrary individuals was first adopted, ironically, under a ruler who would tolerate no opposition to his vision of reform. Napoleon considered law reform to be his most important contribution to society; it was certainly his most lasting.

War and Expansion   As a political leader, Napoleon had taken important steps to restore public order, but the military side of his personality yearned for new challenges and triumphs. He had concluded hostilities with Russia in 1801 and with Britain with the Peace of Amiens in 1802, but Napoleon's ambitions inevitably clashed with Great Britain's desire to maintain the balance of power on the continent. War erupted again in 1803, and within two years Napoleon massed an enormous army for a planned invasion of Britain. He had a large, though poorly trained and commanded fleet at his disposal, but the logistics involved in an amphibious assault were too complicated. On October 21, 1805, British naval forces under the command of Admiral Nelson smashed the combined fleets of France and its Spanish ally, and Napoleon's dream of occupying Britain faded. Instead, Napolean turned to the east and won a string of remarkable victories over Austrian, Russian, and Prussian forces between 1805 and 1807. When the Austrians renewed the struggle in 1809, Napoleon's forces crushed them again.

By 1810, Napoleon and his disciplined, patriotic troops had upset the balance of power and redrawn the political map of Western Europe. The Holy Roman Empire was dismantled in 1806, while Holland and Italy came under French control. Spain was reduced to a client state, and Austria, Russia, and Prussia were forced into the status of French allies. Only Great Britain remained as a viable opponent. In the areas where French forces were triumphant, Napoleon appointed his brothers as monarchs; Joseph held the throne of Naples and then of Spain, Jerome became King of Westphalia in Western Germany, and Louis took the royal office in Holland (see Map 17–2). The reforms previously introduced in France were exported to all occupied lands. Serfdom was abolished, equality before the law and careers open to talents introduced, religious toleration observed, and the Code Napoleon adopted. European liberals and the long-suffering serfs welcomed the reforms, but the spirit of nationalism that French soldiers carried with them was contagious. Before long many Europeans, especially in Spain and parts of Germany, were calling for an end to French control.

Decline and Fall   In 1812 Tsar Alexander I of Russia (r. 1801–1825) broke with Napoleon and joined the British side. In Spain, native guerilla fighters assisted by a British expeditionary force proved to be a constant irritant to Napolean for six years

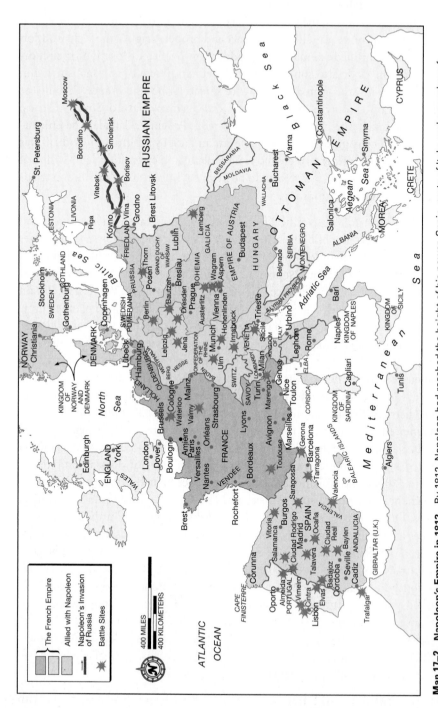

Map 17-2 Napoleon's Empire in 1812 By 1812, Napoleon had reached the height of his power. Spain, parts of Italy, and a number of German states had been incorporated into the French Grand Empire, while Austria and Prussia were forced into alliances with Napoleon. The invasion of Russia signaled the decline of the French Empire.

Question: How did Napoleon attempt to govern his far-flung European territories?

(1808–1814). Napoleon elected to focus his military might on Russia, and in June 1812 an army of half a million men invaded the Russian Empire. Russian imperial troops withdrew into the interior vastness. When Napoleon reached Moscow in September, he found a city set aflame by its residents to deny the French winter quarters. In the countryside the Russians destroyed grain and shelter, leaving the enormous French army without adequate clothing, food, or shelter for the harsh Russian winter. Forced to retreat, Napoleon's army numbered fewer than 100,000 when it finally returned to France. The defeat signaled the broad expansion of Britain's war effort. Prussia, Austria, and Sweden now joined the anti-French alliance. By April 1814, Napoleon's army had been defeated and France occupied. Napoleon abdicated and was exiled to the small Mediterranean island of Elba. He escaped confinement and returned briefly in March 1815 to lead French forces in one last campaign that ended with the famous Battle of Waterloo in Belgium in June. Surrendering again, he was sent to another island exile, but this time far away in the South Atlantic on St. Helena. Having dominated the continent for more than a decade, Napoleon's lasting achievements were only marginally related to his considerable military skills and battlefield victories. Rather, the influence of French—and Napoleonic—ideas, particularly legal, educational, and political ideas built on the twin principles of liberty and equality, would continue to inform the culture of Western Europe into the Industrial Age of the nineteenth century.

The French Revolution and the Americas

The success enjoyed by the independent United States inspired Spanish, French, and Portuguese colonials to seek greater political and economic freedoms for themselves. Many in the United States initially applauded the French Revolution; liberals were encouraged by what appeared to be another effort to implement the principles of the Enlightenment. Inspired by the rhetoric of human equality, a rebellion by black slaves in St. Dominique (Haiti), France's largest sugar-producing colony in the Caribbean, began in 1791. Led by Toussaint L'Ouverture (1743–1803), the rebels claimed equality with whites and independence from France. An independent state was established on the island in 1804, but not before Napoleon attempted (unsuccessfully)

Toussaint L'Ouverture   One of the leaders of the Haitian revolution, which freed the Caribbean island from French rule, abolished slavery, and established an independent repulic. Toussaint (right) became a hero to many blacks and slaves throughout the Americas.

to return the former colony to French control. Haiti quickly became a beacon to black slaves and poor people of color throughout Latin America because the independence struggle there represented a genuine social revolution.

In Spanish Latin America the independence movements were led by the property-owning Creole elite (American-born whites of Spanish descent) who deeply resented the monopoly over political power enjoyed by *peninsulares* (whites from Spain). Like their counterparts in the United States, these landowners, merchants, and traders also wished to put an end to the restrictive mercantilist controls placed on the colonies by Spain. When Napoleon deposed the Spanish Bourbons and placed his brother Joseph on the Spanish throne in 1807, the Spanish colonists in America refused to accept the new king and pledged their allegiance to their legitimate rulers.

The Bourbons were restored to power under Ferdinand VII (r. 1813–1833) after the defeat of Napoleon in 1814. The colonial rebellions ceased at this point, but the Spanish king's reactionary policies soon led to renewed calls for independence. By 1825, all of Spain's mainland colonies in South America had achieved their goals. Jose de San Martin (1778–1850) led armies of liberation from his base in the Rio de la Plata (modern Argentina) across the Andes Mountains into Chile (1817) and Peru (1820). In the north, armies under the direction of Simon Bolivar (1783–1830) defeated forces loyal to Spain in Columbia, Bolivia, Ecuador, and Venezuela. Due to the large sweeps of territory involved in the independence struggles, separate nations emerged across South America during the nineteenth century. Most of these states were led by Creoles who had little interest in popular democracy. In New Spain (modern Mexico, Texas, and California), what began in 1811 as a popular revolt led by Roman Catholic priests who stressed land reform and social equality ended in 1821 as an independence movement firmly under the control of conservative landowners. These men strongly opposed any alteration in economic or social life (see Map 17–3).

When Napoleon invaded Portugal in 1807, the royal family fled to Brazil. Their arrival transformed the city of Rio de Janeiro into a bustling commercial center and imperial capital. King John VI (r. 1816–1824) reluctantly returned to Portugal in 1820, and Brazil achieved formal independence in 1822 after the Portuguese parliament tried to reassert mercantilist controls. Unlike the former Spanish colonies, all of which initially adopted a republican form of government, Brazil remained a monarchy under John VI's son, Pedro I (r. 1822–1831), who had stayed in Brazil, and Pedro's son Pedro II (r. 1831–1888). For several decades Brazil remained the most prosperous and unified state in Latin America. In the United States, fear that other European powers might attempt to take advantage of the new countries, all of which maintained trade relations with Europe, led to the issuance of the Monroe Doctrine in 1823, a warning against the establishment of any new European colonies in the Americas. In practical terms the U.S. government was incapable of backing up its warning with significant military force. However, Britain's commercial interests coincided with the American position. The British wished to trade with each of the newly independent Latin American states, and the reestablishment of Spanish and Portuguese authority would have meant the return of mercantilist restrictions. During the nineteenth century, the British navy, not the Monroe Doctrine, served as the major deterrent to the return of European colonialism in the Americas.

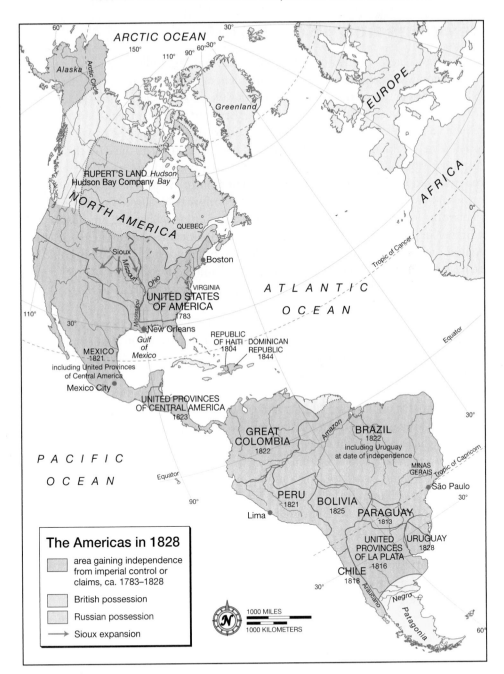

Map 17–3   The Americas in 1828   Between 1811 and 1830, most of South America won its independence from European rule. San Jose de la Martin and Simon Bolivar emerged as the two most powerful leaders of the independence movements.

KEY QUESTION | Revisited

The Estates General opened its first session (May 5, 1789) only five days after George Washington was inaugurated as the first president of the United States of America. The Estates General represented the great medieval divisions of society—nobles, clergy, and commoners—but soon after its convocation, the Third Estate claimed that it alone represented all Frenchmen. Washington had assumed the presidency of a nation that rejected legal distinctions based on status. Now the leaders of the French National Assembly would seek the same reforms in a country, and on a continent, with a centuries-old tradition of social hierarchy based on privilege. The American experiment forwarded political and constitutional patterns inherited from the colonial experience; the French, however, were involved in a revolution whose outcome would have a lasting imprint on modern European history. Political change occurred in North America without social and economic upheaval. In France political change could not be realized without dramatic change in the social and economic order.

Britain's American colonists did not face the combination of hardships that made the situation of Frenchmen so desperate in 1789. The British Empire was at its height after the defeat of the French in 1763, and as late as 1775, most Americans (with the obvious exception of black slaves) were proud to be members of this great empire. A tax system that exempted those most able to pay, widespread social injustices, legal privileges for the clergy and nobility, food shortages and high inflation, government fiscal crisis—Americans suffered under none of these conditions when they repudiated their allegiance to Britain. Instead, Thomas Jefferson claimed in the Declaration of Independence that King George III and Parliament were attempting to undermine traditional English rights with their unprecedented tax schemes. According to Jefferson, "the laws of nature and nature's God" legitimized the American call for independence. Informed by Enlightenment values, the dissolution of Britain's empire in America did not threaten the social or political status quo in the 13 states.

The same cannot be said for developments in France, where the upheaval that began in 1789 altered the basic fabric of political, social, and religious life. The French Revolution was important not only for one country, but for all of Europe. France was the greatest military power on the continent, and in many ways it was the cultural and intellectual leader as well. Fundamental change in Old Regime France was bound to influence conditions elsewhere in Europe. Over the space of two years, the great and lasting changes had been achieved. Between 1789 and 1792 the feudal order was dismantled, and upon its ruins the signposts of modernity were erected. Legal equality, freedom of expression, the sanctity of property, the abolition of serfdom and the right to choose one's career path, popular sovereignty and the separation of executive and legislative powers, a written constitution, religious toleration—these groundbreaking changes ushered in the modern age in Western politics.

Even the language of modern politics finds its roots in the Revolution: The terms *Left* and *Right* emerged from where delegates sat in the Convention. The terms *Conservative* and *Liberal* were not used until the early nineteenth century, but they served to identify where one stood politically on the changes instituted by the French

Revolution. Napoleon's megalomania guaranteed that many of the reforms would reach a Europe-wide audience. Between 1801 and 1814 the Old Regimes across Europe were introduced to French-style legal and administrative reform, to the principle of meritocracy, and, most importantly, to the power of nationalism. The nineteenth century would be a century of nation building and of liberal revolution across Europe. The American and French examples of popular self-government served as the beacon for all who would fight to translate revolutionary ideas into practice.

Review Questions

1. How was "representation" defined by members of Parliament in London and by colonial legislators in America?
2. What were the essential "rights of Englishmen" as understood by English colonists in America?
3. Why did the French monarchy support the American republic, and what problems did this support present for France?
4. What were the causes of France's fiscal difficulties in the 1780s, and what was the major impediment to reform?
5. How could Edmund Burke sympathize with the Americans in 1776 and condemn the French in 1789?
6. What were the permanent social and economic changes that took place in France in the midst of the French Revolution?
7. Was Napoleon a child of the Enlightenment and a champion of the French Revolution, or was he the restorer of absolutist monarchy in France?

Please consult the Suggested Readings at the back of the book to continue your study of the material covered in this chapter. For a list of documents on the Primary Source DVD-ROM that relate to topics in this chapter, please refer to the back of the book.

Part 6
Europe Triumphant, 1815–1914

Gustave Caillebotle, *Paris Street Scene: Rainy Weather,* 1877. *Gustave Caillebotte (French 1848–1894), "Paris Street: Rainy Day." 1877. Oil on Canvas. 83 1/2" × 108 3/4" (212.2 × 276.2 cm). Charles H. and Mary F. S. Worcester Collection, 1964. 336. Photograph © 2006, The Art Institute of Chicago. All Rights Reserved.*

The century between the final defeat and exile of Napoleon Bonaparte and the start of World War I (1815–1914) represented the apogee of European power in the world. After a series of failed revolutions in 1848, middle-class liberals embraced nationalism and began to win new political powers under the leadership of conservative leaders like Otto von Bismarck in Germany and Emperor Louis Napoleon in France. By the start of the twentieth century, universal manhood suffrage had been achieved across most of Western Europe, while women began to organize and press for their political rights.

The birth and rapid growth of industry transformed the material and intellectual landscape of Western Europe during the 1800s. Wherever the factory system emerged, a large migration from rural to urban settings followed. Problems associated with an urban lifestyle served to focus the attention of political leaders and to prompt new responses to pressing public needs. On the global stage, Europe's industrial might enabled a number of countries to extend their political, military, and economic influence. By the last third of the nineteenth century, rival states in Europe began to build extensive overseas empires, each one dedicated to the economic well-being of the imperial heartland.

	ENVIRONMENT AND TECHNOLOGY	SOCIETY AND CULTURE	POLITICS
1815	Manchester-Liverpool railway line (1830)	Romantic era (c.1815–1848)	Congress of Vienna (1814–1815)
1830	Cholera epidemic strikes Europe (1831) First trans-Atlantic steamship crossing (1833) Telegraph (1837) Cunard Lines begins regular trans-Atlantic service (1840) Famine in Ireland (1846–1848)	Death of Beethoven (1827) Majority of Britons live in cities and towns (1830) First factory acts passed in England to regulate labor (1830s) Neo-Gothic Houses of Parliament (1836)	Revolutions in France, Italy, Belgium, and Poland (1830) Reform Bill in England (1832) First Opium War (1839) Marx, *Communist Manifesto* (1848) Revolutions across Europe (1848)
1850	Suez canal opens (1869) Telephone (1876) Electric light (1879)	Crystal Palace exhibition (1851) U.S. forces opening of Japan (1853) Darwin, *Origin of Species* (1859)	Civil War in United States (1861–1865) Austro-Prussian War (1866) Franco-Prussian War (1870) Unification of Germany (1871)
1900	Theory of Relativity (1905) Ford's mass produced autos (1909)	Emancipation of Serfs in Russia (1861) Dreyfus Affair (1897–1899) European population reaches 285 million (1870) Radicalization of British suffragettes (1910)	France becomes a republic (1871) Triple Alliance (1882) Berlin Conference coordinates the carve-up of Africa (1884–1885) Russo-Japanese War (1904–1905) Norway becomes first nation to grant women the vote (1907)
1914			First Balkan War (1912) Start of World War I (1914)

From Rural to Urban Lifestyles in Europe • Agriculture, Demographics, and Labor
• Innovations in Production • The Social Consequences of Industrialization

18 Industry, Society, and Environment

It is not the consciousness of men that determines their being, but, on the contrary, their social being that determines their consciousness.

—Karl Marx (1818–1883)

KEY | Question

How do technology and urbanization influence the relationship between humans and nature?

Karl Marx's friend and collaborator, Friedrich Engels (1820–1895), lived and worked in Britain's first industrial city, Manchester, during the 1840s. Engels was the son of a German manufacturer who owned a textile factory in Manchester, and in 1844 Friedrich published a moving indictment of living conditions in that booming city. Along the Irk River in the heart of the mill district, Engels described how

> . . . the left bank grows more flat and the right bank steeper, but the condition of the dwellings on both banks grows worse rather than better. He who turns to the left here from the main street, Long Millgate, is lost; he wanders from one court to another, turns countless corners, passes nothing but narrow, filthy nooks and alleys, until after a few minutes he has lost all clue, and knows not whither to turn. Everywhere heaps of debris, refuse, and offal; standing pools for gutters, and a stench which alone would make it impossible for a human being in any degree civilized to live in such a district.

Yet thousands of people did live in these conditions, and the overcrowding and filth continued throughout the nineteenth century as masses of displaced rural workers moved to factory towns like Manchester, hoping that the fruits of industrial technology would improve their lives.

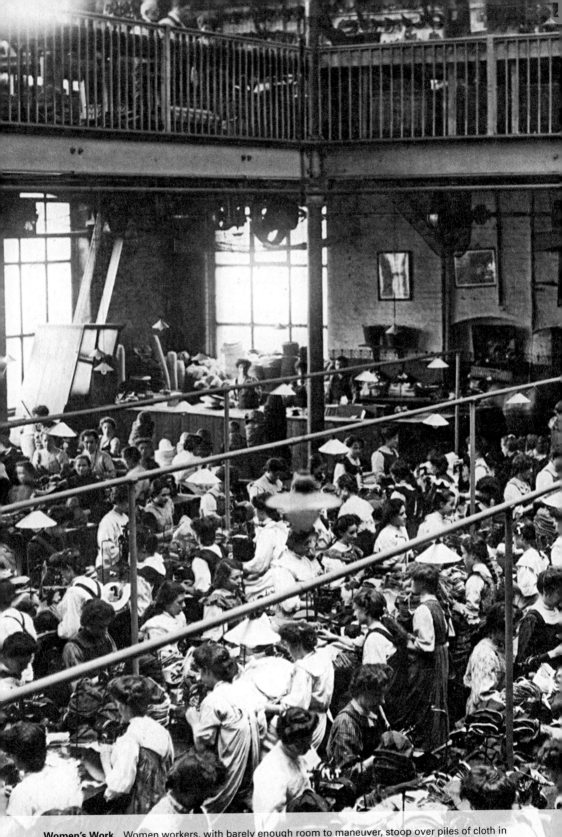

Women's Work   Women workers, with barely enough room to maneuver, stoop over piles of cloth in a vast hat factory in Manchester, England around 1900.

The description of working-class conditions in Manchester offered by Engels might be criticized on the basis of the author's radical political ideology. He did, after all, reject capitalism and, together with Karl Marx, forecast its ultimate destruction in 1848 in *The Communist Manifesto*. However, abundant and compelling evidence of the hardships working people suffered during the industrial era confirms his indictment. Like Manchester, the town of Little Bolton is located in Lancashire, and much of the coal that powered the mills in Manchester came from this nearby source. In 1842 Parliament established a committee of inquiry to investigate conditions of labor in the mines. Betty Harris, aged 37, testified that she first entered the mines at Little Bolton at age 23, having worked as a weaver since she was 12. "I am a drawer" (carrying coal to the surface), she reported. "I have two children, but they are too young to work. I worked at drawing when I was in the family way [pregnant]. I have drawn till I have the skin off me; the belt and chain is worse when we are in the family way."

This testimony, like the stories of many other workers in the mines and factories, suggests that just under two centuries ago a small fraction of the world's population entered into a new relationship with the natural environment. Separation from and dominion over nature became hallmarks of what we call industrial capitalism. At once enormously dynamic and cruelly debilitating, the combination of capitalist market forces and machine technology redefined life and culture in ways that have strained the planet's capacity to sustain life and our ability to solve acute environmental problems. Industrialization has also raised important questions about human nature—about how people ought to live and whether labor that is divorced from basic human needs and is carried out in a large impersonal setting undermines both the dignity of the individual and the integrity of culture and community.

From Rural to Urban Lifestyles in Europe

The widespread shift in labor patterns from farm and household to factory and mine, from human and animal power to machine power, is what French observers in the 1820s first termed the **Industrial Revolution**. Historians still use the term today, and for good reason. We tend to associate the term *revolution* with rapid and sometimes violent political change, but it can also describe a broad economic and social upheaval. Measured by its effect on human life over the past two centuries, this ongoing Industrial Revolution is far more significant than the American, French, or Russian revolutions. It began in Britain around the third quarter of the eighteenth century, spread to Belgium by the early nineteenth century, and gradually affected most of Western Europe and North America by 1900 (see Map 18–1). In a short span of time, the revolution led to the most fundamental alteration in European, and then global, society since early humans replaced their hunter-gather lifestyles with agriculture.

For countless generations, human life had been based on physical toil in nature. Abundant human capital, not precious metals or currency, was the crucial resource that successful landowners and employers coveted. Most people were peasant farmers who worked generation after generation in family and village units on lands owned by a local member of the gentry or aristocracy. The coming of industrial production shattered this age-old pattern. In 1900 relatively few persons in Western Europe were employed in settings that their grandparents would have found familiar, and many workers had no economic interests in common with their employers. Peasant farmers and skilled craftsmen who had worked in or adjacent to their homes had become machine opera-

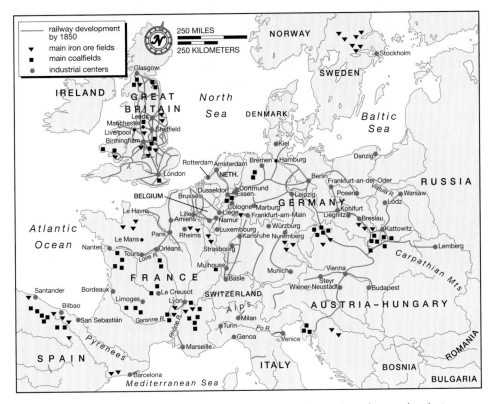

Map 18–1   The Industrial Revolution in Europe   Industrial growth was dependent on abundant supplies of coal and iron ore. Railroads facilitated the movement of raw materials, finished goods, and people. New manufacturing centers emerged across Western Europe during the nineteenth century.

Question: Was political stability essential to industrial growth in nineteenth-century Europe?

tors and clerks within the confines of impersonal factories and offices, and most Europeans had lost their close connection to the natural environment. They had become instead residents of large cities and grim factory towns where food was consumed far away from the farmer that produced it. In 1800 Europe had just 20 cities with populations over 100,000, but by 1900 almost 150 such cities existed in Europe. Industrialization transformed Western Europe economically, socially, and culturally. It altered the social structure and highlighted the importance of class. It fostered new political movements based on the interests of semiskilled and unskilled workers. It emphasized the distinctions between rural and urban lifestyles, between home and workplace, and even between the economic functions of individual family members.

Why the West?   Historians often debate why Europe enjoyed a head start in industry. After all, imperial China seemed poised to become the first great workshop of the world as early as the sixteenth century. European trade with China during this period was driven largely by the popularity of Chinese luxury products in the West. In fact, much of the silver that Europeans extracted from mines in Central and South America eventually found its way to Beijing as payment for Chinese porcelains, silks, and tea. However, China's Confucian culture had elevated the scholar and the rural gentry over the merchant and the artisan. Except for a brief period in the early fifteenth century, the Chinese imperial government did not support the development of manufacture for export or a large merchant fleet to carry products to distant markets. A similar situation existed in the expansive Muslim world, and especially in Mughal India, where trade links with the West beginning in the sixteenth century failed to lead to the development of a Mughal overseas commercial empire.

European heads of state, however, had ample reasons to support commerce, not the least of which involved intra-European political, religious, and military rivalries. War and the threat of war in Europe, and the absence of any Europe-wide centralized authority competent to dictate economic policy, meant that the innovative, entrepreneurial spirit was given free reign. The creation of private wealth enhanced national power, and many European monarchs encouraged and protected overseas trade in the interests of national defense. East India companies, Africa companies, Near East companies, and other "regional" companies were sanctioned by European heads of state and even given monopolies over trade with specific parts of the world.

Why Britain?   The Industrial Revolution began first in Britain thanks to the convergence of a number of key economic, political, and social factors. Abundant capital was available due to profits from two centuries of global trade, including the nefarious trade in slaves. Britain had the world's largest merchant fleet by the 1700s, and its military triumph over France in 1763 enabled it to dominate overseas commerce. Despite the loss of its American colonies in 1783, Britain's colonial empire remained enormous. British investors and traders eagerly brought their risk-taking mentality to the factory floor, while the government encouraged the formation of large investment partnerships. These partnerships were designed to generate profits from domestic production instead of overseas commerce.

Internally, Britain's stable political order, together with a comparatively fluid social structure, an abundant supply of coal and iron ore, a unified and tariff-free internal market, a broad network of navigable rivers and canals for the movement of bulky commodities like coal, a mature financial system, a small military establishment, and comparatively low taxes, all hastened the development of new methods of finance, manufacture, transportation, and distribution. Compared to other European nations, British merchants, manufacturers, bankers, and entrepreneurs were accorded great respect in society. Even the younger sons of the landed aristocracy could take up careers in the business world. Many inventors were religious dissenters, barred from careers in government because of their refusal to accept the official Church of England but allowed to pursue opportunities in business. In France, by contrast, nobles who invested in commercial pursuits normally did so with the short-term goal of purchasing offices, new titles, or land; the business activities themselves remained suspect. Those French entrepreneurs who did invest in manufacturing tended to focus on the luxury goods market, avoiding mass production of cheap goods for the majority of consumers. A tangle of internal tariffs also inhibited investment in industry in France and in most countries on the continent.

Developments in Germany illustrated the close connection between political stability and industrial expansion. Before 1870 Germany was divided into a number of small states, none of which was a major economic power. Only after political unification in 1871 did the German economy begin to compete with its British neighbor, and by 1900 German industrial output in iron, steel, and machinery had overtaken its rival. Similarly in the United States, the North's victory in the bloody and protracted Civil War in 1865 greatly strengthened the American economy. By 1900 it too had surpassed Britain. National unification during the 1860s enhanced opportunities for industrial growth even in Italy, which for centuries had been divided and under the political control of Spain, France, and Austria. In all these countries the creation of uniform laws, currency, tariff policy, and administration created conditions under which investors were more willing to accept long-term risk.

Agriculture, Demographics, and Labor

The domestication of plants and animals that had first taken place some 10,000 years before the Common Era ushered in a new and revolutionary phase in human existence. Nomadic hunter-gatherers became sedentary laborers; kinship social organization gave way to formal institutions of government; tribute was exacted and paid to military, religious, and political elites; and permanent villages, towns, and cities were built and defended against raiders. In the new environment survival increasingly depended upon the production of crops cultivated under labor-intensive conditions. For approximately the next 12,000 years, agricultural productivity set the limits to demographic growth, while attitudes toward land hampered agricultural output.

A Modern Revolution in Agriculture In the late 1700s most Europeans were still subsistence farmers. They cultivated the land in ways that had not changed much since the Middle Ages. Most farmers grew the same crops each year, left between one-third and one-half of their land fallow to avoid soil exhaustion, and kept only enough fodder to preserve a few draft and breeding animals over the long winter months. Large areas of forest and field were left uncultivated as common land where locals could cut wood for fuel and graze their animals. In close contact with the rhythm of nature, Europeans worked the land in a manner that was both physically demanding and technologically unsophisticated. Few peasants believed that they had a choice about how they would feed and shelter themselves and their families. A dramatic enhancement in the soil's ability to produce was neither expected nor encouraged.

A modest but sustained increase in population during the eighteenth century obliged farmers to intensify traditional methods. Marginal land was cleared and put under the plow, swamps were drained, and the owners of large estates in Holland and Britain began to experiment with new crops. The biggest breakthrough came when "improving" landowners began to alternate grain crops like wheat and barley, both of which consumed the soil's nitrogen, with crops like turnips, clover, and alfalfa. These latter crops restored nitrogen to the soil and could be used as fodder. This system basically doubled the amount of land that could be cultivated in a given year and enabled farmers to feed more livestock during the lean winter months. Increased numbers of

Lincolnshire Ox England's "agricultural revolution" of the 1700s enabled it to take the lead in the Industrial Revolution later in the century. The "Lincolnshire Ox" was an enormous, 3,000-pound animal that represented British advances in breeding and other agricultural techniques.

cattle and swine meant more protein-rich foods for humans, while additional horses and oxen meant more productive capacity to work the land and more manure to enrich the soil. The potato, first introduced from America as fodder for animals in the early sixteenth century, began to appear more frequently in the peasant diet during the eighteenth century. Since this highly nutritious root vegetable produced a high yield per acre, it appealed to families with additional mouths to feed.

Technology and science also contributed to agricultural output. Better iron plows and harrows (used for breaking up clods of earth) enabled farmers to dig deeper into richer soils. During the second half of the eighteenth century, inexpensive artificial fertilizers made their appearance thanks to the application of chemistry to agriculture. Surpluses were sold in urban markets at handsome profits, while fewer hands were needed to work the land. The prospect of famine, a constant since the dawn of agriculture, began to fade in lands west of Russia after 1850. Small, independent farmers who did not or would not adopt these new approaches to working the land were unable to compete. Many of them left for the cities, where they became part of a growing pool of urban labor.

Finally, the practice of enclosing common land with fences and hedges to create larger farms dedicated to a single crop accelerated after 1750. Some innovative landowners practiced convertible husbandry. This involved plowing the soil and growing crops when grain prices were high and shifting to pasture, sheep, or cattle when the market price of wool or meat increased. Under this pattern of land use, workers could be hired and dismissed as needed. Enclosure and specialization obviously meant hardship or unemployment for the small landholder, as wage labor in the agricultural sector replaced the more familiar pattern of traditional family links to the manor and village. Land was increasingly treated as a commodity to be exploited for profit in a wider market. Supporters of the changes, mostly wealthy landowners, argued that improved management helped to end the age-old cycle of sufficiency and dearth, which had previously acted as a brake on the rapid and sustained expansion of population. More mouths were fed at lower cost, and increased population created added demand for basic consumer goods. Displaced farmers obviously disagreed with this analysis, but one fact is indisputable: The Industrial Revolution would not have been possible without the efficiencies introduced by new practices in agriculture.

Food and Population   The nineteenth century ushered in the modern age of statistical data. For the first time, governments across Western Europe collected reliable numbers on population trends and other vital information. The collection of birth and death records by civil authorities began in France in 1792, while Britain compiled its first census in 1801. The advent of this age of demographic measurement, so familiar to us today, meant that governments could better assess potential fiscal and human resources when formulating domestic policies. Accurate information about population was key to political decision making. In 1800 approximately 190 million persons lived west of the Ural Mountains in Russia. This figure was up from roughly 100 million a century earlier. By 1914, at the start of World War I, Europe's population had expanded to an amazing 463 million persons.

This extraordinary increase occurred despite massive overseas migration to the Americas, Australasia, and parts of Africa. During the eighteenth century, for example, approximately 2 million Europeans had settled in the Americas. Over the next century, however, the number escalated in dramatic fashion. By 1914, close to 60 million Europeans had departed for opportunities on other continents. Britain alone sent 17 million emigrants to points around the globe. Looking at this demographic data in a global context is helpful. In 1800 roughly one-quarter of all humans lived in Europe; by 1920 the percentage had increased to one-third. Population growth and overseas migration greatly facilitated the emergence of industry in Europe. Europeans abroad often built their regional economies to supply raw materials and foodstuffs to Europe and to import manufactured goods from it.

Increased agricultural output was essential to population growth, but Europe was well positioned for rapid demographic expansion after 1815 for other reasons as well. The general peace that prevailed from 1815 (the defeat of Napoleon) until 1914 meant that most of Europe avoided the civilian hardships associated with military occupation and conflict. The destruction of crops and the breakdown of supply networks were the greatest hardships. Improved transportation systems, beginning with sophisticated canal networks, helped to mitigate food shortages. Beginning in the 1860s, steam-propelled railroads and ships brought down long-distance transport costs. By the end of the century, the United States, Canada, Argentina, Uruguay, Australia, and New Zealand provided grain and livestock to European consumers at competitive rates. Similarly, after 1870 the

Chicago Packinghouse at the Turn of the Century   The meatpacking industry epitomized some of the social ills that accompanied the Industrial Revolution. Social reformers like the American socialist Upton Sinclair brought attention to the dangerous and squalid working conditions in packinghouses.

railroad and steamships on the Black Sea allowed Russian growers to sell their products in Eastern and Western Europe, linking the Russian economy to the wider European market. As food supplies became more secure and predictable, the cost of feeding one's family declined and discretionary spending increased.

In addition to improved nutrition and sanitation, important contributions in medicine led to higher birth rates and lower death rates. Before mid-century, relatively few people survived into their forties. The employment of antiseptics beginning in the 1860s made childbirth safer, while real progress against two fearful killers—tuberculosis and cholera—was made in the 1880s. Other epidemic diseases, such as typhus, typhoid, smallpox, and diphtheria, were effectively treated by medical professionals by the start of the twentieth century. Vaccination and the isolation of infected persons became standard approaches to combating the spread of illnesses. For the first time, hospitalization became an accepted method of addressing serious medical problems. The development of anesthetics, especially ether and chloroform during the 1840s, made surgical procedures less painful. Once viewed as places where poor persons went to die, urban hospitals now became centers of effective treatment and rehabilitation.

Better personal hygiene, cleaner water, and improved nutrition were especially important in reducing child mortality. Before the mid-nineteenth century, one out of every five children died before reaching his or her first birthday. This was true even in advanced countries like Britain and France. In Germany the figure was one in four, while in Eastern Europe one in three perished. This began to change after 1850, as more vegetables, dairy products, and meat became a part of the common person's diet. A rapidly growing population meant that abundant and youthful human resources were available for prospective employers. Increased population also meant new demand for basic infrastructure projects—more housing stock, better transport systems, ready-made clothing, provision for primary education. Each variable—more people, calls for infrastructure, overseas migration, demands for new sources of productive power, capital available from global trade—converged to inspire inventors and entrepreneurs to look for ways to increase productive capacity.

Innovations in Production

Many rural families in early modern Western Europe supplemented their income from the land by taking in wool or linen for spinning and weaving. However, with the enclosure of common lands reducing many farmers to the status of poorly paid wage laborers, the supply of potential workers for basic manufacturing tasks grew rapidly. Responding to greater demand for clothing by a growing population, merchants turned to the countryside to increase textile production. They stimulated "cottage industries," or what was also called the "putting out" system of commercial manufacture. Previously, urban clothing guilds had regulated most textile production. Rural laborers now offered merchants a low-cost alternative. In addition to the raw materials, urban entrepreneurs would often supply rural workers with a spinning wheel and a simple handloom. Because spinning and weaving were relatively unskilled jobs, women and children did much of it, anticipating their crucial role in later factory labor. In the cottage system, merchants paid their employees on the basis of how much finished cloth they produced during a set interval. The work was not dangerous, but it was monotonous and poorly paid. Together with commercial farming, the cottage industries introduced a money economy to the rural sector and integrated the peasant into a broader national and international economy.

Early Advances in Technology   The period and place that historians traditionally identify with the origins of the Industrial Revolution, between 1760 and 1820 in Britain, hardly struck most contemporaries as a significant social or economic age. Their attention was occupied by the conflict with the American colonies and the wars of the French Revolution, not by the emergence of machine-driven manufacture in cities like Glasgow, Manchester, and Leeds. Still, the breakthroughs in machine building that took place during this period had a broad and lasting impact on society. Some of the breakthroughs did not involve a change in power source, but rather tinkering with and constant improvement upon existing technology. During the early stages of the Industrial Revolution, mechanics and solitary inventors who often lacked formal education were the key figures. Cotton production serves as a good illustration. Britain's American colonies provided an abundant source of raw cotton throughout the first three-quarters of the eighteenth century. Female spinners operated wooden wheels to spin the thread, while male weavers ran simple handlooms. The demand for cotton cloth was rising, but output remained flat.

The invention of John Kay's (1704–1764) flying shuttle in 1733 assisted weavers, but the paucity of spun thread created a serious production bottleneck. James Hargreaves (1720–1778) introduced the spinning jenny in 1768, which solved the problem. The jenny consisted of a wooden frame that contained a number of spindles around which the thread was drawn by a hand-operated wheel. Richard Arkwright's (1732–1792) water-powered spinning machine debuted in 1769, and its stronger rollers produced more durable threads for cotton cloth. All of these machines required space, and it was judged more economical to centralize the production in one place rather than divide it among hundreds of separate cottages. The problem was that water provided the main source of power, and useful rivers and hillside streams were often far away from where most people lived. It was also expensive to move goods overland from these water-powered mills.

Steam Technology   The answer to the location and transportation problems was found by applying steam power to the process of spinning and weaving. Thomas Newcomen (1663–1729) had built a primitive machine in 1705, but the first efficient steam engine was pioneered by James Watt (1736–1819) in the 1760s. The earliest "Watt" machines were used to help pump water out of coal mines. Coal had become an important fuel during the eighteenth century, since the traditional practice of burning charcoal to smelt iron ore (a process designed to remove other compounds from iron) had deforested much of Britain. Smelting with coal led to improvements in basic metallurgy, which in turn led to the construction of better steam engines.

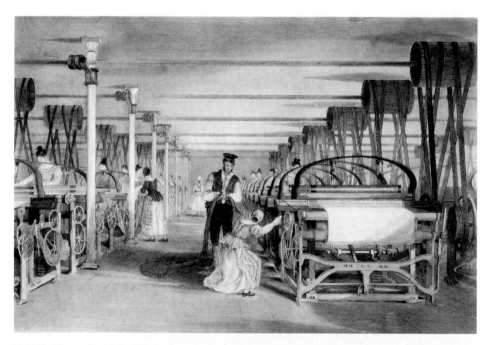

Unskilled Labor Operating Power Looms   By 1830, the cotton industry had become completely mechanized. Women and children were employed at low wages, and hand weavers were supplanted by unskilled workers.

The success of steam engines in draining water from mines led to a number of creative adaptations to power heavier machinery. In particular, the effective employment of coal and steam in place of water power to drive textile machines or operate iron-smelting furnaces meant that centers of production no longer needed to be situated near running water on rural hillsides. Factories were now portable and could be constructed near or within population centers. Overall, the substitution of inanimate fossil fuels (coal and subsequently petroleum products) for water power and human forms of energy greatly increased the ability of Europeans to manipulate and transform their natural environment.

By 1820 the steam-driven power loom had largely overtaken hand weavers in the British cotton industry. Power machinery made spinning jennies that wound fiber into thread and the flying shuttle for weaving enormously efficient. A handful of factory workers could operate many power looms simultaneously, increasing production while simultaneously reducing labor costs and the price of consumer goods. Production of cheap cotton cloth soared during the first half of the nineteenth century. Thanks to the growth of its colonial empire, Britain sold these goods across the globe. By 1850, almost 40% of all British exports consisted of finished cotton products. To keep pace with the insatiable demands of machines that never rested, raw cotton for British factories was imported from India, Egypt, Brazil, and the United States. New industrial cities emerged near abundant sources of coal, dictating new lifestyles and working conditions for thousands of domestic migrants.

The Railway and Steamship Age
Steam power lifted the limits that human, animal, and water power had imposed on productive capacity. While the technology was adapted to different forms of rotary power, none was more ingenious than steam locomotion. Moving bulky coal to factories and moving finished industrial products to markets near and far presented a logistical challenge to ambitious industrialists. All of these manufacturers struggled to satisfy an almost insatiable demand for the products of industry. A canal-building frenzy during the late eighteenth century alleviated some of the difficulties. In England over 2,500 miles of canals were in operation by 1830, and private companies built dozens of hard-surfaced roads.

However, the real breakthrough came in 1830, when a mining engineer named George Stephenson (1781–1848) developed a locomotive, called "the Rocket," that could haul a load three times its own weight on iron rails at the extraordinary speed of almost 30 miles per hour! That same year the industrial city of Manchester was linked to the port city of Liverpool by iron rail. Originally designed to move coal and other heavy goods, the Manchester-Liverpool line became an instant hit with passengers, thousands of whom took passage on the "iron horse" during its first years of operation. One early passenger marveled at "how strange it seemed to be journeying on thus, without any visible cause of progress other than the magical machine, with its flying white breath and rhythmical, unvarying pace. . . ." Subsequent railroad lines were built with both freight and passenger service in mind.

By mid-century, Britain, France, Belgium, and the German states all had extensive rail networks. Speculators eagerly bought shares in railway stocks. The British Parliament authorized thousands of miles of rail construction, while the governments of Germany and

France built rail systems as a part of national economic development policy. In the United States the national government offered free right of way to railroad developers. The train quickly became essential to the movement of coal from its point of extraction to the factory furnace, while rail lines boosted demand for iron and steel, created new employment opportunities for skilled civil and mechanical engineers, and helped to solidify the interdependence of each nation's regional economy. More than any other aspect of industrial technology, the railway linked the rural countryside with the expanding urban centers and port cities. Migrants to the cities and people seeking to emigrate abroad increasingly began their journeys by rail. Rail companies even offered day excursions and short holiday packages to maximize revenues. Travelers could select various levels of service, but as costs declined, even the working-class family could enjoy this revolutionary high-speed transport.

Steam was also applied to water transportation. Here the Americans took the early lead in 1807 when Robert Fulton (1765–1815) experimented with a steamboat on the Hudson River in New York state. The first trans-Atlantic steamship crossing took place in 1833 when the *Royal William* traveled from Nova Scotia to England. By 1840, steam-propelled ships had reduced the time of an Atlantic crossing by half, to an average of two weeks. In 1840 Samuel Cunard's (1787–1865) steamship line announced the beginning of regular trans-Atlantic steamship service and even published dates of departure

The Third Class Carriage   By the mid-nineteenth century, railway travel featured a variety of accommodations. In this 1862 painting, the artist foregrounds the simple dignity of working-class people crowded into cars equipped with hard, wooden benches. *Honore Daumier, French, (1808–79). The Third Class Carriage, Oil on Canvas, H 25.75 × 35.5" (65.4 × 90.2 cm). The Metropolitan Museum of Art, Bequest of Mrs. H. O. Havemeyer Collection 1929, (29.100.129). Photograph © 1992 The Metropolitan Museum of Art, Art Resource, NY*

and arrival beforehand. This information could be communicated across the Atlantic instantly after 1866 thanks to the installation of the first trans-Atlantic electric telegraph cable. By the close of the century, steamships were carrying thousands of migrants at low cost to new homes in the Americas. The same ships that moved people also featured refrigeration compartments that enabled producers to move perishable goods across the oceans for surprisingly low costs.

Second-Generation Power and Industry   The first phase of the Industrial Revolution was based on coal and steam. During the final three decades of the nineteenth century, a second phase, anchored in the chemical, electrical, and petroleum industries, accelerated the process. Instead of solitary inventors, new discoveries and advances tended to emerge from universities, where teams of highly trained specialists worked in formal laboratory settings. The results have become familiar "requirements" of the modern Western lifestyle. During the 1860s, for example, natural gas was used to power an internal combustion engine. These engines were lighter and more portable than the earlier generation steam engines, but since natural gas was difficult to store and transport, the new power plant had to wait until the 1880s, when liquid petroleum was substituted for natural gas as a fuel. After this date the popularity of the portable internal combustion engine in Europe increased demand for oil. Sources as far away as Pennsylvania in the United States and southern Russia met the initial demand for petroleum products. In 1877 the first European pipeline to transport oil was built in Russia; two years later the first oil tanker was put into service.

Another second-generation power source was electricity, with the first electric generator developed in 1870. Countries such as Italy and Switzerland, which lacked large coal reserves, especially favored electric power, since electric current could be produced with the aid of water or wind power. Improved turbines in the 1880s made hydroelectric power production feasible. In America, Thomas Edison's (1847–1931) invention of the incandescent electric light marked the start of a new age of artificial light. Among other uses, the incandescent light helped to inaugurate the round-the-clock shift work in some factories, again reshaping the lives of the **working class**. German scientists took the lead in the electrical and chemical industries, and worldwide sales helped to fund further research into "cutting edge" technologies. The first public electric power station was built in England in 1881, but it was constructed by a German firm, Siemens Brothers.

Key Inventions of the Industrial Revolution	
1733	John Kay's "flying shuttle"
1760s	James Watt modernizes the steam engine
1764	James Hargreaves's "spinning jenny"
1769	Richard Arkwright's "spinning frame"
1807	Robert Fulton's steamboat
1830	George Stephenson's "The Rocket" locomotive

The Social Consequences of Industrialization

Before the Industrial Revolution, most urban centers were located in fertile valleys and flood plains or near rivers and natural ports. The size of cities depended on the ability of the adjacent countryside to provide surplus foodstuffs and on the incidence of disease in crowded, unsanitary surroundings. In general, high mortality rates meant that cities needed a constant influx of migrants from the countryside to maintain their population levels. When plague struck—as it often did in the early 1700s—the well-to-do fled the cities for country retreats, leaving the poor to suffer alone. This pattern changed dramatically during the nineteenth century thanks to advances in agriculture, transportation, medicine, and public health. Clean water supplies, centralized and efficient sewage systems, and improved food preservation techniques, such as canning and refrigeration, were crucial to the demographic shift from countryside to city. After World War I, most Germans, Britons, Belgians, Dutch, and Americans lived in towns and cities; worldwide almost one-fifth of humanity lived in urban settings, a social transformation that was unparalleled in human experience (see Map 18–2).

From Workers to Proletariat   In 1800 the wealthiest members of the middle class were merchants and traders. One century later the middle class was led by captains of industry, the owners of machines and factories, and the employers of propertyless wage workers. Bankers and businessmen involved in commerce continued to make modest gains, but in comparison to the industrialist, the old middle class was under assault. The same relative disadvantage faced the working class. The word *proletariat* refers to a new

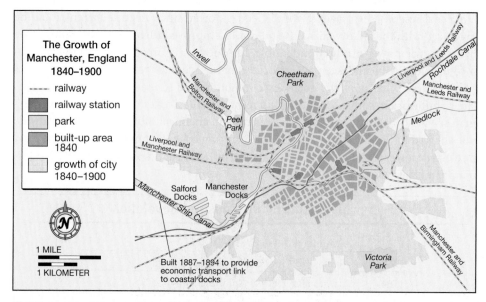

Map 18–2   Manchester, England   A major textile-producing city, Manchester was at the forefront of the Industrial Revolution. In 1800, 75,000 people lived in the city. Fifty years later the population had increased to over 300,000.

Question: Why did Manchester require so many rail lines going in and out of the city?

type of worker who was entirely dependent upon wage labor for his or her survival. In general, the urban proletariat could not afford private homes, did not own land or small businesses, and had nothing to offer for compensation but physical labor. The raw materials that the laborers extracted, the tools that they used, and the power equipment that they operated were owned by the person or persons who had provided the capital to build the factory and purchase the machinery. Skilled and semiskilled artisans, such as weavers, blacksmiths, and glass blowers, found themselves reduced to operatives in huge factories that did not require specialized abilities.

The relationship between the owner of the means of production and the employees became both impersonal and limited to the workplace. In these factories hundreds of workers tended machines that never got tired. Factory owners were well aware that business failures and bankruptcies were widespread and that constant competition threatened their substantial investments. Advanced technology and machinery involved considerable capital investment, and as industry grew, the role of banks and corporations expanded, with shareholders demanding even greater efficiencies in the workplace. Managing the workplace became a high priority. Harsh rules regarding tardiness, drunkenness, theft, and failure to keep pace with the machinery placed the employee—often a recent arrival from the countryside, where the seasons and the weather had regulated the workday—in an unfamiliar and demoralizing situation. This harsh physical environment was what Karl Marx had in mind in the opening quote to this chapter when he stated that mens' social being determined their consciousness.

In the factory, the whistle, the time clock, and the automated machine imposed a new discipline that was oppressive and monotonous. Large work crews in factories were subject to regimentation and to limited, repetitive tasks. Overpopulated cities meant that employers could recruit unskilled machine operatives, even children, from a large pool of potential laborers. Hired to work long (sometimes 16-hour) shifts when demand was high and as easily dismissed when the economy faltered, workers were unlikely to receive a sympathetic hearing from government officials before mid-century, since they did not enjoy the right to vote. Industrialization therefore tended to accentuate economic or class differences in nations where machine production involved a significant percentage of the overall population. In the early nineteenth century skilled English handloom weavers attempted to smash power machinery in a desperate effort to save their traditional form of employment. It was a futile protest. The British Parliament quickly made industrial sabotage a capital offense. Neither Europe's traditional political leaders nor the industrial bourgeoisie were particularly sensitive to the needs of the emerging working class or to those skilled artisans whose livelihoods were destroyed by the coming of the factory. This is not to say that agricultural laborers lived under more gentle superiors in the form of landowners; working conditions in the commercial agricultural sector were also driven by the demands of the market, and rural poverty and child labor remained endemic problems. However, the novel setting for industrial labor, the city environment, and the rules, fines, and lockouts associated with the factory created a special set of challenges for workers.

Consumer Culture   Despite the many hardships associated with industrialization, during the 1800s Europeans and North Americans became wealthier and more comfortable than their counterparts in other societies. Not only more wealth but a greater concentration of the world's wealth in the West marked the age of the machine. Thanks to industry and science broadly defined, Europe was able to feed and employ—or transport overseas—its expanding population. Office employment increased as industries and corporations hired clerks, accountants, and sales and secretarial staff. Highly specialized tasks became the rule in this "white collar" employment sector just as they had on the factory floor, and close supervision of staff by managers ensured maximum productivity. A strong and ever-expanding consumer sector developed, especially within the ranks of the middle class, and advertising in mass circulation newspapers and magazines became an important part of the sales strategy. Buying on credit, market research, enticing window displays, money-back guarantees, and many other modern sales techniques originated in the mid-nineteenth century.

While still largely beyond the reach of the working class, whose disposable income was limited by the high cost of housing, the culture of consumption gained increasing support across Europe and in North America. Large department stores began to encroach on the small specialty shop. In Paris the innovative *Bon Marché* department store opened its doors in 1852 (and is still in business). By the 1890s, the store had over 40 different departments plus a mail-order division. The ideal life was defined in terms of the constant acquisition of material goods and services. Personal identity was increasingly linked to personal possession, the ability to purchase the many fashionable products now available in shops and stores. The English potter Josiah Wedgwood (1730–1795) earned a fortune selling "Queen's ware" table settings to middle-class consumers who wished to associate themselves with the trappings (albeit invented) of royalty. According to Wedgwood, "fashion is superior to merit," and his fabulous commercial success appeared to confirm the maxim.

In the United States pioneering efforts in manufacturing led to the development of interchangeable parts, allowing the production process to become ever more efficient. By the early twentieth century, for example, the automobile manufacturer Henry Ford (1863–1947) instituted the assembly-line technique and the use of interchangeable parts. Ford's factories produced vehicles that were within the financial reach of the workers who built them. Producers like Ford made enormous profits by extending the products of consumer culture to average working families.

Dominion over Nature   Factory life and the use of tireless machines to produce goods changed the relationship between individuals and the natural world. In Britain, 1850 was a watershed year: For the first time in history, more than one-half of a nation's population did not work in agriculture or live in the countryside. As more workers ceased to depend upon the soil for their livelihood, and as technology replaced human power, a sense of human superiority over nature displaced the traditional understanding of the role of humans as dependent on nature. Science and technology offered multiple examples of how nature might be controlled and dominated in the interests of material advancement. Economic "progress" became a principal responsibility of governments during the nineteenth century. Official circles downplayed the potential negative consequences of unimpeded development and industrial expansion. Preservation of the natural environment was not a public priority, and few inventors or entrepreneurs considered the harmful side effects of industry. Cities might be unpleasant, dirty, and dangerous, but in comparison to a life without ready-made clothing, electric lights, and rapid steam transport, the environmental costs seemed relatively minor.

Voices of Dissent   Despite official lack of interest, however, influential writers and poets of the mid-nineteenth century did discuss many of the social and environmental problems associated with rapid industrialization and consumerism. In Britain Charles Dickens (1812–1870) often focused on the shattered lives of industrial workers as they sought to find meaningful work in ugly and unhealthy cities. The fictional "Coketown" of Dickens's *Hard Times* (1854) is inhabited by unscrupulous and callous capitalists and educators who have reduced beauty to production quotas and efficiency goals. In the novel even union leaders fall into the trap of equating wage levels with human happiness. Dickens was writing only three years after Britain hosted a large-scale international celebration of technology—the Crystal Palace exhibition—in London. The spectacular glass and iron exhibit hall attracted millions of visitors from across Europe and America, who were invited to marvel at the latest labor-saving machinery.

Women, Children, and Immigrants   The Industrial Revolution had a profound impact on the role that women played in the larger economy. In the family economy of rural Europe, women worked in and near the home, often alongside their husband and

Interior of Crystal Palace   The exhibit hall of the Crystal Palace (1851) showcased the latest technology and labor-saving devices of the industrial era.

PEOPLE IN CONTEXT *Alfred Krupp*

Alfred Krupp (1812–1887) was a pioneer metallurgist and industrialist who transformed a small steel firm established by his father, Friedrich (1787–1826), into a major producer of sophisticated military hardware. Krupp was born and raised in the city of Essen in the German Rhineland. He assumed control of his father's firm at the age of 14, at a time when sales of steel were modest and when there were only five company employees. By the time of his death in 1887, Alfred Krupp had expanded his labor force to over 20,000, and his firm was a key supplier of military hardware to over 40 nations. Until World War II, the Krupp family company was one of the world's largest steel and weapons manufacturers.

Krupp's early efforts in steel production focused on small domestic products. He manufactured and sold scissors, dies, machine tools, and rolling mills for use in minting coins. In the late 1840s he developed a popular muzzle-loading gun of cast steel for the military while simultaneously working on improved railway components. The firm acquired Europe-wide recognition in 1851 when Krupp displayed heavy cannons and a two-ton steel ingot (mold) at the Crystal Palace exhibition in London. The ingot was nearly twice as heavy as the one produced by its nearest competitor. New orders began to flow to the Essen plant, and in 1852 Krupp designed a seamless steel railway wheel which became an instant commercial success. Profits from these early enterprises enabled Krupp, who was a consummate salesman, to concentrate on securing large mili-

Industrial Empire.   Aerial view of the Krupp armaments factories in Essen, Germany. *Marc Charmet/Picture Desk, Inc./Kobal Collection*

tary contracts from European governments. He sold guns and cannons to Egypt, Belgium, Russia, and Prussia. Once the German states achieved political union in 1871, sales of Krupp ordnance to the new German Empire began to soar. The "cannon king," as he was called, even purchased iron and coalmines across Germany to control the extraction and transport of these essential raw materials.

Some historians have cast an unfavorable light on the Krupp family, seeing them as merchants of death who had no higher interest beyond their firm's profit margin. Krupp armaments were used in many conflicts. Another, more charitable perspective focuses on the firm's special relationship with its workforce. As one of Europe's first self-made industrialists, Alfred Krupp was one of only a handful of large employers to offer his workers a package of comprehensive welfare benefits. In 1836 he started a sickness and burial fund, and in 1855 introduced a pension plan for workers who had become disabled on the job. Krupp then began to construct company houses, and as neighborhoods developed adjacent to the sprawling factory complex, schools, parks, libraries, and churches emerged—all with financial support from the Krupp family. He resisted the "hire and fire" mentality based on swings in the business cycle, working to maintain jobs even during periodic downturns in business. While these innovations were obviously paternalistic and designed to avoid labor disputes that might interrupt production, Krupp did create a dedicated and fiercely loyal workforce.

Question: In light of his success, how did Krupp and men like him contribute to the process of redefining the relationship between humans and their natural environment?

children. In addition to long hours working the land, women were also responsible for housekeeping duties and child care. They might also do piecework, spinning fibers into thread for male handloom weavers under the cottage industry system. The labor was hard and often repetitious, but it allowed family and neighbors to work together. In the industrial city many working-class women became wage laborers in mills and factories separate from the rest of their household. The work discipline of the factory severely limited their ability to care for family members, particularly children. Single women often toiled as domestics in the homes of the middle class. Neither work environment offered much prospect of advancement or of earning a living wage. Income differences between the sexes were significant. In 1900, for example, women in industry earned on average less than half of what their male counterparts earned. As the population of urban centers grew, the cost of housing mounted, making the income secured by women essential to a family's survival. Children and recent U.S. immigrants also played significant roles in the urban workforce. Like women, these two groups were thought to be more compliant than native-born adult males. All could be paid significantly less, and, it was argued, they would also be less likely to unionize.

Middle-class women also experienced the separation of the workplace from the home, but in an entirely different manner. The wives of the bourgeoisie were expected to stay at home, raise the children, and supervise the servants. In the home they would provide hospitality and refuge from the stresses of the new economy in a manner befitting

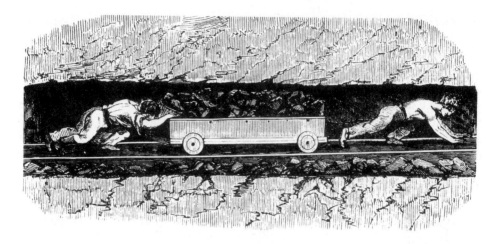

Trolley Boys   Until child labor laws were enacted and enforced, youngsters were employed in factories and mines. Orphans and pauper children were especially vulnerable to this type of exploitation. In this illustration, young children remove coal from a mine shaft on a trolley. The mine shaft is illuminated by candlelight.

their husbands' professional status. These women lived in homes that no longer contributed to the traditional family economy, but were centers of the moral economy, promoting values that were at odds with the competitive spirit of the business world. A unique "domestic sphere" was constructed in which the middle-class home became the focus of the emerging consumer economy. There was no expectation that middle-class women might enter institutions of higher education or train for the professions.

Working-Class Organizations   The factory system destroyed the medieval guild practice of protecting skilled labor while ensuring product quality. A few employers adopted a paternalistic model of management, constructing worker housing and company stores, providing minimal medical care, and occasionally offering basic educational training. In Lowell, Massachusetts, for example, mill owners provided their mostly female (and single) workers with room and board. However, paternalism could quickly deteriorate into coercion, with threats of eviction used against workers who sought to organize for better wages. Even after the advent of factory production, traditional labor organizations, such as mutual aid societies and fraternal organizations, continued to assist workers in their transition to the unfamiliar industrial setting. Formal labor unions were illegal in Britain between 1799 and 1824, when the government finally allowed workers to organize but denied them the right to strike. Normally limited to skilled labor, the first industrial unions focused their attention on incremental change within the framework of the capitalist system.

Early unions for skilled workers offered their members accident insurance, modest retirement benefits, and accidental death and burial payments. After mid-century, however, union organizers shifted their attention to the growing ranks of unskilled workers. In most industrialized countries, wages were creeping up for the average laborer, but working conditions remained poor. The right to strike was finally recognized in Britain in 1875, an important milestone in a nation where factory workers made up more than one-half of the total workforce. Nine years later the French government sanctioned union activity, and by 1900, the French syndicates or labor unions included half a million members. Industrial unions for unskilled workers began to clash openly with employers in the final decades of the century, using strikes as their major weapon. In 1889 a strike at the London docks briefly crippled the movement of goods destined for overseas ports. Despite the sporadic victories of organized workers, however, most of Europe's labor force remained outside of unions at the start of World War I.

Education in the Industrial Age   During the early stages of industrialization, factories did not require educated workers. As late as 1860 most Europeans remained illiterate. The wealthy had always secured their education through tutors or in expensive private institutions. The few primary schools that existed in cities were operated by churches, but they reached only a small fraction of the working class. Most poor families were reluctant to support plans for mandatory education because they needed the income their children earned in the factories. After mid-century, however, industry's growing need for literate clerks, accountants, and men with some technical training led to calls for state-supported and directed schools.

Supporters of compulsory elementary schooling advanced three basic arguments. For those who worried about the potentially disruptive power of large numbers of poorly paid urban dwellers, a carefully managed system of literacy and indoctrination offered the best guarantee of popular loyalty to the state and respect for private property. The virtues of discipline, obedience, and self-help could be communicated by trained professionals. The French statesman (and historian) François Guizot (1787–1874) believed that "the opening of every school house closes a jail." More idealistic supporters focused on the remedial and transforming power of basic education. These proponents were heirs of the Enlightenment tradition, eager to advance equality of opportunity and a new "aristocracy" of talent. Economic progress required state-sponsored schools. Finally, champions of an extended franchise insisted that as more and more men secured the right to vote, it was essential to have an educated citizenry to avoid the rise of demagogues and would-be tyrants.

In 1833 Guizot introduced legislation that called for an elementary school in every French parish. It was an ambitious agenda, and the goal was not fully realized until 1882. The French initiative was also repeated elsewhere in Western Europe. Great Britain began subsidizing its existing religious schools in 1870 while simultaneously supporting the formation of secular institutions at the elementary level. School attendance was first made compulsory for British youth in 1880 and for French children in 1882. Germany, Holland, Belgium, Italy, Switzerland, and Scandinavia all embraced the trend, and by the end of the century, most remaining tuition fees were abolished across Western Europe.

The movement for universal primary education (for children under the age of 14) was strongest in those parts of Europe and America where the process of industrialization was well underway. By World War I, most men and women in these nations could read and write, and many had received specialized technical training. A large corps of

Pupils and Teachers   The Reverend Thomas Guthrie (1803–1873) was an ardent social reformer in Scotland in the middle of the nineteenth century. Among his many causes, he championed the creation of non-sectarian schools. Guthrie can be seen here standing at a blackboard, accompanied by a female aid, instructing young pupils at the Ragged School in Edinburgh, Scotland. One of Guthrie's former pupils said that "he was the only father I ever had."

professional teachers emerged, and pupils from working-class backgrounds were provided with the basic intellectual tools necessary for entry-level white collar employment. Bank clerks, secretaries, machine operators, postal service employees—all needed basic education to carry out their tasks. The schools did promote responsible self-government, but more problematically, they also became training camps for strong and unreflective nationalism in an age of European expansion and imperial rivalry.

The Changing Role of the State   Optimists on both sides of the Atlantic hoped that they could reduce poverty and illness and expand material comforts by alleviating the physical burdens of work through the application of technology. The promises of industry—efficiency, increased productivity, and lower costs for mass-produced goods—all seemed within reach under the appropriate political conditions. Those conditions, at least from the point of view of liberal economists and politicians, involved minimum interference from the state. According to Edward Baines (1800–1890), author of *The History of the Cotton Manufacture in Great Britain* (1835) and an enthusiastic supporter of modernization, "under the reign of just laws [in England], personal liberty and property have been secure; mercantile enterprise has been allowed to reap its reward; capital has accumulated in safety." More controversially, Baines claimed that the working class also benefited from a laissez-faire economic order.

National incomes did increase tremendously in Europe in the century before World War I, and free labor replaced onerous slave systems in the United States and in the British Empire. Yet the income gap between employer and employee appeared to grow wider each decade. Religious organizations like the Salvation Army in Britain, founded in 1878, attempted to assist men and women who faced poverty and despair, but their resources were limited. The fabulous wealth enjoyed by successful businessmen, investors, and owners of large factories, when juxtaposed with the difficult circumstances of workers during the early stages of industrialization, prompted European governments to intervene in a small way in the private sector. Precedents for state action abounded, ironically in the area of government assistance for capitalist ventures. Adam Smith's doctrine of laissez faire (see Chapter 16, "The Age of Enlightenment: Rationalism and Its Uses") was faithfully championed by industrial capitalists when it came to employer–employee relations, but businessmen were aggressive supporters of government investment in infrastructure. Land grants and tax incentives for transport companies (road and bridge building, railroads, harbor projects), together with tariff protection for infant industries facing stiff foreign competition, were all time-honored exceptions to the free market confession of faith.

By 1900, all of the major European states except Russia had adopted less restrictive electoral systems. This process of democratization helped to intensify efforts to improve the lives of the working class. France had universal manhood suffrage in 1848, while Britain extended the franchise to working men in voting reform acts of 1867 and 1884. Germany, Britain's biggest rival in the race for industrial supremacy, instituted universal manhood suffrage in 1871. Amendments to the U.S. Constitution after the Civil War in 1865 called for the enfranchisement of free black males, but that struggle continued well into the 1960s. By the start of World War I, Spain, Belgium, France, Norway, Italy, Switzerland, Austria, and the Netherlands each broadened their franchise to include every adult male, and strenuous efforts were underway to enfranchise women. Norway, in 1907, became the first European state to give the vote to women.

Extending the Enlightenment principle that legitimate governments derive their powers from the consent of the governed, and not from an assumed divine mandate, had the unanticipated effect of enhancing the power of national governments across Western Europe. Patriotic and nationalist rhetoric allowed Europe's democratizing states to cultivate popular support in pursuit of expansionist domestic programs and imperial adventures. Thanks to universal manhood suffrage, serious reform could now take place within the political and economic arenas. Socialist political parties were committed to improving living and working standards for the working class, and conservative and liberal politicians responded by introducing their own programs for social reform. In an economic and cultural environment of rising expectations, where centuries-old assumptions about the inevitability of poverty for the many were no longer accepted, Europe's leaders became increasingly alarmed by the prospect of social conflict. To defuse this potential, governments began to invest heavily in education, housing provision, sanitation, pure water and food supplies, adequate policing, and street lighting.

KEY QUESTION | Revisited

Technology and urbanization had a profound impact on the relationship between humans and nature during the Industrial Revolution. At the time of the French Revolution, Europeans still depended upon wind, water, and animal and human muscle to supply the energy they needed for their daily work. For the most part, that work took place in close connection with the natural environment. The work routine was regulated in large measure by available sunlight, the condition of the soil, and climatic variables. In the nineteenth century this traditional pattern of life and work was gradually replaced by a capital-intensive economy based on manufacturing. Although most people in Southern, Eastern, and Central Europe remained in rural economies at the start of the twentieth century, industrialization had transformed life in Belgium, Britain, France, Germany, the Netherlands, Scandinavia, northern Italy, and in pockets of Austria-Hungary. Across the Atlantic, the United States experienced the full force of the Industrial Revolution after 1865.

In addition to new patterns of organizing human labor, the substitution of factories for small shops and home workrooms, and the emergence of large industrial centers, the Industrial Revolution redefined the relationship between humans and the natural environment. Nonrenewable natural resources such as coal and oil were depleted at a fast pace, while renewable resources such as water and timber were consumed at an unsustainable rate. Trees were felled at an alarming rate to construct houses and factories, create railway lines, and build roads. Factories spewed smoke into the atmosphere and discharged waste products in rivers. Cotton workers were exposed to brown-lung disease, while miners suffered and died from black-lung disease. Poisoning from mercury, lead, and the ingestion of metal shavings became distressing features of industrial life. Traditional sources of drinking water now became convenient dumping points for human and industrial waste, while smoke from coal-fired engines was often the first signal that the traveler was approaching an urban center. Shabby housing in unplanned, overcrowded, and disease-ridden neighborhoods contributed to the overall pattern of environmental degradation.

Still, before 1900, few reformers paid much attention to the environmental consequences of rapid industrialization. Women and men continued to flock to the cities in search of jobs in factories, construction, domestic service, stores, and offices. Despite the pressures of factory discipline, families adjusted to their new environments. The city offered anonymity and freedom of action; traditional values and practices were replaced by new options in personal relations. One's choice of marriage partner, for instance, now transcended the confines of the village. Rates of divorce increased, as did illegitimate births. Even the choice to remain single, always suspect in the rural village, became easier to realize in the city. An increasing emphasis on rights over obligations, especially to social superiors, was perhaps one of the most significant aspects of the new freedoms the large urban setting provided.

By 1914, the condition of the working class in Western Europe was much improved, and some of the conveniences of the expanding consumer economy were within reach of laborers. Adult males had won the right to vote in most countries; children were now afforded primary education at public expense; the disgruntled and the ambitious had the option of cheap passage to the Americas or Australasia. State intervention in the workplace addressed the worst elements of early industrial life. In particular, government-mandated health and safety regulations, better wages, and accident and retirement provisions allowed common people to reach levels of material security never before available. The Western industrial lifestyle was even embraced by colonial peoples who sought both to emulate the West's economic transformation and to free themselves from European control. Unfortunately for people in countries where industry had not taken root and where opportunities for migration were negligible (India and China, for example), acute economic crises, political unrest, and recurrent food shortages became the norm.

Technology and urbanization had redefined the relationship between humans and nature, but in the early nineteenth century, the separation of large numbers of people from the rhythm of life on the land and in small communities seemed, on balance, to have resulted in a better quality of material life for everyone. Industrialization had weakened the influence of both the traditional aristocracy and the official state churches. The middle class rose to political and social power thanks to the economic rewards associated with industrial production. The working class had not been pressed to the limits of physical endurance as the Marxists had predicted at mid-century. Increasing secularization and confidence about the future replaced older, less optimistic assumptions about the possibility and value of change. On the eve of World War I, industrial prowess enabled Europeans to dominate the globe, and few people worried about the capacity of industrialized nations for widespread human and ecological destruction. All of this would change after war began in 1914.

Review Questions

1. How did changes in agriculture expedite the process of early industrialization?
2. Why did governments intervene in the private sector on behalf of industrial workers?
3. Why did Britain become the world's first industrial nation?
4. Why was steam power so central to the early stages of the Industrial Revolution?
5. What were the main objectives of the first industrial unions?
6. What role did manufacturers play in the development of a middle-class consumer culture?
7. How did the roles of working-class and middle-class women change during the Industrial Revolution?

Please consult the Suggested Readings at the back of the book to continue your study of the material covered in this chapter. For a list of documents on the Primary Source DVD-ROM that relate to topics in this chapter, please refer to the back of the book.

Topics in This Chapter

The Congress System and the Conservative Agenda • Ideological Ferment

• The Revolutions of 1848 • Britain and Reform

• The Romantic Movement • Utilitarianism and Utopian Socialism

• The Marxist Challenge

19 The Age of Ideology

Fight on, embattled Russia mine,
Recall the rights of ancient days!
The sun of Austerlitz, decline!
And Moscow, mighty city, blaze!
Brief be the time of our dishonor
The auspices are turning now;
Hail Moscow—Russia's blessings on her!
War to extinction, thus our vow!

—**Alexander Pushkin, "Napoleon" (1821)**

KEY | Question

What leads people to challenge conventional ideas and practices?

In recalling Napoleon's invasion of his homeland in 1812, the Russian poet and dramatist Alexander Pushkin (1799–1837) focused not on the destruction and loss of life caused by the Grand Army led by Bonaparte, but instead on the emergence of Russian national feeling. Pushkin's pride in his country was matched by a strong commitment to political freedom and the advancement of individual rights. Neither goal was realized in Russia during Pushkin's brief lifetime, but the ideals of national autonomy, freedom, and the dignity of the individual became key features of European culture in the three decades following the defeat of Napoleon Bonaparte at Waterloo in 1815.

A wide range of ideological "isms" emerged on the European political scene during these years. Most of these terms and movements are recognizable today—liberalism, conservatism, romanticism, utopianism, industrialism, nationalism, socialism, and Marxism. But most found their definitive modern expression during or in the aftermath of the great

Workers Demonstration This 1902 painting by Ramon Casas (1866–1932) of police in Barcelona dispersing a crowd of striking workers captures the violence that characterized the many conflicts between workers and property owners during the nineteenth century.

French Revolution that began in 1789. Most of them would play decisive roles in shaping the lives of Europeans as they responded to the disruptions caused by two decades of military conflict and the beginnings of an unprecedented change in patterns of labor and production associated with the rise of industry.

Napoleon's imperial dreams may have been shattered decisively at Waterloo, but there was little hope that the intellectual assumptions and beliefs of Old Regime Europe could be restored fully in the nineteenth century. As monarchies were reconstituted and efforts undertaken to affirm the legitimacy of Europe's hereditary rulers, the forces in support of responsible self-government, individual rights, religious pluralism, and civil and legal reform continued to attract additional followers from within the ranks of the expanding middle class. By 1848, a series of liberal and nationalist revolutions across Europe demonstrated the power of ideas first put to the test during the French Revolution. Napoleonic dictatorship and reform by fiat had been rejected in 1815, but no one knew for sure what model of social and political order would take its place. On a continent where the unprecedented forces of industrialization were contributing to a fundamental reordering of established cultural values, ideological commitments repeatedly fueled political action in the streets of Europe's capitals.

The Congress System and the Conservative Agenda

After Napoleon's abdication and banishment to Elba in 1814, Russia, Prussia, Austria, and Britain concluded a lenient "First Peace of Paris" with the defeated French. Louis XVI's young son had been recognized by the other European rulers as Louis XVII after the execution of his father in 1793, but the boy died while being held captive by the revolutionaries and never exercised power. As a result, after the fall of Napoleon, the younger brother of the executed monarch was installed as King Louis XVIII (r. 1814–1824). The restored Bourbon ruler always carried the taint of having been imposed on the French people by the powers who had vanquished Napoleon, but despite this awkward start, the king was welcomed by most of his subjects. The boundaries of the restored monarchy were cut back only to their 1792 dimensions, giving the French territory that they had not held when the French Revolution began in 1789.

After settling affairs in France, the victorious powers agreed to meet again in the Austrian capital of Vienna in September 1814 in order to make additional adjustments to the political map of the continent. As the delegates assembled, the most pressing problems before them involved the re-establishment of political stability and the creation of a balance of power in Europe. The leading figures at the meeting were Austria's chancellor, Prince Clemens von Metternich (1773–1859), British foreign secretary Robert Stewart Viscount Castlereagh (1769–1822), Russian Tsar Alexander I (r. 1801–1825), the aged Baron Hardenberg of Prussia (1750–1822), and France's minister for foreign affairs, Charles Maurice Prince de Talleyrand (1754–1838). They were joined by dozens of rulers who had been summarily dispossessed of their lands by Napoleon and by a host of lesser figures who sought to avenge some slight received during the revolutionary era. Most of the leading figures at Vienna were members of Europe's old aristocracy. They were men who were suspicious of liberal political ideas and who viewed the middle class as troublesome upstarts. The war and chaos of the preced-

Prince Clemens von Metternich The leading figure at the Congress of Vienna, Metternich would remain an important spokesperson for nineteenth-century conservatism until he fled from Vienna during the revolution of 1848.

ing 20 years, they believed, had been occasioned by the dangerous belief in human equality. The delegates were intent upon destroying the revolutionary impulse and reasserting their traditional leadership prerogatives.

Containing the French One of the main principles at the **Congress of Vienna** was monarchical "legitimacy." Many of the rulers abridged or revoked the civil and legal reforms that Napoleon had introduced. As a result, the prerevolutionary dynasties returned to their respective capitals. The Vienna meeting was interrupted by Napoleon's one-hundred-day return to power in March 1815 and defeat at Waterloo in June. In the aftermath of this crisis, France was forced to pay a 700 million franc indemnity, accept the imposition of foreign troops until the indemnity was paid, and retract its eastern frontier to the boundaries of 1789. The creation of strong states along France's eastern border was thought to be in the interest of Europe-wide peace and order; thus, the delegates granted Prussia new lands along the Rhine River while the Protestant Netherlands and Catholic Belgium were joined to make the kingdom of the Netherlands under the rule of William I (r. 1815–1840).

In Italy, where the Napoleonic reforms had taken deep root, the return of the House of Savoy to an expanded kingdom of Piedmont-Sardinia in the northeast, coupled with direct Austrian rule in Venice and Lombardy, led to simmering local discontent. Napoleon, who as a native Corsican was in certain respects more Italian than French, had dismantled the old feudal order and succeeded in winning broad support for the Napoleonic Code. The entire peninsula reverted to rule by more or less reactionary monarchs, including the pope, who returned as ruler of the Papal States.

New Boundaries The leading powers also took the opportunity to expand their own territories. Poland was restored as a state, but under the rule of the Russian tsar and subject to Russian military occupation. Tsar Alexander also won control over Finland, previously ruled by Sweden. The Swedes, in return, acquired Norway, which had been governed by Napoleon's ally Denmark. Prussia acquired part of Saxony and all of the central German province of Westphalia. It emerged from the Congress as the second most powerful state in the former Holy Roman Empire. Not to be outdone, Britain received strategically important naval bases at Helgoland in the North Sea, Malta in the Mediterranean, Cape Colony in South Africa, and the island of Ceylon off the southern coast of India. The Papal States were restored to the Roman Catholic Church under the leadership of Pope Pius VII (r. 1800–1823), and in Spain the Bourbons returned to their capital at Madrid. The defunct Holy Roman Empire was replaced by a loose confederation of 39 German states featuring a federal diet based in Frankfurt. While the "Congress System" was subject to serious strain in the nineteenth century, the Vienna settlement did inaugurate a century in which there was no general European war. The leading states of Western Europe would expand their influence around the globe between the defeat of Napoleon in 1815 and the start of World War I in 1914, but during this period, no one power would come to dominate the continent and threaten its neighbors (see Map 19–1).

Challenging the Peace of Europe   In France the government of Louis XVIII quickly paid its indemnity and was admitted into an alliance of five great states (known as the Quintuple Alliance) that included Russia, Austria, Prussia, and Great Britain. Committed to upholding the territorial and political settlements reached at Vienna, the governments of the restored monarchies cracked down on liberal activists, censored the press, and used their armies to crush revolutionary movements whenever and wherever they emerged. A second and overlapping alliance, the so-called "Holy Alliance," in-

Map 19–1 Europe in 1815 The delegates at the Congress of Vienna dismantled Napoleon's empire and made a wide array of territorial adjustments. The Holy Roman Empire was not restored; instead it was replaced by a new German confederation.

Question: Did the Congress of Vienna acknowledge nationalist sentiments?

volved Russia, Austria, and Prussia. It committed the signatories to upholding the Christian faith throughout the continent.

As early as 1821, Austrian forces overturned a liberal revolution in the southern Italian Kingdom of the Two Sicilies and another in Piedmont. Two years later, 100,000 French troops were sent across the Pyrenees to assist Spanish King Ferdinand VII (r. 1813–1833) against a liberal revolution. The revolutionaries were led by disgruntled soldiers and had forced the king to restore the liberal constitution of 1812, established during the Napoleonic occupation of the country. In Russia, the death of Alexander I in December 1825 led to a revolt by army officers who had been exposed to liberal political ideas and who had founded a number of secret societies dedicated to undermining autocracy in Russia. Lacking broad support, the revolutionaries were easily defeated by troops loyal to the new tsar, Nicholas I (r. 1825–1855). In the aftermath of this "Decembrist" uprising, the tsar inaugurated a rigorous program of censorship and control over foreign travel. The secret police were granted wide powers of surveillance over the Russian population.

There were exceptions to the Vienna consensus. The British were unenthusiastic about Metternich's brand of repression, and they refused to participate in the Holy Alliance. Tsar Alexander's plan to organize a Russian fleet to crush the rebellions that had broken out in Spain's American colonies won little support among the Congress powers. When Greek rebels took up arms against their Turkish overlords in 1821, Britain, France, and Russia supported the revolutionaries despite the protests of the arch conservative Metternich. In 1827 the three powers signed a formal treaty pledging support for the Greek insurgents. European leaders who were educated in the Greek classics and who associated the Greek fighters with the ancient Spartans and Athenians felt compelled to assist in the struggle against the hated Muslim Turk. By 1830, the Greeks had secured their independence. While few Europeans remained alive who had lived through the age of the French Revolution, the memory of reform continued to inspire a new generation.

Ideological Ferment

Conservatism   The Greek struggle for independence during the 1820s was but one of a number of events that highlighted a protracted debate between advocates for change and defenders of tradition and the status quo. Following in the footsteps of Edmund Burke, European conservatives argued that social order and political stability could best be realized in a climate where tradition, hierarchy, and corporate relationships were preserved and respected. For nineteenth-century conservatives, society was made up not just of individuals who had rights—it was a complex organism that had developed slowly over centuries. This organism was best directed by men who had inherited their positions of leadership. Conservatives like the Frenchman Joseph de Maistre (1753–1821) wrote that the state must play an active and directive role in the life of the nation, supporting religious institutions, encouraging educational initiatives, and inculcating a sense of moral authority through example.

According to conservatives, monarchy, aristocracy, and church were the essential anchors of long-term social harmony. Unlike modern conservatives, early conservatism valued the heavy hand of the state because conservatives rejected the Enlightenment faith in universal truths that were applicable to all people in every circumstance. Instead, each state must follow social, religious, and political paths unique to its cultural traditions. The state must be the arbiter of rights that were not universal but were peculiar to one people. Conservatives valued community and duty, by which they meant the obligations that bound individuals to each other and to the state. The experience of the French Revolution and the tyranny of Napoleon were, for conservatives, nearly fatal to the whole concept of civilization. They rejected the Enlightenment's faith in human perfectability and the idea that "all men are created equal." Instead, their picture of human nature and human potential emphasized human frailty and sinfulness.

Liberalism   Nineteenth-century European liberals represented a different point of view. For increasing numbers of bankers, businessmen, traders, manufacturers, lawyers, and other professionals, the defeat of Napoleon did not mean that the values of the American republic or the French Revolution were invalid. Where conservatives stressed duty, tradition, and hierarchy, liberals believed that human beings were individuals who possessed inherent rights. They called for political reform, equality before the law, and economic freedom. They also espoused the sanctity of private property and supported written constitutions that restrained the power of the state.

During the nineteenth century, liberalism appealed most directly to the aspiring middle class. These were men who had acquired significant economic power but who lacked both political rights and social status. They believed that talent, ambition, and material success qualified one for high social status and a role in the political decision-making process. They also held that through education and personal freedom, everyone could live as a rational, self-directed citizen. Maximizing personal autonomy and limiting the power of the state to the basic needs of national defense and law enforcement were, for liberals, key ingredients to personal and corporate happiness. Most liberals were not democrats; they pushed for a moderate extension of the franchise to include men (never women) of property, but did not believe that workers, peasants, the poor, and the uneducated should be given a voice in government.

Political Economy   The personal freedom advocated by liberals after 1815 also included the freedom to fail. With a state limited to protecting the person and property of the individual, and with all monopolies and restrictions on trade lifted, the autonomous citizen would be free to pursue economic advancement without hindrance from the state. However, autonomy and personal responsibility also meant that the state in particular and society as a whole were under no obligation to provide for the destitute or unemployed. Nor was the government charged with overseeing the conditions of labor, regulating wages in the marketplace, or setting minimum standards in housing. Adam Smith had claimed that natural laws existed in the marketplace just as surely as they existed in the heavens, and the first law stated that the economy would remain in balance only if the meddling hand of the state were restricted. The rational self-interest of employers and employees would ensure material well-being for all. Under such an understanding of basic economic forces, those who experienced poverty had no one but themselves to blame.

Some economists, while supportive of Smith's laissez-faire (noninterference) formula, were less optimistic about its impact on the poor. The English clergyman Thomas Malthus (1766–1834) believed that population would always outstrip food supply in a free-market economy. Malthus's *Essay on the Principle of Population* (1798) did not advocate state action in the face of this impending crisis, however. Any effort on the part of the government to raise wages would simply lead Europe's masses to have more children, thus plunging them back to the margins of survival. In the *Principles of Political Economy* (1817), David Ricardo (1772–1823) endorsed the gloomy "Malthusian" prediction, concluding that the wage worker must engage in a constant struggle with his employer for salary increases. Unfortunately, as the population grew, wages would be pushed down due to the inevitable oversupply of labor. According to Ricardo's "iron law of wages," salary deflation was the only force capable of curbing population growth. In the opinion of Europe's expanding **working class,** the theories of Malthus and Ricardo offered a troubling justification for the ongoing callousness and apathy of the wealthy, the owners of the means of production. The "dismal science" of political economy may have pleased middle-class liberals who fought for the right to utilize their property as they saw fit, but for employees, the need for state intervention in the workings of the private sector seemed obvious.

The Revolutions of 1830–1832

By the third decade of the nineteenth century, the Vienna settlement, also known as the Concert of Europe, had been put to the test repeatedly. In most instances it had succeeded in preventing serious upheaval in the major states. In France the restored Bourbon king reluctantly accepted limits on his powers. A constitutional charter established a two-chamber legislative assembly, rights to free expression, and legal equality among all Frenchmen. About 90,000 Frenchmen, or 1 in 300, enjoyed the right to vote for members of the Chamber of Deputies.

Unfortunately, Louis XVIII's younger brother and successor, Charles X (r. 1824–1830), was less pragmatic and forcefully asserted his right to rule without legislative hindrance. Backed by conservative nobles known as "ultras," Charles curbed press freedoms and worked to extend the authority of the Catholic Church. For example, sacrilege against the church was made a crime punishable by imprisonment and even death. Charles also sought to compensate aristocratic families who had lost lands during the revolutionary era. When the king's party failed miserably in the legislative elections of 1830, the monarch dissolved the Chamber of Deputies and instituted a new franchise by decree that was designed to give conservative landowners more electoral power than the wealthy members of the French middle class. The press was also censored. These actions outraged the king's opponents and denied them their only outlet for peaceful political expression at the national level.

These royal decrees coincided with an escalation of food prices throughout the country during the spring of 1830, which created discontent among the urban masses. In a spontaneous uprising in July, barricades were erected in Paris, and clashes between citizens and soldiers ensued. However, the army lost control of the streets, and the urban bourgeoisie abandoned the king. The defiance soon spread to the countryside, and calls for a republic were heard within working-class circles. After Charles X abdicated

Delacroix, *Liberty Leading the People* Eugene Delacroix's famed painting dramatized the French uprising of 1830. This painting helped to popularize the image of Marianne, who symbolizes the French nation and the republican values of liberty, fraternity, and equality. *Eugene Delacroix (1798–1863), "Liberty Leading the People." July 28, 1830. Painted 1830. Oil on canvas, 260 × 325 cm. Photo: Hervé Lewandowski. Musee du Louvre/RMN Reunion des Musees Nationaux, France. SCALA/Art Resource, NY*

and left for a life of exile in Britain, the wealthy middle class, fearful of republican rhetoric, threw their support behind Charles's cousin, the duke of Orleans. Proclaimed King Louis Philippe (r. 1830–1848), the new monarch recognized that he owed his position to the support of the wealthy bourgeoisie. His government consistently supported the interests of this liberal element until another popular revolution overthrew the monarchy in 1848.

In the neighboring Low Counties, the Catholic Belgians were disgruntled by the 1815 union of their state with the mostly Protestant Netherlands. They reacted to the events of 1830 in France by declaring their own independence. A food crisis similar to the one in France triggered the Belgian revolt and call for autonomy. The Belgians stressed the importance of their Catholic traditions, their native language, and their desire for a written constitution. After the Dutch failed to defeat the Belgians, the great powers recognized Belgian independence on the condition that the new state adopt a posture of neutrality. The 1831 constitution that created the Kingdom of Belgium instantly became a beacon of hope for liberals across Europe. Although only 1% of the male population was afforded the right to vote (the franchise was expanded in the 1840s), both houses of the new bicameral legislature were elected (in most countries the upper house was appointed by the crown). Members of the judiciary were granted autonomy from the government, and the Catholic clergy were denied political influence.

Further to the east, revolution in Poland threatened Russia's hold over its western neighbor. The Polish diet had been restored after 1815, but real political power rested with the Russian governor (and the tsar's brother), Grand Duke Constantine (1779–1831). After news of events in Paris reached Warsaw, disgruntled Polish army officers and university students—and even some members of the aristocracy—joined in what became a call for national independence and constitutional government. The uprising began in November 1830, and it took almost one year for the Russian army to crush the insurgency. The Austrians faced similar threats to their control over portions of Italy. Early in 1831 the northwestern Italian states of Parma and Modena attempted to free themselves from Austrian control, and in central Italy's Papal States, nationalists fought to strip the Roman Catholic Church of its political monopoly. In both instances the rebels failed, but Italian nationalists maintained their goals through a number of underground movements that would return to action in 1848.

The Revolutions of 1848

In the spring of 1848 a series of revolutions swept across the continent in dramatic fashion. They threatened the restored regimes of Western Europe and featured a radical dimension that questioned the legitimacy of the monarchical principle. The revolutions also introduced the prospect of a society reordered along more equalitarian lines. Beginning in France, spreading east and south into the small German-speaking states and Italy, and finally engulfing Central Europe, the revolutionary agenda demonstrated that the core ideals of the French Revolution could not be excised by government repression; and in Poland, Italy, Ireland, Hungary, the Czech lands, and Germany, the push for broader political rights and constitutional reform was combined with parallel demands for national autonomy and national unity (see Map 19–2).

The Spread of Ideas   The persistent calls for parliamentary government under a constitutional monarch during the 1830s and 1840s were strengthened by two changes in the intellectual culture of Western Europe. The first force for change involved the universities, where faculty and students for the first time in Western history had a distinct impact on political thought and action. The second involved the expansion of literacy and the resulting growth of the popular press. Newspapers and periodicals became important vehicles for shaping public opinion in the West, especially middle-class opinion. Censorship continued to be applied by governments across the continent, and the further east one traveled, the harsher the controlling arm of the state became. While mass circulation newspapers did not appear until the last decades of the century, the influence of the print media far exceeded its subscription lists. The dissemination of information reached new levels, and papers critical of government policies enjoyed strong popular support. For the first time in Europe, common people, especially urban dwellers, came to understand the importance of politics in their daily lives and began to take direct action to advance their agendas.

The revolutions took place during a period of acute economic hardship. Food shortages across Europe began with the decimation of the potato crop in 1845, affecting

Map 19–2 The Revolutions of 1848 Revolution was widespread in 1848. As this map indicates, the call for political reform and the recourse to violence in order to secure reforms was concentrated in Italy, France, and Germany.

Question: Why did Britain escape revolution in 1848?

peasants from Ireland to Prussia. Famine conditions (the last time that Europe would be faced with a severe food crisis) threatened wide areas of the population. Persistent drought also weakened grain production on the continent. For peasants and urban workers, high food prices and the prospect of malnutrition undermined their innate conservatism and weakened their support for existing regimes. The physical hardship that the unemployed, the malnourished, the bankrupt businessman, and the middle-class investor experienced sharpened the intensity of calls for political reform.

Beginnings in France   For British-controlled Ireland, famine conditions provided ample cause for a popular uprising, but instead of widespread violent revolution against hated British rule, millions of desperate peasants emigrated to England, Canada, and the United States. In France no such outlets for the wretched and the discontented existed. The government of King Louis Philippe had consistently opposed the extension of the franchise to members of the lower middle class, and the police kept a close watch on republican organizations. Restrictions on the press intensified during the 1840s, just as poor harvests and financial reverses pushed the country into an economic crisis. French workers were not allowed to go on strike. Their inability to vent their anger at the ballot box created a situation in which the regime was linked with the narrow economic interests of the urban bourgeoisie.

When protestors began to circumvent the ban on public demonstrations by holding reform banquets, the government tried to proscribe all large meetings. In February 1848 workers in Paris took to the streets, setting up barricades and defying the government's orders. Clashes between soldiers and citizens took place in the capital. In what would become a familiar pattern across Western and Central Europe over the succeeding months, the governing elite panicked and lost confidence in its ability to control the situation. Despite having 40,000 soldiers at his disposal in Paris, King Louis Philippe refused to entertain the prospect of large scale violence. He abdicated on February 24, and a republic was quickly declared by the provisional government that took power after he fled.

Working-Class Demands   Immediately after the king departed, a coalition of moderates who wished to see an extension of the suffrage and radicals who wanted the government to provide extensive social benefits to the workers took control in an uneasy alliance. The government gave the vote to all adult male Frenchmen. The "right to work" radicals succeeded in having a socialist named Louis Blanc (1811–1882) appointed to establish a series of "national workshops" to address the problem of massive unemployment in Paris. The planned workshops drew thousands of unemployed workers from the surrounding countryside into the capital, all desperate to secure a state-sponsored job. Taxes were raised to finance the various work projects, creating peasant discontent in the rural areas. In May 1848 an increasingly conservative government closed the workshops, and this triggered a worker's revolt in Paris the following month.

Barricades reappeared, calls for the redistribution of property were made, and the desperately poor of the capital city demanded a new social order. The republican government, with the overwhelming support of rural France, crushed the rising in three days, but not before some 1,500 people had been killed in fierce street-by-street fighting. The workers' vision of a society where economic equality complemented political equality had been eradicated, but deep class divisions emerged in every major city in France. The radical revolution suppressed, in December 1848 the new mass French electorate chose Louis Napoleon (1806–1873), a nephew of Napoleon Bonaparte, to lead the nation as president of the Second French Republic. Within three years, Louis Napoleon overthrew the republic and declared himself emperor of the French as Napoleon III. His actions were subsequently approved by a majority of Frenchmen in a national plebiscite.

Expanding the Revolution in Germany   Popular demonstrations in favor of constitutional reform, political rights, and civil liberties soon spread to numerous other countries. Between March and April 1848, the rulers of the small German states of Wurttemberg, Bavaria, Saxony, Hanover, and Baden all instituted reforms. These occurred in the wake of vocal protests and uprisings led by middle-class liberals, skilled artisans whose careers were threatened by factory mass production, and university students. Hardline government ministers were quickly dismissed, press freedoms introduced, and legislative assemblies promised. In Prussia King Frederick Wilhelm IV (r. 1840–1861) ordered his troops out of Berlin after clashes with protesters led to the erection of barricades in the city. Overestimating the extent of popular support for the uprising, the king hastened to allow the formation of a Prussian parliament and declared freedom of the press.

Across Germany, liberal politicians worked to forge a pan-German national parliament under the leadership of a single constitutional monarch. An inaugural meeting of the parliament was called for May in Frankfurt with the goal of drafting a unified constitution for all of Germany. Delegates to the assembly were elected on the basis of universal manhood suffrage, but virtually all of those elected came from the professional middle class. In 1849 a majority of delegates offered a new German crown to the Prussian king, who led the largest and most powerful German state, but he refused to accept the title "from the gutter." One year after the initial protests had forced the king's hand in Berlin, Frederick Wilhelm IV gained new determination not to let middle-class reformers dictate the terms of German unification. While he desired a greater role for Prussia within the German Confederation, he wished to lead this effort according to his own timetable and in consort with Prussia's traditional leadership elite of landowning aristocrats and army officers.

The Habsburg Lands   In the Austrian Empire, the revolutionary movement enjoyed a series of initial successes, as liberals and nationalists appeared to win major concessions from the emperor. The Habsburg Empire was especially vulnerable to the rising tide of nationalism in Europe. This multiethnic, multilingual empire stretched from German-speaking Austria in the west to Magyar-dominated Hungary in the east. Poles, Czechs, Serbs, Ruthenians, Croats, Slovaks, Slovenes, Italians, and Romanians all owed allegiance to the weak-minded Emperor Ferdinand I (r. 1835–1848) in Vienna. Metternich, the Austrian chancellor, recognized that the forces of liberalism and nationalism threatened the integrity of the empire. As a result, Austria had some of the most repressive laws in Europe.

Despite the controls, the revolution in France triggered calls for constitutional change across the empire. In the imperial capital of Vienna, large crowds of students and workers demonstrated in the streets. Unwilling to use overwhelming force to end the activities, the emperor and his principal advisors followed the pattern set elsewhere in Europe and made important concessions. By March, Metternich had resigned and fled, a constitutional assembly was established, and serfdom was outlawed in Austria. Disturbances in Hungary and Bohemia placed additional strain on the government. In Hungary ethnic Magyars began the process of creating an autonomous state under the leadership of Louis Kossuth (1802–1894). Kossuth and his allies declared independence for Hungary in the spring of 1848, but the minority Serb, Croatian, and Romanian populations that would be placed under Magyar rule did not support the break and instead backed Austrian efforts to reconquer the territory. The Magyars were defeated by Austrian forces under the command of Count Joseph Jellachich (1801–1859) in the fall of 1848. A second attempt at securing national independence in March 1849 was suppressed with Russian help. Imperial troops also quashed a pan-Slavic insurrection in Prague during June 1848.

Giuseppe Garibaldi (1807–1882)   Seen here toward the end of his life serenely dressed in his trademark poncho (a mode of dress he adopted in the 1830s and 1840s as a freedom fighter in South America), Garibaldi was a forceful and spiritual leader of the movement for Italian unification, which was achieved, after many conflicts, in 1861.

Italian Nationalism
In Italy, where the Habsburgs had exercised significant political control since 1815, a strong nationalist movement led by Giuseppe Mazzini (1805–1872) and Giuseppe Garibaldi (1807–1882) inspired liberal revolutions in Naples, the Papal States, Piedmont-Sardinia, Lombardy, and Venetia. However, like the revolutions in France and Prussia, the initial successes could not be sustained. In mid-March rebels in the city of Milan succeeded in forcing Austrian troops to withdraw, and King Charles Albert of Piedmont (r. 1831–1849) declared war against the Habsburgs. It took the Austrians less than two months to defeat the Piedmontese, but revolutionary activity now shifted south to the Papal States. The revolutionaries had high hopes for the reformist impulses of the new Pope, Pius IX (r. 1846–1878), who had relaxed some restrictions on the press after assuming office in 1846. Radical calls for a Roman Republic, and the assassination of one of the pope's chief ministers, destroyed whatever sympathy the pontiff may have had for political reform. In November 1848 he took refuge in a Neapolitan fortress. The following year, French president Louis Napoleon Bonaparte, eager to court favor with French Catholics, intervened militarily and restored papal authority. Further south, the reactionary King Ferdinand II of Naples (r. 1830–1859) was finally able to crush an uprising that had started in January 1848.

Assessing the Revolution
The initial successes enjoyed by revolutionaries in 1848 were reversed by Europe's dynastic rulers once they recognized that their liberal opponents did not enjoy broad-based popular support. The fragile alliance of middle-class liberals, students, and urban workers was fraught with ideological disagreements. While liberals sought to obtain limited constitutional change and political power for the educated and property-owning middle class, the radicals who enjoyed the support of urban laborers pushed for more basic alterations in the social and economic fabric. The latter wished for a new world, not simply a more responsible government. Once Europe's monarchs recognized that they could count

PEOPLE IN CONTEXT   Giuseppe Mazzini

Giuseppe Mazzini (1805–1872) was one of the principal leaders of the Italian nationalist movement of the mid-nineteenth century. He was born in Genoa and attended the university there, beginning his studies at age 14. Mazzini received a law degree in 1827 and began his association with outlawed reform groups called Carbonari. An informant betrayed Mazzini to the police, and after his arrest and brief imprisonment, Mazzini left for his first period of exile in France. He was impressed by the ideas of Henri de Saint-Simon (1760–1825), the founder of French socialism, especially Saint Simon's faith in progress under enlightened leadership.

In 1831 Mazzini (now living in the French city of Marsailles) founded Young Italy, an association of liberal intellectuals who dedicated themselves to the unification of Italy under a strong central government. The government of King Louis Philippe allowed considerable press freedoms at this time, and Young Italy sought to win support through the dissemination of ideas. The goal was daunting, especially in light of the repressive rulers who controlled most of Italy. However, by 1833, an estimated 50,000 to 60,000 Italians had joined the association. From abroad Mazzini called for the removal of all Austrian influence, an end to the pope's temporal power over the Papal States, and the creation of a republican national government. Rome would serve as the capital of this revolutionary republic, and the Italian people would become the standard bearers of enlightened self-government across Europe, a model society for oppressed peoples everywhere.

A portrait of Giuseppe Mazzini, from about 1865.

When the revolutions of 1848 began in France, Mazzini was living in exile in England (the nation where he spent most of his adult life). During the long years of exile, he had supported a variety of conspirators who attempted to organize popular uprisings in Italy, but all had failed miserably. In March 1848 he reluctantly supported King Charles Albert of Piedmont-Sardinia in the monarch's declaration of war against Austria. Mazzini returned to Italy in April, residing in Milan until the Austrian army retook the city in July. In March 1849 Mazzini relocated to Rome, where a popular revolution had forced Pope Pius IX to abandon his capital. The revolutionaries declared the formation of a republic, and Mazzini moved into the pope's former residence at the Quirinal Palace. The United States was the only country to extend diplomatic recognition to the Roman republic. After five months, Louis Napoleon of France dispatched troops to restore the pope. After two months of fighting, the republic was defeated.

Despite the failed revolutions of 1848, Mazzini's reputation actually grew in international circles. The Roman republic had introduced universal manhood suffrage, instituted government control over clerical salaries, and founded popular political clubs designed to attract the support of the common man. During years of reimposed exile, Mazzini continued to champion republicanism over monarchy, universal manhood suffrage, the end of serfdom, tax credits for the working poor, a progressive income tax, and free education for all citizens. When he died in March 1872, Italy had achieved national unification under a constitutional monarch. Mazzini had dedicated his life to the cause of national unity, but his vision of a democratic republic would not be achieved before the mid-twentieth century.

Question: Why do revolutionaries attract international attention?

on the support of their armies and that the use of force would be supported by the majority peasant population who distrusted the urban working class, the revolutions in the cities were doomed to failure.

Yet the core of the revolutionary agenda—written constitutions, freedom of speech and press, representative political institutions based on an extended franchise, military forces subordinate to civilian authority—was not extinguished by the failure of middle- and working-class insurgency in 1848. The tillers of the soil, still the overwhelming majority of Europe's population in 1848, may not have supported the revolutionaries at mid-century, but over the next 50 years wider political rights were realized and greater government involvement in the economic welfare of the general population was achieved.

Britain and Reform

The only major European power fortunate enough to avoid revolution throughout the period 1815 to 1848 was Great Britain. Given that the country was in the midst of unprecedented social and economic change brought about by rapid industrialization (see Chapter 20, "The Consolidation of Nation-States"), Britain's ability to undertake constitutional reform without recourse to violence was exceptional. While Britons may have enjoyed the broadest political and religious freedoms in Europe, the country was far from tolerant and democratic in 1815, and civil liberties had been sharply curtailed during the Napoleonic wars. The titled aristocracy controlled the House of Lords, while the vast majority of the House of Commons were men of substantial property. Less than 5% of the male population had the right to vote in 1815. In addition, the growth of industrial towns during the early nineteenth century had not led to a reapportionment of seats in Parliament. As a result, densely populated industrial centers in the Midlands and in the north of the country had no members of Parliament, while underpopulated rural areas, dominated by a handful of powerful elites, did. Liberal reformers wished to put an end to these "rotten boroughs" (seats in the House of Commons that had few electors or were owned outright by a single wealthy individual) while simultaneously extending the franchise to members of the commercial and industrial middle class.

Repression at Peterloo

Initial efforts at reform were met with official repression. The end of the Napoleonic wars found returning veterans struggling to find work in a depressed civilian economy. In 1819 workers assembled in St. Peter's fields near the city of Manchester to protest their worsening economic plight and to demand the right to vote. Government forces panicked and attacked the 50,000 unarmed protestors. Hundreds of civilians were injured and 11 killed in what became known as the "Peterloo Massacre" in mock comparison to the great victory over Napoleon at Waterloo. In the aftermath of the attack, the conservative government passed legislation that placed restrictions on public meetings and called for the rigorous prosecution of political radicals.

The Great Reform Bill

The repression did not last for long, however. During the 1820s, the government made a series of important concessions to liberal demands. In 1828 Roman Catholics and Protestant Nonconformists were granted political rights. In British-controlled Ireland, the Catholic Emancipation Act meant that property-owning members of Ireland's Catholic majority could now hold public office. The government also began to back away from some of the more reactionary international policies advocated by Metternich. However, it was not until 1830, when the conservative Tory government was replaced by a more moderate Whig party, that serious discussion over the franchise took place. Sponsored by the Whigs and reluctantly supported by King William IV (r. 1830–1837), the Great Reform Bill of 1832 acknowledged the changing structure of economic power in the country. Britain's ruling elite recognized that the nation's prosperity and international power were made possible by the successes of the middle class.

Under the terms of the Reform Bill, the right to vote in parliamentary elections was extended to the property-owning middle class (especially the wealthy industrial manufacturers) for the first time. This meant the enfranchisement of about 650,000 males, by no means a majority in a nation of some 10 million. Still, the inclusion of Britain's industrial leaders in the political process helped to ensure a large measure of social order in a period of great change resulting from the industrialization of the country. With the precedent established, future Parliaments, in 1867 and again in 1872, would extend the right to vote even further, although Britain would not enjoy universal manhood suffrage until 1918.

Additional Peaceful Reforms

Other important changes followed the passage of the Reform Bill. Slavery was outlawed in all British colonies in 1833. This change was the result of decades of activism on the part of middle-class humanitarians,

House of Commons   With the passage of the Great Reform Bill of 1832, the membership of Britain's House of Commons began to include representatives drawn from new urban centers.

many of whom were associated with the country's evangelical churches. The government compensated slaveowners for the loss of their "property," thereby easing the process of abolition. Towns and cities gained new powers of self-government under the Municipal Corporations Act of 1835, and elected officials were now empowered to address growing social problems associated with the rise of industry. Parliament also turned to the problems faced by industrial laborers. In a series of reform measures taken during the 1830s and 1840s, the conditions of work were ameliorated and the commitment to laissez-faire principles gradually abandoned. The first Factory Act was passed in 1833, limiting the number of hours children under age 13 could work (a 9-hour maximum!) and restricting those under age 18 to 69 hours of labor per week.

Successive laws regulated labor in mines and addressed the conditions of work for women. A parliamentary inquiry into the conditions of labor in the country's numerous coalmines led to swift remedial action. After sometimes harrowing testimony by children before parliamentary committees, the government banned the employment of children under age 10 in the mines while limiting the number of hours to 10 that women and boys under age 18 could work underground. Adult male workers continued to work long hours for another quarter century.

Key Political Developments in Europe, 1815–1848	
1814–1815	Congress of Vienna
1825	"Decembrist" uprising (Russia)
1830	Greek independence
1830	Belgian independence
1830	Revolution in France
1832	Great Reform Bill (Britain)
1830s–1840s	Chartist Movement (Britain)
1848	Revolutions across Europe

The Chartist Movement   The drive for comprehensive political rights after 1830 was led by a coalition of middle-class political radicals and working-class leaders. They called for a new political charter that would guarantee universal manhood suffrage, the secret ballot, annual parliaments, and salaries for members of Parliament. Led by William Lovett (1800–1877) and a group of London-based artisans, most of these "Chartists" embraced peaceful reform, sponsoring rallies and sending petitions with millions of signatures to Parliament. The Charter was presented to Parliament on three separate occasions, and its supporters published a newspaper, *The Northern Star*. Although the movement failed to achieve its main objectives by 1848, it did provide an important outlet for disenfranchised workers to express their many grievances. Chartism represented the first mass political movement in Britain and contributed to a faith in peaceful change through legislative means that enabled the country to avoid revolution at mid-century.

The Romantic Movement

The attention given to reason and natural law during the Enlightenment had informed many of the political transformations in America and France at the end of the eighteenth century. However, it also generated a reaction and the emergence of an alternate perspective on truth, beauty, and the individual during the first half of the nineteenth century. Although it is always difficult to periodize movements in literature and the arts, certain features distinguish what has come to be known as **Romanticism** from the neo-classical style of the mid-eighteenth century. A concern with individual creativity anchored in the emotions, a stress on the unique and even spiritual nature of the creative process, and a celebration of spontaneity informed by imagination as an avenue to truth distinguished aspects of European cultural life in the first half of the nineteenth century. It is appropriate to place these features under the general heading of Romanticism.

Romantic authors, painters, and musicians represented a wide variety of political and religious perspectives, but all of them questioned the value of rational inquiry as the sole avenue to the discovery of universal truths. In France the novelist Victor Hugo (1802–1885); in England the poets William Blake (1757–1827), Samuel Taylor Coleridge

The Chartist Movement A Chartist demonstration in 1842. The Chartists were the first large working-class organization in Britain. Their efforts to extend the right to vote and other political rights contributed to the birth of modern trade unionism and socialism in Europe.

(1772–1834), William Wordsworth (1770–1850), and John Keats (1795–1821); in Russia the poet Alexander Pushkin (1799-1837); and in the German-speaking states the composers Ludwig van Beethoven (1770–1827) and Franz Schubert (1797–1828) all emphasized the importance of the subjective imagination in human expression. The generic concerns of the *philosophes,* especially their unwavering dedication to the principle that progress issued solely from the exercise of reason, struck the Romantics as too simplistic. Such an approach overlooked the multidimensional nature of humans as creative agents. Against the Enlightenment's focus on general rules and features of human nature shared by all, the Romantics dedicated themselves to the celebration of exception, to personal differences, to the unusual and the aberrant. Beethoven, for example, was reluctant to immerse himself in the music of other composers out of fear that it would inhibit or contaminate his own musical ideas. Jean-Jacques Rousseau (1712–1778), who in some respects anticipated the Romantic impulse, believed that in nature humans were pure and good; society—even rationally ordered society—corrupted an otherwise healthy human nature. For Romantics, reason was an insufficient guide to authentic living.

Romantic poets and writers claimed that as a way of knowing truth and penetrating life's deepest mysteries, their method was more productive than formal philosophical inquiry. Indeed, Romantic artists argued that for reason to function at all, it had to be informed by the nonanalytical imagination. The imagination could not be cultivated through the study of rules and manuals, but instead through the experience of nature, the pain of personal loss, the joy of fresh encounters. The poet and artist William Blake believed that it was a focus on the particular, not the general, that enabled great minds to view the sublime. Instinct and feeling were rooted in what would later be labeled the unconscious; for the Romantics, the inner recesses of the soul would find productive expression only if each person's emotional side were allowed free play in the world as experienced. In some respects this feature of Romanticism was anti-egalitarian; the unique genius, the seer, was valued over the ordinary mortal whose only guide was the mundane faculty of reason.

Inspired by the work of Kepler, Galileo, Descartes, and Newton, the Enlightenment had treated the natural environment as a giant clockwork, orderly and predictable. The laws of nature were open to human investigation through the application of the scientific method, and since rationality and predictability governed the cosmos, the same principles ought to guide our terrestrial affairs. Romantics strongly disagreed with this picture of nature. Instead of viewing the environment as a machine whose component parts can be measured and mastered, nature was valued as a spiritual touchstone, a moral teacher, a guide to the emotions, and the principal source of artistic inspiration. It was often the particular in nature, the single example, and not nature as a large system that provided valuable guidance in life's journey. In "The Tables Turned," poet William Wordsworth wrote

> One impulse from a vernal wood
> May teach you more of man,
> Of moral evil and of good,
> Than all the sages can.

While not all Romantics were devout Christians, the symbolic, aesthetic, and otherworldly side of Christian religious expression had great appeal to many poets, artists, writers, and composers. God as nurturer and spiritual force, immanent in nature and receptive to emotional forms of worship and expression, stood in stark opposition to the Enlightenment's picture of the deity as an orderly and disinterested workman. The medieval period, with its great gothic cathedrals, its pilgrimages, and its unified faith tradition, appealed to a generation wearied by decades of war and political upheaval. History, particularly the history of the Middle Ages, fascinated the Roman-tics. The *philosophes* had dismissed the Middle Ages as a protracted period of superstition, intolerance, and economic stagnation. Romantics, in contrast,

William Blake's *Jerusalem* The visionary poet and artist William Blake was a key figure in the Romantic movement. The Romantics did not share the Enlightenment's faith in reason, instead extolling emotion, spontaneity, and human instinct. Blake spent many years on his prophetic book, *Jerusalem* in which he created his own mythological world through etchings and symbolic prose.

were apt to idealize the simple life of the peasantry, the bond of community in medieval agricultural society, the richness of local cultures and languages, and the inherent dignity and originality of folk traditions. The popularity of the novels of Sir Walter Scott (1721–1832), stories of adventure and heroism performed by ordinary people in the Middle Ages, testified to the growing appeal of history for the literate middle class.

The Impact of Romanticism   The aesthetic contributions of Romanticism included a renewed and enhanced respect for human creative impulses rooted in the emotions. While not disparaging the place of reason in the quest for a more humane and just society, the Romantic movement reclaimed the importance of passion, intuition, and will in the creative process. Overall, Romantics did not fall captive to the claim that truth was singular and personal. Most accepted that truth was independent of the seeker, but they wanted the seeker to employ a variety of tools in the search for truth. In addition, Romanticism had an unmistakable impact on political and social developments during the first half of the nineteenth century. Criticism of living and working conditions in the rising industrial towns often found eloquent voice in Romantic novels. Many of the most memorable characters in the novels of Charles Dickens (1812–1870), for example, were those whose lives had been crushed by the factory routine and the logic of laissez-faire economic theory. The strong and deliberate leadership of Napoleon Bonaparte was held up by Romantics as an example of how one man from modest circumstances could transform the continent through force of personality and broad vision. Many of the leaders of nationalist movements in Italy, Poland, France, Prussia, and Austria launched the revolutions of 1848 against enormous odds. Outmanned and outgunned, the insurgents found much of their inspiration in myths created around cultural identity and national destiny. Rational calculation and a balanced assessment of the strength of the opposition would have dictated caution and even inaction in 1848.

Utilitarianism and Utopian Socialism

Early nineteenth-century liberals were not democrats. They were horrified by the excesses of the French Revolution and feared that if political rights were extended to the uneducated masses, the result would be a return to tyranny under the leadership of a despot like Napoleon. To liberals, the uneducated lower classes were incapable of making rational political decisions; given the opportunity, they would advocate policies inimical to the interests of property owners. Poor people, liberals believed, always preferred equality to liberty. The revolutions of the period 1815–1848 may have enjoyed the support of the working classes, but the leaders of these revolutions were deeply suspicious of their allies. As a rule, liberals sought to end revolutionary action as soon as they achieved their limited goals. Only toward the end of the nineteenth century did the twin goals of political democracy and economic justice attract the majority of those who identified themselves as liberals.

Utilitarian Reform   Prior to 1848 a modest number of political radicals moved beyond the liberal camp and supported genuine popular sovereignty. They were convinced that the common man deserved political rights by virtue of his status as citizen. In Britain, Jeremy Bentham (1748–1832) rejected the natural rights philosophy of the Enlightenment and instead maintained that the purpose of all formal institutions, including institutions of government, was to promote the greatest happiness for the greatest number of people. This principle of utility assumed that all humans seek happiness and prefer pleasure to pain. Bentham and his followers argued that the fundamental measure of good laws, good economic systems, good judicial decisions, and good educational endeavors was the extent to which they afforded the greatest happiness to the inhabitants of a particular state. Utilitarianism called for reform based on the immediate needs of the majority—a creed of self-interest—not the abstract principles formulated by an "enlightened" intellectual elite.

Socialist Options   Concern over growing economic disparities and the failure of middle-class reformers to support popular democracy resulted in the emergence of socialist alternatives to the individualistic, competitive, and property-rights orientation of liberal and utilitarian reformers. Early socialism interpreted the Enlightenment's call for a rational society as a mandate for economic equality. In some respects early socialist theory also incorporated elements of the Romantic movement. The socialists believed that a new social and economic order would free individuals to pursue their expressive talents in a setting where everyone's basic needs were met in a community of sharing. In France Henri Count de Saint-Simon (1760–1825) and Charles Fourier (1772–1837) were two of the leading socialist thinkers. Saint-Simon was a member of the aristocracy, but he renounced his title and privileges and called for a new social order led by scientists, industrialists, and other professionals. These specialists would be charged with leading society into a new age of collective abundance through science and technology. Fourier was uncomfortable with the type of large collectives supported by disciples of Saint-Simon. Instead, he believed that human happiness could best be promoted in small communities of about 1,500 citizens. Organized into these small "phalansteries," residents would live a simple lifestyle where agriculture and artisanal enterprises would form the core of economic activity.

Saint-Simon and Fourier were theorists of socialist society; British industrialist Robert Owen (1771–1858) became a practitioner. Born into poverty, Owen went to work at age 9 and rose to become a great textile manufacturer in the city of Manchester. Deeply troubled by the hardships of the factory environment, Owen experimented with socialist alternatives at his cotton mills in New Lanark, Scotland. He became convinced that healthy profits for owners of the means of production could be combined with economic justice for employees in the mills. At New Lanark he improved wages, provided housing for his workers, established pension and sick funds, and built schools for the children of his employees. Owen believed that by providing a healthier lifestyle for working families, his factories would produce more and better quality products. His philanthropic activities attracted the attention of a wide audience. In 1825, for example, Owen was invited to address a special session of the U.S. Congress.

In Britain, Owen urged Parliament to embrace factory reform, but the scale of his proposals frightened fellow industrialists who believed that free-market principles and the sanctity of property offered the best model of industrial organization. Frustrated by his lack of progress at home, Owen spent his entire fortune establishing socialist communities. In New Harmony, Indiana, Owen's cooperative community attracted thousands of sympathizers. Like many other similar ventures in the United States during the 1830s, however, the experiment in cooperative living did not endure. The utilitarian claim that people are motivated solely by self-interest seemed to receive validation in the collapse of the Owenite communities.

The Marxist Challenge

The Revolutions of 1848 were led by middle-class professionals eager to secure constitutional change and political enfranchisement for themselves, but many of their allies within the ranks of the working class demanded more basic social and economic rights. At the midpoint of the nineteenth century, the **Industrial Revolution** had not touched the lives of most Europeans. However, for the inhabitants of the growing cities of Britain, France, and the German states, the harsh conditions of labor within the factory environment would continue so long as working people were denied direct access to political power. The enfranchisement of the bourgeois factory owner, accountant, or lawyer promised little benefit for the uneducated and unskilled city dweller.

Utopian socialists believed that a society based on cooperation instead of competition could be secured in a peaceful manner with the assistance and goodwill of scientists, skilled administrators, and economic managers. Utopian thought minimized the prospect of inevitable violent conflict between economic classes while placing great faith in the willingness of the owners of property to address problems of inequality after a rational assessment of its causes. The German philosopher Karl Marx (1818–1883) was less confident in the ability of self-interested producers to ameliorate the plight of their less fortunate neighbors. The son of a middle-class lawyer, Karl Marx was raised in the city of Trier close to the French border. He attended university to train for the legal profession, but his interest in philosophy led him in new directions.

Marx received a PhD in philosophy from the University of Jena and turned his talents to journalism instead of the academic life. He traveled to Paris in the 1840s and familiarized himself with the socialist ideas of Fourier and Saint-Simon. While in Paris he first met his future collaborator and financial supporter, Friedrich Engels (1820–1895). Like Marx, Engels was of German birth, but his father was a successful textile manufacturer who owned factories in Manchester, England. In

Karl Marx   Marx was deeply affected by the human costs associated with the rise of industry, and his socialist philosophy provided comfort to those who looked forward to the end of capitalist economies.

February 1848 Marx and Engels published a short tract that coincided with the outbreak of revolution across Europe but was destined to have a far greater impact on European—and global—thought than the violent upheavals of that spring. *The Communist Manifesto* called upon the working class to overthrow the capitalist economic system by force. Happiness was to be secured in this life, not in some hoped-for heavenly abode. For Marx and Engels, the religious worldview was the creation of self-interested elites who sought to legitimize their privileged status by creating otherworldly consolation stories for the poor and oppressed.

Like his Enlightenment forebears, Marx believed in the existence of scientific laws of historical development operating in nature. Once these laws were understood, working people could take charge of their destiny. The primary law held that the means of production, the way that goods are produced and wealth is distributed within society, determines the shape of culture, ideas, politics, and even morals. Those who hold material power determine the shape of a culture's dominant ideas and institutions. For example, industrial capitalists and the values of free-market individualism replaced lords of the manor and feudal obligations as soon as machine production deposed cottage manufacture and guild regulations. Throughout the course of the human experience, class conflict stood at the center of material life. It was a conflict between the owners of the means of production and the laborers who, according to Marx, were exploited by their social and economic superiors. From master–slave relationships in the ancient world, to lord and serf in the medieval context, to factory owner and the proletariat, the group that controlled economic power controlled the state. That same group controlled the legal system and the bureaucracy, and forwarded the material and ideological interests of the ruling class.

Despite **Marxism's** emphasis on class conflict throughout history, Marx was an optimist about the future. He believed that in his own day the rise of the industrial middle class or urban bourgeoisie signaled imminent changes in the political system. The urban bourgeoisie were about to break the monopoly over political power enjoyed by the landholding elite for centuries. However, the economic interests of the bourgeoisie—their faith in free markets, free labor, competition, and the sanctity of private property—were deeply at odds with the concerns of the working class. Once the forces of industrial capitalism and the misery of factory conditions had touched the lives of enough people, the final stage in the historical process—the overthrow of the capitalist system—would take place. It would occur under the leadership of men committed to a genuinely equalitarian social and economic system. The start of the revolution would be in Britain, the most advanced industrial nation. Marx even predicted that national differences would fall away once the proletariat understood that **nationalism** and state rivalries were simply productions of the ruling elite.

After the failure of the 1848 revolutions, Marx returned to Germany and briefly edited a newspaper in Cologne. His radical ideas made him an unwelcome figure in the eyes of the authorities, and in 1849 he and his family moved to London, where he would spend the rest of his life writing and preparing for the great revolution that never came. Engels provided much-needed financial support during these years. British authorities were content to let Marx carry out his research and writing in peace at the library of the British Museum. According to Marx, the capitalist stage in history would not endure for long due to the rapid pace of commercial and industrial expansion. As small businessmen were plunged into the ranks of the proletariat due to intensive competition, as wages fell in direct response to the needs of the producer to lower costs, and as members of the burgeoning proletariat recognized their common plight thanks to the aid of communist intellectuals, the few capitalists who remained after eliminating their smaller rivals would be destroyed in a massive popular revolution. In its wake private property would be abolished, and workers would control the material means of production. Only then would new ideas and plans for a society where cooperation replaced competition find their way to the center of human thought.

Marx's belief that material culture determines human consciousness meant that a new consciousness, a new human nature, in fact, would be the final result of the communist revolution. Combining elements of both the Enlightenment and the Romantic traditions, Marx was the author of a secular religion replete with a judgment day in the revolution and an earthly Eden where all would be free to fulfill their potential, "from each according to his abilities, to each according to his needs." In the second half of the nineteenth century, Marx's theory of history was embraced by intellectuals and workers alike as possessing the ring of scientific certainty. By the 1880s, the trend in industry toward greater concentration of economic power, where small competitors were gobbled up by their massive rivals, appeared to legitimize the communist forecast. By this date, a number of European governments began to respond to the horrors of child labor, low wages, and long hours by legislating rules of work and providing minimum employee benefits. These actions belied Marx's prediction that capitalism would collapse under the weight of its own competitive dynamic. Whatever one thought of his theory, however, Marx's basic message provided hope and comfort for large numbers of men and women whose lives were being forever changed by modern capitalism.

KEY QUESTION | Revisited

What leads people to challenge conventional ideas and practices? In the aftermath of the 1848 revolutions, three overriding trends in the intellectual and political life of Europe came into sharper focus. First and foremost, the liberal political agenda, born in the heat of the French Revolution and centered on the establishment of responsible constitutional governments with voting rights for the property-owning middle class, continued to win peaceful incremental victories across the continent. The revolutionaries were defeated by superior force in 1848 to 1849, but Europe's traditional leaders then moved to adopt key elements of the liberal agenda. The liberal economic program evolved from the simple protection of property rights to an acknowledgment that the state had some role to play in protecting the health and well-being of the working public.

Romanticism, with its emphasis on the strengths of unique languages, histories, and cultures, gave an enormous boost to the forces of nationalism, which became one of the most dynamic and destructive forces of the twentieth century. Finally, the social dislocation and sharpening of differences between middle-class liberals and workers, intensified by the advent of large-scale industrial production, set the stage for new political and economic debate during the second half of the century. Calls for universal manhood suffrage and greater economic justice would repeatedly engage the attention of European leaders just as the formation of modern nation-states reached its culmination.

In a global context, Europe's "Age of Ideology" would have a dynamic and formative impact on the world's peoples. The ideas associated with liberalism, embraced by colonial elites studying in European universities, would be turned against authoritarian rulers the world over during the late nineteenth century and against European imperialists themselves during the first half of the twentieth century. Nationalism and the Romantic stress on the integrity of specific cultural identities helped non-European peoples to first resist European expansion and to later win their freedom from European control. Finally, and ironically, the impact of Marxist thought in agrarian Russia, China, and Southeast Asia would change those societies in an integral manner, destroying centuries-old imperial structures and creating new forms of authoritarian rule under leaders who became locked in ideological combat with the West's liberal democracies. Europe's economic and military preeminence around the world by 1900 was prefigured by the ideological struggles of the period 1815 to 1848; the ferment of ideas and the force of revolutionary activity during these decades paved the way for the emergence of strong centralized states. In Western Europe these states would gradually extend political rights to the entire male population while simultaneously intervening in the workplace to prevent the very revolution that Marx had predicted was inevitable.

Review Questions

1. How did the goals of middle-class and working-class revolutionaries differ in 1848?
2. How did Britain manage to avoid revolution in 1848?
3. What were the main features of Romanticism? How would you situate this movement in relation to the Enlightenment?
4. What features of the mid-nineteenth century society did Karl Marx criticize, and what was his view of the industrial middle class?
5. What were the main features of nineteenth-century conservatism?
6. What role did the state play in liberal economic theory?
7. What features distinguished the Austrian Empire from its neighbors in 1848?

Please consult the Suggested Readings at the back of the book to continue your study of the material covered in this chapter. For a list of documents on the Primary Source DVD-ROM that relate to topics in this chapter, please refer to the back of the book.

20 The Consolidation of Nation-States

The Great Decisions of the time will not be resolved by speeches and majority decisions—that was the mistake of 1848 and 1849—but by iron and blood.

—Otto von Bismarck

KEY | Question

Is nationalism a constructive force in the modern age?

The statement previously quoted was from a speech by Otto von Bismarck (1815–1898), Prussian prime minister, to the Prussian Parliament in September 1862. In his speech Bismarck argued that within the German Confederation of States, Prussia was admired as a leader not because of its attachment to liberal political principles but because of its military power. He believed that Prussia must maintain its military readiness in preparation "for the favorable moment" when it could create a larger German state. For Bismarck and for those who supported his policies, the creation of a unified German Empire under one monarch was the prerequisite to future economic progress and social order. Only large unified states, led by men who understood and practiced power politics, could command the respect of the international community.

Modern **nationalism**, defined by loyalty to the state and its abstract ideals, began during the wars of the French Revolution. For the first time in European history, large conscript armies fought bravely on behalf of a set of political ideas, not for a dynasty or a particular ruler. During the second half of the nineteenth century, Europeans and Americans would fight and die to secure the privilege of living in autonomous nation-states. Membership in these states was determined on the basis of a shared language, traditions, and cultural patterns. Early nationalism during the era of the French Revolution tended to promote the values of participatory government, personal freedom, the promotion of universal rights, and

Proclamation of the Third Republic Crowds in Paris celebrate the proclamation of the Third Republic in 1870 during the Franco-Prussian War.

the separation of church and state. After 1850, the rhetoric of national self-determination changed. In a disturbing manner, it began to descend into the realms of power politics, militarism, jingoism, racism, and cultural imperialism. Some of this new spirit can be detected in Bismarck's speech.

The formation of the modern nation-state as the highest expression of political power shattered the universalist ideals that had stood at the core of medieval Christian thought. The conviction that humans owed primary allegiance to a power located outside of the territorial borders of the state in which they lived had first been challenged by the Protestant revolt against the authority of the Roman Catholic Church. The momentum of modern nationalism completely undermined what was left of these universalist ideals. Unsentimental and hostile to the revolutionary impulse, the principal architects of the new nation-states were political realists who sought to win the support of their respective citizenry through measures designed to enhance collective self-esteem. Few of these leaders had much respect for the masses, yet they skillfully adapted themselves to the onset of democratic politics in Western Europe by appealing to the common bond of national identity.

Italian Unification

A Pragmatic Approach   The 1848 revolution in Italy had failed to create a unified state. Giuseppe Mazzini's (1805–1872) dream of a liberal Italian republic designed by idealistic and romantic student revolutionaries was swiftly and decisively rejected by superior military force. The Austrians remained in control of the provinces of Lombardy and Venetia in northern Italy, while a French army guaranteed the integrity of the pope's territories (the Papal States) in the middle of the peninsula. The north-central duchies of Parma, Modena, and Tuscany were under the control of princes allied to the Austrians, and in the south, a reactionary Bourbon monarch ruled the Kingdom of the Two Sicilies. Within 23 years of the failed 1848 revolution, however, full Italian unification had been achieved under the leadership of the northeast Kingdom of Piedmont (officially called the Kingdom of Sardinia).

The path to political union and constitutional government was forged by Count Camillo Cavour (1810–1861), chief minister to King Victor Emmanuel II (r. 1849–1878) of Piedmont-Sardinia. Cavour was a strong monarchist and a political realist who recognized that professional armies would always defeat a mass uprising by untrained revolutionaries. His strategy to achieve Italian unification involved building the power of Piedmont by modernizing its economy. Creating a modern state, he believed, was an essential precondition to removing the Austrians from northern Italy. In 1855 Piedmont joined Britain and France in a war against Russia (the Crimean War) even though the Italians had no strategic interest at stake in the conflict. Cavour believed that Piedmont's participation on the side of the two major Western powers would win their support for Italian unification. The British held back, but Emperor Napoleon III (r. 1852–1870) of France soon became a sympathetic ally. In 1858 Napoleon III and Cavour reached a secret agreement whereby France would come to the aid of Piedmont if Austria attacked the small Italian state. In return for French aid, Cavour was prepared to transfer the Piedmontese territories of Nice and Savoy, which were predominantly French speaking, to France (see Map 20–1).

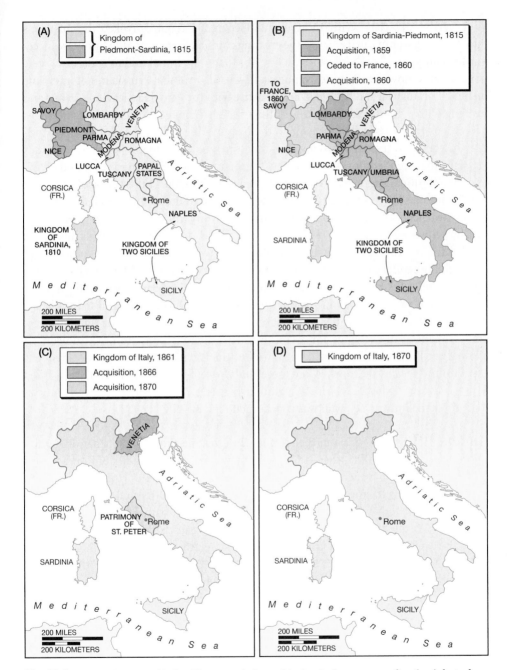

Map 20–1 **The Unification of Italy** The struggle for political unity began soon after the defeat of Napoleon in 1815 and continued until 1870. The northern Kingdom of Piedmont took the lead in the process, aided by a wide range of nationalists from throughout the peninsula.

Question: How was Italian unification complicated by the influence of the Roman Catholic Church?

War with Austria   With an agreement secured, Cavour provoked the Austrians into declaring war in April 1859. In the ensuing conflict, French and Piedmontese forces quickly conquered Lombardy and the city of Milan. The initial military successes were not exploited, however. By June, Napoleon III grew fearful that Prussia might intervene on behalf of Austria, and he signed an armistice with the Austrians, leaving Cavour and his king with a good deal less territory than they had hoped to secure. Unexpectedly, however, revolutionary governments in the neighboring Italian states of Parma, Modena, Tuscany, and the papal provinces of the Romagna voted to join the expanded Italian state, making Piedmont-Sardinia the dominant power in northern Italy and giving Cavour additional support for the overall goal of uniting the entire peninsula.

Piedmont's success against Austria inspired rebels in the southern Italian Kingdom of the Two Sicilies to take action against their Bourbon king, Francis II (r. 1859–1861). Led by Giuseppe Garibaldi (1807–1882), the island of Sicily was quickly liberated. Garibaldi then crossed to the Italian mainland and, welcomed by a jubilant population, captured the capital city of Naples in September 1860 without a fight. With all of southern Italy under his control, Garibaldi decided to attack Rome and its French garrison. This decision provoked Cavour to intervene. Cavour disliked Garibaldi's republicanism, his commitment to gender and racial equality, and his defense of the right of workers to organize. In exchange for a commitment not to occupy Rome, Napoleon III allowed the Piedmontese army to occupy all of the Papal States outside of a small enclave around the city of Rome. When these lands, together with Naples and Sicily, voted for union with Piedmont, Garibaldi voluntarily surrendered his newly won territories to King Victor Emmanuel, who was proclaimed king of Italy.

Venetia and Rome   Cavour died in 1861, but the quest for complete national unity continued. Pope Pius IX (r. 1846–1878) remained in control of the city of Rome thanks to the protection of French troops, while Austria still ruled the northeast province of Venetia. Rome was the most intractable issue. Italian nationalists could not conceive of an independent Italy without Rome as its capital. Church authorities vehemently rejected the idea that the administrative heart of the Roman Catholic Church should become the capital of a Western European nation-state. After 1848, compromise seemed unlikely. A war between Prussia and Austria in 1866 solved the Venetian problem: Italy sided with the victorious Prussians and was rewarded with the contested province. Four years later Italian troops wrested Rome from the pope after Napoleon III was obliged to withdraw his garrison with the outbreak of war between France and Prussia. France's defeat at the hands of the superior Prussian army led to the fall of Napoleon III and the end of centuries of French involvement in Italian affairs.

Unfulfilled Promises   The long struggle for Italian unification had been undertaken with the implicit understanding that a future nation-state would afford its citizens all of the benefits of economic modernization. Hopes were raised that the new government would provide education, jobs, and an improved standard of living. Unfortunately for Italians, the high expectations were never met. Illiteracy rates remained high, especially in the rural south, and only about 2 million males had the right to vote in a country with a total population of almost 28 million. The king appointed the prime minister and the members of the upper house of parliament, who served for life. A lower house was elected, but its members tended to ignore the concerns of the rural peasants, who formed the majority of the population but lacked the right to vote. A great deal of localism remained, with northern industrial workers and illiterate peasants feeling little patriotic allegiance to the state. In addition, the Roman Catholic Church refused to recognize the legitimacy of the new state and warned Catholics not to participate in national politics.

Politicians claimed that Italy had become one of the great powers after the country joined with Germany and Austria in a defensive alliance in 1882. However, an 1896 military disaster in Abyssinia (modern Ethiopia) marked Italy as the only European power to have lost a war to an African opponent. By 1914, Italy had failed to achieve even one-quarter of the industrial strength that Britain enjoyed. Much of the population did not see the benefits of industrialization in their daily lives. On the eve of World War I their sovereign nation was a place where nationalism had yet to transplant centuries of provincialism, conservatism, and poverty.

The Creation of Modern Germany

Otto von Bismarck   Just as the Italian quest for national unity was guided by the pragmatic Cavour after the failed revolutions of 1848, in Prussia an aristocratic practitioner of *Realpolitik* (power politics) took the lead in the broader German struggle to achieve national unity. Otto von Bismarck (1815–1898) was a conservative aristocrat who believed that the king of Prussia, William I (r. 1861–1888), ruled by divine right and that society's natural leaders (landed aristocrats called Junker in Prussia) should determine the shape of any future national German state. Bismarck's appointment as chancellor (prime minister) of Prussia took place at the height of a constitutional struggle between King William I, who wished to reorganize the Prussian army as a counter to Austrian power, and the liberals in the Prussian assembly, who refused to approve the funds to pay for the king's proposal. Bismarck secured the backing of the army

Otto von Bismarck   Bismarck was the most influential European statesman during the period 1850 to 1890. He employed military force in order to unify Germany under Prussian leadership, but worked to maintain peace in Europe after 1871. *Franz von Lenbach (1836–1904) "Prince Otto von Bismark in uniform with Prussian helmet." Canvas. Kunsthistorisches Museum, Gemaeldegalerie, Vienna, Austria. Photograph © Erich Lessing/Art Resource, NY*

and his fellow Junkers, brusquely violated the constitution, and ordered that taxes be raised despite parliament's opposition to fund the reforms. Bismarck was gambling that the liberal members of the Prussian parliament would forgive his extraconstitutional actions if he could create a larger, more prosperous German state under the leadership of Prussia.

Not willing to wait on events, the Prussian chancellor, like Cavour in Piedmont-Sardinia, moved quickly to demonstrate Prussia's new claims to leadership. In 1864 Prussia declared war on Denmark when the Danish government tried to incorporate two formerly autonomous German-speaking territories, Schleswig and Holstein, which had long been ruled by the Danish crown, into the Danish national state. Austria was reluctantly drawn into the quarrel on the side of Prussia when Bismarck skillfully portrayed the conflict as an issue of broader German nationalism. After Denmark was defeated, the two provinces were placed under the joint rule of Prussia and Austria. This proved to be an unworkable situation that was bound to lead to friction between the two powers.

War with Austria   Austria, with its large population and varied territories, viewed itself as the leader of the German Confederation. During the 1830s many member states of the Confederation had entered into a customs union *(Zollverein)* that abolished all tariff barriers. By 1853, Austria was the only German state that did not accept the union, and when the economic benefits of the *Zollverein* began to become apparent, the movement for greater political unity under Prussian leadership intensified. Bismarck began to quarrel with the Austrian leadership over the disposition of Schleswig and Holstein while simultaneously winning support from the Italians by supporting their claim to the province of Venetia and from the Russians by supporting the tsar's suppression of a Polish rebellion.

In 1866 Austria declared war on its ambitious Prussian neighbor, convinced that now was the time to reassert the Habsburg's role as the leader of the German-speaking peoples. It was a gigantic miscalculation. Superior Prussian military technology, greater troop mobility due to more efficient rail transport, and better generalship led to a humiliating defeat for the Austrians after just seven weeks of fighting. Under the terms of the Treaty of Prague, Prussia expelled Austria from the German Confederation and annexed a number of smaller German states that had supported Austria in the conflict. However, unwilling to humiliate the vanquished and thus foster a desire for revenge mentality, Bismarck resisted the call of his king and generals to annex Austrian territories.

In the aftermath of this stunning military triumph, most Prussian legislators forgave Bismarck's earlier anticonstitutional sins. The cause of national unification, once the cornerstone of liberal ideology, had been co-opted by the conservative Bismarck. The government moved to found a new North German Confederation that featured a legislative assembly (the *Reichstag*) whose members were elected by universal manhood suffrage. This concession to democratic forms, however, did little to hide the fact that the Confederation was really an autocratic state in which the chancellor (Bismarck) served at the discretion of the king. The legislature was denied control over the military and, more importantly, over the budget. An important transformation took place in

Map 20–2   The Unification of Germany   Under the leadership of Prussia and guided by Bismarck, the German nation was created in 1871. The new state quickly rose to a preeminent position in Europe, becoming a leader in industry and empire.

Question: Given its location, why did Germany seek to maintain close relations with the Habsburg Empire?

Prussian political culture in the aftermath of the war. Most liberals abandoned their decades-long struggle for responsible constitutional government and joined the call for greater political and cultural unity. While Bismarck's accomplishments were exceptional, his agenda was not yet complete. A number of south German (and Catholic) states remained outside of the Confederation, and Bismarck now focused on strategies that were likely to persuade them to accept Prussian leadership by stirring up a greater sense of German nationalism (see Map 20–2).

War with France   Germany's "Iron Chancellor" did not have to wait long for a new opportunity to further his nation-building goals. Napoleon III and French public opinion were alarmed by the rapid rise of Prussian power. In 1870, when the Spanish crown was offered to a cousin of Prussian King William I, the French, who feared encirclement by German rulers, insisted that the German candidate decline the offer. A diplomatic crisis ensued. Bismarck edited a crucial telegram that made it appear that the Prussian king had insulted the French ambassador (something that had not actually occurred). The telegram was then made public, infuriating French public opinion and provoking France into declaring war on July 19.

As in the case of Bismarck's quarrel with Austria, on paper it looked as though the opposition (in this case France) possessed far greater resources and military might. However, Bismarck's gamble again paid off. The South German states came to the aid of their northern neighbors, putting aside their historic differences with the Protestant North. Rapid German military victories followed, and the French emperor himself was captured after the Prussians encircled a French army at Sedan on September 1. Upon hearing news of the emperor's dilemma, liberals in Paris declared the establishment of a republic and unwisely refused to end the war. Paris was besieged and forced to surrender in January 1871. Meeting at Versailles in the wake of this conquest, the assembled German princes declared that William I was now kaiser (emperor) of a unified German empire.

War and the Nation-State   Given the importance of nationalism as an ideological force during the second half of the nineteenth century, it is surprising that European wars were not more frequent and protracted. Most governments were prepared to go to war to protect or expand their alleged national interests, and new military hardware was readily available to states whose buoyant economies allowed for a more robust international posture. The wars that did occur on the continent in the century after Napoleon's fall in 1815 were comparatively brief affairs (months, not years, in duration) thanks in large measure to the overwhelming military superiority of one of the combatants. Even casualties were relatively light. In 1866, for example, the year when Prussia handily defeated Austria, more people died from cholera than from battlefield injuries. The total number of dead and wounded at the 1870 battle of Sedan (where Emperor Napoleon of France was captured) was 26,000, and only 9,000 of these were German. The only exception to this pattern occurred in America, where more than 600,000 died in a four-year civil war.

The impact of nineteenth-century European wars on civilian populations and on national economies was also generally light. The normal "campaigning" season began in May and ran through September. Despite the use of modern rail transport to move men and material, fighting was normally concentrated in a small geographical area. Most of the population in a country at war was unlikely to experience any immediate disruption of daily life unless they happened to live near the battle zones. Unlike previous centuries, civilians did not suffer at the hands of undisciplined armies bent upon pillaging food and destroying the enemy's transportation and supply network.

Perspectives on the desirability of war tended to reflect class interests and values. Middle-class businessmen were prone to disparage military adventures. They believed that military conflict disrupted normal business channels, manufacture, and opportunities for international trade. With the obvious exception of large arms manufacturers, producers of industrial goods and agricultural products looked upon war as the betrayer of capitalism, ushering in periods of political and economic uncertainty. In particular, international businesses stood to lose money in the event of war between European neighbors. Across the continent, politicians who favored a "peace policy" commanded broad support from the middle class.

Aristocrats and traditional landed elites were less troubled by the prospect of international conflict. These were men who staffed the embassies, served as high-ranking military officers, and held seats in the appointive or hereditary upper chamber of the national legislature. War and training for war had been the special preserve of the aristocracy for centuries, and even with the rise of political democracy in most Western European states by 1900, the politics of deference continued to play an important role in the life of each nation-state. Foreign policy, issues of war and peace, remained the preserve of the monarch and his closest advisors.

These traditional leaders were often joined in their bellicose sentiments by a wide array of intellectuals. According to Walter Bagehot (1826–1877), an influential journalist and interpreter of the British constitution during Queen Victoria's reign, the strongest nations were also the best nations. Samuel Smiles (1812–1904), the author of an immensely popular book called *Self-Help* (1859), sang the virtues of military drill and discipline. Preparation for war transformed complacent citizens into vigilant patriots. Smiles believed that if the entire population were exposed to the rigors of military training, "the country would be stronger, the people would be soberer, and thrift would become much more habitual." The influential Swiss historian Jacob Burckhardt (1818–1897) was convinced that long periods of peace weakened the national spirit. War provided opportunities for heroism, collective moral rejuvenation, and commitment to something higher than bourgeois individualism. Even the novelist George Eliot (born Mary Ann Evans, 1819–1880) remarked that the German victory over France in 1870 represented the triumph of progressive forces over decadent ones.

The widely shared belief that warfare was a legitimate and relatively low-cost means of national advancement continued to inform European consciousness during the high tide of global imperialism. As the great powers extended their territorial and economic sway across Africa and Asia, the willingness to use sophisticated military forces to achieve strategic objectives prepared the way for an increasingly truculent international climate during the first two decades of the twentieth century. The myths of the cleansing value of military conflict and of the tendency of new technology to make wars short would only be dispelled after the outbreak of World War I in 1914.

Bismarck Ascendant, 1870–1890   As the emerging national power in Central Europe, Germany combined autocratic government with industrial prowess and cultural self-assurance. While the German Empire was federal in structure, with certain powers reserved for its member states, the two-chamber legislature did not enjoy significant political power. The franchise was extended to all adult males, but universal manhood suffrage did not translate into democratic rule. Bismarck remained chancellor of the German Empire until 1890. Like the rest of the cabinet, he served at the discretion of the kaiser or emperor. Foreign affairs remained the prerogative of the kaiser, while most important legislative initiatives began with the chancellor. A large conscript army was maintained in peacetime, led by Junker aristocrats. The higher ranks of the civil service also remained the preserve of the aristocracy, which in turn helped to shape a government culture committed to the glorification of the state, not the extension of individual rights and liberties.

The Social Question   With unification secured, Bismarck turned his attention to pressing domestic challenges in a country undergoing rapid industrialization. The chancellor remained disdainful of political democracy, and he viewed political parties

Church-State Conflict   The struggle between the imperial German government and the Catholic Church was one of the most intense cultural conflicts of the late nineteenth century. In this cartoon from the 1870s, Pope Pius IX and Otto von Bismarck, the German chancellor, play a game of political chess. Each piece on the chessboard represents a German church leader whom Bismarck sought to remove from public life. Bismarck is clearly winning the game, while the Pope considers his next move.

as little more than selfish interest groups that were to be manipulated for the benefit of larger state interests. Bismarck's campaign against the Catholic Church during the 1870s, called the *Kulturkampf* (struggle for civilization), was an energetic example of his approach to political alliances. The chancellor was convinced that German Catholics, who constituted almost 40% of the nation's population, owed their first allegiance to the pope. He was joined in this controversial position by German liberals, most of whom objected to the role of the Catholic Church in German political and cultural life. Indeed, for liberals the Church was the enemy of the modern secular state. Bismarck supported liberal legislation that expelled the Jesuits from Germany, instituted civil marriage and state oversight of the Catholic and Protestant churches, and favored secular state education over religious schools. In response, German Catholics fought back by organizing the Center Party, which became one of the largest parties in the *Reichstag*, the elected branch of the German federal parliament.

Bismarck also attacked German socialists, arguing that members of the German Social Democratic Party, or SPD, were, like German Catholics, untrustworthy nationalists, since socialists believed in the international brotherhood of the working class. Three years after its founding in 1875, the chancellor outlawed the party, declaring that its internationalist and anticapitalist views represented a fundamental threat to the security and prosperity of the German Empire. He used the excuse of two assassination attempts against Emperor William I in 1878 to make his case that socialist internationalism had to be destroyed. In a calculated effort to weaken the appeal of socialism among the German working class, Bismarck supported legislation designed to address a number of problems caused by industrialization. During the 1880s, the government approved legislation instituting accident, sickness, and old age insurance. Contributions to the old age and disability plans came from individual workers and employers, but the state organized the plans. Bismarck's brand of paternalistic "state socialism" improved the quality of life for German workers, but it did not succeed in marginalizing the SPD. Despite the chancellor's repressive measures, individual socialist candidates continued to run for and win seats in the *Reichstag*. In 1891 the party adopted an official statement, called the Erfurt Program, which reaffirmed its Marxist faith in the ultimate destruction of capitalism. The party simultaneously pledged to pursue this goal through the existing political process. Similarly, the Catholic Center Party continued to win electoral victories in the wake of the *Kulturkampf*. In 1878 Bismarck quietly entered into negotiations with Pope Leo XIII (r. 1878–1903) and accepted an agreement that put an end to official religious bigotry.

Kaiser William II and German Power

In 1888 William II (r. 1888–1918) succeeded to the throne. The new emperor clashed with Bismarck over foreign policy and over the chancellor's antisocialist campaign. William II believed that the best way to win the allegiance of the German worker was to provide him with tangible evidence of German greatness through an aggressive policy overseas. Within two years of ascending the throne, the kaiser dismissed Bismarck and replaced him with a more pliable chancellor. Antisocialist legislation was allowed to expire, and the SPD became the biggest Marxist political party in Europe. Over the next quarter century, German industrial growth rivaled and in some areas exceeded rates in Britain and the United States, while Germany pursued the kaiser's imperial ambitions in Africa and Asia (see Chapter 21, "Global Empire and European Culture"). The lives of German workers continued to improve during these decades, which strengthened the regime's legitimacy. However, German economic growth and military power were built upon a political foundation that was less responsive to the give and take of the parliamentary process than either its British or American counterparts. The government allied itself firmly with powerful industrial and landowning interests, while the kaiser's desire to build a fleet comparable to Britain's was predicated on the assumption that the German Empire must extend beyond the confines of the German-speaking lands of Europe.

Constitutional Change in France and Britain

The Second French Empire

Louis Napoleon Bonaparte (1808–1873), the nephew of Napoleon I, came to power in France in the aftermath of the failed 1848 revolution. Elected president of the Second French Republic in 1848, he promised to restore order and prosperity to a country torn between urban political radicals and the more conservative peasantry. Within three years of his election, however, Bonaparte dismantled the republic in a *coup d'etat* rather than accept a constitutional requirement that prohibited the president from running for a second term. Resistance to his usurpation of power was light, although the government subsequently deported thousands of opponents. Once firmly in control, Louis Napoleon held two plebiscites in which over 90% of the electorate affirmed his assumption of hereditary power as Emperor Napoleon III (Napoleon I's son had died in 1832) in December 1852.

During the first decade of imperial rule, Napoleon cracked down on opposition groups, censored the press, and denied the national legislature any substantive political power. Controls were relaxed after 1860, however, as the emperor sought to encourage industrialization and economic expansion. Press restrictions were removed, individual liberties guaranteed, unions permitted, and political prisoners pardoned. Paris, once an unsanitary and dangerous city, was rebuilt into a modern urban showpiece, with broad boulevards, parks, and impressive public buildings testifying to the power and prestige of the regime. Napoleon III's advisors were convinced that economic prosperity could eliminate France's social problems and political divisions. Charity hospitals, facilities for the elderly, new housing stock, schools, and a network of railroads and canals all seemed to suggest that quality of life issues were uppermost in the mind of the emperor and his closest advisors.

However, while his domestic improvements won the emperor broad popular support, his ambition extended beyond the boundaries of the nation-state. For the first time since the defeat of Napoleon I, France became a significant military force beyond its own borders. Napoleon joined Britain in the costly Crimean War against Russia in 1853, intervened in Italy on the side of Piedmont and against Austria in 1859, and even attempted to establish the archduke Maximilian, a Habsburg prince, as Emperor of Mexico in 1862. This last venture ended in disaster in 1867 when the French army withdrew and Emperor Maximilian (1832–1867) was executed by Mexican nationalists led by Benito Juarez (1806–1872). The rise of Prussia further eroded Napoleon's prestige. In an effort to bolster his regime, the emperor instituted new reforms and asked the French people to vote on a more liberal constitution. This was overwhelmingly approved in May 1870. Two months later, however, the ailing emperor blundered into a disastrous military conflict with Prussia.

The Third French Republic French national pride was deeply wounded by the humiliation suffered at the hands of the Prussian army in September 1870. The capture of Napoleon at Sedan sealed the fate of the Second Empire. In Paris, what began as a refusal to accept an armistice with the Prussians escalated into a rejection of the new French provisional government. The "Paris Commune" included republicans and socialists who fought a bitter defensive campaign against both the Germans, who cut off supplies to the city and then bombarded it, and their own countrymen. Elections in early 1871 led to the formation of a provisional government that was committed to ending the war and to pacifying the defiant Parisians. To end the war, France ceded Alsace and most of Lorraine to the new German Empire. To regain control of Paris, government forces attacked the city and executed over 20,000 resistance fighters who were hastily buried in mass graves. Humbled by Germany and torn apart by bloody civil war in the capital, France in 1871 was a nation-state divided between monarchists and republicans. Quarrels among the monarchists over who should be king allowed the republicans to set up the Third Republic, but it was an unstable regime with a multitude of parties and shifting political alliances.

Despite the appearance of chronic instability and the reality of a number of embarrassing government scandals, the liberals and conservatives who vied for power nonetheless managed to introduce a number of significant reforms during the 1870s and 1880s. Compulsory public education at the primary level spread a common set of patriotic values, while the historic role of the Catholic Church in education was curbed. A new professional military force was established under a compulsory service law. This helped to bolster national identity and loyalty to the state.

Key Developments in the Rise of European Nationalism	
1848	Revolutions in most of Western and Central Europe
1866	Austro-Prussian War
1870–1871	Franco-Prussian War
1870	Third Republic is proclaimed in France
1871	Unified German Empire proclaimed
1871	Italy is unified

Domestic Crises   The durability of the Third Republic was severely tested by two political crises of the late nineteenth century. The first involved a direct challenge to the integrity of the Republic. When General George Boulanger (1837–1891), backed by disgruntled right-wing supporters, undertook a national campaign to restore authoritarian, one-man rule to France, the defenders of parliamentary government were placed on the defensive. Despite his appeal to monarchists and elements in the military, Boulanger failed to win sufficient popular support, and he fled the country in 1889. The second challenge involved the integrity of the French justice system. In 1894 a Jewish army officer was accused—falsely, as it turned out—of selling military secrets to the Germans. Captain Alfred Dreyfus (1859–1935) was tried for treason in a military court, convicted, and sentenced to a life of solitary confinement at Devil's Island, an overseas penal colony. (This was known as the **Dreyfus Affair**.) In the midst of the trial, a wave of xenophobia and **anti-Semitism** swept across the country. Most of the country seemed satisfied with the conviction, but a number of prominent republicans, including the novelist Emile Zola (1840–1902) and a future prime minister, Georges Clemenceau (1841–1929), argued that the evidence against Dreyfus was fabricated. The political right, however, vociferously defended the conviction. The conviction was overturned in 1906, but not before deep fissures emerged in the political culture of the nation. The anti-Semitism associated with the case continued

Trial of Alfred Dreyfus   Anti-Semitism was widespread in late nineteenth-century Europe. Captain Alfred Dreyfus, standing on the right at his military trial, was convicted in 1894 and exonerated in 1906.

to play a poisonous role in French politics, especially in German-occupied France (1940–1944) during World War II.

In the three decades prior to the outbreak of World War I, France's economy did not match that of Britain and Germany. Although some regions of the country were heavily industrialized, France remained a nation of artisans and peasant farmers. Labor unions, especially those focusing on the unskilled, remained relatively small and decentralized. Despite the efforts of trade unionists and socialists, the country lagged behind in welfare provision and the regulation of workplace conditions. French socialists and anarchists engaged in a number of strikes in the early twentieth century, but in general their deep suspicion of politics limited their ability to influence the formulation of national policy. The church, the army, the unions, and the political parties all appeared to lack appeal much beyond their own particular constituencies. Ironically, the onset of a horrific war in 1914 would finally galvanize the nation under one patriotic banner.

The Advent of Democracy in Britain   Great Britain's mid-century status as the world's leading industrial power was achieved within the context of peaceful political change. While the monarchy under Queen Victoria (r. 1837–1901) remained the symbolic heart of the political system, real power had shifted to the House of Commons, where two major parties, the Liberals and Conservatives, vied for leadership. In 1867 the Conservative Prime Minister Benjamin Disraeli (1804–1881) co-opted a liberal plan and introduced legislation to expand the electorate by approximately 1 million voters, from 1.5 to 2.5 million. Both parties recognized that further democratization was key to economic progress, and Disraeli hoped to win the support of the working and lower middle class with his proposal. His efforts were to bear fruit in the long run for the Conservative Party, but in 1868 the Liberal Party, under William Gladstone (1809–1898), won control of the House of Commons in national elections.

Gladstone's first ministry (1868–1874) marked the high tide of liberal reform in Victorian Britain. The monopoly that members of the state church, the Church of England, had long enjoyed over access to university education, civil service posts, and military appointments was broken. Competitive examinations now determined appointment to government service, Oxford and Cambridge Universities admitted students without reference to religion, and a secret ballot was introduced. Gladstone's reform program sought to create a society in which skill and merit, not patronage or family lineage, determined the bounds of economic, educational, and professional opportunity. While Disraeli and Gladstone were intense rivals, they both sponsored important social legislation. When Disraeli returned to power in 1874 to 1880, for example, public health, housing, and trade union legislation all improved conditions for the working class. As leader of the Conservatives, Disraeli was more sympathetic to the idea of using state power to solve social problems, while the Liberals under Gladstone focused more on individual initiative.

In 1884 Gladstone sponsored another reform bill. Now almost two-thirds of all males, irrespective of whether they owned property, had the right to vote. The extension of democracy transformed the political process. To appeal to the new mass electorate, party leaders now took to the rails and visited cities and towns throughout the country during political campaigns. A new form of political journalism arose, as reporters for serious broadsheet, and less serious tabloid, newspapers began to accompany candidates at mass rallies that drew thousands of supporters. Gladstone also attempted to address the long-standing demands of Irish nationalists who called for the end of British rule in Ireland. The prime minister attempted to pass home rule bills for Ireland in the House of Commons in 1886 and again in 1893, but the legislation was defeated on both occasions. In Northern Ireland, Protestant politicians who opposed home rule feared that the Catholic majority in Ireland would be hostile to the Protestant population, and many of these politicians threatened forceful resistance if Irish home rule became law.

In 1901 Britain's Trades Union Congress founded the Labour Party to advance the political interests of the working class. In the general election of 1906, Labour won 29 seats in the House of Commons. Further to the left of the Labour Party was the Fabian Society, a socialist organization founded in 1884 and led by a number of important non-Marxist intellectuals. Sidney (1859–1947) and Beatrice (1858–1943) Webb, George Bernard Shaw (1856–1950), and H. G. Wells (1866–1946) were among those who sought to convince their countrymen that they could achieve collective ownership of the means of production in a gradualist, peaceful manner. This was the thesis of an influential book called *Evolutionary Socialism* (1899) written by the German author Eduard Bernstein (1850–1932). Bernstein was familiar with the British Fabians, and his book called into question the need for the sort of revolutionary activity required by orthodox Marxists.

The socialists remained a tiny minority in Britain before World War I, in no small part because the major political parties had taken steps to respond to working class demands. When the aristocratic House of Lords objected to the growing cost of government-sponsored welfare plans, the House of Commons, in alliance with the king, passed the Parliament Act of 1911. This was a groundbreaking piece of legislation that limited the legislative veto of the Lords. When large strikes occurred involving the railways, docks, factories, or mines, the government intervened to mediate the dispute. By 1914, most Britons enjoyed free elementary education; minimum wage laws; accident, health, and unemployment insurance; and the enormous psychological advantage of belonging to the world's greatest imperial power. For most British voters and trade union members, political democracy and industrial capitalism appeared to be the key to global power and material prosperity at the start of the twentieth century.

The Waning of the Habsburg, Russian, and Ottoman Empires

Nationalism and Dual Monarchy
Prussia's resounding victory over Austria in 1866 signaled the permanent eclipse of Habsburg leadership within the German Confederation. The military debacle, coming so quickly after defeat at the hands of France and Piedmont-Sardinia in 1859, reflected the corrosive power of modern nationalism in a multilingual, multicultural, and multiethnic empire. Unlike any of the other great powers, the Austrian Empire represented the negation of the modern nation-state with its German, Magyar, Czech, Slovak, Polish, Croat, Italian, Slovene, Serb, and Romanian populations. All owed allegiance to the Habsburg emperor, Francis Joseph (r. 1848–1916). However, during the second half of the nineteenth century, a heightened sense of history and culture led most of the non-German subject groups to challenge the legitimacy of the imperial structure (see Map 20–3).

The usual instruments of repression—a secret police and the military—were utilized in an attempt to quash liberal dissent after the revolutions of 1848, but these blunt instruments swiftly devolved into a rearguard action. Some modest reforms, such as the establishment of a bicameral parliament with an elective lower house, had been agreed to by the conservative Francis Joseph, but no significant steps were taken to integrate non-Germans into the highest levels of administration. Many Austrian Germans were disdainful of the various minorities within the empire. The Roman Catholic Church continued to wield considerable control over education, while the landed aristocracy remained the dominant force in local affairs. Francis Joseph appointed government ministers and the members of the upper chamber of parliament; when the imperial parliament (the *Reichsrat*) was not in session, the emperor could rule by royal decree.

In the immediate aftermath of the Prussian victory in 1866, Emperor Francis Joseph was forced to make significant political concessions to the Magyars of Hungary, the most powerful non-German national group. In 1867 a compromise (*Ausgleich*) was reached whereby Austria and Hungary were split into two territories, a dual monarchy, under Francis Joseph, who was named king of Hungary and emperor of Austria. Joint ministers appointed by the monarch handled foreign affairs, defense, and finance. Beyond this,

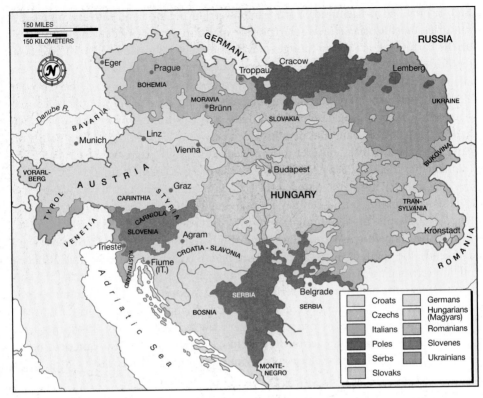

Map 20–3 The Habsburg Multiethnic Empire Nationalism posed a serious problem for the Habsburg rulers of the Austro-Hungarian Empire. While the Magyars of Hungary achieved significant autonomy in 1867, the aspirations of other ethnic groups remained unfulfilled.

Question: How does the Habsburg Empire illustrate the problems of nationalism in the late nineteenth century?

however, the Magyars won complete control over their internal affairs. Henceforth, Austria and Hungary had separate parliaments and prime ministers. The Magyars' success inspired other minorities, especially the Czechs, Romanians, Ruthenians, and Croatians, to press their claims for greater autonomy. By the close of the nineteenth century, the Austrian parliament became a political flashpoint where members disrupted meetings over the question of nationalist self-determination within the empire. The dual monarchy of Austria-Hungary failed to find a satisfactory solution to the dilemma. As a result, the authorities were unable to use the nationalist banner to solidify popular support for the government or promote industrial development. In a Europe of nation-states, Austria-Hungary remained a multiethnic state based on loyalty to a supranational dynasty—the Habsburgs. Ethnic tension and nationalist aspirations within the Habsburg lands would play a crucial role in the outbreak of World War I in 1914.

The Traditional Power: Russia, 1861–1914 Tsar Peter the Great's (r. 1682–1725) efforts to reform Russia from the top down, combined with Catherine the Great's (r. 1762–1796) early interest in Enlightenment ideas, seemed to suggest that the Russian

Empire qualified as a genuinely European power. During the eighteenth and nineteenth centuries, most Russian efforts at territorial expansion were focused, with great success, on the East, whereas Russian thought and Russian high culture looked to the West. After the defeat of Napoleon in 1815, it appeared as though Russian influence in European affairs would expand. Harsh control over Poland, regular bullying of the Ottoman Turks, and claims to a special relationship with the Christian peoples of the Balkans all signaled Russia's ongoing desire to be recognized as a preeminent European power. The hollow nature of the claim was demonstrated between 1854 and 1856, when poorly organized and led British and French forces defeated the Russians in the Crimean War (named after the Black Sea peninsula where the war was largely fought).

The military mismatch revealed the economic and technological backwardness of the Russian empire. At mid-century, more than 90% of the population lived at subsistence level. Despite the abolition of serfdom by Tsar Alexander II (r. 1855–1881) in 1861 (just two years before American President Abraham Lincoln declared that slavery was at an end), the plight of Russia's peasant population continued to deteriorate. While 22 million serfs secured legal freedom, they did not get land. Instead, portions of the land that the peasants had worked as serfs became the property of village communes, and the peasants who made up the communes had to compensate their former lords for whatever they were given. Most poor farmers fell into serious debt. It was not until 1906, in the aftermath of a serious revolution, that the government canceled the remaining debt and allowed the peasants to hold title to their own land.

Assassination and Repression   Tsar Alexander II attempted to appease Russia's small middle class and provincial aristocracy by establishing local political councils called *zemst'va*. He also encouraged the establishment of primary schools and instituted reforms in the military, reducing terms of enlistment to six years (down from 25) and enlisting the support of Western technical advisors. However, the tsar refused to allow the formation of a national legislative assembly. The Russian intellectual elite who were familiar with political developments in Western Europe insisted that genuine modernization required broader political participation. The tsar's intransigence led to the formation of terrorist cells. One of these, known as the People's Will, assassinated Alexander II in March 1881. The murder was the most infamous in a wave of assassinations and terrorist acts that had taken place. The new ruler, Tsar Alexander III (r. 1881–1894), responded to the terror by expanding the powers of the secret police, censoring the press, and rolling back many of his father's modest reforms. The regime sought to strengthen itself by identifying closely with Russian nationalism and by persecuting minority groups within the Russian Empire, especially Jews.

In one area alone did Alexander III demonstrate appreciation for the forces that were shaping the modern world. During the 1890s, the tsar committed his government to a program of rapid industrialization. Under the direction of an innovative finance minister, Sergei Witte (1849–1915), the government sponsored railroads and industrial plants. It also encouraged foreign investment. The French, eager to forge a defensive alliance with Russia, emerged as the key financiers. By 1900, foreigners owned much of the industrial plant in Russia. Yet, while productive capacity grew, the social inequalities and political re-

Russian Peasants after Emancipation   Although serfdom was abolished by Tsar Alexander II in 1861, the condition of the peasantry continued to deteriorate. In this painting peasants wait outside a government building while officials inside finish their lunch.

pression characteristic of absolutist regimes remained. Moscow, St. Petersburg, and a few other cities witnessed the emergence of a small industrial working class. Workers were denied political expression, however, and when a Marxist Social Democratic Party emerged in 1898, the regime drove its leaders into exile. One of the leaders of the Marxist exiles was Lenin (1870–1924), the future leader of the Communist Revolution in Russia. After being exiled to Siberia in 1895 (his brother had been executed by the government in 1887 for participating in a plot to murder the tsar), Lenin spent the years 1900 to 1917 in Switzerland, writing and organizing for revolution. In 1902 he wrote *What Is to Be Done?*, a call to establish a small, elite party of leaders who could guide an overwhelmingly peasant Russia to a proletarian revolution. In 1902 such a revolution seemed unlikely. Since Russia had only 3 million industrial workers out of a total population of 150 million in 1914, the Marxist program had little resonance beyond a few cities. At the start of the twentieth century, it remained to be seen whether Russia's reactionary monarchy could both modernize its economy and assuage worker discontent.

The early signals were not propitious. The new tsar, Nicholas II (r. 1894–1917), was not sympathetic to political reform. His government pursued an expansionist policy in East Asia at the expense of Japan, another rapidly industrializing power. In 1904 the two countries clashed in the Russo-Japanese War, and Russia was defeated on land and at sea. In the midst of these military setbacks, worker discontent, middle-class and student anger over the absence of constitutional government, and mutinies in the navy forced the tsar to set up a national parliament, called the Duma. Elections to the Duma took place, but the tsar retained control of foreign and military affairs, finance, and the appointment of government ministers. The gesture toward constitutional government had been made under duress. Once the embarrassment of defeat at the hands of the Japanese was over, the imperial government muddled along without any vision or long-term program to face the challenges of the modern world.

The Ottoman Failure

The Ottoman Failure Throughout the nineteenth century, the absolutist Ottoman state struggled to maintain its considerable holdings in the Balkans, the Near East, and North Africa. Not unlike its Habsburg neighbor to the north, the sultans ruled over a multiethnic and religiously diverse population numbering some 40 million at the start of the nineteenth century. However, the spread of nationalist ideas, together with the ambitions of the great powers, threatened the territorial integrity of this once-powerful Muslim empire. Centuries of autocratic rule had bred corruption and inefficiency at the highest levels of government in Istanbul. Younger, Western-educated reformers attempted to introduce political and economic reforms in the 1870s, but Sultan Abdul Hamid II (r. 1876–1909) refused to embrace these efforts. His oppressive reign featured a complete rejection of the legal and constitutional changes being adopted in the industrializing states of Western Europe.

Nationalism had its most disruptive impact in the Ottoman Empire's Balkan territories, which were mostly Christian. Beginning with Greece in the 1820s and continuing into the 1870s, a series of Balkan rebellions and wars against Turkish rule placed enormous strain on the fiscal and military resources of the empire. A war between Russia and Turkey (1877–1878) resulted in complete Turkish defeat. Brokered by Bismarck, the European powers then met in Berlin and recognized the full independence of Serbia, Montenegro, and Romania. They also awarded Cyprus to Britain and placed the Turkish provinces of Bosnia and Herzegovina under Austrian administrative protection. In 1885 an autonomous principality of Bulgaria was created, which achieved full independence as a kingdom in 1908 (see Map 20–4).

In the nineteenth century Europe's great powers were a constant threat to the integrity of the Ottoman Empire. There had never been any love lost between Christian Europe and the Muslim Turks. The Muslim intellectual elite were staunchly anti-Western, while the sultans, as leaders of the largest Muslim empire, viewed themselves as caliphs, spiritual heirs of the Prophet Muhammad. Claims to absolute power aside, Ottoman military strength was predicated on the constant acquisition of new territories; once the process of expansion stopped as it did in the seventeenth century, the resources of the empire began to atrophy. The empire lacked a vibrant middle class, and the sultans failed to promote commercial enterprise. To finance its activities, the government contracted loans from Western governments and private financiers. By 1881, however, the empire had become so indebted that the great powers forced the sultan to create the Ottoman Public Debt Administration, an agency staffed by foreigners and empowered to collect revenues from various state monopolies. At the turn of the twentieth century, foreign investors controlled Ottoman banking, railways, mining, and public utilities. For a small core of Turkish nationalists, this situation was intolerable and humiliating.

In 1909 a military coup led by reformist army officers, "the Young Turks," ousted Abdul Hamid II. The rebels installed a compliant successor named Muhammed V (r. 1909–1918), but their efforts to cultivate a sense of Turkish nationalism throughout

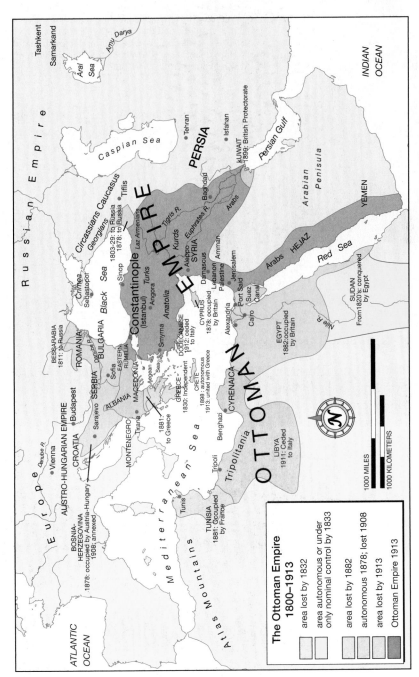

Map 20–4 The Decline of the Ottoman Empire, 1800–1913 Through the seventeenth and eighteenth centuries, the Ottoman Empire was one of the world's largest and most powerful. But by the nineteenth century, competition from Europe, nationalism in the Balkan regions, and autocratic and corrupt rule led to the empire's steady decline.

Question: Approximately what percentage of the Ottoman Empire was lost between 1800 and 1913?

The Ottoman Empire 1800–1913

- area lost by 1832
- area autonomous or under only nominal control by 1833
- area lost by 1882
- autonomous 1878; lost 1908
- area lost by 1913
- Ottoman Empire 1913

1000 MILES
1000 KILOMETERS

Abdul Hamid II, Turkish Sultan The leader of the Ottoman Empire from 1876–1909, Abdul Hamid II presided over the massacre of tens of thousands of Armenians in the mid-1890s. The massacre earned the sultan the nickname, "The Great Assassin." Slow to embrace reform, Abdul Hamid II was overthrown by the military coup of the "Young Turks" in 1909.

the empire failed. As in the Habsburg Empire, a variety of subject peoples resented the centuries-old hegemony of the Turks, be they divine-right caliphs or reformist military men. Albanians, Arabs, Greeks, Armenians, Kurds, and others demanded independence. From 1910 until they decided to cast their lot with the Germans in World War I in 1914, the "Young Turk" leadership found itself in constant crisis and regional war, especially with its remaining Balkan subjects.

The United States and Western Europe

Two Economies During their first 75 years of independence, the former British colonies in North America had adapted their federal system of government to accommodate the economic priorities of two separate economic zones. In the northern states, independent small farmers produced for an internal market, while the inhabitants of coastal cities like Boston, New York, and Philadelphia provided capital and free labor for a vibrant commercial economy. Starting in the 1820s with canal building and shifting by mid-century to railroad development, the northern United States was poised for industrial development. By 1861, the northern states were home to almost 90% of the country's manufacturing establishments. In the southern states, the economy remained predominantly agricultural, with large planters producing cash crops like tobacco and cotton for an overseas market. Labor in the South was divided between poor whites (many of whom were illiterate) and unfree black slaves. Southern leaders, acutely sensitive to antislavery arguments in the North and wary of Britain's efforts after 1815 to interdict the trans-Atlantic slave trade, emphasized the rights of states to control their own affairs. Northern states that wanted federal aid for transportation and infrastructure projects tended to support a more interventionist role for the national government.

Civil War The continuation of chattel slavery in the South was the catalyst for a secession movement that gained force during the 1850s. Southern slaveholders viewed abolitionism as an assault on their economic and political power. They argued that the United States was the states united, a voluntary alliance of sovereign states. When Abraham Lincoln (1809–1865) was elected president in 1860, his opposition to the spread of slavery led to a breakup of the union and to a bloody civil war. Unlike the lightning victories of Prussia over Austria and France in 1866 and 1870, the American conflict turned into a five-year war of attrition in which some 600,000 lives were lost. In the end, the superior numbers and industrial might of the North prevailed. The union was preserved, and the slave system abolished, although free blacks remained subject to appalling discrimination for the next century.

The half century following the Civil War was marked by three significant developments in the United States, all of which affected Western Europe. First and foremost, America's growing industrial power transformed the material and social landscape. Railroad developers enjoyed lavish government subsidies, free right of way over public land, and plentiful European investment capital. By 1914, British, French, and German venture capitalists had invested some $12 billion in American industry. The telegraph, and after 1870 the telephone, began to shrink distances between American cities. Steel, coal, oil, and textile production increased dramatically, employing thousands in ever-expanding production facilities in the North. By the start of the twentieth century, one man or a small group of men dominated most major industries. The Scottish immigrant Andrew Carnegie (1835–1919) controlled the steel industry, John D. Rockefeller (1839–1937) consolidated his hold over oil production and distribution, and J. P. Morgan (1837–1911) was the leading railroad magnate and banker. Income disparities between America's industrial elite and its working class were glaring in 1900. In response, "Progressive" reformers fought to raise wages, limit work hours, and enact health and safety requirements in the workplace. Both major political parties responded to the demand for change. Republican President Theodore Roosevelt (1858–1919) and Democratic President Woodrow Wilson (1856–1924) both incorporated elements of the Progressive agenda in their policies and legislative programs.

The second major development involved the changing demographic profile of the American republic after 1865. Immigration, in terms both of the numbers of new arrivals and the diversity of European countries from which they came, helped to create a truly multicultural society. In 1860 over 80% of all foreigners living in the United States were British, Irish, or German. Thirty years later this majority had shrunk to 64% of the total, and by 1920 that majority had become a minority of only 25%. New arrivals from Italy, Scandinavia, Eastern Europe, the Balkans, and Russia had altered the balance. Most of the new immigrants crowded into America's major coastal and industrial cities, there to become essential, albeit unappreciated, contributors to the nation's unprecedented industrial expansion. Opportunities for public education at the primary and secondary levels expanded after 1900, and the process of assimilating and "Americanizing" these new arrivals proceeded rapidly. As the United States prepared to take its place as one of the world's preeminent economic and military powers, it would make the transition within a democratic political framework where the state protected individual rights. The significance of this connection between great power status and responsible, constitutional government would not be lost on opponents of totalitarian political systems during the twentieth century.

The third development, westward expansion, was closely related to the first two. Westward expansion had been a focus of settlers in British North America since the

Immigrant Labor in the Building of the American Railroads   The extension of railroads was integral to the United States' westward expansion in the 1800s. Immigrant workers, such as the Chinese "coolies" in this photograph, performed much of the labor for railroad construction, usually enduring harsh working conditions.

mid-seventeenth century. Clashes with Native Americans, wars of empire against France and Spain during the eighteenth century, and the expropriation of Mexican lands in the Southwest during the 1840s had all fit the larger pattern of Western territorial aggrandizement. However, during the second half of the nineteenth century, Western railroad-building enabled thousands of Americans and recent immigrants to relocate to regions where they could find new economic opportunities. The mining and cattle industries benefited enormously from the new railroads. As population increased along the eastern seaboard, enterprising Midwestern farmers and cattle ranchers could move their products efficiently and profitably to market.

The obvious losers in the process of Western development were the Native Americans, who despite centuries of abuse still inhabited roughly one-half of the continental United States just before the start of the Civil War. Pressured to cede territory to white settlers and prospectors, the Plains Indians rose up against the government during the Civil War. After 1865, they were dealt with harshly. Forced to settle on reservations and to abandon their hunter-gatherer lives for settled agriculture, the Native American population dwindled. Those who remained were granted citizenship provided, according to the Dawes Severalty Act of 1877, that Indians "adopted the habits of civilized life."

White American attitudes toward native peoples assumed that traditional cultures were stagnant, uncreative, and even uncivilized. Lacking individualistic notions of property, failing to embrace a sedentary lifestyle, and following a spiritual order that did not accord with Western monotheism, the invasion and appropriation of Native American lands was seen as a progressive and enlightened undertaking. The Dawes Act assumed that a federal law could immediately transform an entire culture.

Nationalism and Race

The decline of Native American culture in the late nineteenth century is an important illustration of the diverging nature of nationalism. During the first half of the century, proponents of national identity and autonomy associated the movement with the Enlightenment emphasis on natural rights. Early nationalists such as Guiseppi Mazzini saw no contradiction in their call for human equality within a civil framework of sovereign territorial states.

The rhetoric of nationalism changed sharply in the late nineteenth century, however. An increasing emphasis on the nation as the repository of culture and values began to replace talk about individual rights and freedoms. The glorification of the state as the embodiment of particular racial values, a form of modern tribalism, also found a receptive audience. Extreme nationalists highlighted differences between peoples, not similarities, and it became popular to talk of superior and inferior races. Minority peoples were accused of defiling national culture, while neighboring states were viewed exclusively as rivals. Even democratic political institutions were attacked, especially by nationalists who feared that minority voters would hamper the state's exercise of its powers. Ethnicity became the barometer of good citizenship, and worship of the state and its core values emerged as a new secular religion.

Extremes in Germany   The rapid industrialization and rise to political power of Germany led some extremists to argue that the energy and dynamism of the new state was due to its unique cultural heritage. They maintained that since the days of the late Roman Empire, when the first Germanic peoples had migrated westward, the German *Volk* or people had demonstrated their superior genius for survival and the resilience and creativity of German culture. Many of the *Volkish* propagandists stressed the importance of race in history, claiming that everything from creativity to morality was intimately connected to racial characteristics. Racist thought contributed to an intellectual climate in Germany that fostered imperialism and, more immediately, anti-Semitism.

Disdain for and oppression of Jews had a long and tragic history in Europe. Portrayed as murderers of Christ and as disloyal subjects, Jewish communities throughout Europe were subject to periodic persecution and mob violence. During the Enlightenment, however, a lessening of the bigotry seemed to suggest that a more tolerant, cosmopolitan outlook might emerge. Most European countries eliminated legal restrictions on Jews, although informal discrimination continued. The great German Jewish scholar Moses Mendelssohn (1729–1786) urged his fellow Jews to accept the nation-states in which they lived and to become more active participants in European

Anti-Jewish Pogrom   A violent rampage against Jews in Russia in the 1880s. Jews suffered discrimination and persecution in Europe for many centuries, and in parts of Russia and Poland were still victimized by pogroms well into the twentieth century.

cultural life. Mendelssohn emphasized the connections between Christian and Jewish culture, and he sought to promote a sense of unity between the two traditions. By the 1880s, Jews had become prominent members of most professions and served in a variety of political offices in Western and Central Europe.

The social disruption and insecurity caused by industrialization, urbanization, and class tension, however, provided fertile ground for those who sought to reduce complex problems to simple, all-encompassing myths—and the myth of the evil and disloyal Jew was always close at hand. The worst treatment occurred in Eastern Europe, where over 70% of the world's Jewish population lived. Russian authorities—not for the first time—indulged in pogroms (organized attacks or persecutions against Jews) in the wake of the assassination of Alexander II in 1881. Jews were beaten up and killed, their shops destroyed, and their property confiscated. Millions of Russian Jews, finding no future in the land of their birth, relocated to the United States between 1881 and 1914. In Germany and in German-speaking Austria, late nineteenth-century racial nationalists focused much of their irrational animus on the Jewish community. An anti-Semitic congress held in the German city of Dresden in 1882 called for an end to Jewish influence in political life throughout Europe.

The Birth of Jewish Nationalism   As part of the larger reaction to the wave of persecution Jews experienced in much of Europe, a Jewish nationalist movement called Zionism arose. It held that the Jewish people would never be accorded equal status in

Europe and that they could achieve permanent security only through the creation of a Jewish state in the ancient biblical homeland of Zion (Palestine). The movement was inspired by the success of state-building efforts in Italy and Germany, together with nationalist movements in Ireland, Poland, and the Balkans. Many Jews, led by an Austrian journalist named Theodor Herzl (1860–1904), worked tirelessly to encourage Jewish immigration to Palestine. Despite Ottoman opposition to migration schemes (Palestine was part of the Ottoman Empire until 1918), some 1,000 Jews had settled in Palestine by 1900, with another 3,000 arriving annually until the start of World War I in 1914.

■ ■

PEOPLE IN CONTEXT Theodor Herzl and Jewish Nationalism

Theodor Herzl (1860–1904) was born in Budapest, Hungary, to a family of merchants who had sought to assimilate into the majority culture. He secured a law degree from the prestigious University of Vienna, but his passion for journalism led him into a career as a foreign correspondent. At age 31, Herzl was assigned to Paris, where he witnessed the tide of anti-Semitism surrounding the trial of Captain Alfred Dreyfus. From this point until his death, Herzl focused his energies on the plight of European Jews and on the need for the establishment of a Jewish homeland in Palestine.

In 1895 Herzl published a short pamphlet called *The Jewish State*. Considering the intensification of anti-Semitism during the late nineteenth century, he wrote, "In vain are we loyal patriots, our loyalty in some places running to extremes; in vain do we make the same sacrifices of life and property as our fellow-citizens; in vain do we strive to increase the fame of our native land in science and art, or her wealth by trade and commerce." The so-called Jewish question, he asserted, is neither a social nor religious one, but a national one, and it was now time for Jews all over the world to work in unison for a national homeland in Palestine. "'Next year in Jerusalem' is our old phrase," he recalled. "It is now a question of showing that the dream can be converted into a living reality."

In 1899 Herzl organized and presided over the First Zionist Congress in the Swiss city of Basel. The chief goals of the Congress were to heighten Jewish self-awareness and to coordinate efforts aimed at achieving statehood. Local Zionist organizations emerged wherever Jews had emigrated. Herzl secured meetings with the German kaiser and the Ottoman sultan. In *The*

Theodor Herzl, champion of Zionism

(continued)

Jewish State, Herzl had recommended that in return for Palestine, the Jews might assist the Turks in the regulation of their badly mismanaged fiscal affairs. It was not until the end of World War I, however, when the British ruled Palestine that European Jews were allowed to settle there in considerable numbers.

Herzl's rejection of assimilation was controversial within the European Jewish community. Some of his liberal critics claimed that his skepticism regarding the possibility of assimilation undermined the position of Jews in modern industrial society. On the other hand, his plans for a future state alienated some cultural Zionists who disliked Herzl's secular and Western-oriented focus. They also disliked Herzl's willingness to consider alternative locations for the future state. Between 1901 and his death in 1904, for example, Herzl discussed with British authorities the possibility of claiming the island of Cyprus or the Sinai Peninsula for European Jews. He clearly underestimated the potential for conflict between Arabs and Jewish settlers in Palestine, hoping that both peoples could work together to improve the quality of life for all inhabitants. Unlike the American conquest of the West, he argued, where the "settlers assemble on the frontier, and at the appointed time make a simultaneous and violent rush for their portions," Jewish settlement in Palestine would be orderly and humane. While Herzl's dream of a nation-state for Jews would be realized by the middle of the twentieth century, the process was both difficult and bloody.

Question: How did Zionism complement nationalism?

KEY QUESTION | Revisited

The formation of independent nation-states in Western Europe during the second half of the nineteenth century represented the culmination of efforts begun during the era of the French Revolution and Napoleon. However, the proponents of nationalism after 1850 were often conservative elites who adopted the nationalist agenda to solidify their social and economic privileges. Cavour in Italy, Bismarck in Germany, and Louis Napoleon III in France all promoted the goal of national unity along linguistic and cultural lines from the standpoint of *Realpolitik.* Dismissing the nationalist idealism of an earlier liberal and Romantic tradition, the new architects of the sovereign state were interested in the military, economic, and political advantages that the unified state gave them. They also abandoned the older conservative assumption that governments were distinct from their populations, and instead skillfully portrayed their nation-building crusade as the collective embodiment of and capstone to each citizen's individual genius.

By the closing decades of the nineteenth century, nationalism had become the tool of leaders who cared little for the historic keystones of liberal ideology: individual rights, international cooperation based on the equality of peoples, and the freedom to dissent. National honor and the respect of rival states in a highly competitive state system made the international order increasingly fragile. Although there had been no general European war since the fall of Napoleon Bonaparte in 1815, nationalist politicians dedicated enormous fiscal resources to their military establishments. As we shall see in the next chapter, those military forces were employed repeatedly overseas as Europe's leading powers established huge colonial empires.

In France after 1848, in Italy after 1860, in the United States after 1865, in Britain after 1867, and in Germany after 1871, strong nationalist sentiments developed in concert with an extended franchise and with a more active role for government in labor relations, public health and safety, and education. The great fear of the ruling class that political democracy would mean the end of their ascendancy and perhaps even the overthrow of the existing social order was shown to be misplaced. Instead, universal manhood suffrage, when combined with better material conditions for Europe's working class, became the great bulwarks of the existing order. The bond of national unity proved to be stronger than either the Enlightenment appeal to internationalism or the socialist creed of worker cooperation and class consciousness. The territorial nation-state, sovereign and sacred, the chief object of each citizen's allegiance even to the death, had by 1914 become the new political orthodoxy. The fate of nations and the defense of their honor were about to replace loyalty to a ruling dynasty (even in states with monarchs) as the central concern of the twentieth century.

Is nationalism a constructive force in the modern age? So powerful was the appeal of nationalism after 1900 that those governments, irrespective of their apparent military prowess, that failed to frame their claims to legitimacy in nationalist terms did not survive. From the collapse of the Austrian Habsburg Empire after World War I to the disintegration of the Soviet Empire in the late 1980s, states that did not self-consciously foster nationalism have faltered. The appeal of nationalism, its ability to rally public support around a set of symbols and myths respecting an alleged common culture, has been essential to the formation of the modern state system. However, nationalism also contributed to a disturbing trend after 1870 in which foreigners became "the other," and where the formation, preservation, and expansion of the territorial state bred both distrust and disdain in a global community in which Europe was coming to dominate peoples on every continent.

Review Questions

1. How did approaches to national unification change in Western Europe after the failed revolutions of 1848?
2. How did traditional elites and conservative political leaders use nationalism to strengthen their hold on power after 1850?
3. What role did industry play in the creation of centralized nation-states in Europe and America?
4. How did the rhetoric of nationalism shift during the second half of the nineteenth century?
5. Why did the Austrian Habsburg Empire fail to maintain its leadership within the German Confederation?
6. What internal and external factors undermined the Ottoman Empire during the nineteenth century?
7. How did British nationalism differ from nationalism on the European continent?

Please consult the Suggested Readings at the back of the book to continue your study of the material covered in this chapter. For a list of documents on the Primary Source DVD-ROM that relate to topics in this chapter, please refer to the back of the book.

The New Imperialism: Motives and Methods • The Scramble for Empire: Africa
• The Scramble for Empire: South and East Asia • Imperialism, Intellectual Controversy,
and European Culture • Transformation in the Arts

21 Global Empire and European Culture

Dreamers and visionaries have made civilizations. It is trying to do things that cannot be done that makes life worth while.

—Cecil Rhodes

KEY | Question

How does the projection of power reflect wider cultural values?

In 1877 London-born Cecil Rhodes (1853–1902) published a "Confession of Faith" in which he reflected on the chief good in life. Rhodes had migrated to British-controlled southern Africa in 1870 where he quickly amassed a large fortune in the diamond industry. His company, De Beers Consolidated Mines, Ltd., became the dominant producer and marketer of fine diamonds worldwide. One might expect a self-made man like Rhodes to focus on wealth creation as the greatest good in life, but instead he said that the overseas migration of Britons, "the finest race in the world," provided his greatest personal satisfaction. He asked his readers to consider those parts of the world "that are at present inhabited by the most despicable specimens of human beings" and how much better things would be if these lands "were brought under Anglo-Saxon influence."

In the late nineteenth century, Rhodes was not alone in his estimate of Europe's beneficent impact on the rest of the world, even if it meant the subjection of indigenous peoples by violent means. Europe's industrial and military prowess, its sophisticated transportation and communications networks, its advances in public health and education, and its representative political institutions all seemed to demonstrate that the West deserved to dominate less advanced continents. Coupled with the rise of a body of social thought that carelessly extended Charles Darwin's new theory of biological evolution to social, moral, cultural, intellectual, and political development, Europeans in the late nineteenth century

Imperial Dress Members of the Freemason's Lodge in Freetown, capital of the British colony of Sierra Leone, address the Duke of Connaught, a son of Queen Victoria, in 1910. Dressed in evening suits, the African dignitaries look every bit as formal as their British counterparts.

confidently and aggressively imposed their rule, their institutions, and their values on non-Western peoples around the globe. By 1914, most of Africa and large parts of South and East Asia had come under the direct or indirect control of Western Europe's most powerful nation-states. Indeed, only one-fifth of the world's land mass was not under a European flag when World War I began. The process was so rapid and wide-reaching, and the potential for overseas conflict between rival European states so great, that scholars have described the phenomenon as the "**new imperialism**" to distinguish it from the colonization efforts of the seventeenth and eighteenth centuries.

Most Europeans were supremely confident that global dominance was not at odds with the Enlightenment tradition of inalienable human rights, natural law, the equality of peoples, individual liberty, and rational conduct. Yet, however hard they labored to justify imperialism in terms of spreading Enlightenment ideals, a basic shift in European consciousness occurred during the final decades of the nineteenth century. It emphasized the aggressive and irrational side of human nature, the subconscious impulses and drives that often extolled violence and struggle. Suddenly it seemed to many thinkers that reason was a fragile instrument and that powerful, and little understood, nonrational forces defined human nature. In the late nineteenth century these forces often found their outlet in the cruel quest for empire. During the twentieth century, they would be manipulated by fascist political demagogues who repudiated the liberal tradition of enlightened rationalism.

The New Imperialism: Motives and Methods

Imperialism was not a new feature of European life. Beginning in the late fifteenth century, the kingdoms of Spain and Portugal began a process of global expansion that was to involve every major European power and continue until the end of World War II in 1945. It began with the conquest of the Americas, Siberia, and central Asia, followed by the peopling of these lands with European migrants and, in America, African slaves. During the late eighteenth and early nineteenth centuries, successful revolutions in the Americas transformed most settler colonies into independent nation-states, but Europe's global predominance continued in new directions. By the third quarter of the nineteenth century, European states expanded former slave stations along the coast of Africa, together with trading posts in India, China, and Southeast Asia, into territorial empires. With political control came cultural and economic domination. Even in those areas where the Western powers did not exercise direct political ascendancy—in the Ottoman, Persian, and Chinese empires, for example—Europe's economic superiority dictated the formation of a semicolonial relationship.

Economic Factors   Three features distinguish late nineteenth-century imperialism from all previous forms. The first involves the role of economics. As European states experienced the early stages of industrialization, many politicians and industrialists believed that they needed to secure reliable international markets for their country's manufactured products. It was thought that in a highly competitive capitalist society, the ability of producers to cultivate a transnational consuming public would largely determine success. Earlier proponents of free trade and followers of Adam Smith (see Chapter 16, "The Age of Enlightenment: Rationalism and Its Uses") argued that colonies were unnecessary so long as all producers had equal access to markets. However, national competition within Europe made the free trade argument vulnerable after 1850, especially when countries began to raise tariffs to protect their own industry. Colonies, the argument ran, could absorb Europe's surplus products and investment capital. Proponents of overseas empire also maintained that colonies would serve as potential sources of strategic (and inexpensive) raw materials, such as rubber and petroleum, and as a demographic safety valve for Europe's surplus population. The Russian communist Lenin (1870–1924), a harsh critic of empire, believed that imperialism was inherent in the dynamic of capitalism and that in order to survive, capitalist economies had to find new markets for their surplus products.

Few colonies proved profitable. Most of them turned out to be far more costly to secure, protect, and maintain than anyone anticipated. The healthiest markets for Europe's manufactured products were in other advanced and affluent states, not in underdeveloped and impoverished colonies in Africa or South Asia. Similarly, European investors put little of their capital in overseas possessions that were not populated by European settlers and their descendants. While overseas migration peaked in the late nineteenth century, few white Europeans elected to settle in the many African or East Asian colonies established by the imperial powers.

National Rivalry   The second important feature of the new imperialism involved a self-imposed competition for international prestige engendered by the rise of nationalism. Europe's political leaders, eager to enhance popular support for the state while defusing potential social unrest at home, skillfully directed state resources into the establishment of overseas empires. World powers needed secure ports, coaling stations for their navies, and the ability to raise colonial armies in any potential conflict. The acquisition of new lands overseas would provide these assets and win accolades for politicians who set the ambitious agenda. Governments boasted about the achievements of their armed forces in colonial wars. French acquisitions in North and sub-Saharan Africa and Indochina partly compensated for defeat at the hands of the Germans in 1870; Italy's military adventures in Libya and Somalia provided evidence of that nation's great power status despite the country's relative underdevelopment when compared to its northern neighbors; and Germany's role in Southwest Africa (Namibia) and Tanganyika, and its influence in China, all confirmed Emperor William II's (r. 1888–1918) assertion that his empire was gaining its rightful "place in the sun."

Culture and Race   The final and most pernicious factor undergirding the intensive pace of late nineteenth-century imperialism involved European attitudes toward non-Western, non-Christian cultures. Some apologists for imperialism insisted that territorial expansion was a moral enterprise designed to bring the blessings of a superior civilization to benighted millions. French politician Jules Ferry (1832–1893) argued that "the superior races have a right vis-à-vis the inferior races . . . they have a right to civilize them." British poet Rudyard Kipling's (1865–1936) famed 1898 poem "White Man's Burden" captured this combination of paternalism and racial disdain, referring to the colonized peoples as "half-devil and half-child." However offensive it may seem today, the appeal of what Kipling called the "White Man's Burden" involved an implicit conviction that non-Western peoples had the potential to be like their imperial mentors and that the entire imperialist project was at its core a gigantic educational enterprise, a global extension of the European Enlightenment.

Many advocates of imperialism insisted that evolutionary theory confirmed lingering suspicions about race and cultural development. They argued that just as the animal kingdom was organized hierarchically, so too were human cultures and "races." Depending on their level of cultural and intellectual development, some cultures were deemed superior to others, which made up the essence of **racism**. Race was the defining characteristic in this pseudoscience, which was given an intellectual façade through the efforts of French aristocrat Arthur de Gobineau (1816–1882), Houston Stewart Chamberlain (1855–1927), and others. White European, especially northern European, culture was superior to all others, they argued, and these views were widely accepted throughout the continent by the end of the century. The European conquest and subjection of other races was only the natural working out of the laws of competition and survival where only the fittest would—and should—prevail. Here was a sharp repudiation of the Enlightenment tradition, particularly in the areas of universal human rights and the equality of peoples. This "law of nature" privileged struggle and conflict between peoples and celebrated irrational vitality and a subconscious will to power. The good and the just were reduced to whatever values the victor chose to impose.

Methods of Control   Once they had established their claim to control overseas territories, the European powers adopted a number of strategies to preserve and exploit their acquisitions. Annexation and direct colonial rule using European administrators

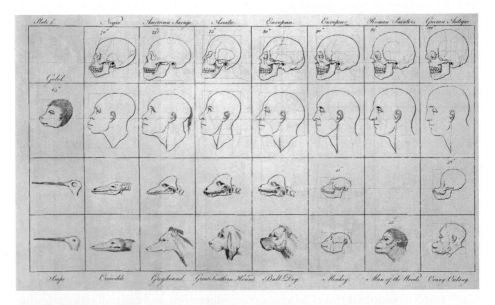

Scientific Racism   This chart purports to show the superiority of white Europeans over other "races." Europeans became obsessed with racial categories in the nineteenth century, and often camouflaged racist ideas with scientific language.

were the most costly options. This was the approach most European powers took in sub-Saharan Africa beginning in the 1880s. An alternative approach was a protectorate arrangement. In a protectorate, the local ruler and his government continued to function, but the Europeans controlled the country's military, foreign affairs, and economy and intervened whenever imperial interests were threatened. This was how the British ran Egypt from 1882 to the 1920s and how the French imposed their authority over Tunisia in 1881. Another approach was referred to as a "sphere of influence." This meant that a non-European country granted a European state certain exclusive economic privileges in part or all of its territory. Europeans living or working in that territory were also exempted from the jurisdiction of the local legal system and resided in their own autonomous sections of foreign cities and towns. Here they attempted to recreate many of the amenities of their home country. These privileges became the norm in Europe's relations with the once powerful Chinese Empire during the nineteenth century.

Educating the Colonial Elite   European colonizers also asserted and maintained their control through the cultivation of an indigenous elite. Recognizing the need for this base of support—and convinced that European culture was vastly superior to anything that was embraced by indigenous peoples—the imperialists undertook to provide a Western-style education for native leaders. Often, the initiative was undertaken by Christian missionaries who viewed the transmission of Western culture as part of a larger civilizing mandate. These initiatives were in general limited to males. A select number of colonial subjects received their university training in Western Europe and upon their return were immediately selected for significant posts in the colonial bureaucracy. It was hoped that these Western-educated intellectuals would begin the process of translating and communicating the "blessings" of Western scientific and philosophical thought to a wider native audience. This would solidify colonial allegiance to the imperial state. Irrespective of their educational accomplishments or their demonstrated loyalty to the empire, however, the members of the new elite were never accepted as genuine equals by white Europeans, for whom the highest appointments in the colonial service were reserved. It was therefore not surprising that many of the Western-educated native elites became the most forceful critics of Western imperialism during the late nineteenth and early twentieth centuries. Their study of European political institutions and Western philosophical ideas spurred the growing call for civil equality and the right to national self-determination. While few of the Western-educated elite actually identified with the illiterate and impoverished majority in their homelands, they began to claim the mantle of leadership in the drive to end colonialism. Their efforts would finally bear fruit in the aftermath of World War II.

The Scramble for Empire: Africa

The most dramatic manifestation of the new imperialism was the division of Africa among the European powers between the 1880s and 1914. Prior to the 1870s, most of the vast African interior was unknown to Europeans (see Map 21–1). Whites had seldom

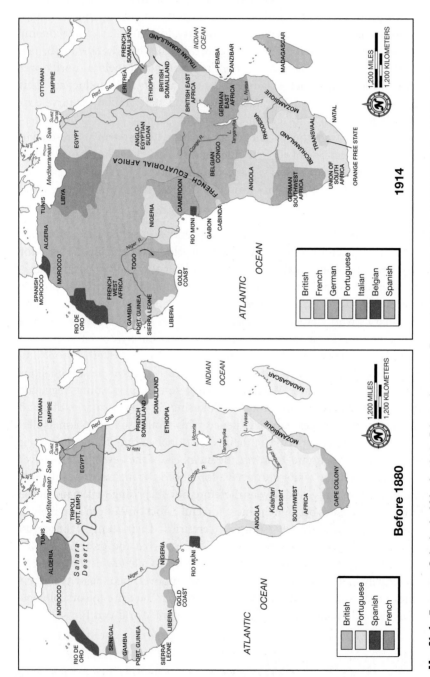

Map 21–1 European Colonies in Africa in 1914 Prior to the 1880s, Europe's presence in Africa was limited to the coastline. Between 1880 and 1914 the continent was divided by the Western powers. Liberia and Ethiopia were the only countries to retain their independence.

QUESTION: How did Europeans determine colonial boundaries in Africa?

penetrated far beyond the coasts. There were scattered forts and former slave stations along the west coast of Africa, and the French had conquered most of Algeria in North Africa during the 1830s. Morocco was independent. Tunisia, Libya, and Egypt were autonomous provinces of the Ottoman Empire. However, the peoples of sub-Saharan Africa continued to follow traditional kinship patterns of social and political organization without interference from the West. European missionaries and explorers like David Livingstone (1813–1873) and Henry Stanley (1841–1904) had visited part of the interior of the continent after mid-century, but their presence had only a nominal impact on local culture.

This situation changed swiftly and dramatically in the mid-1870s as Belgian, French, German, and British interests in sub-Saharan Africa led to a series of territorial disputes. King Leopold II of Belgium (r. 1865–1909) took the lead by securing almost one million square miles of territory in the Congo as his private domain. Leopold's expansive appropriation was based on the work of his personal agent, the formidable Henry Stanley, who secured highly questionable "grants" of land from indigenous leaders. To rule this vast area, Leopold set up the International Association of the Congo, which inaugurated a brutal regime dedicated solely to extracting raw materials, especially rubber and ivory. Germany, Portugal, Britain, and France quickly followed Leopold's lead in the race for prime real estate in central and southern Africa. Each country was eager to reap profits and prestige no matter what the cost to native peoples.

Berlin Conference   In the fall of 1884 German Chancellor Otto von Bismarck (1815–1898) and French Premier Jules Ferry (1832–1893) arranged for a special conference on African affairs to be held in Berlin. Fourteen nations, including the United States, sent delegates, but not a single African leader was invited to attend. The meeting was designed to establish rules for the campaign of empire building. It became the unofficial starting point for a territorial "scramble for Africa" that continued until the entire continent, except for Liberia and Ethiopia, was under European political control. The imperial powers established borders with little regard for the concerns of indigenous peoples. Traditional political and cultural rivals found themselves joined politically within a single European colony, while other tribes were divided among several colonies. Exploitative labor regimes, arbitrary land taxes, and the proselytizing activities of Christian missionaries disrupted centuries-old patterns of social organization.

The Berlin conference stipulated that claims to African territory must be based on actual occupation by an imperial power, but there were frequent clashes over territorial proclamations. Britain and France came close to war over the upper Nile River Valley in 1898 when opposing armies met at Fashoda in southeastern Sudan. Tensions between the French and the Belgians over the Congo and between the British and the Germans respecting claims to territory in southeast Africa each threatened to escalate into armed conflict. In South Africa, where the British had captured Cape Town on the southern tip of the continent from the Dutch during the Napoleonic wars, strains between the British and the descendants of Dutch settlers (called Boers) did result in war in 1898. Many Boers had fled British rule to establish two republics, Transvaal and the Orange Free State, in the 1850s. When gold and diamonds were discovered in Transvaal, however, imperialists

THE RHODES COLOSSUS
STRIDING FROM CAPE TOWN TO CAIRO.

Cecil Rhodes and the New Imperialism   "The Rhodes Colossus," a cartoon depicting English-born Cecil Rhodes striding over the African continent. The views of Rhodes, and many other imperialists, were summed up in his declaration, "I contend that we are the finest race in the world and that the more of the world we inhabit the better it is for the human race."

like Cecil Rhodes called for annexation to Britain. The war lasted until 1902, and although the British prevailed, Germany's public expression of sympathy for the Boers strained relations between the two great powers. An enormous amount of bluster and posturing between the rival powers occurred in the decades before World War I, and the reading and voting public appeared to support the stridency of their respective political leaders. Talk of war over the defense of colonial possessions became stock news stories for the cheap tabloid press. The spirit of internationalism promoted by Enlightenment thinkers was being replaced by a dangerous bellicosity and emotion-laden calls for heroic action.

The Scramble for Empire: South and East Asia

The Indian Raj   British involvement in India began in the early seventeenth century, when commercial agents representing the British East India Company established trade relations with the powerful Mughal Empire. As Mughal power declined during the eighteenth century, the Company began to form commercial and military alliances with rival Indian princes while simultaneously building a large private army of native troops known as *sepoys*. A rebellion against the East India Company took place in 1857, but it was brutally suppressed. In the aftermath Parliament put an end to East India Company rule and declared the entire subcontinent to be a part of the British Empire. Queen Victoria was proclaimed Empress of India in 1877, and the Indian Raj, or rule, quickly became the centerpiece of Britain's global empire.

Under the Raj, a small elite British civil service consisting of roughly 1,000 men was stationed in India to supervise a much larger Indian staff. These bureaucrats governed a population of nearly 300 million. Britain also stationed more than 100,000 British troops in India and raised an Indian army of about 300,000 men under British officers. British rule brought some benefits: Western medical practices and improved agricultural techniques contributed to a rapid rise in overall population. The subcontinent was unified for the first time in its history, and an extensive system of railroads, bridges, and roads was built. However, it is doubtful that the quality of life for average Indians improved much during this period. Moreover, a policy of racial discrimination whereby Indians were denied access to the highest levels of administration and were excluded from British clubs, hotels, and other private venues fanned the resentment of the Indian elite. In the 1880s a group of educated Indians founded the Indian National Congress, a political organization whose members were animated by a strong sense of nationalism. On the eve of World War I, Indian leaders were calling for some degree of autonomy. In a country with hundreds of language groups and a wide variety of religious traditions, the Indian National Congress struggled to forge a common identity using the tools of empire—English language, Western technology, and Western political values, including nationalism, to challenge the Raj.

China and Europe   European demand for China's luxury products—silks, porcelains, teas, spices—had been strong since the early sixteenth century. While eager to trade with China, Western merchants decried the fact that access to China's markets was limited by the authoritarian Ming (1368–1644) and Qing (1644–1912) dynasties. China's rulers had traditionally considered their country to be the most advanced civilization in the world. Since China had no need for Western products (although it did benefit immensely from the introduction of American maize [corn], peanuts, and sweet potatoes), an "unfavorable balance of trade" developed: The West had to pay for Chinese goods with gold and silver. The Chinese considered trade to be a privilege, not a right. The privilege was bestowed on barbarian Westerners according to terms set by the Chinese emperor, the "Son of Heaven." Those terms restricted all foreign trade to the single port of Canton, where a group of Chinese commercial firms, known as *cohongs*, held the exclusive right to interact with Western merchants.

Opium Wars   The West's subordinate association with China changed dramatically with the Industrial Revolution. Beginning in the early 1840s, Britain employed its superior naval might to force the Chinese government to open its markets to foreign products, including opium produced in British India by the East India Company. Opium was illegal in China, but British and American smuggling had produced an enormous addiction problem among the Chinese. The Qing government acted decisively to end the opium trade by destroying stocks of opium that it discovered in Canton, but this bold action precipitated a lopsided war with Britain. After China's defeat in the first Opium War (1839–1842), the Chinese government was obliged to cede the island of Hong Kong to the British (it would not be returned until 1997) and to open up five additional ports to foreign traders.

Another Opium War was fought between 1856 and 1860. This time Britain was joined by France, and the two powers occupied Beijing and forced the Chinese government to grant concessions that further undermined China's sovereignty. Foreign missionaries were now allowed to travel freely throughout the empire, opium was legalized, and Western gunboats were permitted access to many of China's most important rivers. In the late nineteenth century China also fought two more unsuccessful wars against France (1884–1885) and Japan (1894–1895) in which it had to surrender control over Vietnam and Taiwan, respectively. By the 1890s, France, Russia, Germany, Japan, and

Opium Wars in China   Superior naval power enabled the British to defeat the Chinese in two wars fought between 1839 and 1860. In this illustration, the British steamer *Nemesis* attacks Chinese vessels near Canton, China, in 1843.

the United States had all laid claim to spheres of influence on the Chinese mainland. A final Chinese effort to expel foreigners in 1900, called the Boxer Rebellion by Europeans, was crushed by an international force of European, American, and Japanese troops. The Chinese government had become simply another inferior power in a world increasingly dominated by the industrialized West, and in 1912 the ancient dynastic system was abolished (see Map 21–2).

Japan Imitates the West   The first European merchants and missionaries to Japan had arrived in the sixteenth century. However, all except the Dutch had been forced to leave in the seventeenth century. Japan remained an isolated country for the next 200 years, until the American naval commander Matthew Perry (1794–1858) arrived in Tokyo Bay with a fleet in 1853 and demanded the right to trade. Unlike the Chinese, Japan's elite responded to these demands by transforming their country and reorganizing the national government under the titular leadership of the Meiji Emperor. This Meiji Restoration of 1867 included an intensive program of modernization based on a Western model. Universal military service was adopted, the values of nationalism were inculcated, and a new constitution was approved based on that of imperial Germany. Japanese students studied in European and American universities and brought their technical skills to bear in the fields of communications, mining, industry, and infrastructure development.

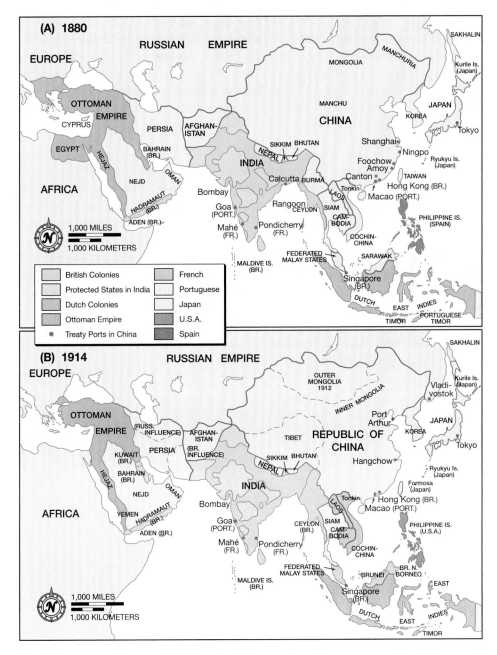

Map 21–2   European Colonies in Asia by 1914   The extension of European power into Asia occurred simultaneously with the carve-up of Africa. Japan and the United States joined the list of imperial powers in Asia prior to World War I.

Question: What role did superior technology play in Europe's Asian empires?

By 1900, a resource-poor state had been transformed into a modern industrial economy. So rapid was Japan's rise to power under its reformist leadership that it became an imperialist aggressor in East Asia. Taiwan was wrested from the Chinese in 1895. In 1905 Japan's surprising military defeat of Russia over the issue of spheres of influence in Manchuria and Korea (which became a Japanese colony in 1910) helped to dispel the notion that the Western powers were invincible. The victory not only strengthened Japanese nationalism but also inspired anti-Western and anti-imperial sentiments throughout Asia.

The Legacy of Empire   The nonindustrial peoples whose homelands Western imperialists intruded upon were forced to alter their traditional patterns of work, thought, and culture. Village life was severely undermined by the introduction of European labor requirements. Large mining operations in Southern Africa, for example, obliged African men to leave their villages for distant work sites to earn enough income to pay newly imposed imperial land taxes. Once colonial peoples began producing cash crops and raw materials for a Western and global market, rural economies became dependent on fluctuating global economic conditions. In terms of material culture, late nineteenth-century imperialism represented the consummation of a process of worldwide economic integration that had begun in the early sixteenth century. The production and consumption of goods within a transnational context were made possible by Europe's control over non-Western peoples. By 1900, the age of independent civilizations was at a close.

The Scramble for Africa   Diamond mining in South Africa in 1872. Africa's rich deposits of such natural resources as diamonds, gold, and rubber made the continent the object of European competition.

Imperialism, Intellectual Controversy, and European Culture

As Europe's power spread around the globe, so too did Western ideas, institutions, and values. English and French became international languages, just as Spanish and Portuguese had in the sixteenth century. Christian missionaries and entrepreneurs worked under the protection of superior military forces, while Western science, medicine, educational theories, and legal forms all found expression in cities where Western-style architecture increasingly replaced indigenous styles. Even Western fashions became commonplace, with educated African and Asian people dressing like Europeans. Not every imposition was exploitative, however. Imperialists played a significant role in the suppression of the Muslim slave trade in Africa, in the abolition of *sati* (the immolation of widows on the funeral pyres of their deceased husbands) in India, and in the elimination of foot binding in China. Most importantly, Western democratic values, especially Enlightenment ideas about responsible self-government, the rule of law, and individual freedom, galvanized educated non-Europeans to work for greater autonomy and, ultimately, national independence.

Ironically, the Enlightenment tradition of natural rights and fixed, natural laws began to take hold in Europe's many colonies just at the moment when that tradition was being undermined by new intellectual trends in the West. The scientific quest for certainty and useful truths was anchored in the Enlightenment assumption that space, time, matter, and energy were independent realities within a fixed and knowable universe. Humans were reasonable creatures capable of investigating the natural laws that governed God's clockwork universe in a dispassionate, objective manner. The continuous improvement of the human condition through the application of the scientific method stood at the core of middle-class ideas of progress. However, during the period of Europe's imperial expansion, these rationalist assumptions were called into question by biologists, physicists, and by professionals (especially psychologists) in the emerging social sciences.

Darwin, Biology, and Deity

The English naturalist **Charles Darwin's** (1809–1882) monumental contributions to biology were the product of years of study, field-based data collection, and rigorous analysis. Untroubled by theological ideas about the status of humans, Darwin's evolutionary theory was as significant to biology as Newton's work had been to physics. The biblical account of humankind's creation remained a compelling and emotionally satisfying story for most Europeans well into the nineteenth century. In less than a week, God had created each species of plant and animal life in its fixed and finished form. Each species was endowed with features designed for a specific purpose, and the entire creative act had taken place a mere 6,000 years ago.

Darwin's *Origin of Species by Means of Natural Selection* (1859) raised fundamental questions about both the timeframe and the process of creation. Instead of a single divine creative act six millennia ago, he introduced a more fluid model in which some creatures came into being and others became extinct and in which the creative process unfolded, and continued to unfold, over millions of years. Darwin's theory, while shocking to traditional religious believers, was in fact the culmination of work carried out by a variety of biologists and geologists for over a century. Darwin's grandfather, Erasmus Darwin (1731–1802), argued in his *Zoonomia, or the Laws of Organic Life* (1794) that Earth existed long before the appearance of humans. In the 1830s Sir Charles Lyell (1797–1875) published his *Principles of Geology,* in which he argued that Earth had evolved over millennia. The discovery of the skeletal remains of extinct species and the extraction of dissimilar fossils at different geological strata indicated a strong connection between the environment and animal forms. Even contemporary experiments in crossbreeding plants and animals suggested that the creative process was much more varied and dynamic than the biblical account allowed for.

Origin of Species was significant because it offered an explanation—the principle of natural selection—for the process of evolution. It even argued for links between extinct and living species. Darwin's path-breaking theory of natural selection maintained that in the ongoing struggle for food and for security against predators, some species are more successful than others at adapting to changes in the environment. Offspring are not exact duplicates of their parents; small and sometimes random variations in speed, strength, color, dexterity, size, and many other features can determine which plants and animals are most likely to reach maturity and have offspring of their own. Those that do survive are apt to pass on their superior attributes to the next generation.

The process was imperceptible, covering millions of years and involving all living organisms, including humans. While Darwin received full credit for the theory of natural selection, his contemporary Alfred Russell Wallace (1823–1913) had reached similar conclusions while working independently. However, neither man could explain the origin of chance variations that gave some organisms an advantage over others in a given species. Not until the work on heredity pioneered by the Austrian monk Gregor Mendel (1822–1884) and expanded by the Dutch botanist Hugo De Vries (1848–1935) became available did scientists solve this puzzle. De Vries asserted that instead of evolution resulting from small variations, as Darwin had claimed, radical change or mutations were key. Genetic mutations that were appropriate for a particular environment enabled the individuals who possessed them to dominate and to pass these qualities along to their descendants.

At one level, the theory of biological evolution conformed nicely with the nineteenth century's ascendant culture of progress. Creation was not an act but a process, and the law governing the process assured that only the best adapted species would survive. Only favorable characteristics emerge and thrive in the race to adapt to an ever-changing natural environment. In 1871 Darwin published his *Descent of Man* in which he explicitly included human beings in the evolutionary paradigm. Darwin insisted that a creator God still had a pivotal role in the process of evolution. However, instead of a solitary act, Darwin's deity provided the physical matter and the form (natural selection) whereby all life emerged. The ability to adapt was the prerequisite for a species' survival over thousands of years.

Such an unconventional perspective on God was cold comfort to many Christians. Darwin's work sparked an intense controversy between traditionalists who accepted Scripture as infallible and members of the scientific community who insisted that the

Charles Darwin and Evolution   Darwin's theory of natural selection represented a significant scientific advance, but provoked opposition among many Europeans, as seen by this cartoon. Although Darwin was not an atheist, his scientific method was rejected by those who believed in a literal interpretation of the Bible. *Private collection/The Bridgeman Art Library*

empirical data in favor of evolution were irrefutable. Critics of Darwin understood that the impersonal process of natural selection stood in bleak opposition to the biblical story of a loving God and to the belief that humankind was a special creation endowed with an immortal soul. Darwinism banished the supernatural and the mysterious from the creation narrative and in the process reconfirmed an argument, first introduced by Galileo in the early seventeenth century, that the Bible had no place in the arena of science. The drama of salvation now stood in stark opposition to uncaring natural processes and chance variations. If nature had no enduring order or design, then could one assume that there were universal rules in the social or political spheres? Could one continue to insist on the existence of a moral order that was applicable to all humans? "Best adapted" seemed to be a morally neutral term. Was there such a thing as fixed truth?

Herbert Spencer   One troubling response to these questions came from the British philosopher Herbert Spencer (1820–1903), who applied evolutionary theory to ethics. According to Spencer, competition and struggle were essential to progress, and those who rose to economic, political, and cultural predominance were justified in imposing their rule over the weak. Spencer coined the term *survival of the fittest*. Policymakers used it to limit state assistance to the poor at home and to oppress colonial peoples abroad. Helping those who had so clearly failed in a competitive environment, these "Social Darwinists" alleged, would undermine the best qualities of the species. Religious scruples about the plight of the poor had no place in a world where compassion became a synonym for cultural decay.

Friedrich Nietzsche and the Will to Power   Influenced by the new trends in biological thought, increasing numbers of European intellectuals began to question the primacy of rationality in human culture, focusing instead on the instinctive, emotional, and unreflective side of human conduct. Imperialist adventures certainly generated a large measure of unreflective and highly emotional jingoism. While some thinkers celebrated the creative potential of the irrational in the arts, religion, and mythology, others cautioned that these forces could easily overwhelm political life. In an increasingly democratic age, the potential for demagogues and unscrupulous politicians to play upon the fears, hopes, and ambitions of the electorate was immense.

The German philosopher Friedrich Nietzsche (1844–1900) was one of the most vehement critics of liberal culture, Christian morality, the ideology of progress, and the belief in reason. Nietzsche viewed mass democratic politics and parliamentary government with contempt. He claimed that the dominant middle-class values were decadent and sterile, committed to materialism and mediocrity. The popular assumption that rational thought was what distinguished human beings from animals, an assumption that could be traced back to the ancient Greeks, was to Nietzsche the grand lie. In fact, he was convinced that the excessive development of reason had led to the enfeeblement of the human species. In a hostile world lacking either divine order or creative purpose, Nietzsche discovered meaning in the simple struggle to create new values through the heroic cultivation of long-submerged instincts and unconscious striving. Since God was a fiction and Christianity was a "slave morality," eternal truths did not exist. Nietzsche was a destroyer of all conventional orthodoxies at the very moment of Europe's material primacy. Three decades after his death, Nazi ideologues distorted his theory of the heroic *Ubermensch* (super-man) to advance their myth of the superior race in Aryan Germany.

Freud and the Unconscious The Viennese physician Sigmund Freud (1856–1939) was an ardent supporter of the Enlightenment tradition. Like the *philosophes* of the eighteenth century, and unlike Nietzsche, he associated reason and science with the highest achievements of civilization. As a doctor who specialized in treating mental disorders, however, Freud's research led him to highlight the role of nonrational and destructive forces in people's lives. Nietzsche celebrated these primal qualities; Freud feared them and worked both to explain their origins and to offer a systematic clinical approach to controlling them. Since he was convinced that nonrational drives threatened civilization, Freud undertook his studies as part of a defense of reason in modern life.

The task before him was daunting because Freud conceded that reason did not regulate most of human behavior. Instead, powerful but little-understood instincts and subconscious drives motivated most decisions and actions. In 1900 he published a controversial book, *The Interpretation of Dreams,* in which he argued that dreams were specific expressions of unconscious desires that the rational, waking self struggles to suppress. By studying irrational phenomena like dreams, the scientist could better explain conscious behavior and help to treat neurotic illnesses. Freud's later work sought to describe the connections between the rational and irrational sides of the mind. He paid particular (and controversial) attention to the role of sexual drives as the strongest human impulse. He used the now famous terms *id* (for the primitive and irrational drives), *superego* (for the faculty that internalizes the moral rules of society), and *ego* (the mediating force) to explain commonplace behavior. According to Freud, within the mind the *ego* was engaged in a constant struggle to repress the destructive features of the *id* while helping the individual to internalize the moral code set by the dominant culture and embodied in the *superego*.

While he believed that the *id* was at odds with the requirements of civilized living, Freud also expressed deep concern that repressing the irrational side of the human per-

Sigmund Freud Freud's exploration of nonrational forces undermined the strength of the Enlightenment tradition in Western thought. Although he championed rationality, Freud alerted his readers to the existence and power of instinctive, aggressive, and amoral drives that could be controlled only through deliberate effort.

sonality contributed to mental disorders. Paradoxically, he also believed that human progress could only occur so long as self-denial and repression were effective. In the aftermath of World War I, Freud published *Civilization and Its Discontents* (1927), a brief but wide-ranging book that placed that horrific experience within the context of his broader psychological theory. Freud interpreted the unprecedented bloodletting of the war as a civilization-wide discharge of aggressive impulses that modern culture had sought to repress. Freud found no solution to humankind's dilemma in religious experience. Like Marx and Nietzsche before him, he dismissed religion as a neurotic manifestation of the immature mind, and he placed his trust in a naturalistic explanation of the universe.

Ironically, Freud's secularized picture of human nature, in which humanity's base instincts and desires must be controlled if civilization is to be preserved, had something in common with the early Christian perspective, where fallen men and women were incapable of obeying God's law and where sacrifice and struggle were essential to the human experience. Freud's most promising student, Carl Jung (1875–1961), did not share his mentor's disdain for religious experience. Jung took issue with Freud's emphasis on the primacy of sexual drives in the formation of the personality and instead emphasized the role that collective memories, which he called archetypes, played in the development of the subconscious. Much to the chagrin of the rationalist Freud, Jung introduced a mystical element into psychoanalysis, legitimizing the role of religion in personality development.

Einstein and the New Physics

The Newtonian picture of the physical universe, where solid objects moved in absolute time and space irrespective of the observer and where humans could discover unchanging, mechanistic, physical laws, suggested the possibility that all of the secrets of nature might one day be discovered. Newton's contribution had inspired eighteenth-century thinkers to draw comparisons between the apparent order and rationality of the physical universe and the disorder and irrationality of Europe's social, religious, and political landscape. The Enlightenment hope for a society ordered by reason was in large measure impelled by the discovery of new truths about God's physical creation.

During the late nineteenth and early twentieth centuries, many of the Newtonian assumptions about physical matter were superceded by a second great revolution in physics, this one associated with the German-born Swiss theoretical physicist Albert Einstein (1879–1955). At the age of 26, while working as a clerk in the Swiss patent office, Einstein published his "Special Theory of Relativity," which included the radical theory that absolute space and time were not fixed realities independent of human experience, as Newtonian physics had long assumed. Einstein demonstrated that there existed no absolute frame of reference in the universe, and that instead space, time, and motion were relative to one another and to the human observer. Probing beneath the surface of experienced reality, Einstein's work appeared to reinforce the antirationalist arguments current in other fields of research.

Einstein's subsequent research revealed the tremendous energy contained in simple matter. By showing that very small amounts of matter could be converted into enormous energy, Einstein broke with the conventional Newtonian treatment of matter and energy as independent quantities. Suddenly, the universe seemed unfamiliar and disorienting. The practical end product of Einstein's path-breaking theoretical work was just as unsettling. The development of the atomic bomb in the 1940s transformed international relations by virtue of the massive destructive power made available to humankind.

The Birth of the Social Sciences
The many tangible benefits of late nineteenth-century science and technology, especially their ability to improve the material quality of life, raised the prestige of those who engaged in scientific activities and encouraged other specialists to claim that their disciplines were also sciences. New and existing fields of study, including sociology, anthropology, economics, history, and archaeology, each proudly declared that it followed the same rigorous empirical and experimental standards as the biological and physical sciences.

In Germany the historical profession was given its specialist credentials early. Leopold von Ranke (1795–1886) argued that each period in the human past was "equidistant from eternity" and must be studied on its own terms; scholars had to reject popular legend and rely on archival source material whenever possible. Dispassionate investigation of social processes also became popular. The word *sociology* was coined by August Comte (1798–1857), and by the end of the century, sociologists concerned themselves with the problem of creating and maintaining social order in a period of rapid urbanization and industrialization. The French scholar Emile Durkheim (1858–1917) was the most influential successor to Comte. Although a defender of modern civilization and an admirer of science, Durkheim warned that some of the main features of modern society, particularly competitive individualism and secularism, could trigger social disintegration. With the loss of communal identity and the weakening of collective spiritual beliefs, modern men and women faced a hostile world without the benefits of companionship. Because people lacked common values and social conventions and were encouraged by popular culture to raise their material expectations, Durkheim believed that a situation of anxiety, or *anomie,* had emerged at the core of advanced Western culture.

The leading social theorist at the turn of the century was the German Max Weber (1864–1920). He too applauded the achievements of rationalism in science, economic and political organization, law, and administration. However, the rationalization of life had unfortunately contributed to the erosion of life-sustaining customs and beliefs. The modern outlook dismissed religion as superstition, emotion as dangerous, and tradition as reactionary. Awash in material abundance, the modern citizen, immersed in the institutions and bureaucracies of his own creation, struggled to find meaning in life. Many sought to find that meaning in the supposed glories of overseas empire. Anticipating some of the darker developments of twentieth-century politics, Weber cautioned that in time of economic crisis, citizens in a society where happiness was equated with possessions would be quick to support charismatic leaders who promised wide-ranging and easy solutions to their plight.

Feminism and Inequality   The calls for equality between the sexes issued by Mary Wollstonecraft and Olympe de Gouges in the 1790s (see Chapter 16, "The Age of Enlightenment: Rationalism and Its Uses") had not been heeded during the first half of the nineteenth century. In the United States, a national women's suffrage movement met at Seneca Falls, New York, in 1848 and issued a *Declaration and Statement of Principles* echoing Thomas Jefferson's Declaration of Independence, but little came out of it. Some intellectual leaders did support the cause of civil equality for women, but these voices were out of the mainstream. In England, John Stuart Mill (1806–1873) published *The Subjection of Women* in 1867 and spoke on behalf of women's suffrage in Parliament, but the proposal was decisively rejected by his colleagues. Even Queen Victoria (r. 1837–1901) rebuked women who agitated for political rights.

The old argument that women were not capable of responsible, rational conduct in the public sphere was strengthened by some of the conclusions of social science and especially by the proponents of Social Darwinism. Women's "nature," it was alleged, was emotional, irrational, unstable, and frivolous. Lacking self-control, women were more likely to make decisions on the basis of those dark irrational forces that adversely affected human life. Since rationality was the one fragile power keeping civilization on its current progressive path, any extension of civil and political rights to women was bound to end badly. Toward the end of the century, as feminists like Emmeline Pankhurst (1858–1928) in England began to engage in acts of civil disobedience, the evidence of women's essential irrationality seemed clear to opponents of equal rights. Reports of arrested feminist militants being force-fed by authorities after going on hunger strikes to protest their status not only shocked the public but in many cases confirmed antifemale prejudice.

Transformation in the Arts

As European states projected their power around the world in the form of territorial and commercial empires, important developments in the arts reflected the broader tension between the Enlightenment heritage and a more subjective and nonrational view of human nature. A general climate of restlessness, directness, and anxiety informed literature as well as the visual and performing arts. Authors and artists emerged as cultural leaders and respected critics; their ability to highlight the pressing issues of the

PEOPLE IN CONTEXT Marie Curie and Modern Physics

M arie Sklodowska Curie (1867–1934) was born in Warsaw, Poland, to parents who were both employed as teachers. Her mother was a devout Catholic, but her father, a mathematics and physics instructor, was an agnostic freethinker. Marie, who shared her father's religious outlook, excelled in school as a child and embraced the dream of becoming a scientist at a time when few women had professional careers. This was especially true in Russian-dominated Poland. After working as a tutor and governess, Marie moved to Paris in 1891. At age 24, she began attending lectures at the Sorbonne, met a number of leading physicists there, and secured a post as laboratory assistant. In 1894, one year after taking her degree in physics, she met Pierre Curie (1859–1906), a shy and introverted man who shared Marie's passion for pure research in the natural sciences. They were married the following year.

Working together in a poorly equipped laboratory, the husband and wife team made a series of important discoveries in physics. In 1896 they discovered the highly radioactive elements polonium and radium, and in 1903 they shared a Nobel Prize in physics with Henri Becquerel (1852–1908) for their joint discovery of natural radioactivity. Although the money from the Nobel Prize freed them from financial worries, the resulting public attention disrupted their personal and professional lives. When World War I began in 1914, Marie Curie was busy establishing the Radium Institute of the University of Paris. She served as the Institute's first director, and during the war she worked on using X-rays to locate shrapnel and bullets so that soldiers might be operated on more effectively. She also pioneered the use of portable X-ray machines in vans to treat the wounded closer to the front.

Family life, including the birth of two daughters in 1897 and 1904, and the tragic death of her husband in an accident in 1906, did not inhibit Curie's professional career. Offered a pension, she refused to accept it, commenting that she was 38 and fully capable of earning a living. After Pierre's death, she was selected

Marie and Pierre Curie   Despite the widespread sexism and anti-Semitism of her day, Marie Curie rose to prominence in physics and chemistry, and is still the only person to win Nobel prizes in two separate scientific fields. She is pictured here with her husband, Pierre, who was also an outstanding scientist—the two were jointly awarded the Nobel Prize in 1903—but who died in a carriage accident in Paris three years later.

to fill his professorship at the Sorbonne. Curie was the first female to hold a faculty position at this leading research institution. In 1911 Curie was awarded a second Nobel Prize, this time in chemistry, for her work on the isolation of pure radium. Just after receiving this unprecedented second prize, Curie was denied admission to France's prestigious Academy of Science. Sexism, anti-Semitism, and disdain for foreigners outweighed the importance of her remarkable scientific work in the eyes of many of her male colleagues. The right-wing press suggested that although Curie was from a Catholic household, her father's name (Sklodowska) suggested that she might be of Jewish origin. The rejection by the Academy deeply wounded Curie.

Exposed to high degrees of radiation during her career, Marie Curie died of leukemia at age 67. She had spent her professional life committed to the belief that science must help lessen human suffering. In 1995 the French government moved the remains of Marie and Pierre Curie to the famous Pantheon mausoleum in Paris.

Question: What conventions did Curie break during her career?

day—poverty, urbanization, women's rights, empire—led Sigmund Freud to describe them as the first psychoanalysts.

Realism and Naturalism   Beginning in the second half of the nineteenth century, many artists and writers rejected the romantic style of expression and adopted a realistic idiom that reflected science and technology's fact-driven, experiential approach to truth. Authors investigated the gritty contours of city life, the personal and the private, the ordinary and the exceptional, in a manner that captured the complexity of living in a society where the forces of industrialization were invalidating traditional norms and values. Mary Ann Evans (1819–1880), who wrote under the name George Eliot in England; Emile Zola (1840–1902) in France; Leo Tolstoy (1828–1910) in Russia; and Henrik Ibsen (1828–1906) in Norway each created characters whose psychological development was detailed within the context of new social forces. In her novel *Middlemarch,* for example, Evans introduced a wide range of fascinating characters, from the idealistic and progressive medical doctor and his ambitious but insecure wife, to the hypocritical banker whose false piety and condescension are betrayed by the revelation of a youthful affair and his abandonment of his mistress and their child. Ibsen's best-known play, *A Doll's House,* detailed the psychological burdens imposed on a woman whose conventional middle-class husband refuses to acknowledge his wife's longing for an independent identity, which shockingly, she chooses anyway.

Modernism   Not surprisingly, the literary and artistic response to the uncertainties introduced by modern biology, physics, and psychology involved a sharp rejection of realism and a vigorous engagement with the subjective, the introspective, the irrational, and the abstract. Conventional literary and artistic forms were deemed inadequate to the task of exploring beneath the surface of rational appearances. Authors such as James Joyce (1882–1941), Thomas Mann (1875–1955), D. H. Lawrence (1885–1930), Virginia Woolf (1882–1941), and Franz Kafka (1883–1924) wrote about the inner psychological conflicts and antisocial penchants of men and women who rejected the conventions of bourgeois existence. A new frankness about the role of sex, a willingness to highlight the power of the instinctive and the primitive, and a penchant for detailing the everyday and often sordid aspects of human life in a world of disorder all distinguished the modern mood in literature.

Major Works of the Nineteenth and Early Twentieth Centuries	
1859	Charles Darwin, *Origin of the Species by Means of Natural Selection*
1867	John Stuart Mill, *The Subjectivity of Women*
1871	Charles Darwin, *Descent of Man*
1878	Leo Tolstoy, *Anna Karenina*
1879	Henrik Ibsen, *A Doll's House*
1886	Friedrich Nietzsche, *Beyond Good and Evil*
1900	Sigmund Freud, *The Interpretation of Dreams*
1905	Albert Einstein, "On the Electrodynamics of Moving Bodies"
1925	Franz Kafka, *The Trial*
1928	D. H. Lawrence, *Lady Chatterley's Lover*

Modern Art and Music   Since the Renaissance, leading artists endorsed the view that art should imitate the world as the senses perceive it. Rules of perspective and proportion set the parameters of what was judged worthy of serious consideration. The finest art would follow a certain structure and attempt to mirror nature, and those who strayed from convention were generally dismissed as insubordinate hacks. Around the middle of the nineteenth century, the French artist Gustave Courbet (1819–1877) inaugurated the Realist movement in landscape and genre painting. Joined by the American Thomas Eakins (1844–1916) and the Englishman Ford Madox Brown (1821–1893), the realists painted what they saw, no matter how appealing or distasteful. Painting the laboring classes instead of the elite, urban slums and factories instead of country estates, the actual conditions of industrial life became the focus of what deserved the attention of the artist.

Some mid-century artists believed that reality was more complex than merely representational. In particular, a group of painters known as Impressionists began to turn away from the deliberate representational form and experiment with personal interpretations, especially the first glance, or "impression," of external reality. Parallel with the development of modern photography, many artists cast off their previous interest in recreating mere surface images. Edouard Manet (1832–1883), Edgar Degas (1834–1917), Claude Monet (1840–1926), and Pierre Auguste Renoir (1841–1919) produced works that mediated between a fascination with nature and a desire to record. Particularly in their treatment of light and form, the Impressionists conveyed a sense of the elusiveness of sensory reality. By the 1890s, post-Impressionist artists

Vincent Van Gogh   *The Night Café* is characteristic of Van Gogh's work in its brilliant and turbulent use of colors. Like many of his late paintings, *The Night Café* leaves the viewer unsettled because of its expressionistic and vaguely nightmarish qualities. *Vincent van Gogh (1853–1890), "Night Cafe (Le Café de nuit)." 1888. Oil on canvas, 28 1/2 × 36 1/4 in. 1961. 18.34. Yale University Art Gallery, New Haven, Connecticut/Art Resource, NY*

like Paul Cézanne (1839–1906) and Vincent van Gogh (1853–1890) worked to portray inner feelings and personal perspectives of reality, largely without regard to the tastes of the public or private patrons.

Modernist artists of the early twentieth century reconstructed their discipline by legitimizing the unconventional and the introspective. Reality was no longer confined within the boundaries of sense experience and rational understanding. **Modernism** heralded the advent of multiple realities, each of which had to be approached in a highly individualistic and personal fashion. The Modernist artist was concerned primarily with the process of expression, the aesthetic experience, and only marginally with the final outcome or outside reality. Similarly, since the finished product no longer depicted a fixed reality, the viewer was invited to share in the highly personal process of interpretation. Reason, order, and clarity were replaced by ambiguity, tension, lack of form, and an appeal to the subconscious. For the modernist, the wellspring of creativity, be it in the artist or the viewer, no longer resided in the rational and conscious mind. With the birth of Cubism just before World War I, artists led by Pablo Picasso (1881–1973) struggled to represent the multiple realities of modern existence on a single canvas.

The same desire to communicate multiple realities inspired the French composer Claude Debussy (1862–1918), who was influenced by the exotic music of Bali in Indonesia when he heard it performed at the Paris Exposition of 1889. His *Prelude to "The Afternoon of a Faun"* (1894) combined a dreamlike melody with innovative chords. The Austrian composer Arnold Schoenberg (1874–1951) and his Russian counterpart Igor Stravinsky (1882–1971) were even bolder. Schoenberg's music employed dissonant chords, abandoning the traditional technique of organizing tones around a musical key and instead treating all 12 notes equally. Stravinsky's ballet *The Rite of Spring* (1913) incorporated a variety of musical styles, including jazz rhythms, to produce a highly dissonant composition that deals with the disturbing theme of primitive Slavonic peoples engaged in human sacrifice. Just as many painters and sculptors of the early twentieth century turned for fresh artistic ideas to the customs and practices of peoples who had avoided modernization, composers sought a new direction in what was termed *primitivism*. Audiences were sometimes outraged. When *The Rite of Spring* was first performed in Paris, the highly discordant and jarring music elicited catcalls, shouts, and boos from members of the audience. The police were called in to restore order, and the composer was obliged to depart through a backstage window. The public was ill-prepared for such a radical challenge to the culture of order, reason, progress, and power that Europeans had projected around the world during the previous quarter century.

KEY QUESTION | Revisited

By 1914, Europe's rapidly expanding population could confidently claim that the West was the dominant global civilization. There was a widespread popular conviction, held most strongly by the middle class, that the great problems of life could and would be successfully addressed. Famine, sickness, ignorance, underemployment, poverty, war—the many ills that had been constants of the human experience for centuries—would be removed with the help of highly educated specialists in education, medicine, sociology, psychology, administration, and politics. More troublesome developments in theoretical science, philosophy, and the arts did not alter the generally confident outlook of most Europeans. Equating science with the benefits of technology, they went about the business of educating themselves, seeking better careers, and consuming new industrial products without giving much thought to the implications of evolutionary theory in biology, Freudian psychology, relativity theory in physics, or modernist art. Even traditional religious forms, while under assault, continued to appeal to millions of Europeans.

Most people maintained their belief in the values and goals of the Enlightenment, including responsible, representative government, the rule of law, protection of individual liberties, religious freedom, the sanctity of property, and a social and economic order responsive to merit and talent.

Overseas empire was commonly justified as the extension of these "universal" values to the peoples who inhabited less-developed areas of the world. At the height of empire, few Europeans questioned the propriety of their nation's overseas conquests; the link between progress and control over non-Western peoples was considered self-evident. Most of the approximately 60 million Europeans who migrated overseas during the nineteenth and early twentieth centuries would have endorsed the claim by Cecil Rhodes respecting the backwardness of indigenous peoples. In the period between 1870 and 1914, the Europeanization of the global community was intimately connected with the gospel of unlimited progress, with a faith in the universality of Western ideas, even when those ideas legitimized the subjection of non-Western peoples.

Review Questions

1. Why did a new European race for imperial possessions begin during the last quarter of the nineteenth century?
2. How did European imperialism contribute to the development of European-style nationalism in India?
3. How did the new physics undermine the Newtonian picture of the universe?
4. What was the nature of Nietzsche's relationship with the Enlightenment tradition?
5. Does Freud's assessment of human rationality have any bearing on Europe's treatment of non-Western peoples?
6. How did views on the role of women in society reflect changing cultural norms?
7. What were the principal goals of Modernist art and how did they differ from earlier aesthetic standards?

Please consult the Suggested Readings at the back of the book to continue your study of the material covered in this chapter. For a list of documents on the Primary Source DVD-ROM that relate to topics in this chapter, please refer to the back of the book.

Part 7
Europe in Crisis, 1914–1945

Pablo Picasso, *Guernica* **(1937).** *Oil on canvas, 350 × 782 cm. Museo Nacional Centro de Arte Reina Sofia, Madrid, Spain. © 2004 Estate of Pablo Picasso/Artists Rights Society (ARS), New York. John Bigelow Taylor/Art Resource, NY.*

No one alive in Europe in the summer of 1914 had ever experienced a general war involving multiple states with well-equipped and well-trained armies. The last time that the continent had been engulfed by conflict on multiple fronts was during the Napoleonic era. There had been a number of regional wars, but the evidence seemed to suggest that modern military conflict involved rapid troop movements, limited casualties, and quick resolution. World War I shattered each of these misconceptions. Plunging from the pinnacle of global power to the depths of financial insolvency and psychological self-doubt, Western Europe failed to find a durable solution to the problem of international rivalry.

A troubled interregnum of 20 years followed the conclusion of World War I and the start of another, more deadly, global conflagration. The Western democracies, especially Britain and France, appeared incapable of responding to the challenge of fascism in Italy and Germany or to the rise of communism in the Soviet Union. The United States retreated into isolationism during the 1920s and 1930s. Those states that repudiated the Enlightenment tradition of responsible, constitutional government, individual rights, and free expression boldly proclaimed the dawn of a new age where race and class were the benchmarks of power.

Between 1939 and 1945, another world war claimed the lives of over 50 million people, combatants and noncombatants alike, around the globe. The unrivaled barbarism of the Jewish Holocaust, together with the inhumanity exhibited by Japanese occupying forces in the Pacific theater, suggested to many in the West that the Enlightenment faith in human rationality had been misplaced. At the end of the war, two great ideological power blocs emerged, one led by the United States and the other dominated by the brutal Stalin regime in the Soviet Union. Western Europe, with its economic base in tatters and its populations wearied by a half-century of distrust and war, surrendered its global primacy in political affairs.

	ENVIRONMENT AND TECHNOLOGY	SOCIETY AND CULTURE	POLITICS
1914	Poison gas, airplanes, and tanks employed in war (1914–1918) Bauhaus school founded (1919) First radio broadcast station opens in France (1920) Electronic television broadcast begins; penicillin discovered (1928)	Spengler, *Decline of the West* (1918) Jazz age in America (1920s) Rampant inflation in Germany (1923) General strike in Britian (1926) Great Depression begins (1929) Holocaust (1941–1945) European population reaches 450 million (1914) Women secure franchise in Britain (1928) Collectivization of Soviet agriculture begins (1928)	Start of trench warfare (1914) U.S. enters World War I; Bolshevik Revolution in Russia (1917) Russian civil war (1918–1921) Treaty of Versailles (1919) Mussolini's "march on Rome" (1922) Stalin consolidates power (1927) Japan invades Manchuria (1931)
1930	Radar technology developed (1935)	Stalin's purges begin (1934) Picasso, *Guernica* (1937)	Hitler becomes chancellor (1933) Civil war in Spain (1936–1939)
1940	Jet engine invented (1941)		World War II begins (1939) Battle of Britain (1940) Germans invade Soviet Union; Pearl Harbor attacked (1941) Atomic bombs dropped on Hiroshima and Nagasaki (1945)

Topics in This Chapter

The Alliance System • The Experience of Modern War

• The Eastern Front and Europe's Empire • Naval War and American Entry

• The Impact of Total War at Home • The Russian Revolution

• The Peace Settlement and European Consciousness

22 World War I: The End of Enlightenment

If in some smothering dreams, you too could pace
Behind the wagon that we flung him in,
And watch the white eyes writhing in his face,
His hanging face, like a devil sick of sin . . .
My friend, you would not tell with such high zest
To children ardent for some desperate glory,
The old Lie: *Dulce et decorum est*
Pro patria mori (it is sweet and proper to die for one's country)

—Wilfred Owen

KEY | Question
Are nation-states inherently adversarial?

The British poet and officer Wilfred Owen (1893–1918) died on the battlefield just a few hours before the armistice ending World War I was signed. Like many young men, Owen had volunteered for military service out of a deep sense of patriotism and commitment to the ideals of the British Empire. When the war began in August 1914, few of the combatants on either side expected it to last more than a few months. Most planned to be home by Christmas, having defeated the enemy in rapid order thanks to the employment of the latest military technology. Their predictions were based on solid empirical evidence. No general European war had been fought for over a century, and those conflicts that had taken place were brief and involved few casualties. There had not been a military clash in Europe between two major powers since 1870, when a better-trained and better-equipped German force triumphed over France in less than six months.

Recruitment Poster When orders for mobilization went up on walls and were broadcast in newspapers across Europe in the summer of 1914, a generation of young men lined up for battle. They went in high spirits, cheered on by their mothers, unaware of the horrors they were about to face.

Many strident European nationalists, encouraged by the easy successes of colonial wars, celebrated military conflict as a heroic, purifying, and liberating experience. They believed that the excitement, emotional intensity, and drama of the battlefield would strengthen the national community and provide a sense of purpose to factory workers, office clerks, and students who found little pleasure or meaning in their dull, repetitive civilian tasks. In the days immediately after the outbreak of World War I, men eagerly lined up at recruiting stations, young soldiers were applauded as they paraded on the way to the front, and serious newspapers praised the renewed sense of national unity and vigor that appeared to affect entire populations. Most socialist politicians abandoned the rhetoric of international working-class solidarity and joined the outpouring of support for the sacred nation-state.

There was an eagerness for war in 1914. The same martial spirit and thirst for glory that gripped the common people of Britain, France, Germany, Austria-Hungary, and Russia also captured the imaginations of Europe's intellectuals, including such well-known scholars as Sigmund Freud. Here was an opportunity to put an end to the complacency of bourgeois life with its focus on getting and spending. The triumph of the nation-state would restore meaning and a sense of collective purpose to modern civilization. Those few voices opposed to the war were treated harshly by their countrymen. In Britain, for example, Ramsey MacDonald (1866–1937) resigned his leadership of the Labour Party in opposition to the war, the plays of pacifist George Bernard Shaw (1856–1950) were boycotted, and the philosopher Bertrand Russell (1872–1970) was jailed. The summer and fall of 1914 were cruel seasons for those who cautioned restraint.

The high expectations were dispelled within a few months. Hopes of rapid victory proved illusory as the anticipated war of movement degenerated into a stalemated and gruesome campaign of attrition. New military technology—machine guns, poison gas, high explosives—magnified the carnage. Military leadership proved to be uninventive and undistinguished, while the bellicose and punitive rhetoric of popularly elected politicians mitigated against diplomatic initiatives and compromise. As the conflict dragged on, disillusionment and despair replaced enthusiasm. Casualty rates were so high that by 1916, the British government was obliged to institute military conscription for the first time in British history to maintain force levels on the continent. The following year French troops mutinied, refusing to follow senseless orders to advance to their deaths across "no-man's land" on the Western Front. The war quickly engaged Europe's colonies in Africa and Asia, involved combat on land and sea, terrorized civilian populations, and led to massive physical destruction in wide stretches of Western and Eastern Europe. By the end of 1917, tsarist Russia had been destroyed, and the American republic had been drawn into the conflagration. European civilization, at the moment of its apogee, decisively forfeited its global primacy in what was akin to a fratricidal civil war. The nation-states of Europe had failed the test of mutual accommodation.

The Alliance System

When a young Serbian terrorist named Gavrilo Princip (1895–1918) assassinated the heir to the throne of Austria-Hungary on June 28, 1914, he also set off a diplomatic crisis in each of Europe's major capitals. Archduke Francis Ferdinand (1863–1914) and his wife were on an official state visit to Sarajevo when they were murdered, and in response the imperial authorities in Vienna decided that now was the moment to crush the Serbian-inspired, pan-Slav separatist movement in Bosnia. The provinces of Bosnia and Herzegovina, nominally part of the Ottoman Empire, had been administered by the Austrians since 1878, and in 1908 they were officially annexed by the multinational

Assassination of Archduke Franz Ferdinand, June 28, 1914   Shortly before this photograph was taken the Austrian archduke and his wife were assassinated by members of a secretive Serbian nationalist group, indirectly sparking the First World War. Here, one of the assailants is captured by police.

Austrian Empire. Since much of the population in these areas were Eastern Orthodox in religion and were ethnically related to the Serbs, the annexation caused consternation in Belgrade, the capital of independent Serbia. A strong nationalist movement had emerged in Serbia during a long and ultimately successful struggle for independence from the Ottoman Empire. Once independence was achieved, Serbia turned its nationalist energies against the Austrians. The Serbs dreamed of a greater union of all South Slavs, including the over 7 million who lived under Austrian rule.

Still, the assassination of Francis Ferdinand need not have led to a general European war. Austrian authorities had been faced with violent secession movements in the past, but they had always been able to address the problem through a combination of military force, political compromise, and the co-option of nationalist leaders. Unfortunately, the Serbian threat had wider international implications. In particular, the Russians had long portrayed themselves as the protectors of their Serb co-religionists. In 1908 Tsar Nicholas II's (r. 1894–1917) government had concluded an informal arrangement with Austria whereby Russia would acquiesce in the Austrian plan to annex Bosnia and Herzegovina in return for Austrian support for Russia's bid to secure naval access from the Black Sea to the Mediterranean through the Ottoman-controlled Dardanelles (adjacent to Istanbul). Austria did annex the provinces, but Britain and France strenuously objected to a Russian fleet in the Mediterranean, and Tsar Nicholas was forced to back down. It was the latest in a string of diplomatic and military humiliations that the Russians had suffered since their defeat by Japan in 1905, and as a result the Russian government was in no mood in 1914 to allow Austria to bully Serbia.

The Triple Alliance and Triple Entente   Otto von Bismarck (1815–1898) had pursued a nonaggressive foreign policy in Europe after Germany was unified in 1871. To solidify his country's position in Europe and prevent an attack by France, Bismarck forged a defensive Triple Alliance in the 1880s with Austria-Hungary and Italy. He also concluded a nonaggression pact with Russia, but this was allowed to expire in 1890 after Bismarck left office. Kaiser William II (r. 1888–1918) disagreed with Bismarck's cautious policy on the continent. The Triple Alliance remained in force, but with strong encouragement from German nationalists, the kaiser began an ambitious naval-building program that was designed to rival the British fleet. William also expanded the size of the German army and inaugurated an expansionist colonial policy. When combined with its industrial, technical, and educational accomplishments, Germany's newly assertive posture on the international front deeply troubled policymakers in Britain, France, and Russia.

In 1893, five years after William assumed the throne and three years after he dismissed Bismarck, Russia and France entered into their own defensive alliance. In 1904, Britain resolved its outstanding differences with France over colonial issues and concluded a defensive understanding, the *Entente Cordiale*. The pact was tested by the German emperor at an international conference held in Algeciras, Spain, in 1906 to decide the fate of Morocco, over which the French were gradually establishing a protectorate. Kaiser William announced that Germany favored independence for Morocco, but only Austria supported its German ally. Britain, Russia, Spain, the United States, and even Italy, which was also still formally a German ally, sided with France. In the aftermath of the conference, the British and French military staffs began to discuss how their forces would cooperate if Germany attacked.

In 1907 the French acted as intermediaries to get Britain and Russia to settle their competing imperial claims in Afghanistan, Tibet, and Persia. The system of alliances that was now in place seemed to represent an important step toward ensuring peace in Europe. No single power would be reckless enough to provoke another state, it was assumed, because any attack could mean war against an entire military partnership. Each country's professional diplomatic corps was charged with settling international disputes. Failing this, the direct intervention of Europe's monarchs, some of whom were relations, would prevent the inconceivable from happening. Rival nation-states appeared capable of establishing formal and adequate mechanisms for avoiding war.

The Balkan Tinderbox   A second Moroccan Crisis occurred in 1911 when a German gunboat arrived in the Moroccan port of Agadir, just as the French were quashing a rebellion. The British feared that the kaiser was seeking to secure a Mediterranean port for Germany's growing navy. The Germans eventually recognized French claims to Morocco, but the dispute bolstered the view in Britain that its security was best served by forging even closer military ties with France. For its part, Germany, recognizing that it could no longer count on Italian support, became even more committed to the support of its one sure ally, Austria-Hungary. Austria's annexation of Bosnia and Herzegovina in 1908 had infuriated Serbian nationalists, while in Vienna key Austrian officials, supported by their German allies, debated strategies for ending Serbian agitation once and for all. In 1912 Serbia joined with Greece, Bulgaria, and Montenegro in a war against the Ottoman Turks that all but expelled the Turks from the Balkans. For a brief moment, the victorious Serbs gained coveted access to the Adriatic coastline, but Austria (with German backing) forced them to surrender this territory and to permit the formation of the independent state of Albania in 1913. After this last Serbian indignity, the Russians concluded that they could not afford to lose any more credibility in the eyes of their Orthodox "little brothers" in Serbia.

Final Breakdown   In the aftermath of this tense situation, the heir presumptive to the Austrian throne made his fateful trip to Sarajevo. Francis Ferdinand, whose wife was a Czech countess, was genuinely interested in seeking political compromise with the empire's Slavic subjects, and his assassination guaranteed that the voice of moderation would no longer prevail in Vienna. The Serbian newspapers reported the murder with satisfaction, and there is evidence that the Serbian government was complicit in the act. With full backing from its German ally, Austria presented Serbia with an ultimatum that included a demand that Austrian authorities conduct an investigation, on Serbian soil, into the murder. The Serbians, afraid of what the Austrians might discover, accepted the other parts of the ultimatum but rejected this last demand as a violation of the rights of a sovereign nation, and Russia supported this interpretation. The Austrian army was then mobilized for action, and on July 28, 1914, the multinational Habsburg Empire declared war on Serbia.

Two days later, Russia began mobilizing its forces. Since most statesmen interpreted full mobilization to be an act of war, Germany sent Russia a 12-hour ultimatum demanding immediate demobilization. When this was ignored, Germany mobilized and formally declared war on Russia on August 1. It was an enormous gamble, but the German army's general staff believed that it was best to fight now rather than to wait for the forces of Slavic nationalism to undermine the integrity of the Austrian Empire, Germany's one reliable ally in Europe. Within 48 hours, the Germans also declared war on France, convinced that the French would honor their pact with Russia and anxious to implement a detailed plan for a two-front war that the German army had drawn up years earlier. The defensive alliance systems, rather than preventing war, actually ensured that a regional conflict would escalate into a continentwide catastrophe. The job of coordinating the movement of men and massive amounts of material via railway networks required strict adherence to preestablished timetables. Any last minute alterations or changes of plan could spell disaster. In the five weeks between the assassination of Francis Ferdinand and the start of war on August 4, military planners on both sides resisted appeals for delay or contingency planning.

The Experience of Modern War

Into the Abyss   Germany's war plan, developed by Count Alfred von Schlieffen (1833–1913) while he was chief of the German general staff, was a desperate gamble to deal with the problems of having to fight a two-front war against France in the west and Russia in the east. The plan envisioned a quick knock-out of France by an invasion through neutral Belgium and Luxembourg, followed by a rapid transfer of troops via railway to the eastern front to rebuff the enormous but slow-moving Russian army. Britain had pledged to guarantee Belgian neutrality in a treaty of 1839, and as German troops rolled through Belgium en route to France during the first three days of August 1914, the British were quick to respond. They entered the war against Germany on August 4, confident of victory and believing that Kaiser William II and his closest military advisors were solely to blame for the conflict. Only the British Foreign Secretary, Sir Edward Grey (1862–1933), appeared to recognize the gravity of what was about to occur. "The lights are going out all over Europe," he commented, "and we shall not see them lit again in our lifetime."

Stalemate in the West   The first few weeks of combat in the Western theater seemed to confirm the predictions of those who had anticipated a short war of movement. The Germans were able to outflank most French defenses by invading from the northeast through Belgium. Their highly mobile troops moved rapidly into French territory, reaching the Marne River, within 40 miles of Paris, during the first month of fighting. The Schlieffen Plan called for German troops to envelop the French defensive forces by sweeping around Paris and attacking the French armies from the rear. At the bloody week-long Battle of the Marne, however, the French, with the assistance of a small British expeditionary force, stopped the German advance and forced the Germans to retreat. In the following weeks, each side desperately tried to outflank the other to secure the ports along the English Channel in what scholars refer to as "the race to the sea." The war now entered an unanticipated phase on the Western Front. Each side began constructing a vast network of defensive trenches stretching from Belgium's North Sea coastline across northern France to the Swiss border in the south. For 400 miles the trench lines snaked their way across devastated countryside. Between the opposing trenches stood nests of barbed wire, shattered trees, and churned up farms. Heavy artillery, poison gas, land mines, and machine guns guaranteed that any assault across this "no man's land" would result in heavy casualties. During the first four months of fighting, 700,000 German, 850,000 French, and 90,000 British troops were either killed or wounded. Again and again over the next four years, however, unimaginative military leaders on both sides disregarded the deadly fact of defensive superiority and sent tens of thousands of men "over the top" of the trenches in repeated efforts to break through the enemy's lines and reignite the war of movement. Most of the troops never returned to the filth and squalor of their defensive positions, having been mowed down by the efficient weaponry of the modern age. The average life expectancy for junior officers who had to lead these attacks was just two months (see Map 22–1).

The psychological strain imposed by life in the trenches was enormous. Months of inactivity amid wounded and dying men, the smell of human and animal excrement and decaying flesh, the cold damp climate, the always expanding rat and lice population, and the sound of heavy bombardments and the cries of the wounded stranded in no man's land all combined to undermine morale. Within one year of the start of the war, the dreams of heroic combat and national glory were dead. The unexpected war of attrition in the heart of Western Europe, where lines of advance were measured in feet and where casualties were counted in hundreds of thousands, contributed to an atmosphere in

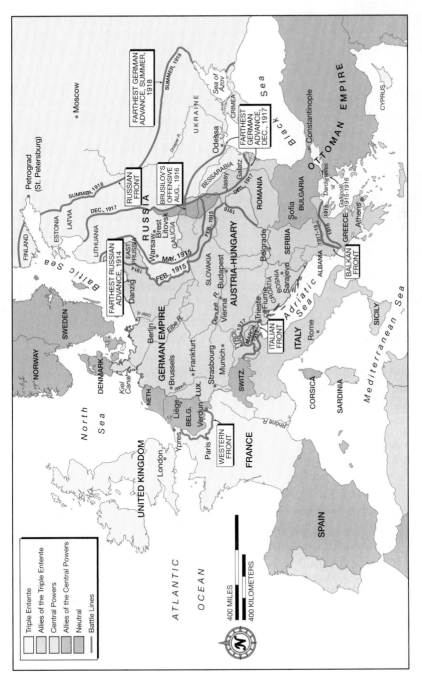

Map 22–1 World War I in Europe The Central Powers were obligated to fight on two fronts after the failure of the Schlieffen Plan in August 1914. Important battles took place across the globe, but the major theater remained in Europe throughout four years of conflict.

Question: Which nation suffered the greatest physical destruction on the Western Front?

The Experience of the Trenches   The stalemate on the Western Front led to four years of trench warfare. Conditions in the trenches were extremely difficult. During long stretches of inactivity, soldiers battled cold, wet, the smell of decaying bodies, and the fear of imminent death from enemy shelling.

which cynicism and despair replaced idealism and courage. "War is hell," wrote Siegfried Sassoon (1886–1967) from the trenches, "and those who institute it are criminals."

Verdun and the Somme   After almost two years of fruitless combat, German commanders decided in February 1916 to concentrate their destructive might against the defenses around the historic French city of Verdun. The plan was simple in its brutality. The Germans expected the French to defend this fortress city to the end. By inflicting massive casualties on the defenders of Verdun, the Germans hoped to break France's will to fight. The French commander, Henri Petain (1856–1951), became a national hero for his success in resisting repeated assaults, but the human cost was astronomical. Before the Germans abandoned the assault in December 1916, over 1 million German and French combatants were either killed or wounded at Verdun. To help the French, the British opened their own offensive against the Germans at the Somme River in northeastern France in July 1916. The assault from the trenches was preceded by a week-long bombardment of the German lines by heavy artillery. This preparatory "softening up" was a complete failure. On the first day of the attack, 60,000 British soldiers were either killed or wounded as they crossed "no man's land" into a hail of German machine gun fire. The battle and the butchery continued at the Somme until November, but neither side capitulated. The British assault at Passchendaele in Flanders during the summer and fall of 1917 followed a similar frontal approach, with disturbingly similar results—this time 300,000 casualties. That same year the French commander General Robert Nivelle (1856–1924) ordered yet another massive assault into the heavily defended German lines. On this occasion the Germans inflicted almost 200,000 casualties on the French over a 10-day period. Mutinies ensued in almost one-half of the French divisions on the front. Thousands of soldiers were eventually court-martialed for refusing to obey orders, but subsequent commanders agreed to forego any future frontal assaults from the trenches.

The Eastern Front and Europe's Empire

One reason the Schlieffen Plan faltered in August 1914 was that the German High Command had redeployed 100,000 troops (four divisions) to the east at a critical moment in the Western campaign. The redeployment was in response to Russia's invasion of East

Prussia and Austrian Galicia. The Germans were able to defeat the enemy at the Battles of Tannenberg and Masurian Lakes, destroying the Russian Second Army and capturing 100,000 Russian soldiers. During the next year the kaiser's forces pushed some 200 miles into Russia's Baltic and Polish territories, inflicting almost 2 million casualties before the end of 1915 and gaining control over 30% of Russia's key industries and 20% of its population.

In the Balkans, the Austrian assault against Serbia was unsuccessful. A battle-hardened Serbian army of 350,000 men forced the Austrians onto the defensive within the first two weeks of fighting. The Germans were obliged to come to the assistance of their ill-prepared allies. After intense fighting, a combined Austrian, Bulgarian, and German force finally eliminated Serbia from the war in October 1915. Ottoman Turkey joined Austria and Germany (now called the Central Powers) in 1914 and repulsed an Anglo-French expeditionary force that attempted an ill-prepared landing at Gallipoli near the Dardanelles. This ill-fated amphibious campaign, planned by Britain's naval chief, Winston Churchill (1874–1965), was designed to break the deadlock on the Western Front by knocking the Turks out of the war and opening up the supply lines to Russia.

Secret Treaties and Broken Promises   After the humiliation of Gallipoli, the British led an effort to arouse Arabs in the Middle East against the Ottoman sultan in return for British assistance in creating an Arab state under the prince of Mecca, Emir Hussein (1853–1931). British forces based in Egypt with Arab troops under the leadership of T. E. Lawrence (1888–1935), "Lawrence of Arabia," gradually pushed back the Turks. Jerusalem fell in 1917 and Damascus in 1918. At the same time that British authorities were making promises to the Arabs, they were also offering assurances to the World Zionist Organization and to the approximately 60,000 Jewish settlers in Palestine. The 1917 Balfour Declaration supported Zionist aspirations for the creation of an independent Jewish homeland in Palestine—so long as it did not interfere with existing Palestinian civil and religious claims. These contradictory commitments resulted in serious problems for British authorities during the 1920s and 1930s.

Italy joined the Allied effort in 1915 after receiving secret promises of Austrian territory. While Italian troops fared poorly against their outnumbered Austrian and German opponents, combat in northern Italy did draw precious German resources away from the Western front. For their part, the Germans attempted to distract British forces by appealing to nationalist sentiments in British-controlled Ireland, to Poles in Russian-dominated Poland, and to Muslims in Egypt and India. A rebellion against British rule in Ireland during Easter week 1916 was put down with dispatch, but it increased London's anxiety about the security of its colonial holdings elsewhere. In the Far East, the Japanese, who had been Britain's ally since 1902, captured German colonies in China and the South Pacific.

The Allies relied heavily on support from their colonial (and former colonial) subjects. More than 1 million Indians, 640,000 Canadians, 330,000 Australians, and 100,000 New Zealand troops fought alongside the British, while hundreds of thousands of Algerians, Indochinese, and black African soldiers from France's colonies served on the Western front. In the aftermath of the war, many of these colonial peoples demanded independence. The war shook European claims to superiority, and colonial leaders based their demands for freedom on the principle of national self-determination first articulated by American President Woodrow Wilson.

India and Britain's Need India's experience in World War I provided a good illustration of the Wilsonian principle in action. When the British declared war against Germany on August 4, 1914, the vast Indian subcontinent, home to over 300 million people and source of enormous material wealth, immediately became embroiled in the struggle. Four years earlier, the King-Emperor George V (r. 1910–1936) presided over an imperial *durbar* (reception) in the new capital at Delhi. Every ruling prince of India was obliged to pay his respects to the newly crowned imperial master. Now, without their consent, the Indians were being asked to contribute their blood and treasure to a war effort that seemed both distant and irrelevant to India itself. Remarkably, most Indian nationalist politicians eagerly supported the British cause, while leaders of the Congress movement firmly believed that cooperation in Britain's hour of need would translate into more freedom for India once the war was concluded. Mohandas Gandhi (1870–1948) organized a field ambulance training corps for use in the war effort. The Indian Viceroy, Lord Hardinge (1858–1944), portrayed the conflict as a global struggle between freedom and slavery. Indians naturally hoped for an extension of the former in the subcontinent once the war was over.

The first Indian expeditionary force left the port city of Karachi (now in Pakistan) for the Western Front on August 24, 1914, reaching Marseilles in southern France on September 26. The troops immediately joined their British and French counterparts in the struggle to rebuff the initial German assault. Within two months over 7,000 Indians had lost their lives in Europe.

The decision of the Ottoman Empire to join the Central Powers in November 1914 caused considerable unrest in India. There were over 60 million Muslims in India, and most considered the Ottoman caliph the leader of the international Islamic community. From the British point of view, however, preventing Germany from accessing Persian Gulf oil justified the use of Indian troops against Ottoman forces in Mesopotamia. By October 1915, over 12,000 British-led Indian troops were within reach of Baghdad before they were pushed back and defeated by Turkish forces in April 1916. Poor leadership and inadequate supplies spelled disaster on this front. In Egypt, almost 30,000 Indian troops stood ready to defend the Suez Canal from Ottoman attack.

Overall, approximately 1.2 million Indian troops and support staff were sent overseas to fight, and just over 100,000 were killed during the war. India also contributed 30 million pounds annually to the British war effort. In return, the British government stated its support for "the gradual development of self-governing institutions, with a view to the progressive realization of responsible government in India as an integral part of the Empire." This was in August 1917, and the proposal appeared to mirror the arrangements already in place in Canada, Australia, South Africa, and New Zealand.

The "Camel Corps"   An Indian military unit that fought on behalf of the British empire during World War I. The British army enlisted more than one million Indian troops during the war. Britain promised that the Indian contribution to the war effort would enhance the colony's prospects for independence, but this would not be achieved for another thirty years.

Unfortunately, immediately after the war, the imperial authorities in India decided to continue wartime measures on press censorship, trial without jury, and internment without trial. India's nationalist leaders raised a storm of protest, and riots ensued in which several British civilians were killed. On April 13, 1919, in the city of Amritsar, as several hundred men, women, and children assembled (in violation of an official ban on public gatherings) for a protest meeting, British-led troops opened fire without warning for 10 minutes—379 unarmed people were killed, and another 1,200 were wounded. This brutal action transformed millions of Indians into strident nationalists; it marked the beginning of the end of Britain's Indian Empire.

Naval War and American Entry

Although the British and German navies were formidable in terms of size, number, and firepower, there was only one large-scale naval battle during World War I. Britain had imposed a tight blockade of all German ports using its large surface fleet, while the Germans employed deadly submarines called U-boats in an effort to prevent food and strategic supplies from reaching Britain. When the German surface fleet finally emerged from its bases in 1916, a large battle ensued off Jutland in the North Sea on May 31, and although Britain lost more battleships than Germany did, the German fleet was obliged to return to port, where it remained for the rest of the war. Ironically, the massive prewar German naval buildup that had so worried British policymakers turned out to be a negligible factor in determining the outcome of World War I.

Early in the war, Germany had declared the waters around Britain off-limits to commercial shipping, and its U-boats attacked neutral vessels with impunity throughout the Atlantic. When the British luxury liner *Lusitania* was torpedoed off the southern coast of Ireland in 1915, resulting in the loss of 1,200 lives (including 128 Americans), pressure from the United States led the German navy to refrain from such attacks without first warning the target vessel. This gave the allies (Britain and France) a temporary advantage in the war of attrition, since the expensive German surface fleet was confined to port. Most trade from the neutral United States now made its way to British and French ports, but no further. Germany and Austria-Hungary began to suffer serious shortages of food and material.

Woodrow Wilson   President Woodrow Wilson (1856–1924) wished to maintain America's neutrality, especially in light of the ethnic diversity of the nation's voters. More than one-third of America's 92 million residents were foreign born. Citizens of English descent tended to support the allied cause, but 4.5 million Irish-Americans and 8 million German or Austrian-Americans sympathized with the Central Powers. In 1914 when the war began, Wilson insisted that Americans must remain neutral in thought and deed, and he naively claimed that neutral nations must be allowed to trade with all belligerents. By 1916, heavy British and French borrowing from American banks, coupled with the fact that America's industries were now producing military and civilian goods primarily for the Allied market, tilted U.S. foreign policy away from neutrality. While commerce with the Central Powers all but disappeared, that with Britain and France rose from $825 million in 1914 to over $3.2 billion in 1916. If Germany won the war, Allied debts would be repudiated and American creditors would be ruined. Germany's cessation of submarine warfare against merchant ships on the Atlantic was clearly undermining the German war effort.

In January 1916 Wilson asked both sides for their peace terms and worked to reach a negotiated settlement. Neither bloc was willing to forego its hopes for victory at this point, however, and the American offer was rejected. By 1917, the situation had changed significantly. The British naval blockade was creating enormous civilian and military hardship in the Central Powers. Acute food shortages were now commonplace, food riots had occurred, and infant mortality rates were rising rapidly. German strategists had concluded that the Allied powers would prevail unless Germany could sever Allied supply lines from America. In early February the Germans announced that they would resume unrestricted submarine warfare, even at the risk of bringing the Americans into the war on the side of the Allies. At the end of February an inter-

"Doughboys"   Though inexperienced, American soldiers—called "doughboys," perhaps in reference to the large buttons on their uniforms, though the exact reasons are unclear—played a critical role in the eventual Allied victory. The photo here shows American machine gunners in action at the second Battle of the Marne in July 1917.

cepted secret telegram from the German government offering to help Mexico recover its "lost territories" in the American Southwest inflamed U.S. public opinion. One month later, the autocratic tsarist government collapsed. Russia was now led by Western-leaning members of the Duma, or national legislature. These three events convinced President Wilson, who viewed the European conflict in moral terms as a war to make the world safe for democracy, that the full military might of the United States must be brought to bear on the side of the Allies. In April 1917 Congress declared war on Germany.

The entry of the United States into the war, with its vast industrial, financial, and human resources, assured that the Allies would eventually prevail. American naval ships now protected trans-Atlantic merchant convoys. U.S. troops were trained and transported across the Atlantic in time to assist weary British and French forces as the German High Command planned and executed a final great offensive in the spring of 1918. In late March, following a plan devised by General Erich Ludendorff (1865–1937), the Germans broke through Allied lines and pushed to within 60 miles of Paris. American soldiers played a key role in what now became the Second Battle of the Marne in mid-July. By this date over 300,000 U.S. troops under the command of General John Pershing (1860–1948) were deployed on the front lines. It had now been four years since the Germans had been first rebuffed at the Marne, upsetting the Schlieffen Plan and inaugurating the long stalemate of **trench warfare**.

Final German Advance   By August, when a final German drive began, a total of 1 million German soldiers had become casualties in the Ludendorff offensive. The Allies, under the overall command of French General Ferdinand Foch (1851–1929), began a dogged counterattack. Lacking adequate reserves and afraid that the war would be carried onto German soil, the German army under Ludendorff advised William II to set up a civilian government along democratic lines. This government asked for peace on the basis of principles put forward by President Wilson in 1917. Ludendorff cynically hoped to pin the blame for defeat on the new civilian government, and during the 1920s and early 1930s this myth that Germany was "stabbed in the back" by civilian defeatists would be a powerful weapon that the Nazis used in their quest for total power. Disorder did break out in Germany, the navy mutinied, and on November 9 Kaiser William II abdicated. Two days later, on November 11, 1918, the civilian, socialist-led government signed the armistice that ended the four years of carnage. The poet Wilfred Owen was one of the last victims.

Assigning Blame By the terms of the **Treaty of Versailles**, which was signed in 1919, Germany and her partners were forced to accept complete responsibility for the war. While this clause in the final treaty was a source of great resentment in Germany, most modern historians believe that Kaiser William II and his advisors did act in a provocative and irresponsible manner in giving Austria a "blank check" to deal with the Serbian problem. According to this interpretation, the Germans realized in 1914 that Austrian military action against Serbia would almost certainly lead to Russian intervention and thus to a wider conflagration. Other scholars see a more complicated picture. Searching for the more systemic and long-term causes, they point to imperial rivalries, angry nationalism, the bombast of elected leaders and hereditary monarchs, and the tendency in Europe to celebrate power and the "cleansing" role of conflict. European civilization, this view concludes, was in serious moral disarray in the early twentieth century, unable to avoid destroying the fabric of material abundance created during the Industrial Age. All of the great European powers, not just Germany, bore some responsibility for the carnage.

The Impact of Total War at Home

World War I was really the first military conflict in history in which almost every member of society and every aspect of the economy became engaged in the struggle for victory. During the first Battle of the Marne in September 1914, the sight of Paris taxicabs rushing troops to the front lines gave an early indication that this war would involve large numbers of civilians. As German airships later flew over London, dropping largely ineffective bombs, the place of innovative technology in combat confirmed that everyone had become a target in this total war. As taxes rose and supplies of food and consumer goods diminished, entire populations were obliged to change their lifestyles. Armies required enormous quantities of machines, armaments, and ammunition, and these were produced by a civilian sector that came under the close scrutiny and control of the state. National governments repeatedly intervened in the private sector to assure that every aspect of business, agriculture, manufacture, and transportation was focused on the war effort. State agencies set aside free-market principles and established production targets, regulated wages and prices, and even imposed rationing. A special Ministry of Munitions was established in Britain under the direction of David Lloyd George (1863–1945) in 1915. In the United States a War Industries Board was established in 1917 and given almost total power to regulate materials, production standards, and prices. Similar state-run agencies appeared in all of the belligerent states. Governments also worked to secure strategic raw materials from neutral nations on favorable terms. This was especially true of Britain's relationship with the United States during the first two years of the war.

Women and Work As casualties mounted, governments recruited new sources of domestic labor, businesses entered into partnership with labor unions, and working hours grew longer to meet the needs of the armed forces. Women entered the industrial workforce in huge numbers, taking positions that previously were reserved for men. By 1918, women constituted approximately one-third of the labor force in most countries. They drove taxis and operated trams; worked as safety officers, firefighters, and nurses; and became key operatives in the steel and munitions industries. Some women even took white collar jobs and supervised office staffs in a wide variety of businesses. In Russia women served in the armed forces. While some female workers experienced new freedoms as full-time employees in crucial sectors of the wartime economy, others struggled to balance work outside the home with their traditional family responsibilities. At the conclusion of the war, the long-standing demands of European suffragists would finally be met as women secured the right to vote at the national level in Britain, Germany, and other countries.

Women Munitions Workers The labor shortage on the home front led to important social changes during World War I. Factories across Europe and in the United States relied heavily on women to build the weapons of war. At the end of the conflict, returning soldiers displaced their female counterparts on the factory floor, but many women retained their jobs outside the home.

Maintaining Morale   Another wartime first involved the official use of mass communications to vilify the enemy and to ensure support for the government's war effort. Press censorship and state-sponsored propaganda became normal aspects of domestic life. As the death tolls mounted, democratically elected politicians assured the voters that the enemy would be punished severely after victory was achieved. Dissent was not tolerated. Police powers were extended, civil liberties abridged, and strikers arrested. In the United States, Congress passed a Sedition Act in 1918 that made it a crime to speak or publish material critical of the government. The law also criminalized opposition to the sale of war bonds. On a more positive note, class distinctions in most European countries began to break down as the priorities of the wartime economy demanded contributions from all citizens, irrespective of their background or training. Aristocrats worked alongside urban laborers in service and volunteer agencies. Under rationing, food allocations were based on need, not social status or income. Nutrition actually improved for the poorest sectors of British and French society, while in Germany the combination of a potato crop failure in 1916 and the strict British blockade reduced the entire population to a "turnip winter" in which caloric intake was halved. Some German soldiers organized attacks simply to raid the enemy's food stores.

The Russian Revolution

Military Failure   The Russians had entered World War I with enormous human resources, but with limited industrial and military capacity. Tsar Nicholas II and his closest advisors hoped that a short conflict in the Balkans on behalf of Serbia would restore Russia's diminished international prestige while simultaneously uniting the tsar's subjects under the banner of nationalism. This was a disastrous miscalculation. Lacking adequate transportation, armaments, and supplies, Russia was not prepared for modern mechanized warfare. Once the Ottomans joined the conflict on the side of the Central Powers, a crucial supply line from the West through the Dardanelles was cut off. In 1915 Tsar Nicholas made a fateful decision to take personal command of the armed forces (the only head of state to do so) while affairs in the capital fell under the baneful influence of his German-born wife Alexandra (1872–1918) and her corrupt advisor, the Orthodox faith healer Grigori Rasputin (1871–1916). Even though the tsar's generals actually ran military affairs, further reverses on the battlefield were bound to be blamed directly on him.

   In June 1916 Russian General Aleksei Brusilov (1853–1926) launched a massive offensive against Austria-Hungary. The attack came close to crippling the enemy, but lack of supplies and military hardware, together with a high rate of desertion, hampered the Russian effort. Soldiers were even sent into battle unarmed, advised to scavenge a rifle from a fallen colleague or dead enemy. A German counteroffensive led to over 1 million Russian casualties. By the spring of 1917, Russian troop morale was awful, and the rate of desertion had skyrocketed. Food shortages in Russia's cities and towns led to strikes and protests, many led by women. By March, the tsarist administration was breaking down. With his leadership discredited and soldiers in the capital mutinying and unwilling to fire on unarmed demonstrators, Nicholas abdicated on March 15 and the Duma organized a provisional government.

While promising civil liberties, universal manhood suffrage, equality before the law, a written constitution, and social reforms, the leaders of the provisional Russian government did not do what the Russian people wanted most—withdraw from the war. Liberal members of the Duma felt that Russia remained obligated to its French and British allies. The collapse of the tsarist autocracy also meant the collapse of traditional authority. As domestic conditions deteriorated during the summer and fall of 1917, calls for peace, bread, and land reform were heard throughout the country. Angry peasants began to seize land and hoard food, exacerbating hardship in the cities. Morale at the front collapsed, and disillusioned soldiers began to return home to make land claims of their own. Radical exiles who had been forced out of the country by the tsar's secret police began reappearing in Russia's major cities, where they formed political organizations of workers and soldiers called soviets. The most influential returnee was Vladimir Ilich Ulyanov (1870–1924), better known by his revolutionary name, Lenin.

The Germans had actually transported Lenin in a sealed train from his exile in Switzerland to the city of Petrograd (St. Petersburg), hoping that he would undermine the ability of the provisional government to maintain its war effort. Their hopes were almost immediately realized. After one failed attempt to overthrow the government (in the aftermath of yet another disastrous military campaign), Lenin and his leading collaborator, Leon Trotsky (1879–1940), led a coalition of workers and soldiers to seize power in Petrograd on November 6, 1917. Trotsky's forces captured the strategic communications and rail hubs as well as key government offices in the city. The leader of the provisional government, Alexander Kerensky (1881–1970), fled the city. The Bolsheviks had come to power in an almost bloodless fashion.

Early Bolshevik Policy   The Bolshevik revolutionaries still had to win the support of Russia's peasants, who made up the vast majority of the population. Lenin had argued that a genuine Marxist revolution could take place in rural Russia even though the country lacked a large proletariat, or industrial working class. Marx had written that a communist revolution could only succeed in a fully industrialized state, where workers had been reduced to the level of landless industrial laborers and where working-class consciousness was strong. Lenin and the Bolsheviks, in contrast, believed that an intellectual vanguard of professional revolutionaries could lead peasants and workers to create a stateless socialist society. Immediately after seizing power in Petrograd, Lenin nationalized land ownership and turned production over to the peasants, repudiated the debts incurred by the tsarist government, and entered into negotiations with the Germans to end the war.

Sensing Bolshevik weakness, the Germans drove a hard bargain. An armistice was signed in December 1917, and under terms of the Treaty of Brest-Litovsk in March 1918, the Bolshevik government surrendered claims to Poland; Finland; the Baltic states

V.I. Lenin and Leon Trotsky The two principal leaders of the Bolshevik revolution of 1917. Trotsky is wearing the uniform of the Red Army, which he led to victory in Russia's brutal civil war.

of Latvia, Lithuania, and Estonia; and Ukraine. The Russians also agreed to pay Germany a large indemnity and to provide enormous supplies of grain and other foodstuffs. Fierce resistance to the newly established communist regime began almost immediately and continued until 1921. Internal opponents of the regime, called the White Army and representing a wide spectrum of political views, were joined by over 100,000 foreign troops from 14 different countries. The foreign forces were led by the United States, Britain, France, and Japan, former Russian allies now intent on destroying the fledgling communist state. During this protracted civil war (1918–1921), Bolshevik armies under Trotsky's leadership repulsed the invading forces. In the midst of the struggle the Bolsheviks murdered the tsar and his family, instituted a reign of terror using the secret police to execute opponents of the new regime, and began the monumental process of transforming an overwhelmingly agrarian and war-torn country of 150 million people into a socialist society.

The Threat of Communism   The overthrow of the tsarist regime in Russia led to widespread fear in European capitals that war-weary citizens might support similar movements in the West. Lenin's Russia may have been excluded from the Versailles peace conference and gripped by civil war, but the ideology of revolutionary Marxism easily transcended geography. Lenin had written that the war was nothing more than a predictable clash of capitalist economies and that true peace would never be achieved until the entire capitalist system was destroyed. In a speech before the Petrograd Soviet, Lenin stated that "it is necessary to overthrow capitalism itself. In this work we shall have the aid of the world labor movement, which has already begun to develop in Italy, England, and Germany."

In the war's aftermath, the communist appeal for a new social order resonated with members of Europe's socialist parties, many of whom had enthusiastically supported their country's war effort in 1914. Each major European postwar democracy soon had a revolutionary communist party and fledgling soviets. In Germany the counterpart of Lenin's Bolsheviks was the Spartacist League, led by Karl Liebknecht (1871–1919) and Rosa Luxemburg (1871–1919). The interim German government was led by moderate socialists, and they used the armed forces to destroy the Spartacists. In December 1919 Liebknecht and Luxemburg were killed, along with a thousand of their supporters. In Hungary, a short-lived Soviet republic was established in March 1919 under the leadership of Bela Kun (1886–1939). That same year Lenin organized an international umbrella organization called the Comintern to provide leadership for the various communist parties in Western Europe. It was a rigidly top-down organization, following Lenin's conviction that the revolutionary vanguard must direct the less enlightened, but it nevertheless attracted support among European communist parties.

As the German and Hungarian examples illustrated, the threat of a communist revolution outside Russia seemed a distinct possibility in the years immediately after the war, and Russian agents fanned across the globe to advance the cause of world revolution. The United States experienced a "Red Scare" in 1919 as government agencies trampled civil liberties in search of radicals, while in Europe fear of communist insurgency led many political moderates to turn toward far right political parties. In particular, emerging Fascist parties were adept at promoting their anticommunist credentials. Less than one year after assuming power in Hungary, Bela Kun's Soviet state was toppled by invading Romanian troops. In its place a rightwing authoritarian government was established with the full support of the anxious Allied powers.

Russian "May Day" Poster   Paraphrasing Karl Marx, this poster declares, "You have nothing to lose but your chains, but the world will soon be yours." The zeal and enthusiasm of the early days of the Russian Revolution is evident in this image, one of many such posters produced at the time. *Museum of the Revolution, Moscow, Russia/Bridgeman Art Library, London.*

■ ■

PEOPLE IN CONTEXT John Reed and Bolshevism

The American journalist John Reed was born in Portland, Oregon, in 1887. He graduated from Harvard University in 1910 and worked as a writer for a variety of leftist and radical magazines, including *The Masses*, for which Reed was reporting in Petrograd when the Bolsheviks seized power in November 1917.

Reed published an eyewitness description of the November Revolution, titled *Ten Days that Shook the World*, in 1919. The book was translated into many languages, with an introduction by Lenin that appeared after Reed's death in 1920. Reed was a partisan journalist, and his sympathies lay with the Bolshevik insurgents. *Ten Days* provided a rare firsthand account of events from the perspective of an American intellectual who found much to admire in Lenin's repudiation of the capitalist West.

Reed returned to the United States at the end of the war. In 1919 he founded the Communist Labor Party during a fractious meeting of the Socialist Party of America in Chicago. To secure recognition for his new party from Lenin's Comintern, he set off again for Russia in the fall of 1919. He left just as the United States attorney general established a new General Intelligence Division in the Department of Justice headed by a young J. Edgar Hoover (1895–1972). The division was charged with collecting information on radical organizations, including communist political groups. In January 1920 police arrested over 6,000 persons in 33 cities across the nation. Many detainees were held without charge for weeks. A handful were deported in this Red Scare. Reed was already back in Russia when the mass arrests took place, but he had been indicted for treason during the panic.

John Reed

In Russia Reed met with Lenin, and he was elected to the Executive Committee of the Comintern. But soon he was struck with typhus. He died in Moscow on October 19, 1920, and was buried with other Bolshevik heroes in the Kremlin. Reed's activities helped arouse deep public suspicion in the West that a handful of dedicated communists were working to overthrow the Western capitalist democracies. Given the success of the small Bolshevik minority in Russia, it was felt that a ruthless cadre could endanger the stability of the postwar West at a moment's notice.

Question: What would an educated young American find appealing about the Russian Revolution of 1917?

■ ■ ■ ■ ■ ■

The Peace Settlement and European Consciousness

What has come to be known as the Great War ended with the armistice signed by Germany on November 11, 1918. The Ottoman, Russian, German, and Austrian empires were dismantled, and the Habsburg, Hohenzollern, Romanov, and Ottoman dynasties abolished. Almost 10 million people had been killed in battle during four years of fighting, and another 15 to 16 million had been wounded. Virtually every family in France, Britain, Russia, Germany, and Austria-Hungary had lost a loved one. In France alone the total population was reduced by one-twentieth, and most of the dead were young men in their most productive years. Millions of civilians also lost their lives during the conflict. As if war-related deaths were not enough, in 1919 a worldwide influenza epidemic killed another 27 million people.

The war severely damaged the national economies of each of the European combatants, with the total direct cost of the conflict estimated at $180 billion. Most governments, unwilling to raise taxes at a time when their populations were making so many other sacrifices, borrowed heavily.

The United States was the biggest lender, and in the process it transformed itself from a debtor to a creditor nation. In 1919 the Europeans owed American creditors $3.7 billion. Europe had suddenly and decisively lost its status as the center of global politics, culture, and economics. Social Darwinist arguments now rang hollow across a continent where once imperial states were reduced to poverty and political instability. The war's savagery had destroyed faith in the inevitability of progress and the primacy of reason in human affairs. Widows, fatherless children, amputees, and the maimed found it hard to resume their broken lives. The poet T. S. Eliot (1888–1965) expressed the sense of alienation brought forward by the conflict in his poem "The Hollow Men," with its haunting depiction of the war's survivors, while the Irishman William Butler Yeats (1865–1939) wrote about the decay of Western civilization. In "The Second Coming" Yeats reflected how

> Things fall apart; the center cannot hold;
> Mere anarchy is loosed upon the world,
> The blood-dimmed tide is loosed, and everywhere
> The ceremony of innocence is drowned;
> The best lack all conviction, while the worst
> Are full of passionate intensity.

In postwar Europe, and especially in Fascist Italy and Nazi Germany during the 1920s and 1930s, the final two lines of this stanza were to be borne out in full measure. After a respite of two decades, "the worst" would lead Europe's nation-states into another, even more costly global struggle (see Map 22–2).

The Versailles Conference   The representatives from 32 victorious states who assembled in the great palace of Versailles outside Paris in January 1919 faced enormous challenges. The leaders of the Big Four—France, Britain, the United States, and

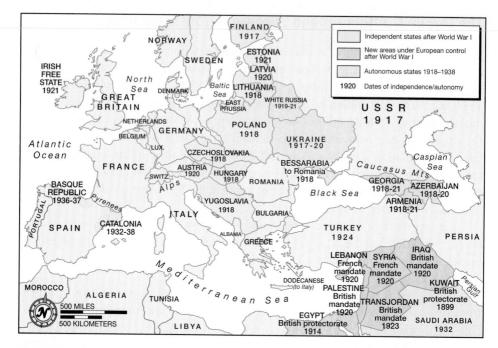

Map 22–2 Postwar Europe While new nations were created at the end of the war, the principle of national self-determination was not applied in a uniform manner. New areas of European control were established in the Middle East, while Africa and South Asia remained under European rule.

Question: How was the principle of national self-determination applied in Eastern Europe after World War I?

Italy—would make the major decisions, and they had promised their peoples compensation for the enormous sacrifices on the battlefield. Germany and Austria-Hungary were excluded from the deliberations, as was Russia, which was now under communist control. Delegates from some of Europe's many colonies also attended in the expectation that their pleas for independence would be acknowledged, especially in light of the fact that millions of colonial troops had fought with distinction to save European civilization.

Two of the leading figures, American President Woodrow Wilson and French Premier Georges Clemenceau (1841–1929), had irreconcilable agendas. The idealistic Wilson, representing a nation that had entered the war late and incurred comparatively few casualties, wished to secure "peace without victors" and to rebuild the continent according to the principle of national self-determination (although no one, including Wilson himself, was sure what self-determination meant). He had first outlined his views one year earlier in his famous "Fourteen Points" speech justifying America's involvement in the war. According to Wilson, secret diplomacy must end, colonial claims for self-governance must be heard, freedom of the seas must be protected and free trade promoted, and armaments must be reduced. Both sides to the conflict had accepted Wilson's outline for an equitable peace before the armistice. Wilson also called on the delegates to establish a permanent League of Nations where future international disputes could be settled without recourse to violence. Clemenceau, in contrast, wished to punish the vanquished states (Germany, Austria, Hungary, Bulgaria, and Turkey). In particular, Clemenceau sought to cripple Germany's war-making capacity. France had been invaded twice by Germany during Clemenceau's lifetime (in 1870 and 1914), and the most brutal fighting in the Western theater during World War I had taken place on French soil. The French had good reason to fear another German invasion. Germany's larger population and greater industrial capacity made the French delegation extremely wary of the principle of peace without victors.

Retribution and Resentment   In the end the delegates settled for a compromise that included a number of punitive elements. The principle of national self-determination, while laudable in theory, was difficult to apply in practice. At what point, for example, was it legitimate to include disgruntled minorities within the boundaries of a new state? One-third of the population of Poland did not speak Polish; Romania contained 1 million Magyars; Czechoslovakia had almost 1 million Germans; Catholic Ireland remained under British rule. Since many areas in Europe contained a mixture of nationalities, redrawing the map on nationalist lines was particularly difficult. No solution was likely to please every interested party.

However, the victors enjoyed distinct advantages. Alsace and Lorraine, lost to Germany in 1871, were restored to France. The Rhineland territories, Germany's industrial heartland, were demilitarized and were to be occupied by Allied troops for 15 years. Germany also forfeited all of its overseas colonies, ceded Polish-speaking areas of eastern Germany to a resurrected Polish state, and accepted the creation of a "Polish corridor," which cut through German territory to provide Poland with an outlet to the sea at the international—but German inhabited—city of Danzig. The German army was limited to 100,000 troops, the powerful navy was scrapped, and a large but undetermined war indemnity imposed. In 1923 the heavy indemnity was set at $33 billion, creating an enormous fiscal burden for the newly established German republic.

Four separate treaties with Germany's wartime allies were concluded during the six months of negotiations at Versailles. The Austrian Empire, home to 50 million subjects of the Habsburgs, had imploded during the final months of the war, and a series of breakaway states were recognized at Versailles. Smaller, independent Austrian and Hungarian states were created, and an independent Czechoslovakia, uniting Czech and Slovak lands, emerged in the heart of Europe. The break-up led to serious economic dislocations as the new states established trade and tariff policies that hindered the movement of raw materials to factories that were once located in the same country. Some Austrians wished to merge with Germany to the north, claiming the primacy of language bonds, but the victors forbade this move. The Serbs realized their goal of a South-Slavic nation with the establishment of Yugoslavia in the Balkans, while the Turks created a republic based on the Turkish-speaking lands of Anatolia. To the north, Finland, Latvia, Estonia, and Lithuania became independent states, while Poland was

Arab Delegates to the Paris Peace Conference, 1919 T.E. Lawrence (middle row, second from the right)—the fabled "Lawrence of Arabia"—with Arab leaders. The British undermined Ottoman control of the Middle East by promising to support local rulers such who sought to break free from the Ottoman Empire.

restored to nation-state status after almost 150 years. The British and French divided the Ottoman Empire's Middle Eastern territories between themselves, with the French claiming Lebanon and Syria while the British took administrative control over Palestine and Mesopotamia (Iraq).

The League of Nations For the first time in history, the Americans wielded direct and decisive influence over European affairs. Woodrow Wilson, discouraged by the punitive features of the Versailles settlement, pushed hard for the establishment of a permanent international body dedicated to the peaceful resolution of international disputes and to the promotion of global health and economic issues. The League of Nations was incorporated into the final peace treaty, but opposition to the League by isolationists in the United States Senate doomed the president's desire that the United States play a larger role in international affairs. In 1920 the Senate refused to ratify the treaty. The absence of the United States, together with the exclusion of Germany and Russia from membership in the League, undermined the League's influence and effectiveness. Lacking a military force of its own, the League council could only apply economic sanctions against future aggressors. France and Britain joined the organization along with 40 other states (26 members of the League were non-European), but there was little enthusiasm in either Britain or France for the League's broadly internationalist agenda. In one area only did the victors support the League, and that was due to the problems of empire. Germany's former colonies, together with former Ottoman lands in the Middle East, were assigned to Britain and France by the League under a "mandate" system. Ostensibly, the imperial powers were charged with preparing their mandated territories for eventual independence under League supervision. In practice, however, these lands were administered as colonial possessions.

A Legacy of Distrust   The war to "make the world safe for democracy"—to use Woodrow Wilson's words—ended in a climate of mutual dissatisfaction and distrust. The French felt betrayed by the failure of their allies to impose a harsher peace on Germany or to ratify a promised alliance to come to the aid of France if Germany attacked again. The Italians resented the Allies' refusal to satisfy their claims to more former Austrian- and Turkish-controlled territories. The German military constructed the myth of civilian betrayal, while the German public resented the "war guilt" clause and the demand that Germany pay reparations. The Americans withdrew into comfortable isolationism while refusing to forgive or even to renegotiate Allied loans taken out during the war. Bolshevik Russia was ostracized by the Western democracies. Colonial peoples in Africa and Asia felt duped by imperial masters who had no intention of extending the right of self-determination beyond the confines of Europe. The Japanese resented the delegates' refusal (at the behest of the United States) to declare formally the equality of all races. In the Middle East, Arabs and Jews quarreled over which duplicitous promise made by the British during the war ought to be honored. Nothing in the treaties addressed the crucial matters of reconciliation and rebuilding. Having barely survived the deluge, the victors could not see their way clear to a better Europe.

In *The Economic Consequences of the Peace*, published in 1919, the young British economist John Maynard Keynes (1883–1946) argued that the new German government was incapable of meeting the reparations demands of Britain and France and that the resulting

Major Events of World War I	
June 28, 1914	Assassination of the Archduke Francis Ferdinand
August 1–3, 1914	Germany declares war on Russia and France
August 4, 1914	Britain declares war on Germany; war begins
September 1914	Battle of the Marne; German retreat signals long stalemate
February 1916	Battle of Verdun begins
July 1, 1916	Battle of the Somme begins
April 1917	United States declares war on Germany
November 1917	Bolshevik revolution in Russia
November 11, 1918	Armistice is signed, ending the war
June 28, 1919	Treaty of Versailles is signed

hardships would make future conflict more likely. Recalling the Roman destruction of Carthage after the Third Punic War (149–146 B.C.E.), Keynes described the Treaty of Versailles as the equivalent of a "Carthaginian peace." At the time of the book's publication, few would have anticipated his forecast that the treaty would lead to future conflict would come to pass in less than 20 years. Like Woodrow Wilson, Keynes recognized that Germany—now a democracy—must be reintegrated into the European state system if the future of the continent was to be peaceful and prosperous. Few Europeans were prepared to be generous and forgiving in 1918. The intensity, longevity, and brutality of the encounter with modern warfare precluded a rational assessment of Europe's predicament.

KEY QUESTION | Revisited

Are nation-states inherently adversarial? Are they doomed to quarrel with each other? The experience of 1914 to 1918 would suggest that they are. Looking at a map of the world in 1920, it appeared that Europe was still the most powerful region in the world. European national flags still flew in scores of colonies around the globe. In the French and British cases their colonial possessions actually increased thanks to their mandates in Africa and the Middle East. The map was misleading, however. World War I had diminished Europe's states economically, militarily, politically, and intellectually. The sense of confidence and superiority that most Europeans felt about their own civilization was consumed by the four long years of carnage, official lies, and punitive settlements. A war that began with widespread public support ended in widespread popular disillusionment and despair. "An old bitch, gone in the teeth," was the American poet Ezra Pound's (1885–1972) diagnosis of Western civilization. The German historian Oswald Spengler (1880–1936) perhaps best captured the mood of the postwar generation with his influential *Decline of the West,* first published in 1920 and premised on the idea that the West had entered an age of "gigantic conflicts." All civilizations, Spengler argued, have natural life cycles, and anyone familiar with the trenches on the Western Front would have been compelled to admit that Europe had reached the end of its primacy.

   While Europe's traditional elite, what historian Barbara Tuchman (1912–1989) called "the Proud Tower," were key players in the decision to go to war, the voting public overwhelmingly supported their elected and hereditary leaders. In light of this fact, the biggest casualty of the war may have been Europeans' faith in the value of traditional political systems, whether parliamentary or monarchical, and in the primacy of rational decision making. Nationalist ideology, the conviction that the sovereign state was master of its own destiny, accountable to no higher authority, had successfully preempted another Enlightenment value: belief in the equality of persons across artificial international boundaries. Late nineteenth-century colonial disputes, intense economic rivalries, and an inflexible system of military alliances all contributed to the breakdown of the European order during four years of total war. For the next two decades, the core values of liberal democracy were called into question in much of Europe. During the interwar years, the subject of the next chapter, parliamentary government, individual rights, and the rule of law would all be challenged by new leaders who publically repudiated the Enlightenment tradition.

Review Questions

1. How would you assess responsibility for World War I?
2. Why was there enthusiasm for war in 1914?
3. What role did military strategy play in prolonging trench warfare?
4. Why did the United States wish to remain neutral, and why did America eventually side with the Allies?
5. What role did propaganda play on the home fronts? How did the war involve Europe's civilian population?
6. What were the main flaws in the Treaty of Versailles?
7. How did tsarist war policy strengthen the Bolshevik cause in Russia?

Please consult the Suggested Readings at the back of the book to continue your study of the material covered in this chapter. For a list of documents on the Primary Source DVD-ROM that relate to topics in this chapter, please refer to the back of the book.

Topics in This Chapter

Postwar Problems in Western Europe • The Price of Victory

• The Great Depression, 1929–1939 • Italy: The First Fascist State

• Authoritarian Regimes in Spain and Eastern Europe • The Emergence of Nazi Germany

• Imperial Japan • The Soviet Union Under Stalin

23 The Troubled Interwar Years

The *völkisch* (racial) state must free all leadership and especially the highest—that is, the political leadership—entirely from the parliamentary principle of majority rule.

—Adolf Hitler

KEY | Question

Can personal liberty be maintained under conditions of material hardship?

Writing from prison in 1923, the leader of Germany's National Socialist (Nazi) Party discussed how to win popular support in a democratic age. Adolf Hitler (1889–1945) placed special emphasis on the role of propaganda in democratic culture. "All propaganda," he insisted, "must be popular and its intellectual level must be addressed to the most limited intelligence among those it is addressed to . . . we must avoid excessive intellectual demands on our public, and too much caution cannot be exerted in this direction." For Hitler and for many others ambitious for political power in postwar Europe, the advent of mass democracy presented a unique opportunity for charismatic leaders to channel popular discontent into political action. By showing contempt for the reasoning power of the average citizen, and by blaming Europe's complex postwar problems on the machinations of traitors, foreign enemies, and inferior races, unprincipled men hoped to destroy liberal democracy and create their own distorted versions of the perfect society.

During the two decades after World War I, Europe's liberal democracies came under increasing pressure from authoritarian, anti-individualistic ideologies on the right and left of the political spectrum. Fascist regimes rose to power by constitutional means in Italy and Germany, while in the Soviet Union the Communist Party wielded absolute and arbitrary authority under the brutal direction of Joseph Stalin (1879–1953). These antidemocratic regimes used propaganda, technology, and large, impersonal bureaucracies to suppress

The Spanish Civil War This poster, created in support of the Nationalist side of the war, provides witness to the intense ideological struggles of the interwar period. The conflict began in July 1936. When it ended in 1939, half a million Spaniards had lost their lives.

individual liberties, rival political parties, the autonomy of the artist, and the security of private property. Their leaders sought to establish complete control over individuals while elevating party ideology and the cult of their own personality to the level of unquestioned truth. In the case of Fascism, the leadership appealed directly to base emotions and the prejudices of the masses to win approval for a variety of inhumane policies. Fascist leaders skillfully exploited democracy in order to secure power, then used that power to destroy democracy once they took office. In the Soviet Union, the Enlightenment inheritance of individual rights and the sanctity of property perished before the forces of state-imposed collectivization, the rejection of the rule of law, and Stalin's megalomania.

By the 1930s, as worldwide economic depression smashed the hopes and dreams of millions in the West, many Europeans lost faith in the ability of liberal democracy to solve life's most pressing daily problems. Two centuries of struggle to achieve political freedoms and civil rights now appeared hollow in the face of hunger and massive unemployment. As the decade wore on, the shrill appeal of leaders who promised jobs, the restoration of national greatness, or the triumph of the international working class began to make headway. Demagogues who appealed to pent-up hatreds and to the darker side of human nature came to power in several European countries and triggered a crisis of confidence in those states that struggled to preserve their democratic institutions.

Postwar Problems in Western Europe

The perceived inadequacies of the Versailles settlement afforded governments across Europe the opportunity to rally popular support for revising the treaties. In democratic states elected politicians were expected to restore prewar prosperity. However, the widespread destruction caused by the Great War and the fact that millions of men in their most productive working years had been killed or maimed on the battlefield undermined efforts to rebuild the continent's economic fabric. Rail systems and industrial plants had been severely damaged or destroyed, especially in areas such as northern France and Belgium, where the most prolonged fighting had taken place. In addition, the creation of new nation-states in central and eastern Europe complicated trade policies and fragmented transportation and production networks. Demand for European manufactures declined as the United States raised tariffs and extended its global market presence. Europe was no longer the financial hub of the global community. That distinction had passed to the Americans, and the enormous debts owed by victor and vanquished alike weakened the ability of postwar European governments to control their own economies.

For those who had fought in the war and survived, a sense of incompleteness and a belief that their sacrifices on behalf of the homeland were not being recognized or properly compensated often accompanied a return to civilian life. High rates of unemployment, continuing food shortages, and the absence of friends and loved ones who had died in the conflagration all contributed to the mood of despondency. The Wilsonian rhetoric of a "world made safe for democracy" meant little to many Europeans in the postwar environment. If anything, they resented the United States' unwillingness to forgive debts that had been incurred during the war. To meet their obligations to repay the United States, the British and the French sought to extract reparations from Germany. Germans in turn resented the terms of what they called the dictated peace of Versailles.

The Price of Victory

Irresolute Britain   The end of the war brought about further democratization in Britain. In 1918 the franchise was extended to all men over the age of 21 and to women who were at least 30 years of age. In 1928 this age discrimination was abolished, and universal suffrage at age 21 became the rule. The Labour Party replaced the Liberals as the main opposition to the Conservatives. Under the leadership of Ramsay MacDonald (1866–1937), Labour successfully fought for reforms to improve the lives of the working class. A general strike came close to provoking social unrest in 1926, but in general, unemployment benefits, housing subsidies, and old-age pensions defused class tensions in a period of economic uncertainty.

Unemployment rates in Britain remained high throughout the 1920s. The economic hard times were in large measure the result of fresh competition from the United States and Japan, which lessened the worldwide demand for British goods. Many of Britain's manufacturing plants had been built in the nineteenth century, and many factories had become outdated by the 1920s, while the destruction of a large portion of the merchant fleet during the war slowed the movement of British goods overseas. Since prewar Germany had been Britain's second best market (the United States was first), political leaders in London were eager to see Germany return to its prewar prosperity so that Germans could afford to buy British goods. Since Germany was now a democratic republic, British policymakers were increasingly sympathetic to the German argument that the Versailles Peace Treaty undermined the very form of political order that the Allies said they had been fighting for.

The Defense of France   French political leaders remained focused on national security. They were troubled by the failure of Britain and the United States to guarantee they would come to France's aid if Germany attacked again. Lacking these guarantees, the French formed defensive alliances with several small Eastern European powers. Poland, Yugoslavia, Czechoslovakia, and Romania joined with France in an effort to further isolate Germany and the Soviet Union. Even in defeat, Germany's growing population of 60 million threatened France's comparatively stagnant 40 million. While the fighting during World War I had devastated France's most industrialized region, Germany's large industrial and transportation infrastructures remained intact, since no fighting had occurred on German soil. In the years immediately after the war, the French government worked continuously to keep Germany weak. Insisting on heavy reparations and the demilitarization of the industrial Rhineland, French politicians remained suspicious of a resurgent German state, even a democratic one.

Weimar Republic   With the Hohenzollern monarchy abolished in November 1918, German liberals and Social Democrats established the Weimar Republic (after the city where it was founded) in August 1919. The new constitution claimed that all political authority "derives from the people." A president, elected by secret ballot on the basis of universal suffrage (women were given the vote in 1919), a Reichstag whose powers included the right to initiate all legislation, a cabinet system that made ministers responsible to the popularly elected legislature, and the protection of civil liberties all reflected enlightened

Hyperinflation in Germany, 1923   A woman in Berlin uses worthless marks (the German currency) to start a fire in her stove. Germany experienced one of the most severe inflations in modern European history in 1923. Germany's severe economic crisis contributed to the political instability that aided Adolf Hitler's rise to power.

liberal ideals. Unfortunately, the new constitution was adopted just as the government, headed by the Social Democrats, was forced to sign the humiliating Versailles Treaty. The Weimar Republic thus began its brief life under the cloud of national defeat and the burden of heavy war reparations. Throughout the 1920s, angry nationalists and their military supporters blamed the republic for everything that went wrong.

Economic problems were the key to popular discontent. Weimar authorities were saddled with the debts that the former government had incurred during the war. The new government elected to honor these commitments and satisfy its reparations obligations by printing additional paper money. The result was hyperinflation and the precipitous collapse of the German mark. During the years 1919 to 1923, pensioners, veterans on disability, government bond holders, mortgage and insurance policyholders, and the owners of personal savings accounts all saw their benefits, finances, and savings evaporate. Many lower- and middle-class Germans were reduced to a barter economy as national wealth was transferred to Britain and France in the form of war reparations.

American Intervention   The economic situation in Germany had become unsustainable by November 1923. New ideas were desperately needed if the German economy was not to collapse entirely. In 1924 British and American authorities, led by American banker Charles Dawes (1865–1951), proposed a plan that reduced and rescheduled Germany's payments while also guaranteeing American loans to the Weimar government. The French were persuaded to agree to the arrangement and pledged not to use military force in the event that Weimar failed to meet its deadlines. Despite the emergency situation, the United States remained unwilling to cancel the wartime debts owed by Britain and France. The imposition of a high tariff by the U.S. Congress made it difficult for any of the European nations to sell their products in America. Since the potential market for European-manufactured products in the United States was strong, the inability of producers to sell in the United States hampered the overall recovery that was in the best interest of every Western capitalist nation.

A Moment of Promise   With the Dawes Plan and American loans, the German currency was at last placed on a firm basis. Germany would use the funds to pay reparations and jump-start its economy. A circular flow of capital began: Germany borrowed from the United States to pay reparations to France and Britain, who used those payments to repay their debts to the United States. This arrangement worked as long as America's economy remained healthy—and it did, at least until the fall of 1929. Germany's economy also seemed to recover. Industrial output grew, foreign investment returned, unemployment fell, and trade grew with other European states. The economic turnaround was matched by a reduction in international tensions. At a meeting in Locarno, Switzerland, in 1925, France, Belgium, and Germany formally agreed to accept their common borders, while Britain and Italy promised to oppose any state that violated the pact. The next year, guided by foreign minister Gustav Stresemann (1878–1929), Germany was admitted to the League of Nations.

Popular Culture and Consumerism   The momentary return of economic stability across most of Western Europe prompted manufacturers to focus on new technologies for a consumer market. Radios, washing machines, refrigerators, vacuum cleaners, and irons all began to appear in middle-class homes. The passion for private transportation spurred the automobile industry and road-building projects. Airplane design improved, and commercial airlines began to appeal to the affluent and adventuresome. The service sector expanded, especially in large towns and cities. Sales jobs in large retail firms, repair services for the myriad new products, travel agencies, gardening centers, telephone operators, home builders, plumbers, electricians, hair stylists, hospital workers, counselors, and therapists all provided new services to a population that for the first time since the war began in 1914 actually could hope for a better future based on material progress. Despite political uncertainties and the financial strain of rebuilding the war-torn north of the country, France remained the acknowledged center of European cultural life during the 1920s. Artists and writers from around the world made their home in Paris. The American expatriate community was especially influential. African-American artists and the new jazz style in music found receptive audiences in the French capital.

For those Europeans with adequate disposable incomes in the 1920s, leisure activities became more diverse and innovative. The motion picture industry blossomed, and movie stars became cultural icons. While most moviegoers sought pure entertainment in the new "movie palaces," some film producers and directors tackled compelling social and intellectual issues. Trends in fashion, often prompted by films, took on added urgency for the middle class. Personal hygiene and beauty products, especially women's cosmetics, were marketed and sold as keys to professional success, psychological well-being, and sexual appeal. Family holidays and shopping excursions became part of middle-class culture. The city became the focal point for new ideas. As skyscrapers began to transform the skyline of major cities in the United States, in Europe the Bauhaus school, established by German architect Walter Gropius (1883–1969), introduced a style that reflected the streamlined efficiencies of the modern factory. Emphasizing function in design and employing the latest synthetic materials, Bauhaus buildings, furniture, and fixtures all shared a stark simplicity. Affordability and utility were hallmarks of what became known as the "international style."

Bauhaus School, Dessau, Germany   Designed by Walter Gropius, this building—the headquarters of the Bauhaus School in the late 1920s—was typical of Bauhaus architecture and graphic design. The Bauhaus style was sleek and modernistic, emphasizing function and simplicity.

The Great Depression, 1929–1939

The optimism of the late 1920s was short-lived, however, and did not survive the **Great Depression** that began with the stock market crash in New York in October 1929. The prosperity of the 1920s rested on shaky foundations. Throughout the decade wages lagged behind rising levels of productivity. This meant that by the late 1920s manufacturers were producing more goods than consumers could afford to purchase, so factories began to slow production and lay off workers. Improvements in farming methods and expanded tillage increased output but had the unintended effect of lowering grain prices.

The combination of rural poverty and flat wage levels for urban workers meant that income disparities were pronounced. In the United States, for example, a mere 5% of the population controlled one-third of total personal wealth. Capital investment and industrial expansion continued, while the potential global market for goods shrank. Non-Western developing countries were unable to buy European manufactures, since high protective tariffs in the West made it nearly impossible for these countries to earn capital through the sale of their agricultural products and raw materials. The reckoning came quickly in October 1929. Within one month of the initial stock market crash, overall stock values dropped by 40%, and the decline continued for the next three years. Suddenly, credit was no longer available for businesses or for foreign governments. Panic spread across borders, and massive layoffs began throughout the industrialized West. American banks, unable to recover loans made before October 1929, failed in

Unemployed Miner   The collapse of the
American stock market and the onset of the
Great Depression led to widespread
unemployment. As workers like this British
coalminer lost their jobs, confidence in
Western liberal democracy began to decline.
Fascists and communists insisted that
liberalism was doomed.

record numbers. One-third of them
had closed by 1932. Even prestigious
European banks declared insolvency,
and by 1933, the international reparations system had broken down completely. Leading Marxist theoreticians
predicted the imminent collapse of
world capitalism under the weight of its
own contradictions.

The Social Impact   The most
crushing feature of the Great Depres-
sion was the loss of millions of jobs. One-fourth of the labor force in Britain and in
the United States were out of work by 1933. Unemployment rates in Germany were
even higher. Productivity plummeted as factories closed. Most governments were ill-
prepared to deal with this crisis. Orthodox economic theory called for cuts in government spending and patience while the market corrected itself. However, as each
nation erected even higher tariffs in a desperate attempt to protect its own producers, the resulting decline in international trade aggravated the overall crisis. The
British economist John Maynard Keynes called for massive deficit spending by leading countries to stimulate their economies, but most policymakers dismissed this option (now commonplace in the West) with contempt. In the meantime, homelessness
and malnutrition mounted, savings accounts were depleted, family farms were fore-
closed, and peoples' confidence in themselves and in their political leaders tumbled.

The Democratic View   The second half of the 1920s had provided a brief respite
for what was an otherwise gloomy economic situation during the interwar period.
In retrospect, the victors had never recovered their momentum after so many millions had died in the period 1914 to 1918. In particular, the multiparty democracies
seemed unable to provide their citizens with a compelling sense of purpose or collective identity. Rifts between right-wing and left-wing parties seemed unbridgeable.
When the French socialist premier, Leon Blum (1872–1959), took office in 1936 and
began a reform program that included a 40-hour work week, right-wing politicians
denounced him as a Jew who was trying to recast France into a communist state. In
Britain, the economic situation was so grim that King George V (r. 1910–1936)
called upon the Labour, Conservative, and Liberal parties to form a joint "national"
government in 1930 to deal with the economic crisis. However, neither the national

government nor the Conservative ministry of Stanley Baldwin (1867–1947) that succeeded it was able to devise a creative solution to Britain's problems. American President Franklin Delano Roosevelt (1882–1945) took a number of modest, although controversial, steps to stimulate the U.S. economy. Centralized planning and a host of new government make-work agencies constituted Roosevelt's "New Deal." Nevertheless, it was not until Britain and the United States began to re-arm in the late 1930s that the worst effects of the depression began to abate (see Map 23–1). Historian William Keylor has noted that one of the tragic ironies of modern history is that "organized violence on a large scale, or the preparation for it, has proved to be the most effective remedy for the economic problems of underconsumption and unemployment."

Map 23–1 The Great Depression in Europe Europe was wracked by instability throughout the 1930s. This map indicates the extent of unemployment and political unrest, as well as the rise of right-wing and left-wing governments.

Question: Which countries were hardest hit by the Depression?

The Totalitarian View   The only governments that appeared to act decisively in the face of the global economic crisis were totalitarian ones under the leadership of a charismatic and intolerant leader. A central tenet of Enlightenment political theory involved the primacy of law over the will of the individual leader. In totalitarian systems, the leader was above the law, and his directives, no matter how irrational and irresponsible they appeared, became the embodiment of the national will. Unquestioning obedience to the leader was required at all times. Any opposition was considered treason and punished accordingly. This leadership principle was combined with an ideology that proclaimed that human history could be reduced to one great myth or higher truth. Often that myth privileged one group of people over others on the basis of culture, race, or class; and the state was dedicated to realizing the triumph of that group.

During the 1920s and 1930s, both Fascism and Soviet communism cast themselves as heroes in a herculean struggle against great evil. For Italian Fascists, that evil was synonymous with the liberal parliamentary state, and for German Nazis, it was with worldwide Jewry. The Soviets under Lenin—and especially under Stalin—associated evil with capitalists, with their parliamentary political systems and meaningless nationalism, both of which prevented the world's working class from recognizing its common interests. Totalitarian regimes need enemies to justify their existence. The totalitarian state can never achieve complete victory, because a world without enemies would remove the justification for pervasive state control. Totalitarian regimes politicized all aspects of life; they recognized no distinctions between the public and the private spheres. Schools, literature, art, scientific inquiry, voluntary associations, religious institutions, and popular culture all were controlled and supervised by the state. Since they viewed themselves as idealists pursuing the goal of social order and harmony, supporters of the totalitarian state felt justified in taking extreme actions against perceived enemies. With the party and its leader defining truth and goodness, individual conscience was nullified, and unspeakable actions in the name of the perfect society were legitimized.

Italy: The First Fascist State

Italy had joined the Allied side in World War I, but Prime Minister Vittorio Emanuele Orlando (1860–1952) walked out of the Paris Peace Conference after it became apparent that Italian demands for former Austrian territories along the Adriatic coast would not be met. Postwar Italian governments were weak and indecisive. Italy continued to wrestle with a deteriorating economy, rural poverty, inflation, and social unrest. Returning veterans could not find work, food shortages were commonplace, industrial strikes disabled production, and peasants began to occupy large estates. Southern Italy became a hotbed of banditry and disorder. Many Italians who had suffered hardships during the war, including relatives of the half-million war dead, began to long for a strong regime.

Benito Mussolini   Into this gathering disorder stepped Benito Mussolini (1833–1945). A veteran of the Great War and an ex-socialist, in 1919 he organized the Fascist Party (from *Fascio di Combattimento,* or League of Combat) in the city of Milan. Recruitment was especially strong among the unemployed ex-soldiers, while industrialists

Benito Mussolini Italy's "Il Duce" in a characteristic pose atop an armored tank. This image conveys the militaristic, aggressive style of Fascist politics. Mussolini's government attacked Ethiopia in 1935, but the Italian army later found itself outmatched in World War II.

and other businessmen who feared a communist revolution provided financial support. For those seeking adventure, Mussolini evoked the history of the Roman Empire; for factory owners and merchants, he promised to fight communist insurgency; and for the middle class, he promised to restore economic security and national purpose. Mussolini's black-shirted street fighters beat up socialists and strikers, often with the connivance of the police and military. In 1922 Mussolini ordered a "march on Rome" to secure national power. When King Victor Emmanuel III (r. 1900–1946) refused to use the military to stop the march, the liberal cabinet resigned. On October 29, 1922, the king named Mussolini prime minister.

Eliminating the Opposition   Once in power, Mussolini consolidated his authority. In 1924 a new election law gave the political party with the largest popular vote two-thirds of the seats in parliament. The Fascists then called new elections and used their majority to pass legislation giving Mussolini the right to rule by decree. Opposition political parties were outlawed, the press was controlled, and Fascist gangs intimidated and in a few cases killed opponents of the regime. By the end of 1926, Mussolini was the unchallenged ruler of Italy with the title *Il Duce* (the leader).

One potential opponent of the regime was the Roman Catholic Church. The Vatican had been at odds with the Italian government since Italy seized the papal city of Rome in 1870. Mussolini shrewdly settled this dispute in 1929. Italy agreed to compensate the Catholic Church for the property it had seized and exempted remaining Church lands from taxation. Mussolini also recognized Vatican City as an independent state, made religious instruction mandatory in schools, and declared Roman Catholicism to be the religion of the nation. In return, Pope Pius XI (r. 1922–1939), who saw Mussolini as a bulwark against communism, recognized the legitimacy of the Italian state and encouraged Roman Catholics to cooperate with the Fascist regime. The Church later took issue with Mussolini's anti-Semitic laws and with his alliance with Germany, but it never broke ties with Italian Fascism.

Domestic Policy   Italian **Fascism** condemned liberalism, socialism, communism, and the equality of peoples. According to Mussolini, "Fascism conceives of the state as an absolute, in comparison with which all individuals and groups are relative, only to be conceived of in their relation to the state." However, when compared with Nazi Germany or Stalin's Russia, the Italian Fascist Party's efforts to control every aspect of life were far from successful. Fascist youth groups were organized to indoctrinate students, but many young Italians did not bother to attend their meetings. Women were encouraged to leave the workplace and remain at home, but this caused great resentment. Italy's military forces remained more loyal to the king than to the Fascist Party. Similarly, the large landowners and industrialists who funded the Fascist Party never fell completely under its control. Independent labor unions and the right to strike were outlawed, but worker unrest persisted, and strikes occurred anyway, even during World War II. Mussolini's attempts to make Italy economically self-sufficient through high import tariffs merely increased the price of domestically produced goods and food.

Fascist Italy remained a relatively poor and backward country where the image of strength and action was more important than reality. The poor remained poor, and corruption grew in the Fascist Party. In the 1930s Mussolini used foreign policy to distract the Italian people. He proclaimed that "war alone . . . puts the stamp of nobility upon the peoples who have the courage to meet it." In October 1935 he defied the League of Nations and invaded Ethiopia, one of only two independent states left in Africa. The stage was set for his fateful alliance with Nazi Germany and the so-called Rome-Berlin "Axis."

Authoritarian Regimes in Spain and Eastern Europe

Spanish Civil War   In 1931 the Spanish monarchy collapsed and Spain became a republic. The domestic policies of the republican government alienated powerful conservative groups across the country, while socialist and anarchist groups grew stronger. Catholics, landowners, business groups, and the army grew increasingly restive, especially after a left-wing "Popular Front" alliance won national elections in February 1936. In July of that year, General Francisco Franco (1892–1975) launched a military revolt that soon led to civil war. The Spanish Civil War became a test case in the ideological struggle between European authoritarianism and democracy. Franco, a conservative Catholic, entered into a tactical alliance with Spain's Fascists, known as the *Falange*. Hitler and Mussolini supported him with troops and weapons. Stalin backed the republic, and by 1937 Soviet agents took over its security forces. Britain, France, and the United States stayed aloof, although tens of thousands of left-wing volunteers from the West joined the beleaguered republican loyalists. The war was bitterly fought, and both sides committed atrocities. After three years of fighting, however, Franco's superior military power, aided by German air power, prevailed. The German bombing of the town of Guernica in northern Spain became emblematic of the horrors of the war, and prompted Pablo Picasso to paint his famous work ("Guernica," 1937), expressionistically depicting the carnage. By the time the republic fell in 1939, almost half a million Spaniards had lost their lives; in the wake of his victory, Franco imprisoned an additional 1 million republican loyalists, many of whom were sent to concentration or labor camps. Pitting the forces of right-wing nationalism and fascism against those of democracy as well as socialism, the Spanish Civil War can now be seen as a dress rehearsal for the world war that would soon begin.

Eastern Europe   In the 1920s and 1930s democratic institutions faltered in the restored state of Poland, in the successor states to the Austro-Hungarian Empire, and in the Balkans. Poland had been divided into Russian, German, and Austrian spheres since the late eighteenth century. When a Polish state was resurrected after World War I, its multiparty system did not produce stable or effective government. In 1926 a military takeover by Marshal Josef Pilsudski (1857–1935) established an authoritarian regime. Similar right-wing governments emerged in Romania, Bulgaria, and Greece.

In Hungary, Admiral Miklos Horthy (1868–1957) took power in 1920. Horthy's conservative royalist government was backed by an alliance of military and church leaders and large landowners. To the south in the new kingdom of Yugoslavia, Orthodox Serbs clashed repeatedly with Roman Catholic Croats and Slovenes, and with Bosnians and Albanians. In 1929, King Alexander I (r. 1921–1934) tried to suppress the disputes by banning political parties. He was assassinated by Croatian fanatics in 1934, but authoritarian rule continued under a regency government for his young son Peter II (r. 1934–1945). The breakup of Yugoslavia in the 1990s was in large measure the product of ethnic and religious divisions that flared up in the 1920s and 1930s. In all of Eastern Europe only Czechoslovakia remained a parliamentary democracy during these years, and even there ethnic tensions among Czechs, Slovenes, Germans, and other groups threatened to break up the state.

The Emergence of Nazi Germany

The Great Depression shattered the stability of the Weimar Republic. As the unemployment lines swelled and the price of basic commodities increased, political parties quarreled over how to address the crisis. To break the stalemate, in 1930 Chancellor Heinrich Bruning (1885–1970) invoked a clause in the Weimar Constitution (Article 48) that allowed the president to issue emergency decrees. The president of Germany was the aged World War I military leader Paul von Hindenberg (1847–1934). When he dissolved the Reichstag in September 1930 and called for new elections, he set the stage for the meteoric rise of the ultraright National Socialist or Nazi Party.

■ ■

PEOPLE IN CONTEXT José Ortega y Gasset

The Spanish philosopher José Ortega y Gasset (1883–1955) was a critic of mass democracy who believed that only the leadership of an intellectual elite could preserve modern civilization. He was educated in Jesuit schools and at the University of Madrid, where he was appointed professor of philosophy in 1910. A liberal in politics, he went into exile during the Spanish Civil War, returning to Spain only after the end of World War II in 1945.

In his most influential work, *The Revolt of the Masses* (1929), Ortega warned that the rise of irrationalism and violence in mass culture was plunging European civilization into a dark period. Ortega believed that mass culture led to conformism and support for mediocre politicians who appealed to base instincts. It would crush "everything that is different, everything that is excellent, individual, qualified and select. Anybody who is not like everybody, who does not think like everybody, runs the risk of being eliminated. . . ." His critique was confirmed during the 1930s, as the Nazis in Germany and Stalin in the Soviet Union used modern communications, surveillance, and terror tactics to eliminate all personal freedoms.

Ortega felt what he called "mass man" was both mentally unassertive and quick to hand over leadership to the undeserving. The ideas of the masses did not represent the best of culture, yet their numbers transformed vulgar ideas into a new orthodoxy. Ortega was convinced that modern mass culture and the primacy of the commonplace undermined the liberal adherence to fixed truths. Under Fascism, "there appears for the first time in Europe a type of man who does not want to give reasons or to be right, but simply shows himself resolved to impose his opinions. This is the new thing: the right not to be reasonable, the 'reason of unreason.'" The rise of communism and Fascism were for Ortega symptoms of unreflective mass society, where immediate and easy solutions to problems replaced any commitment to higher ideals or serious debate in a climate of mutual respect.

José Ortega y Gasset Spanish writer, playwright, and philosopher, in a photograph from the 1940s.

Question: Why is democratic culture susceptible to the lures of antidemocratic politicians?

■ ■ ■ ■ ■ ■ ■ ■

Hitler's Rise to Power   Adolf Hitler, the leader of the Nazis, had served in World War I and returned from the war a deeply embittered man. In 1919 Hitler joined the National Socialist German Workers' Party (Nazis) and rose to the position of its leader, or Fuehrer. In 1923 he tried to overthrow the state government of Bavaria. Imprisoned for nine months, Hitler spent his time behind bars composing his hate-filled autobiography, *Mein Kampf* (My Struggle). Mixing crude Social Darwinism, anticommunism, and anti-Semitism, the book endorsed the myth of the superior German race descended from the ancient Aryans. Hitler called for national renewal through the demolition of the liberal Enlightenment tradition and the expansion of the master race to the east, eliminating inferior Jews and Slavs in the process.

During the 1920s the Nazi Party did poorly at the polls. In 1928 the Nazis had only 12 seats in the Reichstag and little middle-class support. The party's fortunes changed decisively, however, once the Great Depression hit Germany. In the September 1930 elections, Hitler's party won 107 seats in the Reichstag and received 18% of the vote. The Nazis were now attracting the support of more affluent Germans who were worried about the economic crisis. Hitler promised to reestablish confidence in the economy and destroy German communism. He also pledged to undo the hated Versailles Treaty and restore German military greatness.

Hitler was assisted by ever-increasing unemployment. By March 1932, some 6 million Germans were out of work, three times the number in 1930. Some of the unemployed found a sense of purpose and fellowship in the Nazi SA or storm troopers, paramilitary forces who, like their Italian Fascist counterparts, specialized in intimidation and terror tactics. There were 100,000 members of the SA in 1930 and 1 million in 1932. The SA attacked communists and socialists, and staged mass rallies that appealed to German national pride. Still, many Germans who voted for the Nazis did so with little enthusiasm, seeing the Hitler movement as merely the lesser of two evils when compared with the apparent paralysis of Weimar multiparty democracy.

In the presidential election of March 1932, Hitler narrowly lost to Hindenburg. However, in July elections to the Reichstag, the Nazis took 230 seats out of a total of 549, winning almost 40% of the popular vote and becoming the largest party in the legislature. Hoping to control Hitler, the 83-year-old Hindenburg and his conservative advisors offered Hitler the Chancellorship in January 1933. The government was supposed to be a coalition in which most of the ministers were non-Nazis. For years Hitler had been railing against the failings of the Weimar government; now he would be obliged to demonstrate that his policies could pull Germany out of economic depression. To remain in power, it was assumed, the Nazis would be forced to tone down their anti-Semitic, racist, and antidemocratic rhetoric. It was a fatal miscalculation on the part of Hitler's conservative political opponents.

The Nazi State   Chancellor Hitler immediately called for new elections to the Reichstag. Nazi propaganda and bullying frightened many voters who supported anti-Nazi candidates. A few days before the elections, a mysterious fire destroyed the Reichstag building in Berlin. Hitler blamed the communists, suspended civil liberties, and insisted that Germany was under attack from left-wing terrorists. The Nazis and their conservative allies

Key Developments in Hitler's Rise to Power	
1920	Hitler becomes leader of the Nazi Party
1923	Nazis stage "Beer Hall Putsch" in Munich
1924	Hitler writes *Mein Kampf*
1930	Nazis win 107 seats in parliamentary elections
1933	Hitler appointed chancellor
1934	Hitler eliminates SA leaders
1935	Nuremburg Laws
1938	"Kristallnacht"

won a majority of the seats in the elections, and in March 1933 the Reichstag gave Hitler dictatorial power for four years. Without hesitation the Nazi leader outlawed all other political parties, and when Hindenburg died in 1934, Hitler took over complete executive authority. Seeking to secure the support of the German military, whose generals disliked the rival paramilitary SA, Hitler ordered an elite force within the Nazi Party, the SS, to kill the SA leadership. Under Heinrich Himmler (1900–1945), the SS would become a ruthless and murderous organization dedicated to Hitler's world view. The elimination of the SA leaders achieved two goals for Hitler. The German army took a personal oath of allegiance to him as Fuehrer (not to the German state), and Hitler's principal rival within the Party, SA leader Ernst Roehm (1887–1934), was executed.

The Nazis took direct aim at the constitutional liberties guaranteed by Weimar democracy. Freedom of speech, assembly, and press were eliminated, and a secret police force, the Gestapo, rooted out any effective opposition. Nazi officials monopolized key government posts. Schools, professional associations, and even leisure organizations were forced to conform to Nazi directives. The Hitler Youth indoctrinated boys with Nazi ideology while the League of German Girls inculcated young women with the virtues of motherhood and of women's subordination to men. Campaigns were conducted to eliminate birth control, homosexuality, and abortion and to "improve" the German racial stock. Large families received special encouragement from the Nazi state with pensions and medals for women who gave birth to more than four children. Hitler's regime also controlled artistic expression, condemning American jazz and modernist art. University professors and their students publicly burned books thought to be subversive. Faculty who objected lost their posts.

Under the direction of propaganda minister Joseph Goebbels (1897–1945), the print and electronic media (radio and films) emphasized the infallibility of the Fuehrer and the submission of the individual to the totalitarian state and to the greater good of the master race. Goebbels embraced film as a powerful tool in shaping Fascist identity and in highlighting the differences between the harsh realities of Depression-era Germany and the renewal of national life under the Nazis. In 1933 he established the Reich Film Chamber, which became responsible for approving scripts, screening productions, and approving personnel. A state-controlled credit bank provided financing for filmmakers,

Hitler and Propaganda   The Nazis staged large political rallies designed to highlight the dynamism and resolve of state authorities. In this photo from 1938 Hitler salutes from an open vehicle while troops and Nazi banners provide the backdrop.

and in 1934 the Reich Cinema Law outlawed Jewish participation in the industry. Many talented Weimar-era filmmakers fled the Nazi regime for America during the 1930s.

The young actress and filmmaker Leni Riefenstahl (1902–2003) put her talents at the disposal of the Hitler regime, producing masterful propaganda films that recorded the enormous rallies the Nazis held during the 1930s. *The Triumph of the Will* (1934) employed a production crew of 120, more than 30 cameras, and a wide range of techniques, including shots of the Fuehrer in an airplane en route to the Nazi Party rally at Nuremberg. Masses of soldiers formed geometric lines and frames for the long distance shots at the rally, where Hitler strode up the stairs to deliver an emotional speech. Riefenstahl portrayed Hitler as decisive, all-knowing, eternally energetic, and the object of worshipful reverence and respect. Two years later, Riefenstahl produced *Olympia,* an evocative account of the 1936 Berlin Olympics. She emphasized the Nazi concern with physical superiority, using slow motion segments, underwater shots of swimmers, and panoramic scenes. Riefenstahl could not escape her association with Nazi propaganda, and she was briefly imprisoned after World War II. Although most of the approximately 1,100 feature films produced during the 12 years of the Third Reich were entertainment/escapist movies, the 10% that were overt propaganda films centered on the themes of preparation for war, Nazi Party ideology, and anti-Semitism.

Rebuilding the Economy   Unlike most other leaders in Europe during the 1930s, Hitler was willing to engage in deficit spending to jump-start the national economy. His confidence was based on the assumption that Germany would recoup its investments through future military and territorial aggression in Eastern Europe. Large public works, especially the creation of a modern transportation infrastructure, put thousands of Germans back to work. In 1933 Hitler repudiated the military provisions of the Versailles Treaty, withdrew from the League of Nations, and began a massive rearmament program under Hermann Goering (1893–1946). The military buildup led to full employment by the late 1930s. The 6 million Germans who were unemployed when Hitler took office in 1933 now had jobs, and to many the loss of personal freedom and the increasing intolerance of the Nazi regime were a small price to pay for economic security. Hitler had forged a strong sense of national purpose within a few years. Some observers in the Western democracies, still mired in the Great Depression, envied Germany's economic rebound and began to wonder whether a dictatorship was the only viable path to material abundance. Small Fascist movements emerged in France and Britain, while in the United States right-wing demagogues accused the Roosevelt administration of sympathizing with communism.

Anti-Semitism   German Fascism thrived on excluding and demonizing groups it deemed enemies of the German people. Hitler and the Nazi leadership despised leftists, homosexuals, gypsies, and Jehovah's Witnesses; members of these groups were persecuted and imprisoned without trial. In 1939 the regime even approved "euthanasia" programs for the mentally ill and infirm, leading to the murder of tens of thousands of Germans. However, drawing upon 2,000 years of European anti-Jewish prejudice, **Nazism** reserved its deepest animosity for Germany's Jews. For Hitler, Jews were disloyal internationalists who were committed to poisoning the superior "Aryan" racial stock. In 1935 the Nuremberg Laws stripped Jews of their citizenship. They were subsequently denied entry into the medical, legal, educational, and music professions, and were forced to wear a Star of David on their garments. Non-Jews were forbidden to marry or have sexual relations with Jews.

On the night of November 9, 1938, Nazi gangs destroyed thousands of Jewish shops, synagogues, and homes in towns and cities across Germany. Thousands of Jews were imprisoned without trial in concentration camps, and the state seized their property. After this program—which came to be known as Kristallnacht (Night of Broken Glass)—those Jews who could do so emigrated, leaving behind most of their possessions. By the

Kristallnacht   A synagogue burns during the "Night of Broken Glass" (*Kristallnacht*), November 9–10, 1938. This anti-Jewish rampage was an ominous milestone in the Nazis' persecution of German Jews, heralding a more openly violent policy.

start of World War II in September 1939, over one-half of Germany's Jewish population had fled. While a small number of individual Christian clergy spoke out in protest, neither Protestant nor Catholic church leaders publicly opposed Nazi persecution of the Jews. Together with most German intellectual leaders, influential Christians remained loyal to the Nazi regime even after the war began, and they remained silent during the Holocaust. The Nazi goal of stripping individuals of the capacity for independent thought had made enormous headway by the end of the 1930s. Rational thought and humane instincts had crumbled before the forces of intimidation and state-sponsored domestic terror. Few Germans at the time either recognized the full extent of the transformation that had occurred in less than one decade or understood the implications of Nazi policy for the future of European civilization.

Imperial Japan

The rise of authoritarian, antidemocratic government in Western Europe was mirrored by developments in Asia's single industrialized state. Like the United States, Japan had emerged from World War I in a relatively strong position. In the 1920s a vibrant two-party political system developed, with all males over the age of 25 eligible to vote in national elections. A series of social reforms were undertaken, labor unions grew, and military expenditures fell. Japan was the best-educated and most modernized country in Asia. However, since most Japanese were peasants and urban workers who earned low wages, the domestic market for consumer goods was small, and Japanese industry relied heavily on foreign markets to sell its products. When the global depression struck and nations began to raise import tariff barriers to protect domestic industry, Japan's overseas trade, particularly with the United States, plummeted. One-half of all Japanese factories were closed in 1931. As exports dropped by 50% between 1929 and 1931, crop failures in the north of the country led to famine conditions in 1931 and 1932.

Invasion of Manchuria
Ultranationalists and army officers began to argue that economic security required secure Asian markets, preferably in territories that Japan controlled directly or indirectly. It was time to create an Asian Empire under the direction of the military and the emperor. First on the list of potential additions was Manchuria, a fertile and resource-rich region in China's northeast. The attack on Manchuria began in September 1931, and within six months the Japanese had defeated the Chinese Nationalists and installed the former Chinese emperor, Henry P'u Yi (1906–1967), as ruler of a new puppet state named Manchukuo. When the League of Nations condemned the invasion, Japan withdrew from the League. The ease with which Japan flouted the League's authority was not lost on Fascist leaders in Italy and Germany.

Extreme Nationalism
In the spring of 1936 a group of right-wing army officers attempted to overthrow Japan's parliamentary government. They sought to put an end to Western-style democracy and looked with envy on Nazi Germany's accomplishments. They promoted the values of emperor worship and the samurai code of honor. Although the coup failed, the ultranationalists' rhetoric of "Asia for the Asians" and their belief in

Japan's racial superiority resonated with a large segment of the public. Japan continued its aggression against Nationalist China, and by 1938, Japan was selling almost half of its exports to Manchuria, Taiwan, and Korea—all lands under Japanese control. Because Japan still lacked the essential raw materials and fuels that modern industrial economies needed, Japanese military and political leaders now began to consider further expansion in Asia. Of particular interest were the rubber plantations of British Malaya and the oil produced in the Dutch East Indies (Indonesia). Japan's aggression against its Pacific neighbors alarmed Washington. Fear of American opposition proved to be crucial in the military's decision to attack United States naval forces at Pearl Harbor in December 1941.

The Soviet Union Under Stalin

The repressive single-party state that emerged in Russia after the triumph of the Bolsheviks in the civil war against the White Russian forces and their foreign allies (1918–1921) was similar to Europe's Fascist regimes in several important respects. Once in power, the Bolsheviks ruthlessly eliminated their political rivals. They rejected the liberal concept of human rights and the rule of law, created a powerful secret police to root out dissent, and glorified the cult of the all-knowing and all-powerful leader. The good of the state as defined by the Communist Party leadership always took precedence over the economic, political, religious, cultural, and intellectual claims of the individual.

However, the Bolshevik government also rejected some of the key components of the Fascist world view. First and foremost, the leaders of the Soviet Union's Communist Party fervently believed that the revolution in Russia was but the first stage in what would become a global struggle to overthrow the capitalist political and economic order. Their appeal to international worker solidarity and their belief that the Russian Revolution was the dawn of a new age assumed that all human beings were equal. Social Darwinist pseudoscience, racism, and imperialist nationalism, all key components of Fascist thought, never played a significant role in Bolshevik ideology. The Soviet experiment also lasted much longer. The murderous German Third Reich lasted only 12 years, Japanese militarism endured barely a decade, and Mussolini's tenure was less than 25 years. The Soviet Union, by contrast, survived for three-quarters of a century before its demise in 1991.

The Early Soviet Economy   Although the Red Army prevailed during the civil war, conditions in Russia during the early 1920s were desperate. Famine and disease killed between 5 and 7 million people, the economy was in tatters, strikes were commonplace, sailors from the Baltic naval fleet mutinied, and peasants refused to meet government grain requisitions. The promised fruits of a socialist society under the "dictatorship of the proletariat" were nowhere in sight. The Bolsheviks faced an overwhelming economic challenge at home and widespread international hostility. A small group of Communist Party leaders reserved all power to themselves and struggled to turn a backwards economy into a modern, industrialized socialist system. As the head of a seven-man Politburo (political bureau) that set policy for the larger Central Committee of the Communist Party, Lenin decided that he had to postpone his outline for a top-down planned economy. In a strategic retreat in March 1921, he announced the

New Economic Policy (NEP). Peasant farmers were now allowed to manage their own plots of land and sell their surplus grain on the open market in return for the payment of a tax in kind. Similarly, small businesses and retail stores were allowed to operate along market lines. The change in policy had an immediate and positive impact; by 1927, industrial production had returned to pre-World War I levels.

Succession Struggle, 1924–1928

When Lenin died in January 1924 after a series of strokes, a power struggle broke out to succeed him. Leon Trotsky, who advocated worldwide revolution, seemed to be the most likely successor, but the youthful Nikolai Bukharin (1888–1938), a man with wide-ranging interests and a strong supporter of Lenin's NEP, also enjoyed a great deal of influence. One other contender, Joseph Stalin, was not a native Russian but a Georgian from the Caucasus Mountain frontier zone. Raised in poverty, Stalin briefly attended an Orthodox seminary before becoming a Marxist revolutionary and follower of Lenin at the turn of the twentieth century.

Although Lenin had deep reservations about him, Stalin rose quickly to prominence in the Communist Party after the 1917 Revolution. Appointed general secretary of the Central Committee of the Communist Party in 1922, Stalin was no match for either Trotsky or Bukharin as a thinker, nor did he possess much knowledge of the West, having never lived in exile. But Stalin was a masterful propagandist and manager of the Communist Party apparatus. With control over the bureaucracy, which included admission to and promotion within the Communist Party, Stalin built his support within the lower ranks of the administration. He also led a movement to elevate the deceased Lenin to cult hero status and claimed to be Lenin's closest associate. In 1924 Stalin denounced Trotsky's appeal for world revolution and instead called for the creation of "socialism in one country." He also remained unenthusiastic about the NEP, preferring to push for total collectivization of agriculture and rapid industrialization. By 1927, Stalin had effectively marginalized both of his rivals. Trotsky was driven into exile in 1929, eventually finding his way to Mexico, where Stalin's assassins killed him in 1940. Bukharin was ousted from the Politburo and murdered in 1938.

The Stalin Terror State

Between 1928 and the start of World War II in June 1941, Stalin transformed the Soviet Union into one of the world's premier industrial and military powers, but at a cost in human life that is hard to imagine. At least 20 million Soviet citizens died during this frenetic race to modernize an overwhelmingly agrarian empire. Many died from overwork and exhaustion; others were the victims of collectivization of agriculture and the resulting mass starvation. Millions more were shot or died in prison camps, having been arbitrarily defined as opponents of the all-knowing Soviet leader.

Stalin believed that the Soviet Union could not survive in a world of hostile capitalist nation-states unless it could match the West's industrial prowess. Setting aside the gradualist NEP, he established a state planning commission, or *Gosplan,* to oversee a series of Five-Year Plans built around the idea of state ownership in every sphere of economic life. The first target was the collectivization of agriculture. Soviet bureaucrats used the armed forces to put an end to private farming and forced the peasantry to work on large state-owned and managed collective farms. The government set production targets and used surpluses from the sale of farm products to finance industrialization.

Five-Year Plans   Under Joseph Stalin, the Soviet Union embarked upon an accelerated program of industrialization. During the first Five-Year Plan (1933), posters like this encouraged an all-out effort to raise production. The words at the bottom read, "Industrialization is the road to socialism."

There was enormous resistance to collectivization, especially among prosperous peasants. Many farmers even destroyed their own crops and livestock rather than surrender them to the state. However, Stalin was undeterred. Between 1929 and 1933, millions of landowners, called *kulaks* by Soviet authorities, were either killed or exiled to Siberia where they later perished in state-run labor camps. Agricultural output plunged during these years, and famine returned. Millions of people died of starvation, even as Soviet authorities exported grain produced on collectivized farms to raise capital for industrial projects. The greatest brutalities took place in Ukraine, the traditional breadbasket of the Russian Empire. Approximately 7 million people died in Ukraine during the years of forced collectivization, most from starvation, but many at the hands of Soviet officials who killed resisters with impunity.

Forced labor on collectivized state farms eventually ended the famine and raised production levels. Thousands of excess workers were shifted to urban centers where they worked in newly established factories. The picture of Soviet life communicated to the outside world during the first Five-Year Plan (1928–1933) was one of agricultural surpluses, the building of new heavy industries and power plants at astonishing speed, and happy workers exceeding production targets. Carefully crafted media images of inspired workers and well-fed peasants, all committed to the dream of a cooperative socialist society, contrasted sharply with unemployment lines and business failures in the capitalist democracies. Some in the West believed that the Soviet system had avoided the ravages of the global depression. Few observers in the United States and Europe realized the enormous cost in human life resulting from forced collectivization. Nor did they appreciate the scale of Stalin's murderous repression.

Repression and Political Purges   Every sector of Soviet society was mobilized to support the modernization programs. Soviet schools inculcated the virtues of worker discipline, while newspapers, radio, and film applauded Stalin's vision and selflessness. Party officials and the secret police, the *Cheka* (later known as the KGB), ensured that political dissent was swiftly suppressed. Women were recruited into the workforce in large numbers, while mothers were taught to raise their children to serve the state. Soviet authorities imposed an official style in the arts, called "socialist realism," which was dedicated to eliminating decadent bourgeois themes. Artists, musicians, writers, and dramatists were all obliged to have their productions approved by communist bureaucrats. A cult of Stalin developed, and his image appeared on enormous posters, in paintings, in newsreels, and as statues in public places.

Stalin's growing paranoia and crude hunger for absolute power led him to equate debate with betrayal and treason. Beginning in 1934, he began to eliminate most of the old Bolsheviks, the founders and top leaders of the Communist Party, charging them with conspiracy to destroy the Soviet State. In a series of publicized show trials, high-profile defendants confessed (usually after torture and threats of retribution against their families) to a variety of treasonable offenses. All were executed. In parallel secret purges, members of the military high command were condemned and then killed by Stalin's agents. Once the Party and military leadership had been eliminated, Stalin turned against large numbers of middle-class professionals, including scientists, scholars, artists, and engineers. Millions of Soviet citizens, the well-known and the obscure, were killed without the least hesitation. Total conformity and unflinching obedience were required; family members were encouraged to inform on loved ones, and even children were drawn into the net of accusation and denunciation. No one was safe, as this period of the "Great Terror" concluded, and the only truth was that which issued from the diseased mind of the Party leader. By 1938, the Stalinist dictatorship had become a cruel caricature of Karl Marx's stateless communist society. The Russian people, less than two decades removed from tsarist absolutism, were now subject to levels of control and servility of which the tsars had never dreamed.

KEY QUESTION | Revisited

The interwar period failed to achieve either political reconciliation between former adversaries or lasting economic security for the peoples of Europe and the United States. The Versailles Treaty set the stage for future conflict by imposing harsh terms on the vanquished. Europe's fiscal indebtedness to the United States hampered efforts at economic reconstruction across the continent. The Soviet Union repudiated the debts of the tsarist regime, thereby guaranteeing that the West would offer no economic assistance. After a brief period of modest prosperity during the second half of the 1920s, the Great Depression plunged the Western democracies into an unprecedented crisis. As millions of citizens were reduced to the ranks of the unemployed, confidence in the ability of liberal democratic governments to respond effectively to the emergency tumbled. Across Europe the constitutional ideals of the Enlightenment, including responsible elective government, civil rights, equality under the law, and the guarantee of personal liberty, all seemed of minor importance in the face of acute material hardship.

Into this crisis of liberal democracy stepped radical politicians on the right and the left who declared that the Enlightenment tradition was bankrupt and that true greatness and material abundance could be secured only under the direction of charismatic and decisive leaders. Fascist leaders appealed to irrational impulses, ethnic and religious prejudice, hyperbolic nationalism, and aggressive militarism in pursuit of absolute political power. Rejecting parliamentary democracy as a government of weaklings and divisive special interests, authoritarian and Fascist leaders claimed that the future belonged to their movement. Writing at the end of World War II, the exiled German philosopher Ernst Cassirer (1874–1945) described the Fascist phenomenon as the victory of the grand myth over hard reality. The myth was multifaceted, but it was anchored in the rhetoric and action of inhumanity.

Soviet totalitarianism took a different form. The same malignity and repression of the individual was central to the power of both Fascist and communist regimes, but Stalin's call for worker solidarity and the creation of the classless society served as the basis of opposition to Western liberal democracy. Stalin sought supreme power for himself and to make the Soviet Union a modern economic and military power at any cost. By 1939, he had achieved these goals, but Soviet modernization emphasized industrialization for the sole purpose of national defense, while the consumer sector was largely ignored. Soviet citizens lived under a government that put people to work and, by the mid-1930s, offered food and shelter where too often in the past there had been poverty and starvation. However, tens of millions of lives had been lost in the process of building the Soviet economy. A man for whom truth was simply the successful application of power in society, Stalin did not recognize Western liberal definitions of freedom and dignity.

While Western Europe's democratic states maintained personal liberty, defenders of the rationalist-humanist tradition were hard pressed during the interwar period. The appeal of totalitarianism, its simple solutions to complex problems, its call to instinct and action, and its focus on larger collective goals appealed to many Europeans seeking renewal in a deeply troubled postwar culture. In those countries where democracy had taken deep root—Britain, France, Switzerland, Ireland, and in the United States—personal liberties were protected despite acute material hardship. Where democratic practices had not taken root, the promise of material security under authoritarian political systems, while destroying individual autonomy and the right to dissent peacefully through the political process, was too seductive to be ignored. Once seduced, however, the citizen became a subject, the leader became a secular god, and the dignity of the individual evaporated before the shrine of state power.

Review Questions

1. How did the West's liberal democracies respond to the Great Depression? How did Fascist and communist regimes respond?
2. How did the Great Depression assist Hitler's rise to political power?
3. What were the main features of the totalitarian state in the 1930s?
4. How did Stalin modernize the Soviet Union in less than a decade? Why did the Soviet economy appear to be moving forward while Western economies stagnated?
5. How did Mussolini's Fascists manage to secure power in 1922?
6. Why did Japan become more militaristic and imperialistic in the 1930s?
7. How did Nazism repudiate the central tenets of the Enlightenment tradition?

Please consult the Suggested Readings at the back of the book to continue your study of the material covered in this chapter. For a list of documents on the Primary Source DVD-ROM that relate to topics in this chapter, please refer to the back of the book.

Topics in This Chapter

The Process of Appeasement, 1933–1939

• Nazism Triumphant, 1939–1941: Europe and North Africa

• The German Empire • The Home Front and the Role of Women

• War in Asia and the Pacific • The Tide Turns, 1942–1945

• Planning for the Postwar World

24 World War II: Europe in Eclipse

We shall never surrender; and even if, which I do not for a moment believe, this island or a larger part of it were subjected and starving, then our Empire beyond the seas, armed and guarded by the British Fleet, would carry on the struggle, until, in God's good time, the New World, with all its power and might, steps forth to the rescue and liberation of the Old.

—Winston Churchill

KEY | Question

Can the force of ideas sustain a civilization under attack?

In early June 1940, after the conquest of Poland, Denmark, Norway, Belgium, Luxembourg, and Holland by Germany, and as the last troops of the British Expeditionary Force were being hastily evacuated by sea from the beaches at Dunkirk in France, Prime Minister Winston Churchill (1874–1965) addressed the House of Commons and spoke the words just quoted. The defeat of France was now imminent, but Churchill remained defiant. He assured his parliamentary colleagues and the nation that the war against Nazi aggression, what he had earlier termed "a monstrous tyranny, never surpassed in the dark lamentable catalogue of human crime," would continue until victory was achieved.

Churchill seemed to be confident that if Germany invaded the British Isles, the colonial subjects of King George VI (r. 1936–1952) would come to the defense of the Empire. After all, they had done so once before. Churchill took it for granted that Britain's subject peoples would assist Britain in its new moment of peril. Remarkably, most colonials responded positively, again sacrificing their sons for the preservation of a state and a system committed to the principles of liberal democracy, even though those principles had not been extended to the colonies themselves. Churchill also spoke of the New World, with its power and might,

Liberation   The citizens of Palermo, Sicily welcome American forces into their city after it surrendered to Allied forces on July 22, 1943.

coming to the aid of the Old. This too was a bold prediction, especially in light of America's strongly isolationist political culture during the 1930s. But it also came true. The United States entered the war in December 1941 and afforded Britain the material resources to sustain its commitment to democratic culture. With the military support of the United States, Western Europe would reject Nazi absolutism and return to the path of democracy. However, it could no longer follow that path unassisted or unprotected. Europe had been eclipsed.

The Process of Appeasement, 1933–1939

Hitler had stated clearly in *Mein Kampf* that Germany's future greatness was contingent upon war and expansion into Eastern Europe. The Slavic peoples, including the Russians, were from inferior racial stock and needed to be subordinated to the master Aryan inhabitants of Germany. The persecution of German Jews and the destruction of Weimar democracy during the 1930s should have signaled the danger of the Fascist threat to Western civilization. Nazi domestic policy was always formulated in the expectation of future territorial expansion and the inevitability of war. Throughout the 1930s Germany's neighbors, particularly France and Great Britain, failed to recognize the depth of the Nazi commitment to war. They chose instead to believe that if only Hitler's latest territorial demand was met in the best spirit of international cooperation, conflict could be avoided and the Nazi state integrated into the European political system. Appeasing Hitler seemed to be the best way to avoid repeating the horrors of World War I. The memory of that conflict was still fresh in the 1930s, and for many British and French policymakers, **appeasement** was a reasonable, positive approach to international relations on the continent.

Germany's Neighbors Hesitate Hitler's decisions to withdraw from the League of Nations in 1933 and to begin rearming Germany were the first of many calculated gambles that the Nazi leader took, but given the League's failure to act against Japan after that country invaded Manchuria in 1931, it was unlikely that the international organization would intervene. Hitler's assumption was correct. In 1934 the Nazi regime signed a nonaggression pact with Poland, an agreement that increased nervousness in France, which considered Poland a potential ally. It was followed by the restoration of the German air force and the creation of a 500,000-man German army—both violations of the Versailles Treaty.

Instead of a collective response, Germany's neighbors hastened to cut individual deals. Britain, for example, sought to maintain its historic naval superiority by entering into a separate agreement with Hitler. The British approved the construction of a German fleet that would be one-third the size of Britain's Royal Navy. France signed a five-year defensive alliance with the newest member of the League of Nations, the Soviet Union, in May 1935. The French military also constructed a series of defensive installations, called the Maginot Line, to repel any future German attack. The French and British also negotiated regional pacts involving Turkey, Greece, Romania, and Yugoslavia to preserve the status quo in the Balkans. However, none of these agreements or alliances curbed the remilitarization of the German state. Neither did they inhibit Hitler's demands that all German-speaking people be united to Germany or his strident calls for more living space (*Lebensraum*) at the expense of "inferior" Slavic peoples.

The Rhineland Wager   When Mussolini attacked Ethiopia in 1935, the League of Nations imposed weak economic sanctions on Italy but took no military steps to preserve the independence of the African state. In a further blow to League credibility, oil companies in the United States, against the wishes of President Roosevelt, continued to supply the Italian armed forces with fuel. Always the opportunist, Hitler now prepared another strike against the hated Versailles Treaty. He entered into a defense pact with Italy, and both countries were joined by Japan in what was ostensibly an anticommunist alliance. In March 1936 Hitler ordered German troops into the demilitarized Rhineland, the industrial heart of Germany. It was another high-stakes gamble, opposed even by the leaders of his own military who feared that the French would attack and occupy the Rhineland. Hitler's estimate of British and French resolve proved to be on target. British leaders were willing to look the other way, since the Germans were not annexing new territory but simply asserting full sovereignty over a part of Germany itself—and France was unwilling to act without British support.

Austria, Czechoslovakia, and "German" Unity   Hitler was a native Austrian, and he passionately believed that all Germans, especially Austrians, should be united in one state. The idea of unification, or *Anschluss,* between Germany and Austria had been discussed in 1919, but the Versailles Treaty forbade it. By the late 1930s, Austria was weak and divided with a large Nazi Party. In March 1938 Hitler used the pretext of possible civil disturbances in Austria to order the German army to occupy the country. France and Britain took no action. Austria's 6.5 million people became part of the German Reich (empire). Hitler used the rhetoric of national self-determination to legitimize an annexation that was in any case highly popular with the Austrian people.

Almost immediately after his successful Austrian gambit, Hitler took up the question of the 3.5 million Germans living in a region of western Czechoslovakia known as the Sudetenland. Again he used the rhetoric of national self-determination to make a power grab. Although many of the Sudeten Germans disliked Czech rule, Czechoslovakia was the only genuine democracy in Central Europe. Czech authorities stood firm even though Hitler's propaganda machine decried the "persecution" of Czechoslovakia's German minority. By September 1938, war seemed imminent, especially since Czechoslovakia had treaties of alliance with France and the Soviet Union. To avert a European war, British Prime Minister Neville Chamberlain (1869–1940) entered into direct negotiations with Hitler, and Britain and France put pressure on Czechoslovakia to yield to Hitler's demands.

After a series of complicated negotiations, Mussolini called for a four-power conference at Munich. Chamberlain and French Premier Edouard Daladier (1884–1970) met with Hitler and Mussolini at the conference, which ran from September 22 to September 29, 1938. Czechoslovakia and the Soviet Union were not invited to attend. The meeting ended with France and Britain awarding Hitler the Sudetenland. France refused to honor its military commitments to Czechoslovakia, while the Soviets were infuriated by their exclusion from the meeting. Chamberlain represented a nation that was neither prepared for war nor completely unsympathetic to the German claim that the Versailles Treaty had arbitrarily assigned Germans against their will to the new Czech republic. In addition, many British policymakers, while disdainful of the Nazi regime, viewed Hitler as a potential ally against international communism. Chamberlain returned home to announce that with the Munich agreement, Hitler's territorial demands had been satiated. The settlement had achieved "peace in our time." Churchill was less certain. In the House of Commons he stated that Chamberlain had been defeated in Munich and that the German dictator, "instead of snatching the victuals from the table, has been content to have them served to him course by course."

The Destruction of Czechoslovakia   Hitler interpreted the Munich agreement as a further sign of Western weakness. The truncated Czechoslovak state was doomed. Poland and Hungary received parts of it, and in March 1939, on the pretense of protecting the Slovaks who were in revolt against Czech rule, German troops occupied Prague and ended Czech independence (see Map 24–1). This invasion destroyed the pretense that Hitler was simply interested in national self-determination for Germans. It now became apparent that the policy of appeasement, based on the assumption that Hitler was a reasonable statesman who would not recklessly plunge Europe into another world war, was a failure. Britain and France at last began to take steps to resist further Nazi aggression. They did not have long to wait.

Poland and the Resumption of War   For the first time since the Bolshevik Revolution of 1917, the Western democracies and the Soviet Union faced a common threat.

Map 24–1   The Partitions of Czechoslovakia and Poland 1938–1939   Adolf Hitler's obsession with greater "living space" (lebensraum) for the German people led him to steadily encroach upon countries to the east and south of Germany in the late 1930s.

Question: Why were the other European powers unable to stop German expansion?

Hitler's opposition to communism and his stated desire for "living space" in the east posed a long-term challenge to Stalin's totalitarian regime, while the assault on democracy in Central Europe dispelled any lingering Western illusions about the Nazi agenda. Immediately after the carve-up of Czechoslovakia, the Soviets called for a six-nation conference (Britain, France, Russia, Poland, Rumania, and Turkey) to discuss the possibility of joint measures against further Nazi attacks. Most of these states were fearful of Soviet intentions, and the conference was never held. However, when Hitler began to bully Poland in early 1939, Britain and France pledged to come to its aid in the event of a German attack. The Versailles peace settlement had awarded parts of eastern Germany to the Polish state. Hitler now called for a revision of this settlement. His ultimate objective was either to reduce Poland to the status of a puppet state or to destroy it entirely. Poland would not be bullied, and by June 1939, the German army completed plans for an invasion.

Hitler-Stalin Pact   At this critical juncture, the Germans reached a surprise nonaggression pact with the Soviet Union. Stalin was suspicious of the West, and in an attempt to buy Hitler off, he agreed (in secret provisions) to remain neutral while Hitler's forces dismantled Poland. Stalin had never accepted Russia's loss of territory in 1918 and 1919. The pact with Hitler gave the Soviet leader a free hand to reoccupy these lands, including a large part of eastern Poland. The Nazi-Soviet nonaggression pact was signed on August 23, 1939. Less than two weeks later, on September 1, 1939, Germany invaded Poland using tanks and air power. Within one month, this *Blitzkrieg* (lightning war) overwhelmed the Poles. The Soviets invaded eastern Poland, and again the country was wiped off the map of Europe.

War Resumes   The British and the French declared war two days after the German invasion. However, they did nothing to assist the beleaguered Poles and remained passively on the defensive on the Western front. After two decades of uneasy peace, Europeans were once again at war. When it ended six years later, the Western world would be changed forever. Unlike they had in 1914, no one in Britain, France, or Germany rejoiced at the outbreak of the conflict; none of Europe's leading intellectuals mused about the cleansing effects of battle; no parades were organized for the departing troops. After years of hesitation and hope against hope that Hitler would act responsibly once the harsher provisions of the Versailles Treaty were withdrawn, Europe's major constitutional democracies went to war as a last resort against a regime that contemptuously equated truth with power.

Nazism Triumphant, 1939–1941: Europe and North Africa

Germany's swift destruction of Poland was accompanied by Soviet advances from the east. Stalin's Red Army quickly occupied the Baltic states of Latvia, Estonia, and Lithuania, and seized part of Romania. In the winter of 1939 the Red Army attacked Finland, but strong Finnish resistance forced the Soviets to recognize Finland's independence in exchange for territorial concessions. The Western theater, however, was largely quiet between the outbreak of war in September 1939 and the spring of 1940. Often referred to as the "phony war," it was an eerie calm before the great storm. Suddenly, and with overwhelming force, the Nazis occupied Denmark and Norway in April 1940, inflicting heavy damage on

British naval forces and giving Hitler access to key naval and air bases for a future assault against Britain. The next month German troops invaded Belgium, the Netherlands, and tiny Luxemburg. The Blitzkrieg drove through Belgium to the English Channel, forcing a combined British and French army to the beaches at Dunkirk in northern France. Despite German aerial bombardment, over 300,000 French and British troops managed to flee across the Channel aboard everything from small ships to pleasure boats and fishing craft.

Fall of France The German advance had outflanked the well-defended Maginot Line through the Ardennes Forest and into northern France. Well-armed but poorly led French troops quickly lost heart after the Dunkirk disaster. Mussolini, eager to share in the spoils now that a German victory seemed certain, invaded southern France on June 10. The French easily repulsed the Italians, but Paris fell to the Germans on June 13, and French political leaders, after only five weeks of combat, decided to sue for an armistice. It was solemnly signed on June 22, 1940, in the same railway car where Germany had capitulated to the Allies in 1918. Germany occupied northern France and the strategically important coastline. The new French government, led by the aged hero of Verdun, Marshall Henri Philippe Petain (1856–1951), was located in the southern city of Vichy. It agreed to collaborate with the Nazis in areas of France under German occupation. Not all French leaders, however, accepted defeat. General Charles de Gaulle (1890–1970), from exile in London, organized a Free French government and vowed to continue the struggle. For French citizens who remained behind, however, the hard re-

German Troops Occupy Paris French defenses proved to be woefully inadequate against German assault in 1940. In this photo, Hitler's troops march down the Champs-Elysees in the capital city of Paris.

ality of military occupation called for sullen adjustment and resignation. The German juggernaut appeared unstoppable in the summer of 1940, a fact that led Hitler to assume that the British would swiftly accept the new political order on the continent.

Battle of Britain   Winston Churchill became prime minister in May 1940 at the head of a coalition government dedicated to continuing the war. Churchill had been a consistent opponent of appeasement, and he used his oratorical skills to rally the British public for the fight ahead despite seemingly impossible odds. In August the German air force, the *Luftwaffe*, began attacking British naval and military installations in preparation for a cross-Channel invasion. When the British responded by bombing German cities, Hitler began a nightly bombardment of London. For two months, the battle for mastery of the skies over Britain raged between the Royal Air Force (RAF) and the *Luftwaffe*. German losses were twice as high as those incurred by the RAF, and for the first time in the war, Hitler was forced to abandon his offensive plans.

The Battle of Britain united the British public as never before. Although Britain stood alone against the previously unstoppable tyrant, Churchill's leadership and the bravery of a handful of combat pilots had scored an important victory. Referring to those pilots on August 20, Churchill told Parliament that "never in the field of human conflict was so much owed by so many to so few." Even the royal family became a symbol of popular resistance. When large portions of central London were destroyed by Nazi bombs and while other European monarchs were forced to flee their homelands, King George VI (r. 1936–1952) and Queen Elizabeth (1900–2002) remained at their home, Buckingham Palace. The monarchs visited bomb sites across the city on a regular basis, especially the poor districts of the heavily damaged East End. After Buckingham Palace was hit by bombs and rockets, Elizabeth said, "It makes me feel I can look the East End in the Face." The Queen made a point of wearing bright pastel colors and exhibited great warmth on these walkabouts. Her radio addresses, along with those of Churchill, brought comfort and resolve to the nation at its darkest hour. Hitler referred to Elizabeth as the most dangerous woman in Europe.

In the spring of 1941, President Roosevelt, despite strong isolationist sentiment in Congress, established the Lend-Lease Program in which American goods and services, including military hardware, could be transferred to any country whose defense the president deemed vital to the security of the United States. Congress approved the expenditure of $7 billion for war materials under Lend-Lease, and the American navy began patrolling the North Atlantic and assisted the British in tracking down German submarines. From Hitler's perspective, the United States had become an undeclared enemy. Its overwhelming material resources would enable Britain to defy Germany throughout 1941.

North Africa and the Balkans   Eager to match Germany's military feats, in September 1940 Mussolini ordered his forces in the Italian colony of Libya to attack British-controlled Egypt. The Italians also began operations against Greece from bases in occupied Albania. In both assaults the Italians were humiliated. Hitler felt obliged to assist his hapless ally, assigning General Erwin Rommel (1891–1944) to the North African theater. Rommel was a skillful tank commander, and his Afrika Korps armored divisions drove the British back from Libya into Egypt. His goal was to gain control over the

■ ■

PEOPLE IN CONTEXT   Charles de Gaulle and Free France

With much of France under German occupation and collaborationist Vichy France in control of the rest of the country, General Charles de Gaulle (1890–1970) refused to accept France's defeat. Throughout the war de Gaulle lobbied hard with both the British and Americans to provide additional aid to his Free French movement, often infuriating the Americans but always impressing Churchill with his tenacity and patriotism.

De Gaulle was born in Lille, France, the son of a philosophy and literature professor at a Jesuit college. He graduated from a military school in 1912, served in World War I, and was wounded and captured by the Germans in 1916 at Verdun. During the 1930s, he wrote a number of books and articles that criticized the Maginot Line defensive strategy and called for the creation of mechanized armored forces and a modern air force. His advice was not heeded by France's military and political establishment.

When the German assault began in May 1940, de Gaulle was commander of the Fourth Armored Division. In June he was appointed undersecretary of state for war and argued vigorously against surrender. He advised the government to withdraw to Algeria if the Germans overran France. His superiors overruled him, and de Gaulle fled to London. Here, in a radio broadcast to occupied France, he called upon his fellow citizens to continue the struggle against Hitler. On June 28 the British government recognized him as the leader of the Free French. The following month a Vichy court-martial convicted de Gaulle of treason *in absentia*.

A number of the French colonies in sub-Saharan Africa rallied to the Free French. Small Free French units fought alongside the British in North Africa and against Vichy forces in

The Free French   Soldiers fighting at Bir Hakeim, North Africa, May 1942.

Syria and Lebanon. On Bastille Day in 1941 de Gaulle made a strong plea for American entry into the war on behalf of Western democracy and against the Fascist menace. Once the United States was in the war, however, de Gaulle felt betrayed by President Roosevelt's willingness to negotiate with Vichy governments. By 1944, however, de Gaulle's French Committee of National Liberation had become the provisional government of the French Republic, and de Gaulle was its unquestioned leader. Hundreds of thousands of Free French soldiers fought alongside the Allies in the Italian campaign and in the Normandy invasion of June 1944. The Free French Second Armored Division led the Allied advance toward Paris, and on August 26, 1944, de Gaulle entered the city of Paris in triumph.

De Gaulle was elected president of the provisional postwar government in October 1945, but he resigned in January 1946 after failing to secure a constitution that included a strong presidency. However, he returned to power in 1958 and was elected president of the Fifth French Republic under such a constitution. He served as president, pursuing a largely independent course in foreign relations, until his resignation in 1969.

Question: How does de Gaulle's experience in exile relate to the larger issue in this chapter?

Suez Canal, Britain's lifeline to its South Asian Empire. Nazi forces also conquered Greece and Yugoslavia, and forced Hungary and Romania to join the Axis (as the German-Italian alliance was called). Romania's oil fields were crucial to the German war effort, and Hitler needed to secure the Balkans before attacking the Soviet Union. By the spring of 1941, Germany dominated the continent and was poised for an assault against Stalin's totalitarian empire (see Map 24–2).

War in Russia   Hitler had always planned to destroy the Soviet Union despite the nonaggression pact he had signed with Stalin in 1939. He hoped to knock Britain out of the war before turning east, but in June 1941, with Britain still unsubdued, Hitler ordered a massive land and air assault, code named Operation Barbarossa (after the medieval German crusader emperor Frederick Barbarossa), against the communist regime. The invading army consisted of over 3 million men plus thousands of tanks and aircraft. Hoping to repeat Germany's other rapid military successes on the continent, optimistic German generals anticipated the destruction of Soviet forces within six weeks. Hitler apparently believed that by swiftly defeating the Soviet Union, he would convince the British of the futility of continuing the war. In fact, it was imperative that the German campaign reach a successful conclusion before the start of the long Russian winter.

The early stages of the German advance seemed to confirm the original timetable. Despite Stalin's buildup of the Soviet military during the 1930s, Russian forces were caught off guard. The German *Luftwaffe* destroyed thousands of Russian aircraft while they were still on the ground, and over 2 million Russian soldiers were killed, wounded, or captured during the first six months as German tanks repeatedly smashed through Russian lines. Resistance was fierce, however, and when the autumn rains became the snow and sleet of the harsh Russian winter, the invaders found themselves straining to maintain communication and supply lines. The Germans nearly reached Moscow by

Map 24–2 Axis Powers in Europe In the spring of 1941, Nazi Germany and its allies dominated the European continent. The United States had not yet entered the war, and Hitler's forces were poised to invade the Soviet Union.

Question: What were the advantages of Germany's position in 1941? What were the disadvantages?

December 1941, but a bold Russian counterattack saved the city. To the north, the inhabitants of Leningrad found themselves surrounded by German troops but refused to surrender. The Blitzkrieg was over as the war bogged down in conditions that placed the invaders at a severe disadvantage.

The German Empire

By the winter of 1941, Hitler's armed forces had conquered most of Europe, making Hitler master of an empire larger than that of either Charlemagne or Napoleon. The Nazi ruler spoke vaguely of a New Order for Europe and of a thousand-year German Reich. However,

Russian Women Digging Anti-Tank Trenches   The Soviet government enlisted civilian help to prepare for the German assault on Moscow, October 1941. After initial defeats, the Soviet Union rallied to halt and eventually reverse the Nazi advance during the winter of 1941–1942.

the Nazis had no clear blueprint for the future. Instead, Hitler constantly improvised, guided more by racist prejudice than by geopolitical calculation. Where the Nazis did not annex lands and rule directly, they set up puppet regimes and used collaborators to assist their war effort. Foodstuffs, manufactured goods, armaments, oil, and coal flowed into Germany from the defeated and demoralized states of Hitler's continental empire. Millions of forced laborers were brought to Germany to work in factories and mines, on farms, and in other war-related enterprises. The Nazis also looted art treasures and gold from defeated countries and forced them to pay for the troops who were occupying them.

Nazi Brutality   In the occupied lands, hundreds of thousands of innocent people were summarily jailed, tortured, and executed. Some of the worst abuses took place in occupied Poland, where schools and churches were shut down; local political, religious, and community leaders killed; and farmers forced off their land. German soldiers and SS guards reserved their harshest treatment for Russians. As the German army pushed toward Leningrad and Moscow in 1941, captured Soviet leaders were murdered while the civilian population was starved. Hitler believed that the Russian people who survived the war should be either enslaved or forced into central Asia, leaving their fertile lands for German soldier-settlers. The head of the SS, Heinrich Himmler (1900–1945), preferred to eliminate at least 30 million Slavs in order to provide Germany with living space in Eastern Europe.

Resistance to the Nazi regime in Europe was strongest among the various European communist parties after the invasion of the Soviet Union. Other resistance fighters were nationalists who took enormous risks in an effort to free their countries from the Hitler regime. In Vichy France, Norway, Czechoslovakia, and other countries where authorities collaborated with the Nazis, the resistance passed intelligence information to the Allies, engaged in sabotage and assassination, assisted escaped prisoners, and distributed resistance literature. The Croatian communist Josip Broz (1892–1980), who went by the alias Tito, fought a protracted guerilla war against the German and Italian occupiers of Yugoslavia. At the end of the war Tito became the leader of an independent communist Yugoslavia. Many resisters were betrayed and captured by the Nazis, who also tortured and killed the family members of those who dared oppose them.

The Destruction of the Jews   Hitler wished to rid Germany and Europe of its Jews as part of his policy of racial purification, and the war gave him the opportunity to annihilate them. In *Mein Kampf* Hitler decried "the black-haired Jewish youth" who with "satanic joy in his face . . . lurks in wait for the unsuspecting girl whom he defiles with his blood, thus stealing her from her people. With every means he tries to destroy the racial foundations of the people he has set out to subjugate. . . ." Operating on the perverse assumption that an entire people had colluded in a malicious grand design to destroy the German "race," Hitler employed all of the resources of modern technology, bureaucracy, and propaganda to murder an entire people. Himmler was placed in charge of this fiendish business, and he took to his assignment with enthusiasm. In addition to the half million Jews living in German-occupied Western Europe, defeated Poland was home to between 2 and 3 million Jews, while another 3 million lived in the German-controlled areas of the Soviet Union. All were targets of the barbaric Himmler and his faithful subordinates in the SS. Beginning in 1941 with the use of firing squads in Poland and Russia, and then mobile gas vans, the SS-directed genocide (race or nation killing) against the Jews reached new levels of brutal efficiency with the opening of massive extermination camps in Eastern Europe in 1942 (see Map 24–3).

Approximately 6 million Jews perished in the Nazis' "final solution to the Jewish question" before the war ended in 1945. Rounded up and herded into cattle cars for what the Jews were told was "resettlement," many died of dehydration, disease, and starvation en route to the camps. Those who survived the nightmare journey were separated upon arrival into two groups: those fit for slave labor and those to be killed immediately (young children, pregnant women, the old, the debilitated, and the sick). The laborers were then simply worked to death or sent to the gas chambers when they could no longer work. A few became the victims of cruel medical experiments carried out by Nazi physicians. Most died soon after their arrival. In the camp at Auschwitz, one of six major killing factories located in occupied Poland, an estimated 1 million were murdered by gassing, while another half million succumbed to disease and starvation. The entire operation was a model of depraved indifference: Gold was extracted from the teeth of corpses, hair was used to stuff mattresses, bones were crushed for phosphates, and fat was used to make soap. After the corpses were incinerated, the ashes were carried away as fertilizer. The horrors of the camps, the screams, the beatings, the systematic torture, and the starvation were in part pure racism and in part designed to convince the inmates that they were indeed less than human. As the German war effort faltered in 1943 and 1944, the genocide intensified, continuing until the Reich collapsed in 1945.

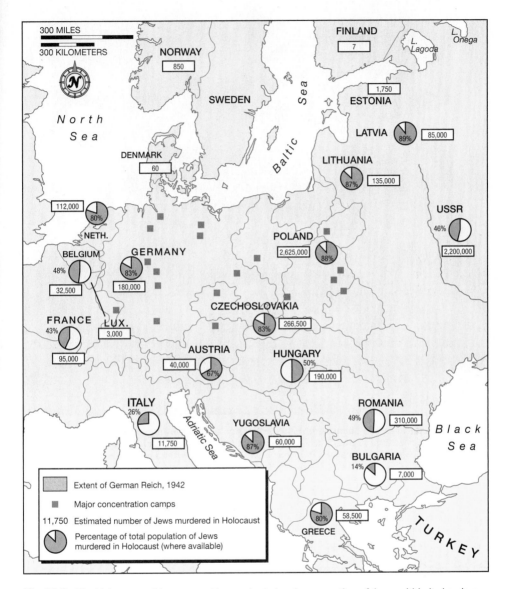

Map 24–3 The Holocaust   After years of increasingly harsh persecution of Jews within its borders, Germany embarked upon the Holocaust—the systematic physical elimination of all Jews, as well as other "undesirables"—during World War II.

Question: Which countries had the largest number of Jewish victims? Which had the fewest?

The Jewish **Holocaust** was the absolute repudiation of the Enlightenment faith in progress and human rationality. Hitler's executioners and the massive bureaucracy that supported them annihilated two-thirds of Europe's Jewish population, and they completed their work with fanatical dedication and moral indifference to human suffering and to the status of civilians during wartime. The Allies could have alleviated some of the horror by bombing rail lines and even the camps themselves, and some Jewish

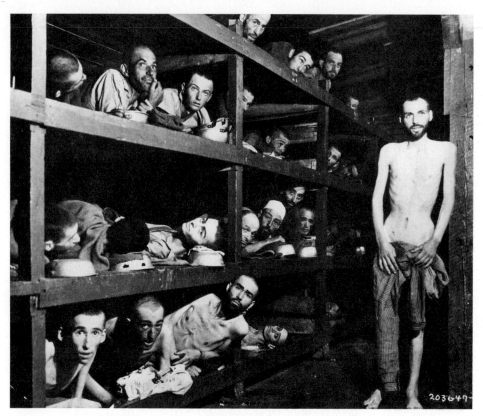

Buchenwald Concentration Camp, April 1945   When American troops arrived at Buchenwald, one of the Nazis' most notorious camps, they found thousands of emaciated, starved inmates. These were among the survivors of the Holocaust, which claimed 6 million Jews and millions of non-Jews.

leaders in the West called for such attacks. However, the military claimed that other targets took priority in the struggle to defeat Nazism.

Some commentators have interpreted the genocide as further evidence of the irrationality and penchant for violence at the core of human personality. Others attribute this callous evil to modern totalitarianism. When combined with the millions of Russians and Ukranians who died to satiate Stalin's megalomania in the 1930s, and with the additional millions who lost their lives under Mao Zedong's (1883–1976) communist dictatorship in China in the 1950s and 1960s, Hitler's depravity appears symptomatic of totalitarian regimes' indifference to human life. Still others see something unique in Western anti-Semitism, a centuries-old sickness that repeatedly spread its hatred across Christian culture. What sets the murders of Nazi Germany apart is the way it applied modern industrial technology to premeditated mass murder.

The Home Front and the Role of Women

Expanding Government   As in World War I, national governments assumed both a directive role over their economies and an intrusive power over the individual citizen. Ironically, Germany was the last major belligerent to interfere directly with civilian life.

For the first two years of the war, German food supplies were adequate and the production of consumer goods continued. Elsewhere, and especially in Britain, the Soviet Union, and the United States, government agencies directed all aspects of industrial production. The type and quantity of goods and conditions of employment—including wage levels and prices—were regulated to further the war effort. Soviet authorities ordered the dismantling and removal to the east of entire manufacturing plants in the fall of 1941 lest the advancing Germans capture them. In the West governments employed scientists from the private sector and universities in weapons production. Rationing became commonplace, and the military was given priority over raw materials. In Britain the use of private automobiles was sharply curbed to conserve fuel, and marginal lands were put under the plow to raise more food. In the United States the federal government spent more money between 1941 and 1945 than it had in the entire history of the country.

Civil liberties were obviously nonexistent in totalitarian countries, but even in the Western democracies the constitutional rights of individuals and groups were violated with impunity during the conflict. The American government, for example, ordered the detention and relocation of about 100,000 Japanese-Americans in 1942 after Japan's attack on Pearl Harbor. Official government-sponsored propaganda portrayed the enemy in the harshest light, engendering racist sentiments in both Axis and Allied countries. The need for a united front against the Nazi menace even led to the propagandistic reinvention of the bloody dictator Stalin into the benevolent "Uncle Joe," the ally of Britain and the United States from late 1941 until 1945. Stalin's communist credentials were replaced by nationalist ones as he met Roosevelt and Churchill in a series of strategic meetings.

Women and War   As the war continued and military conscription depleted the ranks of the civilian workforce, women once again stepped in to meet the military's production needs. Around 6 million women entered the workforce in the United States after 1941, and almost half of them were in the manufacturing sector. In Britain many women served in the armed forces, carrying out essential military duties on the beleaguered home front. Russian women, as they had in the previous war under the tsar, took up arms in defense of their country and accounted for many of the 16 million Russian war dead. Women held one-half of all manufacturing jobs in Russia and constituted three-quarters of all agricultural workers. Only the Nazis continued to insist that women stay at home and bear children. Instead of women, the Nazis used forced laborers and war prisoners to fill vacant industrial and agricultural posts.

U.S. Army Poster   "Join the WAAC"—the Women's Auxiliary Corps—implores this World War II poster. To a greater degree than ever before, women and civilians were encouraged to contribute, in various ways, to the war effort in the United States and Europe.

During World War II it was difficult to draw a clear distinction between the war front and the home front; air power brought the war home to Europe's civilian population in a way that would have been unimaginable 20 years earlier. Close to 600,000 German civilians were killed during Allied bombing raids on German cities; more than half of the victims were women and children. Comparable mortality rates applied wherever heavy bombing occurred. The involvement of women in the war effort and their sacrifices as cities and towns were destroyed enhanced their status as citizens and patriots. At the end of the war in 1945, women in the Western democracies who had played a crucial role in defeating Nazism were not prepared to return to their domestic duties. They had been encouraged, and sometimes forced, to do so after World War I. The post-1945 Western world, with its strong women's movement, would begin the difficult struggle to afford women equality of opportunity in education, the workplace, and especially the professions.

War in Asia and the Pacific

China's Ordeal For the inhabitants of Nationalist China, World War II—or at least the myriad horrors associated with total war—began in 1937, two years before Nazi Blitzkrieg in Poland plunged Western Europe into the abyss. During the late 1920s and early 1930s, Chinese Nationalist leader Chiang Kai-shek (1887–1975) used his Soviet-trained and (after 1927) German-trained army of over 300,000 men to fight various warlords and a small communist movement. After ruthlessly purging the communists in the city of Shanghai in 1927, these troops drove the communists out of their mountain strongholds in the southwest in 1931. Some 90,000 communist troops fled north over 6,000 miles in what has come to be called the "Long March." Only 20,000 survived the ordeal; one of them was Mao Zedong, who managed to win leadership of the Party with a call for revolution based on peasant support and resistance to Japanese aggression in China.

By the mid-1930s, the Nationalists controlled most of China, but Japanese incursions posed a growing threat. In 1936 Chiang reluctantly agreed to form a united front against Japan with Mao's small communist force. A clash between Japanese and Chinese troops outside Beijing in July 1937 precipitated a full-scale Japanese attack. By December, Beijing, Shanghai, and Nanjing (the Nationalist's capital) had all fallen to the Japanese. The attack on Nanjing was particularly barbaric; hundreds of thousands of Chinese civilians were massacred after the city fell. Chiang retreated to the west and established a new capital at Chungking, but with Japan in control of the most populous regions of the country, the credibility of the Nationalist government declined rapidly. Despite receiving military aid and advice from the United States after 1941, Chiang refused to commit his troops to fighting the Japanese. Instead, he chose to preserve his assets for a battle against the communists once the war was over. Mao's communist fighters, however, conducted guerilla operations against the Japanese and won the support of the peasantry due to their efforts to promote literacy and agricultural reform. Their grassroots efforts to assist the peasantry while fighting the Japanese led many Chinese to conclude that Mao's communists were the true Chinese nationalists.

Japan Attacks America The Japanese became allies of Germany and Italy after the outbreak of war in Western Europe. They also signed a treaty of neutrality with Rus-

The "Rape of Nanjing"   Japanese attacks on China culminated in the 1937 takeover of several of China's major cities. Japanese soldiers massacred hundreds of thousands of civilians in Nanjing, an episode that is remembered as one of the great atrocities of the twentieth century. In this photo, Japanese soldiers bayonet helpless civilians.

sia in April 1941. Taking advantage of France's surrender and Britain's weakness, the Japanese military moved into French Indochina and threatened the Dutch East Indies (Indonesia) and British Malaya. In response the United States froze all Japanese assets and imposed a complete economic embargo against Japan in the summer of 1941. Britain and the Netherlands followed with embargos of their own. The cutoff of American and Dutch oil supplies represented a serious threat to Japan's industrial economy. The prowar faction in Japan, led by General Hideki Tojo (1885–1948), decided that a quick but devastating strike against the Pacific naval forces of the United States would allow the Japanese sufficient time to invade and secure the Dutch East Indian oil reserves and the rubber and tin of British Malaya.

On the morning of December 7, 1941, the Japanese launched a surprise attack against Pearl Harbor, America's principal naval base in the Pacific. A large portion of the U.S. fleet and hundreds of airplanes were destroyed. Almost 2,500 military personnel were killed. Fortunately for the Americans, their strategically important aircraft carriers were at sea and missed the attack. Japanese planners knew that they could not win a protracted war against the United States. They hoped that the shock of Pearl Harbor would at least lead the isolationist Americans to acquiesce in Japan's creation of a Southeast Asian sphere of influence. Instead, the attack put an end to American isolationism. On December 11, three days after Congress declared war on Japan, Hitler and Mussolini gratuitously announced that the Axis was at war with the United States. A number of Latin American countries then joined the Allies, and the war assumed truly global proportions.

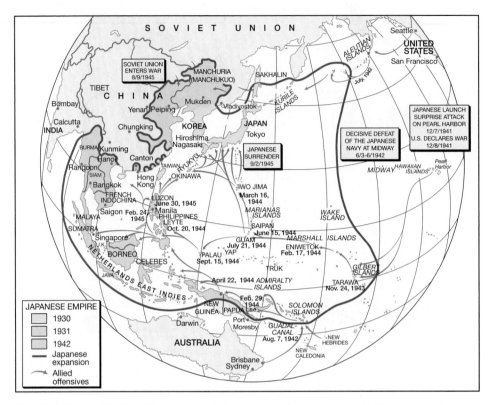

Map 24–4   The Pacific War   The Japanese followed their attack against the United States at Pearl Harbor with a rapid takeover of key areas in Southeast Asia and the Pacific. Allied war efforts in this theater involved protracted and bloody assaults on these positions from 1942 through 1945.

Question: What role did naval power play in the Pacific theater?

The Japanese swiftly "liberated" much of southeast Asia from the forces of Western imperialism, expelling Allied troops and creating what it called the Greater East Asia Co-Prosperity Sphere, a euphemism for a Pacific Empire based in Tokyo. The Americans were forced out of the Philippines, Guam, and Wake Island. Early in 1942, the Japanese overran Hong Kong, Thailand, Burma, Malaya, and the Dutch East Indies. The Japanese forces appeared to be unstoppable, but in May 1942 the Americans slowed the advance and at least temporarily freed Australia from the threat of invasion by defeating the Japanese at the Battle of the Coral Sea. In June, as a large Japanese fleet approached Midway Island, over 1,000 miles northwest of Hawaii, the momentum shifted. In a decisive air battle between planes launched from the decks of aircraft carriers, the Americans sank four of Japan's big carriers. Henceforth, Japan was on the defensive (see Map 24–4).

The Tide Turns, 1942–1945

While the fighting would continue for another three years, America's superior industrial and military capacity would prove to be too much for the aggressors. The Japanese attack on Pearl Harbor solidified public opinion behind President Roosevelt's war policy, and the

American economy shifted quickly to a war footing. The coalition, or Grand Alliance, now opposing the Axis powers (Germany, Italy, Japan) included Britain, the Soviet Union, Nationalist China, and the United States. The Americans began sending huge quantities of military aid in the form of trucks, tanks, planes, and weapons to its beleaguered allies. German submarines sank a great many ships, but a large naval convoy system, together with new sonar and depth-charge capabilities, enabled the Americans to prevail in the protracted Battle of the Atlantic by early 1943. For the duration of the war, the fight for the unconditional surrender of a common enemy overcame most ideological divisions among the Allies.

El Alamein and Stalingrad   The American victory at Midway was one of three decisive battles in the second half of 1942 that changed the tide of the war. The second occurred in North Africa, where in October 1942 the British, under the command of General Bernard Montgomery (1887–1976), were at last able to defeat Rommel at the battle of El Alamein, just 70 miles west of Alexandria, Egypt. The Germans were subsequently pushed back across the desert, and in November a joint Anglo-American army landed in Morocco and Algeria to attack Rommel from the west. The Italians and the Germans, including the famed Afrika Korps, were forced to surrender in May 1943. The British and Americans then used North Africa as a springboard to attack Sicily in July and land in the south of Italy the following month.

The most important battle of 1942 to 1943 occurred on Russian soil. Failing to capture Leningrad and Moscow, Hitler ordered his forces to concentrate on the south in an attempt to deny the Red Army continued access to the oil fields of the Caucasus. The assault began in June 1942, and like the previous summer, the first months were successful as German tanks advanced rapidly across the Russian plains. When German forces reached the Volga River to the north of the city of Stalingrad in August, Soviet troops dug in for a long battle. Hitler's generals wished to bypass Stalingrad, but Hitler overruled them and ordered an attack on the city. The fighting was intense and often at the level of hand-to-hand amid the ruins of the city. In November, two Russian armies counterattacked from the north and the south of Stalingrad, and the Germans suddenly found themselves surrounded in the city. By February, the remnants of the frozen and malnourished German Sixth Army, some 80,000 men, surrendered. By the end of the winter, Soviet troops were advancing along a broad front. Like Japan, Germany too was now on the defensive.

Campaign in Italy   Mussolini had been completely discredited by the disaster in Africa and the subsequent Anglo-American invasion of Sicily. King Victor Emmanuel III (r. 1900–1946), on the advice of dissident Fascists, dismissed *Il Duce,* and a new government coalition under the leadership of Marshal Pietro Badoglio (1871–1956) signed an armistice with the Allies in September 1943. Hitler was unwilling to permit the Allies to secure a base to Germany's immediate south, however, and German troops seized Rome and the northern half of Italy. The Germans set Mussolini up as the puppet ruler of a Fascist republic. For the next year and a half, American and British troops fought a bloody campaign up the Italian peninsula, capturing Rome in June 1944.

The Second Front   Almost as soon as the Americans entered the war, Stalin called for the establishment of a second front in Western Europe to take pressure off Soviet forces in the east. Soviet military and civilian casualties were dramatically higher than those suffered by either Britain or the United States, and despite the infusion of massive American aid beginning in 1942, Stalin resented the Allies' decision to invade North Africa instead of Western Europe in 1942. Nor did he consider the invasion of Italy an adequate substitute. Under the command of General Dwight D. Eisenhower (1890–1969), the Allies finally invaded France in Normandy on June 6, 1944 (D-Day), against heavily defended German positions. That an American commander led this operation from British soil showed how dependent Britain had become on American aid. After establishing a beachhead, the Allies were able to land more than 2 million men over the course of the next few months. In August a second landing in southern France contributed to the rollback of German forces. Paris was liberated on August 25–26, 1944, with the Free French led by General Charles de Gaulle playing a prominent role.

The expulsion of the Nazis from France, after more than four years of occupation, had been preceded by a long and intensive aerial bombing campaign that targeted both German military installations and entire German cities. Most of Germany's cities were leveled, with the loss of almost 600,000 civilian lives, many of them women and children. The morality of these attacks on nonmilitary urban targets was debated at the time within the Allied command and continues to be controversial at the start of the twenty-first century. During 1943 the bombing took place around the clock, with the British flying at night and the Americans attacking during daylight hours. Hundreds of planes and their crews were lost over the skies of Germany, but by early 1945 the German air force had been all but destroyed.

Soviet Advances   While the Allies pushed from the west toward the Rhine River and onto German soil, Russian troops continued their heroic efforts in the east. The Red Army liberated Crimea and Ukraine by spring 1944 and then opened a wide offensive that summer. Poland was taken, and Romania and Bulgaria joined the Soviet side. Fearing that they would be trapped by the advancing Soviet army and its allies, German troops quickly withdrew from the Balkans, leaving resistance fighters like Tito of Yugoslavia in control. The Germans were able to mount one final winter offensive in December 1944 through Belgium's Ardennes Forest (where the Nazis had begun their invasion of France in 1940), but Allied forces prevailed in this Battle of the Bulge and crossed the Rhine River in March 1945.

By April 1945, the Soviets had captured Vienna and were attacking Berlin. Unlike the conclusion to World War I, this time there was no doubt that Germany had been defeated on the battlefield. On the last day of April, Hitler took his life in a Berlin bunker. Two days earlier, Italian partisans had captured and shot Mussolini. On May 7 the last German forces surrendered throughout Europe. The thousand-year Reich had lasted only 12 years, but it had scourged a continent.

The Defeat of Japan   The campaign against Japan in the Pacific theater was difficult and costly. In late 1942 the Americans began a slow and tenacious island-hopping campaign, which drew ever closer to the Japanese mainland. Once they took possession of the Mariana Islands, the Americans could use long-range bombers to attack Japanese positions in the Philippines, on the Chinese mainland, and in Japan itself. Many Japanese soldiers and pilots preferred death to surrender; thus, each American assault on a

Partisans in Yugoslavia The German occupiers were faced with irregular, "guerilla" or partisan warfare in much of Europe. Led by the Communist leader Josip Broz Tito, the Yugoslav partisans—who included a large proportion of women—liberated much of their country from the Nazis.

Japanese-held island involved colossal loss of life on both sides. During the battle for the island of Okinawa, Japanese pilots dive-bombed their planes into Allied ships, killing thousands of sailors on board. Once Iwo Jima and Okinawa fell to the Americans in the spring of 1945, additional bases became available for heavy bombers that now concentrated their destructive payloads against Japan's industrial centers and major cities. The bombing caused huge firestorms that killed hundreds of thousands of civilians.

Despite destruction at home and the steady advance of America's superior military power, the Japanese military refused to surrender. It seemed likely that the United States would have to invade the Japanese home islands with horrific casualties. President Roosevelt had died on April 12, 1945, and the new American president, Harry S Truman (1884–1972), concluded that the projected loss of American life in an invasion of Japan was too great. Instead, he authorized the use of a powerful new weapon. During the war, the government had funded a $2 billion secret research program (the Manhattan Project) to investigate the military uses of atomic energy. Some of the key researchers were refugees from the Hitler regime.

On August 6, 1945, after successful tests in the New Mexico desert, an American aircraft dropped an atomic bomb on the Japanese city of Hiroshima. The initial blast killed approximately 80,000 people, while thousands more perished later from the effects of radiation. On August 9 a second bomb killed 50,000 people in Nagasaki. On August 8 the Soviets declared war on Japan and invaded Manchuria and Korea. The decision to use nuclear weapons has been debated since their first (and thus far only) use. More people died in conventional bombing raids on Dresden, Germany, and Tokyo earlier in 1945 than at Hiroshima and Nagasaki. In July 1943 British and American bombers killed 50,000 people in Hamburg, Germany, most of them women and children. Still, the debate has centered around the necessity of using atomic weapons in 1945. Critics of Truman's decision have argued that a demonstration test on a deserted Pacific island with Japanese observers present would have served the same purpose in speeding a surrender. Others have claimed that a total blockade of Japan, coupled with the precision bombing of its transport infrastructure, would have starved the Japanese into submission within a few months. Whatever the hypothetical arguments, the Japanese people looked for leadership from their emperor. On August 15, 1945, the people of Japan heard the voice of Emperor Hirohito (r. 1926–1989) for the first time. Without once using the word *surrender*, the divine emperor took to the radio to tell his subjects that the war must end. "Should we continue to fight," he warned, "it would not only result in an ultimate collapse and obliteration of the Japanese nation, but also it would lead to the total extinction of human civilization." The emperor's request was heeded immediately. After the deaths of 2.3 million soldiers and 800,000 civilians, the Japanese people accepted a humiliating directive from the man whom they revered as a god. The surrender was made official aboard the U.S. battleship *Missouri* anchored in Tokyo Bay on September 2.

Atomic War   On August 6, 1945, an American bomber dropped an atom bomb on the Japanese city of Hiroshima. Over four square miles of the city were destroyed by the blast. Three days later the United States dropped a second bomb on the city of Nagasaki.

Planning for the Postwar World

In August 1941, four months before the United States entered the war, Roosevelt and Churchill met on a ship off the coast of Newfoundland to agree on a set of principles to guide the future rebuilding of Europe. The principles resembled those put forward by President Wilson at the end of World War I: self-determination of peoples, democratically elected governments, and the creation of an international peacekeeping organization. Once the Grand Alliance was formed, the Soviets were willing to pay lip service to these neo-Wilsonian principles in the interests of wartime solidarity.

The Tehran Conference   The British and the Soviets jointly occupied Iran during the war, and in November 1943 Churchill, Roosevelt, and Stalin met in Tehran, the Iranian capital, to plan for the projected—or in Stalin's view, long delayed—invasion of Western Europe. In return Stalin pledged to join the fight against Japan once the Nazi menace was eliminated. There was little concern raised at the time about the future status of Eastern Europe should Soviet forces roll back the Germans in that area. The next year, however, as Soviet forces entered Poland and then turned south to occupy Romania and Hungary, the British and Americans began to contemplate the possibility of a postwar Soviet Empire in Eastern Europe. The Western allies conceded that innocent Russians had suffered the most at the hands of the invading Germans, but since Britain and France had declared war in 1939 to preserve the territorial and political integrity of Poland, the desire to see democratically elected governments in Eastern Europe was strong.

Meeting in Yalta   The leaders of the Grand Alliance met again in the Russian resort city of **Yalta** on the Crimean peninsula in February 1945. With Soviet and Western forces closing in on Berlin, Stalin was eager to impose a harsh peace on Germany, reminiscent of Versailles. Churchill and Roosevelt, however, feared that the breakup of Germany would lead to a power vacuum in Central Europe—one that the Red Army would quickly fill—and economic instability for the Western democracies. The Yalta Conference did not resolve the question of Germany's future, but the participants did agree to a temporary partition of the country into four military zones under American, British, French, and Soviet administration.

The future of Poland became the major point of dispute at Yalta. In 1943 the Soviets had withdrawn their recognition of the London-based Polish government in exile after its leaders accused the Soviets, justly, of atrocities in eastern Poland. In its place Stalin organized a Russian-based, pro-communist Polish leadership. When the pro-London Polish underground rose up in revolt in Warsaw against the Germans on August 1, 1944, the Red Army, located just a few miles outside the city, refused to help them. The Russians allowed the Germans to crush the rebellion at the cost of thousands of Polish lives. Stalin then recognized the pro-Soviet group as the official government of "liberated" Poland. At Yalta, Stalin agreed to include a few noncommunists in this government and to free elections after the war. Roosevelt returned home from the meeting hopeful that a free and independent Poland could be established. He died soon after reaching the United States. For his part, Stalin returned to Moscow determined to maintain Soviet influence over Poland, the state whose independence had been the occasion for the outbreak of war six years earlier.

The Cost of War Atomic weapons ended the most destructive war in human history. Almost 50 million people had been killed. One-half of the dead were civilians; more than one-third of the total were Russians (20 million). Stalin's postwar policy toward Eastern and Central Europe would be shaped by the overriding desire to protect the Soviet Union from another assault from the West. The physical destruction was in harrowing proportion to the human wreckage: major cities lay in rubble, transportation infrastructures—bridges, waterways, rail lines, roads—were inoperative, and agricultural production was reduced to subsistence levels. Homelessness and forced migration were commonplace, hunger the companion of millions. In China more than 90 million people had abandoned their homes during the Japanese occupation; in Europe millions had fled the Nazis; and in Eastern Europe millions more flooded west to escape the Red Army's advance.

As the historian Roland Stromberg reminds us, many who were alive in 1945 could recall the Bolshevik terror in Russia, the rise of black- and brown-shirted thugs in Germany and Italy, the destruction of republican Spain, the loss of hope in the depths of the Great Depression, death from the air during saturation bombings, the barbarity of the concentration camps, invading armies, and "a European atmosphere heavy with the smell of death." At the end of it all, Europe had been eclipsed, occupied and awaiting its fate at the hands of outsiders. American soldiers were stationed in Western Europe, Japan, and Australia. Soviet troops took up positions in all of Eastern Europe and in northern China, and the two most powerful partners in the Grand Alliance were beginning to quarrel about the contours of the postwar world.

Key Dates for World War II	
March 1935	Germany begins remilitarization
1936–1939	Spanish Civil War
March 1938	Germany annexes Austria
September 1938	Munich conference
August 1939	German-Soviet "nonaggression pact"
September 1939	Germany invades Poland
May 1940	Germany invades Belgium, Holland, and France
July 1940–June 1941	Battle of Britain
June 1941	Germany invades Soviet Union
December 1941	United States enters the war
September 1942–January 1943	Battle of Stalingrad
July 1943	Battle of Kursk
June 1944	D-Day: Allies land in Normandy
May 1945	Germany surrenders
August 6–9, 1945	United States bombs Hiroshima, Nagasaki
August 14, 1945	Japan surrenders

KEY QUESTION | Revisited

World War II in Europe erupted after just 20 years of uneasy peace. Some scholars have referred to the entire period from 1914 to 1945 as the Second Thirty Years' War. It certainly matched and then exceeded its seventeenth-century counterpart in terms of ideological fervor, indiscriminate violence, and physical devastation. In such a climate it was perhaps understandable how the British author H. G. Wells (1866–1946) concluded in *Mind at the End of Its Tether* (1946) that civilization was fast approaching its end. As Churchill indicated in a speech before Parliament, Nazism was "a monstrous tyranny, never surpassed in the dark lamentable catalogue of human crime." For Churchill, the triumph of Hitlerism would have marked the beginning of a new European Dark Age made more malevolent through the power of science and technology.

Can the force of ideas sustain a civilization when threatened by aggression? From the fall of 1939 (1937 in the case of Japanese aggression in China) until the middle of 1942, the Axis powers triumphed over their opponents with remarkable speed and appalling cruelty. Hitler was master of Western Europe, while the Japanese replaced the Western powers as the imperial authority in East and Southeast Asia. The entry of the United States into the war transformed two separate fields of conflict into a truly global war, and once the Americans were fully mobilized, the economic and military might arrayed against the Axis powers would prove to be overwhelming. At some point during the conflict, perhaps as news of the concentration camps began to emerge, World War II became for the Allies a moral conflict, a battle to defend the much-maligned principles of liberal civilization. In the Soviet Union, the ideas of communism and nationalism sustained the Red Army and millions of civilians. The residual power of liberal democracy in the West, and of communism and impassioned nationalism in the Soviet Union, prevailed over the forces of racism and inhumanity.

Review Questions

1. Why did Britain and France appease Hitler during the 1930s?
2. How did science and technology erase the distinction between the war front and the home front during World War II?
3. Why did Stalin agree to a nonaggression pact with the anticommunist Hitler?
4. How were the Allies able to turn the tide of the war?
5. How did the Holocaust change the course of Western civilization?
6. Why did the Japanese decide to attack the United States in 1941?
7. In what respects was European civilization eclipsed during World War II?

Please consult the Suggested Readings at the back of the book to continue your study of the material covered in this chapter. For a list of documents on the Primary Source DVD-ROM that relate to topics in this chapter, please refer to the back of the book.

Part 8
The Postwar Western Community, 1945–2008

Multiculturalism. Turkish women perform a traditional dance in Berlin in 2006. Muslims make up five percent of Germany's population.

The second half of the twentieth century was a period of retreat, retrenchment, and renewal in Western Europe. The United States assisted many countries in their efforts to rebuild after the war, and by the 1950s the idea of greater European integration and cooperation had found powerful supporters. In Soviet-dominated Eastern Europe, authoritarian governments and socialist economies were imposed. The 40-year Cold War (c. 1946–1989) served as a costly focal point around which the world's two nuclear superpowers set their international priorities. A divided Europe was one consequence of the ideological split between the United States and the Soviet Union. Europe played a much-diminished role in international affairs during these decades, withdrawing—largely in a peaceful manner—from colonial commitments and focusing on domestic priorities.

Paradoxically, just as the political might of Western Europe waned, Western civilization's enduring values spread rapidly around the world. The collapse of communism in the late 1980s, in Eastern Europe and by 1991 in the Soviet Union strengthened the appeal of Western democracy and free-market economics in the non-Western world.

Economic and political cooperation were key features of the European Union at the start of the new century, but serious challenges to greater unity remained, especially in southeastern Europe where the collapse of communism led to violent ethnic and religious conflict in the 1990s. Fifty years after the end of World War II, and 10 years after the end of communism, the Western community has again become an important source of power and influence in what is now a multipolar world.

	ENVIRONMENT AND TECHNOLOGY	SOCIETY AND CULTURE	POLITICS
1945	U.S. and Soviet possess hydrogen bombs (1953) Structure of DNA mapped (1954)	Beauvoir, *Second Sex* (1949) Orwell, *1984* (1949) Beckett, *Waiting for Godot* (1953)	United Nations founded (1945) India secures independence (1947) Israel established (1948) Communist Revolution in China (1949) Korean War (1950–53)
1956	Launch of first artificial satellite, Sputnik (1957) First manned space flight (1961) First successful heart transplant (1967) First moon landing (1969) OPEC oil embargo (1973)	Formation of European Common Market (1957) Grass, *The Tin Drum* (1959) Heller, *Catch-22* (1961) The Beatles record their first album (1963) Cultural Revolution begins in China (1966)	Suez Canal Crisis (1956) Cuban missile crisis (1962)
1975	Smallpox eliminated (1977) Personal computers available (1980) AIDS virus identified (1983) Chernobyl accident (1986) Exxon Valdez oil spill (1989) Internet becomes key communications tool (1993) Kyoto Protocol on climate change (1997)	Conflict and ethnic cleansing in the former Yugoslavia (1991–1999) Birth of world's first mammalian clone, Dolly the sheep (1997) Euro currency introduced (1999) World's population exceeds 6 billion (2000) 190 people killed in terrorist bombing in Madrid (2004) Riots in France by young Muslims against discrimination (2006, 2007) Over 100 million iPods sold since its introduction in 2001 (2008)	Americans withdraw from Vietnam (1975) Islamic revolution in Iran (1979) Margaret Thatcher becomes first female Prime Minister of Britain (1979) Gorbachev comes to power (1985) Fall of Communism in Eastern Europe (1989–90) Collapse of Soviet Union (1991) Democratic elections in South Africa (1994) Genocide in Rwanda (1994) Wars in Chechnya (1994, 1999) U.S.-led "War on Terror" begins (2001) U.S. and Britain invade Iraq (2003)

25 Decolonization and the Cold War

At the present moment in world history nearly every nation must choose between alternative ways of life. The choice too often is not a free one.

—Harry Truman, March 12, 1947

KEY | Question

How does ideology shape public policy?

When Harry S Truman (1884–1972) became vice president of the United States in 1945, he knew little about international affairs. He had been abroad only once, as a soldier in France during World War I. He had served in the Senate for 10 years, but he had focused his legislative energies on domestic issues. He knew few of the world's political leaders. During Truman's 83 days as vice president, President Franklin Delano Roosevelt excluded him from all discussions about negotiations with the Soviets and the development of the atomic bomb. When Roosevelt died on April 12, 1945, and Truman succeeded him as president, most of what he knew about Roosevelt's face-to-face meetings with Soviet leader Josef Stalin and of America's wartime weapons program came from what he had read in the newspapers.

Within six months of assuming office, however, Truman had authorized the use of atomic weapons against Japan, confronted the Soviet Union over postwar reconstruction in Eastern Europe, and warned against the dangers of isolationism in foreign affairs in a radio address to the United Nations. The president, who one day after assuming the presidential office confided to a friend that "I'm not big enough for this job," had within months taken the lead in shaping the political contours of postwar Western Europe. Truman's understanding of the Soviet system in general—and of Stalin in particular—would deeply inform American actions around the globe in the decades after 1945.

The End of Empire, 1970   A statue of Queen Victoria is removed in Georgetown, Guyana, in preparation for the former British colony's transition to independence.

The Eclipse of Postwar Optimism

New Directions in Western Thought   In 1945, Europeans were faced with a troubling set of questions regarding the centrality and universality of their Enlightenment heritage. In Africa, South and East Asia, and throughout the Muslim world, the rhetoric of Western cultural superiority had been tested and found wanting during the nightmare of two fratricidal wars. On the material front the continent was a shattered hulk, stripped of prestige and influence and emphatically eclipsed by the upstart Soviet Union and the United States. The "truths" and values that had guided Europeans in their boastful expansion around the planet after 1500 were now thrown into doubt, and a deep sense of the fragility of all civilizations took hold in a variety of intellectual circles.

Perhaps the most unsettling trend was the suspicion that fixed truths—so much a part of historic Western Christian culture—were in fact no more than points of view relative to time and place. For growing numbers of Europeans after World War II, values appeared to be more the product of culture, constructed by humans in response to pressing contingency, than the inflexible result of rational inquiry and discovery. The certainties that had informed Western culture at the turn of the twentieth century had broken down in the aftermath of total war and genocide. Faith in human rationality, or at least the potential for humans to live in a rational manner, was severely tested by the horrors of totalitarianism and the physical destruction wrought by Europeans against their neighbors. For some intellectuals, the years after 1945 represented "the end of ideology," the abandonment of faith in progress. Even scientific specialization and the fruits of technology now appeared under a darker guise, fostering a bland consumer mentality in the West and opening an unbridgeable chasm between the "expert" and the average citizen.

Existentialism   A new and more exacting view of reality known as **existentialism** emerged in the West out of this predicament. Led by the French philosopher Jean-Paul Sartre (1905–1980) and novelist Albert Camus (1913–1960), existentialist writers rejected belief in moral absolutes that existed independent of human agents. Some existentialists went so far as to deny any larger meaning to the human journey outside of birth, existence, and death. If there are to be values worth defending, then these must be constructed by individuals and groups who take full responsibility for their creations. In popular novels such as *The Plague* (1947), Camus portrayed individuals who were attempting to come to grips with a world without purpose or meaning. The playwright Samuel Beckett (1906–1989) captured the spirit of the existentialist school in plays like *Waiting for Godot* in which the main characters are homeless tramps waiting for someone who never arrives—the essential forlorn condition. Sartre's most famous play, *No Exit,* was first performed after the liberation of Paris in 1944. The play depicted hell as a place where people are simply stuck in meaningless isolation.

In a very key respect, existentialism called into question the enormous expansion of state power (and its accompanying ideologies) over the individual that had taken place during the first half of the century. This expansion was captured in disturbing fashion by George Orwell in his widely read novel *1984.* Enormous disenchantment with the intrusion of the state into almost every compartment of life fostered a misplaced assumption

Albert Camus A leader of the existentialist school of literature and philosophy, which came to prominence after World War II. Camus wrote some of the most important novels of the 1940s and 1950s, including *The Plague* and *The Stranger*.

that the parameters of life ought to be defined, regulated, and protected by civil authority. Existentialism insisted on individual responsibility and emphasized personal choice as a moral obligation confronting every person; "following orders" was simply no longer an adequate defense for acts of inhumanity.

Hopeful Beginnings The call to choose came quickly. The official end of World War II in Europe on May 7, 1945, inaugurated a brief period of euphoria and solidarity among the victorious Allies. In particular, the convergence of Soviet and American troops at the Elbe River in Germany, troops that had endured a bloody and protracted struggle against Nazi forces, showed that two hostile political systems could come together to confront a great evil. Soon a peaceful world would be restored, civilian pursuits resumed, and a new international order established on the solid foundations of shared experience in battle. In the summer of 1945 delegates from 51 nations met in San Francisco to establish the United Nations Organization. Its multilateral charter pointed toward a new era of international cooperation that would avoid the mistakes made after World War I. Committed internationalists like Franklin Roosevelt believed that cooperation and reconciliation would replace traditional balance-of-power politics.

The ideological and territorial divisions that hardened into the Cold War were not fixed in 1945. Germany's military and political institutions were, in the estimate of its enemies on all sides, disqualified from playing any role in the reconstruction of Central Europe. New structures of authority were needed straightaway. The de facto force for order became the Soviet and Western armies, each occupying territory it had taken during the fighting. Surprisingly, anticommunist political parties were allowed to operate without hindrance for some time in the Soviet-controlled zone, and noncommunists and communists joined in coalition governments across postwar Eastern Europe. In France, Italy, Belgium, and Greece, communist parties enjoyed considerable strength, with party members even holding cabinet rank. Across the Channel in Britain, a new Labour government committed to the establishment of a wide-ranging socialist economic program replaced a respected wartime coalition headed by Conservative Prime Minister Winston Churchill. The ideological divide separating East and West, the historic barriers between communist and capitalist systems, appeared permeable in the immediate aftermath of the terrible conflict.

Early Tensions and Western Suspicions   Still, there was no denying that underlying disagreements existed among the Allies. First and foremost was Stalin's deep suspicion that the British and Americans had delayed the opening of a western front against Germany until June 1944 in order to undermine Soviet resources. From the moment that Britain and the Soviet Union had signed a pact of mutual assistance in July 1941, Stalin had called for an assault by British forces into occupied France to relieve the strain on the Red Army in the east. Only at a meeting in Tehran, Iran, in November 1943 did Stalin receive assurances from Roosevelt and Churchill that the planned offensive would be centered on northern France. By this date, the Red Army had already begun to expel the Germans from Soviet territory. Historians continue to debate the rationale for the joint Churchill-Roosevelt position on a cross-Channel invasion; what mattered in 1945, of course, was how the paranoid Soviet dictator chose to understand events.

The second area of disagreement involved Stalin's insistence that future Soviet security demanded friendly governments in Eastern Europe. The Soviets had incurred staggering human losses during the war: The Nazis had killed more than 15 million Soviet soldiers and civilians. When we add to this figure deaths related to malnutrition, forced labor, and physical dislocation, a total of 20 to 25 million Soviet citizens perished during the four-year confrontation. Together with the widespread destruction of farms, livestock, agricultural machinery, factories, and homes during the German occupation, it is hardly surprising that the Russians demanded secure frontiers. The Nazi invasion, while certainly the most destructive experience in Russian history, merely reinforced the popular perception that from Napoleon to Kaiser Wilhelm to Hitler, Russia's sorrows originated in the West.

For Stalin, friendly states meant client-states, especially in terms of their political, economic, and military organization. During a summit meeting with Roosevelt and Churchill in the Crimean city of Yalta in February 1945, the Soviet dictator called for the imposition of a harsh peace against Germany, one that would require the country to pay heavy reparations and undergo extreme political reconstruction. While he promised that free elections would take place in Soviet-occupied Poland after the war, Stalin had no intention of allowing Western-style liberal democracies in Soviet-occupied countries. At a July 1945 summit in Potsdam, Germany, he confronted two new and untested leaders: Clement Atlee (1883–1967) of Britain and Harry S Truman of the United States. At this summit, the Soviet leader refused to follow through on his promise to permit elections.

The United States had emerged from the war as the dominant global power, with a monopoly (albeit only until 1949) on atomic weapons, the strongest economy, and the most advanced manufacturing base. Russia may have been a major military power in May 1945, but economically it was poor and backwards. However, the rapid postwar demobilization of American troops in Western Europe, made necessary by political opinion in the United States, meant that a Soviet military force of close to 4 million men was in a strong position to enforce Moscow's dictates on its zone of influence. Thousands of Soviet prisoners of war returned home only to be exiled to forced labor camps or executed for fear that they had been contaminated by anti-Soviet ideas during their imprisonment. Under directions from the Kremlin, the Red Army began to install pro-Soviet puppet regimes across Eastern Europe. Over the next three years, from 1946 to 1948, the countries of Eastern Europe were compelled to adopt Soviet-style political systems and state-dominated command economies, and to support Russian foreign policy. The communists overthrew a coalition government in Czechoslovakia in 1948. In 1956, when the Hungarian communist government of Imre Nagy (1895–1958) attempted to introduce a multiparty political system and withdraw from the Warsaw Pact (the Soviet military alliance), Russian forces invaded Hungary and killed thousands.

The German Dilemma   To policymakers in the West, including those within the new Truman administration, an effective countervailing force was necessary to prevent the extension of Soviet power—indeed, possible Soviet hegemony—throughout the continent. Balance-of-power politics was about to replace internationalism and the hope for greater postwar cooperation. In a famous speech delivered at Fulton, Missouri, in March 1946, Churchill warned his American audience that "there is nothing they [the Russians] admire so much as strength, and there is nothing for which they have less respect than for military weakness." Declaring that an "Iron Curtain" had been established across the continent, Churchill counseled that security depended on an alliance among the Western democracies.

Churchill's speech encapsulated the broader ideological division, or opposing world views, guiding policymakers on both sides. For the Western democracies, Soviet expansion into the European heartland meant the repudiation of the 200-year-old Enlightenment project, with its emphasis on individual rights, the sanctity of property, freedom of thought and expression, self-government, and religious pluralism. From the Russian, and later Chinese, communist perspective, the West had established a long record of global imperialism. Now the United States had become the unrivaled imperialist power in the Pacific basin, establishing a string of military bases with distinctly offensive capabilities. The hostility of the capitalist West toward all communist states demonstrated that those states needed to adopt a strong defensive posture if the Marxist alternative to capitalism were to survive. One month before Churchill's "Iron Curtain" speech, Stalin and Soviet Foreign Minister Vyacheslav Molotov (1890–1986) stated publicly that the Western democracies had become the enemies of the Soviets.

The physical cost of the total war was difficult to calculate, but its punishing nature was apparent to occupying troops. Hitler had exhausted the natural and human resources of occupied countries in his racist bid for mastery, while massive German and Allied bombing of major cities, factories, and communications and transportation networks had crippled Europe's productive capacity. In addition to the millions of war dead, over 50 million refugees wandered across shattered lands, and millions more were homeless and malnourished. The Soviets, along with their Polish, Romanian, and Czechoslovakian clients, expelled more than 13 million ethnic Germans, and most of these people ended their involuntary flight in the western portion of the crippled and divided former Third Reich. Economic collapse was the norm everywhere. Churchill referred to the continent as "A rubble heap, a charnel house, a breeding ground for pestilence and hate." George C. Marshall (1880–1959), the U.S. secretary of state, warned that this situation created "the kind of crisis that communism thrived on." Despite the momentary euphoria of victory in the spring of 1945, Europe's postwar governments faced a monumental task.

At the center of the early Cold War conflict lay the fate of Germany. The victors had established four temporary occupation zones—British, American, French, and Soviet—immediately after the Nazis were defeated. They imposed a similar model on Berlin, located deep in the heart of the Soviet zone. The financial cost of administering each respective zone was high. The Americans, for example, spent $700 million in 1946 alone to provide basic food, clothing, and housing for the desperate population of their zone. The following year, France, Britain, and the United States elected to unify their zones to increase fiscal efficiency. Rather than continue a punitive peace similar to the one adopted at Versailles in 1919, the Western powers, led by the United States, sought to rebuild the continent in general and Germany in particular. Rebuilding meant a democratic political order and free market economics.

The Soviet decision to move natural resources—and even entire factories—from the zone it controlled in Germany to Russia also helped trigger the West's decision. The United States, whose economy had grown during the war and whose land mass no enemy had touched, condemned what it saw as a cynical property grab on Stalin's part. The Soviet leader justified these actions as part of an overall reparations program, but the Western allies interpreted it as a deliberate attempt to permanently impoverish Germany.

The opposing visions reached a crisis point when the United States, Britain, and France introduced a new currency in the western zones of Germany as part of a larger set of incentives to improve the economy. Stalin responded by blocking land access to the Western-controlled sectors of Berlin. For 11 months beginning in June 1948, the United States organized 277,000 airlifts into the city, bringing essential supplies and foodstuffs and circumventing the Soviet land blockade. The Soviets finally reversed their policy, but not before the Western powers decided to unify their three zones in West Germany into a new state: the German Federal Republic. The Soviets responded in October 1949 by forming the German Democratic Republic in their zone, inaugurating what would become a nearly 40-year division of Germany into capitalist and communist spheres.

The Marshall Plan   Crucial to the overall strategy of rebuilding Europe's war-torn economies was the implementation of the **Marshall Plan** for Europe, named after American Secretary of State George C. Marshall. Beginning in 1947, the United States offered massive economic aid to all war-torn countries in Europe, including the Soviet Union and its satellites, but the Soviets rejected the offer and prohibited their client-states from participating. Ostensibly, the Soviets objected to the Plan's requirement that the United States have some supervisory privileges over and access to the budgetary records of the receiving countries. Stalin chose to interpret these conditions as a violation of national sovereignty. The additional requirement that Marshall Plan money be used to purchase American products struck the Soviets as yet another attempt to extend the influence of the capitalist system. The Cominform, the international propaganda wing of the Soviet state, denounced the Marshall Plan as a sinister ploy to "establish the world supremacy of American imperialism." In response, Moscow established in Janu-

Berlin Airlift of 1948   After World War II Berlin was divided into four zones, controlled by the United States, Britain, France, and the Soviet Union. As diplomatic tensions developed between the Western powers and the Soviet Union, the U.S.S.R. cut off land access to western Berlin, prompting the United States to organize airlifts of food and other supplies.

ary 1949 the Council for Mutual Economic Assistance to coordinate the rebuilding of those states under Soviet control.

Sixteen European nations, all outside of the Soviet sphere of influence, welcomed the American offer. Each received a substantial aid package, supervised by the recently formed Organization for European Economic Cooperation. By 1952, the United States had extended over $13 billion in grants and credits (worth perhaps $650 billion in today's money) to participants. The enormous infusion of resources helped to restart Europe's industrial base and modernize its agricultural sector. In West Germany the funds facilitated a remarkable resurrection of its industrial economy; by 1952, German production had climbed more than 50% over prewar levels. The contrast between civilian life in East and West Berlin (especially in the availability of consumer goods and services) became obvious to all visitors and reflected poorly on the Soviet alternative. Overall, the economies of Western European states were growing by 5% annually by 1952. The United States also reaped significant long-term benefits. Almost two-thirds of postwar European imports originated in America, and the reemployment of Europe's laboring population translated into the rapid stabilization of Europe's democratic political systems. The effort to undermine the appeal of the communist alternative through economic revival had passed a crucial test.

The Truman Doctrine   While the Soviet presence in Eastern Europe seemed irreversible short of a major military clash that few in the West welcomed, President Truman and his advisors were eager to foil potential Soviet influence elsewhere. Formal and highly secretive security intelligence gathering and espionage organizations, led by the Central Intelligence Agency (CIA) and the National Security Council (both established in 1948), faced off against their Soviet counterparts in an ever-expanding theater of operations around the world, but most immediately along the southern rim of Asia. The first crisis occurred in Iran, where the Soviet Union encouraged a secessionist movement in the northern province of Azerbaijan. Strong British and American opposition led to the grudging withdrawal of Soviet troops that had been in Iran alongside British forces during the war. In Turkey fear of the growth of communist influence, and in particular Western resentment over Stalin's call for Russian access to the Mediterranean via Turkish waters, led to a swift and dramatic American response. United States naval forces were dispatched to the eastern Mediterranean by President Truman, who announced that they would remain there permanently.

Further to the west, a communist guerilla insurgency against a pro-Western monarchist government in Greece led the American president to announce a new foreign policy priority. During 1946 the Greek government appealed to the United States for financial and material assistance against the rebels. In early 1947 Britain (which had already intervened in the Greek conflict) told the United States that it could no longer afford to give Greece economic or military assistance. It was a watershed diplomatic acknowledgment of the coming end of the British Empire. Henceforth the Americans would have to assume the burden of repulsing communist insurgency. Truman responded in March 1947 in an address before a special joint session of Congress. In what came to be known as the Truman Doctrine, the president stated that "it must be the policy of the United States to support free people who are resisting attempted subjugation by armed minorities or by outside pressures."

In the two years that followed, the United States spent nearly $700 million to shore up the Greek army and provide economic assistance. By 1949, the communists had been defeated, but not before American military trainers had begun to work closely with Greek forces in the field. The Truman Doctrine helped refocus American public opinion about the West's former wartime ally, putting the Soviet Union on notice that the United States would not withdraw from Europe as it had after World War I. A program of "containment," which meant opposing further Soviet expansion, was first articulated by George Kennan (1904–2005), a seasoned foreign service officer stationed at the American embassy in Moscow. After 1949, the idea of containment became central to American foreign policy around the globe.

The Creation of Israel   In 1945 and 1946 many European Jews who survived the Holocaust pressed the international community to recognize their claim to relocate in Palestine. During World War I, the British had promised to establish a Jewish homeland in Arab-inhabited Palestine, and in the interwar years, thousands of European Jews migrated there, buying land and clashing with Muslim inhabitants. In 1947 the British, unable to control fighting, referred the problem to the United Nations, which recommended

Rebuilding Western Europe   President Harry Truman welcomes Secretary of State George Marshall back from a trip to Europe. Both men were instrumental in the establishment of an economic recovery package for Western Europe, and both were leaders in the creation of postwar foreign policy.

dividing Palestine between Jews and Arabs. In the process many Palestinians were driven from lands where they had lived for generations.

In May 1948, Jewish settlers declared the establishment of an independent state called Israel, and the United States quickly recognized the new nation under its first prime minister, David Ben-Gurion (1886–1973). War erupted almost immediately between Israel and its Arab neighbors, and the Israelis were able not only to defeat their opponents but in the process extend the borders of the country beyond the limits established by the U.N. The United States became Israel's staunchest backer during the Cold War, while the Soviet Union increasingly gravitated toward some of the Arab states, such as Egypt, Syria, and Iraq.

Nuclear Arms Race   Soon after the United States employed atomic weapons against Japan, Stalin accelerated the Soviet wartime program of nuclear research and development. The Russian scientific community, assisted by captured German researchers, became part of the Soviet defense establishment. Their work put an end to America's atomic monopoly in 1949; three years later both countries had developed hydrogen bombs, devices with a destructive capacity far exceeding the bombs that had destroyed Hiroshima and Nagasaki in August 1945. Both sides then introduced intercontinental ballistic missile delivery systems (ICBMs) and satellite technology, rounding out the early advances in weapons of mass destruction. Over the next 30 years, the United States and the Soviet

Union spent billions of dollars "enhancing" their stockpiles of weapons and "improving" delivery systems. Inevitably, the technology proliferated, with France, Britain, China, India, Pakistan, and Israel eventually joining the nuclear club. The cycle of weapons development, deployment, and proliferation continued as the superpowers confronted each other around the world.

The End of European Empire

At the conclusion of the war in 1945, almost 750 million people, or nearly one-third of the world's population, lived under the control of a foreign government. Most often these governments were European, and despite their relative weakness after the defeat of Nazism, none of the imperial states was keen to shed itself of its colonial holdings. The United States and the Soviet Union, despite their own efforts to influence domestic politics in developing nations, encouraged European states to grant independence to their colonies (see Map 25–1). It was apparent by the early 1950s that victorious European powers could neither afford the cost of maintaining global empires nor deny the aspirations of colonial peoples without repudiating the very commitment to democracy that stood at the core of the war against Fascism. Pushed by the United States to withdraw from their colonial possessions around the world and stung by Soviet denunciations of old-style imperialism, Western Europe prepared to disengage from its many overseas colonies. By 1985, almost 100 countries had secured their independence—new states that included one-third of the world's total population.

Britain Departs from South Asia   India was by far the largest European colony to gain its independence after the war, raising its national flag for the first time on August 15, 1947. The new country instantly became the world's most populous democracy, adopting a parliamentary system of government that the country's Western-trained elites had learned to admire, despite the fact that British authorities had denied educated Indians access to the highest levels of power in the colonial government. The Indian National Congress had supported Britain during World War I, and Indian troops fought bravely in a number of theaters in the hope that independence would be granted after the conflict. That hope was quickly dashed. A postwar government crackdown against opponents of empire prompted indigenous leaders like Mohandas Gandhi to organize a sophisticated campaign of nonviolent resistance to British rule that won broad-based support during the 1930s. When the British unilaterally announced at the start of World War II that India was also at war with Nazi Germany, the Hindu-dominated Congress Party passed a "Quit India" resolution that led to the banning of the party and the incarceration of leaders like Gandhi and Jawaharlal Nehru.

Prime Minister Winston Churchill was adamantly opposed to Indian independence, but the Labour government that came to power in Britain immediately after the war was committed to a peaceful withdrawal. Sadly, the leaders of India's 95 million Muslims, fearing possible discrimination in a Hindu majority country, demanded the creation of a separate sovereign state that would be majority Muslim. Gandhi and the Congress Party opposed partition, arguing in favor of a nonsectarian state where all faith traditions would

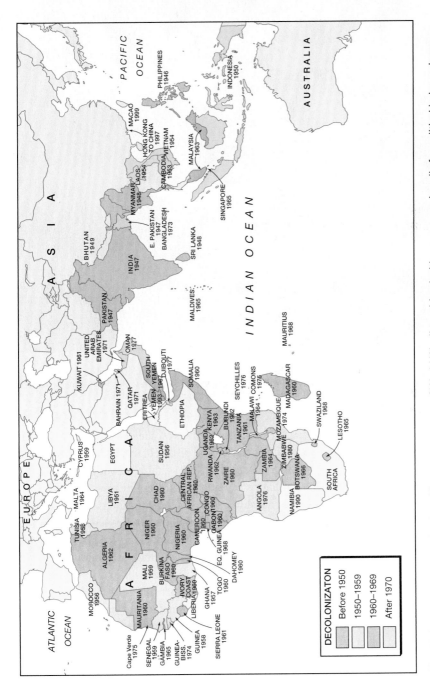

Map 25-1 Postwar Decolonization The enormous cost of World War II combined with an upsurge in calls for political independence after the defeat of Germany and Japan signaled the end of the European empires. In Africa and Asia new nations emerged, each one struggling to achieve economic security and material progress.

Question: Did decolonization mean the end of Western influence in newly independent states?

Jawaharlal Nehru and Mohandas Gandhi   Nehru and Gandhi led India's independence movement, which freed India from British colonial rule in 1947. Gandhi's tactics of non-violent resistance exerted a major influence throughout the world in the second half of the twentieth century.

find a home. When violence between the two communities escalated during 1946, British negotiators scrambled to find a compromise that would be acceptable to both sides. In the end a two-state solution was agreed in the face of terrible sectarian bloodshed. Once the partition took place in August 1947, millions of Hindus fled from northwest India (now Pakistan) while a comparable exodus of Muslims departed India for their new homeland. In the midst of the chaos approximately a quarter of a million people were killed fleeing their homes and crossing the border. Another 17 million became long-term refugees. Under the leadership of Nehru, India emerged as a stable parliamentary democracy, pursued a non-aligned foreign policy, and maintained cordial relations with its former imperial overlord. Pakistan was less fortunate, entering into a long period of troubled democracy and intermittent military rule. Both countries faced enormous economic challenges in the immediate postwar years, and a legacy of distrust soured bilateral relations and led to a series of military conflicts over the disputed territory of Kashmir that further undermined efforts to address pressing domestic needs.

France Withdraws from North Africa   In an effort to retain its considerable

holdings in Africa, France's postwar government conferred metropolitan citizenship on its colonial subjects and attempted to create a wider French Union. The North African colonies of Morocco and Tunisia were committed to full independence, however, and in 1956 the goal was achieved peacefully. The outcome was very different in French Algeria, a colony since the 1830s and home to over 1 million politically powerful French settlers. The Muslim population of 9 million was determined to dislodge the settlers, and a bloody war of national liberation began soon after the French withdrew in defeat from their Southeast Asian colony of Vietnam in 1954. The brutal conflict in Algeria raged for eight years, leading to the collapse of the Fourth Republic and to the return of General Charles de Gaulle as president of a new Fifth Republic. Under de Gaulle's lead, French forces finally withdrew from Algeria in 1962, followed by approximately 1.5 million deeply embittered white settlers. They left behind a war-ravaged country where over 1 million Algerians had died, and where the fledgling government faced an enormous task of reconstruction.

Democratic Promise in Sub-Saharan Africa
India's successful independence struggle set a powerful example for nationalist movements in dozens of sub-Saharan African colonies. There were only three independent African states in 1945 (South Africa, Liberia, and Ethiopia), but as world opinion turned sharply against colonialism in the years immediately after the war, Africa's Western-educated leaders pressed for a complete end to decades of exploitative outside control. During the late 1950s and continuing through the 1960s, more than 30 new nation-states were created on the African continent, with most of the fledgling states maintaining the old colonial boundaries that had been set by Europeans in the late nineteenth century.

The British and the French were the first European countries to accept decolonization in sub-Saharan Africa. For the most part, the process of liberation took place in an orderly and peaceful manner. In the West African British colony of Gold Coast, for example, a charismatic and American-educated leader named Kwame Nkrumah led his Convention People's Party to independence in 1957. Under Nkrumah's guidance, the renamed state of Ghana set out to become a model of African democracy in the postcolonial era. With abundant mineral-ore, hardwood, and cocoa reserves that were in strong demand overseas, and with Nkrumah's vision for stronger pan-African unity and cooperation, initial hopes were high for the rapid social and economic development of West Africa's first independent state.

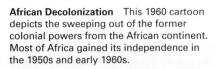

African Decolonization This 1960 cartoon depicts the sweeping out of the former colonial powers from the African continent. Most of Africa gained its independence in the 1950s and early 1960s.

Unfortunately, the high expectations were never realized. Nkrumah's consuming interest in pan-African unity distracted his attention away from pressing domestic issues, and when he began to rule in an increasingly undemocratic manner, restricting press freedoms and detaining critics, popular support eroded. As the mismanaged economy began to falter in the 1960s, the goal of rapid industrialization failed to move forward. Nkrumah was removed from office by the military while the president was on a state visit to China and Vietnam in 1966. It was a pattern of civilian to military rule that became all too familiar on the African continent as the grandiose promises of democratically elected politicians remained unfulfilled in the years immediately after independence. In reality, few of Africa's postwar leaders embraced nationalism as a vehicle for needed social change. In too many cases they had opposed European imperialism because it prevented them from assuming positions of authority at the highest levels.

Independence from the direct control of Western Europe, however exhilarating during the first months and years of freedom, did not set in motion a course of unimpeded progress for new states in South Asia, the Middle East, Africa, and Southeast Asia. Most of these nations found themselves drawn into the Cold War conflict between the superpowers after 1945, often becoming Soviet or American clients in exchange for needed financial and military support. In addition, the economic foundations of nascent postcolonial states frequently rested on the production of single cash crops for a global market. Increasing global economic interdependence often meant that for newly sovereign states in the developing world, the search for autonomy was elusive, with economies disadvantaged in the competition with more mature, industrialized (and usually Western) countries. Finally, the early leaders of former European colonies faced a host of formidable obstacles in their quest to create stable political institutions. Over the last 60 years, nationalist leaders of newly independent states had repeatedly promised significant improvements in the quality of life for their citizens. When these promises were not kept and economies faltered, the recourse to authoritarian and military government followed, inaugurating an unhappy cycle of official corruption, ever-expanding poverty, and civil unrest.

Migration to Europe from the Colonial Periphery   Europe had been the world's principal sending zone since the late sixteenth century. As migrants settled and appropriated lands in the Americas and Australasia, native populations were decimated by a series of infectious diseases introduced inadvertently by Europeans. After 1945 the process of relocation was reversed, with Western Europe becoming a net immigration zone for the first time in over 400 years. As part of the rebuilding of Western Europe's war-torn infrastructure, and in the context of Europe's stagnant or declining birth rate, former colonial subjects and others from less developed regions around the world were invited to become a part of the workforce on what was envisioned as a temporary basis. Immigration authorities were eager to maintain maximum flexibility with respect to residency. Thus, a series of guest worker schemes were devised to control the flow of new arrivals.

West Germany, France, Belgium, Switzerland, the Netherlands, and Britain all recruited temporary laborers after the war, with West Germany facing the most acute shortages in its mines, factories, and construction trades. Between 1945 and 1961, much of the demand for workers was met by migrants fleeing communist-controlled Eastern

Evicting Immigrants   Police in Paris, France in August 2006 evict immigrants from the Ivory Coast and Mali who refused to move into government housing. France has one of the highest immigrant populations in Europe.

Europe. Over 8 million ethnic Germans were forced out of their homes in the east immediately after the war, and a voluntary exodus followed once living conditions in the Soviet Bloc deteriorated. With the erection of the Berlin Wall in 1961, however, the flow westward was arrested and West German authorities were obliged to turn to residents of southern Europe and Turkey for assistance. By the early 1970s many of West Germany's 2.6 million foreign workers were from Turkey, and generous family reunification policies led to the arrival of additional nonworkers. Ethnic enclaves emerged in a number of cities, and anti-immigrant sentiment rose during periods of economic downturn. This was especially true after the oil shocks of the early 1970s, when economies throughout the industrialized West faced inflation and higher levels of unemployment.

In Britain, colonists and citizens of recently independent Commonwealth states were allowed to enter the country and could apply for British citizenship. By the early 1960s over 3.2 million persons had taken advantage of this generous policy. Most settled in the industrial cities of the English midlands where they worked in factories and established small service-oriented businesses. But as racial tensions rose in the early 1960s between native Britons and recent arrivals from India, Pakistan, and sub-Saharan Africa, the government began to place restrictions on immigration. By the early 1980s, only those applicants who possessed specialized skills in targeted sectors found an official welcome. France faced comparable challenges in its efforts to assimilate settlers from its former colonial empire. A National Office of Immigration, created in 1945, regulated the flow of immigrants. In addition to 2 million Europeans who entered the country between the end of the war and 1974, almost 1 million Tunisians, Moroccans,

Map 25–2   Muslim Population of Western Europe, c. 2005   Much of Western Europe saw its Muslim population increase in the 1990s and in the first years of the new century. This growth has generated new social issues related to immigration and anti-Muslim prejudice.

Question: Which European countries have the highest percentage of Muslims? Are there historical factors that account for these trends?

and Algerians gained admittance. Here too tensions between the majority population and migrants from Muslim North Africa, especially during the recession of the 1970s, fueled nativist sentiment and xenophobia. Demographically stagnant Western Europe needed foreign labor resources to rebuild after the war, but seemed reluctant to embrace the multicultural implications of the new immigration (see Map 25–2).

Expanding the Cold War

NATO and the Warsaw Pact   The Western European democracies became central players in the emerging Cold War conflict. Heavily dependent on American economic assistance, France and Britain accepted American forces and weapons systems while also increasing their own military budgets. Given the much larger Soviet ground forces stationed in Europe throughout the Cold War, America's nuclear "umbrella" appeared to be the only guarantee against a potential Soviet incursion. Switzerland, Sweden, Ireland, and Finland managed to follow a neutral course; Austria embraced neutrality after securing independence in 1956; and Marshall Tito's (1892–1980) communist Yugoslavia avoided Soviet domination. Elsewhere, however, Europe's many states felt the pull of American and Soviet power (see Map 25–3).

In 1949 the United States took the unprecedented step of formalizing the military cooperation that already existed among the Western allies. The **North Atlantic Treaty Organization**, or **NATO**, was presented as a defensive alliance in which all the members would regard an attack against one member state as an attack against the entire alliance. In direct response to the formation of NATO, the Soviet Union created its own alliance system, the **Warsaw Pact**. During the 1950s, as the two sides stockpiled weapons and consolidated their positions in Europe, superpower Cold War conflict broadened to embrace peoples around the globe.

East Asia   The first phase of the Cold War ended with the promulgation of the Truman Doctrine and the adoption of containment theory as the basis of America's posture toward the Soviet Union. Abandoning any thought of rolling back the existing Soviet sphere of influence, Western foreign policy and military strategy, led by the United States, would now focus on resisting communist expansion around the globe. Securing reliable allies who embraced the anticommunist position began to take precedence over concerns about the human rights record of these potential allies. During the next 40 years, diplomatic backing of and military assistance to anticommunist regimes often meant American support for repressive regimes whose policies ran counter to the U.S.-professed stand for individual freedom, political democracy, and civilian rule.

The defeat of Japan in August 1945 meant the collapse of an enormous East Asian Empire and created a power vacuum in a number of strategic areas. American forces occupied Japan's main islands, the Soviets took charge in Manchuria, and the two powers organized a temporary partition of Korea between them along the thirty-eighth parallel. However, elsewhere in the former Japanese Empire, the struggles among rival claimants to postwar political power inevitably became part of the Cold War. East Asia,

Map 25–3 The Cold War in Europe The member states of the NATO alliance faced the Soviet-dominated Warsaw Pact from the late 1940s until the late 1980s. Ideological differences between the two superpowers had broad implications for the peace and security of Europe.

Question: To what extent was the Cold War about the future of Europe?

which before the rise of Japanese imperialism had been part of the larger European-dominated world system, was now drawn into the Washington-Moscow rivalry.

The Struggle for China The principal setting for this ideological struggle was China, an enormous nation that had suffered greatly from Japanese invasion and civil conflict between the Nationalist government and rural-based communist insurgents since the late 1920s. In this nation of over 300 million people, the anticommunist Nationalists under the leadership of Chiang Kai-shek (1887–1975) enjoyed the backing of the United States. Chiang's forces were often incompetent and poorly led. Despite an infusion of American military aid, the Nationalists had failed to win a single significant battle against the Japanese.

In the rural areas and along the coast of China, however, an alternative movement under Mao Zedong (1893–1976) had won the support of increasing numbers of resistance fighters. As early as the 1920s, Mao had insisted (in opposition to classical

Marxist-Leninist theory) that the revolutionary potential and leadership capacity of the peasantry were enormous. The communists cultivated the support of the oppressed peasantry by lowering rents and attacking exploitative landlords. By 1945 Mao stood at the head of a communist (mostly peasant) army of over 1 million men. The communist People's Liberation Army (PLA) controlled large sweeps of territory across China, and Mao's call for fundamental land reform, something that the Nationalists had never taken seriously, gave his movement enormous political advantage.

While the Americans continued to send military and financial aid to Chiang Kai-shek, by 1947 it had become obvious that the Nationalists' corruption and complacency could not be reversed. Frustrated by the lack of progress, U.S. forces were withdrawn from China, and American-sponsored mediation efforts between the two sides, led by General George C. Marshall, the future secretary of state, were abandoned. By the spring of 1948, the Nationalists' military situation on the mainland had become untenable, and in 1949 Chiang withdrew to the island of Taiwan. After this stunning military victory, achieved without the support of the Soviet Union and against the American-armed Nationalists, Mao officially announced the formation of the Communist People's Republic of China on October 1, 1949. This momentous victory occurred barely one year after a Soviet takeover in Czechoslovakia and the Berlin blockade, and in the same year that the Soviets successfully tested an atomic bomb. Many Western observers incorrectly linked the rise of Communist China with a Soviet-led worldwide conspiracy.

Mao Zedong This poster from the 1960s stresses the leader principle in Chinese communism. Mao Zedong towers over his peasant supporters, all of whom hold a copy of Mao's teachings, the "Little Red Book." The words at the bottom read, "Be loyal to the great leader, Chairman Mao. Put his ideas into practice."

Conflict in Korea   Superpower differences in the evolving bipolar conflict reached their first flashpoint on the occupied Korean peninsula in 1950, less than a year after the creation of the People's Republic of China. The Soviets and Americans had failed to reach agreement on plans for Korean reunification. After each side installed separate governments in the north and the south (both of which claimed sovereignty over the whole of Korea), the Soviet and American armies had withdrawn in 1948. They left behind a highly volatile stalemate in which neither North nor South was prepared to make tangible concessions to the other. The leader of the U.S.-backed state, the authoritarian Syngman Rhee (1875–1965), vowed to unify Korea by force if necessary. Military and financial assistance flowed into both Koreas over the next two years, and on June 25, 1950, a North Korean army of some 100,000 men, with the endorsement of the Soviet Union, crossed the thirty-eighth parallel to "liberate" the people of the South from their "reactionary" Nationalist government. Stalin and North Korean leader Kim Il Sung (1912–1994) were gambling that the Truman administration would not intervene to save the dictatorial Rhee regime.

The American response, however, conditioned by recent developments in China and by memories of the appeasement of Fascist aggression in 1930s Europe, was immediate. Advocates of containment within the Truman administration insisted that a credible reaction must include military intervention on behalf of the South. President Truman told reporters that the Korean situation represented "the Greece of the Far East," and his advisors were convinced that the invasion was a Soviet-led test of American resolve in the Pacific. Truman dispatched American forces from nearby Japan under the command of General Douglas MacArthur (1880–1964), and the Security Council of the United Nations (in the absence of the Soviets who were protesting the exclusion of Communist China from the United Nations) voted to legitimize the U.S. intervention.

What began as a limited defensive action in Korea quickly developed into a full-scale war. After a series of attacks and counterattacks, a military stalemate ensued along the thirty-eighth parallel. The fighting continued for three years, with the United States incurring over 100,000 casualties as leader of the U.N. army. Chinese and North Korean dead and wounded reached an estimated 1 million soldiers; the same ghastly count applied to South Korean combatants. North Korean cities suffered heavy damage from American bombers, and before an armistice was signed in 1953, the posture of the United States toward both China and Stalin's Soviet Union had hardened into deep disdain.

Southeast Asia   The Philippines, liberated from Japanese occupation in 1944, secured its full independence from the United States in 1946. However in the wake of the Korean conflict, the Philippine government extended long-term leases on military bases and airfields to the Americans, and a defense treaty pledged U.S. assistance in the event of communist aggression. The United States also entered into a mutual defense pact with Australia and New Zealand in 1951 (ANZUS), signaling the replacement of a century of British protection for these European settler countries and former British colonies in the South Pacific. The shadow of one great empire was replaced by the protective military and financial umbrella of a country that for most of its history as an independent nation had eschewed the temptations and burdens of global power.

While the Americans played the predominant role in postwar Japan and South Korea, the British, Dutch, and French returned to their former colonial holdings in Southeast Asia. For Britain and the Netherlands, the reversion was in some cases a temporary measure designed to facilitate the creation of independent, pro-Western, and anticommunist governments. The French were less realistic. In 1946 French soldiers and administrators returned to Indochina, hoping to resume their rule over the region's diverse population. In Vietnam, however, they confronted an indigenous guerrilla movement led by the communist leader Ho Chi Minh (1892–1969).

Vietnam   The United States had originally viewed French operations in Indochina as a misguided attempt to restore an old-style empire. In 1950, however in the wake of the Chinese Revolution and Soviet sponsorship of North Korean aggression, the Truman administration changed its posture. Having "lost" China, the hard-line American policymakers resolved not to repeat the debacle in Southeast Asia. U.S. military hardware and economic aid now began to flow freely to the French.

Despite the infusion of American material assistance, early in 1954 French forces suffered a humiliating defeat at the hands of the communists, with 10,000 French troops surrendering a strategic redoubt at Dien Bien Phu. The French now conceded that they could not win the war; they had already suffered 100,000 casualties, and French public opinion turned decisively against the undertaking. Although of little economic value in terms of its global influence, Vietnam attracted the attention of the superpowers when peace negotiations were opened between communist and noncommunist representatives from Vietnam. The United States, Britain, the Soviet Union, and China all sent delegates to the conference, and once again a disputed land was partitioned pending promised national elections set for 1956. Ho Chi Minh accepted the terms of the accord, confident that the communists would win an overwhelming majority in nationwide balloting.

The elections never took place. The United States recruited a Nationalist leadership for the South, provided military training and funding for a new South Vietnamese army, and spent almost $1 billion to forge a pliable client-state. A communist revolution in Cuba in 1959 influenced the American commitment to remain engaged in Vietnam. The United States interpreted Fidel Castro's victory as a major breach of the containment policy. President John F. Kennedy (1917–1963) was unwilling to allow a similar reversal in Southeast Asia. As early as 1956, while he was still a U.S. senator, Kennedy had stated that "Vietnam represents the cornerstone of the Free World in Southeast Asia." By the time of Kennedy's assassination in 1963, over 15,000 American military advisors were stationed in South Vietnam. The new president, Lyndon

■ ■

PEOPLE IN CONTEXT Ho Chi Minh

Like his Chinese counterpart Mao Zedong, Ho Chi Minh believed strongly in the revolutionary potential of the peasantry, and his insistence upon the need for fundamental land reform attracted many impoverished Vietnamese to his guerilla insurgency against the French.

Ho was born in 1890, the youngest of three children. He spent his youth in central Vietnam and participated in local tax revolts against the French. In 1911 he traveled to Paris and worked as a photo restorer. In 1919, still living in France, Ho joined the Communist Party. He hoped that French rule would end after World War I, but the peace conference at Versailles declined to address the issue of French colonialism in Vietnam.

In the 1920s Ho served as a covert Soviet agent in Asia. In 1929 he established the Indochinese Communist Party. When the Japanese invaded Vietnam in 1940, Ho began to organize the Vietnam Independence League, or Vietminh. He brought to the movement a sense of dedication and purpose unrivaled by other anticolonial groups. When the French refused to recognize Vietnamese independence after World War II, Ho's resistance organization withdrew to the countryside and formed a guerilla movement similar to the one previously established by Mao Zedong in the north of China.

In the late 1950s Ho had warned that the insurgency against colonial rule might last for another 30 years. Unconventional guerilla tactics shortened the struggle, but not before millions had lost their lives. When Ho died in 1969, his armies still faced years of conflict before the country was reunified. However, his refusal to compromise with the French and Americans, and his disagreements with Chinese communists, marked his movement as a nationalist struggle first and a communist revolution second.

Ho Chi Minh   Meeting with advisors in 1954, Ho Chi Minh (center) directs the insurgency against French colonial forces. The North Vietnamese fought an unconventional guerilla war against both the French and Americans.

Question: What role did traditional forms of nationalism play in Ho Chi Minh's struggle against France and America?

■ ■ ■ ■ ■ ■

Johnson (1908–1973), inherited a rapidly deteriorating and chaotic situation in Saigon. Over the next two years, South Vietnamese generals struggled for mastery as more of the countryside fell to communist forces. The social and economic disorder visited upon the civilian population, both North and South, was without precedent in the history of the region (see Map 25–4).

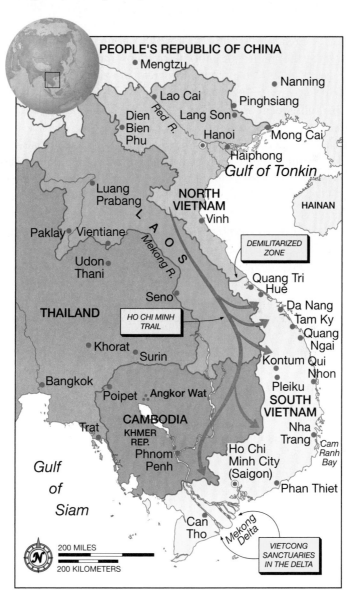

Map 25–4   War in Vietnam   Southeast Asia became a flashpoint in the Cold War as French and subsequently American forces tried (unsuccessfully) to defeat communist insurgents in Vietnam. For American strategists in the 1950s and 1960s, the fall of Vietnam would have strengthened the global reach of communism.

Question: How did Vietnam's proximity to China affect the way the United States viewed it?

The Cold War and Nuclear Threat

Cuban Missile Crisis   During the early 1950s, Cuban dictator Fulgencio Batista (1901–1973) banned the Communist Party and established close relations with the United States in return for military aid and business investment. In a small island nation of 7 million people, a tiny Cuban middle class benefited greatly from its economic ties to the American colossus to the north. Sugar exports and the tourist trade stood at the heart of the relationship, but improved economic conditions for some could not compensate for the absence of political freedoms under a regime that did little to improve the lives of most Cubans. A youthful reform-oriented opponent of U.S. influence in Cuba, Fidel Castro (b. 1926), staged a successful revolt against the Batista regime in 1958. In his subsequent assumption of political power, Castro was able to unite disparate ideological forces: communists, socialists, and anti-Batista liberals who advocated social justice and land reform for the rural poor. U.S. officials, pleased to see the end of the corrupt and ineffective Batista dictatorship, held out modest hope that the coalition would hold, especially since Castro himself seemed to have no clear agenda beyond a call for national renewal.

Within three years of his initial victory, however, Castro had broken with most of his allies over the issue of free elections, erected a one-party state, began to create a Soviet-style command economy, and turned to the Soviet Union for essential foreign aid. Political dissent, press freedoms, foreign ownership of established business enterprises, and landed estates were all forbidden. By the end of the Eisenhower presidency in 1960, Castro had seized the property of all U.S.-owned businesses in Cuba, worth several billion dollars, and the United States had adopted a full embargo on trade with the island. As Castro turned to the Soviets for technical advice, economic assistance, and trade agreements, the new Kennedy administration prepared to fight the Cold War in its own hemisphere.

In April 1961 a U.S.-organized and funded group of 1,400 Cuban exiles disembarked from American naval vessels at the Bay of Pigs on the Cuban coast. Their assault was short-lived, with Cuban authorities arresting sympathizers and Cuban troops quickly defeating the rebel contingent on the landing beaches. In the aftermath of this debacle, Castro proclaimed his adherence to the Marxist-Leninist community of anti-imperialist nations. While he did not secure the formal military alliance with the Soviet Union that he desired, Russian leader Nikita Khrushchev (1894–1971) did offer Castro medium- and intermediate-range ballistic missiles on the condition that the Soviets install and control the weapons in Cuba. Castro consented, and in the fall of 1962 the lethal hardware, together with thousands of Russian technicians and military personnel, began to arrive at its destination less than 100 miles off the southern coast of Florida (see Map 25–5).

Speculation continues to this day over the Soviet decision to confront the Americans in their own hemisphere. Khrushchev may have hoped to use the missiles as a bargaining chip to eliminate the Western enclave in Berlin or to remove American ballistic missiles stationed near the Soviet border in Turkey, but no single motive is clear. What is clear is that the subsequent Cuban Missile Crisis brought the world's two superpowers to the edge of nuclear war just 17 years after they had been allies in defeating Nazism in Europe.

Map 25–5 The Cuban Missile Crisis   The Soviet Union and the United States avoided armed conflict with each other throughout the Cold War, but in 1962 the two superpowers came close to nuclear warfare.

Question: Why did the United States feel threatened by the events in Cuba of the early 1960s?

With missiles in Cuba, America's major cities were vulnerable to a direct Soviet nuclear strike. In October the United States began an air and naval blockade of Cuba and insisted that the Soviets withdraw the missiles. Kennedy received NATO backing for his position and declared that any missile launched from Cuba against any nation in the Western hemisphere would result in American nuclear retaliation against the Soviet Union.

A tense week of threats and counterthreats ensued as 19 American warships prepared to stop and board Russian cargo ships bound for Havana. Without consulting Castro, Khrushchev finally agreed to remove the weapons in return for a U.S. pledge not to attempt the overthrow of the Castro government. The Soviet leader also requested the removal of the U.S. missiles in Turkey; while Kennedy officially refused, the weapons were quietly removed from their forward positions in 1963. The world had narrowly avoided a violent conclusion to the Cold War that no one would have survived.

Divisions and Detente The political and ideological divisions that emerged within the larger family of Marxist states belied Western fear that communism represented a monolithic force committed to the overthrow of capitalist democracies. Mao's relations with Stalin were always icy, and in the 1960s the Soviets began withholding economic and technological aid that they had promised to the Chinese. Nor did communism diminish the historic and deeply rooted animosity between the Vietnamese and their Chinese neighbors to the north. In the 1970s, while the United States was still deeply engaged in the Vietnam conflict, China and the United States began to normalize diplomatic and commercial relations. In February 1972 Richard Nixon (1913–1994) became the first American president to visit China. In Cuba, while Castro's regime continued to receive substantial economic assistance from the Soviets until the late 1980s, the resolution of the missile crisis demonstrated how unequal the relationship between Castro and his Soviet patrons was throughout the years.

Despite the many tensions Cold War rivalries generated, the United States and the Soviet Union were able on occasion to use their diplomatic power to diffuse potentially dangerous military situations. In 1956, for example, Egyptian President Gamel Abdel Nasser (1918–1970) nationalized the Suez Canal, precipitating a British and French invasion designed to protect their interests and influence in North Africa and the Near East. The United States forced its European allies into a humiliating withdrawal, while the Soviets loudly supported Egypt, one of its Arab allies. Israel, which had invaded Egypt's Sinai and Gaza Strip in conjunction with the British and French, was also forced to withdraw. The incident demonstrated that the two superpowers could restrain their respective allies from military adventures that might easily escalate into wider conflicts.

During the height of the Cold War, the threat of nuclear annihilation led both superpowers to seek ways to regulate the production and deployment of weapons of mass destruction. Under the 1963 Nuclear

Suez Canal Votes In an attempt to prevent Egyptian leader Gamal Naser from nationalizing the Suez Canal in 1956, Britain, France, and Israel intervened militarily. This provoked a furious response from the U.S. which led to a worldwide condemnation of the assault and a debate on the issue at the U.N. Security Council. In the photograph here, the contrasting votes of the U.S. and British ambassadors are starkly constrasted.

Test Ban Treaty, over 100 nations agreed to stop testing nuclear devices in the atmosphere, under the oceans, and in space. In 1968 the Nuclear Non-Proliferation Treaty obliged more than 100 signatories to refrain from developing these weapons. Although China, Israel, France, and India refused to sign the U.N.-sponsored treaty and proceeded to develop their own nuclear capabilities, the two superpowers continued to work toward greater regulation of their respective weapons arsenals. President Nixon visited Moscow in May 1972, just three months after his visit to China. He met with Soviet leader Leonid Brezhnev (1906–1982) and signed an interim arms control agreement. It placed limits on the number of intercontinental ballistic missiles (ICBMs), antiballistic missiles (ABMs), and submarine-launched missiles each side could deploy. At the end of the meeting, a confident Brezhnev told his aids, "You can do business with Nixon." This period of U.S.-Soviet relations, often referred to as *detente*, continued until 1979. A series of agreements reached at Helsinki, Finland, in 1975 committed Europe, the United States, and the Soviet Union to recognize the existing borders in Central Europe, thus bringing to a close debates that had been ongoing since the end of World War II. The signatories also agreed to share technical and scientific information in an effort to reduce Cold War tensions.

Power and Principle Committed first and foremost to stopping the expansionism thought to be inherent in capitalism and communism respectively, both sides in the Cold War too often pursued strategic goals with a disregard for their own ideals. The Soviet, Chinese, North Korean, North Vietnamese, and Cubans sacrificed the quest for a just social and economic order in the name of party discipline, military preparedness, and the cult of leadership. The Marxist ideal of the classless society in which human potential would at last be realized under conditions of genuine majority rule was repeatedly subordinated to the territorial and nationalist ambitions of the leadership elite. The very concept of the nation-state, so anathema to the Marxist ideal of international proletarian solidarity, emerged as the central focus of the communist bloc. The strained relations that emerged within the family of communist states after 1945 testified to this ideologically awkward reality.

On the other side of the ideological divide, the United States advertised itself as the defender of the Enlightenment tradition of liberalism, including the defense of individual liberty, national self-determination, and the right to overthrow repressive regimes. Along with its West European allies, the Americans claimed the moral high ground over the Soviets by virtue of their respect for the will of the majority and the right of minorities to freely dissent. Unfortunately, as Cold War suspicions intensified, policymakers in the United States interpreted postcolonial nationalist revolts through the lens of containment theory. Alliances predicated solely on a state's anticommunist credentials undermined America's reputation throughout the developing world. From Korea and Southeast Asia in the Pacific theater to Cuba, Guatemala, and Nicaragua in Central America, the United States repeatedly propped up undemocratic and brutal regimes in the interest of anticommunist solidarity.

Key Dates in the Cold War and Decolonization	
1946	Churchill gives "Iron Curtain" speech
1947	India gains independence
1947	Truman Doctrine
1948	Marshall Plan
1949	Formation of NATO
1954	Battle of Dien Bien Phu
1954–1962	Algerian war of independence
1955	Formation of Warsaw Pact
1956	Suez Canal crisis
1961	Berlin Wall is built
1962	Cuban Missile Crisis

KEY QUESTION | Revisited

It has been argued that disagreement between the Soviet Union and the United States after the defeat of Fascism was the predictable outcome of great power relations. Throughout history, major states have distrusted each other; while occasionally avoiding outright war, they have taken rivalry and rhetorical sparring for granted. What one side may consider essential to its defense often strikes the other as insidious expansionism, while the formation of extensive alliance systems and friendship pacts merely makes the other side uneasy.

Another interpretation sees the postwar U.S.-Soviet antagonism in starkly ideological terms. Two opposing systems of political, social, and economic organization, both "revolutionary" in terms of the long sweep of global history, each viewed the collapse of Nazi totalitarianism and the end of colonial empires as an opportunity to rebuild the world in their own image. For the United States, the heir of a liberal democratic revolution that was 200 years old, humanity's best hope centered on the primacy of the individual. Freedom to pursue one's material goals in a market economy, to seek social change within a democratic polity, and to differ without fear from one's neighbor under conditions of free expression were the benchmarks of civilized living. They were also the inalienable rights for which so many millions had already sacrificed their lives during the first half of the twentieth century, the bloodiest half-century in history.

For the Soviet Union, heir to a more recent Marxist revolution, the promises of liberal capitalism, of markets, and of selfish individualism rang hollow in light of the class conflict and economic inequality that characterized societies that the Enlightenment project had spawned. According to this world view, liberal capitalism would never lead to true human dignity and material sufficiency. Lenin had identified the natural tendency of capitalist states to foster a competitive culture that in the end would consume them; communists believed that it was time to escape from the grip of a system whose inherent dynamic was to guarantee the misery of the majority. That the Soviet system had not evolved into the noncoercive classless social order Marx envisioned was due solely, its defenders argued, to the ongoing hostility of the Western capitalist states to the socialist experiment.

The dangerous dynamic of great power rivalry, of ideological confrontation, not only informed political and military decisions but also shaped economic priorities on both sides, fostering what President Dwight D. Eisenhower (1890–1969) lamented as the "military-industrial complex" in the West. This same complex denied Soviet citizens a genuine consumer sector as Stalin and his successors doggedly pursued military parity with the United States. The struggle, and particularly their failure to honor the aspirations embodied in the founding ideas of their respective systems, diminished both sides.

Review Questions

1. How justified were Stalin's suspicions of the Western democracies after World War II?
2. Why did the Soviets refuse to accept Marshall Plan funding?
3. How did the Truman Doctrine help to redefine America's role in the global community?
4. Why did China's Nationalist government fail to defeat communism?
5. What was containment policy?
6. What was the purpose of NATO and the Warsaw Pact?
7. How did both sides in the Cold War violate their founding principles?

Please consult the Suggested Readings at the back of the book to continue your study of the material covered in this chapter. For a list of documents on the Primary Source DVD-ROM that relate to topics in this chapter, please refer to the back of the book.

The End of Communism • United Europe?

• Science, Technology, and the Environment • Women and the Struggle for Equality

• Religious Divides and Ethnic Nationalism • The Postindustrial West

26 Western Civilization and the Global Community

Politicians are rightly worried by the problem of finding the key to ensure the survival of a civilization that is global and at the same time clearly multicultural. How can generally respected mechanisms of peaceful coexistence be set up, and on what set of principles are they to be established?

—Vaclav Havel

KEY | Question

Has the West defined the process of globalization?

Former president of the Czech Republic Vaclav Havel (b. 1936) spent five years in prison during the period when Czechoslovakia was under communist control. The dissident and playwright was first elected president of Czechoslovakia in December 1989, and during the 1990s he became a leading voice in discussions about the West's role in a new global community. The speech just quoted was delivered at Independence Hall in Philadelphia on July 4, 1994. Havel called for all humans to transcend their individual national identities and "start from what is at the root of all cultures." By this he meant that all peoples must recognize "that we are not here alone nor for ourselves alone" but instead are part of a larger "miracle of Being." Survival depends on our ability to engage in a constructive manner with "what we ourselves are not" and on our ability to value coexistence with people from different cultures and traditions.

With the end of the Cold War and the collapse of the Soviet empire, Western political, economic, and cultural values have begun to exercise enormous influence around the globe. European economic integration has made the continent an economic force as powerful as the United States. Both the Americans and the Europeans have had an inordinate influence on non-Western civilizations. This influence is especially felt in the developing world, where

Smokestacks at Drax Power Station, England   Industrial chimneys belch smoke at the Drax power station in northern England. Its coal fired plants emit over 20 million tons of carbon dioxide a year—an amount that exceeds the yearly CO_2 emissions of over 100 countries.

Western values are reflected in everything from popular music, dress, and architecture to political and economic priorities.

Instantaneous communication through faxes, emails, mobile phones, and the Internet has lessened the importance of state borders and highlighted global interdependence. However, globalization has also threatened traditional societies and challenged cultural pluralism. Resistance to **globalization** has manifested itself in many forms. In particular, the Western model of development, a model that emphasizes material comfort and consumerism, is being questioned both in the West and in non-Western civilizations. Some opponents of Western culture have even resorted to violence in protest against what they see as a Western, and particularly American, drive for world domination.

The End of Communism

The ideological conflict between the communist and capitalist worlds, led by the Soviet Union and the United States, respectively, came to an abrupt halt in the late 1980s and early 1990s. The conflict had been responsible for an unprecedented arms buildup between the two superpowers; it had ignited and fueled proxy wars in Korea, Southeast Asia, Latin America, and Africa, and it contributed to an enormous waste of human and material resources. The policy of mutually assured destruction (MAD), for example, where a nuclear first strike by one side would be met by massive retaliation, cost the Americans and the Soviets billions of dollars over a 40-year period. That money might have been invested in any number of more productive and certainly more humane public enterprises from improved health care to literacy programs. Rarely before in history had two wartime allies descended so quickly into so costly a confrontation. By 1980, this confrontation seemed to be a permanent fixture of international life. Suddenly, however, during the second half of the 1980s, new leadership in the Kremlin began a process of reform that was initially designed to strengthen and update the Soviet system but ended up destroying it.

Soviet Economic Troubles
The heavily bureaucratized and centralized Soviet system did not respond well to technical innovations in industry. By the late 1970s, factories were failing to keep pace with the changing needs of the consumer. Few starved, but consumer goods were often shoddy and monotonous, and long waits in line outside understocked shops had become a way of life for the average Soviet citizen. Moreover, the Soviet state, which put a premium on controlling access to information, was highly suspicious of the new information technology sector. The controlled Soviet economy neither allowed nor rewarded flexibility or risk taking.

Soviet workers had little incentive to work harder, since the state guaranteed their positions for life, while managers were reluctant to challenge the decisions of Party leaders regarding economic priorities. The same inefficiencies plagued the agricultural sector. Private ownership of land was forbidden, and farmers had to labor on collective farms. As a result, Soviet economic growth rates declined; by the late 1910s, the government had to import grain from the capitalist West to feed an increasingly disgruntled population. Only the Communist Party elite was exempt from the growing economic problems, living lavishly and enjoying access to the latest in Western goods and services.

A few Soviet citizens became active in dissident movements, but most sank into apathy and resignation, convinced that the Marxist ideal had been a cruel hoax.

When Ronald Reagan (1911–2004) became president of the United States in 1981, he accelerated the pace and cost of the Cold War arms race. The Soviet invasion of Afghanistan in 1979, together with earlier Soviet efforts to aid Marxist regimes in Ethiopia and Angola, confirmed American fears of Soviet global expansionism. Reagan publicly described the Soviet state as an "evil empire," and the United States pumped billions of additional dollars into its defense budget. In an effort to keep pace, Soviet leaders diverted precious fiscal resources away from the struggling civilian economy. Leonid Brezhnev (1906–1982) failed to recruit younger Party members for leadership posts, and his death was followed by a period of drift under two sickly and uninspiring elderly leaders, Yuri Andropov (1900–1984), and Constantin Chernenko (1914–1985). Corruption and mismanagement became commonplace, while political dissidents were hounded and exiled. The Soviet Union appeared to be losing its way under a bureaucracy that seemed dedicated to propping up a failing ideological status quo.

Rise of Gorbachev   To the surprise of many, after the death of Chernenko in 1985, Mikhail Gorbachev (b. 1931) emerged as the new Soviet leader. Committed to reform in the interests of saving the Soviet system, Gorbachev implemented an economic program called *perestroika* (restructuring) that reduced the size and power of central bureaucracies and introduced limited free-market principles. Not unlike Lenin's New Economic Policy of the 1920s, **perestroika** aimed to increase production levels while rewarding those workers and factory managers who were able to meet pent-up consumer demand for goods and services. Shortages continued during the transition, however, and Gorbachev took a further step to bolster confidence in the system by allowing public discussion and criticism of the Communist Party. This policy of *glasnost* (openness) introduced unprecedented freedoms. National minorities began to express their dissatisfaction with the Soviet federal system, and dissidents won political office.

In 1989 Gorbachev was able to extract Soviet troops from Afghanistan, a costly and demoralizing imperial misadventure begun under Brezhnev. The Soviet leader also took steps to end the ruinous arms race with the United States. The growth of nuclear stockpiles, coupled with the advent of new technologies that allowed the superpowers to achieve even more lethal advantages without violating existing treaties, seemed to make the world less secure during the early 1980s. Of particular concern was the development of multiple independently targeted reentry vehicles (MIRVs). These were single rockets that could carry multiple nuclear warheads, each one targeted on a different location. The advent of radar-evading cruise missiles and neutron bombs that were capable of killing people without damaging physical infrastructure also increased levels of uncertainty. When President Reagan proposed building an elaborate nuclear defense system, called "star wars" by its critics, Gorbachev vigorously objected on the grounds that the proposed shield would actually increase the likelihood that a nation in possession of such technology would be more apt to consider a first strike. The Soviet leader was also concerned about the enormous cost involved in trying to match any potential American "star wars" system.

Mikhail Gorbachev and Ronald Reagan   The diplomacy between the Soviet and American leaders helped to ease Cold War tensions and reduce the threat of nuclear war. Gorbachev's reforms also contributed to the demise of Communist rule in Eastern Europe as well as the Soviet Union.

Both Reagan and Gorbachev had much to gain from improved bilateral relations, and in their early meetings a surprising level of trust developed that enabled them to move forward. In 1988 the two leaders were able to reach an agreement on reducing the number of nuclear weapons deployed in Europe. Gorbachev also shrunk the size of the armed forces and agreed to withdraw troops stationed in Eastern Europe. Many Europeans had long feared that a nuclear exchange between the United States and the Soviet Union might begin in Europe, where the West's conventional forces were thought to be inferior to Warsaw Pact capabilities. Gorbachev also withdrew Soviet support for communist regimes in the Third World and canceled further nuclear weapons tests. By 1991, the United States and the Soviet Union agreed to reduce both their nuclear and conventional forces. The Cold War was over, and the specter of nuclear annihilation resulting from a superpower confrontation receded.

All of these actions made Gorbachev immensely popular in the West, but at home he was viewed less favorably. The Soviet government planned to shift some of the anticipated savings from military cutbacks to the domestic sector, but as the media were now free to report, evidence of substantive change in the economy was hard to detect by the late 1980s. Persistent economic stagnation, mismanagement, shortages of consumer goods, and rising unemployment persuaded some Russians that *glasnost* was a failure. Some were nostalgic for the days of empire and guaranteed employment, and even for the era of Stalin and Brezhnev.

Peaceful Revolutions in Eastern Europe   Greater openness in Moscow shook the regimes in its Eastern European satellite states which suffered from the same economic hardships that hampered the Soviet Union. The communist leaders of these countries came under enormous popular pressure to institute democratic political and economic reforms. When Gorbachev indicated that the Soviet Union would no longer interfere in their internal affairs, the political floodgates opened across the Eastern Bloc.

Poland was the first country to jettison its hidebound communist leadership. In 1980 a noncommunist union of shipyard workers had been formed under the name **Solidarity.** The following year the government began a harsh crackdown, banning Solidarity and arresting its leader, Lech Walesa (b. 1937). As the Polish economy continued to deteriorate during the 1980s, however, the Communist Party felt obliged to reopen discussions with the union. In 1989 Solidarity was legalized; with the approval of the Soviet Union, nationwide elections were called. The influential Roman Catholic Church threw its support behind reform efforts, and Solidarity candidates won a stunning victory in the elections. Unwilling to use force against his own people, the communist Polish president, General Wojciech Jaruzelski (b. 1923), asked the victors to form a new government. The following year, the once-jailed Walesa was elected president of democratic Poland.

Anticommunist reformers in Hungary were the next to take action against the Iron Curtain status quo. The Soviets had intervened once before in Hungary (in 1956), but Moscow took no action in the fall of 1989 as a multiparty political system emerged and free elections were held. Janos Kadar (1912–1989), the communist leader whom the Soviets had installed in 1956, was forced to step down. In neighboring Czechoslovakia, also the scene of a brutal Soviet crackdown in 1968, student and worker demonstrators filled the streets night after night demanding greater political and personal freedoms. In December the communist government suddenly resigned, and the noted playwright (and dissident) Vaclav Havel (b. 1936), together with the leader of the 1968 movement for reform, Alexander Dubcek (1921–1992), emerged as the new leaders of the country.

Similar events occurred in East Germany where demonstrations against the government began in October 1989. Once again the communist government capitulated. In November the East German authorities ordered that the Berlin Wall, long the symbol of Cold War and divided Europe, be opened. Civilians from both sides of the divided city began to dismantle it brick by brick. In 1990 East and West Germany united, ending 45 years of Cold War division.

The remaining communist states in Eastern Europe quickly followed the lead of their neighbors. Bulgarian dissidents ousted their aging Stalinist head of state without violence, but in Romania Nicholae Ceausescu (1918–1989) was the one communist dictator who refused to go peacefully. Although he ordered troops to fire on unarmed demonstrators, he lost the support of the army, and fierce fighting broke out in the capital Bucharest. Ceausescu and his wife fled but were captured and executed in December 1989. Further south, communist Yugoslavia adopted a multiparty political system in January 1990. By this date, in just

The Fall of the Berlin Wall The collapse of the Berlin Wall was the most dramatic moment during the disintegration of Eastern Europe's communist systems. Thousands of demonstrators from both East and West Berlin converged on the Wall on November 9, 1989, and began to dismantle this hated symbol of European and German division.

over one year, all of Eastern Europe had freed itself from Soviet control, formed democratic governments after holding free and open elections, and started to make the difficult transition from command economies to free markets.

The Soviet Union Implodes   None of the historic events in Eastern Europe could
have taken place without the acquiescence of Soviet authorities. Gorbachev was convinced that reform in the Soviet Union was best served by permitting the satellite states to
pursue their own political futures. After enabling these states to break free from Soviet
control, he then called for ending the Communist Party's monopoly of power at home.
He sincerely believed that by embracing political pluralism, the communists would
strengthen their mandate to rule in a period of rapid economic change. It did not work
out that way. After 1990, Gorbachev faced a number of serious challenges. Proponents of
rapid democratization, led by Boris Yeltsin (1931–2007), the president of the Russian Republic, pushed Gorbachev to accelerate the transition to a market economy and loosen
central government control over the Soviet Union's constituent republics. Communist
hard-liners wanted to restore the dictatorial supremacy of the Communist Party. Finally,
nationalism was growing rapidly in a number of the Soviet republics, in particular the
Baltic states of Latvia, Lithuania, and Estonia. They had never acknowledged their absorp-
tion by Stalin in 1940, and they demanded independence. When further unrest occurred
in some of the Islamic republics of central Asia, Gorbachev was forced to negotiate new
arrangements between Moscow and the constituent republics.

These negotiations were ongoing when in August 1991 hard-line communist members of the government who had been appointed by Gorbachev ordered the armed
forces to occupy Moscow. Gorbachev was arrested and detained in the Crimea. However, Yeltsin defied the plotters, and after two days the coup collapsed. Russia's pro-
democracy forces had achieved a crucial victory. The coup attempt had totally
discredited the Communist Party. Even Gorbachev rejected it. The coup also doomed
the Soviet Union. In December 1991 a new Commonwealth of Independent States replaced it, and Gorbachev was out of office (see Map 26–1).

Continued Russian Reforms   The chief heir of Soviet power was Boris Yeltsin's
Russia, which began a rapid but difficult transition to democratic government and free-
market capitalism. His government had some important successes, particularly in the
area of disarmament. The member states of the new Commonwealth of Independent
States turned over their nuclear stockpiles to Russia. The United States pledged to assist
the Russians in handling and decommissioning these stockpiles, and by the mid-1990s
both nations agreed to stop targeting each other. But developments on the domestic
front were not reassuring. Skyrocketing prices placed most consumer goods beyond the
reach of the average citizen. As inefficient government factories were closed, unemployment rates climbed. A 1993 standoff between Yeltsin and his hard-line communist opponents led Yeltsin to authorize a military assault on the Russian parliament building.
The president was able to consolidate his power after Russians elected a new Parliament
in December 1993, but subsequent government reform efforts were compromised by
the outbreak of war between the central government and the predominantly Muslim
province of Chechnya in the south.

Map 26–1   The End of the Soviet Union   At the end of 1991, the Soviet Union dissolved into 15 separate republics. The experiment in communist rule had failed to provide Soviet citizens with a standard of living remotely comparable to that enjoyed in Western Europe.

Question: Can the breakup of the Soviet Union be considered a form of decolonization?

An ailing Yeltsin managed to win reelection as president in 1996, but his popularity continued to slump in the face of deepening economic problems and charges of political corruption at the local and national levels. A large black-market economy developed in Russia's cities, crime rates escalated, and many Russians began to lose hope that political democracy would lead to economic betterment. Increasing levels of alcohol and drug abuse were but two indicators of a larger disquiet afflicting post-Soviet Russian society. For many citizens in democratic Russia, newly secured freedoms included the freedom to fail, to be unemployed, and to be without much hope for the future. Vladimir Putin was elected president in 2000, and while his administration continued to endorse free-market reforms and closer relations with the United States, Putin began to emphasize Russian nationalism and the need for greater state control in the face of escalating terrorism by Chechen separatists. By 2007, diplomatic relations with Europe and the United States began to cool, with President Bush expressing public concern over the erosion of personal freedoms in Russia, and with President Putin taking strong exception to plans by the Bush administration to place a missile defense system in former East Bloc countries. Putin even suggested that implementation of the plans would lead to a new arms race.

The Fate of Communism   A few states—North Korea, Vietnam, Laos, China, and Cuba—retained their official commitment to Marxism after the swift collapse of the Soviet Union. However, in reality, most of them had degenerated into cynical dictatorships or oligarchies long before Gorbachev came to power. With the collapse of the Soviet Union, Fidel Castro lost his main financial backer, and the Cuban economy nose-dived. The secretive North Korean state spiraled toward economic collapse in the 1990s, and famine or its prospect became a constant of everyday life there. North Korea was reduced to blackmailing the West; it repeatedly threatened to begin producing nuclear weapons unless the United States provided it with energy assistance and food. By 2007 the secretive North Korean leadership agreed to end its nuclear program in return for massive economic assistance and food imports, but verification that North Korea held up their promises remained difficult.

In Communist China, the Party leadership under Deng Xiaoping (1905–1997) used military force to suppress a student-led democracy movement in 1989 in Beijing.

Repression   Despite the pursuit of market-based economic reforms in the 1980s and 1990s, China's authoritarian communist government has maintained its monopoly over political power. A student-led democracy movement was crushed in May 1989. Here a lone protester defies a row of tanks in Beijing.

Yet Deng's government nonetheless introduced market reforms that mirrored practices in the capitalist West. Inefficient industries were closed down, Western companies invested in China, and a widespread push for economic modernization informed all aspects of government policy. Deng sought to preserve the Communist Party's exclusive hold on political power, creating a Western-oriented economic order. It was a difficult balancing act, and it remains to be seen whether, as some Western leaders hope, economic liberalization in China will lead to political liberalization.

By the mid-1990s, some political theorists in the West declared that liberal democracy and free-market capitalism were about to triumph around the globe, unchallenged by any other social, economic, or political systems. Marxist claims about the inevitable collapse of capitalism seemed discredited, while a new enthusiasm for free-market principles and pluralistic democracy spread across the globe. Capitalist Hong Kong continued to flourish one decade after its reintegration into China in 1997, communist Vietnam slowly opened up its economy to Western companies, and, despite a sharp economic downturn in the late 1990s, Asia's "economic tigers"—Singapore, Thailand, Hong Kong, Malaysia, Taiwan, South Korea, and Japan—continued to serve as models for developing states throughout Asia. Western models seemed to be defining *globalization* on the political and economic fronts.

United Europe?

Strength in Unity   The end of the global conflict in 1945 presented war-torn Western European nation-states with an opportunity to lower some of the political, economic, and ideological divisions that had divided peoples for centuries. Now that the era of colonialism was coming to a close, European leaders began to entertain the prospect that a wider European union, absent since the fall of Rome in the fifth century, might facilitate the recovery of the entire continent and promote the movement of goods, capital, and labor over a wide geographical area.

Democracy and the Welfare State   Multiparty democratic government was quickly restored across Western Europe after the defeat of Nazism. Thirteen billion dollars of Marshall Plan assistance boosted economic recovery efforts, and governments took control of key industries and services, including transportation, utilities, and some financial institutions. With economic recovery well underway by the early 1950s, the promise of a better life under democratically elected governments captured the imagination of millions. Citizens who had become familiar with widespread government direction of the economy during wartime expected the anticipated benefits of peace to be distributed more equitably. Social services were expanded in almost every Western European country after the war as governments struggled to insulate their respective populations from acute material hardship. The "welfare state" offered its citizens healthcare benefits, more generous unemployment and accident insurance, housing subsidies, and expanded educational opportunities. Among Western countries, only the United States resisted the trend toward "cradle to grave" assistance, remaining wary of the high tax requirements of these innovative programs.

Innovations in Health Care   Polio was a major health concern for Europeans until the discovery of penicillin in 1941. Its containment is an important example of the advances made in public health in the twentieth century, as Western European governments devoted greater resources to scientific research and health care. This 1955 photograph shows mothers and children in London waiting in line for the newly developed vaccine.

Employment opportunities remained abundant during a long period of unparalleled growth that moderated only after 1973. In Western Europe, gross domestic product per capita increased dramatically in the half-century after the war while the average hours worked per year declined, allowing a growing middle class additional leisure time and greater opportunity for holiday travel. In general Europeans at the start of the twenty-first century were better off in terms of income and the material quality of life than at any earlier time in history. The longer the prosperity continued, the more typical it became for them to take such growth as normative rather than exceptional. People invested in their homes, in their children's education, and most readily in all manner of durable goods. Women entered the workforce in large numbers, while younger adults were more apt to relocate and change jobs repeatedly in search of professional advancement. A general mood of optimism, even in the face of the Cold War insecurities, characterized the domestic scene.

European Integration   From an American perspective, one key objective of Marshall Plan aid was to initiate greater economic cooperation *among* European nations. In particular, a German state that was dependent upon economic contacts with its immediate neighbors would be unlikely to pose another threat to the stability of the continent. In 1950 West Germany and France took the first steps on the long road to economic union when a joint coal and steel authority was formed with the goal of eliminating tariff barriers while streamlining mineral extraction and industrial production. Two years later four additional countries (Italy, Luxembourg, Belgium, and the Netherlands) joined the alliance, known as the European Coal and Steel Authority. In 1957 the member states signed the much broader Treaty of Rome, an agreement that established the European Economic Community (EEC) or Common Market. In addition to ending discriminatory national tariffs, the EEC abolished restrictions on the movement of labor and capital across international borders.

As productivity and trade increased during the prosperous 1950s, supporters of the economic union looked forward to the day when the emerging European community would stand as an economic, military, and political rival to the American and Soviet superpowers. This projected autonomy won additional support after a French and British military intervention in Egypt was condemned by both the Soviets and the Americans. The Suez Crisis of 1956 proved a great humiliation for the French and British and strengthened the case for political and economic union. In 1948 through 1949 a multistate forum for the exchange of ideas on common problems had been organized as the Council for Europe. While this body had no enforcement powers, it served as an early clearinghouse for crossborder political dialogue.

By 1967 a host of smaller cooperative bodies joined with the EEC to form the European Community (EC), an umbrella organization dedicated to the establishment of a free-trade zone embracing all member states. An executive headquarters was located in Brussels, and European Parliament was established with over 500 members elected for five-year terms. While not superseding the sovereign lawmaking authority of the member states, the European Parliament represented an incipient legislative assembly for the community. Soon after the breakup of the Soviet Union in 1991, the 12 member states of the European Economic Community (EEC) redefined themselves as the **European Union**. They voted to create an inclusive free-trade zone and to permit their nationals to live and work in any member nation. By the end of the decade, the majority of EU countries had adopted a common currency, the Euro, and established a central bank to oversee the transition to a transnational financial system. Eastern European countries like Poland, the Czech Republic, Hungary, Romania, and Bulgaria were welcomed into the European Union, and additional countries applied for membership (see Map 26–2). By 2000, Europe had become the most affluent region of the world after the United States.

Europeans also demonstrated greater cooperation in military affairs. The U.S.-led North Atlantic Treaty Organization (NATO) had been established after World War II to defend Western Europe against potential Soviet aggression. After the Cold War, NATO was promoted as a Europe-wide security umbrella. In 1999 Poland, the Czech Republic, and Hungary joined NATO, although this caused great consternation in Russia. After the Europeans joined forces with their North American NATO allies in a military campaign against Serbia in 1999, the possibility of a joint European Union military establishment of over 50,000 troops moved closer to reality. A few countries, especially

Map 26–2 **The Growth of the European Union** After the devastation of two world wars, Europeans were determined to reduce the threats of nationalism and competition. Beginning in 1957, European governments formed a succession of political and economic alliances, leading to the establishment of the European Union (EU).

Question: How does the eastward expansion of the European Union affect its relations with Russia?

Great Britain, expressed reservations over the potential loss of national identity and fiscal autonomy implied by these steps, but overall most states welcomed concrete plans designed to eclipse centuries of rivalry, suspicion, and conflict in Europe.

Preserving National Identities Chancellor Helmut Kohl (b. 1930) of the West German government pledged to improve living standards in the former communist East Germany after unification, and under his leadership Germany launched a costly renewal effort in former communist-controlled areas. Inefficient state-owned industries were privatized, the nation's capital was moved from Bonn to Berlin, and infrastructure and social services were improved. United Germany, with over 80 million inhabitants, became Europe's most populous country and its leading economic power in the 1990s. While economic downturns have led to the reappearance of neo-Nazi elements, both Kohl and his successors, Gerhard Schroeder (b. 1944) and Angela Merkel (b. 1954), worked to assimilate refugees and new immigrants. They also strengthened Germany's relationship with France, recognizing the value of strong bilateral relations with the continent's largest state.

France, with a population of just over 50 million, supported the European Union while at the same time emphasizing the dangers of cultural homogenization. Of all the Western European states, France remained the most skeptical about the projection of American political and military power worldwide. Under the leadership of Presidents Francois Mitterrand (1916–1996) and Jacques Chirac (b. 1932), France maintained a relatively strong economy despite periods of high unemployment. The French, like the Germans, experienced challenges from right-wing political movements, but in national elections these extremist movements, most often associated with anti-immigrant sentiment, have only received nominal support. In the 2007 presidential race, conservative Nicholas Sarkozy (b. 1954) campaigned on a platform of economic renewal, and his election signaled the rise of a new generation of national leaders born after World War II.

In Britain both the Conservative governments of Margaret Thatcher (b. 1925) and John Major (b. 1944) and, since 1997, the Labour-led governments of Tony Blair (b. 1953) and Gordon Brown (b. 1953) have been much more supportive of America in the international arena. The Labour Party moved to the center of the political spectrum during the 1990s, deemphasizing its socialist roots and adopting pro-business economic policies. Blair's government devolved political authority onto newly created regional legislative assemblies in Scotland and Wales. The Labour Party also returned considerable political power to local authorities in Northern Ireland, forwarding the peace process between Catholic and Protestant communities in that troubled region. Although generally supportive of European economic cooperation, Britain has not adopted the Euro currency, and Euro-skeptics continue to play an important role in politics.

While each of Europe's major states has taken strides to balance national sovereignty with the proven benefits of greater integration, Europe as a whole has not wielded the same level of international influence that the United States has since the end of the Cold War. Europe's economy, while unquestionably stronger under a single market, also faces challenges ranging from the high cost of labor and benefits to the rise of multinationals that enjoy access to cheap labor markets in developing countries. The emergence of the global economy has the potential of undermining consumer confidence at home as more jobs are relocated overseas. At the start of the new century, Europe's enthusiasm for the spread of the global economy has been a mixed blessing for its own citizens.

Private Lives and Consumer Culture   The quality of life for most residents of Western Europe improved dramatically during the final decades of the twentieth century. Birth rates boomed after World War II, perhaps one measure of the resilience of humans in the aftermath of the most horrific conflict in history. From approximately

New Housing Development, Dublin Beginning in the 1980s, the Irish economy enjoyed unprecedented growth, spurred in part by foreign investment from such high-tech firms as Dell and Google. This influx of wealth has transformed Irish society. For decades, the country was a net exporter of people, but it is now the destination for many immigrants from Africa and eastern Europe. The success of the "Celtic tiger" has also radically altered the Irish landscape. Farmland is increasingly being converted to golf courses, or, as in the photo here, turned into housing developments.

250 million in 1945, Europe's population climbed to over 300 million before the economic recession of the 1970s. Birth rates then began to decline, and today Europe's population is barely at replacement level (defined as 2.3 children per mother) with women and men electing to have fewer children while focusing on professional and leisure activities outside of the home. Divorce rates have continued to increase, and the role of organized religion has waned, but the family has remained a valued unit of social, emotional, and economic order. Single-parent households became more commonplace throughout the Western world, and many children often spent time in formal day-care programs, since there was no longer a caregiver at home during business hours. Once at home, family members placed a premium on private space, and new construction increasingly featured separate rooms for sleeping, entertainment, and meals.

Housing stock expanded in most Europeans countries, but increasing numbers of workers followed the American pattern of suburban living and long commutes on congested motorways and public transport. Cities continued to attract rural migrants, while retailing lost its regional and personal flavor. Where once the homemaker shopped in locally owned stores on the high street, by the 1980s new suburban shopping centers anchored by large conglomerate retailers had become the norm. Standardized sizes and product lines replaced items made by craftspeople for individual clients. By the start of the twenty-first century the Internet internationalized the buying experience with on-line or e-commerce vendors, blurring regional and national distinctions. In Western Europe, as in North America, the consumer service sector grew as jobs in traditional manufacturing areas migrated to cheaper labor markets in the developing world. Many educated professionals in the services industry found themselves reduced to "blue collar" wages, while top managers were paid high salaries and lucrative bonuses on the basis of their ability to impose new efficiencies.

On the broader consumer front, reservations about the increasing "Americanization" of Europe's national cultures grew sharply during the final quarter of the twentieth century. Before the fall of the Berlin Wall, American youth culture was seen by authorities in the East as an imminent threat to socialist values. The reservations expressed in the West were more subtle, focusing on topics like the dangers of homogenization and planned obsolescence in product development. Youth culture became increasingly product-oriented across Europe, with American movies, computer software, music, and fashion all setting the benchmarks for standardization. The controversial opening of a Disney theme park outside of Paris in the mid-1990s highlighted the omnipresence of American leisure entertainment in Europe. Getting and spending became an end in itself, a lifestyle that was aggressively promoted by advertisers with advanced university degrees in applied subjects like marketing and "entrepreneurship." These trends were lamented by a number of journalists, artists, and intellectuals, inspiring new forms of dissent that challenged widely held assumptions in the dominant culture.

The Fear of Terrorism   Perhaps an even greater threat to the security of Western democracies at the start of the twenty-first century came from international terrorist groups, especially those associated with radical Islamist movements. Carefully planned terrorist attacks against the United States on September 11, 2001, led to a broad-based international response against the Islamist Taliban regime in Afghanistan. A military coalition led by the United States ousted the Taliban, but the terrorist leader (and Saudi national) Osama bin Laden eluded capture. Still, the early fight against international terrorists enhanced cooperation among countries as ideologically diverse as China and the United States.

Unfortunately, the spirit of cooperation did not last. Soon after the establishment of a new government in Afghanistan, the administration of George W. Bush turned its attention to Iraq, whose leader Saddam Hussein was thought to be producing weapons of mass destruction. Inspectors from the United Nations had been assigned to Iraq after the Gulf War of 1991, but Hussein's regime was reluctant to cooperate with the inspectors, who were eventually withdrawn from the country. In the spring of 2003, American and British forces invaded Iraq and ousted Hussein, but the occupying troops found no evidence of weapons of mass destruction. Subsequent reports and Congressional inquiries revealed that the administration had acted on deeply flawed "intelligence" information. The invasion had not been endorsed by the United Nations, and many of America's strongest allies in the fight against terrorism criticized the military action in Iraq. Much of the sympathy and support that America received after the tragedy of September 11th evaporated in the lead-up to the Iraq war. Contrary to the optimistic predictions of the Bush administration, the postwar occupation of Iraq showed few signs that a beacon of Arab democracy in the

Middle East would be established at any time in the near future. A civil war in all but name, the divisions between Iraq's Shiite majority and the Sunni minority were deep and lasting. Thousands of civilians lost their lives in sectarian bloodletting after 2003, while hundreds of thousands of additional Iraqis fled the violence, becoming long-term refugees in neighboring Arab states. Europeans turned against the American-led occupation, and in Britain, Prime Minister Tony Blair left office in the summer of 2007 with his reputation much diminished because of his support of the Bush administration's policies in Iraq.

Many experts argued that the type of state-sponsored terrorism alleged against Iraq was not the principal threat facing the West at the start of the new century. Instead, the danger was much more insidious precisely because it could not be identified with a state. Most of the September 11th suicide hijackers, not to mention bin Laden, were Saudi nationals who were as contemptuous of the Saudi monarchy as they were of America. A 2005 terrorist attack in London's underground was organized and carried out by British-born Muslim youths. Fears that well-armed terrorist cells might secure materials to construct and plant a "dirty" nuclear bomb in a major city led to a heightened emphasis in the West on espionage and intelligence gathering. Difficult as it has been to prevent nuclear escalation at the state level, it may be even more difficult to keep nuclear, chemical, and biological weapons out of the hands of shadowy but well-financed terrorist groups who are determined to inflict as much harm as possible on the West. The fight has obliged Western democracies to re-evaluate their commitment to civil liberties. Just as democratic states abridged freedoms during the two world wars,

War in Afghanistan   In the aftermath of the September 11, 2001, terrorist attacks, the United States led a NATO invasion of Afghanistan, ousting the Taliban regime, which had sheltered al-Qaeda. Here, a Turkish soldier in a NATO unit patrols the capital city of Kabul.

they found it difficult after September 11th to establish an acceptable balance between the need for enhanced domestic security and the preservation of personal autonomy. Reports of secret CIA detention centers in Eastern Europe, where suspects were held without charge for long periods, exacerbated the growing divide between Europe and the United States over the appropriate response to terrorist threats.

Science, Technology, and the Environment

Innovation and Health   Like residents of every developed country, Europeans benefited from a wide range of advances in the applied sciences. During the war years, basic laboratory research assumed a level of strategic importance equal to military operations in the field. Specialists in physics, engineering, biology, chemistry, metallurgy, and electronics were encouraged—and fully funded—to take risks and to innovate. The solitary genius or inventor of an earlier age was displaced by the collaborative team working in large research institutes and corporations. National governments continued their role as the principal patrons of scientific research during the Cold War, citing national security priorities and partnering with leading universities and private institutes to develop new technologies.

The output was impressive. Beginning in the 1950s, wartime research into radar navigation and jet aircraft engines transformed the civilian aeronautics industry. The collaboration of American, British, and German refugee scientists on atomic weapons set the stage for the commercialization of nuclear power for peaceful purposes. By the 1960s Europe's nuclear power stations had become key to the electricity generation industry. Transistors replaced unreliable vacuum tubes in the early 1950s, inaugurating the age of miniaturization and anticipating the computer age. The latter technology, while again a spin-off from wartime research, reached its full commercial potential with the advent of the personal desktop computer in the 1980s.

The health services offered broader state-funded programs as part of the postwar promise to enhance the lives of all citizens. Government stressed the importance of prevention, health education, and infant care, and specialist doctors worked closely with researchers to better treat patients. Improved housing, sanitation, and rules of cleanliness reduced the incidence of disease, but the advent of "killer bacterias" played an even greater role in extending life. During the 1930s scientists recognized that sulfa drugs were effective against a range of infectious diseases. Plant research at Oxford University, for example, led to the discovery of the plant mold penicillin in 1941, which was used effectively during and after the war to treat the onset of septicemia. The scourge of polio was eradicated in the 1950s through new vaccines, and a measles vaccine in the 1960s eliminated a recurring epidemic that had been most dangerous for young children. An expanding range of new antibiotic drugs was made commercially available after the war, and by the 1970s traditional scourges like tuberculosis and smallpox had been eliminated. At the turn of the twenty-first century infectious communicable diseases had ceased to be the leading cause of death in the developed world.

Physicians and researchers then turned their attention to the treatment of chronic non-communicable organ disease. New surgical procedures and chemical interventions reduced cancer and cardiovascular mortality. Organ and bone marrow transplants, together with heart bypass operations, became commonplace at major hospitals. New machines for diagnosis and treatment, including ultrasound, dialysis, and MRI (magnetic resonance imaging) machines, offered doctors additional life-saving tools. Even patients suffering from chronic psychiatric conditions were helped by the advent of new psychotropic drugs. In genetics, the structure of DNA (deoxyribonucleic acid) was discovered in 1953 by the British research team of Francis Crick and James Watson. By the final decade of the century scientists were beginning to clone animal and plant products and organs, prompting medical ethicists to debate the implications of this research for human culture. Overall the medical breakthroughs were welcome, but by the close of the century the escalating cost of treatment and professional services placed enormous strains on national health systems and the governments that funded them.

Environmental Challenges Before the outbreak of World War I in 1914, few people in the West thought in terms of common global problems or threats whose resolution was of interest to governments and people everywhere on Earth. At the end of the twentieth century, a wide array of challenges had global implications, from resource use to global warming to pollution. The unprecedented mastery of nature that has been one of the signal features of Western civilization over the past 200 years may have improved the quality of life for the inhabitants of industrially advanced nations, but it has also led to serious and perhaps irreversible environmental degradation on a global scale. As developing nations raced to "catch up" with the West, the pace of degradation accelerated.

Overgrazing on land, soil exhaustion resulting from intensive agriculture, deforestation on every continent, disposal of nuclear waste, and the exhaustion of fisheries all contributed to an emerging ecological crisis that transcended national borders. When coupled with the reckless discharge of industrial waste leading to contamination of water resources and air pollution from coal-burning factories and the ubiquitous automobile, the planet's ability to accommodate the needs of the world's rising population was cast into doubt. The burning of fossil fuels greatly increased the carbon dioxide in the atmosphere, and many scientists claimed that the resultant **global warming** increased average temperatures around the world. It is feared that this may cause ocean levels to rise, which would flood low-lying coastal areas, increase the number of destructive storms, and cause havoc with world agriculture. Since many people in the developing world understandably aspire to a "Western" quality of life, the current indulgent path to modernization may accelerate harmful processes.

International Meetings Since the impact of environmental degradation reaches well beyond the borders of the nation-state, addressing the problem requires international cooperation. In 1992 the United Nations hosted an international earth summit in Rio de Janeiro. However, it quickly became obvious that it would be extremely difficult to convince developed nations in Western Europe, Asia, and North America to take measures that might adversely affect the lifestyles of their citizens and reduce the levels of resources they consumed. Nor did developing nations wish to accept restraints on

Global Warming   Protests at U.N. Climate Change Conference, Montreal, December 2005. Global warming has emerged as a major environmental issue and political challenge in recent years.

their modernization plans, especially since the West had reached its industrial primacy absent any restraints. In 1997 the United Nations hosted another important meeting, this time on global warming, in Kyoto, Japan. Again, leading industrial states were reluctant to commit to enforcing the recommendations that emerged from the meeting. Despite recent successes in lowering harmful emissions levels from automobiles and factories, the strength of modern industrial economies continues to depend on the ever-increasing consumption of nonrenewable resources.

North Versus South   The image of a North-South divide is based on the fact that most of the world's wealthiest nations and regions (the United States, Japan, Europe, Canada) are situated north of the equator, while the poorest regions (sub-Saharan Africa, South Asia, Latin America) are in the southern hemisphere. The northern hemisphere contains about one-quarter of the world's population, but most of the world's goods and services originate here. In the United States, approximately 300 million people (4.5% of the world's total) consume over a quarter of the world's resources.

The problem of global economic inequality, of rich nations growing richer and consuming more and more of Earth's resources while poor nations continue to struggle with overpopulation, poor health care, lack of education, economic underdevelopment, and political instability, has become *the* great global challenge of the early twenty-first century. It is also the problem with the most serious ethical implications for the modern West. In 1800, just as the Industrial Revolution was beginning to spread from England to North America, the world's richest societies (all in the West) were about twice as affluent as the poorest. Two centuries later, the gap had widened considerably. The richest countries are now perhaps 100 times better off than the poorest. Income disparities between the richest and the poorest nations continue to expand even as the world's economy becomes more integrated and interdependent. Thanks to modern electronic communications, many of the poor have instant access to the sounds and images of Western affluence. Radio, television, and the Internet have transformed expectations. The more than 1 billion people (20% of the world's population) who live on less than $500 per year are well aware of lifestyles in the West and Japan (see Map 26–3).

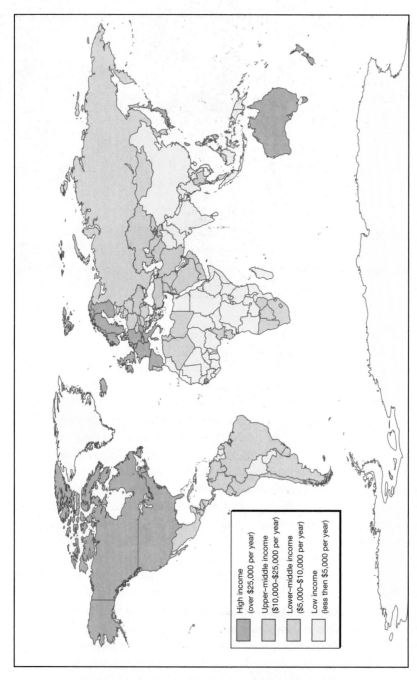

Map 26-3 Comparative World Wealth, c. 2004 In the first years of the new millennium, global inequalities showed no signs of abating, as many poor countries found themselves trapped in a cycle of debt and underdevelopment.

Question: What factors might help explain the disparity in wealth between the northern and southern hemispheres?

High income
(over $25,000 per year)

Upper-middle income
($10,000–$25,000 per year)

Lower-middle income
($5,000–$10,000 per year)

Low income
(less then $5,000 per year)

Population Growth

When World War I started in 1914, there were just under 2 billion people on Earth. At the beginning of the twenty-first century, that number skyrocketed to just over 6 billion. Much of the growth was made possible by the spread of Western medical technology, especially in disease prevention and nutrition. In the industrialized West, population levels are either stagnant or declining, whereas in the world's poorest nations, rapid growth is the norm. During the twenty-first century, the peoples of China, South Asia, and Africa will make up an ever-increasing percentage of the global population. If current demographic trends continue, many of these people will live in sprawling urban concentrations. Mexico City, with almost 16 million residents, and Mumbai (Bombay) in India, with 14 million, are examples of cities whose governments struggle mightily with housing and sanitation crises. Still, internal migrants continue to relocate to urban centers around the world in ever-larger numbers, hoping for adequate employment and a better standard of living.

Figure 26–1

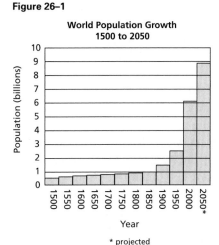

The South Seeks Redress

Global inequality became a contentious political issue during the final three decades of the twentieth century. Industrial producers in the West were exporting vast quantities of goods to developing countries, but as these countries fell deeper into debt, Western lending institutions began to lose faith in the ability of government leaders in the southern hemisphere to manage their economies. In the mid-1980s, for example, 80% of Sudan's total export earnings were being used merely to pay interest on the country's foreign debt. The leaders of many postcolonial states had the misfortune of attempting to raise living standards and provide jobs for a public that was well aware of conditions in the modern West.

Beginning in the 1970s, developing nations sought to win a series of concessions from the advanced industrialized countries through the United Nations. In this international forum, political leaders from the southern hemisphere argued that decades of imperialism and colonial domination had facilitated Europe's head start in the process of modernization. Calling for a New International Economic Order (NIEO), countries that had recently achieved political independence from Europe demanded substantive economic concessions from the northern hemisphere. These concessions would take the form of lower tariffs on goods imported from developing countries, and prices for their exports that were indexed to the cost of exports from developed nations. In this way, developing nations hoped to close the enormous and ever-widening gap between industrial capacity in the northern and southern hemispheres. Poor states also called for a more generous foreign aid formula. The United Nations had set a standard of 0.7% of gross national product as the benchmark for annual foreign aid contribution, but in the early 1980s only a handful of northern hemisphere states had met this minimum. Finally, developing countries requested a larger voice in international financial agencies like the World Bank and the International Monetary Fund, where decisions typically reflected the interests of the northern hemisphere, and especially the United States.

The North Dissents   Proponents of NIEO hoped to redistribute wealth through structured policies endorsed by the United Nations. Economic decision making would shift from strict market criteria into the hands of an international body where all nations would have an equal vote. Not surprisingly, developed nations, particularly those in the West, resented the implication that their success was due to centuries of exploitation and unfair trade policies carried out during the colonial era. In rebuttal, the Western industrialized democracies claimed that most of the economic problems of postcolonial states were due to internal domestic failings: fiscal mismanagement, poor planning, and political corruption. In the late 1980s and early 1990s successful examples of development in countries like South Korea and Malaysia seemed to prove that a country's previous colonial status was not a barrier to economic health. The shattered Japanese economy of 1945 had by the early 1980s become one of the world's leaders, and Japan's gross domestic product was second only to that of the United States. Even communist China experienced record economic growth in the 1980s and 1990s. In India, despite ongoing poverty for the majority, a vibrant middle class of between 100 and 200 million suggested that under competent governments, market-based economics could transform the lives of millions.

Oil Shocks   The only instance of rapid postwar development in the southern hemisphere during the 1970s occurred in the oil rich nations of the Middle East. When member states of the Organization of Petroleum Exporting Countries (OPEC) quadrupled the price of oil in 1973, Western industrialized economies suffered a severe economic shock, with recession, high levels of unemployment, and inflation causing significant distress. In the years following the original spike in oil prices, the biggest and fastest transfer of wealth in history took place. Some oil-producing states, particularly Saudi Arabia, began modernizing their economies on the strength of exceptional export earnings. Because of their new affluence, Arab leaders were reluctant to support the NIEO call for radical adjustments to the market economy.

Women and the Struggle for Equality

The rebuilding of Western Europe after the catastrophe of World War II had important consequences for the women's movement. The United Nations Universal Declaration of Human Rights, set forth as a nonbinding resolution in 1948, set a high standard for all of the signatory states, many of whom continued to exclude women from full civil equality. In Western Europe universal suffrage was finally realized after the war. However, women's access to equality in education and employment remained unrealized. The early hope that voting rights would lead swiftly to the implementation of civil and personal equality through the power of the ballot box was not realized.

During the 1960s, the women's movement assumed a more determined stance across Western Europe and North America. Although political rights had been secured, women continued to shoulder responsibilities that narrowed their opportunities outside of the home. Still regarded as the principal caregiver in the family, responsible for household and children, feminists like Betty Friedan (1921–2006) in the United States and Simone de Beauvior (1908–1986) in France called for a reconceptualization of gender roles. For those women in the West who did manage to secure an education and entry into the professions, inequalities in compensation and access to promotion (the so-called "glass ceiling") demonstrated that the quest for equality had to be fought on a large number of fronts against considerable, and sometimes subtle, opposition. By the mid-1990s, women's participation in paid employment outside of the household exceeded 70% in Britain, 66% in Germany, and over 85% in Sweden, but percentages of women in supervisory positions remained minimal.

The Role of the United Nations   One of the most difficult challenges facing Western feminists during the late twentieth century involved the tension between the ideals of universality and cultural diversity. In 1967 the United Nations adopted a Universal Declaration of Women's Rights that was heavily influenced by European and American standards. Many of the specific freedoms included in the Declaration, such as "equal rights with men during marriage and at its dissolution," were alien to cultures outside the West. For example, in Western Europe and the United States, the postwar feminist movement placed great emphasis on women's right to choose to work, breaking the "cult of domesticity" that had been imposed on middle-class women in the nineteenth century. This agenda was irrelevant to most women outside of the West, where women worked out of necessity and where most of that work was in the agricultural sector. Again, the West seemed to be defining the process of globalization.

Both the U.N. declarations of Human Rights and of Women's Rights embraced the Enlightenment conviction that certain human values can and must be shared irrespective of cultural claims. Many political leaders in non-Western settings rejected this position, especially in the Muslim world. In the oil-rich Arab states, for example, where the infusion of export revenues in the 1970s supported extensive infrastructure development, the new affluence did little to alter the status of women. Some Muslim women even defended strict Islamic codes as a way to express their dissent from the harmful effects of Western popular culture. In India the ancient tradition of dowry, where the bride's family would pay an agreed sum to the family of the groom, continued despite having been outlawed by the national government. Critics of dowry have argued persuasively that the practice leads to the devaluation of female children, and in extreme cases to infanticide, by impoverished families who cannot afford to pay.

Western Values?   Authoritarian and absolutist regimes around the globe continued to restrict women to the domestic sphere at the close of the century, often appropriating the language of cultural diversity to legitimize their policies. Two important measures of the status of women, access to education and to contraception, indicate that the gap between the West and the developing world remains immense. By the

■ ■

PEOPLE IN CONTEXT Simone de Beauvoir

Simone de Beauvoir (1908–1986) was raised in a middle-class Roman Catholic household and completed a degree in philosophy in 1929. While in college at the Sorbonne, she fell in love with the existentialist philosopher Jean-Paul Sartre. Although they rejected conventional marriage, they remained together for the next 50 years. During the 1930s, de Beauvoir taught high school and generally avoided politics. During the Nazi occupation of France, she lived in Paris and dedicated herself to full-time writing. In 1949 she published *The Second Sex,* a groundbreaking study of the condition of women in the modern West. It quickly became a foundational text for the women's movement.

The Second Sex argues that women are not biologically predetermined to serve solely as mothers and wives, but instead are free to determine their own fate in the world. "No biological, psychological, or economic fate determines the figure that the human female presents in society; it is civilization as a whole that determines this creature." For too long women had been culturally defined by men as "the other." *The Second Sex* called upon women to reject all views that attempted to define their essential nature. The book had a wide readership in the West; in the United States, Betty Friedan's (b. 1921) *The Feminine Mystique,* first published in 1963, drew many of its ideas from de Beauvoir.

Simone de Beauvoir avoided active involvement in the women's movement during the 1950s and 1960s. She thought that the advance of socialism throughout the West

Simone de Beauvoir In the 1970s Beauvoir became active in France's women's liberation movement. In 1972 she signed the Manifesto of the 343, a list of famous women who claimed, mostly falsely, to have had an abortion. In this photo, de Beauvoir is arriving for the famous 1972 trial in Bobigny of a woman and her friend who were accused of performing an abortion on the woman's sixteen-year old daughter. The minor was acquitted; the two adults were fined and given suspended sentences.

would have a greater impact in advancing the goal of human equality. She was a strong opponent of colonialism and criticized France's efforts to retain control over Vietnam and Algeria. During the last 15 years of her life, her growing disillusionment with socialism led her to take a more active role in the women's movement. She served as president of the French League of Women Voters and became involved in a number of journals dedicated to women's issues.

Question: Is feminism a uniquely Western phenomenon?

mid-1990s, enrollment levels for boys and girls in primary schools were equal in Western Europe, North America, and the former Soviet Union, but opportunities for boys were greater in Africa, South Asia, and the Middle East. Almost three-quarters of women of childbearing age in the West were using contraception, whereas the figure was only two-fifths in South Asia, the Middle East, and North Africa. Access to contraception was lowest in sub-Saharan Africa. At the start of the twenty-first century, prospects were not good that the core elements of the U.N. Declaration of Women's Rights would be adopted outside of the industrialized West.

Religious Divides and Ethnic Nationalism

The Fate of Christianity
In the aftermath of global war, the Holocaust, and the use of atomic weapons, many Europeans lost faith in centuries-old traditional forms of Christianity. Church attendance decreased and the authority once exercised by priests and pastors was called into question. In response, some influential Protestant thinkers turned away from the reliance upon reason that had characterized mainstream religious thought since the late nineteenth century. The Swiss theologian Karl Barth (1886–1968) was the leader of a neo-orthodox movement within Protestantism that emphasized humankind's inability to know God through reason. Barth unapologetically returned to traditional concepts of original sin, the Trinity, and the transformative power of the Resurrection. The German-born theologian Paul Tillich (1886–1965), who had served as an army chaplain during World War I but who fled Nazi Germany for the United States in 1933, insisted in his post-World War II writings that human existence was meaningless without God. One must make the "leap of faith" to escape from the banality and cruelty of modern existence. The German-Jewish religious philosopher Martin Buber (1878–1965), himself a 1938 refugee from Nazi Germany, authored a groundbreaking work titled *I and Thou* in 1923 that continued to influence Western thought after 1945. Buber, who became a leading intellectual in the new state of Israel, maintained that the relationship between the individual and God, characterized by mutuality and trust, must also direct human-to-human relations. Too often humans adopt an I-It relationship with each other, treating fellow humans as objects for their own use and advancement.

Within the Roman Catholic tradition, Pope John XXIII (r. 1958–1963) launched an important reform movement that was subsequently carried forward by the Second Vatican Council between 1962 and 1965. The Church approved the use of vernacular languages in the mass, extended opportunities for lay participation in religious services, and,

Pentecostals in Brazil   Evangelical Christianity has won millions of new converts in impoverished regions of Latin America and Africa in recent years. Pentecostalism has proven especially popular among poor urban dwellers.

most importantly, reached out to non-Catholic denominations in an effort to build ecumenical bridges. The Catholic Church also worked to improve its relationship with the Jewish community, acknowledging and repudiating a tragic history of anti-Semitism and coercion. Perhaps most significantly, the spirit of Vatican II began to transform the relationship between the Catholic Church and the conservative political establishment in Latin America. A new **liberation theology** inspired clergy to champion the right of poor people and linked the Christian message with calls for greater social and economic justice. Pope John Paul II (r. 1978–2005) championed efforts to end Soviet control over Eastern Europe, but he was wary of liberation theology and warned priests against taking too great a role in political activities at the national level. The reputation of the Roman Catholic Church also suffered at the start of the new century as charges of pedophilia dominated the news in more developed countries. Massive victim compensation packages placed enormous strain on the fiscal resources of more than a few influential Roman Catholic dioceses. In the worldwide Anglican communion, debates over the propriety of female priests, same-sex marriages, and the ordination of homosexuals pitted the more conservative African episcopate against bishops in the more liberal European and North American churches.

Militant Islam   One-fifth of the world's population were Muslims at the end of the twentieth century, and Islam continues to attract new converts. Living in countries around the globe, Muslims, like believers in the other great world religions, hold a wide range of political views. But during the final three decades of the twentieth century, a new form of militant politicized Islam, known as **Islamism** began to win converts from North Africa to Southeast Asia. Angered by Western (particularly American) support for Israel, by the painful memory of colonial rule, and by the growing influence of Western cultural forms, new antidemocratic leaders in countries like Libya, Syria, Iraq, and Iran called for Muslim unity and vigorous resistance to all manifestations of Western culture. More recently, Islamic fundamentalism has become a serious challenge to the Western-dominated process of globalization.

In addition to militant Muslim political leaders, a more popular, grassroots Islamic fundamentalism developed in a number of regions. These Islamists decried Western secularism and commercialism, and called for a return to traditional Islamic cultural and religious forms, including the imposition of harsh restrictions on women. In 1979 militant fundamentalists overthrew the American-backed Shah Reza Pahlavi (1919–1980) of Iran. The Shah had sponsored a program of rapid economic modernization, but his repressive monarchy cracked down hard on all forms of dissent.

Iranian Revolution   The emergence of Ayatollah Ruholla Khomeini (1900–1989), who was living in exile in France, as the de facto ruler of Iran symbolized the rejection of Western values and cultural influence at the heart of the Islamist movement. Ironically, however, Khomeini's return from exile and successful rise to power would have been impossible without the aid of Western technology. While still living in France, he was able to foster dissent against the Iranian monarchy by smuggling audiotapes of his sermons into Iran. Once in power, Khomeini employed the same brutal methods of repression and torture against his opponents that the Shah had used (but now on "religious" grounds). Khomeini built and maintained his regime around the idea of opposition to the United States, "the Great Satan," while simultaneously employing all of the technologies developed first in the West in order to strengthen his hold on power.

The success of the Islamic political revolution in Iran inspired opponents of moderate Muslim regimes throughout the Middle East. In November 1979, some 400 radical Muslims seized the Grand Mosque in Mecca, Saudi Arabia, and declared the end of the Saudi monarchy. It took the embarrassed Saudi government three weeks to reestablish control over Islam's holiest site. In 1981 Egyptian fundamentalists opposed to normalized relations with Israel assassinated President Anwar Sadat (1917–1981). His successor, Hosni Mubarak (b. 1928) has continued to struggle against anti-Western extremism ever since. Islamic fundamentalists' view of Israel as a product of Western imperialism and the ongoing Israeli-Palestinian dispute serves as a rallying point for radicals who wish to reclaim the Middle East for Islam.

Western powers have grown deeply suspicious of governments that are committed to fundamentalist Islam. In 1991, for example, France and the United States supported the Algerian army's decision to suspend democratic elections in that former French colony to prevent the anticipated victory of a militantly Islamic government, an event that sparked terrorist killings in France and contributed to wholesale slaughter of civilians in Algeria. More recently, Europe joined with the United States in demanding the government of Iran open its nuclear research program to a comprehensive U.N. inspections

Islamic Fundamentalism Three decades after the 1979 Iranian revolution, the country is split between advocates of reform and supporters of a strict, repressive interpretation of Islam imposed by the country's conservative clerics and "supreme leaders" of the country, Ayatollah Ali Khamenei (left) who currently is in power, and Ayatollah Ruhollah Khomeini (right), the father of the revolution.

protocol. European leaders strongly suspected that Iran was trying to develop nuclear weapons, something that the Iranian government vehemently denied. Some observers in the West saw Islamic fundamentalism taking the place of communism as the chief global challenge to liberal democracy at the start of the new century. When terrorism is organized into cells that have no specific geographical location, states find it difficult to respond to the threat.

Ethnic Cleansing in Yugoslavia One of the key features of globalization at the close of the twentieth century was the emphasis of international economic cooperation and the irrelevance of national borders when it came to the production and distribution of goods. By the close of the twentieth century, Poland, Hungary, and the Czech Republic had made a successful transition to democracy and economic reform despite the hardships involved when inefficient industries were shut down. They had been granted NATO membership, and they had applied for membership in the expanding European Union. In rural Bulgaria, Romania, and Albania, the transition was more difficult, but democratic political institutions continued to function. Further south in the Balkans, the decade of the 1990s was filled with horror and destruction. Here, just as Western Europe moved toward greater economic integration in the 1990s, heightened nationalism, ethnic tension, and war marked every aspect of daily life.

Yugoslavia was established immediately after World War I, but the new country was, like the pre–World War I Austrian Empire, a multiethnic and multilingual territorial entity. Over the centuries, there had been little love lost among the Serbs, Croatians, Slovenes, Montenegrins, Bosnians, Albanians, and Macedonians who now made up Yugoslavia. The greatest tensions were those between Orthodox Christian Serbs and Roman Catholic Croats, and between both of these groups and Muslims. While each ethnic and religious group had a particular region as its homeland, the population of Yugoslavia was mixed, with members of each group living in lands dominated by another group.

Marshal Josef Tito (1892–1980) had managed to repress ethnic rivalries during his 35 years as leader of Yugoslavia, but after his death in 1980, tensions increased in the wake of a downturn in the economy. In particular, the strident nationalist leader of Serbia, Slobodan Milosevic (1941–2006), alleged that Serbs residing in regions where they were in the minority were discriminated against by their neighbors. In the summer of 1990, less than one year after the collapse of communism in Eastern Europe, predominantly Catholic Slovenia and Croatia withdrew from the Yugoslav federation and were quickly recognized by the member states of the European Community.

The Serb leadership, responding to appeals from the Serb minority in Croatia, attacked Croatia in 1991 in an effort to preserve a Serb-dominated Yugoslav state. When the fighting spread to Bosnia and Herzegovina in the following year, Serb forces began a policy of "ethnic cleansing" aimed at the Muslim inhabitants of Bosnia. Muslim civilians were attacked, raped, and killed, and Serbs also established a series of concentration camps to house (and starve) those Bosnians who were captured in the fighting. The city of Sarajevo, host city of the 1984 Winter Olympics, was bombed incessantly by Serbian

Ethnic Nationalism   The Bosnian capital of Sarajevo was repeatedly bombed by Serbian forces in the early 1990s. The remains of a Roman Catholic Church highlight the fact that civilians were often the victims of ethnic hatred in the Balkans.

artillery. Finally, in 1994 NATO forces threatened retaliation unless the Serbs withdrew from their positions around the city. The opposing sides met in Dayton, Ohio, in 1995 to work out a complicated peace agreement. However, the end of hostilities in Bosnia did not mean the end of the suffering for civilians elsewhere in the former Yugoslavia.

Beginning in 1999, Milosevic ordered Serb troops to drive mostly Muslim ethnic Albanians from their homes in the southern province of Kosovo. After reports of mass killings of unarmed civilians, NATO responded with an intensive bombing campaign against Serbian targets. It was the largest military campaign in Europe since the end of World War II, and it succeeded in forcing the Serbians out of Kosovo. Milosevic was later arrested and sent to the International Court in the Hague to stand trial for human rights violations. Thousands died during these conflicts. While American and European military and political cooperation in the face of Serbian aggression affirmed the trend toward international cooperation, ethnic nationalism in the Balkans pointed in the opposite direction. Conflict in the Balkans belied the trend toward global understanding and cooperation across borders. Instead, it pointed toward a future where ethnicity and religion became tragic pretexts for political division and bloodshed.

Ethnic Nationalism in Russia   The Commonwealth of Independent States (CIS) had replaced the defunct Soviet Union in 1991, but within many of the successor states religious and ethnic minorities began to call for greater autonomy. Russians living in independent Ukraine and the Baltic states remained restive, while ethnic minorities in Armenia and Georgia threatened the stability of those fledgling governments. The most serious challenge to the Russian Republic was centered in the Caucasus, where insurgents in the Muslim-dominated region of Chechnya clashed with Russian authorities in the mid-1990s. Russian military forces withdrew from the region in 1996 without settling the issue of Chechnya's independence. However, Russian President Vladimir Putin (b. 1948) resumed military operations in 1999 after a series of terrorist attacks against apartment buildings in central Moscow were blamed on Chechen rebels. Almost a quarter of a million refugees fled the region in the wake of intensive Russian air strikes. Although initially condemned by the West, Russian actions in Chechnya were viewed with greater tolerance by some European and American political leaders after the September 2001 terrorist attacks against the United States.

The Postindustrial West

By the final decade of the twentieth century it was becoming clear that the West's manufacturing age was nearing an end; it was not for lack of skill, but simply a matter of making things cheaper elsewhere. New economic trends, fueled by rapidly changing technology, positioned the world's first industrial countries to assume a new profile. Where once there were large factories, labor unions, and long careers for men with a single company that offered a generous pension program, now there was the "information age" and the "knowledge economy." Financial and consumer services, health care, information technology, all twinned with short-term, project-oriented contracts, absence of defined benefits, and maximum mobility across the EU, had become the new growth sectors in professional employment. Women as well as men entered these "white collar" professions, and for married couples the advent of two incomes made the attractions of consumer life possible. Birth rates in the developed countries are now at or below replacement levels, and advanced birth control procedures allow couples to delay or avoid the responsibilities of childbearing while they pursue professional goals.

Low wage and low skill jobs still existed, of course, but they were increasingly relegated to newcomers from abroad fleeing even greater economic hardship in their home countries. Some arrived illegally from former Soviet Bloc countries like Ukraine and Moldova; others were smuggled into the EU from China by unscrupulous entrepreneurs. Many of the legal immigrants worked in the agricultural sector, where mechanization, together with improved fertilizers and seed, made possible huge surpluses. Still others lived in substandard housing and formed segregated communities on the outskirts of major cities. Few enjoyed access to proper medical care or employer-provided benefits. The "Three D" jobs—dull, dirty, and dangerous—were assumed by society's "others," at the very time when the presence of immigrant communities heightened anxiety about the impact of growing multiculturalism on national identity. Europe and the United States had yet to come to terms with changing demographics. Both a traditional sending area (Europe) and a traditional receiving area (U.S.) were equally reluctant to embrace newcomers who were essential to the postindustrial economy.

Europe and the United States were also committed, in principle at least, to strengthening international cooperation, consultation, and economic interdependence. This had been the goal of postwar rebuilding efforts from the Marshall Plan forward, and the accomplishments had been significant. In terms of fundamental social, political, and economic values, the West continued to serve as a bulwark of individual freedoms. How those freedoms were best protected and extended, however, were matters of considerable friction the wake of the 2003 Iraq invasion. The trans-Atlantic unity that was so much in evidence in the months after September 11th unraveled precipitously once the American-led war against terrorism shifted into an unprecedented pre-emptive mode. There was little sympathy in Europe for the "with us or against us" tone of rhetoric that emanated from the Bush White House, especially after it was demonstrated that there was no connection between al-Qaeda and the oppressive regime of Saddam Hussein.

The postindustrial West continued to dominate the global economy in the early years of the twenty-first century. Non-Western states aspired to comparable levels of prosperity, but as the chasm between rich and poor areas of the world grew larger, resentment and frustration intensified. Immigrants sought to redress the balance on the micro level by relocating to the affluent states. Others lashed out against the Western powers, the old colonial masters, by denouncing the capitalist and secularized states, and by appealing to the disaffected to attack these states by whatever means possible. Many in the West recognized that the problem of terrorism would never be addressed effectively by military means alone. In a globalizing world, the images of affluence were available instantly through the wonders of electronic communications in all of its forms. Extending a modicum of that affluence to others, while simultaneously protect-ing a fragile natural environment, demanded much more than force of arms and blue-prints for the export of Western-style democracy.

KEY QUESTION | Revisited

The defense of cultural pluralism has become one of the principal rallying points for critics of modern Western civilization and globalization at the end of the twentieth cen-tury. The criticism takes many forms, but three approaches stand out. In the postcolo-nial age, it is argued, the omnipresence of Western values, tastes, products, and popular culture undermine the cultural integrity of peoples and societies around the world. Western technology—movies, television, radio, the Internet, recordings, fax transmissions—floods world markets with the overriding idea that consumption represents the highest human good. The world has been overwhelmed with consumer-oriented capitalist ideology, a monolithic cultural perspective that can tolerate no rivals. Having aban-doned the old imperialism of territorial control and no longer facing a hostile Soviet Union, the West has fashioned a new and more insidious form of domination. Instead of forcing colonial peoples to abandon their traditional social and religious patterns, Western technology lures them to cast off their traditions for the environmentally fatal attractions of capitalist consumer culture.

Religious critics argue that modern Western civilization has marginalized faith tra-ditions for an emotionally and intellectually sterile form of secular rationalism. The fo-cus in the West has turned away from consideration of the transcendent. According to these critics, the focus is now on the production of goods and services, efficiency, com-petition with one's neighbor, and development and mastery of the physical environ-ment without proper consideration of long-term consequences. The end of the Cold War has afforded the West a precious opportunity to put its enormous material re-sources at the service of higher moral standards; instead, the end of superpower rivalry has led to the acceleration of cultural trends that satisfy narrow material interests absent any reference to a spiritual compass. In part, the rise of Islamic fundamentalism is due to this perception that Western culture has repudiated its former concern with religious values.

Finally, late twentieth-century criticism of Western civilization from within the ac-ademic community emphasizes the West's association with various forms of exploita-tion. Slavery, racism, sexism, imperialism, degradation of the natural environment, and class conflict have all been a part of the West's rise to economic and military primacy over the past three centuries. Western achievements were made possible through the ex-ploitation of indigenous peoples, women, the poor, and the enslaved. Western capital-ist culture, with its emphasis on rationality and efficiency, continues to strengthen inequalities while buttressing the power of traditional elites.

While the debate over the impact of Western culture in a global context is valuable, criticism of Western civilization runs the risk of forgetting that change and reform have also been at the heart of Western culture. The Enlightenment tradition, anchored in the rationalist heritage of ancient Greece and the equalitarian assumptions at the core of

Jewish and Christian thought, provided the intellectual underpinning for the West's critical approach to life. From antislavery to women's rights, in the struggle for political democracy and in the establishment of free universal education, Western civilization at its best has been self-reflective and tolerant, open to change, and committed to the dignity of the individual. This is the type of civilization celebrated by Vaclav Havel at the opening of this chapter.

As the values of democracy and freedom find voice around the world in the twenty-first century, it is crucial, as Havel reminds us, to preserve the richness and diversity of cultural expression. Those who protest the globalization of culture provide timely reminders that no single world view can satisfy the human quest for meaning in existence. Creative expression, scientific ingenuity, moral inquiry, and spiritual exploration all remained vibrant in diverse settings despite the spread of Western cultural forms. Cultural isolation has diminished thanks to modern communications and travel, but pluralism has survived, assuring that new solutions to future problems will originate out of a rich variety of intellectual contexts.

Review Questions

1. Why did Mikhail Gorbachev permit the Soviet satellites in Eastern Europe to break away from Soviet rule?
2. How has the nuclear dilemma changed since the end of the Cold War?
3. Is Western-style capitalism's focus on consumption and growth sustainable?
4. Why did ethnic conflict grip the former Yugoslavia during the 1990s, and how did Europe respond?
5. What are the key components of global culture, and why do many Muslims reject them?
6. Can Europe's post-World War II recovery be replicated in the developing world? What, in your view, does the northern hemisphere owe the southern hemisphere?
7. How has the role of women and the family changed in the postmodern world, and what are its consequences?

Please consult the Suggested Readings at the back of the book to continue your study of the material covered in this chapter. For a list of documents on the Primary Source DVD-ROM that relate to topics in this chapter, please refer to the back of the book.

Glossary

Absolutism A form of government in the seventeenth and eighteenth centuries in which the ruler possessed complete and unrivalled power.

Act of Supremacy Act passed by the English Parliament in 1534 that severed England's ties with the papacy and established the king as the head of the Church in England.

Alimenta An endowment established by Rome's emperors to support and educate the children of poverty stricken Italians.

Amarna Capital of Egypt during the reign of the pharaoh Akhenaten (1352–1338 B.C.E.); seat of his religious reform and a unique era in the history of Egyptian art.

Anti-Semitism Prejudice, hostility, or legal discrimination against Jews.

Appeasement British diplomatic and financial efforts to stabilize Germany in the 1920s and 1930s in hopes of avoiding a second world war.

Areopagus Council of the Areopagus, the oldest political body in Athens, the seat of aristocratic influence before the rise of the Athenian democracy.

Axial Age A characterization of the seventh and sixth centuries B.C.E. as a time of major religious and philosophical developments throughout the ancient world.

Babylonian Captivity Critical characterization of the era (1378–1415) in which the popes left Rome and resided in Avignon; reference to the exile of the ancient Jews from Jerusalem by the Chaldaeans of Babylon.

Barracks Emperors Characterization of the period in Roman history from 235 to 285 C.E. when there was a rapid turnover of claimants to the imperial throne; most were men "from the barracks" (i.e., ordinary soldiers who rose through the ranks).

Bishop The *episcopus* or "overseer," the title given to the religious official who oversaw the clergy working in a district called a diocese.

Boule The representative assembly central to the organization of Athens' democracy; founded by Solon and reorganized by Cleisthenes.

Bourgeoisie Term for the people who lived in a medieval *bourg*, a fortified settlement; a designation for the new middle class that appeared in medieval Europe.

Caliph "Successor," office of the heir to Muhammad's role not as prophet, but as leader of the *umma*.

Carolingians The dynasty of Frankish kings that succeeded the Merovingians; their most famous member, Charlemagne, ruled the territory of modern France, much of Germany, and part of Italy.

Church "Lord's House," term for the communities established by the early Christians.

Cluniac Reform A movement originating at the French monastery of Cluny that sought to elevate the level of conduct of the medieval clergy by establishing the church's independence of the laity.

Code of Hammurabi Collection of laws issued by the Amoritic ruler of Babylon, Hammurabi (1792–1750 B.C.E.); earliest major collection of legal materials.

Coloni Tenant farmers who, late in the history of the Roman Empire, became tied to the lands they worked.

Comitatus A band of German warriors that was created by the oaths of personal loyalty that members took to their leader.

Compurgation A legal procedure by which an accused person could clear his or her name by finding a certain number of people who would swear to his or her integrity.

Conciliarism A legal argument for recognizing universal councils, not popes, as the supreme authorities for determining the faith and practice of the Catholic Church.

Condottiere Commander of an army of mercenaries; when hired to defend one of Italy's towns, the risk was that he would use his soldiers to take over and make his power permanent.

Congress of Vienna A conference of the major powers of Europe in 1814 to 1815 to establish a new balance of power at the end of the Napoleonic wars.

Constitutions of Clarendon A decree issued by England's King Henry II that sought to bring clergy who were convicted of crimes in church courts under the jurisdiction of royal courts for their punishment.

Copernicus Polish astronomer (1473–1543) who promulgated the now-accepted theory that Earth and the other planets move around the sun (the Copernican System).

Council of Trent A church council, meeting from 1545 to 1563, that was charged with the responsibility of strengthening the Roman Catholic Church to equip it to respond to the challenge of the Protestant Reformation.

Courtly Love A modern term for a medieval aristocratic fad, a game of courtship in which a man exalted a woman as a paragon of beauty and virtue and pledged to endure any hardship in exchange for a sign of her favor.

Crusade "War of the cross," term commonly applied to the military offensives that medieval European Christians launched against Muslim opponents.

Cuneiform A script or system of writing devised by the Sumerians; its elements were composed of the wedge-shaped impressions that a stylus makes in the surface of a mud tablet.

Danegeld A tax levied by the Anglo-Saxon kings of England to purchase peace from Viking invaders.

Darwin, Charles (1809–1882) Scientist associated with the theory that highlights the role of variation and natural selection in the evolution of a species.

Decolonization Withdrawal of Western nations from colonies in Africa and Asia after World War II.

Deism Seventeenth- and eighteenth-century belief that God created the universe and established immutable laws of nature but did not subsequently intervene in the operation of nature or in human affairs.

Delian League A defensive alliance Athens organized following the Persian Wars; became the basis for the construction of an Athenian Empire.

Demagogue Politician who acquires power and influence by manipulating the emotions of the masses.

Demesne The fields on a medieval manor from which its lord derived his income; the primary obligation of the peasants who lived on the manor was to work these fields for the lord who provided their protection.

Dialectic The academic discipline that, during the Middle Ages, focused on methods for the construction and critique of logical arguments.

Diet A German political assembly.

Divine Right Political theory that held the institution of monarchy had divine origin and that the monarch functioned as God's representative on Earth.

Dominate A system of government headed by a *Dominus*, lord; the autocratic system that took hold during the reign of the Roman emperor Diocletian.

Donation of Constantine A document forged in the eighth century to enhance the political authority of the papacy; it claimed that the ancient Roman Emperor Constantine had ceded control over the Roman Empire to Pope Sylvester I.

Donation of Pepin Gift to the pope of Italian land that the Frankish king Pepin (r. 741–768) took from the Lombards; a step in the creation of the Papal States.

Dreyfus Affair The trials of Captain Alfred Dreyfus on treason charges, which dominated French political life in the decade after 1894 and revealed fundamental divisions in French society.

Dynasty A ruling family; transmission of monarchical authority through lines of descent within a family.

Edict of Nantes A decree that King Henry IV issued in 1598 that established places in France where Protestants could legally worship.

Enlightened Despots The term assigned to absolute monarchs who initiated a series of legal and political reforms in an effort to realize the goals of the Enlightenment.

Enlightenment An international intellectual movement of the eighteenth century that emphasized the use of reason and the application of the laws of nature to human society.

European Union A successor organization to the EEC; the organization attempted to integrate European political, economic, cultural, and military structures and policies.

Existentialism Twentieth-century philosophy that emerged in the interwar era and influenced many thinkers and artists after World War II. Existentialism emphasizes individual freedom in a world devoid of meaning or coherence.

Exodus The pivotal event in the history of the Hebrew people, their departure from Egypt under Moses, their covenant with God, and the beginning of the fulfillment of God's pledge to Abraham.

Fair A regularly scheduled time for merchants and customers to gather at a particular place for the purpose of conducting business; frequently corresponded with a holiday (a *feria*, "feast day").

Fascism Twentieth-century political ideology that rejected the existing alternatives of conservatism, communism, socialism, and liberalism. Fascists stressed the authoritarian power of the state, the efficacy of violent action, the need to build national community, and the use of new technologies of influence and control.

Fertile Crescent An arc of cultivated land stretching from the Persian Gulf up the Tigris and Euphrates Rivers across Syria to the Mediterranean and south through Palestine to and including Egypt; the seat of the earliest civilizations.

Feudum The income that a medieval government provided to support the agents that served it; in the absence of a monetary economy and a system of taxation, it was often a piece of land.

Foederati "Allies," Latin term for the German tribes that were permitted to occupy land within the Roman Empire in exchange for a pledge to assist with its defense.

Friar A new religious invocation that emerged in Europe in the late twelfth century; a Christian who took monastic vows of poverty and celibacy but who stayed in the world rather than retreat to a monastery.

Fyrd A peasant army unique to Anglo-Saxon England.

Gaugamela The decisive battle, at a site north of Babylon, at which Alexander the Great defeated Darius and went on to consolidate his hold on the Persian Empire.

Ghibelline A medieval political faction founded by the dukes of Swabia that sought to extend the authority of the German kings into Italy.

Global Warming An increase in the average temperature of the Earth's atmosphere, especially a sustained increase great enough to cause changes in the global climate. The present warming is generally attributed to an increase in the greenhouse effect, brought about by increased levels of greenhouse gases, largely due to the effects of human activity.

Globalization The tendency of capital and trade flows to move beyond domestic and national markets to other markets around the globe, thereby increasing the interconnectedness of these flows. Globalization also refers to the increasing interconnectedness of culture, music, art, food, dress, and ideas that has been increasing in recent times.

Gothic A style of medieval architecture that utilized pointed or broken arches and flying buttresses; it emphasized vertical lines and sought to create buildings flooded by light.

Great Depression Calamitous drop in prices, reduction in trade, and rise in unemployment that devastated the global economy beginning in 1929.

Great Dionysia Spring festival in honor of the god Dionysus, origin of the tradition of Greek theater.

Great Schism The period from 1378 to 1415 during which there were multiple claimants to the papacy.

Guelf A medieval political faction founded by the dukes of Saxony and subsequently a movement in Italy that opposed the efforts of German kings to extend their authority into Italy.

Guild A medieval union or corporation that monopolized the production of a product with the intent of sustaining a healthy market.

Hadith "Traditions" handed down about the Prophet Muhammad's acts and teachings; material supplementary to the Qur'an.

Hanseatic League An alliance of cities in northern Germany (established in 1359) that enabled them to dominate commerce in the Baltic and North Seas.

Hieroglyph "Sacred writing," a script or system of writing devised by the ancient Egyptians utilizing pictographs.

Hijra "Departure," Muhammad's relocation from Mecca to Medina and organization of the first Muslim community; the pivot point for the Muslim calendar.

Holocaust Adolf Hitler's effort to murder all the Jews in Europe during World War II.

Hoplite Name for a Greek infantryman, derived from his unique bowl-shaped shield; fought in a tightly packed company called a phalanx.

Hundred Years' War An era of occasionally renewed conflict between England and France in the fourteenth and fifteenth centuries that culminated in England's retreat from the continent.

Imperium The authority to command armies during the era of the Roman Republic and Empire.

Indo-European A family of languages that extends from Ireland across Europe and Persia to India; spread by a major migration at the start of the second millennium that established major new peoples in the ancient world (e.g., Greeks, Romans, Hittites, Persians, etc.).

Indulgence A papal dispensation from the obligation to perform a penance.

Industrial Revolution Sustained period of economic growth and change brought on by technological innovations in the process of manufacturing; began in Britain in the mid-eighteenth century.

Inquisition A church court established by the papacy to root out heresy in Catholic countries.

Investiture Controversy A dispute between the papacy and Europe's kings in 1075 over the right of kings to appoint candidates to offices in the church and participate in the ceremonies that invested clergy with their authority and properties.

Islamism Islamic radicalism or *jihadism*, this ideology insists that Islam demands a rejection of Western values and that violence in this struggle against the West is justified.

Jacobins A French political party supporting a democratic republic that found support in political clubs throughout the country and dominated the National Convention from 1792 until 1794.

Latifundia Latin term for a plantation, staffed by slaves and specializing in crops raised for market.

Liberation Theology The effort by certain Roman Catholic theologians to combine Marxism with traditional Christian concern for the poor.

Line of Demarcation A longitudinal line decreed by the pope in 1494 to divide territories in the western hemisphere between Spain and Portugal.

Linear B Script developed by the Mycenaeans following the example of the Minoans (Linear A); earliest recorded specimens of the Greek language.

Manor A medieval agricultural cooperative; it combined private ownership of land with common ownership of the tools that worked the land.

March A frontier district held by an army to provide protection for a country and a base for potential conquest and expansion.

Marshall Plan The use of U.S. economic aid to restore stability to Europe after World War II and so undercut the appeal of communist ideology.

Martyr "Witness," in particular someone who suffers or dies to testify to a religious belief.

Marxism The theory of Karl Marx (1818–1883) and Friedrich Engels (1820–1895) that stated history is the result of class conflict, which will end in the inevitable triumph of the industrial proletariat over the bourgeoisie and the abolition of private property and social class.

Merovingians The descendants of the Frankish king Clovis (466–511 C.E.); the first dynasty of French kings.

Messiah "Anointed"; in Hebrew tradition, an agent commissioned to act for God to bring about fulfillment of God's covenant with Abraham; in Christian tradition, the role that Jesus of Nazareth played in history.

Middle Kingdom The era in Egyptian history (2025–1630 B.C.E.) characterized by public works, literary production, and the shift of the seat of government to Thebes.

Missi dominici "Emissaries of the Lord," title granted to the agents who toured Charlemagne's empire to hear complaints against local governors.

Modern Devotion A religious revival originating in northern Europe during the fourteenth and fifteenth centuries that promoted education and charitable work.

Modernism Term applied to artistic and literary movement from the late nineteenth century through the 1950s. Modernists sought to create new aesthetic forms and values.

Monist The thesis argued by Thales, the first philosopher (640–546 B.C.E.), and his followers; suggested that the world was a coherent place because everything in it was the product of a single substance.

Monk "Solitary"; a Christian who chose to live apart from family and society in order to devote himself exclusively to prayer and acts of faith.

Mufti A specialist in the interpretation of Islamic religious law.

Nationalism The belief that the people who form a nation should have their own political institutions and that the interests of the nation should be defended and promoted at all costs.

NATO NATO (North Atlantic Treaty Organization) is the defensive anti-Soviet alliance of the United States, Canada, and the nations of Western Europe established in 1949.

Nazism Twentieth-century political ideology associated with Adolf Hitler that adopted many Fascist ideas but with a central focus on racism and particularly anti-Semitism.

Neolithic Era "The New Stone Age," the final phase in prehistoric cultural development; characterized by a farming economy, domestication of wild plant and animal species, and semi-permanent village settlements.

New Comedy Popular theatrical genre that thrived during the Hellenistic era; unlike Old Comedy (e.g., the plays of Aristophanes), which usually had a serious message, it was pure entertainment.

New Imperialism The third phase of modern European imperialism, which occurred in the late nineteenth and early twentieth centuries and extended Western control over almost all of Africa and much of Asia.

New Kingdom "The Egyptian Empire" (1550–1075 B.C.E.), the era when the ancient Egyptians abandoned their traditional isolationism and expanded south into Nubia and east into Palestine and Syria.

New Model Army A Protestant military organization established by Oliver Cromwell in 1645 that enabled the English Parliament to depose King Charles I and govern England as a Puritan republic.

Nominalism The philosophical claim that words for categories of things are only names that people invent for convenience of communication; such words do not correspond to anything that actually exists.

Old Kingdom "The Pyramid Age" (2700–2200 B.C.E.), the formative phase in the development of ancient Egyptian civilization.

Optimates Roman political faction that hoped to stabilize the Roman Republic by preserving traditions that empowered the Senatorial classes.

Oratory of Divine Love An organization of Catholic clergy and laity that was established in the sixteenth century to work for religious renewal.

Ostracism A vote to determine whether any individual should be exiled from Athens as a suspected threat to the city.

Paleolithic Era "The Old Stone Age," the first period in the evolution of human culture; characterized by a hunter-gather economy and pressure-chipped tool manufacture.

Pantheon A roster of the ancient gods, particularly those associated with Zeus-Jupiter.

Parliament The political body that began to evolve in England in the thirteenth century; it brought together representatives of all the propertied classes in England and provided them with an opportunity to negotiate with their king, but it did not represent the peasant majority.

Parthenon Athenian temple on the Acropolis in the Doric style; most famous specimen of Classical Greek architecture.

Patrician Term for a man from one of the politically empowered families that originally controlled the Roman Republic.

Peace of Augsburg A truce that was declared between Protestant and Catholic factions in Germany in 1555 and which prevented religious conflict in Germany until 1618.

Peace of Westphalia The international agreement concluded in 1648 that ended the Thirty Years' War and resolved numerous boundary disputes.

Peloponnesian War A Greek civil war (432–404 B.C.E.) that led to the decline of Hellenic civilization, opposing sides led by Athens and Sparta.

Perestroika "Restructuring." The attempt in the 1980s to reform the Soviet government and economy.

Perspective The techniques developed by painters during the era of the Renaissance to create the illusion of three-dimensional space on a flat surface.

Philosophes The writers and thinkers of the Enlightenment, especially in France.

Plantagenet The name by which England's Norman dynasty ultimately came to be known; it derives from the father of King Henry II (r. 1154–1189).

Plebeian Term for a man from a citizen family that originally had no right to participate in the government of the Roman Republic.

Pluralist Term for the ancient Greek thinkers who suggested that the world was a product of a variety of things (e.g., elements or atoms).

Podestà A neutral stranger who was brought in to rule and mediate among factions when conflict caused the government of an Italian town to break down.

Polis A Greek city-state that undertook a program of social engineering to influence the development of its citizens.

Populares Roman political faction that sought influence by appealing to the Roman masses.

Pragmatic Sanction of Bourges An agreement in 1438 between the king of France and the pope that extended the authority of the French monarchy over the Catholic Church in France.

Predestination Belief, primarily associated with the Swiss theologian John Calvin, that the absolute sovereignty of God implies that a person's conduct cannot alter God's decision about his or her ultimate fate.

Pre-Socratics Greek philosophers prior to Socrates (469–399 B.C.E.) who studied the external world and natural science, whereas later Greek thinkers focused on the internal world of human psychology, rationality, and values.

Princeps "First Citizen," title of honor the Romans bestowed on Octavian (63 B.C.E.–14 C.E.) to thank him for his alleged restoration of their Republic.

Ptolemy Friend of Alexander the Great who won control of Egypt after Alexander's death and found the last dynasty of pharaohs to rule that country.

Puritan Name for a radical Protestant faction that drew its inspiration from the Swiss Reformation. It temporarily overthrew the monarchy and established a Republican government in England.

Quadrivium The secondary portion of the medieval student's curriculum; instruction in arithmetic, geometry, astronomy, and music.

Racism The pseudoscientific theory that biological features of race determine human character and worth.

Realism The philosophical claim that words for categories of things are not arbitrary conventions of speech, but refer to fundamental metaphysical realities.

Reform Protestantism Protestant churches that trace their origin less to Martin Luther and Germany than to the work of the Swiss reformers Ulrich Zwingli and John Calvin.

Reign of Terror A purging of alleged enemies of the French state between 1793 and 1794, organized by the Committee of Public Safety, that resulted in the execution of 17,000 people.

Republicanism A political theory first developed by the ancient Greeks, especially the philosopher Plato, but elaborated on by the ancient Romans and rediscovered during the Italian Renaissance. The fundamental principle of Republicanism as developed during the Italian Renaissance was that government officials should be elected by the people or a portion of the people.

Romanesque A style of medieval architecture that utilized round arches, heavy masonry walls, small windows, and attached buttresses.

Romanitas The customs, traditions, and values that the ancient Romans regarded as the source of their unique strengths and virtues as a people.

Romanticism An artistic and literary movement of the late eighteenth and nineteenth centuries that involved a protest against classicism, appealed to the passions rather than the intellect, and emphasized the beauty and power of nature.

Rule The name for the constitution that the church approved to govern the lives of an order of monks or nuns.

Russian Revolution Revolution in Russia in 1917 that overthrew the tsar and eventually brought the Bolsheviks, a Communist party led by Lenin, to power.

Sans-cullotes Literally, "those without knee-britches"; working-class revolutionaries who initiated the radical stage of the French Revolution in 1792.

Schism A split or division within a community or organization.

Scholasticism The dominant philosophy of the High Middle Ages; drew heavily on the teachings of Aristotle and the construction of dialectical arguments.

Scientific Revolution In the sixteenth and seventeenth centuries, a period of new scientific inquiry, experimentation, and discovery that resulted in a new understanding of the universe based on mathematical principles and led to the creation of the modern sciences, particularly astronomy and physics.

Sea Peoples Collective term for the wave of invaders who spread throughout the eastern Mediterranean about 1200 B.C.E.

Seleukos Macedonian soldier who seized control of Babylon after Alexander the Great's death; his descendants formed a dynasty that held the central portion of that empire until ousted by the Parthians and Romans.

Serfs During the Middle Ages, serfs were agricultural laborers who worked and lived on a plot of land granted to them by a lord to whom they owed a certain portion of their crops. They could not leave the land, but they had certain legal rights that were denied to slaves.

Shari'a "Required path," the religious law that governs some Muslim communities.

Shi'a "Party," the branch of Islam that springs from the supporters of Ali, Muhammad's son-in-law, in his struggle for the caliphate.

Solidarity Trade union and political party in Poland that led an unsuccessful effort to reform the Polish communist state in the early 1980s; it survived state persecution to lead Poland's first non-communist government since World War II in 1989.

Spanish Armada The great fleet that Philip II launched in 1588 in what proved to be a futile attempt to conquer England and subdue Protestant resistance in the Netherlands.

St. Bartholomew's Day Massacre A surprise attack that the French monarchy launched (August 24, 1572) on Protestants who had gathered in Paris to celebrate the wedding of a daughter of queen regent Catherine de Medicis to Henry of Navarre, a Protestant leader.

Stalin's Purges (or Great Terror) Period of mass arrests and executions particularly aimed at Communist Party members. Lasting from 1934 to 1938, the Great Purge enabled Stalin to consolidate his one-man rule over the Soviet Union.

Studia humanitas The mission of the intellectual leaders of Italy's Renaissance, a search for methods to discover and realize the potentials of human nature.

Sultan Title of the leader of the Seljuk Turks who rose to power in the domain of the Abbasid caliph in the eleventh century.

Summa An attempt to sum up in a logically coherent system an entire field of knowledge; for example, the works of the medieval theologian Thomas Aquinas.

Suras The divine messages revealed to Muhammad that, taken together, constitute the Qur'an, Islam's sacred text.

Theme A region within the Byzantine Empire assigned to a military commander.

Thirty Years' War A devastating war fought on German territory from 1618 to 1648; originating as a conflict between Germany's Protestants and Catholics, concern for the balance of power ultimately encouraged French and Scandinavian monarchs to intervene.

Tholos Unique pseudo-domed tomb structures erected by the Mycenaeans.

Torah The first five books of the Hebrew Scriptures: Genesis, Exodus, Numbers, Leviticus, and Deuteronomy.

Treaty of Versailles Peace settlement with Germany at the end of World War I; included the War Guilt Clause fixing blame on Germany for the war and requiring massive reparations.

Trench Warfare Warfare marked by slow wearing down of the opposing forces and piecemeal gains at heavy cost. The term applies especially to World War I.

Triumvirate An arrangement among three men to share governmental authority; Rome's First Triumvirate was a private agreement among Julius Caesar, Pompey, and Crassus; Rome's Second Triumvirate was a formal legal arrangement whereby Octavian, Mark Anthony, and Lepidus were to work for the restoration of the Roman Republic.

Trivium The elementary portion of the medieval student's curriculum; instruction in basic literacy: grammar, dialectic, rhetoric.

Troubadour "Inventor," a kind of lyric poet that appeared in Europe in the eleventh century; who departed from the earlier warrior epic tradition by concentrating on themes of love and intimate personal feelings.

Umma "Community," the new principle of unity that Muhammad created to bind people together through faith in his role as prophet.

Urbanization The social process whereby cities grow and societies become more urban.

War of the Roses Civil war in England (1455–1485) in which the families of the dukes of York and Lancaster struggled for the throne; ended with the establishment of the Tudor dynasty.

Warsaw Pact The military alliance of the Soviet Union and its Eastern European satellite states in the Cold War era.

Wergeld A provision in Germanic law that allowed an individual who harmed someone to pay a fine equivalent to the seriousness of the injury he had inflicted; a method of avoiding socially disruptive vendettas.

Working Class People who work for wages, especially low wages, including unskilled and semiskilled laborers and their families.

Yalta A resort city in Crimea in the southern Ukraine on the Black Seas that was the site of the Allied conference between Roosevelt, Stalin, and Churchill in February 1945.

Ziggurat A multistory mound of sun-dried brick erected as a platform for a temple by the Sumerians and Babylonians.

Suggested Resources

Introduction

The increasing interconnectedness of the modern world has produced numerous reflections on the nature of history and the importance of understanding the interrelatedness of global peoples.

J. M. Hobson, *The Eastern Origins of Western Civilization* (2004); D. Landes, *The Wealth and Poverty of Nations* (1998); R. Royal, "Who Put the West in Western Civilization?" *The Intercollegiate Review* (Spring 1998); F. Fukuyama, *The End of History and the Last Man* (1993); J. Roberts, *The Triumph of the West* (1985).

Chapter 1

Scholars who study the transition from the prehistorical to the historical eras must infer a great deal from scanty evidence. Archaeologists have made some lucky discoveries at widely scattered sites, but only a few key locales have been intensively explored. Anthropological studies of modern tribal peoples have suggested theoretical models that might shed light on the remote past. The dramatic progress that ecologists have been making in uncovering information about Earth's climate cycles has also yielded valuable information about the environments to which early human cultures adapted and spawned theories about the demise of some ancient civilizations.

R. Desalle & I. Tattersall, *Human Origins* (2007); C. Zimmer, *Smithsonian Intimate Guide to Human Origins* (2007); C. Gamble, *Origins and Revolutions: Human Identity in Earliest Prehistory* (2007); R. Gabriel, *The Ancient World* (2007); B. Kemp, *Ancient Egypt: An Anatomy of a Civilization*, 2nd ed. (2006); J. Diamond, *Collapse: How Societies Choose to Fail or Succeed* (2005); R. Chadwick, *First Civilizations: Ancient Mesopotamia and Ancient Egypt*, 2nd ed. (2005); J. McIntosh, *Ancient Mesopotamia: New Perspectives* (2005); H. Crawford, *Sumer and Sumerians* (2004); N. B. Hunt, *Historical Atlas of Ancient Mesopotamia* (2004); D. Lambert, *Encyclopedia of Prehistory* (2002); S. Sanderson, *The Evolution of Human Sociality: A Darwinian Conflict Perspective* (2001); M. Isler, *Sticks, Stones, and Shadows: Building the Egyptian Pyramids* (2001); E. Delson et al., *Encyclopedia of Human Evolution and Prehistory* (2000); R. Rudgley, *The Lost Civilizations of the Stone Age* (2000); R. J. Werke, *Prehistory: Humankind's First Three Million Years* (1999); S. Pollock, *Ancient Mesopotamia: The Eden That Never Was* (1999); R. Ardrey, *The Territorial Imperative: A Personal Inquiry into the Animal Origins of Property and Nations* (1997); J. Diamond, *Guns, Germs, and Steel: The Fates of Human Societies* (1997); D. C. Snell, *Life in the Ancient Near East* (1997); C. Freeman, *Egypt, Greece, and Rome* (1996); A. Cherry, *The Socializing Instincts: Individual, Family, and Social Bonds* (1994); A. J.

Spencer, *Early Egypt: The Rise of Civilization in the Nile Valley* (1993); J. N. Postgate, *Early Mesopotamia* (1992); M. Ehrenberg, *Women in Prehistory* (1989); D. O. Henry, *From Foraging to Agriculture* (1989); H. W. F. Saggs, *Civilization Before Greece and Rome* (1989); N. Grimal, *A History of Ancient Egypt* (1988); S. Lloyd, *The Archaeology of Mesopotamia* (1984); S. N. Kramer, *History Begins at Sumer* (1959); H. Frankfort et al., *The Intellectual Adventure of Ancient Man* (1946).

Chapter 2

The invention of writing made it possible for human beings to document their lives in unprecedented detail. Ancient peoples produced both intentional and unintentional records—that is, archival documents that they expected to survive and incidental jottings whose survival has been totally fortuitous. From these things it is possible, for the first time, to infer something about the intellectual lives and thought processes of human beings. The following items survey some of this intriguing work.

B. Fagan, *Return to Babylon: Travelers, Archaeologists, and Monuments in Mesopotamia* (2007); R. Gabriel, *The Ancient World* (2007); M. Chavalas, *The Ancient Near East: Historical Sources in Translation* (2006); P. Esler, *Ancient Israel: The Old Testament in Its Social Context* (2006); W. Grajetzki, *The Middle Kingdom of Ancient Egypt* (2006); D. Silverman, *Akhenaten and Tutankhamon: Revolution and Restoration* (2006); M. Van de Mieroop, *King Hammurabi of Babylon: A Biography* (2005); C. Roehrig, *Hatshepsut: From Queen to Pharaoh* (2005); M. Smith, *The Memoirs of God: History, Memory, and the Experience of the Divine in Ancient Israel* (2004); C. Scarre & B. M. Fagan, *Ancient Civilizations*, 2nd ed. (2003); V. Matthews, *A Brief History of Ancient Israel* (2002); I. Finkelstein, *The Bible Unearthed: Archaeology's New Vision of Ancient Israel and the Origin of Its Sacred Texts* (2001); J. & D. Oates, *Nimrud: An Assyrian City Revealed* (2001); I. Shaw, *The Oxford History of Ancient Egypt* (2000); O. Eliezer, *The Sea Peoples and Their World: A Reassessment* (2000); B. Brier, *The Murder of Tutankhamen* (1998); K. R. Nemet-Nejat, *Daily Life in Ancient Mesopotamia* (1998); A. Kuhrt, *The Ancient Near East, c. 3000–330 B.C.* (1995); H. W. F. Saggs, *Babylonians* (1995); G. Robbins, *Women in Ancient Egypt* (1993); N. Grimal, *A History of Ancient Egypt* (1988); D. Redford, *Akhenaten* (1987); O. R. Gurney, *The Hittites* (1954/81); S. Moscati & N. Sanders, *The Sea Peoples: Warriors of the Ancient Mediterranean* (1978); S. Moscati, *Ancient Semitic Civilizations* (1960); J. B. Pritchard, *The Ancient Near East: An Anthology of Texts and Pictures* (1958); H. Frankfort et al., *The Intellectual Adventure of Ancient Man* (1946).

Chapter 3

The classical Greek civilization that arose in the Aegean was incredibly inventive and potent. It permanently changed life in the West, and its influence continues to be felt today. Scholars, however, debate explanations for its origin. Some emphasize its originality and others stress its indebtedness to other cultures.

L. Schofield, *The Mycenaeans* (2007); H. A. Shapiro, *The Cambridge Companion to Archaic Greece* (2007); D. Kyle, *Sport and Spectacle in the Ancient World* (2007); P. Cartledge, *Thermopylae: The Battle that Changed the World* (2006); J. Ducat, *Spartan Education: Youth and Society in the Classical Period* (2006); R. Castleden, *Mycenaeans* (2005); M. Schmidt, *The First Poets: Lives of the Ancient Greek Poets* (2005); J. Foley, *A Companion to Ancient Epic* (2005); T. Holland, *Persian Fire: The First World Empire and the Battle for the West* (2005); A. Lloyd, *Marathon: The Story of Civilizations on Collision Course* (2004); T. Figueira, *Spartan Society* (2004); P. Cartledge, *The Spartans: The World of the Warrior-Heroes of Ancient Greece, From Utopia to Crisis and Collapse* (2003); P. De Souza, *The Greek and Persian Wars, 499–386 B.C.* (2003); J. Lesley Fittor, *Minoans* (2002); F. Braudel, *Memory and the Mediterranean* (2002); J. M. Camp, *The Archaeology of Athens* (2002); N. Lunaghi, *The Historian's Craft in the Age of Herodotus* (2001); J. A. MacGillivray, *Minotaur: Sir Arthur Evans and the Archaeology of the Minoan Myth* (2000); S. B. Pomeroy, S. M. Burstein, W. Donlan, & J. T. Roberts, *Ancient Greece: A Political, Social, and Cultural History* (1999); L. G. Mitchell & P. J. Rhodes, Eds., *The Development of the Polis in Archaic Greece* (1997); O. Dickinson, *The Aegean Bronze Age* (1994); R. Drews, *The End of the Bronze Age: Changes in Warfare and Catastrophes, ca. 1200 B.C.* (1993); V. D. Hanson, *The Western Way of War* (1989); J. Boardman, J. Griffin, & O. Murray, *Greece and the Hellenistic World* (1988); R. Drews, *The Coming of the Greeks: Indo-European Conquests in the Aegean and Near East* (1988); W. Bernal, *Black Athena: The Afroasiatic Roots of Classical Civilization* (1987); R. Osborne, *Demos* (1985); A. R. Burn, *Persia and the Defense of the West*, rev. ed. (1984); J. Boardman, *The Greeks Overseas*, rev. ed. (1980); W. Forrest, *A History of Sparta, 950–121 B.C.*, 2nd ed.(1980); J. Griffin, *Homer* (1980); M. I. Finley, *The World of Odysseus*, rev. ed. (1979); J. Chadwick, *The Mycenaean World* (1976); A. C. Brackman, *The Dream of Troy* (1974); A. Andrews, *Greek Tyrants* (1963).

Chapter 4

The artistic and literary monuments of classical Greek civilization were created over the span of only a few generations—and against a background of frequent military activity. Wars tested Greece's institutions but apparently did not divert Greek intellectuals from thinking deeply about the phenomena of the natural world and the mysteries of human self-awareness. The result was the production of a body of philosophical, scientific, and artistic work of unsurpassed importance.

L. Samons, *The Cambridge Companion to the Age of Pericles* (2007); D. Shangke, *Thucydides and the Philosophical Origins of History* (2007); J. Hurwit, *The Acropolis in the Age of Pericles* (2007); L. Navia, *Socrates: A Life Examined* (2007); M. Linck, *The Ideas of Socrates* (2007); J. Warren, *Presocratics: Natural Philosophers Before Socrates* (2007); A. Saxonhouse, *Free Speech and Democracy in Ancient Athens* (2006); N. Bagnall, *The Peloponnesian War: Athens, Sparta, and the Struggle for Greece* (2006); J. Morrison, *Reading Thucydides* (2006); P. Connolly, *The Ancient City: Life in Classical Athens and Rome* (2006); G. Ley, *A Short Introduction to the Ancient Greek Theater* (2006); V. Hanson, *A War Like No Other: How the Athenians and Spartans Fought the Peloponnesian War* (2005); D. Kagan, *The Peloponnesian War* (2003); J. Annas, *Plato: A Very Short Introduction* (2003); J. Barnes, *Aristotle: A Very Short Introduction* (2000); S. B. Pomeroy et al., *Ancient Greece: A Political, Social and Cultural History* (1999); M. M. Henry, *Prisoner of History: Aspasia of Miletus and Her Biographical Tradition* (1995); A. Shapiro, *Women in the Classical World* (1994); J. K. Davies, *Democracy and Classical Greece* (1993); C. W. Fornara & L. J. Samons, *Athens from Cleisthenes to Pericles* (1991); D. Kagan, *Pericles of Athens and the Birth of Athenian Democracy* (1991); I. F. Stone, *The Trial of Socrates* (1989); J. Boardman et al., *Greece and the Hellenistic World* (1988); S. Woodford, *An Introduction to Greek Art* (1986); Y. Garlan, *Slavery in Ancient Greece* (1988); W. Burkert, *Greek Religion* (1985); J. D. Romilly, *A Short History of Greek Literature* (1985); J. Boardman, *Greek Art* (1985); A. Burn, *Persia and the Greeks: The Defense of the West*, 2nd ed. (1984); K. J. Dover, *Greek Homosexuality* (1978); R. Meigs, *The Athenian Empire* (1972); J. J. Pollitt, *Art and Experience in Classical Greece* (1972); M. Grant, *The Ancient Historians* (1970); G. E. R. Lloyd, *Early Greek Science* (1970); W. K. Guthrie, *History of Greek Philosophy* (1962–1981); E. Hamilton, *The Greek Way* (1930).

Chapter 5

Roman civilization was a Hellenistic civilization. That is, Rome adopted and adapted the cosmopolitan Greek culture that spread throughout the West in the wake of Alexander the Great's conquests. The Romans were, however, also innovators and pioneers—particularly in the arenas of law and politics. America's "founding fathers" were greatly attracted to the study of Roman history, and their idealized visions of ancient Rome influenced the formation of the early American republic.

C. Thomas, *Alexander the Great in His World* (2007); A. Goldsworthy, *Caesar: Life of a Colossus* (2006); N. Cantor, *Alexander the Great: Journey to the End of the Earth* (2005); A. Fraschetti, *The Foundation of Rome* (2005);

D. Kleiner, *Cleopatra and Rome* (2005); M. Grant, *Cleopatra* (2004); L. Burn, *Hellenistic Art from Alexander the Great to Augustus* (2004); H. Flower, *The Cambridge Companion to the Roman Republic* (2004); C. Mackay, *Ancient Rome: A Military and Political History* (2004); F. Borrelli, *The Etruscans: Art, Architecture, and History* (2004); G. Irby-Massie, *Greek Science of the Hellenistic Era: A Sourcebook* (2002); R. Seager, *Pompey the Great: A Political Biography* (2002); H. Mouritsen, *Plebs and Politics in the Late Roman Republic* (2001); P. Horden, *The Corrupting Sea: A Study of Mediterranean History* (2000); A. Goldsworthy, *The Punic Wars* (2000); S. Haynes, *Etruscan Civilization: A Cultural History* (2000); A. W. Lintott, *The Constitution of the Roman Republic* (1999); T. J. Cornell, *The Beginnings of Rome: Italy and Rome from the Bronze Age to the Punic Wars* (1995); M. H. Crawford, *The Roman Republic*, 2nd ed. (1993); F. W. Walbank, *The Hellenistic World* (1993); R. A. Bauman, *Women and Politics in Ancient Rome* (1992); P. Green, *Alexander of Macedon* (1991); N. Bagnall, *The Punic Wars* (1990); J. Boardman et al., *The Roman World* (1990); E. N. Borza, *In the Shadow of Olympus: The Emergence of Macedon* (1990); R. E. Mitchell, *Patricians and Plebeians: The Origin of the Roman State* (1990); N. G. L. Hammond & F. W. Walbank, *A History of Macedonia* (1988); A. B. Bosworth, *Conquest and Empire: The Reign of Alexander the Great* (1988); A. D. Long, *Hellenistic Philosophy: Stoics, Epicureans, Skeptics*, 2nd ed. (1986); J. J. Pollitt, *Art in the Hellenistic Age* (1986); G. Alföldy, *The Social History of Rome* (1985); E. S. Gruen, *The Hellenistic World and the Coming of Rome* (1984); H. H. Scullard, *A History of the Roman World, 753–146 B.C.E.*, 4th ed. (1980); M. Pallottino, *The Etruscans* (1975); P. M. Fraser, *Ptolemaic Alexandria* (1972); M. Grant, *Cleopatra* (1972); R. M. Errington, *The Dawn of Empire: Rome's Rise to World Power* (1971); B. H. Warmington, *Carthage*, 2nd ed. (1969); R. Syme, *The Roman Revolution* (1960).

Chapter 6

The Roman Empire was a remarkably successful and long-lived institution. It maintained order and stability throughout the entire Western world for over two centuries, a record that no subsequent government has equaled. The empire was not, however, sustained by a single set of unchanging institutions. To preserve the empire, Rome's leaders had to constantly adapt and reorganize it. Eventually, it changed so much that its core identity was threatened.

W. Eck, *The Age of Augustus* (2007); J. B. Rives, *Religion in the Roman Empire* (2007); D. S. Potter, *A Companion to the Roman Empire* (2006); E. Fantham, *Julia Augusti: The Emperor's Daughter* (2006); J. Osgood, *Caesar's Legacy: Civil War and the Emergence of the Roman Empire* (2006); P. Matyszak, *The Sons of Caesar: Imperial Rome's First Dynasty* (2006); K. Galinsky, *The Cambridge Companion to the Age of Augustus* (2005); J. Malitz, *Nero* (2005); R. Seager, *Tiberius* (2005); E. Speller, *Following Hadrian: A Second-Century Journey Through the Roman Empire* (2004); J. Carcopino, *Daily Life in Ancient Rome: The People and the City at the Height of the Empire* (2003); A. Barrett, *Livia: First Lady of Imperial Rome* (2002); J. Grubbs, *Women and the Law in the Roman Empire* (2002); J. Boardman, *The Oxford Illustrated History of the Roman World* (2001); R. Thomas, *Virgil and the Augustan Reception* (2001); J. C. Coulston, *Ancient Rome: The Archaeology of the Eternal City* (2000); M. Boatwright, *Hadrian and the Cities of the Roman Empire* (2000); K. Galinsky, *Augustan Culture* (1996); M. Grant, *The Antonines: The Roman Empire in Transition* (1994); T. Wiedemann, *Emperors and Gladiators* (1992); H. C. Boren, *Roman Society*, 2nd ed. (1992); D. Shotter, *Augustus Caesar* (1991); A. Ferrill, *Caligula: Emperor of Rome* (1991); R. P. Saller, *The Roman Empire: Economy, Society and Culture* (1987); M. Grant, *The Roman Emperors* (1985); B. Campbell, *The Emperor and the Roman Army* (1984); P. MacKendrick, *The Mute Stones Speak: The Story of Archeology in Italy*, 2nd ed. (1983); T. Barnes, *The New Empire of Diocletian and Constantine* (1982); R. Duncan-Jones, *The Economy of the Roman Empire* (1982); F. G. B. Millar, *The Emperor in the Roman World, 31 B.C.–A.D. 337* (1977); E. N. Luttwak, *The Grand Strategy of the Roman Empire* (1976); E. T. Salmon, *A History of the Roman World, 30 B.C. to A.D. 138* (1968); R. Syme, *The Roman Revolution* (1960).

Chapter 7

As the Roman Empire declined, its eastern and western halves separated. This foreshadowed the split that has emerged in the modern era between a Christian "West" and a Muslim "East." During the Middle Ages, however, the civilization that spread throughout Europe was transformed by surges of influences from the Middle East. The most significant of these was, of course, Christianity. But the brilliant Byzantine and Islamic cultures that also arose in the Middle East were particularly instrumental in helping Europe emerge from its Dark Age and restore its civilized institutions.

S. Mitchell, *A History of the Later Roman Empire, A.D. 284–641: The Transformation of the Ancient World* (2007); A. Casiday, *Constantine to c. 600* (2007); R. van Dam, *The Roman Revolution of Constantine* (2007); M. Kulikowski, *Rome's Gothic Wars:From the Third Century to Alaric* (2007); A. Barbero, *The Day of the Barbarians: The Battle that Led to the Fall of the Roman Empire* (2007); I. Zeitlin, *The Historical Muhammad* (2007); H. Halm, *The Arabs: A Short History* (2007); B. Rogerson, *The Heirs of Muhammad: Islam's First Century and the Origins of the Sunni-Shia Split* (2007); W. A. Goffart, *Barbarian Tides: The Migration Age and the Later Roman Empire* (2006); C. T. R. Hewer, *Understanding Islam* (2006); G. E. M. De Ste. Croix, *Christian Persecution, Martyrdom, and Orthodoxy* (2006); R. Horsley, *Christian Origins* (2005); P. Heather, *The Fall of the Roman Empire*

(2005); D. Catchpole, *Jesus People: The Historical Jesus and the Beginning of Community* (2006); M. White, *From Jesus to Christianity* (2004); C. Kelly, *Ruling the Later Roman Empire* (2004); D. S. Potter, *The Roman Army at Bay, A.D. 180–395* (2004); M. Salzman, *The Making of a Christian Aristocracy: Social and Religious Change in the Western Roman Empire* (2002); W. Stagemann, *The Social Setting of Jesus and the Gospels* (2002); P. Southern, *The Roman Empire from Severus to Constantine* (2001); G. Dawes, *The Historical Jesus Quest: Landmarks in the Search for the Jesus of History* (2000); F. E. Peters, *Muhammad and the Origins of Islam* (1994); J. Morehead, *Justinian* (1995); K. Armstrong, *Muhammad: A Biography of the Prophet* (1992); A. Schimmel, *Islam: An Introduction* (1992); A. H. Hourani, *A History of the Arab Peoples* (1992); R. Browning, *The Byzantine Empire* (1992); P. J. Heather, *Goths and Romans, 332–489* (1991); T. Barnes, *The New Empire of Diocletian and Constantine* (1982); W. Goffart, *Barbarians and Romans, A.D. 418–584: The Techniques of Accommodation* (1980); M. Grant, *The Fall of the Roman Empire* (1990); C. H. Lawrence, *Medieval Monasticism*, 2nd ed. (1989); H. St. L. B. Moss, *The Birth of the Middle Ages, 395–814*, 2nd ed. (1972); P. Brown, *The World of Late Antiquity, C.E. 150–750* (1971); G. Ostrogosky, *History of the Byzantine State*, 2nd ed. (1969); P. Brown, *Augustine of Hippo* (1967).

Chapter 8

Early medieval Europe was characterized by a diversity of peoples and cultures. Several attempts were made to overcome its political fragmentation and restore the unity it had enjoyed during the Roman era, but none succeeded for very long. The resulting period in history is difficult to generalize with any accuracy. A rich mix of peoples and movements contributed to Europe's reorganization and its gradual emergence as an original and influential civilization.

R. A. Hall, *The World of the Vikings* (2007); M. Arnold, *The Vikings: Wolves of War* (2007); J. Sypeck, *Becoming Charlemagne: Europe, Baghdad, and the Empires of A.D. 800* (2006); C. Corning, *The Celtic and Roman Traditions: Conflict and Consensus in the Early Medieval Church* (2006); C. McClendon, *The Origins of Medieval Architecture:Building in Europe, A.D. 600–900* (2005); A. Clot, *Harun al-Rashid and the World of the Thousand and One Nights* (2005); A. D. M. Forte, *Viking Empires* (2005); T. Glick, *Islamic and Christian Spain in the Early Middle Ages* (2005); T. Gregory, *A History of Byzantium* (2005); A. Barbero, *Charlemagne: Father of a Continent* (2004); C. Backman, *The Worlds of Medieval Europe* (2003); J. Moorhead, *The Roman Empire Divided, 400–700* (2001); P. Fouracre, *The Age of Charles Martel* (2000); N. Christie, *The Lombards, the Ancient Longobards* (1995); I. N. Wood, *The Merovingian Kingdoms, 450–751* (1994); R. McKitterick, *Carolingian Culture: Emulation and Innovation* (1994); S. Reynolds, *Fiefs and Vassals: The Medieval Evidence Reinterpreted* (1994); R. W. Mathisen, *Roman Aristocrats in Barbarian Gaul: Strategies for Survival in an Age of Transition* (1993); J. P. Ply & E. Bournazel, *The Feudal Transformation, 900–1200* (1991); F. D. Logan, *The Vikings in History*, 2nd ed. (1991); L. Bitel, *Isle of the Saints: Monastic Settlement and Christian Community in Early Ireland* (1990); P. J. Geary, *Before France and Germany: The Creation and Transformation of the Merovingian World* (1988); H. R. Loyn, *The Governance of Anglo-Saxon England, 500–1087* (1984); J. D. Randers-Pherson, *Barbarians and Romans: The Birth Struggle of Europe, A.D. 400–700* (1983); R. McKitterick, *The Frankish Kingdoms under the Carolingians, 751–987* (1983); R. Collins, *Early Medieval Spain: Unity in Diversity, 400–1000* (1983); O. Chadwick, *The Making of the Benedictine Ideal* (1981); J. Richards, *The Popes and the Papacy in the Early Middle Ages, 476–752* (1979); L. White, *Medieval Technology and Social Change* (1972); J. Boussard, *The Civilization of Charlemagne* (1971); P. H. Blair, *The World of Bede* (1970); G. Duby, *Rural Economy and Country Life in the Medieval West* (1968).

Chapter 9

Europe entered the Middle Ages as the weakest of the Mediterranean world's three civilizations. Its Byzantine and Muslim neighbors were far more culturally sophisticated and had richer economies and more thriving urban institutions. Not surprisingly, therefore, Europe languished on the defensive, struggling with successive waves of invasion and migration. By the eleventh century, however, European societies had begun to stabilize, and Europeans were able to reverse course and take the offensive. The wars of conquest—which they inaugurated—and the crusades both signaled and promoted the revival of European civilization, but these wars have left a legacy of hate that continues to the present day.

A. Cameron, *The Byzantines* (2006); C. Tyenman, *God's War: A New History of the Crusades* (2006); D. Horspool, *King Alfred: Burnt Cakes and Other Legends* (2006); S. Friedman, *A History of the Middle East* (2006); R. H. Bloch, *A Needle in the Right Hand of God: The Norman Conquest of 1066 and the Making of the Bayeux Tapestry* (2006); M. Angold, *Eastern Christianity* (2006); N. Oikonomidès, *Society, Culture, and Politics in Byzantium* (2005); R. Huscroft, *Ruling England, 1042–1328* (2005); A. Clot, *Harun al-Rashid and the World of the Thousand and One Nights* (2005); T. Ashridge, *The First Crusade: A New History* (2004); J. P. Berkey, *The Formation of Islam: Religion and Society in the Near East, 600–1800* (2003); K. Armstrong, *Holy War: The Crusades and Their Impact on Today's World*, rev. ed. (2001); M. Gervens, *Tolerance and Intolerance: Social Conflict in the Age of the Crusades* (2001); R. Barber, *Henry Plantagenet* (2001); M. Brett, *The Rise of the Fatimids: The World of the Mediterranean and the Middle East in the 4th Century of the Hijra, 10th Century C.E.* (2001);

E. Hallam, *Capetian France, 987–1328* (2001); G. A. Loud, *The Age of Robert Guiscard: Southern Italy and the Norman Conquest* (2000); R. I. Moore, *The First European Revolution* (2000); D. Crouch, *The Reign of King Stephen, 1135–1154* (2000); J. Haldon, *Byzantium: A History* (2000); R. Hodges, *Towns and Trade in the Age of Charlemagne* (2000); D. Webb, *Pilgrims and Pilgrimage in the Medieval West* (1999); C. Hillenbrand, *The Crusades: Islamic Perspectives* (1999); J. Rathbone, *The Last English King* (1999); J. Riley-Smith, *The First Crusaders, 1095–1131* (1997); J. Riley-Smith, Ed., *The Oxford Illustrated History of the Crusades* (1997); R. Bartlett, *The Making of Europe: Conquest, Colonization and Cultural Change, 950–1350* (1993); W. Roesener, *Peasants in the Middle Ages* (1992); W. Treadgold, *The Byzantine Revival, 780–842* (1988); U. R. Blumenthal, *The Investiture Controversy: Church and Monarchy from the Ninth to the Twelfth Century* (1988); H. Kennedy, *The Prophet and the Age of the Caliphates: The Islamic Near East from the Sixth to the Eleventh Century* (1986); S. Reynolds, *Kingdoms and Communities in Western Europe, 900–1300* (1984); E. M. Hallam, *Capetian France, 987–1328* (1980); E. Ennen, *The Medieval Town* (1979); G. Barraclough, *The Crucible of Europe, the Ninth and Tenth Centuries in European History* (1976); R. S. Lopez, *The Commercial Revolution of the Middle Ages, 950–1350* (1971); B. Hill, *Church and State in the Middle Ages* (1970); R. Jenkins, *Byzantium: The Imperial Centuries, 610–1071* (1969); D. C. Douglas, *William the Conqueror: The Norman Impact Upon England* (1964); S. Runciman, *A History of the Crusades* (1964).

Chapter 10

During the High Middle Ages, the contours of some of Europe's major nation-states began to appear on the map and strides were made toward the development of their characteristic political and cultural institutions. This was a period of intellectual and artistic inventiveness. Great cathedrals—wonders of engineering and architectural vision—were erected. Universities appeared, literacy spread, and Europeans engaged in lively (often contentious) debates that produced breakthroughs in philosophy and science.

C. Lindberg, *A Brief History of Christianity* (2006); R. Horrox, *A Social History of England, 1200–1500* (2006); J. Flori, *Richard the Lionheart: King and Knight* (2006); R. Huscroft, *Ruling England, 1042–1328* (2005); M. McCarthy, *Classical and Gothic: Studies in the History of Art* (2005); P. Strafford, *Romanesque Churches of France; A Traveller's Guide* (2005); R. Begley, *Medieval Education* (2005); R. M. Holt, *The Crusader States and their Neighbors* (2004); J. Brower, *The Cambridge Companion to Abelard* (2004); R. Rubenstein, *Aristotle's Children: How Christians, Muslims, and Jews Rediscovered Ancient Wisdom and Illuminated the Dark Ages* (2003); A. Nichols, *Discovering Aquinas: An Introduction to His Life, Work and Influence* (2002); D. Spoto, *Reluctant Saint: The Life of Francis of Assisi* (2002); D. Burr, *The Spiritual Franciscans* (2001); R. Barber, *Henry Plantagenet* (2001); D. Crouch, *The Reign of King Stephen, 1135–1154* (2000); M. Kitchen, *The Cambridge Illustrated History of Germany* (2000); M. Barber, *The Cathars: Dualist Heretics in Languedoc in the High Middle Ages* (2000); R. Bartlett, *England Under the Norman and Angevin Kings, 1075–1225* (2000); C. H. Berman, *The Cistercian Evolution: The Invention of a Religious Order in Twelfth-Century Europe* (2000); J. Gillingham, *Richard I* (1999); R. N. Swanson, *The Twelfth-Century Renaissance* (1999); L. B. Glick, *Abraham's Heirs: Jews and Christians in Medieval Europe* (1999); M. T. Clanchy, *Abelard: A Medieval Life* (1997); M. D. Costen, *The Cathars and the Albigensian Crusade* (1997); C. H. Lawrence, *The Friars: The Impact of the Early Mendicant Movement on Western Society* (1994); H. Schulze, *States, Nations and Nationalism* (1994); H. de Ridder-Symoens, Ed., *Universities in the Middle Ages* (1992); W. S. Stoddard, *Art and Architecture in Medieval France* (1990); D. Abulafia, *Frederick II: A Medieval Emperor* (1988); M. R. Menocal, *The Arabic Role in Medieval Literary History: A Forgotten Heritage* (1987); J. Marenbon, *Later Medieval Philosophy (1150–1350): An Introduction* (1987); J. B. Baldwin, *The Government of Philip Augustus: Foundations of French Royal Power in the Middle Ages* (1986); S. C. Ferruolo, *The Origins of the University* (1985); S. Reynolds, *Kingdoms and Communities in Western Europe, 900–1300* (1984); J. Bony, *French Gothic Architecture of the Twelfth and Thirteenth Centuries* (1983); E. M. Hallam, *Capetian France, 987–1328* (1980); W. C. Jordan, *Louis IX and the Challenge of the Crusade: A Study in Rulership* (1979); K. J. Conant, *Carolingian and Romanesque Architecture, 800–1200,* 2nd ed. (1979); W. L. Warren, *Henry II* (1973); J. W. Baldwin, *The Scholastic Culture of the Middle Ages, 1000–1300* (1971); J. R. Strayer, *On the Medieval Origins of the Modern State* (1970); P. Munz, *Frederick Barbarossa: A Study in Medieval Politics* (1969).

Chapter 11

The late medieval world was tested in many ways, and, over all, it confronted its challenges successfully. Despite failures of leadership and what was sometimes an all-consuming preoccupation with a struggle to survive, Europe's cultural creativity was undiminished. Europeans weathered their crises, restored their institutions, and emerged from their trials prepared for a new era of invention and expansion.

J. Aberth, *Disease in Human History* (2007); D. Morgan, *The Mongols* (2007); D. Green, *Edward the Black Prince: Power in Medieval Europe* (2007); D. Spoto, *Joan: The Mysterious Life of the Heretic Who Became a Saint* (2007); R. Blumenfeld-Kosinski, *Poets, Saints, and Visionaries of the Great Schism, 1378–1417* (2006); M. Prawdin, *The Mongol Empire: Its Rise and Legacy* (2006); S. Haw, *Marco Polo's China: A Vene-tian in the Realm of Khubilai Khan* (2006); M. Livingstone, *The Road to Crécy: The English*

Invasion of France (2005); P. Jackson, *The Mongols and the West* (2005); A. Ayton, *The Battle of Crécy* (2005); R. J. Knecht, *The Valois: Kings of France, 1328–1589* (2004); J. Philips, *The Fourth Crusade and the Sack of Constantinople* (2004); J. Byrne, *The Black Death* (2004); A. Curry, *The Hundred Years' War* (2003); J. C. Moore, *Pope Innocent III: To Root Up and to Plant* (2003); K. Fowler, *Medieval Mercenaries, Vol. 1: The Great Companies* (2001); N. Cantor, *In the Wake of the Plague: The Black Death and the World It Made* (2001); J. Larner, *Marco Polo and the Discovery of the World* (1999); J. Moore, *Innocent III and His World* (1999); R. Brown-Grant, *Christine de Pizan and the Moral Defense of Women: Reading Beyond Gender* (1999); J. Poole, *Joan of Arc* (1998); D. Herlihy, *The Black Death and the Transformation of the West* (1997); W. C. Jordan, *The Great Famine: Northern Europe in the Early Fourteenth Century* (1996); R. Frame, *The Political Development of the British Isles, 1100–1400* (1995); J. Schatazmiller, *Jews, Medicine, and Medieval Society* (1994); P. Stump, *The Reforms of the Council of Constance, 1414–1418* (1994); A. Curry, *The Hundred Years' War* (1993); J. H. Burns, Ed., *The Cambridge History of Medieval Political Thought* (1988); C. Allmand, *The Hundred Years' War: England and France at War* (1988); R. Gottfried, *The Black Death: Natural and Human Disaster in Medieval Europe* (1983); N. W. Warner, *Joan of Arc: Image of Female Heroism* (1981); M. G. A. Vale, *War and Chivalry: Warfare and Aristocratic Culture in England, France, and Burgundy at the End of the Middle Ages* (1981); J. R. Strayer, *The Reign of Philip the Fair* (1980); F. Oakley, *The Western Church in the Later Middle Ages* (1979); T. S. R. Boase, *Death in the Middle Ages: Mortality, Judgment, and Remembrance* (1972); Y. Renouard, *The Avignon Papacy, 1305–1403* (1970); J. P. Morrall, *Political Thought in Medieval Times* (1962).

Chapter 12

Europe's Renaissance and Age of Exploration mark a turning point in global history. Many of the key developments that have shaped life in the modern world can be traced to this era: mass literacy, global exchanges of goods and cultures, widening divergence of Christian and Muslim peoples, and the resurgence of influences from the ancient phase in Western civilization.

C. L. Frommel, *The Architecture of the Italian Renaissance* (2007); R. Jacoff, *The Cambridge Companion to Dante* (2007); N. R. Havely, *Dante* (2007); K. A. Simon Eliot, *A Companion to the History of the Book* (2007); E. Enenkel, *Petrarch and His Readers in the Renaissance* (2006); L. Fusco, *Leonardo de' Medici* (2006); R. Crum, *Renaissance Florence: A Social History* (2006); H. Kamen, *Spain, 1469–1714: A Society in Conflict* (2005); J. Reston, *Dogs of God: Columbus, the Inquisition, and the Defeat of the Moors* (2005); S. Füssel, *Gutenberg and the Impact of Printing* (2005); J. Snyder, *Northern Renaissance Art* (2005); R. Mackenney, *Renaissances: The Cultures of Italy, c. 1300–1600* (2005); H. Thomas, *Rivers of*

Gold: The Rise of the Spanish Empire, from Columbus to Magellan (2004); J. C. Smith, *The Northern Renaissance* (2004); J. Najemy, *Italy in the Age of the Renaissance, 1300–1550* (2004); J. Edwards, *Ferdinand and Isabella* (2004); P. Strathern, *The Medicis:Godfathers of the Renaissance* (2003); B. Lewis, *What Went Wrong? Western Impact and Middle Eastern Response* (2002); H. Beinart, *The Expulsion of the Jews from Spain* (2002); P. Russell, *Prince Henry "the Navigator": A Life* (2000); S. Bemrose, *A New Life of Dante* (2000); M. Greene, *A Shared World: Christians and Muslims in the Early Modern Mediterranean* (2000); P. Johnson, *The Renaissance: A Short History* (2000); P. Dollinger, *The German Hansa* (1999); P. Burke, *The European Renaissance: Centers and Peripheries* (1998); B. Thompson, *Humanists and Reformers* (1996); L. Jardine, *Worldly Goods: A New History of the Renaissance* (1996); C. G. Nauert, *Humanism and the Culture of the Renaissance* (1995); B. G. Kohl & A. A. Smith, *Major Problems in the History of the Italian Renaissance* (1995); J. Hale, *The Civilization of Europe in the Renaissance* (1994); J. Huizinga, *The Autumn of the Middle Ages* (1924/1996); G. Holmes, *Renaissance* (1996); F. Fernandez-Armesto, *Columbus* (1991); M. L. King, *Women of the Renaissance* (1991); G. V. Scammell, *The First Imperial Age: European Overseas Expansion, c. 1400–1715* (1989); L. Martins, *Power and Imagination: City-States in Renaissance Italy* (1989); A. W. Crosby, *The Biological Expansion of Europe* (1986); J. N. Hillgarth, *The Spanish Kingdoms, 1250–1516* (1978); E. L. Eisenstein, *The Printing Press as an Agent of Change* (1978); G. Leff, *The Dissolution of the Medieval Outlook, an Essay on Intellectual and Spiritual Change in the Fourteenth Century* (1976); H. Inalcik, *The Ottoman Empire: The Classical Age, 1300–1600* (1973); D. Waley, *The Italian City Republics* (1969); B. Lewis, *Istanbul and the Civilization of the Ottoman Empire* (1963).

Chapter 13

Despite the confident predictions of many secularists, religion has not faded as a significant factor influencing the behavior of modern peoples and states. The history of the era of Europe's Reformation and religious wars may, therefore, be of special interest to students of current world affairs. It is also important for the study of American history, for the religious ideologies that emerged at this time were transplanted to America and shaped the American way of life.

R. Shaughnessy, *The Cambridge Companion to Shakespeare and Popular Culture* (2007); S. Ronald, *The Pirate Queen: Queen Elizabeth I, Her Pirate Adventurers, and the Dawn of Empire* (2007); R. Rex, *Henry VIII and the English Reformation* (2006); M. Bennett, *Oliver Cromwell* (2006); G. W. Bernard, *The King's Reformation: Henry VIII and the Remaking of the English Church* (2005); P. Oswald, *Mary Stuart* (2005); L. DeLisle, *After Elizabeth: The Rise of James of Scotland and the Struggle for the Throne of En-gland* (2005); M. Holt, *The French*

Wars of Religion, 1562–1629 (2005); C. V. Wedgwood, *The Thirty Years' War* (2005); L. Picard, *Elizabeth's London: Everyday Life in Elizabethan London* (2004); H. Kleinschmidt, *Charles V: The World Emperor* (2004); H. Kamen, *Golden Age Spain* (2004); P. Collinson, *The Reformation: A History* (2004); M. Mullett, *Martin Luther* (2004); D. McKim, *The Cambridge Companion to Martin Luther* (2003); C. Levin, *Elizabeth I, Always Her Own Free Woman* (2003); B. Pursell, *The Winter King: Frederick V of the Palatinate and the Coming of the Thirty Years' War* (2003); L. Frieda, *Catherine de Medici, Renaissance Queen of France* (2003); A. Levi, *Renaissance and Reformation: The Intellectual Genesis* (2002); G. Parker, *Philip II* (2002); M. Kitchen, *The Cambridge Illustrated History of Germany* (2000); R. J. Knechy, *Catherine de' Medici* (1998); C. Haigh, *Elizabeth I*, 2nd ed. (1998); S. Greenblatt, Ed., *The Norton Shakespeare* (1997); B. Thompson, *Humanists and Reformers: A History of Renaissance and Reformation* (1996); P. Gaunt, *Oliver Cromwell* (1996); C. Lindberg, *The European Reformations* (1996); M. P. Holt, *The French Wars of Religion, 1562–1629* (1995); R. Ashton, *Counter-Revolution: The Second Civil War and Its Origin, 1646–1648* (1995); W. P. Stephens, *Zwingli* (1994); A. McGrath, *Reformation Thought: An Introduction*, 2nd ed. (1993); G. H. Williams, *The Radical Reformation*, 2nd ed. (1992); H. A. Oberman, *Luther* (1992); S. Ozment, *Protestants: The Birth of a Revolution* (1992); J. Wormald, *Mary Queen of Scots: A Study in Failure* (1991); J. McConica, *Erasmus* (1991); H. Kamen, *Spain 1469–1714: A Society of Conflict*, 2nd ed. (1991); S. J. Lee, *The Thirty Years' War* (1991); E. Cameron, *The European Reformation* (1991); R. Bonney, *The European Dynastic States, 1494–1660* (1991); A. McGrath, *A Life of John Calvin: A Study in the Shaping of Western Culture* (1990); P. Caravan, *Ignatius Loyola: A Biography of the Founder of the Jesuits* (1990); A. G. Dickens, *The English Reformation*, 2nd ed. (1989); W. J. Bouwsma, *John Calvin: A Sixteenth-Century Portrait* (1988); P. Collinson, *The Religion of Protestants: The Church in English Society, 1559–1625* (1982); S. Ozment, *The Age of Reform, 1250–1550: An Intellectual and Religious History of Late Medieval and Reformation Europe* (1980); R. S. Dunn, *The Age of Religious Wars, 1559–1715*, 2nd ed. (1979); F. Braudel, *The Mediterranean and the Mediterranean World in the Age of Philip II*, 2 vols. (1976); M. R. O'Connell, *The Counter Reformation, 1559–1610* (1974); P. Gay & R. K. Webb, *Modern Europe to 1815* (1973); A. Wandruszka, *The House of Habsburg* (1965).

Chapter 14

The sixteenth-century Reformation set the stage for the formation of strong centralized states in Europe. No longer competing with church authorities for the allegiance of their subjects, state sovereignty and dynastic power reached new heights during the seventeenth and eighteenth centuries. Recent scholarly literature has focused on the limits of absolutism during this period, highlighting the importance of economic and political checks on the power of monarchs who claimed to rule by divine right, and contrasting European monarchical power with its more absolutist forms in non-Western civilizations.

M. S. Anderson, *Europe in the Eighteenth Century, 1713–1783* (1987); J. Black, *Eighteenth-Century Europe, 1700–1789* (1990); J. Black, *European Warfare, 1660–1815* (1994); J. Blum, *The End of the Old Order in Rural Europe* (1978); F. Braudel, *The Structures of Everyday Life* (1982); J. Brewer, *The Sinews of Power: War, Money and the English State, 1688–1783* (1989); G. Burgess, *Absolute Monarchy and the Stuart Constitution* (1996); J. C. D. Clark, *English Society, 1688–1832* (1985); I. Madariaga, *Catherine the Great: A Short History* (1990); W. Doyle, *The Old European Order* (1992); M. W. Flinn, *The European Demographic System, 1500–1820* (1981); P. Goubert, *The Ancient Regime: French Society, 1600–1750* (1974); L. Hughes, *Russia in the Age of Peter the Great* (1998); J. I. Israel, *The Dutch Republic: Its Rise, Greatness, and Fall, 1477–1806* (1995); D. McKay & H. M. Scott, *The Rise of the Great Powers, 1648–1815* (1983); A. Pagden, *Lords of All the World: Ideologies of Empire in Spain, Britain and France, 1492–1830* (1995); D. J. Sturdy, *Louis XIV* (1998).

For primary sources illustrating the theory and practice of absolutism, see:
http://lcweb.loc.gov/exhibits/bnf/bnf0005.html

For documents on everyday life in early modern Europe, see:
http://www.fordham.edu/halsall/mod/modsbook04.html

Chapter 15

The Scientific Revolution of the sixteenth and seventeenth centuries provided an important backdrop to the Enlightenment. Traditionally, the advance of scientific inquiry has been interpreted in terms of expanding human rationality and a knowable deity who was also a supreme architect. More recently, historians have emphasized the importance of an earlier magical and alchemical tradition to scientific inquiry. Scholars have also worked to highlight the limits of reason during these centuries by examining the persistence of religious intolerance and the persecution of women accused of witchcraft.

H. Butterfield, *The Origins of Modern Science* (1949); C. M. Cipolla, *Before the Industrial Revolution: European Society and Economy, 100–1700*, 2nd ed. (1980); R. Hall, *Scientific Revolution, 1500–1800* (1945); M. Jacob, *The Cultural Meaning of the Scientific Revolution* (1988); H. Kearney, *Science and Change, 1500–1700* (1971); T. S. Kuhn, *The Copernican Revolution* (1957); L. Schiebinger, *The Mind Has No Sex? Women in the Origins of Modern Science* (1990); W. M. Spellman, *John Locke* (1997); W. M. Spellman, *European Political Thought, 1600–1700* (1998); R. S. Westfall, *Never at Rest: A Biography of Isaac Newton* (1981); R. S. Westman, *The Copernican Achievement* (1975); B. Willey, *The Seventeenth Century Background* (1949); M. E. Wiesner, *Women and Gender in Early Modern Europe* (1994); P. Zagorin, *Francis Bacon* (1998).

For sources on the life and work of Galileo, see the Galileo Project at:
http://galileo.rice.edu/lib/catalog.html

Oxford's Museum of the History of Science offers online exhibits at:
http://www.mhs.ox.ac.uk

Chapter 16

Most studies of the European Enlightenment concentrate on the ideas of a small intellectual elite. While it is important to recognize the significance of the many social, political, and religious reform efforts that emerged during the eighteenth century, it is also useful to acknowledge the practical limits of the Enlightenment. Studies of slavery, the condition of women, and the lives of common people during this era have increased dramatically. This new scholarship has alerted us to the complexity and variety of eighteenth-century thought and lived experience.

C. Becker, *The Heavenly City of the Eighteenth-Century Philosophers* (1935); G. Cragg, *The Church and the Age of Reason* (1966); L. Crocker, *An Age of Crisis: Man and World in Eighteenth-Century French Thought* (1959); R. Darnton, *The Business of Enlightenment: A Publishing History of the Encyclopedia* (1979); P. Gay, *The Enlightenment: An Interpretation*, 2 vols. (1969); N. Hampson, *A Cultural History of the Enlightenment* (1968); P. Hazard, *The European Mind, 1680–1715* (1935); R. Houston, *Social Change in the Age of the Enlightenment* (1995); M. Jacob, *The Radical Enlightenment: Pantheists, Freemasons and Republicans* (1980); L. Krieger, *An Essay on the Theory of Enlightened Despotism* (1975); J. Lough, *The Encyclopedia* (1971); F. Manuel, *The Eighteenth Century Confronts the Gods* (1959); G. Ritter, *Frederick the Great: A Historical Profile* (1968); H. Scott, *Enlightened Absolutism* (1990); R. Shackleton, *Montesquieu: A Critical Biography* (1961); J. Shklar, *Men and Citizens: A Study of Rousseau's Social Theory* (1969); S. Spencer, Ed., *French Women and the Age of Enlightenment* (1984); I. Wade, *The Intellectual Origins of the French Enlightenment* (1957).

For documents on the Enlightenment and additional web links, see:
http://www.fordham.edu/halsall/mod/modsbook10.html

Chapter 17

The institutions and values of Old Regime Europe, including monarchy, aristocracy, and legal inequality, were challenged and overturned during the final quarter of the eighteenth century. The changes brought about by the American Revolution were modest in comparison to the events that began in Paris in 1789. On the American side, the break from Britain was comparatively bloodless, and the prerevolutionary social structure remained in place after independence. In France, however, fundamental restructuring took place during the 1790s, and the rise of Napoleon Bonaparte to power signaled the extension of revolutionary principles across Europe. Some recent studies have emphasized the social implications of the French Revolutions for all of Europe.

B. Bailyn, *The Ideological Origins of the American Revolution* (1967); R. Cobb, *The People's Armies* (1987); F. Furet, *Interpreting the French Revolution* (1981); P. Gay, *The Enlightenment*, 2 vols., (1978); J. Godechot, *The Counter-Revolution: Doctrine and Action* (1971); J. Landes, *Women and the Public Sphere in the Age of the French Revolution* (1988); M. Lyons, *Napoleon Bonaparte and the Legacy of the French Revolution* (1994); G. Lefebvre, *The Coming of the French Revolution*, trans. R. R. Palmer (1947); R. Middlekauff, *The Glorious Cause: The American Revolution, 1763–1789* (1982); E. Morgan, *The Stamp Act Crisis* (1953); R. R. Palmer, *The Age of Democratic Revolution,* 2 vols. (1941); C. Robbins, *The Eighteenth-Century Commonwealthmen* (1959); D. G. Sutherland, *France, 1789–1815: Revolution and Counterrevolution* (1986); B. Stone, *The Genesis of the French Revolution* (1994); W. Stinchcombe, *The American Revolution and the French Alliance* (1969); G. Wood, *The Radicalism of the American Revolution* (1990).

For scholarly essays and additional texts on the American Revolution, see:
http://odur.let.rug.nl/~usa/

For scholarly essays, images, maps, and documents on the French Revolution, see:
http://chnm.gmu.edu/revolution/

Chapter 18

The defeat of Napoleon meant the end of French domination of Europe, but the ideas of the French Revolution could not be extinguished. Conservative regimes attempted to restore the prerevolutionary political and social order in the West, but liberal reformers, spurred by the changes introduced by the early stages of industrialization, pushed for constitutional, representative government and the inclusion of the middle class in the political process. At the same time, the plight of the new urban working class was championed by socialist and Marxist thinkers.

A. Arblaster, *The Rise and Decline of Western Liberalism* (1984); M. Brock, *The Great Reform Act* (1974); A. Briggs, *The Making of Modern England* (1959); I. Deak, *The Lawful Revolution: Louis Kossuth and the Hungarians, 1848–1849* (1979); J. Droz, *Europe Between Revolutions,*

1815–1848 (1967); J. Elster, *An Introduction to Karl Marx* (1985); J. F. C. Harrison, *Quest for the New Moral World: Robert Owen and the Owenites in Britain and America* (1969); E. J. Hobsbawm, *The Age of Revolution, 1789–1848* (1962); R. Porter & M. Teich, Eds., *Romanticism in National Context* (1999); R. Price, *The Revolutions of 1848* (1989); J. Sperber, *The European Revolutions, 1848–1851* (1994); D. Thompson, *The Chartists: Popular Politics in the Industrial Revolution* (1984).

The Yale Law School Avalon Project provides additional documents at:
http://www.yale.edu/lawweb/avalon/19th.htm

Chapter 19

The factory age began in Britain during the late eighteenth century and spread rapidly to Western Europe and North America during the first half of the nineteenth century. Industrialization had a major impact on social and economic life. The impact of the factory on the natural environment was not a major concern of early industrialists, most of whom equated the advanced machine technology and urbanization with human progress. However, the social and environmental costs of industrialization are now part of the large body of scholarship on this broad topic.

C. Chinn, *Poverty Amidst Prosperity: The Urban Poor in England, 1834–1914* (1995); P. Deane, *The First Industrial Revolution* (1965); G. Himmelfarb, *The Idea of Poverty: England in the Early Industrial Age* (1983); D. Landes, *The Unbound Prometheus: Technological Change and Industrial Development in Western Europe from 1750 to the Present* (1969); P. Mathias, *The First Industrial Revolution* (1983); C. Nardinelli, *Child Labor and the Industrial Revolution* (1990); I. Pinchbeck, *Women Workers and the Industrial Revolution, 1750–1850* (1930, reprinted 1969); S. Pollard, *Peaceful Conquest: The Industrialization of Europe, 1760–1970* (1981); E. P. Thompson, *The Making of the English Working Class* (1964); P. Stearns, *The Industrial Revolution in World History* (1993); L. Tilly & J. Scott, *Women, Work and Family* (1978).

For additional sources on the Industrial Revolution, see:
http://history.evansville.net/industry.html

Chapter 20

The American and French revolutionaries skillfully appealed to the ideas of citizenship, equality before the law, and the rights of man as central components of national identity. Initially, nationalism was situated within the broader context of human freedom. By the second half of the nineteenth century, however, nationalism had become an exclusive rather than an inclusive phenomenon. New nation-states emerged, with leaders accentuating the unique cultural features of the citizenry. Historians have emphasized the role played by conservatives in redefining nationalism in this more parochial manner.

R. F. Bensel, *Yankee Leviathan: The Origins of Central State Authority in America* (1990); D. Blackbourn, *The Long Nineteenth Century: A History of Germany, 1780–1918* (1998); G. Chapman, *The Dreyfus Affair: A Reassessment* (1955); F. J. Coppa, *The Wars of Italian Independence* (1992); G. Craig, *Germany, 1866–1945* (1978); S. Elwitt, *The Making of the Third Republic: Class and Politics in France, 1868–1884* (1975); R. A. Kann, *The Multinational Empire, 1875–1914* (1950); W. B. Lincoln, *The Great Reforms: Autocracy, Bureaucracy, and the Politics of Change in Imperial Russia* (1990); G. Mosse, *The Crisis of German Ideology* (1964); B. F. Pauley, *The Habsburg Legacy, 1867–1939* (1972); O. Pflanze, *Bismarck and the Development of Germany,* 3 vols. (1990); H. Rogger, *Russia in the Age of Modernization and Revolution, 1881–1917* (1983); A. Sked, *The Decline and Fall of the Habsburg Empire, 1815–1918* (1989); D. M. Smith, *The Making of Italy, 1796–1870* (1968); N. Stone, *Europe Transformed* (1984); J. P. Taylor, *The Struggle for Mastery in Europe, 1848–1918* (1974); T. Zeldin, *France, 1848–1945,* 2 vols. (1973, 1977).

Helpful scholarly analysis of the Victorian era is available at:
http://www.victoriandatabase.com

Chapter 21

The imperial expansion of the West during the late nineteenth century sharply accelerated a process that began just prior to 1500. Europe's industrial power facilitated the new age of empire in Africa and Asia, while Western cultural developments, especially ideas concerning race, strengthened arguments in favor of empire. The impact of Western ideas in a global setting, and the incongruity between European democratic politics and colonial administration, are topics that have interested scholars of this period.

C. Allen, *The Human Christ: The Search for the Historical Jesus* (1998); F. Baumer, *Modern European Thought* (1977); P. Bowler, *Evolution: The History of an Idea* (1989); O. Chadwick, *The Secularization of the European Mind in the Nineteenth Century* (1975); A. Danto, *Nietzsche as Philosopher* (1965); M. Doyle, *Empires* (1986); A. Desmond & J. Moore, *Darwin* (1992); B. Farrington, *What Darwin Really Said* (1966); P. Gay, *Freud: A Life for Our Time* (1988); J. C. Greene, *The Death of Adam* (1961); E. Hobsbawm, *The Age of Empire, 1875–1914* (1987); T. Pakenham, *The Scramble for Africa* (1991); A. Hochschild, *King Leopold's Ghost: A Story of Greed, Terror, and Heroism in Colonial Africa* (1999); G. Fredrickson, *Racism: A Short History* (2003); P. Roazen, *Freud's Political and Social Thought* (1968); R. Stromberg, *European Intellectual History Since 1789* (1986); N. Wilson, *God's Funeral* (1999).

Primary sources from the age of imperialism can be found at:
http://www.fordham.edu/halsall/mod/modsbook36.html

Chapter 22

Western Europe's global dominance was short-lived. At the start of the twentieth century Europe's great powers afforded their citizens a quality of life that could scarcely be imagined one century earlier. However, four years of devastating warfare shattered the self-confidence of the West, undermining economic security and calling into question many of the optimistic assumptions about human rationality first articulated during the Enlightenment.

V. Dedijer, *The Road to Sarajevo* (1966); F. Fischer, *Germany's Aims in the First World War* (1967); S. Fitzpatrick, *The Russia Revolution, 1917–1932* (1994); P. Fussell, *The Great War and Modern Memory* (1975); J. Winter, *Sites of Memory, Sites of Mourning: The Great War in European Cultural History* (1998); M. Gilbert, *The First World War* (1994); O. Hale, *The Great Illusion, 1900–1914* (1971); L. Hart, *The Real War, 1914–1918* (1964); H. Holborn, *The Political Collapse of Europe* (1951); J. Jole, *The Origins of the First World War* (1984); J. Keegan, *The First World War* (1999); J. Keynes, *The Economic Consequences of the Peace* (1920); L. Lafore, *The Long Fuse* (1971); A. Mayer, *The Politics and Diplomacy of Peacemaking* (1967); H. Nicholson, *Peacemaking* (1965); K. Robbins, *The First World War* (1984); D. Stevenson, *The First World War and International Politics* (1988); A. Walworth, *Wilson and His Peacemakers* (1986); J. Williams, *The Homefronts: Britain, France, and Germany, 1914–1918* (1972); J. Winter, *The Experience of World War I* (1988).

Documents related to the rise of Fascism can be found at:
http://www.lib.byu.edu/~rdh/eurodocs/germ/1945. html

Chapter 23

The democratic liberal tradition was placed squarely on the defensive during the years between World War I and World War II. A successful communist revolution in Russia, the emergence of authoritarian rule in Spain and Japan, and the ominous rise of Fascism in Italy and Germany challenged the viability of responsible self-government around the world. Scholars have examined the crisis of Western liberal values during these years in a variety of studies that range from the more traditional fields of diplomatic and political history, to more recent efforts in cultural and social studies.

K. D. Bracher, *The German Dictatorship* (1970); I. Kershaw, *Hitler: 1889–1936 Hubris* (1998) and *Hitler: 1936–1945 Nemesis* (2000); R. J. B. Bosworth, *Mussolini's Italy: Life Under the Fascist Dictatorship* (2007); R. Conquest, *The Great Terror: Stalin's Purges of the Thirties* (1968); I. Deutscher, *Stalin: A Political Biography* (1967); S. Fitzpatrick, *Stalin's Peasants: Resistance and Survival in the Russian Village After Collectivization* (1994); K. Galbraith, *The Great Crash* (1979); N. Greene, *From Versailles to Vichy: The Third Republic, 1919–1940* (1970); R.

Hamilton, *Who Voted for Hitler?* (1982); M. Jackson, *Fallen Sparrows: The International Brigades in the Spanish Civil War* (1994); B. Kent, *The Spoils of War: The Politics, Economics, and Diplomacy of Reparations, 1918–1932* (1993); C. Kindleberger, *The World in Depression, 1929–1939* (1986); M. Kitchen, *Europe Between the Wars: A Political History* (1988); E. Nolte, *Three Faces of Fascism* (1965); S. Payne, *A History of Fascism, 1914–1945* (1995); D. Peukert, *Inside Nazi Germany: Conformity, Opposition, and Racism in Everyday Life* (1987); D. P. Silverman, *Reconstructing Europe After the Great War* (1982); D. M. Smith, *Mussolini* (1982); R. J. Sontag, *A Broken World, 1919–1939* (1971); E. G. Walters, *The Other Europe: Eastern Europe to 1945* (1988); R. Tucker, *Stalin in Power* (1990).

Documents related to the rise of Fascism can be found at:
http://www.lib.byu.edu/~rdh/eurodocs/germ/1945. html

Chapter 24

The massive destruction of World War II effectively put an end to Europe's position of global dominance. Shattered economies, demoralized civilian populations, and the moral turpitude of the Holocaust left Europe in a state of dependency in 1945. Yet the war also marked the triumph of liberal democratic principles over a hate-filled Nazi world view. On the home front, the war transformed the role of women in the workplace, energized whole populations around a broad set of humane values associated with the Enlightenment tradition, and fostered a strong movement in favor of international cooperation.

R. Adams, *British Politics and Foreign Policy in the Age of Appeasement, 1935–1939* (1993); P. Bell, *The Origins of the Second World War in Europe* (1986); B. Calber, *The Battle of Britain* (1962); B. Collier, *The War in the Far East* (1970); T. Des Pres, *The Survivors* (1976); H. Feis, *Churchill, Roosevelt, Stalin* (1957); A. Iriye, *Power and Culture: The Japanese-American War, 1941–1945* (1981); J. Keegan, *The Second World War* (1989); M. Knox, *Mussolini Unleashed* (1982); A. Beevor, *The Battle for Spain: The Spanish Civil War 1936–1939* (2006); H. Liddell Hart, *History of the Second World War* (1970); M. Marrus, *The Holocaust in History* (1987); C. Browning, *The Origins of the Final Solution* (2004); R. Overy, *Why the Allies Won* (1995); J. Remak, *The Origins of the Second World War* (1976); W. Rock, *British Appeasement in the 1930s* (1977); M. Sherwin, *A World Destroyed: The Atomic Bomb and the Grand Alliance* (1975); D. Watts, *How War Came* (1989); G. Weinberg, *A World at Arms: A Global History of World War II* (1994); G. Weinberg, *The Foreign Policy of Hitler's Germany*, 2 vols. (1970, 1979); G. Wright, *The Ordeal of Total War, 1939–1945* (1968); E. Wiesel, *Night* (1958).

Primary sources from World War II are available at:
http://www.yale.edu/lawweb/wwii/wwii.htm

Chapter 25

The Grand Alliance of the United States, Great Britain, and the Soviet Union during World War II raised expectations that a new international order might be realized after the defeat of Nazi Germany and imperial Japan. However, despite the fact that a new international organization, the United Nations, was established in 1945, deep ideological differences between the world's two "superpowers" led to the emergence of a "Cold War" that lasted until the late 1980s. While European decolonization led to the emergence of new nation-states around the globe, many of these states were alternately courted and coerced by the superpowers into joining the Cold War struggle. Recent scholarship has examined the overall cost of this rivalry in terms of lost opportunities in the areas of education, medicine, food production, environmental protection, and balanced economic development in the non-Western world.

M. Beschloss, *The Crisis Years: Kennedy and Khrushchev, 1960–1963* (1991); L. Davis, *The Cold War Begins* (1974); A. DePorte, *Europe Between the Superpowers* (1979); L. Freedman, *The Evolution of Nuclear Strategy* (1989); J. Gaddis, *The United States and the Origins of the Cold War, 1941–1947* (1972); J. Gaddis, *We Know Now: Rethinking the Cold War* (1998); R. Garthoff, *The Great Transition: American-Soviet Relations and the End of the Cold War* (1994); J. Gimbel, *The Origins of the Marshall Plan* (1976); L. Halle, *The Cold War as History* (1967); S. Karnow, *Vietnam: A History* (1984); M. Young, *The Vietnam Wars 1945–1990* (1991); P. Kenez, *A History of the Soviet Union from the Beginning to the End* (1999); W. LaFeber, *America, Russia, and the Cold War* (1976); G. Partos, *The World that Came in from the Cold* (1993); A. Rubenstein, *Soviet Foreign Policy Since World War II* (1981); M. Walker, *The Cold War* (1993); T. Judt, *Postwar: A History of Europe Since 1945* (2005); E. J. Hobsbawm, *The Age of Extremes: A History of the World, 1914–1991* (2001).

Cold War documents and an additional bibliography are available at:
http://wwics.si.edu/index.cfm?fuseaction= topics_id=1409

Chapter 26

Despite being eclipsed by the United States and the Soviet Union after World War II, Western Europe rebounded quickly thanks to massive economic aid from the United States. Economic stagnation in Soviet-controlled areas contrasted sharply with high standards of living in the democratic West. The end of the Soviet Union and the reintegration of Europe has raised the prospect of greater economic, military, and political union in Europe. Europe stands poised as one of the world's great economic powerhouses. During the last decade, an abundance of literature has emerged on the New Europe.

E. Bottome, *The Balance of Terror: Nuclear Weapons and the Illusions of Security, 1945–1985* (1986); A. Brown, *The Gorbachev Factor* (1996); J. Chafetz & A. Dworkin, *Female Revolt: Women's Movement in World Historical Perspective* (1986); D. Hiro, *Holy Wars: The Rise of Islamic Fundamentalism* (1989); R. Khalidi, *Resurrecting Empire: Western Footprints and America's Perilous Path in the Middle East* (2004); A. Rashid, *The Taliban: Militant Islam, Oil and Fundamentalism in Central Asia* (2000); L. Johnson, *Central Europe: Enemies and Neighbors and Friends* (1996); J. Keep, *Last of the Empires: A History of the Soviet Union, 1945–1991* (1995); P. Kennedy, *Preparing for the Twenty-First Century* (1993); M. Milani, *The Making of Iran's Islamic Revolution* (1994); J. Newhouse, *Europe Adrift* (1997); R. Pells, *Not Like Us: How Europeans Have Loved, Hated, and Transformed American Culture Since World War II* (1997); D. Remnick, *Lenin's Tomb* (1993); L. Silber & A. Little, *Yugoslavia: Death of a Nation* (1996); G. Stokes, *The Walls Came Tumbling Down: The Collapse of Communism in Eastern Europe* (1993); P. Kenney, *A Carnival of Revolution: Central Europe 1989* (2002); H. Turner, *Germany from Partition to Reunification* (1992); S. Weart, *Nuclear Fear: A History of Images* (1988); D. Yergin, *The Prize: The Epic Quest for Oil, Money, and Power* (1992).

For recent scholarly articles on the European Union, see:
http://www.mtholyoke.edu/acad/intrel/eu.htm

Index

Note: Page numbers ending in "f" refer to figures. Page numbers ending in "m" refer to maps. Page numbers ending in "t" refer to tables.

A

1984 (Orwell), 686
Aachen, 222, 223, 280
Abbas, 205
Abbasid dynasty, 205, 214, 222–223, 225, 238–239
Abd al-Rahman, 238
Abdul Hamid II (Ottoman Empire), 566, 568
Abelard, Peter, 270–271
Abraham, 51–52, 53, 54, 56, 198
Absolutism, 390
    France, 399–404
    Russia, 408–409
Abu Bakr, 201, 204
Abyssinia, 551
Academic guilds, 271–273
Academie des Sciences, 423
Acharnians, The, 115
Achilles, 62, 70, 122
Acropolis, 94, 95, 111
Actium, 144
Act of Supremacy, 370
Adams, Abigail, 440, 455
Adams, John, 440, 455, 470
Adelard of Bath, 268
Administration. *See* Bureaucracy
Adrianople, 190
Adriatic Sea, 261
Adultery, 154, 170
Advancement of Learning, The (Bacon), 428
Aegean civilizations, 62–64
    Aegean Dark Age, 70–72
    Athens, 81–84
    Minoans, 64–67
    Mycenaeans, 67–70
    Persian Wars, 84–88
    Sparta, 79–81
    See also Hellenic era; Hellenistic era; *specific civilizations*
Aegean Dark Age, 70–72
Aegean Sea, 62, 64, 129, 195
Aeneas, 129, 158
Aeneid, 158
Aeschylus, 114
Aëtius, 193, 210
Afghanistan, 608, 717, 729
Africa (poem), 332
Africa
    decolonization of, 696–698
    new imperialism and, 576–578, 579, 581–584, 588
    Portuguese exploration of, 348
    postcolonial migrations from, 698, 699, 700m, 701
    slave trade in, 457–458
    See also specific countries
African soldiers, in World War I, 613–614
Afrika Korps, 663, 675
Agadir, 608
Against the Robbing and Murdering Hordes of Peasants, 360
Agamemnon, 63, 67, 70

Age of Anxiety, 294–296, 320
    Middle East turmoil and, 300–305
    natural environment, challenges from, 296–300
    spiritual crises, 305–311
    wars, 312–319
Age of Reason. *See* Enlightenment
Aghlabid dynasty, 225, 238–239
Agincourt, 317, 318
Agriculture, 4, 31
    1920s, 638
    Aegean civilizations, 64, 71, 72, 79, 81, 82
    Augustan era, 153
    early modern era, 393–395
    Egyptian civilization, 23–24
    Enlightenment, 449
    famines, 296–297
    Industrial Revolution and, 497–501
    medieval Europe, 229–231, 261, 346–347
    prehistoric cultures, 9, 11, 12*m*
    Roman Empire, 138
    Scientific Revolution and, 429–430
    Second Intermediate Period (Egypt), 37–38
    slave trade, 457
    Soviet Union, 651–653
    Sumer, 14, 15, 23
    World War I, 620
Agrippina the Younger, 161
Agronomy, 430
A'isha, 200
Akhenaten, 40–41, 42, 43, 54
Akhetaten, 40
Akkad, 22, 23, 34
Alaric, 190, 191
Albania/Albanians, 609, 644, 663, 743, 744
Albert of Brandenburg, 357
Alberti, Leon Battista, 324, 334
Albigensians, 277
Alboin, 214
Alcibiades, 99–100
Alcmaeonids, 83
Alcuin, 210, 233–234
Alembert, Jean le Rond d', 446
Alexander I (Hungary), 644
Alexander I (Russia), 483, 520, 521, 523
Alexander II (Russia), 564, 572
Alexander III (Russia), 564
Alexander IV (Persia), 125
Alexander VI (pope), 367
Alexander the Great, 25, 118, 121–125
Alexandra (wife of Nicholas II), 620
Alexandria, 126, 128–129, 156
Alexius Comnenus (Byzantine Empire), 255, 258
Alfred the Great (Wessex), 243
Algebra, 268
Algeria/Algerians, 613–614, 664, 675, 697, 701, 741
Ali, 204
Alighieri, Dante, 330–331
Alimenta, 165–166
Al-Khwarizmi, 268
Allah, 197, 198–199, 200, 202
Alliance system, in World War I, 606–609
Al-Mansur, 254
Al Qaeda, 745

Al-Rashid, Harun, 239, 241
Alsace, 558, 627
Altar of Peace, 148, 150, 158
Amarna Period, 40–44
Ambrose of Milan (bishop), 231
Amenhotep III, 40
Amenhotep IV, 40
Americanization, 569, 729
American Revolution, 462–470, 488
American War for Independence, 468–469
Americas, slave trade in, 457. *See also* Latin America; *specific countries*
Amish, 363
Amorites, 23, 34, 37
Amphitheaters, 112–114
Amritsar, 616
Amun-Ra, 40, 42
Anabaptists, 363, 380
Anatolia, 11, 45, 627
Anaximander, 102
Anaximenes, 102, 105
Ancient Greece, 25, 57. *See also* Aegean civilizations; Hellenic era; Hellenistic era
Andropov, Yuri, 717
Anesthetics, 500
Angevin Empire, 247
Angles, 191, 216
Anglican Church (Church of England), 371, 382, 384, 386, 404, 405, 434, 458, 561
Anglo-Saxons, 216, 217, 233, 243, 245
Angola, 717
Ankhesenpaaten, 42, 43
Anne of Cleves, 371
Anomie, 594
Anschluss, 659
Anthony (Egyptian hermit), 188
Anthropology, 594
Antiballistic missiles (ABMs), 711
Antibiotics, 731
Antigone, 114
Antigonus the One-Eyed, 125
Antiochus III, 137–138
Anti-Semitism, 413
    Catholic Church and, 740
    German nationalism and, 571, 572
    Hitler, Adolf, 646
    Holocaust, 668–670
    Nazi Germany, 646, 648, 649–650
    Third French Republic, 559, 560
Antiseptics, 500
Antoinette, Marie, 456, 477–478
Antoninus Pius, 167
Anu, 15, 21
ANZUS, 704
Apennine Mountains, 130*m*
Aphrodite, 133
Apocalyptic preaching, 184–185
Apollo, 133, 260
Appeasement (1933–1939), 658–661
Aqueducts, 155
Aquinas, Thomas, 274, 421
Aquitaine, 247, 251
Arabia, 197–198. *See also* Islam; Muslims/Muslim Empire
Aragon, 413
Aral Sea, 302
Aramaeans, 47
Arcadius, 190

Archaeology, 594
Archaic period, in Hellenic era, 72–76
Archaic states, 13
Archetypes, 593
Archimedes of Syracuse, 128
Architecture
  Augustan era, 155
  Bauhaus School, 637, 638
  Enlightenment, 459–461
  European High Middle Ages,
    278–283
  Hellenic era, 112–113
  Hellenistic era, 126
  Muslim Empire, 204
  Renaissance, 333, 335–336, 339
  See also Infrastructure; Pyramids;
    Temples; *specific buildings and*
    types of architecture
Arch of Constantine, 187
Archons, 81, 82
Arden, Mary, 378
Areopagus, 81, 82, 83
Ares, 133
Arian Christians, 191, 211, 214
Aristarchus of Samos, 128, 424
Aristocracy
  Athens, 81, 82, 83
  Black Death and, 300
  conservatism and, 524
  Europe (early modern era), 392–393
  Homeric era, 72
  Hundred Years' War and, 315
  Pliny the Elder and Pliny the
    Younger, 164–165
  Roman Empire, 169
  Roman hereditary succession,
    159–163
  See also Hereditary succession;
    specific individuals and dynasties
Aristocratic *salons*, 446–447
Aristophanes, 115, 126
Aristotle, 109–110, 121, 273–274, 309,
  421, 422
Arius, 187
Arkwright, Richard, 502
Armenia, 49, 203, 302
Armies. *See* War/militarization
Armor, 315
Arms race. *See* Nuclear arms race
Arouet, Francois Marie. *See* Voltaire
Artemis, 133
Arthur (King Arthur), 216–217
Articles of Confederation, 469
Artifacts
  archaic states, 13
  prehistoric, 7
  Sumerian, 5, 19
Artillery, 342
Artistic life, Hellenic era, 101–115
Art of Love, The, 159
Artois, count of, 475
Arts
  Augustan era, 155–159
  Bauhaus School, 637, 638
  Black Death and, 299
  Byzantine Empire, 196
  Enlightenment, 459–461
  European High Middle Ages, 278–283
  Hellenic era, 110–115
  Hellenistic era, 126–127
  Italian Renaissance, 330–338
  Medici family and, 328
  Minoans, 66
  modernism, 597–600
  Muslim Empire, 204
  new imperialism and, 595, 597–600

Northern Renaissance, 339–340
prehistoric, 7–9
Roman Empire, 149, 170–172
Spanish Golden Age, 375–376
Sumerian, 5, 19
Asceticism, 188–189, 217
Ashurnasirpal II, 47
Asia
  Cold War events and issues in,
    701–707
  decolonization of, 694, 696
  new imperialism and, 578, 584–588
  World War II, 672–674
  See also specific countries
Aspasia, 96–97
Assassinations, Alexander II (Russia), 564
Assignats, 474
Assurbanipal, 48, 50
Assyria, 34, 47–48, 49–50, 56, 84
Astrology, 36
Astronomy, 36, 128, 424–427
Asturias, 214
Aten, 40–41, 42, 54
Athena, 94, 133
Athens, 81–84, 116
  intellectual and artistic life, 101–115
  Macedonia and, 121
  Peloponnesian War, 94–101, 120
  Persian Wars, 84, 86, 87–88, 93
Atlantic, battle of, 675
Atlantic exploration, 346–351
Atlee, Clement, 688
Atomic bombs, 594, 677–678, 684. *See*
  also Nuclear arms race; Nuclear
  threats
Attica, 88, 95, 97, 98, 100
Attila, 191, 193
Attributes, 269–270
Augsleich, 562
Augustan era, 150–159
Augustine of Hippo, 180, 182, 191,
  231, 233
Augustus, 150–159, 166m, 169–170, 173
Auschwitz, 668
Australia, 613, 614, 674m, 704
Austrasia, 211, 215–216, 218, 223
Austria
  Cold War and, 701
  Nazi Germany and, 659–660
  Treaty of Versailles and, 627
Austrian Empire (Habsburg
    Empire), 415
  anti-Semitism in, 572
  Catherine the Great and, 410
  Charlemagne and, 220
  Charles V and, 361
  Congress System and, 520–523
  decline of, 562–568
  dual monarchy, 562–563
  early modern era, 415
  French absolutism and, 399,
    402, 403
  French Revolution and, 475, 478
  German Confederation and,
    562–563
  German war (nineteenth century),
    552–553
  Habsburg-Valois wars, 368–369
  Holy Alliance, 522–523
  Italian unification and, 548, 550
  Joseph II, 452–453
  Napoleon and, 483, 485, 520
  Napoleon III and, 558
  Netherlands, 369, 373–374, 414
  Otto I and, 249
  Poland and, 413

Quintuple Alliance, 522
Renaissance, 338–339
revolution (1830–1832), 527–528
revolution (1848), 530, 532
Thirty Years' War, 379–380
Treaty of Versailles and, 625–627
voting rights, 515
War of Austrian Succession,
  407–408
War of the Spanish Succession, 414
  See also World War I
Authoritarianism, in Spain and eastern
  Europe, 643–644, 645
Authority
  Europe (early modern era), 392
  reason and, 270–271
Autocracy, 146
Autonomy, personal, 524
Auxiliaries, 152
Avaris, 38
Avars, 220
Avicenna, 273
Avignon, 307, 308
Axial Age, 57
Ay, 42, 43
Ayyubid Empire, 302
Azerbaijan, 692
Azores, 348
Aztecs, 351

B

Babylon, 22, 23, 34–36, 45, 50, 53, 123,
  124
Babylonian captivity, 307
Bacchus, 133
Bacon, Francis, 428, 447–448
Bacon, Roger, 421
Baden, 529
Badoglio, Pietro, 675
Bagehot, Walter, 555
Baghdad, 205, 239, 302, 304
Baines, Edward, 514
Baldwin, Stanley, 640
Balfour Declaration, 613
Balkans, 153, 194, 223, 241. *See also*
  specific countries
Bank of France, 482
Banks, Great Depression and,
  638–639
Barbados, 406
Barbarians, 75, 190
Barcelona, 220
Barracks Emperors, 168, 173–174, 176,
  185
Barter, 182
Barth, Karl, 739
Basel, 311, 364
Basil I (Byzantine Empire), 242
Basil II (Byzantine Empire), 242
Basilicas, 279–280
Basil of Caesarea, 189
Basilikon Doron (Royal Gift)
  (James I), 398
Basques, 220
Bastille, fall of, 473
Baths, in Rome, 155
Batista, Fulgencio, 708
Battle of Bouvines, 285, 286
Battle of Britain, 663
Battle of Crécy, 295, 313
Battle of Lepanto, 412
Battle of Masurian Lakes, 613
Battle of Naseby, 385
Battle of Plassey, 408
Battle of Tannenberg, 613
Battle of the Atlantic, 675

Battle of the Bulge, 676
Battle of the Coral Sea, 674
Battle of the Marne, 610
Battle of Waterloo, 485, 518, 520, 521
Bauhaus architecture, 637, 638
Bavaria, 249, 289, 530, 646
Bay of Pigs invasion, 708–709
Bayle, Pierre, 444, 445
Beccaria, Cesare, 450, 451
Becket, Thomas, 284–285
Beckett, Samuel, 686
Becquerel, Henri, 596
Bede, 233
Bedouins, 197
Beethoven, Ludwig van, 537
Beijing, 672
Belgium
    Congress System and, 521
    European unity and, 725
    French wars against, 402, 403
    imperialism, 583
    Industrial Revolution, 503, 513
    postcolonial migrations to, 698–699
    revolution in, 526
    Spain and, 415
    voting rights, 515
    World War I, 610
    World War I aftermath, 637
    World War II, 662, 676
    World War II aftermath, 687
Belgrade, 607
Belisarius, 194
Bellini, Gentile, 342, 343
Benedict of Nursia, 189, 231
Benedict XI (pope), 307
Benedictines, 251, 252–253, 274
Ben-Gurion, David, 693
Bentham, Jeremy, 540
Berber Muslims, 225, 238, 239
Berengar of Tours, 269
Berlin, 676, 690, 691
Berlin Airlift (1948), 691
Berlin Conference, 583–584
Berlin Olympics (1936), 648
Berlin Wall, 699, 719
Bern, 339
Bernard of Chartres, 266
Bernard of Clairvaux, 278
Bernini, Gianlorenzo, 336
Bernstein, Eduard, 561
Bible, 51–58
    Age of Anxiety and, 309
    Anabaptists and, 363
    Calvinists and, 364
    Darwinism and, 591
    Genesis, 52
    humanism and, 341
    Islam and, 202
    King James Version, 382, 398
    Lutheran Reformation and, 357, 358–359
    Noah's ark, 16
    Vulgate, 231
    See also New Testament
Biblical faith, 56–58
Bill of Rights (England), 405
Bill of Rights (United States), 469
Bin Laden, Osama, 729
Biology, 430–431, 589–591
Bishops, 186, 187–188
Bismarck, Otto von, 546, 548, 551–554, 555–557, 566, 583, 608
Bithynia, 165
Black Death, 297–300, 429
Black Friars. *See* Dominicans
Black Sea, 195, 261, 409, 410

Black-figure pottery, 111
Blair, Tony, 727, 730
Blake, William, 536, 537
Blanc, Louis, 529
Blanche of Castile, 287
Blatic Sea, 261
Blenheim, 402–403
Blitzkrieg, 661–662, 665–666
Blum, Leon, 639
Boccaccio, Giovanni, 330–331, 332
Boers, 583–584
Boethius, 193, 231, 269
Bohemia, 339, 380, 530
Boleyn, Anne, 370, 371, 373
Bolivar, Simon, 486, 487*m*
Bolivia, 486
Bologna, 272
Bolshevik Revolution, 621–624
Bonaparte, Jerome, 483
Bonaparte, Joseph, 483, 486
Bonaparte, Louis, 483
Bonaparte, Napoleon. *See* Napoleon Bonaparte
Bonaventure, Saint, 278
Bondone, Giotto di, 336
Boniface VIII (pope), 306–307, 311
Bon Marché (department store), 508
Book of Common Prayer, The, 371
Book of Ezra, 56
Book of Kells, 217
Book of the Courtier, The, 334
Bordeaux, 312
Borgia, Cesare, 367
Bosnia/Bosnians, 606–607, 608, 644, 743
Boston Massacre, 467
Boston Tea Party, 468
Boulanger, George, 559
Boule, 82, 83
Bourbons, 377, 486, 520, 522
Bourgeoisie, 263. *See also* Middle class
Bouts, Dirk, 338
Bouvines, battle of, 285, 286
Boyle, Robert, 418, 432
"Boyle Lectures," 418
Brahe, Tycho, 425–426
Brain, Hellenistic-era science and, 128
Bramante, Donato, 336
Brandenburg, 410
Brazil, 406, 486
Brethren of the Common Life, 340–341
Brezhnev, Leonid, 711, 717
Bribes, in Augustan era, 157
Bridges. *See* Infrastructure
Bridget of Sweden, 307
Britain, 191
    American Revolution and, 462–470
    appeasement (1933–1939), 658–661
    Bolshevik Revolution and, 622
    colonialism (post-World War II), 705
    Congress System and, 521–522, 523
    constitutional reform in, 533–536
    Crimean War, 548, 558, 564
    decolonization, 694, 697
    democracy in, 560–562
    elementary education, 513
    empirical wars and global markets (early modern era), 406, 407–408
    European Union and, 725–726
    French Revolution and, 478
    Great Depression, 639, 640
    Industrial Revolution, 449, 496–497, 499, 501, 502, 503, 507, 509, 512
    Iraq war (2003–), 729, 730
    Israel, creation of, 692–693

Julio-Claudians and, 161
League of Nations, 628–629
medieval, 214, 216–217
Monroe Doctrine, 486
Napoleon and, 480, 483, 485, 520
NATO, 701
North American colonies, 449
nuclear arms race, 694
occupation zones (post-World War II), 690
Opium Wars, 585–586
postcolonial migrations to, 698, 699, 701
Quintuple Alliance, 522
right-wing movements in, 649
Suez Canal, 710
Treaty of Versailles, 625–628
U.S. industrialization and, 569
Vietnam, 705
voting rights, 515
War of the Spanish Succession, 414
women's movement and, 737
World War I aftermath, 634, 635, 636, 637
World War II aftermath, 688
See also England; World War I; World War II
Britannicus, 161
British East India Company, 584, 585
British imperialism, 587*m*
    Africa, 576, 581, 583–584
    China, 585–586
    India, 584–585
    India, 614–615
British Malaya. *See* Malaya
British Parliament. *See* English Parliament
Britons, 214
Brittany, 216
Bronze, 13
Bronze Age, 66. *See also* Minoan civilization
Brown, Ford Madox, 598
Brown, Gordon, 727
Broz, Josip. *See* Tito
Brunelleschi, Filippo, 335, 337
Brunhild, 215–216, 217, 233
Bruning, Heinrich, 644
Bruno, Giordano, 434
Brusilov, Aleksei, 620
Brutus, 144
Buber, Martin, 739
Bubonic plague, 297–300
Buchenwald, 670
Buckingham Palace, 663
Buddha, 57
Buddhism, 420
Buildings. *See* Architecture; Infrastructure; *specific buildings*
Bukharin, Nikolai, 652
Bulgaria, 609, 613, 627, 644, 676, 719
Bulgars, 241, 242
Bulge, battle of, 676
Burckhardt, Jacob, 555
Bureaucracy
    Augustan era, 153
    Byzantine Empire, 196
    France (early modern era), 402
    Julio-Claudians, 160
    Ottoman Empire, 411, 412
    Roman Empire, 174
    Tiberius and, 170
Burgundians, 191, 211, 318, 319
Burials. *See* Tombs
Burke, Edmund, 476–477, 523
Burma, 674
Bush, George W., 721–722, 729, 745

Butterfield, Herbert, 422
Buyids, 239
Byblos, 55
Byzantine Empire, 193–197, 206
　Age of Anxiety, 300, 301
　Charlemagne and, 221–223
　Constantinople, 241–242
　Germany and, 249
　Islam and, 203
　medieval Italy and, 214
　medieval, 241–242
　Muslims and, 239, 241
　Ottoman Empire and, 341–342
　trade, 261
　Venice and, 326

C

Cabot, John, 349, 351
Caernarfon Castle, 287
Caesar, Julius, 142–143, 150, 155
Cairo, 239
Calais, 319
Calculus, 128
Calicut, 348
California, 406
Caligula, 160, 161
Caliphates/caliphs, 201, 204–205, 238–241
Calisthenes, 122
Callias, 97
Calonne, Charles Alexandre de, 471
Calvin, John, 363–365
Calvinism, 364–365, 371, 379, 380
Cambridge University, 561
Camelot, 216–217
Campania, 129, 130*m*
Camus, Albert, 686, 687
Canaan, 54
Canaanites, 20, 54
Canada, 349, 351, 406, 448, 613, 614
Canals, 503
Canary islands, 348
Cancer, 732
Candied (Voltaire), 445
Cannons, 315, 342, 347
Canterbury, 233, 284–285
Canterbury Tales, The, 332
Canton, 585
Cape Colony, 521
Cape of Good Hope, 414
Capet, Hugh, 248
Cape Town, 583
Capitalism, 262
　Bolshevik Revolution and, 622–623
　British democracy and, 562
　China market reforms, 723
　Erfurt Program and, 557
　Great Depression, 638
　industrial, 494
　Marx, Karl, 542, 543
　new imperialism and, 578–579
　power versus principle, 711
　World War II aftermath, 687
　See also Cold War; Industrial Revolution
Capri, 160
Caracella, 169
Carcassonne, France, 263
Cardinals (Catholic), 307, 308
Caribbean islands, 349, 351, 406–407, 457, 485
Carloman, 219
Carnegie, Andrew, 569
Carolingian era, 217–225, 226*m*, 231
Carolingian Renaissance, 233–235

Carter, Howard, 42
Carthage, 135, 136, 138, 191, 204–205
Carthaginian empire, 135, 136–137, 138
Carthusian Order, 274
Cartier, Jacques, 351
Cartography, 105
Casas, Ramon, 519
Caspian Sea, 302
Cassiodorus, 193
Cassirer, Ernst, 655
Cassius, 144
Castel, Etienne de, 316
Castiglione, Baldassare, 334, 335
Castro, Fidel, 705, 708–709, 710, 722
Çatahöyük, 11–13
Catalonia, 413
Cathars, 277–278, 286, 305
Cathedral of Cordoba, 239
Catherine of Aragon, 369–370
Catherine of Siena, 307
Catherine the Great (Russia), 394–395, 410
Catholic Church, 196
　Anabaptists and, 363
　Arian Christians and, 211, 214
　Aristotle and, 274
　Bismarck, Otto von, 556, 557
　Calvin, John, 363, 364, 365
　Carolingian era, 218, 219–220
　Congress System and, 522
　early modern era, 397
　England (early modern era), 405
　Enlightenment and, 447–448
　European High Middle Ages, 269
　French religious wars and, 376–377
　French Revolution and, 474–475
　globalization and, 739–740
　humanism and, 341
　Italian Fascism and, 643
　Italian unification and, 548, 550, 551
　Louis XIV, 400
　Lutheran Reformation and, 357–358, 361
　Merovingian Kingdom, 211
　Napoleon and, 481
　nation-states and, 548
　Nazi Germany, 650
　Northern Ireland, 561
　Ottoman Empire and, 343, 344
　Reformation-era politics and, 372–377
　revolution (1830–1832), 526, 527
　revolution (1848), 531
　Richelieu, Cardinal, 399, 400
　Scientific Revolution and, 424–425, 434, 436
　Solidarity and, 719
　superstition and, 436–437
　Swiss Reformation and, 362
　Third French Republic and, 559
　Thirty Years' War, 379–380
　Tudors and, 370, 371
　Visigoths and, 211, 214
　See also Christianity; Papacy; *specific popes*
Catholic Emancipation Act, 534
Catholic League, 379
Catholic Reformation, 365–368
Cato the Elder, 155
Catullus, 156
Cavaliers, 384
Cavalry, 315
Cave paintings, 8–9
Ceausescu, Nicholae, 719

Celtic tribes, 129
Celts. *See* Romano-Celts
Censorship, in France (Enlightenment), 448
Census data, during Industrial Revolution, 499
Center Party (Germany), 556, 557
Central America, 349
Central Committee of the Communist Party, 651, 652
Central Europe, 408–411
Central Intelligence Agency (CIA), 692, 731
Centralized states, 392, 396–399
Central Powers, 613
Ceres, 133
Cervantes, Miguel de, 375–376
Ceuta, 348
Ceylon, 521–522
Cézanne, Paul, 599
Chaeronea, 121
Chalcidice, 97, 99
Chaldaean empire, 50, 52, 53, 56, 84
Chalres of Valois, 313
Chamberlain, Houston Stewart, 580
Chamberlain, Neville, 659–660
Chambers, Ephraim, 445
Chance, 107
Charlemagne, 208, 210, 224
　Aachen churh, 280
　bust of, 233
　Carolingian empire, 217, 219–223, 224
　Carolingian Renaissance, 234–235
　European reorganization, 242–243
　statue of, 209
Charles Albert (Piedmont), 531
Charles I (England), 383–384, 404
Charles II (England), 386, 404, 405
Charles II (Spain), 414
Charles IV (France), 313
Charles IV (Germany), 339
Charles V (France), 315, 316
Charles V (Holy Roman Emperor), 358, 359*m*, 360–361, 362, 368–369, 370
Charles VI (Austrian Empire), 415
Charles VI (France), 316, 317, 318
Charles VII (Charles "the Dauphin" of France), 318–319
Charles VIII (France), 328, 368
Charles IX (France), 377, 397
Charles X (France), 525
Charles of Anjou, 288, 290, 340, 368
Charles the Bald, 224
Charles the Simple, 243
Charter of Liberties, 246
Charters, 266–268
Chartism, 536
Chartres Cathedral, 267
Châtelet, Émilie de, 455
Chaucer, Geoffrey, 332
Chauvet Cave, 8
Chechnya, 720, 721, 744
Checks and balances, 469
Cheka. See K.G.B.
Chemical industry, 503
Cheops (Khufu), 28
Chernenko, Constantin, 717
Chiang Kai-shek, 672, 702, 703
Childebert II, 215, 216
Child labor reforms, in Britain, 535
Children
　European unity and, 728
　Industrial Revolution and, 509, 511–512
　Sparta, 79–80

Chile, 486
Chilperic, 215
China
  Black Death and, 298
  Cold War, 702–703
  communist revolution in, 702–703
  Confucius and Lao-tzu, 57
  democracy movement, suppression of, 722–733
  Genghis Khan and, 302
  globalization and, 736
  Huns and, 190
  Industrial Revolution and, 495–496
  innovations in, 347
  Japanese imperialism and, 650–651
  market reforms in, 723
  Muslims and, 205
  new imperialism and, 578, 579, 581, 585–586, 588
  Nixon, Richard M., 710
  nuclear arms race, 694
  Polo, Marco, 302–303
  Portuguese exploration and, 348
  Rome and, 173
  Shang Dynasty, 13
  Soviet Union and, 710
  technological innovations, 421
  Vietnam, 705
  World War I, 613
  World War II, 672, 675, 676, 680
Chirac, Jacques, 727
Chlotar II, 213, 215, 216
Choice, existentialism and, 687
Choruses, 114
Christ. *See* Jesus of Nazareth
Christian missionaries
  Atlantic exploration, 351
  Magyars and, 249
  medieval Europe, 183, 185–186, 189–190, 217, 233
  new imperialism and, 581, 583
Christianity, 51
  Age of Anxiety, spiritual crises during, 305–311
  Alfred the Great, 243
  Arian, 191, 211, 214
  Aristotle and, 110, 273, 274
  Augustine of Hippo, 182
  Black Death and, 298–299
  Byzantine Empire, 195–197, 206, 242
  Carolingian era, 218, 219–220, 225
  church architecture, 278–283
  Cluny, 251
  Darwinism and, 589, 590–591
  dialectics and, 269
  Divine Comedy, The, 331
  Enlightenment and, 448, 458
  European High Middle Ages, 274–278
  Freud, Sigmund, 593
  Germany and, 189–193
  globalization and, 739–740
  Greek language and, 125
  Hroswitha of Gandersheim, 252–253
  Investiture Controversy, 253–254
  Islam and, 202–203, 205, 206–207
  Louis IX (France), 288
  medieval European culture, 231, 232–233, 235
  medieval Germany, 251
  medieval Ireland, 217
  Merovingian Kingdom, 211
  Modern Devotion, 340–341
  nation-states and, 548
  Nazi Germany, 650
  Nero and, 162

  new imperialism and, 581
  Nietzsche, Friedrich, 592
  nominalism and, 270
  Normandy/Normans, 243, 245
  Ottoman Empire and, 343, 344, 346, 566
  Perpetua, Vibia, 180, 182
  Pliny the Younger, 165
  Roman Empire and, 182–189, 206
  Scientific Revolution and, 420–421, 434, 436
  Urban II (pope), 236
  Yugoslavian ethnic cleansing, 742–744
  See also Crusades
Churches, 183, 185–186, 278–283. *See also* Christianity
Churchill, John (duke of Marlborough), 402
Churchill, Winston, 613
  Chamberlain, Neville, 660
  decolonization, 694
  Iron Curtain, 689
  Tehran Conference, 679, 688
  World War II, 656, 663, 664, 671
  World War II aftermath, 687
  Yalta, 679, 688
Church of England (Anglican Church), 371, 382, 384, 386, 404, 405, 434, 458, 561
Church of Holy Wisdom. *See* Hagia Sophia
Church of the Holy Sepulcher, 222
Cicero, 156–157, 329, 330
Cimabue, 336
Cimon, 93
Ciompi Revolt, 328
Cistercians, 274
Cities. *See specific cities and city-states*
Citizenship, 96
  Augustan era, 152
  Hellenic era, 108
  Hellenistic era, 127
  Roman Empire, 169
  See also Democracy; Politics
City-states
  Augustan era, 153
  Italy, 324–326
  See also Athens; *Polis*; Rome; Sparta
Civil Code. *See* Code Napoleon
Civilization, 2
  archaic states, 13
  community and environment, 4, 6, 30–31
  prehistoric cultures, 6–13
  Sumer, 14–23
  timelines, 3, 62
  unity versus divisiveness, 32, 34, 58
  Western civilization, 62, 64, 88
  See also Aegean civilizations; Age of Anxiety; American Revolution; Byzantine Empire; Cold War; Decolonization; Egypt; European High Middle Ages; French Revolution; Hellenic era; Hellenistic era; Ideology; Industrial Revolution; Interwar years (1919–1939); Medieval civilizations; Medieval Europe; Muslims/Muslim Empire; Nation-states; New imperialism; Politics; Reformation; Renaissance; Roman Empire; Rome; Scientific Revolution; War/militarization; World War I; World War II
Civilization and Its Discontents (Freud), 593

Civil War (United States), 568–571
Class conflict, 542
Classical architecture, 282
Classical civilization. *See* Hellenic era
Classical music, 459
Classicism, 112
Claudius, 160–161, 166*m*, 170
Claudius Nero, 160
Cleisthenes, 83–84
Clemenceau, Georges, 559, 626
Clement V (pope), 307
Clement VI (pope), 298
Clement VII (pope), 307, 369, 370
Cleopatra VII, 38, 142, 143, 144
Climate change, during Little Ice Age, 296–297, 429
Clive, Robert, 408
Clocks, 347
Cloisters. *See* Monks/monasticism
Cloning, 732
Clovis, 210, 211–212, 214, 231
Cluniac Reform, 251, 253
Cluny, 251, 255, 274
Coal, 502, 503, 504
Code Napoleon, 482–483, 521
Code of Civil Procedure (France), 482
Code of Hammurabi, 34–36
Cohongs, 585
Colbert, Jean-Baptiste, 402
Cold War, 682, 702*m*
  China, 702–703
  decolonization and, 694–701
  east Asia, 701–702
  Germany and, 689–690
  Israel, creation of, 692–693
  Korean War, 704
  Marshall Plan, 690–691
  NATO and Warsaw Pact, 701
  nuclear arms race, 693–694
  nuclear threats, 708–711
  southeast Asia, 704–705
  Truman Doctrine, 692
  Vietnam War, 705–707
Coleridge, Samuel Taylor, 536
Collectivization, in Soviet Union, 652–653
College of Cardinals, 307, 308
Coloni, 169
Colonial elite, education of, 581
Colonization
  Hellenic era, 73*m*, 75
  slave trade and, 457
  See also Decolonization; Imperialism; New imperialism
Colosseum, 162
Columba (monk), 233
Columbia, 486
Columbus, Christopher, 348–349, 351
Comedia. See *Divine Comedy, The*
Comedies, 114, 115
Cominform, 690
Comintern, 623, 624
Comitatus, 227–228
Commercial Code (France), 482
Committee of Public Safety (France), 478
Commodus, 167
Common good, 454
Common law, 284
Common Sense (Paine), 468
Commonwealth of Independent States (CIS), 720, 744
Commonwealthmen, 467
Communes, 325
Communication technology, 716, 733

Communism
Bolshevik Revolution, 621–624
China, 672, 702–703
Cuba, 705, 708–711
fall of, 716–723
Korea, 704
"mass man" and, 645
Nazi Germany and, 659, 661
post-Soviet, 722–723
power versus principle, 711
Tito, 668
Vietnam, 705–707
World War II aftermath, 687
See also China; Cold War; Soviet
Union
Communist Labor Party (United
States), 624
Communist Manifesto, The (Marx and
Engels), 494, 542
Communist Party (Soviet Union), 651,
652, 654, 716, 717, 720
Communist Revolution, 565
Communities. See specific cities and
city-states
Compasses, 347
Compostela, 254
Compurgation, 284
Comte, August, 594
Concentration camps, 649, 668–670
Conciliarism, 308–311
Condottiere, 328
"Confession of Faith" (Rhodes), 576
Confucius, 57
Congo, 583
Congress of Vienna, 521–523
Congress Party (India), 694
Congress System, 520–523
Conrad (duke of Franconia), 249
Conrad III (Germany), 258, 260
Conservatism, 476, 523–524
Conservative agenda, 520–524
Conservative Party (England), 560–561,
639, 640
Constance, council of, 310
Constantine
agriculture and, 230
bust of, 181
Byzantine culture and, 195,
196–197
Christianity and, 182, 183,
186–189, 206
Sylvester I and, 220
Constantine the African, 268
Constantine XI (Byzantine Empire), 342
Constantinople, 195
Age of Anxiety, 300, 301, 305
Carolingians and, 218–219
medieval, 241–242
Muslims and, 203
Ottoman Empire and, 342
Roman Empire and, 190, 192m, 193
trade, 261
Venice and, 326
See also Byzantine Empire
Constantius I, 189, 210
Constitution
France, 474
United States, 454, 469, 515
Constitutional conflicts, preceding
American Revolution, 466–468
Constitutionalism
England, 404–405
liberalism and, 524
Constitutional reform, in Britain,
533–536
Constitutions of Clarendon, 284

Consumerism
1920s, 637
European unity and, 727–729
Industrial Revolution and, 508
Continental Congress, 468, 469
Continuity, in Roman Empire,
159–163, 165–168
Contracts, in medieval Europe, 228
Convention People's Party (Ghana), 697
Cooper, Anthony Ashley, 435
Copernicus, Nicholas, 424–425
Copper, 13, 49
Coral Sea, battle of, 674
Corcyra, 97
Corday, Charlotte, 477
Corinth, 94–95, 97, 121, 138
Corinthian architecture, 112
Cornelia, 140–141
Corpus juris civilis (Body of Civil
Law), 195
Cortes (Spanish aristocratic
assemblies), 413
Cortés, Hernán, 351
Corvée system, 394, 399
Cosmology, 421–422, 424
Cottage industry system, 501, 511
Cotton industry, 501, 502, 503
Council for Mutual Economic
Assistance, 691
Council of Constance, 310
Council of Trent, 367, 447
Counter-Reformation. See Catholic
Reformation
Counts, 223
Courbet, Gustave, 598
Courtly love, 276–277
Court of Inquisition, 367, 369
Cranmer, Thomas, 370
Crassus, 142
Creation story (biblical), 589
Crécy, battle of, 295, 313
Creoles, 486
Crete, 64–65, 66, 67, 68, 346
Crick, Francis, 732
Crime
Enlightenment ideas about, 450
Russia (post-Soviet), 721
World War I and, 620
Crimea, 298, 676
Crimean War, 548, 558, 564
Crimes and Punishments
(Beccaria), 450
Croatia/Croatians, 531, 563,
644, 743
Cromwell, Oliver, 384, 385, 404
Cromwell, Richard, 385
Cromwell, Thomas, 371
Crossbows, 315
Crusades, 238, 304
First Crusade, 301
Fourth Crusade, 301
Holy Land and, 255–260
Innocent III, 305
Louis IX (France), 288
Spanish and Sicilian, 254–255
Third Crusade, 285, 289
Crystal Palace, 509, 510
Ctesiphon, 203, 205
Cuba, 406, 705, 708, 722
Cuban Missile Crisis, 708–711
Cubism, 599
Cults, 184
Culture and society
1920s, 637
archaic states, 13
Athens, 81

Augustan era, 152, 153, 155–157
Black Death and, 298–300
Byzantine Empire, 195–197
consumerism and globalization,
727–729
Enlightenment, 442–443, 449
European early modern states,
392–396
Hellenic era, 101–115
Hellenistic era, 126–129
Holy Land (medieval), 260
hoplite, 77–79
Industrial Revolution and, 494–497,
506–515
"mass man" and, 645
medieval Europe, 231–235, 260
new imperialism and, 579–580,
589–595, 598–600
New Kingdom (Egypt), 44–45
Ottoman Empire, 344, 346
Renaissance, 329–338
Roman Empire, 169–172, 174–175
See also specific cultures
Cunard, Samuel, 504
Cuneiform, 20–21, 23, 41–41, 46
Curie, Marie, 596–597
Curie, Pierre, 596, 597
Cursus honorum, 134
Curtin, Philip, 457
Cute, 243
Cyclopes, 69
Cylon, 82
Cynics, 127–128
Cyrus the Great, 56, 84
Czech lands, revolutions in, 527
Czechoslovakia, 627, 635, 644, 659–660,
668, 689, 714, 719
Czech Republic, 725
Czechs, 563, 644

D

Dacia, 165
Dagobert, 213, 218
Daladier, Edouard, 659
Damascus, 204, 205, 304, 613
Dance, in Hellenic era, 111
Danegeld, 243
Danelaw, 243
Dante Alighieri, 421
Danube River, 191
Danube Valley, 153, 220
Danzig, 627
Darius I, 84, 86
Darius III, 122–123
Dark Ages. See Aegean Dark Age; Age
of Anxiety; European High
Middle Ages; Medieval
civilizations; Medieval
Europe
Darwin, Charles, 576, 589–591
Darwin, Erasmus, 590
David (sculpture), 333
David, 55, 56, 57m
David, Jacques-Louis, 460, 477
Dawes, Charles, 636
Dawes Plan, 636–637
Dawes Severalty Act (1877), 570–571
Dayton Accords (1995), 744
D-Day, 676
Death/mortality
Black Death and, 299
Egyptian civilization and, 27–28
Europe (early modern era),
395–396
Industrial Revolution, 500–501
Middle Kingdom (Egypt), 37

Mycenaeans, 68–69
 Scientific Revolution and, 429–430
 World War II, 677–678, 680
Death of Socrates, The (painting), 460
Debate, 170
De Beauvior, Simone, 737, 738–739
De Beers Consolidated Mines, Ltd., 576
Debussy, Claude, 599–600
Decameron, 332
Decembrist uprising, 523
Decius, 185
Declaration and Statement
 of Principles, 595
Declaration of Independence, 468
Declaration of the Rights of Man and
 Citizen, 455, 464, 473–474
Declaration of the Rights of Women
 and Citizen (Gouges), 455,
 456, 474
Declaratory Act (1766), 466
Decolonization, 694, 695*m*
 Europe, migration to, 698–701
 Guyana, 685
 North Africa, 696–697
 South Asia, 694, 696
 sub-Saharan Africa, 697–698
Defenestration of Prague, 380
Defense of Liberty Against Tyrants, 397
Degas, Edgar, 598
De Gaulle, Charles, 664–665,
 676, 697
De Gouges, Olympe, 455, 456, 474,
 478, 595
Deir el-Bahri, 38–39
Deism, 448–449
Delhi, 304
Delian League, 93, 95*m*, 97
Delos, 93
Demagogues, 98, 141. *See also specific*
 individuals
Demes, 83
Demesne, 230, 264
Demeter, 133
Democracy
 Aegean civilizations, 84
 Britain, 560–562
 European "welfare states" and,
 723–724
 Great Depression and, 639–640
 Hellenic era, 98–99, 100, 108, 109,
 110, 115
 mass, 645
 Nazi Germany and, 660, 661
 Nietzsche, Friedrich, 592
Democratization, during Industrial
 Revolution, 515
Democritus of Abdera, 103–104
Demographics
 globalization and, 733, 734*m*, 735
 Industrial Revolution, 497–501
 U.S. immigration, 569
Demosthenes, 99, 121
Deng Xiaoping, 722–723
Denmark, 243, 380, 521, 552, 661
Departements, 474, 478
Department stores, 508
Descartes, René, 419, 428–429, 448
Descent of Man (Darwin), 590
Deschamps, Eustache, 294, 296
Desiderius, 219
Despots, enlightened, 451–453. *See also*
 specific rulers
Détente, 710–711
De Vries, Hugo, 590
De vulgari eloquentia, 331
Dhimma status, 205

Dialectics, 269–270, 271, 278
Dialogue on the Two Great Systems of
 the World (Galilei), 426
Dialogues (Gregory I), 232–233
Diana (Roman goddess), 133
Dias, Bartolomeu, 348
Diaspora, 56
Dickens, Charles, 509, 539
Dictators. *See specific dictators*
Diderot, Denis, 445–446, 449
Didymus of Alexandria, 128
Diet, 358
Diocletian, 173–174, 175*m*, 182,
 186–187
Diogenes of Sinope, 127–128
Dionysus, 113, 133, 156
Directory government (France), 479–480
Discourse on Method (Descartes), 428–429
Discourse on the Origin of Inequality
 (Rousseau), 453
Diseases. *See* Black Death; Health
 issues
Disraeli, Benjamin, 560–561
Dissent
 Industrial Revolution, 509
 World War I, 620
Divine Comedy, The (Dante Alighieri),
 331, 421
Divine-right monarchy, 433
Divorce
 Code Napoleon and, 483
 European unity and, 728
 Roman Empire, 170
Djoser, 28
DNA, 732
Dnieper River, 261
Doctrine, in Byzantine Empire, 196
Doll's House, A (Ibsen), 597
Dominate, 173–174
Dominican Republic, 406
Dominicans, 275, 277
Domitian, 163
Donatello, 333
Donation of Constantine, 219–220
Donation of Pepin, 219
Donatists, 186–187
Don Quixote, 375–376
Dorian dialect (Greek), 71, 79
Doric architecture, 112, 113
Dowry, 737
Draco, 82
Drama, 112–114
Dresden, 572, 677
Dreyfus, Alfred, 559, 560
Dreyfus Affair, 559–560
Droughts, revolutions caused by, 529
Dubcek, Alexander, 719
Dublin, 728
Dukes, 223, 249. *See also specific dukes*
Duma, 565, 621
Dürer, Albrecht, 340
Durkheim, Emile, 594
Dutch East India Company, 414
Dutch East Indies. *See* Indonesia
Dynasties. *See specific dynasties*

E

Eakins, Thomas, 598
Early Dynastic Period, in Egyptian
 civilization, 25–26
Early Minoan Period, 66
Early modern states. *See* Nation-states,
 early modern
Earth
 age of, 2
 Hellenistic-era science and, 128

Earth summit (1992), 732–733
East Asia, Cold War events and issues
 in, 701–702
Eastern Europe, 408–411
 authoritarian regimes in,
 643–644, 645
 revolutions (anti-communist),
 718–720
 Soviet Union and, 688, 689
 See also specific countries
Eastern front, in World War I, 612–615
Eastern Roman Empire. *See* Byzantine
 Empire
East March, 220
East Prussia, 612–613
Ecclesiastical History of the English
 People, The, 233
Eclogues, 157
Economic Consequences of the Peace, The
 (Keynes), 629–630
Economics
 anti-immigrant sentiments
 and, 699
 China market reforms, 723
 discipline of, 594–595
 Enlightenment, 449, 450
 European unity and, 724–726, 727
 globalization and, 733, 734*m*,
 735–736
 Great Depression, 638–641
 Italian Fascism and, 643
 laissez-faire, 450, 524–525
 Marxism, 541–543
 mercantilism, 402, 406–408,
 449, 486
 Napoleon and, 482
 Nazi Germany, 648–649
 new imperialism, 578–579 (*see also*
 New imperialism)
 political economy, 524–525
 postindustrial age, 744–746
 post-World War I, 625, 634
 Soviet Union, 651–652, 716–717
 United States, 568
 World War I, 619
 World War I aftermath, 636–637
 See also Industrial Revolution;
 Trade/economy
Ecuador, 486
Edessa, 258
Edict of Nantes, 377, 400
Edict of Prices, 174
Edison, Thomas, 505
Education
 Athenian theater and, 115
 Augustan era, 153
 Byzantine Empire, 195
 Carolingian Renaissance, 234–235
 colonial elite, 581
 European High Middle Ages, 269,
 270–271
 immigrant Americanization, 569
 Industrial Revolution, 513–514
 Jesuit, 447–448
 Locke, John, 444
 women (Enlightenment),
 455, 457
 See also Scholasticism; Universities;
 Writing
Edward I (England), 286, 312
Edward II (England), 312
Edward III (England), 312, 313
Edward IV (England), 319
Edward VI (England), 371
Edward the Black Prince (England),
 315, 317

Edward the Confessor, 243, 245
Ego, 592
Egypt, 203, 204
    Cold War, 710–711
    Early Dynastic Period, 25–26
    environment, 23–24
    First Crusade and, 301
    First Intermediate Period, 25, 30
    First Triumvirate and, 142, 143
    Hellenic-era Greeks and, 75
    Indo-Europeans and, 45–50
    Islam and, 239, 241
    Middle Kingdom, 25, 36–37
    Minoans and, 66
    new imperialism and, 581, 583
    New Kingdom, 38–45
    Old Kingdom, 25, 26–30
    political development, 24–25
    Ptolemy I, 125, 128
    rise of, 23–30
    Second Intermediate Period, 37–38
    Second Triumvirate, 144
    Soviet Union and, 693
    transition states, 34–38
    World War I and, 613
    World War II, 663, 675
Einhard, 208, 210, 222, 234, 235
Einstein, Albert, 427, 593–594
Eisenhower, Dwight D., 676, 713
El Alamein, 675
Elamites, 23, 34
Elba, 485, 520
Eleanor of Aquitaine, 246–247,
    248–249, 260, 277, 283, 285
Elective monarchy, in Poland, 413
Electrical power technologies, 503
Elementary education, 513
Elements of Geometry, 268
Eliot, George, 555, 597
Eliot, T. S., 625
Elizabeth I (England), 355, 372–373,
    375, 377, 382, 404, 663
Emile (Rousseau), 453, 458
Empedocles of Agrigentum, 103, 104
Empirical wars, in early modern era,
    406–408
Empiricism/environmentalism,
    444–445. See also Scientific
    Revolution
Encyclopedia (Diderot), 445–446,
    455, 458
Engels, Friedrich, 492, 494, 541–542, 543
Engineering, in Rome, 155
England
    absolutism, 397, 398–399
    aristocracy (early modern era), 393
    civil wars, 404
    constitutionalism in, 404–405
    Elizabeth I, 372–373
    exploration by, 349, 350m, 351
    French religious wars and, 377
    Glorious Revolution, 391, 405, 467
    High Middle Ages, 283–286
    Hundred Years' War, 312–319
    James I, 397, 398–399
    medieval, 214, 216–217, 233, 243,
        244m, 245–249, 261
    papacy and, 308, 309
    peasants and serfs in, 394
    Reformation, 369–372
    religious civil war, 382–386
    Spanish Golden Age and, 375
    Thirty Years' War, 379
    William III, 391
    See also Britain
English Channel, 142

English Parliament, 246, 286, 319,
    371–372, 382, 383, 384, 385–386,
    404, 405, 466, 467, 534–536
Enheduana, 22
Enki, 21
Enkidu, 21
Enlightened despots, 451–453
Enlightenment, 440–442, 461
    arts, 459–461
    Code Napoleon and, 483
    conservatism and, 523–524
    critiquing, 453–458
    Deism, 448–449
    despots during, 451–453
    empiricism/environmentalism,
        444–445
    French Revolution and, 471
    Jesuit education, 447–448
    Jews and, 571
    Masonic lodges and aristocratic
        salons, 446–447
    material conditions, formulas for
        improving, 449–450
    new imperialism and, 578, 580, 584,
        589, 592, 593, 595
    philosophers, community of, 443–444
    reform literature, 445–446
    religion and, 448
    Romanticism and, 537, 538
    socialism and, 540
    traditional life and, 442–443
Enlil, 21
Enmebaragesi, 16
Enquêteurs, 288
Entente Cordiale, 608
Environment
    community and, 4, 6, 30–31
    Egyptian civilization, 23–24
    globalization and, 731–736
    Hellenistic era, 125–126
    Industrial Revolution and, 508–509
    Italian, 129
    medieval challenges from, 296–300.
        See also Climate Change
    Romanticism and, 538
Epaminondas, 101
Ephesus, 126
Ephors, 80
Epic of Gilgamesh, The, 6, 21
Epictetus, 156
Epicurean philosophy, 156
Epicureans, 127, 128
Epicurus, 127
Epidemics, 297–298
Epigrams (Martial), 171
Equality, women's struggle for,
    736–739
Equestrian class, 151, 152, 153, 157, 162
Erasistratus of Ceos, 128
Erasmus, Desiderius, 341, 354, 359
Eratosthenes of Cyrene, 128
Erfurt Program, 557
Eridu, 15, 22
Esarhaddon, 48
Essay Concerning Human Understanding
    (Locke), 433, 435, 444
Essay on the Principle of Population
    (Malthus), 525
Essen (Germany), 510
Estates General (France), 306, 319,
    471–472
Estonia, 409, 622, 661, 720
Ethelred the Unready, 243
Ethics (Spinoza), 449
Ethics, evolutionary theory and, 591
Ethiopia, 583, 643, 659, 697, 717

Ethnic cleansing, in Yugoslavia, 742–744
Ethnic nationalism, 739–744
Etruria, 129, 130m, 131
Etruscans, 131–132
Etymologiae, 233
Euboea, 109
Eucharist. See Transubstantiation
Euclid, 128, 268
Euphrates River, 12m, 14, 15, 22, 24
Eurasians, 13
Euripides, 115, 121
Euro, 725, 727
Europe
    American Revolution and, 470
    central and eastern, 408–411
    post-colonization migration to,
        698–701
    postindustrial age, 745
    World War I aftermath, 634–637
    See also Age of Anxiety; Cold War;
        Decolonization; Enlightenment;
        European High Middle Ages;
        Ideology; Industrial Revolution;
        Interwar years (1919–1939);
        Medieval Europe; Nation-states;
        Reformation; Renaissance;
        Scientific Revolution; World War
        I; World War II; specific countries
        and empires
European Coal and Steel Authority, 725
European Community (EC), 725
European Economic Community
    (EEC), 725
European High Middle Ages, 266–268,
    290–291
    artistic vision of, 278–283
    nation-states, 283–290
    political leaders, 291
    religious revival and diversity of
        opinion, 274–278
    renaissance of twelfth century,
        268–271
    universities and scholasticism,
        271–274
European imperialism. See New
    imperialism
European Parliament, 725
European Union (EU), 725–726
European unity (post-World War II),
    723–731
Eurotas River, 79
Evans, Mary Ann, 597. See also Eliot,
    George
Evolutionary Socialism (Bernstein), 561
Evolutionary theory, 589–591
Exile, 56
Existentialism, 686–687
Exodus, 54
Exploration
    Atlantic, 346–351
    Phoenicians, 55
Exports, 503
Eyck, Hubert van, 339
Eyck, Jan van, 338, 339

F

Fabian Society, 561
Factories, 503, 506. See also Industrial
    Revolution
Factory Act (1833), 535
Fairs, 262–263
Faith
    biblical, 56–58
    private, 311
Falange, 644
Fallow farming, 230

Family
  Europe (early modern era), 395
  European unity and, 728
  Nazi Germany, 647
  Renaissance perspective on, 334
  Roman Empire, 169–170
  Rome, 133–134
Famines, 296–297, 528–529, 651, 653
Farming. *See* Agriculture
Fascism, 632, 634, 641–643, 645
Fascist Party (Italy), 641–642, 643
Fashion, in 1920s, 637
Fatima, 198, 239
Fatimid dynasty, 239, 241, 301
Fayum, 36
Feminine Mystique, The (Friedan), 738
Feminism, 595, 736–739. *See also*
  Women
Ferdinand, Francis, 606, 607, 609
Ferdinand (Habsburg Emperor), 361
Ferdinand I (Austria), 530
Ferdinand II (Holy Roman Empire), 380
Ferdinand II (Naples), 531
Ferdinand V of Aragon, 349, 367, 369
Ferdinand VII (Spain), 486, 523
Ferrara, 326
Ferry, Jules, 579
Fertile Crescent, 14*m*
Festivals, Augustan era, 157
Feudalism, 227
Ficino, Marsilio, 424
Fiefs (feudum), 225, 227, 251, 256
Fifth Crusade, 304, 305
Fifth French Republic, 665, 697
Finland, 521, 621, 627, 661, 711
*First Blast of the Trumpet Against the
  Monstrous Regiment of Women,
  The*, 372–373
First Continental Congress, 468
First Crusade, 238, 257, 258, 260,
  301, 304
First Estate, 472
First Intermediate Period, in Egyptian
  civilization, 25, 30
First Punic War, 135
First Triumvirate, 142–144
First Vatican Council, 311
Five-Year Plans, 652, 653
Flanders, 312, 612
Flavian dynasty, 162–163, 169,
  171–172, 176
Floods, in Sumer, 16
Florence, 324, 326, 328
Florida, 406
Flying buttresses, 282
Foederati, 190, 191, 214
Fontenelle, Bernard de, 443
Food issues. *See* Agriculture
Food shortages, revolutions caused by,
  528–529
Food supplies, during Scientific
  Revolution, 429–430
Ford, Henry, 508
Ford Motor Company, 508
Forms, 108–109
Fortunatus, 232
Forum, 132, 163, 171
Fourier, Charles, 540
"Fourteen Points" speech, 626
Fourth Crusade, 301, 304, 305
Fourth French Republic, 697
Fourth Lateran Council, 306
France, 205
  absolutism in, 397, 399–404
  Alexander III (Russia), 564
  Algeria and, 741

American Revolution and,
  462–464, 469
appeasement (1933–1939), 658–661
aristocracy (early modern era), 393
Bolshevik Revolution and, 622
Charles X, 525–526
Clavin, John, 364
Congress System and, 521–522, 523
Crimean War, 548, 558, 564
crusades and, 255, 258, 260
decolonization, 696–697
elementary education, 513
Elizabeth I (England) and, 373
empirical wars and global markets
  (early modern era), 406, 407–408
Enlightenment, 443, 445, 448, 454
European High Middle Ages,
  266–268
European unity and, 725
exploration by, 350*m*, 351
Fifth French Republic, 665
German war (nineteenth century),
  553–554
Great Depression, 640*m*
Habsburg-Valois wars, 368–369
High Middle Ages, 279, 281, 285,
  286–288, 290
Hundred Years' War, 312–319
imperialism, 579, 583, 585–586, 587*m*
Industrial Revolution, 496, 499,
  503–504, 508
Italian city-states and, 328
Italian unification and, 548, 550
League of Nations, 628–629
Louis XVIII, 520
Lutheran Reformation and, 361
France, *continued*
  medieval, 243, 245–249, 251, 261
  Muslim Empire and, 225
  national identity, preservation of, 727
  NATO, 701
  Normandy/Normans, 243, 245
  nuclear arms race, 694
  occupation zones (post-World
    War II), 690
  papacy and, 306–307
  peasants and serfs in, 394
  postcolonial migrations to, 698,
    699, 701
  Quintuple Alliance, 522
  religious wars, 376–377
  Renaissance, 340
  revolutions of 1848, 532
  right-wing movements in, 649
  Second French Empire, 557–558
  Spain and, 414
  Spanish Golden Age and, 374–375
  Suez Canal, 710–711
  Third Crusade, 285
  Third French Republic, 558–560
  Thirty Years' War, 379, 380
  Treaty of Versailles, 625–628
  U.S. industrialization and, 569
  Vietnam and, 705, 706, 707*m*
  voting rights, 515
  women's movement and, 737,
    738–739
  World War I aftermath, 634, 635,
    636, 637
  World War II aftermath, 687
  See also Francia; Franks; French
    Revolution; Gaul; World War I;
    World War II
Francesca, Piero della, 336
Francia, 210, 212, 214, 215. *See also*
  Franks; Merovingian Kingdom

Francis I (France), 340, 364,
  368–369, 376
Francis II (Austria), 550
Francis II (France), 373, 375, 377
Franciscans, 275, 277, 302
Francis Joseph (Austria), 562
Francis of Assisi, 275, 306
Francogallia (Hotman), 397
Franconia, 249
Frankfurt, 522, 530
Franklin, Benjamin, 470
Franks, 191, 211–213, 214. *See also*
  Carolingian era
Fratricide, 342–343
Fredegund, 215–216
Frederick I "Barbarossa," 285, 288–289
Frederick II (Germany), 289–290,
  339–340, 368
Frederick II (Prussia), 390, 407, 411,
  413, 415
Frederick IV (Palatinate ruler), 380
Frederick V (Palatinate ruler), 380
Frederick the Wise (Elector
  of Saxony), 358
Frederick Wilhelm IV (Prussia), 530
Frederick William (Elector
  of Prussia), 410
Frederick William I (Prussia), 411
Frederick William II (Prussia), 475
Freedom, 148, 150, 176, 264, 524
Freedom of religion, 180, 182, 205–207
Free French movement, 662, 664–665, 676
Free-market economics, 525
Freemasonry, 446–447, 577
Free trade
  China market reforms, 723
  new imperialism and, 578–579
  See also Capitalism
French and Indian War, 464, 466, 470
French Committee of National
  Liberation, 665
French Revolution, 488–489
  1830–1832, 525–526
  1848, 527, 528–529
  American Revolution and, 462–464
  Americas and, 485–486, 487*m*
  Bastille, fall of, 473
  Burke, Edmund, 476–477
  Catholic Church and, 474–475
  constitution, 474
  *Declaration of the Rights of Man and
    Citizen*, 473–474
  Directory government, 479–480
  Enlightenment and, 452, 455
  Estates General and National
    Assembly, 471–472
  ideology and, 518, 520
  Jacobin rule and Reign of Terror,
    478–479
  Napoleon Bonaparte, 480–485
  Old Regime crisis, 470–471
  radical (1792–1794), 475–478
French Union, 696
Frequens, 310
Freud, Sigmund, 592–593
Friars, 275
Friedan, Betty, 737, 738
Fronde, 400
Fulton, Robert, 504
Fyrd, 245

G

Gaius Gracchus, 139, 141
Gaius Marius, 139
Galen, 430–431
Galicia, 413, 613

Galilee, 183
Galilei, Galileo, 426–427, 434
Gallicanism, 400
Gallic Wars, 142
Gallipoli, 341, 613
Galswinth, 215
Gama, Vasco da, 348
Gandersheim, 252–253
Gandhi, Mohandas, 614, 694, 696
Garibaldi, Giuseppe, 531, 550
Garonne River, 211
Gascony, 312, 317
Gaugamela, 123
Gaul, 129, 130*m*, 191, 193, 194, 210,
 211–212, 216. *See also* Franks;
 Merovingian Kingdom
Gaza Strip, 710
Gdansk, 413
Gedrosian Desert, 124
Gelasius I (pope), 220
Gender *See* Women
General Intelligence Division (United
 States), 624
General will, 454
Genesis, 52
Genetics, 732
Geneva, 365, 453, 454
Genghis Khan, 302
Genoa, 261, 301, 324, 326, 342
Genocide, 668–670
Gens, 133
Gentiles, 183, 184
Geoffrin, Marie-Therese, 447
Geometric pottery, 111
Geometry, 128
George, David Lloyd, 618
George III (England), 464, 466,
 467, 468
George V (England), 614, 639
George VI (England), 656, 663
Georgia, 744
Georgics, 158
Gerbert of Aurillac, 269
German Bible, 359
German Confederation of States, 530,
 546, 551–557, 562
German Democratic Republic, 690
German Federal Republic, 690
Germany, 153, 243
 Berlin Wall, 699
 Black Death and, 300
 Bolshevik Revolution and,
 621–622, 623
 Charlemagne and, 220
 Cold War, 689–690
 Congress System and, 522
 crusades and, 258, 260
 elementary education, 513
 European unity and, 725
 Great Depression, 639
 Habsburg-Valois wars, 368–369
 High Middle Ages, 288–290
 imperialism, 579, 583, 584,
 585–586
 Industrial Revolution, 497, 501,
 503–504, 510–511
 Innocent III and, 305
 Italian city-states and, 325, 328
 Keynes, John Maynard, 629–630
 League of Nations and, 628, 629
 Lutheran Reformation, 356–361
 Marcus Aurelius and, 167
 Marshall Plan and, 691
 medieval, 249–254
 nationalism in, 571–572
 peasants and serfs in, 393–394

 postcolonial migrations to,
 698–699
 Renaissance politics, 338–339
 revolutions in, 527, 530
 Roman Empire and, 172, 189–193
 social sciences, 594–595
 Soviet Union and, 719
 Swiss Reformation and, 362–363
 Third Crusade, 285
 Third French Republic and,
 558–559
 Thirty Years' War, 379–380
 Treaty of Versailles, 625–627,
 629–630
 U.S. industrialization and, 569
 unification of, 551–557, 719,
 726–727
 voting rights, 515
 Weimar Republic, 635–637
 women's movement and, 737
 World War I aftermath, 634,
 635–637
 World War II aftermath, 687, 688,
 689–690
 See also Franks; Nazi Germany;
 World War I; World War II
Gerousia, 80
Ghana, 697–698
Ghibellines, 288
Gibraltar, 214
Gilgamesh, 6, 15, 17, 21
Girondins, 478
Gladiatorial combat, 157
Gladstone, William, 561
Glasnost, 717, 718
Globalization, 714–716, 746–747
 communism, fall of, 716–723
 European unity, 723–731
 postindustrialism, 744–746
 religious divides and ethnic
 nationalism, 739–744
 science, technology, and
 environment, 731–736
 women and equality, 736–739
Global markets, early modern era and,
 406–408
Global warming, 732
Globe (theater), 379
Glorious Revolution, 391, 405, 467
Gnosticism, 277
Gobineau, Arthur de, 580
God (Christian), 420–421, 422, 434,
 436, 589–592
Gods. *See* Pantheons; Religions;
 specific gods
Godwin, 245
Godwinson, Harold, 245
Goebbels, Joseph, 647
Goering, Herman, 648
Gold Coast, 697
Golden Age, of Spain, 373–376
Golden Bull, 339
Golden Horde, 303
Golden House, 162
Gonzaga, Elisabetta, 334–335
"Good Emperors," 165–167, 176
Gorbachev, Mikhail, 717–718, 720
Gospel of John, 183
Gospel of Luke, 183
Gospel of Mark, 183
Gospel of Matthew, 183, 186
Gospels, 183, 184, 186. *See also* New
 Testament
Gosplan, 652
Gothic architecture, 280, 281–283, 339
Goths. *See* Ostrogoths; Visigoths

Government, 118, 120
 limited, 433–434
 See also Politics; *specific governments*
Government reform
 Enlightenment ideas about, 450, 454
 Napoleon, 481–482
 Paine, Thomas, 477
 See also American Revolution;
 French Revolution
Gracchi family, 138–139, 140–141
Gracchus, Gaius, 139, 141
Gracchus, Tiberius, 138–139, 140
Granada, 349, 368
Grand Alliance, 406, 675
Granikos River, 122
Gratian, 190
Gravity, 427
Great Awakening, 458
Great Britain. *See* Britain
Great Depression, 638–641
Great Dionysia, 113, 114
Greater East Asia Co-Prosperity
 Sphere, 674
Great Pestilence, 326
Great Pyramid at Giza, 28–29
Great Reform Bill (1832), 534–535
Great Schism, 308, 309, 365
Great Terror, 653–654
Greco, El, 375
Greece
 appeasement (1933–1939), 658
 Augustan era and, 155, 156, 157
 authoritarianism in, 644
 Congress System and, 523
 Julio-Claudians and, 161
 Roman Empire and, 137–138
 Second Triumvirate and, 144
 Truman Doctrine and, 692
 World War I, 609
 World War II, 663, 665
 World War II aftermath, 687
 See also Aegean civilizations;
 Ancient Greece; Hellenic era;
 Hellenistic era
Greek Christian Byzantium. *See*
 Byzantine Empire
Greek civilization, origin of, 68
Greek language, 67, 71, 75, 79
Greek New Testament, 341
Greenland, 298
Gregory I (pope), 232–233
Gregory VII (pope), 253
Gregory X (pope), 339
Gregory XI (pope), 307, 308
Gregory of Tours, 232
Gregory the Great (pope), 215
Grenville, George, 466
Grey, Sir Edward, 610
Gropius, Walter, 637, 638
Guadeloupe, 406
Guam, 674
"Guernica" (painting), 644
Guesclin, Bertrand du, 315
Guilds, 262
Guillotine, 477, 479
Guiscard, Robert, 255
Guizot, F., 513
Gulf of Corinth, 94, 344
Gulliver's Travels (Swift), 445
Gunpowder, 315, 347
Gustavus Adolphus (Sweden), 380, 399
Gutenberg, Johannes, 340, 347
Guyana, 685
Guzmán, Dominic de, 275
Gymnos, 77

H

Habsburg Empire. *See* Austrian Empire
Habsburg-Valois wars, 368–369
Hades, 133
Hadiths, 198, 200
Hadrian, 166–167, 214
Hagar, 198
Hagia Sophia, 194
Haiti. *See* Saint Dominique
Hamburg, bombing of, 678
Hamilcar Barca, 136
Hammurabi, 34–36, 53
Hannibal, 136–137
Hannibalic War, 136–137, 138
Hanover, 530
Hanseatic League, 338
Harappan civilization, 13
Hardenberg, Baron, 520
Hardinge, Lord, 614
Hardrada, Harold, 245
Hard Times (Dickens), 509
Hargreaves, James, 502
Harris, Betty, 494
Harun al-Rashid, 222–223, 239, 241
Harvey, William, 432, 434
Hathaway, Anne, 378
Hatsheput, 38–39
Hattusas, 46
Hauteville, Tancred de, 255
Havel, Vaclav, 714, 719
Haydn, Franz Joseph, 459
Health issues
    globalization and, 731–732
    Industrial Revolution, 500
    post–World War I, 625
    Scientific Revolution and, 429–432
    Soviet Union, 651
    See also Black Death;
        Death/mortality; Medicine
Hebrews, 51–58. *See also* Jews
Hebrew Scriptures, 56
Hecataeus of Miletus, 105, 106
Hedonism, 127–128
Helgoland, 521
Heliocentric theory, 424, 425, 426, 427
Hellenic era, 72, 116–117
    archaic period, 72–76
    Aspasia, 96–97
    Athens, 81–84
    end of, 125
    hoplite culture, 77–79
    hoplite infantry, 76–77
    intellectual and artistic life,
        101–115
    Peloponnesian War, 94–95, 97–101
    Pericles, 90, 92
    Persian Wars, 84–88, 92–93
    Sparta, 79–81
Hellenism, 75
Hellenistic era, 118, 120, 146
    Alexander the Great, 121–125
    culture, 126–129
    environment, 125–126
    Macedonia and, 120–121
Heloise, 270–271
Helots, 80
Helsinki Accords (1975), 711
Henry I (England), 246, 283
Henry I "the Fowler (duke
    of Saxony)," 249
Henry II (England), 246–247, 249,
    283–285, 312
Henry II (France), 369, 376
Henry III (England), 285–286
Henry III (France), 377
Henry III (Germany), 251

Henry IV (England), 317
Henry IV (France), 377, 399
Henry IV (Germany), 251, 253
Henry V (England), 317, 318
Henry V (Germany), 288
Henry VI (England), 318, 319
Henry VI (Germany), 289
Henry VII (England), 319, 349, 369, 375
Henry VII (Germany), 339
Henry VIII (England), 369–371,
    373, 374
Henry of Lancaster, 317
Henry of Navarre, 377
Henry the Lion (Germany), 288
Henry the Navigator (Portuguese
    prince), 347–348
Hephaestus, 133
Hera, 133
Heracleitus of Ephesus, 102, 103
Heraclius, 203, 241
Herculaneum, 163
Herding. *See* Agriculture
Hereditary succession
    absolutism and, 397
    Merovingian Kingdom, 212–213,
        215–216
    Roman Empire, 159–163
    Tudors, 371–372
    See also specific rulers and dynasties
Heresy/heretics, 211, 277–278. *See also*
    Cathars
Hermes, 133
Hermits. *See* Monks/monasticism
Herodotus, 28–29, 88
Herodotus of Halicarnassus, 105, 106
Herophilius of Chalcedon, 128
Herzegovina, 606–607, 608, 743
Herzl, Theodor, 573
Hesiod, 74–75, 128
Hestia, 133
Hetairae, 78–79
Hierakonpolis, 25
Hieroglyphs, 26
High Middle Ages. *See* European High
    Middle Ages
Hijra, 199
Hildgeard of Bingen, 278
Himalayan Mountains, 124
Himmler, Heinrich, 647, 667, 668
Hindenberg, Paul von, 644, 646, 647
Hindus/Hinduism, 420, 694, 696
Hipparchus, 83
Hipparchus of Nicaea, 128
Hippias, 83, 84
Hippocrates of Cos, 104–105
Hirohito, 678
Hiroshima, 677–678
Hispaniola, 406
Histor, 105
Historical and Critical Dictionary
    (Bayle), 444, 445
History
    discipline of, 594
    Hellenic era, 105–107
    Minoan, 66–67
*History of the Cotton Manufacture in
    Great Britain, The* (Baines), 514
History of the Franks, 232
Hitler, Adolf, 632
    anti-Semitism, 649–650
    appeasement (1933–1939), 658,
        659–660, 661
    economic crisis and, 636
    economic rebuilding, 648–649
    Franco, Francisco, 643
    Holocaust, 668–670

Mein Kampf, 646, 658, 668
Nazi Germany, 646–648
rise of, 646, 647
World War II, 662, 663, 665,
    666–667, 673, 675, 676
Hitler Youth, 647
Hittites, 36, 45–46, 53
Hobbes, Thomas, 433, 434
Ho Chih Minh, 705, 706
Hogarth, William, 461
Hohenstaufen dynasty, 288–289,
    338–339, 340
Hohenzollern dynasty, 410, 625
Holbach, Baron d', 449
"Hollow Men, The" (Eliot), 625
Holocaust, 650, 668–670
Holstein, 552
Holy Alliance, 523
Holy Land, 255–260. *See also* Crusades
Holy Roman Empire, 339, 358,
    379–380, 415, 483, 522. *See also*
    Germany
Holy Synod, 409
Homer, 67, 70–71, 72, 106, 129, 330
Homeric era, 71–72
Hominids, 13
Homo sapiens sapiens, 6, 7
Homosexuality, of Alexander the
    Great, 125
Hong Kong, 585, 674, 723
Honorius, 190–191
Hoover, J. Edgar, 624
Hoplite culture, 77–79
Hoplite infantry, 76–77
Hoplos, 76
Horace, 158, 170
Horemheb, 43
Hortensian Law, 134
Horthy, Miklos, 644
Hospitalization, 500
Hotman, Francois, 397
House of Commons, 404, 533–534,
    560–561, 562
House of Lords, 404, 533, 562
House of Savoy, 521
Housing, in Sumer, 18
Howard, Catherine, 371
Hroswitha of Gandersheim, 252–253
Hudson Bay, 406
Hugo, Victor, 536
Huguenots, 376, 377, 400
Humanism
    Gonzaga, Elisabetta, 334–335
    Italian Renaissance, 330, 331–332,
        333, 334–335
    Northern Renaissance, 340–341
    Reformation and, 356
    See also Renaissance
Hume, David, 448–449, 455
Hundred Years' War, 312–319
Hungary
    authoritarianism in, 644
    Bolshevik Revolution and, 623
    Czechoslovakia and, 660
    Dual monarchy, 562–563
    European Union membership, 725
    Lutheran Reformation and, 369
    Ottoman Empire, 342, 344
    papacy and, 249
    peasants and serfs in, 393
    Renaissance, 328
    revolution in, 527, 530
    Soviet Union and, 689, 719
    World War I, 627
    World War II, 665, 679
    See also Austrian Empire

Huns, 190s, 191, 193
Hunter-gatherers, 7, 9
Hurrians of Mitanni, 45
Hus, John, 310, 361, 380
Hussein, Emir, 613
Hussein, Saddam, 729, 745
Hussites, 310
Hutterites, 363
Hybris, 116
Hydroelectric power, 505
Hydrogen bombs, 693
Hyksos, 37–38, 45, 52
Hyperinflation, 636

I

I and Thou (Buber), 739
Ibn Khaldun, 457
Ibsen, Henrik, 597
Ice Age, 9
Iceman, 10
Icons/iconoclasm, 197, 242
Id, 592
Ideas, 109, 110
Ideology, 518–520, 544
   Britain and constitutional reform,
      533–536
   Cold War, 710–711, 716
   congress system and conservative
      agenda, 520–523
   conservatism, 523–524
   liberalism, 524
   Marxism, 541–543
   political economy, 524–525
   post–World War II, 686, 687
   revolutions, 525–533
   Romanticism, 537–539
   utilitarianism and utopian socialism,
      539–541
   See also Capitalism; Communism;
      Philosophy
Ides of March, 143
Iliad, 67, 70, 101, 129
Imams, 203, 204
Imhotep, 28
Immigrants/immigration
   globalization and, 745
   Industrial Revolution and, 509,
      511–512
   Roman Empire, 189–190
   U.S. Industrial Revolution and,
      569–570
Imperialism
   Japan (1919–1939), 650–651
   Soviet Union, 688–689
   United States (post–World
      War II), 688–689
   World War I and, 612–615
   See also Decolonization; New
      imperialism; Roman Empire
Imperium, 150–151
Imports, 503
Impressionism, 598–599
Inanna, 15, 21
Inca, 351
Index of Prohibited Books, 368
India, 57, 173
   decolonization of, 694, 696
   imperial wars and global markets, 407
   Industrial Revolution and, 496
   new imperialism and, 578, 584–585,
      587m
   nuclear arms race, 693–694
   Portuguese exploration, 348
   postcolonial migrations from, 699
   Timur "the Lame," 304
   World War I and, 613, 614, 615

Indian National Congress, 585, 694
Indian Ocean, 344, 348, 415
Indian Raj, 584–585
Individualism, 594
Indochinese soldiers, in World War I,
   613–614
Indo-Europeans, Egyptian civilization
   and, 45–50
Indonesia (Dutch East Indies), 407,
   415, 651, 673, 674
Indulgences, 357
Indus River Valley, 13, 124, 205
Industrial capitalism, 494. *See also*
   Industrial Revolution
Industrialization
   pollution and, 732
   Soviet Union, 652, 653
Industrial production, during World
   War II, 670–671
Industrial Revolution, 449, 490–494,
   495m, 516–517
   agriculture, demographics, and
      labor, 497–501
   Bismarck, Otto von, 555, 557
   Napoleon III, 558
   new imperialism and, 578, 585, 586,
      588, 594, 597, 598
   production innovations, 501–505
   rural and urban lifestyles, 494–497
   Russia, 564–565
   social consequences of, 506–515
   United States, 568, 569
Industry. *See* Trade/economy
Inequality, feminism and, 595
Infantries. *See* Hoplite infantry
Inflation, anti-immigrant sentiments
   and, 699, 701
Information age, 744–745
Infrastructure
   Augustan era, 152, 155
   India, 584
   Napoleon and, 482
   Vespasian, 162
   See also Architecture; *specific works*
Innocent III (pope), 285, 289, 305–306
Innocent VII (pope), 367
Inquisition, 367, 369, 414, 448
*Institutes of the Christian Religion,
   The,* 364
Intellectual life
   Carolingian Renaissance, 233–235
   Hellenic era, 101–115
   new imperialism and, 589–595,
      596–597
   Roman Empire, 170–172
   Sumer, 19–21
   See also Arts; Culture and society;
      Medicine; Philosophy; Science;
      Scientific Revolution; Writing
Intendants, 402
Intercontinental ballistic missile delivery
   systems (ICBMs), 693, 711
International Association of the
   Congo, 583
International Monetary Fund (IMF), 736
International style, 637, 638
Internet, 733
Interpretation of Dreams, The
   (Freud), 592
Interwar years (1919–1939), 632–634,
   654–655
   appeasement process (1933–1939),
      658–661
   Great Depression, 638–641
   Italy, fascism in, 641–643
   Japan, imperialism of, 650–651

Nazi Germany, emergence of, 644,
   646–650
   post–World War I aftermath,
      635–638
   Soviet Union, 651–654
   Spain and eastern Europe,
      authoritarian regimes in,
      643–644, 645
   Western Europe, problems in, 634
Investiture Controversy, 253–254
Iona, 233
Ionia, 84–86, 100, 101, 102
Ionic architecture, 112, 113
Iran, 204, 692, 741–742
Iranian Revolution, 741–742
Iraq, 204, 628, 693, 741
Iraq war (2003–), 729–730, 745
Ireland, 214, 217, 283, 385, 527, 528,
   534, 561, 613, 627, 728
Iron, 49
Iron Age
   Bible, 51–58
   Indo-Europeans and, 45–50
   Middle Kingdom, 25, 36–37
   New Kingdom, 38–45
   Second Intermediate Period, 37–38
   transition states, 34–38
   unity versus divisiveness, 32, 34, 58
Iron Curtain, 689
Iron law of wages, 525
Irrigation, 31
   Egyptian civilization, 23, 24
   Sumer, 14, 15, 16, 17, 23
   See also Agriculture
Isaac, 52, 198
Isabella I of Castile, 349, 367, 369
Isaurian dynasty, 241
Ishmael, 198
Ishtar. *See* Inanna
Isidore of Seville, 233
Isis, 37, 184
Islam, 51, 206–207
   Age of Anxiety, 300–305
   caliphs and sultans, 238–241
   crusades and, 254–60, 285, 288, 289
   European High Middle Ages and, 268
   militant, 740–742
   Muslim Empire, 197–205
   Ottoman Empire, 343, 344
   See also Muslims/Muslim Empire;
      Ottoman Empire
Islamic fundamentalism, 740–742
Islamism, 741
Isocrates, 120
Isolationism, 673
Israel, 51, 54, 56
   Cold War, 711
   creation of, 692–693
   Iran and, 741
   nuclear arms race, 694
Israelites, 51—58
Issos River, 122
Istanbul, 193, 346, 411
Isthmus of Corinth, 86–87, 88, 94
Italian environment, 129
Italian Renaissance, 296
   context for, 324–329
   culture of, 329–338
   See also Renaissance
Italy, 97
   Augustan era, 152, 154
   Austrian Habsburg Empire and, 415
   Carolingians and, 218–219
   Carthage and, 135, 137
   city-states in, 135, 324–326
   crusades and, 255

elementary education, 513
European unity and, 725
fascism in, 641–643
Habsburg-Valois wars, 368–369
High Middle Ages, 288–290
Holy Roman Empire and, 339
imperialism, 579
Industrial Revolution, 497, 505
Lombards and, 194, 213–214
medieval, 249–254
Napoleon and, 483, 521
Napoleon III and, 558
Nazi Germany and, 659
political development during Renaissance, 326–329
revolution (1830–1832), 527
revolution (1848), 531–533
Theodoric and, 193
trade (medieval), 260–261
Trajan, 165
Treaty of Versailles, 625–627
unification of, 548–551
Vespasian and, 162
Visigoths and, 190–191
voting rights, 515
World War I, 608, 613
World War II, 663, 665, 675, 676
See also Roman Empire; Rome
Ivan III "the Great" (Russia), 303
Ivan the Terrible (Russia), 409
Iwo Jima, 677

J
Jacob, 52
Jacobin rule, 478–479
Jacquerie rebellions, 300
Jamaica, 406
James (brother of Jesus), 183
James I (England), 375, 382, 397, 398–399, 404. *See also* James VI (Scotland)
James II (England), 405
James VI (Scotland), 375, 382, 398. *See also* James I (England)
Janissaries, 343–344
Jansenism, 400
Japan, 348, 349
Bolshevik Revolution and, 622
Cold War, 701–702
globalization and, 723, 736
Japan, *continued*
imperialism, 585–586, 587*m*, 588, 650–651
World War I and, 613
World War II, 672–674, 676–678, 680
Japanese-Americans, World War II relocation of, 671
Jaxartes River, 239
Jazz, 637
Jefferson, Thomas, 440, 441, 444, 468, 470
Jellachich, Joseph, 531
Jericho, 11
Jerome (scholar), 231
Jerome, Saint, 359
"Jerusalem" (Wordsworth), 538
Jerusalem
Assyria and, 50
Bible and, 51, 55–56
Charlemagne and, 222
Christianity and, 183
crusades and, 255–260
Islam and, 199, 203
Saladin and, 301
World War I and, 613
Jesuit education, 447–448

Jesuits, 367, 379
Jesus of Nazareth, 172
Constantine and, 183–184, 186
Francis of Assisi and, 275
Islam and, 197, 199, 202, 203
Peter and, 218
Jewish nationalism, 572–573
Jews
Arabia and, 198
Assyria and, 50
Bible and, 51–58
Black Death and, 298
Catholic Church and, 740
Christianity and, 183–184
crusades and, 257–258
France (High Middle Ages), 288
German nationalism and, 571–572
Hitler, Adolf, 646
Holocaust, 668–670
Israel, creation of, 692–693
Lutheran Reformation and, 360
medieval Spain and, 233
Muhammad and, 199
Muslim Empire and, 205
Napoleon and, 481
Nazi Germany, 649–650
Ottoman Empire and, 343, 344, 346
Poland, 413
Third French Republic, 559, 560
Titus and, 163
Jews and Their Lies, The, 360
Jihad, 201–202
Joan of Arc, 317, 318–319
John. *See* Gospel of John
John (England), 249, 285
John II "the Good" (France), 315
John VI (Portugal), 486
John XXIII (pope), 739
John of Gaunt, 317
John of Montecorvino, 302
John of Piancarpino, 302
John of Salisbury, 266
John of the Cross, Saint, 368
John Paul II (pope), 740
John the Fearless (France), 318
Johnson, Lyndon B., 705–706
Jordan River, 54
Joseph, 52
Joseph II (Austrian Habsburg Empire), 415, 452–453
Josephus, 172
Joshua, 54
Joyce, James, 597–598
Juarez, Benito, 558
Judah, 50, 51, 56
Judaism, 51, 183, 184, 203, 207, 449. *See also* Jews
Julia (daughter of Augustus), 151, 155, 160
Julian "the Apostate," 189
Julio-Claudians, 160–162, 176
Julius II (pope), 367
Julius Caesar. *See* Caesar, Julius
Jung, Carl, 593
Junkers, 551, 552, 555
Juno, 133
Jurisdiction, 227
Justin, 193
Justinian, 193–195, 203, 211, 213–214
Jutland, 616

K
Ka'aba, 198, 199
Kadar, Janos, 719
Kafka, Franz, 597–598
Kamerernebti, 27

Kant, Immanuel, 444, 455
Karachi, 614
Karnak, 40, 43
Kashmir, 696
Kassites, 47, 53
Kay, John, 502
Keats, John, 537
Kennan, George, 692
Kennedy, John F., 705, 707, 709
Kent, 233
Kepler, Johannas, 425–426, 427, 434
Kerensky, Alexander, 621
Keylor, William, 640
Keynes, John Maynard, 629–630, 639
KGB, 653
Khadija, 198
Khamenei, Ayatollah Ali, 742
Khomeini, Ayatollah Ruholla, 741–742
Khufu. *See* Cheops
Khurasan, 239
Khusro I, 194
Khwarazm, 302
Kiev, 242, 261, 303
King and the Education of the King, The (Molina), 397
Kingdom of the Two Sicilies, 523, 548
King James Bible, 382, 398
King Tut, 42–33
Kipling, Rudyard, 579–580
Kish, 16
Kiya, 42
Kleros, 79, 80
Knights, 228–229, 256–257, 315
Knights of St. John, 344
Knights Templar, 280, 307
Knossos, 64–65, 66, 67, 68, 69
Knowledge economy, 744–745
Knox, John, 365, 372–373, 375
Kohl, Helmut, 726–727
Korea, 347, 588, 651, 701, 676
Korean War, 704
Kosovo, 342, 744
Kossuth, Louis, 531
Kouros, 104
Kristallnacht, 649
Krupp, Alfred, 510–511
Krupp, Friedrich, 510
Krushchev, Nikita, 708–709, 710
Krypteia, 80
Kulaks, 653
Kulturkampf, 556, 557
Kun, Bela, 623
Kuraish, 198
Kyoto Protocol, 733

L
Labor
early modern era, 394
globalization and, 728
Great Depression, 638, 639
Holocaust, 668
Industrial Revolution and, 492–494, 497–501, 502, 505, 506–507, 512–513, 515
information age, 744–745
Marxism and, 542–543
political economy and, 525
revolutions of 1848, 529–530
Russian Marxism and, 565
slave trade and, 457
Soviet Union, 653
U.S. Civil War and, 568
U.S. Industrial Revolution and, 569
working class (proletariat), 505, 506–507, 511
World War I, 619

Labor reforms, in Britain, 535–536
Labor unions, 512–513
Labour Party (England), 561, 635, 639, 687, 694, 727
Labrador, 349
Lafayette, Marquis de, 462–464, 473, 475, 480
Laissez-faire economics, 450, 524–525
Lancastrians, 319
Lances, 229
Land management, 430
Landscape painting, 338
La Mattrie, Julian, 449
Lanfranc of Bec, 269–270
Language
    dialectics and, 269
    Latin, 152, 155, 212
    nominalism and, 270
    See also Writing; *specific cultures*
Laocoön, 127
Laos, 722
Lao-tzu, 57
Late Minoan Period, 66–67
Latifundia, 138, 169
Latin America
    American Revolution and, 470
    French Revolution and, 485–486, 487*m*
    See also specific countries
Latin Christian Europe, 182
    church organization, 185–186
    Constantine and imperial Christianity, 186–189
    early history, 184–185
    Germany, 189–193
    origins, 183–184
    See also Medieval Europe
Latin high culture, 155–157
Latin language, 152, 155, 212
Latins, 129
Latinus, 129
Latium, 129, 130–131
Latvia, 409, 622, 627, 661, 720
Laud, William, 383
Lavinia, 129
La Vita Nuova (*The New Life*), 331
Law of the Maximum (France), 478
Lawrence, D. H., 597–598
Lawrence, T. E., 613
Laws
    Athens, 82
    Byzantine Empire, 195, 242
    Code of Hammurabi, 34–36
    common law, 284
    Frankish, 211–212
    Hortensian Law, 134
    Roman, 169–170
    shari'a, 203
    Twelve Tables, 134
    See also Politics
League of German Girls, 647
League of Nations, 627, 628–629, 637, 643, 650, 658, 659
Lebanon, 628, 665
Legal reforms
    Britain, 533–536
    Enlightenment ideas about, 450, 454
    Napoleon and, 482–483
Legionnaires, 152
Legislative Assembly (France), 474, 477
Leisure activities, in 1920s, 637
Lend-Lease Program, 663
Lenin, Vladimir, 565, 579, 621, 622, 624, 651, 651–652
Leningrad, 666, 667
Leo III (Byzantine Empire), 241

Leo III (pope), 222
Leo IX (pope), 251
Leo X (pope), 357, 367
Leo XIII (pope), 557
Leonardo da Vinci, 340
Leonidas, 86, 88
Leopold I (Austria), 415
Leopold II (Austria), 475
Leopold II (Belgium), 583
Lepanto, 344, 412
Lepidus, 144
Lesbos, 98–99, 101
Letter Concerning Toleration, A (Locke), 434
Letters on the English (Voltaire), 445
Levelers, 385
Leviathan (Hobbes), 433
Liberalism, 524
Liberal Party (England), 560–561, 639
Liberation theology, 740
Liberia, 583, 697
Liberty, order versus, 148, 150, 176
Libya, 579, 583, 663, 741
Liebknecht, Karl, 623
Limited government, 433–434
Lincoln, Abraham, 568–569
Lincolnshire Ox, 498
Line of Demarcation, 351
Linear A, 66, 67, 69
Linear B, 66, 67, 69–70
Literacy, 423–424
Literature. *See* Writing
Lithuania, 304, 622, 627, 661, 720
Little Ice Age, 296–297, 429
Liverpool (England), 503
Livestock. *See* Agriculture
Livia (wife of Augustus), 151, 160
Living conditions, during Industrial Revolution, 492–497
Livingstone, David, 583
Livy, 159, 161, 170
Locke, John, 405, 427, 433–434, 444, 454, 455
Locomotives, 503
Logic, 110, 269–270, 273
Loire Valley, 211
Lollards, 309
Lombard, Peter, 271
Lombards, 194, 213–214, 218–219, 220
Lombardy, 214, 289, 521, 531, 548, 550
London, 300, 730
Longbows, 315, 317
Long March, 672
Long Parliament, 384
Lords, 264
Lorenzo "the Magnificent," 328
Lorraine, 558, 627
Lothair, 224
Louis (Duke of Orleans), 318
Louis VI (France), 248, 281
Louis VII (France), 249, 258, 260, 281
Louis VIII (France), 286–287
Louis IX (France), 287–288, 302
Louis X (France), 313
Louis XII (France), 368
Louis XIII (France), 380, 399
Louis XIV (France), 392, 399–404, 415
Louis XV (France), 408
Louis XVI (France), 456
    American Revolution, 462, 464, 469, 470
    French Revolution, 470, 471, 473, 475, 476, 477
Louis XVII (France), 520
Louis XVIII (France), 520, 522
Louis Napoleon. *See* Napoleon III

Louis Philippe (France), 526, 529
Louis the Pious, 224
Love. *See* Courtly love
Lovett, William, 536
Loyola, Ignatius, 367, 368
Lucan, 171
Lucca, 326
Lucretia, 133
Lucretius, 156
Ludendorff, Erich, 617
Luftwaffe, 663, 665
Luke. *See* Gospel of Luke
Lusitania, 616
Luther, Martin, 356–358, 361, 362, 363, 364, 367, 370
Lutheran Reformation, 356–361
Lutherans/Lutheranism, 363, 379, 380
Luxembourg, 339, 610, 662, 725
Luxemburg, Rosa, 623
Luxor, 40
Lyceum, 109
Lycurgos, 79
Lydia, 84
Lyell, Sir Charles, 590
Lysander, 100
Lysistrata, 115

M

MacArthur, Douglas, 704
MacDonald, Ramsey, 606, 635
Macedonia/Macedonians, 120–125, 137–138, 242, 743
Machiavelli, Niccolò, 328–329, 432–433
Machinery, 501–505
Madeira islands, 348
Madrid (Spain), 522
Maecenas, 157, 158
Magdeburg Ivories, 252
Magellan, Ferdinand, 349
Magic, 436–437
Maginot Line, 658, 664
Magistrates, 134–135, 138, 150
Magna Carta, 246, 285
Magna Mater, 184
Magnus, Albertus, 274, 421
Magyars, 225, 238, 243, 249, 530, 562–564
Mainz diocese, 357
Maistre, Joseph de, 523
Major, John, 727
Malaya, 651, 673, 674
Malaysia, 723, 736
Malta, 344, 521
Malthus, Thomas, 525
Mamluks, 302, 344
Manchester (England), 492–494, 503, 506*m*
Manchuko, 650
Manchuria, 588, 650, 651, 677, 701
Manet, Edouard, 598
Manhattan Project, 677
Mann, Thomas, 597–598
Manors, 230
Mantua, 326
Manufacturing technology, during Industrial Revolution, 501–502
Manzikert, 242, 255
Mao Zedong, 672, 702–703, 706
Marat, Jean Paul, 477
Marathon, 84–86
March, 220
Marcus Aurelius, 156, 167
Mardonius, 88
Maria Teresa (Austria), 407, 415, 453
Marius, Gaius, 139
Mark. *See* Gospel of Mark

Mark Antony, 143, 144, 150, 154, 157
Markets, global (early modern era),
    406–408. *See also* Economics;
    Trade/economy
Marne River, battles of, 610, 617, 618
Marriage
    Augustan era, 154
    Code Napoleon and, 482–483
    Egyptian civilization, 44–45
    Roman Empire, 134, 169–170
    See also specific rulers and dynasties
Mars, 129, 133
Marshall, George C., 689–690, 703
Marshall Plan, 690–691, 723, 724
Marsiglio of Padua, 309
Martel, Charles, 214, 218, 229
Martial, 171
Martin V (pope), 310
Martinique, 406
Martyrs/martyrdom, 185, 187
Marx, Karl, 492, 494, 507, 541–543, 621
Marxism, 541–543, 561–562, 565,
    622–623. *See also* Communism;
    Socialism
Marxist Social Democratic Party
    (Russia), 565
Mary I (England), 370, 371–372
Mary II (England), 391, 405
Mary of Guise, 372, 374–375
Mary Queen of Scots, 398
Masaccio, 336
Mask of Agamemnon, 63
Masonic lodges, 446–447, 577
Massachusetts colony, 468
Mass democracy, 645
Masses, The (magazine), 624
"Mass man," 645
Mastaba, 28
Masurian Lakes, battle of, 613
Material conditions, formulas for
    improving, 449–450
*Mathematical Principles of Natural
    Philosophy, The* (Newton), 427
Mathematics, 36, 128, 268–269, 424,
    426, 427, 428–429, 438
Matilda, 246, 283
Matthew. *See* Gospel of Matthew
Maximian, 174
Maximilian (Mexico), 558
Maximilian of Bavaria, 380
Mazarin, Cardinal, 400
Mazzini, Giuseppe, 531, 532–533, 571
McNeill, William, 432
Meaning, Weber on, 595
Measles, 298, 731
Mecca, 198, 199, 204, 344, 741
Medes, 50
Medical practitioners, during Scientific
    Revolution, 431–432
Medical technology, 732
Medical thought and training, during
    Scientific Revolution, 430–432
Medici, Cosimo de, 328, 333
Medici, Giovanni de, 328
Medici, Marie de, 399
Medici family, 326
Medicine, 104–105, 128. *See also* Health
    issues
Medicis, Catherine de, 369, 372,
    376–377
Medieval civilizations, 178
    Byzantine Empire, 193–197
    Christianity, 182–189
    freedom of religion and, 180, 182,
        205–207
    Germany, 189–193

Islam, 197–205
    timeline, 179
Medieval Europe, 208–210, 235,
    264–265, 292
    Brunhild and Fredegund, 215–216
    Carolingian era, 217–225, 226*m*
    Cathedral of Cordoba, 239
    culture, 231–235
    eleventh-century turning point,
        254–264
    England, 214, 216–217
    Ireland, 217
    Italy and Lombards, 213–214
    Merovingian Kingdom, 210–213
    reorganization of, 243–254
    retrenchment and reorganization,
        225, 227–231
    Spain, 214
    timeline, 293
    Urban II (pope), 236, 238
    See also Age of Anxiety; European
        High Middle Ages
Medieval society, Romanticism and,
    538–539
Medieval world view, 420–422
Medina, 204, 344
Meditations (Marcus Aurelius), 167
Megara, 94, 98
Mehmed II "the Conqueror (Ottoman
    Empire)," 342–343
Meiji Emperor, 586
Meiji Restoration of 1867, 586
Mein Kampf (Hitler), 646, 658, 668
Melos, 99, 115
Memphis, 26, 36
Mendel, Gregor, 590
Mendelssohn, Moses, 571–572
Menkaure, 27
Mennonites, 363
Mercantilism, 402, 406–408, 449, 450, 486
Mercenaries, 315
Merchants, 262–264. *See also*
    Trade/economy
Mercury (Roman god), 133
Merkel, Angela, 727
Merneptah, 54
Merovech, 215
Merovingian Kingdom, 210–213,
    215–216, 218, 231–232
Mesoamerica, 13
Mespotamian civilization. *See* Egypt;
    Sumer
Messana, 135
Messiah, 183–184
Metalworking, 13, 24, 31, 49
Metamorphoses, 159
Methodism, 458
Metics, 96
Metternich, Clemens von, 520, 523,
    530, 534
Mexico, 351, 617
Michael (Russian tsar), 409
Michelangelo, 333, 336, 367
Middle Ages, Romanticism and, 538–539.
    See also Age of Anxiety; European
    High Middle Ages; Medieval
    civilizations; Medieval Europe
Middle class (bourgeoisie), 506, 511–512
    1920s pop culture and
        consumerism, 637
    Charles X and, 525
    liberalism and, 524
    Louis Philippe and, 526, 529
    Marxism and, 542–543
    medieval Europe, 262–264
    political economy, 525

Middle East, medieval turmoil in,
    300–305. *See also* Islam;
    Muslims/Muslim Empire;
    Ottoman Empire; *specific
    cultures, kingdoms, empires,
    and countries*
Middle Kingdom, 25, 36–37, 53, 66
Middlemarch (Evans), 597
Middle Minoan Period, 66
Midway Island, battle of, 674, 675
Milan, 190, 324, 326, 328, 368, 531
Miletus, 84, 96, 102
Militant Islam, 740–742
Militarization/militarism. *See* War/
    militarization
Military technology
    Assyrians, 49
    China, 347
    Hellenic era, 76–77
    Hundred Years' War, 315
    medieval Europe, 229
    Ottoman Empire, 342
    Sea Peoples and, 47
    Second Intermediate Period (Egypt),
        37–38
    World War I, 606
    See also Atomic bombs; Nuclear
        arms race; War/militarization
Military-industrial complex, 713
Mill, John Stuart, 595
Mills, 502, 512
Milosevic, Slobodan, 743, 744
Miltiades, 84, 86
Mind at the End of Its Tether
    (Wells), 681
Minerva, 133
Ming dynasty (China), 348, 585
Mining, 502, 503
Mining reforms, in Britain, 535
Minoan civilization, 64–67, 68, 111
Minos, 64, 68
Mirandola, Pico della, 424
Missi dominici, 223
Missionaries. *See* Christian missionaries
Mitannian Empire, 45, 47, 49, 53
Mitterand, Francois, 727
Modena, 326, 527, 548, 550
Modern art and music, 598–600
Modern Devotion, 340–341
Modernism, 597–600
Modern states, early. *See* Nation-states,
    early modern
Moldova, 745
Molina, Juan de, 397
Molotov, Vyacheslav, 689
Mona Lisa (painting), 340
Monarchy
    Augustan era, 150–151
    Austria-Hungary, 562–563
    conservatism and, 523–524
    divine-right, 433
    elective, 413
    England (early modern era),
        392, 405
    French Revolution and, 475–478
    post-French Revolution, 520
    See also specific rulers
Monet, Claude, 598
Money, in Roman Empire, 174, 182
Mongolia, 190
Mongols, 298, 302–305
Monist philosophers, 102
Monks/monasticism
    Cluny, 251
    European High Middle Ages,
        274–275

Ireland, 217
medieval civilizations, 188–189
scholarship, 231, 233
universities and scholasticism, 271–274
Monotheism, 180, 185, 202. *See also* Christianity; Islam
Monroe Doctrine, 486
Montefeltro, Guidobaldo da, 334
Montenegro/Montenegrins, 609, 743
Montesquieu, Baron de, 445, 454, 455
Montfort, Simon de, 286
Montgomery, Bernard, 675
Morale, during World War I, 610, 620
Morality, in Augustan era, 153–155
Moravians, 458
More, Thomas, 329, 341
Morgan, J. P., 569
Morocco, 583, 608, 675, 697, 699
Mortality. *See* Death/mortality
Mortimer, Isabella, 312
Mortimer, Roger, 312
Moscow, 303, 485, 667
Moses, 54
Mosques, 203, 205
Movies, 1920s, 637
Mozart, Wolfgang Amadeus, 459
Mu'awiya, 204
Mubarak, Hosni, 741
Muftis, 344
Mughal Empire, 584
Muhammad, 197, 198–202, 203–204, 206, 344
Muhammad V (Ottoman Empire), 566, 568
Munich agreement (1938), 659–660
Municipal Corporations Act (1835), 535
Münster, 363
Müntzer, Thomas, 360
Murad I (Ottoman Empire), 343
Murad II (Ottoman Empire), 342
Muses, 128
Museum, 128, 156
Music
    Enlightenment, 459
    Hellenic era, 111
    jazz, 637
    modernist, 599–600
Muslims/Muslim Empire, 199, 201–202, 203–205
    Age of Anxiety, 300–305
    Black Death, 298
    caliphs and sultans, 238–241
    Carolingian era and, 220, 222–223, 225
    Charlemagne and, 243
    crusades and, 254–60, 285, 288, 289
    European High Middle Ages and, 268–269
    India decolonization and, 694, 696
    Industrial Revolution and, 496
    militant Islam, 740–742
    postcolonial migrations of, 700m, 701
    scientific advancements, 421
    slavery, 457
    Spain, 214, 233
    terrorism and, 729, 730
    women's rights and, 737
    World War I and, 613, 614–615
    Yugoslavian ethnic cleansing, 742–744
    See also Islam; Ottoman Empire
Mussolini, Benito, 641–643, 644, 659, 673, 675, 676

Mutually assured destruction (MAD), 716
Mycenae/Mycenaeans, 67–71, 111
Mystery cults, 184
Mysticism, 278, 311, 344
Myths, in Hellenic era, 101

N

Nagasaki, 677–678
Nagy, Imre, 689
Namibia, 579
Nanjing, 672
Naples, 129, 289, 290, 326, 328, 340, 368, 478, 483, 531, 550
Napoleon Bonaparte, 480–485, 486, 518, 520, 521, 539
Napoleon III (Louis Napoleon)
    French Revolution, 529, 531, 532
    German war (nineteenth century), 553
    Italian unification, 548, 550, 551
    Second French Empire, 557–558
Narmer, 25
Naseby, battle of, 385
Nasser, Gamel Abdel, 710
National Assembly (France), 464, 471–472, 474, 475, 476
National Convention (France), 477, 478, 479, 480, 482, 488
National identity, preservation of, 726–727
Nationalism
    China, 672
    Code Napoleon and, 483
    democratization and, 515
    ethnic, 739–744, 744
    French Revolution and, 478
    Habsburg Empire and, 562–563
    Italian, 531, 532–533
    Japan, 586, 588, 650–651
    nation-state consolidation and, 546–548, 573, 575
    new imperialism and, 579
    Ottoman Empire and, 566
    race and, 571–573, 574–575
    Russia, 564
    Spanish Civil War, 643–644
    war and, 554
    World War I and, 606–607, 609
    See also Nation-states
National Office of Immigration (France), 699
National Security Council, 692
National self-determination, 614, 626, 627, 659, 679
Nation-states
    conservatism and, 523
    European High Middle Ages, 283–290
    Industrial Revolution and, 514–515
    war and, 554–555
    See also specific nations
Nation-states, early modern, 390–392, 416
    Austrian Habsburg Empire, 415
    central and eastern Europe, 408–411
    centralized states, 396–399
    empirical wars and global markets, 406–408
    English constitutionalism, 404–405
    European society, 392–396
    French absolutism, 399–404
    James I (England), 398–399
    Netherlands, 414–415
    Ottoman Empire, 411–413
    Poland, 413
    Spain, 413–414

Nation-states, nineteenth century
    British democracy, 560–562
    Germany, 551–557
    Habsburg Empire, decline of, 562–563
    Italian unification, 548–551
    nationalism and, 546–548, 571–573, 574–575
    Ottoman Empire, decline of, 566–568
    race and nationalism, 571–573, 574–575
    Russian Empire, decline of, 563–566
    Second French Empire, 557–558
    Third French Republic, 558–560
    U.S. Civil War, 568–571
Native Americans, 570–571
NATO (North Atlantic Treaty Organization), 701, 725, 730, 742, 744
Natural environment, medieval challenges from, 296–300
Natural gas, 505
Naturalism, 597
Natural philosophy, 422, 443. *See also* Scientific Revolution
Natural rights, 477, 589
Natural selection, 590
Nature
    Industrial Revolution and, 508–509
    Romanticism and, 538
    See also Environment
Naval war/navies
    Byzantine Empire, 241
    Persian Wars, 87–88
    World War I, 616–618
    World War II, 663
    See also War/militarization
Navarre, 254–255
Nazi Germany, 632
    appeasement (1933–1939), 658–661
    emergence of, 644, 646–650
    homefront and role of women, 670–672
    Italian fascism and, 643
    Japanese imperialism and, 650–651
    Nietzsche and, 592
    Spanish Civil War and, 643–644
    totalitarianism, 641
    World War I and, 618
    World War II empire, 667–670
Nazi SA (storm troopers), 646, 647
Nazi SS, 647, 667, 668
Neanderthals, 7
Nefertiti, 41, 42, 43
Nehru, Jawaharlal, 694, 696
Nelson, Horatio, 480, 483
Neoclassical architecture, 460
Neolithic era, 9, 11
Neptune, 133
Nero, 161–162, 170–171
Nerva, 165
Netherlands
    Belgian revolution against, 526
    colonialism (post-World War II), 705
    Congress System and, 521
    Cromwell, Oliver, 385
    early modern era, 414–415
    elementary education, 513
    empirical wars and global markets (early modern era), 406–408
    European unity and, 725
    French Revolution and, 478
    Habsburg, 369, 373–374
    imperialism, 583–584, 587m
    Lutheran Reformation and, 361
    Napoleon and, 483
    postcolonial migrations to, 698

Renaissance, 338, 340
Spain and, 375, 413
Thirty Years' War, 379, 380
World War II, 662, 673
Neustria, 211, 212, 215–216
New Astronomy, The (Kepler), 426
New Atlantis, The (Bacon), 428
New Comedy, 126
Newcomen, Thomas, 502
New Deal, 640
New Economic Policy (NEP), 651–652
Newfoundland, 406
New France (Canada), 406, 448
New Harmony, Indiana, 541
New Heloise, The (Rousseau), 458
New imperialism, 576–578, 600–601
Africa, 581–584
arts, 595, 597–600
Asia, 584–588
culture and intellectual controversy, 589–595, 596–597
motives and methods, 578–581
New International Economic Order (NIEO), 735, 736
New Kingdom, in Egyptian civilization, 38–45, 53
New Logic, 273
New Mexico, 406
New Model Army, 384–385
New Orleans, 406
New Spain, 486
Newspapers, revolutions of 1848, 527
New Testament, 125, 183, 341, 358–359, 361, 362. *See also* Bible; Gospels
Newton, Isaac, 427, 434, 444, 593–594
New Zealand, 613, 614, 704
Nicaea, 187, 341
Nicaean Creed, 187–188
Nicholas I (Russia), 523
Nicholas II (pope), 251, 253
Nicholas II (Russia), 565, 607, 620–621
Nicholas V (pope), 335, 366–367
Nicholas of Cusa, 424
Nicias, 99, 100
Nietzsche, Friedrich, 591–592
Nike, statue of, 119
Nile River/Nile River Valley, 12*m*, 23–24, 25, 26, 27–28, 37, 583
Nimrud, 47
Ninety-Five Theses, 358
Nineveh, 47, 50
Ninhursaga. *See* Inanna
Nivelle, Robert, 612
Nixon, Richard M., 710, 711
Nkrumah, Kwame, 697–698
Noah's ark, 16
Nobility, French Revolution and, 474
No Exit (Sartre), 686
Nominalism, 270
Nonaggression pact (Nazi Germany and Soviet Union), 661
Normandy (Normans), 243, 245–246, 255, 312, 313
Normandy invasion (World War II), 676
Norsemen, 225
North Africa
decolonization of, 696–697
postcolonial migrations from, 701
World War II and, 663, 664–665, 675
See also specific countries
North American colonies, 449
North Atlantic Treaty Organization. *See* NATO
North Briton, The (newspaper), 467

Northern Ireland, 561, 727
Northern Renaissance, 338–341
Northern Star, The (newspaper), 536
North German Confederation, 552
North Korea, 704, 722
North Sea, 616
Norway, 243, 245, 515, 521, 661, 668
Nova Scotia, 406
Novgorod, 261
Novum Organum (Bacon), 428
Nubia, 36, 38, 39, 40, 48
Nuclear arms race, 693–694, 717, 718
Nuclear defense system, 717
Nuclear energy, 731
Nuclear Test Ban Treaty, 710–711
Nuclear threats, during Cold War, 708–712
Nuclear weapons, 677–678, 684
Numidia, 137, 139
Nuremberg, 340
Nuremberg rallies, 648

O

Oath of the Horatii (painting), 460
Oaths, 228
Observation, 101, 110
Occupation zones, post-World War II, 690
Octavian, 143–145, 148, 150. *See also* Augustus
Odovacer, 193
Odysseus, 62
Odyssey, 70, 101
Oedipus Rex, 114
Office employment, 508
Ohio River Valley, 407, 468
Oil, 505
anti-immigrant sentiments and, 699
globalization and, 736
Italian Fascism and, 659
women's rights and, 737
World War I, 614
World War II, 665, 667, 673, 675
Oil painting, 338, 339
Okinawa, 677
Old Comedy, 126
Old Kingdom, in Egyptian civilization, 25, 26–30
Old Logic, 269, 270
Old Regime (France), crisis in, 470–471
Oligarchy, 81
Olmecs, 13
Olympia (Nazi propaganda film), 648
Olympians (gods), 112, 113, 184
Olympics (1936), 648
Olympus, 112
On the Restoration and Opposition of Numbers, 268
On the Revolutions of the Heavenly Orbs (Copernicus), 424–425
Opera, 459
Operation Barbarossa, 665
Opinion, in European High Middle Ages, 274–278
Opium Wars, 585–586
Optics (Descartes), 419
Optimates, 139, 141, 142
Oral tradition, during Aegean Dark Age, 70
Orange Free State, 583
Oratory of Divine Love, 365
Orchestra, 459
Order
liberty versus, 148, 150, 176
Roman Empire, 159–163, 165–168
Order of Preachers. *See* Dominicans

Order of the Garter, 312
Oresteia, 114
Organization for European Economic Cooperation, 691
Organization of Petroleum Exporting Countries (OPEC), 736
Origin of Species (Darwin), 589, 590
Orlando, Vittorio Emanuele, 641
Orléanists, 318
Ortega y Gasset, Jose, 645
Orthodox Christianity, 196–197
Orwell, George, 686
Osiris, 37
Osman, 341
Ostia, 161
Ostmark, 220
Ostracism, 83–84
Ostrogoths, 190, 193, 194, 213–214
Otto I "the Great" (Germany), 249, 252
Otto II (Germany), 249, 251
Ottokar II (Germany), 339
Ottoman Empire, 193, 328, 339, 341–346, 369
Catherine the Great and, 410
decline of, 566–568
early modern era, 411–413
new imperialism, 587*m*
Peter the Great and, 409
World War I and, 606, 607, 609, 613, 614–615, 620, 625
Zionism and, 573
Ottoman Public Debt Administration, 566
Ottoman Turks. *See* Ottoman Empire
Ottonian Renaissance, 249, 252–253
Otto of Brunswick, 285, 289
Ovid, 158–159, 170
Owen, Robert, 540–541
Owen, Wilfred, 604, 618
Ownership, working class and, 506–507
Oxford University, 561

P

Pachomius, 188
Pacific theater (World War II), 672–674, 676–678
Pagans/paganism, 180, 182, 184–185, 189, 191, 211
Pahlavi, Reza, 741
Paine, Thomas, 458, 468, 477
Painting
cave, 8–9
Enlightenment, 459–461
Hellenic era, 111–112
modernist, 598–599
Renaissance, 336–338, 339, 340
Pakistan, 205, 694, 696, 699
Palace, 163
Palace of Versailles, 400–402
Palaeologus, Michael, 301
Palatinate, 380
Paleolithic era, 7–9
Palestine, 11, 20, 38, 39, 48, 52, 54, 55–56, 57*m*, 184, 573, 613, 628, 692–693
Pamela (Richardson), 458
Pan-Hellenic shrines and festivals, 75
Pankhurst, Emmeline, 595
Pan-Slav separatist movement, 606
Pantheons, 133, 167
Papacy
Age of Anxiety, 305–311
Charlemagne and, 219–220
European High Middle Ages, 277
High Middle Ages, 289
Italian city-states and, 328

Papacy, *continued*
  Italian Renaissance and, 325
  medieval Germany and Italy,
    249–254
  Renaissance, 365–368
  Tudors and, 369, 370, 371
  See also Catholic Church; *specific*
    popes
Papal monarchy, 305–306
Papal schism. *See* Great Schism
Papal States, 219, 289, 307, 308
  Congress System and, 521, 522
  Italian unification and, 548
  revolutions and, 527, 531, 532
Paracelsus, 431
Parelements, 474
Paris, 211, 270–271, 324, 473
  1920s culture, 637
  French Revolution and, 473, 474, 475
  German war (nineteenth
    century), 554
  liberation of, 676
  revolutions of 1848, 529
  World War II, 662
Paris Commune, 558
Paris National Guard, 473
Paris Peace Conference, 641
Parlements, 399, 400, 408, 471
Parliament Act (1911), 562
Parliaments
  Hundred Years' War and, 319
  medieval, 246, 286, 288
  Reformation and, 371–372, 382
  See also English Parliament
Parma, 527, 548, 550
Parmenides of Elea, 102, 103
Parr, Catherine, 371
Parthenon, 94
Parthian Empire, 142, 144, 167, 168, 172
Pascal, Blaise, 436
Passchendaele, 612
Paterfamilias, 134
Patrician families, in Rome, 133–134
Patrick, Saint, 217
Patriotism
  democratization and, 515
  French Revolution and, 478
  See also Nationalism
Paul (apostle of Jesus), 357
Paul (formerly Saul of Tarsus), 183
Paul III (pope), 367
Paul VII (pope), 481
Paul the Deacon, 234
Pausanias, 88, 92
Pavia, 214
Peace (play), 115
Peace of Amiens, 483
Peace of Augsburg, 361, 379
Peace of God, 236
Peace of Lodi, 328
Peace of Westphalia, 380, 381*m*
Pearl Harbor, 651, 671, 673, 674
Peasants
  Europe (early modern era), 393–395
  French Revolution and, 471
Peasants' Crusade, 258
Peasants' Revolt, 300
Pedantry, 128
Pedophilia, in Catholic Church, 740
Pedro I (Portugal), 486
Pegae, 94
Peisistratus, 82–83
Pella, 121
Peloponnese, 69, 88
Peloponnesian League, 97

Peloponnesian War, 94–95, 96, 97–101,
  116, 120
Penal Code (France0, 482
Penances, 357
Penicillin, 731
Peninsulares, 486
People's Liberation Army (PLA), 703
People's Republic of China, 703, 704
People's Will, 564
Pepin III, 218, 219, 220
Pepin of Heristal, 218
Perdiccas III, 121
Perestroika, 717
Pericles, 90, 92, 94, 96–97, 98, 99,
  116, 141
Periodicals, revolutions of 1848, 527
Perpetua, Vibia, 180, 182
Perpindicular Gothic architecture, 339
Perry, Matthew, 586
Persecution, 185, 186, 187
Persepolis, 123
Perses, 74
Pershing, John, 617
Persia, 608
Persian Empire
  Alexander the Great and, 122,
    123–124
  Athenian Empire and, 95*m*, 97
  Byzantine Empire and, 194
  Hellenistic era and, 120
  Jews and, 56
  Peloponnesian War and, 100
  Zoroaster, 57
Persian Gulf, 15
Persian Letters (Montesquieu), 445
Persian Wars, 84–88, 92–93, 106
Personal autonomy, 524
Personal identity, 508
Perspective, 334, 336–337
Peru, 351, 486
Petain, Henri Philippe, 612, 662
Peter (apostle of Jesus), 186, 218
Peter II (Hungary), 644
Peterloo Massacre, 534
Peter the Great (Russia), 394–395,
  409–410, 451 ▬
Peter the Hermit, 257–258
Petrarch, 330–332
Petrograd, 621
Petroleum, 503, 505
Petronius, 171
Phaistos, 66
Phalanx, 76
Pharaohs, 26–27, 38–44. *See also specific*
  pharaohs
Pharsalus, battle of, 142
Philip II (England), 249, 285, 286
Philip II (Macedonia), 121
Philip II (Spain), 361, 372, 373–376,
  413, 414
Philip III (France), 288
Philip IV (France), 288, 306, 307,
  311, 313
Philip V (France), 313
Philip V (Macedonia), 137
Philip V (Spain), 403
Philip VI (France), 313
Philip of Anjou, 402, 414
Philip of Hesse, 362
Philip of Swabia, 289
Philippi, 144
Philippines, 674, 676, 704
Philip the Good of Burgundy,
  317–318, 319
Philistines, 54, 55

Philosophes
  community of, 443–444
  despots and, 451
  French Revolution and, 480
  Jesuit education and, 448
  Montesquieu, Baron de, 454
  religious tolerance, 448
  romanticism and, 537, 538
  Roussea, Jean-Jacques, 453–454
  slavery and, 457–458
  women, 455
  writing, 445–446
Philosophical Dictionary (Voltaire), 448
Philosophy
  asceticism, 188
  Augustan era, 156
  Enlightenment, 443–444
  European High Middle Ages, 268,
    273–274
  existentialism, 686–687
  Hellenic era, 101–104, 107–110
  Hellenistic era, 127–128
  Marcus Aurelius, 167
  medieval world view and, 422–423
  new imperialism and, 591–592
Phintias, 111
Phoenicia/Phoenicians, 20, 55, 135
Phoenician War, 135
Physical education, in Hellenic era, 77
Physics, 424–427, 593–594, 596–597
Physiocrats, 449
Picasso, Pablo, 599, 603, 644
Pico della Mirandola, Giovanni,
  322, 324
Piedmont, 523, 531, 548, 550, 558
Piedmont-Sardinia, 521, 531,
  548, 550
Pietism, 458
Pikes, 315
Pilgrims, 238
Pilsudski, Josef, 644
Piraeus, 95
Pisa, 261, 310, 326
Pisano, Giovanni, 333
Pisano, Nicola, 333
Pithom, 54
Pitt, William, 408
Pius II (pope), 311
Pius VII (pope), 522
Pius IX (pope), 531, 532, 550
Pius XI (pope), 643
Pizan, Christine de, 316–317
Pizarro, Francisco, 351
Plague, The (Camus), 686
Plague. *See* Black Death
Plains Indians, 570
Plantagenet dynasty, 285–286, 319
Plantation slavery, 457
Plassey, battle of, 408
Plataea, 88, 92, 98
Plato, 108–109, 110, 120, 330, 424
Plautus, 155
Plays. *See* Theater
Pleasure, 127
Plebeians, 133, 134, 139
Plebiscites, 134
Plessis, Armand Jean de (Cardinal
  and duc de Richelieu), 380,
  399, 400, 442
Pliny the Elder, 164–165
Pliny the Younger, 164–165
Pluralist philosophers, 103
Plutarch, 172
Pluto, 133
Podesta, 325

Poetry
  Age of Anxiety, 316–317
  ancient Greece, 101
  Augustan era, 156, 157–159
  crusades and, 260
  Hellenic era, 105–106
  Hellenistic era, 128
  medieval Europe, 232
  Renaissance, 330–332
  Roman Empire, 170, 171
  William IX (duke of Aquitaine and
    count of Poitou), 276–277
Pogroms, 572
Poitiers, 315
Poland
  authoritarianism in, 644
  Bolshevik Revolution and, 621
  Catherine the Great and, 410
  Congress System and, 521
  Czechoslovakia and, 660
  elective monarchy in, 413
  European Union membership, 725
  peasants and serfs in, 393–394
  revolutions in, 527
  Solidarity, 718–719
  Soviet Union and, 689
  Treaty of Versailles and, 627–628
  World War I, 613
  World War I aftermath, 635
  World War II, 660–661, 667,
    676, 679
Police power, during World War I, 620
Polio, 731
Polis, 75–78
  decline of, 125
  Hellenistic era and, 126, 127
  intellectual and artistic life, 101–115
  Peloponnesian War and, 94
  Persian Wars and, 84, 86–87
  See also Athens; Hellenic era;
    Hellenistic era; Sparta
Politburo, 651, 652
Political economy, 524–525
Political leaders. *See specific leaders and
  rulers*
Political purges, in Soviet Union,
  653–654
Political Testament (Frederick II), 390
Political theory, states and, 397–399
Politics
  Alexander the Great, 124
  Arabia (pre-Islamic), 197
  Athens, 81, 82–84, 93
  Augustan era, 150–153
  Black Death and, 300
  Byzantine Empire, 196
  centralized states in early modern
    era, 396–399
  Constantinople, 188
  Diocletian, 173–175
  Egyptian civilization, 24–25
  England (medieval), 246, 283–284
  First Triumvirate, 142–144
  France (High Middle Ages), 286
  Hellenic culture and, 107–115
  Hellenistic era, 125–126
  Hobbes, Thomas, 433
  Italian city-states, 325
  Italian Renaissance, 326–329
  Locke, John, 433–434, 435
  Lutheran Reformation, 358–361
  Machiavelli, Nicoolo, 432–433
  medieval Europe, 227–229
  Montesquieu, Baron de, 454
  Persian Empire, 124

Reformation, 372–377
Roman emperors, 159–168, 176
Rome and Roman Empire, 134–135,
  138–141
Roussea, Jean-Jacques, 454
science of, 432–434, 435
Second Triumvirate, 144–145
Sparta, 80
  See also American Revolution; Cold
    War; Decolonization; French
    Revolution; Ideology; Interwar
    years (1919–1939); World War I;
    World War II
Pollution, 732
Polo, Marco, 302–303
Polybius, 118, 120
Polycarp of Smyrna, 185
Polytheism, 180
Pompadour, Madame de, 455
Pompeii, 163, 164
Pompey, 141–142, 155
Pontifex maximus, 151
Popes, Congress System and, 521
Popular culture
  1920s, 637
  "mass man" and, 645
Popular Front, 643
Populares, 139, 141, 142
Population growth, in twentieth and
  twenty-first centuries, 735. *See
  also* Demographics
Po River, 129
Portrait, from Roman Empire, 149
Portugal
  French Revolution and, 478
  imperialism, 344, 347–348, 349,
    350*m*, 351, 578, 583, 587*m*
  Napoleon and, 486
  Netherlands and, 414
  slave trade, 457
  Spain and, 413
Poseidon, 91, 133
Post-Impressionism, 598–599
Postindustrialism, 744–746
Potidaea, 97
Potsdam Conference, 688
Pottery, 13
Pottery painting, in Hellenic era, 111–112
Poverty
  early modern era, 393–395
  Enlightenment and, 442
  Great Depression, 638–641
  Industrial Revolution, 507, 515
  laissez-faire economics and, 450
  North-South divide, 733, 734*m*,
    735–736
Power, 107, 109, 134, 400–402, 711
Power technology, 503–505
Praetorian Guard, 152, 160
Pragmatic Sanction, 369, 415
Prague, 380, 530, 660
Praise of Folly, 341
Predestination, 364
Predynastic Era, in Sumer, 15–16
Prehistoric cultures, evolution of, 6–13
Prelude to "The Afternoon of a Faun"
  (Debussy), 600
Presbyterian Church, 404
Pre-Socratics, 107
Press, revolutions of 1848, 527
Primary education, 513
Primitivism, 600
Primogeniture, 256
Prince, The (Machiavelli), 328–329,
  432–433

Princeps, 156–157
Princeps civitatis, 151
Princip, Gavrilo, 606
Principals of Political Economy
  (Ricardo), 525
Principate, 151
Principles of Geology (Lyell), 590
Printing press, 340, 347
Private appropriation, 449
Private life, European unity and,
  727–729
Procopius, 195
Production
  Industrial Revolution, 501–505
  World War II, 670–671
Professors, 272
Progress, 331–332
Progressive era, 569
Proletariat. *See* Working class
Promised Land, 56, 58
Propaganda
  Augustan era, 157–159
  Nazi Germany, 647, 648
  Stalin, Joseph, 652, 653–654
  World War II, 671
Property rights
  Code Napoleon, 483
  Enlightenment ideas about, 454, 455
  liberalism and, 524
  political economy and, 525
  Sumer, 17
Prophets, 56, 57–58
Prose, 106
  Augustan era, 159
  Renaissance, 330–332
  See also Writing
Prostitution, 170
Protagoras, 107
Protectionism. *See* Mercantilism
Protestant Nonconformists, 534
Protestant Reformation, 277, 397
  Catholic Reformation and, 367, 368
  England, 369–372
  final religious upheavals, 377,
    379–386
  literacy and, 423–424
  Lutheran, 356–361
  politics and, 372–377
  Scientific Revolution and, 424–425
  Swiss, 361–365
Protestants/Protestantism
  England (early modern era), 404, 405
  Enlightenment, 448, 458
  globalization and, 739
  Napoleon and, 481
  nation-states and, 548
  Nazi Germany, 650
  Northern Ireland, 561
  witchcraft and, 437
Protestant Union, 379
Provence, count of, 475
Prussia
  Austrian Habsburg Empire and, 415
  Catherine the Great and, 410
  Congress System and, 521, 522, 523
  Frederick II, 390
  Frederick the Great, 451–452
  French Revolution and, 475, 478
  German unification and, 551–557
  Holy Alliance, 523
  Italian unification and, 550
  militarism in, 410–411
  Napoleon and, 483, 485, 520
  Napoleon III and, 558
  Poland and, 413

Prussia, *continued*
  Quintuple Alliance, 522
  revolutions of 1848, 530
Psychoanalysis, 593
Psychology
  Freud, Sigmund, 592–593
  Hellenic era, 107–110
Ptolemy, 421
Ptolemy I, 125, 128
Ptolemy of Alexandria, 128
Publius Cornelius Scipio, 137
Publius Cornelius Scipio Aemilianus
  Africanus Numantinus, 118,
  134, 137
Publius Cornelius Scipio Africanus,
  134, 137, 140
Puerto Rico, 406
Punishment, Enlightenment ideas
  about, 450
Purgatory, 357
Puritans, 371, 382–384, 385, 386,
  404, 424
Pushkin, Alexander, 518, 537
Putin, Vladimir, 721–722, 744
P'u Yi, Henry, 650
Pylos, 69, 99
Pyramids, 28–30
Pyrataneis, 83
Pyrenees, 214
Pythagoras, 104

Q

Qadesh, 45
Qing dynasty (China), 585
Quadrivium, 234, 272
Quebec Act (1774), 468
Quebec City, 408
Quesnay, Francois, 449
Quintessence, 422
Quintillian, 165
Quintuple Alliance, 522
Qur'an, 198, 202, 260, 344

R

Race
  nationalism and, 571–573, 574–575
  new imperialism and, 579–580
  postcolonial migrations and, 699
Racism, 580, 668–670. *See also* anti-
  Semitism; Ethnic cleansing;
  Holocaust
Radical revolution, in France
  (1792–1794), 475–478
Radio, 733
Radium Institute of the University of
  Paris, 596
Railways, 503–505, 570
Raj, 584–585
Ramadan, 202
"Ram Caught in a Thicket" (Sumerian
  artifact), 5
Ramillies, 403
Ramses (city), 54
Ramses I, 43
Ramses II, 33, 43–44, 54
Ranke, Leopold von, 594
Raphael, 367
Rasputin, Grigori, 620
Rationalism. *See* Enlightenment;
  Reason/rationalism; Scientific
  Revolution
Ravenna, 190–191, 194, 196, 214,
  218–219, 222, 326
Reagan, Ronald, 717–718
Realism, 597, 598

Reason/rationalism, 156, 274, 311
  Aristotle and, 274
  authority and, 270–271
  dialectics and, 269–270
  Freud, Sigmund, 592
  Hellenic era, 110
  Latin high culture and, 156
  "mass man" and, 645
  mysticism and, 278, 311
  Nietzsche, Friedrich, 592
  Weber, Max, 594–595
  See also Enlightenment; Scientific
  Revolution
Reasonableness of Christianity, The
  (Locke), 434
Red-figure pottery, 111–112
Red Scare (1919), 623, 624
Red Sea, 195, 344
Reed, John, 624
Reflections on the Revolution in France
  (Burke), 476–477
Reform congregations, 365
Reform literature (Enlightenment),
  445–446
Reformation, 366m, 386–387
  Catholic, 365–368
  England, 369–372
  final religious upheavals, 377,
  379–386
  Habsburg-Valois wars, 366m,
  368–369
  literacy and, 423–424
  Lutheran, 356–361
  politics (foreign and domestic),
  372–377
  Scientific Revolution and, 424–425
  Shakespeare and, 378–379
  Swiss, 361–365
Reich Cinema Law, 648
Reich Film Chamber, 647
Reichsrat, 562
Reichstag, 552, 556, 557, 635, 644,
  646–647
Reign of Terror, 478–479
Reims, 319
Relativism, 107–108
Religion
  Amarna Period, 40–43
  Arabia (pre-Islamic), 197–198
  Aristotle and, 110
  Augustan era, 156
  Bible and, 51–58
  Byzantine Empire, 242
  Celts and, 211
  conservatism and, 524
  Darwin, Charles, 589, 590–591
  early modern era, 397
  Enlightenment and, 448–449, 458
  European High Middle Ages,
  274–278
  freedom of, 180, 182, 205–207
  Freud, Sigmund, 593
  Hellenic era, 75, 112
  Industrial Revolution and, 515
  Locke and, 434
  Middle Kingdom (Egypt), 37
  Modern Devotion, 340–341
  Netherlands (early modern era), 415
  Nietzsche, Friedrich, 592
  Ottoman Empire, 344
  Pantheons (Greek and Roman), 133
  post-World War II divisions,
  739–744
  Scientific Revolution and, 418–421,
  434, 436

spiritual crises (medieval Europe),
  305–311
  Sumer, 16–17, 18, 19–21
  Weber, Max, 596
  World War I and, 606–607
  See also Catholic Church;
  Christianity; Islam; Latin
  Christian Europe; Reformation
Remus, 129
Renaissance, 296, 322–324, 327m, 352
  Atlantic exploration and, 346–351
  context for, 324–329
  culture of, 329–338
Renaissance, *continued*
  northern Europe, 338–341
  Ottoman Empire, 341–346
  papacy, 365–368
  scientific advancements, 423
  twelfth-century, 268–271
  See also Reformation
Renoir, Pierre Auguste, 598
Representation, 466–468
Repression, in Soviet Union, 653–654
Republicanism, 464
Republics. *See specific republics*
Responsibility, existentialism and, 687
Revere, Paul, 467
Revolutions
  1830–1832, 525–527
  1848, 527–533
  eastern Europe (anti-communist),
  718–720
  See American Revolution; French
  Revolution; Glorious Revolution
Rhee, Syngman, 704
Rhetoric, 170
Rhineland militarization (1936), 659
Rhine River, 142, 153, 191, 210, 211
Rhodes, 126, 344
Rhodes, Cecil 576, 584
Ricardo, David, 525
Richard I (England), 249, 285
Richard II (England), 317
Richard III (England), 319, 369
Richardson, Samuel, 458
Richelieu, Cardinal. *See* Plessis,
  Armand Jean de
Riefenstahl, Leni, 648
Rights. *See* Bill of Rights
Rights of Man, The (Paine), 477
Rio de Janeiro, 486
Rio de Janeiro earth summit (1992),
  732–733
Rio de la Plata, 486
Ripuarian Franks, 210
Rite of Spring, The (ballet), 600
Rivers. *See specific rivers*
Roads. *See* Infrastructure
Robert "Curthose," 245
Robert of Chester, 268
Robespierre, Maximilien, 456, 478–479
Rockefeller, John D., 569
Roehm, Ernst, 647
Roger II (Normandy), 255
Rollo, 243
Romagna, 550
Roman baths, 155
Roman Catholic Church. *See* Catholic
  Church
Roman Empire, 120, 135–139
  Augustan era, 150–159
  basilicas, 279–280
  Byzantine Empire and, 193–197
  Charlemagne and, 221–222
  Christianity and, 182–189, 206

decline of, 172–175
dynasties, 159–163, 176
elective option for continuity and
    order, 163, 165–168
Germany and, 189–193
imperial economy, 168–169
intellectual life, 170–172
Islam and, 197–205
liberty versus order, 148, 150, 176
medieval Europe and, 210
Pliny the Elder and Pliny the
    Younger, 164–165
social developments, 169–170
Roman Republic, 120, 132
    Augustan era and, 150–159
    Roman Empire and, 135–138
    Roman revolution, 132–135
    stresses in, 138–139
    See also Roman Empire
Romanesque architecture, 280–281
Romania/Romanians
    appeasement (1933–1939), 658
    authoritarianism in, 644
    interwar years (1919–1939), 635
    nationalism, 562, 563
    revolutions (1848), 530
    Soviet Union and, 689
    World War I, 623, 627
    World War II, 661, 665, 676, 679
Romano-Celts, 211, 212, 214
Romanov dynasty, 409, 625
Romanticism, 536–539
Romanus IV Diogenes (Byzantine
    Empire), 242
Rome, 118, 120, 146
    civil war, 139, 141–145
    Cornelia, 140–141
    Habsburg-Valois wars, 369
    Italian unification and, 550
    kingdom of, 129–131
    origin of, 129–132
    papacy and, 307, 308
    revolution of, 132–135
    rise of, 130m
    Roman Republic, 120, 132–139
    Visigoths and, 191
    See also Roman Empire
Rommel, Erwin, 663, 675
Romulus (Augustulus), 129–130, 193
Roosevelt, Franklin Delano, 640, 659
    death of, 677
    internationalism, 687
    Tehran Conference, 679, 688
    Truman, Harry S., 684
    World War II, 663, 665, 671,
        674–675
    Yalta, 679, 688
Roosevelt, Theodore, 569, 649
Roundheads, 384
Rousseau, Jean-Jacques, 451, 453–454,
    455, 458, 537
Rouvroy, Louis de (Duc de Saint-
    Simon), 401
Royal Air Force (RAF), 663
Royal bureaucrats, in France (early
    modern era), 402
Royal Society for Promoting Natural
    Knowledge, 423
Royal Society for the Advancement of
    Knowledge, 427, 435
Royal William (steamship), 504
Rudolf II (Holy Roman Emperor), 426
Rudolf of Habsburg, 339
Rules, Christian, 189
Rump Parliament, 385

Rural lifestyles, during Industrial
    Revolution, 494–497
Ruric, 242
Rus, 242
Russell, Bertrand, 606
Russia, 242, 261, 303–304
    absolutism in, 408–409
    anti-Semitism in, 572
    Catherine the Great, 410, 451
    Congress System and, 521, 522, 523
    Crimean War, 548, 558, 564
    ethnic nationalism in, 744
    Holy Alliance, 523
    imperialism, 585–586
    Industrial Revolution and, 499,
        500, 505
    Japan and, 588
    League of Nations and, 628
    Napoleon and, 483, 485, 518, 520
    peasants and serfs in, 393–395
    Peter the Great, 409–410
    Poland and, 413
    Polish revolution against, 527
    Quintuple Alliance, 522
    reform (post-Soviet), 720–722
    See also Soviet Union; World War I
Russian Empire, decline of, 563–566
Russian Orthodox Church, 409
Russian Revolution, 620–624
Russo-Japanese War, 565
Ruthenians, 563

S

SA (storm troopers), 646, 647
Sacraments, 187
Sacrosancta, 310
Sadat, Anwar, 741
Saddles, 229
Safavid Empire, 344
Sailing. *See* Atlantic exploration
St. Bartholomew's Day Massacre,
    377, 397
St. Denis (monastery), 281
Saint Dominique (Haiti), 406, 485–486
St. Lawrence River Valley, 406, 407
St. Peter's (church), 335–336
St. Petersburg, 410
Saints, 185, 307. *See also specific saints*
Saint-Simon, Henri de, 532, 540
Sais, 49
Saite dynasty, 49
Saladin, 285, 301
Salamis, 86–88, 92
Salian dynasty, 210, 251, 253–254, 288
Salian Law, 313
Salons, 446–447
Salvation, 364
Salvation Army, 515
Samarkand, 298
Samothrace, 119
Sancho III "the Great" (Navarre),
    254–255
San Martin, Jose de, 486, 487m
Sans-culottes, 475, 477, 478
Sappho, 101
Sara (wife of Abraham), 198
Sarajevo, 609
Sarcophagus, 131, 132
Sardinia, 136, 478. *See also* Piedmont-
    Sardinia
Sargon, 22, 25
Sargon II, 48
Sarkozy, Nicholas, 727
Sartre, Jean-Paul, 686, 738
Sassanid Empire, 194

Sassoon, Siegfried, 612
Satellite technology, 693
Satire, 171
Satires (Juvenal), 171
Satrapies, 124
Satyricon, The, 171
Satyrs, 113
Saul, 55
Saul of Tarsus. *See* Paul
Saxons, 191, 216, 249, 251, 288
Saxony, 220, 289, 521, 529
Scandinavia, 224, 513
Schism, 255, 308, 309, 365
Schleswig, 552
Schlieffen, Alfred von, 609
Schlieffen Plan, 610, 612, 617
Schliemann, Heinrich, 63, 70
Schmalkaldic League, 361
Schoenberg, Arnold, 600
Scholarship, in medieval Europe,
    231–233. *See also* Education;
    Universities; Writing
Scholasticism, in European High
    Middle Ages, 271–274
Schools. *See* Universities
Schroeder, Gerhard, 727
Schubert, Franz, 537
Science, 36
    Enlightenment and, 444–445
    European High Middle Ages,
        268, 269
    globalization and, 731–736
    Hellenic era, 101–104
    Hellenistic era, 128
    Industrial Revolution and, 498
    new imperialism and, 589–591,
        592–595, 596–597
    Roman Empire, 173
Scientific method, 420, 428, 589
Scientific racism, 580
Scientific Revolution, 418–420, 438
    anticipation of, 422–424
    astronomy and physics, 424–427
    Enlightenment and, 444
    medieval world view and, 420–422
    politics as science, 432–434, 435
    religion and, 434, 436
    superstition, 436–437
    theory and application, 429–432
    truth, new approaches to, 427–429
Scotland, 214, 313, 365, 374–375, 382,
    384, 385, 398
Scots, 312
Scott, Sir Walter, 539
Sculpture
    Enlightenment, 459–461
    Hellenic era, 112
    Hellenistic era, 126–127
    Renaissance, 333
SDP, 557
Sea Peoples, invasion of, 46–47of,
    54, 84
Seafaring, 65
Second Battle of the Marne, 617
"Second Coming, The" (Yeats), 625
Second Continental Congress, 468
Second Crusade, 258, 260, 304
Second Estate, 472
Second French Empire, 557–558
Second French Republic, 529, 557–558
Second Intermediate Period, in Egyptian
    civilization, 37–38, 45, 53
Second Punic War, 137
Second Sex, The (de Beauvoir), 738
Second Triumvirate, 144–145, 157

Second Vatican Council, 739–740
Secret societies, 184
Secularism, 433
  Durkheim, Emile, 594
  England (early modern era), 405
  Freud, Sigmund, 593
  Nietzsche, Friedrich, 592
Security Council of the United
  Nations, 704
Sedan, battle of, 554
Sedition Act (1918), 620
Seleukos, 125
Self-Help (Smiles), 555
Self-interest, 524–525
Selim I (Ottoman Empire), 344
Seljuks, 239, 242, 255, 302, 344. *See also*
  Ottoman Empire
Senate (Roman), 131, 132, 134, 139
  Augustan era, 150–152, 153–154,
    156–157
  Domitian and, 163
  First Triumvirate and, 143–144
  Flavian dynasty, 162
  "Good Emperors" and, 165, 167
  Julio-Claudians, 160
  Sulla and, 141–142
Seneca, 330
Seneca the Younger, 170–171
Senenmut, 38
Separation of powers, 454, 469
Sepoys, 584
September 11 (2001) terrorist attacks,
  729, 730, 731, 745
Septimus Severus, 168
Serapis, 184
Serbia/Serbs
  authoritarianism, 644
  ethnic cleansing, 742–744
  ideology, 530
  NATO and, 725
  World War I, 606, 607–609, 613,
    620, 627
Serfs, 230, 264, 299
  Catherine the Great and, 410
  enlightened despots and, 451, 453
  Europe (early modern era), 393–395
  Napoleon and, 483
  Peter the Great and, 410
Servetus, Michael, 365
Seti, 43
Seventh Crusade, 304
Seven Years' War, 407, 408, 411
Severans, 168, 169, 176
Sextus, 132–133
Seymour, Jane, 371
Sforza, Francesco, 328
Shah, 741
Shakespeare, John, 378
Shakespeare, William, 378–379
Shang Dynasty, 13
Shanghai, 672
Shari'a, 203
Shariah, 344
Shaw, George Bernard, 561, 606
Shechem, 56
Shi'a/Shi'ites, 204, 238–239, 241, 344, 730
Ships. *See* Atlantic exploration
Shires, 283
Shopping. *See* Consumerism
Short Parliament, 384
Siberia, 408–409
Sic et Non, 271
Sicilian crusades, 254–255, 304
Sicily
  Black Death, 298
  Byzantine Empire and, 194

Charles of Anjou, 340
  High Middle Ages, 289, 290
  Italian political development
    and, 326
  Italian unification and, 550
  Muslim Empire and, 225, 239
  Peloponnesian War, 97, 99–100
  Roman Empire and, 191
  Roman Republic and,
    135–136, 137
  scientific advances, 421
  World War II, 675
Sidon, 55
Siemens Brothers, 505
Siena, 326
Sierra Leone, 577
Sigibert, 215, 216
Sigibert II, 216
Silesia, 407, 415
Silver Age (Rome), 170–171
Sinai, 38, 52, 54, 710
Singapore, 723
Sins, 187
Sistine Chapel, 336, 367
Sixth Crusade, 304
Sixtus IV (pope), 336, 367
Skepticism, 107–108, 269–270,
  311, 436
Skyscrapers, 126, 637
Slavery
  Atlantic exploration and, 351
  Babylon, 35
  British abolition of, 534–535
  Christianity and, 184
  Enlightenment and, 457–458
  Hellenistic era, 129
  Islam and, 239
  Ottoman Empire, 344
  Portuguese exploration and, 348
  Roman Empire, 169
  Saint Dominique (Haiti), 486
  Sparta, 93
  Sumer, 17
  U.S. Civil War and, 568–569
  War of the Spanish Succession
    and, 414
Slavs, 194, 241
Slovenes, 644, 743
Smallpox, 298, 731
Smiles, Samuel, 555
Smith, Adam, 444, 524, 525, 578
Social Contract, The (Rousseau), 453
Social Darwinism, 591, 595, 625
Socialism
  Bismarck, Otto von, 557
  British democracy and, 561–562
  utopian, 539, 540–541
  See also Marxism
Social sciences, origins of, 449–450,
  589, 594–595
Society. *See* Culture and society
Society of Jesus. *See* Jesuit education;
  Jesuits
Sociology, 594
Socrates, 107, 108
Solidarity, 718–719
Solomon, 55, 56, 57*m*
Solon, 82, 93, 106
Somalia, 579
Some Thoughts Concerning Education
  (Locke), 444
Somme River, 211, 612
Song of Roland, The, 220, 256, 260
Sophists, 107–108
Sophocles, 114
Sorbonne, 597

Sorcery, 436
South Africa, 521, 614, 697–698
South America, Napoleon and, 486. *See
  also specific countries*
South Asia, decolonization of, 694, 696.
  See also specific countries
Southeast Asia
  Cold War events and issues, 704–705
  new imperialism and, 578, 584–588
  See also specific countries
South Korea, 704, 723, 736
Soviet Union, 632, 634
  appeasement (1933–1939), 658,
    660–661
  Berlin Wall, 699
  China and, 710
  Cold War beginnings, 689–690
  Cuban Missile Crisis, 708–709
  decolonization and, 694
  détente, 710–711
  dissolution of, 720
  eastern Europe and, 688, 689
  eastern European revolutions,
    718–720
  economic troubles, 716–717
  Germany and, 689–690
  Gorbachev, Mikhail, 717–718
  Iron Curtain, 689
  Israel, creation of, 693
  Marshall Plan and, 690–691
  nuclear arms race, 693–694, 717, 718
  occupation zones (post-World War
    II), 690
  Stalin, Joseph, 651–654
  Truman, Harry S., 684
  Truman Doctrine and, 692
  Vietnam, 705
  Warsaw Pact, 701
  World War I aftermath, 635
  World War II aftermath, 687, 688
  See also Cold War; World War II
Spain
  authoritarian regimes in, 643–644, 645
  Black Death and, 300
  Byzantine Empire and, 194
  Catholic Reformation and, 368
  Charlemagne and, 220
  Congress System and, 522, 523
  early modern era, 413–414
  Elizabeth I (England) and, 373
  empirical wars and global markets
    (early modern era), 406
  Enlightenment, 448
  exploration by, 348, 349, 350*m*, 351
  First Punic War, 136
  French religious wars and, 377
  French Revolution and, 478
  French wars against, 402, 403
  Golden Age, 373–376
  Habsburg-Valois wars, 369
  imperialism, 578, 587*m*
  Italian city-states and, 328
  Lutheran Reformation and, 361
  Mary I (England) and, 371, 372
  medieval, 214, 233
  Muslims and, 205, 239
  Napoleon and, 483, 486
  Roman Empire and, 191
  scientific advances, 421
  Second Punic War, 137
  slave trade, 457
  Thirty Years' War, 379, 380
  voting rights, 515
  World War I, 608
Spanish Armada, 375
Spanish Bourbons, 486

Spanish Civil War, 633, 643–644, 645
Spanish crusades, 254–255, 304
Spanish Inquisition, 367, 369, 414, 448
Spanish march, 220
Sparta, 79–81
    Athenian Empire and, 95*m*
    Attica and, 97
    Peloponnesian War, 98, 99–101, 120
    Persian Wars, 84, 86–87, 88, 92–93
Spartacist League, 623
"Special Theory of Relativity"
    (Einstein), 594
"Speech on Conciliation with the
    Colonies" (Burke), 475
Spencer, Herbert, 591
Spinning, 501–502, 503, 511
Spinoza, Baruch, 449
Spirit of the Laws, The (Montesquieu), 454
Spiritual crises, in medieval Europe,
    305–311
Spiritual Exercises, 368
Spirituals, 361
SS, 647, 667, 668
Stalin, Joseph, 632, 634
    Cold War beginnings, 689, 690
    eastern Europe and, 688
    post-World War II policies, 680
    Potsdam Conference, 688
    Soviet economy, 651–654
    Tehran Conference, 679, 688
    totalitarianism, 641
    Truman Doctrine and, 692
    World War II, 661, 665, 671
    Yalta, 679, 688
Stalingrad, battle of, 675
Stamp Act (1765), 466
Stanley, Henry, 583
Starry Messenger, The (Galilei), 426, 427
"Star wars" defense system, 717
States. *See* Nation-states
Status, in Europe (early modern era), 392
Steam technology, 502–503
Steamship age, 503–505
Steel production, 510–511
Stephen (English king), 246
Stephen (Hungarian king), 249
Stephen II (pope), 219
Stephenson, George, 503
Stewart, Robert, 520
Stilicho, 190, 191
Stirrups, 229, 315
Stock market crash (1929), 638
Stoics/Stoicism, 127, 128, 156, 167,
    169, 170
Stone Age. *See* Prehistoric cultures
Storm troopers. *See* Nazi SA
Straits of Gibraltar, 191, 347
Strasbourg, 402
Strategos, 83, 84, 93
Stravinsky, Igor, 600
Stresemann, Gustav, 637
Strikes, 512–513
Stromberg, Roland, 680
Structure of the Human Body, The
    (Vesalius), 432
Stuart, Mary, 372, 374, 375
Stuart dynasty, 404, 404
Students, in medieval universities, 272
Studia humanitatis, 330
Subconscious, 592, 593
Subjection of Women, The (Mill), 595
Submarines, 616, 675, 711
Sub-Saharan Africa
    decolonization of, 697–698
    postcolonial migrations from, 699, 701
    See also specific countries

Substances, 269–270
Sudan, 735
Sudetenland, 659
Suetonius, 161, 172
Suez Canal, 614, 665, 710
Suez Crisis (1956), 725
Suffrage. *See* Voting rights
Sufism, 344
Sugar Act (1764), 466
Suger, 281
Suleiman I (Ottoman Empire), 411, 412
Süleyman (Ottoman Empire), 344, 369
Sulla, 141–142, 155
Sultans
    Muslim Empire, 238–241
    Ottoman Empire, 342–343
    See also specific sultans
Sumer, 4, 6, 14–15
    city life, 17–18
    dynastic eras, 16–17
    history, 22–23
    Predynastic Era, 15–16
    trade and industry, 18–19
    writing, religions, and intellectual
        life, 19–21
Sumerian artifact, image of, 5
Summa, 268, 274
Sun, Hellenistic-era science and, 128
Sunni Muslims, 204, 239, 344, 730
Superego, 592
Superstition, during Scientific
    Revolution, 436–437
Suppiluliuma, 43
Suras, 198
Surgery, 500
Surinam, 406
Survival of the fittest, 591
Susa, 123
Sussition, 79
Swabia, 249, 288
Sweden, 243, 380, 409, 485, 521, 737
Swift, Jonathan, 445
Swiss Brethren, 363
Swiss Reformation, 361–365
Switzerland, 228, 505, 513, 515, 698
Sylvester I (pope), 220
Symbolism, prehistoric, 7–9
Symphonies, 459
Syracuse, 97, 100, 135
Syria, 11, 34, 39, 45, 47, 52, 203, 204,
    301, 628, 665, 693, 741

T
"Tables Turned, The" (Wordsworth), 538
Tacitus, 148, 150, 153, 171, 329
Taille, 402
Taiwan, 585, 588, 651, 703, 723
Taliban, 729
Talleyrand, Charles Maurice Prince
    de, 520
Tanganyika, 579
Tannenberg, battle of, 613
Tarde, Sumer, 17
Tariffs, 638, 639, 643
Tarik, 214
Tarquinia, 132
Tarquinius Superbus (Tarquin the
    Proud), 132
Taxation
    American Revolution and, 465–466
    Augustan era, 153, 154
    Danegeld, 243
    early modern era, 393
    English religious civil war and,
        383, 384
    French Revolution and, 471, 474, 476

medieval Europe, 227
Muslim Empire, 205
Ottoman Empire, 343
papacy and, 306
Peter the Great, 410
Puritans and, 404
revolutions of 1848, 529
U.S. Constitution, 469
Technology
    globalization and, 731–736
    Industrial Revolution, 501–505, 514
    nuclear arms race, 693–694
    See also Industrial Revolution;
        specific technological innovations
Tehran Conference, 679, 688
Television, 733
Tell el-Amarna. *See* Akhetaten
Tempera, 337–338
Templar. *See* Knights Templar
Temujin. *See* Genghis Khan
Ten Days that Shook the World
    (Reed), 624
Terence, 155
Teresa of Avila, 368
Terrorism
    globalization and, 729–731
    postindustrial age, 745
    Russian nationalism and, 564
Tetrarchy, 174
Tetzel, Johann, 357
Textbooks, in Carolingian
    Renaissance, 234
Thailand, 674, 723
Thales, 102
Thatcher, Margaret, 727
Theater
    Augustan era, 155
    Hellenic era, 111, 112–115
    Hellenistic era, 126
    Shakespeare, William, 378–379
Thebes, 36, 42, 43, 98, 99, 100–101,
    120, 121
Themistocles, 87–88, 92, 93
Theodora, 194
Theodoric the Ostrogoth, 193, 213, 231
Theodosius, 190
Theogony, 74
Theophano, 249
Theory, during Scientific Revolution,
    429–432
Thermopylae, 86–88
Theses, 272
"Theseus and the Minotaur," 68
Thespis, 114
Theuderic, 216
Third Crusade, 285, 289, 304
Third Dynasty of Ur, 22, 25, 34, 52
Third Estate, 471–472
Third French Republic, 547, 558–560
Third Punic War, 138
Third Reich. *See* Nazi Germany
Thirty Years' Peace, 97
Thirty Years' War, 361, 399, 415
Tholoi, 68–69
Thucydides, 99, 106–107
Thutmose I, 39
Thutmose III, 39–40
Tiberius, 160, 170, 183
Tiberius Gracchus, 138–139, 140
Tiber River, 129, 130
Tibet, 608
Tiglath-Pileser I, 47
Tiglath-Pileser III, 47–48
Tigris River, 12*m*, 14, 15, 24, 34
Tillich, Paul, 739
Time of Troubles, 409

Timur the Lame (Tamerlane), 303–304, 342
Tin, 49
Tito, 668, 676, 677, 701, 743
Titus, 162–163
Tojo, Hideki, 673
Tokyo, bombing of, 678
Toledo, 255
Tolstoy, Leo, 597
Tombs, 28, 37, 38–39, 131
Tools
    archaic states, 13
    prehistoric cultures, 7, 9, 11
Topkapi Palace, 343
Torah, 56
Tories, 469
Torture, Enlightenment ideas about, 450
Totalitarianism, 641, 670. *See also* Fascism; Nazi Germany; Soviet Union
Tournai, 211
Toussaint L'Ouverture, 485
Towns, in medieval Europe, 262–264
Townshend, Charles, 467
Trade/economy
    Athens, 81, 82
    Atlantic exploration and, 351
    Bedouins, 197
    Byzantine Empire, 195
    Diocletian, 182
    early modern era, 406–408
    empirical wars and global markets (early modern era), 406–408
    Great Depression and, 638, 639
    Hanseatic League, 338
    Italian city-states, 325
    Italian Renaissance, 326, 329
    medieval Europe, 229–231, 260–264
    Minoans, 65–66
    Netherlands (early modern era), 414
    Ottoman Empire, 344, 346
    Phoenicians, 55
    Roman Empire, 168–169, 172–173
    Sparta, 80
    Sumer, 18–19
    World War I, 616–617
    See also Economics; Industrial Revolution; New imperialism
Trades Union Congress, 561
Tragedies, 113–114
Trains, 503–505
Trajan, 165–166
Transition states, 34–38
Transubstantiation, 269, 306, 362
Transvaal, 583
Treaty of Brest-Litovsk, 621
Treaty of Câteau-Cambrésis, 369
Treaty of Nystad, 409–410
Treaty of Radstadt, 415
Treaty of Rome, 725
Treaty of Utrecht, 406
Treaty of Verdun, 224
Treaty of Versailles, 618, 625–630, 636, 659, 661
Treaty of Westphalia, 415
Trench warfare, 610, 612, 617
Tribunes, 134, 138–139
Trigonometry, 268
Triple Alliance, 608
Triumph of the Will, The (Nazi propaganda film), 648
Trivium, 234, 272
Trojan War, 70, 115
Trolley boys, 511

Trotsky, Leon, 621, 622, 652
Troubadours, 260, 276–277
Troy, 70–71, 115, 122, 129
Truce of God, 236
True Law of Free Monarchies, The (James I), 382, 397, 398
Truman, Harry S., 677, 678, 684, 688, 692, 693, 704, 705
Truman Doctrine, 692
Truth, 108–109
    Locke and, 433–434
    post-World War II, 686
    Scientific Revolution and, 418–420, 427–429
Tuberculosis, 731
Tudor, Henry, 319
Tudor, Mary, 373
Tudor dynasty, 319, 369–372, 382
Tunisia, 301–302, 581, 583, 697, 699
Turkey
    appeasement (1933–1939), 658
    nationalism in, 566–567
    nuclear missiles in, 708, 709
    postcolonial migrations from, 699
    Treaty of Versailles, 627
    Truman Doctrine and, 692
    World War I, 613, 614
    See also Ottoman Empire
Turks, 239, 242, 255, 298. *See also* Ottoman Empire
Tuscany, 548, 550
Tutankhamun (Tutenkhaten), 42–43
Twelve Tables, 134
Two Treatises of Government (Locke), 434, 455
Tyrants, in Athens, 81, 83
Tyre, 55

U

Übermensch, 592
U-boats, 616. *See also* Submarines
Ukraine, 408, 653, 676, 744, 745
"Ultras," 525
Ulyanov, Vladimir, Ilich. *See* Lenin, Vladimir
Umar, 204
Umayyad caliphs, 204–205, 238, 239, 254
Umma, 199, 201, 202, 203–204, 238, 241
Unemployment
    anti-immigrant sentiments and, 699, 701
    Great Depression, 634, 639, 640*m*
    Nazi Germany, 646
    revolutions of 1848, 529
    Soviet Union and, 653
    World War I aftermath, 634
Unions. *See* Labor unions
United Nations, 687
    earth summit (1992), 732–733
    globalization and, 735–736
    Israel, creation of, 692–693
    Korean War, 704
    Kyoto Protocol, 733
    U.S. invasion of Iraq, 729
    Universal Declaration of Human Rights, 736, 737
    Universal Declaration of Women's Rights, 737, 739
United Provinces, 374
United Provinces of Holland, 402
United States
    American Revolution, 462–470, 488
    ANZUS, 704
    Bolshevik Revolution and, 622, 623

China and, 710
Chinese communist revolution and, 702, 703
Cold War beginnings, 689
Cuban Missile Crisis, 708–710
decolonization and, 694
détente, 710–711
Great Depression, 638–640
Industrial Revolution, 504, 508
Iranian Revolution and, 741
Iraq war (2003–), 729–730, 745
Israel, creation of, 693
Japan and, 650
Korean War, 704
League of Nations and, 628
Marshall Plan, 690–691
Monroe Doctrine, 486
NATO, 701
new imperialism, 583, 586, 587*m*
nuclear arms race, 693–694, 717, 718
occupation zones (post-World War II), 690
postindustrial age, 745
Red Scare (1919), 623, 624
right-wing movements in, 649
Russian reform (post-Soviet), 720
social services, resistance to, 723
Treaty of Versailles, 625–627
Truman Doctrine, 692
Vietnam War, 705–707, 707*m*
voting rights, 515
women's movement and, 737
World War I, 608, 615–617, 625
World War I aftermath, 634, 635, 636–637
World War II aftermath, 688
See also Cold War; World War II
U.S. Civil War, 568–571
U.S. Constitution, 454, 469, 515
Universal Declaration of Human Rights, 736, 737
Universal Declaration of Women's Rights, 737, 739
Universities
    British democracy and, 561
    European High Middle Ages, 271–274
    revolutions of 1848, 527
University of Bologna, 316
University of Paris, 341, 596
Ur, 16, 19, 22–23, 34, 52, 53
Urban II (pope), 236, 238, 255, 257, 301
Urban VI (pope), 308
Ur-Nammu, 22, 34
Uruk, 6, 15–16, 19, 20, 22
Uthman, 204
Utilitarianism, 539–541
Utopia (More), 329
Utopian socialism, 539, 540–541

V

Vaccines, 731
Valens, 189, 190
Valentinian I, 189
Valentinian II, 190
Valentinian III, 193
Valley of the Kings, 39
Valois dynasty, 377. *See also* Habsburg-Valois wars
Values, post-World War II, 686
Vandals, 191, 194
Van Gogh, Vincent, 599
Varna, battle of, 342
Vassals, 227, 230, 248, 305
Vassus, 223

Vatican City, 325, 643
Vatican II, 739–740
Velázquez, 375
Venetia, 548, 550
Venezuela, 486
Venice, 260–261, 301, 302, 324, 326, 328, 338, 342, 454, 521
Venus, 133
Verdun, 612. *See* Treaty of Verdun
Versailles, 400–402, 471, 472, 554
Versailles Conference, 625–627
Verus, Lucius, 167
Vesalius, Andreas, 432
Vespasian, 162
Vespucci, Amerigo, 349
Vesta, 133
Vesuvius, 163, 164
Vichy government, 662, 664, 665, 668
Victor Emmanuel II (Piedmont-Sardinia), 548, 550
Victor Emmanuel III (Italy), 642, 675
Victoria (England), 561, 584, 595
Vienna, 303, 339, 344, 346, 369, 520, 530, 676. *See also* Congress of Vienna
Vietnam, 585, 697, 722, 723
Vietnam Independence League (Vietminh), 706
Vietnam War, 705–707, 707*m*
Vikings, 224–225, 238, 242, 243, 244*m*, 245, 261
Vindication of the Rights of Women, A (Wollstonecraft), 455
Vindobona (Vienna), 167
Virgil, 157–158, 170, 331
Virgin Mary, 202, 278
Virginia House of Burgesses, 465
Visigoths, 190–191, 211, 214
Visionaries, in European High Middle Ages, 278
Vitruvius, 333
Vladimir (Russian city), 303
Vladimir I (Russia), 242
Volk, 571
Voltaire, 444, 445, 448, 451, 458
Voluntary intellectual associations, 423
Voting rights (suffrage)
Britain, 561
Industrial Revolution and, 515
Weimar Republic, 635
women's suffrage movement, 595
Vulcan, 133
Vulgate, 231

W

Wages, 525
Waiblingens. *See* Ghibellines
Waiting for Godot (Beckett), 686
Wake Island, 674*m*
Waldo, Peter, 277, 361
Wales, 312, 315
Walesa, Lech, 718–719
Wallace, Alfred Russell, 590
War/militarization
Aegean civilizations, 76–79
Alexander the Great, 121–125
American War for Independence, 468–469
Assyrians, 49–50
Athens, 87–88, 93, 95
Augustan era, 152–153
Barracks Emperors, 168
Boer War, 583–584
Byzantine Empire, 241, 242
Charlemagne, 220

Charles of Anjou, 340
Crimean War, 548, 558, 564
Diocletian, 173–174
empirical (early modern states), 406–408
English civil wars, 404
English religious civil war, 382–386
European High Middle Ages, 285, 286, 288
First Triumvirate, 142, 143–144
Flavian dynasty, 162–163
French and Indian War, 464, 466, 470
French religious wars, 376–377
German-Austrian (nineteenth century), 552–553
German-French (nineteenth century), 553–554
Habsburg-Valois wars, 368–369
Hadrian, 166
Hellenic era, 77–78
Hellenistic era, 120
Honorius, 190–191
Hundred Years' War, 312–319
Iraq war (2003–), 729–730, 745
Italian unification, 550
Japan, 586, 588
justifications for, 354, 356
Justinian, 194
Korean War, 704
Louis XIV, 402–404
Marcus Aurelius, 167
medieval wars, 216, 228–229, 245, 312–319
Merovingians, 215
Muslim caliphs and sultans, 239
Muslim Empire, 203
Napoleon and, 483
nationalism and, 554–555
nation-states and, 554–555
Nazi Germany, 647, 648
Nero, 162
Normandy, 243, 245
Opium Wars, 585–586
Ottoman Empire, 341–344, 346, 411–412
Peter the Great, 409
Prussia (early modern era), 410–411
Rome, 134, 139, 141–145
Russo-Japanese War, 565
Second Triumvirate, 144–145
Septimus Severus, 168
Seven Years' War, 407, 408, 411
Sicily, 135
Spanish Civil War, 633, 643–644, 645
Spanish exploration, 351
Sparta, 79–81
Thirty Years' War, 379–380, 399, 415
Trajan, 165
Vietnam War, 705–707, 707*m*
Visigoths and Ostrogoths, 190
War of Austrian Succession, 407–408
War of the League of Augsburg, 402
War of the Roses, 319, 369
War of the Spanish Succession (1714), 406, 407, 414
See also American Revolution; Cold War; Crusades; French Revolution; World War I; World War II; *specific wars*
War of Austrian Succession, 407–408
War of the League of Augsburg, 402
War of the Roses, 319, 369

War of the Spanish Succession (1714), 406, 407, 414
Warsaw Pact, 689, 701
Washington, George, 462, 464, 469
Water power, 502, 503
Waterloo, battle of, 485, 518, 520, 521
Watson, James, 732
Watt, James, 502
Wealth
Enlightenment ideas about, 449, 450
globalization and, 733, 734*m*, 735–736
Industrial Revolution and, 508, 515
Wealth of Nations, The (Smith), 450
Weapons trade, 511
Weaving, 501–502, 503, 511
Webb, Beatrice, 561
Webb, Sidney, 561
Weber, Max, 594–595
Wedgwood, Josiah, 508
Weimar Constitution, 644
Weimar Republic, 635–636, 644, 646, 647
"Welfare states" (European), 723–724
Welfs. *See* Guelfs
Wells, H. G., 561, 681
Wergeld, 211–212
Wesley, Charles, 458
Wesley, John, 458
Wessex, 243
West Indies, 407
Western civilization, 62, 64
Western front, in World War I, 606, 609–612
Western Roman Empire. *See* Roman Empire
Westphalia, 483, 521
Westward expansion, in United States, 569–570
What Is to Be Done? (Lenin), 565
Whigs, 476, 534
White Army, 622
White collar employment sector, 508, 514, 744–745
Whitefield, George, 458
"White Man's Burden," 579–580
Wilkes, John, 467
William I (England), 245, 283
William I (Netherlands), 521
William I (Prussia), 551, 553, 554, 557
William II (England), 245–246, 283
William II (Germany), 557, 579, 608, 610, 618
William III (England), 391, 405
William IV, 534
William IX (duke of Aquitaine and count of Poitou), 276–277
William of Ockham, 309, 311
William of Orange, 374, 405
William of Ruybroek, 302
Wilson, Woodrow, 569, 614, 616–617, 626–627, 628, 629
Winged Victory of Samothrace, 119
Wisdom literature, 74
Witchcraft, 436–437
Witte, Sergei, 564
Wollstonecraft, Mary, 455, 457, 595
Women
Aristophanes and, 115
Aristotle and, 110
Aspasia, 96–97
Assyria, 50
Christianity and, 184
Code Napoleon and, 482
Curie, Marie, 596–597
early modern era, 395

Women, *continued*
Enlightenment, 455–457
equality struggle (post-World War II), 736–739
Etruscans, 131, 132
French Revolution, 474
Gonzaga, Elisabetta, 334–335
Hellenic era, 78–79
Hesiod and, 75
Hroswitha of Gandersheim, 252–253
Industrial Revolution and, 509, 511–512
Islam and, 200
Merovingians, 215
Minoans, 66
mystics and visionaries, 278
Nazi Germany, 647
New Kingdom (Egypt), 38, 45
Ottoman Empire, 343
Pizan, Christine de, 316–317
Roman Empire, 169
Sparta, 80
suffrage movement, 595
Sumer, 17
voting rights, 515
Weimar Republic, 635
witchcraft and, 437
World War I, 619
World War II, 670–672
See also specific women
Women's Auxiliary Corps, 671
Women's clubs, during Enlightenment, 456
Women's movement, 736–739
Woolf, Virginia, 597–598
Wordsworth, William, 537, 538
Work and Days, 74–75
Working class (proletariat)
Chartism, 536
Industrial Revolution, 505, 506–507, 511, 569
Marxism and, 542–543
political economy and, 525
revolutions of 1848, 529
Russia, 565
U.S. Industrial Revolution and, 569
See also Labor
Working-class organizations, 512–513
Working conditions, early modern era, 394
World Bank, 736

World War I, 602, 604–606, 630
aftermath of, 635–638
alliance system, 606–609
domestic impact of, 618–620
Eastern front and imperialism, 612–615
experience of, 609–612
naval war and U.S. entry, 615–618
peace settlement and European consciousness, 625–630
Russian Revolution and, 620–624
World War II, 656–658, 660*m*, 666*m*, 681
1939–1941, 661–666
1942–1945, 674–678
appeasement process (1933–1939), 658–661
Asia and Pacific war, 672–674
German Empire, 666–670
homefront and role of women, 670–672
postwar planning, 679–680
World Zionist Organization, 613
Worms, 358
Writing
Age of Anxiety, 316–317
Alfred the Great, 243
Augustan era, 155–156, 157–159
Byzantine Empire, 195
Carolingian Renaissance, 234
crusades and, 260
Egyptian civilization, 26
Enlightenment, 445–446
European High Middle Ages, 268
Hellenic era, 74, 105–106
Hellenistic era, 128
Writing, *continued*
Hroswitha of Gandersheim, 252–253
Industrial Revolution, 509
Ireland (medieval), 217
medieval Europe, 231–233
Middle Kingdom (Egypt), 37
Minoans, 66
modernism, 597–598
Mycenaeans, 69–70
Pliny the Elder, 164
Pliny the Younger, 165
realism and naturalism, 597
Renaissance, 329–332
Roman Empire, 170–172
Shakespeare, William, 378–379
Spanish Golden Age, 375–376
Sumer, 19–21

William IX (duke of Aquitaine and count of Poitou), 276–277
See also Bible; New Testament; *specific works*
Writs, 284
Wurttemberg, 529
Wyclif, John, 309, 310, 361

X
Xenophobia, 559
Xenophon, 120
Xerxes, 85*m*, 86, 88, 92
X-rays, 596

Y
Yalta, 679, 688
Yarmuk, 203
Yathrib, 199
Yeats, William Butler, 625
Yellow River, 13
Yeltsin, Boris, 720–721
Yorkists, 319
Young Italy, 532
Young Turks, 566
Youth culture, 729
Yugoslavia
appeasement (1933–1939), 658
Cold War, 701
ethnic cleansing in, 742–744
interwar years (1919–1939), 627, 635, 644
Soviet Union and, 719–720
World War II, 665, 668, 676

Z
Zacharias (pope), 219
Zagros Mountains, 15, 36
Zananza, 43
Zealots, 184
Zemst'va, 564
Zeno, 127
Zenobia, 168
Zeus, 68, 112
Ziggurats, 18, 19
Zionism, 572–573
Zola, Emile, 559, 597
Zollverein, 552
Zoonomia, or the Laws of Organic Life (Darwin), 590
Zoroaster, 57
Zuccari, Federico, 355
Zurich, 362
Zwingli, Ulrich, 362–363

DVD Table of Contents

1 The Birth of Civilization

Text Sources
- Ptahhotep, excerpt from the *Egyptian Book of Instructions*
- Excerpts from The Epic of Gilgamesh
- The Code of Hammurabi
- David Rindos, from "Symbiosis, Instability, and the Origins and Spread of Agriculture: A New Model"
- Charles Darwin, "Cultivated Plants: Cereal and Culinary Plants" from *The Variation of Animals and Plants under Domestication*
- An Egyptian Hymn to the Nile
- Marshall Sahlins, "The Original Affluent Society," from *Stone Age Economics*
- Jane Goodall, from "The Challenge Lies in All of Us"

Visual Sources
- Hominid tools
- The Standard of Ur
- Dolmen of Kerhan
- Cuneiform tablet
- Assyrian King list

2 The Rise of Empires and the Beginning of the Iron Age

Text Sources
- Hittite Law Code: Excerpts from The Code of the Nesilim
- The Book of Job and Jewish Literature
- The "Cyrus Cylinder: The First Declaration of Religious Freedom

Visual Sources
- Egyptian obelisks
- Assyrian winged bull
- Assyrian warriors
- Abu Simbel

3 Aegean Civilizations

Text Sources
- Tyrtaeus: *The Spartan Creed*, c. 650 B.C.E.
- Lyric Poetry: Archilochus and Sappho, 650–590 B.C.E.
- Homer: Debate Among the Greeks at Troy, c. 750 B.C.E.
- Herodotus: Themistocles' Cleverness at the Battle of Salamis, c. 430 B.C.E.
- Herodotus: Demaratus Explains Greek "Freedom" to Xerxes, c. 430 B.C.E.
- Herodotus: "The Beginning of Evils for the Greeks" in the Ionian Revolt, c. 430 B.C.E.
- Education and the Family in Sparta, c. 100 C.E.

- "Aristotle": The Creation of the Democracy in Athens, c. 330 B.C.E.

Visual Sources
- Greek athletics

4 The Hellenic Era

Text Sources
- Thucydides: The Debate on the Sicilian Expedition, c. 420 B.C.E.
- Socrates' *Apology*, as Reported by Plato, c. 390 B.C.E.
- On the Murder of Eratosthenes: A Husband's Defense, c. 403 B.C.E.
- Drama: *Antigone*, by Sophocles, c. 441 B.C.E.
- Aristophanes: Lysistrata Argues Against the War, 411 B.C.E.
- *Pericles' Funeral Oration* by Thucydides, c. 420 B.C.E.

Visual Sources
- Thucydides
- The Parthenon
- Illustration of a paradox of Zeno and Elea
- Detail of a statue from Delphi

5 The Hellenistic Era and the Rise of Rome

Text Sources
- *Maccabees: Resistance to Hellenization in the Hellenistic Period*, c. 100 B.C.E.
- Women in Roman Politics: Manipulators or Manipulated?, c. 100 C.E.
- The "Laudatio Turiae": A Grieving Husband's Tribute to His Remarkable Wife, c. 15 B.C.E.
- Slaves in the Roman Countryside, c. 150 B.C.E.–50 C.E.
- Polybius: "Why Romans and Not Greeks Govern the World," c. 140 B.C.E.
- Livy: The Rape of Lucretia and the Origins of the Republic, c. 10 B.C.E.
- Appian of Alexandria, "War, Slaves, and Land Reform: Tiberius Gracchus," c. 150 C.E.

Visual Sources
- Archimedes' mirror
- Ptolemaic world map

6 Rome's Empire and the Unification of the Western World

Text Sources
- Traditional Roman Religious Practices, 382
- Juvenal: A Satirical View of Women, c. 100

- Augustus' Moral Legislation: Family Values, 18 B.C.E.
- Priscus Panites at the Court of Attila the Hun, c. 450

Visual Sources
- Statue of Caesar Augustus
- Roman Forum
- Roman aqueduct

7 The West's Medieval Civilizations

Text Sources
- Tertullian: "What Has Jerusalem to Do with Athens?", c. 200
- Perpetua: The Autobiography of a Christian Martyr, c. 203
- Gnostic Teachings on Jesus, According to Irenaeus, c. 170
- Eusebius of Caesarea on the Nicaean Council and the Creed, c. 330
- The Qur'an
- Prologue of the *Corpus Juris Civillis*, c. 530
- Liutprand of Cremona, Report of His Mission to Constantinople, 968
- Benedict of Nursia: *The Rule*, c. 530
- Baghdad: City of Wonders, c. 800
- *The Confession of Saint Patrick*, c. 450
- *The Acts of the Apostles: Paul Pronounces the "Good News" in Greece*, c. 100

Visual Sources
- The interior of Hagia Sophia
- The Dome of the Rock
- Qur'an's first chapter
- Medina
- Mecca
- Jvari Monastery, Georgia
- Armenian Monastery
- Al Quibla schematic map

8 The Emergence of Europe

Text Sources
- Excerpts from *Feudal Contracts*, c. 1200
- Doom and Gloom in the Ninth Century: *The Annals of Xanten*, c. 850
- *The Book of Emperors and Kings: Charlemagne and Pope Leo III*, c. 1150

Visual Sources
- Norse ship
- T-O Map from Isidore of Seville

9 Europe Turns Outward

Text Sources
- Science and Mathematics: Al-Ghazzali, "On the Separation of Mathematics and Religion"
- Philip II Augustus Expels the Jews from France, 1182
- Christian Armies Besiege Lisbon, 1147
- Behâ ed-Din: Richard I Massacres Prisoners After Taking Acre, c. 1195

- Benjamin of Tudela, from *Book of Travels*
- Anna of Comnena, from the *Alexiad*
- Excerpts from the *Life and Travels of Rabban Bar Sawma*

Visual Sources
- View of Acre
- Vardzia monastery complex, Georgia
- The Tondo of St. Mamai
- Tamar, ruler of Georgia
- Saladdin
- Byzantines fighting the Bulgarians
- Medieval Islamic map of the world
- Islamic world map

10 Europe's High Middle Ages

Text Sources
- The Penitentials, c. 1575
- Letter of Pope Gregory VII to the Bishop of Metz, 1081
- A Brief Description of the Seven Sacraments of the Church, 1438
- *Unam Sanctam: Pope Boniface VIII on the Two Swords*, 1302
- St. Thomas Aquinas: *Faith and Reason in the Summa Against the Gentiles*, 1259–1264
- Sports in the City of London, 1180
- Professor Abelard Confronts Bernard of Clairvaux, c. 1140
- Manorial Court Records, 1246–1247
- Guilds: Regulating the Craft, 1347
- College Life: Letters Between Students and Their Fathers, c. 1200

Visual Sources
- St. John the Evangelist from a twelfth-century manuscript
- Mosque of al-Azhar
- Medieval medicine
- Extract from the *Domesday Book*
- Eleventh-century illuminated Gospel manuscript
- The Book of Adam
- Islamic science and alchemy
- Islamic astronomy and astrology
- Illustration from *The Properties of Things*
- Illustration from *Die Proprietatibus Rerum*
- Wheel of Fortune
- Medieval world view
- Medieval medical illustration
- Medieval depiction of Adam and Eve
- Image of the universe, from the Nuremberg Chronicle

11 Challenges to the Medieval Order

Text Sources
- Excerpt from William of Rubruck's *Account of the Mongols*
- The Ideal Merchant's Wife, c. 1450

- Marco Polo, excerpts from *Travels*, c. 1300
- "For the Honor of the Guild": Social and Civic Responsibilities, 1421–1425
- The Lollard Conclusions, 1394
- The Execution of Heretics: Saints and Witches, 1389–1427
- Propositions of John Wycliffe, as described in the Church's Condemnation, 1415
- Marco Polo at the Court of Kublai Khan, c. 1300
- How They Died: Coroner's Rolls from the Fourteenth Century, 1322–1337
- Flagellants Attempt to Ward Off the Black Death, 1349
- Boccaccio's Decameron: The Tale of the Three Rings, c. 1350

Visual Sources
- Mongol yurt
- The First Horseman of the Apocalypse
- The Black Death
- The baptism of Clovis
- Illustrations from *The Travels of Sir John of Mandeville*
- Illustration from *The Life of Christ*
- French customary laws I
- French customary laws II
- French customary laws III
- French customary laws IV
- First printed medical text with illustrations
- 1551 Edition of Maimonides' *Guide for the Perplexed*

12 Renaissance and Exploration

Text Sources
- Giorgio Vasari on the Life of Michelangelo, 1550
- Petrarch: Rules for the Successful Ruler, c. 1350
- Niccolò Machiavelli: From the *Discourses on Livy*, 1513–1517
- Marriage in the Renaissance: A Serious Business, 1464–1465
- Lorenzo Valla Skewers the Supposed "Donation of Constantine," c. 1440
- Benvenuto Cellini: The Life of an Artist, 1558–1562
- Advice to Lorenzo de Medici: *On Wifely Duties*, 1416
- Letters from the Kings of Portugal to the King of Kongo
- René Laudonnière, A Notable History of Florida
- Bartolomé Las Casas, *Very Brief Report on the Destruction of the Indians*
- Bartolomé Las Casas, "A Right with Roots in the Bible"
- Christopher Columbus, "The Letters of Columbus to Ferdinand and Isabel"
- Cieza de León, "The Chronicle of Peru"

Visual Sources
- Woodcut by Albrecht Dürer showing perspective
- Sketches by Leonardo da Vinci for fortifying cities
- Printers and booksellers I
- Printers and booksellers II
- Printers and booksellers III
- Leonardo da Vinci's Vitruvian Man
- Illustrations for *The Emperor's Astronomy*
- Dürer, Adam and Eve
- Drawing from Leonardo da Vinci's *Codice Atlantico*
- Cupola of Santa Maria del Fiore Church, Florence
- First book printed in the New World
- Views of Cuzco
- View of Hormuz
- Vespucci's encounter with Indians
- Mixtec creation myth
- Indians planting corn
- Illustrations from Jacques Le Moyne and Theodore de Bry of Indians I
- Illustrations from Jacques Le Moyne and Theodore de Bry of Indians II
- Illustrations from Jacques Le Moyne and Theodore de Bry of Indians III
- Illustrations from Jacques Le Moyne and Theodore de Bry of Indians IV
- Hispania slaying Leviathan
- Francis Drake's encounter with Indians
- Founding of Tenochtitlan
- Early European depiction of the banana
- Columbus's encounter with the Indians
- American cannibals
- Illustration from de Sahagun's "History of the Conquest of New Spain"
- Sixteenth-century world map
- Sixteenth-century portolan
- Sixteenth-century map of the Atlantic
- Samuel de Champlain's map of eastern North America
- Fifteenth-century portolan from Majorca

13 Reformation, Religious Wars, and National Conflicts

Text Sources
- Catherine Zell, "Letter to Ludwig Rabus," 1556–1558
- *The Act of Supremacy*, 1534
- Martin Luther's "*Ninety-Five Theses*", 1517
- Desiderius Erasmus, "Pope Julius Excluded from Heaven," 1513–1514
- John Calvin, *Ecclesiastical Ordinances*, 1533
- Anonymous, "The Execution of Archbishop Cranmer," 1556
- Anonymous Government Agent, "Arrest of Edmund Campion and His Associates," 1581
- *The Edict of Nantes*, 1598
- *The Council of Trent*, 1545–1563
- *Acts of Uniformity*, 1559
- The Poor Laws
- Swabian Peasants, "The Twelve Articles"
- Martin Luther, "Against the Robbing Murdering Hordes of Peasants"
- Glückel of Hamlen, *Memoirs*
- Jamestown Charter
- Richard Frethorne, "Letter to Father and Mother"

- Anonymous, "The English Describe Pawatah's People"
- "The Code Noir"
- Miguel de Cervantes, *Don Quixote*
- John Bunyan, *Pilgrim's Progress*

Visual Sources
- St. Francis Xavier and other Jesuit missionaries
- Johann Tetzel selling indulgences
- Jesuit martyrs in Japan
- Jesuit baptizing an Indian
- Heretic burning at the stake
- Safavid battle tunic
- Ottoman naval attack on the island of Gerbi
- Seal of Connecticut
- Powhatan
- Pocahontas
- King Philip's War
- John Smith
- First national atlas of England
- First Dutch national atlas

14 The Early Modern State

Text Sources
- Louis de Rouvroy, duc de Saint-Simon, *Mémoires*
- Cardinal Richelieu, *Political Testament*
- Peter the Great, "Correspondence with Alexis"
- Louis XIV, *Mémoires, for the Instruction of the Dauphin*
- Jean Bodin, *Six Books of the Commonwealth*, "The True Attributes of Sovereignty"
- Hugo Grotius, selections from *On the Law of War and Peace*
- Thomas Hobbes, *The Leviathan*
- Jacques-Benigne Bossuet, *Politics Drawn from the Very Words of the Holy Scripture*
- *The Peace of Westphalia*
- La Colonie, "The Battle of Schellenberg"
- Jean Baptiste Colbert, "Mercantilism: Dissertation on Alliances"
- Charles Perrault, *Little Red Riding-Hood*
- Hannah More, "The Carpenter"
- Jacques-Louis Ménétra, *Journal of My Life*

Visual Sources
- Hobbes, *Leviathan* I
- Hobbes, *Leviathan* II
- Ottoman law book
- View of Loango
- Don Alvaro of Kongo
- Title page from Vico, *Principii di una Scienza Nuova*
- View of St. Petersburg from the first Russian newspaper
- The New York fur trade
- New England primer
- View of Gibraltar
- View of Cape Town
- The Cape of Good Hope
- Seventeenth-century Portuguese trading posts in the Indian Ocean

- Plan of San Antonio, Texas
- Map of the country of Georgia
- Map of Kongo, Angola to Benguela
- Map of East Indies

15 New World Views: Europe's Scientific Revolution

Text Sources
- Witchcraft: *Malleus Maleficarum*
- William Harvey, Address to the Royal College of Physicians
- René Descartes, *The Discourse on Method and Metaphysical Meditations*, "I Think, Therefore I Am"
- Nicolaus Copernicus, excerpt from *On the Revolutions of the Heavenly Spheres*
- Isaac Newton, from *Opticks*
- Galileo Galilei, "Third Letter on Sunspots"
- Galileo Galilei, "Letter to Madame Christine of Lorraine, Grand Duchess of Tuscany"
- Francis Bacon, from *Novum Organum*
- Wortley Montagu, "Letter Regarding the Small Pox Vaccination"
- Auguste Tissot, "Midwives"

Visual Sources
- The Copernican solar system
- Principles of magnetism
- Title page from Francis Bacon, *Novum Organum*
- Sixteenth-century anatomical drawings, I
- Sixteenth-century anatomical drawings, II
- Pascal's *Traitez*
- Newton's *Opticks*
- Illustration showing the properties of a vacuum
- Galileo's views of the moon
- Frontispiece from Andreas Vesalius, *On the Fabric of the Human Body*
- Descartes, illustration from *Optics*
- Descartes' view of the universe
- Anton von Leeuwenhoek
- Jewish medical text
- Illustrations from Adam Olearius, *Voyages*
- Illustration from *Poor Richard's Almanack*
- Seventeenth-century Portuguese map of the Indian Ocean
- Map of Africa from the *Cedid Atlas*

16 The Age of Enlightenment: Rationalism and Its Uses

Text Sources
- The *Encyclopédie* "Bakers (*Boulanger*)"
- Jonathan Swift, "A Description of a City Shower"
- Marquis de Condorcet, passage from *Sketch for a Historical Picture of the Progress of the Human Mind*
- James Lind, from *A Treatise of the Scurvy*
- Voltaire, *Letters on England*
- The Execution of Damiens
- Adam Smith, *The Wealth of Nations*

- Jean-Jacques Rousseau, *Emile*
- Baron de Montesquieu, excerpt from *The Spirit of the Laws*
- John Locke, *Essay Concerning Human Understanding*
- Denis Diderot, Preliminary Discourse from *The Encyclopedia*
- Catherine the Great, "Instructions for a New Law Code"
- Cesare Beccaria, *On Crimes and Punishments*
- Abu Taleb Khan, *A Muslim Indian's Reactions to the West*

Visual Sources
- Russian views of "People of the Empire"
- Russian charter granted to the nobility
- Prussian soldiers
- View of Isfahan
- Torah scroll
- Title page from Japanese anatomy text, c. 1775
- The Peking observatory
- Study of the Aztec calendar stone
- Blake's image of the creation
- Aztec calendar wheel
- Armenian missal
- Armenian creation myth
- American magnolia tree, 1731

17 Rebellion and Revolution: American Independence and the French Revolution

Text Sources
- Willem Bosman, from *A New and Accurate Description of the Coast of Guinea Divided into the Gold, the Slave, and the Ivory Coasts*
- Phillis Wheatly, "To the Right Honourable William, Earl of Dartmouth..."
- Thomas Paine, "Common Sense"
- Olaudah Equiano, "Atlantic Crossing on a Slave Ship"
- Benjamin Franklin and the British Parliament, "Proceedings Regarding the Stamp Act"
- Five African American spirituals
- Bryan Edwards, excerpt from "Observations on the...Maroon Negroes of the Island of Jamaica"
- Alexander Telfair, *Instructions to an Overseer in a Cotton Plantation*
- John Adams, *Thoughts on Government*
- "Newspaper Ads: Slavery in Rio de Janeiro"
- The National Convention, "Law on Suspects (1793)" and "Law of 22 Prairial Year II (1794)"
- Emmanuel Joseph Sieyès, *What Is the Third Estate?*
- Maximillien Robespierre, "Speech to National Convention: The Terror Justified"
- Thomas Paine, *Rights of Man*
- National Assembly, "The Declaration of the Rights of Man and Citizen"
- Louis XVI, "A Royal Reform Proposal"
- French Peasants, *Cahiers de doléances*

- Olympe de Gouges, "Declaration of the Rights of Woman"
- Edmund Burke, *Reflections on the Revolution in France*
- "Petition of Women of the Third Estate"
- William Wordsworth, *Tintern Abbey*
- Sir Harry Smith, *Autobiography*
- Charles Parquin, "Napoleon's Army"
- Mary Shelley, excerpt from *Frankenstein*
- Johann Wolfgang von Goethe, *Prometheus*
- François René Chateaubriand, *The Genius of Christianity*
- Louis Antoine Fauvelet de Bourrienne, *Memoirs of Napolean Bonaparte*

Visual Sources
- View of Nanjing
- Cod fishing
- Eighteenth-century powderhorn
- View of the Guinea coast
- View of Guangzhou (Canton)
- View of Cape Town
- The slave ship *Brookes*
- Sugar plantation, Brazil
- Revolutionary ladies, North Carolina
- Portrait of Olaudah Equiano
- Pirate attack on Panama City
- Illustrations from *Voyages and Travels* I
- Illustrations from *Voyages and Travels* II
- Illustration from "American Magazine," 1758
- House in Benin
- Gold coast dress
- Captain Cook in the Sandwich Islands
- Buccaneers
- Boston Tea Party Revolution
- Boston Harbor
- Battle of Yorktown
- Advertisement for a slave auction
- 1755 Battle Between British and Indians
- "Tea-Tax Tempest," by Carl Guttenberg
- Origins of the French monarchy
- French Revolution
- Death of Marat
- "Cult of the Supreme Being," French Revolution
- A Beethoven sonata
- Ohio River Valley

18 Industry, Society, and Environment

Text Sources
- Leeds Woolen Workers, "Petition"
- Richard Guest, *The Creation of the Steam Loom*
- David Ricardo, excerpt from *Principles of Political Economy and Taxation*
- David Ricardo, *On Wages*, "The Iron Law of Wages"
- Daniel Defoe, selection from *The Complete English Tradesman*
- Andrew Ure, from *The Philosophy of Manufactures*
- The Sadler Report: Child Labor in the United Kingdom, 1832

- Karl Marx and Friedrich Engels, from *The Communist Manifesto*
- Léon Faucher, "Prison Rules"
- Edwin Chadwick, Summary from the *Poor Law Commissioners*
- Parliamentary Report on English Female Miners, 1842
- British Parliament, "Inquiry: Child Labor"
- Michael Bakunin, "Principles and Organization of the International Brotherhood"

Visual Sources
- Mill on the Brandywine
- Logging in Minnesota, 1893
- Illinois Central Railroad poster
- Homestead steel mill
- Excelsior Iron Works
- Cotton plantation
- Child textile worker
- Calcutta water dispenser
- Bolivian child laborers
- Architectural iron works
- Gas-smoothing iron
- Map of Mauritius, nineteenth century
- Map of Greenland

19 The Age of Ideology

Text Sources
- Alexis de Tocqueville, *Democracy in America*
- T. B. Macaulay, Speech on Parliamentary Reform
- José María Morelos, *Sentiments of the Nation*
- Karl von Clausewitz, *On War, Arming the Nation*
- Simon Bolivar, "Address to Second National Congress"
- Chartist Movement: The People's Petition of 1838

Visual Sources
- Sequoyah
- Nineteenth-century globe
- Cherokee Constitution
- "Parade on Tsarina's Meadow"
- *Birds of America* by John Audubon I
- *Birds of America* by John Audubon II

20 The Consolidation of Nation-States

Text Sources
- Joseph Mazzini, *Life and Writings of Joseph Mazzini*

Visual Sources
- Reconstruction in the American South
- Lincoln remembrance
- Black soldier, United States Civil War
- Battle of Kinburn, 1855
- View of Charleston, ca. 1870

- Slaves carrying cotton and picking cotton I
- Slaves carrying cotton and picking cotton II
- Slave shackles
- Nineteenth-century whale chart
- *Uncle Tom's Cabin* advertisement
- Map of the western United States

21 Global Empire and European Culture

Text Sources
- John Stuart Mill, excerpts from *On Liberty*
- W. E. B. DuBois, from "Souls of Black Folk"
- Doris Viersbeck, "Life Downstairs: A Servant's Life"
- George Bernard Shaw, *Mrs. Warren's Profession*
- Seneca Falls Convention, "Declaration of Sentiments"
- Adelheid Popp, "Finding Work: Women Factory Workers"
- Pope Leo XIII, *Rerum Novarum* (Of New Things)
- John Stuart Mill, *The Subjection of Women*
- George Eliot, "Review: Margaret Fuller and Mary Wollstonecraft"
- Booker T. Washingtons, "Industrial Education for the Negro"
- Emile Zola, *Nana*
- William James, from *Pragmatism*
- Thorstein Veblen, excerpt from *The Theory of Leisure Class*
- Friedrich Nietzsche, *Beyond Good and Evil*
- Richard Freiherr von Krafft-Ebing, *Psychopathia Sexualia*
- Frederick Winslow Taylor, "A Piece Rate System"
- Charles Darwin, *Autobiography*
- Auguste Comte, "Course of Positive Philosophy"
- Cecil Rhodes, "Confession of Faith"
- Carl Peters, "A Manifesto for German Colonization"
- Edward D. Morel, *The Black Man's Burden*
- Lin Zexu, *Letter to Queen Victoria*
- Mary Kingsley, *Travels in West Africa*
- Raden Ayu Kartini, *Letters of a Javanese Princess*
- Jules Ferry, from *Le Tonkin et La Mere-Patrie*

Visual Sources
- Great Zimbabwe
- Women suffrage parade
- The "New Europes": Sydney
- The "New Europes": New York City
- The "New Europes": Johannesburg
- The "New Europes": Detroit
- The "New Europes": Cape Town
- Tbilisi in the late nineteenth century
- Street scenes, Germany
- Singer sewing machine advertisement
- San Francisco earthquake
- Italian immigrants in USA

- Inuit family, 1918
- Indian School, Pennsylvania
- Immigrants sailing to USA
- Georgian musicians
- Georgian (Caucasus) peasants
- Dead horse in New York street
- Chinese immigrants in USA
- Frontispiece from *Martin Chuzzlewit*
- Pygmies, 1904 World's Fair
- Pinel's skull types
- Muybridge photos
- Frontispiece to *al-Muqtataf*
- Egyptian statues
- Edison's Vitascope
- de Ovi Mamalian, by Karl von Baer
- Christian missionaries in Africa, late nineteenth century
- Chinese pavilion, 1904 World's Fair
- Africans being baptized, South Africa, nineteenth century
- Unloading coffee in Brazil
- The Portsmouth Treaty, 1905
- Tattooed Polynesian
- Tattooed native of Nukahiwa
- Quito textile factory, circa 1910
- Portrait of Jose Rizal
- Port of Valparaiso, Chile
- Plague hospital, Bombay
- Pears' soap advertisement
- North–South reconciliation through the Spanish–American War
- Mandan Sioux offering
- Machine exhibit, 1904 World's Fair
- Kimberley mine, South Africa
- Japanese views of Commodore Perry's mission, 1853, I
- Japanese views of Commodore Perry's mission, 1853, II
- Japanese views of Commodore Perry's mission, 1853, III
- Japanese views of Commodore Perry's mission, 1853, IV
- Japanese views of Commodore Perry's mission, 1853, V
- Japanese views of Commodore Perry's mission, 1853, VI
- Filipino insurgents, ca. 1900
- Field hospital, Philippines
- Early churches in Hawaii I
- Early churches in Hawaii II
- Dinizulu, king of the Zulus
- Chinese destroying opium
- Ceylonese tea picker
- Caucasian warriors wearing chain mail
- Araucanian chief
- Apache Indian prisoners, 1886
- Americans in Yokohama, 1855
- Afrikaaner guerrillas
- African women protest white rule in South Africa
- A Muslim view of the Russian Empire

22 World War I: The End of Enlightenment

Text Sources

- Woodrow Wilson, *The Fourteen Points*
- *The Balfour Declaration*
- Sofia Pavlova, "Taking Advantage of New Opportunities"
- Sir Henry McMahon, *Letter to Ali ibn Husain*
- Siegfried Sassoon, *They*
- Nadezhda Krupskaya, "What a Communist Ought to Be Like"
- Isaac Rosenberg, "Dead Man's Dump"
- International Congress of Women, "Manifesto"
- Huda Shaarawi, "Europe on the Eve of War"
- Anna Eisenmenger, "A German Soldier Returns Home"
- George Clemenceau, "French Demands at the Peace Conference"
- "A French Bakery During the War"

Visual Sources

- Women shipyard workers
- Women munitions workers
- Trench warfare, I
- Trench warfare, II
- Pancho Villa
- French tanks
- Black American soldiers
- Austro-Hungarian soldiers wearing gas masks
- Arab delegates to the Versailles conference
- American World War I poster
- American machine gunners
- Woodrow Wilson on his way to Versailles
- Victory parade, Paris
- Spartacist demonstration, Germany
- Looted food shop, Germany
- Anti-Spartacist demonstration, Germany

23 The Troubled Interwar Years

Text Sources

- Virginia Woolf, from *A Room of One's Own*
- Werner Heisenberg, "Uncertainty"
- Soviet Union "Law Code on Marriage" and "Law Code on Motherhood"
- Joseph Stalin, *Five Year Plan*
- John Maynard Keynes, from *The End of Laissez-Faire*
- Irina Kniazeva, "A Life in a Peasant Village"
- Heinrich Hauser, "With Germany's Unemployed"
- Gertrud Scholtz-Klink, "Speech to the Nazi Women's Organization"
- Constancia de la Mora, from *In Place of Splendor*
- Chicago Commission on Race Relations, "The Negro in Chicago: A Study of Race Relations and a Race Riot"
- Benito Mussolini, "The Political and Social Doctrine of Fascism"

- Adolf Hitler, *Mein Kampf*
- A. Dubova, "Living Someone Else's Life"

Visual Sources
- Yugoslavs at well
- Women bathers, 1920s
- Stalinist poster
- Spanish Civil War poster
- Soviet poster
- Shanghai in the 1920s
- Russian factory, 1939
- Rape of Nanjing
- Poverty, southern United States
- Nazi rally
- Nazi party congress, Nuremberg
- Movie theater, New York, 1920s
- Migrant mother, Great Depression
- Mexican migrants in USA, 1936
- London stock exchange, 1920s
- Ku-Klux-Klan rally
- Japanese in Tsingtao, China, 1920s
- Inflation in Germany
- Hoover Dam
- Herbert Hoover speaks to a television audience, 1927
- German persecution of the Jews
- Execution by guillotine, France, 1929
- Chinatown, San Francisco, 1920s
- Cars on Daytona Beach, 1920s
- British Empire poster, "Growing Markets for Our Goods"
- Bread line, 1930s
- Bolshevik Revolution poster
- Automobile advertisement, 1920s
- Anti-Japanese sentiment, California, 1920s
- 1936 Berlin Olympics
- "There's no way like the American way" billboard
- Tin Mining, Indonesia

24 World War II: Europe in Eclipse

Text Sources
- Winston Churchill, "Their Finest Hour"
- Transcript of the Rape of Nanjing Sentencing
- The Effects of Atomic Bombs on Hiroshima and Nagasaki
- The Charter of the United Nations
- *The Buchenwald Report*
- Neville Chamberlain, *In Search of Peace*
- Marc Bloch, from *Strange Defeat*
- Heinrich Himmler, "Speech to SS Officers"
- Franklin D. Roosevelt, "Call for Sacrifice"
- Franklin D. Roosevelt and Winston Churchill, "The Atlantic Charter"
- Emmanuel Ringelblum, "Notes from the Warsaw Ghetto"
- Anna Petrovna Ostroumova-Lebedeva, "Leningrad Diary"
- Adolf Hitler, "The Obersalzberg Speech"
- A. Philip Randolph, "A Call to March on Washington"

Visual Sources
- Warsaw ghetto
- U.S. troops before D-Day
- U.S. air bombing of Bologna
- Tokyo shanty town, September 1945
- Tokyo and Nuremberg war crimes trials, I
- Tokyo and Nuremberg war crimes trials, II
- The war in the Pacific
- The internment of Japanese Americans, I
- The internment of Japanese Americans, II
- The internment of Japanese Americans, III
- The Holocaust, I
- The Holocaust, II
- The destruction of Europe
- Summits of the Allied leaders, I
- Summits of the Allied leaders, II
- Rosie the Riveter
- Nazis executing Russian civilians
- Japanese surrender aboard the *USS Missouri*
- Japanese bombing of Pearl Harbor
- Hitler and Chamberlain
- Hiroshima after the dropping of the atomic bomb
- France surrenders to the Germans
- D-Day
- Civilian refugees in Europe
- Atomic bomb mushroom cloud
- American workers at B-17 bomber plant
- American propaganda poster
- American GIs in Holland
- "United We Win" poster
- U.S. and Soviet forces meet, 1945

25 Decolonization and the Cold War

Text Sources
- Winston Churchill, from "The Iron Curtain Speech"
- Helga Schütz, "The Wall in My Back Yard"
- Robert Schuman, "The Schuman Declaration"
- *Ladies Home Journal*, "Young Mother"
- Nikita S. Krushchev, "Address to the Twentieth Congress"
- Joseph Stalin, excerpts from the "Soviet Victory" Speech
- John F. Kennedy, Address Before the General Assembly of the United Nations
- James B. Stockdale, excerpt from *A Vietnam Experience: Ten Years of Reflection*
- Henry A. Myers, "East Berliners Rise Up Against Soviet Oppression"
- Harry S Truman, "The Truman Doctrine"
- George Kennan, "The United States and Russia"
- George C. Marshall, "The Marshall Plan"
- Francois Mitterand, Speech to the United Nations
- United Nations, "Universal Declaration of Human Rights"
- United Nations, "Declaration on the Granting of Independence to Colonial Countries and Peoples"
- Palestinian Declaration of Independence
- Jawaharlal Nehru, "Why India Is Non-Aligned"
- Mohandas Ghandi, from *Hind Swaraj*

- Kwame Nkrumah, from *I Speak of Freedom: A Statement of African Ideology*
- Jomo Kenyatta, from *Facing Mt. Kenya: The Tribal Life of the Gokuyu*
- Jawaharlal Nehru, from *The Autobiography of Jawaharlal Nehru*
- Israel's Proclamation of Independence
- Ho Chi Minh, "Declaration of Independence of the Democratic Republic of Vietnam"
- Gamal Abdel Nasser, Speech on the Suez Canal
- Frantz Fanon, from *The Wretched of the Earth*
- Martin Luther King, Jr., Letter from Birmingham City Jail

Visual Sources
- Bulgarian labor brigade
- Vietnamese refugees
- U.S. and British votes in the UN on the Suez Canal crisis, 1956
- UN sprays DDT over Seoul
- The "Kitchen Debate" between Nixon and Khrushchev
- Stalin monument, Prague
- Soviet collective agriculture
- Soviet agriculture
- Segregation USA, 1950s, I
- Segregation USA, 1950s, II
- Polio vaccination
- Outdoor market, Soviet Central Asia
- Nixon in China
- Nikita Khrushchev visiting an Albanian factory
- Newspaper headline showing the "Red Scare," 1950s, USA
- Mossadegh supporters
- Meeting between the Chinese, Soviet, and Indian foreign ministers, 1962
- Koreans in Japan mark homeland
- Korean child receiving food aid
- Kennedy in Berlin, 1963
- Hungarian uprising, 1956
- H-Bomb shelter
- French nurse inoculating Indochinese baby
- Chinese Communist guerrillas
- Chinese artillery class
- Cardinal Francis Spellman conducting mass in New York
- Asian games, Tokyo, 1958
- Anti-Vietnam protesters
- Albanian-Chinese ties
- 1955 designer kitchen
- Midwifery class, Burma
- Mahatma Gandhi
- Kwame Nkrumah and Julius Nyerere
- Iranian students protest
- Indonesian political rallies
- Indonesian guerillas
- Governor's residence of Indonesia
- Female Irgun recruits, Israel

- Construction of the Aswan Dam, Egypt
- Cocoa harvesting in Ghana
- Cairo traffic
- Moroccan health care worker
- Moroccan child receiving immunization
- March on Washington, 1963
- Man on the moon
- Levittown, New York
- Latino rights
- Indian women receiving military training
- Disabled Italians demand more government aid
- Civil rights march, USA

26 Western Civilization and the Global Community

Text Sources
- Mikhail Gorbachev, Speech to the 27th Congress of the Communist Party of the Soviet Union
- Helmut Kohl, Speech to the American Council on Germany
- Nelson Mandela, from *Freedom, Justice and Dignity for All South Africa*
- Zlata Filipovi, from *Zlata's Diary: A Child's Life in Sarajevo*
- Vaclav Havel, "The Need for Transcendence in the Postmodern World"
- Treaty on European Union
- The Kyoto Protocol to the United Nations Framework Convention on Climate Change, Article 2
- Statement from Chancellor Schröder on the Iraq Crisis
- Sayyid Qutb, from *Milestones*
- Pope John Paul II, from *Centesimus Annus*
- Osama bin Laden, "World Islamic Front Statement"
- National Organization for Women, *Statement of Purpose*
- Justin Vaïsse, from "Veiled Meaning"
- Jörg Haider, from *The Freedom I Mean*
- George W. Bush, Addresses
- Deng Xiaoping, on introducing capitalist principles to China
- Alain Destexhe, from *Rwanda and Genocide in the Twentieth Century*
- A Constitution for Europe

Visual Sources
- Smog in Los Angeles, 1954
- Ozone poster
- Operation Desert Storm
- Mayan religious ceremony
- International space station
- Hurricane Katrina
- Earth at night